P9-CQW-977

financial management
principles and practice

Canadian Edition

financial management
principles and practice

Timothy J. Gallagher
Colorado State University

Joseph D. Andrew, Jr.
BIA Financial Network, Inc.

Darek J. Klonowski
Brandon University

Steven M. Landry
John Abbott College

Canadian Edition

Toronto

Library and Archives Canada Cataloguing in Publication

Financial management : principles and practice / Timothy J. Gallagher ... [et al.].—
Canadian ed.

Includes index.
ISBN 0-13-124567-8

1. Corporations—Finance—Textbooks. I. Gallagher, Timothy James, 1952– II. Title.

HG4026.F52 2006 658.15 C2004-905856-8

0-13-124567-8

Vice President, Editorial Director: Michael J. Young
Senior Acquisitions Editor: Gary Bennett
Marketing Manager: Jeff Clarke
Developmental Editor: Maurice Esses
Production Editor: Jennifer Handel
Copy Editor: Bonnie DiMalta
Proofreader: Rodney Rawlings
Production Coordinator: Deborah Starks
Manufacturing Coordinator: Susan Johnson
Permissions Research: Beth McAuley
Page Layout: Gerry Dunn
Art Director: Julia Hall
Interior and Cover Design: Gillian Tsintziras
Cover Image: Photonica

Statistics Canada information is used with the permission of the Minister of Industry, as Minister responsible for Statistics Canada. Information on the availability of the wide range of data from Statistics Canada can be obtained from Statistics Canada's Regional Offices, its World Wide Web site at http://www.statcan.ca, and its toll-free access number 1-800-263-1136. The Statistics Canada CANSIM II database can be accessed at http://cansim2.statcan.ca/cgi-win/CNSMCGI.EXE.

1 2 3 4 5 10 09 08 07 06

Printed and bound in the United States of America.

To Susan and Emily
—T.J.G. and J.D.A.

To my parents, Wieslawa and Roman
—D.J.K.

To Amy and Tony, my mother and father, and to my supportive wife, Jennifer
—S.M.L.

Brief Contents

Contents

Preface

The Challenge

The introductory finance course can cause anxiety in many students. Often, students have the mistaken belief that it requires high-level mathematics. Many students also mistakenly believe that finance is an area in which they will not need competency. Finance concepts often seem far removed from daily life. Nevertheless, almost every major in a business college and many majors in other colleges have to take a principles-of-finance course. As a result, many students who find themselves sitting in finance class on the first day of a semester do not want to be there.

We do not believe that this needs to be the case. Finance is important, dynamic, interesting, and fun. The challenge we take head-on in *Financial Management: Principles and Practice*, Canadian Edition, is to convince students of this. In order to learn, students must want to learn. If they can see the usefulness of what is presented to them, they will work hard and they will learn.

Our many years of teaching experience have taught us that an introductory financial management course can be one that students enjoy and see as having added considerable value to their educational experiences. Finance is, after all, central to any business entity. More CEOs have come up through the finance ranks than any other discipline. Students need to know that the principles and practices of financial management apply to any business unit, from the very largest multinational corporation to the very smallest proprietorship, including the family. Financial ratios tell a story: they are not numbers to be calculated as ends unto themselves. Risk is important and can be managed. Time value of money has meaning and is the central tool of valuation. Funds have a cost, and different sources of funds have different costs. Financial performance and condition can be assessed. Amortized loan payments, rates of return on investment, future value of investment programs, and present value of payments to be received from bonds and stocks can be calculated. The opportunities and special challenges of international operations can be understood.

Our Approach

We believe that students should walk out of the room after the final exam for a finance course believing they have learned something useful. They should see a direct benefit to themselves personally, rather than just the belief that they have mastered some set of necessary job skills; although if students have truly understood the material, then they will indeed have some valuable job skills.

In *Financial Management: Principles and Practice*, Canadian Edition, we start with the student in mind and then present finance material so that students (1) want to learn and (2) can readily learn the necessary material. We do this because finance is not medicine, and it should not be administered as such. Instead, we believe students should be engaged in such a way that they develop the desire to learn. There are those who approach the task of teaching finance with the philosophy, "Here is the finance knowledge you need. Learn it!" These are not the people we had in mind when we wrote this book.

Two key characteristics of *Financial Management: Principles and Practice*, Canadian Edition, are currency and relevance. The authors have various backgrounds, and this combination results in a text that presents the latest in financial theory while retaining a strong "real-world" connection. No other textbook on the market enjoys this balance of academic and practitioner perspectives.

There are a few cartoons in this book. Do not allow their presence to mislead you. This book is serious about learning and the cartoons serve a serious purpose. They tend to "lighten up" the presentation in order to capture students' interest. Although our style is lighthearted, the writing itself is substantive, concise, clear, and easy to understand.

Distinctive Focus

Although there are many other introductory financial management books on the market, none contains the unique style and content of *Financial Management: Principles and Practice*, Canadian Edition. Many texts focus mostly on accounting, with little presentation of the economic theory that underlies the financial techniques presented. Others assume that students remember everything from the accounting course that is usually a prerequisite for this course. Still others claim to take a "valuation approach" but present their topics in a straight accounting framework. In this book, we are serious about focusing on what creates value. We are consistent throughout the book, addressing issues such as what creates value, what destroys it, how value is measured, and how value and risk are related. In so doing, we maximize the value of the finance course to the student.

The Canadian Edition

In preparing the Canadian edition, we have retained the following key characteristics of the U.S. book:

- A student-friendly style and a concise, easy-to-understand presentation.
- The level of rigour that professors demand.
- Coverage of all the current topics you would expect from a book of this type, including:
  - Real options with numeric examples.
  - EVA, MVA, and EBITDA.
  - A value added (NPV) approach to inventory and accounts receivable investment rather than the outmoded return on investment ratio approach.
- Exclusion of topics most likely taught in a second financial management course; students should not have to buy more than what they need.

At the same time, we made some modifications to the book so that Canadian students could relate to and appreciate how finance works within Canada.

- Instead of a separate chapter on international finance, we have incorporated boxes about international finance in most chapters.
- In response to reviewers' suggestions, we added a number of new end-of-chapter problems. Our approach was to create more comprehensive problems, enhancing the student's ability to think beyond the number crunching.
- To make the book more relevant to Canadian students, we revised the chapter openers, and changed the part openers to include a written vignette featuring specific Canadian companies.
- We created *Financial Management and You* boxes, *Finance at Work* boxes, and *Ethical Connections* boxes to reflect current Canadian issues.
- We added Comprehensive Cases at the end of each part, tying in several topics for students to display a practical application of knowledge.
- We added a section on options in Chapter 15.
- As the U.S method of tax is dramatically different from ours, we made significant modifications to the treatment of taxes.
- We also cover the structure of financial intermediaries in Canada and the important role of the Bank of Canada.

Organization of the Text

The book is organized into five major parts as follows:

Part I. **The World of Finance** contains chapters on the structure and goals of firms, the role of financial managers, and an examination of the financial environment.

Part II. **Essential Concepts in Finance** presents chapters on accounting statements and their interpretation, forecasting, risk and return, and the time value of money.

Part III. **Capital Budgeting and Business Valuation** contains chapters on measuring a firm's cost of capital, capital budgeting decision methods, incremental cash flow estimation, and business valuation.

Part IV. **Long-Term Financing Decisions** contains chapters on capital structure basics, corporate bonds, preferred shares, leasing, common shares, and dividend policy.

Part V. **Short-Term Financing Decisions** includes chapters on working capital policy, cash and marketable securities, accounts receivable and inventory, and short-term financing.

Special Features in the Text

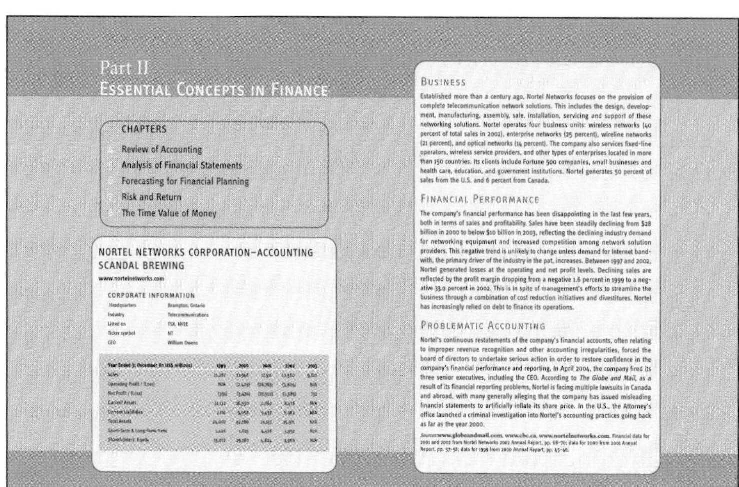

Part II
Essential Concepts in Finance

CHAPTERS

Review of Accounting
Analysis of Financial Statements
Forecasting for Financial Planning
Risk and Return
The Time Value of Money

NORTEL NETWORKS CORPORATION–ACCOUNTING SCANDAL BREWING

www.nortelnetworks.com

CORPORATE INFORMATION

Headquarters	Brampton, Ontario
Industry	Telecommunications
Listed on	TSX, NYSE
Ticker symbol	NT
CEO	William Owens

Year Ended 31 December (in US$ millions)	1999	2000	2001	2002	2003
Sales	[illegible]	[illegible]	17,511	10,560	[illegible]
Operating Profit / (Loss)	N/A	[illegible]	[illegible]	[illegible]	N/A
Net Profit / (Loss)	[illegible]	[illegible]	[illegible]	[illegible]	732
Current Assets	[illegible]	[illegible]	[illegible]	[illegible]	N/A
Current Liabilities	[illegible]	9,058	[illegible]	[illegible]	N/A
Total Assets	[illegible]	42,180	[illegible]	15,971	N/A
Short-Term & Long-Term Debt	[illegible]	[illegible]	[illegible]	[illegible]	N/A
Shareholders' Equity	[illegible]	[illegible]	[illegible]	[illegible]	N/A

BUSINESS

Established more than a century ago, Nortel Networks focuses on the provision of complete telecommunication network solutions. This includes the design, development, manufacturing, assembly, sale, installation, servicing and support of these networking solutions. Nortel operates four business units: wireless networks (40 percent of total sales in 2002), enterprise networks (25 percent), wireline networks (21 percent), and optical networks (14 percent). The company also services fixed-line operators, wireless service providers, and other types of enterprises located in more than 150 countries. Its clients include Fortune 500 companies, small businesses and health care, education, and government institutions. Nortel generates 50 percent of sales from the U.S. and 6 percent from Canada.

FINANCIAL PERFORMANCE

The company's financial performance has been disappointing in the last few years, both in terms of sales and profitability. Sales have been steadily declining from $28 billion in 2000 to below $10 billion in 2003, reflecting the declining industry demand for networking equipment and increased competition among network solution providers. This negative trend is unlikely to change unless demand for Internet bandwith, the primary driver of the industry in the pat, increases. Between 1997 and 2002, Nortel generated losses at the operating and net profit levels. Declining sales are reflected by the profit margin dropping from a negative 1.6 percent in 1999 to a negative 33.9 percent in 2002. This is in spite of management's efforts to streamline the business through a combination of cost reduction initiatives and divestitures. Nortel has increasingly relied on debt to finance its operations.

PROBLEMATIC ACCOUNTING

Nortel's continuous restatements of the company's financial accounts, often relating to improper revenue recognition and other accounting irregularities, forced the board of directors to undertake serious action in order to restore confidence in the company's financial performance and reporting. In April 2004, the company fired its three senior executives, including the CEO. According to *The Globe and Mail*, as a result of its financial reporting problems, Nortel is facing multiple lawsuits in Canada and abroad, with many generally alleging that the company has issued misleading financial statements to artificially inflate its share price. In the U.S., the Attorney's office launched a criminal investigation into Nortel's accounting practices going back as far as the year 2000.

Sources: **www.globeandmail.com, www.cbc.ca, www.nortelnetworks.com.** Financial data for 2001 and 2002 from Nortel Networks 2002 Annual Report, pp. 68–70; data for 2000 from 2001 Annual Report, pp. 57–58; data for 1999 from 2000 Annual Report, pp. 45–46.

Part-Opening Vignettes

Each part of *Financial Management: Principles and Practice*, Canadian Edition, opens with a vignette that explores the financial issues at some of Canada's most prominent companies. This helps relate the course material to real-world examples that are a part of students' everyday lives.

Chapter Objectives

At the start of each chapter, the objectives are clearly outlined to help students focus on the material and evaluate their learning progress.

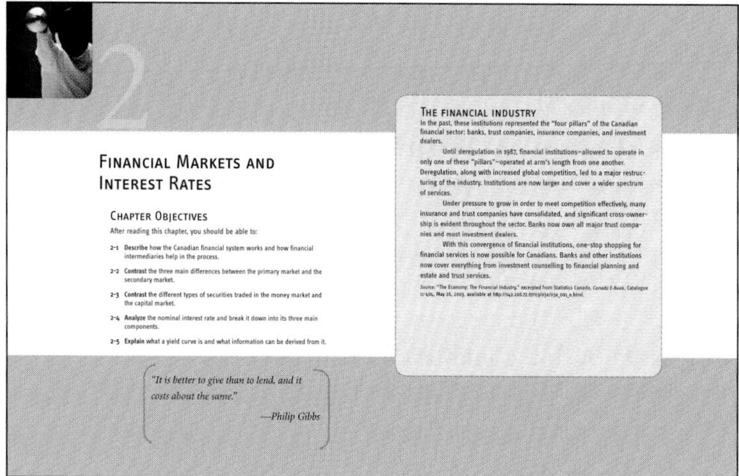

2

FINANCIAL MARKETS AND INTEREST RATES

CHAPTER OBJECTIVES

After reading this chapter, you should be able to:

2-1 **Describe** how the Canadian financial system works and how financial intermediaries help in the process.

2-2 **Contrast** the three main differences between the primary market and the secondary market.

2-3 **Contrast** the different types of securities traded in the money market and the capital market.

2-4 **Analyze** the nominal interest rate and break it down into its three main components.

2-5 **Explain** what a yield curve is and what information can be derived from it.

"It is better to give than to lend, and it costs about the same."

—Philip Gibbs

THE FINANCIAL INDUSTRY

In the past, these institutions represented the "four pillars" of the Canadian financial sector: banks, trust companies, insurance companies, and investment dealers.

Until deregulation in 1987, financial institutions—allowed to operate in only one of these "pillars"—operated at arm's length from one another. Deregulation, along with increased global competition, led to a major restructuring of the industry. Institutions are now larger and cover a wider spectrum of services.

Under pressure to grow in order to meet competition effectively, many insurance and trust companies have consolidated, and significant cross-ownership is evident throughout the sector. Banks now own all major trust companies and most investment dealers.

With this convergence of financial institutions, one-stop shopping for financial services is now possible for Canadians. Banks and other institutions now cover everything from investment counselling to financial planning and estate and trust services.

Source: "The Economy: The Financial Industry," excerpted from Statistics Canada, *Canada E-Book*, Catalogue 11-404, May 26, 2003, available at http://142.206.72.67/03/03e/03e_001_e.html.

Chapter-Opening Vignettes

Each chapter in *Financial Management: Principles and Practice*, Canadian Edition, begins with a real-world example that illustrates the concepts to be addressed in that chapter. This gives the student a reason to learn this material and to show its practical application.

Chapter Overview

A Chapter Overview previews the chapter for students, preparing them for the material ahead.

Special Boxes

- **Ethical Connections**—*Ethical Connections* boxes identify many financial decisions that have ethical dimensions to them. We don't give easy answers, but we don't pull punches either. Cop-outs, such as "being ethical is good business," are avoided. This may be true, up to a point, but sometimes doing the right thing costs you.

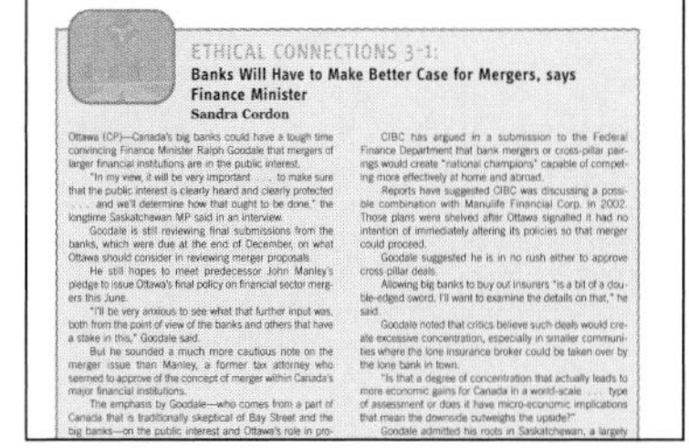
ETHICAL CONNECTIONS 3-1:
Banks Will Have to Make Better Case for Mergers, says Finance Minister
Sandra Cordon

- **Financial Management and You**—*Financial Management and You* boxes take the financial management concepts intended for use within a firm and show how they can be used by individuals for personal financial decision making. This gives students the context they need to understand such concepts.

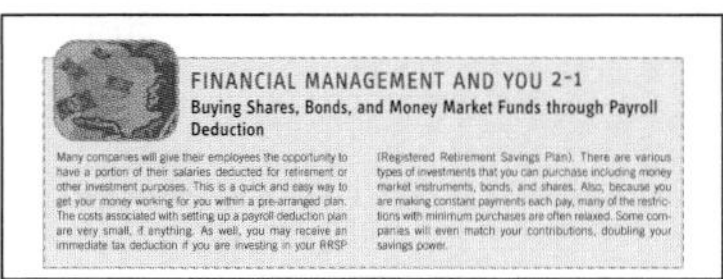
FINANCIAL MANAGEMENT AND YOU 2-1
Buying Shares, Bonds, and Money Market Funds through Payroll Deduction

- **Finance at Work**—*Finance at Work* boxes are designed to demonstrate how finance relies on, contributes to, and interacts with other functional areas of the firm. Understanding the role of finance within the firm is important for all students, even those that do not major in finance.

FINANCE AT WORK 1-1
Sales Retail Sports Media Technology Public Relations Production Exports
BRAD FORD, SENIOR ACCOUNTANT–INVENTORY CONTROL

- **International Perspectives in Finance**—*International Perspectives in Finance* boxes, new to the Canadian edition, put Canada into a global context. Living in a global community, we should know how Canada relates to the rest of the world.

INTERNATIONAL PERSPECTIVES IN FINANCE 4-1
Accounting Boards Pledge to Work on Common Rules

Take Note Marginalia

Margin notes provide students with important tips along the way.

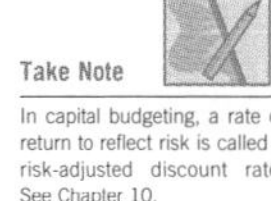

Take Note

In capital budgeting, a rate of return to reflect risk is called a risk-adjusted discount rate. See Chapter 10.

Calculator Solutions

Financial calculator solutions are included for all problems dealing with the general time value of money and specific security valuation. This material is presented in a way that accommodates professors' differing preferences about the use of financial calculators.

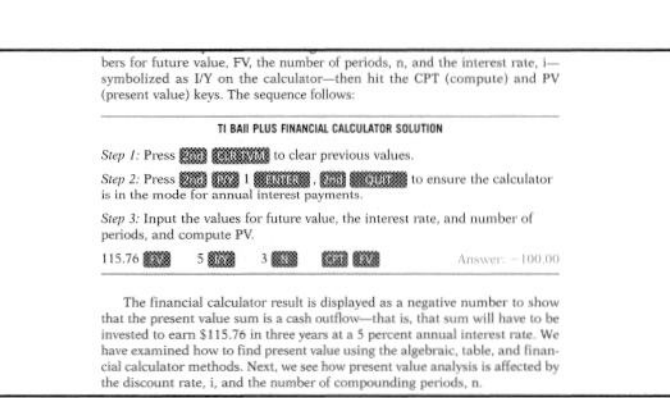
TI BAII PLUS FINANCIAL CALCULATOR SOLUTION

Equations Introduced in This Chapter

At the end of each chapter, a compiled list of equations provides students with a helpful reference when completing practice problems and preparing for tests.

Summaries

The summary for each chapter specifically describes how the learning objectives have been achieved.

Key Terms

Each chapter has key terms in **bold** that are defined in the chapter and in the glossary.

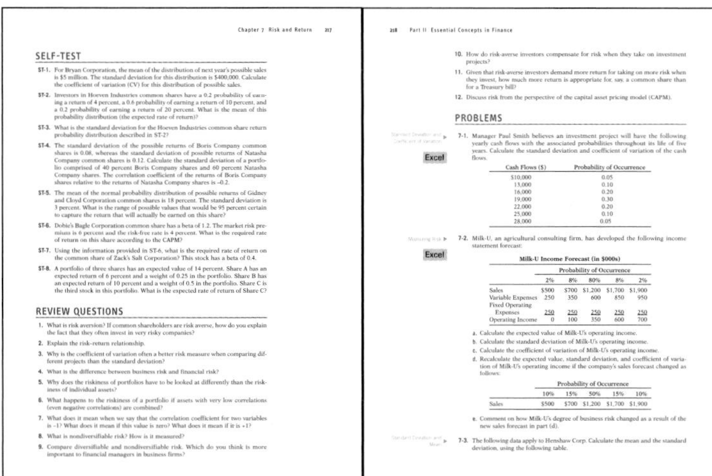

Chapter 7 Risk and Return 217

SELF-TEST

ST-1. For Bryan Corporation, the mean of the distribution of next year's possible sales is $5 million. The standard deviation for this distribution is $400,000. Calculate the coefficient of variation (CV) for this distribution of possible sales.

ST-2. Investors in Hoeven Industries common shares have a 0.2 probability of earning a return of 4 percent, a 0.6 probability of earning a return of 10 percent, and a 0.2 probability of earning a return of 20 percent. What is the mean of this probability distribution (the expected rate of return)?

ST-3. What is the standard deviation for the Hoeven Industries common share return probability distribution described in ST-2?

ST-4. The standard deviation of the possible returns of Boris Company common shares is 0.08, whereas the standard deviation of possible returns of Natasha Company common shares is 0.12. Calculate the standard deviation of a portfolio comprised of 40 percent Boris Company shares and 60 percent Natasha Company shares. The correlation coefficient of the returns of Boris Company shares relative to the returns of Natasha Company shares is –0.2.

ST-5. The mean of the normal probability distribution of possible returns of Gidney and Cloyd Corporation common shares is 18 percent. The standard deviation is 3 percent. What is the range of possible values that would be 95 percent certain to capture the return that will actually be earned on this share?

ST-6. Dobie's Bagle Corporation common share has a beta of 1.2. The market risk premium is 6 percent and the risk-free rate is 4 percent. What is the required rate of return on this share according to the CAPM?

ST-7. Using the information provided in ST-6, what is the required rate of return on the common share of Zack's Salt Corporation? This stock has a beta of 0.4.

ST-8. A portfolio of three shares has an expected value of 14 percent. Share A has an expected return of 6 percent and a weight of 0.25 in the portfolio. Share B has an expected return of 10 percent and a weight of 0.5 in the portfolio. Share C is the third stock in this portfolio. What is the expected rate of return of Share C?

REVIEW QUESTIONS

1. What is risk aversion? If common shareholders are risk averse, how do you explain the fact that they often invest in very risky companies?
2. Explain the risk-return relationship.
3. Why is the coefficient of variation often a better risk measure when comparing different projects than the standard deviation?
4. What is the difference between business risk and financial risk?
5. Why does the riskiness of portfolios have to be looked at differently than the riskiness of individual assets?
6. What happens to the riskiness of a portfolio if assets with very low correlations (even negative correlations) are combined?
7. What does it mean when we say that the correlation coefficient for two variables is –1? What does it mean if this value is zero? What does it mean if it is +1?
8. What is nondiversifiable risk? How is it measured?
9. Compare diversifiable and nondiversifiable risk. Which do you think is more important to financial managers in business firms?

218 Part II Essential Concepts in Finance

10. How do risk-averse investors compensate for risk when they take on investment projects?
11. Given that risk-averse investors demand more return for taking on more risk when they invest, how much more return is appropriate for, say, a common share than for a Treasury bill?
12. Discuss risk from the perspective of the capital asset pricing model (CAPM).

PROBLEMS

7-1. Manager Paul Smith believes an investment project will have the following yearly cash flows with the associated probabilities throughout its life of five years. Calculate the standard deviation and coefficient of variation of the cash flows.

Excel

Cash Flows ($)	Probability of Occurrence
$10,000	0.05
13,000	0.10
16,000	0.20
19,000	0.30
22,000	0.20
25,000	0.10
28,000	0.05

7-2. Milk-U, an agricultural consulting firm, has developed the following income statement forecast:

Excel

Milk-U Income Forecast (in $000s)

	Probability of Occurrence				
	2%	8%	80%	8%	2%
Sales	$500	$700	$1,200	$1,700	$1,900
Variable Expenses	250	350	600	850	950
Fixed Operating Expenses	250	250	250	250	250
Operating Income	0	100	350	600	700

a. Calculate the expected value of Milk-U's operating income.
b. Calculate the standard deviation of Milk-U's operating income.
c. Calculate the coefficient of variation of Milk-U's operating income.
d. Recalculate the expected value, standard deviation, and coefficient of variation of Milk-U's operating income if the company's sales forecast changed as follows:

	Probability of Occurrence				
	10%	15%	50%	15%	10%
Sales	$500	$700	$1,200	$1,700	$1,900

e. Comment on how Milk-U's degree of business risk changed as a result of the new sales forecast in part (d).

7-3. The following data apply to Hemshaw Corp. Calculate the mean and the standard deviation, using the following table.

Self-Test Questions with Answers

Self-test questions and problems at the end of chapters, along with their solutions, enable students to check their grasp of the material presented.

Review Questions and Problems

Review questions and an abundant number of end-of-chapter problems are included in the appropriate chapters. Notes in the margins connect the problems to the relevant topics in the chapter.

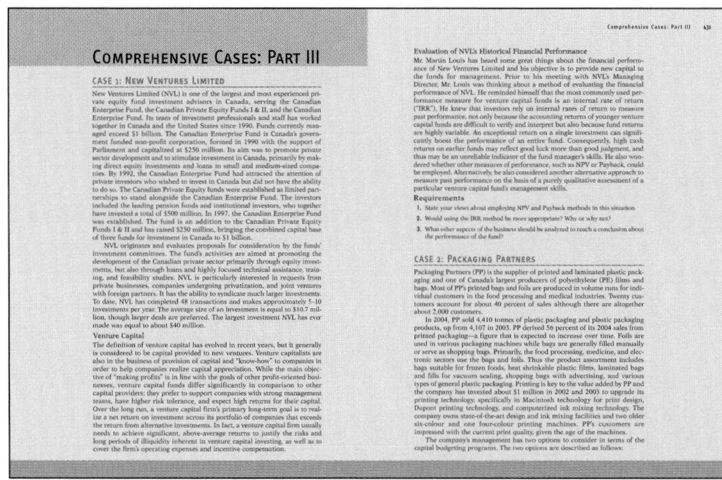

COMPREHENSIVE CASES: PART III

CASE 1: NEW VENTURES LIMITED

New Ventures Limited (NVL) is one of the largest and most experienced private equity fund investment advisors in Canada, serving the Canadian Enterprise Fund, the Canadian Private Equity Funds I & II, and the Canadian Enterprise Fund. Its team of investment professionals and staff has worked together in Canada and the United States since 1990. Funds currently managed exceed $1 billion. The Canadian Enterprise Fund is Canada's government funded non-profit corporation, formed in 1990 with the support of Parliament and capitalized at $250 million. Its aim was to promote private sector development and to stimulate investment in Canada, primarily by making direct equity investments and loans to small and medium-sized companies. By 1992, the Canadian Enterprise Fund had attracted the attention of private investors who wished to invest in Canada but did not have the ability to do so. The Canadian Private Equity funds were established as limited partnerships to stand alongside the Canadian Enterprise Fund. The investors included the leading pension funds and institutional investors, who together have invested a total of $500 million. In 1997, the Canadian Enterprise Fund was established. The fund is an addition to the Canadian Private Equity Funds I & II and has raised $250 million, bringing the combined capital base of three funds for investment in Canada to $1 billion.

NVL originates and evaluates proposals for consideration by the funds' investment committees. The fund's activities are aimed at promoting the development of the Canadian private sector primarily through equity investments, but also through loans and highly focused technical assistance, training, and feasibility studies. NVL is particularly interested in requests from private businesses, companies undergoing privatization, and joint ventures with foreign partners. It has the ability to syndicate much larger investments. To date, NVL has completed 48 transactions and makes approximately 5–10 investments per year. The average size of an investment is equal to $10.7 million, though larger deals are preferred. The largest investment NVL has ever made was equal to about $40 million.

Venture Capital

The definition of venture capital has evolved in recent years, but it generally is considered to be capital provided to new ventures. Venture capitalists are also in the business of provision of capital and "know-how" to companies in order to help companies realize capital appreciation. While the main objective of "making profits" is in line with the goals of other profit-oriented businesses, venture capital funds differ significantly in comparison to other capital providers; they prefer to support companies with strong management teams, have higher risk tolerance, and expect high returns for their capital. Over the long run, a venture capital firm's primary long-term goal is to realize a net return on investment across its portfolio of companies that exceeds the return from alternative investments. In fact, a venture capital firm usually needs to achieve significant, above-average returns to justify the risks and long periods of illiquidity inherent in venture capital investing, as well as to cover the firm's operating expenses and incentive compensation.

Comprehensive Cases: Part III 431

Evaluation of NVL's Historical Financial Performance

Mr. Martin Louis has heard some great things about the financial performance of New Ventures Limited and his objective is to provide new capital to the funds for management. Prior to his meeting with NVL's Managing Director, Mr. Louis was thinking about a method of evaluating the financial performance of NVL. He reminded himself that the most commonly used performance measure for venture capital funds is an internal rate of return ("IRR"). He knew that investors rely on internal rates of return to measure past performance, not only because the accounting returns of younger venture capital funds are difficult to verify and interpret but also because fund returns are highly variable. An exceptional return on a single investment can significantly boost the performance of an entire fund. Consequently, high cash returns on earlier funds may reflect good luck more than good judgment, and thus may be an unreliable indicator of the fund manager's skills. He also wondered whether other measures of performance, such as NPV or Payback, could be employed. Alternatively, he also considered another alternative approach to measure past performance on the basis of a purely qualitative assessment of a particular venture capital fund's management skills.

Requirements

1. State your views about employing NPV and Payback methods in this situation.
2. Would using the IRR method be more appropriate? Why or why not?
3. What other aspects of the business should be analyzed to reach a conclusion about the performance of the fund?

CASE 2: PACKAGING PARTNERS

Packaging Partners (PP) is the supplier of printed and laminated plastic packaging and one of Canada's largest producers of polyethylene (PE) films and bags. Most of PP's printed bags and foils are produced in volume runs for individual customers in the food processing and medical industries. Twenty customers account for about 40 percent of sales although there are altogether about 2,000 customers.

In 2004, PP sold 4,410 tonnes of plastic packaging and plastic packaging products, up from 4,107 in 2003. PP derived 56 percent of its 2004 sales from printed packaging—a figure that is expected to increase over time. Foils are used in various packaging machines while bags are generally filled manually or serve as shopping bags. Primarily, the food processing, medicine, and electronic sectors use the bags and foils. Thus the product assortment includes bags suitable for frozen foods, heat shrinkable plastic films, laminated bags and fills for vacuum sealing, shopping bags with advertising, and various types of general plastic packaging. Printing is key to the value added by PP and the company has invested about $1 million in 2002 and 2003 to upgrade its printing technology, specifically in Macintosh technology for print design, Dupont printing technology, and computerized ink mixing technology. The company owns state-of-the-art design and ink mixing facilities and two older six-colour and one four-colour printing machines. PP's customers are impressed with the current print quality, given the age of the machines.

The company's management has two options to consider in terms of the capital budgeting programs. The two options are described as follows:

Comprehensive Cases

Comprehensive Cases, new to the Canadian edition, provide a capstone to each part, allowing students to integrate their new knowledge with critical thinking skills, and make connections between the chapters.

Computer Spreadsheet–Supported Problems

A number of end-of-chapter problems are marked with the special computer-problem logo shown here. This indicates that a downloadable Excel spreadsheet template for the problem is available on the Companion Website at www.pearsoned.ca/gallagher.

Excel

Cartoons

Cartoons are added for fun—and occasionally to make a financial point.

Supplements

For the Student

- **Student Workbook and Study Guide**—The Student Workbook and Study Guide outlines the chapters, explains key points and terms, and provides additional problems (with solutions) for practice.
- **Companion Website**—The Companion Website can be accessed at www.pearsoned.ca/gallagher and includes the following: Excel spreadsheet files containing templates that facilitate solving designated end-of-chapter problems, Internet exercises, and online quizzes that provide students with immediate feedback.

For the Professor

- **Instructor's Manual**—The Instructor's Manual provides the professor with chapter outlines and suggestions for alternative ways to present the material. Key points are identified and a variety of types of assistance for class preparation are presented.
- **Solutions Manual**—Detailed solutions, not just final answers, are presented for each end-of-chapter question and problem. These have all been personally checked by the authors, in addition to two other levels of accuracy checks.
- **TestGen**—This computerized test bank enables instructors to view and edit the existing questions, add questions, generate tests, and print the tests in a variety of formats. Powerful search and sort functions make it easy to locate questions and arrange them in any order desired. With over 1,000 multiple-choice, essay, and problem-based questions to choose from, the TestGen allows for complete customization of an exam according to chapters covered, type of problem, and level of difficulty.
- **PowerPoint Slides**—Animated slides covering all main topics in the text are available to assist the professor during class.

In Conclusion

We believe that students will understand the very important finance concepts and master necessary problem-solving skills when they complete the course in which this text is used because it is founded upon our "Students First" philosophy. We also believe that a professor's own classroom experience is more rewarding when students are enthusiastic and grasp the conceptual content and the problem-solving techniques. If we have helped to make this happen, we have succeeded in achieving our vision for *Financial Management: Principles and Practice*, Canadian Edition.

Acknowledgments

We gratefully appreciate all the contributions made by those who helped make this book a reality. It has been a dream of ours to be involved with the creation of a textbook of which we could be proud. Our success at this endeavour comes with many thanks to many people.

To all those who provided formal reviews for the Canadian edition, we greatly appreciate your input and suggestions; they have been a huge help to us.

David E. Allwright, *Mount Royal College*

Cecile Ashman, *Algonquin College*

Elisabeth Carter, *Douglas College*

John Currie, *Humber College*

Brian Hobson, *Georgian College*

Susan Graydon Kelsall, *Humber College*

Marie Madill-Payne, *George Brown College*

Anna Schiavi, *Vanier College*

Judith Watson, *Capilano College*

We would also like to thank the entire Pearson Team, especially those behind the scenes. Special thanks go to Gary Bennett, Senior Acquisitions Editor, who gave both of us this opportunity and showed us the ropes along the way; to Rema Celio, Associate Editor, who patiently dealt with all our problems; to Rachel Stuckey, Assistant Editor, who took over during Rema's leave; to Maurice Esses, Supervising Developmental Editor, for stepping up to the plate and giving us his vast experience; to Jen Handel, Production Editor, for helping us make our work a reality; to Beth MacAuley, Permissions Editor, who tackled all the difficult permission issues; and to Bonnie DiMalta, copy-editor, for the time she spent within this process.

Finally, we would like to give our sincere thanks to those who supported us throughout this endeavour. This includes friends, business colleagues—especially Torben Andersen from Red Deer College and David Taylor from Brandon University—and, of course, our families. Without your emotional support, we could never have done it. Thanks to Jennifer, Amy, Tony, and Norma Landry, as well as Wieslawa, Roman, Ela, and Adam Klonowski.

About the Authors

Timothy J. Gallagher (Tim) is professor of finance and chair of the Department of Finance & Real Estate at Colorado State University. Tim received his Ph.D. in finance in 1978 from the University of Illinois at Urbana–Champaign.

Tim has taught undergraduate and graduate finance courses for 24 years, including courses in financial management, markets and institutions, and investments. He has taught traditional and nontraditional students at all levels, including executive MBAs, and in all types of classroom settings—large lecture, small seminar, and distance learning.

Tim has published in journals such as *The Journal of Money, Credit, and Banking*, *The Journal of Portfolio Management*, *Financial Management*, and *The Financial Review*, among others.

Joseph D. Andrew Jr. (Joe) is a financial analyst with BIA Financial Network, Inc., a financial consulting firm specializing in the analysis and appraisal of broadcasting, cable, and telecommunications companies and in preparation of bank presentations for communications clients. As a senior telecom analyst with BIA, Joe performs asset and stock appraisals, business plan analyses, industry studies, and litigation support functions for communications companies, primarily in the local, long distance, wireless, specialized mobile radio, and Internet industries. He also participates in specialized strategic research projects and impact studies covering various aspects of the communications industry. Joe is a member of the American Society of Appraisers and has been with BIA since April 1997.

Prior to joining BIA, Joe served as chief financial officer for X-Change Software, Inc., a start-up software development firm in Oakton, Virginia. As CFO, he was responsible for corporate investment analysis, cash flow planning, forecasting and analysis, receivables and payables management, and supervision of bookkeeping and accounting functions.

In addition to managing corporate finances, Joe teaches graduate courses for Webster University of St. Louis, Missouri, dividing his time between the university's Washington, D.C., campus and its international campus in Hamilton, Bermuda. His published works include this book and *Effective Writing: A Handbook for Finance People*, with Dr. Claire May of the Art Institute of Atlanta and Dr. Gordon May of the University of Georgia.

Joe's past experience includes teaching assignments for National-Louis University in McLean Virginia, the University of Southern Colorado in Colorado Springs, and McMurry College in Abilene, Texas. He also served 23 years as a missile maintenance specialist in the U.S. Air Force, retiring at the rank of chief master sergeant in 1982.

Darek J. Klonowski, Ph.D., is an Associate Professor of Business Administration at Brandon University in Manitoba, and teaches courses in corporate finance, investments and venture capital.

Darek has worked in the venture capital industry for over ten years, making investments throughout Central and Eastern Europe, most recently as Managing Director of Copernicus Capital Management, a venture capital fund affiliated with Boston-based Advent International, focusing on investments in the region. Previously, he worked for Enterprise Investors, the largest and most successful venture capital fund in Poland. Darek has also advised several clients, including the European Bank for Reconstruction and Development, on asset allocation strategies for Eastern Europe. He has participated in numerous industry conferences as guest speaker and discussion panel member.

Steven M. Landry (Steve) is a professor at John Abbott College in Quebec. Having two degrees from McGill University, Steve also proudly retains the right to use the Chartered Financial Analyst (CFA) designation.

Steve has diverse experience in teaching, from finance to martial arts. For over ten years, Steve has worked with various age groups, from the young to the not-as-young. Steve's strategy of instruction has always been to use the student's own experience to explain complicated topics, a strategy he employed while writing the Canadian edition of *Financial Management*.

Tim, Joe, Darek, and Steve's partnership in this book's creation represents a unique opportunity for readers to experience the best of both worlds—Tim and Steve's development of the theory and logic of financial principles and Joe and Darek's real-world financial orientation. Their combined experience with students ensures that readers will learn theory and practice in an innovative, up-to-date, and accurate manner.

The Pearson Education Canada **COMPANION WEBSITE**

A Great Way to Learn and Instruct Online

The Pearson Education Canada Companion Website is easy to navigate and is organized to correspond to the chapters in this textbook. Whether you are a student in the classroom or a distance learner you will discover helpful resources for in-depth study and research that empower you in your quest for greater knowledge and maximize your potential for success in the course.

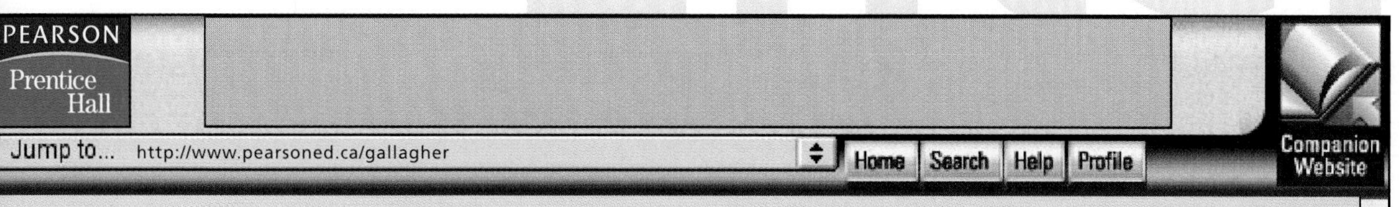

PEARSON Prentice Hall

Jump to... http://www.pearsoned.ca/gallagher | Home | Search | Help | Profile

Companion Website

Home >

PH Companion Website

Financial Management: Principles and Practice, Canadian Edition, by Gallagher, Andrew, Klonowski, and Landry

Student Resources

The modules in this section provide students with tools for learning course material. These modules include:

- Quizzes
- Internet Exercises
- Excel Spreadsheet Templates
- Glossary Flashcards

In the quiz modules, students can send answers to the grader and receive instant feedback on their progress through the Results Reporter. Coaching comments and references to the textbook may be available to ensure that students take advantage of all available resources to enhance their learning experience.

Instructor Resources

A link to this book on the Pearson online catalogue (www.pearsoned.ca) provides instructors with additional teaching tools. Downloadable PowerPoint Presentations and an Instructor's Solutions Manual are just some of the materials that may be available. The catalogue is password protected. To get a password, simply contact your Pearson Education Canada Representative or call Faculty Sales and Services at 1-800-850-5813.

Part I
The World of Finance

CHAPTERS

ROYAL BANK OF CANADA—A STRONG CANADIAN FINANCIAL INSTITUTION

www.rbc.com

CORPORATE INFORMATION

Headquarters	Toronto, Ontario
Industry	Financial Services
Number of Employees	60,812
Number of Branches	1,297
Listed on	TSX, NYSE
Ticker symbol	RY
President & CEO	Gordon Nixon

Year Ended 31 October (In $ millions)	1999	2000	2001	2002	2003
Revenue	11,140	12,731	15,805	17,060	16,947
Profit before Tax	2,707	3,640	3,892	4,421	4,592
Net Profit	1,725	2,208	2,435	2,898	3,036
Loans (Assets)	144,793	156,184	171,177	171,523	172,547
Deposits (Liabilities)	187,897	206,237	235,687	245,040	260,518
Total Assets	273,406	294,173	362,562	382,000	412,591
Cash Resources	23,042	16,408	17,516	21,293	17,520
Shareholders' Equity	12,408	13,297	18,205	18,755	18,117

Business

The Royal Bank of Canada (RBC) is one of Canada's premier diversified financial services institutions. RBC has three businesses, which are structured around client and geographic needs. These businesses are: a consumer business for clients in Canada, which includes banking, investments, and insurance; a consumer business for U.S. and international clients, which includes banking and investments in the U.S., banking in the Caribbean, and Global Private Banking internationally; and a wholesale business for clients around the globe, which includes capital markets and corporate and commercial banking. RBC serves more than 12 million personal, business, and public sector clients worldwide from offices in more than thirty countries. In Canada, the Company operates a network of 1,297 branches and 4,400 ATMs. In terms of international presence, RBC has focused on expansion in the United States, where it focuses on personal and commercial banking, mortgage origination, insurance, full-service brokerage, and corporate and investment banking services. RBC also maintains a retail network in the Caribbean, as well as in the Bahamas. Outside North America, the Company provides corporate and investment banking, trade finance, correspondent banking, treasury and securities custody services to business clients, and private banking services to individuals. RBC also has a major presence in the global reinsurance market.

Financial Performance

RBC's historical financial performance is best described as solid, reflecting a 10-year compound annual rate of return to shareholders of 20 percent between 1993 and 2003, which was the third highest return among the leading North American financial services companies. In 2003, the Company reached revenues of $17 billion and net profit of $3 billion, the largest amount of net profit in the history of the Canadian financial services industry.

International Expansion

RBC's international expansion plans are perhaps best captured in a direct quote from RBC's CEO Gordon Nixon, which comes from an ROB TV interview given earlier this year:

> We've made it very clear to the marketplace that we want to continue to invest in the personal and commercial financial services businesses, and particularly in the Southeast, and if we can grow that franchise, it will not only increase our presence and brand in the United States; it will facilitate our other businesses in the United States, like insurance and wealth management, where we'll have an increased distribution channel off which we can sell more insurance and more wealth management products as well. The challenge that we have, and it comes back to the size issue, is we have to grow very cautiously and very conservatively in the United States because we just don't have the size and scale to acquire larger financial institutions in the United States which would get us there more quickly, without potentially compromising our fundamentals or taking more risks than we're willing to take.

Source: Adapted from rbc.com, globeandmail.com, cbc.ca, and tsx.com. Reprinted with permission of RBC Financial Group.

1

Finance and the Firm

Chapter Objectives

After reading this chapter, you should be able to:

1-1 **Describe** the field of finance.

1-2 **Summarize** five of the main duties of financial managers.

1-3 **Identify** the basic goal of a business firm.

1-4 **List** three important factors that affect the value of a firm.

1-5 **Summarize** three main legal and ethical challenges faced by financial managers.

1-6 **Identify** three of the different forms of business organization.

"It may be that the race is not always to the swift, nor the battle to the strong, but that is the way to bet."

—Damon Runyon

Finance Grabs the Business Headlines

Headlines from the front page of some recent *Globe and Mail* editions.*

- Strong dollar hits Imperial Oil
- Appliance, furniture sales boost Sears Canada profits
- EnCana lands U.S.-based gas producer Tom Brown for $2.3-billion (U.S.)
- Branson's Virgin teams with Bell
- RBC cracks $3-billion profit
- Excellent results expected for Telus
- Bombardier to shake up European units
- Rogers to launch Internet phones
- U.S. banks strike $58-billion mega deal
- JPMorgan sees earlier rate hike
- Record high for Canadian dollar

What do all these stories have in common? They deal with finance. Companies cutting costs, companies reporting profits or losses, governments concerned about interest rates—these are just a sampling of business stories involving finance that appear every day in the press.

Finance is at the heart of business management. No business firm—or government, for that matter—can exist for long without following at least the basic principles of financial management.

This book is designed to introduce you to basic financial management principles and skills. Some of these concepts and skills are surprisingly straightforward; others are quite challenging. All, however, will help you in the business world, no matter what career you choose.

**Source of headlines:* www.globeandmail.com.

Chapter Overview

In this chapter, we will introduce financial management basics that provide a foundation for the rest of the course. First, we will describe the field of finance and examine the role of financial management within a business organization. Then we will investigate the financial goal of a business firm and the legal and ethical challenges that are faced by financial managers. We will end with a description of the most common forms of business in the economy: sole proprietorships, partnerships, and corporations.

The Field of Finance

In business, financial guidelines determine how money is raised and spent. Although raising and spending money may sound simple, financial decisions affect every aspect of a business—from how many people a manager can hire, to what products a company can produce, to what investments a company can make.

For example, when EnCana, Canada's largest oil and gas producer, decided to expand its operations and become one of the world's leading companies in the industry, it acquired a Denver-based firm, Tom Brown, for US$2.3 billion. EnCana executives knew that Tom Brown had valuable long-term reserves of gas properties in the U.S. Rockies, which was one of EnCana's regions of operation. One of EnCana's goals achieved by the acquisition was to shift away from a production business to a resource-based business. In addition, EnCana planned to dispose of some of the non-core assets valued at US$1.5 billion. In purchasing Tom Brown's shares, EnCana offered a 24 percent premium over Tom Brown's closing price on the New York Stock Exchange.[1]

Money continually flows through businesses. It may flow in from banks, from the government, from the sale of shares, and so on; and it may flow out for a variety of reasons—to invest in bonds, to buy new equipment, or to hire top-notch employees. Businesses must pay constant attention to ensure that the right amount of money is available at the right time for the right use.

In large firms, it may take a whole team of financial specialists to understand the financial impact of an acquisition. When Maple Leaf Foods purchased a Virginia-based company Schneider Corporation from its U.S. parent company Smithfield Food Incorporated for US$378 million, Maple Leaf became one of the largest meat companies in North America. During this time, teams of financial specialists worked on issues related to valuing the acquired business, developing a set of financial projections for the combined businesses post-acquisition, and finalizing financing plans and cost reduction initiatives.[2] This acquisition concluded a period of effort to acquire Schneider undertaken by Maple Leaf in 1997.

---

[1]Jang, B., and Brethour, P. (2004, April 16). EnCana Lands Gas Producer Tom Brown for $2.3-billion (U.S.). *The Globe and Mail.*

[2]Chow, J. (2002, September 26, FP1). Maple Leaf, Schneider in Merger. *The Financial Post.*

Finance Career Paths

Finance has three main career paths: financial management, financial markets and institutions, and investments. Financial management, the focus of this text, involves managing the finances of a business. Financial managers—people who manage a business firm's finances—perform a number of tasks. They analyze and forecast a firm's finances, assess risk, evaluate investment opportunities, decide when and where to find money sources and how much money to raise, and decide how much money to return to the firm's investors.

Bankers, stockbrokers, and others who work in financial markets and institutions focus on the flow of money through financial institutions and the markets in which financial assets are exchanged. They track the impact of interest rates on the flow of that money. People who work in the field of investments locate, select, and manage income-producing assets. For instance, security analysts and mutual fund managers both operate in the investment field. In certain circumstances, even general managers or directors have to resolve financial issues. See International Perspectives in Finance 1-1 on page 14 for such an example.

Table 1-1 summarizes the three main finance career paths.

Financial Management

Financial management is essentially a combination of accounting and economics. First, financial managers use accounting information—balance sheets, income statements, and so on—to analyze, plan, and allocate financial resources for business firms. Second, financial managers use economic principles to guide them in making financial decisions that are in the best interest of the firm. In other words, finance is an applied area of economics that relies on accounting for input. Some financial specialists argue that finance links economics and accounting.

Because finance looks closely at the question of what adds value to a business, financial managers are central to most businesses. Let's take a look at what financial managers do.

Table 1-1 Careers in the Field of Finance

Career Area	Function
Financial management	Manage the finances of a business firm. Analyze, forecast, and plan a firm's finances; assess risk; evaluate and select investments; decide where and when to find money sources, and how much money to raise; and determine how much money to return to investors in the business.
Financial markets	Handle the flow of money in financial markets and institutions, and focus on the impact of interest rates on the flow of that money.
Investments	Locate, select, and manage money-producing assets for individuals and groups.

The Role of the Financial Manager

Financial managers measure the firm's performance, determine what the financial consequences will be if the firm maintains its present course or changes it, and recommend how the firm should use its assets. Financial managers also locate external financing sources and recommend the most beneficial mix of financing sources, and they determine the financial expectations of the firm's owners.

All financial managers must be able to communicate, analyze, and make decisions based on information from many sources. To do this, they need to be able to analyze financial statements, forecast and plan, and determine the effect of size, risk, and timing of cash flows. We will cover all of these skills in this text. Finance at Work 1-1 on pages 8–9 illustrates the skills needed by financial managers in the retail food industry.

Finance in the Organization of the Firm Financial managers work closely with other types of managers. For instance, they rely on accountants for raw financial data and on marketing managers for information about products and sales. Financial managers coordinate with technology experts to determine how to communicate financial information to others in the firm. Financial managers also provide advice and recommendations to top management.

Figure 1-1 shows how finance fits into a typical business firm's organization.

The Organization of the Finance Team In most medium-to-large businesses, a chief financial officer (CFO) supervises a team of employees who manage the financial activities of the firm. One common way to organize a finance team in a medium-to-large business is shown in Figure 1-2.

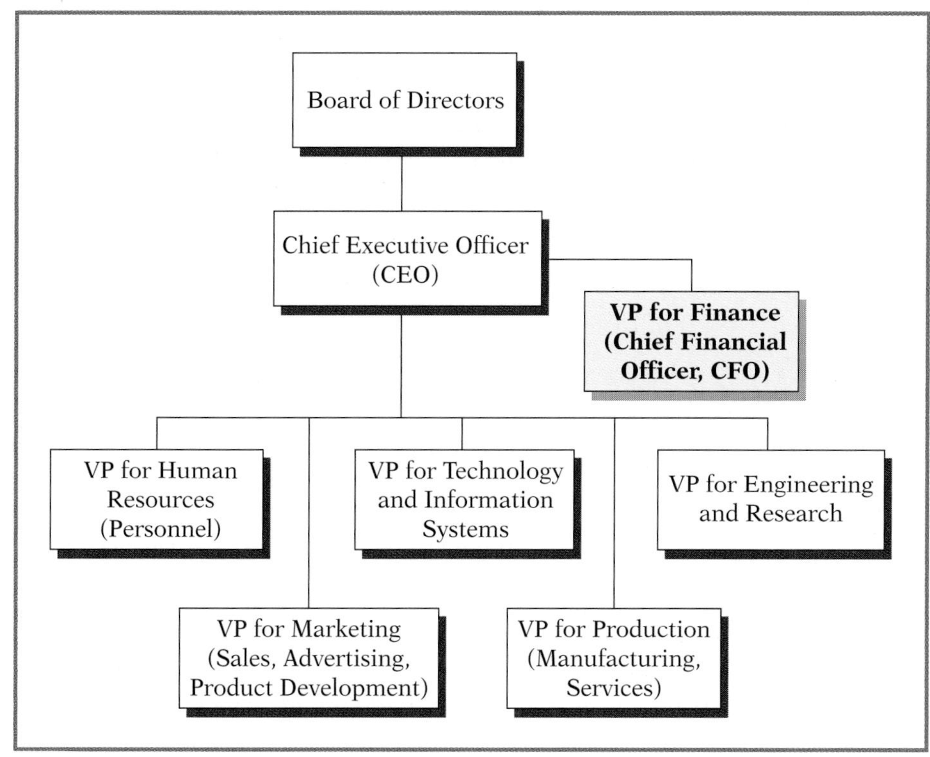

Figure 1-1 The Organization of a Typical Corporation
Figure 1-1 shows how finance fits into a typical business organization. The vice president for finance, or chief financial officer, operates with the vice presidents of the other business teams.

FINANCE AT WORK 1-1

Sales Retail Sports Media Technology Public Relations Production Exports

BRAD FORD, SENIOR ACCOUNTANT–INVENTORY CONTROL

BRAD FORD

Brad Ford, senior accountant for inventory control for Eagle Food Centers, is always amazed when he visits one of the local Eagle supermarkets. There are so many different types of items available, yet people continually ask him questions such as, "Why doesn't Eagle carry this brand of wine cooler?" or "How can you be out of Jiffy Pop popcorn?" As an accounting major, Brad never thought he would have to learn about different types of spices and vegetables, and he found it to be quite a challenge.

Q. As an accounting major, you must find it interesting that you became an inventory control specialist for a grocery store chain. How did that occur?

I originally graduated with a finance degree. With this degree, I gained experience as a banking examiner for the federal government. I then went back to school to earn an accounting degree. With these additional credentials, I went to work for a nationally known mortgage-banking firm before joining Eagle Foods in 1998. I have found the financial experience I have gained in my previous positions to be invaluable in performing my current job responsibilities.

Q. What are your responsibilities at Eagle Food Centers?

I have varied responsibilities, including inventory control, gross margin reporting, contract maintenance, and income statement allowance reporting. The major portion of my time is spent reporting and analyzing store gross margin results for our 64 stores.

Q. How important is inventory in the retail food business?

Just walk into your neighbourhood grocery store and this question pretty much answers itself. Inventory is the core of our business and industry. A typical Eagle store carries over 23,000 items, including food, health and beauty care, and specialty department items such as floral, deli, and pharmacy. Our job is to make sure that the customer is presented with a top-quality image of our merchandise that keeps them returning to our stores often. The food retailing business is highly competitive. Being able to provide the widest variety and the freshest selection is extremely important, though doing this profitably can be a challenge.

Q. How do you monitor store performance?

We monitor the sales of our stores daily through "flash sal reporting. This information is entered into a system along w the costs of purchasing inventory to arrive at key profitab measures such as sales, cost of sales, and gross margin. information is reported to top management and sales pers nel weekly to ensure that any problems and concerns addressed in a timely manner and corrected. We also hav contract with an inventory service to provide professional i counts at each store on a quarterly basis. Based on the c tractor's count information, we determine how much "shri (spoilage, theft) has occurred in the current cycle. Along w increasing sales and maintaining customer service, reduc shrink is a critical factor contributing to the bottom line of company and increasing shareholder value.

Q. What are some things average people may not rea about the grocery industry when they go on their we shopping trip?

There is much more going on behind the scenes than the ical customer realizes. For example, in some cases, suppl pay grocery stores to display the supplier's products. A sup may come in and say, "I will give you US$2 million to ex sively display our product over a five-year period." If the s agrees, then a contract is signed, the product is displayed, the $2 million is amortized over the life of the contract. provides a source of revenue beyond that achieved at checkout lane. Another example is how bananas are prepa for sale. First, they are brought into our warehouse, where are passed through a gas chamber to ripen them. Then are shipped by truck to our stores, displayed for sale for a s period of time, and then replaced due to their highly perish nature.

Q. How does a store end up being out of Jiffy Pop or w out a customer's favourite brand of pop?

Products come in many different brands and flavours that constantly changing. For us to carry an item there first ne to be demand for it in order to warrant shelf space. The p uct then must be ordered and tracked by store personn ensure that there is always an adequate supply but no excessive buildup of inventory. This is a delicate balancing Also, many items are seasonal, which makes it even more ficult. For example, Jiffy Pop popcorn is especially pop during heavy camping weekends. That factor must be ta into account when determining order volumes to meet tomer demand.

Q. From your perspective, what are the most important skills that college students in accounting or finance should learn?

is very important to learn the basics. In my position, a thor-gh understanding of general ledger accounts and the fects they have on the income statement are critical to the conciliation and publishing of financial statements. Further, cause our company is a public corporation, it is essential to mplete the closing process in a timely manner so that SEC-imposed guidelines are met. For this reason, one of the most important characteristics I look for in recent college graduates is the ability to complete tasks accurately and on time. A second characteristic that I look for is a strong sense of ethics. This is important because of the large volume of sensitive information that finance professionals are faced with every day.

Source: Interview with Brad Ford

In Figure 1-2, we see that the **chief financial officer** (CFO) directs and coordinates the financial activities of the firm. The CFO supervises a treasurer and a controller. The **treasurer** generally is responsible for cash management, credit management, and financial planning activities, whereas the **controller** is responsible for cost accounting, financial accounting, and information system activities. The treasurer and the controller of a large corporation are both likely to have a group of junior financial managers reporting to them.

At a small firm, one or two people may perform all the duties of the treasurer and controller. In very small firms, one person may perform all functions, including finance.

The Basic Financial Goal of the Firm

The financial manager's basic job is to make decisions that add value to the firm. When asked what the basic goal of a firm is, many people will answer, "to make a lot of money" or "to maximize profits." Although no one would argue that profits are not important, the single-minded pursuit of profits is not necessarily good for the firm and its owners. We will explain why this is so in the following sections. For now, let's say that a better way to express the primary financial goal of a business firm is to "maximize the wealth of the firm's owners." This is an extremely important, even crucial, point, so we will say it again: *The primary financial goal of the business firm is to maximize the wealth of the firm's owners.*

Figure 1-2 An Example of How to Organize a Finance Team
This chart shows how to organize a finance team in a medium-to-large business. Most teams include both a finance function (on the left) and an accounting function (on the right). The chief financial officer usually reports to the CEO, as shown in Figure 1-1.

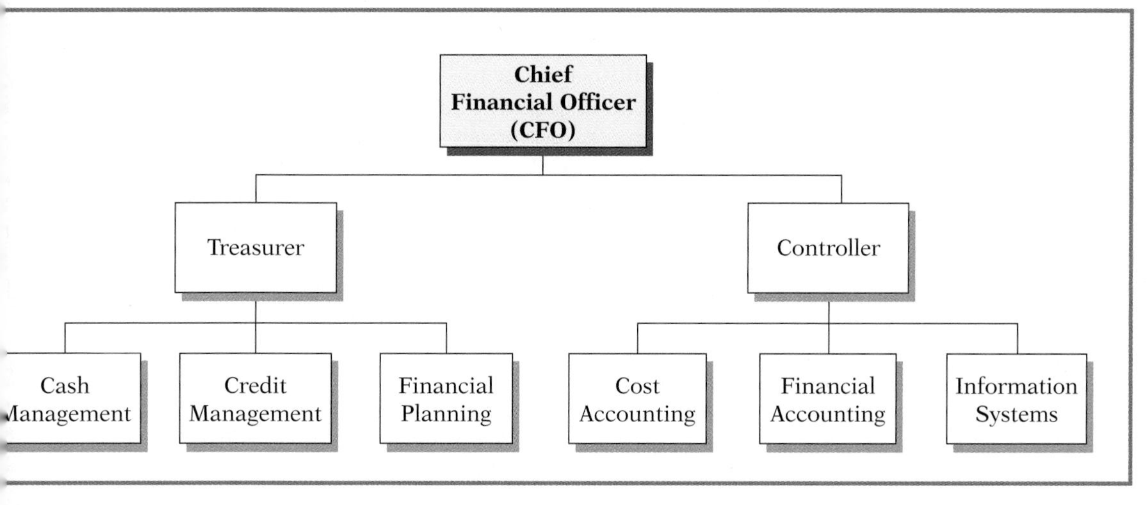

Everything the financial manager does—indeed, all the actions of everyone in the firm—should be directed toward this goal, subject to legal and ethical considerations that we will discuss in this chapter and throughout the book.

Now, what do we mean by wealth? **Wealth** refers to value. If a group of people owns a business firm, the contribution that firm makes to that group's wealth is determined by the market value of that firm.

This is a very important point: We have defined wealth in terms of *value*. The concept of value, then, is of fundamental importance in finance. Financial managers and researchers spend a lot of time measuring value and figuring out what causes it to increase or decrease.

In Search of Value

We have said that the basic goal of the business firm is to maximize the wealth of the firm's owners—that is, to maximize the value of the firm. The next question, then, is how to measure the value of the firm.

The value of a firm is determined by whatever people are willing to pay for it. The more valuable people think a firm is, the more they will pay to own it. Then the existing owners can sell it to investors for more than their original purchase price, thereby increasing current owner wealth. The financial manager's job is to make decisions that will cause people to think more favourably about the firm and, in turn, to be willing to pay more to purchase the business.

For companies that sell shares to the general public, the price can indicate the value of a business because *shareholders*—people who purchase corporate shares—become part owners of the corporation. (We will discuss shares in greater detail in Chapter 2.) People will pay a higher price for shares—that is, part ownership of a business—if they believe the company will perform well in the future. For instance, Yahoo, a developer of Internet access software, originally sold its shares for US$3.25 (adjusted for two 2–1 splits). (A share is one unit of ownership.) Because of the potential of its Internet services, it was worth more than US$152 per share in February 1999. This was not too bad for a company that had losses for most of its history until it turned a slight quarterly profit in 1998. Investors were betting on a bright future for Yahoo.

For businesses that sell shares publicly, then, the financial manager's basic role is to help make the firm's shares more valuable. Although some businesses do not sell shares to the general public, we will focus on share price as a measure of the value of the firm. Keep in mind, however, that investing in one share (one unit) means the investor only owns one small piece of a firm. Many firms sell hundreds of thousands or millions of shares, so the total value of the firm is the equivalent of the sum of all the shares' values.

Next, let us look closely at three factors that affect the value of a firm's share price: cash flow, timing, and risk.

The Importance of Cash Flow In business, cash is what pays the bills. It is also what the firm receives in exchange for its products and services. Cash is, therefore, of ultimate importance, and the expectation that the firm will generate cash in the future is one of the factors that gives the firm its value.

We use the term *cash flow* to describe cash moving through a business. Financial managers concentrate on increasing cash *in*flows—cash that flows into a business—and decreasing cash *out*flows—cash that flows away from a business. Cash outflows will be approved if they result in cash inflows of sufficient magnitude and if those inflows have acceptable timing and risk.

It is important to realize that sales are not the same as cash inflows. Businesses often sell goods and services on credit, so no cash changes hands at the time of the sale. If the cash from the sale is never collected, the sale cannot add any value to the firm. Owners care about actual cash collections from sales—that is, cash inflows.

Likewise, businesses may buy goods and services to keep firms running but may make the purchases on credit, so no cash changes hands at that time. However, bills always come due sooner or later, so owners care about cash expenditures for purchases—cash outflows. For any business firm (assuming other factors remain constant), the higher the expected cash inflows and the lower the expected cash outflows, the more positive impact there will be on the firm's share price.

Take Note

The point about cash received sooner being better than cash received later works in reverse, too: It is better to pay out cash later rather than sooner (all other factors being equal, of course).

The Effect of Timing on Cash Flows The timing of cash flows also affects a firm's value. To illustrate, consider this: Would you rather receive $100 cash today and $0 one year from now, or would you rather receive $0 cash today and $100 one year from now? The two alternatives follow:

	Today	*One Year from Now*
Alternative A	+$100	$0
Alternative B	$0	+$100

Both alternatives promise the same total amount of cash, but most people would choose Alternative A because they realize they could invest the $100 received today and earn interest on it during the year. By doing so, they would end up with more money than $100 at the end of the year. For this reason, we say that—all other factors being equal—cash received sooner is better than cash received later.

Owners and potential investors look at when firms can expect to receive cash and when they can expect to pay out cash. All other factors being equal, the sooner a company expects to receive cash and the later it expects to pay out cash, the more valuable the firm and the higher its share price will be.

The Influence of Risk We have seen that the size of a firm's expected cash inflows and outflows and the timing of those cash flows influence the value of the firm and its share price. Now let us consider how risk affects the firm's value and its share price.

Risk affects value because the less certain owners and investors are about a firm's expected future cash flows, the lower they will value the company. The more certain owners and investors are about a firm's expected future cash flows, the higher they will value the company. In short, companies in which expected future cash flows are doubtful will have lower values than companies in which expected future cash flows are virtually certain.

What is not nearly as clear as the *way* risk affects value is *how much* risk affects value. For example, if one company's cash flows are twice as risky as another company's cash flows, is its share worth half as much? We cannot say. In fact, we have a tough time quantifying just how risky the companies are in the first place.

Table 1-2 Accomplishing the Primary Financial Goal of the Firm

The Goal:	Maximize the wealth of the firm's owners
Measure of the Goal:	Value of the firm (measured by the price of the share on the open market for corporations)
Factor	**Effect on Share Price**
Size of expected future cash flows	Larger future cash inflows raise the share price. Larger cash outflows lower the share price. Smaller future cash inflows lower the share price. Smaller future cash outflows raise the share price.
Timing of future cash flows	Cash inflows expected sooner result in a higher share price. Cash inflows expected later result in a lower share price. (The opposite effect occurs for future cash outflows.)
Riskiness of future cash flows	When the degree of risk associated with future cash flows goes down, share price goes up. When the degree of risk associated with future cash flows goes up, share price goes down.

We will examine the issue of risk in some detail in Chapter 7. For now, it is sufficient to remember that risk affects share price—as risk increases, share price goes down; and conversely, as risk decreases, share price goes up.

Table 1-2 summarizes the influences of cash flow size, timing, and risk on share prices.

Profits versus Share Value Earlier in the chapter, we said that the single-minded pursuit of profits is not necessarily good for the firm's owners. Indeed, the firm's owners view share value, not profit, as the appropriate measure of wealth. Share value depends on future cash flows, their timing, and their riskiness. Profit calculations do not consider these three factors. Profit, as defined in accounting, is simply the difference between sales revenue and expenses. If all we were interested in were profits, we could simply start using high-pressure sales techniques, cut all expenses to the bone, and then point proudly to the resulting increase in profits. For the moment, anyway. In all probability, managers practising such techniques would find their firm out of business later when the quality of the firm's products, services, and workforce dropped, eventually leading to declining sales and market share.

It is true that more profits are generally better than fewer profits. But when the pursuit of short-term profits adversely affects the size of future cash flows, their timing, or their riskiness, then these profit maximization efforts are detrimental to the firm. Concentrating on share value, not profits, is a better measure of financial success.

Legal and Ethical Challenges in Financial Management

Several legal and ethical challenges influence financial managers as they pursue the goal of wealth maximization for the firm's owners. Examples of legal considerations include environmental statutes mandating pollution control equipment, workplace safety standards that must be met, human rights that must be obeyed, and intellectual property laws that regulate the use of others' ideas.

Ethical concerns include fair treatment of employees, customers, the community, and society as a whole. Indeed, many businesses have written ethics codes that articulate the ethical values of the business organization.

Three legal and ethical influences of special note include the agency problem, the interests of non-owner stakeholders, and the interests of society as a whole. We will turn to these issues next.

Agency Issues

The financial manager and the other managers of a business firm are agents for the owners of the firm. An agent is a person who has the implied or actual authority to act on behalf of another. The owners whom the agents represent are the principals. For example, the board of directors and senior management of Telus, a well-known Canadian telecommunications company, are agents for the Telus shareholders, the principals. Agents have a legal and ethical responsibility to make decisions that further the interests of the principals.

The interests of the principals are supposed to be paramount when agents make decisions, but this is often easier said than done. For example, the managing director of a corporation might like the convenience of a private jet that is on call 24 hours a day, but do the common shareholder owners of the corporation receive enough value to justify the cost of a jet? It looks like the interests of the managing director (the agent) and the interests of the common shareholder owners (the principals) of the corporation are in conflict in this case.

The Agency Problem When the interests of the agents and principals conflict, an agency problem results. In our jet example, an agency problem occurs if the managing director buys the jet, even though he knows the benefits to the shareholders do not justify the cost.

Another example of an agency problem occurs when managers must decide whether to undertake a project with a high potential payoff but high risk. Even if the project is more likely to be successful than not, managers may not want to take a risk that owners would be willing to take. Why? An unsuccessful project may result in such significant financial loss that the managers who approved the project lose their jobs—and all the income from their paycheques. The owners, however, may have a much smaller risk because their investment in company share represents only a small fraction of their financial investment package. Because the risk is so much larger to the manager as compared to the shareholder, a promising but somewhat risky project may be rejected even though it is likely to benefit the firm's owners.

The agency problem can be lessened by tying the managers' compensation to the performance of the company and its share price. This tie brings the interests of the managers and those of the firm's owners closer together. That is why companies often make shares a part of the compensation package offered to managers, especially top executives. If managers are also shareholders, then the agency problem should be reduced.

Agency Costs At times, firms spend time and money to monitor and reduce agency problems. These outlays of time and money are **agency costs**. One common example of an agency cost is an accounting audit of a corporation's financial statements. If a business is owned and operated by the same person, the owner does not need an audit—she can trust herself to report her finances accurately. Most companies of any size, however, have agency costs because managers, not owners, report the finances. Owners audit the company financial statements to see whether the agents have acted in the owners' interests by reporting finances accurately.

The Interests of Other Groups

Shareholders and managers are not the only groups that have a stake in a business firm. There are also nonmanager workers, creditors, suppliers, customers, and members of the community where the business is located. These groups are also **stakeholders**—people who have a "stake" in the business. Although the

INTERNATIONAL PERSPECTIVES IN FINANCE 1-1

Melanie Rosen, Electronic Media, *The New York Times*

MELANIE ROSEN

Melanie Rosen is the director of Electronic Media for The New York Times Informational Services Group. She runs a new company within The New York Times *that produces educational products for schools. One product is called* Live from the Past. *Live from the Past takes historical articles from* The New York Times *and converts them to digital format so articles and videotapes from actual events can be used in the classroom, online, from a CD, or in any other electronic format. Melanie is a natural for this type of endeavour because she was a communications/graphics major in college and then earned an MBA.*

Q. What are some of your daily responsibilities?

Two main aspects of my business are production and finance. Production involves figuring out how to combine many types of media to create the best product possible. To create such a product, though, I have to know the financial impact of what I invest in—will the company benefit from my production decisions?

Q. In effect, you are starting a new company within The New York Times. How would you describe what you do?

I function as a general manager, financial manager, product manager, and sales manager, all under one hat. About 50 percent to 60 percent of my time is devoted to financial management. That is, I constantly evaluate the finances of the product line. I try to assess how much money it will cost to design and produce a product, how much it will cost to m ket it, how much of the product we will produce, what risks are, and what our revenues will be.

I budget and monitor my group's performa against its budgeted, or forecasted, performance. I'm responsible for keeping management informed about much money our group has invested so far, how much m we expect to invest, how much money we expect to ge ate, and when.

Q. How supportive is The New York Times of your " company"?

When a product like *Live from the Past* is in start-up m the company is always supportive. Management tries to vide the opportunity to make as much money as poss but there are constraints. Most corporations like to see businesses become profitable in the third year. In fact, m corporations try to push for a two-year time frame. Th because companies are concerned about cash flowing investments without seeing an accompanying return f the investment.

Q. What basic financial "tools" would you suggest fu business people should master?

I'd recommend students should understand some b financial concepts when they leave college. Business pe need to be able to read and understand financial stateme including the cash flow statement. Only then will they un stand how much money the business has before and taxes, where the money is going, and what the timing those cash flows. Too many businesses fail because of cash flow.

Source: Interview with Melanie Rosen.

primary financial goal of the firm is to maximize the wealth of the owners, the interests of these other stakeholders can influence business decisions.

One example of outside stakeholder influence is pressure from political lobbyists or consumer groups. For instance, Magic Johnson, basketball star of the Los Angeles Lakers partnered with Sony to assist a neighbourhood in Los Angeles that had been severely damaged in the events following the original Rodney King beating trial. No company was willing to run the risk of operating a movie theatre in the area because the risk of property damage was so high.[3] So—despite the risk of monetary loss—Magic Johnson and Sony built a clean, safe movie theatre in the neighbourhood, offering job opportunities as well as first-run films.

It was such a successful venture, both for the L.A. neighbourhood and its founders, that Magic and Sony plan to build similar theatres in the inner cities of Atlanta, New York, Chicago, Washington, and Houston.[4] In March 1998, Magic, singer Janet Jackson, and music executive Jheryl Busby bought a majority interest in Founders National Bank of Los Angeles. They paid $2.5 million. This black-owned bank is seeking deposits from African American leaders and from residents of minority communities.[5]

The Interests of Society as a Whole

Sometimes the interests of a business firm's owners are not the same as the interests of society. For instance, the cost of properly disposing of toxic waste can be so high that companies may be tempted to simply dump their waste in nearby rivers. In so doing, the companies can keep costs low and profits high, and drive their share prices higher at least in the short term (if they are not caught). However, many people suffer from the polluted environment. This is why we have environmental and other similar laws—so that society's best interests take precedence over the interests of individual company owners.

When businesses take a long-term view, the interests of the owners and society often (but not always) coincide. When companies encourage recycling, sponsor programs for disadvantaged young people, run media campaigns promoting the responsible use of alcohol, and contribute money to worthwhile social causes, the goodwill generated as a result of these activities can lead to long-term increases in the firm's sales and cash flows. These actions translate into additional wealth for the firm's owners.

Although the traditional primary economic goal of the firm is to maximize shareholder wealth, the unbridled pursuit of value is too simplistic a view of this goal. Firms often take into account ethical factors, the interests of other stakeholders, and the long-term interests of society.[6] (See Figure 1-3.)

---

[3]Interview with Taylor Brangh, public relations director of Magic Johnson Enterprises, Inc., January 10, 1996; Kenneth Noble (January 8, 1996), "Magic Johnson Finding Success in a New Forum," *The New York Times*, 8.

[4]Noble, Magic Johnson, 8.

[5]Brown, A. (August 1988). Creating a Little "Magic" at Founders. *Black Enterprise*, 17.

[6]Not everyone agrees with this approach. Milton Friedman, Nobel laureate in economics, claims that any action taken by a manager that is not legally mandated and that reduces the value available to the owners, is theft.

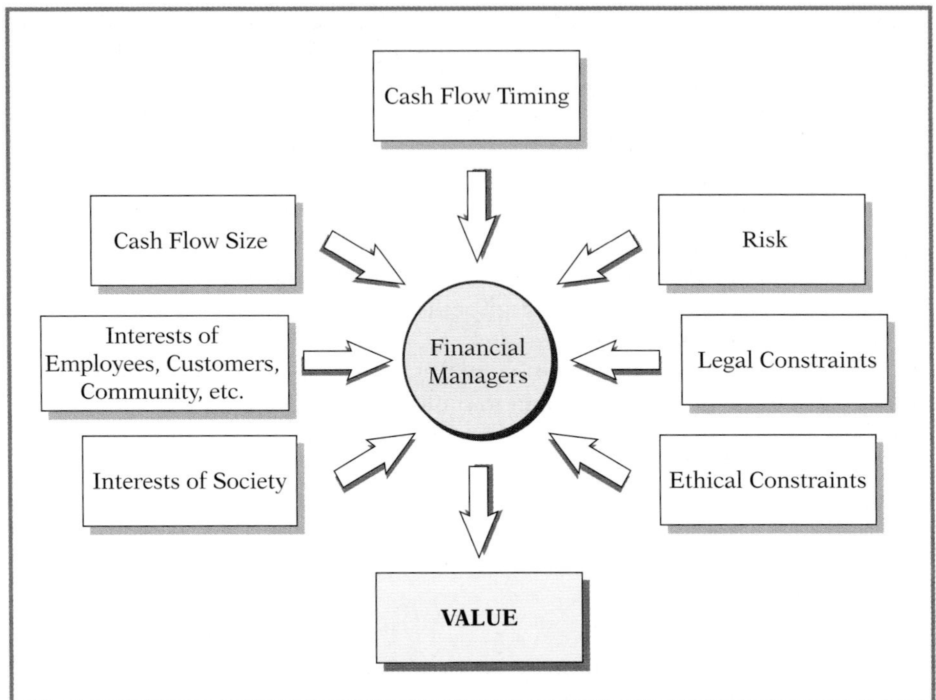

Figure 1-3
Influences on Financial Managers
This figure summarizes the various influences that financial managers may consider in their pursuit of value.

Forms of Business Organization

Businesses can be organized in a variety of ways. The three most common types of organization are proprietorships, partnerships, and corporations. The distinguishing characteristics give each form its own advantages and disadvantages.

The Proprietorship

The simplest way to organize a business is to form a **proprietorship**, a business owned by one person. An individual raises some money, finds a location from which to operate, and starts selling a product or service. A profit and loss statement for the business is included as a part of the owner's personal tax return. The sole proprietor is responsible for any tax liability generated by the business, and the tax rates are those that apply to an individual. Sole proprietorships represent the most common form of business organization in Canada.

The sole proprietor has *unlimited liability* for matters relating to the business. This means that the sole proprietor is responsible for all the obligations of the business, even if those obligations exceed the amount the proprietor has invested in the business. If a customer is injured on the company premises and sues for $1 million, the sole proprietor must pay that amount if the court awards it to the plaintiff customer. This is true even if the total amount invested by the sole proprietor in the business is only $10,000.

Although unlimited liability is a major disadvantage of a proprietorship, liability insurance is often available to reduce the risk of losing business and non-business assets. However, the risk always remains that the business will be unsuccessful and that the losses incurred will exceed the amount of money invested by the proprietor. The other assets owned by the proprietor will then be at risk.

The Partnership

Two or more people may join together to form a business as a **partnership**. This can be done on an informal basis without a written partnership agreement, or a contract can spell out the rights and responsibilities of each partner. This written contract is called the *partnership agreement* and is strongly recommended in order to lessen the likelihood of disputes between partners.

The partnership agreement generally spells out how much money each partner will contribute to the business, what the ownership share of each partner will be, how profits and losses will be allocated among partners, who will perform what work for the business, and other matters of concern to the partners. The percent of ownership for each partner does not have to be the same as the percent each partner invests in the partnership.

Each partner in a partnership is usually liable for the activities of the partnership as a whole. This also means in the event that the partnership assets are insufficient to cover partnership liabilities, personal assets of all partners may be seized and liquidated.[7] This is an important point. Even if there are 100 partners, each one is technically responsible for all the debts of the partnership. If 99 partners declare personal bankruptcy, the hundredth partner still is responsible for all the partnership's debts. This is known as joint liability.

Special Kinds of Partnerships There are two types of partnerships: the limited partnership (LP) and the limited liability partnership (LLP). Many provinces such as Ontario, Alberta, Saskatchewan, Manitoba, Quebec, and Nova Scotia have amended their incorporation acts to allow for these types of partnerships. However, these business forms cannot be created informally and require written partnership agreements, which need to be filed at appropriate provincial offices. The purpose of filing is to provide a notice to the public about the partnership structure and identify the party responsible for its daily operations (i.e., the general partner).

In a **limited partnership**, there are two classes of partners: general partners and limited partners. The general partners usually actively participate in the management of the business whereas limited partners do not. Limited partners usually contribute capital and share in the profits but take no part in running the business—they are passive investors. As a result, general partners usually contract for a more favourable allocation of ownership and profits compared with limited partners. General partners have unlimited liability for the partnership activities. Limited partners are only liable for the amount they invest in the partnership. If you are a limited partner who invests $5,000 in the business, then $5,000 is the most you can lose. For this reason, every partnership must have at least one general partner (a partnership could have all general partners, but it could not have all limited partners). This business form has been mostly used as an investment vehicle where limited partners provide capital into the business and the general partner manages and operates the investment for a fixed compensation. These types of partnerships are common in real estate development and fund management.

Another form of the partnership is the **limited liability partnership**. This business form was designed for situations where partners seek to limit their

[7]See the discussion that follows on general and limited partners.

liabilities but for whatever reason are not able to form a corporation. This form of business organization is simply a general partnership that is allowed to operate like a corporation with limited liability features much like those of a corporation. Professionals such as lawyers, accountants, or medical doctors commonly use this business form. Let's take an example here to better make the distinction between LLP and other types of partnerships. Let's imagine that medical doctors form a limited liability partnership. Under the LLP agreement, all partners (all medical doctors) have unlimited liability for ordinary business debts or obligations accumulated by an LLP during its regular course of business. However, compared to other types of partnerships, a partner (a medical doctor) may not be liable for the negligence or malpractice of another doctor. You can imagine how useful this protection can be.

The partnership is not considered as a separate legal entity and it does not pay any taxes. A partner will pay taxes on her or his share of the profits and file an individual tax return. The partners pay any taxes owed. The partnership itself is not taxed because the income merely passes through the partnership to the partners where it is taxed.

The Corporation

The third major form of business organization is the corporation. Unlike proprietorships and partnerships, corporations are legal entities separate from their owners. To form a corporation, the owners specify the governing rules for the running of the business in a contract known as the *articles of incorporation*, or the memorandum of association, or the letters patent, depending on the province of incorporation. They submit the articles or their equivalent to the appropriate government office or agency in which the corporation is formed, and the government issues the corporation's "birth certificate" or its certificate of incorporation that creates the separate legal entity. Companies may choose to be incorporated provincially under applicable provincial statutes or federally under the Canada Business Corporations Act.

Corporations are taxed as separate legal entities. That is, corporations must pay their own income tax just as if they were individuals. This is where the often-discussed "double taxation" of corporate profits comes into play. First, a corporation pays income tax on the profit it earns. Then the corporation may distribute to the owners the profits that are left after paying taxes. These distributions, called dividends, count as investment income for the owners and are taxed on the individual owners' income tax returns. Thus, the Canada Revenue Agency collects taxes twice on the same income. However, the CRA recognizes the double taxation issue and therefore offers a dividend tax credit to reduce the taxes otherwise payable on these dividends.

Double taxation of dividends is bad news for the owners of corporations, but there is good news as well. Shareholders, the corporation's owners, have limited liability for the corporation's activities. They cannot lose more than the amount they paid to buy the shares. This makes the corporate form of organization very attractive to owners who desire to shelter their personal assets from creditors of the business.

Corporations have other benefits too. For example, because they exist separately from their owners, they can "live" beyond the death of their original owners. Another benefit of the corporate form of business is that corporations generally have a professional management team and board of directors, elected by the owners. It is the board's job to look out for the interests of the owners (the shareholders). Shareholders, especially in the case of large corporations, usually do not take an active role in the management of the business, so it is the board of directors' job to represent them.

Table 1-3 summarizes the advantages and disadvantages of the various forms of business organization.

Special Kinds of Corporations There are two variations of the corporation: private and public.

A **private corporation** is generally owned by a small group of shareholders, such as employees, family members or management and it is often regarded as closely held. These corporations are not allowed to offer shares for sale to the general public. Other restrictions may also apply: there may be restrictions on the transfer of shares and the number of shareholders may be limited. Many new corporations begin their life in this manner due to lower incorporation

Table 1-3
Characteristics of Business Ownership Forms

	Sole Proprietorship	**Partnerships**		**Corporations**	
		Limited (LP)	**Limited Liability (LLP)**	**Public**	**Private**
of formation	Easy	Relatively easy, but written agreement needed	Relatively easy	Complex—articles of association or equivalent and additional documentation needed	Less complex than for public corporation
of desired nation	Settling debts	More complex depending on partnership agreement	Same as in LP	Difficult and complex	Less complex and difficult than for public corporation
f firm	Terminates on death or sale	Terminates on death or withdrawal of general partner	Terminates on death or withdrawal of partner	In perpetuity	In perpetuity
r's liability	Unlimited	Unlimited for general partners, limited to invested capital to limited partners	Limited to invested capital	Limited	Limited
ate legal entity	No	No	No	Yes	Yes
e of control	Complete	Strong for general partners, weaker for limited partners	Partners' decision	Management control—separation of ownership and control	Management control—separation of ownership and control
	Based on personal income taxes	Based on personal income taxes	Based on personal income taxes	Corporate income tax and additional tax on dividends	Corporate income tax with potential for reduction on the first $200,000. Additional tax on dividends
fer of ship	Limited	Requires agreement of partners	Requires agreement of partners	Unlimited	May be restricted

costs and documentation simplicity while taking advantage of limited liability. Smaller companies that do not intend to raise additional external financing in the foreseeable future use these corporations. An added advantage for these corporations is that the *Income Tax Act* allows for a reduction of the income tax rate on the first $200,000 of taxable income. In effect, a private corporation may pay half of the regular corporate rate on this income but a normal tax rate on the remaining amount of taxable income. Examples of private corporations may be McCain Foods, Irving, Ledcor, and Holt Renfrew.

A **public corporation**, often referred to as a widely held corporation, issues shares to the public and is subject to the relevant provincial securities regulations. These shares trade on a public stock exchange. The corporation has flexibility to issue additional shares through the initial public offering (IPO) or private placement. A public corporation may trade on more than one exchange. Examples of public corporations are WestJet, EnCana, Nortel Networks, and Barrick Gold Corporation.

SUMMARY

1-1 Describe the field of finance.

Finance is important to business people. Financial decisions about how to raise, spend, and allocate money can affect every aspect of a business—from personnel to products. Finance also offers career opportunities in three main areas: financial management, financial markets and institutions, and investments. Financial management focuses on managing the finances of a business.

1-2 Summarize five of the main duties of financial managers.

Financial managers use accounting information and economic principles to guide their financial decisions. They measure the firm's financial condition, forecast, budget, raise funds, and determine the financial goals of the firm's owners. They also work closely with other managers to further the firm's goals.

In medium and large firms, more than one person usually handles the financial management duties. In some firms, a chief financial officer (CFO) supervises the financial activities including cash and credit management, financial planning, and accounting.

1-3 Identify the basic goal of a business firm.

The basic goal of the business firm is to maximize the wealth of the firm's owners by adding value; it is not to maximize profits. The value of a firm is measured by the price investors are willing to pay to own the firm. For businesses that sell shares to the general public, share price indicates the firm's value because shares are units of ownership. So the basic financial goal of such firms is to maximize the price of the firm's shares.

1-4 List three important factors that affect the value of a firm.

The value of a firm is affected by the size of future cash flows, their timing, and their riskiness.

- Cash inflows increase a firm's value, whereas cash outflows decrease it.
- The sooner cash flows are expected to be received, the greater the value. The later those cash flows are expected, the less the value.
- The less risk associated with future cash flows, the higher the value. The more risk, the lower the value.

1-5 Summarize three main legal and ethical challenges faced by financial managers.

Legal and ethical considerations include the agency problem, the interests of other stakeholders, and the interests of society as a whole.

- The agency problem exists when the interests of a firm's managers (the agents) are in conflict with those of the firm's owners (the principals).
- Other stakeholders whose interests are often considered in financial decisions include employees, customers, and members of the communities in which the firm's plants are located.
- Concerns of society as a whole—such as environmental or health problems—often influence business financial decisions.

1-6 Identify three of the different forms of business organization.

The three most common forms of business organization are the proprietorship, the partnership, and the corporation.

- Proprietorships are businesses owned by one person. The owner is exposed to unlimited liability for the firm's debts.
- Partnerships are businesses owned by two or more people, each of whom is responsible for the firm's debts. The exception is a limited partner, a partner who contracts for limited liability.
- Corporations are separate legal entities. They are owned by shareholders that are responsible for the firm's debts only to the extent of their investment. A corporation can be private or public. Only public corporations are listed on stock exchanges.

SELF-TEST

ST-1. What are the three main areas of career opportunities in finance?

ST-2. What are the primary responsibilities of a person holding the title of treasurer at a large corporation?

ST-3. Who is a "principal" in an agent–principal relationship?

ST-4. What legal and ethical factors may influence a firm's financial decisions?

ST-5. What is an LLP?

ST-6. What is a private corporation? Give an example of a Canadian private corporation.

REVIEW QUESTIONS

1. How is finance related to the disciplines of accounting and economics?
2. List and describe the three career opportunities in the field of finance.
3. Describe the duties of the financial manager in a business firm.
4. What is the basic goal of a business?
5. List and explain the three financial factors that influence the value of a business.
6. Explain why striving to achieve accounting profits and maximizing share value are not the same.
7. What is an agent? What are the responsibilities of an agent?
8. Describe how society's interests can influence financial managers.
9. Briefly define the terms *proprietorship, partnership,* and *corporation.*
10. Compare and contrast the potential liability of owners of proprietorships, partnerships (general partners), and corporations.

PROBLEMS

The Field of Finance ▶

1-1. Explain the difference between what an accountant does and what a financial analyst does.

Financial Management ▶

1-2. Describe the basic role of a financial manager in a firm that sells shares publicly.

The Basic Financial Goal of the Firm ▶

1-3. How would the value of a firm be affected by the following events?

a. The introduction of a new product designed to increase the firm's cash inflows is delayed by one year. The size of the expected cash flows is not affected.

b. A firm announces to the press that its cash earnings for the coming year will be 10 percent higher than previously forecast.

c. A utility company acquires a natural gas exploration company. After the acquisition, 50 percent of the new company's assets are from the original utility company and 50 percent are from the new exploration company.

Legal and Ethical Challenges in Financial Management ▶

1-4. Tornado Capital is an investment firm located in Montreal. The fund has made over 30 investments in companies, mostly in Eastern Canada. The investment firm uses a standard template as the basis for an agreement between the owners of the companies they invest in and the venture capital fund. These agreements are also used for the basis of creating company by-laws governing the relationship between the shareholders and management. Please note that in many of the companies Tornado Capital invests in, senior managers are also owners of the company. Tornado Capital's agreements contain the following clause: "Special Board Approval: The consent of a majority of the Board including at least one member appointed by Tornado Capital will be required for the following:

a. Setting up and modifying compensation program and employment agreements for top management;

b. Approval of any share option program;

c. Granting of loans or financial assistance to, or entering into any contracts not in the normal course of business with, employees, directors, or related parties;

d. Any change to the operating authorities of any bank account including the appointment of any signatories."

Why are such clauses standardly used by Tornado Capital? Why would it be important to use these clauses in company by-laws?

Legal and Ethical Challenges in Financial Management ▶

1-5. In a corporate setting, should owners or shareholders be allowed the appointment as CEO? Discuss.

Legal and Ethical Challenges in Financial Management ▶

1-6. Should the chairman of the board of directors be allowed to be appointed as CEO? Discuss possible conflicts of interest as well as advantages and disadvantages of such an arrangement.

Forms of Business Organization ▶

1-7. John Kudelski is a portfolio manager at one of the leading investment firms on Bay Street. He has over 20 years of experience and a successful track record of investments in companies in Canada and abroad. He focuses specifically on smaller firms with a high growth potential. Recently, John got together for coffee with Mark Scott, his old-time friend and fellow student from the University of Alberta. The two of them graduated from the University of Alberta with an MBA degree specializing in finance. Mark has been pursuing a career in the investment field as well but focused on larger companies. It turns out that Mark is in the process of establishing an investment firm and has already secured some financing from external sources—people who would be willing to provide anywhere from $1 million to $5 million for management. These individuals do not wish to take an active role in day-to-day management of the venture capital fund but trust Mark's investment talents. Mark decided to invite John to participate in the newly created firm. John would not be expected to bring any cash into the venture either, but he would be co-responsible for the firm's investment strategy. What would be the most suitable form of business organization for the new venture? Please provide your reasons.

1-8. David O'Brien wishes to start another business venture that focuses on provision of high speed Internet services to private businesses. David is expecting that the venture will require an initial investment of $5 million. He also estimates that in order to roll out his program of setting up a network of Internet services throughout Canada, the firm is likely to need another round of financing equal to $20 million. He expects that his venture, being a newly started company, is unlikely to get bank financing. David has also tried to raise additional capital from wealthy individuals but was not successful in his attempt. He expected that the company would need to be listed on a stock exchange. What type of corporation should he plan to organize (public or private) and why?

◀ Forms of Business Organization

1-9. Discuss the advantages and disadvantages of a sole proprietorship.

◀ Forms of Business Organization

1-10. Discuss the advantages and disadvantages of a limited partnership. Describe circumstances where this form of organization is most appropriate. In what types of industries are you likely to see this type of business organization being used?

◀ Forms of Business Organization

ANSWERS TO SELF-TEST

ST-1. Financial management, financial markets and institutions, and investments.

ST-2. The treasurer of a large corporation is responsible for cash management, credit management, and financial planning.

ST-3. A principal in an agent–principal relationship is the person who hires the agent to act on the principal's behalf. The principal is the person to whom the agent owes a duty.

ST-4. Legal and ethical factors influence businesses. Examples of legal constraints include environmental, safety, and common rights laws. Examples of ethical considerations include fair treatment of workers, environmental sensitivity, and support for the community.

ST-5. An LLP, or a limited liability partnership, is a form of partnership that allows its owners to limit its liabilities. In many respects, an LLP has many features of a corporation.

ST-6. A private corporation, often regarded as closely held, is generally owned by a small group of shareholders such as family members, members of a management team, or employees. The shares of this type of corporation are not allowed to be publicly traded. Other restrictions to share transfer also apply. An example of such a private corporation could be McCain Foods.

2

Financial Markets and Interest Rates

Chapter Objectives

After reading this chapter, you should be able to:

2-1 **Describe** how the Canadian financial system works and how financial intermediaries help in the process.

2-2 **Contrast** the three main differences between the primary market and the secondary market.

2-3 **Contrast** the different types of securities traded in the money market and the capital market.

2-4 **Analyze** the nominal interest rate and break it down into its three main components.

2-5 **Explain** what a yield curve is and what information can be derived from it.

"It is better to give than to lend, and it costs about the same."

—Philip Gibbs

THE FINANCIAL INDUSTRY

In the past, these institutions represented the "four pillars" of the Canadian financial sector: banks, trust companies, insurance companies, and investment dealers.

Until deregulation in 1987, financial institutions—allowed to operate in only one of these "pillars"—operated at arm's length from one another. Deregulation, along with increased global competition, led to a major restructuring of the industry. Institutions are now larger and cover a wider spectrum of services.

Under pressure to grow in order to meet competition effectively, many insurance and trust companies have consolidated, and significant cross-ownership is evident throughout the sector. Banks now own all major trust companies and most investment dealers.

With this convergence of financial institutions, one-stop shopping for financial services is now possible for Canadians. Banks and other institutions now cover everything from investment counselling to financial planning and estate and trust services.

Source: "The Economy: The Financial Industry," excerpted from Statistics Canada, *Canada E-Book*, Catalogue 11-404, May 26, 2003, available at http://142.206.72.67/03/03e/03e_001_e.html.

Chapter Overview

One of the central duties of a financial manager is to acquire capital—that is, to raise funds. Few companies are able to fund all their activities solely with funds from internal sources. Most find it necessary at times to seek funding from outside sources. For this reason, all business people need to know about financial markets.

As we see in this chapter, there are a number of financial markets and each offers a different kind of financial product. In this chapter, we discuss the relationship between firms and the financial markets and briefly explain how the financial system works including the role of *financial intermediaries*—investment bankers, brokers, and dealers. Next, we explore the markets themselves and describe financial products ranging from government bonds to corporate shares. Finally, we examine interest rates.

The Financial System

The current Canadian financial system attempts to bring together both suppliers and demanders of capital in a mutually beneficial manner. The major participants in this financial system are individuals, businesses, and governments where suppliers of funds are defined as those that have a greater income than they spend and demanders of funds are defined as those that spend more than their income can provide.

The financial system also makes it possible for participants to adjust their holdings of financial assets as their needs change. This is the *liquidity function* of the financial system—that is, the system allows funds to flow with ease.

To enable funds to move through the financial system, funds are exchanged for financial products called *securities*. A clear understanding of securities is essential to understanding the financial system, so before we go further, let's examine what securities are and how they are used.

Securities

Securities are documents that represent the right to receive funds in the future. The person or organization that holds a security is called a **bearer**. A security certifies that the bearer has a *claim* to future funds. For example, if you lend $100 to someone and the person gives you an IOU, you have a security. The IOU is your "claim check" for the $100 you are owed. The IOU may also state *when* you are to be paid, which is referred to as the **maturity date** of the security. When the date of payment occurs, we say the security matures.

Securities have value because the bearer has the right to be paid the amount specified, so a bearer who wanted some money right away could sell the security to someone else for cash. Of course, the new bearer could sell the security to someone else too, and so on down the line. When a security is sold to someone else, the security is being *traded*.

Business firms as well as municipalities, provinces, and the federal government sell securities to the public to raise money. After the initial sale, investors may sell the securities to other investors. As you might suspect, this can become a complicated business. Financial intermediaries facilitate this process. Markets are available for the subsequent traders to execute their transactions.

Financial Intermediaries

Financial intermediaries act as the grease that enables the machinery of the financial system to work smoothly. They specialize in certain services that would be difficult for individual participants to perform such as matching buyers and sellers of securities. Three types of financial intermediaries are investment bankers, brokers, and dealers.

Investment Bankers Institutions called **investment-banking firms** exist to help businesses, institutions, and governments sell their securities to the public.

Investment bankers arrange securities sales on either an *underwriting basis* or a *best efforts basis.* The term **underwriting** refers to the process by which an investment banker (usually in cooperation with other investment banking firms) purchases all the new securities from the issuing company and then resells them to the public.

Investment bankers who underwrite securities face some risk because occasionally an issue is overpriced and cannot be sold to the public for the price anticipated by the investment banker. The investment banker has already paid the issuing company or municipality its money up front, and so it must absorb the difference between what it paid the issuer and what the security actually sold for. To alleviate this risk, investment bankers sometimes sell securities on a **best efforts basis.** This means the investment banker will try its best to sell the securities for the desired price, but there are no guarantees. If the securities must be sold for a lower price, the issuer collects less money.

Brokers Brokers—often account representatives for an investment-banking firm—handle orders to buy or sell securities. **Brokers** are agents who work on behalf of an investor. When investors call with orders, brokers work on their behalf to find someone to take the other side of the proposed trades. If investors want to buy, brokers find sellers. If investors want to sell, brokers find buyers. Brokers are compensated for their services when the person they represent—the investor—pays them a commission on the sale or purchase of securities.

Dealers **Dealers** make their living buying securities and reselling them to others. They operate just like car dealers who buy cars from manufacturers for resale to others. Dealers make money by buying securities for one price, called the *bid price,* and selling them for a higher price, called the *ask* (or *offer*) *price.* The difference, or *spread,* between the bid price and the ask price represents the dealer's fee.

Financial Markets

As we have pointed out, the financial system allows suppliers and demanders of capital to trade together. The trades are carried out in the financial markets.

Financial markets are categorized according to the characteristics of the participants and the securities involved. In the *primary market,* for instance, issuers sell new securities directly to the public. In the *secondary market,* investors trade securities among themselves. Primary and secondary markets can be further categorized as to the maturity of the securities traded. Short-term securities—securities with a maturity of one year or less—are traded in the *money market;* and long-term securities—securities with a maturity of more than one year—are traded in the *capital market.* A number of other financial markets exist, but we are mainly concerned with these four. In the following sections, we examine each of these markets in turn.

Take Note

Do not confuse financial markets with financial institutions. A financial market is a forum in which financial securities are traded (it may or may not have a physical location). A financial institution is an organization that takes in funds from the public or other institutions and makes them available to others.

The Primary Market

When a security is created and sold for the first time in the financial marketplace, this transaction takes place in the **primary market**. CIBC World Markets helped Shoppers Drug Mart sell shares to the public in 2001. This was a primary market transaction. In this market, the issuing business or entity sells its securities to investors (the investment banker simply assists with the transaction).

The Secondary Market

Once a security has been issued, it may be traded from one investor to another. The **secondary market** is where previously issued securities—or "used" securities—are traded among investors. Suppose you called your stockbroker to request that she buy 100 shares for you. The shares would usually be purchased from another investor in the secondary market. Secondary market transactions occur thousands of times daily as investors trade securities among themselves. These transactions may occur on an exchange or on the over-the-counter market.

The Money Market

Short-term securities (a maturity of one year or less) are traded in the **money market**. Networks of dealers operate in this market. They use phones and computers to make trades rapidly among themselves and with the issuing organizations. The specific securities traded in the money market include Treasury bills, negotiable certificates of deposit, commercial paper, and other short-term debt instruments. Often, investors (suppliers of capital) will use the money market to park cash temporarily. This may be due to a lag in time between other investment opportunities, or simply that there was a surplus of cash that may be needed at any given time. The money market is valuable in this sense because it is highly liquid. Liquidity refers to the speed at which an investment can be converted to cash. In terms of money market instruments, you should be able to convert a money market instrument into cash within one business day. The downside to money market instruments, from an investor's perspective, is that your potential return will be significantly lower than if you were to invest your money in a capital market.

The Capital Market

Long-term securities (maturities over one year) trade in the **capital market**. Federal, provincial, and municipal governments, as well as large corporations raise long-term funds in the capital market. Firms usually invest proceeds from capital market securities sales in long-term assets such as buildings, production equipment, and so on. Initial offerings of securities in the capital market are usually large deals put together by investment bankers, although after the original issue, the securities may be traded quickly and easily among investors. The two most widely recognized securities in the capital market are bonds and shares. Investors (suppliers of capital) are willing to give money to demanders of capital within the capital market because the potential returns are much greater than are those that can be found within the money market. Unlike the money market, where only high-quality investments can be purchased, the capital market can provide investments with varying risks. Investors must be more careful when choosing which company to lend to (bonds) or buy into (shares).

Security Exchanges

Security exchanges such as the Toronto Stock Exchange (TSX) are organizations that facilitate trading of shares and bonds among investors. Corporations arrange for their shares or bonds to be *listed* on an exchange so that investors may trade the company's shares and bonds at an organized trading location. Corporations list their securities on exchanges because they believe that having their securities traded at such a location will make them easier to trade and, therefore, boost the price. Exchanges accept listings because they earn a fee for their services.

Each exchange-listed share is traded at a specified location on the trading floor called *the post.* Specialists who act either as brokers (bringing together buyers and sellers) or as dealers (buying or selling the shares themselves) supervise the trading.

Prominent international securities exchanges include the New York Stock Exchange (NYSE), the American Stock Exchange (AMEX), and major exchanges in Tokyo, London, Amsterdam, Frankfurt, Paris, Hong Kong, and Mexico.

The Over-the-Counter (OTC) Market

In contrast to the organized exchanges, which have physical locations, the **over-the-counter market** has no fixed location—or, more correctly, it is everywhere. The over-the-counter market, or OTC, is a network of dealers around the world who maintain inventories of securities for sale. Say you wanted to buy a security that is traded OTC. You would call your broker who would then shop among competing dealers who have that security in their inventory. After locating the dealer with the best price, your broker would buy the security on your behalf.

Most dealers in the OTC market are connected through a computer network called Nasdaq. Many securities issued by very small companies are simply bought and sold over the telephone.

International Perspectives in Finance 2-1 on page 30 displays the history of how some companies originated with the Dow Jones Industrial Average, which is a very prominent average in the United States.

Market Efficiency

The term **market efficiency** refers to the ease, speed, and cost of trading securities. In an efficient market, securities can be traded easily, quickly, and at low cost. Markets lacking these qualities are considered inefficient.

The major stock markets are generally efficient because investors can trade thousands of dollars worth of shares in minutes simply by making a phone call and paying a relatively small commission. In contrast, the real

INTERNATIONAL PERSPECTIVES IN FINANCE 2-1

Dow Jones History

The Dow Jones Industrial average, an index used to evaluate American stock performance, h been around for a long time. The following outlines the listings of the companies on the ind throughout the years as provided by http://www.djindexes.com.

July 3, 1884–

Chicago & North Western
Delaware, Lackawanna & Western
Lake Shore
Louisville & Nashville
Missouri Pacific
New York Central
Northern Pacific pfd.
Pacific Mail
St. Paul
Union Pacific
Western Union

May 26, 1896–

American Cotton Oil
American Sugar
American Tobacco
Chicago Gas
Distilling & Cattle Feeding
General Electric
Laclede Gas
National Lead
North American
Tennessee Coal & Iron
U.S. Leather
U.S. Rubber

January 29, 1930–

Allied Chemical
American Can
American Smelting
American Sugar
American Tobacco B
Atlantic Refining
Bethlehem Steel
Chrysler
Curtiss-Wright
General Electric Company
General Motors Corporation
General Railway Signal
Goodrich
International Harvester
International Nickel
Johns-Manville
Mack Truck
Nash Motors
National Cash Register
Paramount Publix
Postum Incorporated
Radio Corporation
Sears Roebuck & Company
Standard Oil (NJ)
Texas Company
Texas Gulf Sulphur
Union Carbide
U.S. Steel
Westinghouse Electric
Woolworth

April 22, 1959–

Allied Chemical
Aluminum Company of America
American Can
American Tel. & Tel.
American Tobacco B
Anaconda Copper
Bethlehem Steel
Chrysler
Du Pont
Eastman Kodak Company
General Electric Company
General Foods
General Motors Corporation
Goodyear
International Harvester
International Nickel
International Paper Company
Johns-Manville
Owens-Illinois Glass
Procter & Gamble Company
Sears Roebuck & Company
Standard Oil of California
Standard Oil (NJ)
Swift & Company
Texaco Incorporated
Union Carbide
United Aircraft
U.S. Steel
Westinghouse Electric
Woolworth

April 8, 2004–

3M Company
Alcoa Incorporated
Altria Group, Incorporated
American Express Company
American International Group Inc.
Boeing Company Incorporated
Caterpillar Incorporated
Citigroup Incorporated
Coca-Cola Company
Du Pont
Exxon Mobil Corporation
General Electric Company
General Motors Corporation
Hewlett-Packard Company
Home Depot Incorporated
Honeywell International Inc.
Intel Corporation
International Business Machines
J. P. Morgan Chase & Company
Johnson & Johnson
McDonald's Corporation
Merck & Company, Incorporated
Microsoft Corporation
Pfizer Incorporated
Procter & Gamble Company
SBC Communications
United Technologies Corporation
Verizon Communications Inc.
Wal-Mart Stores Incorporated
Walt Disney Company

estate market is relatively inefficient because it might take you months to sell a house and you would probably have to pay a real estate agent a large commission to handle the deal.

The more efficient the market, the easier it is for investors to buy and trade securities. In an inefficient market, price listings can be extremely misleading, creating a difficult situation in order to trade at true market value. As well, it may be difficult to match trading partners in inefficient markets thereby reducing liquidity. When trades are not made efficiently, losses can occur through actual monetary losses or through missed opportunities.

Financial markets help firms and individual investors buy and sell securities efficiently. So far, we have discussed the various markets in which securities are traded. Now let's turn to the securities themselves.

SECURITIES IN THE FINANCIAL MARKETPLACE

Securities are traded in both the money and capital markets. Money market securities include Treasury bills, negotiable certificates of deposit, commercial paper, Eurodollars, and banker's acceptances. Capital market securities include bonds and shares. We describe each of these securities briefly in the following discussion.

Securities in the Money Market

Governments, corporations, and financial institutions that want to raise money, for a short time, issue money market securities. Buyers of money market securities include governments, corporations, and financial institutions that want to park surplus cash for a short time and other investors who want the ability to alter or cash in their investments quickly.

T-Bills (or Treasury bills) **T-Bills** or **Treasury Bills** are the federal government's way of financing short-term financial requirements. T-Bills are distributed through an auction where the Bank of Canada acts on the government's behalf. The auction usually takes place bi-weekly on the Tuesday of that week. Banks and other institutions will place bids where the highest bid will receive the T-Bill. T-Bills are extremely safe due to their short-time horizon and their guarantee from the Canadian federal government. The way the buyers of the T-Bills make money is by making bids that are less than the face value of the T-Bill. That is to say, if the Bank of Canada auctioned off a $25,000 T-Bill maturing in 91 days, a bidder may ask to pay $24,850. If successful in the bid, the bidder would have paid $24,850 for a T-Bill that would convert to $25,000 in 91 days. Generally, the maturities of T-Bills are 3, 6, or 12 months.

Negotiable Certificates of Deposit You may already be familiar with the certificates of deposit (CDs) that you can purchase from your local bank. They are simply pieces of paper that certify you have deposited a certain amount of money in the bank to be paid back on a certain date with interest. Small-denomination consumer CDs are very safe investments and they tend to have low interest rates.

Large-denomination CDs (of $100,000 to $1 million or more), with maturities of two weeks to a year, are **negotiable CDs** because they can be traded in the secondary market after they are initially issued by a financial institution. Large corporations and other institutions buy negotiable CDs when they have cash they wish to invest for a short period of time. They sell negotiable CDs when they want to raise cash quickly.

Commercial Paper **Commercial paper** is a type of short-term promissory note—similar to an IOU—issued by large corporations with strong credit ratings. Commercial paper is *unsecured,* meaning that the issuing corporation does not provide any property as collateral that the lender (the one who buys the commercial paper note) can take instead of a payment if the issuing corporation defaults on the note. That is why commercial paper is only issued by financially strong, reliable firms.

Commercial paper is considered to be a safe place to put money for a short period of time. The notes themselves are issued and traded through a network of commercial paper dealers. Most of the buyers are large institutions.

Banker's Acceptances A **banker's acceptance** is a short-term debt instrument that is guaranteed for payment by a commercial bank (the bank "accepts" the responsibility to pay). Banker's acceptances thus allow businesses to avoid problems associated with collecting payment from reluctant debtors. They are often used when firms are doing business internationally because they eliminate the worry that the lender will have to travel to a foreign country to collect on a debt.

Securities in the Capital Market

When governments, corporations, and financial institutions want to raise money for a long period of time, they issue capital market securities. In contrast to money market securities, capital market securities may not be very liquid or safe. They are not generally suitable for short-term investments.

The two most prominent capital market securities are bonds and shares (see Financial Management and You 2-1 on page 34). We will examine these two securities in some depth now.

Bonds **Bonds** are essentially IOUs that promise to pay their owners a certain amount of money on some specified date in the future—and in most cases, interest payments at regular intervals until maturity. When companies want to borrow money (usually a fairly large amount for a long period of time), they arrange for their investment bankers to print up the IOUs and sell them to the public at whatever price they can get. In essence, a firm that issues a bond is borrowing the amount that the bond sells for on the open market.

Bond Terminology and Types.

Although many types of bonds exist, most bonds have three special features: face value, maturity date, and coupon interest.

- *Face value:* The amount that the bond promises to pay its owner at some date in the future is called the bond's **face value**, or **par value**, or **principal**. Bond face values range in multiples of $1,000 all the way up to more than $1 million. Unless otherwise noted, assume that all bonds we discuss from this point forward have a face value of $1,000.
- *Maturity date:* The date on which the issuer is obligated to pay the bondholder the bond's face value.

- *Coupon interest:* The interest payments made to the bond owner during the life of the bond.[1] Some bonds pay coupon interest once a year, but most pay it twice a year. Some bonds do not pay any interest at all. These bonds are called **zero-coupon bonds** or **strip bonds**.

The percentage of face value that the coupon interest payment represents is called the *coupon interest rate.* For example, assuming the face value of the bond was $1,000, a bond owner who received $80 interest payments each year would own a bond paying an 8 percent coupon interest rate:

$$\$80/\$1{,}000 = 0.08 \text{ or } 8\%$$

The major types of bonds include Treasury bonds and notes and are issued by the federal government. Provincial bonds, municipal bonds, and corporate bonds are issued by provincial and municipal governments and corporations. The significant differences among these types of bonds are described in the following sections.

Treasury Bonds.

As of 1995, all Government of Canada Marketable bonds must be sold through a participant of the Debt Clearing Service. Most of the big banks are associated directly or indirectly. The bonds are sold in denominations of $1,000 face value. Prior to 1993, bonds were sold in denominations of anywhere from $1,000 to $1,000,000 and could have been non-registered (whoever holds the bond owns the bond). Canadian government bonds are currently ranked with the highest credit rating possible, both within Canada and outside of Canada. A high credit rating is very important because with it, the federal government's cost for financing the bonds will be much lower. In other words, the federal government is rewarded for having a high credit rating and will need to pay less in terms of interest to its bondholders. This means that tax dollars, which are used in part to pay back the federal debt, can be distributed to other projects instead of paying the higher interest rate.

Corporate Bonds.

Corporate bonds are similar to Government of Canada bonds except that corporations issue them. Like Government of Canada bonds, they pay their owner interest during the life of the bond and repay the principal at maturity. Unlike Government of Canada bonds, however, corporate bonds sometimes carry substantial risk of default. As a last resort, the Canadian government can print money to pay off its Canadian bond obligations, but when private corporations run into trouble, they have no such latitude. Corporations' creditors may get paid late or not at all.

Relatively safe bonds are called *investment-grade bonds.* Many financial institutions and money management firms are required to invest only in those corporate bonds that are investment grade. Relatively risky bonds are called

[1]The name originated decades ago when holders of bearer bonds would actually tear off coupons from their bond certificates and mail them to the bond issuer to get their interest payments, hence, the name *coupon* interest. Today, bonds are sold on a "registered" basis, which means the bonds come with the owner's name printed on them. Interest payments are sent directly to the owner.

FINANCIAL MANAGEMENT AND YOU 2-1

Buying Shares, Bonds, and Money Market Funds through Payroll Deduction

Many companies will give their employees the opportunity to have a portion of their salaries deducted for retirement or other investment purposes. This is a quick and easy way to get your money working for you within a pre-arranged plan. The costs associated with setting up a payroll deduction plan are very small, if anything. As well, you may receive an immediate tax deduction if you are investing in your RRSP (Registered Retirement Savings Plan). There are vari types of investments that you can purchase including mo market instruments, bonds, and shares. Also, because are making constant payments each pay, many of the rest tions with minimum purchases are often relaxed. Some co panies will even match your contributions, doubling y savings power.

junk bonds.[2] Junk bonds are generally issued by troubled companies, but they may be issued by financially strong companies that later run into trouble.

This completes our introduction to bonds. Now let's turn our attention to the other major security in the capital market, corporate shares.

Corporate Shares Rather than borrowing money by issuing bonds, a corporation may choose to raise money by selling shares of ownership interest in the company. Those shares of ownership are **stock**. Investors who buy stock or shares are called stockholders or shareholders.

As a source of funds, shares have an advantage over bonds: The money raised from the sale of shares does not ever have to be paid back and the company does not have to make interest payments to the shareholders.

A corporation may issue two types of corporate shares: *common shares* and *preferred shares*. Let's look at their characteristics.

Common Shares.

Common shares are so called because there is nothing special about them. The holders of a company's common shares are simply the owners of the company. Their ownership entitles them to the firm's earnings that remain after all other groups having a claim on the firm (such as bondholders) have been paid.

Each common shareholder owns a portion of the company represented by the fraction of the whole that the shareholder's shares represent. Thus, if a company issued 1 million common shares, a person who holds one share owns one-millionth of the company.

Common shareholders receive a return on their investment in the form of common share **dividends**, distributed from the firm's profits and **capital gains** realized when they sell the shares.[3]

Preferred Shares.

Preferred shares are so called because if the board of directors of a business declares dividends, they are paid to preferred shareholders first. If any funds

---

[2]The term *junk bond* is a slang term that is now widely accepted. Firms trying to sell junk bonds hate the term, of course. They would prefer to call such bonds *high yield*.

[3]Of course, there is no guarantee that a common shareholder's shares will increase in price. If the price goes down, the shareholder will experience a capital loss.

are left over, they may be paid to the common shareholders. So why would anyone buy common shares? First, preferred shareholders normally do not get to vote on how the firm is run. Second, common shares normally provide a slightly higher expected return because it is a more risky investment—that is, dividends are not guaranteed. However, common shareholders—as owners—are entitled to all the residual income of the firm and there is no upper limit on how great the residual income of the firm might be. Preferred shares have a fixed dividend.

INTEREST

No one lends money for free. When people lend money to other people, a number of things could happen that might prevent them from getting all their money back. Whenever people agree to take risk, compensation is required before they will voluntarily enter into an agreement. In financial activities, we refer to this compensation as interest. **Interest** represents the return or compensation a lender demands before agreeing to lend money. When we refer to interest, we normally express it in percentage terms, called the *interest rate.* Thus, if you lend a person \$100 for one year, and the return you require for doing so is \$10, we would say that the interest rate you are charging for the loan is \$10/\$100 = 0.10, or 10 percent.

Determinants of Interest Rates

The prevailing rate of interest in any situation is called the **nominal interest rate.** In the preceding example, the nominal interest rate for the one-year \$100 loan was 10 percent. The nominal interest rate is actually the total of a number of separate components as shown in Figure 2-1. We will explore each of these components in the following sections.

The Real Rate of Interest Lenders of money must postpone spending during the time the money is loaned. Lenders, then, lose the opportunity to invest

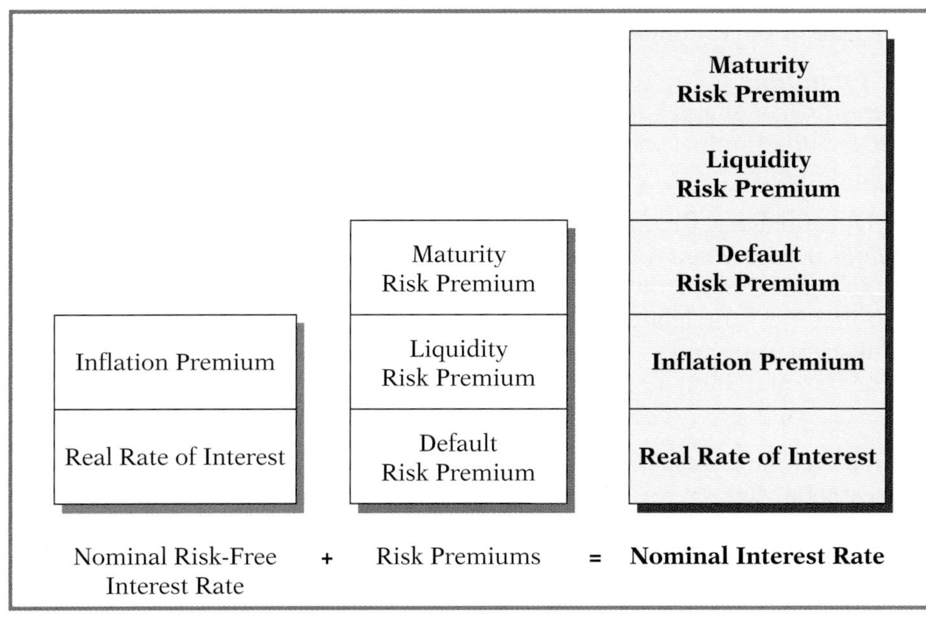

Figure 2-1 Components of the Nominal Interest Rate
The nominal interest rate is composed of the real interest rate plus a number of premiums. The nominal risk-free interest rate is the real rate plus an inflation premium. When risk premiums are added, the result is the total nominal interest rate.

their money for that period of time. To compensate for the cost of losing investment opportunities while they postpone their spending, lenders demand and borrowers pay a basic rate of return—the **real rate of interest**. The real rate of interest does not include adjustments for any other factors such as the risk of not getting paid back. We will describe this in a moment.

Let's continue with the example on page 35 in which you lent a person $100. The total interest rate that you charged was 10 percent (the nominal interest rate). The portion of the total nominal rate that represents the return you demand for forgoing the opportunity to spend your money now is the real rate of interest. In our example, assume the real rate of interest is 2 percent.

Additions to the real rate of interest are called *premiums*. The major premiums are the inflation premium, the default risk premium, the liquidity risk premium, and the maturity risk premium.

The Inflation Premium Inflation erodes the purchasing power of money. If inflation is present, the dollars that lenders get when their loans are repaid may not buy as much as the dollars that they lent to start with. Therefore, lenders who anticipate inflation during the term of a loan will demand additional interest to compensate for it. This additional required interest is the **inflation premium**.

If, when you lent $100, you thought that the rate of inflation was going to be 4 percent a year during the life of the loan, you would add 4 percent to the 2 percent real rate of interest you charged for postponing your spending. The total interest rate charge—so far—would be 6 percent.

The Nominal Risk-Free Rate The interest rate that we have built so far, containing the real rate of interest and a premium to cover expected inflation, is often called the **nominal risk-free rate of interest**, as shown earlier in Figure 2-1. It is called this because it does not include any premiums for the uncertainties associated with borrowing or lending. The yield on short-term Canadian Treasury bills is often used as a proxy for the risk-free rate because the degree of uncertainty associated with these securities is very small.

Take Note

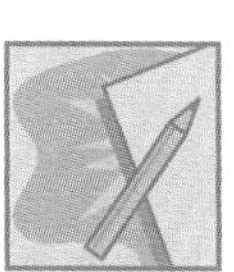

You can find the history of the Canadian T-Bill yields by going to the Bank of Canada's website, www.bankofcanada.ca. Then, select the link addressing historical yields of T-Bills.

Risk Premiums The remaining determinants of the nominal interest rate represent extra charges to compensate lenders for taking risk. Risks in lending come in a number of forms. The most common are default risk, liquidity risk, and maturity risk.

The Default Risk Premium.

A *default* occurs when a borrower fails to pay the interest and principal on a loan on time. If a borrower has a questionable reputation or is having financial difficulties, the lender faces the risk that the borrower will default. The **default risk premium** is the extra compensation lenders demand for assuming the risk of default.

In our $100 loan example, if you were not completely sure that the person to whom you had lent $100 would pay it back, you would demand extra compensation—let's say, two percentage points to compensate for that risk. The total interest rate demanded so far would be 2 percent real rate of interest + 4 percent inflation premium + 2 percent default risk premium = 8 percent.

The Liquidity Risk Premium.

Sometimes lenders sell loans to others after making them. (This happens often in the mortgage business in which investors trade mortgages among themselves.) Some loans are easily sold to other parties and others are not. Those that are easily sold are *liquid* and those that are not sold easily are considered *illiquid.* Illiquid loans have a higher interest rate to compensate the lender for the inconvenience of being stuck with the loan until it matures. The extra interest that lenders demand to compensate for the lack of liquidity is the **liquidity risk premium.** Because this premium is greater the *less* liquid the security, some would call this an illiquidity risk premium.

> You will probably not be able to sell your $100 loan to anyone else and will have to hold it until maturity. Therefore, you require another 1 percent to compensate for the lack of liquidity. The total interest rate demanded so far is 2 percent real rate of interest + 4 percent inflation premium + 2 percent default risk premium + 1 percent liquidity risk premium = 9 percent.

The Maturity Risk Premium.

If interest rates rise, lenders may find themselves stuck with long-term loans paying the original rate prevailing at the time the loans were made, whereas other lenders are able to make new loans at higher rates. On the other hand, if interest rates go down, the same lenders will be pleased to find themselves receiving higher interest rates on their existing long-term loans than the rate at which other lenders must make new loans. Lenders respond to this risk that interest rates may change in the future in two ways:

1. If lenders think interest rates might rise in the future, they may increase the rate they charge on their long-term loans now and decrease the rate they charge on their short-term loans now to encourage borrowers to borrow short term.
2. Conversely, if lenders think interest rates might fall in the future, they may decrease the rate they charge on their long-term loans now and increase the rate they charge on their short-term loans now to encourage borrowers to borrow long term (locking in the current rate).

This up or down adjustment that lenders make to their current interest rates to compensate for the uncertainty about future changes in rates is called the **maturity risk premium.** The maturity risk premium can be either positive or negative.

> In our example, if you thought interest rates would probably rise before you were repaid the $100 you lent, you might demand an extra percentage point to compensate for the risk that you would be unable to take advantage of the new higher rates. The total rate demanded is now 10 percent (2 percent real rate of interest + 4 percent inflation premium + 2 percent default risk premium + 1 percent liquidity risk premium + 1 percent maturity risk premium = 10 percent, the nominal interest rate).

The total of the real rate of interest, the inflation premium, and the risk premiums (the default, liquidity, and maturity risk premiums) is the nominal interest rate, the compensation lenders demand from those who want to borrow money. See Ethical Connections 2-1 on the next page for a discussion of extremes in interest rates.

Next, we will consider the *yield* curve—a graph of a security's interest rates depending on the time to maturity.

The Yield Curve

A yield curve is a graphical depiction of interest rates for securities that differ only in the time remaining until their maturity. Yield curves are drawn by plotting the interest rates of one kind of security with different maturity dates. The curve depicts the interest rates of these securities at a given point in time.

Yield curves of Canadian Treasury securities are most common because with Treasury securities it is easiest to hold constant the factors other than maturity. All Treasury securities have essentially the same default risk (almost

ETHICAL CONNECTIONS 2-1

Part I—Government Targets Alternative Banking Industry

Friday, January 16, 2004

Winnipeg—Ottawa and the provinces agreed Friday to study the burgeoning short-term credit industry, which they say has left some Canadians drowning under exorbitant interest rates.

Federal and provincial ministers responsible for consumer protection concluded their one-day meeting by creating a committee to come up with a plan in the coming months to better protect the public.

"We're in a situation now where we have to look at what legislative alternatives are available, what mechanisms there are to get the banks better involved and make sure the consumers have the information they need not to be taken advantage of when they use those services," Manitoba Finance Minister Greg Selinger told a news conference.

The ministers will target so-called payday loan companies, pawnshops, and cheque-cashing stores—referred to collectively as the alternative banking industry.

One company, for example, will give an advance to most customers equal to about 30 per cent of their net pay until their next paycheque. The interest rate is 89 cents per $100, per week.

In some cases, interest rates can reach more than 1,000 per cent when all fees are taken into account, said Selinger.

Selinger said a provision in the Criminal Code prohibits annual interest rates in excess of 60 per cent, but it is not always enforced.

Financial alternatives need to be identified for people who find themselves in trouble and unable to get a small loan from a chartered bank, said Quebec Citizenship Minister Michelle Courchesne.

"It has to be a wider responsibility," said Courchesn "It addresses mostly the most vulnerable people who will g and ask for those loans. There's a social aspect where w have to . . . make sure we go through each component ar aspect of this complex file."

Part II—Identity Theft

The ministers also agreed to harmonize efforts to bett inform consumers about identity theft.

They released an information kit, which is also availab on the internet, that tells Canadians how to reduce the ris of being victimized.

A federal government-funded study released last fa concluded identity theft is growing "explosively" in Canad and consumers need better protection.

The study's recommendations included better enforc ment of existing laws and new rules making it illegal to ho identity documents under more than one name.

Questions to Consider

1. *What sort of premium is a "Payday" loan compar analyzing when selecting its rate?*
2. *Who are "Payday" loan companies attracting? What sc of ethical issue arises?*
3. *What arguments do you think the Government will mak What arguments do you think the "Payday" loan comp nies will make?*

Sources: "Government Targets Alternative Banking Industry," Janua 16, 2004. http://www.canada.com/montreal/specials/business/story.html?id=FE598316-F283-4CEF-9F9A-A327EC3462EF. Reprinted with the permission of The Canadian Press.

none) and about the same degree of liquidity (excellent). Any differences in interest rates observed in the yield curve, then, can be attributed to the maturity differences among the securities because other factors have essentially been held constant. Figure 2-2 shows a Treasury securities yield curve for January 21, 2004.

Making Use of the Yield Curve The shape of the yield curve gives borrowers and lenders useful information for financial decisions. Borrowers, for example, tend to look for the low point of the curve, which indicates the least expensive loan maturity. Lenders tend to look for the highest point on the curve, which indicates the most expensive loan maturity.

Finding the most advantageous maturity is not quite as simple as it sounds because it depends on more factors than cost. For instance, the least expensive maturity is not always the most advantageous for borrowers. If a firm borrows short term, for example, it may obtain the lowest interest rate, but the loan may mature in a short time and have to be renewed at a higher rate if interest rates have risen in the interim. Borrowing for a longer term may cost a borrower more at the outset but less in the long run because the interest rate is locked in.

Lenders face the opposite situation. Granting long-term loans at relatively high interest rates may look attractive now; but if short-term rates rise, the lenders may miss profitable opportunities because their funds have already been invested. Both borrowers and lenders must balance their desire for return with their tolerance for risk.

Figure 2-2
Government of Canada Interest Rate Yield Curve as at January 21, 2004

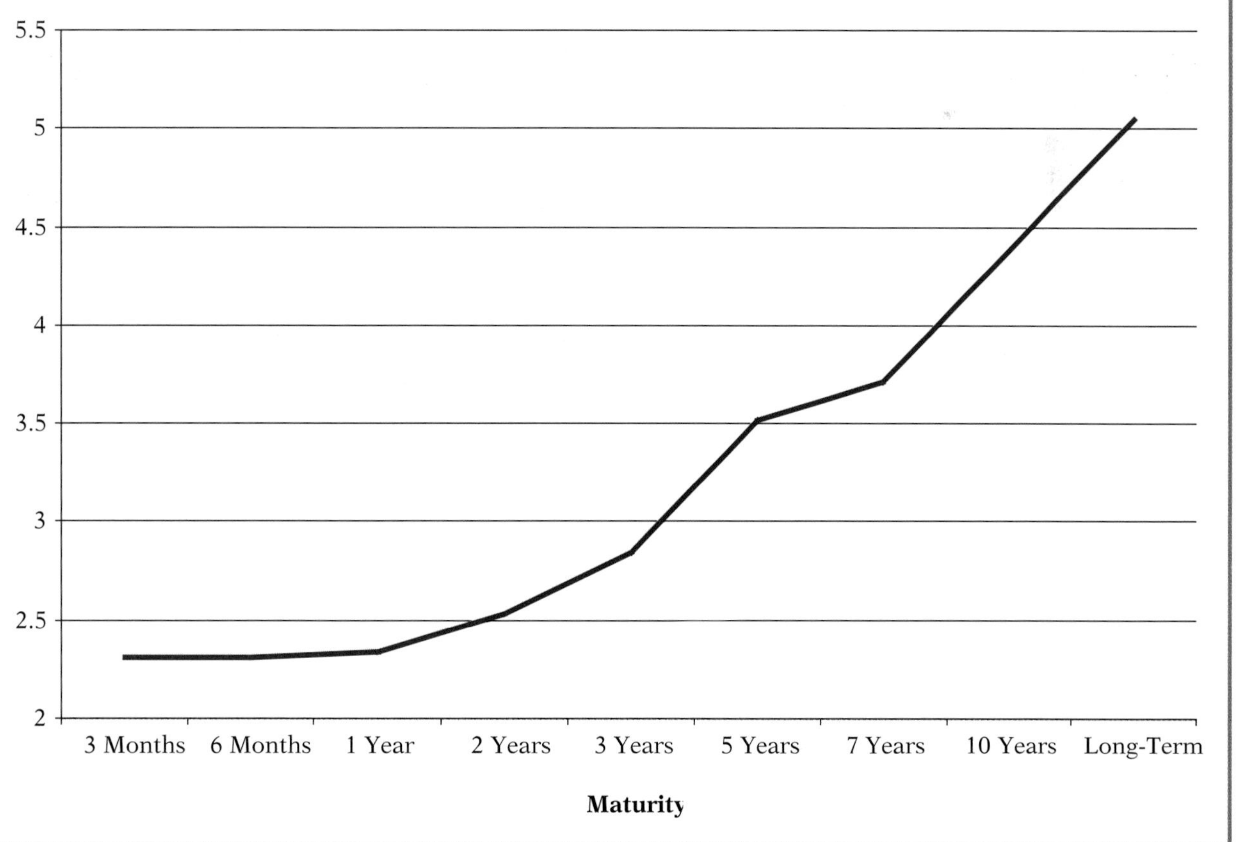

SUMMARY

2-1 Describe how the Canadian financial system works and how financial intermediaries help in the process.

The financial system is made up of suppliers of capital, entities and individuals that have excess funds, and demanders of capital, entities and individuals that need to acquire additional funds. The financial system provides the network that brings these two groups together.

Financial intermediaries act to put those in need of funds in contact with those who have funds available. Investment banking firms help businesses acquire funds from the public by issuing securities in the financial marketplace. Brokers help members of the public trade securities with each other. Dealers buy and sell securities themselves.

2-2 Contrast the three main differences between the primary market and the secondary market.

The financial markets include the primary market, in which new securities are issued for the first time and the secondary market, in which previously issued securities are traded among investors. The investment banker has much more influence on bringing the security to the primary market, while the stockbroker deals with trades within the secondary market. Once a security is sold within the primary market, it is traded within the secondary market for further trades; this creates the potential for an infinite amount of subsequent trades.

2-3 Contrast the different types of securities traded in the money market and the capital market.

Securities traded in the money market include:

- *Treasury bills:* short-term debt instruments issued by the Canadian Treasury that are sold at a discount and pay face value at maturity.
- *Negotiable certificates of deposit (CDs):* certificates that can be traded in financial markets and represent amounts deposited at banks that will be repaid at maturity with a specified rate of interest.
- *Commercial paper:* unsecured short-term promissory notes issued by large corporations with strong credit ratings.
- *Banker's acceptances:* documents that signify a bank has guaranteed payment of a certain amount at a future date if the original promissor does not pay.

The two major securities traded in the capital market include:

- *Bonds:* long-term securities that represent a promise to pay a fixed amount at a future date usually with interest payments made at regular intervals. The Canadian federal government issues Canadian government bonds and corporate bonds are issued by firms.
- *Shares:* shares of ownership interest in corporations. Preferred shares come with promised dividends but usually no voting rights. Common shares may come with dividends, paid at the discretion of the board, but do have voting rights. Common shareholders share in the residual profits of the firm.

2-4 Analyze the nominal interest rate and break it down into its three main components.

The nominal interest rate has three main components:

- *The real rate of interest:* the basic rate lenders require to compensate them for forgoing the opportunity to spend money during the term of the loan.
- *An inflation premium:* a premium that compensates for the expected erosion of purchasing power due to inflation over the life of the loan.

- *Risk premiums:* premiums that compensate for the risks of default (the risk that the lender will not be paid back), liquidity (the risk that the lender will not be able to sell the security in a reasonable time at a fair price), and maturity (the risk that interest rates may change adversely during the life of the security).

2-5 Explain what a yield curve is and what information can be derived from it.

A yield curve is a graphical depiction of interest rates on securities that differ only in the time remaining until their maturity. Lenders and borrowers may use a yield curve to determine the most advantageous loan maturity.

SELF-TEST

ST-1. To minimize risk, why do most firms not simply finance their growth from the profits they earn?

ST-2. What market would a firm most probably go to if it needed cash for 90 days? if it needed cash for 10 years?

ST-3. If your company's shares were not listed on the Toronto Stock Exchange, how could investors purchase the shares?

ST-4. What alternatives does General Motors of Canada, a very large and secure firm, have for obtaining $3 million for 60 days?

ST-5. Assume Treasury security yields for today are as follows:

One-year government bond 5.75%
Two-year government bond 5.50%
Three-year government bond 5.25%
Five-year government bond 5.00%
Ten-year government bond 4.75%
Twenty-year government bond 4.00%
Thirty-year government bond 3.25%

Draw a yield curve based on these data.

REVIEW QUESTIONS

1. What are financial markets? Why do they exist?
2. What is a security?
3. What are the characteristics of an efficient market?
4. How are financial trades made on an organized exchange?
5. How are financial trades made in an over-the-counter market? Discuss the role of a dealer in the OTC market.
6. What is the role of a broker in security transactions? How are brokers compensated?
7. What is a Treasury bill? How risky is it?
8. Would there be positive interest rates on bonds in a world with absolutely no risk (no default risk, maturity risk, and so on)? Why would a lender demand, and a borrower be willing to pay, a positive interest rate in such a no-risk world?

PROBLEMS

The Financial System ▶

2-1. **a.** What are "suppliers of capital?" Give two examples of entities in the financial system that typically would be classified as suppliers of capital.

b. What are "demanders of capital?" Give two examples of entities in the financial system that typically would be classified as demanders of capital.

Financial Markets ▶

2-2. Answer the following as true or false:

a. Trades among investors at the Toronto Stock Exchange are primary market transactions.

b. The money market is where firms go to obtain funding for long-term projects.

c. Your firm has $2,000,000 of excess funds that will not be needed for one month. You would most likely go to the capital market to invest the money until needed.

d. Gold and international currencies are traded in the money market.

Financial Markets ▶

2-3. **a.** Arrange the following markets in order from most efficient to least efficient.

i. The real estate market
ii. The money market
iii. The secondary market (Toronto Stock Exchange)
iv. The over-the-counter market

b. Explain the rationale you used to order the markets the way you did in part a.

Securities in the Financial Marketplace ▶

2-4. **a.** What characteristics must a security have to be traded in the money market?

b. Give two examples of securities that are traded in the money market.

Securities in the Financial Marketplace ▶

2-5. Public Service Company of Quebec issued $150 million worth of bonds this year. The bonds had a face value of $1,000 each and each came with a promise to pay the bearer $66.25 a year in interest during the life of the bond. What is the coupon interest rate of these bonds?

Interest ▶

2-6. The real rate of interest is 2 percent, inflation is expected to be 3 percent during the coming year, and the default risk premium, liquidity risk premium, and maturity risk premium for the Bonds-R-Us corporation are 1 percent each. What would be the yield on a Bonds-R-Us bond?

Interest ▶

Excel

2-7. Assume Treasury security yields for today are as follows:

Three-month T-Bill 4.50%
Six-month T-Bill 4.75%
One-year government bond 5.00%
Two-year government bond 5.25%
Three-year government bond 5.50%
Five-year government bond 5.75%
Ten-year government bond 6.00%
Thirty-year government bond 6.50%

Draw a yield curve based on these data. Discuss the implications if you are:

a. a borrower

b. a lender

2-8. Anita was the owner of a company that had been in the family for several decades. The company was having financial difficulties and Anita was being forced to make a decision. Fortunately, the debt load was very minimal because the company had always followed the policy, "If you don't have it, then you shouldn't spend it." This meant that they had never borrowed money before but relied on family investments and the massive earning power of the company itself. However, the company had not been earning what it used to earn, and though still profitable, was not profitable enough to invest in future projects. Anita had already forecasted the cost for new equipment and vehicles, which totalled $24 million. Last year's earnings were only $14 million. ◀ Financing New Projects

a. In terms of financing new projects, use your knowledge from Chapter 2 to suggest several ideas that could finance new projects. What do you think the advantages are? What do you think the disadvantages are?

b. Someone suggested that Anita should use short-term financing to finance the company's projects and when the short-term debts became due, refinance the debt with more short-term borrowing. They told Anita that by looking at the yield curve, you could see that short-term borrowing would always be less expensive than long-term borrowing. In terms of borrowing short-term versus long-term, what are some of the drawbacks to the above-mentioned short-term rollover strategy.

c. What do you think the disadvantages would be to borrowing money in this case? What do you think the advantages would be?

2-9. Franco was on the verge of retiring and had always been a very conservative investor. Most of his money had been placed under his mattress or in a savings account at one of the big banks. Unfortunately, Franco has been forced to retire because arthritis has affected his ability to create shoes. His boss, being the caring person that she is, gave him a sizeable severance (retirement allowance) for his outstanding service throughout the years. With this money and Franco's savings, he could live comfortably but not without some sort of investment restructuring. Being 67 years old, Franco did not need a high rate of return, but he did need something other than the current 0.25 percent return from his savings account. Franco has asked you for help. ◀ Financial Markets

a. Is Franco a demander or supplier of capital? Assuming Franco's risk tolerance, where do you think he should invest his money so that it would best suit his interests?

b. What types of investments do you think would match Franco's situation? Why?

c. When you ask Franco if he would put a small percentage of his money into shares, Franco said he hated the Internet and believed all deals should be done face to face. If you followed Franco's logic, which exchange would it be more difficult to trade in? Franco asked for your thoughts on his reasoning. What do you think?

2-10. A recent expansion team to the NHL (National Hockey League), the Yukon Caribou, needed money to finance the construction of a new arena. The Canadian government has partially supplied the financial needs through a government grant. ◀ Financial Markets and Interest

a. With current interest rates as they are, would debt financing be a relatively inexpensive solution? The following are the Bank of Canada's historic trend interest rates. The Yukon Caribou can expect to pay 2 percent above the current trend rate from the Bank of Canada.

1970	1971	1972	1973	1974	1975	1976	1977	1978	1979
6.00%	4.75%	4.75%	7.25%	8.75%	9.00%	8.50%	7.50%	10.75%	14.00%
1980	**1981**	**1982**	**1983**	**1984**	**1985**	**1986**	**1987**	**1988**	**1989**
17.26%	14.66%	10.26%	10.04%	10.16%	9.49%	8.49%	8.66%	11.17%	12.47%
1990	**1991**	**1992**	**1993**	**1994**	**1995**	**1996**	**1997**	**1998**	**1999**
11.78%	7.67%	7.36%	4.11%	7.43%	5.79%	3.25%	4.50%	5.25%	5.00%
2000	**2001**	**2002**	**2003**						
6.00%	2.50%	3.00%	3.00%						

Source: Bank of Canada, "Historic Trend Interest Rates," data derived from www.bankofcanada.ca/pdf/annual_page1_page2. pdf. Reprinted with perm[ission] of the Bank of Canada.

b. The financial manager of the team does not know the difference between the money market and the capital market. Can you make an argument for the market that will be the most appropriate in raising funds for the new arena?

c. The government of British Columbia is contemplating whether or not to guarantee the loan for the Yukon Caribou. If the guarantee was made, the bond rating would be considered investment grade. Without the guarantee, the bond rating would be considered speculative. In terms of financing, why would this issue be important?

Interest ▶ **2-11.** Li has recently heard of a great deal at a local bank. A friend of his went to get a business loan the other day and they offered him a rate of 4.5 percent to be paid back within one year. Li was considering going on vacation this year and thought a 4.5 percent rate was a fabulous deal that he could pay back within 7 years. Unfortunately, when Li went to the bank to get a loan quote, the bank quoted him almost double what his friend had received. Li was furious and demanded to know the reason why.

a. You are the bank representative and your job is to show Li the reasons why he has to pay a higher interest rate. What sort of differences can you read from the problem or naturally assume that make Li's and his friend's situations different?

b. How would you explain each of these in terms of the different components of the nominal return?

c. After hearing your reasoning, Li offered to put up his house, which is fully paid for as collateral on the loan. How would this change the quoted rate from the bank, if any? Why?

Financial Markets ▶ **2-12.** You were listening to your friend brag about a great return he achieved from a stock market tip. The following is what was said: "You know, yours truly is the smartest person in the world. I just made a 50 percent return from this stock tip I picked up. All I did was go to that fancy NASDAQ exchange and told the floor trader to buy it for me. Who knew? Trading in the Money Market is the place to be. That's where I made this 50 percent return. Boy, don't you feel silly that you didn't listen to me when you had the chance? You could have made a killing like me if you started investing in the Primary market like me. This is the market where you buy low and sell high. I mean, before I used to be big into Canadian T-Bills. If you hold onto them for at least 3 years, you could get an above-average return, but now it is all about the risk-free corporate bonds from small emerging companies. Better yet, each year I get to vote on company issues. I tell you, you really messed up. You should have followed my lead."

a. After listening to your friend, you realized that your friend really did not invest any money and did not get rich. What made you realize that your friend was full of "hot air"?

b. Rewrite your friend's speech so that it makes more sense.

Financial Markets and Securities in the Financial Marketplace

2-13. Bettina, Kelly, and Shawna operated a privately owned fashion house. Always being in touch with what people want, these three women were able to create popular fashions for both males and females. Feeling that their company was worth several million dollars, the three founders decided that they wanted to cash in some of this money by selling shares in their company. However, they did not want to sell so many shares that they would lose control of the company to outside buyers. Being their friend, the three founders have come to you concerning some questions they have about going public (the act of taking a private company and selling its shares for the first time to a much larger population of buyers).

a. Their first question was about the roles of financial intermediaries. They wanted to know what they were, and what functions they performed. Which type of financial intermediary would the women most likely be interested in?

b. The second question dealt with the financial markets. They wanted to know the differences among the markets. Which market do you think the founding women would be the most interested in?

c. The third question had to do with selling and repurchasing. They wanted to know what percentage of their shares they should keep in order to retain full control of the company. They also wanted to know if sometime in the future they wanted to buy their shares back, where they could do so.

ANSWERS TO SELF-TEST

ST-1. In most cases, profits are insufficient to provide the funds needed, especially with large projects. Financial markets provide access to external sources of funds.

ST-2. To obtain cash for 90 days, a business firm would most probably go to the money market in which it would sell a 90-day security. To obtain cash for 10 years, a firm would sell a security in the capital market.

ST-3. Investors would simply purchase the shares on another exchange or over the counter from a dealer. (Investors simply call their brokers to purchase shares. Brokers decide where to get it.)

ST-4. General Motors of Canada could:

a. Obtain a 60-day loan from a financial institution.
b. Delay payments to its suppliers.
c. Sell commercial paper notes in the money market.

ST-5. The yield curve follows:

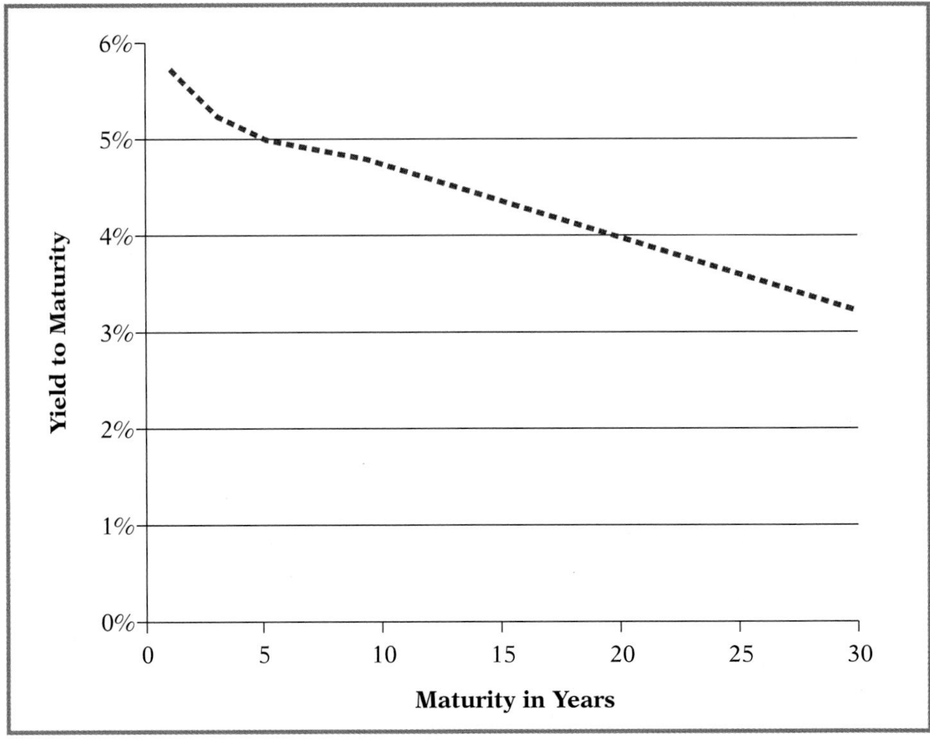

Notice that this yield curve is downward sloping, which indicates that lenders expect interest rates to fall in the future. (See the discussion about the maturity risk premium on page 37). A downward sloping curve such as this one is called an *inverted* yield curve.

3

Financial Institutions

Chapter Objectives

After reading this chapter, you should be able to:

3-1 Explain financial intermediation and the three main roles of financial institutions.

3-2 Define chartered banks.

3-3 Describe the most influential way the Bank of Canada controls the money supply.

3-4 Explain two similarities and the main difference between trust companies and chartered banks.

3-5 Explain how credit unions and caisses populaires are similar in the way they work.

3-6 Compare and contrast finance companies, insurance companies, and pension funds.

"A banker is a fellow who lends his umbrella when the sun is shining and wants it back the minute it begins to rain."

—Mark Twain

Spyware Aims to Profit from You

The threat of spyware hackers probing your finances on your computer is growing.

Maryanna Lewyckyj, Special to The Free Press, 2004-04-28 03:05:25

Toronto—You don't have to be the keeper of top-secret military data to be the target of espionage these days. Anyone with a computer and Internet access is vulnerable to a sophisticated new breed of cyber spies that can wreak havoc on your computer and your finances.

The dangers of the rapidly growing spyware threat were highlighted last year after the arrest of a prolific hacker.

In July 2003, 24-year-old Juju Jiang of Flushing, N.Y., pleaded guilty to computer fraud and software piracy.

Jiang had secretly installed software that logs individual keystrokes in at least 14 Kinko's stores with public-access computer terminals.

He then captured more than 450 user names and passwords, using them to access banking data, set up new accounts online and transfer other people's money to the unauthorized accounts.

The threat of such cybercrime is growing, as security experts estimate about 90% of personal computers with Internet access have been infiltrated by spyware.

"Spyware is an electronic stalker, secretly watching the online activities of millions of unsuspecting Canadians daily," says Alex Leslie, V-P of Technology for AOL Canada Inc.

Spyware installs itself invisibly and lurks in the background, opening up potentially serious security holes, putting even experienced computers at risk, he says.

There are many forms of spyware, ranging from benign adware that tracks buying and surfing habits, to programs designed to make money off stolen identities.

While virus writers typically get a thrill from wreaking havoc on computer users for the sheer challenge of it, spyware is designed to cash in on security flaws.

"Viruses have never really been used for financial gain purposes, whereas with spyware it's the complete opposite," notes Jack Sebbag of Network Associates, which makes McAfee Anti-Virus and AntiSpyware utilities.

Chapter Overview

In this chapter, we will examine how financial institutions help channel available funds to those who need them. We will also see the important role the Bank of Canada plays in regulating the financial system, protecting both suppliers and demanders of capital.

Financial Intermediation

The financial system makes it possible for individuals, businesses, and governments to come together, exchanging funds for securities, to their mutual benefit. When funds flow from suppliers of capital to a financial institution to demanders of capital, the process is known as **intermediation**. The financial institution acts as an intermediary between the two parties.

Suppliers of capital can channel their funds into financial institutions by purchasing savings accounts, chequing accounts, life insurance policies, casualty insurance policies, or claims on a pension fund. The financial institutions can then pool the funds received and use them to purchase claims issued by demanders of capital such as Treasury or corporate bonds and common or preferred shares. (The institutions may purchase real assets too such as real estate or gold.)

At first glance it might seem that intermediation complicates things unnecessarily. Why is a middle person needed? The answer is that financial institutions can do things for both that they often cannot do for themselves. Here are some examples of the services that financial institutions provide.

Denomination and Maturity Matching

Members of the household sector often have only a small amount of funds available to invest in securities. Although, as a group, they are net suppliers of funds and have a large amount of funds available, this is often not the case for individuals or families. Businesses and government entities usually need large amounts of funds. Thus, it is often difficult for individuals, businesses, and governments to come together on their own to arrange a mutually beneficial exchange of funds for securities. Individuals typically want to supply a small amount of funds whereas businesses and governments typically want to obtain a large amount of funds.

A financial institution can step in and save the day. A bank, trust company, or insurance company can take in small amounts of funds from many individuals, form a large pool of funds, and then use that large pool to purchase securities from individual businesses and governments. This pooling of funds is depicted in Figure 3-1.

The typical individual likes to make funds available to others for a short period of time. Most people, for example, would like to get their money back on short notice if the need were to arise. They would prefer to buy securities that have a short maturity. Most businesses and government entities, on the other hand, want to make use of funds for a long period of time. The new plants, roads, airports, and the like that businesses and governments buy and build are long-term projects that often require long-term financing. They would prefer to sell securities that have a long maturity.

Here's the problem: How can exchanges agreeable to both sides be arranged when the individuals want the right to get their funds back quickly? Remember, a financial institution has many different individuals buying its

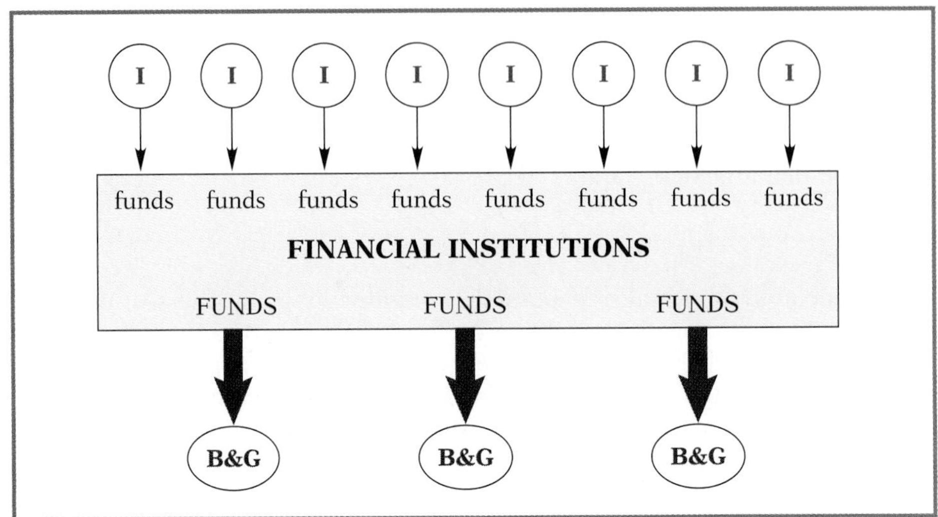

Figure 3-1
Maturity Matching
Figure 3-1 shows how small amounts of funds from many individuals (I) can be pooled and channelled into the hands of a relatively small number of businesses or governments (B&G). The financial institution provides each what it needs.

securities (savings accounts, chequing accounts, insurance policies, and so on). The number that will want their funds back on any given day is likely to be small and they will probably withdraw only a very small percentage of the total funds held in the financial institution. So a large percentage of the funds held by the financial institution can be invested in long-term securities with little danger of running out of funds.

Absorbing Credit Risk

Credit risk is the risk that the issuer of a security may fail to make promised payments to the investor at the times specified. Individuals do not usually have the expertise to determine whether businesses and governments can and will make good on their obligations, so it is difficult for them to predict when an institution will fail to pay what it owes. Such a failure is likely to be devastating to an individual that has lent a proportionately large amount of money. In contrast, a financial institution is in a better position to predict who will pay and who will not. It is also in a better position, having greater financial resources, to occasionally absorb a loss when someone fails to pay.

Now let us turn to the various types of financial institutions. We will start with commercial banks, more commonly known as chartered banks in Canada, which are regulated by various government entities. We will also discuss the Bank of Canada's role in bank regulation and in overseeing the financial system.

Chartered Banks

Commercial banks are financial institutions that exist primarily to lend money to businesses. Unlike other countries, commercial banks in Canada are referred to as chartered banks because historically Canadian commercial banks needed to be chartered in order to operate. Banks also lend to individuals, governments, and other entities, but the bulk of their profits typically come from business loans. Chartered banks make money by charging a higher interest rate on the money they lend than the rate they pay on money lent to them in the form of deposits. This rate charged to borrowers minus the rate paid to depositors is known as the **interest rate spread**.

Banking is different from many other types of business in that it must have a charter before it can open its doors. A bank charter—much more difficult to obtain than a city license needed to open another type of business—is an authorization from the government granting permission to operate. The federal government issues commercial bank charters. You cannot just rent some office space, buy a vault and some office furniture, put up a sign that says, "Joe's Bank," and begin taking in deposits and making loans.

Banks cannot operate without a charter because banking is a business intimately involved in the payment system and money supply of the economy. To protect individuals and the economy as a whole, the government has decided to control entry into this business and to regulate it too. See Figure 3-2 for a graphic description of the soundness of various banks by country.

Regulations

The power to regulate banking was given to the federal government through Section 91 of the BNA Act. Although this is the case, due to the expanding nature of banks, some of their functions actually fall under provincial supervision. That being said, all banks are required by law to be regulated through what is called the **Bank Act**. Historically, banks were classified as Schedule I and II banks. Schedule I banks were mostly Canadian-owned, while Schedule II banks were mostly foreign-owned. This was changed in 2001, where the size of the bank replaced the old regime. If any bank in Canada has over $5 billion in equity, no one person has the right to own more than 20 percent of the bank's voting shares. The regulations become less strict as the bank's equity amount falls. If the bank has less than $1 billion in equity, the bank has no ownership limitations. Currently, banks account for over 70 percent of the total assets of the financial service sector and have been given a very high score in terms of security worldwide.

The Office of the Superintendent of Financial Institutions (OSFI) is the federal agency principally responsible for supervising all federally regulated financial institutions, including chartered banks. Its primary function is to ensure that the banks are running smoothly and that any potential problems can be easily detected. The OSFI sets up risk standards and other policies that

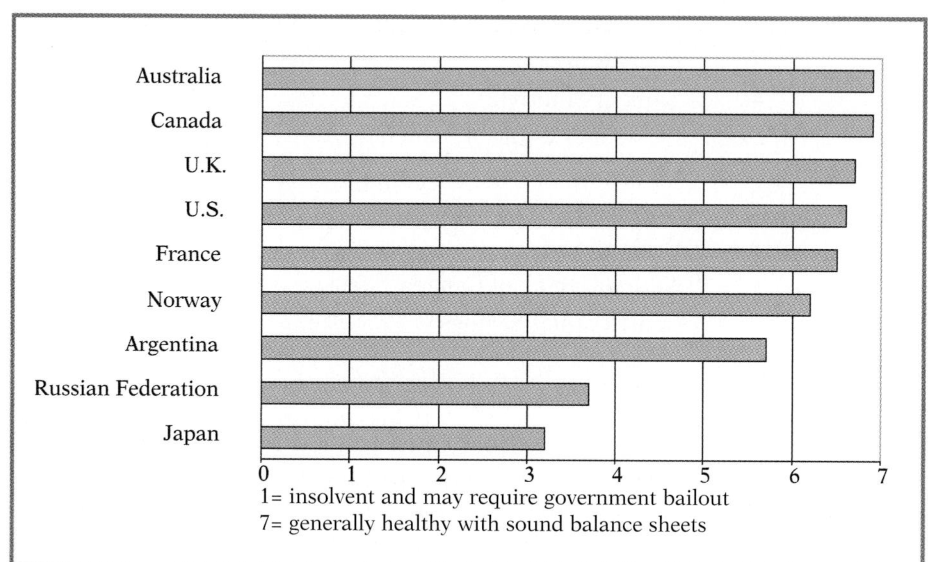

Source: World Economic Forum, *The Global Competitiveness Report 2001–2002*. Used with permission.

Figure 3-2 **Soundness of Banks, 2001–2002**

will reduce the risks involved in Canadian banking. To further reduce risk, the Canadian Deposit Insurance Corporation was created and is federally owned. It guarantees deposits up to $60,000 per account in the unlikely but possible event that a bank should collapse.

Chartered Bank Operations

Chartered banks operate with more government oversight than most businesses, but they are managed just like other companies. Chartered banks have shareholders, employees, managers, equipment, and facilities and the primary financial goal of such banks is to maximize value for their shareholders. The banks do most of their business by receiving funds from depositors and lending the funds to those who need them. Chartered banks also occasionally issue long-term bonds to raise funds, borrow from the Bank of Canada, or borrow deposits kept by other financial institutions.

Online Banking

Online banking consists of using the Internet to link your personal computer to your bank account. Online banks offer a full range of services including chequing accounts, savings accounts, loans, mortgages, credit cards, and online bill paying. About the only thing you cannot do (so far!) with an online bank is have it send you cash over the Internet.

Online banking requires special software, which is either provided by the bank itself or by financial programs such as Quicken® or Microsoft Money®. Online customers use their own personal identification number (PIN) to access their accounts. Using a 128-bit, Secure Socket Layer (SSL) encryption enhances security.

Most major banks in Canada offer some form of online banking today. The following table shows the top 10 online banks in Q3 of 2003 according to gomezcanada.com, a popular online consumer buying guide.

	Firm	*Score (out of 10)*
1.	Scotiabank	7.58
2.	TD Canada Trust	7.52
3.	Royal Bank	7.47
4.	Bank of Montreal	7.06
5.	President's Choice Financial	6.93
6.	CIBC	6.70
7.	Citizens Bank of Canada	6.61
8.	Desjardins	6.49
9.	National Bank of Canada	6.47
10.	Coast Capital Savings	6.39

Source: Watchfire GomezPro Banker—Canada Scorecard (Score out of 10) Q3 2003. www.gomezpro.watchfire.com.

Although our banking system has been ranked fairly highly in recent years, it has been argued that our banks are too small to compete in the emerging global market. The merger of some noted banks has been debated for some time. One argument is for better global competition, while the other side argued that fewer banks would affect quality and competition. See Ethical Connections 3-1 for further discussion.

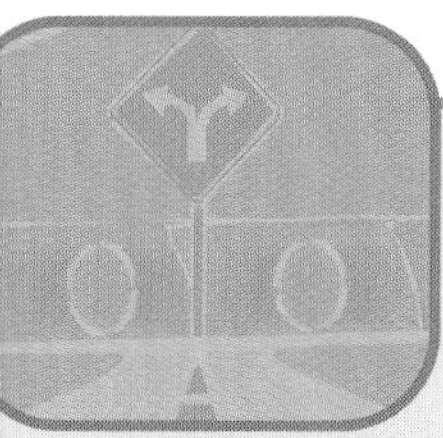

ETHICAL CONNECTIONS 3-1

Banks Will Have to Make Better Case for Mergers, Says Finance Minister

By Sandra Cordon

ttawa (CP)—Canada's big banks could have a tough time onvincing Finance Minister Ralph Goodale that mergers of rger financial institutions are in the public interest.

"In my view, it will be very important . . . to make sure at the public interest is clearly heard and clearly protected . . and we'll determine how that ought to be done," the ngtime Saskatchewan MP said in an interview.

Goodale is still reviewing final submissions from the anks, which were due at the end of December, on what ttawa should consider in reviewing merger proposals.

He still hopes to meet predecessor John Manley's edge to issue Ottawa's final policy on financial sector merg-s this June.

"I'll be very anxious to see what that further input was, oth from the point of view of the banks and others that have stake in this," Goodale said.

But he sounded a much more cautious note on the erger issue than Manley, a former tax attorney who eemed to approve of the concept of merger within Canada's ajor financial institutions.

The emphasis by Goodale—who comes from a part of anada that is traditionally skeptical of Bay Street and the g banks—on the public interest and Ottawa's role in pro-cting that could unnerve some in the banking sector.

Bankers have acknowledged concerns about public terest but have cautioned Ottawa not to overburden them ith regulation.

The major banks have been closely watching the new overnment of Prime Minister Paul Martin for signals on how views the issue.

It was Martin who shot down the first two merger pro-osals floated by Royal Bank with Bank of Montreal and BC with Toronto Dominion Bank in 1998 when he was inister of finance.

With a federal election looming in the spring, the timing ay still not be right for mergers that have never been a pop-ar idea with the public.

Small business and consumer groups have opposed ergers, fearing they will lead to local bank branch closures, yoffs, higher fees and possibly more difficulty for entrepre-eurs seeking loans.

Some of the banks have recently shifted tactics to press tawa to change regulations that now bar them from merg-g with insurance companies.

They have argued that such "cross-pillar" deals would duce competition concerns because they wouldn't elimi-ate banking competitors.

CIBC has argued in a submission to the Federal Finance Department that bank mergers or cross-pillar pairings would create "national champions" capable of competing more effectively at home and abroad.

Reports have suggested CIBC was discussing a possible combination with Manulife Financial Corp. in 2002. Those plans were shelved after Ottawa signalled it had no intention of immediately altering its policies so that merger could proceed.

Goodale suggested he is in no rush either to approve cross-pillar deals.

Allowing big banks to buy out insurers "is a bit of a double-edged sword. I'll want to examine the details on that," he said.

Goodale noted that critics believe such deals would create excessive concentration, especially in smaller communities where the lone insurance broker could be taken over by the lone bank in town.

"Is that a degree of concentration that actually leads to more economic gains for Canada in a world-scale . . . type of assessment or does it have micro-economic implications that mean the downside outweighs the upside?"

Goodale admitted his roots in Saskatchewan, a largely rural province, have a strong influence on the way he considers issues in financial services.

That background gives "a useful perspective" in balancing the concerns of average citizens on main street alongside Toronto's Bay Street banking sector, said the finance minister.

"There are a whole bunch of factors that have to be weighed carefully, but in terms of the completeness of the perspective—having been on main street, having lived there—does help to make sure that whatever decision is ultimately made, it is in fact in the public interest."

Questions to Consider

1. *In terms of being a customer of banks, how might you be hurt from Canadian bank mergers?*
2. *In terms of competition, what do you think the argument is for bank mergers?*
3. *Can you think of any possible compromise?*

Source: Sandra Cordon, "Banks Will Have to Make Better Case for Mergers, Says Finance Minister." Reprinted with permission of The Canadian Press.

The Reserve System The Bank of Canada serves as the central bank for Canada. It regulates the nation's money supply, makes loans to member banks and other financial institutions, and regulates the financial system as described in the previous section.

Open-market purchases of government securities, making loans to financial institutions, and decreasing the Target Overnight Rate all lead to an increase in the money supply. Open-market sales of government securities, receiving payments on loans made to financial institutions, and increasing the Target Overnight Rate all lead to a decrease in the money supply.

Controlling the Money Supply

Why, you might ask, would the Bank of Canada want to increase or decrease the money supply? The answer is simple: to influence economic activity. When the economy is growing too slowly, the Bank of Canada increases the money supply, thus increasing liquidity in the economy and stimulating growth. When the economy is growing too fast and inflation seems imminent, the Bank of Canada decreases the money supply (or slows down its growth). This causes the economy to "cool off" because liquidity has decreased.

Open-Market Operations

Open-market operations are purchases and sales of government securities. When the Bank of Canada *buys* government securities or currencies, it increases bank reserves and the money supply. When the Bank of Canada *sells* government securities or currencies, it decreases bank reserves and the money supply.

When the Bank of Canada wishes to increase the money supply, it buys government securities (primarily government bonds) on the open market. The Bank of Canada contacts government securities dealers (that are mostly banks) around the country and buys the required amount of securities. When the Bank of Canada buys government securities from a dealer, it credits that dealer's account. This action increases the amount of funds held by the dealer banks and enables them to make additional loans and investments. When the additional loans and investments are made, the supply of money in circulation increases, thus accomplishing the Bank of Canada's objective.

The exact opposite occurs when the Bank of Canada wishes to decrease the money supply. The Bank of Canada contacts government securities dealers around the country and sells the required amount of securities to them. When the dealers receive their securities, their accounts are debited and the amount of funds held by these banks decreases. The amount of loans and investments, then, that these banks can support also decreases. Some maturing loans are not renewed and some marketable security investments are not replaced because of the loss of funds. The result is a decrease in the supply of money in circulation.

Although the government securities and currency markets are very large and efficient, the Bank of Canada is like a large elephant: People notice when it enters the market. It buys and sells in huge amounts; so when the Bank of Canada buys or sells securities, its actions cannot help but affect prices (and interest rates) across the whole market.

Target for the Overnight Rate

It used to be that the Bank Rate was the trend-setting rate in Canada. This was the rate that the Bank of Canada would charge chartered banks for loans. It was very closely tied to the 3-month T-Bill rate, being set one-quarter of one percent above it. Further, the prime rate—the rate given by banks to its best customers—was usually set a couple of percentages above the Bank Rate. This made the Bank of Canada's involvement in open market transactions a more important role than it is today.

Today, the Bank of Canada uses a different mechanism to control the economy's money supply. It is known as the Target Overnight Rate, the rate at which the Bank of Canada wants to see institutions loan each other overnight. Similar to the way other rates used to adjust themselves according to the Bank Rate, they now adjust themselves according to the Target Overnight Rate. The way the system works is as follows:

Financial institutions routinely trade billions of dollars with each other each day. At the end of the day, some institutions will have surplus funds while others will not have enough funds to cover the day's transactions. The transactions are done through the Large Value Transfer System (LVTS). At the end of the day, those institutions not having enough money will be charged a rate (equivalent to the Bank Rate), and those institutions having a surplus of money will be given a rate one-half of a percent lower than the borrowing rate. This is known as the operating band. The top of the band is the borrowing rate, while the bottom of the band is the lending rate. The upper and lower bands are separated by one-half of a percentage. The Target Overnight Rate is said to be the rate exactly in-between the upper and lower band. The higher the Target Rate is, the higher the prime rate and other important rates will be. This will reduce the desire for people and business to take out loans, which lowers the money supply, which will in turn slow down inflation because people and business are not buying as much anymore. If the Bank of Canada decreases the Target Rate, this will decrease the prime rate and other important rates, which will in turn stimulate the economy.

One of the reasons the Target Overnight Rate is used, as opposed to the use of the Bank Rate, is that the Target Overnight Rate is comparable to the U.S. Federal Reserve's Target Federal Funds Rate and the Bank of England's two-week Repo Rate.

Zero Reserve Ratio

At no time do banks hold all deposits in the bank. The fact is that most of a bank's profits come from loaning out deposits that people make. The difference in interest between the loan amount and the deposit amount is the profit spread that the bank will gain on each dollar they loan out. This means that at any given time only a fraction of our money is actually in the bank, while most of it has been loaned out. The original thinking was that if some sort of legal requirement were not created to force the banks to retain some of the deposit money, they would loan out too large an amount. Being overextended could affect the stability of banking in Canada and could jeopardize an industry that was supposed to be as safe as possible. Originally, in 1935, the Bank of Canada required that all banks hold a daily cash reserve of 5 percent of their Canadian deposits. This was an attempt to control the amount that banks could lend out at any given time. Effectively the Bank of Canada could increase the money supply by reducing the reserve rate and decrease the money supply by increasing the reserve rate. The logic was that if reserve rates were high, for example, banks could not make as many loans, which would decrease the money supply. As time went on, it became apparent to the Bank of Canada that setting reserve rates was not the most effective way of dealing with the problem of the over-extension of loans.

In 1991, attempts began to reduce reserve requirements. Under that system, banks that over-extended themselves would have to borrow money from the Bank of Canada in order to cover the deficit, borrowing at the Bank Rate. This was a loan from the Bank of Canada. As mentioned before, the Bank Rate was the target rate set by the Bank of Canada. However, the Target Overnight Rate is now used where the Bank of Canada will set this rate, and the Bank Rate is now made to equal the upper limit of the operating band.

Moral Suasion

In the past, the Bank of Canada has occasionally attempted to make the economy react in a certain manner without a direct action. The following is an example. Pretend that the economy is in an inflationary period and the Bank of Canada wants to cool the economy off. We know from our previous readings that the Bank most likely will increase the Target for the Overnight Rate. However, the Bank could instead announce its intention to increase the Target for the Overnight Rate. The economy, believing that the rates will increase, may adjust accordingly by increasing the prime rate and other rates, adjusting spending forecasts, et cetera. In this sense, the economy has reacted to something that the Bank of Canada intended to do but never did.

The following article discusses a situation where moral suasion could be used. Greenspan is notorious for using this method.

INTERNATIONAL PERSPECTIVES IN FINANCE 3-1

Fed's Balanced on a Knife Edge

By Mathew Ingram

Tuesday, Aug. 12, 2003

It would be easy to see today's Federal Reserve meeting as a non-event. After all, the U.S. economy seems to be picking up steam, and most economists expect the central bank to hold its benchmark lending rate steady. Beneath the surface, however, there is a lot going on—and most of it has to do with whether the bond market has lost its faith in Fed chairman Alan Greenspan. If it has, the consequences could be serious.

As most people know, the U.S. central bank tries to promote economic growth by raising or lowering its overnight lending rate (the rate banks charge other banks). In theory, this affects interest rates throughout the entire financial system, helping to stimulate or retard the advance of t U.S. economy, depending on what the Fed wants.

Stories about Mr. Greenspan often make him sound l an almost omniscient being, a master engineer who pu this or that lever, tinkering with the settings on the cent bank engine until the U.S. economy is humming along just the right speed. The reality, however, is that the financ markets are a wild and unruly beast, driven by a broad ran of short- and long-term factors—both real and perceived

That's why the Fed spends a lot of time trying to co municate its intentions to the market, through the statem released with each Fed meeting, as well as its "Beige Boo and Mr. Greenspan's appearances before the U.S. Congre In economic terms, this is known as using "moral suasio ut many traders call it "jawboning the market." Mr. reenspan is seen as a master of this art, but even the laestro makes mistakes.

One of the biggest burrs under the Fed's saddle during e economic downturn has been the way longer-term inter- st rates stayed relatively high, even as short-term rates fell to 0-year lows. While homeowners were happy to ramp up their ortgage-refinancing activity thanks to low short-term rates, gh longer-term rates kept business spending muted. The entral bank's problem was how to bring long rates down.

Earlier this year, the Fed started talking openly—for the rst time—about the risk of deflation, and the various ways e central bank could offset that risk. Some Federal eserve officials even mused about going outside the Fed's sual practice and buying long-term bonds directly, to try to elp drive longer-term interest rates down (rates move in ndem with bond yields, which fall when bond prices rise).

These musings did the trick. Long-bond yields went into eefall, dropping by the largest amount in 20 years. Traders ought in for a variety of reasons: Some thought the Fed ight actually make good on its bond-buying speculation if rther rate cuts weren't enough; others saw even the dis- ussion of such a move by the central bank as a sign that the conomy was still weak, making bonds still look attractive.

Unfortunately for the bond bulls, however, Mr. reenspan didn't follow through on any of those expecta- ons at the Fed's June meeting. In fact, he cut rates by only quarter of a percentage point rather than the half-point cut any traders were expecting; then, in July, the central bank aid measures such as bond purchases were unlikely. And here did bond prices go? Into the tank, sending yields rock- ing higher.

In fact, U.S. 30-year mortgage rates have climbed to e point where some economists are concerned that the mortgage-refinancing boom could be choked off, removing what has been one of the pillars of the U.S. recovery. Mortgage refinancing rates have dropped by about 60 per cent. High long-term rates could also imperil a broad recovery in business spending, which economists have been waiting for since 2000.

In other words, the dramatic yo-yo effect that the Fed's comments produced in the bond market has had a very real impact on the economy, an impact that is the exact opposite of the one the central bank was hoping for (although the bond selloff may have been accelerated by other factors). That means Mr. Greenspan probably will be choosing his words with even more care than he usually does, for fear of exacerbating the problem. It's not so much about rate cuts right now—it's about perception.

If the Fed seems to be too positive about the strength of the economy, for example, bond prices are likely to suffer because this would suggest no more rate cuts, and possibly even rate increases. As a result, yields will rise, pushing long-term rates higher. If the Fed comes out with a pessimistic report about the economy, meanwhile, the bond market may not believe it, given what some traders see as the about-face in June.

In the end, the Fed's job depends as much on expectations and trust as it does on the actual mechanics of setting the central bank rate. Today's meeting—and the fallout from it—will put those factors to the test, regardless of whether there is a rate cut or not.

Mathew Ingram writes analysis and commentary for globeandmail.com.

Source: http://globeandmail.ca/servlet/ArticleNews/TPStory/LAC/20030812/RMATH/TPColumnists. Excerpt from Matthew Ingram, "Fed's Balanced on a Knife Edge," 12 August 2003. Reprinted with permission of *The Globe and Mail.*

Trust Companies

Like chartered banks, trust companies are in business to take in deposits and lend money, primarily in the form of mortgage loans. *Mortgage loans* are loans that are secured by real property such as real estate. If a borrower defaults on a mortgage loan, the lender can take legal possession of the property. The property can then be sold and the lender keeps the proceeds from the sale up to the amount owed. Trust companies make a profit by charging a higher interest rate on the money they lend than the rate paid on deposits they take in. Like banks, trust companies can borrow from the Bank of Canada and from other financial institutions.

Trust Legislation

Trust companies were originally created because, under common law, corporations were not allowed to act as trustees. First beginning in the United States in the 1820s, trust companies became more popular in Canada as time went on. They operate very similarly to chartered banks, having branches, setting up chequing accounts, and giving out loans. However, due to their legislation, trust companies can also administer estates, trusts, and pension plans. Banks cannot do this. However, today, nothing prevents a bank from owning a trust company.

In the beginning of the 1980s, real estate and construction projects were going up. To satisfy the needs of the people, regulators allowed trust companies to increase their loaning power. Unfortunately, interest rates went up (the problem with this is discussed in the following sections) and some scandals took place, undermining the credibility of trust companies. This led to a relatively large amount of trust companies ceasing operations.

Regulations Trust Companies

Trust companies must operate under provincial or federal legislation and are regulated by the Federal Trust and Loan Companies Act. Their deposits are eligible for deposit insurance through the Canada Deposit Insurance Corporation.

Take Note

GICs (Guaranteed Investment Certificates) are relatively low risk investments offered by banks and other financial institutions like trust companies. The terms can vary; most falling between 1 and 5 years. The terms are fixed when purchased, meaning a buyer's money is theoretically locked in until the GIC matures.

The Problem of Matching Loan and Deposit Maturities

Most of the mortgage loans made by trust companies have very long maturities (the 25-year mortgage is most common). However, most of the deposits that provide the money for these loans have zero or short maturities (passbook savings accounts have zero maturity because the depositor can withdraw at any time; GICs come in maturities of up to five years). This gap between the 25-year maturity of the trust's major assets and the zero- to five-year maturity of their deposits creates a problem if market interest rates rise. Consider the following example.

Suppose a trust wanted to make a 25-year, fixed-rate mortgage loan for $100,000 at 7 percent interest. To raise cash for the loan, the trust sells a one-year $100,000 GIC at 3 percent interest. This creates a favourable spread (7% – 3% = + 4%) as long as interest rates stay where they are. Table 3-1 shows the trust's profit during the first year of the loan.

Table 3-1 First-Year Profit for a Trust with a 7% Loan Financed by a 3% GIC

Interest received from the loan	$\$100,000 \times 0.07 = \$7,000$
Interest paid out to the GIC holder	$\$100,000 \times 0.03 = \$3,000$
	Net Income: $4,000

Note: For simplicity in this example, we assume the loan's terms allow the borrower to make only interest payments each year, deferring payment of the principal until the end of the loan's term.

At the end of the first year, the GIC matures and the trust must pay the GIC holder $100,000 plus 3 percent interest ($3,000). So the trust sells another one-year GIC for $100,000, giving the proceeds to the first GIC holder. Then it uses $3,000 of its interest income from the loan to pay the interest due on the first GIC. At the end of the second year and thereafter, the cycle repeats itself with the trust selling a new one-year GIC each year and using the profits from the loan to pay the interest due on the old GICs. You can see that as long as each new GIC is issued for 3 percent interest, the trust will net a yearly profit of $4,000 ($7,000 income from the loan minus $3,000 paid to the GIC holder).

What happens, however, if interest rates rise during the first year, such that at the end of the year the trust must pay 9 percent to get anyone to buy a new one-year GIC? Now the trust is in trouble. It has to sell a new GIC to pay the $100,000 owed to the holder of the first GIC, but it can only do so by offering an interest rate two points higher than its mortgage loan is paying. So at the end of the second year, when the trust must pay the interest to the GIC holder, it must pay $9,000 instead of $3,000 and suffers a $2,000 loss for the year. Table 3-2 summarizes the situation.

Table 3-2 **Second-Year Loss for a Trust with a 7% Loan Financed by a 9% GIC**

Interest received from the loan	$100,000 × 0.07 = $7,000
Interest paid out to the GIC holder	$100,000 × 0.09 = $9,000
	Net Income: ($2,000)

Of course, market interest rates can go down too, creating extra profits for the trust, but trusts face a risk of loss when market interest rates move against them.

Credit Unions

Credit unions are member-owned financial institutions. They pay interest on shares bought by, and collect interest on loans made to, the members. Members are individuals rather than businesses or government units.

Credit unions are able to make relatively low interest loans to their members because they are cooperative organizations. Also, they make loans *only* to members who are presumed to be somewhat better credit risks than the general population.

The Common Bond Requirement

To help ensure that credit union members actually are better credit risks than the general population, credit union members must have a *common bond* with one another. This could mean that all members work for the same company, belong to the same labour union, or perhaps just live in the same town as the other members. The theory is that people, who all belong to the same group, sharing common values, will be less likely to default on loans supported by money from their fellow group members.

Members as Shareholders

Credit unions are owned by their members, so when credit union members put money in their credit union, they are not technically "depositing" the money. Instead, they are purchasing *shares* of the credit union.

Like owners of other businesses, credit union members are entitled to any income the credit union has after debts and expenses have been paid. This residual income may be distributed in the form of extra dividends paid on the members' shares or by a rebate on interest paid on loans.

Credit Unions Compared with Banks

Traditionally, credit unions were small institutions that did not compete much with banks. However, they have grown rapidly in recent years and now provide most of the same services as chartered banks.

Caisses Populaires

Caisses populaires are Quebec's response to the idea of a credit union. They were founded on the principal belief that banks were too profit-oriented and were not as in touch with their customers as they should be. Caisses operate in a similar fashion as credit unions where members are actual owners of the financial institution and each member has the right to speak about the institution's financial decisions. However, caisses populaires are not as strict on common bond requirements. The movement began through Desjardins in the 1900s. Although caisses populaires work independently of each other, they do sometimes combine assets for more resource-heavy products such as selling insurance. Both caisses populaires and credit unions are provincially regulated.

Finance Companies, Insurance Companies, and Pension Funds

Finance companies are nonbank firms that make short-term and medium-term loans to consumers and businesses. They often serve those customers who do not qualify for loans at other financial institutions.

Like banks and trust companies, finance companies operate by taking in money and lending it out to their customers at a higher interest rate. A major difference between finance companies and other financial institutions, however, lies in the source of finance company funds. Banks and trust companies receive most of their funds from individuals and businesses that deposit money in accounts at the institutions. Finance companies generally get their funds by borrowing from banks or by selling commercial paper.

Types of Finance Companies

There are three main types of finance companies: consumer, commercial, and sales. In the following sections, we will explain the characteristics and functions of each type.

Consumer Finance Companies Consumer finance companies, sometimes known as small-loan companies, make small loans to consumers for car purchases, recreational vehicles, medical expenses, vacations, and the like. Consumer finance companies often make loans to customers with less than perfect credit. Because the customers are a higher risk, the interest rates charged on loans are usually a little higher to compensate for the greater risk.

Commercial Finance Companies These firms concentrate on providing credit to other business firms. A special type of commercial finance company is called a *factor.* Factoring is the buying of a business firm's accounts receivable, thus supplying needed funds to the selling firm. Commercial finance companies also make loans to businesses, usually with accounts receivable or inventory pledged as collateral. This type of financing will be examined in detail in the latter chapters.

Sales Finance Companies The mission of sales finance companies is to help the sales of some corporation (indeed, many are subsidiaries of the corporation the sales of which they are promoting). In the automotive industry, for example, customers are more likely to buy cars from dealers that offer financing on the spot than from dealers who have no financing programs.

A finance company generally gives its retail dealers a supply of loan contract forms, which the dealers fill out at the time of sale. The contract is immediately sold to the finance company (at a slightly reduced price, of course, to allow for the finance company's profit). General Motors Acceptance Corporation (GMAC) and the Ford Motor Credit Company are prominent examples of sales finance companies.

Insurance Companies

Insurance companies are firms that, for a fee, will assume risks for their customers. They collect fees, called premiums, from a large number of customers. Then they draw on the pool of funds collected to pay those customers who suffer damages from the perils they have insured against.

There are two main types of insurance companies: life insurance companies and property and casualty insurance companies.

Life Insurance Companies *Life insurance companies* sell policies that pay the beneficiaries of the insured when the insured person dies. You might ask how life insurance companies make any money because *everybody* dies sooner or later. If the risk life insurance companies were taking in return for the premium received were the risk of their customers dying, it is true that none of them would make any money. The real risk they are taking, however, is that the insured person will die *sooner than expected.*

To help assess this risk, insurance companies employ actuaries. **Actuaries** help calculate the premium for a life insurance policy for a person of a given age, gender, and state of health, so that the insurance company can pay the insurance benefit, cover expenses, and make a profit. Actuaries cannot tell specifically *who* is going to die when, but they can predict, with a high degree of accuracy, *how many* in a group of 100,000 healthy 40-year-old males will die during the coming year.

Life insurance companies function as financial intermediaries essentially the same way as chartered banks or trust companies. They take money in the form of policy premiums and channel it to investments in common shares, corporate bonds, mortgages, and real estate. Their payout can be predicted with a high degree of accuracy, so they need only a small amount of liquid assets.

Property and Casualty Insurance Companies *Property and casualty insurance companies* insure against a wide range of hazards associated with person and property. These include theft; weather damage from hurricanes, tornadoes, floods, and ice storms; fire; and earthquakes. Two close relatives of property and casualty companies are health insurance companies, which insure people against injuries and illnesses, and disability insurance companies, which insure people against loss of income from being unable to work.

One special hazard that these companies insure against is a policyholder's own negligence. This kind of insurance is called **liability insurance**. Most people are familiar with automobile liability insurance, but liability coverage can also be purchased for such things as medical malpractice, dog bites, and falls by visitors on your property.

The risks protected against by property and casualty companies are much less predictable than the risks insured by life insurance companies. Hurricanes, fires, ice storms, floods, and trial judgments are all much more difficult to predict than the number of 60-year-old females who will die this year among a large number in this risk class. This means that property and casualty insurance companies must keep more liquid assets than life insurance companies.

Pension Funds Pension funds are set up by companies, governments, and unions to pay retirement benefits for their employees. They are essentially savings plans. Employees generally contribute money to the funds now in order to draw it out later, on retirement. Employers usually contribute money on behalf of the employees, too. All the money is pooled and invested and the investment returns are added to the pot. It is always possible, of course, that the sponsor (the company, government, or union) will not be able to pay promised benefits. If this happens, the pension fund is said to have failed and the worker may not collect all the promised benefits.

Pension funds invest so much money that they are the country's greatest source of long-term capital. They have *billions* of dollars invested in a wide range of securities and other assets such as real estate. Pension fund officials often hire money management firms just to manage the fund's investments. Bank trust departments and insurance companies also manage pension fund money.

Pension funds generally use one of two types of procedures for determining benefits for retired workers: a defined benefit plan and a defined contribution plan. In a defined benefit plan, retirement benefits are determined by a formula that usually considers the worker's age, salary, and years of service. The employee and/or the firm contribute the amounts necessary to reach the goal. In a defined contribution plan, the contributions to be made by the employee and/or employer are spelled out, but retirement benefits depend on the total accumulation in the individual's account at the retirement date.

Annuities An *annuity* is a series of equal payments that are made at regular time intervals, such as monthly, for a specified period of time. Pension fund benefits are often paid out in the form of annuities. Sometimes the sponsor of a pension fund will use the funds accumulated during the retiring person's working years to purchase an annuity from an insurance company. This provides the retired person's benefits. Insurance companies also sell annuities to investors. In return for the amount paid to the insurance company, the investor receives payments (usually monthly) for the remainder of his or her life. A person who receives annuity payments is called an annuitant. The size of the payments depends on how much money is paid to the insurance company at the time of the employee's retirement, along with factors such as the age, gender (if allowed by law), and state of health of the annuitant. If the pension fund investments made on behalf of a given employee earned a high return, a large amount of money will be available to purchase a large annuity.

If the defined contribution pension fund investments performed poorly, the retired employee will be able to purchase only a small annuity.

Sometimes the investments made on an employee's behalf will be paid out in a lump sum at retirement. It is then up to the retired employee to invest this money wisely to generate the needed income during retirement.

FINANCIAL MANAGEMENT AND YOU 3-1

Canada Pension Plan and Quebec Pension Plan

ost of us are participants in the Canada Pension Plan (or ebec Pension Plan*). It is the largest pension vehicle in nada. Ironically, it is not a pension fund, but a system in ich those contributing money today are paying the retire- ent and disability benefits for those collecting today. hough in years past the fund has ran a surplus, that will t be the case for much longer.

With a pension fund, you put in money that is set aside pay future claims. With the CPP (or QPP), in essence, you t in babies who will become taxpayers to provide the eded funds for beneficiaries having claims in the future. ien the older generation collecting benefits is very large d the younger generation paying the taxes funding those benefits is very small, some difficult choices have to be made. Taxes on the young have to be increased or benefits to the old have to be decreased. Contributors versus beneficiaries will continue to decline as the "baby-boomer" generation retires and stops paying into the CPP (or QPP) and begins collecting from it.

What does this suggest to you about your own financial planning? Polls show that more young adults believe in flying saucers than believe that CPP (or QPP) will be there when they retire. Other polls show that young people are beginning to save more money when they start working than their parents' generation did at the same age.

*Quebec residents.

SUMMARY

3-1 Explain financial intermediation and the three main roles of financial institutions.

Financial institutions act as intermediaries between suppliers and demanders of capital. They coordinate the flow of funds, absorbing differences between the amount of funds offered and needed, between the length of time funds are offered and needed, and between the degree of risk that individuals are willing to bear and the risk that is inherent in the securities offered by businesses and governments.

3-2 Define chartered banks.

Chartered banks are financial institutions that are owned by shareholders, that take in deposits, and that make loans (primarily to businesses). They are regulated by the Bank Act and are strictly monitored.

3-3 Describe the most influential way the Bank of Canada controls the money supply.

The Bank of Canada usually uses its ability to set the Target Overnight Rate to influence monetary policy. If the Bank of Canada wants to increase the money supply, it will lower this target rate and if it wants to decrease the money supply, it will increase the target rate. Because transactions are done through the Large Value Transfer System (LVTS), participating members are easily monitored in terms of daily cash deficits and surpluses. The Bank of Canada can also influence the money supply through moral suasion and open market trading. However, this is less favoured when compared to influencing the Target Overnight Rate.

3-4 Explain two similarities and the main difference between trust companies and chartered banks.

Trust companies are financial institutions that take in deposits and mainly make mortgage loans. Trust companies are regulated by the Federal Trust and Loan Companies Act. Trust companies primarily make mortgage loans (to consumers). Banks primarily make commercial loans to businesses.

3-5 Explain how credit unions and caisses populaires are similar in the way they work.

Credit unions and caisses populaires are financial institutions that take in funds by selling shares to members and make loans to those members. People are eligible for membership in a credit union if they meet the requirement of having a common bond with the other members while caisses populaires are not as strict with this requirement. This might be working for a given company, belonging to a certain union, or living in a specified area. Credit unions operate throughout Canada while caisses populaires are mostly located in Quebec.

3-6 Compare and contrast finance companies, insurance companies, and pension funds.

Finance companies take in funds, primarily by selling commercial paper, and make personal loans. Insurance companies sell policies, collecting premiums and paying beneficiaries if the insured-against event the insurance covers occurs. Pension funds take in funds, usually contributed by both the employer and the employee, and invest those funds for future payment to the worker when he or she retires. This retirement benefit may be determined by a formula (a defined benefit plan) or by how much is in the investment fund at the time of retirement (a defined contribution plan).

SELF-TEST

ST-1. Why is intermediation sometimes needed to bring together suppliers and demanders of capital?

ST-2. Discuss how the Bank of Canada can control the money supply through changing the Target Overnight Rate.

ST-3. What is the common bond requirement that credit union members must have to be eligible for membership?

ST-4. Where is the Bank Rate currently set?

REVIEW QUESTIONS

1. Define *intermediation*.
2. What can a financial institution often do for individuals that the individuals would have difficulty doing for themselves if the individuals were to deal directly with businesses or governments?
3. What can a financial institution often do for businesses or governments that they would have difficulty doing for themselves if the businesses and governments were to deal directly with an individual?
4. What are a bank's reserves? When the Bank of Canada sets reserve requirements, what is its primary goal? What is the current reserve requirement?
5. Who owns a credit union? Explain.
6. Which type of insurance company generally takes on the greater risks: a life insurance company or a property and casualty insurance company?

7. Compare and contrast a *defined benefit* and a *defined contribution* pension plan.
8. What tools are used in online banking to ensure the security of transactions?

PROBLEMS

3-1. Assume that society is made up of 100 individuals that have $10 each and three businesses that need $100 each. With that in mind, describe ◀ Financial Intermediation

a. how the society would have to operate if there were no financial institutions present to perform financial intermediation.

b. how financial institutions help overcome the problems you described.

3-2. a. Assume that the Goodfellows National Bank pays 5 percent interest on depositors' accounts and charges 10 percent interest on loans it makes to businesses. What is Goodfellows' interest rate spread? ◀ Chartered Banks (interest rate spread)

b. To make the problem a little more challenging, assume that Goodfellows pays 5 percent interest on depositors' savings accounts, which make up 50 percent of all funds on hand and 7 percent interest on all GICs, which make up the other 50 percent of funds received. Next, assume that Goodfellows charges 10 percent interest on short-term loans, which make up 50 percent of all loans outstanding and 12 percent interest on long-term loans, which make up the other 50 percent of all loans outstanding. What is Goodfellows' interest rate spread?

3-3. Assume that Goodfellows National Bank has $60 million in transaction accounts, $20 million in nonpersonal time deposits, and $10 million in Eurocurrency liabilities. Given the current reserve requirements, how much must Goodfellows keep on hand in reserve funds? ◀ Chartered Banks (required reserve ratio)

3-4. There is great concern that the economy is in a recessionary trend. ◀ The Bank of Canada System

a. What would you recommend that the Bank of Canada do to stimulate the economy?

b. Explain the chain of events that occurs when the Bank of Canada takes the action that you recommended in part (a)?

3-5. Goodfellows National Bank has decided to compete with trust companies by offering 25-year, fixed rate mortgage loans at 8 percent annual interest. It plans to obtain the money for the loans by selling one-year 6 percent GICs to its depositors. During the first year of operation, Goodfellows sells its depositors $1,000,000 worth of 7 percent one year GICs, and homebuyers take out $1,000,000 worth of 8 percent 25-year fixed rate mortages. ◀ Matching Loan and Deposit Maturities

a. Considering only the information above, what is Goodfellows' gross profit for the first year of operation?

In its second year of operation, Goodfellows must sell $1,000,000 worth of new GICs to replace the ones that mature. However, interest rates have gone up during the year and now the rate the bank must pay to get people to buy new GICs is 9 percent.

b. Assuming that Goodfellows does sell $1,000,000 worth of new GICs at 9 percent interest in the second year, and assuming the $1,000,000 worth of 8 percent mortgage loans are still outstanding, what is Goodfellows' gross profit during the second year?

(Note: For the purposes of this problem, assume that the mortgage holders make only interest payments each year.)

Bank of Canada ▶

3-6. You have just become the Prime Minister of Canada and you noticed that the economy seems to be falling in terms of economic output. You are very concerned with the situation and you would like to see the economy recover before the forthcoming election. You have suggested that the Bank of Canada sell more government T-Bills in order to stimulate the economy.

a. The Bank of Canada puts down your idea for two reasons. What are they? Explain them.

b. You realize your error and instead suggest that the Bank of Canada decrease the Bank Rate. Again, the Bank of Canada shakes it head in disagreement. Why? Explain the process for setting the Bank Rate.

c. You make a final suggestion to lower the current required reserve ratio for chartered banks. The Bank of Canada again shakes its head and suggests that what you ask is impossible. Why? Explain the Bank of Canada's current position on the required reserve ratio.

Financial Intermediaries ▶

3-7. You are looking to buy a house and a new car. You have shopped around for the best rates and have found several options. You expect your mortgage needs to be about $150,000 and you will need a loan for $15,000 for a new car. Your current credit rating is okay but not great. You should have no problems getting a mortgage loan anywhere because you plan on putting down a sizeable down payment. However, the car loan may be difficult. Your friend suggests that you borrow only from a finance company.

a. What other borrowing options may you have? What are the drawbacks of borrowing from a finance company? Can you think of any potential problems with your friend's idea? Can you formulate a better solution?

b. You are now considering borrowing money from a trust company or from a chartered bank. Your friend, speaking again, tells you to be careful; trust companies are much more risky in terms of borrowing than chartered banks. What is the history of trust companies and their past failure? Does that have any reflection on your current situation? Explain.

c. Finally deciding, you go to a credit union outside of town to borrow the full $165,000. Your application was rejected on the spot. What could be the possible reasons?

Banking Regulation ▶

3-8. You decide to start your own bank. You want to call it "The Bank of Give Me Money" (GMM for short). You decide to loan out funds at the Bank Rate and, being non-discriminating, you decide that money should be available to anybody who wants a loan. Your grandfather was rich (really rich) and gave you $5 billion to start off your bank. Fearful of your decision to give loans out to anybody, you put a no-guarantee clause on all deposits, compensating the increased risk with a higher deposit interest rate. Your first month of operation is a disaster. A government official visited you, you were pestered by nagging customers and, to top it off, you lost money.

a. During your first day of operation a government official came to your bank and began criticizing your bank, suggesting that it had several flaws. What flaws do you think can be found? Is there a way to correct the situation?

b. As expected, several people default on their loans, which creates a severe cash flow problem for your bank. Several people are demanding their deposit money, despite your no-guarantee policy. If your bank were operating under normal conditions, how could this situation be averted? What other mechanism(s) are in place to secure deposits?

c. Having no cash, you are forced to borrow money for the difference. Further, you have to borrow money in order to satisfy loan needs. Even when the best rate is found, it is still very difficult for your bank to make money. Why? What do you think is the logical way banks would normally set their interest rates?

3-9. Kara and Mikeal, married for 25 years, were planning for their retirement. Their mutual company began the process of converting their defined benefit program to a defined contribution program. The company has offered all the current employees the option of staying within the old program or converting to the new one, but all new employees will only be eligible for the new defined contribution program. You are a friend of Kara and Mikeal's and you want to give them some advice. Kara and Mikeal are going to retire in about 7 years when they turn 65 and 68 respectively.

◀ Defined Benefit versus Defined Contribution

a. Firstly, Kara and Mikeal have no idea what a defined contribution plan is or what a defined benefit program is. Can you explain it to them? What are the pros and cons and why do you think the company is trying to change systems?

b. Concerning Kara and Mikeal's current situation, which program do you think would be the most favourable?

c. Would your answer change if you knew that the pension plan was solely operated through the company (i.e., the company was responsible for all aspects of the pension fund)? Why?

3-10. Alan Greenspan, Chairman of the Federal Reserve Board of the United States of America, has been called, by some, the most important person in the world. In his speeches to the public, he will make both general and indirect comments. For example, he may say something like "in the foreseeable future, it is more likely that one could see the effects of previous stimulus."

◀ Money Supply Tools

a. What do you think previous stimulus implies? What sort of economic situation needs a stimulus? Explain how this stimulus works.

b. Assuming that the above quote was accurate, how may the market interpret the need for further stimulus in the future? How is this important to capital markets and money markets for both suppliers and demanders of capital?

c. If Greenspan is hopeful that the public reacts solely on the quote alone, what type of strategy is being used? What does it depend on in order to be successful?

d. Why do you think that what the Chairman of the Federal Reserve Board of the United States of America says should be of any concern to us in Canada?

3-11. The Bank of Canada has recently changed its Target for the Overnight Rate. They have dropped the rate by 0.25 percent. You have several holdings and liabilities. You own several GICs. You also have a fixed-rate mortgage and a variable loan taken out through a line of credit. You should be able to pay off your $25,000 mortgage or your $25,000 loan on your line of credit within 5 years. The Bank of Canada has announced that it does not foresee any inflationary situations within the next 4 years.

◀ Bank of Canada Analysis

a. After the rate dropped, what has happened to your GICs? To your fixed-rate mortgage? To your variable loan?

b. Why might a mortgage loan company be happy with the future of interest rates?

c. If you had the option to pay off either your line of credit loan or your mortgage by borrowing from the other, what could you do to save money? How important is the Bank of Canada's economic forecast to your decision?

ANSWERS TO SELF-TEST

ST-1. Intermediation is sometimes needed when suppliers and demanders of capital cannot agree about the denomination, maturity, and risk of the security offered and bought. Financial intermediaries can often give each side what it needs by stepping into the middle of the exchange of funds for securities.

ST-2. The Bank of Canada can change the money supply by either increasing or decreasing the Target Overnight Rate. If the Bank of Canada wishes the economy to expand, it will lower the rate and it will increase the rate if it wants the economy to slow down.

ST-3. Credit union members are required to have some common bond with the other members before the request for membership is approved. Examples of common bonds include working for a given company, belonging to a certain union, or living in a certain area.

ST-4. The Bank Rate is currently set at 0.25 percent above the Target Overnight Rate.

Comprehensive Cases: Part I

Case 1: Computer Land Canada (CLC)

Computer Land Canada (CLC) is a computer dealer, value-added reseller (VAR), and systems integrator that has the license to operate in Canada under the internationally recognized umbrella of the Computer Land Europe Corporation. The company began operations in early 2001. CLC was formed by a Swedish investment group comprising entrepreneurs with experience in the computer industry in Sweden. By late 2002, the company began opening sales offices throughout Canada to better serve its customers. By the end of 2004, the company had been able to transform from selling mostly personal computers (PCs) to offering a greater percentage of sales of more sophisticated computer hardware, peripherals, and services. CLC's strategy behind making this transition was to pattern itself after U.S. computer resellers that developed a significant percentage of service sales in their business in an effort to maintain higher profitability and cultivate a repeat-customer base over time.

Thomas Sehl manages the company, which has a total staff of 70 people. He holds a M.Sc. Eng. in electronics and computer science. Before joining CLC, he worked as a software engineer and eventually executive vice-president for Kamel, a diversified company with wide ranging activities, including computer software design to trading of commodities. He joined CLC in March 2001 as the manager of the Toronto office. He was appointed President of CLC in early 2002. Mr. Sehl is currently a 10 percent shareholder in CLC. His desire is to own more of the company in the future. He also has the incentive, provided by a management stock option program, to acquire up to an additional 5 percent over the next five years (1 percent per year) based on achieving an increase in sales above the budget and the company share value in the market.

CLC, under the direction of its president, is looking to acquire ProSoft. ProSoft segregates its activities into two areas: software development and modification and systems procurement and integration. ProSoft's revenues are similar to that of CLC's. ProSoft is headquartered in Calgary and therefore competes very heavily with the CLC Calgary office. ProSoft has representative offices in Toronto and Vancouver as well. CLC is looking to acquire ProSoft for a price well above the company's market value. A recent valuation of ProSoft performed by a prestigious Calgary-based consulting firm confirmed that CLC would be paying approximately 50 percent more for ProSoft than its market value. CLC's price is also 60 percent above the latest offer made to ProSoft by a company competing with CLC.

Dr. Adam Ela is a member of the board of directors of CLC and a 25 percent owner of the company. Dr. Ela decided to review Mr. Sehl's share option and bonus program and discovered that Mr. Sehl would receive a handsome bonus at the end of the year if the acquisition of ProSoft went through. The president would also be entitled to an accelerated scheme on his share option program as a consequence of this acquisition. In effect, the president's right to acquire an additional 5 percent of the company would accelerate—he would be able to acquire his 5 percent in two tranches over the next two years. While

Dr. Ela always trusted Mr. Sehl's business judgment, he did not understand Mr. Sehl's reasons to argue so vigorously about the acquisition of ProSoft at the last board meeting in Toronto. He wondered whether Mr. Sehl had another motivation.

Requirements

1. Summarize the sound business arguments in this case.
2. Summarize the personal interests that Mr. Sehl may have.
3. Create a remedy if a potential conflict exists.

CASE 2: THE BARBER SHOP

Sally Ross has been exploring the idea of expanding her small business. Currently, Sally operates a men's hair salon with two chairs for cutting hair. Both she and an employee work 6 days a week, 10 hours a day. Fatigued with the amount of work she is doing, Sally figures that if she expands, she would actually be able to work less because she would be able to offset the extra cost of help with the increased revenue. Because it is a hair salon, the only significant assets that Sally owns through the business are the two chairs, which are worth $50,000 each. As for her personal finances, Sally owns her house, has $5,000 in investments, and has $25,000 in RRSPs. The investments and her RRSPs were made several years ago in a big lump sum. Since then she has not been able to save further, putting all her money into the business start-up. Her financial assets, both business and personal, are summarized as follows. A summary of how much Sally makes from the business is also included.

	Market Value	Book Value	Years Held
House	240,000	25,000	25
2 Barber chairs	100,000	150,000	5
RRSP (no dividends)	25,000	24,500	8
Investments (no dividends)	5,000	7,500	8

Summary Income Statement

Revenue	
Hair cuts	$125,000
Expenses	
Staff	$20,000
Products	20,000
Rent	18,000
Utilities	5,000
Other	2,000
Income before Taxes	**$60,000**
Tax 20%	12,000
Net Income	**$48,000**

The statement of income has been fairly consistent over the last five years.

Sally would like to move to a new location, doubling her size. However, doubling her size would also double her rent and utilities. She would like to buy three more chairs for a total of five chairs, and hire four more people to cut hair while paying them at the same low wage she has been paying her original employee. Sally has always thought little of her employees in terms of compensation believing that if people really wanted to make money, they would become self-employed as she had done. Sally charges $13.50 per haircut and expects to be able to raise the price to $15.00. She thinks people will pay the extra because she plans on making the new place look more prestigious. Sally expects revenue to be proportional to the number of chairs she has, as it has been in the past. To summarize, she needs the following in up-front capital if she wishes to continue with her expansion project:

Summary

	Up-Front Capital
New Chairs	$300,000
Renovations	100,000
Moving	5,000
Cancel Current Lease	4,500
Additional Working Capital	50,000
Total Up-Front Capital Needed	**$459,500**

She has gone to the local bank to get a loan for the $459,500. The current going rate for business loans that have relatively no risk is 5 percent. Currently, inflation has been floating below historic norms and it is expected to rise (in absolute terms) by 50 basis points (0.5 percent). Further, due to several accounting scandals, banks have been forced to scrutinize their loans much more and have been requiring higher collateral for secured loans. Previously, banks could loan a person 80 percent of the value of their secured assets; now that amount has fallen to 75 percent. The amount has fallen even further for loans that have a maturity greater than five years, down to 65 percent.

Sally has exhausted all sources of financing and borrowing from the bank is her only possible solution. She does not like the idea of putting her house up as collateral, but she will do it if need be. Further, Sally has just found out that her wage rate is way too low. She knows that she has to increase it but does not feel that the bank will give her a loan if the bank sees more money going to others first instead of it. Sally is not able to borrow against her RRSPs and if she decides to take the money out, it will be taxed at 40 percent. Further, she is not sure what rate of interest she can afford. Sally needs at least $40,000 each year to live and needs to know that she can pay all her obligations off even if her revenue forecasts are off by one-third.

Requirements

1. Assess Sally's current position.
2. Develop strategies in whatever legal manner possible to make the financial situation more favourable for getting the bank loan.
3. Make recommendations and summarize the course of action.

CASE 3: READING THE HEADLINES

It was a long day for Mark Wong who worked for MCD Mortgage Company. Although MCD Mortgage Company is exclusive to mortgage loans, it was actually incorporated under the Bank Act and has the full abilities and obligations of a bank. The last couple of years had been great as business was going very smoothly. The following are last year's financial statements.

MCD Mortgage Company
Balance Sheet As at October 31
(C$ millions)

Assets		**Liabilities**	
Cash	$1,500	Deposits	
Deposits with banks or BOC	4,000	Personal	$50,000
Short-term investments	15,000	Government	5,000
Loans		Other banks	1,000
Residential mortgage	50,000	**Total Liabilities**	$56,000
Allowance for loan losses	–500	**Shareholders' equity**	
	$70,000	Preferred shares	
Other		(200,000 outstanding)	20
Other assets	5,000	Common shares	
Total assets	$75,000	(1,000,000,000 outstanding)	7,000
		Retained earnings	11,980
		Total shareholders' equity	$19,000
		Total liabilities and shareholders' equity	$75,000

MCD Mortgage Company
Income Statement
For the year ended October 31
(C$ millions)

Interest Income	
Mortgage loans	$ 4,000
Investment	600
Deposits with banks or BOC	150
	$ 4,750
Interest Expense	
Deposits	$ 1,680
Net interest income	$ 6,642
Other	3,358
Total revenues	$ 10,000
Bad debt	50
Other expenses	2,500
Net income before income taxes	$ 7,450
Income taxes	1,863
Net income	$ 5,588
Preferred share dividends	1
Net income available to common shareholders	$ 5,587
Average number of common shares (in thousands)	1,000,000
Earnings per share (in dollars)	$5.5865
Dividends per share (in dollars)	$2

MCD has grown very quickly over the last several years, but last year's equity was only $4,900 million. The relative nature of each account remained constant, every account growing at the same percentage rate. Mark Wong has been the sole common shareholder for MCD since its inception and originally sold preferred shares to his family and friends. One of the bank's strengths has been its family-run attitude, which really complemented the community in which it operated. Interest rates had been falling for the last couple of years and Wong took advantage of this. However, the following newspaper articles made Wong feel a little uneasy.

The Tribune

BOC TO TAKE ACTION AGAINST INFLATION

It was announced today that the Bank of Canada (BOC) will be taking action to slow down the potential for inflation. The Bank of Canada is thinking of several ways of doing this, including revising the current zero-reserve ratio policy. The BOC is toying with the idea of stating that each bank must keep at least 3% of all deposits in cash or in bank deposits. Further measures will also be taken, which seem to suggest that the Target for the Overnight Rate may be increased as well.

GREENSPAN SPEAKS ON THE GREENBACK

Alan Greenspan, Chairman of the Federal Reserve Board, has seen the U.S. dollar shrink in the last several months. U.S productivity has fallen due to this, and the Board has decided to take measures to increase the value of the greenback . . . .

BANK RUN EXPECTED; NOT LIKELY

The CDIC insurance company has decided to increase its deposits insurance from $60,000 of eligible deposits to $100,000 of eligible deposits. The CDIC stated that it was proud of its banking and wanted to curb some of the enthusiasm of Canadians investing in offshore accounts.

Wong is feeling very uneasy right now and would like to know what to do.

Requirements

1. Identify all the salient issues at hand that exist for MDC and Mark Wong (include legal, structural, ethical, and various other problems). If interest rates rise, what will happen to MCD Mortgage Company?
2. Try to explore and create a solution for each of your identified issues.

Part II
Essential Concepts in Finance

CHAPTERS

NORTEL NETWORKS CORPORATION—ACCOUNTING SCANDAL BREWING

www.nortelnetworks.com

CORPORATE INFORMATION

Headquarters	Brampton, Ontario
Industry	Telecommunications
Listed on	TSX, NYSE
Ticker symbol	NT
CEO	William Owens

Year Ended 31 December (in US$ millions)	1999	2000	2001	2002	2003
Sales	21,287	27,948	17,511	10,560	9,810
Operating Profit / (Loss)	N/A	(2,429)	(26,763)	(3,804)	N/A
Net Profit / (Loss)	(351)	(3,470)	(27,302)	(3,585)	732
Current Assets	12,132	16,530	11,762	8,476	N/A
Current Liabilities	7,101	9,058	9,457	6,982	N/A
Total Assets	24,007	42,180	21,137	15,971	N/A
Short-Term & Long-Term Debt	1,426	1,623	4,476	3,952	N/A
Shareholders' Equity	13,072	29,180	4,824	1,960	N/A

Business

Established more than a century ago, Nortel Networks focuses on the provision of complete telecommunication network solutions. This includes the design, development, manufacturing, assembly, sale, installation, servicing and support of these networking solutions. Nortel operates four business units: wireless networks (40 percent of total sales in 2002), enterprise networks (25 percent), wireline networks (21 percent), and optical networks (14 percent).

Financial Performance

The company's financial performance has been disappointing in the last few years, both in terms of sales and profitability. Sales have been steadily declining from $28 billion in 2000 to below $10 billion in 2003, reflecting the declining industry demand for networking equipment and increased competition among network solution providers. Between 1997 and 2002, Nortel generated losses at the operating and net profit levels. Nortel has increasingly relied on debt to finance its operations. The level of short- and long-term debt more than doubled between 1999 and 2002. The liquidity position also deteriorated as current assets continued to decline. Evidence for these trends can be seen in the declining current ratio, which was equal to 1.7 in 1999 and 1.2 in 2002.

Problematic Accounting

Nortel's continuous restatements of the company's financial accounts, often relating to improper revenue recognition and other accounting irregularities, forced the board of directors to undertake serious action in order to restore confidence in the company's financial performance and reporting. In April 2004, the company fired its three senior executives, including the CEO. According to *The Globe and Mail*, as a result of its financial reporting problems, Nortel is facing multiple lawsuits in Canada and abroad, with many generally alleging that the company has issued misleading financial statements to artificially inflate its share price. In the U.S., the Attorney General's office launched a criminal investigation into Nortel's accounting practices going back as far as the year 2000. The Ontario Public Services Employee Union Pension Trust took legal action not only against the company, but also against its former senior executives, alleging that executives benefited from the company's inflated financial performance through stock option programs. Nortel is also facing charges by securities regulators in Canada and the U.S.

Sources: www.globeandmail.com, www.cbc.ca, www.nortelnetworks.com. Financial data for 2001 and 2002 from Nortel Networks 2002 *Annual Report*, pp. 68–70; data for 2000 from 2001 *Annual Report*, pp. 57–58; data for 1999 from 2000 *Annual Report*, pp. 45–46.

4

Review of Accounting

Chapter Objectives

After reading this chapter, you should be able to:

4-1 Describe a main function for each of the four accounting financial statements: the income statement, the retained earnings statement, the balance sheet, and the cash flow statement.

4-2 Discuss how amortization affects cash flow and two major methods used to compute amortization expense.

4-3 Explain a major difference between amortization and capital cost allowance.

4-4 Explain the basics of corporate taxation and know how to apply taxes.

"Anyone who isn't confused here doesn't really understand what is going on."

—Anonymous

Credibility Gap Threatens World Financial Reporting

Financial reporting is suffering an abysmal credibility gap, and the problem is serious, systemic and global, according to the author of a report just issued by the International Federation of Accountants.

"We have confirmed that this is serious," said John Crow, chair of IFAC's task force on rebuilding confidence in financial reporting, and a former governor of the Bank of Canada. "We looked into each other's eyes, thought about our experiences around the world, and decided that the U.S. isn't unique even though the size of its cases dwarfs everyone else's. We also decided that the problem of credibility, which is a problem with perception, is serious."

Crow said the lack of confidence in financial information is leading to market volatility and an increase in the cost of capital. Unfortunately, he said, the overall increase cannot be measured because of myriad complicating and counterbalancing factors.

Low interest rates offset the heightened cost of capital by supporting market growth. The true cost of the credibility gap is therefore unknowable.

In individual cases, however, where distorted reports result in restatements—Crow calls them "uncontrolled experiments"—the market quickly demonstrates the cost of inaccurate financial statements.

Crow said that it's important to read the whole report, not just part, because the causes of the problem are interlinked through the entire "information supply chain" that stretches from company management to the potential investor or other final user of the information. Along this chain are CA firms, lawyers, bankers, financial analysts, credit rating agencies, regulators, standard-setters, internal auditors, boards of directors and the media.

All of these participants operate under continuous pressure, the report said. Management wants to report profit and performance that meets expectations. Standards-setters face "political pressures" from industry and government. Auditors and rating agencies face the pressure of producing opinions on the companies that hire them.

Source: Excerpt from Glenn Cheney, "Credibility Gap Threatens World Financial Reporting." Reprinted with permission from *Accounting Today* 9/22/03–10/05/03.

Chapter Overview

Accounting plays an important role in a firm's financial success. Accountants prepare financial statements that financial managers use to analyze the condition of a firm and to plan for its future. Financial managers must understand, then, how to analyze and interpret financial statements as they make decisions. It is important that the financial manager be versed in the use of financial statements in order to help create value for the firm's owners.

In this chapter, we will review the four financial statements: the income statement, the retained earnings statement, the balance sheet, and the cash flow statement. We will also study how amortization and taxes affect a firm's cash flows.

Review of Accounting Fundamentals

Financial statements for public companies are generally prepared in accordance with Generally Accepted Accounting Principles, or "GAAP." The Canadian Accounting Standards Board (abbreviated AcSB), a private professional accounting body, which is a part of the Canadian Institute of Chartered Accountants, establishes and develops financial reporting standards and guidance on how businesses account for their activities. These rules are published in the form of the *CICA Handbook*, which acts as a compendium of accounting recommendations or rules in the regulation of business corporations.

We do not have a central securities regulatory body (similar to the Securities and Exchange Commission in the United States) although there has been a lot of debate on the subject in recent years. In effect, provinces operate their own securities regulations, which govern underwriting, distribution, and disclosure requirements for listing companies. In terms of the provision of financial information, public companies are generally required to provide a detailed set of financial and management information to their shareholders. For example, the Ontario Securities Commission, the leading securities regulator in Canada, requires that public companies file an *Annual Information Form* (AIF), which contains the *Management's Discussion and Analysis of Financial Condition and Results of Operations* (MD&A). Annual financial statements are accompanied by a report of a financial auditor. Ethical Connections 4-2 on page 91 discusses some issues related to financial reporting.

The following basic accounting equation is central to understanding the financial condition of a firm:

$$\text{Assets} = \text{Liabilities} + \text{Equity}$$

Assets are the items of value a business owns. *Liabilities* are claims on the business by nonowners and equity is the owners' claim on the business. The sum of the liabilities and equity is the total **capital** contributed to the business. Capital contributions come from three main sources: creditors (including bondholders and banks), preferred shareholders, and common shareholders.

BASIC ACCOUNTING FINANCIAL STATEMENTS

You can get a good picture of how a firm is doing by looking at its financial statements. The four financial statements are the *income statement,* the *retained earnings statement,* the *balance sheet,* and the *cash flow statement.* Each of these statements gives a slightly different view of the firm. Let's look at these financial statements and how they interrelate.

The Income Statement

We can compare the **income statement** to a video: It measures a firm's profitability over a period of time. The firm can choose the length of the reporting time period. It can be a month, a quarter, or a year. (By law, a publicly traded corporation must report its activities at least quarterly.) Sometimes, companies may generate the income statement combined with the retained earnings statement instead of presenting two different statements. An example of such a combined statement is presented in Chapter 5.

The income statement shows *revenues, expenses,* and *income.* Revenues represent gross income that the firm earned during a particular period of time (usually from sales). Expenses represent the cost of providing goods and services during a given period of time. Net income is what is left after expenses are subtracted from revenues.

Figure 4-1 shows an income statement for Canadian Auto Parts (CAP), a firm that distributes auto parts for European import vehicles in the province of Nova Scotia. The income statement is for the year ended December 31, 2004. This income statement describes sales, expenses, and net income for CAP from the beginning of the business day on January 1, 2004, until the end of the business day on December 31, 2004.

Revenues As Figure 4-1 shows, CAP's sales totalled $90 million during 2004. Generally, the income statement does not distinguish between cash and credit sales. As a result, we are not sure how much actual *cash* came into the firm from the $90 million in reported sales.

Net Sales	$90,000,000
Cost of Goods Sold	64,000,000
Gross Profit	26,000,000
Selling and Administrative Expenses	13,000,000
Amortization	2,300,000
Operating Income (EBIT)	10,700,000
Interest Expense	450,000
Earnings before Taxes (EBT)	10,250,000
Income Taxes (40%)	4,100,000
Net Income (NI)	6,150,000

Figure 4-1
Canadian Auto Parts Income Statement for the Year Ended December 31, 2004

Expenses Expenses include costs incurred while conducting the operations of the firm and financial expenses such as interest on debt and taxes owed. These items are matched to the revenues that were generated as the expenses were incurred.

Cost of Goods Sold.

The first expense subtracted from sales is *cost of goods sold,* which consists of the company's purchases of goods sold during the year.

Subtracting cost of goods sold of $64 million from sales of $90 million gives CAP's *gross profit,* which equals $26 million.

Take Note

Notice that *cost of goods sold* is not called *cost of goods produced.* Only cost of goods sold is reported on this year's income statement. Goods purchased or produced but not sold are considered inventory.

Selling and Administrative Expenses.

From gross profit, we next subtract CAP's *selling and administrative expenses* ($13 million). Selling expenses include marketing and salespeople's salaries. Administrative expenses encompass such items as office support, insurance, security, rent, office supplies, and overhead.

Amortization Expense.

Amortization expense is subtracted next—$2.3 million for CAP in 2004. Amortization expense is the year's allocation of the cost of distribution centres that have been built or acquired this year and in previous years. Because assets provide their benefits to the firm over several years, accountants subtract the cost of long-lived assets a little at a time over a number of years. The allocated cost of a firm's assets for the income statement's period of time is the amortization expense.[1] Amortization expense is a noncash expense. However, because it is a tax-deductible expense, it increases the cash flows of the business.

Operating Income and Interest Expense.

When we subtract selling and administrative expenses and amortization expense from gross profit, we are left with CAP's *earnings before interest and taxes (EBIT),* also known as operating income. This figure is $10,700,000.

Gross Profit	= 26,000,000
Selling and Administrative Expenses	– 13,000,000
Amortization Expense	– 2,000,000
Earnings before Interest and Taxes (EBIT, or Operating Income)	= 10,700,000

EBIT is the profit that the firm receives from its business operations before subtracting any financing expenses and, subsequently, taxes. From EBIT, we then subtract *interest expense* associated with any debts of the company to arrive at CAP's *earnings before taxes (EBT).* CAP has $450,000 in interest expense. When we subtract this figure from the $10,700,000 EBIT figure, we find CAP had earnings before taxes (EBT) of $10,250,000. Income taxes will be discussed in detail later in the chapter.

Net Income Finally, after we subtract all operating expenses, financing expenses, and taxes from revenues, we arrive at the firm's *net income* (NI). For CAP, net income in 2004 was $6,150,000. This is the firm's accounting net profit for the year.

One of the important profit lines of the income statement that is widely used by analysts and financial managers is EBITA or EBITDA. More about

[1]We will discuss the role of amortization and amortization methods later in this chapter.

the importance of this profit line is discussed in Financial Management and You 4-1.

Let's make one note here. In various accounting jurisdictions, like the U.S., you are likely to see the terms, "depreciation" and "amortization." The term "depreciation" would be equivalent to the Canadian term "amortization" and the term "amortization" used outside of Canada may describe the writing off of intangible assets. Consequently, the income statement in various countries may have a line called EBITDA (pronounced "ee-bid-dah"), earnings before interest, taxes, depreciation, and amortization. You will also see the term EBITDA used in annual reports of some Canadian public companies (i.e., Canadian Tire, www.canadiantire.ca). The good news is, however, that due to efforts to standardize financial reporting across the globe, the term "amortization" is likely to be the prevalent one.

Earnings per Share (EPS).

CAP's shareholders are very interested in their individual share of the corporation's earnings. Therefore, we can calculate *earnings per share* (EPS) when earnings available to common shareholders is divided by the number of common shares outstanding. The earnings available to common shareholders figure comes straight from the income statement.

Net Income (NI)	=	6,150,000
Preferred Share Dividends Paid	−	1,000,000
Earnings Available to Common Shareholders	=	5,150,000
Earnings per Share (EPS) (1,750,000 shares)	=	$2.94

The number of common shares outstanding comes from the balance sheet. CAP has 1,750,000 common shares outstanding.

FINANCIAL MANAGEMENT AND YOU 4-1

A Special Earnings Category—EBITA or EBITDA

nancial analysts often make use of another measure of a mpany's earnings called earnings before interest, taxes, d amortization, or EBITA (pronounced "ee-bid-tah"). 3ITA is found by adding amortization expense back to 3IT. Because amortization is a noncash expense, which will discussed later in this chapter, the result of adding amorization back into EBIT is a figure that represents revenues inus cash expenses or approximately the amount of cash rned by the daily operations of a business.

Although EBITA is of great interest to financial analysts, s not required to be reported by the Canadian Accounting andards Board and, thus, is not usually shown as a specific line item on most income statements. As a result, it usually must be calculated manually. CAP's EBITA for 2004 is:

Operating Income (EBIT)	$10,700,000
+ Amortization	2,300,000
= EBITA	$13,000,000

Having made this calculation, a financial analyst would proceed with the knowledge that CAP's normal business operations threw off approximately $13 million in cash during 2004.

To calculate EPS, divide earnings available to common shareholders by the number of outstanding common shares. For CAP, we calculate EPS as follows:

$$\text{EPS} = \frac{\text{Earnings Available to Common Shareholders}}{\text{Number of Common Shares Outstanding}}$$

$$= \frac{\$5,150,000}{1,750,000}$$

$$= \$2.94$$

Take Note

If the amount remaining after paying dividends had been *negative,* then we would have *subtracted* our number from retained earnings instead of adding to it. For CAP, there is a positive number to add to retained earnings—$4,712,000.

The Retained Earnings Statement

A company has two options as to what it will do with its net income. It can pay dividends to its shareholders or it can retain the net income. Retaining the net income will likely lead to a greater future growth in sales and net income as new assets are purchased or existing liabilities are paid. In 2004, CAP has chosen to pay $438,000 (7.1 percent of its net income) in dividends to its common shareholders and pay $1,000,000 (16.3 percent of its net income) in dividends to preferred shareholders. The company's addition to retained earnings in 2004 is equal to $4,712,000 ($6,150,000 − $438,000 − $1,000,000 = $4,712,000).

Many firms prepare the retained earnings statement, as shown in Figure 4-2. This financial statement records dividend and retained earnings information for the company for a given year. Assuming that CAP's beginning-of-2004 retained earnings were $14,748,000, CAP's accountants add the 2004 net income and subtract the 2004 dividends paid to common and preferred shareholders. The result is the figure of $19,460,000 in retained earnings at the end of 2004.

Sometimes, in spite of management's efforts to provide a true and accurate description of the company's financial standing, financial statements are re-done time and time again. Ethical Connections 4-1 discusses potential problems related to financial disclosure.

The Balance Sheet

If the income statement is like a video, a balance sheet is like a still photograph. The **balance sheet** shows the firm's assets, liabilities, and equity at a given point in time. This snapshot of a company's financial position tells us nothing about the firm's financial position before or after that point in time.

Figure 4-2
Canadian Auto Parts Retained Earnings for the Year Ended December 31, 2004

Retained Earnings, January 1, 2004		$14,748,000
Net Income in 2004	+	6,150,000
Common Share Dividends in 2004	−	438,000
Preferred Share Dividends in 2004	−	1,000,000
Retained Earnings, December 31, 2004	=	$19,460,000

ETHICAL CONNECTIONS 4-1

Nortel Puts Money Men on Leave

ortel Networks Corp. was rocked again yesterday as it put chief financial officer and its controller on paid leave until second review of the company's financial results is finhed, driving its stock down nearly 20 percent.

The move "is an indication that accounting problems ould be more serious than we had thought," analyst Ehud elblum of JPMorgan Securities Inc. said in a report.

Nortel surprised investors last week when it said it ould likely have to restate its financial results for the sec- d time in several months.

The first review was conducted internally, producing nall changes to the numbers from the start of 2000 rough mid-2003. The second review, conducted inde- endently by an external law firm and Nortel's audit com- ittee, is continuing.

Regulators in Canada and the United States are now aking inquiries as well.

Following the massive accounting frauds at Enron Corp. d WorldCom Inc., the mere hint of scandal makes vestors worry. Such concern slashed $6.8-billion from the arket value of Nortel yesterday, which is Canada's fourth ost valuable company and is among the most widely held ocks in the country. The shares fell $1.60 or 18.6 per- nt—one of Nortel's worst percentage declines to date—to .98 on the Toronto Stock Exchange.

The Ontario Securities Commission has asked Nortel to pply "further information regarding the likely revisions that ere identified by the company," OSC spokeswoman Wendy ey said. She would not elaborate.

The U.S. Securities and Exchange Commission had no mment. Nortel said it had received inquiries from the SEC d the OSC and that it is co-operating.

The first indication of accounting problems arose last ovember, when Nortel first filed restated numbers with the C.

On page 83 of that document, Nortel said its external ditor, Deloitte & Touche LLP, had found some "material eaknesses in internal control" of the company's account- g, relating to accruals and provisions. These items are at e centre of the second review.

Nortel also revealed that some accruals were booked en though they "were not supported by adequate docu- entation." Accruals recognize income and expenses as ey occur, even if actual cash isn't received or paid. In sev- al other cases related to accruals and provisions, Nortel said documentation to support them "did not exist at the time."

"Many of you may feel disheartened," Frank Dunn, Nortel president and chief executive officer, said in a letter to Nortel's 35,500 workers. But he said the independent review "needs to be as diligent and thoughtful as possible" and is "reflective of what world class companies do," even if putting the CFO and controller on leave "may seem challenging."

Douglas Beatty, Nortel chief financial officer, and Michael Gollogly, controller, are on paid leave pending the completion of the second review. William Kerr, a former Nortel controller, was hired as interim CFO and MaryAnne Pahapill, a former Nortel finance official, was installed as interim controller, effectively the company's chief accountant.

The Brampton, Ont.–based communications equipment maker said it had put the employees on paid leave in order to complete the second review as quickly as possible, suggesting conflict between Mr. Beatty, Mr. Gollogly and the independent review.

The first accounting restatement covered 2000, 2001, 2002 and the first half of 2003. Mr. Dunn was chief financial officer for more than half of the restated period. Asked whether the inquiry might affect Mr. Dunn, spokeswoman Tina Warren said she could not "speculate because the independent review is not complete."

The second review will likely lead to the restatement of unaudited 2003 results, and possibly prior periods.

Nortel doesn't know when the process will conclude. It will miss a March 30 deadline to file its audited 2003 results with the SEC, a possibility raised last week. The company's annual general meeting, scheduled for April 29 in Mississauga, could also be delayed. Missing the SEC deadline puts Nortel in technical default on $3.6-billion (U.S.) of debt and convertible debentures, as well as $334-million in commitments from Export Development Canada.

At the end of this month, EDC could demand cash from Nortel to cover the amount the Crown corporation has put up to support Nortel's business. Nortel wants EDC to waive its rights. Negotiations are continuing, EDC spokeswoman Daniela Pizzuto said.

Michel Magnan, an accounting professor at Concordia University in Montreal, said the fact that Nortel cut its work force by about two-thirds from early 2001 through 2003 could have contributed to the accounting problem.

In such a situation, Mr. Magnan said that, because of the cutbacks, some finance workers could have ended up doing two jobs, sometimes at cross purposes, such as making estimates for accruals, and then also authorizing the accruals.

"Controls cost money," he said.

Bay and Wall Street financial analysts mostly ignored last year's restatement, describing it as a housecleaning. Last week, analysts were once again largely unconcerned, saying a second restatement would probably be minor and wouldn't affect Nortel's prospects.

Some analysts expressed more apprehension yesterday.

"The news could get worse before it gets better," said analyst Vivian Mamelak of Natexis Bleichroeder Inc., wondering, "What if a broad problem does emerge?"

Ms. Mamelak said the problems may have been discovered following the U.S. Sarbanes-Oxley Act, which became effective last summer. The Act requires a company's top officers to certify financial statements for accuracy, as well as the effectiveness of underlying internal cc trols for accounting.

Putting the CFO and controller on leave "is a muc stronger statement on the potential [second] restatemen Merrill analyst Pat Chiefalo said in a report.

"Our concern relates to what these measures sugg about the magnitude and the actions behind the resta ment."

Questions to Consider

1. *How would you summarize the major issues at Nor contributing to accounting problems?*
2. *Was it an appropriate action by Nortel to send its C and controller on a paid leave during the accounti investigation and why?*

Source: Dave Ebner, "Nortel Puts Money Men on Leave," 16 March 2004. Reprinted with permission of *The Globe and Mail.*

Let's examine the end-of-2004 balance sheet for CAP. Figure 4-3 shows the balance sheet for CAP as of the end of the business day, December 31, 2004.

On the balance sheet, the firm's assets are listed in order of their liquidity. Liquidity is the ease with which you can convert an asset to cash. This means that cash and near-cash assets called **current assets** are listed first. Assets that are difficult to convert to cash are listed later. On the other side of the balance sheet, the liabilities that are due earliest, **current liabilities,** are listed first. Current liabilities are almost always due within one year. The liabilities due later, such as long-term debt, are listed later on the balance sheet.

The equity section lists the claims of the owners (CAP's common shareholders). The owners' claims include both the amount the owners contributed when the common share was first issued and the total cumulative earnings retained by the firm since inception.

The Asset Accounts CAP has current assets and property, plant, and equipment (P.P. & E.). Current assets provide short-term benefits whereas property, plant, and equipment provide long-term benefits to the firm.

Current Assets.

CAP has $3.3 million in *cash* at the end of 2004. *Marketable securities*—securities that can quickly and easily be converted to extra cash—are listed next. CAP has $1 million in these securities. Customers owe the company $10 million, the amount of *accounts receivable.*

The company has $9 million of *inventory* and $0.8 million in *prepaid expenses.* The inventory figure reflects the amount of goods in CAP's distribution centres but not yet sold to customers. The prepaid expense figure represents future expenses that have been paid in advance. An example of a prepaid expense is the premium paid on an insurance policy. You pay the premium in

Assets	
Cash	$ 3,310,000
Marketable Securities	1,000,000
Accounts Receivable	10,000,000
Inventory	9,000,000
Prepaid Expenses	800,000
Total Current Assets	24,110,000
Property, Plant, and Equipment, Gross	23,000,000
Less Accumulated Amortization	(12,200,000)
Property, Plant, and Equipment, Net	10,800,000
Total Assets	$34,910,000

Liabilities and Equity	
Accounts Payable	$ 8,000,000
Notes Payable	500,000
Accrued Expenses	700,000
Total Current Liabilities	9,200,000
Long-Term Debt	4,000,000
Total Liabilities	13,200,000
Preferred Shares	500,000
Common Shares (1,750,000 shares)	1,750,000
Retained Earnings	19,460,000
Total Equity	21,710,000
Total Liabilities and Equity	$34,910,000

Figure 4-3
Canadian Auto Parts Balance Sheet as of December 31, 2004

advance, so the insurance coverage is "owed" to you until the term of coverage expires. Because prepaid expenses such as insurance premiums have been paid for but not yet received, they are owed to the company and are considered assets.

The sum of all current assets including cash, marketable securities, net accounts receivable, inventory, and prepaid expenses is often referred to as working capital. For CAP, this figure is $24.1 million.

Property, Plant, and Equipment.

Next to be listed are the property, plant, and equipment of the firm. Property, plant, and equipment are assets that are expected to provide a benefit to the firm for more than one year. These assets are generally less liquid than the current assets. CAP has $23 million of gross buildings and equipment, which are listed at the original cost of these assets. The *accumulated amortization* figure is the sum of all the amortization expenses ever taken on the firm's income statements for the assets still carried on the books. CAP's accumulated amortization figure is $12.2 million. To find the net buildings and equipment figure—or net property, plant and equipment—subtract the amount of accumulated amortization from gross fixed assets ($23 million minus $12.2 million). The result is $10.8 million.

The $24.1 million in current assets plus the $10.8 million in net property, plant, and equipment are the total assets of the firm. At the end of 2004, CAP's total assets were nearly $35 million.

The Liabilities and Equity Accounts The liabilities and equity section of the balance sheet shows how the company's assets were financed. The funds come from those who have liability (debt) claims against the firm or from those who have equity (ownership) claims against the firm.

Liabilities.

In the liability section of the balance sheet, current liabilities are listed first. CAP has accounts payable at the end of 2004 of $8 million. *Accounts payable* represent money a business owes to suppliers that have sold the firm materials on account.

Notes payable are $0.5 million for this company. Notes payable are legal IOUs that represent the debt of the borrower (CAP) and the claim the lender has against that borrower. CAP also has accrued expenses of $0.7 million. Accrued expenses are business expenses that have not been paid yet. For example, universities often make professors work for a full month before they are paid. The universities accrue wages payable for the month before the payroll cheques are finally issued. CAP's accounts payable, notes payable, and accrued expenses add up to $9.2 million in current liabilities.

Net working capital is current assets minus current liabilities. For CAP, this would be $14.9 million ($24.1 million current assets – $9.2 million current liabilities).

Next, long-term liabilities are listed. Long-term liabilities are liabilities that do not mature within twelve months. Capital leases, term loans, or corporate debt papers may be examples of long-term debt instruments. In this case, CAP has $4 million in long-term bonds payable that mature in 2015. The $4 million figure listed on the balance sheet refers only to the principal on these bonds.

Take Note

Do not fall into the trap of thinking that the retained earnings account contains cash. Remember, equity accounts, including this one, represent owners' *claims* on assets. They are not assets themselves. The earnings not paid out as dividends have already been used to accumulate additional assets or to pay off liabilities.

Preferred Shares, Common Shares, and Retained Earnings.

The equity section of the balance sheet, often called Share Capital, shows that CAP has *preferred share equity* of $0.5 million. The common share equity section of the balance sheet contains two items: common shares and retained earnings. The common share entry shows that CAP's *common share equity* is $1,750,000, reflecting the 1,750,000 shares issued to investors.

The second entry in the common share equity section is retained earnings. The *retained earnings* figure represents the sum of all the earnings available to common shareholders of a business during its entire history, minus the sum of all the common and preferred share dividends that it has ever paid.[2] Those earnings that were not paid out were, by definition, retained. The retained earnings figure for CAP at the end of 2004 is $19.5 million.

---

[2]There are exceptions. If a company pays a dividend in the form of new common shares instead of cash, then there would be a transfer from retained earnings to the other common share equity accounts. We will skip this exception for now. The use of stock dividends instead of cash dividends, and the resulting accounting treatment, will be examined in Chapter 16.

The Cash Flow Statement

The third major financial statement is the *cash flow statement*. This statement, like the income statement, can be compared to a video: It shows how cash flows into and out of a company over a given period of time.

We construct the cash flow statement by adjusting the income statement to distinguish between *income* and *cash flow* and by comparing balance sheets at the beginning and end of the relevant time period. The cash flow statement shows cash flows in operating, investing, and financing activities, as well as the overall net increase or decrease in cash for the firm. You can see CAP's cash flow statement for 2004 in Figure 4-4. The cash flow statement is presented in accordance with the indirect method, which is most common for public and private companies.

Take Note

Be careful not to confuse the cash flow statement with the income statement. The income statement lists *revenues* and *expenses* over a period of time. The cash flow statement lists where *cash* came from and what it was used for during a period of time.

Cash Received from (Used in) Operating Activities	
Net Income	$6,150,000
Amortization	2,300,000
Decrease (Increase) Marketable Securities	(200,000)
Decrease (Increase) Accounts Receivable	(2,000,000)
Decrease (Increase) Inventory	(1,500,000)
Decrease (Increase) Prepaid Expenses	(100,000)
Increase (Decrease) Accounts Payable	1,500,000
Increase (Decrease) Accrued Expenses	100,000
Total Cash from Operations	**$6,250,000**
Cash Received from (Used for) Investment Activities	
New Property, Plant, and Equipment Purchases	($2,000,000)
Total Cash from Investments	**($2,000,000)**
Cash Received from (Used for) Financing Activities	
Repayment of Long-Term Debt Issue	($2,000,000)
Proceeds from New Common Share Issue	1,650,000
Short-Term Notes Paid Off	(250,000)
Preferred Share Repurchases	(250,000)
Preferred Dividends	(1,000,000)
Common Dividends	(438,000)
Total Cash from Financing	**($2,288,000)**
Net Change in Cash Balance	**$1,962,000**
Beginning Cash Balance	**$1,348,000**
Ending Cash Balance	**$3,310,000**

Figure 4-4
Canadian Auto Parts Cash Flow Statement for the Year Ended December 31, 2004

Operating Activities Operating activities on the cash flow statement shows that CAP had $6,150,000 in net income for 2004. This number represents what was left after CAP paid all the firm's expenses for that year. We adjust that number to determine the operating cash flows for 2004.

Adjustment for Amortization Expense Although amortization expense is a legitimate reduction of income for accounting purposes, it is not a cash outlay. In other words, firms record amortization expense on financial statements but do not write cheques to pay it. We must add the $2.3 million in amortization expense because net income was reduced by this amount—even though amortization is a noncash expense.

Changes in Balance Sheet Accounts Changes in asset accounts on the balance sheet indicate changes in the company's cash flow. Because firms must pay cash to accumulate new assets, any increase in an asset account between the time one balance sheet is published and the time the next balance sheet is published indicates a cash outflow. Likewise, because firms sell assets to raise cash, any decrease in an asset account indicates a cash inflow. For CAP, balance sheet changes in marketable securities, accounts payable, accounts receivable (net), and inventory are shown in the operations section of Figure 4-4.

Changes in the liabilities and equity section of the balance sheet also signal cash flow changes. Because firms must use cash to pay off obligations, any decrease in liability, preferred share, or common share equity accounts between the time one balance sheet is published and the time the next balance sheet is published indicates a cash outflow during those time periods. To raise additional cash, firms can incur debt or equity obligations. Therefore, any increase in liability, preferred share, or common share items indicate a cash inflow.

Figure 4-5 shows two balance sheets for CAP side by side. We can compare them and note where the cash inflows and outflows that appear on the cash flow statements came from.

Operating Activities In the asset section of the balance sheet, we see that accounts receivable rose from $8 million to $10 million, a $2 million increase. In effect, CAP had a cash outflow of $2 million in the form of funds recognized as revenue but not collected from its credit customers. Inventory *increased* from $7.5 million to $9 million, which represents a $1.5 million use of cash, a cash outflow, in the form of inventory items bought. Similarly, marketable securities increased by $200,000 signalling that CAP bought some marketable securities and generated a cash outflow of $200,000.

In the liabilities and equity section of the balance sheet, observe that accounts payable increased by $1.5 million. CAP's suppliers must have further extended their credit to CAP in the amount of $1.5 million; therefore, this represents a cash inflow. Likewise, the accrued expenses account increased by $100,000, indicating that CAP "received" $100,000 in cash by not paying them.

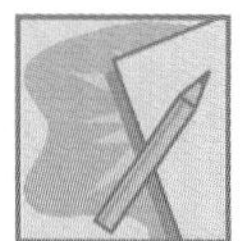

Take Note

We do not mention the change in accumulated amortization in the cash flow statement. The additional accumulated amortization of $2.3 million is already included in the amortization expense figure on the income statement. We do not want to count this twice.

Investment Activities The investments section of the cash flow statement shows investing activities in long-term securities or property, plant, and equipment. Increasing investments require a cash outflow and decreasing investments signal a cash inflow. For instance, observe in Figure 4-5 that CAP's property, plant, and equipment increased to $23 million in 2004, up from $21 million in 2003. This $2 million increase reflects a cash outlay used to buy additional assets.

Assets	12/31/03	12/31/04	Change
Cash	$ 1,348,000	$ 3,310,000	$1,962,000
Marketable Securities	800,000	1,000,000	200,000
Accounts Receivable	8,000,000	10,000,000	2,000,000
Inventory	7,500,000	9,000,000	1,500,000
Prepaid Expenses	700,000	800,000	100,000
Total Current Assets	18,348,000	24,110,000	5,762,000
Property, Plant, and Equipment, Gross	21,000,000	23,000,000	2,000,000
Less Accumulated Amortization	9,900,000	12,200,000	(2,300,000)
Property, Plant, and Equipment, Net	11,100,000	10,800,000	(300,000)
Total Assets	$29,448,000	$34,910,000	$5,462,000

Liabilities and Equity			
Accounts Payable	$ 6,500,000	$ 8,000,000	$1,500,000
Notes Payable	750,000	500,000	(250,000)
Accrued Expenses	600,000	700,000	100,000
Total Current Liabilities	7,850,000	9,200,000	1,350,000
Long-Term Debt	6,000,000	4,000,000	(2,000,000)
Total Liabilities	13,850,000	13,200,000	(650,000)
Preferred Shares	750,000	500,000	(250,000)
Common Shares	100,000	1,750,000	1,650,000
Retained Earnings	14,748,000	19,460,000	4,712,000
Total Equity	15,598,000	21,710,000	6,112,000
Total Liabilities and Equity	$29,448,000	$34,910,000	$5,462,000

Figure 4-5
Canadian Auto Parts Balance Sheet Changes between December 31, 2003 and December 31, 2004

Financing Activities The financing section of the cash flow statement shows financing activities related to the sales and retirement of notes, bonds, preferred and common shares, and other corporate securities. The retirement (i.e., buying back) of previously issued securities signals a cash outflow. The issuing of securities is a cash inflow. On the CAP balance sheet, for example, preferred share equity decreased from $750,000 to $500,000. The decrease shows that the firm spent $250,000 to retire outstanding preferred shares.

Further down in the liabilities and equity section of the balance sheet (Figure 4-5), we see that the common share equity account increased by $1,650,000. This increase is the result of $1,650,000 in cash received from a new issue of 1,650,000 common shares.

In the common share equity section of the balance sheet, we see that retained earnings increased from $14.7 million to $19.5 million. Although this $4,712,000 increase in retained earnings represents a cash inflow to the firm, it is not recorded on the cash flow statement. Why? Because the cash inflow it represents was recorded on the cash flow statement as net income ($6,150,000) less preferred share dividends ($1 million) less common share dividends ($438,000). To include the increase in retained earnings again would result in double counting.

Net Cash Flow during the Period We have now completed the adjustments necessary to convert CAP's net income for 2004 into actual cash flows. Figure 4-4 shows that the cash inflows exceeded the cash outflows, resulting in a net cash inflow of $1,962,000 for CAP in 2004. (Notice in Figure 4-5 that CAP's cash balance of $3,310,000 on December 31, 2004 is $1,962,000 higher than it was on December 31, 2003.)

AMORTIZATION

Amortization is important to financial managers because it directly affects a firm's tax liabilities, which, in turn, affect cash flows. Here is how: Taxes paid are negative cash flows. Tax savings realized by deducting expenses generate more cash for the firm—the equivalent of a cash inflow.

Accounting amortization is the allocation of an asset's initial cost over time. Let's look at why it is important to amortize property, plant, and equipment over time. Suppose CAP bought a piece of equipment in 2004 that was expected to last ten years. If CAP paid $10 million cash for the asset and the entire cost were charged as an expense in 2004, the transaction would wipe out all but $250,000 of CAP's earnings before taxes for the year ($10,250,000 earnings before taxes − $10,000,000 property, plant, and equipment). Nothing would show that CAP had acquired an asset worth $10 million. Then, for the next nine years, CAP's income statements would show increases in profits generated by the asset, but there would be no corresponding accounting for the cost of that asset. In effect, it would look like CAP spent a lot of money in 2004, which provided no immediate benefit and, unaccountably, led to increased profits for the next nine years. This clearly would be misleading.

To get around the problem, accountants apply the *matching principle:* Expenses should be matched to the revenues they help generate. In other words, if you buy an asset and the asset is expected to last for ten years, then you should recognize the cost of the asset over the entire ten-year period. The cost is *amortized,* or spread out, over the ten-year period. In that way, the value of the asset will be properly shown on the financial statements in proportion to its contribution to profits.

Accounting amortization is very different from economic amortization. The latter attempts to measure the change in the value of an asset. Because this involves making value estimates that may turn out to be incorrect, accountants use an established set of rules to determine the amount of amortization to allocate to a certain time period.

We have already stressed the importance of proper and accurate disclosure of the company's financial information, but full financial disclosure does not only mean showing numbers. In the annual reports, information related to the market, the industry, and the competition is discussed. More importantly, the company's management needs to discuss any changes that they made to accounting policies, including any changes to the amortization methods they used.

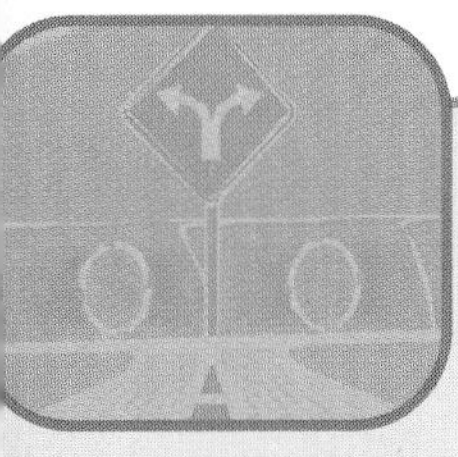

ETHICAL CONNECTIONS 4-2
Bar Set Higher for Annual Reports

ast year was a tough one in the fertilizer business.

You can read all about it in Potash Corp.'s latest annual ›port, along with some details that many companies would ather not divulge—like how the Saskatoon-based company tacked up against its own performance targets.

Publishing those metrics is a bold step. Most Canadian ompanies aren't that open in their annual reports, says Bill uchanan, overall judging co-ordinator for the annual report wards held yearly by a group of financial experts, including ıe Canadian Institute of Chartered Accountants.

"The best reports tell you things like their bottom-line ırgets for next year, how they're going to get there and what appened last year. They'll hold themselves accountable, ut it isn't that common. The really good ones stand out," ays Mr. Buchanan, whose committee screens about 150 nnual reports a year from companies listed on the Toronto tock Exchange.

Some companies are afraid of divulging too much, for ompetitive reasons, or managers don't want to be on record etting goals in case they don't make them, says Ron Blunn, ead of Blunn & Co. Inc., an investor relations and commuications firm in Toronto, which has worked with Potash.

"When companies make that argument, it's a copout. ou get a lot more marks for being honest and you gain credıility in the market," responds Betty-Ann Heddie, Potash's enior vice-president of corporate relations.

Potash sends out 30,000 to 40,000 copies of its annual ›port a year, at a cost of about $315,000. Depending on the ze of the report and the print run, companies can spend as ıuch as $1-million on the yearly exercise, says Bev udhope, co-chief executive officer of Interbrand Tudhope in oronto, which produces annual reports for firms.

While most companies may not be as upfront as otash, more are realizing the importance of laying out their sion and strategy in their annual report, Mr. Tudhope says.

"What's called for now is more disclosure, greater transarency. People don't just want to know where the company as been but where it's going, in plain language, without the orporate speak."

In recent years, "because of budgets and some legal aranoia, some companies stripped their annual reports own to what looked like regulatory documents," Mr. Blunn ays.

Along with content, photographs and graphics were hittled away, and cheaper paper was used, he says.

The pendulum has now swung back, says Mr. Tudhope. Though many annual reports still aren't as glossy as they once were, they're much more polished and user-friendly, he says.

One of the biggest developments in recent years is the growth in the management discussion and analysis (MD&A) section, the hard nut that, along with the financial statements, lies at the core of the annual report. The size and style of the MD&A have expanded, as companies try to make the nitty-gritty numbers less impenetrable, says Mr. Buchanan.

In fact, the CICA issued new guidelines last year for the MD&A, to encourage more disclosure of financial information and potentially contentious issues such as off-balance sheet arrangements. It is only the MD&A, financial statements and auditor's report that companies are required, by law, to make public.

This past year, Potash used more graphs, plain language and explanatory information to try to put its financial figures into context for the average stakeholder, Ms. Heddie says.

But though companies are moving to more open MD&As, they're doing it with some trepidation.

"There can be a battle with the lawyers over this because the legal department wants to be sure you don't say something you can get sued over," Mr. Blunn says.

The CICA guidelines are more "forward-looking" than those in the United States, which is a legitimate concern for an inter-listed company like Potash, Ms. Heddie says.

"The U.S. is a lot more litigious and I thought we'd have a hard time with our U.S. counsel. I thought they'd be nervous and, frankly, they were."

But when one of the company's largest U.S. institutional investors gave the report top marks, Ms. Heddie says it was a big vote of confidence. The next annual report will likely go even further to explain the financials, she says.

Another recent trend is for corporations to put their annual reports on-line. It isn't yet legal for them to provide the information to an investor via the Web alone, but a regulatory change permitting that is in the offing. Even still, the paperbound copy isn't going away, investment experts say.

"A big deal was made about on-line reports a few years ago, but the fact is most people want a hard copy as well that they can read in their living room, at their leisure," says Mr. Tudhope.

A common complaint is that many companies post the print version of the report on their site, in a cumbersome PDF version that is far from intuitive. The on-line version must contain the same information but make the most of dynamic Web technology, including hyperlinks, says Mr. Blunn. Highlights should be pulled out and featured separately, so people don't have to search for them, he suggests.

Analysts use annual reports for reference all year long, says Mr. Buchanan and, if anything, they're becoming longer due to MD&A expansion and more disclosure.

"It's probably the most valuable hard-copy report that a corporation produces in a year," says Mr. Buchanan.

For a company like Potash, which doesn't put out a lot of marketing material, the annual report is a chance to tell its story to employees, customers, suppliers and investors, says Ms. Heddie. The story has to be told in a compelling way to compete for attention with Web sites stacked with information, fast-paced television and glitzy publications, Ms. Heddie says.

Part of what makes the story compelling, of course, telling it like it is.

Questions to Consider

1. *Should companies disclose any "bad news" in the reports?*
2. *Would it be important for shareholders to see how the company's actual financial performance compared wi budget?*
3. *Is it fair to the shareholders not to disclose all releva information?*

Source: Ann Kerr, "Bar Set Higher for Annual Reports." *The Glob and Mail*, 22 October 2003. Reprinted with permission of the author.

Calculating the Amount of Amortization Expense

Amortization expense (a term commonly used for financial reporting purposes) for a given period is determined by calculating the total amount to be amortized (the amortization *basis*) and then calculating the percentage of that total to be allocated to a given time period (the *amortization rules*).

The total amount to be amortized over the accounting life of the asset is known as the **amortization basis**. It is equal to the cost of the asset plus any setup or delivery costs that may be incurred.[3]

Amortization Methods The cost of an asset can be allocated over time by using any of several sets of amortization rules. The two most common amortization approaches used by public and private companies are the straight-line method and the declining balance method, both consistent with GAAP. Other methods (such as the sum-of-years-digits method) are also available but are less frequently used. In some special circumstances, a company may develop and use its own amortization method, reflecting the unique nature of the company, its industry, or its manufacturing process. The key principle, however, is that the cost of the asset is allocated throughout its useful life on a consistent basis (i.e., no change in amortization methodology).

Straight-Line Method.

The simplest and most transparent method of amortization is the *straight-line amortization (SL)* method. To use the **straight-line amortization method**, you divide the cost of the asset by the number of years of life for the asset, according to classification rules, and charge the result off as amortization expense each year. Under this method, an equal amount of amortization expense is charged to each period. For instance, if the managers at CAP bought a $1 million piece of equipment that belonged to the ten-year-asset class and had no

[3]Although in financial statements prepared by public corporations for reporting purposes, salvage value—the value of the asset if sold for salvage—may be subtracted in arriving at the amortization basis, it is not considered part of the amortization basis for tax reporting purposes.

residual value, then straight-line amortization for the asset would be computed as follows:

Asset's initial cost	$1,000,000
Divided by length of service	10 years
Equals amortization expense each year	$100,000[4]

Declining Balance Method.

Under the **declining balance method**, a fixed amortization rate is multiplied by the book value of an asset in order to determine the amortization expense in that period. In subsequent years, the same amortization rate is again applied to the declining net book value (asset minus accumulated amortization) to determine the amount of amortization expense in the subsequent period.

If you were to apply the declining balance method to the straight-line example ($1 million piece of equipment that belonged to the ten-year-asset class), the amortization rate under the declining balance method would be 20 percent on each year's book value. In the first year, the $1 million equipment would be amortized at 20 percent and the amortization expense would equal $200,000. In the second year, the remaining balance ($800,000) amortized at 20 percent is equal to $160,000. By the end of ten years, there is an unamortized balance of $107,374. The calculation is presented in Table 4-1.

Note also that the declining balance method may be viewed as an accelerated amortization method—greater amounts of the amortization basis are subtracted from income in the early years compared with the amount applied

Table 4-1 **Amortization Expense Under the Declining Balance Method**

Year-End	Amortization Expense	Net Book Value
1	200,000	800,000
2	160,000	640,000
3	128,000	512,000
4	102,400	409,600
5	81,920	327,680
6	65,536	262,144
7	52,429	209,715
8	41,943	167,772
9	33,554	134,218
10	26,844	107,374

[4]To be more precise, we would use what is known as the *half-year convention* in determining the annual amortization. One-half a year's amortization would be taken the year the asset was put into service and one-half in the final year. For example, for the preceding asset with a stated ten-year life, amortization would in fact be spread over eleven years. In this case, $50,000 in years 1 and 11, and $100,000 in years 2 through 10.

in the later years. The acceleration is important because the more quickly firms can write off the cost of an asset, the sooner they save taxes from the tax-deductible expenses.

So far we have discussed the two main methods of accounting for amortization. The amortization expense is a term used by financial accountants for the purposes of financial reporting. Now, it is a good time to look at what the Canada Revenue Agency (CRA) views as appropriate procedures for dealing with the amortization expense.

Under the terms of the *Income Tax Act*, a company is not permitted to use the amortization expense calculated by financial accountants for the purposes of calculating taxable income. Even though the overall approach and goal of the *Income Tax Act* is to allow a company to allocate the cost of an asset across its useful life, the CRA's mechanics of applying amortization principles differ from those charged to the income statement under GAAP. Under CRA rules, a company is allowed to claim capital cost allowance (CCA) as specified by the *Act*. Capital cost allowance is used in calculating taxable income regardless of the method chosen by the company for the purpose of financial reporting. This means that the amount of amortization expense developed for financial reporting purposes will differ from capital cost allowance calculated for tax purposes. Consequently, income taxes actually paid will vary from taxes declared in the net income statement. An exception would be a situation where the company chooses to adopt CRA's capital cost allowance rates and procedures for its reporting purposes. Smaller companies may adopt this approach. In most cases, capital cost allowance will exceed the amount of amortization expense, especially in the early years.

Let's see how capital cost allowance works in practice. The procedure is similar to an accelerated amortization scheme (such as a double declining balance method) where the net book value or Undepreciated Capital Cost (UCC), a term used for taxation purposes, refers to the cost of the asset less any amounts of amortization expense already charged to revenue in previous years. Additionally, the half-year rule applies where a company is only allowed to claim one-half of its normal amortization in the first year of its application. Let's assume that we want to purchase a fleet of trucks for use in the distribution system and we pay $1 million in cash for the asset. Since the asset falls into Class 10, the applicable CCA rate is equal to 30 percent and we apply the declining balance procedures. We also use the half-year rule. In the first year, capital cost allowance is equal to $150,000 ($1 million times 50 percent times 30 percent). The Undepreciated Capital Cost is equal to $850,000 ($1 million less $150,000). In the second year, allowable capital cost allowance is equal to $255,000 ($850,000 times 30 percent). At this point, the UCC is equal to $595,000 and so on.

The *Income Tax Act* has forty-three classes of assets. Table 4-2 summarizes some of the main asset classes, capital cost allowance rates, and methods to be used for different types of assets. In two of these classes (13 and 14), the calculation is more complex than applying a simple capital cost allowance rate.

Table 4-2 Main Capital Cost Allowance Classes and Rates

Class	Capital Cost Allowance Rate	Methods to Be Used	Examples of Assets in the Class
1	4%	Declining Balance	Buildings, Bridges, Subways, Tunnels
3	5%	Declining Balance	Buildings (acquired before 1988), Docks, Windmills, Telephone Poles
8	20%	Declining Balance	Machinery, Equipment, Advertising Posters, Furniture
10	30%	Declining Balance	Most Vehicles, Automotive Equipment, Trailers, Computer Hardware, and System Software
12	100%	100% Write-off in Year of Purchase	Books, Dishes, Cutlery, Uniforms and Costumes, Linen
13	Complex	Straight-line	Leasehold Improvements
14	Complex	Straight-line	Some Intangible Assets (excluding patents)
43	30%	Declining Balance	Manufacturing Equipment

Source: Data adapted from C. Byrd and I. Chen, *Canadian Tax Principles* (Toronto: Prentice Hall, 2003), pp. 217–218. Reproduced with permission of Clarence Byrd Inc.

INCOME TAXES

Tax policies are set by Parliament. The federal government imposes taxes through a complex and long document called the *Income Tax Act*. In addition, provincial income tax statutes enact provincial income tax policies. The federal government, through the Canada Revenue Agency, generally collects federal and provincial income tax. CRA is responsible for administering and enforcing the Act. CRA also enforces its claims against the taxpayers.

Federal and provincial corporate taxes are based on the flat tax rate applied to corporate taxable income. All corporations earning income in a Canadian jurisdiction are initially subject to the same basic federal tax rate, which is equal to 28 percent. The basic federal tax rate is further influenced by the general rate reduction percentage and corporate surtax. The "effective" federal tax rate is equal to 24.12 percent. Similarly, provincial income taxes are calculated from the application of a flat tax rate applied to taxable income. They are computed as an additional tax rate, generally ranging from 12 to 17 percent. Please note that you can calculate the tax rate in a province by deducting the federal tax rate from the combined provincial/federal tax rate shown in Table 4-3. For example, a provincial corporate tax rate in Manitoba is equal to 16 percent (40.12% − 24.12%). Note from Table 4-3 that taxes differ from province to province. For example, combined federal and provincial taxes in Quebec equal 33.02 percent while in Saskatchewan they equal 41.12 percent. So, if a corporation is registered in Manitoba and earned $400,000 in corporate taxable income, its combined federal and provincial taxes would equal $160,480 ($400,000 × 40.12% = $160,480).

The federal and provincial governments wish to encourage entrepreneurship, manufacturing activity, and scientific research through incentive tax

Table 4-3
Combined Federal and Provincial Tax Rates

	General Tax Rate (in percent)	Small Business Tax (in percent)	Manufacturing and Processing Tax Rate (in percent)
Federal Tax	24.12	13.12	22.12
Alberta	36.12	17.12	26.12
British Columbia	37.62	17.62	35.62
Manitoba	40.12	18.12	27.12
New Brunswick	37.12	16.12	35.12
Newfoundland and Labrador	38.12	18.12	27.12
Northwest Territories	36.12	17.12	34.12
Nova Scotia	40.12	18.12	38.12
Nunavut	36.12	17.12	34.12
Ontario	36.62	18.12	27.62
Quebec	33.02	20.62	29.62
Prince Edward Island	40.12	22.02	31.02
Saskatchewan	41.12	19.12	32.12
Yukon	39.12	15.62	24.62

Source: Reprint of Figure 15.3 from C. Byrd and I. Chen, *Canadian Tax Principles* (Toronto: Prentice Hall, 2003), p. 553. Reproduced with permission of Clarence Byrd Inc.

credits, which may result in a significant reduction of the corporate tax paid. For example, to encourage small business development, the federal government offers a tax credit, which provides a deduction against taxable income on the first $300,000 (the amount may vary from province to province) of corporate income. In addition, there are numerous tax credits that can be applied against tax payables. Their extent and application may vary from province to province. A list of most common tax credits is presented here:

1. Foreign tax credit—credit for taxes paid by a corporation to another country.
2. Political contributions tax credit—corporations can claim contributions made to registered political parties, registered district associations, and registered, non-affiliated candidates as defined under the *Elections Act*.
3. Research and development tax credit—corporations can claim this credit if they make eligible expenditures for research and development.
4. Film and video industry tax credit—a tax credit is obtained by corporations that produce an eligible film or video.
5. Corporate investment tax credit—allowed for corporations that have acquired qualified property.

We have already stressed the importance of proper financial disclosure. One area in finance that has also received a lot of attention is the world-wide standardization of accounting rules. While it is not possible to standardize taxes across the globe, it is possible to set the principles of financial accounting so that financial accounting and reporting are consistent from country to country. International Perspectives in Finance 4-1 discusses this problem.

INTERNATIONAL PERSPECTIVES IN FINANCE 4-1

Accounting Boards Pledge to Work on Common Rules

ernational and U.S. accounting standard setters pledged . to continue their efforts to develop common rules and d they will sit down . . . to set an agenda for change in coming three years.

Indeed, after . . . joint meetings between the key counting groups, the head of the International Accounting ndards Board, Sir David Tweedie, said he envisages a day en there will be just one global accounting standard-set- "I think some time in the future—not in my professional —there will be just one board, ultimately, many, many rs down the road. You can see it happening," he said fol- ing the meetings in Toronto.

In such a world, he said, national standard setters, such Canada's Accounting Standards Board, would play a key e by providing research and feedback on emerging issues heir respective countries.

The IASB is developing a set of global accounting stan- ds for international adoption by 2007. Members of the European Union have already pledged to start using the common standard by 2005, and many other countries have pledged to begin using the international target by 2007. Australia and New Zealand have said they will adopt the standard by the 2005 deadline.

Robert Herz, chairman of the U.S. Financial Accounting Standards Board, said the joint meetings made significant headway on the issue of global convergence of standards and said FASB will put out exposure drafts in the next month on issues such as the handling of changes in accounting policy, asset exchanges and inventory costing that will bring U.S. rules in line with international standards.

So far, Canada is not planning to adopt the global rules in 2007.

Source: Elizabeth Church and Janet McFarland, "Accounting Boards Pledge to Work on Common Rules," 24 October 2003. Reprinted with permission of *The Globe and Mail.*

SUMMARY

4-1 Describe a main function for each of the four accounting financial statements: the income statement, the retained earnings statement, the balance sheet, and the cash flow statement.

Financial managers need to understand the key elements of financial statements to analyze a firm's finances and plan for its future.

- The income statement shows the amount of revenues, expenses, and income a firm has earned over a specified period of time.
- The retained earnings statement records dividend, net income, and retained earnings information.
- The balance sheet describes the assets, liabilities, and equity values for a company at a specific point in time.
- The cash flow statement describes a firm's cash inflows and outflows over a period of time.

4-2 Discuss how amortization affects cash flow and two major methods used to compute amortization expense.

Amortization is a noncash, tax-deductible expense. Because amortization is tax deductible, it affects cash flow—the greater a firm's amortization, the greater its cash flow. Cash flow, in turn, affects the value of the firm. The more cash a firm has, the greater its value.

To allocate the cost of an asset over time, accountants use different amortization methods, such as straight-line amortization or the declining balance method. Whatever method is used, accountants must first find the amortization basis—the total cost of the asset plus setup and delivery costs. Then they calculate the percentage of that total allocated for the time period at issue, as determined by either the straight-line amortization method or the declining balance method.

4-3 Explain a major difference between amortization and capital cost allowance.

Reporting for financial and tax purposes is likely to differ. Financial accountants, for the purpose of financial reporting, use the term amortization expense and appropriate methods for its calculation. Under the terms of the *Income Tax Act*, a company is not allowed to use the amortization expense calculated by financial accountants. Instead, a company may claim capital cost allowance (CCA) for assets falling into specific asset classes as declared by the Act. This generally means that the amount of amortization expense developed for financial reporting purposes will differ from CCA calculated for tax purposes. Consequently, income taxes paid will vary from taxes declared in the income statement.

4-4 Explain the basics of corporate taxation and know how to apply taxes.

Corporate taxes are set by Parliament and administered by the Canada Revenue Agency (CRA) through the *Income Tax Act*. CRA also collects the tax and is responsible for enforcement.

Federal and provincial taxes are based on a flat rate applied to the corporate taxable income. The basic federal tax rate is equal to 24.12 percent. The amount of taxes owed by a firm is calculated by multiplying the combined federal and provincial tax rate by the amount of taxable income. Taxes differ among provinces, with the lowest combined tax in Quebec (33.02 percent) and the highest in Saskatchewan (41.12 percent).

SELF-TEST

ST-1. Brother Mel's Bar-B-Q Restaurant has $80,000 in assets and $20,000 in liabilities. What is the equity of this firm?

ST-2. Cantwell Corporation has sales revenue of $2 million. Cost of goods sold is $1,500,000. What is Cantwell Corporation's gross profit?

ST-3. Adams Computer Store had accumulated amortization of $75,000 at the end of 2002, and at the end of 2001 this figure was $60,000. Earnings before interest and taxes for 2002 were $850,000. Assuming that no assets were sold in 2002, what was the amount of amortization expense for 2002?

ST-4. Shattuck Corporation had operating income (EBIT) of $2,500,000 in 2002, amortization expense of $500,000, and dividends paid of $400,000. What is Shattuck's operating cash flow (EBITDA) for 2002?

ST-5. Bubba's Sporting Goods Company had retained earnings of $3 million at the end of 2001. During 2002, the company had earnings available to common shareholders of $500,000 and, of this, paid out $100,000 in dividends. What is the retained earnings figure for the end of 2002?

ST-6. Ron's In-Line Skating Corporation had retained earnings at the end of 2002 of $120,000. At the end of 2001, this figure was $90,000. If the company paid $5,000 in dividends to common shareholders during 2002, what was the amount of earnings available to common shareholders?

ST-7. Hayes Company recently bought a new computer system. The total cost, including setup, was $8,000. What would be the amount of amortization expense taken on this system in year 2 if the asset falls into a 20 percent capital cost allowance rate using the declining balance method? Use the half-year rule.

ST-8. If Burns Corporation has taxable income of $800,000, how much federal and provincial income taxes are owed? The company is located in Alberta and is classified as a small business. What is the average tax rate?

ST-9. If Badeusz Quarry Corporation located in Manitoba has taxable income of $4 million, how much federal and provincial taxes are owed? Badeusz is not a small business and is not eligible for manufacturing and processing tax rate.

ST-10. If Parmenter Corporation located in British Columbia has taxable income of $20 million, how much federal and provincial taxes are owed? The company is classified as a manufacturing and processing concern.

REVIEW QUESTIONS

1. Why do total assets equal the sum of total liabilities and equity? Explain.
2. What are the time dimensions of the income statement, the balance sheet, and the cash flow statement? (Hint: Are they videos or still pictures?) Explain.
3. Define amortization expense as it appears on an income statement. How does amortization affect cash flow?
4. What are retained earnings? Why are they important?
5. Explain how earnings available to common shareholders and common share dividends paid, as shown on the current income statement, affect the balance sheet item, retained earnings.
6. What is accumulated amortization?
7. What are the three major sections of the cash flow statement?
8. How do financial managers calculate the amount of taxes owed?
9. Are taxes the same across provinces in Canada?
10. Identify whether the following items belong on the income statement or the balance sheet.

    a. Interest Expense
    b. Preferred Share Dividends Paid
    c. Property, Plant, and Equipment
    d. Sales
    e. Notes Payable
    f. Common Shares
    g. Accounts Receivable
    h. Accrued Expenses
    i. Cost of Goods Sold
    j. Preferred Shares
    k. Long-Term Debt
    l. Cash
    m. Operating Expense
    n. Amortization Expense
    o. Marketable Securities
    p. Accounts Payable
    q. Prepaid Expenses
    r. Inventory
    s. Net Income
    t. Retained Earnings

11. Indicate to which section the following balance sheet items belong (current assets, property, plant, and equipment, current liabilities, long-term liabilities, or equity).

a. Cash
b. Notes Payable due within 1 year
c. Common Shares
d. Accounts Receivable
e. Accrued Expenses
f. Preferred Shares
g. Property, Plant, and Equipment
h. Marketable Securities
i. Accounts Payable
j. Prepaid Expenses
k. Inventory
l. Retained Earnings

PROBLEMS

Financial Statement Connections ▶

4-1. You are interviewing for an entry-level financial analyst position with Zeppelin Associates. Monte Rutledge, the senior partner, wants to be sure all the people he hires are very familiar with basic accounting principles. He gives you the following data and asks you to fill in the missing information. Each column is an independent case. Month and day references are for the current year.

	Case A	Case B
Revenues	200,000	________
Expenses	________	70,000
Net Income	________	________
Retained Earnings, Jan 1	300,000	100,000
Dividends Paid	70,000	30,000
Retained Earnings, Dec 31	270,000	________
Current Assets, Dec 31	80,000	________
Noncurrent Assets, Dec 31	________	180,000
Total Assets, Dec 31	________	410,000
Current Liabilities, Dec 31	40,000	60,000
Noncurrent Liabilities, Dec 31	________	________
Total Liabilities, Dec 31	140,000	________
Share Capital, Dec 31	520,000	100,000
Total Shareholders' Equity, Dec 31	________	210,000

Financial Statement Connections ▶

4-2. Fill in the following missing income statement values. The cases are independent.

	Case A	Case B
Sales	________	250,000
COGS	200,000	________
Gross Profit	________	150,000
Operating Expenses	60,000	60,000
Operating Income (EBIT)	________	________
Interest Expense	10,000	________
Income before Taxes (EBT)	________	80,000
Tax Expense (40%)	92,000	________
Net Income	________	________

Tax Rates ▶

4-3. Lightning, Inc. has earnings before taxes of $500,000. The company is located in Alberta and is classified as a small business.

a. Calculate the tax obligation for Lightning, Inc.
b. What is Lightning's average tax rate?

4-4. Thunder, Inc. has earnings before taxes of $150,000. Thunder's headquarters are located in Manitoba. Calculate the tax obligation for Thunder, Inc. ◀ Tax Rates

4-5. Jetaire's EBT is $3,200,000. The company is located in Nova Scotia and qualifies as a manufacturing and processing concern. What is the average tax rate? ◀ Tax Rates

4-6. The following is a portion of Hitchcock Haven, Inc.'s balance sheet. ◀ Equity

Share Capital (400,000 shares authorized; 200,000 shares issued)	$200,000
Retained Earnings	$500,000

What was the market price per share when it was originally sold?

4-7. This year the Simon and Pieman Corporation had $10 million in sales, $5.2 million in operating costs, and $200,000 in interest expense. It also paid 40 percent of its pre-tax income to the government as income tax expense. What was Simon's net after-tax income for the year? ◀ After-Tax Earnings

4-8. A portion of Hitchcock Haven, Inc.'s comparative balance sheet follows. What is the amount of amortization expense you would expect to see on the 2004 income statement? No assets that were on the books at the end of 2003 were sold or otherwise disposed of in 2004. ◀ Amortization

Hitchcock Haven, Inc.
Balance Sheet as of December 31

	2003	2004
Property, Plant, and Equipment	$200,000	$250,000
Less: Accumulated Amortization	($60,000)	($70,000)
Property, Plant, and Equipment, Net	$140,000	$180,000

4-9. Use the following table to calculate (a) current assets, (b) net property, plant, and equipment, (c) current liabilities, and (d) net working capital. ◀ Balance Sheet

Notes Payable	4,000,000
Cash	11,000,000
Long-Term Debt	16,000,000
Marketable Securities	9,000,000
Amortization	8,000,000
Inventory	11,000,000
Accounts Receivable	3,000,000
Accrued Expenses	2,000,000
Property, Plant, and Equipment	30,000,000
Prepaid Expenses	1,000,000

4-10. The following financial data correspond to Callahan Corporation's 2004 operations. ◀ Income Statement

Cost of Goods Sold	$200,000
Selling and Administrative Expenses	40,000
Amortization Expense	85,000
Sales	440,000
Interest Expense	40,000
Applicable Income Tax Rate	40%

Calculate the following income statement items.

a. Gross Profit

b. Operating Income (EBIT)
c. Earnings before Taxes (EBT)
d. Income Taxes
e. Net Income

Net Worth ▶ **4-11.** Simon and Pieman began the year with $1,000,000 in total assets and ended the year with $1,500,000 in total assets. It had no debt at the beginning of the year, but it had $200,000 at the end of the year. What was Simon's net worth (i.e., total shareholders' equity) at the end of the year?

Amortization ▶ **4-12.** The Exotic Perfume Company (EPC), a profit-making company, purchased a process line for $131,000 and spent another $12,000 on its installation. The line was commissioned in January 2003 and it is amortized at 10 percent under the straight-line method. Applicable income tax rate for EPC is 40 percent and there is no investment tax credit. Calculate the following:

a. 2004 amortization expense for this process line
b. Amount of tax savings due to this investment

EBITA ▶ **4-13.** Refer to the following income statement for Target Telecom (TT):

Total Revenue	$4,125,000
Cost of Goods Sold	1,237,500
Gross Profit	2,887,500
Operating Expenses	
Marketing	825,000
Amortization	57,000
General and Administrative	1,237,500
Total Operating Expenses	2,119,500
Operating Profit	768,000
Interest Expense	10,000
Before-Tax Profit	758,000
Taxes	265,300
After-Tax Profit	492,700

What was TT's Earnings before Interest, Taxes, and Amortization (EBITA) for the year?

Taxes ▶ **4-14.** In 2004, Goodwill Construction Company purchased $130,000 worth of construction equipment. Goodwill's taxable income for 2004 without considering the new construction equipment would have been $400,000. The new equipment is amortized at 10 percent using the straight-line method. Assume the applicable income tax rate is 34 percent.

a. What is the company's 2004 taxable income?
b. How much income tax will Goodwill pay?

Income Statement ▶ **4-15.** Last year Johnson Flow Measurement Systems, Inc. had an operating profit of $600,000 and paid $50,000 in interest expenses and $63,000 in preferred share dividends. The applicable income tax rate for the year was 34 percent. The company had 100,000 common shares outstanding at the end of last year.

a. What was the amount of Johnson's earnings per share last year?
b. If the company paid $1.00 per share to its common shareholders, what was the addition to retained earnings last year?

Use the comparative figures of Pinewood Company and Subsidiaries that follow to answer questions 4-16 through 4-20.

Pinewood Company and Subsidiaries
As of December 31

	2003	2004
Assets		
Cash	$ 5,534	$ 9,037
Marketable Securities	952	1,801
Accounts Receivable, Gross	14,956	16,110
Less: Allowance for Bad Debts	211	167
Accounts Receivable, Net	14,745	15,943
Inventory	10,733	11,574
Prepaid Expenses	3,234	2,357
Property, Plant, and Equipment, Gross	57,340	60,374
Less: Accumulated Amortization	29,080	32,478
Property, Plant, and Equipment, Net	28,260	27,896
Land	1,010	1,007
Long-Term Investments	2,503	4,743
Liabilities		
Accounts Payable	3,253	2,450
Notes Payable	—	—
Accrued Expenses	6,821	7,330
Bonds Payable	2,389	2,112
Shareholders' Equity		
Common Shares	8,549	10,879
Retained Earnings	45,959	51,587

4-16. Compute the following totals for the end of 2003 and 2004. ◀ Balance Sheet

a. Current Assets
b. Total Assets
c. Current Liabilities
d. Total Liabilities
e. Total Shareholders' Equity

4-17. Show whether the basic accounting equation is satisfied in problem 4-16. ◀ Basic Accounting Equation

4-18. Calculate the cash flows from the changes in the following from the end of 2003 to the end of 2004. Indicate inflow or outflow. ◀ Cash Flows

a. Accumulated Amortization
b. Accounts Receivable
c. Inventories
d. Prepaid Expenses
e. Accounts Payable
f. Accrued Expenses
g. Property, Plant, and Equipment
h. Marketable Securities
i. Land
j. Long-Term Investments
k. Common Shares
l. Bonds Payable

4-19. Prepare a cash flow statement in proper form using the inflows and outflows from problem 4-18. Assume net income (earnings after taxes) from the 2004 income statement was $10,628 and $5,000 in common share dividends were paid. Ignore the income tax effect on the change in amortization. ◀ Cash Flow Statement

4-20. Show whether your net cash flow matches the change in cash between the end-of-2003 and end-of-2004 balance sheets. ◀ Financial Statement Corrections

Income Statement Values ▶

4-21. Fill in the missing income statement values for Edelen Enterprises.

Sales	900,000
COGS	______
Gross Profit	600,000
Operating Expenses	______
Operating Income (EBIT)	400,000
Interest Expense	______
Income before Taxes (EBT)	300,000
Tax Expense (30%)	______
Net Income	______

Dividends Paid ▶

4-22. Flannery Pharmaceuticals' retained earnings at the end of 2003 was $8,000,000, 2004 earnings available to common shareholders was $1,500,000, and retained earnings for the end of 2004 was $8,700,000. What was the amount paid in dividends to common shareholders in 2004?

Amortization ▶

4-23. The Shaggy Dog Microbrewery bought a new mash tun in 2003 for $385,000. The mash tun is expected to last for 10 years, but the asset is amortized at 20 percent under the declining balance method. Calculate the amortization expense for the new mash tun that should be recorded during each of the next 10 years.

Income Statement, Cash Flow ▶

4-24. Thunder Bay Distributors has provided you with its income statement and some parts of the balance sheet. The owner of the company, Mr. John Real, has asked you to interpret the financial information for him. Mr. Real is quite excited about the situation in which the company had losses, but more cash appears in the company's bank account. Use the following information to answer to Mr. Real's specific questions.

Income Statement for 2004

	2004
Net Sales	5,000,000
Cost of Goods Sold	3,000,000
Selling and Administrative Expenses	500,000
Amortization	1,800,000
Operating Income	(300,000)
Interest Expense	400,000
Earnings Before Taxes	(700,000)
Income Tax	0
Net Income	(700,000)

Selected balance sheet items for 2003 and 2004

	2003	2004
Accounts Receivable	10,000,000	8,500,000
Inventory	3,000,000	3,300,000
Prepaid Expenses	1,000,000	1,200,000
Account Payable	6,000,000	7,000,000
Accrued Expenses	300,000	250,000

a. How it is possible to have losses from operations at the net income level but generate cash from operations? Prepare a simplified cash flow statement showing the cash flow generated by operating activities in 2004.

b. What were the major factors that contributed to the cash flow from operations being positive or negative?

c. Can you make any generalizations about the relationship between the net income line and the cash flow from operating activities?

d. What is the net working capital in 2004?

e. Does the net income figure matter?

4-25. Rogers Communications Incorporated (NYSE: RG) is one of Canada's leading providers of communications, entertainment, and information. The company predominantly consists of three business units: Rogers Cable (cable service provider), Rogers Wireless (wireless service provider), and Rogers Media (radio stations, TV). The company's annual report for 2002 contained the following financial information (in thousands of dollars):

◀ Cash Flow

	2002	2001
Issue of long-term debt	2,977,330	2,187,200
Repayment of long-term debt	2,445,131	1,248,367
Proceeds on termination of cross-currency interest rate exchange agreements	225,210	0
Premium on early repayment of long-term debt	21,773	0
Funds received from non-controlling shareholders	0	167,302
Financing costs incurred	27,399	27,102
Repurchase of preferred and collaterized equity instruments	1,317,040	0
Issue of equity instruments	0	245,632
Issue of shares	5,729	18,795
Dividends on Preferred Shares and distribution on Convertible Preferred Securities	33,000	33,014

Based on the information included above, prepare the cash flow from financing activities for Rogers Communications Incorporated for the years 2001 and 2002. (Hint: Determine which of the financial elements or items listed above have a negative or positive impact on the company's financing activities and determine the net amount.)

4-26. Canadian Tire (TSX: CTR.NV) is a complex business. In addition to 451 retail stores operated from coast to coast in Canada, it also provides gasoline through its network of 212 independently operated gasoline sites. Canadian Tire also owns Mark's Work Warehouse, one of the largest specialty retailers, which operates a chain of 306 corporate and franchise stores. An annual report for 2002 includes the following information (in millions of dollars) for the years 2001 and 2002:

◀ Cash Flow

	2002	2001
Information from Income Statement		
Net Earnings	202.4	176.7
Amortization	158.5	136.3
Information from Balance Sheet		
Accounts Receivable	584.1	433.9
Inventories	503.0	440.9
Prepaid Expenses and Other Current Assets	19.1	14.3
Accounts Payable	1,294.7	1,009.7
Income Tax Payable	80.7	70.4

a. Based on the information given, compute the cash flow from operating activities for 2002.

b. Please discuss the major factors that contributed to the cash flow from operations being either positive or negative.

Cash Flow ▶ **4-27.** Nortel Networks Corporation (TSX: NT; NYSE: NT) is a well-known Canadian provider of telecommunication network solutions and services to fixed-line operators and wireless service providers as well as other enterprises. The company's main clients include Fortune 500 companies, small business, health care, education, and government institutions. The annual reports for the years 2000, 2001, and 2002 include the following information (in millions of U.S. dollars):

	2000	2001	2002
Information from Income Statement			
Net Earnings	(2,539)	(24,474)	(3,535)
Amortization	6,792	5,691	701
Information from Balance Sheet			
Accounts Receivable	8,198	2,926	1,911
Inventories	4,336	1,586	889
Income tax receivable	0	796	58
Other current assets	1,662	858	496
Trade and other accounts payable	3,102	1,375	893
Payroll and benefits-related liabilities	917	638	521
Other accrued liabilities	3,973	3,926	2,895

a. Based on the information given, compute the cash flow from operating activities for both 2001 and 2002.

b. Discuss the company's financial position at the operating level in view of the continued losses at the net earnings' level. Has Nortel's situation deteriorated or improved?

Cash Flow ▶ **4-28.** Green Booth is one of the leading manufacturers of ice cream in Ontario. The products are sold in the retail market throughout Canada in the form of tubs, buckets, scoops, and ice-cream sticks. The company also services the institutional market: The main clients are major international retail operators who sell their products through chains. Green Booth is one of the best-known consumer brands in Ontario and throughout Canada. In 1988, the company was founded by a local entrepreneur from a family with a long tradition in the production of handmade bakery products, pastry products, and ice cream. He continues the family tradition by industrially producing ice cream in a modern facility. The income statement and balance sheet for the years 2002, 2003, and 2004 follow:

Income Statement
Green Booth
2002–2004

	2002	2003	2004
Net Sales	45,000,000	62,000,000	84,000,000
Cost of Goods Sold	32,000,000	45,000,000	60,000,000
Selling and Administrative Expenses	5,000,000	6,000,000	8,000,000
Amortization	1,500,000	1,800,000	2,200,000
Operating Income	6,500,000	9,200,000	13,800,000
Interest Expense	600,000	650,000	550,000
Earnings before Taxes	5,900,000	8,550,000	13,250,000
Income Tax	2,360,000	3,420,000	5,300,000
Net Income	3,540,000	5,130,000	7,950,000

Balance Sheet
Green Booth
2002–2004

	2002	2003	2004
Assets			
Cash	11,540,000	11,520,000	11,270,000
Marketable Securities	500,000	800,000	1,000,000
Accounts Receivable	6,000,000	7,000,000	8,000,000
Inventory	8,500,000	9,000,000	10,000,000
Prepaid Expenses	400,000	500,000	500,000
Property, Plant, and Equipment, Gross	15,000,000	18,000,000	22,000,000
Less: Accumulated Amortization	7,500,000	9,300,000	11,500,000
Property, Plant, and Equipment, Net	7,500,000	8,700,000	10,500,000
Liabilities			
Accounts Payable	7,000,000	8,000,000	10,000,000
Notes Payable	1,000,000	1,500,000	1,500,000
Accrued Expenses	1,000,000	1,200,000	1,000,000
Long-Term Debt	5,000,000	5,000,000	4,000,000
Shareholders' Equity			
Preferred Shares	4,000,000	4,000,000	4,000,000
Common Shares	6,000,000	6,000,000	6,000,000
Retained Earnings	10,440,000	11,820,000	14,770,000

a. Calculate the amount of dividends for 2003 and 2004.

b. Generate a cash flow statement for 2003 and 2004.

ANSWERS TO SELF-TEST

ST-1. \$80,000 assets − \$20,000 liabilities = \$60,000 equity

ST-2. Gross profit = \$2,000,000 sales revenue − \$1,500,000 cost of goods sold = \$500,000

ST-3. \$75,000 end-of-2002 accumulated amortization − \$60,000 end-of-2001 accumulated amortization = \$15,000 amortization expense for 2002

ST-4. \$2,500,000 EBIT + \$500,000 = \$3,000,000 cash flow from operations (Dividend payments are not operating cash flows. They are financial cash flows.)

ST-5. \$3,000,000 end-of-2001 retained earnings + \$500,000 earnings available to common shareholders − \$100,000 dividends paid = \$3,400,000 end-of-2002 retained earnings

ST-6. Beginning retained earnings + net income − dividends paid = ending retained earnings. Therefore: Net income = ending retained earnings − beginning retained earnings + dividends paid. So, for Ron's In-Line Skating Corporation: Net income = \$120,000 − \$90,000 + \$5,000 = \$35,000.

ST-7. First year amortization: \$8,000 × 0.2 × 0.5 = \$800. Second year amortization: \$7,200 × 0.2 = \$1,440.

ST-8. \$300,000 × 17.12% = \$51,360 + \$500,000 × 36.12% = \$180,600 = \$231,960. The amount of taxes owed is equal to \$231,960. The average tax rate is equal to 29.00% (\$231,960 ÷ \$800,000).

ST-9. \$4,000,000 × 40.12% = \$1,604,800. Badeusz Quarry owes \$1,604,800 in taxes.

ST-10. \$20,000,000 × 35.62% = \$7,124,000. Parmenter Corporation owes \$7,124,000 in taxes.

5

Analysis of Financial Statements

Chapter Objectives

After reading this chapter, you should be able to:

5-1 **Explain** two ways in which financial ratio analysis helps financial managers assess the health of a company.

5-2 **Define** what profitability, liquidity, debt, asset activity, and market value ratios measure.

5-3 **Name** and **describe** three types of analyses that compare financial information over time and among companies.

5-4 **Name** four sources that can be used to locate ratio value data for specific companies and industries.

"Money is better than poverty, if only for financial reasons."

—Woody Allen

Financial Ratios and Rules of Thumb

Analysts, inexperienced finance students, and non-finance professionals often search for quick-and-easy yardsticks to assess the historical financial performance of a company. A common question is whether there are any ratios that may be used to ascertain financial performance at a glance. The answer is simple: No. A number of reasons explain this. Firstly, there are different types of companies with fundamentally different business models. For example, companies in the telecommunication, natural gas, and energy sectors—often referred to as utilities—have large amounts of fixed assets and are highly leveraged. They also have steady cash flows due to a large and steady customer base, and their profits are stable and less influenced by business cycles. In comparison, industrials have the opposite characteristics, manufacturing products for consumption by end-users or as input by other companies or delivery services. Companies in these sectors often present more potential for growth and appreciation in value. Secondly, businesses go through cycles where financial performance deteriorates or improves with no immediate implication for the viability of the business. This implies that performance measures are needed for both good and bad times, a scenario that could prove difficult.

The ratios listed below, however, yield themselves to the most common generalizations. Financial analysts in their preliminary analysis of a company's financial performance often use these rules of thumb.

	Definition	Industrials	Utilities
Current Ratio	$\frac{\text{Current Assets}}{\text{Current Liabilities}}$	>2	>2
Quick Ratio	$\frac{\text{Current Assets} - \text{Inventory}}{\text{Current Liabilities}}$	>1	>1
Times Interest Earned	$\frac{\text{Operating Profit (EBIT)}}{\text{Interest Expense}}$	>3	>2
Debt to Equity	$\frac{\text{Total Liabilities}}{\text{Common Shareholders' Equity}}$	<0.5	<1.5

Source: www.westjet.com.

Chapter Overview

In Chapter 4, we reviewed the major financial statements, the primary sources of financial information for a business. In this chapter we will learn how to interpret these financial statements in greater detail. All business owners, investors, and creditors use financial statements and ratio analysis to investigate the financial health of a firm. We will see how financial managers calculate ratios that measure profitability, liquidity, debt, asset activity, and market performance of a firm. We will then explore how financial experts use ratios to compare a firm's performance to managers' goals, the firm's past and present performance, and the firm's performance to similar firms in the industry. We will also discuss sources of financial information.

Assessing Financial Health

Medical doctors assess the health of people. Financial managers assess the health of businesses. When you visit a doctor for an examination, the doctor may check your blood pressure, heart rate, cholesterol, and blood sugar levels. The results of each test should fall within a range of numbers considered "normal" for your age, weight, gender, and height. If they do not, the doctor will probably run additional tests to see what, if anything, is wrong.

Like doctors, financial managers check the health of businesses by running basic tests—such as a financial ratio analysis—to see whether a firm's performance is within the normal range for a company of that type. If it is not, the financial manager runs more tests to see what, if anything, is wrong.

Misleading Numbers

Both medical doctors and financial managers must interpret the information they have and decide what additional information they need to complete an analysis. For instance, suppose a doctor examines a six-foot, 230-pound, 22-year-old male named Dirk. The doctor's chart shows that a healthy male of that age and height should normally weigh between 160 and 180 pounds. Because excess weight is a health risk, the numbers do not look positive.

Before the doctor prescribes a diet and exercise program for Dirk, she asks follow-up questions and runs more tests. She learns that Dirk, a starting fullback for his college football team, has only 6 percent body fat, can bench-press 380 pounds, runs a 40-yard dash in 4.5 seconds, has a blood pressure rate of 110/65, and a resting heart rate of 52 beats per minute. This additional information changes the doctor's initial health assessment. Relying on incomplete information would have led to an inaccurate diagnosis.

Like doctors, financial managers need to analyze many factors to determine the health of a company. Indeed, for some firms, the financial statements do not provide the entire picture.

On occasion, accounting conventions may prevent factors affecting a firm's finances from appearing on financial statements. Just as Dirk's doctor looked beyond the obvious, financial managers using ratio analysis must always seek complete information before completing an analysis. In the sections that follow, we discuss ratios based on financial statements, ratios that use market information, and outside information sources.

Financial Ratios

Financial managers use ratio analysis to interpret the raw numbers on financial statements. A **financial ratio** is a number that expresses the value of one financial variable relative to another. Put more simply, a financial ratio is the result you get when you divide one financial number by another. Calculating an individual ratio is simple, but each ratio must be analyzed carefully to effectively measure a firm's performance.

Ratios are comparative measures. Because the ratios show relative value, they allow financial analysts to compare information that could not be compared in its raw form.[1] Ratios may be used to compare:

- one ratio to a related ratio
- the firm's performance to management's goals
- the firm's past and present performances
- the firm's performance to similar firms

For instance, say a company reaped huge revenues from one investment, but the cost of the investment was high. A financial manager could use a ratio to compare that investment to another that did not generate such high revenues but had low cost. Take James Cameron's *Titanic*. This blockbuster movie grossed more than $1.75 billion—the number-one grossing movie for 1998. Compare *Titanic's* total revenues to the $23.6 million revenues that Ang Lee's *The Wedding Banquet* generated.[2] Looking only at the total revenue figures, *Titanic* looks like a better investment than *The Wedding Banquet*.

Dogbert points out to the pointy headed boss how bad news can sometimes come from your auditor when actual financial performance and condition are not what was reported by internal accountants.

Source: DILBERT © 1996 United Features Syndicate. Reprinted by permission.

However, analysts in the movie industry use a return-on-cost ratio (total revenues divided by total cost) to find a movie's net return per $1 invested. Using that ratio we see that *Titanic*, at a cost of $200 million, had a return-on-cost ratio of 8.75 ($1,750,000,000 ÷ $200,000,000 = 8.75). *The Wedding*

[1]Financial managers who analyze the financial condition of the firms they work for act as financial analysts. The term *financial analyst*, however, also includes financial experts who analyze a variety of firms.

[2]*Colorado Springs Gazette-Telegraph* (January 15, 1994), p. A2.

Banquet, at a cost of $1 million, had a return-on-cost ratio of 23.6 ($23,600,000 ÷ $1,000,000 = 23.6). Although *Titanic* made more total revenue, *The Wedding Banquet* made more money relative to its cost than *Titanic*.

Financial managers, other business managers, creditors, and shareholders all use financial ratio analysis. Specifically, creditors may use ratios to see whether a business will have the cash flow to repay its debt and interest. Shareholders may use ratios to see what the long-term value of their shares will be. In October 2003, Nortel Networks announced that it expected to make a profit after many years of losses. At the same time, Nortel announced a restatement of its financial results for the years 2000, 2001, and 2002. In spite of the positive news on the profit side for the year 2003, some analysts questioned whether the company "has actually turned the corner."[3]

The Basic Financial Ratios

Financial ratios are generally divided into five categories: profitability, liquidity, debt, asset activity, and market value. The ratios in each group give us insights into different aspects of a firm's financial health.

- *Profitability ratios* measure how much company revenue is eaten up by expenses, how much a company earns relative to sales generated, and the amount earned relative to the value of the firm's assets and equity.
- *Liquidity ratios* indicate how quickly and easily a company can obtain cash for its needs.
- *Debt ratios* measure how much a company owes to others.
- *Asset activity ratios* measure how efficiently a company uses its assets.
- *Market value ratios* measure how the market value of a company's shares compares with its accounting values.

Calculating the Ratios

We will use the financial statements for the Canadian Auto Parts (CAP) presented in Chapter 4 as the basis for our ratio analysis. Figure 5-1 shows CAP's statement of income and retained earnings for 2004. Figure 5-2 shows its December 31, 2004, balance sheet.

Note that this form of the statement combines the more typical income statement and the retained earnings statement into one presentation. This format is common in public and private companies, hence its presentation here. One of the distinguishing features of the statement of income and retained earnings is that it includes information on earnings available to common shareholders and earnings per share. The line earnings to common shareholders is important as it truly represents the income or earnings, which can be either used for reinvestment purposes in the business or paid out to common shareholders, or some combination of the two options. The amount of dividends paid to preferred shareholders, which often represents a fixed obligation on the part of the company, is subtracted from the net income figure. This earnings line is often used in the ratio analysis.

---

[3]David Ebner, "Nortel Posts Profits, Restates," 24 October 2003. *The Globe and Mail.*

Now let's analyze CAP's financial health by calculating its profitability, liquidity, debt, asset utilization, and market value ratios.

Profitability Ratios Profitability ratios measure how the firm's returns compare with its sales, asset investments, and equity. Shareholders have a special interest in the profitability ratios because profit ultimately leads to cash flow, a primary source of value for a firm. Managers, acting on behalf of shareholders, also pay close attention to profitability ratios to ensure that the managers preserve the firm's value.

Take Note

All profitability ratios and other ratios use net sales rather than gross sales.

We will discuss five profitability ratios: gross profit margin, operating profit margin, net profit margin, return on assets, and return on equity. Some of the profitability ratios use figures from two different financial statements.

Net Sales	$90,000,000
Cost of Goods Sold	64,000,000
Gross Profit	26,000,000
Selling and Administrative Expenses	13,000,000
Amortization	2,300,000
Operating Income (EBIT)	10,700,000
Interest Expense	450,000
Earnings Before Taxes	10,250,000
Income Taxes (40%)	4,100,000
Net Income	6,150,000
Preferred Share Dividends	1,000,000
Earnings Available to Common Shareholders	5,150,000
Earnings per Share (1,750,000 shares)	$2.94
Common Dividends Paid	438,000
Increase in Retained Earnings	$ 4,712,000

Figure 5-1
Canadian Auto Parts Statement of Income and Retained Earnings for the Year Ended December 31, 2004

Gross Profit Margin.

The *gross profit margin* measures how much profit remains out of each sales dollar after the cost of the goods sold is subtracted. The ratio formula follows:

$$\text{Gross Profit Margin} = \frac{\text{Gross Profit}}{\text{Sales}} = \frac{\$26{,}000{,}000}{\$90{,}000{,}000} = 0.29, \text{ or } 29\%$$

This ratio shows how well a firm generates revenue compared with its costs of goods sold. The higher the ratio, the better the cost controls compared with the sales revenues.

To find the gross profit margin ratio for CAP, look at Figure 5-1, CAP's statement of income and retained earnings. We see that CAP's gross profit for the year was $26 million and its sales revenue was $90 million. Dividing $26 million by $90 million yields CAP Corporation's gross profit margin of 0.29 or 29 percent. This ratio shows that CAP's cost of products and services sold was 71 percent of sales revenue, leaving the company with 29 percent of sales revenue to use for other purposes.

Figure 5-2
Canadian Auto Parts Balance Sheet as of December 31, 2004

Assets	
Cash	$3,310,000
Marketable Securities	1,000,000
Accounts Receivable	10,000,000
Inventory	9,000,000
Prepaid Expenses	800,000
Total Current Assets	24,110,000
Property, Plant, and Equipment, Gross	23,000,000
Less Accumulated Amortization	(12,200,000)
Property, Plant, and Equipment, Net	10,800,000
Total Assets	$34,910,000

Liabilities and Equity	
Accounts Payable	$8,000,000
Notes Payable	500,000
Accrued Expenses	700,000
Total Current Liabilities	9,200,000
Long-Term Debt	4,000,000
Total Liabilities	13,200,000
Preferred Shares	500,000
Common Shares (1,750,000 shares)	1,750,000
Retained Earnings	19,460,000
Total Equity	21,710,000
Total Liabilities and Equity	$34,910,000

Operating Profit Margin.

The *operating profit margin ratio* measures the cost of goods sold, as reflected in the gross profit margin ratio, as well as all other operating expenses. This ratio is calculated by dividing earnings before interest and taxes (EBIT or operating income) by sales revenue.

$$\text{Operating Profit Margin} = \frac{\text{Earnings before Interest and Taxes}}{\text{Sales}}$$

$$= \frac{\$10,700,000}{\$90,000,000} = 0.12, \text{ or } 12\%$$

CAP's EBIT, as shown on its statement of income and retained earnings (see Figure 5-1), is $10,700,000. Dividing $10.7 million by its sales revenue of $90 million gives an operating profit margin of 12 percent (10,700,000 ÷ 90,000,000 = 0.12 or 12%). CAP's operating profit margin indicates that 12 percent of its sales revenues remain after subtracting all operating expenses.

Net Profit Margin.

The *net profit margin* measures how much profit out of each sales dollar is left after all expenses are subtracted—that is, after all operating expenses, interest, tax expenses, and preferred share dividends are subtracted. Please note again that preferred share dividends are deducted from the company's net income. Net earnings available to common shareholders represent the company's income, which could be "used" by common shareholders. The preferred share dividends often represent a fixed obligation on the part of the company. The net profit margin is computed by dividing net earnings available to common shareholders by sales revenue. CAP's net earnings available to common shareholders for the year was \$5.150 million. Dividing \$5.150 million by \$90 million in sales yields a 5.72 percent net profit margin. Here's the computation:

$$\text{Net Profit Margin} = \frac{\text{Net Earnings Available to Common Shareholders}}{\text{Sales}}$$

$$= \frac{\$5,150,000}{\$90,000,000} = 0.0572, \text{ or } 5.72\%$$

Net earnings available to common shareholders and the net profit margin ratio are often referred to as "bottom-line" measures. The net profit margin includes adjustments for nonoperating expenses such as interest and taxes and operating expenses. We see that in 2004, Canadian Auto Parts had nearly 6 percent of each sales dollar remaining after all expenses were paid.

Return on Assets.

The return on assets (ROA) ratio indicates how much income each dollar of assets produces on average. It shows whether the business is employing its assets effectively. The ROA ratio is calculated by dividing net earnings available to common shareholders by the total assets of the firm. For CAP, we calculate this ratio by dividing \$5.150 million in net income (see Figure 5-1, CAP statement of income and retained earnings) by \$34.9 million of total assets (see Figure 5-2, CAP balance sheet) for a return on assets (ROA) of 14.75 percent. Here's the calculation:

$$\text{Return on Assets} = \frac{\text{Net Earnings Available to Common Shareholders}}{\text{Total Assets}}$$

$$= \frac{\$5,150,000}{\$34,910,000} = 0.1475, \text{ or } 14.75\%$$

In 2004, each dollar of CAP's assets produced, on average, income of nearly \$0.15. Although this return on assets figure may seem low, it is not unusual for certain types of companies, such as commercial banks, to have low ROA ratios.

Return on Equity.

The return on equity (ROE) ratio measures the average return on the firm's capital contributions from its owners (for a corporation that means the contributions of common shareholders). It indicates how many dollars of income were produced for each dollar invested by the common shareholders.

ROE is calculated by dividing net earnings available to common shareholders by common shareholders' equity. To calculate ROE for Canadian Auto Parts, divide \$5.150 million in net earnings available to common shareholders by \$21.210 million in total common shareholders' equity (see Figure 5-2, CAP balance statement). CAP's ROE is 24.28 percent, shown as follows:

Take Note

Do not confuse the ROE ratio with the return earned by the individual common shareholders on their common share investment. The changes in the market price of the shares and dividends received determine the total return on an individual's common share investment.

$$\text{Return on Equity} = \frac{\text{Net Earnings Available to Common Shareholders}}{\text{Common Shareholders' Equity}}$$

$$= \frac{\$5{,}150{,}000}{\$21{,}210{,}000} = 0.2428, \text{ or } 24.28\%$$

The ROE figure shows that in 2004 Canadian Auto Parts returned, on average, 24.28 percent for every dollar that common shareholders invested in the firm.

Mixing Numbers from Income Statements and Balance Sheets. When financial managers calculate the gross profit margin, operating profit margin, and net profit margin ratios, they use only income statement or statement of income and retained earnings variables. In contrast, analysts use both income statement or statement of income and retained earnings and balance sheet variables to find the return on assets and return on equity ratios. A **mixed ratio** is a ratio that uses both income statement or statement of income and retained earnings and balance sheet variables as inputs.

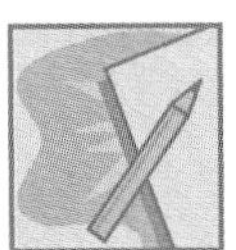

Take Note

Note that Common Shareholders' Equity does not include Preferred Shares. Hence, the amount of Preferred Shares needs to be deducted from the amount of Total Equity.

Because income statement or statement of income and retained earnings variables show values over a period of time and balance sheet variables show values for one moment in time, using mixed ratios poses the question of how to deal with the different time dimensions. For example, should the analyst select balance sheet variable values from the beginning, the end, or the midpoint of the year? If there is a large change in the balance sheet account during the year, the choice could make a big difference. Consider the following situation:

Total Assets January 1, 2002	$1,000,000
Total Assets December 31, 2002	2,000,000
Net Income in 2002	100,000

Return on assets based on January 1 balance sheet:

100,000/1,000,000 = 0.10 or 10%

Return on assets based on December 31 balance sheet:

100,000/2,000,000 = 0.05 or 5%

Which figure is correct? There is no black-and-white answer to this problem. Some analysts add the beginning-of-the-year balance sheet figure to the end-of-the-year figure and divide by two to get an average figure.

Logic and common sense suggest that analysts should pick figures that best match the returns to the assets or to the equity. Say that CAP purchased a large amount of assets early in the year. The middle- or end-of-year balance sheet figures would probably match the returns to the assets more effectively than beginning-of-the-year figures because assets can only affect profit if they have been used. For simplicity, we used end-of-year balance sheet figures to calculate CAP's mixed profitability ratios.

Liquidity Ratios

Liquidity ratios measure the ability of a firm to meet its short-term obligations. These ratios are important because failure to pay such obligations can lead to bankruptcy. Bankers and other lenders use liquidity ratios to see whether to extend short-term credit to a firm. Generally, the higher the liquidity ratio, the more able a firm is to pay its short-term obligations. Shareholders, however, use liquidity ratios to see how the firm has invested in assets. Too much investment in current—as compared with long-term—assets indicates inefficiency.

The two main liquidity ratios are the current ratio and the quick ratio.

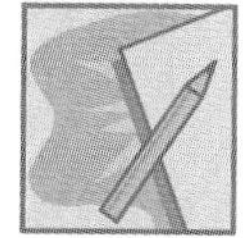

Take Note

Note that the current ratio or working capital ratio describes a relationship between current assets and current liabilities while working capital is the sum of all current assets. Net working capital is equal to current assets less current liabilities.

The Current Ratio.

The *current ratio* compares all the current assets of the firm (cash and other assets that can be easily converted to cash) with all the company's current liabilities (liabilities that must be paid with cash soon). At the end of 2004, CAP's current assets were $24.1 million and its current liabilities were $9.2 million. Dividing CAP's current assets by its current liabilities, we see that:

$$\text{Current Ratio} = \frac{\text{Current Assets}}{\text{Current Liabilities}} = \frac{\$24,110,000}{\$9,200,000} = 2.62$$

CAP's current ratio value, then, is 2.62. The ratio result shows that CAP has $2.62 of current assets for every dollar of current liabilities, indicating that CAP could pay all its short-term debts by liquidating about a third of its current assets.

The Quick Ratio.

The *quick ratio*, often referred to as the acid-test ratio, is similar to the current ratio but is a more rigorous measure of liquidity because it excludes inventory from current assets. To calculate the quick ratio, divide current assets less inventory by current liabilities.

$$\text{Quick Ratio} = \frac{\text{Current Assets Less Inventory}}{\text{Current Liabilities}} = \frac{\$24,110,000 - \$9,000,000}{\$9,200,000} = 1.6$$

This conservative measure of a firm's liquidity may be useful for some businesses. To illustrate, suppose a computer retail store had a large inventory of personal computers with out-of-date Intel 486® microprocessors. The computer store would have a tough time selling its inventory for much money.

At the end of 2004, the balance sheet figures show that CAP's current assets less inventory are worth $15.1 million ($24,110,000 − $9,000,000). Its current liabilities are $9.2 million. Dividing $15.1 million by $9.2 million, we see that its quick ratio is 1.64. A quick ratio of 1.64 means that CAP could pay off 164 percent of its current liabilities by liquidating its current assets, excluding inventory.

If CAP's inventory is hard to liquidate, the quick ratio is more important. If the company being analyzed had very liquid inventory, such as a government securities dealer, the quick ratio would not be a useful analysis tool compared with the current ratio.

Even though the current and quick ratios are commonly used to ascertain the firm's ability to meet its short-term obligations, these ratios are not without problems. See Finance at Work 5-1 for a discussion of imperfections in these ratios and Finance at Work 5-2 for an analysis of one company's financial performance.

FINANCE AT WORK 5-1

Sales Retail Sports Media Technology Public Relations Production Exports

THE CURRENT AND QUICK RATIO—DO THEY STAND UP TO SCRUTINY?

The two most popular ratios that people use to measure a firm's liquidity are the current and quick ratio. The intent of these ratios is to provide measures of the margins of safety that a firm has in meeting obligations that will mature during the current period. Because these ratios are easy to calculate, many people rely on them.

Credit analysts look at current assets as resources invested in assets that are closely linked to day-to-day operations. They expect any item included in current assets to turn into cash within the firm's operating cycle or one year, whichever is longer.

Some Ratios Do Not Measure Up

The point is that the current ratio and quick ratio can be easily window dressed. Here is a simple example to expose the shortcomings of these two ratios. Suppose that a firm has a loan from a bank and the debt covenant requires that the firm maintain a current ratio of 2:1. If the current ratio falls below 2:1, the bank can call the loan. Currently, management is in the process of closing the firm's accounting books for the year. After looking at a trial balance, the finance manager notices that current assets are $1,000,000 and current liabilities are $750,000. Clearly, the current ratio is below the necessary 2:1 level. People in the accounting function are busily trying to figure out what to do, so there is no violation of the loan covenant. However, since there is not much time to resolve the problem, they eliminate many alternatives from consideration. The ledger keeper suggests either reclassifying some current liabilities as long-term liabilities or reclassifying some of the long-term assets as short-term assets. The finance officer rejects both suggestions because the auditors would not accept them under the umbrella of generally accept accounting principles. The finance manager quickly reject suggestion to raise new long-term financing and put the p ceeds into the cash account. There is not enough time to p suade a new lender to supply funds.

After a period of silence, a junior account analyst sa "Why not take $500,000 of cash and use it to pay off t amount of current liabilities? The current assets will then $500,000 and the current liabilities will be $250,000 result in a current ratio of 2:1. This action will not violate any gen ally accepted accounting principles and, thus, will not conc the auditors." The finance manager embraces the idea.

If management wants to become more creative, it c simply write $500,000 worth of cheques to suppliers, but a them to return the cheques uncashed. Alternatively, mana ment could request that some suppliers cancel their invoi and reissue them at a later date. Another ploy is to write cheques, crediting cash and debiting account payable, but not mail them until the invoices are actually due. I think y get the idea—the possibilities are unlimited!

So, what is the moral of the story as it relates to a cre analyst? If a firm can make its financing condition appear b ter with a bank, then it can also make it appear better to a s plier in an effort to secure a trade credit line. Credit analy must realize limitations of the current and quick ratios a should not simply accept these ratios at face value.

Source: George W. Gallinger, "The Current and Quick Ratios: Do They Stand Up to Scrutiny?" May 1997. Reprinted from *Busines. Credit* magazine with permission from the National Association of Credit Management.

Debt Ratios The financial analyst uses debt ratios to assess the relative size of a firm's debt load and the firm's ability to pay off the debt. The three primary debt ratios are the debt to total assets, debt to equity, and times interest earned ratios.

Current and potential lenders of long-term funds, such as banks and bondholders, are interested in debt ratios. When a business's debt ratios increase significantly, bondholder and lender risk increases because more creditors compete for that firm's resources if the company runs into financial trouble. Shareholders are also concerned with the amount of debt a business has because bondholders are paid before shareholders.

The optimal debt ratio depends on many factors, including the type of business and the amount of risk lenders and shareholders will tolerate. Generally, a profitable firm in a stable business can handle more debt and a higher debt ratio than a growth firm in a volatile business.

INANCE AT WORK 5-2

ales Retail Sports Media Technology Public Relations Production Exports

NALYZING THE COMPANY'S HISTORICAL FINANCIAL PERFORMANCE

e have asked Mr. Curtis Johnson, managing director of lead-
g Canadian venture capital firm Crimson Capital, one of the
ading Canadian venture capital firms, to comment on the
y he analyzes companies' historical financial performance.

Crimson Capital has over $1 billion under management d employs eleven investment professionals. The company s a strong record of successful investments and exits (i.e., alization or divestments). It has been able to achieve an erage of 20 percent return for each of the years it has been operation. This is what Mr. Johnson said:

"At Crimson we developed a way to analyze the com-ny's financial performance in a systematic manner. We have ccessfully used this approach for many years and we know at other firms in the industry are using a similar technique.

"We must first look at the company's liquidity. Basic ancial ratios, quick ratio, and current ratio can be used for s purpose. The level of cash available at hand must also be mpared to the company's immediate cash needs. The times erest coverage ratio is also useful in determining whether e company is able to service its interest payments. Beyond s ratio, we must also look at the timing of interest payments d the repayment of the principal. We use this information to dge whether the company will be in business tomorrow, next onth, or next quarter. Obviously, if a company has troubles the area of liquidity, it may have some fundamental prob-ns pertaining to the management of its customers or suppli-s or another critical area of business. We often tend not to rsue these types of companies, especially if problems with uidity are persistent and long-term. On occasion, a liquidity oblem will prove to be temporary and can be easily plained and dealt with.

"Let's now discuss a specific example. We recently ana-ed a company in the construction industry and located in nnipeg. It had a current ratio of 1.4 in 2001, 2.0 in 2002, 4 in 2003 and 2.6 in 2004. Even though the company had current ratio below our expectations in 2001 (being less than it has been able to improve it in subsequent years to a sat-actory level. This positive trend is what we would like to see.

"If the liquidity test is passed, we move toward assessing e company's cash generating ability. This is critical for a firm e Crimson Capital, which wishes to support high-growth sinesses, since companies are often valued on the back of eir cash generating capabilities. The basic rule here is: the ore cash companies generate, the more valuable they are. e therefore focus on the level of cash flow generated from operating activities (i.e., net income plus amortization plus changes in working capital) and the net cash flow at year-end. In the case of the construction company from Winnipeg, there was a nice trend of cash from operating activities increasing from $23 million in 2001 to $37 million in 2004. A similar positive trend was observed with respect to the net cash flow figure in spite of a significant capital expenditure program undertaken by the company between 2001 and 2004.

"Once we understand the company's cash generating ability and we confirm that there is a strong potential to generate cash in the future, we focus on another area, namely profitability. Here, we ask questions about how profitable the company is compared to its competitors and how profitable it could become on a stand-alone basis. We try to determine whether there are additional measures that could be undertaken to improve its profitability. We check profitability at different levels, such as gross, operating, and net, expressed as a percentage of sales. Each of these figures tells a slightly different story. The key figure, however, is the company's profitability at the EBITDA level. We would like to see positive trends across the board here. Generally, declining margins are a sign of increased competition in the market, the product or service being commoditized, or an over-capacity in the industry. Compared to other areas of our analysis, (which are relatively quick), explaining the company's level of profitability is not an easy task. Trying to determine the company's margin levels for the future is even more difficult. Our example company had strong growth in its EBITDA margins over the years. They achieved 6.5 percent in 2001 and 12.6 percent in 2004. This came as a result of cost cutting initiatives, including the streamlining of operations, a reduction in labour force, and efficient raw material planning and purchasing.

"Lastly, we assess the company's growth dynamics, mainly in sales, but also in other areas (i.e., profit). In terms of sales growth, we compare how the company did versus the market and other competitors. We know that when the company is growing above its industry average growth rates, it is taking market share away from other companies in the industry or its market. This is very good news for us. In the case of the construction business, the company's annual average growth rate was equal to 23 percent, while the market had grown by 11 percent in the same time period."

Source: Interview with Mr. Curtis Johnson from Crimson Capital, August 12, 2004.

Debt to Total Assets.

The *debt to total assets* ratio measures the percentage of the firm's assets that is financed with debt. CAP's total liabilities at the end of 2004 were \$13.2 million. Its total assets were \$35 million. The calculation for the debt to total assets ratio follows:

$$\text{Debt to Total Assets} = \frac{\text{Total Liabilities}}{\text{Total Assets}} = \frac{\$13,200,000}{\$34,910,000} = 0.38, \text{ or } 38\%$$

CAP's debt to total assets ratio value is 38 percent, indicating that the other 62 percent of financing came from equity investors (the common and preferred shareholders).

Debt to Equity.

The *debt to equity* ratio measures the relationship between total liabilities and the total value of common shareholders' equity. CAP's total value of common shareholders' equity in 2004 was equal to \$21,210,000. The calculation for the debt to equity follows:

$$\text{Debt to Equity} = \frac{\text{Total Liabilities}}{\text{Common Shareholders' Equity}} = \frac{\$13,200,000}{\$21,210,000} = 0.62, \text{ or } 62\%$$

CAP's debt to equity ratio value is equal to 62 percent, indicating that there were 0.62 dollars of liabilities for every dollar of common shareholders' equity. Generally, the higher the ratio, the higher the risk of the company being subject to excessive leverage.

Times Interest Earned.

The times interest earned ratio is often used to assess a company's ability to service the interest on its debt with operating income from the current period. The *times interest earned* ratio is equal to earnings before interest and taxes (EBIT) divided by interest expense. Canadian Auto Parts has EBIT of \$10.7 million and interest expense of \$0.45 million for 2004. CAP's times interest earned ratio is as follows:

$$\text{Times Interest Earned} = \frac{\text{EBIT}}{\text{Interest Expense}} = \frac{\$10,700,000}{\$450,000} = 23.78$$

CAP's times interest earned ratio value of 23.78 means that the company earned \$23.78 of operating income (EBIT) for each \$1 of interest expense incurred during that year.

A high times interest earned ratio suggests that the company will have ample operating income to cover its interest expense. A low ratio signals that the company may have insufficient operating income to pay interest as it becomes due. If so, the business might need to liquidate assets or raise new debt or equity funds to pay the interest due. Recall, however, that operating income is not the same as cash flow. Operating income figures do not show the amount of *cash* available to pay interest. Because interest payments are made with cash, the times interest earned ratio is only a rough measure of a firm's ability to pay interest with current funds.

Asset Activity Ratios Financial analysts use asset activity ratios to measure how efficiently a firm uses its assets. They analyze specific assets and classes of assets. The three asset activity ratios we will examine here are the average collection period (for accounts receivable), the inventory turnover, and the total asset turnover ratios.

Average Collection Period.

The *average collection period* ratio measures how many days, on average, the company's credit customers take to pay their accounts. Managers, especially credit managers, use this ratio to decide to whom the firm should extend credit. Slow payers are not welcome customers.

To calculate the average collection period, divide accounts receivable by the company's average credit sales per day. (This, in turn, is the company's annual credit sales divided by the number of days in a year, 365.)

$$\text{Average Collection Period} = \frac{\text{Accounts Receivable}}{\text{Average Daily Credit Sales}} = \frac{\$10,000,000}{\$90,000,000 \div 365} = 41 \text{ days}$$

Canadian Auto Parts had $10 million in accounts receivable and average daily credit sales of $246,575.34 (i.e., $90 million total credit sales divided by 365 days in one year). Dividing $10 million by $246,575.34 gives a value of 40.56. The ratio shows that in 2004, CAP's credit customers took an average of 40.56 days to pay their account balances.

Notice that, in calculating the ratio, we used CAP's total sales figure for 2004 in the denominator, assuming that all of CAP's sales for the year were made on credit. We made no attempt to break down CAP's sales into cash sales and credit sales. Financial analysts usually calculate this ratio using the total sales figure when they do not have the credit-sales-only figure.

Inventory Turnover.

The *inventory turnover* ratio tells us how efficiently the firm converts inventory to sales. If the company has inventory that sells well, the ratio value will be high. If the inventory does not sell well due to lack of demand or if there is excess inventory, the ratio value will be low.

The inventory turnover formula follows:

$$\text{Inventory Turnover} = \frac{\text{Sales}}{\text{Inventory}} = \frac{\$90,000,000}{\$9,000,000} = 10 \text{ times}$$

Canadian Auto Parts had sales of $90 million and inventory of $9 million in 2004. Dividing $90 million by $9 million, we see that the inventory turnover value is 10. This number means that in 2004 CAP "turned" its inventory into sales 10 times during the year.[4]

Total Asset Turnover.

The *total asset turnover* ratio measures how efficiently a firm utilizes its assets. Shareholders, bondholders, and managers know that the more efficiently the firm operates the better the returns.

[4]Many financial analysts define the inventory turnover ratio using *cost of goods sold* instead of *sales* in the numerator. They use cost of goods sold because sales are defined in terms of *sales price* and inventory is defined in terms of *cost*. We will use *sales* in the numerator of the inventory turnover ratio to be consistent with the other turnover ratios.

If a company has many assets that do not help generate sales (such as fancy offices and corporate jets for senior management), then the total asset turnover ratio will be relatively low. A company with a high asset utilization ratio suggests that its assets help promote sales revenue.

To calculate the asset turnover ratio for CAP, divide sales by total assets as follows:

$$\text{Total Asset Turnover} = \frac{\text{Sales}}{\text{Total Assets}} = \frac{\$90,000,000}{\$34,910,000} = 2.58$$

The 2004 total asset turnover ratio for Canadian Auto Parts is its sales of \$90 million divided by its total assets of \$35 million. The result is 2.58, indicating that CAP's sales were 2.58 higher than its assets. Put another way, 2.58 dollars of sales were generated by each dollar of assets.

Market Value Ratios The ratios examined so far rely on financial statement or statement of income and retained earnings figures. However, market value ratios mainly rely on financial marketplace data such as the market price of a company's common share. Market value ratios measure the market's perception of the future earning power of a company as reflected in the share price. The two market value ratios we discuss are the price to earnings ratio and the market to book value ratio.

Price to Earnings Ratio.

The price to earnings (P/E) ratio is defined as:

$$\text{P/E Ratio} = \frac{\text{Market Price per Share}}{\text{Earnings per Share}}$$

To calculate earnings per share (EPS), we divide earnings available to common shareholders by the number of common shares outstanding.

Investors and managers use the P/E ratio to gauge the future prospects of a company. The ratio measures how much investors are willing to pay for a claim to one dollar of the earnings per share of the firm. The more investors are willing to pay over the value of EPS for the share, the more confidence they are displaying about the firm's future growth—that is, the higher the P/E ratio, the higher are investors' growth expectations. Consider the following marketplace data for CAP:

Current Market Price of CAP's Shares	\$25.00
2004 EPS	\$2.94

$$\text{P/E Ratio} = \frac{\text{Market Price per Share}}{\text{Earnings per Share}} = \frac{\$25}{\$2.94} = 8.50$$

We see that the \$25 per share market price of CAP's common shares is 8.5 times the level of its 2004 earnings per share (\$2.94 EPS). The 8.5 result indicates that stock exchange traders predict that CAP has average future earnings potential. It would take just under 9 years, at CAP's 2004 earnings rate, for the company to earn net profits of \$25 per share, the amount an investor would pay today to buy this share.

Market to Book Value.

The *market to book value* (M/B) ratio is the market price per share of a company's common shares divided by the accounting book value per share (BPS) ratio. The book value per share ratio is the amount of common share equity on the firm's balance sheet divided by the number of common shares outstanding.

The book value per share is a proxy for the amount remaining per share after selling the firm's assets for their balance sheet values and paying the debt owed to all creditors and preferred shareholders. We calculate CAP's BPS ratio based on the following information:

Total Common Share Equity at Year-End 2004	$21,210,000
Number of Common Shares Outstanding	1,750,000

$$\text{BPS} = \frac{\text{Common Share Equity}}{\text{Number of Common Shares Outstanding}} = \frac{\$21{,}210{,}000}{1{,}750{,}000} = \$12.12$$

Now that we know the book value per share of CAP's shares is $12.12, we can find the market to book value ratio as follows:

$$\text{Market to Book Value Ratio} = \frac{\text{Market Price per Share}}{\text{Book Value per Share}} = \frac{\$25}{\$12.12} = 2.06$$

We see that CAP's M/B ratio is 2.06. This value indicates that the market price of a CAP's common share ($25) is 2.06 times its book value per share ($12.12).

The phenomenon of having a book value per share being below the market price per share is a common occurrence in businesses. This may be due to a number of reasons. Firstly, assets, especially those long-term like property, plant, and equipment, are recorded in accounting books in terms of their historical costs. Moreover, these long-term assets are amortized on an annual basis, which further reduces their net value. In reality, the amortized assets may be worth much more than is accounted for in the company's books. Secondly, the net book value per share may not reflect some intangible assets that the company may have. For example, a company operating in the high technology industry has developed cutting edge software, which translates into handsome profits now and is likely to continue in the future. This value is not reflected in the company's balance sheet and its net book value per share. The market value, on the other hand, reflects the market perception of the company's worth. It reflects the company's ability to generate profits and cash in the future and may have less to do with actual assets and liabilities of the balance sheet even though these items are very important for financial analysis purposes.

When the market price per share is greater than the book value per share, analysts often conclude that the market believes the company's future earnings are worth more than the firm's liquidation value. The value of the firm's future earnings minus the liquidation value is the **going concern value** of the firm. The higher the M/B ratio, when it is greater than 1, the greater the going concern value of the company seems to be. In our case, Canadian Auto Parts seems to have a positive going concern value.

Companies that have a market to book value of less than 1 are sometimes considered to be "worth more dead than alive." Such an M/B ratio suggests that if the company liquidated and paid off all creditors and preferred shareholders, it would have more left over for the common shareholders than what the common share could be sold for in the marketplace.

The M/B ratio is useful, but it is only a rough approximation of how liquidation and going concern values compare. This is because the M/B ratio uses an accounting-based book value. The actual liquidation value of a firm is likely to be different than the book value. For instance, the assets of the firm may be worth more or less than the value at which they are currently carried on the company's balance sheet. In addition, the current market price of the company's bonds and preferred shares may also differ from the accounting value of these claims.

Economic Value Added and Market Value Added.

Two new financial indicators that have become popular are *economic value added* (EVA) and *market value added* (MVA). These indicators were developed by Stern Stewart & Company, a consulting firm in New York City. EVA is a measure of the amount of profit remaining after accounting for the return expected by the firm's investors, whereas MVA compares the firm's current value with the amount the current owners paid for it. According to Stern Stewart, the use of the EVA and MVA indicators can help add value to a company because they help managers focus on rewards to shareholders instead of traditional accounting measures.[5] In the following paragraphs, we discuss EVA and MVA individually.

Economic Value Added (EVA).

As we mentioned previously, **EVA** is a measure of the amount of profit remaining after accounting for the return expected by the firm's investors. As such, EVA is said to be an "estimate of true economic profit or the amount by which earnings exceed or fall short of the required minimum rate of return investors could get investing in other securities of comparable risk."[6] The formula to calculate EVA is as follows:

$$\text{EVA} = \text{EBIT}(1 - \text{TR}) - (\text{IC} \times \text{Ka})$$

where EBIT = earnings before interest and taxes (i.e., operating income)

TR = the effective or average income tax rate

IC = invested capital (explained later)

Ka = investors' required rate of return on their investment (explained later)

Invested capital (IC) is the total amount of capital invested in the company. It is the sum of the *market values* of the firm's equity, preferred shares, and debt capital. Ka is the weighted average of the rates of return expected by the suppliers of the firm's capital, sometimes called the weighted average cost of capital or WACC.

---

[5]http://www.sternstewart.com.

[6]Ibid.

To illustrate how EVA is calculated, assume that one of CAP's common shares is currently selling for $25 a share and the weighted average return expected by investors (Ka) is 12 percent. Also assume that the book values of debt and preferred shares on CAP's balance sheet are the same as the market values.[7] Also recall from Figures 5-1 and 5-2 that CAP's EBIT for 2004 is $10,700,000, its effective income tax rate is 40 percent, and there are 1,750,000 common shares outstanding.

The last term we need before calculating CAP's EVA is invested capital (IC). Remember that it is the sum of the *market values* of the firm's equity, preferred shares, and debt capital. CAP's IC is found as follows:

$$\text{Market Value of Common Equity} = 1{,}750{,}000 \text{ shares} \times \$25$$

$$= \$43{,}750{,}000$$

$$\text{Market Value of Preferred Shares} = \text{Book Value}$$

$$= \$500{,}000$$

$$\text{Market Value of Debt Capital} = \text{Book Value}$$

$$= \text{Notes Payable} + \text{Long-Term Debt}^{8}$$

$$= \$500{,}000 + \$4{,}000{,}000$$

$$= \$4{,}500{,}000$$

$$\text{Total Invested Capital (IC)} = \$43{,}750{,}000 + 500{,}000 + 4{,}500{,}000 = \$48{,}750{,}000$$

Now we have all the amounts necessary to solve the EVA equation for Canadian Auto Parts:

$$\text{EVA} = \text{EBIT}(1 - \text{TR}) - (\text{IC} \times \text{Ka})$$

For CAP in 2004:

$$\text{EVA} = \$10{,}700{,}000(1 - 0.40) - (\$48{,}750{,}000 \times 0.12)$$

$$= \$6{,}420{,}000 - \$5{,}850{,}000$$

$$= \$570{,}000$$

CAP's EVA for 2004 is positive, indicating that the company earned a sufficient amount during the year to provide the return expected by all those who contributed capital to the firm. CAP had $10,700,000 of operating income and $6,150,000 of net income in 2004, which was enough to provide the 12 percent return expected by CAP's creditors and shareholders.

---

[7]This assumption is frequently made in financial analysis to ease the difficulties of locating current market prices for debt and preferred securities. Because prices of debt and preferred securities do not tend to fluctuate widely, the assumption does not generally introduce an excessive amount of error into the EVA calculation.

[8]Take note that total debt capital is *not* the same as total liabilities. Liabilities that are spontaneously generated, such as accounts payable and accrued expenses, are not generally included in the definition of debt capital. True debt capital is created when a specified amount of money is lent to the firm at a specified interest rate.

Market Value Added (MVA).

Market value added (MVA) is the market value of the firm, debt plus equity, minus the total amount of capital invested in the firm. MVA is similar to the market to book ratio (M/B). MVA focuses on total market value and total invested capital, whereas M/B focuses on the per share price and invested equity capital. The two measures are highly correlated.

For CAP in 2004:

$$\begin{aligned} \text{MVA} &= (\$43{,}750{,}000 + \$5{,}000{,}000) - (\$21{,}710{,}000 + \$4{,}500{,}000) \\ &= \$48{,}750{,}000 - \$26{,}210{,}000 \\ &= \$22{,}540{,}000 \end{aligned}$$

Companies that consistently have high EVAs would normally have a positive MVA. If a company consistently has negative EVAs, it should have a negative MVA too.

In this section, we examined the key profitability, liquidity, debt, asset activity, and market value ratios. The value of each ratio tells part of the story about the financial health of the firm. Next we explore relationships among ratios.

Relationships among Ratios: The Du Pont System As we discussed earlier, ratios may be used to compare one ratio to another related ratio. Financial analysts compare related ratios to see what specific activities add to or detract from a firm's performance.

The Du Pont system of ratio analysis is named for the company whose managers developed the general system. It first examines the relationships between earnings available to common shareholders relative to sales and sales relative to total assets. The product of the net profit margin and the total asset turnover is the return on assets (or ROA). This equation, known as the Du Pont equation, follows:

Du Pont Equation

$$\text{Return on Assets} = \text{Net Profit Margin} \times \text{Total Asset Turnover}$$

$$\frac{\text{Earnings Available to Common Shareholders}}{\text{Total Assets}} = \frac{\text{Earnings Available to Common Shareholders}}{\text{Sales}} \times \frac{\text{Sales}}{\text{Total Assets}} \tag{5-1}$$

Sales, on the right side of the equation, appear in the denominator of the net profit margin and in the numerator of the total asset turnover. These two equal sales figures would cancel each other out if the equation were simplified, leaving earnings available to common shareholders over total assets on the right. This, of course, equals earnings available to common shareholders over total assets, which is on the left side of the equal sign, indicating that the equation is valid.

This version of the Du Pont equation helps us analyze factors that contribute to a firm's return on assets. For example, we already know from our basic ratio analysis that CAP's return on assets for 2004 was 14.75 percent. Now suppose you wanted to know how much of that 14.75 percent was the result of CAP's net profit margin for 2004 and how much was the result of the activity of CAP's assets in 2004. Equation 5-1, the Du Pont equation, provides the following answer:

$$\text{Return on Assets} = \text{Net Profit Margin} \times \text{Total Asset Turnover}$$

$$\text{ROA} = \frac{\text{Earnings Available to Common Shareholders}}{\text{Sales}} \times \frac{\text{Sales}}{\text{Total Assets}}$$

For CAP:

$$0.1475\text{, or } 14.75\% = \frac{\$5{,}150{,}000}{\$90{,}000{,}000} \times \frac{\$90{,}000{,}000}{\$34{,}910{,}000}$$

$$0.1475 = 0.0572 \times 2.58$$

or

$$14.75\% = 5.72\% \times 2.58$$

We see that Canadian Auto Parts has a good net profit margin equal to 5.72 percent and strong total asset turnover equal to 2.58 times its sales. The 2.58 total asset turnover multiplier has the effect of magnifying the 5.72 percent net profit margin such that ROA shows a healthy figure of 14.75 percent.

We might see a relatively lower net profit margin and a high total asset turnover in a distribution business such as CAP is involved in. Similarly, a grocery store would sell low net profit margin products at a high total asset turnover (volume) because many items are sold every day, but little profit is made on each dollar of sales. Conversely, we may see a low total asset turnover and high net profit margin in a jewellery store where few items are sold each day, but a high profit is made on each item.

Another version of the Du Pont equation, called the Modified Du Pont equation, measures how net profit margin, asset activity, and debt financing affect the return on equity (ROE). As shown in Equation 5-2, in the modified Du Pont equation, ROE is the product of net profit margin, total asset turnover, and the **equity multiplier** (the ratio of total assets to common equity).

Modified Du Pont Equation

$$\text{ROE} = \text{Net Profit Margin} \times \text{Total Asset Turnover} \times \text{Equity Multiplier}^{9}$$

$$\frac{\text{Earnings Available to Common Shareholders}}{\text{Common Equity}} = \frac{\text{Earnings Available to Common Shareholders}}{\text{Sales}} \times \frac{\text{Sales}}{\text{Total Assets}} \times \frac{\text{Total Assets}}{\text{Common Equity}} \quad (5\text{-}2)$$

[9]Notice that sales and total assets appear in both a numerator and a denominator on the right side of the equation and would cancel out if the equation were simplified, leaving earnings available to common shareholders over equity on both the right and the left of the equal sign.

$$\frac{\text{Earnings Available to Common Shareholders}}{\text{Common Equity}} = \frac{\text{Earnings Available to Common Shareholders}}{\cancel{\text{Sales}}} \times \frac{\cancel{\text{Sales}}}{\cancel{\text{Total Assets}}} \times \frac{\cancel{\text{Total Assets}}}{\text{Common Equity}}$$

$$\frac{\text{Earnings Available to Common Shareholders}}{\text{Common Equity}} = \frac{\text{Earnings Available to Common Shareholders}}{\text{Common Equity}}$$

For Canadian Auto Parts:

$$0.2428 = 24.28\% = \frac{\$5{,}150{,}000}{\$90{,}000{,}000} \times \frac{\$90{,}000{,}000}{\$34{,}910{,}000} \times \frac{\$34{,}910{,}000}{\$21{,}210{,}000}$$

$$0.2428 = 0.0572 \times 2.58 \times 1.65$$

$$24.28\% = 5.72\% \times 2.58 \times 1.65$$

Examining the preceding equation, we see that CAP's net profit margin of 5.72 percent is lower than its 24.28 percent ROE. However, CAP's high productivity of assets ($2.58 in sales for every dollar of assets employed) increases the effect of the profit margin—5.72% × 2.58 = 14.75%. If no other factors were present, CAP's ROE would be 14.75 percent.

Now the equity multiplier comes into play. The equity multiplier indicates the amount of financial leverage a firm has. A firm that uses only equity to finance its assets should have an equity multiplier that equals 1.0. To arrive at this conclusion, recall the basic accounting formula—total assets = liabilities + equity. If a firm had no debt on its balance sheet, its liabilities would equal zero, so equity would equal total assets. If equity equalled total assets, then the equity multiplier would be 1. Multiplying 1 times any other number has no effect so, in such a situation, ROE would depend solely on net profit margin and total asset turnover.

If a firm does have debt on its balance sheet (as CAP does), it will have greater assets than equity and the equity multiplier will be greater than 1. This produces a multiplier effect that drives ROE higher (assuming net income is positive) than can otherwise be accounted for by net profit margin and asset turnover.

CAP's equity multiplier of 1.65 indicates that CAP has assets that are 1.65 times its equity. This has the effect (called the **leverage effect**) of boosting CAP's return on equity from 14.75 percent to 24.28 percent. The leverage effect, caused by debt of $4.5 million shown on CAP's balance sheet, significantly alters CAP's ROE.[10]

In this section, we reviewed basic ratios and analyzed relationships of one ratio to another to assess the firm's financial condition. Next we will investigate how ratio analysis can be used to compare trends in a firm's performance and to compare the firm's performance to other firms in the same industry.

Trend Analysis and Industry Comparisons

Ratios are used to compare a firm's past and present performance and its industry performance. In this section, we will examine trend analysis and industry comparison. Comparing a ratio for one year with the same ratio for other years is known as **trend analysis**. Comparing a ratio for one company with the same ratio for other companies in the same industry is **industry comparison**.

Trend Analysis

Trend analysis helps financial managers and analysts see whether a company's current financial situation is improving or deteriorating. To prepare a trend analysis, compute the ratio values for several time periods (usually years) and compare them. Table 5-1 shows a five-year trend for CAP's ROA.

[10]We will discuss leverage in more detail in Chapter 13.

ETHICAL CONNECTIONS 5-1

Financial Restatement "The Right Thing To Do"

Vhen you say restatement, a lot of people go 'whoa,'" rank Dunn, Nortel president and chief executive officer, aid in an interview yesterday. "It was the right thing to do. It as something we have to put behind us. The real focus is at Nortel will make money this year."

The restatement flows from a financial review that was rst announced in July and is still being conducted. Nortel stimated the major change will be a reduction of liabilities about $900-million (U.S.), representing 7 percent of those sted on its balance sheet as of June 30.

This should reduce stated losses for the years 2000, 001, 2002, Nortel said. For those three years, the company ad previously reported total sales of $56.03-billion and ombined losses of $33.3-billion, which are set to come own to about $32.5-billion.

The changes in part overshadowed the company's sults for the July–September period, which were published skeleton form and called "preliminary." More complete formation is expected in mid-November. The full restatement should be completed by the end of the year.

"The outlook isn't strong enough to help people feel omfortable," said Tom Lauria, an independent analyst at tera Management LLC in New Jersey.

Mr. Dunn spoke with a positive tone on the company's onference call. He asked analysts not to be distracted by e restatement. He said Nortel is doing well selling dvanced network equipment, such as those for new mobile etworks and fixed-line equipment that runs data and voice n a single network.

"I'm very pleased with our prospects," he said, adding that there's been "a lot of great progress" as he cited the predicted 2003 profit.

"That will be the first time in six years," he said. Nortel's last annual profit, in 1997, was $829-million.

The company didn't issue a balance sheet. It said cash was about $3.6-billion as of Sept. 30, down from $4.31-billion at June 30. Nortel said it repaid debt, contributed to its pension fund and covered some restructuring.

There are about 35,500 workers, slightly fewer than the about 36,000 three months ago.

Gross margin—sales minus cost of goods sold—was 52.1 percent, well higher than 43.7 percent last quarter. Nortel said the mid-40-percent range is more realistic longer term, though that is higher than a previous estimate of the low-40-percent range. Mr. Dunn said the change is occurring as Nortel sells less big boxes and more software.

Questions to Consider

1. *As a potential investor in Nortel, how would you distinguish between an honest error and poor accounting practices?*
2. *When should company presidents announce errors in accounting practices, early or late, never, or when companies have "good news" to tell?*

Source: David Ebner, "Nortel Posts Profits, Restates," 24 October 2003. Reprinted with permission from *The Globe and Mail.*

As Table 5-1 shows, CAP's ROA has risen steadily over this five-year period with the largest growth occurring between 2002 and 2003. Overall, the trend analysis indicates that CAP's 2004 ROA of 14.75 percent is strong compared to earlier years.

Table 5-1 **Canadian Auto Parts Five-Year Return on Assets (ROA) Trend Analysis**

	2000	2001	2002	2003	2004
ROA	−7.22%	0.29%	2.84%	9.63%	14.75%

Usually, analysts plot ratio value trends on a graph to provide a picture of the results. Figure 5-3 is a graph of CAP's 2000–2004 ROA ratios. The graph also shows the industry averages for these years (in blue). The five-year

Figure 5-3
Canadian Auto Parts Five-Year Trend in ROA
This figure shows the trend in the return on assets ratio from 2000 to 2004 for Canadian Auto Parts.

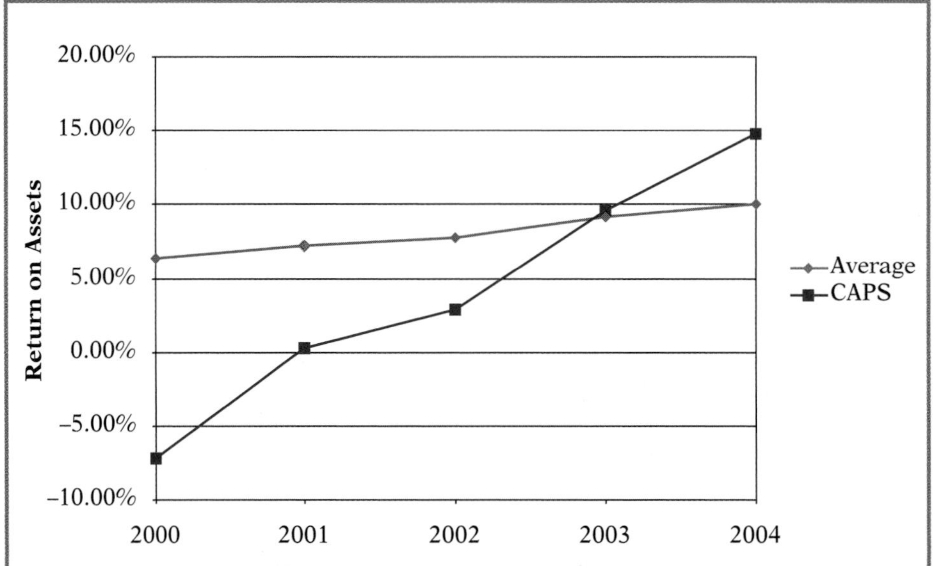

upward trend in ROA, depicted in Figure 5-3, indicates that Canadian Auto Parts increased the amount of profit it generated from its assets.

Trend analysis is an invaluable part of ratio analysis. It helps management spot a deteriorating condition and take corrective action, or identify the company's strengths. By assessing the firm's strengths and weaknesses and the pace of change in a strength or weakness, management can plan effectively for the future.

Financial ratios generally become meaningful in two circumstances. In the first circumstance, the financial ratios are compared externally to financial ratios of similar companies or industry averages on an absolute basis. In the second circumstance, financial ratios are tracked over time (ratios calculated for one year only have limited usefulness) for the same company and compared to previous years (such trend lines may also be compared to trend lines of comparable companies or industry averages). This latter technique refers to developing a trend line. A trend line or just a trend is generally developed by establishing a base year, usually represented as the figure 100, and then dividing any numbers in subsequent years by the value of the base year.

Vertical and Horizontal Analysis

Financial analysts often perform a comparative analysis of financial statements over time. This is often referred to as **horizontal analysis**. This normally entails an analysis of the items in the financial statements from year-to-year or over a period of time. The increases or decreases in certain items of the financial statements are expressed in dollar and percentage terms. While we are not planning to provide a complete version of this analysis, it may be useful to provide a short example. We will use the financial performance of WestJet between 2002 and 2003 to demonstrate our points. Let's recall these numbers. Sales increased from $680 million in 2002 to $794.4 million, an increase of $114.4 million from year-to-year, which also represents a 16.8

percent increase. Similarly, the operating profit figure increased from $86.4 million in 2002 to $119.5 million, a $33.1 million increase in dollar terms and a 38.3 increase in percentage terms over the same time period.

(in $ millions)	*2002*	*2003*	*Change in $*	*Change in %*
Sales	680.0	794.4	114.4	16.8
Operating Profit	86.4	119.5	33.1	38.3

Another way to gain insight into a financial statement is to conduct a common-size analysis of financial statements, also referred to as **vertical analysis.** In this case, we would express a particular financial statement in percentage terms. For example, when we use this approach to a balance sheet, we would express total assets as 100 percent but express other items comprising the total asset in a percentage form. Let's continue with our WestJet example. If in 2003, total assets for WestJet were equal to $1,476.9 million and accounts receivable were equal to $19.9 million, we would express accounts receivable as a percentage of total assets, which would equal 1.3 percent.

The vertical analysis is beneficial in understanding the composition of financial statements over time and inter-company comparisons.

Industry Comparisons

Another way to judge whether a firm's ratio is too high or too low is to compare it with the ratios of other firms in the industry (this is sometimes called **cross-sectional analysis**, or *benchmarking*). This type of comparison pinpoints deviations from the norm that may indicate problems.

Table 5-2 shows a comparison between CAP's ROA ratio and the average ROA in CAP's industry for 2004. It shows that, compared with other firms in CAP's industry, CAP achieved an above average ROA in 2004. Only Company B managed to do better than CAP.

Benchmarking allows analysts to put the value of a firm's ratio in the context of its industry. For example, CAP's ROA of 14.75 percent is higher than average for its industry, thus CAP would be looked upon favourably. In another industry, however, the average ROA might be 20 percent, causing CAP's 14.75 percent to appear much lower. Whether a ratio value is good or bad depends on the characteristics of the industry. By putting the ratio in context, analysts compare apples to apples and not apples to oranges.

Note—do not fall into the trap of thinking that a company does not have problems just because its ratios are equal to the industry averages. Maybe the whole industry is in a slump! When a ratio equals the industry average, it simply means that the company is average in the area the ratio measures.

Company	**ROA**
Canadian Auto Parts	14.75%
Company A	7.1%
Company B	18.2%
Company C	4.6%
Industry Average: (CAP + A + B + C) ÷ 4	11.2%

Table 5-2 Canadian Auto Parts Cross-Sectional Analysis of ROA 2004

Summary Analysis—Trend and Industry Comparisons Together

A complete ratio analysis of a company combines both trend analysis and industry comparisons. Table 5-3 shows all the ratios presented in this chapter for Canadian Auto Parts for 2000 through 2004, along with the industry averages for those ratios.

First, let's review CAP's profitability ratios compared with the industry average for 2000 to 2004. In 2000, Canadian Auto Parts had negative net income. This is typical for young and rapidly growing companies that need to invest financial resources into operations and expansion. This gave a negative value to the net profit margin, return on assets, and return on equity for 2000 (because the net income is the numerator for each ratio). There was steady improvement, however, in the profit ratios from 2002 to 2004. In fact, Canadian Auto Parts achieved a better financial performance compared to the industry averages.

Canadian Auto Parts had lower gross profit, operating profit, and net profit margins than the industry norm for the first three years of our analysis (2000–2002). As CAP's sales grew, it has been able to cover its operating costs more effectively. Its increasing sales also contributed to a slight improvement in gross margin as a result of more purchasing power vis-à-vis its suppliers. For 2000, 2001, and 2002, CAP also had a lower return on assets ratio than the industry average. As the summary analysis shows, the rapidly growing ROA are the result of higher asset turnover ratios and increasing net profit margins.

The return-on-equity figures paint a telling story over this five-year period. From 2000 to 2002, Canadian Auto Parts had a much lower return on equity than the average firm in its industry. In 2000, these figures even had negative values, but the industry norm was positive. Since 2003, however, Canadian Auto Parts has had a much higher return on equity than the average firm in its industry, much to the satisfaction of its shareholders.

CAP has continued to have a high debt load. Look at the debt to assets and debt to equity ratio values. The debt to total assets ratio is consistently above 50 percent whereas the industry norm for this ratio oscillates around 30 percent. A high debt load magnifies the changes in return on equity ratio values.

The times interest earned ratio shows that Canadian Auto Parts has been able to cover its interest expense with its operating income. This value appeared well above industry averages. CAP has significantly improved its ability to pay its interest payment in the year 2003. The situation could become problematic for CAP if interest rates dramatically increase.

Next, we examine the liquidity ratios: the current and quick ratios. The current ratio has been above 2 each year except 2001. It has been growing steadily since then. It reached a level of 2.62 by 2004. Having two times or more the amount of current assets as current liabilities is a good target for most companies. Because the industry norm for the current ratio was around the value Canadian Auto Parts had in each of these years, CAP had a comparatively good liquidity position.

The quick ratio stayed near the industry average throughout the five-year period. This means that when inventory is subtracted from total current assets, CAP's liquidity looked steady.

Now, let's look at the asset activity ratios: average collection period, inventory turnover, and asset turnover. The average collection period was generally

Table 5-3 Five-Year Ratio Analysis for Canadian Auto Parts

		2000	2001	2002	2003	2004
Profitability Ratios						
Gross Profit Margin	CAP	21.67%	24.00%	25.81%	28.00%	28.89%
	Industry	27.90%	26.50%	26.40%	25.60%	26.70%
Operating Profit Margin	CAP	5.00%	6.40%	8.39%	10.53%	11.89%
	Industry	11.80%	12.40%	11.50%	10.20%	11.10%
Net Profit Margin	CAP	24.33%	0.12%	1.13%	3.78%	5.72%
	Industry	5.20%	4.90%	4.80%	5.10%	5.50%
Return on Assets	CAP	27.22%	0.29%	2.84%	9.63%	14.75%
	Industry	6.40%	7.20%	7.80%	9.20%	10.10%
Return on Equity	CAP	215.29%	0.71%	6.58%	19.09%	24.28%
	Industry	7.20%	6.70%	7.20%	6.20%	7.20%
Liquidity Ratios						
Current Ratio	CAP	1.75	2.33	2.06	2.34	2.62
	Industry	2.20	2.40	2.50	2.40	2.50
Quick Ratio	CAP	0.87	1.50	1.21	1.38	1.64
	Industry	1.50	1.60	1.70	1.60	1.50
Debt Ratios						
Debt/Equity Ratio	CAP	120.00%	129.41%	122.21%	93.28%	61.94%
	Industry	43.20%	43.20%	44.50%	42.10%	42.20%
Debt/Total Assets	CAP	60.10%	52.38%	52.77%	47.03%	37.76%
	Industry	30.00%	32.20%	34.20%	33.70%	33.80%
Times Interest Earned	CAP	4.0	5.3	7.4	11.7	23.8
	Industry	4.3	4.6	5.2	4.9	4.6
Asset Activity Ratios						
Average Collection Period (Days)	CAP	30	37	32	39	41
	Industry	45	44	45	45	45
Inventory Turnover (Days)	CAP	10.5	10.0	10.3	10.0	10.0
	Industry	5.4	4.8	5.2	5.6	6.1
Total Asset Turnover	CAP	2.6	2.4	2.5	2.5	2.6
	Industry	1.4	1.5	1.7	1.8	1.6
Market Value Ratios						
P/E Ratio	CAP	—	83.3	21.4	9.0	8.5
	Industry	7.5	7.8	8.8	8.2	8.1
Market to Book Value	CAP	0.4	0.6	1.4	1.7	2.1
	Industry	2.6	3.1	2.8	3.2	3.4

lower for CAP than for the average firm in the industry. It appears that CAP did a better than average job of collecting its accounts receivable.

The inventory turnover ratio was very stable over this five-year period. This suggests that CAP did a good job matching its inventory to its demand for products. The numbers suggest that CAP's managers have done a very good job in projecting a future market demand and adjusting its inventory control policies. More about this topic in Chapter 19.

The total asset turnover ratio was consistently higher than the industry norm. This helped the return on assets ratio during the years when net income was positive, as described earlier.

Finally, we turn to the market value ratios. CAP had no meaningful P/E ratio for 2000 because net income was negative and, therefore, EPS were negative. The P/E ratio of 21.4 in 2002 shows that investors had high expectations about CAP's future growth, but these expectations moderated in the next two years as the company matured. The market to book value ratio shows an upward trend over the five-year period indicating that investors increasingly valued CAP's future earnings potential above the company's asset liquidation value.

We have just finished a complete ratio analysis for Canadian Auto Parts including examination of the company's profitability, liquidity, debt management, asset activity, and market value ratios. To conclude this analysis, we combined trend and industry analysis so that we could see how Canadian Auto Parts performed over time and how it performed relative to its industry. Managers inside the company can use the results of the analysis to support proposed changes in operations or organizations. Creditors and investors outside the company can use the results to support decisions about lending money to the company or buying its shares.

Locating Information about Financial Ratios

Ratio analysis involves a fair amount of research. Before analysts can calculate all the ratios, they must locate the underlying, raw financial data. Analysts can gather information about publicly traded corporations at most libraries, on CD-ROM databases, and on the Internet.

A number of organizations publish financial data about companies and industries. Many publications contain ratios that are already calculated. Table 5-4 contains a list of publications that financial analysts find useful when they are researching companies and industries. Many of them are available at local libraries.

SUMMARY

5-1 *Explain two ways in which financial ratio analysis helps financial managers assess the health of a company.*

Just as doctors assess a patient's health, financial managers assess the financial health of a firm. One of the most powerful assessment tools is financial ratio analysis. Financial ratios are comparative measures that allow managers to interpret raw accounting data and identify strengths and weaknesses of the firm.

5-2 *Define what profitability, liquidity, debt, asset activity, and market value ratios measure.*

Profitability, liquidity, debt, asset activity, and market value ratios show different aspects of a firm's financial performance. Profitability, liquidity, debt, and asset activity ratios use information from a firm's income statement or balance sheet to compute the ratios. Market value ratios use market and financial statement information.

Table 5-4 Sources of Financial Information

rmation	Medium	Source
siness news; articles; market a; stock, investment fund ce quotes	Newspapers	*The Globe and Mail* *Financial Post* *Wall Street Journal*
siness news, articles	Magazines	*Business Week* *Fortune* *Forbes* *Entrepreneur* *Small Business Canada Magazine* *Maclean's* *The Economist*
ta on economic industries; ny financial statistics terest rates, inflation)	Publications	Statistics Canada Industry Canada Bank of Canada
mmary data about industries, npanies; advice on industries, cks; analysis and forecasts	Computer databases and publications	http://www.globeinvestor.com Ebscohost Business Source Premier Winspear Canadian Industry Database http://www.corporateinformation.com
ta on companies and ustries	Computer databases	Ebscohost Business Source Premier Winspear Canadian Industry Database http://www.corporateinformation.com
mpany performance: rporate financial data	Various	SEDAR database EDGAR database
ormation about bonds	Computer databases	http://www.bank-banque-canada.ca
ormation about estment funds	Computer databases	http://www.globefund.com
riety of business and ancial news and ormation (some require d subscription)	Computer databases	http://www.bloomberg.com http://www.strategis.ic.gc.ca http://www.bank-banque-canada.ca http://www.chamber.ca http://www.fin.gc.ca http://www.globalinsight.com http://www.fraserinstitute.ca http://www.id.ca

Profitability ratios measure how the firm's returns compare with its sales, asset investments, and equity. Liquidity ratios measure the ability of a firm to meet its short-term obligations. Debt ratios measure the firm's debt financing and its ability to pay off its debt. Asset activity ratios measure how efficiently a firm uses its assets. Finally, market value ratios measure the market's perception about the future earning power of a business.

The Du Pont system analyzes the sources of ROA and ROE. Two versions of the Du Pont equation were covered in this chapter. The first analyzes the contributions of net profit margin and total asset turnover to ROA. The second version analyzes how the influences of net profit margin, total asset turnover, and leverage affect ROE.

INTERNATIONAL PERSPECTIVES IN FINANCE 5-1

Vodafone–The King in International Mobile Communications

Vodafone is the largest mobile telecommunications network company in the world, with equity interests in 26 countries and Partner Networks in a further 13 countries. At the end of 2003, Vodafone had over 130.4 million customers worldwide. The Company's ordinary shares are listed on the London Stock Exchange and other types of securities are listed on the New York Stock Exchange. The Company had a total market capitalization of approximately £86 billion in 2003, making it the second largest company in the Financial Times Stock Exchange 100 index, or FTSE 100, and the eleventh largest company in the world based on market capitalization at that date.

Vodafone Group Plc (further the "Group") provides an extensive range of mobile telecommunications services, including voice and data communications, with a significant presence in Continental Europe, the United Kingdom, the United States and the Far East through the Company's subsidiary undertakings, associated undertakings and investments. The Group presently operates in 26 countries worldwide, with its mobile subsidiaries operating under the brand name "Vodafone." In the United States the Group's associated undertaking operates as Verizon Wireless. During the last two financial years, the Group has also entered into arrangements with network operators in countries where the Group does not hold an equity stake. The Group and its partner networks co-operate in the development and marketing of global services under dual brand logos. Through these agreements, the Group has extended its brand reach into 13 further countries.

The Company was formed in 1984 as a subsidiary of Racal Electronics Plc. Then known as Racal Telecom Limited, approximately 20% of the Company's capital w offered to the public in 1988. It was fully demerged fr Racal Electronics Plc and became an independent compa in 1991, at which time it changed its name to Vodafo Group Plc. Following its merger with AirTouch Communic tions, Inc., the Company changed its name to Vodafo AirTouch Plc in 1999 and reverted to its former nam Vodafone Group Plc in 2000. The Company is a public li ited company incorporated in England and Wales.

The Group's financial highlights are included below:

In £ millions	2001	2002	2003
Group Turnover	15,004	22,845	30,375
Operating Loss	(6,438)	(10,377)	(5,541)
Loss after Taxation	(9,885)	(16,155)	(9,819)
Total Assets	147,428	131,534	207,692
Current Assets	17,960	9,438	8,951
Current Liabilities	6,546	4,017	5,702

Questions to Consider

1. *How would you rate the Group's liquidity situatio What information would you need to do a complete ana sis of the Group's liquidity?*

2. *The Group estimated that in 2003 its EBITDA w equal to £12,700 million, which increased by 26 perce from the 2002 level. How would you use this informati to assess the company's financial strength?*

Source: "Vodafone — The King in International Mobile Communica tion." Adapted from Vodafone House. www.vodafone.com. Reprinte

5-3 *Name and describe three types of analyses that compare financial information over time and among companies.*

Trend analysis compares past and present financial ratios to see how a firm has performed over time. Industry analysis compares a firm's ratios with the ratios of companies in the same industry. Summary analysis, one of the most useful financial analysis tools, combines trend and industry analysis to measure how a company performed over time in the context of the industry.

5-4 *Name four sources that can be used to locate ratio value data for specific companies and industries.*

A number of organizations publish financial data about companies and industries. Many publications contain ratios that are already calculated. Table 5-4 contains a list of publications that financial analysts find useful when they are researching companies and industries.

EQUATIONS INTRODUCED IN THIS CHAPTER

Profitability Ratios

$$\text{Gross Profit Margin} = \frac{\text{Gross Profit}}{\text{Sales}}$$

$$\text{Operating Profit Margin} = \frac{\text{Earnings before Interest and Taxes}}{\text{Sales}}$$

$$\text{Net Profit Margin} = \frac{\text{Net Earnings Available to Common Shareholders}}{\text{Sales}}$$

$$\text{Return on Assets} = \frac{\text{Net Earnings Available to Common Shareholders}}{\text{Total Assets}}$$

$$\text{Return on Equity} = \frac{\text{Net Earnings Available to Common Shareholders}}{\text{Common Shareholders' Equity}}$$

Liquidity Ratios

$$\text{Current Ratio} = \frac{\text{Current Assets}}{\text{Current Liabilities}}$$

$$\text{Quick Ratio} = \frac{\text{Current Assets Less Inventory}}{\text{Current Liabilities}}$$

Debt Ratios

$$\text{Debt to Total Assets} = \frac{\text{Total Liabilities}}{\text{Total Assets}}$$

$$\text{Times Interest Earned} = \frac{\text{Earnings before Interest and Taxes}}{\text{Interest Expense}}$$

$$\text{Debt to Equity} = \frac{\text{Total Liabilities}}{\text{Common Shareholders' Equity}}$$

Asset Activity Ratios

$$\text{Average Collection Period} = \frac{\text{Accounts Receivable}}{\text{Average Daily Credit Sales}}$$

$$\text{Inventory Turnover} = \frac{\text{Sales}}{\text{Inventory}}$$

$$\text{Total Asset Turnover} = \frac{\text{Sales}}{\text{Total Assets}}$$

Market Value Ratios

$$\text{P/E Ratio} = \frac{\text{Market Price per Share}}{\text{Earnings per Share}}$$

$$\text{Market to Book Value Ratio} = \frac{\text{Market Price per Share}}{\text{Book Value per Share}}$$

Equation 5-1: The Du Pont Formula

$$\text{ROA} = \text{Net Profit Margin} \times \text{Total Asset Turnover}$$

$$= \frac{\text{Earnings Available to Common Shareholders}}{\text{Sales}} \times \frac{\text{Sales}}{\text{Total Assets}}$$

Equation 5-2: The Modified Du Pont Formula

$$\text{ROE} = \text{Net Profit Margin} \times \text{Total Asset Turnover} \times \text{Equity Multiplier}$$

$$= \frac{\text{Earnings Available to Common Shareholders}}{\text{Sales}} \times \frac{\text{Sales}}{\text{Total Assets}} \times \frac{\text{Total Assets}}{\text{Common Equity}}$$

SELF-TEST

ST-1. De Marco Corporation has total assets of \$5 million and an asset turnover ratio of 4. If earnings available to common shareholders are \$2 million, what is the value of the net profit margin?

ST-2. Francisco Company has current assets of \$50,000. Total assets are \$200,000 and long-term liabilities, preferred shares, and common shares collectively total \$180,000. What is the value of the current ratio?

ST-3. If one-half the current assets in ST-2 consist of inventory, what is the value of the quick ratio?

ST-4. Sheth Corporation has a return on assets ratio of 6 percent. If the debt to total assets ratio is 0.5, what is the firm's return on equity?

ST-5. Mitra Company has a quick ratio value of 1.5. It has total current assets of \$100,000 and total current liabilities of \$25,000. If sales are \$200,000, what is the value of the inventory turnover ratio?

ST-6. Yates Corporation has total assets of \$500,000. Its equity is \$200,000. What is the company's debt to total asset ratio?

ST-7. Pendell Company has total sales of \$4 million. One-fourth of these are credit sales. The amount of accounts receivable is \$100,000. What is the average collection period for the company? Use a 365-day year.

REVIEW QUESTIONS

1. What is a financial ratio?
2. Why do analysts calculate financial ratios?

3. Which ratios would a banker be most interested in when considering whether to approve an application for a short-term business loan? Explain.

4. In which ratios would a potential long-term bond investor be most interested? Explain.

5. Under what circumstances would market to book value ratios be misleading? Explain.

6. Why would an analyst use the Modified Du Pont system to calculate ROE when ROE may be calculated more simply? Explain.

7. Why are trend analysis and industry comparisons important to financial ratio analysis?

PROBLEMS

5-1. The 2002 income statement for TeleTech is shown here: ◀ Profit Ratios

Net Sales	$35,000,000
Cost of Goods Sold	15,000,000
Gross Profit	20,000,000
Selling and Administrative Expenses	1,000,000
Amortization	3,000,000
Operating Income (EBIT)	16,000,000
Interest Expense	2,500,000
Income before Taxes (EBT)	13,500,000
Taxes (40%)	5,400,000
Net Income	8,100,000

Calculate the following:

a. Gross profit margin

b. Operating profit margin

c. Net profit margin

5-2. Rally's has notes payable of $500, long-term debt of $1,900, inventory of $900, total current assets of $5,000, accounts payable of $850, and accrued expenses of $600. What is Rally's current ratio? What is its quick ratio? ◀ Liquidity Ratios

5-3. XYZ Corporation has annual credit sales equal to $5 million and its accounts receivable account is $500,000. Calculate the company's average collection period. ◀ Asset Activity Ratios

5-4. In 2002, TeleTech had sales of $35 million. Its current assets are $15 million. Of this amount, $12 million is in cash, accounts receivable are $600,000, and net fixed assets are $20 million. What is TeleTech's inventory turnover? What is its total asset turnover? ◀ Asset Activity Ratios

5-5. The following data apply to Ramchander Corporation: ◀ Various Ratios

Total Common Share Equity at Year-End 2002	$4,500,000
Number of Common Shares Outstanding	650,000
Market Price per Share	$25

Calculate the following:

a. Book value per share

b. Market to book value ratio

Problems 5-6 to 5-11 refer to the consolidated statement of income and retained earnings and consolidated balance sheet of Pinewood Company and Subsidiaries that follow.

Pinewood Company and Subsidiaries
Income Statement for 2004 ($000s)

Sales	$94,001
Cost of Goods Sold	46,623
Gross Profit	47,378
Selling and Administrative Expenses	28,685
Amortization and R&D Expense (both tax deductible)	5,752
EBIT or Operating Income	12,941
Interest Expense	48
Interest Income	427
Earnings before Taxes (EBT)	13,320
Income Taxes	4,700
Net Income (NI)	8,620
Preferred Dividends	—
Earnings Available to Common Shareholders	8,620
Earnings per Share	1.72

Pinewood Company and Subsidiaries
Balance Sheet as of End of 2004 ($000s)

Assets	
Cash	$ 5,534
Accounts Receivable, Gross	14,956
Less: Allowance for Bad Debts	211
Accounts Receivable, Net	14,745
Inventory	10,733
Marketable Securities	952
Prepaid Expenses	3,234
Property, Plant, and Equipment, Gross	57,340
Less: Accumulated Amortization	29,080
Property, Plant, and Equipment, Net	28,260
Land	1,010
Long-Term Investments	2,503
Total Assets	66,971
Liabilities	
Accounts Payable	3,253
Notes Payable	—
Accrued Expenses	6,821
Bonds Payable	2,389
Shareholders' Equity	
Common Shares	8,549
Retained Earnings	45,959
Total Liabilities and Equity	66,971

Profit Ratios ▶

5-6. Calculate the following profitability ratios for 2004.

a. Gross profit margin

b. Operating profit margin

c. Net profit margin

d. Return on assets

e. Return on equity

Comment on net profit margin and return on assets ratios if the industry average for these two ratios is 5 percent and 14 percent, respectively.

5-7. Calculate the following liquidity ratios for the end of 2004. ◀ Liquidity Ratios

a. Current ratio

b. Quick ratio

Comment on the company's ability to pay off short-term debts.

5-8. Calculate the following debt ratios for the end of 2004. ◀ Debt Ratios

a. Debt to total assets

b. Times interest earned

Would a banker agree to extend a loan to Pinewood? Explain.

5-9. Calculate the following asset activity ratios for the end of 2004. ◀ Asset Activity Ratio

a. Average collection period

b. Inventory turnover

c. Total asset turnover

Comment on Pinewood's asset utilization.

5-10. Construct and solve Pinewood's Modified Du Pont equation for 2004. Use the end of 2004 asset figures. Comment on the company's sources of ROE. ◀ Modified Du Pont Equation

5-11. a. Calculate the economic value added (EVA) for Pinewood, assuming that the firm's income tax rate is 35 percent, the weighted average rate of return expected by the suppliers of the firm's capital is 10 percent, and the market price of the firm's share is $15. There are 5 million shares outstanding. ◀ EVA, MVA

b. Comment on your results. What does the EVA value that you calculated indicate?

c. Calculate the market value added (MVA) for Pinewood.

d. Comment on your results. What does the MVA value that you calculated indicate?

5-12. Refer to the following financial statements for the Eversharp Drilling Company. ◀ EVA, MVA

Eversharp Drilling Company
Financial Statements, 2004
Income Statement
For the Year Ended Dec. 31, 2004

Net Sales	$11,000
Operating Expenses	3,000
Operating Income (EBIT)	8,000

Balance Sheet
Dec. 31, 2004

Assets	
Total Assets	$21,000
Liabilities & Equity	
Long-Term Debt	$6,000
Total Common Equity	$15,000
Total Liabilities and Equity	$21,000

a. Calculate the EVA for Eversharp, assuming that the firm's income tax rate is 35 percent, the weighted average rate of return expected by the suppliers of the firm's capital is 12 percent, and the market price of the firm's share is $9. There are 3,000 shares outstanding.

b. Comment on your results. What does the EVA value that you calculated indicate?

c. Calculate the MVA for the Eversharp Drilling Company.

d. Comment on your results. What does the MVA value that you calculated indicate?

EVA, MVA ▶ **5-13.** Refer to the following financial statements for the T & J Corporation.

T & J Corporation
Financial Statements, 2004
Income Statement
For the Year Ended Dec. 31, 2004

Net Sales	$10,000
Cost of Goods Sold	3,000
Gross Profit	7,000
Amortization	200
S&A Expenses	300
Operating Income (EBIT)	6,500
Interest Expense	584
Income before Taxes	5,916
Income Taxes (35%)	2,071
Net Income	$3,845
Earnings per Share (3,000 shares)	$1.28

Balance Sheet
Dec. 31, 2004

Assets	
Cash	$350
Accounts Receivable	400
Inventory	680
Marketable Securities	300
Prepaid Expenses	200
Total Current Assets	1,930
Property, Plant, and Equipment, Gross	63,000
Less Accumulated Amortization	(42,000)
Property, Plant, and Equipment, Net	21,000
Total Assets	$22,930
Liabilities & Equity	
Accounts Payable	$740
Notes Payable	630
Accrued Expenses	350
Total Current Liabilities	1,720
Long-Term Debt	6,000
Total Liabilities	7,720
Common Shares	9,610
Retained Earnings	5,600
Total Common Equity	15,210
Total Liabilities and Equity	$22,930

The total invested capital of the firm is $33,630.

a. Calculate the EVA for T & J Corporation, assuming that the firm's income tax rate is 35 percent, the weighted average rate of return expected by the suppliers of the firm's capital is 12 percent, and the market price of the firm's share is $9.

b. Comment on your results. What does the EVA value that you calculated indicate?

c. Calculate the MVA for the T & J Corporation.

d. Comment on your results. What does the MVA value that you calculated indicate?

5-14. The following financial data relate to ABC Textile Company's business in 2004. ◀ Du Pont Equation

Sales	=	$1,000,000
Net Income	=	$80,000
Total Assets	=	$500,000
Debt to Total Assets Ratio	=	0.5 or 50%

a. Construct and solve the Du Pont and Modified Du Pont equations for ABC.

b. What would be the value of the ROE ratio if the debt to total asset ratio were 70 percent?

c. What would be the value of the ROE ratio if the debt to total asset ratio were 90 percent?

d. What would be the value of the ROE ratio if the debt to total asset ratio were 10 percent?

5-15. From the values of the different ratios that follow, calculate the missing balance sheet items and complete the balance sheet. ◀ Financial Relationships

Sales	$100,000
Average Collection Period	55 days
Inventory Turnover	15
Debt to Assets Ratio	0.4 or 40%
Current Ratio	3
Total Asset Turnover	1.6
Fixed Asset Turnover	2.9

Assets		Liabilities + Equity	
Cash	$6,000	Accounts Payable	6,000
Accounts Receivable	_____	Notes Payable	_____
Inventory	_____	Accrued Expenses	600
Prepaid Expenses	_____	Total Current Liabilities	_____
Total Current Assets	_____	Bonds Payable	_____
Property, Plant, & Equipment	_____	Common Shares	16,000
		Retained Earnings	_____
Total Assets	_____	Total Liabilities + Equity	_____

5-16. Given the partial financial statement information from La Strada Corporation, a circus equipment supplier, calculate the return on equity ratio. ◀ Financial Relationships

Total Assets	$10,000
Total Liabilities	6,000
Total Sales	5,000
Net Profit Margin	10%

Liquidity Ratios ▶ **5-17.** What is the current ratio of Ah, Wilderness! Corporation, given the following information from its end of 2002 balance sheet?

Current Assets	$ 5,000
Long-Term Liabilities	18,000
Total Liabilities	20,000
Total Equity	30,000

Du Pont Equation ▶ **5-18.** Rocinante, Inc. manufactures windmills. What is Rocinante's total asset turnover if its return on assets is 12 percent and its net profit margin is 4 percent?

Use the following information to answer questions 5-19 to 5-25.

In 2002, Iron Jay opened a small sporting goods retail store called Iron Jay's Sports Stuff (IJSS). It immediately became very popular and growth was only limited by the amount of capital Jay could generate through profits and loans. Jay's financial manager advised him to incorporate. His manager said that by selling shares, Jay would have the necessary capital to expand his business at an accelerated pace. Answer the following questions relating to Iron Jay's Sports Stuff.

Profitability Ratios ▶ **5-19.** The management team at IJSS is looking toward the future. They want to maintain a gross profit margin of 50 percent. If the estimate for net sales in 2003 is $5 million, how much gross profit will be necessary in 2003 to maintain this ratio?

Profitability Ratios ▶ **5-20.** Using the data in 5-19, if the management team estimated $200,000 in selling and administration expenses and $50,000 in amortization expenses for 2003, with net sales of $5 million, what operating profit margin can they expect?

Profitability Ratios ▶ **5-21.** What must net income be in 2003 if IJSS also wants to maintain a net profit margin of 20 percent on net sales of $5 million?

Financial Relationships ▶ **5-22.** What will IJSS's return on assets be if its total assets at the end of 2003 are estimated to be $20 million? Net sales are $5 million and the net profit margin is 20 percent in that year.

Profitability Ratios ▶ **5-23.** IJSS management knows that the astute owners of IJSS shares will sell their shares if the return on shareholders' equity investment (return on equity ratio) drops below 10 percent. Total shareholders' equity for the end of 2002 is estimated to be $15 million. How much net income will IJSS need in 2003 to fulfill the shareholders' expectation of the return on equity ratio of 10 percent?

Liquidity Ratios ▶ **5-24.** Of the $20 million in total assets estimated for the end of 2003, only $2 million will be classified as noncurrent assets. If current liabilities are $4 million, what will IJSS's current ratio be?

Liquidity Ratios ▶ **5-25.** Inventory on the balance sheet for the end of 2003 is expected to be $3 million. With total assets of $20 million, noncurrent assets of $2 million, and current liabilities of $4 million, what will be the value of IJSS's quick ratio?

Debt Ratios ▶ **5-26.** Given $20 million in total assets, $14 million in total shareholders' equity, and a debt to total asset ratio of 30 percent for Folson Corporation, what will be the debt to equity ratio?

Asset Activity Ratios ▶ **5-27.** If total assets are $20 million, noncurrent assets are $2 million, inventory is $3 million, and sales are $5 million for Toronto Brewing Company, what is the inventory turnover ratio?

Debt Ratios ▶ **5-28.** If the net profit margin of Dobie's Dog Hotel is maintained at 20 percent and total asset turnover ratio is 0.25, calculate return on assets.

5-29. The following data are from Saratoga Farms, Inc. 2004 financial statements. ◀ Du Pont Equation

Sales	$2,000,000
Net Income	200,000
Total Assets	1,000,000
Debt to Total Asset Ratio	60%

a. Construct and solve the Du Pont and Modified Du Pont equations for Saratoga Farms.

b. What would be the impact on ROE if the debt to total asset ratio were 80 percent?

c. What would be the impact on ROE if the debt to total asset ratio were 20 percent?

5-30. The following financial information is from two successful retail operations in Niagara Falls. Rose and George Loomis own Notoriously Niagara, a lavish jewellery store that caters to the "personal jet-set" crowd. The other store, Niagara's Notions, is a big hit with the typical tourist. Polly and Ray Cutler, the owners, specialize in inexpensive souvenirs such as postcards, mugs, and T-shirts. ◀ Various Ratios

Notoriously Niagara		Niagara's Notions	
Sales	$ 500,000	Sales	$500,000
Net Income	100,000	Net Income	10,000
Assets	5,000,000	Assets	500,000

a. Calculate the net profit margin for each store.

b. Calculate the total asset turnover for each store.

c. Combine the preceding equations to calculate the return on assets for each store.

d. Why would you expect Notoriously Niagara's net profit margin to be higher than Niagara's Notions, considering both stores had annual sales of $500,000 and the same figure for return on assets?

5-31. Thunder Alley Corporation supplies parts for Indianapolis-type race cars. Current market price per share of Thunder Alley's common share is $40. The latest annual report showed net income of $2,250,000 and total common share equity of $15 million. The report also listed 1,750,000 common shares outstanding. No common share dividends are paid. ◀ Various Ratios

a. Calculate Thunder Alley's earnings per share (EPS).

b. Calculate Thunder Alley's price to earnings (P/E) ratio.

c. Calculate Thunder Alley's book value per share.

d. What is Thunder Alley's market to book ratio?

e. Based on this information, does the market believe that the future earning power of Thunder Alley justifies a higher value than could be obtained by liquidating the firm? Why or why not?

5-32. Carrie White, the new financial analyst of Golden Products, Inc. has been given the task of reviewing the performance of her company over three recent years against the following industry information (figures in $000s): ◀ Industry Comparisons

Year	Net Income	Current Assets	Current Liabilities	Total Assets	Total Liabilities	Sales
2002	$400	$500	$530	$3,800	$2,600	$4,000
2003	425	520	510	3,900	2,500	4,500
2004	440	550	510	4,000	2,400	4,700

The industry averages are:

NI/Sales	Current Ratio	Total Asset Turnover
9.42%	1.13	2.00

Should Carrie be critical of her company's performance?

Industry Comparisons ▶ **5-33.** Johnny Hooker, another financial analyst of Golden Products, Inc. is working with the same yearly figures shown in 5-32, but he is trying to compare the performance trend using another set of industry averages:

The industry averages are:

Fixed Asset Turnover	Return on Assets	Debt to Equity Ratio	Return on Equity
1.33	11.00%	1.8	26%

Assume that the company has no long-term assets other than property, plant, and equipment. Should Johnny be appreciative of his company's performance?

Profitability Ratios ▶ **5-34.** Vernon Pinkby, the financial analyst reporting to the chief financial officer of Alufab Aluminum Company, is comparing the performance of the company's four separate divisions based on profit margin and return on assets. The relevant figures follow (figures in $000s):

	Mining	Smelting	Rolling	Extrusion
Net Income	$ 500	$ 2,600	$ 7,000	$ 2,500
Sales	15,000	30,000	60,000	25,000
Total Assets	12,000	25,000	39,000	18,000

a. Compare profit margin ratios of the four divisions.

b. Compare return on assets ratios of the four divisions.

c. Compute profit margin of the entire company.

d. Compute return on assets of the entire company.

Challenge Problem ▶ **5-35.** From the values of the different ratios given, calculate the missing balance sheet and statement of income and retained earnings items of National Glass Company.

Average Collection Period	48.67 days
Inventory Turnover	9×
Debt to Asset Ratio	0.4 or 40%
Current Ratio	1.625
Total Asset Turnover	1.5
Fixed Asset Turnover	2.647
Return on Equity	0.1933 or 19.33%
Return on Assets	0.116 or 11.6%
Operating Profit Margin	13.33%
Gross Profit Margin	48.89%

National Glass Company
Statement of Income and Retained Earnings for 2004
($000s)

Sales	$45,000
Cost of Goods Sold	______
Gross Profit	______
Selling and Administrative Expenses	______

Amortization	3,000
Operating Income (EBIT)	______
Interest Expense	______
Earnings before Taxes (EBT)	______
Income Taxes (T = 40%)	2,320
Net Income (NI)	______
Preferred Share Dividends	0
Earnings Available to Common Shareholders	______

National Glass Company
Balance Sheet as of End of 2004
($000s)

Assets	
Cash	$______
Accounts Receivable	______
Inventory	______
Property, Plant, and Equipment, Net	______
Land	1,000
Liabilities	
Accounts Payable	2,000
Notes Payable	______
Accrued Expenses	3,000
Bonds Payable	______
Shareholders' Equity	
Common Shares	4,000
Retained Earnings	______

5-36. Kingston Tools Company (KTC) manufactures various types of high-quality punching and deep-drawing press tools for kitchen appliance manufacturers. Horner Smith, the finance manager of KTC, has submitted a justification to support the application for a short-term loan from the Alberta Savings Bank (ASB) to finance increased sales. The consolidated statement of income and retained earnings and balance sheet of KTC, submitted with the justification to ASB, follow:

◀ Comprehensive Problem

Kingston Tools Company
Income Statement for 2002 and 2003 ($000s)

	2002	2003
Sales	$40,909	$45,000
Cost of Goods Sold	20,909	23,000
Gross Profit	20,000	22,000
Selling and Administrative Expenses	11,818	13,000
Amortization	2,000	3,000
Operating Income (EBIT)	6,182	6,000
Interest Expense	400	412
Earnings before Taxes (EBT)	5,782	5,588
Income Taxes (@ 40%)	2,313	2,235
Net Income (NI)	3,469	3,353
Preferred Share Dividends	—	—
Earnings Available to Common Shareholders	3,469	3,353
Dividends Paid (@ 21.86%)	758	733

Kingston Tools Company
Balance Sheet as of End of 2002 and 2003 ($000s)

	2002	2003
Assets		
Cash	$ 2,000	$ 1,800
Accounts Receivable, Net	6,000	7,600
Inventory	5,000	5,220
Property, Plant, and Equipment, Gross	26,000	31,000
Less: Accumulated Amortization	10,000	13,000
Property, Plant, and Equipment, Net	16,000	18,000
Land	1,000	1,000
Liabilities		
Accounts Payable	2,000	2,600
Notes Payable	3,000	3,300
Accrued Expenses	3,000	3,100
Bonds Payable	4,000	4,000
Shareholders' Equity		
Common Shares	4,000	4,000
Retained Earnings	14,000	16,620

You are the loan officer at ASB responsible for determining whether KTC's business is strong enough to be able to repay the loan. To do so, accomplish the following:

a. Calculate the following ratios for 2002 and 2003, compare with the industry averages shown in parentheses, and indicate if the company is doing better or worse than the industry and whether the performance is improving or deteriorating in 2003 as compared to 2002.
   i. Gross profit margin (50 percent)
   ii. Operating profit margin (15 percent)
   iii. Net profit margin (8 percent)
   iv. Return on assets (10 percent)
   v. Return on equity (20 percent)
   vi. Current ratio (1.5)
   vii. Quick ratio (1.0)
   viii. Debt to total asset ratio (0.5)
   ix. Times interest earned (25)
   x. Average collection period (45 days)
   xi. Inventory turnover (8)
   xii. Total asset turnover (1.6)
b. Calculate the EVA and MVA for Kingston Tools, assuming that the firm's income tax rate is 40 percent, the weighted average rate of return expected by the suppliers of the firm's capital is 10 percent, and the market price of the firm's shares is $20 per share. There are 1.2 million shares outstanding.
c. Discuss the financial strengths and weaknesses of KTC.
d. Determine the sources and uses of funds and prepare a cash flow statement for 2003.
e. Compare and comment on the financial condition as evident from the ratio analysis and the cash flow statement.
f. Which ratios should you analyze more critically before recommending granting of the loan and what is your recommendation?

5-37. Refer to the following financial statements of Super Dot Com, Inc. ◀ Ratio Analysis

Super Dot Com, Inc.
Statement of Income and Retained Earnings
(In $000s, except EPS)

	2002	2003	2004
Net Sales	$2,100	$3,051	$3,814
Cost of Goods Sold	681	995	1,040
Gross Profit	1,419	2,056	2,774
Selling & Administrative Expenses	610	705	964
Operating Profit	809	1,351	1,810
Interest Expense	11	75	94
Income before Tax	798	1,276	1,716
Income Tax (T = 35%)	279	447	601
Net Income	$519	$829	$1,115
Dividends Paid	$0	$0	$0
Increase in Retained Earnings	$535	$855	$1,150
Common Shares Outstanding	2,500	2,500	2,500
EPS	$0.21	$0.33	$0.45

Super Dot Com, Inc.
Balance Sheets
(In $000s)
As of Dec. 31, Years Ended

	2002	2003	2004
Assets			
Cash & Equivalents	$224	$103	$167
Accounts Receivable	381	409	564
Inventories	307	302	960
Other Current Assets	69	59	29
Total Current Assets	981	873	1,720
Property, Plant, and Equipment, Gross	1,901	3,023	3,742
Less Accumulated Amortization	(81)	(82)	(346)
Property, Plant, and Equipment, Net	1,820	2,941	3,396
Other Assets	58	101	200
Total Assets	$2,859	$3,915	$5,316
Liabilities & Equity			
Accounts Payable	$210	$405	$551
Short-Term Debt	35	39	72
Total Current Liabilities	245	444	623
Long-Term Debt	17	19	91
Total Liabilities	262	463	714
Common Shares	2,062	2,062	2,062
Retained Earnings	535	1,390	2,540
Total Equity	2,597	3,452	4,602
Total Liabilities & Equity	$2,859	$3,915	$5,316

a. How long, on average, was Super Dot Com taking to collect on its receivable accounts in 2004? (Assume all of the company's sales were on credit.)

b. Was Super Dot Com more or less profitable in 2004 than in 2002? Justify your answer by examining the net profit margin and return on assets ratios.

c. Was Super Dot Com more or less liquid at the end of 2004 than it was at the end of 2002? Justify your answer using the current and quick ratios.

Challenge Problem ▶ **5-38.** IT Solutions (ITS) is one of the leading Canadian IT services companies focusing primarily on IT consulting services and ERP software implementation. The company is currently owned by five shareholders who are also involved in day-to-day operations of the company. ITS has grown significantly in the recent years in terms of sales and has expanded its breadth and depth of product offerings. Multinational companies account for over 75 percent of the company's revenues. There are 500,000 common shares and 1,000,000 preferred shares outstanding. The company paid an annual dividend of $0.01 per common share in 2001 and $0.05 per common share between 2002 and 2004. The dividend on preferred shares was equal to $0.05 in 2001, $0.1 in 2002, and $0.25 in 2003 and 2004. Refer to the financial statements of IT Solutions.

Income Statement
IT Solutions
2001–2004

	2001	2002	2003	2004
Net Sales	14,000,000	17,000,000	24,000,000	35,000,000
Cost of Goods Sold	9,100,000	10,880,000	15,360,000	21,000,000
S&A Expenses	3,000,000	3,500,000	4,000,000	7,000,000
Amortization	400,000	400,000	400,000	400,000
Operating Income	1,500,000	2,220,000	4,240,000	6,600,000
Interest Expense	500,000	500,000	500,000	500,000
Earnings before Taxes	1,000,000	1,720,000	3,740,000	6,100,000
Income Tax	400,000	688,000	1,496,000	2,440,000
Net Income	600,000	1,032,000	2,244,000	3,660,000

Additional information is included in the table below:

	2001	2002	2003	2004
Common shareholders' equity	$4,800,000	$5,707,000	$7,676,000	$11,061,000
Total Assets	$14,500,000	$15,407,000	$17,376,000	$20,761,000

The industry averages for selected financial ratios are included below:

	2001	2002	2003	2004
Gross Profit Margin	34.1%	35.2%	37.0%	37.2%
Operating Profit Margin	14.2%	15.2%	16.3%	17.4%
Net Profit Margin	5.4%	5.7%	6.2%	7.4%
Return on Assets	7.2%	7.8%	9.2%	10.1%
Return on Equity	10.7%	10.2%	11.2%	12.7%

a. Prepare a statement of income and retained earnings for the company for the years 2001, 2002, 2003, and 2004 showing addition to the retained earnings line.

b. Using the information above, calculate the following financial ratios for each of the years (2001 to 2004):

   i. Gross profit margin

   ii. Operating profit margin

   iii. Net profit margin

   iv. Return on assets

   v. Return on equity

c. Compare your calculations in (b) to the industry average in the period between 2001 and 2004. Discuss the company's strengths and weaknesses compared to the industry averages.

5-39. Northwest Publishing (NP) is the publisher of business journals in Canada with a combined distribution of over 200,000 copies per week. The company has grown its business journal publication and, at the same time, developed other complementary business publications such as book of lists and city guides. In addition, management recently introduced their first travel publication, Travel On-line, a high-end travel magazine. In 2002, the company increased its capital from 10 million common shares at $1 per share to 20 million common shares at $1 per share. In addition, there are 6 million preferred shares. Every year the company paid an annual dividend of $0.10 per common share and $0.20 per preferred share. Refer to the following statements of Northwest Publishing. ◀ Challenge Problem

Income Statement
Northwest Publishing
2001–2004

	2001	2002	2003	2004
Net Sales	120,000,000	150,000,000	180,000,000	200,000,000
Cost of Goods Sold	54,000,000	69,000,000	84,600,000	96,000,000
S&A Expenses	32,000,000	40,000,000	45,000,000	50,000,000
Amortization	1,300,000	2,800,000	4,300,000	6,300,000
Operating Income	32,700,000	38,200,000	46,100,000	47,700,000
Interest Expense	2,600,000	1,700,000	1,000,000	1,000,000
Earnings before Taxes	30,100,000	36,500,000	45,100,000	46,700,000
Income Tax	12,040,000	14,600,000	18,040,000	18,680,000
Net Income	18,060,000	21,900,000	27,060,000	28,020,000

Balance Sheet
Northwest Publishing
2001–2004

	2001	2002	2003	2004
Assets				
Cash	3,000,000	6,500,000	660,000	6,780,000
Marketable Securities	6,000,000	7,000,000	8,000,000	5,000,000
Accounts Receivable	20,000,000	20,000,000	25,000,000	30,000,000
Inventory	40,000,000	47,000,000	50,000,000	60,000,000
Prepaid Expenses	10,000,000	8,000,000	7,000,000	6,000,000
P.P. & E., Gross	13,000,000	28,000,000	43,000,000	63,000,0000
Less: Accum. Amort.	6,000,000	8,800,000	13,100,000	19,400,000
P.P. & E., Net	7,000,000	19,200,000	29,900,000	43,600,000
Total Assets	86,000,000	107,700,000	120,560,000	151,380,000
Liabilities				
Accounts Payable	35,000,000	40,000,000	35,000,000	40,000,000
Notes Payable	6,000,000	7,000,000	5,000,000	5,000,000
Accrued Expenses	7,000,000	4,000,000	5,000,000	6,000,000
Long-Term Debt	20,000,000	10,000,000	5,000,000	5,000,000
Shareholders' Equity				
Preferred Shares	6,000,000	6,000,000	6,000,000	6,000,000
Common Shares	10,000,000	20,000,000	20,000,000	20,000,000
Retained Earnings	2,000,000	20,700,000	44,560,000	69,380,000
Total Liabilities and Shareholders' Equity	86,000,000	107,700,000	120,560,000	151,380,000

a. Prepare the cash flow statement for the company for 2002, 2003, and 2004.

b. Calculate the following financial ratios for each of the years 2001 to 2004. (Hint: Generate a statement of income and retained earnings to help with calculations.)

- **i.** Return on assets
- **ii.** Return on equity
- **iii.** Current ratio
- **iv.** Quick ratio
- **v.** Debt to equity
- **vi.** Debt to total assets
- **vii.** Times interest earned
- **viii.** Average collection period
- **ix.** Inventory turnover
- **x.** Total asset turnover

c. Discuss the results of your calculations above for the period between 2001 and 2004. What do you see as trends in each of the ratios and explain why they are changing (improving or deteriorating)?

d. Discuss the strengths and weaknesses of the company in view of the above analysis.

Challenge Problem ▶

5-40. Fast Food Enterprises Canada is a wholly owned subsidiary of Fast Food Enterprises, a privately owned Delaware registered company. The Canadian company, which develops and operates its own brands of fast food restaurants in Canada, has its headquarters in Mississauga. Its most established brand is "Italian Small Pizza." Two new complementary concepts, "Burger Time" and "Chinatown Express," are being introduced to expand the product offering. The company operates thirty units in Ontario, which share sites with service stations / grocery stores and supermarkets. The company was founded in 1999 by Peter Rozen, who is currently President and CEO. Mr. Rozen has been actively developing fast food concepts in Asia, Central and Eastern Europe, and South America. Refer to the following financial statements of Fast Food Enterprises Canada.

Statement of Income and Retained Earnings
Fast Food Enterprises Canada
2001–2004

	2001	2002	2003	2004
Net Sales	15,000,000	21,000,000	25,000,000	28,000,000
Cost of Goods Sold	6,750,000	9,660,000	11,750,000	13,440,000
Selling and Administrative Expenses	6,400,000	8,000,000	9,400,000	10,000,000
Amortization	1,300,000	1,500,000	1,700,000	1,700,000
Operating Income	550,000	1,840,000	2,150,000	2,860,000
Interest Expense	600,000	700,000	700,000	800,000
Earnings before Taxes	(50,000)	1,140,000	1,450,000	2,060,000
Income Tax	0	456,000	580,000	824,000
Earnings after Tax	(50,000)	684,000	870,000	1,236,000
Preferred Dividends	150,000	150,000	150,000	150,000
Earnings Available to Common Shareholders	(200,000)	534,000	720,000	1,086,000
Common Dividends Paid	50,000	62,000	75,000	88,000
Addition to Retained Earnings	(250,000)	471,000	645,000	998,000

Balance Sheet
Fast Food Enterprises Canada
2001–2004

	2001	2002	2003	2004
Assets				
Cash	3,000,000	2,922,000	4,967,000	8,565,000
Marketable Securities	500,000	400,000	800,000	1,000,000
Accounts Receivable	5,000,000	7,000,000	9,500,000	11,000,000
Inventory	5,000,000	5,500,000	5,700,000	6,500,000
Prepaid Expenses	500,000	400,000	300,000	200,000
P.P. & E., Gross	13,000,000	15,000,000	17,000,000	17,000,000
Less: Accumulated Amortization	6,000,000	7,500,000	9,200,000	10,900,000
P.P. & E., Net	7,000,000	7,500,000	7,800,000	6,100,000
Total Assets	21,000,000	23,722,000	29,067,000	33,365,000
Liabilities				
Accounts Payable	4,500,000	4,000,000	7,000,000	7,700,000
Notes Payable	1,000,000	2,000,000	2,000,000	4,000,000
Accrued Expenses	500,000	500,000	450,000	300,000
Long-Term Debt	5,000,000	5,000,000	5,000,000	4,000,000
Shareholders' Equity				
Preferred Shares	1,500,000	1,500,000	1,500,000	1,500,000
Common Shares	7,000,000	8,750,000	10,500,000	12,250,000
Retained Earnings	1,500,000	1,972,000	2,617,000	3,615,000
Total Liabilities and Shareholders' Equity	21,000,000	23,722,000	29,067,000	33,365,000

a. Prepare the cash flow statement for the company for each of the years between 2002 and 2004.

b. Calculate the following financial ratios for each of the years (2001 to 2004):
   i. Return on assets
   ii. Return on equity
   iii. Current ratio
   iv. Quick ratio
   v. Debt to equity
   vi. Debt to total assets
   vii. Times interest earned
   viii. Average collection period
   ix. Inventory turnover
   x. Total asset turnover

c. Discuss the results of your calculations. What do you see as trends in each of the ratios and explain why they are changing (improving or deteriorating)?

d. Discuss the strengths and weaknesses of the company in view of the above analysis.

5-41. You are an analyst working for a major investment bank in Toronto. Your boss asked you to prepare an analysis of the balance sheet for Durum Drive Limited, one of the two major telecommunication companies in Manitoba. As you start to work on the assignment at home, you realize that you forgot to take your entire file from your office and the balance sheet for 2004 for Durum Drive is missing. You soon discover that in your briefcase there is a copy of the cash flow statement for that year. "What a relief!" you think to yourself. Using the information below, construct the balance sheet for Durum Drive for 2004. ◀ Challenge Problem

Balance Sheet
Durum Drive Limited
2001–2003

	2001	2002	2003
Assets			
Cash	3,000,000	884,000	5,700,000
Marketable Securities	12,000,000	14,000,000	14,000,000
Accounts Receivable	50,000,000	56,000,000	62,000,000
Inventory	45,000,000	60,000,000	67,000,000
Prepaid Expenses	7,000,000	8,000,000	9,000,000
P.P. & E., Gross	76,000,000	96,000,000	117,000,000
Less: Accumulated Amortization	6,000,000	15,600,000	27,300,000
P.P. & E., Net	70,000,000	80,400,000	89,700,000
Total Assets	187,000,000	219,284,000	247,400,000
Liabilities			
Accounts Payable	20,000,000	25,000,000	27,000,000
Notes Payable	7,000,000	12,000,000	13,000,000
Accrued Expenses	3,000,000	4,000,000	3,500,000
Long-Term Debt	25,000,000	28,000,000	34,000,000
Shareholders' Equity			
Preferred Shares	17,000,000	17,000,000	17,000,000
Common Shares	113,500,000	113,500,000	113,500,000
Retained Earnings	1,500,000	19,784,000	39,400,000
Total Liabilities and Shareholders' Equity	187,000,000	219,284,000	247,400,000

Cash Flow Statement
Durum Drive Limited
2004

	2004
Cash Received from (Used in) Operating Activities	
Net Income	23,880,000
Amortization	14,200,000
Decrease (Increase) Marketable Securities	(2,000,000)
Decrease (Increase) Accounts Receivable	(12,000,000)
Decrease (Increase) Inventory	(7,000,000)
Decrease (Increase) Prepaid Expenses	0
Increase (Decrease) Accounts Payable	6,000,000
Increase (Decrease) Accrued Expenses	(500,000)
Total Cash from Operations	22,580,000
Cash Received from (Used for) Investment Activities	
P.P. & E., Purchases	(25,000,000)
Total Cash from Investments	(25,000,000)
Cash Received from (Used for) Financing Activities	
Proceeds from New Long-Term Debt Issue	9,000,000
Short-Term Notes Issued	2,000,000
Preferred Dividends	(850,000)
Common Dividends	(2,250,000)
Total Cash from Financing	7,900,000
Net Change in Cash Balance	**5,480,000**
Beginning Cash Balance	**5,700,000**
Ending Cash Balance	**11,180,000**

ANSWERS TO SELF-TEST

ST-1. Sales ÷ \$5,000,000 = 4 ∴ sales = \$20,000,000
\$2,000,000 earnings available to common shareholders ÷ \$20,000,000 sales = 0.1 = 10% net profit margin

ST-2. Current liabilities = \$200,000 total assets − \$180,000 LTD, PS, & CS = \$20,000
\$50,000 current assets ÷ \$20,000 current liabilities = 2.5 current ratio

ST-3. Current assets − inventory = \$50,000 − (0.5 × \$50,000) = \$25,000
\$25,000 ÷ \$20,000 current liabilities = 1.25 quick ratio

ST-4. Debt ÷ assets = 0.5 ∴ equity ÷ assets = 0.5 ∴ assets ÷ equity = 1 ÷ 0.5 = 2
Return on equity = Return on assets × assets ÷ equity = 0.06 × 2 = 0.12, or 12%

ST-5. (\$100,000 current assets − inventory) ÷ \$25,000 = 1.5 quick ratio ∴ inventory = \$62,500
\$200,000 sales ÷ \$62,500 inventory = 3.2 inventory turnover ratio

ST-6. Debt = \$500,000 assets − \$200,000 equity = \$300,000
\$300,000 debt ÷ \$500,000 assets = 0.6 = 60% debt to total asset ratio

ST-7. Credit sales = \$4,000,000 ÷ 4 = \$1,000,000 Average collection period = accounts receivable ÷ average daily credit sales = \$100,000
Accounts receivable ÷ (\$1,000,000 annual credit sales ÷ 365 days per year) = 36.5 days

6

Forecasting for Financial Planning

Chapter Objectives

After reading this chapter, you should be able to:

6-1 **Explain** why forecasting is vital to business success.

6-2 **Describe** three main approaches to the financial statement forecasting process.

6-3 **Explain** how *pro forma* (projected) financial statements are produced.

6-4 **Explain** the importance of analyzing forecasts.

"An economist's guess is liable to be as good as anybody else's."

—Will Rogers

The Cash Budget—A Useful Forecasting Tool

Management of cash is paramount to any business success. If cash shortages occur, the business will not be able to settle its debts and may ultimately face bankruptcy.

A cash budget is a financial tool. The cash budget often consists of three parts: cash receipts, cash disbursements, and financing. In the cash receipts or cash collections section, it must be determined what percentage of sales will occur as cash sales (i.e., cash received at the moment the sale is made) and what sales are likely to be collected in the future. The percent of cash received immediately and in later periods can be estimated from history on the basis of the past collection record. For example, an owner of a small restaurant in Red Deer, Alberta knows that about 80 percent of the sales are made on a cash basis, while 20 percent are made on credit—these sales relate to the restaurant hosting corporate events. The owner estimates that she receives payment for hosting these events within 10 business days from the date of the event. Estimating the amount of cash disbursements is an opposite exercise. The restaurant owner from Red Deer attempts to estimate how quickly she would need to pay her bills (raw materials, wages, utilities, etc.) and settle tax payments. By putting together a schedule of cash receipts and cash disbursements, the business owner is able to forecast her cash position for some time in the future. Depending on the outcome of such an exercise, the business may or may not need any external cash. If a need for further cash arises, the business owner would be able to address this in the financing section of her cash budget. The cash budget is very popular for a number of reasons. First, it is simple to prepare. The business owner does not need to prepare a full set of financial statements that include the income statement, balance sheet, cash flow, and the retained earnings statement. Instead, the owner prepares one statement, which captures the essence of the business—proper accounting for revenues, cost, and their appropriate timing. Second, the cash balance is highly intuitive for large corporations and small business owners. Preparation of the cash balance does not require any education or background in finance. In many respects, the cash balance is similar to the balance in a personal chequebook; both consist of credits and debits.

Chapter Overview

A business owner who wants to run a successful business must be able to answer many questions about the future, including the following:

- How much profit will the business make?
- How much demand will there be for the product or service?
- How much will it cost to produce the product or offer the service?
- How much money will need to be borrowed and when and how will it be paid back?

Business people must estimate the future all the time. The task of estimating future business events is daunting and nearly impossible, but in business, it is necessary. Without some idea of what is going to happen in the future, it is impossible to plan and to succeed in business.

We will look first at the forecasting task, discuss why it is important, and explain what forecasting approaches business people use. Then, step by step, we will build a set of projected financial statements. We will conclude with a discussion of how to analyze forecasts to plan for the financial success of the company.

Why Forecasting Is Important

Every day you make decisions based on forecasts. When you go shopping, for example, you decide how much money to spend based on your forecast of how much money you need for other reasons. When you plan trips, you decide how much money to take along based on your forecast of the trip's expenses. You choose what to wear in the morning based on the weather forecaster's prediction of good or bad weather.

The situation is similar in business—particularly in finance. Financial decisions are based on forecasts of situations that a business expects to confront in the future. Businesses develop new products, set production quotas, and select financing sources based on forecasts about the future economic environment and the firm's condition. If economists predict interest rates will be relatively high, for example, a firm may plan to limit borrowing and defer expansion plans. Forecasting in business is especially important because failing to anticipate future trends can be devastating.

Firms often spend a large amount of time, effort, and money to obtain accurate forecasts. Financial forecasting is also a highly personalized process. Even though, at the end of the process, the objective is that the two sides of the balance sheet agree, there are various ways of preparing a full set of financial projections. Some financial analysts like to start by projecting the income statement and the balance sheet, and the cash flow statement is a by-product of the first two. On the other hand, other financial analysts prepare the income statement and the cash flow statement, and develop the balance sheet last. Our intention is not to cover all these possible approaches but provide you with a sample methodology of how financial projections may be done. Some of the complexities behind financial forecasts are discussed in Finance at Work 6-2 on page 170.

Let's take a look at some of the ways forecasters approach the forecasting task.

Forecasting Approaches

Forecasting simply means making projections about what we think will happen in the future. To make these projections, forecasters use different approaches depending on the situation. Financial managers concentrate on three general approaches: *experience, probability,* and *correlation.*

Experience Sometimes we think things will happen a certain way in the future because they happened that way in the past. For instance, if it has always taken you 15 minutes to drive to the grocery store, then you will probably assume that it will take you about 15 minutes the next time you drive to the store. Similarly, financial managers often assume sales, expenses, or earnings will grow at certain rates in the future because that is how the rates grew in the past. The disadvantage of this method, as you can imagine, is that the past does not equal the present or the future. Finance at Work 6-1 on page 169 discusses financial forecasting in this light.

Probability Sometimes we think things will happen a certain way in the future because the laws of probability indicate that they will be so. For example, let's say insurance company statisticians calculate that male drivers under 25 years of age during a one-year period will have a 0.25 probability of having an accident. The company insures 10,000 male drivers under 25, so the company's financial manager—based on probability figures—will forecast that 2,500 of the firm's under-25 male policyholders ($0.25 \times 10{,}000 = 2{,}500$) will have an accident during the coming year. Financial managers use probabilities to forecast the number of customers who will not pay their bills, the number of rejects in a production process, and so on. The drawback here is that statistics also defines a term called "an outlier," which means that events occur beyond what reasonably could be expected.

Correlation Sometimes we think things will happen a certain way in the future because there is a high correlation between the behaviour of one item and the behaviour of another item that we know more about. For example, if you knew that most people buy new cars right after they graduate from college, you could forecast new-car sales to recent graduates fairly accurately. You would base your plans on the amount of correlation between the number of people graduating and new-car sales. In a similar manner, financial managers forecast more sales for snow tires in the winter and more sales of lawn mowers in the summer. The disadvantage of this approach is that there is often a limited causal relationship between events. This means that one event may not necessarily cause another.

Why Forecasts Are Sometimes Wrong

In general, forecasting the future is based on what has happened in the past (either past experience, past probability, or past correlation). However, just because something has occurred in the past does not *ensure* that it will happen the same way in the future, which is why forecasts are sometimes spectacularly wrong. No one can forecast the future with absolute precision. For example, the attacks on the World Trade Center and on the Pentagon in 2001 or accession of the former Soviet bloc countries to the European Union in 2004 were completely unforeseen.

The approaches to forecasting range from being quite simple to complex and sophisticated, depending on what is being forecast and how much the business needs to rely on an accurate forecast. In the sections that follow, we will examine some of the approaches that business people use to predict future sales and the way that finance people predict their firms' future.

Forecasting Sales

Producing a sales forecast is not purely a financial task. Estimates of future sales depend on the demand for the firm's products and the strength of the competition. Sales and marketing personnel usually provide assessments of demand and the competition. Production personnel usually provide estimates of manufacturing capacity and other production constraints. Top management will make strategic decisions affecting the firm as a whole. Therefore, sales forecasting is a group effort. Financial managers coordinate, collect, and analyze the sales forecasting information. They also provide valuable input to top management on whether available financial resources are sufficient to finance the company's plans or additional financing needs to be secured in the form of debt or equity. Figure 6-1 shows a diagram of the process.

Sometimes financial analysts make a quick estimate of a company's future sales by extending the trend of past sales. Figure 6-2 illustrates this technique with the sales record of Esoteric Enterprises, Inc. for 1999 to 2004.

The graph in Figure 6-2 shows that Esoteric's sales have been somewhat constant during the five-year period. A forecaster, by extending the past trend, would estimate that Esoteric's sales in the next year are likely to be about $220,000. The technique of extending a past trend works well when the past trend is discernible and no outside factors, such as new competition, act to change the trend.

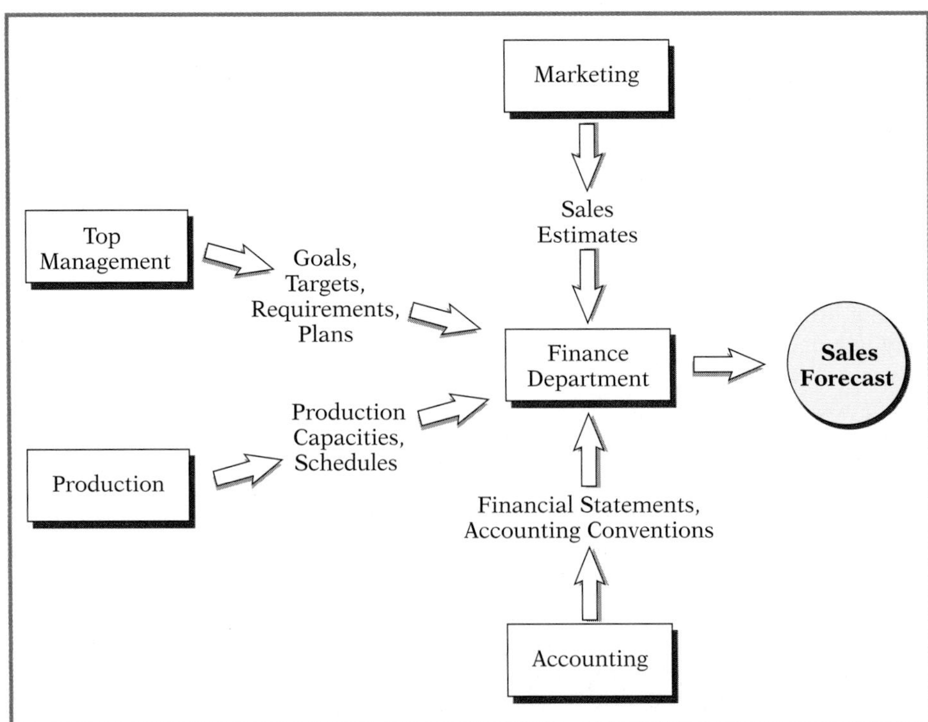

Figure 6-1 The Sales Forecasting Process
This chart shows how a company's sales forecast is developed from many different sources. Marketing data, company goals, production capabilities, and accounting data are analyzed, weighed, and combined to produce the final sales estimate.

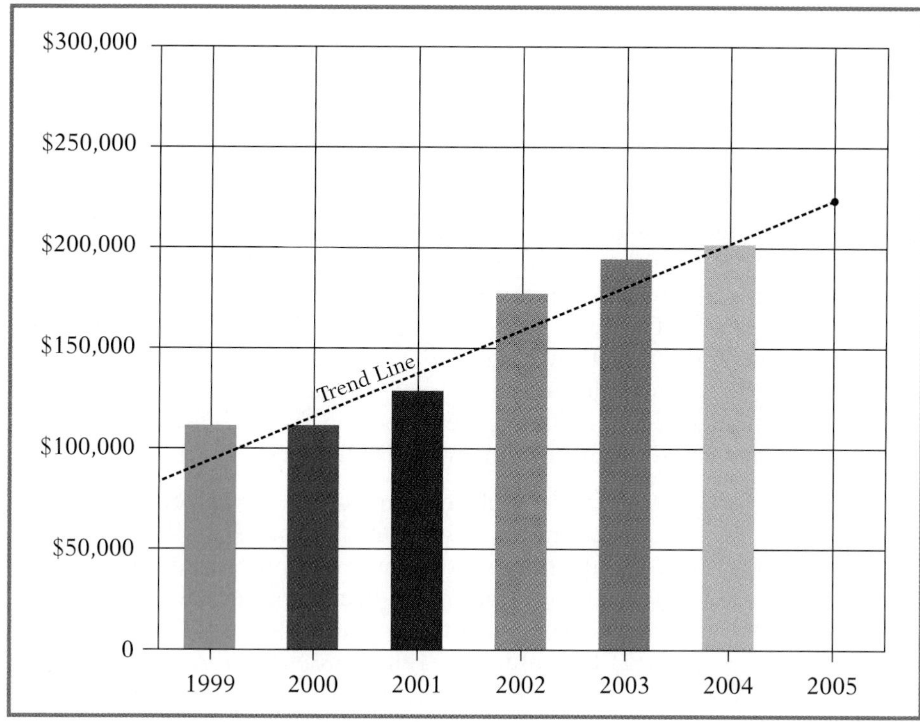

Figure 6-2
Sales Record, Esoteric Enterprises
This graph shows the sales record for Esoteric Enterprises, Inc. during 1999 to 2004. Sales growth has been fairly constant during the five-year period. By extending the sales trend, an analyst might estimate Esoteric's sales in 2005 to be about $220,000.

Forecasting Financial Statements

After the sales forecast is complete, financial managers determine whether the firm can support the sales forecast financially. They do this by extending the firm's financial statements into future time periods. These forecasted financial statements are commonly referred to as **pro forma financial statements.**[1] *Pro forma* financial statements show what the firm will look like if the sales forecasts are indeed realized and management's plans carried out. By analyzing the projected financial statements, managers can tell if funds needed to make purchases will be available, if the firm will be able to make loan payments on schedule, if external financing will be required, what return on investment the shareholders can expect, and so on.

Budgets

Financial managers use a variety of budgets to help produce *pro forma* financial statements. Budgets contain estimates of future receipts and expenditures for various activities. Financial managers produce *pro forma* statements that assume the budget figures will, in fact, occur.

Two budgets are particularly important to forecasters. These are the *cash budget* and the *capital budget.* The **cash budget** shows the projected flow of cash in and out of the firm for specified time periods. The **capital budget** shows planned expenditures for major asset acquisitions. In the sections that follow, we will see how forecasters incorporate data from these budgets into *pro forma* financial statements.

Take Note

Developing a cash budget and a capital budget is a complex matter. We discuss cash budgets in Chapter 18, and capital budgets in Chapters 10 and 11.

[1]*Pro forma* is a Latin term meaning "as a matter of form." *Pro forma* financial statements show what the business will look like (its form) if expected events take place.

Producing *Pro Forma* Financial Statements

Now that we have reviewed the sales forecast and the budgets from which data are drawn to produce *pro forma* financial statements, we can discuss how to produce *pro forma* financial statements. In the following sections, we explore the step-by-step process of creating both a *pro forma* income statement and a *pro forma* balance sheet for Esoteric Enterprises, Inc.

Esoteric Enterprises makes one product: a rechargeable lithium battery used in industrial facilities to power emergency lights. The company's statements of income and retained earnings and balance sheet for 2004 are shown in the first column of Figures 6-3a and 6-3b. We will create a *pro forma* statement of income and retained earnings and balance sheet for 2005 by filling in the blanks in the second column of Figures 6-3a and 6-3b.

For convenience, assume that we are preparing this forecast on January 1, 2005. (Being dedicated, we have come in on New Year's Day to do this.)

Choosing the Forecasting Basis Before we make *pro forma* forecasts of each statement of income and retained earnings and balance sheet line item, let's consider our procedure. Unfortunately, no universal procedure applies to all line items on *pro forma* financial statements because forecasters choose values for a variety of reasons. There are three main reasons: (1) management specifies a target goal, (2) the value is taken from either the cash or capital budgets, or (3) the value is an extension of a past trend. If management does not specify a target value and if no value from a budget is available, then forecasters must evaluate how the item has behaved in the past and estimate a future value based on experience, probability, or correlation as discussed earlier in the chapter.

As we consider each financial statement item on Esoteric's *pro forma* statements, we will determine its value by seeing whether management has a target goal or whether a budget sets the value for the item. If not, we will extend the trend based on experience, probability, or correlation.

Figure 6-3a
Esoteric Enterprises Statement of Income and Retained Earnings
The first column in this figure shows Esoteric Enterprises' statement of income and retained earnings for 2004. The *pro forma* forecast for 2005 will be inserted in the second column.

	2004	Forecast for 2005
Net Sales	$201,734	______
Cost of Goods Sold	107,280	______
Gross Profit	94,454	______
Operating Expenses		
Selling and Marketing Expenses	32,392	______
General and Administrative Expense	10,837	______
Amortization	4,500	______
Operating Income	46,725	______
Interest Expense	2,971	______
Before-Tax Income	43,754	______
Income Taxes (tax rate = 40%)	17,502	______
Net Income	$26,252	______
Dividends Paid	23,627	______
Addition to Retained Earnings	2,625	______

Let's begin with Esoteric Industries' *pro forma* statement of income and retained earnings for 2005.

	Actual Dec. 31 2004	Forecast for Dec. 31 2005
Assets		
Current Assets		
Cash and Marketable Securities	$ 65,313	______
Accounts Receivable	13,035	______
Inventory	21,453	______
Total Current Assets	99,801	______
Property, Plant, and Equipment, Gross	133,369	______
Less Accumulated Amortization	(40,386)	______
Property, Plant, and Equipment, Net	92,983	______
Total Assets	$192,784	______
Liabilities and Equity		
Current Liabilities		
Accounts Payable	$ 4,733	______
Notes Payable	302	______
Total Current Liabilities	5,035	______
Long-Term Debt	37,142	______
Total Liabilities	42,177	______
Common Shares (35 million shares)	35,000	______
Retained Earnings	115,607	______
Total Shareholders' Equity	150,607	______
Total Liabilities and Equity	$192,784	______

Figure 6-3b
Esoteric Enterprises Balance Sheets
The first column in this figure shows Esoteric Enterprises' balance sheet as of December 31, 2004. The *pro forma* forecast for December 31, 2005 will be inserted in the second column.

The Pro Forma Income Statement To prepare the *pro forma* statement of income and retained earnings, we project the values of the following items: sales, costs and expenses associated with sales, general and administrative expenses, amortization, interest, taxes, dividends paid, and addition to retained earnings. We will examine how to project each value next.

The Sales Projection.

At the top of our *pro forma* statement of income and retained earnings for 2005 (shown in Figure 6-3a), we need a figure for sales. Assume that our analysis of marketing, production, finance, and management information results in a sales forecast of $221,907. Enter this figure in the "Forecast for 2005" column of Figure 6-3a, as shown:

	Forecast for 2005
Net Sales	$221,907

Cost of Goods Sold (COGS) and Selling and Marketing Expenses.

After sales, the next two items are cost of goods sold (COGS) and selling and marketing expenses. We do not have a management target or budget figure for these expenses, so we will forecast them based on past experience. For Esoteric Enterprises, experience suggests that over time both these items have remained a constant percentage of sales. That is, over the years, COGS has been about 53 percent of sales and selling and marketing expenses have been about 16 percent of sales. So we conclude that in 2005, these items will be 53 percent and 16 percent of sales, respectively, shown as follows:

	Forecast for 2005
Cost of Goods Sold	$221,907 × 0.53 = $117,611
Selling and Marketing Expenses	$221,907 × 0.16 = $ 35,505

General and Administrative Expenses.

General and administrative expenses are closely related to the size of Esoteric's manufacturing plant. For our 2005 forecast, we assume that Esoteric's property, plant, and equipment will not change. This means that our projected value for general and administrative expenses is $10,837, the same value as in the previous year:

	Forecast for 2005
General and Administrative Expenses	$10,837

Take Note

For simplicity, we use the straight-line amortization method instead of the double declining method to determine amortization expense for 2005. As a result, we obtain a constant amortization expense value as long as no equipment is replaced.

Amortization Expense.

For our amortization expenses forecast, let us say that Esoteric Enterprises' capital budget does not include the purchase of any additional property, plant, or equipment, and that no equipment is near the end of its projected useful life. The projected amortization expense, then, will be $4,500, the same value as it was for 2004.

	Forecast for 2005
Amortization Expense	$4,500

Interest Expense.

The amount of interest to be paid in 2005 depends on the amount of debt outstanding in that year. That has not been determined yet because it is part of the balance sheet forecast. At this point, we have no information indicating new debt will be obtained or old debt paid off, so we will project that interest expense in 2005 will be $2,971, the same as its 2004 value.

	Forecast for 2005
Interest Expense	$2,971

As we see in Figure 6-4, Esoteric's before-tax income is expected to be $50,483.

	Forecast for 2005
Net Sales	$221,907
Cost of Goods Sold	117,611
Gross Profit	104,296
Operating Expenses	
Selling and Marketing Expenses	35,505
General and Administrative Expenses	10,837
Amortization	4,500
Operating Income	53,454
Interest Expense	2,971
Before-Tax Income	50,483
Income Taxes (tax rate = 40%)	20,193
Net Income	$ 30,290
Dividends Paid	27,261
Addition to Retained Earnings	3,029

Figure 6-4
Esoteric Enterprises *Pro Forma* Statement of Income and Retained Earnings for 2005
This figure shows Esoteric Enterprises' anticipated 2005 values for each statement of income and retained earnings line item. Each forecast value was calculated separately according to the forecasting assumptions given.

Income Taxes.

Esoteric's effective 2004 combined federal and provincial tax rate, shown in Figure 6-3a, is 40 percent. We assume no changes in the tax law for 2005, so to obtain income tax expense for 2005, multiply the 2005 before-tax income by 40 percent as follows:

	Forecast for 2005
Income Tax Expense	$50,483 × 0.40 = $20,193

Dividends Paid and Additions to Retained Earnings.

Esoteric's management plans to continue the current dividend policy of paying 90 percent of net income in dividends and retaining 10 percent in 2005. We forecast net income in 2005 as $30,290 (see Figure 6-4), so dividends paid and the addition to retained earnings will be as follows:

	Forecast for 2005
Dividends Paid	$30,290 × 0.90 = $27,261
Addition to Retained Earnings	$30,290 × 0.10 = $ 3,029

This completes our *pro forma* statement of income and retained earnings. The results are summarized in Figure 6-4. Now let's turn to the *pro forma* balance sheet.

The Pro Forma Balance Sheet Now we will create the *pro forma* balance sheet for 2005 (December 31) by examining each individual line item account. If no target value is specified by management and if no value from a budget is available, then we will evaluate the item's past performance and estimate its future value based on experience, probability, or correlation.

Cash and Marketable Securities.

The forecast value for cash and marketable securities is normally drawn from the company's *cash budget* as discussed earlier. Let's assume that financial managers at Esoteric have prepared a cash budget that predicts the amount of cash on hand at the end of 2005 as $71,853.

Accounts Receivable and Inventory.

Experience has shown that the accounts receivable and inventory accounts tend to remain the same percentage of sales, similar to the cost of goods sold and selling and marketing expenses on the income statement. In the past, accounts receivable has been 6 percent of sales and inventory has been 11 percent of sales. Therefore, we will assume that these items will be 6 percent and 11 percent of 2005 sales, respectively, at the end of 2005:

	Forecast for 2005 *12/31/05*
Accounts Receivable	$221,907 × 0.06 = $13,314
Inventory	$221,907 × 0.11 = $24,410

Property, Plant, and Equipment.

Esoteric's capital budget does not include any provision for purchasing production equipment, buildings, or land. In our statement of income and retained earnings forecast, we assumed that in 2005 Esoteric Enterprises will not need any additional equipment, no equipment will be disposed of, and no equipment will reach the end of its useful life. Property, plant, and equipment gross at the end of 2005, then, will be the same as its end of 2004 value of $133,369. Property, plant, and equipment net will be the 2004 gross value less the additional amortization expense ($4,500) accumulated during 2005. Here are the calculations:

		Forecast for 2005 *12/31/05*
Property, Plant, and Equipment, Gross (Same as 12/31/04)		$133,369
Less Accumulated Amortization	$40,386 + $4,500 =	$44,886
[end of 2004 accumulated amortization ($40,386) plus 2005 amortization expense ($4,500)]		
Property, Plant, and Equipment, Net		$88,483

Accounts Payable.

Experience has shown that, like accounts receivable and inventory, accounts payable tends to remain the same percentage of sales. In the past, accounts payable has been about 2 percent of sales. Therefore, we will assume that accounts payable at the end of 2005 will be 2 percent of 2005 sales. Here is the calculation:

	Forecast for 2005 *12/31/05*
Accounts Payable	$221,907 × 0.02 = $4,438

Notes Payable.

We assume, based on experience and management policy, that any notes outstanding at the end of a year will be paid off by the end of the following year, resulting in a zero balance in the notes payable account. Accordingly, Esoteric's notes payable value for the end of 2005 will be $0 shown as follows:

	Forecast for 2005 *12/31/05*
Notes Payable	$0

Long-Term Debt.

We will assume that no principal payments on Esoteric's long-term debt are due in 2006 and no new debt financing arrangements have been made yet. Therefore, the long-term debt value at the end of 2005 will be the same as the end of 2004 value, $37,142.

	Forecast for 2005 *12/31/05*
Long-Term Debt (same as 2004 value)	$37,142

Common Shares.

Esoteric's management has no plans to issue or to buy back shares in 2005. The common share equity, then, will remain the same at the end of 2005 as it was at the end of 2004, $35,000. The forecast follows:

	Forecast for 2005 *12/31/05*
Common Shares (same as 2004 value)	$35,000

Retained Earnings.

As discussed in Chapter 4, the retained earnings account represents the sum of all net income not paid out in the form of dividends to shareholders.[2]

At the end of 2005, the retained earnings value will be the total of the end of 2004 figure ($115,607) plus the 2005 addition to retained earnings ($3,029), as shown on the statement of income and retained earnings forecast.

	Forecast for 2005 *12/31/05*
Retained Earnings	$115,607 + $3,029 = $118,636

This completes our *pro forma* balance sheet. Figure 6-5 summarizes the results.

Now both our *pro forma* financial statements for Esoteric Enterprises are complete. Figures 6-6a and 6-6b on pages 172–173 contain the complete 2005

[2]Esoteric has no preferred shares and, therefore, no preferred share dividends paid. This means that its net income is the same as its earnings available to common shareholders, which was discussed in Chapters 4 and 5.

Figure 6-5
Esoteric Enterprises *Pro Forma* Balance Sheet for December 31, 2005
This figure shows Esoteric Enterprises' projected end of 2005 values for each balance sheet line item. Each forecasted value was calculated separately by assessing management goals, budget figures, or past trends.

	Forecast for 12/31/05
Assets	
Current Assets	
Cash and Marketable Securities	$ 71,853
Accounts Receivable	13,314
Inventory	24,410
Total Current Assets	109,577
Property, Plant, and Equipment, Gross	133,369
Less Accumulated Amortization	(44,886)
Property, Plant, and Equipment, Net	88,483
Total Assets	$198,060
Liabilities and Equity	
Current Liabilities	
Accounts Payable	$ 4,438
Notes Payable	0
Total Current Liabilities	4,438
Long-Term Debt	37,142
Total Liabilities	41,580
Common Shares	35,000
Retained Earnings	118,636
Total Shareholders' Equity	153,636
Total Liabilities and Equity	$195,216

forecast, including source notes explaining the reasons for each forecasted item's value.

Additional Funds Needed When the *pro forma* balance sheet is completed, total assets and total liabilities and equity will rarely match. Our forecast in Figure 6-6b on page 173 in which total assets are forecast to be $198,060, but total liabilities and equity are forecast to be only $195,216 is typical. The discrepancy between forecasted assets and forecasted liabilities and equity ($2,844 in our example) results when either too little or too much financing is projected for the amount of asset growth expected. The discrepancy is called **additional funds needed** (AFN) when forecasted assets exceed forecasted liabilities and equity. It is called **excess financing** when forecasted liabilities and equity exceed forecasted assets. Our forecast indicates that $2,844 of additional funds are needed to support Esoteric's needed asset growth.

The determination of additional funds needed is one of the most important reasons for producing *pro forma* financial statements. Armed with the knowledge of how much additional external funding is needed, financial managers can make the necessary financing arrangements in the financial markets before a crisis occurs. Esoteric only needs a small amount, $2,844, so the company would probably obtain the funds from a line of credit with its bank. When large amounts are required, other funding sources include a new bond or share issue.

A Note on Interest Expense.
According to Esoteric's *pro forma* financial statements, the company needs \$2,844 of new external financing in 2005. If it borrows the money (as we implied it would), then Esoteric will incur new interest charges that were not included in the original *pro forma* statement of income and retained earnings. To be accurate, forecasters should revise the *pro forma* statement of income and retained earnings to include the new interest. However, if they make the

INANCE AT WORK 6-1

ales Retail Sports Media Technology Public Relations Production Exports

INANCIAL FORECASTING

'ery company has planned business activities to some gree—even if the plan is not committed to paper. However, tting it down in black and white formalizes the process and stills a discipline upon the corporation; it forces action and volvement at all levels of the company.

Preparing a financial forecast represents a unique oppor-nity for a company: the process articulates the vision of all vels of management, and adds real-world input from nkers, accountants, and outside advisors. A well-prepared recast reflects your views, tempers it with reality, and tells u where you're going and how to get there.

The financial plan ties the whole thing together. Here u're looking at forecasted monthly balance sheets, depart-ental operating statements, overhead schedules, income atements, monthly cash flows, working capital, and available nk credit. Supporting your financial plan should be details d commentary for sales, expenses and capital costs.

etting Started: Looking Down the Road

ne strategic plan for the company is the starting point in any dgeting process. Where is the company headed during the xt five years? Where are the markets? The growth opportu-ies? What products will be in demand? What do you want to complish between now and then? This exercise involves cre-ve thinking, but not wishful thinking—the long-range objec-e must be realistic. They serve as the foundation for the mpany's shorter range annual planning.

Long-range goals, once set, should be reviewed and stated annually. What are the new factors to consider? What ppened during the last year? What are the new opportuni-s and threats the company should be considering?

The next step in the planning exercise follows hard on the els of long-range goal setting: An assessment of the com-ny's current strengths and weaknesses. What are the things e company does well, and what are the areas that need provement? There is little point in building a plan on a weak ındation; weaknesses should be identified and corrective tion implemented. Some hard decisions may be required.

In addition to software, your budget toolkit involves a process to review and update your progress. The reviews should take the form of quarterly meetings and include submissions from each manager comparing the actuals with the budget to date and a recast for the remainder of the year, along with a full year variance.

Presenting the Package

Whichever route you take, here is what bankers and boards of directors are looking for in your forecast:

- Include a narrative description of last year's performance along with a narrative description for the coming year. Ensure there is consistency between dollars and descriptions.
- Narrate the changes in your financial position. A financial statement to this effect should be included.
- Avoid pie-in-the-sky forecasts. Any knowledgeable person will spot undue optimism, particularly when opening and closing balance sheets are compared.
- Make sure your numbers are attainable. Budget failures don't sit well with stakeholders. It can make your advisors look foolish for approving and accepting the numbers.
- Present a full set of financial statements including the balance sheet and cash flows. Include a ratio analysis. Presenting only the income statement won't cut it.
- If five-year forecasts are presented, include a summary comparing annual balance sheets, income statements, overhead schedules, cash flows and ratios. Have the supporting details available for scrutiny.
- Be prepared to make revised submissions promptly.

When the presentation is over and the approvals are in place, the financial plan will serve as a reminder of the direction your company has chosen to take. The package will allow you to adapt quickly to changes and take advantage of opportunities.

FINANCE AT WORK 6-2

Sales Retail Sports Media Technology Public Relations Production Exports

FINANCIAL FORECASTING—A COMPLICATED PROCESS

As we mentioned, preparing financial projections is a highly personalized process. Even though the two sides of the balance sheet have to agree at the end of the forecasting process, there are various ways of preparing a full set of forecasted financial statements.

We spoke to Mrs. Andrea Messier, a top employee in a leading Montreal consulting firm, and asked her about the process of preparing financial forecasts. Mrs. Messier's firm advises private and public companies in the areas of finance, corporate strategy, and distribution. She is responsible for converting the company's strategy into financial forecasts and has been doing this successfully for the last fifteen years. Her approach is summarized as follows. It certainly outlines the point that financial forecasting could be a complicated process.

Income Statement Forecasting

We initially look at the top line, sales and we try to determine what the company's growth rate is likely to be. If the company has many different business units, we try to estimate the growth rates in all business units. We usually try to focus on two or three drivers of revenue (i.e., a number of customers in the company's target market—the price the company can charge) and try to be precise in our estimations. We generally focus on the major areas or assumptions rather than trying to focus on every possible "revenue driver" and we compare the company's revenue growth rates with those projected for the entire market.

In terms of estimating cost, we usually determine whether specific costs are variable or fixed. For example, if the cost of goods sold, which are generally *variable costs*, were historically equal to 45 percent of sales, we assume that these costs are likely to continue at this level as a percentage of sales. Then, we speak to the company's management to determine whether management estimates an improvement or deterioration in this area. Whatever the answer is, we question management to provide appropriate explanations. We either accept or reject their explanations. We also discuss fixed costs. For example, administrative costs can generally be treated as fixed and not changing with the level of sales. However, management knows when they will need to hire extra senior management to deal with business expansion. We then make certain assumptions and focus on the timing of these new cost items. In this way, we proceed to discuss other cost items.

There are some items on the income statement that we would not be able to project immediately because they are connected with other decisions. These items are amortization expense and interest expense. The amortization expense relates to the level of capital expenditures the managem plans and the interest expense relates to the amount of d the company undertakes. While we can project the desired needed level of capital expenditure for the company and level of sales associated with capital expenditure, project the level of debt is more difficult. We generally wait with decision on debt financing once a cash flow and a balar sheet have been built to determine the necessary level external financing (whether debt or equity) and a managea level of leverage. Nevertheless, for the sake of having a sta ing point, we assume a level of debt similar to the debt le the company has had in the past. We would adjust the int est expense line as the cash flow is built and the level of ext nal financing is known with more precision.

Cash Flow Forecasting

Once a preliminary income statement has been generated, proceed to build a cash flow statement. However, before we that, we make some assumptions about certain working ca tal items, namely the number of days in which we conv accounts receivable into cash, the number of days it takes pay our suppliers, and the number of days it takes to conv raw materials into ready products. The standard formulas the accounts receivable collection period can be manipulat to establish the year-end balance in this area once we ha assumed the appropriate number of days it takes to conv accounts receivable into cash. We proceed to find year-e balances for the level of inventory, accounts payable, a other working capital items in this manner.

Once the end balances of working capital items are ge erated, we can build the portion of the cash flow statem that deals with cash from operating activities. We would kn the level of net income (from the preliminary income sta ment) and the level of amortization expense given that a p ticular level of capital expenditure has been assumed. At t point, we are also in a position to estimate the desired or o gated level of dividends that the company needs to pay (in t case of preferred share dividends). By this point in t process, the level of cash generated from operating activit is known as well as investment activities and a portion of t financing activities section. The preliminary result shows t level of financing necessary for the company so that the ye end cash balance (the cash balance from the previous y plus a net change in cash flow) is positive. If the figure is n ative, the business is out of cash, which is problematic. adjust the financing section (the composition of debt a equity financing) in such a way that the year-end cash balar is positive.

We need to remember that if our assumptions are anged with regard to the level of debt financing, the level of erest expense also needs to be changed. This, in turn, anges the level of profit before tax and profit after tax and is changes the level of cash generated by operating activi-s. Similar changes would occur if we were to change the el of capital expenditure; this would impact the level of ortization expense. The process is highly iterative until a sired result is achieved.

lance Sheet Forecasting

ce we have prepared the cash flow statement and deter-ned the level of year-end balances in major items, the ocess of putting a balance sheet together is highly mechan-l. We already know the level of year-end balance for the past ars, and also the year-beginning balances. Once the changes in certain items, as demonstrated by the cash flow, are known it is easy to figure out the year-end balance for the forecasted year. The items that require some attention are the level of accumulated amortization, which is the sum of the accumulated amortization from the previous year plus the expense in the forecasted year, and the level of retained earnings, which is the sum of the previous year's retained earnings plus the forecasted net income less dividends.

Financial forecasting is a complicated and iterative process. The most frustrating moment in financial forecasting is the situation when the balance sheet does not balance. This is usually the result of some mathematical or logistical error, but it feels satisfying when you get the balance sheet to balance.

Source: An interview with Mrs. Andrea Messier, December 2004.

revision, it will reduce 2005's net income, which, in turn, will reduce 2005's retained earnings on the balance sheet forecast. This will change the total liabilities and equity figure for 2005, throwing the balance sheet out of balance again and changing the amount of additional funds needed!

In forecasting circles, this is known as the *balancing problem.* If the forecast is done on an electronic spreadsheet, it is not difficult to recast the financial statements several times over until the additional amount of interest expense becomes negligible. In this chapter, however, to avoid repeating the forecast over and over, we will simply stay with our original interest expense figure.

When analyzing the *pro forma* statements, financial managers often see signs of emerging positive or negative conditions. If forecasters discover positive indicators, they will recommend that management continue its current plans. If forecasters see negative indicators, they will recommend corrective action.

To illustrate, let's see how Esoteric Enterprises' financial managers would analyze the company's *pro forma* financial statements and plan for the future.

Analyzing Forecasts for Financial Planning

The most important forecasting task begins after the *pro forma* financial statements are complete. At that time, financial managers must analyze the forecast to determine:

1. What current trends suggest will happen to the firm in the future
2. What effect management's current plans and budgets will have on the firm
3. What actions to take to avoid problems revealed in the *pro forma* statements

Scanning the first column in Figure 6-6a, we calculate Esoteric Enterprises' 2004 net profit margin (net income divided by sales) as follows:

$$\text{Current Net Profit Margin} = \$26{,}252/\$201{,}734 = 0.1301 \text{ or } 13.01\%$$

Using the figures from the *pro forma* forecast (see Figure 6-6a, column 2), Esoteric's forecasted net profit margin in 2005 is as follows:

Figure 6-6a
Esoteric Enterprises Statements of Income and Retained Earnings
The first column in this figure shows Esoteric Enterprises' statement of income and retained earnings for 2004. The second column shows the *pro forma* forecast for 2005. The last column contains notes on where each line item value was obtained.

	2004	Forecast for 2005	Source Notes
Net Sales	$201,734	$221,907	Sales forecast
Cost of Goods Sold	107,280	117,611	53% of sales
Gross Profit	94,454	104,296	
Operating Expenses			
Selling and Marketing Expenses	32,392	35,505	16% of sales
General and Administrative Expenses	10,837	10,837	Keep same
Amortization	4,500	4,500	Keep same
Operating Income	46,725	53,454	
Interest Expense	2,971	2,971	Keep same
Before-Tax Income	43,754	50,483	
Income Taxes (tax rate = 40%)	17,502	20,193	Same tax rate
Net Income	26,252	30,290	
Dividends Paid	23,627	27,261	Same payout policy (90%)
Addition to Retained Earnings	$2,625	$3,029	Net income – dividends paid

$$\text{Forecasted Net Profit Margin} = \$30{,}290/\$221{,}907 = 0.1365 \text{ or } 13.65\%$$

The expected increase in the net profit margin from 13.01 percent to 13.65 percent is a desirable trend, so Esoteric's financial managers will probably recommend that the business maintain its current course of action.

However, if the analysis had shown a projected decline in the net profit margin to 11 percent, the financial managers would try to determine the cause of this decline (perhaps administrative expenses are too high or asset productivity is too low). After the financial managers found the cause, they would recommend appropriate corrective action. Once the company adjusted its plans to correct the problem, the financial managers would prepare a new set of *pro forma* financial statements that reflected the changes.

We presented a brief example to illustrate the process of analyzing *pro forma* financial statements. A complete analysis would involve calculating profitability ratios, asset productivity ratios, liquidity ratios, and debt management ratios, as described in Chapter 5.

	Actual 12/31/04	Forecast 12/31/05	Source Notes
Assets			
Current Assets			
Cash and Marketable Securities	$ 65,313	$ 71,853	Cash budget
Accounts Receivable	13,035	13,314	6% of sales
Inventory	21,453	24,410	11% of sales
Total Current Assets	99,801	109,577	Capital budget
Property, Plant, and Equipment, Gross			(keep same)
Less Accumulated Amortization	(40,386)	(44,886)	2004 plus amortization expense
Property, Plant, and Equipment, Net	92,983	88,483	
Total Assets	$192,784	$198,060	
Liabilities and Equity			
Current Liabilities			
Accounts Payable	$ 4,733	$ 4,438	2% of sales
Notes Payable	302	0	Pay off
Total Current Liabilities	5,035	4,438	
Long-Term Debt	37,142	37,142	Keep same
Total Liabilities	42,177	41,580	
Common Shares (35 million shares)	35,000	35,000	Keep same
Retained Earnings	115,607	118,636	2004 end-of-year retained earnings + 2005 addition to retained earnings
Total Shareholders' Equity	150,607	153,636	
Total Liabilities and Equity	$192,784	$195,216	2005 AFN = $2,844

Figure 6-6b
Esoteric Enterprises Balance Sheets
The first column in this figure shows Esoteric Enterprises' balance sheet for December 31, 2004. The second column shows the *pro forma* forecast for December 31, 2005. The last column contains notes on where each line item value was obtained.

SUMMARY

6-1 Explain why forecasting is vital to business success.

Business planning is based on forecasts of the company's future financial performance. Without forecasting, a business cannot succeed. Incorrect forecasts can be costly—so costly, in some cases, that the mistakes lead to failure.

6-2 Describe three main approaches to the financial statement forecasting process.

Forecasting means making assumptions about what will happen in the future. The three main approaches to making these assumptions are:

- *Experience.* We assume things will happen a certain way in the future because they have happened that way in the past.
- *Probability.* We assume things will happen a certain way in the future because the laws of probability indicate that they will be so.
- *Correlation.* We assume things will happen a certain way in the future because of a high correlation between the thing we are interested in and another thing we know more about.

Financial managers use the sales forecast, a variety of budgets, and past trend information to produce financial statements for periods in the future. These projected financial statements are *pro forma* financial statements. *Pro forma* financial statements show what assets, liabilities, and equity a firm is expected to have in the future.

6-3 Explain how pro forma *(projected) financial statements are produced.*

Pro forma financial statements are based on a company's current financial statements. The forecasted value of each current financial statement line item is determined by a target specified by management, a value extracted from a budget, or an extension of a past trend. In *pro forma* financial statement preparation, no general rule can be applied universally to all line items. Instead, each item must be examined individually. If no target value is specified by management and if no value from a budget is available, then forecasters must evaluate the past performance of the account and estimate a future value based on experience, probability, or correlation.

On the *pro forma* balance sheet, the forecasted values for total assets and total liabilities and equity rarely match. When forecasted assets exceed forecasted liabilities and equity, the difference is called additional funds needed (AFN). When forecasted liabilities and equity exceed forecasted assets, the difference is called excess financing. Additional funds needed are the additional external financing required to support projected asset growth. Excess financing means that too much funding has been set aside for expected asset growth.

6-4 Explain the importance of analyzing forecasts.

Once the *pro forma* financial statements are complete, financial managers must analyze them to determine if the company should continue with its current plans (as in the case of *pro forma* statements that show a growth in revenues), or if plans need to be modified to avoid problems in the future. Financial managers analyze the *pro forma* statements by using the ratio analysis techniques described in Chapter 5.

SELF-TEST

ST-1. For the last five years, cost of goods sold (COGS) for the Heaven's Gate Corporation has averaged 60 percent of sales. This trend is expected to continue in the foreseeable future. If sales for 2005 are expected to be $2.5 million, what would be the forecast 2005 value for COGS?

ST-2. In 2004, the Ishtar Corporation had $180,000 in retained earnings. During 2005, the company expects net income to be $750,000. What will the value of retained earnings be on the company's *pro forma* balance sheet for Dec. 31, 2005 if the company continues its policy of paying 50 percent of net income in dividends?

ST-3. The Far and Away Irish Import Company's *pro forma* balance sheet for Dec. 31, 2005 indicates that total assets will be $8,420,000, but total liabilities and equity will be only $7,685,000. What should Far and Away do to resolve the discrepancy between assets and liabilities?

ST-4. Refer to the *pro forma* financial statements for Esoteric Enterprises, Figures 6-6a and 6-6b. Calculate Esoteric's return on equity (ROE) ratio for 2004 and 2005. Comment on the results.

REVIEW QUESTIONS

1. Why do businesses spend time, effort, and money to produce forecasts?
2. What is the primary assumption behind the experience approach to forecasting?

3. Describe the sales forecasting process.
4. Explain how the cash budget and the capital budget relate to *pro forma* financial statement preparation.
5. Explain how management goals are integrated into *pro forma* financial statements.
6. Explain the significance of the term *additional funds needed.*
7. What do financial managers look for when analyzing *pro forma* financial statements?
8. What action(s) should be taken if analysis of *pro forma* financial statements reveals positive trends? Negative trends?

PROBLEMS

6-1. Miniver Corporation grows flowers and sells them to retail flower shops. Mrs. Miniver has asked you to prepare a forecast of expected future sales. The following chart shows the Miniver Corporation's sales record for the last six years. Make an estimate of 2005 sales by extending the trend. Justify your estimate to Mrs. Miniver. ◀ Sales Forecasts

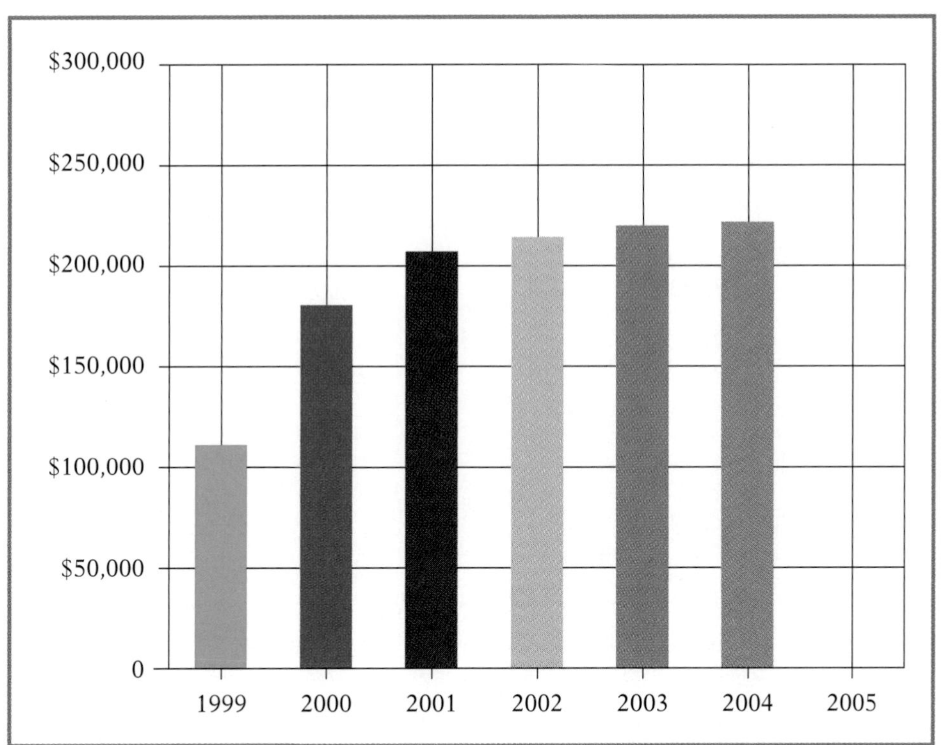

6-2. Complete the following *pro forma* financial statements. Use the forecasting assumptions in the far right-hand column. ◀ Additional Funds Needed

	This Year	Next Year	Forecasting Assumption
Sales	100	_______	Sales will grow 20%
Variable Costs	50	_______	Constant % of sales
Fixed Costs	40	_______	Remains the same
Net Income	10	_______	

Dividends	5	_______	Keep 50% payout ratio
Current Assets	60	_______	Constant % of sales
Property, Plant, & Equipment	100	_______	Remains the same
Total Assets	160	_______	
Current Liabilities	20	_______	Constant % of sales
Long-Term Debt	20	_______	Remains the same
Common Shares	20	_______	Remains the same
Retained Earnings	100	_______	
Total Liabilities and Equity	160	_______	
	AFN =	_______	

Additional Funds Needed ▶

6-3. Jolly Joe's Pizza has just come out with a new pizza that Joe is sure will cause sales to double between 2004 and 2005. Using the following worksheet, complete Joe's *pro forma* financial forecast and answer the related questions.

You may assume the COGS, current assets, and current liabilities will maintain the same percentage of sales as in 2004. Furthermore, you may assume that no new property, plant, and equipment will be needed in 2005 and the current dividend policy will be continued in 2005.

Jolly Joe's Pizza, Inc.
Financial Status and Forecast

	2004	Estimate for 2005
Sales	\$10,000	_______
COGS	4,000	_______
Gross Profit	6,000	_______
Fixed Expenses	3,000	_______
Before-Tax Profit	3,000	_______
Tax @ 33.33%	1,000	_______
Net Profit	\$ 2,000	_______
Dividends	\$0	_______
Current Assets	\$25,000	_______
Property, Plant, and Equipment, Net	15,000	_______
Total Assets	\$40,000	_______
Current Liabilities	\$17,000	_______
Long-Term Debt	3,000	_______
Common Shares	7,000	_______
Retained Earnings	13,000	_______
Total Liabilities and Equity	\$40,000	_______

Will Joe be able to get by without any additional funds needed in 2005? If not, how much will he need?

Pro Forma Statement of Income and Retained Earnings ▶

6-4. Jose Tine owns Sugar Cane Alley, a small candy shop in Aspen, Colorado. He would like to expand his business and open a second store in Vail. Mr. Tine does not have the capital to undertake this project and would like to borrow the money from the local bank. He knows that the banker will need a projected statement of income and retained earnings for his current store when considering his loan application. Net sales for 2004 were \$90,000. Considering previous growth rates in his business and the anticipated increase in tourism projected net sales for 2005 are \$110,000. Answer the questions based on the following assumptions. Cost of goods sold and selling and marketing expenses will remain the same percentage of sales as 2004. General and administration expenses will remain the same value as 2004 at $5,000. Mr. Tine uses the straight-line method of amortization, so last year's amortization expense figure of $2,000 can also be applied to 2005.

a. The 2004 cost of goods sold was $48,000. What is the forecasted value of the cost of goods sold for 2005?

b. What is the forecasted gross profit for 2005?

c. Selling and marketing expenses for 2004 were $13,000. What is the forecasted value for 2005?

d. Calculate the forecasted operating income for 2005.

e. Assume the interest expense for 2005 will be $800 and the tax rate is 30 percent. Calculate earnings before taxes (EBT) and net income expected for 2005 to the nearest dollar.

f. If $10,000 is distributed in dividends in 2005, what will be 2005's addition to retained earnings?

◀ *Pro Forma* Balance Sheet

6-5. After completing the *pro forma* income statement in problem 6-4, Mr. Tine now realizes he should also complete a *pro forma* balance sheet. Net sales in 2004 were $90,000 and his forecasted sales for 2005 are $110,000. All of Sugar Cane Alley's current assets will remain the same percentage of sales as they were in 2004. Mr. Tine does not plan to buy or sell any equipment, so his gross property, plant, and equipment amount will remain the same as 2004. In the liabilities and equity section, only accounts payable will remain the same percentage of sales as 2004. Except for retained earnings, the other accounts are expected to remain the same value as 2004. The following balances were taken from Sugar Cane Alley's end-of-2004 balance sheet:

Cash	$10,000
Accounts Receivable	2,220
Inventory	8,000
Property, Plant, and Equipment, Gross	25,000
Accumulated Amortization	4,000
Property, Plant, and Equipment, Net	21,000
Accounts Payable	1,380
Long-Term Notes Payable	8,000
Retained Earnings	5,000
Common Shares	26,840

a. Calculate the forecasted end-of-2005 values for each of the current asset accounts.

b. Amortization expense for 2005 is estimated to be $2,000. Calculate the estimated total assets for the end of 2005.

c. Forecast the accounts payable for the end of 2005.

d. What will total liabilities be at the end of 2005?

e. Assuming the forecasted net income for 2005 is $19,351 and cash dividends paid equal $10,000, what total will be forecasted for the end-of-2005 total liabilities and equity?

f. Based on these calculations of the *pro forma* balance sheet, are additional funds needed?

g. Net income for 2004 was $14,840. What was Sugar Cane Alley's net profit margin for 2004? The forecasted net income for 2005 is $19,351. What is Sugar Cane Alley's forecasted 2005 net profit margin.

Pro Forma Balance Sheet ▶

6-6.

Marsh, Inc.
Balance Sheet, Dec. 31, 2004
(Thousands of Dollars)

Assets		Liabilities	
Cash	$10,000	Accounts Payable	$10,500
Accounts Receivable	25,000	Notes Payable	10,000
Inventory	20,000	Accrued Expenses	11,000
Prepaid Expenses	2,000	Long-Term Debt	15,000
Total Current Assets	57,000	Common Shares	38,500
Property, Plant, and Equipment	32,000	Total Liabilities & Equity	85,000
Accumulated Amortization	4,000		
Total Assets	85,000		

Marsh's net sales for 2004 were $150 million. Sales growth is expected to be 25 percent in 2005 and all current asset and current liability accounts will have the same percentage of sales as in 2004. Net property, plant, and equipment will remain the same dollar amount. There is a 100 percent dividend payout ratio. Prepare a *pro forma* balance sheet for 2005.

Pro Forma Statement of Income and Retained Earnings ▶

6-7. Fill in the missing values for the 2005 *pro forma* statement of income and retained earnings. Sales will increase by 25 percent and the dividend payouts will increase from 40 percent to 55 percent. Variable costs will be 5 percentage points less than the original percentage of sales.

	2004	**2005**
Sales	1,000	____
Variable Costs	500	____
Fixed Costs	160	____
Net Income	340	____
Dividends	136	____

Pro Forma Balance Sheet ▶

6-8. The balance sheet of Free Enterprises, Inc. at the end of 2004 follows:

Free Enterprises, Inc.
Balance Sheet, Dec. 31, 2004
(Thousands of Dollars)

Assets		Liabilities + Equity	
Cash	$ 4,000	Accounts Payable	$ 4,400
Accounts Receivable	10,000	Notes Payable	4,000
Inventory	13,000	Accrued Expenses	5,000
Prepaid Expenses	400	Total Current Liabilities	13,400
Total Current Assets	27,400	Bonds Payable	6,000
Property, Plant, and Equipment	11,000	Common Equity	19,000
Total Assets	$38,400	Total Liabilities & Equity	$38,400

Net sales for 2004 were $85,000,000. The average, annual sales growth rate is expected to be 10 percent every year for the next three years. Over the past several years, the earnings before taxes (EBT) were 11 percent of net sales and are expected to remain the same over the next three years. The company's tax rate is 40 percent and it plans to maintain the dividend payout ratio (dividends paid/net income) at 60 percent.

Prepare a *pro forma* balance sheet for Free Enterprises, Inc. for December 31, 2005. Assume the accounts that are not a function of sales (property, plant, and equipment, and bonds payable) remain the same as in 2004. Current assets and current liabilities will remain the same percentage of sales as 2004. Assume the only change to common share equity is for the addition to retained earnings.

6-9. Consider the current and *pro forma* financial statements that follow: ◀ Forecasting Ratio Values

	2004	2005
Sales	200	220
Variable Costs	100	110
Fixed Costs	80	80
Net Income	20	30
Dividends	10	22
Current Assets	120	132
Property, Plant, and Equipment	200	200
Total Assets	320	332
Current Liabilities	40	44
Long-Term Debt	40	40
Common Shares	40	40
Retained Earnings	200	208
Total Liabilities and Equity	320	332
		AFN = 0

Compute the following ratios for 2004 and 2005:

Excel

	2004	2005
Current Ratio	____	____
Debt to Assets Ratio	____	____
Sales to Assets Ratio	____	____
Net Profit Margin	____	____
Return on Assets	____	____
Return on Equity	____	____

Comment on any trends revealed by your ratio analysis.

6-10. 1.Develop a *pro forma* income statement and balance sheet for the Bright Future Corporation. The company's 2004 financial statements begin on page 180. Base your forecast on the financial statements and the following assumptions: ◀ Challenge Problem

- Sales growth is predicted to be 20 percent in 2005.
- Cost of goods sold, selling and administrative expense, all current assets, accounts payable, and accrued expenses will remain the same percentage of sales as 2004.
- Amortization expense, interest expense, property, plant, and equipment, notes payable, long-term debt, and equity accounts *other than retained earnings* in 2005 will be the same as 2004.
- The company's tax rate in 2005 will be 40 percent.
- The same dollar amount of dividends will be paid to the preferred and common shareholders in 2005 as 2004.
- Bad debt allowance in 2005 will be the same percentage of accounts receivable as it was in 2004.

2. a. Calculate Bright Future's additional funds needed, or excess financing. If additional funds are needed, add them to long-term debt to bring the balance sheet into balance. If excess financing is available, increase common share dividends paid and, therefore, decrease 2005 retained earnings until the balance sheet is in balance.

b. Calculate Bright Future's current ratio for the end of 2004 and 2005.

c. Calculate Bright Future's total asset turnover and inventory turnover ratios for 2004 and 2005.

d. Calculate Bright Future's total debt to total assets ratio for 2004 and 2005.

e. Calculate Bright Future's net profit margin, return on assets, and return on equity ratios for 2004 and 2005.

3. Comment on Bright Future's liquidity, asset productivity, debt management, and profitability based on the results of your ratio analysis in (b) through (e) in problem 2.

4. What recommendations would you provide to management based on your forecast and analysis?

Bright Future Corporation
Statement of Income and Retained Earnings for 2004

Sales	$10,000,000
Cost of Goods Sold	– 4,000,000
Gross Profit	= 6,000,000
Selling and Administrative Expenses	– 800,000
Amortization Expense	– 2,000,000
Earnings Before Interest and Taxes (EBIT, or Operating Income)	= 3,200,000
Interest Expense	– 1,350,000
Earnings before Taxes (EBT)	= 1,850,000
Taxes (40%)	– 740,000
Net Income (NI)	= 1,110,000
Preferred Share Dividends Paid	– 110,000
Earnings Available to Common Shareholders	= 1,000,000
Earnings per Share (EPS) (1 million shares) = $1.00	
Common Share Dividends Paid	– 400,000
Addition to Retained Earnings	= 600,000

Bright Future Corporation
Balance Sheet Dec. 31, 2004

Assets			
Current Assets			
Cash		$ 9,000,000	
Marketable Securities		8,000,000	
Accounts Receivable, Gross	$1,200,000		
Less Allowance for Bad Debts	200,000		
Accounts Receivable, Net		1,000,000	
Inventory		20,000,000	
Prepaid Expenses		1,000,000	
Total Current Assets			$39,000,000
Property, Plant and Equipment, Gross	20,000,000		
Less Accumulated Amortization	9,000,000		
Property, Plant, and Equipment, Net		11,000,000	

Total Fixed Assets			11,000,000
Total Assets			$50,000,000
Liabilities and Equity			
Current Liabilities			
Accounts Payable	$12,000,000		
Notes Payable	5,000,000		
Accrued Expenses	3,000,000		
Total Current Liabilities		$20,000,000	
Long-Term Debt			
Bonds Payable (5%, due 2015)	20,000,000		
Total Long-Term Debt		20,000,000	
Total Liabilities			$40,000,000
Equity:			
Preferred Shares		1,000,000	
Common Shares			
(1 million shares, $1 par)		1,000,000	
Retained Earnings		8,000,000	
Total Equity			10,000,000
Total Liabilities And Equity			$50,000,000

6-11. You have been helping a friend prepare a business plan. Since he has been growing his business nicely and is in need of further financing, he needs to prepare a business plan to present to potential financiers. These potential financiers would like to receive a full set of financial projections, but you decide to start by understanding the dynamics of the income statement. You have the income statement for 2004 and interviewed your friend for additional information. Now, there is enough information to put in the following table. In addition, you have been given the following information about the company: ◀ Challenge Problem

- The annual interest payments equal 10 percent of the outstanding amount of debt at the end of each year, including Notes Payable and Long-Term Debt.
- The company uses a straight-line amortization method and amortizes property, plant, and equipment at the rate of 10 percent per annum. The beginning balance of Gross Assets for the year 2004 was equal to $76,000.
- The company pays taxes at the rate of 40 percent per annum.

Income Statement
Advent Ventures
2004

	2004
Net Sales	200,000
Cost of Goods Sold	130,000
Gross Profit	70,000
Selling and Administrative Expenses	50,000
Amortization	7,600
Operating Income (EBIT)	12,400
Interest Expense	3,200
Earnings before Taxes (EBT)	9,200
Tax	3,680
Net Income	5,520

Key Assumptions for 2005, 2006, and 2007

	2005	2006	2007
Increase in sales from previous year (in %)	20	15	10
Cost of Goods Sold as a percentage of Sales (in %)	62	61	60
Increase in S&A expense from previous year (in %)	15	10	5
Balance of Notes Payable at year end (in $)	12,000	13,000	15,000
Balance of Long-Term Debt at year end (in $)	28,000	34,000	43,000
Investments in the year (in $)	20,000	21,000	25,000

a. Develop financial projections of the income statement for the company for the years 2005, 2006, and 2007 by using the data and assumptions given.

b. Comment on the company's profitability at the gross, EBIT, and net profit margins for these years. Can you account for changes in cost that were responsible for increases or decreases of profitability at these levels?

Challenge Problem ▶ **6-12.** Given information regarding the Red Deer Cougars, respond to parts (a) and (b).

- The annual interest payments equal 5 percent of the outstanding amount of debt at the end of each year, including Notes Payable and Long-Term Debt.
- The Red Deer Cougars use a straight-line amortization method and amortize property, plant, and equipment at the rate of 10 percent per annum. The beginning balance of Gross Assets for the year 2004 was equal to $10,000.
- The Red Deer Cougars pay taxes at the rate of 40 percent per annum.

Income Statement
Red Deer Cougars
2004

	2004
Net Sales	54,000
Cost of Goods Sold	27,000
Gross Profit	27,000
Selling and Administrative Expenses	10,000
Amortization	1,000
Operating Income (EBIT)	16,000
Interest Expense	550
Earnings before Taxes (EBT)	15,450
Tax	6,180
Net Income	9,270

Key Assumptions for 2005, 2006, and 2007

	2005	2006	2007
Increase in sales from previous year (in %)	40	45	50
Cost of Goods Sold as percentage of Sales (in %)	55	60	65
Increase in S&A expense from previous year (in %)	15	10	5
Balance of Notes Payable at year end (in $)	1,000	1,000	1,000
Balance of Long-Term Debt at year end (in $)	12,000	14,000	16,000
Investments in the year (in $)	3,000	4,000	6,000

a. Develop financial projections of the income statement for the years 2005, 2006, and 2007 by using the data and assumptions given.

b. Comment on the company's profitability at the gross, EBIT, and net profit margins for these years. Can you account for changes in cost that were responsible for increases or decreases of profitability at these levels?

6-13. Given the information regarding the Ottawa Reds, respond to parts (a) and (b). ◀ Challenge Problem

- The annual interest payments equal 15 percent of the outstanding amount of debt at the end of each year, including Notes Payable and Long-Term Debt.
- Ottawa Reds uses a straight-line amortization method and amortizes property, plant and equipment at the rate of 10 percent per annum. The beginning balance of Gross Assets for the year 2004 was equal to $120,000.
- Ottawa Reds pays taxes at the rate of 35 percent per annum.
- The company has 10,000 common shares and 15,000 preferred shares. The Ottawa Reds plans to pay a dividend of $0.01 per common share and $0.05 per preferred share in the next three years.

Income Statement
Ottawa Reds
2004

	2004
Net Sales	150,000
Cost of Goods Sold	75,000
Gross Profit	75,000
S&A Expenses	10,000
Amortization	12,000
Operating Income (EBIT)	53,000
Interest Expense	2,250
Earnings before Taxes (EBT)	50,750
Tax	17,763
Net Income	32,987

Key Assumptions for 2005, 2006, 2007

	2005	2006	2007
Increase in sales from previous year (in %)	40	45	50
Cost of Goods Sold as percentage of Sales (in %)	55	60	65
Increase in S&A expense from previous year (in %)	15	10	5
Balance of Notes Payable at year end (in $)	6,000	7,000	8,000
Balance of Long-Term Debt at year end (in $)	10,000	10,000	10,000
Investments in the year (in $)	25,000	15,000	10,000

a. Develop financial projections of the statement of income and retained earnings for the years 2005, 2006, and 2007 by using the data and assumptions given. Please show the addition to retained earnings line.

b. Comment on the company's profitability at the gross, EBIT, and net profit margins for these years. Can you account for changes in cost that were responsible for increases or decreases of profitability at these levels?

6-14. You have been asked by your boss to participate in an interview with a business owner, Mr. Doer. He owns a leading video rental chain in Saskatoon, called Doer Movies. He wants to hire consultants that would advise him on his strategic decisions and prepare a full set of financial projections for 2007. Your boss has asked you to take careful notes during the discussion so that you will be able to prepare a full set of financial statements for Mr. Doer's business. Your notes include the following: ◀ Challenge Problem

- Mr. Doer estimates sales in 2007 to be equal to $18,000, but the company's gross margin will decline by 1 percentage point from the year 2006.
- Mr. Doer's selling and administrative cost will increase by 10 percent from its 2006 level. Mr. Doer does not plan any further investments in fixed assets.

- The amortization rate reflects the straight-line amortization scheme equal to 10 percent per annum.
- The annual interest payments equal 10 percent of the outstanding amount of debt at the end of each year, including Notes Payable and Long-Term Debt.
- The tax rate is equal to 40 percent.
- Mr. Doer expects to pay $238 in dividends ($150 in preferred share dividends and $88 in common share dividends).
- The ending balances of certain balance sheet items for 2007 are expected to be as follows: marketable securities – $1,000; accounts receivable – $11,000; inventory – $6,500; prepaid expenses – $200; accounts payable – $7,700; accrued expenses – $300; long-term debt – $4,000; notes payable – $4,000.
- The company is expected to raise an additional $1,750 in external financing by issuing an additional 250 common shares at $7 par share.

Income Statement
Doer Movies
2004–2006

	2004	2005	2006
Net Sales	12,000	14,000	16,000
Cost of Goods Sold	5,400	6,440	7,520
Gross Profit	6,600	7,560	8,480
Selling & Administrative Expenses	4,000	4,500	5,000
Amortization	1,300	1,500	1,700
Operating Income (EBIT)	1,300	1,560	1,780
Interest Expense	600	700	700
Earnings before Taxes (EBT)	700	860	1,080
Tax	280	344	432
Net Income	420	516	648

Balance Sheet
Doer Movies
2004–2006

	2004	2005	2006
Assets			
Cash	3,000	2,754	4,577
Marketable Securities	500	400	800
Accounts Receivable	5,000	7,000	9,500
Inventory	5,000	5,500	5,700
Prepaid Expenses	500	400	300
Property, Plant, and Equipment, Gross	13,000	15,000	17,000
Less: Accumulated Amortization	6,000	7,500	9,200
Property, Plant, and Equipment, Net	7,000	7,500	7,800
Liabilities			
Accounts Payable	4,500	4,000	7,000
Notes Payable	1,000	2,000	2,000
Accrued Expenses	500	500	450
Long-Term Debt	5,000	5,000	5,000
Shareholders' Equity			
Preferred Shares	1,500	1,500	1,500
Common Shares	7,000	8,750	10,500
Retained Earnings	1,500	1,804	2,227

a. Prepare the statement of income and retained earnings for the company for 2007. Show the value of the addition to retained earnings line.
b. Prepare the cash flow statement for 2007. (Hint: This will help you generate the cash line of the balance sheet.)
c. Prepare the balance sheet for 2007. Confirm whether the two sides of the balance sheet are equal (Assets = Liabilities + Shareholders' Equity) and the balance sheet equation is satisfied.
d. Calculate the following financial ratios for the years between 2004 and 2007 and discuss the strengths and weaknesses of the company's financial position:
   i. gross profit margin
   ii. operating profit margin
   iii. net profit margin
   iv. return on assets
   v. return on equity
   vi. current ratio
   vii. quick ratio
   viii. debt to equity ratio
   ix. times interest earned.

ANSWERS TO SELF-TEST

ST-1. If COGS is expected to remain 60 percent of sales, then in 2005, COGS will be 60 percent of 2005's sales:

$$0.60 \times \$2{,}500{,}000 = \$1{,}500{,}000$$

ST-2. If Ishtar earns $750,000 in 2005 and pays 50 percent of it to shareholders as dividends, then the other 50 percent, or $375,000, will be retained and added to the existing retained earnings account. Therefore, retained earnings on Ishtar's December 31, 2005 *pro forma* balance sheet will be:

$$\$180{,}000 + \$375{,}000 = \$555{,}000$$

ST-3. Far and Away's total liabilities and equity are forecast to be $735,000 less than total assets. This means Far and Away must arrange for $735,000 in additional financing to support expected asset growth. Possible sources of this financing include bank loans, a bond issue, a share issue, or perhaps lowering the 2005 dividend (if any).

ST-4.

$$\text{ROE} = \frac{\text{Net Income}}{\text{Common Shareholders' Equity}}$$

For Esoteric in 2004 (from the 2004 financial statements):

$$\text{ROE} = \frac{\$26{,}252}{\$150{,}607} = 0.1743, \text{ or } 17.43\%$$

For Esoteric in 2005 (from the 2005 *pro forma* financial statements):

$$\text{ROE} = \frac{\$30{,}290}{\$153{,}636} = 0.1972, \text{ or } 19.72\%$$

Note that this is a favourable forecast. The gain of over two percentage points in an already respectable ROE value should be particularly pleasing to the shareholders. Esoteric's financial managers should recommend that the company continue with its current plans, assuming that the increase in ROE does not signal an excessive increase in risk.

Take Note

Remember that risk and return go hand in hand. The financial managers at Esoteric Enterprises must evaluate the risk associated with the ROE figures before concluding that current plans will lead to desirable results.

7

Risk and Return

Chapter Objectives

After reading this chapter, you should be able to:

7-1 **Define** risk, risk aversion, and the risk-return relationship.

7-2 **Describe** how risk can be measured using the standard deviation and the coefficient of variation.

7-3 **Identify** three main types of risk that business firms encounter.

7-4 **Describe** three methods of risk reduction.

7-5 **Discuss** a major way that firms can compensate for assuming risk.

7-6 **Explain** how the capital asset pricing model (CAPM) relates risk and return.

"Believe me! The secret of reaping the greatest fruitfulness and the greatest enjoyment from life is to live dangerously!"

—Friedrich Wilhelm Nietzsche

Venture Capital Investing—A Risky Business

Venture capital can be most simply defined as risk-equity investing. It is an activity by which corporate investors support entrepreneurial ventures with finance and business skills to exploit market opportunities and, therefore, obtain long-term capital gains. The definition of venture capital has changed somewhat over the years in Western countries and even varies from firm to firm, but it is generally understood as capital provided to new ventures. *The Webster Dictionary*, a popular American English language dictionary, defined "venture" as "an undertaking involving chance, risk or danger, especially a speculative business enterprise" and "venture capital" as "money invested or available for investment in shares, especially of new or speculative enterprises." *The Gilpin Dictionary*, a dictionary of economic terms, describes "venture capital" as "financing which is subject to considerable risk."

In comparison to other types of financing, venture capital has many important features. It is equity-oriented, usually highly selective in the choice of businesses in order to minimize risk, makes a medium- to long-term commitment of finance, requires an identifiable exit route, and has some degree of active "hands-on" involvement in the management of a company receiving capital. Venture capital firms make their money from growth (selling shares in a company that has grown significantly in size and profitability since the initial investment) rather than from pre-negotiated percentage-return agreements. Venture capital is frequently subordinated to other types of financing and is not secured by the personal assets of the entrepreneur. Therefore, if the company fails, the venture capital firms may recover very little of the capital invested. The venture capital community is generally not regulated by federal authorities, unlike the securities and banking industries.

Venture capital is a big business in Canada. According to Canadian Venture Capital Association, an average of $2 billion per year is invested by venture capital funds in Canadian businesses. The majority of funds are invested in manufacturing, communications, and computer-related businesses.

Chapter Overview

Business firms face risk in nearly everything they do. Assessing risk is one of the most important tasks financial managers perform. In this chapter, we will discuss *risk, risk aversion,* and the *risk–return relationship.* We will measure risk using *standard deviation* and the *coefficient of variation.* We will identify types of risk and examine ways to reduce risk exposure or compensate for risk. Finally, we will see how the capital asset pricing model (CAPM) explains the risk–return relationship.

Risk

The world is a risky place. For instance, if you get out of bed in the morning and go to class, you run the risk of getting hit by a bus. If you stay in bed to minimize the chance of getting run over by a bus, you run the risk of getting coronary artery disease because of a lack of exercise. In everything we do—or do not do—there is a chance that something will happen that we did not expect. **Risk** is the potential for unexpected events to occur.

Risk Aversion

Most people try to avoid risks if possible. Risk aversion does not mean that some people do not enjoy risky activities such as skydiving, rock climbing, or automobile racing. In a financial setting, however, evidence shows that most people avoid risk when possible. Faced with financial alternatives that are equal except for their degree of risk, most people will choose the less risky alternative.

Risk aversion is the tendency to avoid additional risk. Risk-averse people will avoid risk if they can, unless they receive additional compensation for assuming that risk. In finance, the added compensation is a higher expected rate of return.

The Risk–Return Relationship

The relationship between risk and the required rate of return is known as the **risk–return relationship**. It is a positive relationship because the more risk assumed, the higher the required rate of return that most people will demand. It takes compensation to convince people to suffer.

Suppose, for instance, that you were offered a job in the Sahara Desert working long hours for a boss everyone describes as a tyrant. You would surely be averse to the idea of taking such a job. But think about it: Is there any way you would take this job? What if you were told that your salary would be $1 million per year? This compensation might cause you to sign up immediately. Even though there is a high probability you would hate the job, you would take that risk because of the high compensation.[1]

[1]We do not wish to suggest that people can be coaxed into doing anything they are averse to doing merely by offering them a sufficient amount of compensation. If people are asked to do something that offends their values, there may be no amount of compensation that can entice them.

Not everyone is risk averse, and among those who are, not all are equally risk averse. Some people would demand $2 million before taking the job in the Sahara Desert, whereas others would do it for a more modest salary.

People sometimes engage in very risky financial activities, such as buying lottery tickets or gambling in casinos. This suggests that they like risk and will pay to experience it. Most people, however, view these activities as entertainment rather than financial investing. The entertainment value may be the excitement of being in a casino with all sorts of people or being able to fantasize about spending the multimillion-dollar lotto jackpot. However, in the financial markets, where people invest for the future, they almost always seek to avoid risk unless they are adequately compensated.

Risk aversion explains the positive risk–return relationship. It explains why risky bonds carry a higher market interest rate than essentially risk-free Canadian Treasury bills. Hardly anyone would invest $5,000 in a risky bond if the interest rate on the risky bond were lower than that of Canadian Treasury bills having the same maturity.

MEASURING RISK

We can never avoid risk entirely. That is why businesses must make sure that the anticipated return is sufficient to justify the degree of risk assumed. To do that, however, firms must first determine how much risk is present in a given financial situation. In other words, they must be able to answer the question, "How risky is it?"

Measuring risk quantitatively is a rather tall order. We all know when something feels risky, but we do not often quantify it. In business, risk measurement focuses on the degree of **uncertainty** present in a situation—the chance, or probability, of an unexpected outcome. The greater the probability of an unexpected outcome, the greater the degree of risk.

Using Standard Deviation to Measure Risk

In statistics, *distributions* are used to describe the many values variables may have. A company's sales in future years, for example, is a variable with many possible values. So the sales forecast may be described by a distribution of the possible sales values with different probabilities attached to each value. If this distribution is symmetric, its mean—the average of a set of values—would be the expected sales value. Similarly, possible returns on any investment can be described by a *probability distribution*—usually a graph, table, or formula that specifies the probability associated with each possible return the investment may generate. The mean of the distribution is the most likely, or expected, rate of return.

The graph in Figure 7-1 shows the distributions of forecast sales for two companies, Company Calm and Company Bold. Note how the distribution for Company Calm's possible sales values is clustered closely to the mean and how the distribution of Company Bold's possible sales values is spread far above and far below the mean.

The narrowness or wideness of a distribution reflects the degree of uncertainty about the expected value of the variable in question (sales, in our example). The distributions in Figure 7-1 show, for instance, that although the most probable value of sales for both companies is $1,000, sales for Company Calm

Figure 7-1
Sales Forecast Distributions for Companies Calm and Bold
This graph illustrates possible future sales distributions for two companies. Calm has a relatively "tight" distribution and Bold has a relatively "wide" distribution. Note that sales for Company Bold has many more possible values than sales for Company Calm.[2]

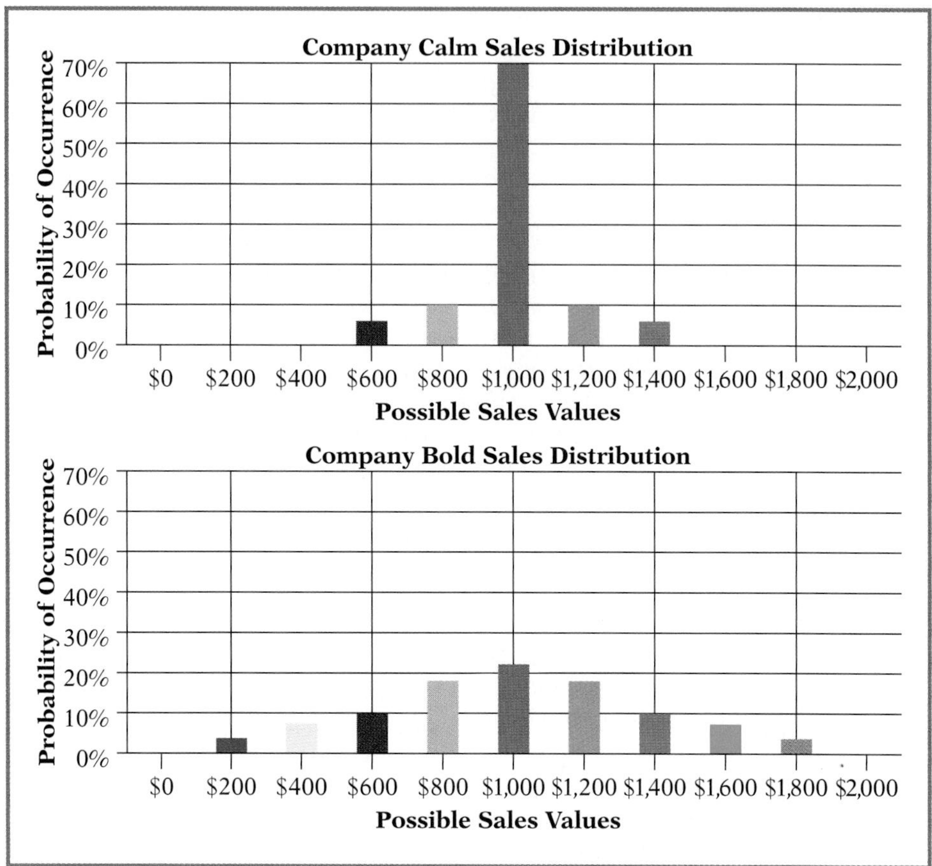

could vary between $600 and $1,400, whereas sales for Company Bold could vary between $200 and $1,800. Company Bold's relatively wide variations show that there is more uncertainty about its sales forecast than about Company Calm's sales forecast.

One way to measure risk is to compute the standard deviation of a variable's distribution of possible values. The **standard deviation** is a numerical indicator of how widely dispersed the possible values are around a mean. The more widely dispersed a distribution is, the larger the standard deviation, and the greater the probability that the value of a variable will be greatly different than the expected value. The standard deviation, then, indicates the likelihood that an outcome different from what is expected will occur.

Let's calculate the standard deviations of the sales forecast distributions for Companies Calm and Bold to illustrate how the standard deviation can measure the degree of uncertainty, or risk, that is present.

Calculating the Standard Deviation To calculate the standard deviation of the distribution of Company Calm's possible sales, we must first find the expected value, or mean, of the distribution using the following formula:

[2]These two distributions are *discrete*. If sales could take on any value within a given range, the distribution would be *continuous* and would be depicted by a curved line.

Formula for Expected Value or Mean (μ)

$$\mu = \Sigma\,(V \times P) \tag{7-1}$$

where μ = the expected value, or mean
Σ = the sum of
V = the possible value for some variable
P = the probability of the value V occurring

Applying Equation 7-1, we can calculate the expected value, or mean, of Company Calm's forecasted sales. The following values for *V* and *P* in Table 7-1 are taken from Figure 7-1:

Table 7-1 Calculating the Mean (μ) of Company Calm's Possible Future Sales Distribution

Possible Sales Value (V)	Probability of Occurrence (P)	V × P
$600	0.05	30
$800	0.10	80
$1,000	0.70	700
$1,200	0.10	120
$1,400	0.05	70
	Σ = 1.00	Σ = 1,000 = μ

Each possible sales value is multiplied by its respective probability. The probability values, taken from Figure 7-1, may be based on trends, industry ratios, experience, or other information sources. We add together the products of each value times its probability to find the mean of the possible sales distribution.

We now know that the mean of Company Calm's sales forecast distribution is $1,000. We are ready to calculate the standard deviation of the distribution using the following formula:

The Standard Deviation (σ) Formula

$$\sigma = \sqrt{\Sigma\, P(V - \mu)^2} \tag{7-2}$$

where σ = the standard deviation
Σ = the sum of
P = the probability of the value V occurring
V = the possible value for a variable
μ = the expected value

To calculate the standard deviation of Company Calm's sales distribution, we subtract the mean from each possible sales value, square that difference, and then multiply by the probability of that sales outcome. These differences squared, times their respective probabilities, are then added together and the square root of this number is taken. The result is the standard deviation of the distribution of possible sales values.

This standard deviation result, 155, shown in Table 7-2, serves as the measure of the degree of risk present in Company Calm's sales forecast distribution.

Table 7-2 Calculating the Standard Deviation (σ) of Company Calm's Possible Future Sales Distribution

Possible Sales Value (V)	Probability of Occurrence (P)	V − μ	(V − μ)²	P(V − μ)²
$600	0.05	– 400	160,000	8,000
$800	0.10	–200	40,000	4,000
$1,000	0.70	0	0	0
$1,200	0.10	200	40,000	4,000
$1,400	0.05	400	160,000	8,000
				Σ = 24,000
				$\sqrt{24,000} = 155 = \sigma$

Take Note

In the following procedure, we combine two steps: (1) finding the mean of the distribution with Equation 7-1; and (2) calculating the standard deviation with Equation 7-2.

Let's calculate the standard deviation of Company Bold's sales forecast distribution.

As you can see in Table 7-3, Company Bold's standard deviation of 385 is over twice that of Company Calm. This reflects the greater degree of risk in Company Bold's sales forecast.

Table 7-3 Mean (μ) and Standard Deviation (σ) of Company Bold's Possible Future Sales Distribution

Possible Sales Value (V)	Probability of Occurrence (P)	Mean calculation V × P	V − μ	(V − μ)²	P(V − μ)²
$200	0.04	8	–800	640,000	25,600
$400	0.07	28	–600	360,000	25,200
$600	0.10	60	–400	160,000	16,000
$800	0.18	144	–200	40,000	7,200
$1,000	0.22	220	0	0	0
$1,200	0.18	216	200	40,000	7,200
$1,400	0.10	140	400	160,000	16,000
$1,600	0.07	112	600	360,000	25,200
$1,800	0.04	72	800	640,000	25,600
		Σ = 1,000 = μ			Σ = 148,000
					$\sqrt{148,000} = 385 = \sigma$

Interpreting the Standard Deviation Estimates of a company's possible sales or a proposed project's future possible cash flows can generally be thought of in terms of a *normal* probability distribution. The normal distribution is a special type of distribution. It allows us to make statements about how likely it is that the variable in question will be within a certain range of the distribution.

Figure 7-2 shows a normal distribution of possible returns on an asset. The vertical axis measures probability density for this continuous distribution

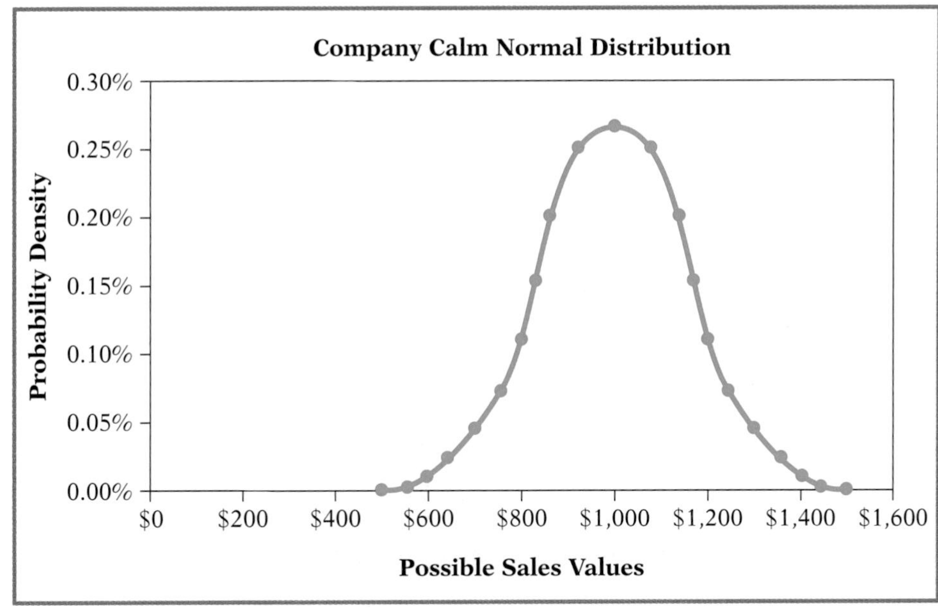

Figure 7-2
Normal Distribution
This normal probability distribution of possible returns has a mean, the expected value of $1,000.

so that the area under the curve always sums to one. Statistics tells us that when a distribution is normal, there is about a 67 percent chance that the observed value will be within one standard deviation of the mean. In the case of Company Calm, if sales were normally distributed, there would be a 67 percent probability that the actual sales will be $1,000 plus or minus $155 (between $845 and $1,155). For Company Bold, it means that if sales were normally distributed, there would be a 67 percent probability that sales will be $1,000 plus or minus $385 (between $615 and $1,385).

Another characteristic of the normal distribution is that approximately 95 percent of the time, values observed will be within two standard deviations of the mean. For Company Calm, this means that there would be a 95 percent probability that sales will be $1,000 plus or minus $155 × 2 or $310 (between $690 and $1,310). For Company Bold, it means that sales will be $1,000 plus or minus $385 × 2 or $770 (between $230 and $1,770). These relationships are shown graphically in Figure 7-3, on page 194.

The greater the standard deviation value, the greater the uncertainty about what the actual value of the variable in question will be. The greater the value of the standard deviation, the greater the possible deviations from the mean.

Using the Coefficient of Variation to Measure Risk

Whenever we want to compare the risk of investments that have different means, we use the *coefficient of variation*. We were safe in using the standard deviation to compare the riskiness of Company Calm's possible future sales distribution with that of Company Bold because the mean of the two distributions was the same ($1,000). Imagine, however, that Company Calm's sales were 10 times that of Company Bold. If that was the case and all other factors remained the same, then the standard deviation of Company Calm's possible future sales distribution would increase by a factor of 10 to $1,550. Company Calm's sales would appear to be much more risky than Company Bold's, in which the standard deviation was only $385.

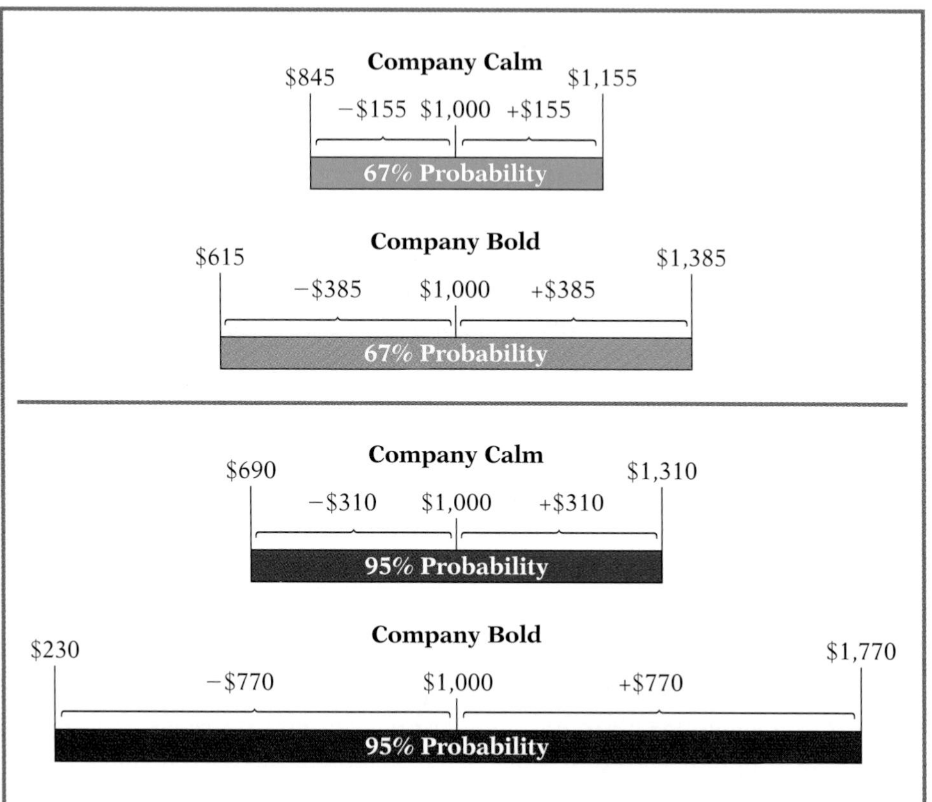

Figure 7-3 The Degree of Risk Present in Company Calm's and Company Bold's Possible Future Sales Values as Measured by Standard Deviation
The standard deviation shows there is much more risk present in Company Bold's sales probability distribution than in Company Calm's. If the distributions are normal, then there is a 67% probability that Company Calm's sales will be between $845 and $1,155 and a 95% probability that those sales will be between $690 and $1,310. For Company Bold, there is a 67% probability that sales will be between $615 and $1,385 and a 95% probability that sales will be between $230 and $1,770.

To compare the degree of risk among distributions of different sizes, we should use a statistic that measures *relative* riskiness. The **coefficient of variation** (CV) measures relative risk by relating the standard deviation to the mean. The formula follows:

Coefficient of Variation (CV)

$$CV = \frac{\text{Standard Deviation}}{\text{Mean}} \tag{7-3}$$

The coefficient of variation represents the standard deviation's percentage of the mean. It provides a standardized measure of the degree of risk that can be used to compare alternatives.

To illustrate the use of the coefficient of variation, let's compare the relative risk depicted in Company Calm's and Company Bold's possible sales distributions. When we plug the figures into Equation 7-3, we see:

$$\text{Company Calm } CV_{sales} = \frac{\text{Standard Deviation}}{\text{Mean}} = \frac{155}{1{,}000} = 0.155, \text{ or } 15.5\%$$

$$\text{Company Bold } CV_{sales} = \frac{\text{Standard Deviation}}{\text{Mean}} = \frac{385}{1{,}000} = 0.385, \text{ or } 38.5\%$$

Company Bold's coefficient of variation of possible sales (38.5 percent) is more than twice that of Company Calm (15.5 percent). Furthermore, even if Company Calm were 10 times the size of Company Bold—with a mean of its possible future sales of \$10,000 and with a standard deviation of \$1,550—it would not change the coefficient of variation. This would remain 1,550/10,000 = 0.155, or 15.5 percent. We use the coefficient of variation instead of the standard deviation to *compare* distributions that have means with different values because the CV adjusts for the difference, whereas the standard deviation does not.

The Types of Risks Firms Encounter

Risk refers to uncertainty—the chance that what you expect to happen *will not* happen. The forms of risk that businesses most often encounter are *business risk, financial risk,* and *portfolio risk.*

Business Risk

Business risk refers to the uncertainty a company has with regard to its operating income (also known as earnings before interest and taxes, or EBIT). The more uncertainty about a company's expected operating income, the more business risk the company has. For example, if we assume that grocery prices remain constant, the only grocery store in a small town probably has little business risk—the store owners can reliably predict how much their customers will buy each month. In contrast, a gold mining firm has a lot of business risk. Because the owners have no idea when, where, or how much gold they will strike, they cannot predict how much they will earn in any period with any degree of certainty.

Measuring Business Risk The degree of uncertainty about operating income (and, therefore, the degree of business risk in the firm) depends on the volatility of operating income. If operating income is relatively constant, as in the grocery store example, then there is relatively little uncertainty associated with it. If operating income can take on many different values, as is the case with the gold mining firm, then there is a lot of uncertainty about it.

We can measure the variability of a company's operating income by calculating the standard deviation of the operating income forecast. A small standard deviation indicates little variability and, therefore, little uncertainty. A large standard deviation indicates a lot of variability and great uncertainty.

Some companies are large and others small. So to make comparisons among different firms, we must measure the risk by calculating the coefficient of variation of possible operating income values. The higher the coefficient of variation of possible operating income values, the greater the business risk of the firm.

Table 7-4 shows the expected value (μ), standard deviation (σ), and coefficient of variation (CV) of operating income for Company Calm and Company Bold, assuming that the expenses of both companies vary directly with sales (i.e., neither company has any fixed expenses).

This table shows the comparison of the standard deviation and coefficient of variation of possible operating income values for Company Calm (top) and Company Bold (bottom) *when all expenses are variable***.** The table indicates Company Bold's operating income is more than twice as volatile as the operating income of Company Calm.

Table 7-4 Expected Value (μ), Standard Deviation (σ), and Coefficient of Variation (CV) of Possible Operating Income Values for Companies Calm and Bold, Assuming All Expenses Are Variable

Company Calm

	Probability of Occurrence				
	5%	**10%**	**70%**	**10%**	**5%**
Sales	$600	$800	$1,000	$1,200	$1,400
Variable Expenses	516	688	860	1,032	1,204
Operating Income	84	112	140	168	196

μ of Possible Operating Income Values per Equation 7-1: $140

σ of Possible Operating Income Values per Equation 7-2: $21.69

CV of Possible Operating Income Values per Equation 7-3: 15.5%

Company Bold

	Probability of Occurrence								
	4%	**7%**	**10%**	**18%**	**22%**	**18%**	**10%**	**7%**	**4%**
Sales	$200	$400	$600	$800	$1,000	$1,200	$1,400	$1,600	$1,800
Variable Expenses	172	344	516	688	860	1,032	1,204	1,376	1,548
Operating Income	28	56	84	112	140	168	196	224	252

μ of Possible Operating Income Values per Equation 7-1: $140

σ of Possible Operating Income Values per Equation 7-2: $53.86

CV of Possible Operating Income Values per Equation 7-3: 38.5%

The Influence of Sales Volatility Sales volatility affects business risk—the more volatile a company's sales, the more business risk the firm has. Indeed, when no fixed costs are present—as in the case of Company Calm and Company Bold—sales volatility is equivalent to operating income volatility. Table 7-4 shows that the coefficients of variation of Company Calm's and Company Bold's operating income are 15.5 percent and 38.5 percent, respectively. Note that these coefficient numbers are exactly the same numbers as the two companies' coefficients of variation of expected sales.

The Influence of Fixed Operating Costs In Table 7-4 we assumed that all of Company Calm's and Company Bold's expenses varied proportionately with sales. We did this to illustrate how sales volatility affects operating income volatility. In the real world, of course, most companies have some fixed expenses as well, such as rent, insurance premiums, and the like. It turns out that fixed expenses magnify the effect of sales volatility on operating income volatility. In effect, fixed expenses intensify business risk. The tendency of fixed expenses to magnify business risk is called **operating leverage**. To see how this works, refer to Table 7-5, in which we assume that all of Company Calm's and Company Bold's expenses are fixed.

Table 7-5
Expected Value (μ), Standard Deviation (σ), and Coefficient of Variation (CV) of Possible Operating Income Values for Companies Calm and Bold, Assuming All Expenses Are Fixed

Company Calm

	Probability of Occurrence				
	5%	10%	70%	10%	5%
Sales	$600	$800	$1,000	$1,200	$1,400
Fixed Expenses	(860)	(860)	(860)	(860)	(860)
Operating Income	(260)	(60)	140	340	540

μ of Possible Operating Income Values per Equation 7-1: $140

σ of Possible Operating Income Values per Equation 7-2: $155

CV of Possible Operating Income Values per Equation 7-3: 110.7%

Company Bold

	Probability of Occurrence								
	4%	7%	10%	18%	22%	18%	10%	7%	4%
Sales	$200	$400	$600	$800	$1,000	$1,200	$1,400	$1,600	$1,800
Fixed Expenses	(860)	(860)	(860)	(860)	(860)	(860)	(860)	(860)	(860)
Operating Income	(660)	(460)	(260)	(60)	140	340	540	740	940

μ of Possible Operating Income Values per Equation 7-1: $140

σ of Possible Operating Income Values per Equation 7-2: $385

CV of Possible Operating Income Values per Equation 7-3: 275.0%

As Table 7-5 shows, the effect of replacing each company's variable expenses with fixed expenses increased the volatility of operating income considerably. The coefficient of variation of Company Calm's operating income jumped from 15.5 percent when all expenses were variable to over 110 percent when all expenses were fixed. When all expenses are fixed, a 15.5 percent variation in sales is magnified to a 110.7 percent variation in operating income. A similar situation exists for Company Bold.

Table 7-5 shows the comparison of the standard deviation and coefficient of variation of possible operating income values for Company Calm (top) and Company Bold (bottom) *when all expenses are fixed*. The table indicates that the volatility of both firms' operating income is increased by the presence of fixed expenses.

The greater the fixed expenses, the greater the change in operating income for a given change in sales. Capital-intensive companies, such as electric generating firms have high fixed expenses. Service companies such as consulting firms often have relatively low fixed expenses. For a description of some of the business risks related to international expansion, see the feature Finance at Work 7-1.

FINANCE AT WORK 7-1

Sales Retail Sports Media Technology Public Relations Production Exports

DOORMAKER TO THE WORLD

Think of the number of doors in your home. Not just the front door but all those doors that lead into all those rooms and enclosed spaces in the house.

In fact, go to your favourite spot in your home and there's probably a door attached to it—and the odds are four in 10 that door was manufactured by Masonite International Corp., a Canadian company Philip Orsino has built into doormaker to the world.

Mr. Orsino is Canada's Outstanding CEO of the Year, an award sponsored by The Caldwell Partners International, CTV Inc. and the *National Post.* Over the past 20 years, he has grown the Toronto-based company into the world's largest doormaker, with $2.5-billion in annual sales and customers in more than 70 countries.

Doors seem to have been his destiny. "I'll tell you a funny story," says the 49-year-old. "The person in charge of all our component manufacturing is Jim Morrison. We've worked together for years and he runs our plants all over the world."

What's more, Mr. Orsino remembers years ago watching the *Ed Sullivan Show* and the band playing was The Doors. "They were actually lowering doors behind the band [as part of the set]," he laughs. "I never realized one day I would be working at selling doors for a living."

Mr. Orsino originally got into the building products industry because he liked the fact it appealed to basic needs, namely shelter. "Doors are a product that is used on a worldwide basis, and have been used since they started building walls. As long as there have been walls, there have been doors. If people want security, they need a door," says Mr. Orsino.

In 1982, he established a private company called Century Wood Door Ltd. Seven years later, the firm merged with Premdor Inc., which had gone public three years earlier. The management of Century ran the combined company, with Mr. Orsino at the helm.

Two years ago, the company made another major leap in size. It purchased Chicago-based Masonite Corp., its largest supplier, for US$500-million. The acquisition almost doubled its assets.

From the start, Mr. Orsino saw an opportunity in concentrating solely on doors, as opposed to being a conglomerate of building products. "It allowed us to be highly focused but expand the product line."

It worked. The company focused on existing homes a specifically on building doors that changed the look of roo without much cost or hardship to consumers.

"When you think of all the homes built in 1940s, '5 '60s, '70s, '80s, all those people want to change their do because their doors are worn out or they want to change t look of the interior," he says.

That's why Masonite's competition is not just other d companies; it's other renovation projects. "I don't want you build a new deck, renovate your kitchen, put in a new carp I want you to change the doors," says Mr. Orsino.

The average home has between 20 and 30 interior do and the number is growing. "People are working from hom says Mr. Orsino, "and they want more separate rooms."

While interior doors have been the company's bread a butter, Masonite's share of the exterior door market is grow as well. It has 20% of that segment in North America. The fi is also active in the commercial sector, building doors hotels, offices and hospitals.

Today, Masonite has more than 12,000 employees wo ing in 70 facilities in 12 countries around the world. Shipp costs dictate products be made close to local markets. "It' logistical business. Doors take up a lot [of] space and can't shipped a [long] distances."

Masonite's geographic diversity means Mr. Orsino nee people on the ground around the world he can trust. And says he has them. "You develop a management team t develops the same values. We are a big company, but t company moves as a single force. And it makes a big diff ence when you can establish that type of culture."

Questions to Consider

1. *Identify the key business decisions Mr. Orsino has und taken in developing Masonite International Corp.*
2. *Rank the key business decisions in terms of their p sonal risk.*
3. *Develop a risk-return profile for these decisions.*

Source: Garry Marr, "Doormaker to the World," *National Post*, 4 November 2003. Material reprinted with the express permission o "The National Post Company," a Canwest Partnership.

External risks relate to two main external risk factors that businesses do not control, namely foreign exchange and inflation. While we are not planning to discuss the impact of these external risks on a company's financial performance in depth, they are important to mention. In reality, the company's finan-

NANCE AT WORK 7-2

les Retail Sports Media Technology Public Relations Production Exports

SKS IN PROPORTION TO OPPORTUNITIES

de with the United States is serious business for Canadian npanies. Exports to the south totalled $167.4-billion in the t half of 2003, down marginally from a year earlier, accord- to Statistics Canada. That compares with the $122.6-bil- worth of goods the United States shipped to Canada in the iod.

The business is not handled exclusively by behemoths of corporate world. More than 30,000 Canadian companies h export between $30,000 and $5-million in goods or serv- s every year, placing them firmly in the category of small to dium-sized businesses, says Team Canada Inc.

However, smaller volumes do not necessarily equate to aller risks.

Nowhere were potential pitfalls of cross-border trade re apparent than in this year's rising value of the Canadian ar, which has slashed export-related profit margins.

However, risks can be mitigated. The solution to volatile rency markets, Mr. Scott says, is to "hedge, hedge, hedge. 're better to lock in and know you're getting $1.40 with every $1 instead of taking a gamble. The banks are always betting Canadian dollar will drop," he says, referring to the process vhich a business sells U.S. currency at predetermined rates.

Opportunities to leverage the stronger loonie also should be missed, says Gavin Semple, president of Regina-based ndt Industries Ltd., which makes agricultural equipment. the dollar strengthens, we have an opportunity to source re raw materials and components in the U.S. for our man- cturing plants."

Warwick Jones, president of the Coppley Apparel Group, amilton-based manufacturer that specializes in made-to- asure suits, says it is dangerous to build a business plan ed on population alone.

"We originally made an assumption that, because of our population, the potential market in the U.S. was 10 times the size of the Canadian market. It turned out to be 5.5 [times]." U.S. buyers simply have different needs, he says. Department stores play a larger role in U.S. suit sales, whereas Coppley sells most of its wares through specialty retailers.

He warns against attempting to tackle the entire market at once. "That American market is still very large. In Canada, the market is served by five major metropolitan centres. In the U.S., you have 17. We decided we were going to target a 500-mile radius from Hamilton," he says. "The cost of doing business there was much more manageable. It was driveable if you wanted to do that."

Still, doing business further afield can increase the risks of biting into your receivables. "If your customer doesn't want to pay you down there, you have an enormous problem," Mr. Scott says. Legal action requires a U.S. lawyer and personal trips. So it is important to work out a letter of credit, or take a deposit on an order, he says. "You can't drive in front of the guy's door to yell at him."

Questions to Consider

1. *What kind of business risks are involved with exporting activities?*
2. *How can you "hedge" against these risks?*

Source: Excerpted from John G. Smith, "Risks in Proportion to Opportunities," *The Financial Post*, 20 October 2003. Material reprinted with the express permission of "The National Post Company," a Canwest Partnership.

cial statements can be influenced, either positively or negatively, by movements in exchange rates and inflation and the effects of these external factors need to be analyzed and understood.

As you perhaps already read in the article, "Risk in Proportion to Opportunities," businesses need to deal with fluctuating exchange rates. This is particularly important for exporters of products or services abroad or importers of raw materials from abroad. The exchange rate fluctuations are likely to impact receivables collection and accounts payable. As mentioned in the article, proper management of foreign exchange risk is a key factor that will determine a company's overall profitability. In many cases, a company needs to use hedging techniques in order to counter the possibly damaging effects of exchange rate fluctuations by entering into sophisticated financial contracts such as currency swaps or future or forward contracts. Read the feature Finance at Work 7-2 for a discussion of foreign exchange risk.

Inflation is another external risk factor that can distort the evaluation of the company's financial performance. Let's just imagine we did not know that a company operated in a market where inflation was equal to 15 percent. Without this knowledge, we could have interpreted that the company's sales were increasing by 15 percent perhaps due to increasing unit sales. In reality, our analysis needs to separate the increase in unit sales from an external impact of inflation.

Financial Risk

When companies borrow money, they incur interest charges that appear as fixed expenses on their income statements. (For business loans, the entire amount borrowed normally remains outstanding until the end of the term of the loan. Interest on the unpaid balance, then, is a fixed amount that is paid each year until the loan matures.) Fixed interest charges act on a firm's net income in the same way that fixed operating expenses act on operating income—they increase volatility. The additional volatility of a firm's net income caused by the fixed interest expense is called **financial risk**, or **financial leverage**.

Take Note

For simplicity, Table 7-6 assumes that neither firm pays any income taxes. Income tax is not a fixed expense, so its presence would not change the volatility of net income.

Measuring Financial Risk Financial risk is the additional volatility of net income caused by the presence of interest expense. We measure financial risk by noting the difference between the volatility of net income when there is no interest expense and when there is interest expense. To measure financial risk, we subtract the coefficient of variation of net income without interest expense from the coefficient of variation of net income with interest expense. The coefficient of variation of net income is the same as the coefficient of variation of operating income when no interest expense is present. Table 7-6 shows the calculation for Company Calm and Company Bold assuming (1) all variable operating expenses and (2) $40 in interest expense.

Table 7-6 illustrates the effect of financial risk. Compare the CVs of possible net income values in this table to those of operating income in Table 7-4. Note Company Calm's CV is increased by 6.5 percentage points and Company Bold's CV is increased by 15.5 percentage points as a result of the *presence of fixed interest expense*.

Take Note

One group of businesses that is exposed to an extreme amount of financial risk because they operate almost entirely on borrowed money are banks and other financial institutions. Banks get almost all the money they use for loans from deposits—and deposits are liabilities on the bank's balance sheet. Banks must be careful to keep their revenues stable. Otherwise, fluctuations in revenues would cause losses that would drive the banks out of business. Now you know why the government regulates financial institutions so closely!

Financial risk, which comes from borrowing money, compounds the effect of business risk and intensifies the volatility of net income. Fixed operating expenses increase the volatility of operating income and magnify business risk. In the same way, fixed financial expenses (such as interest on debt or a noncancellable lease expense) increase the volatility of net income and magnify financial risk.

Firms that have only equity financing have no financial risk because they have no debt on which to make fixed interest payments. The exception may be companies, which have preferred shares in their capital structure. Payments to preferred shareholders may be viewed as fixed. Conversely, firms that operate primarily on borrowed money are exposed to a high degree of financial risk.

Portfolio Risk

A **portfolio** is any collection of assets managed as a group. Most large firms employ their assets in a number of different investments. Together, these make up the firm's portfolio of assets. Individual investors also have portfolios containing many different shares or other investments. Firms (and individuals for

Table 7-6
Expected Value (μ), Standard Deviation (σ), and Coefficient of Variation (CV) of Possible Net Income Values for Companies Calm and Bold

Company Calm

	Probability of Occurrence				
	5%	**10%**	**70%**	**10%**	**5%**
Sales	$600	$800	$1,000	$1,200	$1,400
Variable Expenses	516	688	860	1,032	1,204
Operating Income	84	112	140	168	196
Interest Expense	40	40	40	40	40
Net Income	44	72	100	128	156

μ of Possible Net Income Values per Equation 7-1: $100

σ of Possible Net Income Values per Equation 7-2: $22

CV of Possible Net Income Values per Equation 7-3: 22.0%

Summary

CV of Possible Net Income Values When Interest Expense Is Present:	22.0%
CV of Operating Income When Interest Expense Is *Not* Present (from Table 7-4):	15.5%
Difference (financial risk):	6.5%

Company Bold

	Probability of Occurrence								
	4%	**7%**	**10%**	**18%**	**22%**	**18%**	**10%**	**7%**	**4%**
Sales	$200	$400	$600	$800	$1,000	$1,200	$1,400	$1,600	$1,800
Variable Expenses	172	344	516	688	860	1,032	1,204	1,376	1,548
Operating Income	28	56	84	112	140	168	196	224	252
Interest Expense	40	40	40	40	40	40	40	40	40
Net Income	(12)	16	44	72	100	128	156	184	212

μ of Possible Net Income Values per Equation 7-1: $100

σ of Possible Net Income Values per Equation 7-2: $54

CV of Possible Net Income Values per Equation 7-3: 54.0%

Summary

CV of Possible Net Income Values When Interest Expense Is Present:	54.0%
CV of Operating Income When Interest Expense Is *Not* Present (from Table 7-4):	38.5%
Difference (financial risk):	15.5%

that matter) are interested in portfolio returns and the uncertainty associated with them. Investors want to know how much they can expect to get back from their portfolio compared with how much they invest (the portfolio's expected return) and what the chances are that they will not get that return (the portfolio's risk).

We can easily find the expected return of a portfolio, but calculating the standard deviation of the portfolio's possible returns is a little more difficult. For example, suppose Company Cool has a portfolio that is equally divided between two assets, Asset A and Asset B. The expected returns and standard deviations of possible returns of Asset A and Asset B are as follows:

	Asset A	*Asset B*
Expected Return E(R)	10%	12%
Standard Deviation σ	2%	4%

Finding the expected return of Company Cool's portfolio is easy. We simply calculate the weighted average expected return, $E(R_p)$, of the two-asset portfolio using the following formula:

Expected Rate of Return of a Portfolio, $E(R_p)$

Composed of Two Assets, A and B

$$E(R_p) = [w_A \cdot E(R_A)] + [(w_B \cdot E(R_B)] \qquad (7\text{-}4)$$

where $E(R_p)$ = the expected rate of return of the portfolio composed of Asset A and Asset B

w_A = the weight of Asset A in the portfolio

$E(R_A)$ = the expected rate of return of Asset A

w_B = the weight of Asset B in the portfolio

$E(R_B)$ = the expected rate of return of Asset B

According to Equation 7-4, the expected rate of return of a portfolio containing 50 percent Asset A and 50 percent Asset B is

$$\begin{aligned} E(R_p) &= (0.50 \times 0.10) + (0.50 \times 0.12) \\ &= (0.05 + 0.06) \\ &= 0.11 \text{ or } 11\% \end{aligned}$$

Now let's turn to the standard deviation of possible returns of Company Cool's portfolio. Determining the standard deviation of a portfolio's possible returns requires special procedures. Why? Because gains from one asset in the portfolio may offset losses from another, lessening the overall degree of risk in the portfolio. Figure 7-4 shows how this works.

Figure 7-4 shows that even though the returns of each asset vary, the timing of the variations is such that when one asset's returns increase, the other's decrease. Therefore, the net change in the Company Cool portfolio returns is very small—nearly zero. The weighted average of the standard deviations of returns of the two individual assets, then, does not result in the standard deviation of the portfolio containing both assets. The reduction in the fluctuations of the returns of Company Cool (the combination of Assets A and B) is called the **diversification effect**.

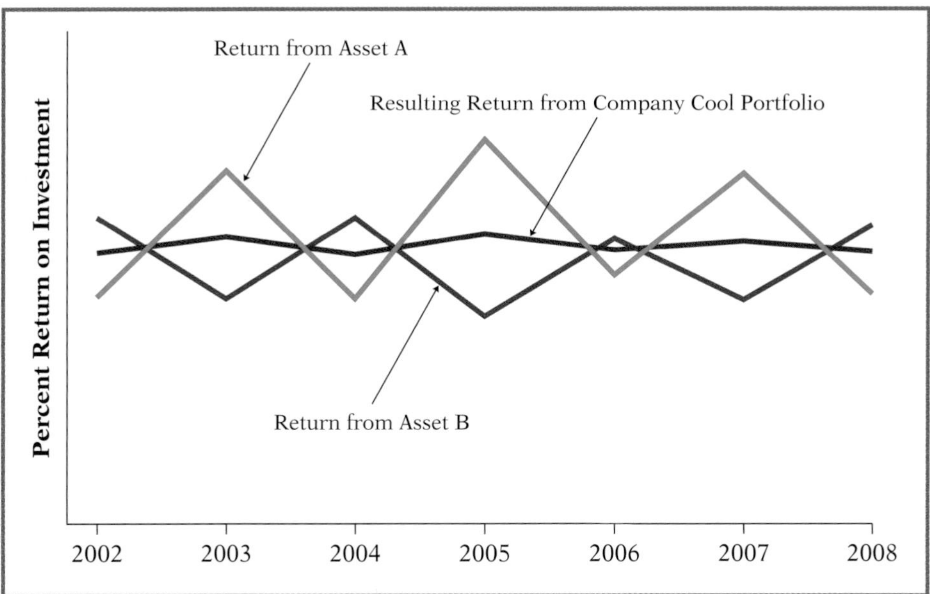

Figure 7-4 The Variation in Returns over Time for Asset A, Asset B, and the Combined Company Cool Portfolio
Figure 7-4 shows how the returns of Asset A and Asset B might vary over time. Notice that the fluctuations of each curve are such that gains in one almost completely offset losses in the other. The risk of the Company Cool portfolio is small due to the offsetting effects.

Correlation How successfully diversification reduces risk depends on the degree of correlation between the two variables in question. **Correlation** indicates the degree to which one variable is linearly related to another. Correlation is measured by the **correlation coefficient**, represented by the letter *r*. The correlation coefficient can take on values between +1.0 (perfect positive correlation) to –1.0 (perfect negative correlation). If two variables are perfectly positively correlated, it means they move together—that is, they change values proportionately in the same direction at the same time. If two variables are perfectly negatively correlated, it means that every positive change in one value is matched by a proportionate corresponding negative change in the other. In the case of Assets A and B in Figure 7-4, the assets are negatively correlated.

The closer *r* is to +1.0, the more the two variables will tend to move with each other at the same time. The closer *r* is to –1.0, the more the two variables will tend to move opposite each other at the same time. An *r* value of zero indicates that the variables' values are not related at all. This is known as *statistical independence.*

In Figure 7-4, Asset A and Asset B had perfect negative correlation ($r = -1.0$). So the risk associated with each asset was nearly eliminated by combining the two assets into one portfolio. The risk would have been completely eliminated had the standard deviations of the two assets been equal.

Calculating the Correlation Coefficient.

Determining the precise value of *r* between two variables can be extremely difficult. The process requires estimating the possible values that each variable could take and their respective probabilities, simultaneously.

We can make a rough estimate of the degree of correlation between two variables by examining the nature of the assets involved. If one asset is, for instance, a firm's existing portfolio and the other asset is a replacement piece of equipment, then the correlation between the returns of the two assets is probably close to + 1.0. Why? Because there is no influence that would cause the returns of one asset to vary any differently than those of the other. A Coca-

Take Note

Any time the correlation coefficient of the returns of two assets is less than + 1.0, then the standard deviation of the portfolio consisting of those assets will be less than the weighted average of the individual assets' standard deviations.

Cola® Bottling company expanding its capacity would be an example of a correlation of about +1.0.

What if a company planned to introduce a completely new product into a new market? In that case, we might suspect that the correlation between the returns of the existing portfolio and the new product would be something significantly less than +1.0. Why? Because the cash flows of each asset would be due to different, and probably unrelated, factors.

Calculating the Standard Deviation of a Two-Asset Portfolio To calculate the standard deviation of a portfolio, we must use a special formula that takes the diversification effect into account. Here is the formula for a portfolio containing two assets.[3] For convenience, they are labelled Asset A and Asset B:

Standard Deviation of a Two-Asset Portfolio

$$\sigma_p = \sqrt{w_a^2\sigma_a^2 + w_b^2\sigma_b^2 + 2w_a w_b r_{a,b}\sigma_a\sigma_b} \tag{7-5}$$

where σ_p = the standard deviation of the returns of the combined portfolio containing Asset A and Asset B

w_a = the weight of Asset A in the two-asset portfolio

σ_a = the standard deviation of the returns of Asset A

w_b = the weight of Asset B in the two-asset portfolio

σ_b = the standard deviation of the returns of Asset B

$r_{a,b}$ = the correlation coefficient of the returns of Asset A and Asset B

The formula may look scary, but do not panic. Once we know the values for each factor, we can solve the formula rather easily with a calculator. Let's use the formula to find the standard deviation of a portfolio composed of equal amounts invested in Asset A and Asset B (i.e., Company Cool).

To calculate the standard deviation of expected returns of the portfolio for Company Cool, we need to know that Company Cool's portfolio is composed of 50 percent Asset A ($w_a = 0.5$) and 50 percent Asset B ($w_b = 0.5$). The standard deviation of Asset A's expected returns is 2 percent ($\sigma_a = 0.02$), and the standard deviation of Asset B's expected returns is 4 percent ($\sigma_b = 0.04$). To begin, assume the correlation coefficient (*r*) is –1.0, as shown in Figure 7-4.

Now we're ready to use Equation 7-5 to calculate the standard deviation of Company Cool's returns.

$$\begin{aligned}
\sigma_p &= \sqrt{w_a^2\sigma_a^2 + w_b^2\sigma_b^2 + 2w_a w_b r_{a,b}\sigma_a\sigma_b} \\
&= \sqrt{(0.50^2)(0.02^2) + (0.50^2)(0.04^2) + (2)(0.50)(0.50)(-1.0)(0.02)(0.04)} \\
&= \sqrt{(0.25)(0.004) + (0.25)(0.0016) - 0.0004} \\
&= \sqrt{0.0001 + 0.0004 - 0.0004} \\
&= \sqrt{0.0001} \\
&= 0.01, \text{ or } 1\%
\end{aligned}$$

[3]You can adapt the formula to calculate the standard deviations of the returns of portfolios containing more than two assets, but doing so is complicated and usually unnecessary. Most of the time, you can view a firm's existing portfolio as one asset and a proposed addition to the portfolio as the second asset.

The diversification effect results in risk reduction. Why? Because we are combining two assets with returns that are negatively correlated (r = –1.0). The standard deviation of the combined portfolio is much lower than that of either of the two individual assets (1 percent for Company Cool compared with 2 percent for Asset A and 4 percent for Asset B).

Nondiversifiable Risk Unless the returns of one-half the assets in a portfolio are perfectly negatively correlated with the other half, which is extremely unlikely, some risk will remain after assets are combined into a portfolio. The degree of risk that remains is **nondiversifiable risk**, the part of a portfolio's total risk that cannot be eliminated by diversifying.

Nondiversifiable risk is one of the characteristics of market risk because it is produced by factors that are shared, to a greater or lesser degree, by most assets in the market. These factors might include inflation and real gross domestic product changes. Figure 7-5 illustrates nondiversifiable risk.

In Figure 7-5, we assumed that the portfolio begins with one asset with possible returns having a probability distribution with a standard deviation of 10 percent. However, if the portfolio is divided equally between two assets, each with possible returns having a probability distribution with a standard deviation of 10 percent, and correlation of the returns of the two assets is, say +0.25, then the standard deviation of the returns of the portfolio drops to about 8 percent. If the portfolio is divided among greater numbers of shares, the standard deviation of the portfolio will continue to fall—as long as the newly added shares have returns that are less than perfectly positively correlated with those of the existing portfolio.

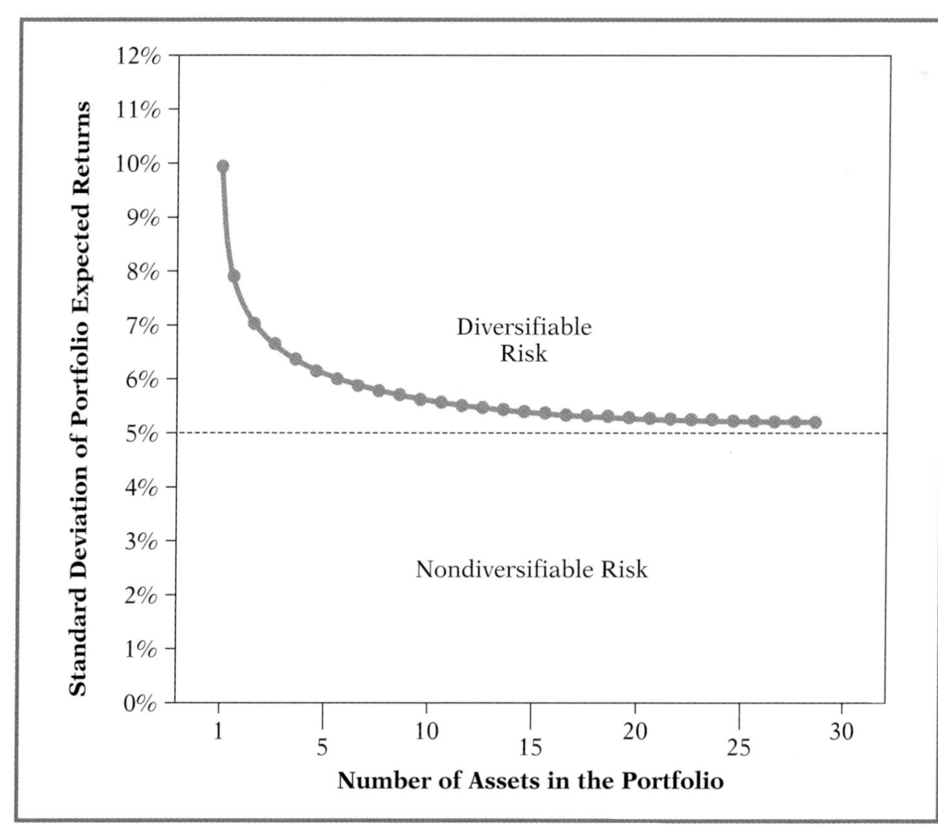

Figure 7-5 The Relationship between the Number of Assets in a Portfolio and the Riskiness of the Portfolio
The graph shows that as each new asset is added to a portfolio, the diversification effect causes the standard deviation of the portfolio to decrease. After about 20 assets have been added, however, the effect of adding further assets is slight. The remaining degree of risk is nondiversifiable risk.

Note in Figure 7-5, however, that after about 20 assets have been included in the portfolio, adding more has little effect on the portfolio's standard deviation. Almost all the risk that can be eliminated by diversifying is gone. The remainder, about 5 percent in this example, represents the portfolio's nondiversifiable risk.

Measuring Nondiversifiable Risk.

Nondiversifiable risk is measured by a term called **beta** (β). The ultimate group of diversified assets, the market, has a beta of 1.0. The betas of portfolios, and individual assets, relate their returns to those of the overall stock market. Portfolios with betas higher than 1.0 are relatively more risky than the market. Portfolios with betas less than 1.0 are relatively less risky than the market. (Risk-free portfolios have a beta of zero.) The more the return of the portfolio in question fluctuates relative to the return of the overall market, the higher the beta, as shown graphically in Figure 7-6.

Figure 7-6 shows that returns of the overall market fluctuated between about 8 percent and 12 percent during the 10 periods that were measured. By definition, the market's beta is 1.0. The returns of the average-risk portfolio fluctuated exactly the same amount, so the beta of the average-risk portfolio is also 1.0. Returns of the low-risk portfolio fluctuated between 6 percent and 8 percent, half as much as the market. So the low-risk portfolio's beta is 0.5, only half that of the market. In contrast, returns of the high-risk portfolio fluctuated between 10 percent and 16 percent, one and a half times as much as the market. As a result, the high-risk portfolio's beta is 1.5, half again as high as the market.

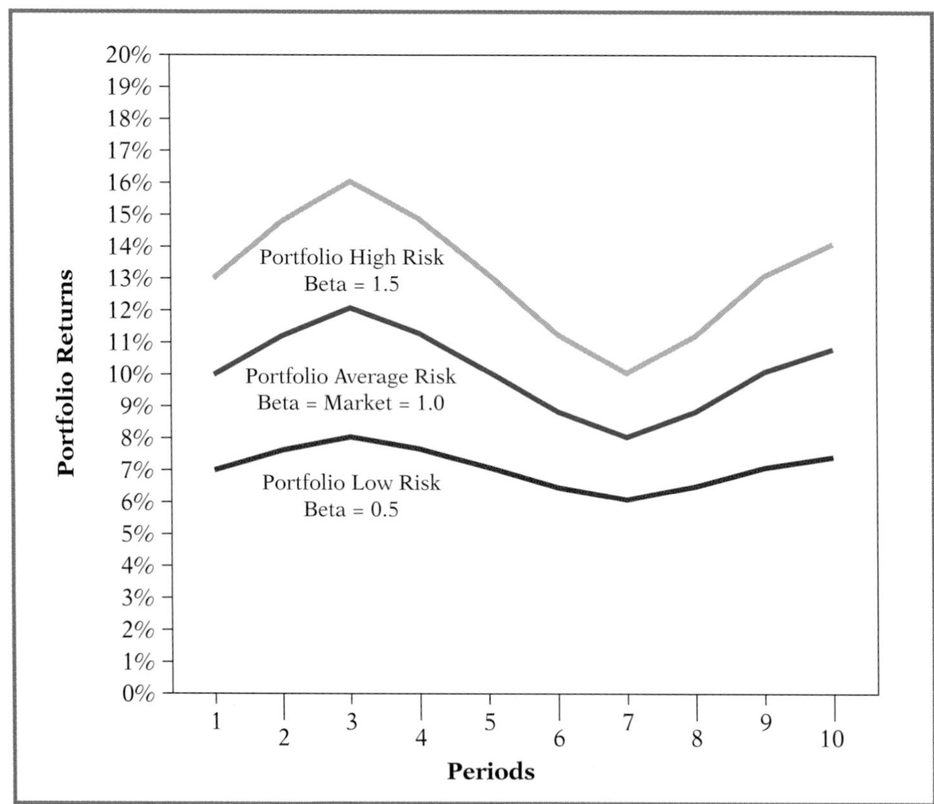

Figure 7-6
Portfolio Fluctuations and Beta
These graphs show the relative fluctuation in returns for portfolios of different betas. The higher the beta, the more the portfolio's returns fluctuate relative to the returns of the overall market. The market itself has a beta of 1.0.

Companies in low-risk, stable industries like public utilities will typically have low beta values because returns of their shares tend to be relatively stable. (When the economy goes into a recession, people generally continue to turn on their lights and use their refrigerators; and when the economy is booming, people do not splurge on additional electricity consumption.) Recreational boat companies, on the other hand, tend to have high beta values. This occurs because demand for recreational boats is volatile. (When times are tough, people postpone the purchase of recreational boats. During good economic times, when people have extra cash in their pockets, sales of these boats take off.)

Dealing with Risk

Once companies determine the degree of risk present, what do they do about it? Suppose, for example, a firm determined that if a particular project were adopted, the standard deviation of possible returns of the firm's portfolio of assets would double. So what? How should a firm deal with the situation?

There are two broad classes of alternatives for dealing with risk. First, you might take some action to reduce the degree of risk present in the situation. Second (if the degree of risk cannot be reduced), you may compensate for the degree of risk you are about to assume. We will discuss these two classes of alternatives in the following sections.

Risk-Reduction Methods

One way companies can avoid risk is simply to avoid risky situations entirely. Most of the time, however, refusing to get involved is an unsatisfactory business decision. Carried to its logical conclusion, this would mean that everyone would invest in risk-free assets only, and no products or services would be produced. Edward Rogers, founder of Rogers Communications, did not get rich by avoiding risks. To succeed, businesses must take risks.

If we assume that firms (and individuals) are willing to take some risk to achieve the higher expected returns, which accompany that risk, then the task is to reduce the degree of risk as much as possible. The following three methods help to reduce risk: reducing sales volatility and fixed costs, insurance, and diversification.

Reducing Sales Volatility and Fixed Costs Earlier in the chapter, we discussed how sales volatility and fixed costs contribute to a firm's business risk. Firms in volatile industries in which sales fluctuate widely are exposed to a high degree of business risk. That business risk is intensified even further if they have large amounts of fixed costs. Reducing the volatility of sales and the amount of fixed costs a firm pays, then, will reduce risk.

Reducing Sales Volatility.

If a firm could smooth out its sales over time, then the fluctuation of its operating income (business risk) would also be reduced. Businesses try to stabilize sales in many ways. For example, retail ski equipment stores sell tennis equipment in the summer, summer vacation resorts offer winter specials, and movie theatres offer reduced prices for early shows to encourage more patronage during slow periods.

Insurance Insurance is a time-honoured way to spread risk among many participants and thus reduce the degree of risk borne by any one participant. Business firms insure themselves against many risks such as flood, fire, and liability. However, one important risk—the risk that an investment might fail—is uninsurable. To reduce the risk of losing everything in one investment, firms turn to another risk-reduction technique, diversification.

Diversification Review Figure 7-4 and the discussion following the figure. We showed in that discussion how the standard deviation of returns of Asset A (2 percent) and Asset B (4 percent) could be reduced to 1 percent by combining the two assets into one portfolio. The diversification effect occurred because the returns of the two assets were not perfectly positively correlated. Any time firms invest in ventures in which returns are not perfectly positively correlated with the returns of their existing portfolios, they will experience diversification benefits. Read Financial Management and You 7-1 for a description of how the mutual fund industry has taken advantage of the concept of diversification.

Compensating for the Presence of Risk

In most cases it is not possible to avoid risk completely. Some risk usually remains even after firms use risk-reduction techniques. When firms assume risk to achieve an objective, they also take measures to receive compensation for assuming that risk. In the sections that follow, we discuss these compensation measures.

Take Note

In capital budgeting, a rate of return to reflect risk is called a risk-adjusted discount rate. See Chapter 10.

Adjusting the Required Rate of Return Most owners and financial managers are generally risk averse. So for a given expected rate of return, less risky investment projects are more desirable than more risky investment projects. The higher the expected rate of return, the more desirable the risky venture will appear. As we noted earlier in the chapter, the risk–return relationship is positive. That is, because of risk aversion, people demand a higher expected rate of return for taking on a higher-risk project.

Although we know that the risk–return relationship is positive, an especially difficult question remains, How much return is appropriate for a given degree of risk? Say, for example, that a firm has all assets invested in a chain of convenience stores that provides a stable return on investment of about 6 percent a year. How much more return should the firm require for investing some assets in a baseball team that may not provide steady returns[4]—8 percent? 10 percent? 25 percent? Unfortunately, no one knows for sure, but financial experts have researched the subject extensively.

Take Note

Diversification is a hotly debated issue among financial theorists. Specifically, theorists question whether a firm provides value to its shareholders if it diversifies its asset portfolio to stabilize the firm's income. Many claim that individual shareholders can achieve diversification benefits more easily and cheaply than a firm, so firms that diversify actually do a disservice to their shareholders. What do you think?

One well-known model used to calculate the required rate of return of an investment is the **capital asset pricing model (CAPM)**. We discuss CAPM next.

Relating Return and Risk—The Capital Asset Pricing Model

Financial theorists William F. Sharpe, John Lintner, and Jan Mossin worked on the risk–return relationship and developed the capital asset pricing model,

[4]Some major league baseball teams are losing money and others make a great deal. Television revenues differ greatly from team to team as do ticket sales and salary expenses.

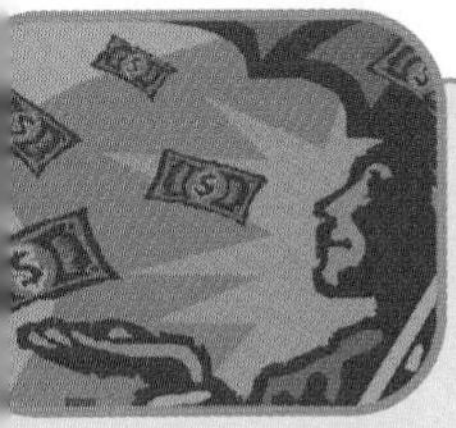

FINANCIAL MANAGEMENT AND YOU 7-1

What Is a Mutual Fund and What Are the Risks of Investing in a Mutual Fund?

nutual fund is a pool of investments made on behalf of ople with a similar investment objective. When you invest a mutual fund, your money is working together with that of ny other investors. A professional investment manager ests this money on behalf of the whole group.

Investors share a mutual fund's income, expenses, ns and losses in proportion to their interest in the mutual d. Mutual funds can give individuals the advantages of a npler, more accessible, less expensive and less time-nsuming method of investing in a portfolio of securities.

Mutual funds own different kinds of investments, pending on their objectives. These include equities like ares, fixed income securities like bonds and cash or cash uivalents like Treasury bills.

sk and Return

an investor, there is always a risk you could lose money. ıtual funds are no exception, but the degree of risk varies nsiderably from one mutual fund to the next. As a general e, investments with the greatest risk also have the great- potential return.

For example, Canada Savings Bonds are nearly risk-free cause the Government of Canada has promised to pay estors back, but they generally earn a rate of interest at e more than the rate of inflation. Shares in companies his-ically have offered the potential to provide returns signifi-ntly above the rate of inflation over the long term but are ly to be volatile. The key is to recognize the risk involved n the investment, understand it, and decide whether it is isk you are comfortable accepting.

A longer time horizon allows you to take on more short-m risk. Although the value of your investments may drop the short term, longer investment horizons will help to sen the effects of short-term market volatility. A shorter investment horizon may result in you having to sell your investments in adverse conditions. Ideally, investors in equity funds have a five- to 10-year investment horizon, which should provide enough time for their investments to over-come any short-term volatility and grow.

The following chart shows the relationship between risk and potential return. As you can see, money market funds are the least volatile and generally have the lowest returns. At the other end of the scale, international equity funds are usu-ally the most risky, but also tend to have the highest potential return. Global equity funds invest in markets around the world, combining Canadian, U.S., and international invest-ments to provide investors with geographic diversification.

Source: Excerpted from RBC Funds, *Simplified Prospectus*, July 15, 2004, pp. 3–4. Reprinted with the permission of RBC Financial Group.

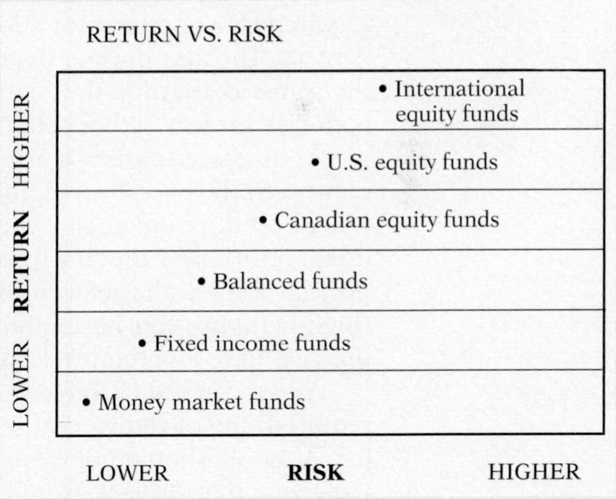

or CAPM. We can use this model to calculate the appropriate required rate of return for an investment project given its degree of risk as measured by beta (β).[5] The formula for CAPM is presented in Equation 7-6.

---

[5]Sharpe, W. (1964). Capital Asset Prices: A Theory of Market Equilibrium. *Journal of Finance*; Lintner, J. (1965). The Valuation of Risk Assets and the Selection of Risky Investments in Stock Portfolios and Capital Budgets. *Review of Economics and Statistics*; and Mossin, J. (1966). Equilibrium in a Capital Asset Market. *Econometrica*.

CAPM Formula

$$k_p = k_{RF} + (k_M - k_{RF}) \times \beta \tag{7-6}$$

where k_P = the required rate of return appropriate for the investment project
k_{RF} = the risk-free rate of return
k_M = the required rate of return on the overall market
β = the project's beta

The three components of the CAPM include the risk-free rate of return (k_{RF}), the market risk premium ($k_M - k_{RF}$), and the project's beta (β). The **risk-free rate of return (k_{RF})** is the rate of return that investors demand from a project that contains no risk. Risk-averse managers and owners will always demand at least this rate of return from any investment project.

The required rate of return on the overall market minus the risk-free rate ($k_M - k_{RF}$) represents the additional return demanded by investors for taking on the risk of investing in the market itself. The term is sometimes called the **market risk premium**. In the CAPM, the term for the market risk premium, ($k_M - k_{RF}$), can be viewed as the additional return over the risk-free rate that investors demand from an "average share" or an "average-risk" investment project. The S&P/TSX 60 stock market index is often used as a proxy for the market.

Table 7-7 shows three examples of how the CAPM is used to determine the appropriate required rate of return for projects of different degrees of risk.

Given that the risk-free rate of return is 4 percent and the required rate of return on the market is 12 percent, the CAPM indicates the appropriate required rate of return for a low-risk investment project with a beta of 0.5 is 8 percent. The appropriate required rate of return for an average-risk project is the same as that for the market, 12 percent, and the appropriate rate for a high-risk project with a beta of 1.5 is 16 percent.

As discussed earlier, a project's beta (β) represents a project's degree of risk relative to the overall stock market. In the CAPM, when the beta term is multiplied by the market risk premium term, ($k_M - k_{RF}$), the result is the additional return over the risk-free rate that investors demand from that individual project. Beta is the relevant risk measure according to the CAPM. High-risk (high-beta) projects have high required rates of return and low-risk (low-beta) projects have low required rates of return.

As we can see in Table 7-7, Project High Risk, with its beta of 1.5, has a required rate of return that is twice that of Project Low Risk, with its beta of 0.5. After all, should not we ask for a higher rate of return if the risk is higher? Note also that Project Average Risk, which has the same beta as the market, 1.0, also has the same required rate of return as the market (12 percent). The risk–return relationship for these three projects is shown in Figure 7-7.

Remember that the beta term in the CAPM reflects only the nondiversifiable risk of an asset, not its diversifiable risk. Diversifiable risk is irrelevant because the diversity of each investor's portfolio essentially eliminates (or should eliminate) that risk. (After all, most investors are well diversified. They will not demand extra return for adding a security to their portfolios that contains diversifiable risk.) The return that well-diversified investors demand when they buy a security, as measured by the CAPM and beta, relates to the degree of nondiversifiable risk in the security.

Table 7-7 Using the CAPM to Calculate Required Rates of Return for Investment Projects

Given:

The risk-free rate, $k_{RF} = 4\%$

The required rate of return on the market, $k_M = 12\%$

Project Low Risk's beta = 0.5

Project Average Risk's beta = 1.0

Project High Risk's beta = 1.5

Required rates of return on the projects per the CAPM:

Project Low Risk: $k_p = 0.04 + (0.12 - 0.04) \times 0.5$
$= 0.04 + 0.04$
$= 0.08$ or 8%

Project Average Risk: $k_p = 0.04 + (0.12 - 0.04) \times 1.0$
$= 0.04 + 0.08$
$= 0.12$ or 12%

Project High Risk: $k_p = 0.04 + (0.12 - 0.04) \times 1.5$
$= 0.04 + 0.12$
$= 0.16$ or 16%

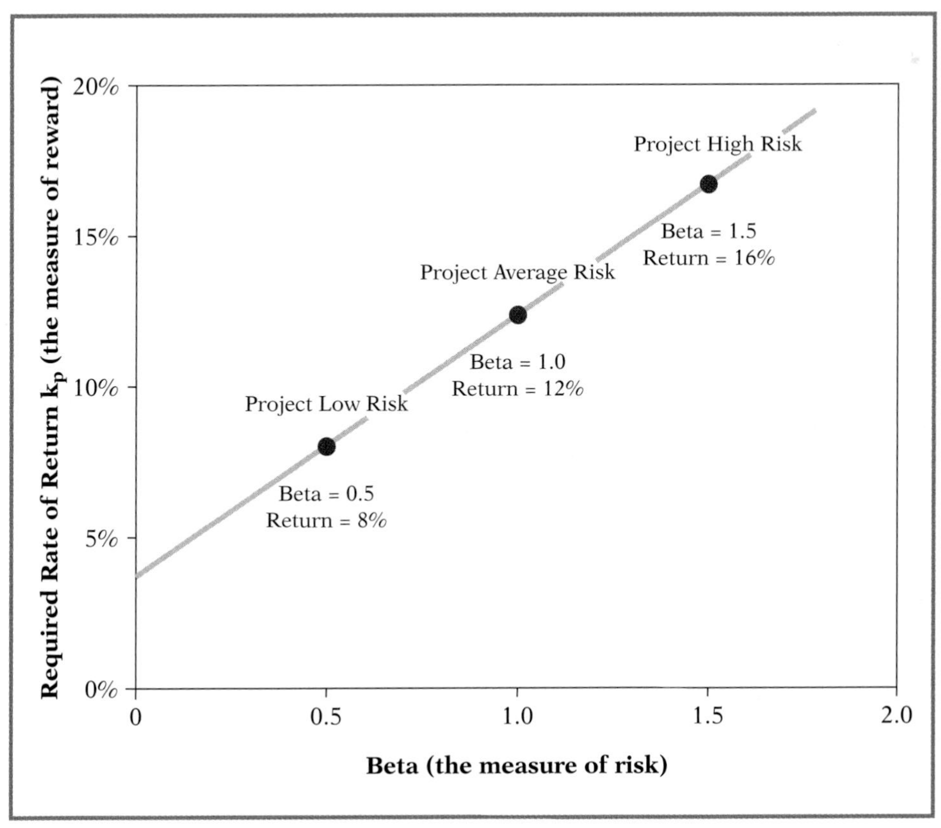

Figure 7-7 CAPM and the Risk–Return Relationship This graph illustrates the increasing return required for increasing risk as indicated by the CAPM beta. This graphical depiction of the risk–return relationship according to the CAPM is called the security market line (SML).

You have probably been wondering where betas come from? In the stock market, betas reflect the historical relationship between a security's return and the market return. Let's just imagine that we are trying to determine beta for Nortel. In order to do that, we need to find out the return on Nortel and the market (i.e., S&P/TSX 60) in a particular time (i.e., day, week, quarter). Let's say that on the 30th of December 2004, the return on the market was 4.5 percent and the return on Nortel was 6 percent. On the next day, the return on the market was 1 percent and on Nortel 2 percent. We could continue our observations of the return of the market and Nortel for a long period of time and could eventually plot these observations on the graph, where the horizontal (x) axis measures the historical market returns and the vertical (y) axis measures Nortel historical returns. We could then use statistical techniques to generate the characteristic line that describes the relationship between the Nortel-return and market-return. The slope of this line (i.e., a rise over run) is known as Nortel's beta. This is presented in Figure 7-8.

We could use the same technique for finding betas of other types of investment projects that we have done in the past by charting returns from historical projects against returns from comparable market projects in order to determine beta. We could then apply the statistically derived beta to determine the required rates of returns from newly planned investment projects.

Figure 7-8
Determining Beta for Nortel

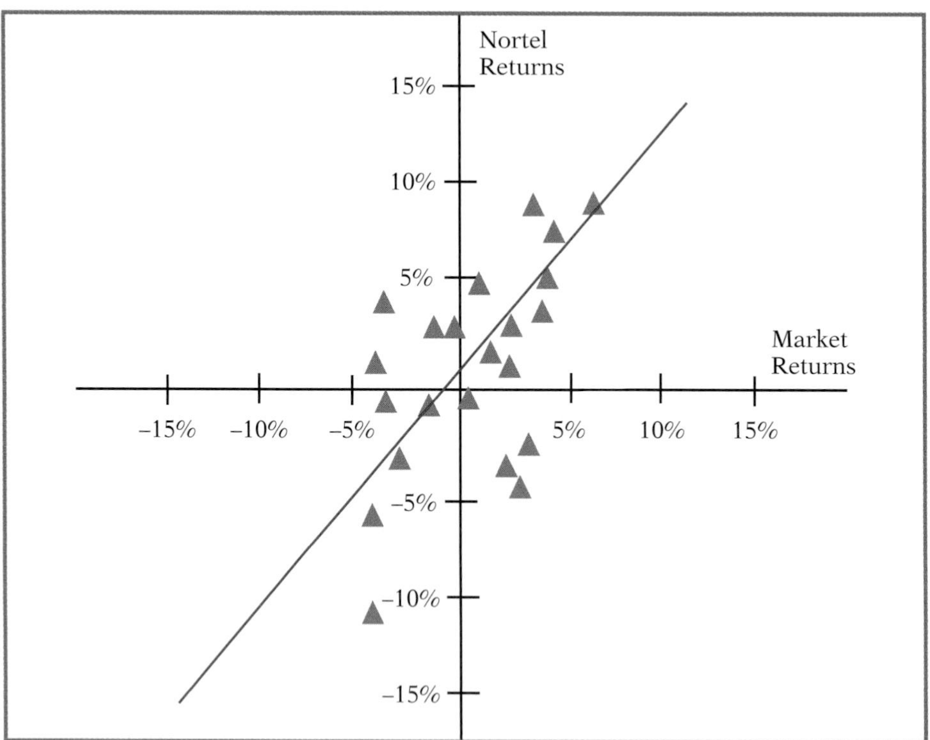

SUMMARY

7-1 Define risk, risk aversion, and the risk–return relationship.

In everything you do, or do not do, there is a chance that something will happen that you did not count on. Risk is the potential for unexpected events to occur.

Given two financial alternatives that are equal except for their degree of risk, most people will choose the less risky alternative because they are risk averse. Risk aversion is a common trait among almost all investors. Most investors avoid risk if they can, unless they are compensated for accepting risk. In an investment context, the additional compensation is a higher expected rate of return.

The risk–return relationship refers to the positive relationship between risk and the required rate of return. Due to risk aversion, the higher the risk, the more return investors expect.

7-2 Describe how risk can be measured using the standard deviation and coefficient of variation.

Risk is the chance, or probability, that outcomes other than what is expected will occur. This probability is reflected in the narrowness or width of the distribution of the possible values of the financial variable. In a distribution of variable values, the standard deviation is a number that indicates how widely dispersed the possible values are around the expected value. The more widely dispersed a distribution is, the larger the standard deviation, and the greater the probability that an actual value will be different than the expected value. The standard deviation, then, can be used to measure the likelihood that some outcome substantially different than what is expected will occur.

When the degrees of risk in distributions of different sizes are compared, the coefficient of variation is a statistic used to measure *relative* riskiness. The coefficient of variation measures the standard deviation's percentage of the expected value. It relates the standard deviation to its mean to give a risk measure that is independent of the magnitude of the possible returns.

7-3 Identify three main types of risk that business firms encounter.

Business risk is the risk that a company's operating income will differ from what is expected. The more volatile a company's operating income, the more business risk the firm contains. Business risk is a result of sales volatility, which translates into operating income volatility. Business risk is increased by the presence of fixed costs, which magnify the effect on operating income of changes in sales.

Financial risk occurs when companies borrow money and incur interest charges that show up as fixed expenses on their income statements. Fixed interest charges act on a firm's net income the same way fixed operating expenses act on operating income—they increase volatility. The additional volatility of a firm's net income caused by the presence of fixed interest expense is called financial risk.

Portfolio risk is the chance that investors will not get the return they expect from a portfolio. Portfolio risk can be measured by the standard deviation of possible returns of a portfolio. It is affected by the correlation of returns of the assets making up the portfolio. The less correlated these returns are, the more gains on some assets offset losses on others, resulting in a reduction of the portfolio's risk. This phenomenon is known as the *diversification effect*. Nondiversifiable risk is risk that remains in a portfolio after all diversification benefits have been achieved. Nondiversifiable risk is measured by a term called beta (β). The market has a beta of 1.0. Portfolios with betas greater than 1.0 contain more nondiversifiable risk than the market, and portfolios with betas less than 1.0 contain less nondiversifiable risk than the market.

7-4 Describe three methods of risk reduction.

Firms can reduce the degree of risk by taking steps to reduce the volatility of sales or their fixed costs. Firms also obtain insurance policies to protect against many risks, and they diversify their asset portfolios to reduce the risk of income loss.

7-5 Discuss a major way that firms can compensate for assuming risk.

Firms almost always demand a higher rate of return to compensate for assuming risk. The more risky a project, the higher the return firms demand.

7-6 Explain how the capital asset pricing model (CAPM) relates risk and return.

When investors adjust their required rates of return to compensate for risk, the question arises as to how much return is appropriate for a given degree of risk. The capital asset pricing model (CAPM) is a model that measures the required rate of return for an investment or project, given its degree of nondiversifiable risk as measured by beta (β).

EQUATIONS INTRODUCED IN THIS CHAPTER

Equation 7-1: The Expected Value, or Mean (μ), of a Probability Distribution

$$\mu = \Sigma\,(V \times P)$$

where
μ = the expected value, or mean
V = the possible value for some variable
P = the probability of the value V occurring

Equation 7-2: The Standard Deviation

$$\sigma = \sqrt{\Sigma\, P(V - \mu)^2}$$

where
σ = the standard deviation
V = the possible value for a variable
P = the probability of the value V occurring
μ = the expected value

Equation 7-3: The Coefficient of Variation of a Probability Distribution

$$CV = \frac{\text{Standard Deviation}}{\text{Mean}}$$

Equation 7-4: The Expected Rate of Return of a Portfolio, $E(R_p)$, Composed of Two Assets, A and B

$$E(R_p) = [w_a \times E(R_a)] + [(w_b \times E(R_b)]$$

where
w_a = the weight of Asset A in the portfolio
$E(R_a)$ = the expected rate of return of Asset A
w_b = the weight of Asset B in the Portfolio
$E(R_b)$ = the expected rate of return of Asset B

Equation 7-5: The Standard Deviation of a Two-Asset Portfolio

$$\sigma_p = \sqrt{w_a^2\sigma_a^2 + w_b^2\sigma_b^2 + 2w_a w_b r_{a,b}\sigma_a\sigma_b}$$

where
σ_p = the standard deviation of the returns of the combined portfolio containing Asset A and Asset B
w_a = the weight of Asset A in the two-asset portfolio
σ_a = the standard deviation of the returns of Asset A
w_b = the weight of Asset B in the two-asset portfolio
σ_b = the standard deviation of the returns of Asset B
$r_{a,b}$ = the correlation coefficient of the returns of Asset A and Asset B

Equation 7-6: The Capital Asset Pricing Model (CAPM)

$$k_p = k_{RF} + (k_M - k_{RF}) \times \beta$$

where
k_p = the required rate of return appropriate for the investment project
k_{RF} = the risk-free rate of return
k_M = the required rate of return on the overall market
β = the project's beta

SELF-TEST

ST-1. For Bryan Corporation, the mean of the distribution of next year's possible sales is \$5 million. The standard deviation for this distribution is \$400,000. Calculate the coefficient of variation (CV) for this distribution of possible sales.

ST-2. Investors in Hoeven Industries common shares have a 0.2 probability of earning a return of 4 percent, a 0.6 probability of earning a return of 10 percent, and a 0.2 probability of earning a return of 20 percent. What is the mean of this probability distribution (the expected rate of return)?

ST-3. What is the standard deviation for the Hoeven Industries common share return probability distribution described in ST-2?

ST-4. The standard deviation of the possible returns of Boris Company common shares is 0.08, whereas the standard deviation of possible returns of Natasha Company common shares is 0.12. Calculate the standard deviation of a portfolio comprised of 40 percent Boris Company shares and 60 percent Natasha Company shares. The correlation coefficient of the returns of Boris Company shares relative to the returns of Natasha Company shares is –0.2.

ST-5. The mean of the normal probability distribution of possible returns of Gidney and Cloyd Corporation common shares is 18 percent. The standard deviation is 3 percent. What is the range of possible values that would be 95 percent certain to capture the return that will actually be earned on this share?

ST-6. Dobie's Bagel Corporation common share has a beta of 1.2. The market risk premium is 6 percent and the risk-free rate is 4 percent. What is the required rate of return on this share according to the CAPM?

ST-7. Using the information provided in ST-6, what is the required rate of return on the common share of Zack's Salt Corporation? This share has a beta of 0.4.

ST-8. A portfolio of three shares has an expected value of 14 percent. Share A has an expected return of 6 percent and a weight of 0.25 in the portfolio. Share B has an expected return of 10 percent and a weight of 0.5 in the portfolio. Share C is the third share in this portfolio. What is the expected rate of return of Share C?

REVIEW QUESTIONS

1. What is risk aversion? If common shareholders are risk averse, how do you explain the fact that they often invest in very risky companies?
2. Explain the risk–return relationship.
3. Why is the coefficient of variation often a better risk measure when comparing different projects than the standard deviation?
4. What is the difference between business risk and financial risk?
5. Why does the riskiness of portfolios have to be looked at differently than the riskiness of individual assets?
6. What happens to the riskiness of a portfolio if assets with very low correlations (even negative correlations) are combined?
7. What does it mean when we say that the correlation coefficient for two variables is –1? What does it mean if this value is zero? What does it mean if it is +1?
8. What is nondiversifiable risk? How is it measured?
9. Compare diversifiable and nondiversifiable risk. Which do you think is more important to financial managers in business firms?

10. How do risk-averse investors compensate for risk when they take on investment projects?

11. Given that risk-averse investors demand more return for taking on more risk when they invest, how much more return is appropriate for, say, a common share than for a Treasury bill?

12. Discuss risk from the perspective of the capital asset pricing model (CAPM).

PROBLEMS

Standard Deviation and Coefficient of Variation ▶

Excel

7-1. Manager Paul Smith believes an investment project will have the following yearly cash flows with the associated probabilities throughout its life of five years. Calculate the standard deviation and coefficient of variation of the cash flows.

Cash Flows ($)	Probability of Occurrence
$10,000	0.05
13,000	0.10
16,000	0.20
19,000	0.30
22,000	0.20
25,000	0.10
28,000	0.05

Measuring Risk ▶

Excel

7-2. Milk-U, an agricultural consulting firm, has developed the following income statement forecast:

Milk-U Income Forecast (in $000s)

	Probability of Occurrence				
	2%	8%	80%	8%	2%
Sales	$500	$700	$1,200	$1,700	$1,900
Variable Expenses	250	350	600	850	950
Fixed Operating Expenses	250	250	250	250	250
Operating Income	0	100	350	600	700

a. Calculate the expected value of Milk-U's operating income.

b. Calculate the standard deviation of Milk-U's operating income.

c. Calculate the coefficient of variation of Milk-U's operating income.

d. Recalculate the expected value, standard deviation, and coefficient of variation of Milk-U's operating income if the company's sales forecast changed as follows:

	Probability of Occurrence				
	10%	15%	50%	15%	10%
Sales	$500	$700	$1,200	$1,700	$1,900

e. Comment on how Milk-U's degree of business risk changed as a result of the new sales forecast in part (d).

Standard Deviation and Mean ▶

7-3. The following data apply to Henshaw Corp. Calculate the mean and the standard deviation, using the following table.

Possible Sales ($)	Probability of Occurrence
1,000	0.10
5,000	0.20
10,000	0.45
15,000	0.15
20,000	0.10
	Σ = 1.00

7-4. As a new loan officer in the Bulwark Bank, you are comparing the financial riskiness of two firms. Selected information from *pro forma* statements for each firm follows:

◀ Measuring Risk

Excel

Equity Eddie's Company
Net Income Forecast (in $000s)

	Probability of Occurrence				
	5%	10%	70%	10%	5%
Operating Income	$100	$200	$400	$600	$700
Interest Expense	0	0	0	0	0
Before-Tax Income	100	200	400	600	700
Taxes (28%)	28	56	112	168	196
Net Income	72	144	288	432	504

Barry Borrower's Company
Net Income Forecast (in $000s)

	Probability of Occurrence				
	5%	10%	70%	10%	5%
Operating Income	$110	$220	$440	$660	$770
Interest Expense	40	40	40	40	40
Before-Tax Income	70	180	400	620	730
Taxes (28%)	19.6	50.4	112	173.6	204.4
Net Income	50.4	129.6	288	446.4	525.6

a. Calculate the expected values of Equity Eddie's and Barry Borrower's net incomes.

b. Calculate the standard deviations of Equity Eddie's and Barry Borrower's net incomes.

c. Calculate the coefficients of variation of Equity Eddie's and Barry Borrower's net incomes.

d. Compare Equity Eddie's and Barry Borrower's degrees of financial risk.

7-5. George Taylor, owner of a toy manufacturing company, is considering the addition of a new product line. Marketing research shows that gorilla action figures will be the next fad for the six- to ten-year-old age group. This new product line of gorilla-like action figures and their high-tech vehicles will be called Go-Rilla. George estimates that the most likely yearly incremental cash flow will be $26,000. There is some uncertainty about this value because George's company has never before made a product similar to the Go-Rilla. He has estimated the potential cash flows for the new product line along with their associated probabilities of occurrence. His estimates follow:

◀ Standard Deviation and Coefficient of Variation

Excel

Go-Rilla Project

Cash Flows	Probability of Occurrence
$20,000	1%
$22,000	12%
$24,000	23%
$26,000	28%
$28,000	23%
$30,000	12%
$32,000	1%

a. Calculate the standard deviation of the estimated cash flows.

b. Calculate the coefficient of variation.

c. If George's other product lines have an average coefficient of variation of 12 percent, what can you say about the risk of the Go-Rilla Project relative to the average risk of the other product lines?

Portfolio Risk ▶

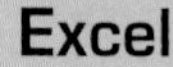

7-6. Assume that a company has an existing portfolio A with an expected return of 9 percent and a standard deviation of 3 percent. The company is considering adding an Asset B to its portfolio. Asset B's expected return is 12 percent with a standard deviation of 4 percent. Also assume that the amount invested in A is $700,000 and the amount to be invested in B is $200,000. If the degree of correlation between returns from portfolio A and Asset B is zero, calculate:

a. The standard deviation of the new combined portfolio and compare it with that of the existing portfolio.

b. The coefficient of variation of the new combined portfolio and compare it with that of the existing portfolio.

Coefficient of Variation ▶

7-7. Zazzle Company has a standard deviation of 288 and a mean of 1,200. What is its coefficient of variation (CV)?

Expected Rate of Return ▶

7-8. What is the expected rate of return on a portfolio that has $4,000 invested in Share A and $6,000 invested in Share B? The expected rates of return on these two shares are 13 percent and 9 percent, respectively.

Standard Deviation ▶

7-9. A two-share portfolio has 30 percent in Share A with an expected return of 21 percent and a standard deviation of 5 percent. The remainder is in Share B with an 18 percent expected return and a standard deviation of 2 percent. The correlation coefficient is 0.6. Determine the standard deviation for this portfolio.

Challenge Problem ▶

7-10. A firm has an existing portfolio of projects with an expected return of 11 percent a year. The standard deviation of these returns is 4 percent. The existing portfolio's value is $820,000. As financial manager, you are considering the addition of a new project, PROJ1. PROJ1's expected return is 13 percent with a standard deviation of 5 percent. The initial cash outlay for PROJ1 is expected to be $194,000.

a. Calculate the coefficient of variation for the existing portfolio.

b. Calculate the coefficient of variation for PROJ1.

c. If PROJ1 is added to the existing portfolio, calculate the weight (proportion) of the existing portfolio in the combined portfolio.

d. Calculate the weight (proportion) of PROJ1 in the combined portfolio.

e. Assume the correlation coefficient of the cash flows of the existing portfolio and PROJ1 is zero. Calculate the standard deviation of the combined portfolio. Is the standard deviation of the combined portfolio higher or lower than the standard deviation of the existing portfolio?

f. Calculate the coefficient of variation of the combined portfolio.

g. If PROJ1 is added to the existing portfolio, will the firm's risk increase or decrease?

7-11. Assume the risk-free rate is 5 percent, the expected rate of return on the market is 15 percent, and the beta of your firm is 1.2. Given these conditions, what is the required rate of return on your company's share per the capital asset pricing model? ◀ CAPM

7-12. Calculate the required rates of return for the low-, average-, and high-risk shares. The risk-free rate is 4.5 percent and the market risk premium is 12.5 percent. ◀ CAPM

a. Low-risk beta = 0.5

b. Average-risk beta = 1.0

c. High-risk beta= 1.6

7-13. Your firm has a beta of 1.5 and you are considering an investment project with a beta of 0.8. Answer the following questions assuming that short-term Treasury bills are currently yielding 5 percent and the expected return on the market is 15 percent. ◀ Challenge Problem

a. What is the appropriate required rate of return for your company per the capital asset pricing model?

b. What is the appropriate required rate of return for the investment project per the capital asset pricing model?

c. If your firm invests 20 percent of its assets in the new investment project, what will be the beta of your firm after the project is adopted? (Hint: Compute the weighted average beta of the firm with the new asset using Equation 7-4.)

The following problems (7-14 to 7-18) relate to the expected business of Power Software Company (PSC) in 2003 ($000s):

(for problems 7-14 through 7-18)

Excel

Power Software Company Forecasts

	Probability of Occurrence						
	2%	8%	20%	40%	20%	8%	2%
Sales	$800	$1,000	$1,400	$2,000	$2,600	$3,000	$3,200

7-14. Calculate the expected value, standard deviation, and coefficient of variation of sales revenue of PSC. ◀ Measuring Risk

7-15. Assume that PSC has no fixed expense but has a variable expense that is 60 percent of sales as follows: ◀ Business Risk

Power Software Company Forecasts

	Probability of Occurrence						
	2%	8%	20%	40%	20%	8%	2%
Sales	$800	$1,000	$1,400	$2,000	$2,600	$3,000	$3,200
Variable Expense	480	600	840	1,200	1,560	1,800	1,920

Calculate PSC's business risk (coefficient of variation of operating income).

Business Risk ▶ **7-16.** Now assume that PSC has a fixed operating expense of $400,000, in addition to the variable expense of 60 percent of sales, shown as follows:

Power Software Company Forecasts

	Probability of Occurrence						
	2%	8%	20%	40%	20%	8%	2%
Sales	$800	$1,000	$1,400	$2,000	$2,600	$3,000	$3,200
Variable Expense	480	600	840	1,200	1,560	1,800	1,920
Fixed Operating Expense	400	400	400	400	400	400	400

Recalculate PSC's business risk (coefficient of variation of operating income). How does this figure compare with the business risk calculated for variable cost only?

Various Statistics and Financial Risk ▶ **7-17.** Assume that PSC has a fixed interest expense of $60,000 on borrowed funds. Also assume that the applicable tax rate is 30 percent. What are the expected value, standard deviation, and coefficient of variation of PSC's net income? What is PSC's financial risk?

Business and Financial Risk ▶ **7-18.** To reduce the various risks, PSC is planning to take suitable steps to reduce volatility of its operating and net income. PSC has projected that fixed expenses and interest expenses can be reduced. The revised figures follow:

Power Software Company Forecasts

	Probability of Occurrence						
	1%	6%	13%	60%	13%	6%	1%
Sales	$800	$1,000	$1,400	$2,000	$2,600	$3,000	$3,200
Variable Expense	480	600	840	1,200	1,560	1,800	1,920
Fixed Operating Expense	250	250	250	250	250	250	250
Interest Expense	40	40	40	40	40	40	40

Recalculate PSC's business and financial risks and compare these figures with those calculated in problems 7-16 and 7-17. The tax rate is 30 percent.

CAPM ▶ **7-19.** Mark Johnson is a portfolio manager for Toronto Securities Incorporated. He has been looking to construct a portfolio consisting of three securities. He has selected three securities described below, which are listed on the Toronto Stock Exchange.

Security	Beta
Alberta Gas	–0.6
Wheat Pool	1.5
Red Deer Door Maker	1.75

Answer the following questions assuming that Canadian Treasury bills are currently yielding 7 percent and the market risk premium is equal to 10 percent.

a. What is the appropriate required rate of return for each of the securities under CAPM?

b. If Mark invests 20 percent of his assets in Alberta Gas, 30 percent in Wheat Pool, and 50 percent in Red Deer Door Maker, what will the beta of the combined portfolio be?

c. If Mark was to limit his asset allocation to two securities and split the investment into them on a 50/50 basis and he knew that the market was expected to increase, which securities should he choose? What would the beta of the combined portfolio be?

7-20. As an analyst for Scotia Investment Banking division, you have been following Hamilton Steel Corporation. You have been able to estimate that the company may have a 60 percent probability to return 21 percent, a 30 percent probability to return 18 percent, and a 10 percent probability to return 32 percent. From the historic information of the security's performance versus the market, you have been able to estimate the company's beta using regression analysis. Hamilton's beta is equal to 2.0. The market required rate of return is 17 percent and the Canadian Treasury bills currently yield 7 percent. ◀ CAPM

a. What is the expected rate of return for the company?

b. What is the required rate of return for the company?

c. Based on the information given, would your recommendation be to buy or to sell?

7-21. You are considering four securities in four international markets. Using the CAPM, calculate the required rate of return for each security using the information below. Which security or securities would you recommend to someone to buy if his or her expected rate of return was equal to 17 percent? ◀ CAPM

Security	Risk Free Rate for Local Treasury Bills	Market Return	Beta
Copernicus Capital	7%	14%	1.2
Troika Internet	12%	23%	0.9
Toronto Retailers	6%	12%	1.7
Texas Oil	12%	14%	–1.0

7-22. Using the CAPM, calculate the required rate of return for each security using the following information. Which security or securities would you recommend if the expected rate of return were equal to 11 percent? ◀ CAPM

Security	Risk Free Rate for Local Treasury Bills	Market Return	Beta
A	6%	12%	1.0
B	18%	25%	1.9
C	7%	15%	0.7
D	11%	15%	1.0

ANSWERS TO SELF-TEST

ST-1. $CV = \sigma \div \mu = \$400{,}000 \div \$5{,}000{,}000 = 0.08 = 8\%$

ST-2. $\mu = (0.2 \times 0.04) + (0.6 \times 0.10) + (0.2 \times 0.20) = 0.108 = 10.8\%$

ST-3. $\sigma = ([0.2 \times (0.04 - 0.108)^2] + [0.6 \times (0.10 - 0.108)^2] + [0.2 \times (0.20 - 0.108)^2])^{0.5} = [(0.2 \times 0.004624) + (0.6 \times 0.000064) + (0.2 \times 0.008464)]^{0.5} = 0.002656^{0.5} = 0.0515 = 5.15\%$

ST-4. $\sigma_p = [(0.4^2 \times 0.08^2) + (0.6^2 \times 0.12^2) + (2 \times 0.4 \times 0.6 \times -0.2 \times 0.08 \times 0.12)]^{0.5} = [(0.16 \times 0.0064) + (0.36 \times 0.0144) + (-0.0009216)]^{0.5} = 0.0052864^{0.5} = 0.0727 = 7.27\%$

ST-5. $0.18 + (2 \times 0.03) = 0.24 = 24\%$ $0.18 - (2 \times 0.03) = 0.12 = 12\%$ $\therefore$ We are 95% confident that the actual return will be between 12% and 24%.

ST-6. $k_s = 0.04 + (0.06 \times 1.2) = 0.112 = 11.2\%$

ST-7. $k_s = 0.04 + (0.06 \times 0.4) = 0.064 = 6.4\%$

ST-8. WT of Share C must be 0.25 for the total of the weights to equal 1

$0.14 = (0.06 \times 0.25) + (0.10 \times 0.5) + [E(R_C) \times 0.25]$

$0.14 = 0.065 + [E(R_C) \times 0.25]$

$0.075 = E(R_C) \times 0.25$

$E(R_C) = 0.30 = 30\%$

8

The Time Value of Money

Chapter Objectives

After reading this chapter, you should be able to:

8-1 **Define** the time value of money and its importance in the business world.

8-2 **Explain** how to calculate the future value and present value of a single amount.

8-3 **Describe** how to calculate the future and present values of an annuity.

8-4 **Explain** how to solve time value of money problems with uneven cash flows.

8-5 **Describe** how to solve for the interest rate, number or amount of payments, or the number of periods in a future or present value problem.

"Time is money."

—Benjamin Franklin

Hockey, Financial Contracts, and Present Value

A Calgary Flames hockey player sits at a table in Adriano's, his favourite Italian coffee shop. He has reflected on the season and the fact that the team made the Stanley Cup Finals, a feat achieved after a fifteen-year absence from post-season play. On the way to the finals, the team was able to beat the Vancouver Canucks, Detroit Red Wings, and San Jose Sharks. The player thought about his own accomplishments throughout the season. He had scored over twenty goals in the regular season and was one of the top scorers in the play-offs. But now, he has a dilemma.

He has just received an offer from the New York Rangers, one of the all-time great teams and one-time home to many of his hockey heroes (Mark Messier, Wayne Gretzky, Jaromir Jagr, etc.). He is having some problems evaluating the financial offer he has received and in comparing it to the one he enjoys now. He has therefore invited his friend, an accountant and an old fan of the Calgary Flames, to help him with the decision. The player is also considering the non-monetary aspects of the deal. He has always enjoyed New York and all the entertainment opportunities it offers but is worried about the family transition to such a big city. Then again, he and his family have already moved a few times from city to city.

Before his friend arrives, the player makes a brief summary of the alternatives he has:

1. The New York Rangers offered a 7-year contract paying an annual salary of $2 million and a bonus of $500,000 if the team makes the play-offs.
2. The Calgary Flames offered a 5-year contract paying an annual salary of $1.5 million, but a $1 million bonus if the team makes the play-offs. An additional $1 million is paid if the team wins the Stanley Cup.

As he is thinking about the financial offers, the player sees his accountant colleague come into the coffee shop. He is confident that the accountant will help him make the appropriate financial decision, at least with respect to the financial aspects of the offer.

CHAPTER OVERVIEW

A dollar in hand today is worth more than a promise of a dollar tomorrow. This is one of the basic principles of financial decision making. Time value analysis is a crucial part of financial decisions. It helps answer questions about how much money an investment will make over time and how much a firm must invest now to earn an expected pay-off later.

In this chapter, we will investigate why money has time value, as well as learn how to calculate the *future value* of cash invested today and the *present value* of cash to be received in the future. We will also discuss the present and future values of an *annuity*—a series of equal cash payments at regular time intervals. Finally, we will examine special time value of money problems such as how to find the rate of return on an investment and how to deal with a series of uneven cash payments.

WHY MONEY HAS TIME VALUE

The **time value of money** means that the money you hold in your hand today is worth more than the money you expect to receive in the future. Similarly, money you must pay out today is a greater burden than the same amount paid in the future.

In Chapter 2, we learned that interest rates are positive in part because people prefer to consume now rather than later. Positive interest rates indicate, then, that money has time value. When one person lets another borrow money, the first person requires compensation in exchange for reducing current consumption. The person who borrows the money is willing to pay to increase current consumption. The cost paid by the borrower to the lender for reducing consumption, known as an *opportunity cost,* is the real rate of interest.

The real rate of interest reflects compensation for the **pure time value of money**. The real rate of interest does not include interest charged for expected inflation or the risk factors discussed in Chapter 2. Recall from the interest rate discussion in Chapter 2 that many factors—including the pure time value of money, inflation, default risk, liquidity risk, and maturity risk—determine market interest rates.

The required rate of return on an investment reflects the pure time value of money, an adjustment for expected inflation, and any risk premiums present.

MEASURING THE TIME VALUE OF MONEY

Financial managers adjust for the time value of money by calculating the *future value* and the *present value.* Future value and present value are mirror images of each other. **Future value** is the value of a present amount at a future point in time, given the rate of growth per period and the number of periods until that future time. How much will $1,000 invested today at a 10 percent interest rate grow to in 15 years? **Present value** is the value of a future amount today, assuming a specific required interest rate for a number of periods until that future amount is realized. How much should we pay today to obtain a promised payment of $1,000 in 15 years if investing money today would yield a 10 percent rate of return per year?

The Future Value of a Single Amount

To calculate the future value of a single amount, we must first understand how money grows over time. Once money is invested, it earns an interest rate that compensates for the time value of money and, as we learned in Chapter 2, for default risk, inflation, and other factors. Often, the interest earned on investments is **compound interest**—interest earned on interest *and* on the original principal. In contrast, *simple interest* is interest earned only on the original principal.

To illustrate compound interest, assume the financial manager of Alta Gas decided to invest $100 of the firm's excess cash in an account that earns an annual interest rate of 5 percent. In one year, Alta Gas will earn $5 in interest, calculated as follows:

$$\begin{aligned}\text{Balance at the End of One Year} &= \text{Principal} + \text{Interest}\\ &= \$\,100 + (100 \times 0.05)\\ &= \$\,100 \times (1 + 0.05)\\ &= \$\,100 \times 1.05\\ &= \$105\end{aligned}$$

The total amount in the account at the end of year 1, then, is $105.

But look what happens in years 2 and 3. In year 2, Alta Gas will earn 5 percent of *105*. The $105 is the original principal of $100 *plus* the first year's interest—so the interest earned in year 2 is $5.25, rather than $5. The end of year 2 balance is $110.25—$100 in original principal and $10.25 in interest. In year 3, Alta Gas will earn 5 percent of $110.25, or $5.51, for an ending balance of $115.76, shown as follows:

	Beginning Balance	×	*(1 + Interest Rate)*	*= Ending Balance*	*Interest*
Year 1	$100.00	×	1.05	= $105.00	$5.00
Year 2	$105.00	×	1.05	= $110.25	$5.25
Year 3	$110.25	×	1.05	= $115.76	$5.51

In our example, Alta Gas earned $5 in interest in year 1, $5.25 in year 2 ($110.25 – $105), and $5.51 in year 3 ($115.76 – $110.25) because of the compounding effect. If the Alta Gas deposit earned interest only on the original principal, rather than on the principal and interest, the balance in the account at the end of year 3 would be $115 ($100 + ($5 × 3) = $115). In our case, the compounding effect accounts for an extra $0.76 ($115.76 – $115 = 0.76).

The simplest way to find the balance at the end of year 3 is to multiply the original principal by 1 plus the interest rate per period, 1 + i, raised to the power of the number of compounding periods, n.[1] Here is the formula for finding the future value—or ending balance—given the original principal, interest rate per period, and number of compounding periods:

[1]The compounding periods are usually years but not always. As you will see later in the chapter, compounding periods can be months, weeks, days, or any specified period of time.

THE FAR SIDE By GARY LARSON

Einstein brings together the theory of relativity and the theory of finance.

Source: THE FAR SIDE © 1985, 1992 FARWORKS, Inc. Dist. by UNIVERSAL PRESS SYNDICATE. Reprinted with permission.

Future Value of a Single Amount

Algebraic Method

$$FV = PV \times (1 + i)^n \tag{8-1a}$$

where

FV = Future Value, the ending amount

PV = Present Value, the starting amount, or original principal

i = Rate of interest per period (expressed as a decimal)

n = Number of time periods

In our Alta Gas example, PV is the original deposit of \$100, i is 5 percent, and n is 3. To solve for the ending balance, or FV, we apply Equation 8-1a as follows:

$$FV = PV \times (1 + i)^n = \$100 \times (1.05)^3 = \$100 \times 1.1576 = \$115.76$$

We may also solve for future value using a financial table. Financial tables are a compilation of values, known as interest factors, that represent a term, $(1 + i)^n$ in this case, in time value of money formulas. Table I in the Appendix at the end of the book is developed by calculating $(1 + i)^n$ for many combinations of i and n.

Table I is the **future value interest factor (FVIF)** table. The formula for future value using the FVIF table follows:

Future Value of a Single Amount

Table Method

$$FV = PV + (FVIF_{i,\,n}) \tag{8-1b}$$

where

FV = Future value, the ending amount

PV = Present value, the starting amount

$FVIF_{i,n}$ = Future value interest factor given interest rate, i, and number of periods, n, from Table I

In our Alta Gas example, in which $100 is deposited in an account at 5 percent interest for three years, the ending balance, or FV, according to Equation 8-1b, is as follows:

$$\begin{aligned} FV &= PV + (FVIF_{5\%,\,3}) \\ &= \$100 \times 1.1576 \\ &= \$115.76 \end{aligned}$$

To solve for FV using a financial calculator, we enter the numbers for PV, n, and i (i is depicted as I/Y on the TI BAII PLUS calculator; on other calculators it may be symbolized by i or I), and ask the calculator to compute FV. The keystrokes follow.

Take Note

Because future value interest factors are rounded to four decimal places in Table I, you may get a slightly different solution compared to a problem solved by the algebraic method.

TI BAII PLUS FINANCIAL CALCULATOR SOLUTION

Step 1: First press 2nd CLR TVM . This clears all the time value of money keys of all previously calculated or entered values. Always perform this function before you begin new calculations.

Step 2: Press 2nd P/Y 1 ENTER , 2nd QUIT . This sets the calculator to the mode where one payment per year is expected, which is the assumption for the problems in this chapter. This is important to do, especially when you just purchased your calculator.

Step 3: Input values for principal (PV), interest rate (i or I/Y on the calculator), and number of periods (n).

100 +/– PV 5 I/Y 3 N CPT FV Answer: 115.76

In the Alta Gas example, we input –100 for the present value (PV), 3 for the number of periods (n), and 5 for the interest rate per year (I/Y). Then we ask the calculator to compute the future value, FV. The result is $115.76. Our TI BAII PLUS is set to display two decimal places. You may choose a greater or lesser number if you wish.

We have learned three ways to calculate the future value of a single amount: the algebraic method, the financial table method, and the financial calculator method. This is very useful to know and, therefore, you can always crosscheck your calculations in real life and during finance exams. In the next section, we see how future values are related to changes in the interest rate, i, and the number of time periods, n.

The Sensitivity of Future Values to Changes in Interest Rates or the Number of Compounding Periods

Future value has a positive relationship with the interest rate, i, and with the number of periods, n. That is, as the interest rate increases, future value increases. Similarly, as the number of periods increases, so does future value. In contrast, future value increases by smaller amounts with decreases in i and n values.

It is important to understand the sensitivity of future value to i and n because increases are exponential, as shown by the $(1 + i)^n$ term in the future value formula. Consider this: A business that invests $10,000 in a savings account at 5 percent for 20 years will have a future value of $26,532.98. If the interest rate is 8 percent for the same 20 years, the future value of the investment is $46,609.57. We see that the future value of the investment increases as i increases. Figure 8-1a shows this graphically.

Now let's say that the business deposits $10,000 for 10 years at a 5 percent annual interest rate. The future value of that sum is $16,288.95. Another business deposits $10,000 for 20 years at the same 5 percent annual interest rate. The future value of that $10,000 investment is $26,532.98. Just as with the interest rate, the higher the number of periods, the higher the future value. Figure 8-1b shows this graphically.

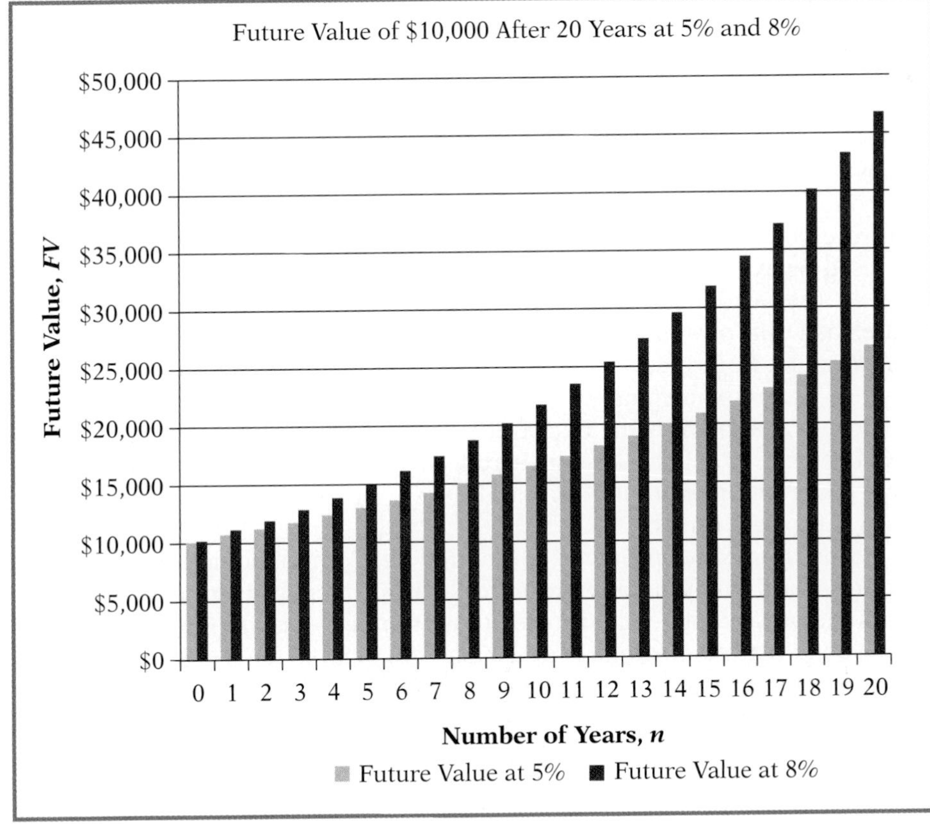

Figure 8-1a
Future Value at Different Interest Rates
Figure 8-1a shows the future value of $10,000 after 20 years at interest rates of 5 percent and 8 percent.

Figure 8-1b
Future Value at Different Times
Figure 8-1b shows the future value of $10,000 after 10 years and 20 years at an interest rate of 5 percent.

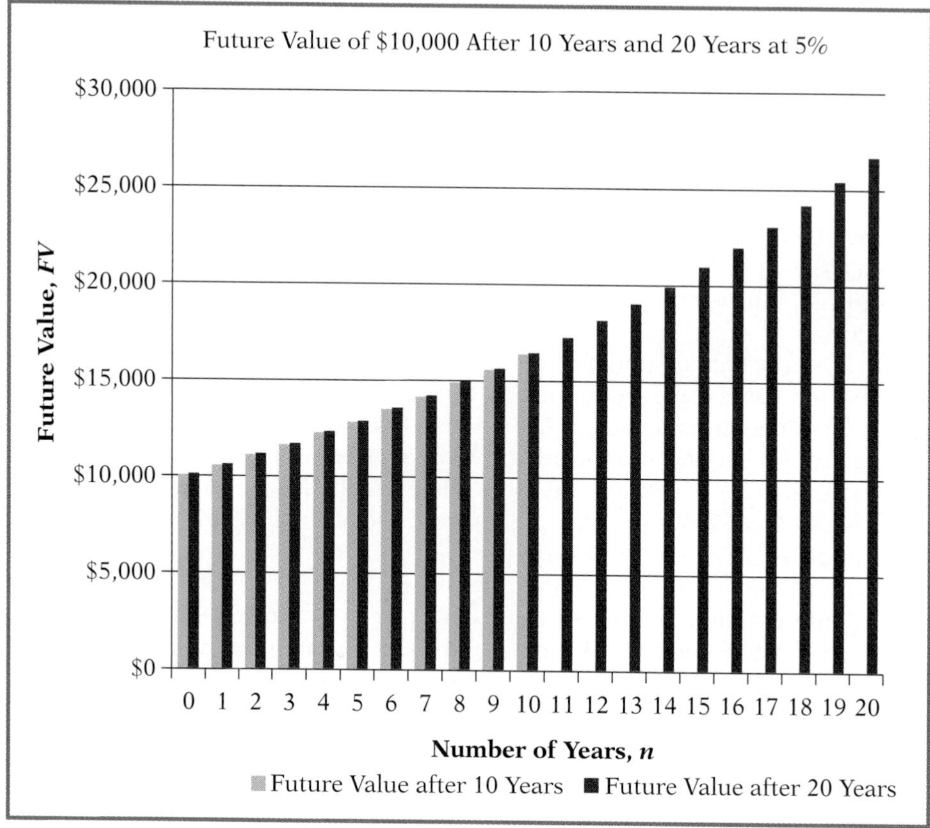

The Present Value of a Single Amount

Present value is today's dollar value of a specific future amount. With a bond, for instance, the issuer promises the investor future cash payments at specified points in time. With an investment in new plant or equipment, certain cash receipts are expected. When we calculate the present value of a future promised or expected cash payment, we discount it (mark it down in value) because it is worth *less* if it is to be received later rather than now. Similarly, future cash outflows are less burdensome than present cash outflows of the same amount. Future cash outflows are similarly discounted (made less negative). In present value analysis, then, the interest rate used in this discounting process is known as the discount rate. The **discount rate** is the required rate of return on an investment. It reflects the lost opportunity to spend or invest now (the opportunity cost) and the various risks assumed because we must wait for the funds.

Discounting is the inverse of compounding. Compound interest causes the value of a beginning amount to increase at an increasing rate. Discounting causes the present value of a future amount to decrease at an increasing rate.

To demonstrate, imagine the Alta Gas financial manager needed to know how much to invest *now* to generate $115.76 in three years, given an interest rate of 5 percent. Given what we know so far, the calculation would look like this:

$$FV = PV \times (1 + i)^n$$
$$\$115.76 = PV \times 1.05^3$$
$$\$115.76 = PV \times 1.157625$$
$$PV = \$100$$

To simplify solving present value problems, we modify the future value for a single amount equation by multiplying both sides by $1/(1 + i)^n$ to isolate PV on one side of the equal sign. The present value formula for a single amount follows:

Present Value of a Single Amount

Algebraic Method

$$PV = FV \times \frac{1}{(1+i)^n} \tag{8-2a}$$

where

PV = Present value, the starting amount

FV = Future value, the ending amount

i = Discount rate of interest per period (expressed as a decimal)

n = Number of time periods

Applying this formula to the Alta Gas example, in which its financial manager wanted to know how much the firm should pay today to receive $115.76 at the end of three years, assuming a 5 percent discount rate starting today, the following is the present value of the investment:

$$PV = FV \times \frac{1}{(1+i)^n}$$
$$= \$115.76 \times \frac{1}{(1+0.05)^3}$$
$$= \$115.76 \times .86384$$
$$= \$100$$

Alta Gas should be willing to pay $100 today to receive $115.76 three years from now at a 5 percent discount rate.

To solve for PV, we may also use the Present Value Interest Factor Table in Table II in the Appendix at the end of the book. A **present value interest factor**, or PVIF, is calculated and shown in Table II. It equals $1/(1 + i)^n$ for given combinations of i and n. The table method formula, Equation 8-2b, follows:

Present Value of a Single Amount

Table Method

$$PV = FV \times (PVIF_{i,n}) \tag{8-2b}$$

where

PV = Present value, the starting amount

FV = Future value, the ending amount

$PVIF_{i,n}$ = Present value interest factor given discount rate, i, and number of periods, n, from Table II

In our example, Alta Gas's financial manager wanted to solve for the amount that must be invested today at a 5 percent interest rate to accumulate \$115.76 within three years. Applying the present value table formula, we find the following solution:

$$\begin{aligned} PV &= FV \times (PVIF_{5\%,\,3}) \\ &= \$115.76 \times 0.8638 \text{ (from the PVIF table)} \\ &= \$99.99 \text{ (slightly less than \$100 due to the rounding to four places in the table)} \end{aligned}$$

The present value of \$115.76, discounted back three years at a 5 percent discount rate, is \$100.

To solve for present value using our financial calculator, enter the numbers for future value, FV, the number of periods, n, and the interest rate, i—symbolized as I/Y on the calculator—then hit the CPT (compute) and PV (present value) keys. The sequence follows:

TI BAII PLUS FINANCIAL CALCULATOR SOLUTION

Step 1: Press 2nd CLR TVM to clear previous values.

Step 2: Press 2nd P/Y 1 ENTER , 2nd QUIT to ensure the calculator is in the mode for annual interest payments.

Step 3: Input the values for future value, the interest rate, and number of periods, and compute PV.

115.76 FV 5 I/Y 3 N CPT PV Answer: −100.00

The financial calculator result is displayed as a negative number to show that the present value sum is a cash outflow—that is, that sum will have to be invested to earn \$115.76 in three years at a 5 percent annual interest rate. We have examined how to find present value using the algebraic, table, and financial calculator methods. Next, we see how present value analysis is affected by the discount rate, i, and the number of compounding periods, n.

The Sensitivity of Present Values to Changes in i and n

In contrast with future value, present value is inversely related to i and n values. In other words, present value moves in the opposite direction of i and n. If i increases, present value decreases; if i decreases, present value increases. If n increases, present value decreases; if n decreases, present value increases.

Consider this: A business that expects a 5 percent annual return on its investment ($i = 5\%$) should be willing to pay \$3,768.89 today (the present value) for \$10,000 to be received 20 years from now. If the expected annual return is 8 percent for the same 20 years, the present value of the investment is only \$2,145.48. We see that the present value of the investment decreases as i increases. The way the present value of the \$10,000 varies with changes in the required rate of return is shown graphically in Figure 8-2a.

Now let's say that a business expects to receive \$10,000 ten years from now. If its required rate of return for the investment is 5 percent annually, then it should be willing to pay \$6,139 for the investment today (the present value

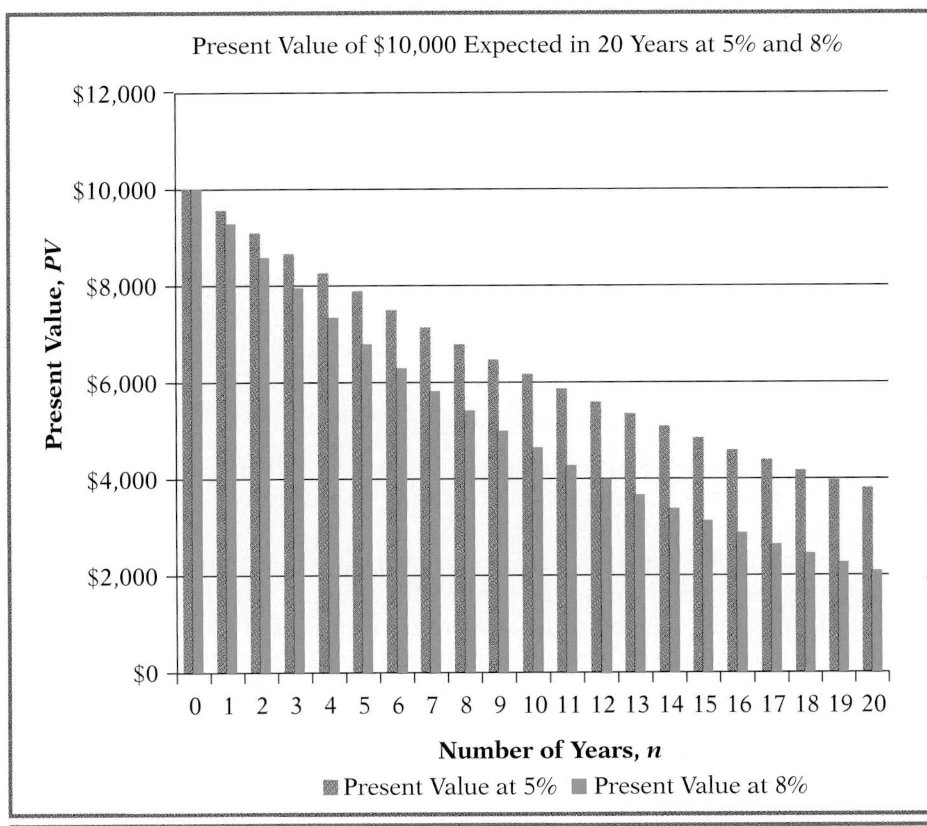

Figure 8-2a
Present Value at Different Interest Rates
Figure 8-2a shows the present value of $10,000 to be received in 20 years at interest rates of 5 percent and 8 percent.

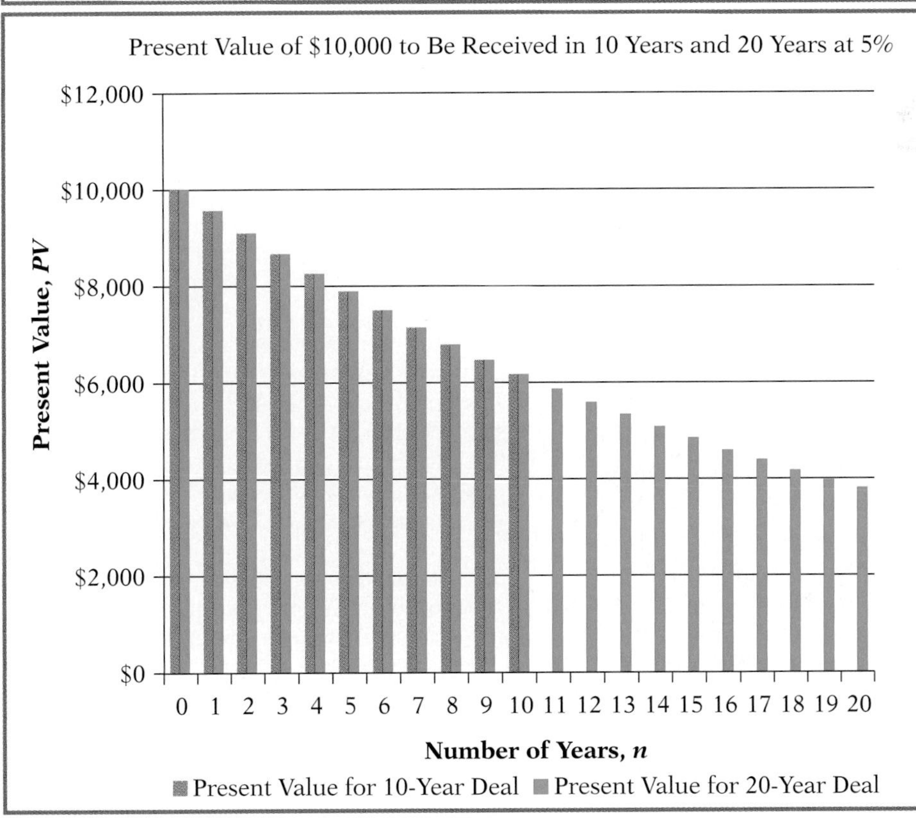

Figure 8-2b
Present Value at Different Times
Figure 8-2b shows the present value of $10,000 to be received in 10 years and 20 years at an interest rate of 5 percent.

is \$6,139). If another business expects to receive \$10,000 twenty years from now and it has the same 5 percent annual required rate of return, then it should be willing to pay \$3,769 for the investment (the present value is \$3,769). Just as with the interest rate, the greater the number of periods, the lower the present value. Figure 8-2b shows how it works.

In this section, we have learned how to find the future value and the present value of a single amount. Next, we will examine how to find the future value and present value of several amounts. Now, let's see if we can apply our knowledge of PV to a life situation again. Financial Management and You 8-1 discusses the application of PV principles in determining the value of your MBA education.

Working with Annuities

Financial managers often need to assess a series of cash flows rather than just one. One common type of cash flow series is the **annuity**—a series of equal cash flows, spaced evenly over time.

Professional athletes often sign contracts that provide annuities for them after they retire, in addition to the signing bonus and regular salary they may receive during their playing years. Consumers can purchase annuities from insurance companies as a means of providing retirement income. The investor pays the insurance company a lump sum now in order to receive future payments of equal size at regularly spaced time intervals (usually monthly). Another example of an annuity is the interest on a bond. The interest payments are usually equal dollar amounts paid either annually or semiannually during the life of the bond.

Annuities are a significant part of many financial problems. You should learn to recognize annuities and determine their value, future or present. In

FINANCIAL MANAGEMENT AND YOU 8-1

What's the Net Present Value of Your MBA Diploma?

Let's imagine that your studies as an undergraduate business student are coming to an end. Let's further assume that you are considering two options: to go to the U.S. and enter one of the top business schools in the world as measured by international ranking or to enter one of the top business schools in Canada, also ranked highly in international rankings. After an initial search on the Internet, you find out that you would need to pay around \$50,000 in tuition and living expenses per annum if you were to attend the U.S. university and you would attend for two years. Alternatively, your tuition and living expenses in Canada would be equal to approximately \$17,000 per annum and you would also attend the university for two years.

Upon completion of your cost investigation, you say to yourself, "What a big difference in costs!" Then, you discover that MBA graduates from the top U.S. university are able earn an average salary of \$150,000 per annum while grac ates from a top Canadian university can earn an avera salary of \$100,000—still a handsome payout. You could u these figures as approximations of your potential earni power for the next forty years. Suppose you knew that t average interest rate would be equal to 5 percent per annu in the next two years but only around 3 percent for t remaining time until your retirement. How would you use t principles of PV to solve this problem?

There are many other examples in life where PV can used to help solve real-life problems. While life challeng often go beyond the simple techniques of PV mathematic using PV techniques is usually a good start.

this section we will explain how to calculate the future value and present value of annuities in which cash flows occur at the end of the specified time periods. Annuities in which the cash flows occur at the end of each of the specified time periods are known as *ordinary annuities.* Annuities in which the cash flows occur at the beginning of each of the specified time periods are known as *annuities due.*

Future Value of an Ordinary Annuity

Financial managers often plan for the future. When they do, they often need to know how much money to save on a regular basis to accumulate a given amount of cash at a specified future time. The future value of an annuity is the amount that a given number of annuity payments, n, will grow to at a future date, for a given periodic interest rate, i.

For instance, suppose the Alta Gas Company plans to invest $500 in a money market account at the end of each year for the next four years, beginning one year from today. The business expects to earn a 5 percent annual rate of return on its investment. How much money will Alta Gas have in the account at the end of four years? The problem is illustrated in the timeline in Figure 8-3. The t values in the timeline represent the end of each time period. Thus, t_1 is the end of the first year, t_2 is the end of the second year, and so on. The symbol t_0 is *now,* the present point in time.

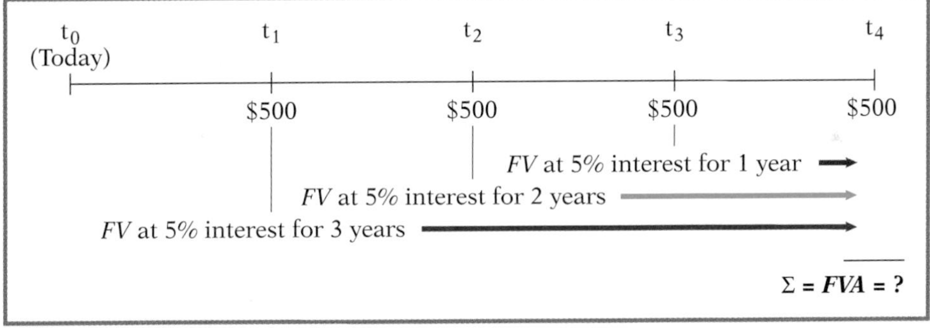

Figure 8-3 Alta Gas Annuity Timeline

Because the $500 payments are each a single amount, we can solve this problem one step at a time. Looking at Figure 8-4, we see that the first step is to calculate the future value of the cash flows that occur at t_1, t_2, t_3, and t_4 using the future value formula for a single amount. The next step is to add the four values together. The sum of those values is the annuity's future value.

As shown in Figure 8-4, the sum of the future values of the four single amounts is the annuity's future value, $2,155.05. However, the step-by-step process illustrated in Figure 8-4 is time-consuming even in this simple example. Calculating the future value of a 20- or 30-year annuity, such as would be the case with many bonds, would take an enormous amount of time. Instead, we can calculate the future value of an annuity easily by using the following formula:

Future Value of an Annuity

Algebraic Method

$$FVA = PMT \times \left[\frac{(1+i)^n - 1}{i}\right] \quad (8\text{-}3a)$$

Figure 8-4
Future Value of the Alta Gas Annuity

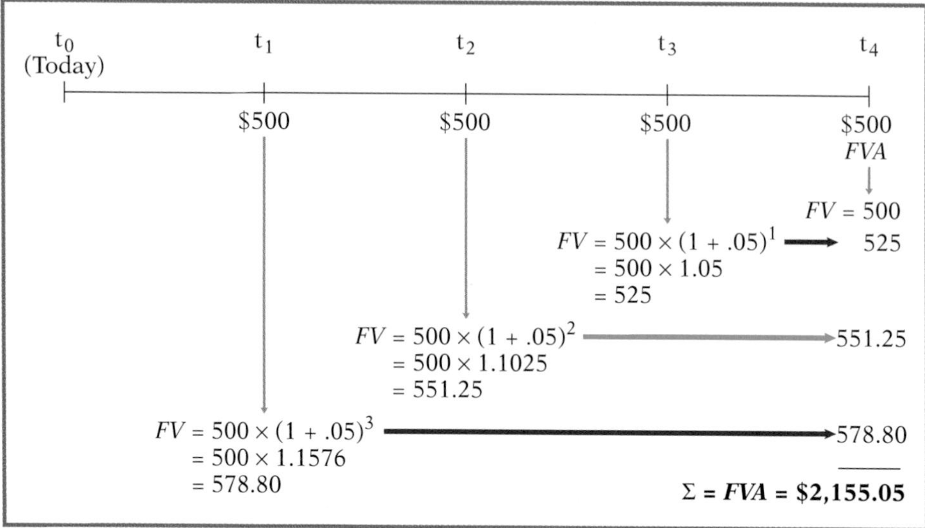

where

FVA = Future value of an annuity
PMT = Amount of each annuity payment
i = Interest rate per time period
n = Number of annuity payments

Using Equation 8-3a in our Alta Gas example, we solve for the future value of the annuity at 5 percent interest (i = 5%) with four $500 end-of-year payments (n = 4 and PMT = $500), as follows:

$$\begin{aligned} FVA &= 500 \times \left[\frac{(1+0.05)^4 - 1}{0.05}\right] \\ &= 500 \times 4.3101 \\ &= \$2{,}155.05 \end{aligned}$$

For a $500 annuity with a 5 percent interest rate and four annuity payments, we see that the future value of the Alta Gas annuity is $2,155.05.

To find the future value of an annuity with the table method, we must find the **future value interest factor for an annuity** (FVIFA) found in Table III in the Appendix at the end of the book. The $FVIFA_{i,n}$ is the value of $[(1 + i)^n - 1] \div i$ for different combinations of i and n.

Future Value of an Annuity

Table Method

$$FVA = PMT \times FVIFA_{i,\,n} \tag{8-3b}$$

where

FVA = Future value of an annuity
PMT = Amount of each annuity payment
$FVIFA_{i,\,n}$ = Future value interest factor for an annuity from Table III
i = Interest rate per period
n = Number of annuity payments

In our Alta Gas example, then, we need to find the FVIFA for a discount rate of 5 percent with four annuity payments. Table III in the Appendix shows that the $FVIFA_{i = 5\%, n = 4}$ is 4.3101. Using the table method, we find the following future value of the Alta Gas annuity:

$$\begin{aligned} FVA &= 500 \times FVIFA_{5\%, 4} \\ &= 500 \times 4.3101 \text{ (from the FVIFA table in Table III)} \\ &= \$2,155.05 \end{aligned}$$

To find the future value of an annuity using a financial calculator, key in the values for the annuity payment (PMT), n, and i (remember that the notation for the interest rate on the TI BAII PLUS calculator is I/Y, not i). Then compute the future value of the annuity (FV on the calculator). For a series of four \$500 end-of-year (ordinary annuity) payments where n = 4 and i = 5 percent, the computation is as follows:

TI BAII PLUS FINANCIAL CALCULATOR SOLUTION

Step 1: Press 2nd CLR TVM to clear previous values.

Step 2: Press 2nd P/Y 1 ENTER , 2nd BGN , 2nd SET . Repeat 2nd SET until END shows in the display, 2nd QUIT to set the annual interest rate mode and to set the annuity payment to end of period mode.

Step 3: Input the values and compute.

0 PV 5 I/Y 4 N 500 +/− PMT CPT FV Answer: 2,155.06

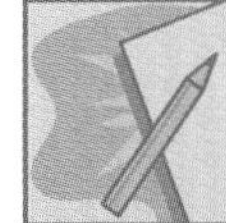

Take Note

Note that slight differences occur between the table method, algebraic method, and calculator solution. This is because our financial tables round interest factors to four decimal places whereas the other methods generally use many more significant figures for greater accuracy.

In the financial calculator inputs, note that the payment is keyed in as a negative number to indicate that the payments are cash outflows—the payments flow out from the company into an investment.

The Present Value of an Ordinary Annuity

Because annuity payments are often promised (as with interest on a bond investment) or expected (as with cash inflows from an investment in new plant or equipment), it is important to know how much these investments are worth to us today. For example, assume that the financial manager of Niagara Digital learns of an annuity that promises to make four annual payments of \$500, beginning one year from today. How much should the company be willing to pay to obtain that annuity? The answer is the present value of the annuity.

Because an annuity is nothing more than a series of equal single amounts, we could calculate the present value of an annuity with the present value formula for a single amount and sum the totals, but that would be a cumbersome process. Imagine calculating the present value of a 50-year annuity! We would have to find the present value for each of the 50 annuity payments and total them.

Fortunately, we can calculate the present value of an annuity in one step with the following formula:

Present Value of an Annuity

Algebraic Method

$$PVA = PMT \times \left[\frac{1 - \frac{1}{(1+i)^n}}{i} \right] \tag{8-4a}$$

where

PVA = Present value of an annuity
PMT = Amount of each annuity payment
i = Discount rate per period
n = Number of annuity payments

Using our example of a four-year ordinary annuity with payments of $500 per year and a 5 percent discount rate, we solve for the present value of the annuity as follows:

$$PVA = 500 \times \left[\frac{1 - \frac{1}{(1+.05)^4}}{.05} \right]$$

$$= 500 \times 3.54595$$

$$= \$1,772.98$$

The present value of the four-year ordinary annuity with equal yearly payments of $500 at a 5 percent discount rate is $1,772.98.

We can also use the financial table for the **present value interest factor for an annuity (PVIFA)** to solve present value of annuity problems. The PVIFA table is found in Table IV in the Appendix at the end of the book. The formula for the table method follows:

Present Value of an Annuity

Table Method

$$PVA = PMT \times PVIFA_{i, n} \tag{8-4b}$$

where

PVA = Present value of an annuity
PMT = Amount of each annuity payment
$PVIFA_{i, n}$ = Present value interest factor for an annuity from Table IV
i = Discount rate per period
n = Number of annuity payments

Applying Equation 8-4b, we find that the present value of the four-year annuity with $500 equal payments and a 5 percent discount rate is as follows:[2]

$$PVA = 500 \times PVIFA_{5\%, 4} = 500 \times 3.5460 = \$1,773.00$$

[2]The $0.02 difference between the algebraic result and the table formula solution is due to differences in rounding.

We may also solve for the present value of an annuity with a financial calculator. Simply key in the values for the payment, PMT, number of payment periods, n, and the interest rate, i—symbolized by I/Y on the TI BAII PLUS calculator—and ask the calculator to compute PVA (PV on the calculator). For the series of four $500 payments where n = 4 and i = 5 percent, the computation follows:

TI BAII PLUS FINANCIAL CALCULATOR SOLUTION

Step 1: Press 2nd CLR TVM to clear previous values.

Step 2: Press 2nd P/Y 1 ENTER , 2nd BGN , 2nd SET . Repeat 2nd SET until END shows in the display, 2nd QUIT to set to the annual interest rate mode and to set the annuity payment to end of period mode.

Step 3: Input the values and compute.

5 I/Y 4 N 500 PMT CPT PV Answer: −1,772.98

The calculations relating to PV of an annuity can be very helpful in solving many financial problems, especially when we deal with multiple alternatives. An example of such a case in the United States is discussed in Ethical Connections 8-1.

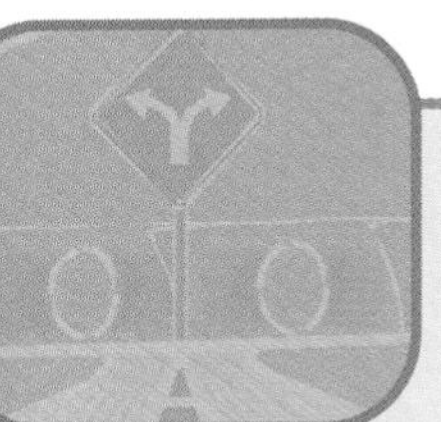

ETHICAL CONNECTIONS 8-1

When a Million Isn't a Million: Taking a Chance on the Time Value of Money

ou've won the lottery: $1 million. Congratulations! You're ch. No, wait a minute—maybe not.

"I wish they would stop *calling* us millionaires," whisers Cindy, who doesn't want to give out her last name. You e, Cindy, a recent lottery winner, has faced an awful truth: e time value of money.

In fact, most lottery winners wish the news media would ll the truth about those "millions." Those huge prizes that e media report are usually doled out over 20 years (25 in olorado). The annual cheque for a million-dollar winner is 50,000—before taxes. They also take any student loans u haven't paid out of the cheque.

Michael Ondrish, a "millionaire" winner who thought 'd won a real, lump sum million in 1982, tried suing the izona lottery for fraud and deception because lottery offials never mentioned the drawn-out payment scheme. He st his case and received a good lesson in the time value of oney.

A million dollars paid out over 20 years is an annuity. ke any other million-dollar annuity, it actually costs about 450,000 to buy because that is its present value. epending on interest rates, taxes, and inflation, the value of the yearly cheque dwindles over time. Again, it's what financial experts call the time value of money. In fact, investors willing to buy those annuities from winners who need cash offer about 40 cents on the dollar.

But you won't see the time value of money in any lottery commercial. "You Could Win an Annuity Spread over Twenty Years" just doesn't have the same appeal as "You've Won a Million." But look on the bright side. When you win the lottery, you'll know the truth. Especially after reading this chapter.

Questions to Consider

1. *Do you think it is ethical to advertise the lottery without explaining that the winnings are an annuity? Explain.*
2. *Is it ethical to fail to disclose that the jackpot winnings are the future value of the jackpot, not the present value?*
3. *Why do you think that Michael Ondrish lost his case against the Arizona lottery?*

Source: Gould, L. (1995). Ticket to Trouble, *New York Times Magazine.*

The financial calculator present value result is displayed as a negative number to signal that the present value sum is a cash outflow. In other words, $1,772.98 will have to be invested to earn a 5 percent annual rate of return on the four future annual annuity payments of $500 each to be received.

Future and Present Values of Annuities Due

Sometimes we must deal with annuities in which the annuity payments occur at the *beginning* of each period. These are known as annuities *due,* in contrast to *ordinary* annuities in which the payments occur at the end of each period, as described in the preceding section.

Annuities due are more likely to occur when doing future value of annuity (FVA) problems than when doing present value of annuity (PVA) problems. Today, for instance, you may start a retirement program, investing regular equal amounts each month or year. Calculating the amount you would accumulate when you reach retirement age would be a future value of an annuity due problem. Evaluating the present value of a promised or expected series of annuity payments that began today would be a present value of an annuity due problem. This is less common because car and mortgage payments almost always start at the end of the first period, making them ordinary annuities.

Whenever you run into an FVA or a PVA of an annuity due problem, the adjustment needed is the same in both cases. Use the FVA or PVA of an ordinary annuity formula shown earlier, then multiply your answer by (1 + i). We multiply the FVA or PVA formula by (1 + i) because annuities due have annuity payments earning interest one period sooner. So, higher FVA and PVA values result with an annuity due. The first payment occurs sooner in the case of a future value of an annuity due. In present value of annuity due problems, each annuity payment occurs one period sooner, so the payments are discounted less severely.

In our Alta Gas example, the future value of a $500 ordinary annuity, with i = 5 percent and n = 4, was $2,155.06. If the $500 payments occurred at the *beginning* of each period instead of at the end, we would multiply $2,155.06 by 1.05 (1 + i = 1 + 0.05). The product, $2,262.81, is the future value of the annuity due. In our earlier Niagara Digital example, we found that the present value of a $500 ordinary annuity, with i = 5 percent and n = 4, was $1,772.98. If the $500 payments occurred at the *beginning* of each period instead of at the end, we would multiply $1,772.98 by 1.05 (1 + i = 1 + 0.05) and find that the present value of Niagara Digital's annuity due is $1,861.63.

The financial calculator solutions for these annuity due problems are shown next.

Future Value of a Four-Year, $500 Annuity Due, i = 5%

TI BAII PLUS FINANCIAL CALCULATOR SOLUTION

Step 1: Press 2nd CLR TVM to clear previous values.

Step 2: Press 2nd P/Y 1 ENTER , 2nd BGN , 2nd SET . Repeat the 2nd SET command until the display shows BGN, 2nd QUIT to set to the annual interest rate mode and to set the annuity payment to beginning of period mode.

Step 3: Input the values for the annuity due and compute.

5 I/Y 4 N 500 PMT CPT FV Answer: −2,262.82

Present Value of a Four-Year, $500 Annuity Due, i = 5%

TI BAII PLUS FINANCIAL CALCULATOR SOLUTION

Step 1: Press 2nd CLR TVM to clear previous values.

Step 2: Press 2nd P/Y 1 ENTER, 2nd BGN, 2nd SET. Repeat the 2nd SET command until the display shows BGN, 2nd QUIT to set to the annual interest rate mode and to set the annuity payment to beginning of period mode.

Step 3: Input the values for the annuity due and compute.

5 I/Y 4 N 500 PMT CPT PV Answer: −1,861.62

In this section, we discussed ordinary annuities and annuities due and learned how to compute the present and future values of the annuities. Next, we will learn what a perpetuity is and how to solve for its present value.

Perpetuities

An annuity that goes on forever is called a perpetual annuity or a **perpetuity**. Perpetuities contain an infinite number of annuity payments. An example of a perpetuity is the dividends typically paid on a preferred share issue.

The future value of perpetuities cannot be calculated, but the present value can be. We start with the present value of an annuity formula, Equation 8-3a.

$$PVA = PMT \times \left[\frac{1 - \frac{1}{(1+i)^n}}{i} \right]$$

Now imagine what happens in the equation as the number of payments (n) gets larger and larger. The $(1 + i)^n$ term will get larger and larger, and as it does, it will cause the $1/(1 + i)^n$ fraction to become smaller and smaller. As n approaches infinity, the $(1 + i)^n$ term becomes infinitely large, and the $1/(1 + i)^n$ term approaches zero. The entire formula reduces to the following equation:

Present Value of a Perpetuity

$$PVP = PMT \times \left[\frac{1-0}{i} \right]$$

$$PVP = PMT \times \left(\frac{1}{i} \right) \quad (8\text{-}5)$$

where

PVP = Present value of a perpetuity

PMT = Amount of each perpetual annuity payment

i = Discount rate

Neither the table method nor the financial calculator can solve for the present value of a perpetuity. This is because the PVIFA table does not contain values for infinity and the financial calculator does not have an infinity key.

Suppose you had the opportunity to buy a preferred share that pays $70 per year forever. If your required rate of return is 8 percent, what is the present value of the promised dividends to you? In other words, given your required rate of return, how much should you be willing to pay for the preferred share? The answer, found by applying Equation 8-5, follows:

$$\text{PVP} = \text{PMT} \times \left(\frac{1}{\text{i}}\right) = \$70 \times \left(\frac{1}{0.08}\right) = \$875$$

The present value of the preferred share dividends, with an i of 8 percent and a payment of $70 per year forever, is $875.

Present Value of an Investment with Uneven Cash Flows

Unlike annuities that have equal payments over time, many investments have payments that are unequal over time. That is, some investments have payments that vary over time. When the periodic payments vary, we say that the cash flow streams are uneven. For instance, a professional athlete may sign a contract that provides for an immediate $7 million signing bonus, followed by a salary of $2 million in year 1, $4 million in year 2, then $6 million in years 3 and 4. What is the present value of the promised payments that total $25 million? Assume a discount rate of 8 percent. The present value calculations are shown in Table 8-1.

As we see from the table, we calculate the present value of an uneven series of cash flows by finding the present value of a single amount for each series and sum the totals.

We can also use a financial calculator to find the present value of this uneven series of cash flows. The worksheet mode of the TI BAII PLUS calculator is especially helpful in solving problems with uneven cash flows. The C

Table 8-1 The Present Value of an Uneven Series of Cash Flows

t_0	\$7,000,000	$\$7{,}000{,}000 \times \frac{1}{1.08^0} = \$7{,}000{,}000$
t_1	\$2,000,000	$\$2{,}000{,}000 \times \frac{1}{1.08^1} = \$1{,}851{,}851.85$
t_2	\$4,000,000	$\$4{,}000{,}000 \times \frac{1}{1.08^2} = \$3{,}429{,}355.28$
t_3	\$6,000,000	$\$6{,}000{,}000 \times \frac{1}{1.08^3} = \$4{,}762{,}993.45$
t_4	\$6,000,000	$\$6{,}000{,}000 \times \frac{1}{1.08^4} = \$4{,}410{,}179.12$
		Sum of the PVs = \$21,454,379.70

display shows each cash payment following CF_0, the initial cash flow. The F display key indicates the frequency of that payment. The keystrokes follow.

Take Note

We used the NPV (net present value) key on our calculator to solve this problem. NPV will be discussed in Chapter 10.

TI BAII PLUS FINANCIAL CALCULATOR PV SOLUTION
Uneven Series of Cash Flows

Keystrokes	*Display*
CF	CF_0 = old contents
2nd CLR Work	CF_0 = 0.00
7000000 ENTER	7,000,000.00
↓ 2000000 ENTER	C01 = 2,000,000.00
↓	F01 = 1.00
↓ 4000000 ENTER	C02 = 4,000,000.00
↓	F02 = 1.00
↓ 6000000 ENTER	C03 = 6,000,000.00
↓ 2 ENTER	F03 = 2.00
NPV	I = 0.00
8 ENTER	I = 8.00
↓ CPT	NPV = 21,454,379.70

We see from the calculator keystrokes that we are solving for the present value of a single amount for each payment in the series except for the last two payments, which are the same. The value of F03, the frequency of the third cash flow after the initial cash flow, was 2 instead of 1 because the $6 million payment occurred twice in the series (in years 3 and 4).

We have seen how to calculate the future value and present value of annuities, the present value of a perpetuity, and the present value of an investment with uneven cash flows. Now we turn to time value of money problems in which we solve for i, n, or the annuity payment.

Special Time Value of Money Problems

Financial managers often face time value of money problems even when they know both the present value and the future value of an investment. In those cases, financial managers may be asked to find out what return an investment made—that is, what the interest rate is on the investment. Still other times, financial managers must find either the number of payment periods or the amount of an annuity payment. In the next section, we will learn how to solve for i and n. We will also learn how to find the annuity payment (PMT).

Finding the Interest Rate

Financial managers frequently have to solve for the interest rate, i, when firms make a long-term investment. The method of solving for i depends on whether the investment is a single amount or an annuity.

Finding i of a Single-Amount Investment Financial managers may need to determine how much periodic return an investment generated over time. For example, imagine that you are head of the finance department of Brandon Contractors. Say that Brandon Contractors purchased a house on prime land 20 years ago for \$40,000. Recently, Brandon Contractors sold the property for \$106,131. What average annual rate of return did the firm earn on its 20-year investment?

First, the future value—or ending amount—of the property is \$106,131. The present value—the starting amount—is \$40,000. The number of periods, n, is 20. Armed with those facts, you could solve this problem using the table version of the future value of a single amount formula, Equation 8-1b, as follows:

$$FV = PV \times (FVIF_{i,\,n})$$

$$\$106{,}131 = \$40{,}000 \times (FVIF_{i\,=\,?,\,n\,=\,20})$$

$$\$106{,}131 \div \$40{,}000 = 2.6533 = (FVIF_{i\,=\,?,\,n\,=\,20})$$

Now find the FVIF value in Table I, part of which is shown in Table 8-2. The whole table is in the Appendix at the end of the book. You know n = 20, so find the n = 20 row on the left-hand side of the table. You also know that the FVIF value is 2.6533, so move across the n = 20 row until you find (or come close to) the value 2.6533. You find the 2.6533 value in the i = 5% column. You discover, then, that Brandon Contractor's property investment had an interest rate of 5 percent.

Table 8-2 Future Value Interest Factors, Compounded at i Percent for n Periods, Part of Table I

	Interest Rate, i										
Number of Periods, n	**0%**	**1%**	**2%**	**3%**	**4%**	**5%**	**6%**	**7%**	**8%**	**9%**	**10%**
18	1.0000	1.1961	1.4282	1.7024	2.0258	2.4066	2.8543	3.3799	3.9960	4.7171	5.5599
19	1.0000	1.2081	1.4568	1.7535	2.1068	2.5270	3.0256	3.6165	4.3157	5.1417	6.1159
20	1.0000	1.2202	1.4859	1.8061	2.1911	2.6533	3.2071	3.8697	4.6610	5.6044	6.7275
25	1.0000	1.2824	1.6406	2.0938	2.6658	3.3864	4.2919	5.4274	6.8485	8.6231	10.8347

Solving for i using the FVIF table works well when the interest rate is a whole number, but it does not work well when the interest rate is not a whole number. To solve for the interest rate, i, we rewrite the algebraic version of the future value of a single-amount formula, Equation 8-1a, to solve for i:

The Rate of Return, i

$$i = \left(\frac{FV}{PV}\right)^{\frac{1}{n}} - 1 \qquad (8\text{-}6)$$

Let's use Equation 8-6 to find the average annual rate of return on Brandon Contractors' house investment. Recall that the company bought it 20 years ago for \$40,000 and sold it recently for \$106,131. We solve for i applying Equation 8-6 as follows:

$$k = \left(\frac{FV}{PV}\right)^{\frac{1}{n}} - 1 = \left(\frac{\$106,131}{\$40,000}\right)^{\frac{1}{20}} - 1 = 2.653275^{.05} - 1 = 1.05 - 1$$
$$= .05 \text{ or } 5\%$$

Equation 8-6 will find any rate of return or interest rate given a starting value, PV, an ending value, FV, and a number of compounding periods, n.

To solve for i with a financial calculator, key in all the other variables and ask the calculator to compute i (depicted as I/Y on your calculator). For Brandon Contractors' house-buying example, the calculator solution follows:

TI BAII PLUS FINANCIAL CALCULATOR SOLUTION

Step 1: Press 2nd CLR TVM to clear previous values.

Step 2: Press 2nd P/Y 1 ENTER , 2nd QUIT .

Step 3: Input the values and compute.

40000 +/– PV 106131 FV 20 N CPT I/Y Answer: 5.00

Remember when using the financial calculator to solve for the rate of return, you must enter cash outflows as a negative number. In our example, the $40,000 PV is entered as a negative number because Brandon Contractors spent that amount to invest in the house.

Finding i for an Annuity Investment Financial managers may need to find the interest rate for an annuity investment when they know the starting amount (PVA), n, and the annuity payment (PMT), but they do not know the interest rate, i. For example, suppose Brandon Contractors wanted a 15-year, $100,000 amortized loan from a bank. An amortized loan is a loan that is paid off in equal amounts that include principal as well as interest.[3] According to the bank, Brandon Contractors' payments will be $12,405.89 per year for 15 years. What interest rate is the bank charging on this loan?

To solve for i when the known values are PVA (the $100,000 loan proceeds), n (15), and PMT (the loan payments $12,405.89), we start with the present value of an annuity formula, Equation 8-3b, as follows:

$$PVA = PMT \times (PVIFA_{i,\,n})$$
$$\$100,000 = \$12,405.89 \times (PVIFA_{i\,=\,?,\,n\,=\,15})$$
$$8.0607 = (PVIFA_{i\,=\,?,\,n\,=\,15})$$

Now refer to the PVIFA values in Table IV, shown in part as Table 8-3. You know n = 15, so find the n = 15 row on the left-hand side of the table. You have also determined that the PVIFA value is 8.0607 ($100,000/$12,405.89 = 8.0607), so move across the n = 15 row until you find (or come close to) the

[3]*Amortize* comes from the Latin word *mortalis,* which means "death." You will kill off the entire loan after making the scheduled payments.

value of 8.0607. In our example, the location on the table where n = 15 and the PVIFA is 8.0607 is in the i = 9% column, so the interest rate on Brandon Contractors' loan is 9 percent.

To solve this problem with a financial calculator, key in all the variables but i, and ask the calculator to compute i (depicted as I/Y on the TI calculator) as follows:

TI BAII PLUS FINANCIAL CALCULATOR SOLUTION

Step 1: Press 2nd CLR TVM to clear previous values.

Step 2: Press 2nd P/Y 1 ENTER , 2nd BGN , 2nd SET . Repeat 2nd SET until END shows in the display, 2nd QUIT .

Step 3: Input the values and compute.

100000 PV 15 N 12405.89 +/– PMT CPT I/Y Answer: 9.00

In this example, the PMT was entered as a negative number to indicate that the loan payments are cash outflows, flowing away from the firm. The missing interest rate value was 9 percent, the interest rate on the loan.

Table 8-3 Present Value Interest Factors for an Annuity, Discounted at i Percent for n Periods, Part of Table IV

Number of Annuity Payments, n	Discount Rate, i										
	0%	1%	2%	3%	4%	5%	6%	7%	8%	9%	10%
13	13.0000	12.1337	11.3484	10.6350	9.9856	9.3936	8.8527	8.3577	7.9038	7.4869	7.1034
14	14.0000	13.0037	12.1062	11.2961	10.5631	9.8986	9.2950	8.7455	8.2442	7.7862	7.3667
15	15.0000	13.8651	12.8493	11.9379	11.1184	10.3797	9.7122	9.1079	8.5595	8.0607	7.6061
16	16.0000	14.7179	13.5777	12.5611	11.6523	10.8378	10.1059	9.4466	8.8514	8.3126	7.8237

Finding the Number of Periods

Suppose you found an investment that offered you a return of 6 percent per year. How long would it take you to double your money? In this problem, you are looking for n, the number of compounding periods that it will take for a starting amount, PV, to double in size (FV = 2 × PV).

To find n in our example, start with the formula for the future value of a single amount and solve for n as follows:

$$FV = PV \times (FVIF_{i,\,n})$$

$$2 \times PV = PV \times (FVIF_{i = 6\%,\, n = ?})$$

$$2.0 = (FVIF_{i = 6\%,\, n = ?})$$

Now refer to the FVIF values, shown in Table 8-4 in part of Table I. You know i = 6 percent, so scan across the top row to find the i = 6 percent column.

Number of Periods, n	Interest Rate, i										
	0%	1%	2%	3%	4%	5%	6%	7%	8%	9%	10%
11	1.0000	1.1157	1.2434	1.3842	1.5395	1.7103	1.8983	2.1049	2.3316	2.5804	2.8531
12	1.0000	1.1268	1.2682	1.4258	1.6010	1.7959	2.0122	2.2522	2.5182	2.8127	3.1384
13	1.0000	1.1381	1.2936	1.4685	1.6651	1.8856	2.1329	2.4098	2.7196	3.0658	3.4523
14	1.0000	1.1495	1.3195	1.5126	1.7317	1.9799	2.2609	2.5785	2.9372	3.3417	3.7975

Table 8-4 Future Value Interest Factors, Compounded at i Percent for n Periods, Part of Table I

Knowing that the FVIF value is 2.0, move down the i = 6% column until you find (or come close to) the value 2.0. Note that it occurs in the row in which n = 12. Therefore, n in this problem, and the number of periods it would take for the value of an investment to double at 6 percent interest per period, is 12.

This problem can also be solved on a financial calculator quite quickly. Just key in all the known variables (PV, FV, and I/Y) and ask the calculator to compute n.

TI BAII PLUS FINANCIAL CALCULATOR SOLUTION

Step 1: Press 2nd CLR TVM to clear previous values.

Step 2: Press 2nd P/Y 1 ENTER , 2nd QUIT .

Step 3: Input the values and compute.

1 +/– PV 2 FV 6 I/Y CPT N Answer: 11.90

In our example, n = 12 when $1 is paid out and $2 received with a rate of interest of 6 percent. That is, it takes 12 years to double your money at a 6 percent annual rate of interest.

Solving for the Payment

Lenders and financial managers frequently have to determine how much each payment—or installment—will need to be to repay an amortized loan. For example, suppose you are a business owner and you want to buy an office building for your company that costs $200,000. You have $50,000 for a down payment and the bank will lend you the $150,000 balance at a 6 percent annual interest rate. How much will the annual payments be if you obtain a 10-year amortized loan?

As we saw earlier, an amortized loan is repaid in equal payments over time. The period of time may vary. Let's assume in our example that your payments will occur annually, so that at the end of the 10-year period you will have paid off all interest and principal on the loan (FV = 0).

Because the payments are regular and equal in amount, this is an annuity problem. The present value of the annuity (PVA) is the $150,000 loan amount, the annual interest rate (i) is 6 percent, and n is 10 years. The payment amount (PMT) is the only unknown value.

Because all the variables but PMT are known, the problem can be solved by solving for PMT in the present value of an annuity formula, Equation 8-4a, as follows:

$$PVA = PMT \times \left[\frac{1 - \frac{1}{(1+i)^n}}{i}\right]$$

$$\$150{,}000 = PMT \times \left[\frac{1 - \frac{1}{(1.06)^{10}}}{0.06}\right]$$

$$\$150{,}000 = PMT \times 7.36009$$

$$\frac{\$150{,}000}{7.36009} = PMT$$

$$\$20{,}380.19 = PMT$$

We see, then, that the payment for an annuity with a 6 percent interest rate, an n of 10, and a present value of \$150,000 is \$20,380.19.

We can also solve for PMT using the table formula, Equation 8-4b, as follows:

$$PVA = PMT \times (PVIFA_{i,\ n})$$

$$\$150{,}000 = PMT \times (PVIFA_{6\%,\ 10\ years})$$

$$\$150{,}000 = PMT \times 7.3601 \text{ (look up PVIFA, Table IV)}$$

$$\frac{\$150{,}000}{7.3601} = PMT$$

$$\$20{,}380.16 = PMT \text{ (note the \$0.03 rounding error)}$$

The table formula shows that the payment for a loan with the present value of \$150,000 at an annual interest rate of 6 percent and an n of 10 is \$20,380.16.

With the financial calculator, simply key in all the variables but PMT and have the calculator compute PMT as follows:

TI BAII PLUS FINANCIAL CALCULATOR SOLUTION

Step 1: Press 2nd CLR TVM to clear previous values.

Step 2: Press 2nd P/Y 1 ENTER , 2nd BGN , 2nd SET . Repeat the 2nd SET command until the display shows END, 2nd QUIT to set to the annual interest rate mode and to set the annuity payment to end of period mode.

Step 3: Input the values and compute the payment.

150000 PV 6 I/Y 10 N CPT PMT Answer: −20,380.19

The financial calculator will display the payment, \$20,380.19, as a negative number because it is a cash outflow.

Loan Amortization

As each payment is made on an amortized loan, the interest due for that period is paid, along with a repayment of some of the principal that must also be "killed off." After the last payment is made all the interest and principal on the loan have been paid. This step-by-step payment of the interest and principal owed is often shown in an *amortization table.* The amortization table for the ten-year 6 percent annual interest rate loan of $150,000 that was discussed in the previous section is shown in Table 8-5. The annual payment, calculated in the previous section, is $20,380.19.

We see from Table 8-5 how the balance on the $150,000 loan is killed off a little each year until the balance at the end of year 10 is zero. The payments reflect an increasing amount going toward principal and a decreasing amount going toward interest over time.

Table 8-5 Amortization Table $150,000 Loan, 6 percent Annual Interest Rate, 10 Years

Loan Amortization Schedule

ount Borrowed $150,000
erest Rate 6.0%
m 10 years
quired Payments $20,380.19 (found using Equation 8-4a)

	Col. 1	Col. 2	Col. 3 Col. 1 × 0.06	Col. 4 Col. 2 − Col. 3	Col. 5 Col. 1 − Col. 4
ear	Beginning Balance	Total Payment	Payment of Interest	Payment of Principal	Ending Balance
1	$150,000.00	$20,380.19	$9,000.00	$11,380.19	$138,619.81
2	$138,619.81	$20,380.19	$8,317.19	$12,063.00	$126,556.81
3	$126,556.81	$20,380.19	$7,593.41	$12,786.78	$113,770.03
4	$113,770.03	$20,380.19	$6,826.20	$13,553.99	$100,216.04
5	$100,216.04	$20,380.19	$6,012.96	$14,367.23	$85,848.81
6	$85,848.81	$20,380.19	$5,150.93	$15,229.26	$70,619.55
7	$70,619.55	$20,380.19	$4,237.17	$16,143.02	$54,476.53
8	$54,476.53	$20,380.19	$3,268.59	$17,111.60	$37,364.93
9	$37,364.93	$20,380.19	$2,241.90	$18,138.29	$19,226.64
0	$19,226.64	$20,380.24	$1,153.60	$19,226.59	$0.05

Compounding More Than Once per Year

So far in this chapter, we have assumed that interest is compounded *annually.* However, there is nothing magical about annual compounding. Many investments pay interest that is compounded semiannually, quarterly, or even daily. Most banks, for example, compound interest on their deposits more frequently than annually.

Suppose you deposited $100 in a savings account that paid 12 percent interest, compounded *annually.* After one year, you would have $112 in your account ($\$112 = \$100 \times 1.12^1$).

Now, however, let's assume the bank used *semiannual* compounding. With semiannual compounding you would receive half a year's interest (6 percent) after six months. In the second half of the year, you would earn interest both on the interest earned in the first six months *and* on the original principal. The total interest earned during the year on a $100 investment at 12 percent annual interest would be:

$ 6.00	(interest for the first six months)
+ $ 0.36	(interest on the $6 interest during the second 6 months)[4]
+ $ 6.00	(interest on the principal during the second six months)
= $12.36	total interest in year 1

At the end of the year, you will have a balance of $112.36 if the interest is compounded semiannually, compared to $112 with annual compounding—a difference of $0.36.

Here is how to find answers to problems in which the compounding period is less than a year: Apply the relevant present value or future value equation, but adjust i and n so they reflect the actual compounding periods.

To demonstrate, let's look at our example of a $100 deposit in a savings account at 12 percent for one year with semiannual compounded interest. Because we want to find out what the future value of a single amount will be, we use that formula to solve for the future value of the account after one year. Next, we divide the *annual* interest rate, 12 percent, by two because interest will be compounded twice each year. Then, we multiply the number of *years*, n (one in our case), by two because with semiannual interest there are two compounding periods in a year. The calculation follows:

$$\begin{aligned} FV &= PV \times (1 + i/2)^{n \times 2} \\ &= \$100 \times (1 + 0.12/2)^{1 \times 2} \\ &= \$100 \times (1 + 0.06)^2 \\ &= \$100 \times 1.1236 \\ &= \$112.36 \end{aligned}$$

The future value of $100 after one year, earning 12 percent annual interest compounded semiannually, is $112.36.

To use the table method for finding the future value of a single amount, find the $FVIF_{i,n}$ in Table I in the Appendix at the end of the book. Then, divide i by two and multiply n by two as follows:

$$\begin{aligned} FV &= PV \times (FVIF_{i/2,\, n \times 2}) \\ &= \$100 \times (FVIF_{12\%/2,\, 1 \times 2 \text{ periods}}) \\ &= \$100 \times (FVIF_{6\%,\, 2 \text{ periods}}) \\ &= \$100 \times 1.1236 \\ &= \$112.36 \end{aligned}$$

[4]The $0.36 was calculated by multiplying $6 by half of 12%: $\$6.00 \times 0.06 = \$0.36$.

To solve the problem using a financial calculator, divide the i (represented as I/Y on the TI BAII PLUS calculator) by two and multiply the n by two. Next, key in the variables as follows:

TI BAII PLUS FINANCIAL CALCULATOR SOLUTION

Step 1: Press 2nd CLR TVM to clear previous values.

Step 2: Press 2nd P/Y 1 ENTER , 2nd QUIT .

Step 3: Input the values and compute.

100 +/– PV 6 I/Y 2 N CPT FV Answer: 112.36

The future value of \$100 invested for two periods at 6 percent per period is \$112.36.

Note that we "lied" to our TI BAII PLUS calculator. It asks us for the interest rate per year (I/Y). We gave it the semiannual interest rate of 6 percent, not the annual interest rate of 12 percent. Similarly, n was expressed as the number of semiannual periods, two in one year. As long as we are consistent in expressing the i and n values according to the number of compounding or discounting periods per year, the calculator will give us the correct answer.

Other compounding rates, such as quarterly or monthly rates, can be found by modifying the applicable formula to adjust for the compounding periods. With a quarterly compounding period, then, annual i should be divided by four and annual n multiplied by four. For monthly compounding, annual i should be divided by twelve and annual n multiplied by twelve. Similar adjustments could be made for other compounding periods.

Annuity Compounding Periods Many annuity problems also involve compounding or discounting periods of less than a year. For instance, suppose you want to buy a car that costs \$20,000. You have \$5,000 for a down payment and plan to finance the remaining \$15,000 at 6 percent annual interest for four years. What would your *monthly* loan payments be?

First, change the stated annual rate of interest, 6 percent, to a monthly rate by dividing by 12 (6%/12 = 1/2% or 0.005). Second, multiply the four-year period by 12 to obtain the number of months involved (4 × 12 = 48 months). Now solve for the annuity payment size using the annuity formula.

In our case, we apply the present value of an annuity formula using equation 8-4a as follows:

$$\text{PVA} = \text{PMT} \times \left[\frac{1 - \dfrac{1}{(1+\text{i})^{\text{n}}}}{\text{i}} \right]$$

$$\$15{,}000 = \text{PMT} \times \left[\frac{1 - \dfrac{1}{(1.005)^{48}}}{0.005} \right]$$

$$\$15{,}000 = \text{PMT} \times 42.5803$$

$$\frac{\$15{,}000}{42.5803} = \text{PMT}$$

$$\$352.28 = \text{PMT}$$

The monthly payment on a $15,000 car loan with a 6 percent annual interest rate (0.5 percent per month) for four years (48 months) is $352.28.

Solving this problem with the PVIFA table in Table IV in the Appendix at the end of the book would be difficult because the 0.5 percent interest rate is not listed in the PVIFA table. If the PVIFA were listed, we would apply the table formula, make the adjustments to reflect the monthly interest rate and the number of periods, and solve for the present value of the annuity.

On a financial calculator, we would first adjust the i and n to reflect the same time period—monthly, in our case—and then input the adjusted variables to solve the problem as follows:

TI BAII PLUS FINANCIAL CALCULATOR SOLUTION

Step 1: Press 2nd CLR TVM to clear previous values.

Step 2: Press 2nd P/Y 1 ENTER , 2nd BGN , 2nd SET . Repeat the 2nd SET command until the display shows END, 2nd QUIT to set to the annual interest rate mode and to set the annuity payment to end of period mode.

Step 3: Input the values and compute.

15000 PV .5 I/Y 48 N CPT PMT Answer: −352.28

Note that once again we have lied to our TI BAII PLUS financial calculator. The interest rate we entered was not the 6 percent rate per year but rather the 0.5 percent rate per month. We entered not the number of years, four, but rather the number of months, 48. Because we were consistent in entering the i and n values in monthly terms, the calculator gave us the correct monthly payment of −352.28 (an outflow of $352.28 per month).

Continuous Compounding The effect of increasing the number of compounding periods per year is to increase the future value of the investment. The more frequently interest is compounded, the greater the future value. The smallest compounding period is used when we do **continuous compounding** —compounding that occurs every tiny unit of time (the smallest unit of time imaginable).

Recall our $100 deposit in an account at 12 percent for one year with annual compounding. At the end of year 1, our balance was $112. With semiannual compounding, the amount increased to $112.36.

When continuous compounding is involved, we cannot divide i by infinity and multiply n by infinity. Instead, we use the term e, which you may remember from your math class. We define e as follows:

$$e = \lim_{h \to \infty} \left[1 + \frac{1}{h}\right]^h \approx 2.718\,28$$

The value of e is the natural antilog of 1 and is approximately equal to 2.71828. This number is one of those like pi (approximately equal to 3.14159), which we can never express exactly but can approximate. Using e, the formula for finding the future value of a given amount of money, PV, invested at an annual rate, i, for n years, with continuous compounding, is as follows:

Future Value with Continuous Compounding

$$FV = PV \times e^{(i \times n)} \tag{8-7}$$

where i and n are expressed in annual terms.

Applying Equation 8-7 to our example of a \$100 deposit at 12 percent annual interest with continuous compounding, we would have the following balance at the end of one year:

$$FV = \$100 \times 2.71828^{(0.12 \times 1)}$$
$$= \$112.75$$

The future value of \$100, earning 12 percent annual interest compounded continuously, is \$112.75.

As this section demonstrates, the compounding frequency can impact the value of an investment. Investors, then, should look carefully at the frequency of compounding. Is it annual, semiannual, quarterly, daily, or continuous? Other things being equal, the more frequently interest is compounded, the more interest the investment will earn.

SUMMARY

8-1 Define the time value of money and its importance in the business world.

Money grows over time when it earns interest. Money expected or promised in the future is worth less than the same amount of money in hand today. This is because we lose the opportunity to earn interest when we have to wait to receive money. Similarly, money we owe is less burdensome if it is to be paid in the future rather than now. These concepts are at the heart of investment and valuation decisions of a firm.

8-2 Explain how to calculate the future value and present value of a single amount.

To calculate the future value and the present value of a single dollar amount, we may use the algebraic, table, or financial calculator methods. Future value and present value are mirror images of each other. They are compounding and discounting, respectively. With future value, increases in i and n result in an exponential increase in future value. Increases in i and n result in an exponential decrease in present value.

8-3 Describe how to calculate the future and present values of an annuity.

Annuities are a series of equal cash flows. An annuity that has payments that occur at the end of each period is an ordinary annuity. An annuity that has payments that occur at the beginning of each period is an annuity due. A perpetuity is a perpetual annuity.

To find the future and present values of an ordinary annuity, we may use the algebraic, table, or financial calculator method. To find the future and present values of an annuity due, multiply the applicable formula by $(1 + i)$ to reflect the earlier payment.

8-4 Explain how to solve time value of money problems with uneven cash flows.

To solve time value of money problems with uneven cash flows, we find the value of each payment (each single amount) in the cash flow series and total each single amount. Sometimes the series has several cash flows of the same amount. If so, calculate the present value of those cash flows as an annuity and add the total to the sum of the present values of the single amounts to find the total present value of the uneven cash flow series.

8-5 Describe how to solve for the interest rate, number or amount of payments, or the number of periods in a future or present value problem.

To solve special time value of money problems, we use the present value and future value equations and solve for the missing variable such as the loan payment, i, or n. We may also solve for the present and future values of single amounts or annuities in which the interest rate, payments, and number of time periods are expressed in terms other than a year. The more often interest is compounded, the larger the future value.

EQUATIONS INTRODUCED IN THIS CHAPTER

Equation 8-1a: Future Value of a Single Amount—Algebraic Method

$$FV = PV \times (1 + i)^n$$

where

FV = Future value, the ending amount
PV = Present value, the starting amount, or original principal
i = Rate of interest per period (expressed as a decimal)
n = Number of time periods

Equation 8-1b: Future Value of a Single Amount—Table Method

$$FV = PV + (FVIF_{i,\,n})$$

where

FV = Future value, the ending amount
PV = Present value, the starting amount
$FVIF_{i,\,n}$ = Future value interest factor given interest rate, i, and number of periods, n, from Table I

Equation 8-2a: Present Value of a Single Amount—Algebraic Method

$$PV = FV \times \frac{1}{(1+i)^n}$$

where

PV = Present value, the starting amount
FV = Future value, the ending amount
i = Discount rate of interest per period (expressed as a decimal)
n = Number of time periods

Equation 8-2b: Present Value of a Single Amount—Table Method

$$PV = FV \times (PVIF_{i,\,n})$$

where

PV = Present value, the starting amount
FV = Future value, the ending amount
$PVIF_{i,n}$ = Present value interest factor given discount rate, i, and number of periods, n, from Table II

Equation 8-3a: Future Value of an Annuity—Algebraic Method

$$FVA = PMT \times \left[\frac{(1+i)^n - 1}{i}\right]$$

where

FVA = Future value of an annuity
PMT = Amount of each annuity payment
i = Interest rate per time period
n = Number of annuity payments

Equation 8-3b: Future Value of an Annuity—Table Method

$$FVA = PMT \times FVIFA_{i,\,n}$$

where

FVA = Future value of an annuity
PMT = Amount of each annuity payment
$FVIFA_{i,\,n}$ = Future value interest factor for an annuity from Table III
i = Interest rate per period
n = Number of annuity payments

Equation 8-4a: Present Value of an Annuity—Algebraic Method

$$PVA = PMT \times \left[\frac{1 - \dfrac{1}{(1+i)^n}}{i} \right]$$

where

PVA = Present value of an annuity
PMT = Amount of each annuity payment
i = Discount rate per period
n = Number of annuity payments

Equation 8-4b: Present Value of an Annuity—Table Method

$$PVA = PMT \times PVIFA_{i,\,n}$$

where

PVA = Present value of an annuity
PMT = Amount of each annuity payment
$PVIFA_{i,\,n}$ = Present value interest factor for an annuity from Table IV
i = Discount rate per period
n = Number of annuity payments

Equation 8-5: Present Value of a Perpetuity

$$PVP = PMT \times \left(\frac{1}{i} \right)$$

where

PVP = Present value of a perpetuity
PMT = Amount of each perpetual annuity payment
i = Discount rate

Equation 8-6: Rate of Return

$$i = \left(\frac{FV}{PV} \right)^{\frac{1}{n}} - 1$$

where

i = Rate of return
FV = Future value
PV = Present value
n = Number of compounding periods

Equation 8-7: Future Value with Continuous Compounding

$$FV = PV \times e^{(i \times n)}$$

where

FV = Future value
PV = Present value
e = Natural antilog of 1
i = Stated annual interest rate
n = Number of years

SELF-TEST

ST-1. Jed is investing $5,000 in an eight-year certificate of deposit (CD) that pays 6 percent annual interest with annual compounding. How much will he have when the CD matures?

ST-2. Tim has found a 1999 Toyota 4-Runner on sale for $19,999. The dealership says that it will finance the entire amount with a one-year loan and the monthly payments will be $1,776.89. What is the interest rate on the loan?

ST-3. Heidi's grandmother died and in her will provided that Heidi will receive $100,000 from a trust when Heidi turns 21 years of age, 10 years from now. If the appropriate discount rate is 8 percent, what is the present value of this $100,000 to Heidi?

ST-4. Zack wants to buy a new Ford Mustang automobile. He will need to borrow $20,000 to go with his down payment in order to afford this car. If car loans are available at a 6 percent annual interest rate, what will Zack's monthly payment be on a four-year loan?

ST-5. Bridget invested $5,000 in a growth mutual fund and in 10 years her investment had grown to $15,529.24. What annual rate of return did Bridget earn over this 10-year period?

ST-6. If Tom invests $1,000 a year *beginning today* in a portfolio that earns a 10 percent return per year, how much will he have at the end of 10 years? (Hint: Recognize that this is an annuity due problem.)

REVIEW QUESTIONS

1. What is the time value of money?
2. Why does money have time value?
3. What is compound interest? Compare compound interest to discounting.
4. How is present value affected by a change in the discount rate?
5. What is an annuity?
6. Suppose you are planning to make regular contributions in equal payments to an investment fund for your retirement. Which formula would you use to figure out how much your investments will be worth at retirement time, given an assumed rate of return on your investments?
7. How does continuous compounding benefit an investor?
8. If you are doing PVA and FVA problems, what difference does it make if the annuities are ordinary annuities or annuities due?
9. Which formula would you use to solve for the payment required for a car loan if you know the interest rate, length of the loan, and the borrowed amount? Explain.

PROBLEMS

Future Value ▶ **8-1.** What is the future value of $1,000 invested today if you earn 7 percent annual interest for five years?

Future Value ▶ **8-2.** Calculate the future value of $50,000 ten years from now if the annual interest rate is

a. 0 percent
b. 5 percent
c. 10 percent
d. 20 percent

8-3. How much will you have in 10 years if you deposit $5,000 today and earn 8 percent annual interest? ◀ Future Value

8-4. Calculate the future value of $100,000 fifteen years from now based on the following interest rates: ◀ Future Value

a. 3 percent
b. 6 percent
c. 9 percent
d. 12 percent

8-5. Calculate the future values of the following amounts at 10 percent for twenty-five years: ◀ Future Value

a. $50,000
b. $75,000
c. $100,000
d. $125,000

8-6. Calculate the future value of $60,000 at 12 percent for the following years: ◀ Future Value

a. 5 years
b. 10 years
c. 15 years
d. 20 years

8-7. What is the present value of $20,000 to be received ten years from now using a 12 percent annual discount rate? ◀ Present Value

8-8. Calculate the present value of $60,000 to be received twenty years from now at an annual discount rate of ◀ Present Value

a. 0 percent
b. 5 percent
c. 10 percent
d. 20 percent

8-9. Norton is going to receive a graduation present of $9,000 from his grandparents in four years. If the discount rate is 8 percent, what is this gift worth today? ◀ Present Value

8-10. Calculate the present value of $25,000 to be received in ten years using the following annual discount rates: ◀ Present Value

a. 3 percent
b. 6 percent
c. 9 percent
d. 12 percent

8-11. Calculate the present values of the following using a 6 percent discount rate at the end of 15 years: ◀ Present Value

a. $50,000
b. $75,000
c. $100,000
d. $125,000

Present Value ▶ **8-12.** Calculate the present value of $80,000 at a 9 percent discount rate to be received in

a. 5 years
b. 10 years
c. 15 years
d. 20 years

Present Value of an Ordinary Annuity ▶ **8-13.** What is the present value of a $500 ten-year annual ordinary annuity at a 6 percent annual discount rate?

Present Value of an Ordinary Annuity ▶ **8-14.** Calculate the present value of a $10,000, thirty-year annual ordinary annuity at an annual discount rate of:

a. 0 percent
b. 10 percent
c. 20 percent
d. 50 percent

Present Value of an Ordinary Annuity ▶ **8-15.** What is the present value of a ten-year ordinary annuity of $20,000, using a 7 percent discount rate?

Present Value of an Ordinary Annuity ▶ **8-16.** Find the present value of a five-year ordinary annuity of $10,000, using the following discount rates:

a. 9 percent
b. 13 percent
c. 15 percent
d. 21 percent

Future Value of an Ordinary Annuity ▶ **8-17.** What is the future value of a five-year annual ordinary annuity of $500, using a 9 percent interest rate?

Future Value of an Ordinary Annuity ▶ **8-18.** Calculate the future value of a twelve-year, $6,000 annual ordinary annuity, using a discount rate of:

a. 0 percent
b. 2 percent
c. 10 percent
d. 20 percent

Future Value of an Ordinary Annuity ▶ **8-19.** What is the future value of a ten-year ordinary annuity of $5,000, discounted at 6 percent?

Future Value of an Ordinary Annuity ▶ **8-20.** What is the future value of an eight-year ordinary annuity of $5,000, using an 11 percent discount rate?

Future Value of an Ordinary Annuity ▶ **8-21.** Find the future value of the following five-year ordinary annuities, using a 10 percent discount rate.

a. $1,000
b. $10,000

c. $75,000
d. $125,000

8-22. Starting today, you invest $1,200 a year into your retirement account. If your retirement account earns 12 percent a year, how much will be available at the end of 40 years?

◀ Future Value of an Annuity Due

8-23. John will deposit $500 at the beginning of each year for five years into an account that has an interest rate of 8 percent. How much will John have to withdraw in five years?

◀ Future Value of an Annuity Due

8-24. An account manager has found that the future value of $10,000, deposited at the end of each year, for five years at a discount rate of 6 percent will amount to $56,370.93. What is the future value of this scenario if the account manager deposits the money today?

◀ Future Value of an Annuity Due

8-25. If your required rate of return is 12 percent, how much will an investment that pays $80 a year at the beginning of each of the next 20 years be worth to you today?

◀ Present Value of an Annuity Due

8-26. Sue has won the lottery and is going to receive $30,000 for 25 years; she received her first cheque today. The current discount rate is 9 percent. Find the present value of her winnings.

◀ Present Value of an Annuity Due

8-27. Kelly pays a debt service of $1,300 a month and will continue to make this payment for 15 years. What is the present value of these payments discounted at 7 percent if she mails her first payment in today?

◀ Present Value of an Annuity Due

8-28. You invested $50,000, and 10 years later the value of your investment has grown to $185,361. What is your compounded annual rate of return over this period?

◀ Solving for i

8-29. You invested $1,000 five years ago and the value of your investment has *fallen* to $773.78. What is your compounded annual rate of return over this period?

◀ Solving for i

8-30. What is the rate of return on an investment that grows from $50,000 to $246,795 in 10 years?

◀ Solving for i

8-31. What is the present value of a $50 annual perpetual annuity using a discount rate of 8 percent?

◀ Present Value of a Perpetuity

8-32. A payment of $80 per year forever is made with a discount rate of 9 percent. What is the present value of these payments?

◀ Present Value of a Perpetuity

8-33. You are valuing a preferred share that makes a dividend payment of $65 per year and the current discount rate is 8.5 percent. What is the value of this preferred share?

◀ Perpetuity

8-34. What is the future value of $10, earning 8 percent annual interest, 200 years later?

◀ Future Value

8-35. Joe's Dockyard is financing a new boat with an amortizing loan of $24,000, which is to be repaid in 10 annual installments of $4,247.62 each. What interest rate is Joe paying on the loan?

◀ Solving for the Loan Interest Rate

8-36. On June 1, 2002, Sue purchased a home for $220,000. She put $20,000 down on the house and obtained a 30-year fixed-rate mortgage for the remaining $200,000. Under the terms of the mortgage, Sue must make payments of $1,330.61 a month for the next 30 years starting June 30. What is the effective annual interest rate on Sue's mortgage?

◀ Solving for Monthly Interest Rate on a Mortgage

Present Value ▶ **8-37.** What is the amount you have to invest today at 7 percent annual interest to be able to receive $10,000 after

a. 5 years?
b. 10 years?
c. 20 years?

Future Value ▶ **8-38.** How much money would Ruby Carter need to deposit in her savings account at Great Western Bank today in order to have $16,850.58 in her account after five years? Assume she makes no other deposits or withdrawals and the bank guarantees an 11 percent annual interest rate, compounded annually.

Future Value ▶ **8-39.** If you invest $20,000 today, how much will you receive after

a. 7 years at a 5 percent annual interest rate?
b. 10 years at a 7 percent annual interest rate?

Solving for i ▶ **8-40.** The Microsoft share you purchased twelve years ago for $55 a share is now worth $67.73. What is the compounded annual rate of return you have earned on this investment?

Solving for n ▶ **8-41.** Amy Jolly deposited $1,000 in a savings account. The annual interest rate is 10 percent, compounded semiannually. How many years will it take for her money to grow to $2,653.30?

Present Value of an Annuity ▶ **8-42.** Beginning a year from now, Bernardo O'Reilly will receive $20,000 a year from his pension fund. There will be fifteen of these annual payments. What is the present value of these payments if a 6 percent annual interest rate is applied as the discount rate?

Future Value of a Payment ▶ **8-43.** If you invest $4,000 per year into your pension fund, earning 9 percent annually, how much will you have at the end of twenty years? You make your first payment of $4,000 today.

Future Value of an Annuity ▶ **8-44.** What would you accumulate if you were to invest $100 every quarter for five years into an account that returned 8 percent annually? Your first deposit would be made one quarter from today. Interest is compounded quarterly.

Future Value of an Annuity ▶ **8-45.** If you invest $2,000 per year for the next ten years at an 8 percent annual interest rate, beginning one year from today compounded annually, how much are you going to have at the end of the tenth year?

Challenge Problem Present Value of an Annuity ▶ **8-46.** It is the beginning of the quarter and you intend to invest $300 into your retirement fund at the end of every quarter for the next thirty years. You are promised an annual interest rate of 8 percent, compounded quarterly.

a. How much will you have after thirty years upon your retirement?
b. How long will your money last if you start withdrawing $6,000 at the end of every quarter after you retire?

Solving for Payment ▶ **8-47.** A $30,000 loan obtained today is to be repaid in equal annual installments over the next seven years starting at the end of this year. If the annual interest rate is 10 percent, compounded annually, how much is to be paid each year?

Present Value of a Perpetuity ▶ **8-48.** Allie Fox is moving to Central America. Before he packs up his wife and son, he purchases an annuity that guarantees payments of $10,000 a year in perpetuity. How much did he pay if the annual interest rate is 12 percent?

8-49. Matt and Christina Drayton deposited $500 into a savings account the day their daughter, Joey, was born. Their intention was to use this money to help pay for Joey's wedding expenses when and if she decided to get married. The account pays 5 percent annual interest with continuous compounding. Upon her return from a graduation trip to Hawaii, Joey surprises her parents with the sudden announcement of her planned marriage to John Prentice. The couple set the wedding date to coincide with Joey's twenty-third birthday. How much money will be in Joey's account on her wedding day? ◀ Future Value

8-50. You deposit $1,000 in an account that pays 8 percent interest, compounded annually. How long will it take to double your money? ◀ Time to Double Your Money

8-51. Upon reading your most recent credit card statement, you are shocked to learn that the balance owed on your purchases is $4,000. Resolving to get out of debt once and for all, you decide not to charge any more purchases and to make regular monthly payments until the balance is zero. Assuming that the bank's credit card interest rate is 19.5 percent and the most you can afford to pay each month is $200, how long will it take you to pay off your debt? ◀ Solving for n

8-52. Joanne and Walter borrow $14,568.50 for a new car before they move to Toronto. They are required to repay the amortized loan with four annual payments of $5,000 each. What is the interest rate on their loan? ◀ Solving for i

8-53. Norman Bates is planning for his eventual retirement from the motel business. He plans to make quarterly deposits of $1,000 into a retirement plan starting three months from today. The guaranteed annual interest rate is 8 percent, compounded quarterly. He plans to retire in 15 years. ◀ Challenge Problem Future Value of an Annuity

a. How much money will be in his retirement account when he retires?

b. Norman also supports his mother. At Norman's retirement party, Mother tells him they will need $2,000 each month in order to pay for their living expenses. Using the preceding interest rate and the total account balance from part (a), for how many years will Norman keep Mother happy by withdrawing $6,000 at the end of each quarter? It is very important that Norman keep Mother happy.

8-54. Jack Torrance comes to you for financial advice. He hired the Redrum Weed-N-Whack Lawn Service to trim the hedges in his garden. Because of the large size of the project (the shrubs were really out of control), Redrum has given Jack a choice of four different payment options. Which of the following four options would you recommend that Jack choose? Why? ◀ Challenge Problem

Option 1. Pay $5,650 cash immediately.

Option 2. Pay $6,750 cash in one lump sum two years from now.

Option 3. Pay $800 at the end of each quarter for two years.

Option 4. Pay $1,000 immediately plus $5,250 in one lump sum two years from now.

Jack tells you he can earn 8 percent interest, compounded quarterly, on his money. You have no reason to question his assumption.

8-55. Sarah has $30,000 for a down payment on a house and wants to borrow $120,000 from a mortgage banker to purchase a $150,000 house. The mortgage loan is to be repaid in monthly installments over a thirty-year period. The annual interest rate is 9 percent. How much will Sarah's monthly mortgage payments be? ◀ Solving for Payment

Solving for Payment ▶

8-56. The Robinsons have found the house of their dreams. They have $50,000 to use as a down payment and they want to borrow $250,000 from the bank. The current mortgage interest rate is 6 percent. If they make equal monthly payments for fifteen years, how much will their monthly mortgage payment be?

Solving for Payment ▶

Excel

8-57. Slick has his heart set on a new Miata sportscar. He will need to borrow $18,000 to get the car he wants. The bank will loan Slick the $18,000 at an annual interest rate of 6 percent.

a. How much would Slick's monthly car payments be for a four-year loan?

b. How much would Slick's monthly car payments be if he obtains a six-year loan at the same interest rate?

Challenge Problem
Value of Missing Cash Flow ▶

Excel

8-58. Assume the following set of cash flows:

Time 1	Time 2	Time 3	Time 4
$100	$150	?	$100

At a discount rate of 10 percent, the total present value of all the cash flows above, including the missing cash flow, is $320.74. Given these conditions, what is the value of the missing cash flow?

Loan Amortization Table ▶

8-59. You are considering financing the purchase of an automobile that costs $22,000. You intend to finance the entire purchase price with a five-year amortized loan with an 8 percent annual interest rate.

a. Calculate the amount of the *monthly* payments for this loan.

b. Construct an amortization table for this loan using the format shown in Table 8-5. Use monthly payments.

c. If you elected to pay off the balance of the loan at the end of the thirty-sixth month, how much would you have to pay?

Challenge Problem ▶

8-60. You have won a lottery. When you call to claim your $5,000 reward, the lottery agent points out that you will receive $5,000, but the payment will be spread out over time. He proposes four scenarios for your consideration. You are somewhat surprised. You expected to collect the entire $5,000 to pay down your student loan, pay for your reading week winter holiday in Hawaii, and make a small investment in a company that you have followed for many years, but have never had sufficient cash to invest in. You are told that you have 24 hours to make your decision. Please review the options below and decide which one you would choose.

a. Receive $3,000 immediately.

b. Receive five equal installments of $1,000 at the end of each year.

c. Receive a payment of $2,000 right now, the next one equal to $1,000 one year from now, and $3,000 at the end of year five.

d. Receive 10 equal installments of $750 for the next ten years. Payments occur at the end of each year. After observing the market, you estimate that the going market interest rate is equal to 10 percent compounded annually.

Challenge Problem ▶

8-61. Jack Wheel is thinking about developing a delivery business and estimates that he would need to invest approximately $30,000 in a small transportation vehicle. He approached three banks and received the following proposals:

	Bank A	Bank B	Bank C
Amount	30,000	30,000	30,000
Annual interest rate	10%	8%	12%
Time period	5 years	4 years	3 years
Compounding	Monthly	Semiannually	Annually

The loan is to be repaid in equal installments over the proposed time period starting at the end of each year. Given the annual interest rates and other loan terms, how much will Jack pay each year for the proposed loans? If Jack can only afford less than $8,000 in annual payments, which bank should he choose?

8-62. You are planning to retire in the next 10 years. You estimated that you would like to have $1.5 million when you retire. Since you have a good paying job at a prestigious Toronto investment-banking firm, you are convinced it is possible, especially since you already have $350,000 in your savings account. You collect 2 percent interest per annum on that amount. To accumulate the planned amount you wonder about two possible strategies you can adopt: ◀ Challenge Problem

a. You could deposit an equal amount of $20,000 at the bank at the end of each quarter, which would earn 3 percent interest per annum compounded quarterly; or

b. You could just deposit a bonus of $400,000 at the end of the fifth year, which you plan to collect as a partner in the firm. You expect to receive an interest rate of 4 percent on this deposit.

Which one of the scenarios would get you closer to your financial goal of retiring with $1.5 million in savings?

8-63. You are collecting cash to purchase a dream car, a 1965 Ford Mustang and you plan to purchase it in 10 years on your 30th birthday. The value of the car is to increase on an annual basis by 5 percent and it currently costs $20,000. How much would you need to deposit at the beginning of each of the next ten years to pay for the car if you can earn 5 percent of your deposit? ◀ Challenge Problem

ANSWERS TO SELF-TEST

ST-1. FV = $5,000 × 1.06^8 = $7,969.24 = Jed's balance when the eight-year CD matures

ST-2. $19,999 = $1,776.89($PVIFA_{i = ?, n = 12}$)
11.2551 = $PVIFA_{i = ?, n = 12}$
i = 1% monthly (from the PVIFA Table at the n = 12 row, i = 1%)
Annual rate = 1% ×12 = 12%

ST-3. PV = $100,000 × 1 / 1.08^{10} = $46,319.35
= the present value of Heidi's $100,000

ST-4. $20,000 = PMT × [1 – (1 / 1.005^{48})]/0.005
$20,000 = PMT × 42.5803
PMT = $469.70 = Zack's car loan payment

ST-5. $5,000 × $FVIF_{i = ?, n = 10}$ = $15,529.24
$PVIF_{i = ?, n = 10} = 3.1058$ ∴ i = 12% = Bridget's annual rate of return on the mutual fund (from the FVIF Table at the n = 10 row, i = 12%)

ST-6. FV = PMT($FVIFA_{i\%, n}$) × (1 + i)
= $1,000($FVIFA_{10\%, 10}$) × (1 + 0.10)
= $1,000(15.9374) × 1.10
= $17,531.14

Comprehensive Cases: Part II

Case 1: Alberta Printing House

Alberta Printing House (APH) is a private company, which prints paper labels (through offset printing), mainly for local soft drink manufacturers and breweries. The rapid growth of the company since 1992 has been limited by inadequate capital to finance sufficient expansion in production capacity to meet the market demand. Substantial growth of the company's major clients is anticipated, which includes Coca-Cola, PepsiCo, and leading Canadian breweries.

APH, based in Red Deer, is one of the leading Canadian companies involved in offset printing of paper labels. Two printing experts started the company as a 50/50 private partnership. Initially, the company used second-hand renovated machinery and employed four people, including the owners.

MARKET

APH is currently active in three major segments: soft drink manufacturers, breweries, and distillers. APH has started manufacturing for two additional types of industries: food processing and confectionery companies. Printing promotional materials is a seasonal activity to utilize short-term excess manufacturing capacity.

The soft drink market segment represents 51 percent of APH's sales in 2003 and is the second biggest segment in Canada in terms of the total demand for labels. APH estimates that this segment will be 1.1 billion pieces in 2004, of which Coca-Cola alone is expected to purchase 400 million pieces. Only about 15 percent of the labels used domestically are imported. Demand is expected to continue to grow at the rate of 10 percent per annum due to significant investments in Canada by leading soft drink producers. The beer market segment represents 33 percent of APH's sales in 2003 and is the biggest segment of the market with total demand in 2004 estimated to be at 1.6 billion pieces. Approximately 45 percent of that production is imported. All major market players foresee further growth in the domestic demand, but no reliable data seems to exist. The distillers' market segment represents 13 percent of the company's sales. APH estimates the total demand to be 350 million sets of labels annually. About 35 percent of those are imported. APH supplies the biggest clients in this segment. The food processing and confectionery market segments are currently a very small percent of APH's sales (3 percent of sales in 2003). The company produces about 20 million sets of labels for a food processing company in Hamilton and about 5 million chocolate wrappers for a producer based in Vancouver. APH's management believes that the company has a significant opportunity to penetrate these market segments. Over 50 percent of the labels and wrappers used by food processing and confectionery companies in Canada are imported.

The label printing market in Canada is a very competitive business, with a large number of relatively small private companies providing between 50 percent and 85 percent of all labels printed in Canada. The remaining labels used in the domestic market are imported, usually from the United States and Europe. Only a few private Canadian companies managed to establish long-term relationships with major corporate clients.

APH's management believes that the company has many opportunities to grow because of APH's marketing skills and customer contacts. Management believes that there are some other interesting market segments, which, due to a lack of production capacity, the business has not been able to address. These segments include household chemicals, cosmetics, toiletries, et cetera. These segments should grow significantly as a result of increased foreign and domestic investment and increased promotion and consumer spending.

FINANCIAL DATA

The historical financial results for 2002 and 2003 and management's projections are presented below. The financials have been prepared according to Canadian GAAP and appear to accurately reflect the operating results.

Financial projections prepared by management assume a very significant growth of sales from 2004 to 2007. The sales growth can primarily be attributed to a significant growth in production capacity (approximately 75 percent in 2005 as well as a further increase of approximately 50 percent in 2006 and approximately 20 percent in 1997). Management's discussions with major customers and their evaluation of potential market opportunities indicate that such a significant growth of sales may be achievable. The projected increase in the gross margin results mainly from an assumed reduction of raw material costs compared to 2003 levels. This increase is due to importing raw material without trade intermediaries and cost reductions after the installation of new machinery and because employment is not expected to increase significantly over the 2003 levels. Operating profit should increase as the company generates more revenues in the same organizational form as in 2003. Amortization was always at a relatively high level as a percentage of net sales due to continuous investments and accelerated amortization schedules.

	Historical		Forecasts			
(In $000s)	**2002**	**2003**	**2004**	**2005**	**2006**	**2007**
Net Sales	**5,624**	**21,495**	**70,361**	**122,240**	**183,360**	**220,032**
Cost of Goods Sold	**4,547**	**17,113**	**54,859**	**85,889**	**123,671**	**146,195**
Raw materials	3,389	12,128	42,258	69,000	103,205	123,847
Wages	417	1,361	5,149	6,376	7,332	8,432
Energy and transport	155	839	1,709	2,542	3,746	3,937
Other services	228	1,514	2,464	3,326	4,990	5,489
Other costs	358	1,271	3,279	4,645	4,398	4,490
Gross Profit	**1,077**	**4,382**	**15,502**	**36,351**	**59,689**	**73,837**
S&A Expenses	105	994	1,860	3,600	3,974	4,338
Amortization	681	1,753	3,648	12,608	13,977	12,076
Operating Margin	**291**	**1,635**	**9,994**	**20,143**	**41,738**	**57,423**
Financial Revenues	7	16	38	1,207	100	120
Financial Costs	4	534	1,231	2,263	879	227
Profit before Tax	**294**	**1,117**	**8,801**	**19,087**	**40,959**	**57,316**
Income Tax	103	392	3,457	7,572	16,320	22,863
Net Profit	**191**	**725**	**5,344**	**11,515**	**24,639**	**34,453**

Mr. John Turner, President and Chief Operating Officer of APH, was just reviewing the financial forecasts for the company for the next four years. While he has always been an optimist, he wondered if the financial projections are too aggressive. After all, APH's sales are expected to increase 10-fold between 2003 and 2007. In the same period, net profits increased by more than 35 times. He decided to go over the financial plans one more time and to focus on the key revenue and cost assumptions.

Requirements

1. Assess the viability of financial projections for APH. (Hint: concentrate on sales growth and margin analysis in the past and in the future.)
2. Do these financial projections look aggressive? Why or why not?

CASE 2: RUBBERCAN

Mr. John Harris, a new financial analyst at Stone Resources, a leading Canadian plastic processor, was planning his time to conduct the analysis of RubberCan. Stone Resources was looking to acquire RubberCan, but Stone's management wanted to have a good assessment of RubberCan's historical financial performance. They were also particularly interested in RubberCan's cash generating abilities. As Mr. Harris planned the format of his financial report, he had reminded himself that he had to look at other areas of the business in order to arrive at a comprehensive report.

THE BUSINESS

RubberCan is a major Canadian manufacturer of technical rubber goods based in southeastern Ontario. RubberCan is involved in the manufacture and distribution of a wide range of technical rubber goods: molded goods (primarily seals, gaskets, rings and other articles, and spare parts for the automotive and household appliances industries); extruded rubber products (including sealing profiles and insulations); and different types of rubber belts. The company is organized in five stand-alone centres corresponding to the main production units (molded products, extruded products, belts, mixing) and a central office, which handles marketing, finance, and administration. Mr. Henry Krawczyk wholly owns the business. His business philosophy is based on reinvesting profits—no dividends have been paid in the past.

Capacity utilization varies in different plants. For example, the mixing plant has a capacity of 20,400 tonnes per year, while present capacity utilization is estimated at 50 percent. Extrusion lines are 100 percent utilized, while the line for the production of rubber belts is currently operating at 40 percent capacity. Management plans to make new investments that will enable RubberCan to increase its production capacity for those products for which demand is highest. Current capacity and the planned capital investments should allow RubberCan to achieve its growth projections for the next few years.

THE MARKETS

Domestic Market.

RubberCan mainly supplies original equipment manufacturers (OEMs) and sells to the replacement markets with rubber components in the automotive, agricultural, construction, and household appliances, industrial, and pharmaceutical markets. The company also sells excess rubber band.

According to management estimates, the total Canadian rubber goods' market (composed of six market segments) represented 7,600 tonnes of finished products in 2004. RubberCan supplied the total volume of 4,645 tonnes domestically, resulting in a 61.1 percent market share. Management projects the growth of the total market to 13,802 tonnes in 2008 with RubberCan production increasing to 7,645 tonnes and the total market share decreasing to 58.4 percent.

The automotive market segment is composed of a relatively small number of high volume customers, including major vehicle manufacturers in Canada. The largest clients by volume are Ford and Chrysler. The agricultural market segment includes rubber belts and the replacement market. The demand and production of agricultural machines is stable and the company continues to increase its sales through its own network of distributors. The construction market segment is a new market for the company. In 2004, the company introduced two new extruded products designed to save energy (pipewrap thermal insulation and window draft seals). The group of thirty customers in this market segment includes manufacturers of window frames as well as insulation companies. The household appliance market segment comprises only molded products for a limited number of OEMs, which account for 78 percent of total sales. The remaining amount is sold through a distribution network to the replacement market. The industrial market segment includes a vast array of products supplied to a few hundred customers from such industries as machine tools, food processing machinery, paper, furniture and wood processing, and mining. The largest percentage of sales is rubber belts for industrial use. The pharmaceutical market segment is a relatively small niche, which includes molded products sold to three pharmaceutical companies.

Exports.

While RubberCan's export revenue is not a significant part of the business (8 percent) versus domestic sales, it is important to note that RubberCan has substantially changed its export business. The company was traditionally selling the majority of its export products to the United States, but the collapse of this market through trade barriers forced the management to look for new customers. RubberCan currently exports its products to Germany, Italy, Spain, Sweden, Denmark, and Finland. The company has concluded distribution agreements with strong partners in these countries and is in the process of negotiating agreements with a potential British partner.

FINANCIAL DATA

The historical financial results of RubberCan are presented below. The financials have been prepared in accordance with generally accepted accounting principles.

Income Statement

(In $000s)	2001	2002	2003	2004
Net Sales	557,265	636,413	688,223	734,000
Cost of Goods Sold	310,084	348,321	374,193	386,699
Selling and Admin. Expenses	116,390	135,165	139,232	146,973
Amortization	110,223	122,723	132,723	142,723
Operating Income	20,568	30,204	42,075	57,605
Interest Expense	4,200	4,000	3,000	2,000
Earnings before Taxes	16,368	26,204	39,075	55,605
Income Tax	6,547	10,482	15,630	22,242
Net Income	9,821	15,722	23,445	33,363

Balance Sheet

(In $000s)	2001	2002	2003	2004
Assets				
Cash	3,000	9,193	51,881	115,203
Marketable Securities	1,000	1,000	1,000	1,000
Accounts Receivable	66,453	74,315	79,780	82,990
Inventory	44,408	50,652	53,928	56,056
P.P. & E., Gross	1,102,232	1,227,232	1,327,232	1,427,232
Less: Accumulated Amortization	600,428	723,151	855,874	998,598
P.P. & E., Net	501,804	504,081	471,358	428,634
Total Assets	**616,665**	**639,241**	**657,946**	**683,883**
Liabilities				
Accounts Payable	71,370	80,224	85,484	88,058
Notes Payable	22,000	12,000	10,000	5,000
Long-Term Debt	20,000	28,000	20,000	15,000
Shareholders' Equity				
Preferred Shares	17,000	17,000	17,000	17,000
Common Shares	55,000	55,000	55,000	55,000
Retained Earnings	431,295	447,017	470,462	503,825
Total Liabilities and Equity	**616,665**	**639,241**	**657,946**	**683,883**

Requirements

1. Assess the Company's historical financial performance. As a part of the analysis prepare the following:

   a. the statement of income and retained earnings

   b. the cash flow statement

   c. ratio analysis.

2. What are the strengths and weaknesses of the company, given your analysis above?

3. Should your financial analysis be limited to the analysis of financial statements only? What else should you analyze as a part of your general assessment of the company's historical financial performance?

CASE 3: INTER-TEAM

Inter-Team (IT) is one of the most respected distributors of automotive parts in Central Alberta. The key to its success has been a commitment to developing a province-wide distribution system, customer service, and heavy marketing. IT became a parts distributor after running a Ford dealership. Encouraged by its initial success in selling cars and Ford parts, it began distributing parts for a wider range of vehicles. It is based in Airdrie and has a 150 × 200 metre warehouse. The company initially focused on high-quality parts, but recently it began to introduce parts from alternative, less expensive suppliers. Sales are generated from the central warehouse and seven regional branches, located in the major centres throughout Alberta. These branches are known to maintain a relatively low level of inventory (well below the optimal level of 25,000 stock lines) and they are supplied by the central warehouse only once per week.

Mr. John Smith who is no longer actively involved in day-to-day operations owns Inter-Team. Two managers who are well known to be quite aggressive and expansion-oriented manage the business. The company employs 60–70 people.

The key financial indicators for Inter-Team between 2001 and 2004 are presented below.

(In $ millions)	2001	2002	2003	2004
Net Sales	13.9	21.3	29.8	36.4
Cost of Sales	10.4	15.4	21.8	26.4
Gross Profit	3.5	5.9	8.0	10.0
EBITDA	1.9	3.8	4.7	5.5
EBIT	1.8	3.6	4.5	5.1
EAT	0.8	1.7	2.1	3.1

Mr. Smith was very proud of the company's historical financial performance. He also wondered about how the growth dynamics and profitability would compare to other leading companies in the sector. This would provide him with information about how much he and his management team still has to do in the future in order to be considered one of the industry leaders.

COMPARABLE COMPANIES

Automotive Group Limited (Canada)

The principal activity of the group is the distribution and sale of automotive components for the vehicle aftermarket. The group operates through approximately 195 sites. In all the regions of the automotive market in which the company operates, it is either the number 1 or number 2 company. The company has been able to grow its business considerably, especially in 1997 and 1998 post acquisitions. These acquisitions enhanced gross and operating margins and improved the company's operating efficiencies. Benefits of improved buying terms, inter-company trading, and volume growth through increased market share should translate into further improvement in profitability. Key financial indicators between 2001 and 2004 are presented below.

(In $ millions)	2001	2002	2003	2004
Net Sales	98.1	107.9	228.9	388.1
Gross Profit	15.7	17.6	39.6	76.1
EBIT	7.9	9.0	20.2	35.3
EAT	4.8	5.8	13.3	19.7

Part Co-operatives Limited

The principal activities of the PartCo are the distribution of components to the automotive aftermarket, primarily in the northern United States and Western Canada. The group also manufactures and packages automotive parts and components. The company specifically deals with automotive paints, refinishing materials, and machinery, tools and equipment for vehicle workshops, radiators, and engine cooling components and supplies. It further services automotive and related air conditioning in the United States. The company has been able to grow its business through a combination of acquisitions and organic growth. Gross margins were maintained at around 36 percent while operating margins increased from 5 percent to 7 percent beginning 2002. Net profit margin has been maintained at 4 percent in spite of additional debt. The key financial indicators between 2001 and 2004 are presented below.

(In $ millions)	2001	2002	2003	2004
Net Sales	136.4	164.4	204.2	286.0
Gross Profit	48.0	59.3	75.2	104.4
EBIT	6.9	7.5	13.4	26.2
EAT	6.8	7.8	7.9	14.4

Auto Fit Holdings Canada

Auto Fit Holdings Canada is the holding company for a group of companies that operate approximately 1,097 specialist tire, exhaust, and brake repair services centres in Canada. The group also provides mobile fitting services and operates wholesale automotive parts distribution centres. A strong brand and considerable purchasing power gives Auto Fit Holdings an ability to maintain its leading market position in Canada. The Speedy acquisition also gave the group a major presence and a strong base in Europe. European fast-fit is less developed than in Canada and thus presents a major growth opportunity for the group. The company's core skill is in retailing and its key assets are the company's brand name and its wealth of customer information. Its intense customer focus has meant that the group has become adept at reorganizing new market opportunities. The summary of key financial indicators is included below. The company has been able to improve its gross and operating profitability.

(In $ millions)	2001	2002	2003	2004
Net Sales	297.6	365.4	426.9	472.8
Gross Profit	37.2	49.0	54.9	69.8
EBIT	25.3	34.7	43.2	58.0
EAT	20.5	25.4	30.3	39.5

Requirements

1. Perform the comparative analysis of the financial performance of Inter-Team versus other industry players.
2. What are the key components of such an analysis?
3. What are the main conclusions of the analysis above?

Part III
Capital Budgeting and Business Valuation

CHAPTERS

HUDSON BAY COMPANY—A CAPITAL EXPENDITURE PROGRAM IN MOTION

www.hbc.com

CORPORATE INFORMATION

Headquarters	Toronto, Ontario
Industry	Retail
Number of Stores	448
Listed on	TSX
Ticker symbol	HBC
President & CEO	George Heller

Year Ended 31 January (In $ millions)	2001	2002	2003	2004
Sales	7,400	7,446	7,384	7,400
Operating Profit	300	185	161	199
Net Profit	125	73	69	111
Current Assets	2,372	2,558	2,409	2,344
Current Liabilities	1,228	1,085	1,261	1,053
Total Assets	4,376	4,534	4,276	4,111
Capital Expenditure	241	143	133	115
Short-Term & Long-Term Debt	822	806	510	672
Shareholders' Equity	2,303	2,529	2,394	2,431

Business

The Hudson Bay Company (HBC) is one of Canada's largest multi-channel department store retailers. Established in 1670, the company provides a wide selection of goods and services and consists of three complementary retail business units: The Bay (a department store), Zellers (a mass merchandise store), and Home Outfitters (a kitchen, bed, and bath specialty store). The Bay operations consist of 99 department stores across Canada, with the largest amount of stores (38) in Ontario, and provides products appealing to middle- and upper-income customers. Zellers operates 312 units and offers national and private brand merchandise at prices that provide value to customers. Home Outfitters consists of a network of 37 units and has a strong presence in Ontario (19 units).

Financial Performance

The level of sales has been flat in the last four years while industry sales have grown by 3–4 percent. The operating profit declined between 2001 and 2003, but recovered in 2004 when HBC posted a profit of $111 million. Current assets ranged between $2.3 billion and $2.5 billion while current liabilities were steady at the $1.1–1.2 billion level, yielding to the current ratio of about 2. In the fiscal year ended in January 2003, HBC dedicated a significant portion of its cash flow towards reducing its debt burden, consequently constraining its capital expenditure program. The company reduced its level of debt from $822 million in 2001 to $510 million in 2004. This trend was reversed in the following fiscal year when the company took on additional debt.

A Capital Budget Program for Renovations —A "Must" to Compete with Wal-Mart

In the last four years, HBC spent $632 million in capital expenditures. The capital outlay was dedicated towards new store openings, store renovations, and improvements to technology infrastructure. The expenditures in software are expected to translate into cost cutting and better inventory management.

In 2004, HBC embarked on an ambitious capital expenditure program to renovate 175 out of 312 existing Zellers stores, increase capacity in the Bay and Home Outfitter stores, and continue the technological upgrades. The total capital budget is expected to cost between $200 million and $250 million, of which more than half will be dedicated towards renovating Zellers stores. According to Management, Zellers' expansion and renovation is critical to the Company's ability to effectively compete against Wal-Mart. The cost-benefit analysis performed by management determined that in spite of incremental depreciation expense, net profit is likely to increase due to an incremental increase in revenue and a decrease in some of the other operating cost items.

Sources: Data for 2004 and 2003 from 2003 HBC *Annual Report* (pp. 41–43, 12–30); data for 2002 from 2002 *Annual Report* (pp. 30–32); data for 2001 from 2001 *Annual Report* (pp. 31–33).

9

The Cost of Capital

Chapter Objectives

After reading this chapter, you should be able to:

9-1 **Describe** four main sources of capital and how firms raise capital.

9-2 **Explain** how to estimate the cost of capital for each of the four main financing sources.

9-3 **Define** the estimated weighted average cost of capital (WACC).

9-4 **Describe** how to use the marginal cost of capital (MCC) schedule to make capital budgeting decisions.

9-5 **Explain** the importance of the marginal cost of capital (MCC) schedule in financial decision making.

"There's no such thing as a free lunch."

—Milton Friedman

Royal Bank Takes Steps to Reduce Its Cost of Capital

Royal Bank of Canada, one of the largest financial institutions in Canada, announced in June 2002 that it will buy back some of its common shares. In a news release issued by the bank, it said that "the purchase of common shares under the normal course issuer bid will enable the bank to balance the imperatives of maintaining strong capital ratios with the ongoing need to generate shareholder value." Royal Bank would also consider issuing debt to execute the share buyback program while interest rates were low.

Why would Royal Bank of Canada be interested in buying back its shares, and why would the program reduce the bank's cost of capital? The answer is that buying back shares changes the relative amount of debt and equity financing to fund the bank's assets. As you will see from your study of the chapter ahead, debt financing is less expensive than equity financing, so using relatively more debt financing and relatively less equity financing tend to lower the overall cost of the bank's capital. Naturally, therefore, the bank's managers would be interested in buying the banks' shares as long as the increase in the percentage of debt capital was not seen as increasing the bank's risk too much.

CHAPTER OVERVIEW

In capital budgeting decisions, financial managers must analyze many factors to determine whether a project will add value to a firm, including estimated incremental cash flows, the timing of those cash flows, risk, and the project's required rate of return.

One of the key components of the capital budgeting decision is the cost of capital. **Capital** is the term for funds that firms use. Businesses, such as Royal Bank, raise capital from creditors and owners. All capital raised has a cost because the suppliers of capital demand compensation for the funds provided.

In this chapter, we examine the costs of different types of capital. We see how to estimate the cost of capital from a particular source, as well as the overall cost of capital for a firm. We also see how estimating a firm's cost of capital affects a firm's financing and investment decisions.

THE COST OF CAPITAL

To properly evaluate potential investments, firms must know how much their capital costs. Without a measure of the cost of capital, for example, a firm might invest in a new project with an expected return of 10 percent even though the capital used for the investment cost 15 percent. If a firm's capital costs 15 percent, then the firm must seek investments that return at least that much. It is vital, then, that managers know how much their firm's capital costs *before* committing to investments.

Suppliers and users of capital use cost estimates before making short- or long-term financial decisions. Investors must determine their required rate of return, k, to value either a bond or shares before they invest. The required rate of return, k, for each type of security issued is the cost of capital for that source. Overall, the cost of capital is the compensation investors demand of firms that use their funds, adjusted for taxes and transaction costs in certain cases, as we will explain later in this chapter.

In Chapter 10, we will see that firms determine their required rate of return before deciding whether to accept a capital budgeting project. The discount rate or hurdle rate, k, is the firm's cost of capital for that project. Investors supply capital, so they require a return, and firms use capital, so they must pay suppliers of capital for the use of those funds.

SOURCES OF CAPITAL

Its creditors and owners supply a firm's capital. Firms raise capital by borrowing it (issuing bonds to investors or promissory notes to banks), or by issuing preferred or common shares. The overall cost of a firm's capital depends on the return demanded by each of these suppliers of capital.

To determine a firm's overall cost of capital, the first step is to determine the cost of capital from each supplier. The cost of capital from a particular source, such as bondholders or common shareholders, is known as the **component cost of capital**.

In the following sections, we estimate the cost of debt capital, k_d; the cost of capital raised through a preferred share issue, k_p; and the cost of equity capital supplied by common shareholders, k_s for internal equity and k_n for new external equity.

The Cost of Debt

When a firm borrows money at a stated rate of interest, determining the cost of debt, k_d, is relatively straightforward. As shown in Figure 9-1, the lender's cost of capital is the required rate of return on either a company's new bonds or a promissory note. The firm's **cost of debt** when it borrows money by issuing bonds is the interest rate demanded by the bond investors. When borrowing money from an individual or financial institution, the interest rate on the loan is the firm's cost of debt.

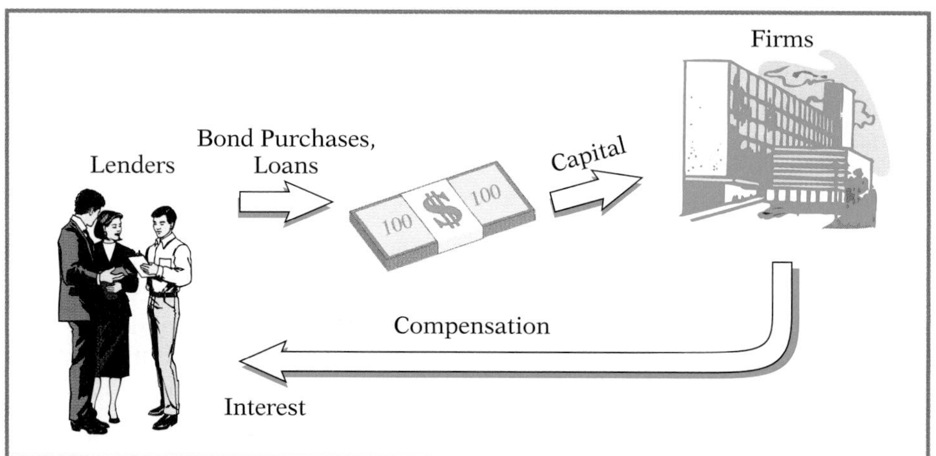

Figure 9-1 The Flow of Debt Capital from Investors to Firms
Figure 9-1 shows how debt investors supply capital to and receive interest from the firm.

The After-Tax Cost of Debt (AT k_d) The **after-tax cost of debt, AT k_d**, is the cost to the company of obtaining debt funds. Because the interest paid on bonds or bank loans is a tax-deductible expense for a business, a firm's AT k_d is less than the required rate of return of the suppliers of debt capital. For example, suppose Ellis Industries from Edmonton borrowed $100,000 for one year at 10 percent interest paid annually. The interest rate on the loan is 10 percent, so Ellis must pay the lender $10,000 in interest each year the loan is outstanding (10 percent of $100,000). However, look at what happens when Ellis takes its taxes for the year into account:

	Before Borrowing	*After Borrowing*
Operating Income	$50,000	$50,000
Interest Expense	0	10,000
Before-Tax Income	50,000	40,000
Income Tax (40% rate)	20,000	16,000
Net After-Tax Income	30,000	24,000

The $10,000 interest charge caused a $6,000 decrease in Ellis's net after-tax income ($30,000 – $24,000 = $6,000). Therefore, assuming a tax rate of 40 percent, the true cost of the loan is only $6,000 (6 percent), not $10,000 (10 percent).

The following formula converts k_d into AT k_d, the true after-tax cost of borrowing:

Formula for the After-Tax Cost of Debt

$$AT\ k_d = k_d(1 - T) \tag{9-1}$$

where

k_d = The before-tax cost of debt

T = The firm's marginal tax rate

To solve for AT k_d in our Ellis Industries example, recall that Ellis's before-tax cost of debt is 10 percent and its tax rate is 40 percent. The after-tax cost of debt, according to Equation 9-1, follows:

$$\begin{aligned} \text{AT } k_d &= 0.10(1 - 0.40) \\ &= 0.10 \times 0.60 \\ &= 0.06 \text{ or } 6\% \end{aligned}$$

Our calculations show that for Ellis Industries the after-tax cost of debt on a \$100,000 loan at a 10 percent rate of interest is 6 percent.

We have seen that the cost of using borrowed money is the interest rate charged by the lender. In addition, we discussed how the tax deductibility of interest lowers the firm's true cost of debt. Next, we turn to the cost of preferred shares and common share equity.

The Cost of Preferred and Common Share Funds

When corporations raise capital by issuing preferred or common shares, these investors expect a return on their investments. If that return is not realized, investors will sell their shares, driving the share price down. Although the claim of preferred and common shareholders may not be contractual, as it is for bondholders, there is a cost nonetheless. To calculate the cost of using preferred and common shareholders' money, then, the firm must estimate the rate of return that these investors demand. Figure 9-2 shows how firms raise capital from, and compensate, equity investors.

The Cost of Preferred Shares (k_p) The **cost of preferred shares (k_p)** is the rate of return investors require on a company's new preferred shares, plus the cost of issuing the shares. Therefore, to calculate k_p, a firm's managers must estimate the rate of return that preferred shareholders would demand and add in the cost of the share issue. Because preferred share investors normally buy preferred shares to obtain the stream of constant preferred share

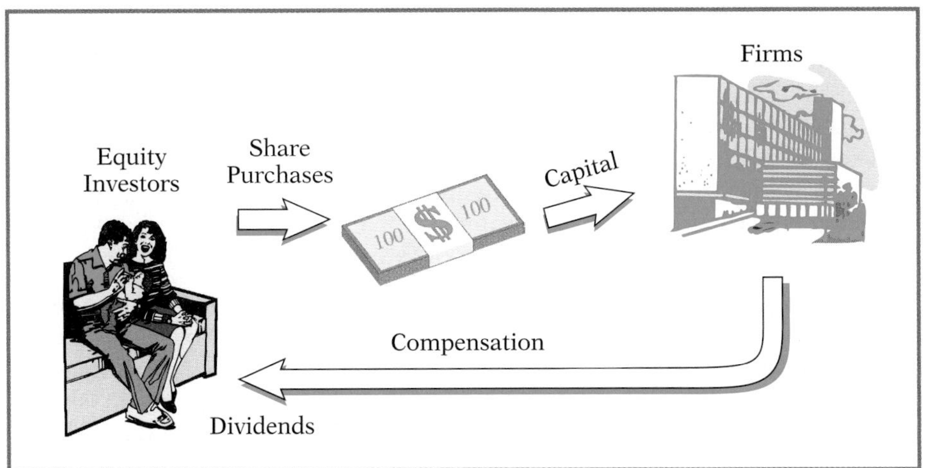

Figure 9-2 The Flow of Capital from Equity Investors to Firms
Figure 9-2 shows how equity investors supply capital to the firm and receive dividends from it.

dividends associated with the preferred share issue, their return on investment can normally be measured by dividing the amount of the firm's expected preferred share dividend by the price of the preferred shares. The cost of issuing the new securities, known as **flotation cost**, includes investment bankers' fees and commissions, and lawyers' fees. These costs must be deducted from the preferred share price paid by investors to obtain the net price paid to the firm. Equation 9-2 shows how to estimate the cost of preferred shares:

Formula for the Cost of Preferred Shares (k_p)

$$k_p = \frac{D_p}{(P_p - F)} \tag{9-2}$$

where

k_p = The cost of the preferred share issue; the expected return
D_p = The amount of the expected preferred share dividend
P_p = The current price of the preferred shares
F = The flotation cost per share

The cost of using the company's preferred shares is k_p. The value of k_p, the expected return from the preferred share issue, is the minimum return the firm's managers must earn when they use the money supplied by preferred shareholders. If they cannot earn this return, the preferred shareholders will sell their shares, causing the preferred share's price to fall. This means the firm must issue more preferred shares before the share price fell to raise the same amount of funds.

Suppose Ellis Industries has issued preferred shares that have been paying annual dividends of \$2.50 per share and that are expected to continue to do so indefinitely. The current price of Ellis's preferred shares is \$22 a share, and the flotation cost is \$2 per share. According to Equation 9-2, the cost of Ellis's preferred shares is as follows:

$$k_p = \frac{\$2.50}{(\$22 - \$2)}$$
$$= .125, \text{ or } 12.5\%$$

We see that Ellis Industries' cost of new preferred shares, assuming that a preferred share pays dividends of \$2.50 per year, has a market price of \$22, and has a flotation cost of \$2, is 12.5 percent.

The cost of preferred shares, k_p, is higher than the before-tax cost of debt, k_d, because a company's bondholders and bankers have a prior claim on the earnings of the firm and on its assets in the event of a liquidation. Preferred shareholders, as a result, take a greater risk than bondholders or bankers and demand a correspondingly greater rate of return.

Take Note 

There is no tax adjustment in the cost of preferred share calculation. Unlike interest payments on debt, firms may not deduct preferred share dividends on their tax returns. The dividends are paid out of after-tax profits.

The Cost of Internal Common Equity (k_s) The **cost of internal common equity (k_s)** is the required rate of return on funds supplied by existing common shareholders. The cost of equity depends on the rate of return the common shareholders demand for holding the company's common shares. Calculating k_s is tougher than calculating k_p because common shareholders do not receive a constant stream of dividends. Instead, investors own the firm, including the corporate earnings left over after other claimants on the firm have been paid. Neither creditors nor preferred shareholders have a claim on these residual earnings. Corporations may either retain the residual earnings or return them in the form of common share dividends. Retained earnings have a cost, however. The cost of retained earnings, another name for the cost of internal equity, is the rate of return that the company must earn to justify retaining the earnings instead of paying them as dividends. These are internally generated (within the firm) equity funds.

As noted, common share dividend payments change from year to year or may not be paid at all. Ultimately, however, dividends are the only payments a corporation makes to its common shareholders. The corporation may pay regular dividends, or it may pay a liquidation dividend some time in the future. For companies that pay regular dividends, which grow at a constant rate, the constant dividend growth model may be used to estimate the cost of equity. For companies that do not pay regular dividends, or when the market approach to risk is more appropriate, the CAPM may be used to estimate the cost of equity.

Using the Dividend Growth Model to Estimate k_s.

The dividend growth model (sometimes called the Gordon Model after its developer, financial economist Myron Gordon) uses the time value of money concepts in Chapter 8 to calculate the present value of a continuing stream of future dividends:

$$P_0 = \frac{D_1}{k_s - g}$$

where

P_0 = The current price of the common share

D_1 = The dollar amount of the common share dividend expected one period from now

k_s = Required rate of return per period on this common share investment

g = Expected constant growth rate per period of the company's common share dividends[1]

Rearranging the terms in the dividend growth model to solve for k_s, we rewrite the formula as follows:

Formula for the Cost of Common Share Equity (k_s)

$$k_s = \frac{D_1}{P_0} + g \qquad (9\text{-}3)$$

By making use of Equation 9-3, we can solve for k_s, assuming we know the values of the terms P_0, D_1, and g. The term D_1/P_0 in Equation 9-3 represents the share's *dividend yield,* and the g term represents the dividend growth

[1]This is the *constant growth version* of the dividend growth model. It assumes that the company's dividends grow at the same rate indefinitely.

rate from year to year. We can often obtain historic values of these terms from analyst reports, which can be used as the basis for determining their future values.

To apply Equation 9-3, suppose that Ellis Industries' common share is selling for \$40 a share. Next year's common share dividend is expected to be \$4.20, and the dividend is expected to grow at a rate of 5 percent per year indefinitely. Given these conditions, Equation 9-3 tells us that the expected rate of return on Ellis's common shares is as follows:

$$k_s = \frac{\$4.20}{\$40} + 0.05$$
$$= 0.105 + 0.05$$
$$= 0.155, \text{ or } 15.5\%$$

At a common share price of \$40, a dividend of \$4.20, and an expected dividend growth rate of 5 percent, the expected return from Ellis's common shares is 15.5 percent. The expected return of 15.5 percent is the minimum return the firm's managers must earn when they use money supplied by common shareholders. If they cannot achieve this return, common shareholders will sell their shares, causing the share's price to fall. This will make it necessary to sell more shares to raise the desired amount of funds. The cost of using money supplied by the company's common shareholders, then, is 15.5 percent. Because dividends paid are not tax deductible to the corporation, there is no tax adjustment to the k_s calculation.

The CAPM Approach to Estimating k_s.

A firm may pay dividends that grow at a changing rate; it may pay no dividends at all; or the managers of the firm may believe that market risk is the relevant risk. In such cases, the firm may choose to use the capital asset pricing model (CAPM) to calculate the rate of return that investors require for holding common shares. The CAPM solves for the rate of return that investors demand for holding a company's common shares according to the degree of nondiversifiable risk[2] present in the shares. The CAPM formula, Equation 9-4, follows:

CAPM Formula for the Cost of Common Share Equity (k_s)

$$k_s = k_{RF} + (k_M - k_{RF}) \times \beta \tag{9-4}$$

where

k_s = The required rate of return from the company's common share equity

k_{RF} = The risk-free rate of return

k_M = The expected rate of return on the overall stock market

β = The beta of the company's common shares, a measure of the amount of nondiversifiable risk

[2]According to the CAPM, common shareholders hold well-diversified portfolios, so the only relevant risk measure is nondiversifiable (market) risk.

Suppose Ellis Industries has a beta of 1.39, the risk-free rate as measured by the rate on short-term Canadian Treasury bills is 3 percent, and the expected rate of return on the overall stock market is 12 percent. Given those market conditions, according to Equation 9-4, the required rate of return for Ellis's common shares is as follows:

$$\begin{aligned} k_s &= 0.03 + (0.12 - 0.03) \times 1.39 \\ &= 0.03 + 0.09 \times 1.39 \\ &= 0.03 + 0.1251 \\ &= 0.1551 \text{ or about } 15.5\% \end{aligned}$$

According to the CAPM, we see that the cost of using money supplied by Ellis's common shareholders is about 15.5 percent, given a company beta of 1.39, a risk-free rate of 3 percent, and an expected market rate of return of 12 percent.

Deciding How to Estimate k_s.

Should you use the dividend growth model, Equation 9-3, or the CAPM, Equation 9-4, to estimate a firm's cost of common share equity? The choice depends on the firm's dividend policy, available data, and management's view of risk. As a financial manager, if you were confident that your firm's dividends would grow at a fairly constant rate in the future, you could apply the dividend growth model to calculate k_s. If your firm's growth rate were erratic or difficult to determine, you might use the CAPM instead, assuming that you agreed with the CAPM's underlying hypothesis that common shareholders hold well-diversified portfolios and that nondiversifiable risk is what is priced in the market. When possible, practitioners apply both models and use their business judgment to reconcile differences between the two outcomes.

The Cost of Equity from New Common Shares (k_n) The cost incurred by a company when new common shares are sold is the **cost of equity from new common shares (k_n)**. In the preceding section, we discussed the cost of using funds supplied by the firm's existing shareholders. Capital from existing shareholders is internal equity capital. That is, the firm already has these funds. In contrast, capital from issuing new shares is external equity capital. The firm is trying to raise new funds from outside sources.

New shares are sometimes issued to finance a capital budgeting project. The cost of this capital includes not only shareholders' expected returns on their investment but also the flotation costs incurred to issue new securities. Flotation costs make the cost of using funds supplied by new shareholders slightly higher than using retained earnings supplied by the existing shareholders. To estimate the cost of using funds supplied by new shareholders, we use a variation of the dividend growth model that includes flotation costs:

Formula for the Cost of New Common Equity (k_n)

$$k_n = \frac{D_1}{P_0 - F} + g \qquad (9\text{-}5)$$

where

k_n = The cost of new common share equity

P_0 = The price of one common share

D_1 = The amount of the common share dividend expected to be paid in one year

F = The flotation cost per share

g = The expected constant growth rate of the company's common share dividends

Equation 9-5 shows mathematically how the cost of new common shares, k_n, is greater than the cost of existing common share equity, k_s. By subtracting flotation costs, F, from the common share price in the denominator, the k_n term becomes larger.

Let's look at the cost of new common shares for Ellis Industries. Suppose again that Ellis Industries' anticipated dividend next year is $4.20 a share, its growth rate is 5 percent a year, and its existing common shares are selling for $40 a share. New shares can be sold to the public for the same price, but to do so, Ellis must pay its investment bankers 5 percent of the share's selling price or $2 per share. Given these conditions, we use Equation 9-5 to calculate the cost of Ellis Industries' new common equity as follows:

$$\begin{aligned} k_n &= \frac{\$4.20}{\$40 - \$2} + 0.05 \\ &= 0.1105 + 0.05 \\ &= 0.1605, \text{ or } 16.05\% \end{aligned}$$

Because of $2 flotation costs, Ellis Industries keeps only $38 of the $40 per share paid by investors. As a result, the cost of new common shares is higher than the cost of existing equity—16.05 percent compared to 15.5 percent.

If the cost of new common equity is higher than the cost of internal common equity, the cost of preferred shares, and the cost of debt, why use it? Sometimes corporations have no choice. Take Duramed Pharmaceuticals. Duramed issued new shares to raise $25 million to invest in a promising project to develop a new generic version of a drug used to fight osteoporosis and the effects of menopause. In addition, Duramed needed new funds to pay $7 million it owed to Provident Bancorp. If Duramed did not repay Provident within a month, the interest rate would leap from 10.75 percent to 36.5 percent. With further delays, that rate could increase to 53.6 percent. Facing skyrocketing interest rates, Duramed had to raise capital through a new share issue.[3]

Also, if the amount of debt a firm has incurred continues to increase and internal equity funds have run out, it may be necessary to issue new common shares to bring the weight of debt and equity on the balance sheet into line.[4]

We have examined the sources of capital and the cost of each capital source. Next, we investigate how to measure the firm's overall cost of capital.

---

[3]Norris, N. (1995, November 16). Duramed Pharmaceuticals Faces Some Harsh Terms to Raise Cash. *The New York Times*, D10.

[4]This issue will be discussed in detail in Chapter 13.

The Weighted Average Cost of Capital (WACC)

To estimate a firm's overall cost of capital, the firm must first estimate the cost for each component source of capital. The component sources include the after-tax cost of debt, AT k_d; the cost of preferred shares, k_p; the cost of common share equity, k_s; and the cost of new common share equity, k_n. In the following section, we first discuss all component sources except k_n, which we discuss separately.

To illustrate the first step in estimating a firm's overall cost of capital, let's review Ellis Industries' component costs of capital. From our previous calculations, we know the following costs of capital:

$$\text{AT } k_d = 6\%$$

$$k_p = 12.5\%$$

$$k_s = 15.5\%$$

The next step in finding a firm's overall cost of capital is assessing the firm's *capital structure*. In practice, the assets of most firms are financed with a mixture of debt, preferred shares, and common equity. The mixture of capital used to finance a firm's assets is called the **capital structure** of the firm. To analyze the capital structure of a business, we must find the percentage of each type of capital source.

To illustrate how to assess a firm's capital structure, assume that Ellis Industries finances its assets through a mixture of capital sources, as shown on its balance sheet.[5]

Total Assets	$1,000,000
Long- and Short-Term Debt	$400,000
Preferred Shares	100,000
Common Equity	500,000
Total Liabilities and Equity	$1,000,000

In percentage terms, then, the mixture of capital used to finance Ellis's $1 million worth of assets is as follows:

Debt	400,000/1,000,000 = 0.40 or 40%
Preferred Shares	100,000/1,000,000 = 0.10 or 10%
Common Equity	500,000/1,000,000 = 0.50 or 50%

Our calculations show that Ellis Industries' capital structure consists of 40 percent debt, 10 percent preferred shares, and 50 percent common equity. If Ellis Industries thinks that this mixture is optimal and wants to maintain it, then it will finance new capital budgeting projects with a mixture of 40 percent debt, 10 percent preferred shares, and 50 percent common equity. This mixture might not be used for each and every project, but in the long run, the firm is likely to seek this capital structure if it is believed to be optimal.

[5]Ideally, the percentage of each component in the capital structure would be measured on the basis of market values instead of accounting values. For the sake of simplicity, we use accounting values here, as do many real-world companies.

The final step in estimating a firm's overall cost of capital is to find the weighted average of the costs of each individual financing source. The **weighted average cost of capital (k_a or WACC)** is the mean of all component costs of capital, weighted according to the percentage of each component in the firm's optimal capital structure. We find the WACC by multiplying the individual source's cost of capital times its percentage of the firm's capital structure, then adding these results. For Ellis Industries, the weighted average of the financing sources follows:

$$\begin{aligned}(0.40 \times \text{AT } k_d) + (0.10 \times k_p) + (0.50 \times k_s) \\ &= (0.40 \times 0.06) + (0.10 \times 0.125) + (0.50 \times 0.155) \\ &= 0.024 + 0.0125 + 0.0775 \\ &= 0.114 \text{ or } 11.4\%\end{aligned}$$

Ellis Industries' weighted average cost of capital is 11.4 percent. The general formula for any firm's WACC is shown in Equation 9-6:

Formula for the Weighted Average Cost of Capital (WACC)

$$k_a = (WT_d \times \text{AT } k_d) + (WT_p \times k_p) + (WT_s \times k_s) \tag{9-6}$$

where

k_a = The weighted average cost of capital (WACC)

WT_d = The weight, or proportion, of debt being used to finance the firm's assets

AT k_d = The after-tax cost of debt

WT_p = The weight, or proportion, of preferred shares being used to finance the firm's assets

k_p = The cost of preferred shares

WT_s = The weight, or proportion, of common share equity being used to finance the firm's assets

k_s = The cost of common share equity

A firm must earn a return equal to the WACC to pay suppliers of capital the return they expect. In the case of Ellis Industries, for instance, its average-risk capital budgeting projects must earn a return of 11.4 percent to pay its capital suppliers the return they expect.

To illustrate how earning the WACC ensures that all capital suppliers will be paid their required cost of capital, let's return to our example. Suppose Ellis Industries undertakes a plant expansion program that costs \$1 million and earns an annual return of 11.4 percent, equal to Ellis's WACC. Capital for the project is supplied as follows:

- 40 percent of the \$1 million, or \$400,000, is supplied by lenders expecting a return equal to before-tax k_d, 10 percent.
- 10 percent of the \$1 million, or \$100,000, is supplied by preferred shareholders at a cost equal to k_p, 12.5 percent.[6]

---

[6]In this example, the firm sold 5,000 preferred shares at \$22 a share for a total of \$110,000; \$2 a share, or \$10,000, went to the investment bankers and lawyers in the form of flotation costs, leaving \$100,000 for the capital budget.

- 50 percent of the $1 million, or $500,000, is supplied by common shareholders expecting a return equal to k_s, 15.5 percent.

If the project does in fact produce the expected 11.4 percent return, will all these suppliers of capital receive the return they expect? The computations that follow show how Ellis will pay its capital suppliers:

First-year return from the project	$1,000,000 × 0.114 = $114,000
Interest at 10 percent paid to the bondholders	$400,000 × 0.10 = $40,000
Less tax savings on interest expense	$40,000 × firm's tax rate of 40% = $16,000
Net interest cost to the firm	$40,000 – $16,000 = $24,000
Amount remaining to repay other sources of capital	$114,000 – $24,000 = $90,000
Preferred dividend paid to preferred shareholders	5,000 shares × $2.50 = $12,500
Amount remaining for common shareholders	$90,000 – $12,500 = $77,500
Summary	
Return realized by lenders	$40,000/$400,000 = 0.10 or 10%
Return realized by preferred share investors	$12,500/$100,000 = 0.125 or 12.5%[7]
Return realized by common shareholders	$77,500/$500,000 = 0.155 or 15.5%

We see that Ellis was able to pay all its capital suppliers by earning an overall return of 11.4 percent, its WACC.

In the long run, companies generally try to maintain an optimal mixture of capital from different sources. In the short run, however, one project may be financed entirely from one source. Even if a particular project is financed entirely from one source, the WACC should still be used as the required rate of return for an average-risk project. Say, for instance, such a project is entirely financed with debt, a relatively cheap source of capital. The cost of debt should not be used as that project's cost of capital. Why? Because the firm's risk would increase with the increase in debt, and the costs of all sources of capital would increase.

THE MARGINAL COST OF CAPITAL (MCC)

A firm's weighted average cost of capital will change if one component cost of capital changes. Often, a change in WACC occurs when a firm raises a large amount of capital. For example, lenders may increase the interest rate they charge, k_d, if they think the firm's debt load will be too heavy. Or a firm's cost of equity may increase when new shares are issued after new retained earn-

[7]To be precise, 12.5 percent is the return to the preferred shareholders plus the investment bankers' and lawyers' fees for issuing the shares ($2). The net return realized by the preferred share investors is the preferred dividend they receive ($2.50) divided by the price they paid for the share ($22), which is 11.36 percent.

ings run out. This is because of the flotation costs incurred when new shares are issued.

Firms, then, must consider how increasing component costs of capital affect the WACC. The weighted average cost of the next dollar of capital to be raised is the **marginal cost of capital (MCC)**. To find the MCC, financial managers must (1) assess at what point a firm's cost of debt or equity will change the firm's WACC, (2) estimate how much the change will be, and (3) calculate the cost of capital up to and after the points of change. See Finance at Work 9-1 for the discussion of raising capital and its cost for a business owner.

FINANCE AT WORK 9-1

Sales Retail Sports Media Technology Public Relations Production Exports

INTERVIEW WITH FRED HIGGINS—MINIT MART FOODS, INC., CEO

FRED HIGGINS

Fred Higgins was a law student when he launched his first Minit Mart. He owned six stores by the time he was out of law school. Now his company owns over a hundred Minit Marts. Fred realized the importance of raising capital and assessing its cost as he built his Minit Mart empire.

Q. *Tell us about your first experience in trying to raise capital.*
When I was in law school trying to build my first Minit Mart, I had convinced the people who owned the land to build and then lease the building back to me. I was convinced the site had a great location because of its heavy traffic count and apartments nearby. And it was a great location; it's still making money today.

However, I needed capital to buy inventory, so I went to a bank. I explained the whole scenario to the banker. Then the banker asked what assets I had. I said, "Me." The banker threw me out of his office. I was lucky, though. I was finally able to obtain financing with the help of my father, who knew another banker.

If someone is starting in business, he or she needs credibility. The first time I talked with a banker, I had no credibility, no track record. The banker didn't know me from a hole in the ground. Today when I walk into the bank, the bankers can accurately judge the risk of loaning money to me because they can look at my past experience.

Q. *How do you raise debt capital now?*
Aside from bank loans, I sometimes use insurance companies for long-term debt financing, particularly when I want to buy some real estate. But as a small business, it's tough to ha insurance companies work with you. It costs them the same loan millions of dollars as it does $100,000. They'd rat make a big loan and be done with it. Again, I was luc because I knew people who could provide introductions insurance company lenders.

Q. *Why is it important to measure your capital costs?*
At Minit Mart, we want our projects to generate a posit return. We need to be able to estimate how much the cost our capital is to be sure that our investments earn a cert amount of dollars, after all the costs, including capital, ha been deducted. There are a lot of projects out there, and if can't get our desired rate of return with one, we will bypas and move on to the next one.

Q. *What outside factors affect your cost of capital?*
So many outside factors can increase your cost of debt ca tal. A few years ago, Circle K went bankrupt, and Seve Eleven and several other convenience store chains were performing as well as they had been. The financial mark became very leery of our industry, and that raised the cost debt capital.

Another time our cost of capital increased due to Environmental Protection Agency. The EPA started clos scrutinizing businesses that sold gas for potential environm tal violations. Minit Marts sell gas, so because of the EPA's r scrutiny, banks either wouldn't loan to us or demande higher interest rate.

Source: Interview with Fred Higgins.

The Firm's MCC Schedule

The marginal cost of the *first* dollar of capital a firm raises is the same as the firm's basic WACC. However, as the firm raises more capital, a point is reached at which the marginal cost of capital changes. Why? Because one of the component sources of capital changes. This point is the *break point* in the firm's MCC schedule. Capital above the break point can only be raised at a higher cost.

Finding the Break Points in the MCC Schedule To find break points in the MCC schedule, financial managers determine what limits, if any, there are on the firm's ability to raise funds from a given source at a given cost. Suppose that Ellis Industries' financial managers, after consulting with bankers, determined that the firm can borrow up to $300,000 at an interest rate of 10 percent, but any money borrowed above that amount will cost 12 percent. To calculate Ellis Industries' after-tax cost of debt, assume the firm's tax rate is 40 percent. We apply Equation 9-1 as follows:

$$\begin{aligned} \text{AT } k_d &= k_d(1 - T) \\ \text{AT } k_d &= 0.10 \times (1 - 0.40) \\ &= 0.06 \text{ or } 6\% \end{aligned}$$

We see that at an interest rate of 10 percent and a tax rate of 40 percent, Ellis's after-tax cost of debt is 6 percent. However, if Ellis Industries borrows more than $300,000, then its interest rate increases to 12 percent. At a tax rate of 40 percent and an interest rate of 12 percent, the firm's after-tax k_d for amounts borrowed over $300,000 is:

$$\begin{aligned} \text{AT } k_d \text{ (over \$300,000 borrowed)} &= 0.12 \times (1 - 0.40) \\ &= 0.072 \text{ or } 7.2\% \end{aligned}$$

Because Ellis's AT k_d increases when it borrows more than $300,000, its MCC will also increase when it borrows more than $300,000. (We'll see how much it increases in the next section.) The financial managers at Ellis Industries want to know how much total capital they can raise before the debt portion reaches $300,000, causing an increase in the AT k_d and the MCC.

Ellis Industries' marginal cost of capital break point is not $300,000 because the firm's capital structure is 40 percent debt, 10 percent preferred shares, and 50 percent common shares. At $300,000, then, only 40 percent of that capital is debt. Instead, the financial managers of Ellis Industries must figure out at what point the firm will use $300,000 of debt capital.

To find a firm's marginal cost of capital break point, we use Equation 9-7:

Formula for the Marginal Cost of Capital (MCC) Break Point

$$BP = \frac{\text{Limit}}{\text{Proportion of Total}} \tag{9-7}$$

where

BP = The capital budget size at which the MCC changes (break point)

Limit = The point at which the cost of the source of capital changes

Proportion of Total = The percentage of this source of capital in the firm's capital structure

In our Ellis Industries example, we know that the firm has a \$300,000 debt limit before its after-tax cost of debt will increase and that the debt is 40 percent of the firm's capital structure. Applying Equation 9-7 to our Ellis example, we see that its debt break point is the following:

$$BP_d = \frac{\$300{,}000}{0.04}$$
$$= \$750{,}000$$

We find that Ellis Industries' break point is \$750,000. By applying Equation 9-7, Ellis's financial managers know that they may raise up to \$750,000 in capital before their borrowing costs will rise from 6 percent to 7.2 percent. Any capital raised over \$750,000 will reflect the higher cost of borrowing, as shown in Figure 9-3.

Notice we used a subscript d with BP in Equation 9-7. That was to identify the break point as a *debt break point*. There could be other debt break points for Ellis Industries. If, for instance, the company's lenders set additional limits on the company's borrowing, the debt break points would be denoted as BP_{d1}, BP_{d2}, and so on. For our example, let's assume that Ellis's bankers will lend the firm an unlimited amount of money over \$300,000 at 7.2 percent, so there are no further debt break points.

The Equity Break Point.

The equity break point is the point at which the MCC changes because the cost of equity changes. Equity costs may change because firms exhaust the supply of funds from the firm's existing common shareholders—that is, they exhaust additions to retained earnings. After firms exhaust their supply of internal equity, which has a capital cost of k_s, they will have to raise additional equity

Figure 9-3 Ellis Industries Debt Break Point
Figure 9-3 shows how Ellis Industries can raise up to \$750,000 of total capital before the \$300,000 of lower-cost debt is exhausted.

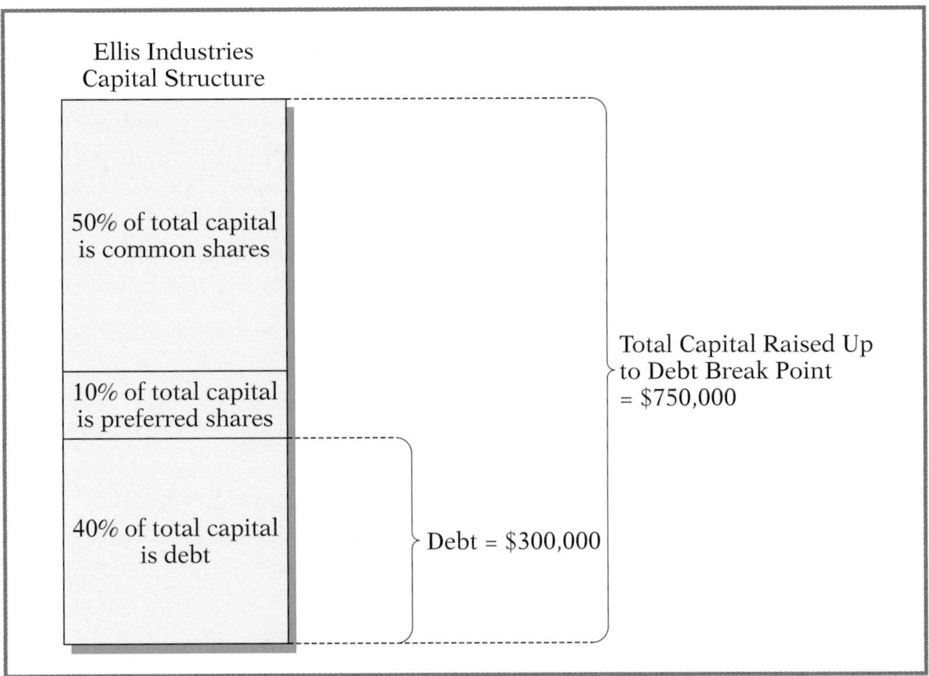

funds by issuing new shares, which has a higher cost, k_n. This additional equity is external equity capital. The MCC increases accordingly.

Let's illustrate how the MCC increases because of changes in the cost of equity. We will assume that Ellis Industries expects to realize $600,000 in income this year after it pays preferred shareholders their dividends. The $600,000 in earnings belong to the common shareholders. The firm may either pay dividends or retain the earnings. Let's assume Ellis retains the $600,000. The finite supply of capital from the existing common shareholders is the $600,000 addition to retained earnings. To find the equity break point, then, Ellis's managers must know at what point the firm will exhaust the common equity capital of $600,000, assuming existing common share equity is 50 percent of the firm's capital budget. Figure 9-4 graphically depicts the Ellis equity break point analysis.

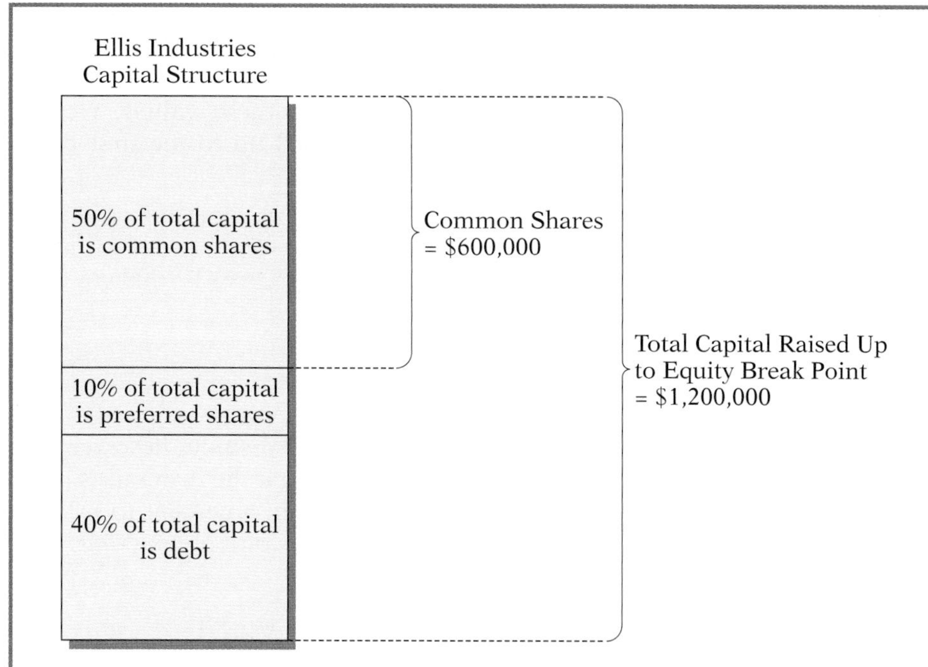

Figure 9-4 Ellis Industries Equity Break Point

Figure 9-4 shows how Ellis Industries can raise up to $1,200,000 of total capital before the $600,000 of lower-cost internal equity is exhausted.

To find the equity break point, we apply Equation 9-7, the MCC break point formula. We know that the existing common share capital limit is $600,000 and that common equity finances 50 percent of the total capital budget. Using Equation 9-7, we solve for the equity break point, BP_e, as follows:

$$BP_e = \frac{\$600{,}000}{0.50}$$
$$= \$1{,}200{,}000$$

Our calculations show that the Ellis equity break point is $1,200,000. If the capital budget exceeds $1,200,000, the portion financed with common equity will exceed $600,000. At that point, Ellis will need to issue new common shares to raise the additional capital. The new common share's cost, k_n, will be greater than the cost of internal common equity, k_s, so the MCC will rise when the capital budget exceeds $1,200,000, as shown in Figure 9-4.

Calculating the Amount the MCC Changes To calculate MCC changes, we must first identify the break points. In our Ellis Industries example, we identified two break points at which the firm's MCC will change:

$$\text{Debt Break Point, } BP_d = \$750{,}000$$

$$\text{Equity Break Point, } BP_e = \$1{,}200{,}000$$

The next step in the MCC analysis is to estimate how much the change in the MCC will be for varying amounts of funds raised.

The MCC Up to the First Break Point.
Because the MCC is simply the weighted average cost of the next dollar of capital to be raised, we can use the WACC formula, Equation 9-6, to calculate the MCC as well.

We assume that Ellis Industries wants to maintain its current capital structure of 40 percent debt, 10 percent preferred shares, and 50 percent common equity. We assume further that its after-tax cost of debt, AT k_d, is 6 percent; its cost of preferred share equity, k_p, is 12.5 percent; and its cost of internal common equity, k_s, is 15.5 percent. With these values, we use Equation 9-6 to find the Ellis MCC for capital raised up to the first break point, BP_d, as follows:

$$\begin{aligned}\text{MCC up to } BP_d\ (\$750{,}000) &= (0.40 \times \text{AT } k_d) + (0.10 \times k_p) + (0.50 \times k_s)\\ &= (0.40 \times 0.06) + (0.10 \times 0.125) + (0.50 + 0.155)\\ &= 0.024 + 0.0125 + 0.0775\\ &= 0.114 \text{ or } 11.4\%\end{aligned}$$

We see from our calculations that up to the first break point, the Ellis MCC is 11.4 percent—the WACC we calculated earlier. We know, however, that the Ellis lenders will raise the interest rate to 12 percent if the firm raises more than \$750,000, at which point the AT k_d increases from 6 percent to 7.2 percent. So between the first break point, BP_d, and the second break point, BP_e, the MCC is:

$$\begin{aligned}\text{MCC between } BP_d\ (\$750{,}00) &= (0.40 \times \text{AT } k_d) + (0.10 \times k_p) + (0.50 \times k_s)\\ \text{and } BP_e\ (\$1{,}200{,}000)\\ &= (0.40 \times 0.072) + (0.10 \times 0.125) + (0.50 \times 0.155)\\ &= 0.0288 + 0.0125 + 0.0775\\ &= 0.1188 \text{ or } 11.88\%\end{aligned}$$

Our calculations show that the MCC between the first and second break points, \$750,000 and \$1,200,000, is 11.88 percent.

At the second break point, BP_e, we know from our earlier Ellis discussion that k_s of 15.5 percent changes to k_n, which has a value of 16.05 percent. Applying Equation 9-6, the MCC for amounts raised over \$1,200,000 follows:

$$\begin{aligned}\text{MCC over } BP_e\ (\$1{,}200{,}000) &= (0.40 \times \text{AT } k_d) + (0.10 \times k_p) + (0.50 \times k_n)\\ &= (0.40 \times 0.072) + (0.10 \times 0.125) + (0.50 \times 0.1605)\\ &= 0.0288 + 0.0125 + 0.08025\\ &= 0.1216 \text{ or } 12.16\%\end{aligned}$$

We find that the Ellis MCC with a capital budget exceeding $1,200,000 is 12.16 percent. A graph of Ellis Industries' marginal cost of capital is shown in Figure 9-5. Now that we have learned to estimate the MCC for a firm, we examine how MCC estimates affect capital budgeting decisions.

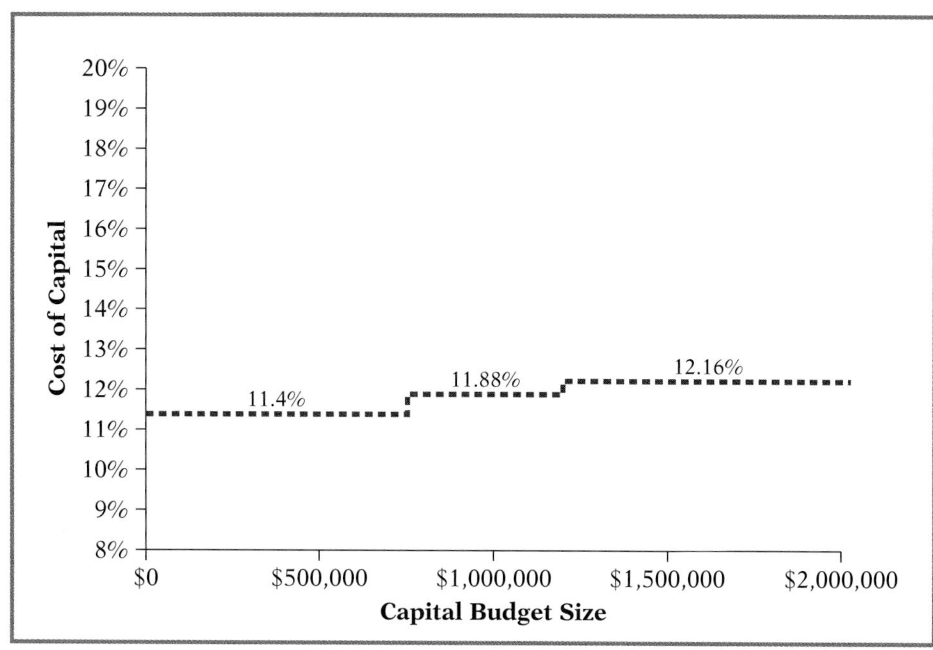

Figure 9-5 Ellis Industries Marginal Cost of Capital Schedule
Figure 9-5 shows the marginal cost of capital (MCC) schedule that reflects the cost of debt and cost of equity break points.

The MCC Schedule and Capital Budgeting Decisions

Firms use the MCC schedule to identify which new capital budgeting projects should be selected for further consideration and which should be rejected. For example, assume that Ellis Industries has identified the following projects for possible adoption:

Project	*Initial Investment Required*	*Project's Expected Rate of Return*
A	$500,000	18.00%
B	$300,000	14.00%
C	$200,000	12.05%
D	$300,000	11.50%
E	$700,000	9.00%

The projects are ranked from highest to lowest expected rate of return. The list of proposed capital budgeting projects ranked by expected rate of return is the firm's investment opportunity schedule (IOS). To determine which proposed projects should be accepted, the Ellis financial managers determine which projects have expected rates of return that exceed their respective costs of capital. To compare the projects' expected rates of return to the firm's cost of capital, the financial managers plot the IOS on the same graph as the MCC. Figure 9-6 shows this technique.

Figure 9-6 Ellis Industries MCC and IOS Schedules
Figure 9-6 shows the MCC and IOS schedules. Those projects on the IOS schedule above the MCC schedule are accepted.

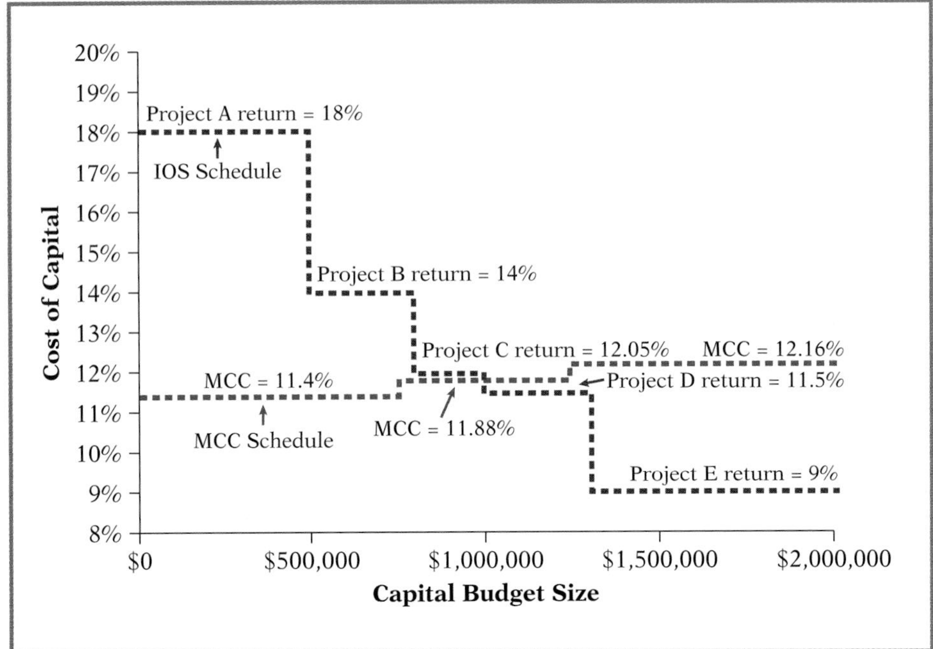

The projects with the highest expected rates of return are plotted first. The Ellis financial managers should start with Project A, which has an expected rate of return of 18 percent. This project requires a capital investment of $500,000. Next, they should add Project B, a project with an expected rate of return of 14 percent and an investment of $300,000. The total capital budget with Projects A and B is $800,000. Then Project C, with an expected rate of return of 12.05 percent, should be added. Project C's investment requirement of $200,000 increases the capital budget to $1,000,000.

The addition of Project D, a project with an expected rate of return of 11.5 percent and investment of $300,000, results in a capital budget of $1,300,000.

Notice, however, that Project D's expected rate of return is less than the marginal cost of capital at the point at which it is added. If Project D were adopted, Figure 9-6 shows that it would have to be financed with capital that costs 11.88 percent, even though the project's expected rate of return is only 11.5 percent. The Ellis financial managers, then, should reject Project D. Project E has a lower expected rate of return of 9 percent and requires a capital investment of $700,000. Project E is also rejected. Combining the IOS and MCC schedules is an effective tool to see whether a firm should accept or reject a project.

The Optimal Capital Budget

When we integrate the IOS and the MCC schedules, as shown in Figure 9-6, we see that Ellis Industries' optimal capital budget is $1 million, consisting of Projects A, B, and C. The **optimal capital budget** is the list of all accepted projects and the total amount of initial cash outlays for these projects. All projects on the IOS schedule that are above the MCC schedule are accepted; the rest are rejected.

Table 9-1 summarizes the seven steps to calculate the optimal capital budget.

Table 9-1 **Determining the Optimal Capital Budget**

Steps	Actions
Step 1	Calculate the costs of the firm's sources of capital: AT k_d, k_p, k_s, and k_n. Record any borrowing limits and the resulting changes in AT k_d with those limits.
Step 2	Calculate the break points in the capital budget size at which the MCC will change. There will always be an equity break point, BP_e, and there may be one or more debt break points, BP_{d1}, BP_{d2}, and so on.
Step 3	Calculate the MCC up to, between, and above all the break points. The MCC increases at each break point. Record the MCC values before and after each break point.
Step 4	Plot the MCC values on a graph, with the capital budget size on the *X* axis and cost of capital/IRR on the *Y* axis.
Step 5	Identify the firm's potential investment projects. Record each investment project's initial investment requirement and expected rate of return. Make an investment opportunity schedule (IOS) by lining up the projects from highest return to lowest.
Step 6	Plot the IOS on the same graph as the MCC.
Step 7	Note the point at which the IOS and MCC schedules cross. Projects on the IOS line above the MCC line should be accepted, and those below the MCC line should be rejected.

The Importance of MCC to Capital Budgeting Decisions

Analyzing the combined IOS and MCC schedules allows financial managers to examine many projects at once, rather than each project in isolation. This way they choose the best projects.

To demonstrate how important the MCC schedule is to capital budgeting decisions, look at Figure 9-6 again. Notice that Project D is rejected because it is below the MCC line. The graph shows us that if Project D is accepted, it will have to be financed in part with capital costing 11.88 percent and in part with capital costing 12.16 percent. Because Project D's expected rate of return is only 11.5 percent, it is a poor investment. However, this statement is only true because Projects A, B, and C were already considered before Project D. Together, Projects A, B, and C require $1 million of capital investment. Given that $1 million has already been spent for Projects A, B, and C, the $300,000 required for Project D can only be raised at costs of 11.88 percent (the first $200,000) and 12.16 percent (the last $100,000).

If Project D were considered by itself, as if it were Ellis Industries' only capital budgeting project, then the $300,000 investment the project requires could have been raised at the company's initial WACC of 11.4 percent. Because the project's expected rate of return of 11.5 percent exceeds that WACC rate by

0.1 percent, the project looks like a good investment. However, because its expected rate of return was lower than those of Projects A, B, and C, Project D is not a good investment, given the changes in Ellis's cost of capital due to the MCC break points.

This example illustrates the importance of using a firm's MCC, not the firm's initial WACC, to evaluate investments. If all investment projects are treated in isolation and evaluated using the firm's initial WACC, then some of them may be overvalued. The discrepancy will become apparent when the firm tries to raise the entire amount of capital to support the complete capital budget and finds that the cost of the last dollar raised exceeds the expected rate of return of the last project adopted.

SUMMARY

9-1 *Describe four main sources of capital and how firms raise capital.*

Firms raise debt capital from lenders or bondholders. They also raise funds from preferred shareholders, from current shareholders, and from investors who buy newly issued shares. All suppliers of capital expect a rate of return proportionate to the risk they take. To ensure a supply of capital to meet their capital budgeting needs, firms must pay that return to capital suppliers. To compensate creditors, firms must pay the interest and principal on loans. For bondholders, firms must pay the market required interest rate. For preferred shareholders, the dividend payments serve as compensation. To compensate common share investors, firms pay dividends or reinvest the shareholders' earnings.

9-2 *Explain how to estimate the cost of capital for each of the four main financing sources.*

To find a firm's overall cost of capital, a firm must first estimate how much each source of capital costs. The after-tax cost of debt, AT k_d, is the market's required rate of return on the firm's debt, adjusted for the tax savings realized when interest payments are deducted from taxable income. The before-tax cost of debt, k_d, is multiplied by one minus the tax rate (1 – T) to arrive at the firm's after-tax cost of debt.

The cost of preferred shares, k_p, is the investor's required rate of return on that security. The cost of common share equity, k_s, is the opportunity cost of new retained earnings, the required rate of return on the firm's common shares. The cost of new common shares, k_n, (external equity) is the required rate of return on the firm's common shares, adjusted for the flotation costs incurred when new common shares are sold in the market.

9-3 *Define the estimated weighted average cost of capital (WACC).*

The weighted average cost of capital, k_a or WACC, is the overall average cost of funds considering each of the component capital costs and the weight of each of those components in the firm's capital structure. To estimate WACC, we multiply the individual source's cost of capital times its percentage of the firm's capital structure and then add the results.

9-4 *Describe how to use the marginal cost of capital (MCC) schedule to make capital budgeting decisions.*

A firm's WACC changes as the cost of debt or equity increases as more capital is raised. Financial managers calculate the break points in the capital budget size at which the MCC will change. There will always be an equity break point, BP_e, and there may be one or more debt break points, BP_{d1}, BP_{d2}, and so on. Financial managers then calculate the MCC up to, between, and above all the break points and plot the MCC values on a graph showing how the cost of capital changes as capital budget size changes.

Financial managers create an Investment Opportunity Schedule (IOS) by ranking all potential capital budgeting projects from the highest internal rate of return to the lowest and then plotting the IOS on the same graph with the MCC. To increase the value of the firm, projects on the IOS line above the MCC line should be accepted and those below the MCC line rejected.

9-5 Explain the importance of the marginal cost of capital schedule in financial decision making.

The MCC schedule forces financial managers to match a project's rate of return with the cost of funds for that specific project. This marginal analysis prevents financial managers from estimating a project's value incorrectly because of faulty cost of capital estimates that fail to consider how a larger capital budget increases capital costs.

EQUATIONS INTRODUCED IN THIS CHAPTER

Equation 9-1: Formula for the After-Tax Cost of Debt (AT k_d)

$$AT\ k_d = k_d(1 - T)$$

where

k_d = The before-tax cost of debt
T = The firm's marginal tax rate

Equation 9-2: Formula for the Cost of Preferred Shares (k_p)

$$k_p = \frac{D_p}{(P_p - F)}$$

where

k_p = The cost of the preferred share issue; the expected return
D_p = The amount of the expected preferred share dividend
P_p = The current price of the preferred shares
F = The flotation cost per share

Equation 9-3: Formula for the Cost of Common Share Equity (k_s)

$$k_s = \frac{D_1}{P_0} + g$$

where

k_s = The required rate of return from the company's common share equity
P_0 = The current price of the common share
D_1 = The amount of the common share dividend expected one period from now
g = The expected constant growth rate of the company's common share dividends

Equation 9-4: CAPM Formula for the Cost of Common Share Equity (k_s)

$$k_s = k_{RF} + (k_M - k_{RF}) \times \beta$$

where

k_s = The required rate of return from the company's common share equity
k_{RF} = The risk-free rate of return
k_M = The expected rate of return on the overall stock market
β = The beta of the company's common shares, a measure of the amount of nondiversifiable risk

Equation 9-5: Formula for the Cost of New Common Share Equity (k_n)

$$k_n = \frac{D_1}{P_0 - F} + g$$

where

k_n = The cost of new common share equity
P_0 = The price of one common share
D_1 = The amount of the common share dividend expected to be paid in one year
F = The flotation cost per share
g = The expected constant growth rate of the company's common share dividends

Equation 9-6: Formula for the Weighted Average Cost of Capital (WACC)

$$k_a = (WT_d \times AT\ k_d) + (WT_p \times k_p) + (WT_s \times k_s)$$

where

k_a = The weighted average cost of capital (WACC)
WT_d = The weight, or proportion, of debt being used to finance the firm's assets
$AT\ k_d$ = The after-tax cost of debt
WT_p = The weight, or proportion, of preferred shares being used to finance the firm's assets
k_p = The cost of preferred shares
WT_s = The weight, or proportion, of common share equity being used to finance the firm's assets
k_s = The cost of common share equity

Equation 9-7: Formula for the Marginal Cost of Capital (MCC) Break Point

$$BP = \frac{\text{Limit}}{\text{Proportion of Total}}$$

where

BP = The capital budget size at which the MCC changes (break point)
Limit = The point at which the cost of the source of capital changes
Proportion of Total = The percentage of this source of capital in the firm's capital structure

SELF-TEST

ST-1. Jules' Security Company can issue new bonds with a market interest rate of 14 percent. Jules' tax rate is 32 percent. Compute the after-tax cost of debt, AT k_d, for this company.

ST-2. Mr. White's company, The Problem Solvers, wants to issue new preferred shares. The preferred share dividend is \$3.00 per share, the share can be sold for \$30, and the flotation costs are \$1. What is the cost of preferred share, k_p?

ST-3. Vincent's Dance Studio, Inc. has a beta of 1.9. The risk-free rate of interest is 4 percent. The market portfolio has an expected rate of return of 10 percent. What is the cost of internal equity, k_s, for this company using the CAPM approach?

ST-4. Marsalis's Entertainment Corporation has an after-tax cost of debt of 8 percent, a cost of preferred shares of 12 percent, and a cost of common equity of 16 percent. What is the WACC, k_a, for this company? The capital structure of Marsalis's company contains 20 percent debt, 10 percent preferred shares, and 70 percent common equity.

ST-5. Quinten's Movie Company has been told by its investment-banking firm that it could issue up to $8 million in bonds at an after-tax cost of debt of 10 percent. However, after that, additional bonds would have a 12 percent after-tax cost. Quinten's company uses 40 percent debt and 60 percent equity for major projects. How much money could this company raise, maintaining its preferred capital structure, before the after-tax cost of debt would jump to 12 percent?

REVIEW QUESTIONS

1. Which is lower for a given company: the cost of debt or the cost of equity? Explain. Ignore taxes in your answer.
2. When a company issues new securities, how do flotation costs affect the cost of raising the capital?
3. What does the "weight" refer to in the weighted average cost of capital?
4. How do tax considerations affect the cost of debt and the cost of equity?
5. If dividends paid to common shareholders are not legal obligations of a corporation, is the cost of equity zero? Explain your answer.
6. What is the investment opportunity schedule (IOS)? How does it help financial managers make business decisions?
7. What is a marginal cost of capital (MCC) schedule? Is the schedule always a horizontal line? Explain.
8. For a given IOS and MCC, how do financial managers decide which proposed capital budgeting projects to accept and which to reject?

PROBLEMS

9-1. **a.** What would be the after-tax cost of debt for a company with the following yields to maturity for its new bonds, if the applicable tax rate were 40 percent? ◀ Cost of Debt

i. YTM = 7%
ii. YTM = 11%
iii. YTM = 13%

b. How would the cost of debt change if the applicable tax rate were 34 percent?

9-2. Calculate the after-tax cost of debt for loans with the following effective annual interest rates and corporate tax rates. ◀ Cost of Debt

a. Interest rate, 10%; tax rate, 0%
b. Interest rate, 10%; tax rate, 22%
c. Interest rate, 10%; tax rate, 34%

9-3. What would be the cost of debt for the following companies given their yields to maturity (YTM) for new bonds and the applicable corporate tax rates? ◀ Cost of Debt

Company	YTM	Tax Rate
A	8%	34%
B	11%	40%
C	14%	30%

Cost of Debt ▶

9-4. Mary Lynn Eatenton is the chief financial officer of Magnolia Steel, Inc. She has asked Trudy Jones, one of the financial analysts, to calculate the after-tax cost of debt based on different bond yield to maturity rates. Magnolia Steel's current tax rate is 34 percent, but increasing sales and profits will put them in the 40 percent tax bracket by the end of the year. Calculate the after-tax, cost-of-debt figures that will be shown in Ms. Jones's report at each tax rate for the following YTM rates.

a. Yield to maturity, 8%

b. Yield to maturity, 14%

c. Yield to maturity, 16%

Cost of Debt ▶

9-5. A firm is issuing new bonds that pay 8 percent annual interest. The market required annual rate of return on these bonds is 13 percent. The firm has a tax rate of 40 percent.

a. What is the before-tax cost of debt?

b. What is the after-tax cost of debt?

Cost of Debt ▶

9-6. A company's creditors charge 9.5 percent annual interest on loans to the company. The company's tax rate is 35 percent. What is the company's after-tax cost of debt?

Cost of Preferred Shares ▶

9-7. A company can sell preferred shares for $26 per share and each share is expected to pay a dividend of $2. If the flotation cost per share is $0.75, what would be the estimate of the cost of capital from this source?

Cost of Preferred Shares ▶

9-8. Leo Bloom, the treasurer of a manufacturing company, thinks that debt (YTM = 11%, tax rate = 40%) will be a less expensive option for acquiring funds compared to issuing new preferred shares. The company can sell preferred shares at $61 per share and pay a yearly preferred dividend of $8 per share. The cost of issuing preferred shares is $1 per share. Is Leo correct?

Cost of Preferred Shares ▶

9-9. One-Eyed Jacks Corporation needs money to fund a new production line of playing cards. Rio Longworth, manager of the finance department, suggests they sell preferred shares for $50 per share. They expect to pay annual preferred share dividends of $6 per share. What is the estimate of the cost of preferred shares if the flotation cost is $2.25 per share?

Cost of Preferred Shares ▶

9-10. El Norte Industries will issue $100 par, 12 percent preferred shares. The market price for the share is expected to be $89 per share. El Norte must pay flotation costs of 5 percent of the market price. What is El Norte's cost for a preferred share?

Cost of Preferred Share Financing ▶

9-11. A company's investment bankers say that a proposed new issue of 7.5 percent cumulative preferred shares with a par value of $10 a share can be sold to the public for $27 a share. The transaction costs will be $1 a share. What is the company's cost of preferred share financing?

Cost of Equity ▶

9-12. Twister Corporation is expected to pay a dividend of $7 per share one year from now on its common shares, which has a current market price of $143. Twister's dividends are expected to grow at 13 percent.

a. Calculate the cost of the company's retained earnings.

b. If the flotation cost per share of new common shares is $4, calculate the cost of issuing new common shares.

9-13. Amy Jolly is the treasurer of her company. She expects the company will grow at 4 percent in the future and debt securities (YTM = 14%, tax rate = 30%) will always be a less expensive option to finance the growth. The current market price per common share is $39 and the expected dividend in one year is $1.50 per share. Calculate the cost of the company's retained earnings and check if Amy's assumption is correct.

◀ Cost of Retained Earnings

9-14. Free Willy, Inc. has a beta of 1.4. If the rate on Canadian Treasury bills is 4.5 percent and the expected rate of return on the stock market is 12 percent, what is Free Willy's cost of common equity financing?

◀ Cost of Equity CAPM Approach

9-15. Pedro Muzquiz and Tita de la Garza are the CEOs of a large bakery chain, Chocolates, Inc. The common shares sell on the stock exchange with a current market price of $65 per share. A $7 dividend is planned for one year from now. Business has been good and they expect the dividend growth rate of 10 percent to continue.

◀ Challenge Problem

a. Calculate the cost of the corporation's retained earnings.

b. At the beginning of the year, 1 million shares were authorized with 500,000 issued and outstanding. They plan to issue another 200,000 shares. Calculate the cost of capital of the new common shares if the flotation cost per share is $3. Do you expect the cost of new common equity (external) to be higher than the cost of the internal equity? Why?

9-16. Margo Channing, the financial analyst for Eve's Broadway Production Company, has been asked by management to estimate a cost of equity for use in the analysis of a project, which was under consideration. In the past, dividends declared and paid have been very sporadic. Because of this, Ms. Channing elects to use the CAPM approach to estimate the cost of equity. The rate on the short-term Canadian Treasury bills is 3 percent and the expected rate of return on the overall stock market is 11 percent. Eve's Broadway Production Company has a beta of 1.6. What will Ms. Channing report as the cost of equity?

◀ Cost of Equity CAPM Approach

9-17. African Queen River Tours, Inc. has capitalized on the renewed interest in riverboat travel. Charlie Allnut, the lone financial analyst, estimates the firm's earnings, dividends, and share price will continue to grow at the historical 5 percent rate. AQRT's common shares are currently selling for $30 per share. The dividend just paid was $2. They pay dividends every year. The rate of return expected on the overall stock market is 12 percent.

◀ Cost of Common Equity Financing

a. What is AQRT's cost of equity?

b. If they issue new common shares today and pay flotation costs of $2 per share, what is the cost of new common equity?

c. If AQRT has a risk-free rate of 3 percent and a beta of 1.4, what will be AQRT's cost of equity using the CAPM approach?

9-18. Alvin C. York, the founder of York Corporation, thinks that the optimal capital structure of his company is 30 percent debt, 15 percent preferred shares, and the rest common equity. If the company pays 40 percent tax, compute its weighted average cost of capital given that:

◀ Weighted Average Cost of Capital

- YTM of its debt is 10 percent.
- New preferred shares will have a market value of $31, a dividend of $2 per share, and flotation costs of $1 per share.
- Price of common shares is currently $100 per share and new common shares can be issued at the same price with flotation costs of $4 per share. The expected dividend in one year is $4 per share and the growth rate is 6 percent.

Assume the addition to retained earnings for the current period is zero.

Weighted Average Cost of Capital ▶

9-19. A company has an optimal capital structure as follows:

Total Assets	\$600,000
Debt	\$300,000
Preferred Shares	\$100,000
Common Equity	\$200,000

What would be the minimum expected return from a new capital investment project to satisfy the suppliers of the capital? Assume the applicable tax rate is 40 percent, YTM of its debt is 11 percent, flotation cost per preferred share is \$0.75, and flotation cost per share of common shares is \$4. The preferred and common shares are selling in the market for \$26 and \$143 a share, respectively, and they are expected to pay a dividend of \$2 and \$7, respectively, in one year. The company's dividends are expected to grow at 13 percent per year. The firm would like to maintain the foregoing optimal capital structure to finance the new project.

Weighted Average Cost of Capital ▶

9-20. Great Expectations, a wedding and maternity clothing manufacturer, has a cost of equity of 16 percent and a cost of preferred shares of 14 percent. Its before-tax cost of debt is 12 percent and its tax rate is 40 percent. Assume that the most recent balance sheet shown here reflects the optimal capital structure. Calculate Great Expectations' after-tax WACC.

Great Expectations Balance Sheet Dec. 31, 2002

Assets		Liabilities and Equity	
Cash	\$ 50,000		
Accounts Receivable	90,000	Long-Term Debt	\$ 600,000
Inventories	300,000	Preferred Shares	250,000
Plant and Equipment, Net	810,000	Common Shares	400,000
Total Assets	\$1,250,000	Total Liabilities and Equity	\$1,250,000

Weighted Average Cost of Capital ▶

9-21. Puppet Masters is considering a new capital investment project. The company has an optimal capital structure and plans to maintain it. The yield to maturity on Puppet Masters' debt is 10 percent and its tax rate is 35 percent. The market price of the new issue of preferred shares is \$25 per share with an expected per share dividend of \$2 at the end of this year. Flotation costs are set at \$1 per share. The new issue of common shares has a current market price of \$140 per share with an expected dividend in one year of \$5. Flotation costs for issuing new common shares are \$4 per share. Puppet Masters' dividends are growing at 10 percent per year and this growth is expected to continue for the foreseeable future. Selected figures from last year's balance sheet follow:

Total Assets	\$1,000,000
Long-Term Debt	300,000
Preferred Shares	100,000
Common Shares	600,000

Calculate the minimum expected return from the new capital investment project needed to satisfy the suppliers of the capital.

Weighted Average Cost of Capital ▶

9-22. Jay Lo Enterprises finances its assets with 60 percent debt, 10 percent preferred shares, and 30 percent common shares. Jay Lo's after-tax cost of debt is 5 percent, its cost of preferred shares is 8 percent, and its cost of common share equity financing is 12 percent. Given these conditions, what is Jay Lo's WACC?

9-23. The investment firm of Dewey, Cheatem, and Howe (DCH) has the following balance sheet:

◀ Weighted Average Cost of Capital

Assets		Liabilities and Equity	
Cash	$110,000	Accounts Payable	$ 70,000
Receivables	240,000	Long-Term Debt	160,000
Office Equipment	80,000	Preferred Shares	100,000
Total Assets	$430,000	Common Shares	100,000
		Total Liabilities and Equity	$430,000

DCH's creditors charge 9.5 percent annual interest on loans to the company. It can sell preferred shares with a $10 per share dividend to the public for $50 a share (net to the company after commissions). The company's combined federal and provincial tax rate is 35 percent, its beta is 1.1, the risk-free rate is 4 percent, and the expected rate of return on the stock market is 12 percent. Given these conditions, what is DCH's WACC?

9-24. Fans By Fay Company has a capital structure of 60 percent debt and 40 percent common equity. The company expects to realize $200,000 in net income this year and will pay no dividends. The effective annual interest rate on its new borrowings increases by 3 percent for amounts over $500,000.

◀ Marginal Cost of Capital Schedule

a. At what capital budget size will Fans By Fay's cost of equity increase? In other words, what is its equity break point?

b. At what capital budget size will its cost of debt increase (debt break point)?

9-25. Babe's Dog Obedience School, Inc. wants to maintain its current capital structure of 50 percent common equity, 10 percent preferred shares, and 40 percent debt. Its cost of common equity is 13 percent and the cost of preferred shares is 12 percent. The bank's effective annual interest rate is 11 percent for amounts borrowed that are less than or equal to $1 million and 13 percent for amounts between $1 million and $2 million. If more than $2 million is borrowed, the effective annual interest rate charged is 15 percent. Babe's tax rate is 40 percent. The firm expects to realize $2,750,000 in net income this year after preferred dividends have been paid.

◀ Marginal Cost of Capital Schedule

Excel

a. Calculate the MCC if $900,000 is needed for an upcoming project.

b. Calculate the MCC if $1,500,000 is needed for the project instead.

c. If a different project is adopted and $2,005,000 is needed for it, what is the MCC?

9-26. Stone Wood Products has a capital structure of 35 percent debt and 65 percent common equity. The managers consider this mix to be optimal and want to maintain it in the future. Net income for the coming year is expected to be $1.2 million. Duke Mantee, the loan officer at the local bank, has set up the following schedule for Stone Wood Products' borrowings. There are 40,000 common shares outstanding. The firm's tax rate is 40 percent.

◀ Comprehensive Problem

Loan Amount	Interest Rate
$0 to $750,000	10%
> $750,000	12%

The market price per share of Stone Wood Products' common shares is $50 per share. They have decided to pay a $5 dividend in one year. The company's expected growth rate is 9 percent. The flotation costs for new common shares issued are set at 8 percent of the market price.

The managers are considering several investment opportunities for the upcoming year. They have asked the senior financial analyst, Gabrielle Maple, to recommend which of the following projects the firm should undertake. Because you are the newest member of her team and need the experience, she has passed this management request on to you.

Investment Opportunities

Project	Initial Investment (in millions)	Rate of Return
A	$0.5	16%
B	$1.6	12%
C	$0.6	15%
D	$1.5	18%

a. Calculate all of Stone Wood Products' component costs of capital (after-tax cost of debt, cost of equity, and cost of new equity).

b. Calculate all of the MCC break points.

c. Calculate all of the MCC figures.

d. Make an IOS by listing the projects from the highest to the lowest internal rates of return.

e. Plot the MCC values and the IOS values on the same graph.

f. Which projects will you recommend management adopt for the next year?

Challenge Problem ▶ **9-27.** The CEO of Hamilton Aluminum Processors considers building a $10 million processing plant. The CEO estimates that the future inflows from the project would be as follows: Year 1 – $5 million; Year 2 – $7 million; Year 3 – $5 million; Year 4 – $2 million. The CEO needs to make a decision to finance this capital budgeting project and he considers three alternatives.

Option 1: The company may be able to raise $10 million in debt with an annual interest rate of 10 percent.

Option 2: The company may be able to issue preferred shares, which would pay an annual dividend of $1 per share and the shares are expected to do so indefinitely. The stock market specialists tell the CEO that the price for preferred shares may be equal to $15 per share. The flotation cost is expected to be $1 per share.

Option 3: The company may be able to finance its expansion by issuing common share equity. The company shares are likely to trade around the $45 price point. The next year's common share dividend is expected to be $2.1 per share. The dividend is expected to grow by 5 percent per annum for the foreseeable future.

Given that the company's tax rate is expected to be 40 percent, calculate PV of cost and PV of benefits of the intended capital budgeting project under each of the financing scenarios. Which financing option would you recommend and why?

Challenge Problem ▶ **9-28.** Ontario Media Broadcasting, the holding conglomerate, comprises four business units, portfolio companies, each of them listed separately on the Toronto Stock Exchange. Management of the holding company estimates that each of the portfolio companies has a different business risk profile and, therefore, the shareholders of these companies have different expectations in terms of required rates of return. Calculate WACC of the combined portfolio of businesses given the information below.

Company	Market Capitalization (In $ millions)	Required Rate of Return (In percent)
A	12	5
B	8	17
C	27	34
D	15	11

9-29. Given the following information, calculate WACC. ◀ Challenge Problem

Company	Market Capitalization (In $ millions)	Required Rate of Return (In percent)
W	10	15
X	20	7
Y	30	6
Z	40	18

9-30. You have collected information relating to Brick Enterprises. Given the information that follows, calculate the company's WACC. ◀ Challenge Problem

1. The company has 1 million outstanding common shares currently trading at $48 per share.
2. The company's expected dividend in the past was equal to $3 per share. Due to the company's anticipated strong financial performance, the dividend is expected to grow by 20 percent next year. Thereafter, management expects dividends to grow by 5 percent.
3. The company has $13 million of Long-Term Debt, which carries an annual interest rate of 12 percent.

ANSWERS TO SELF-TEST

ST-1. $0.14 \times (1 - 0.32) = 0.0952 = 9.52\%$ AT k_d

ST-2. Using equation 9-2, $k_p = D_p/(P_p - F)$ $\$3/(\$30 - \$1) = 0.1034$ or 10.34%

ST-3. $0.04 + (0.10 - 0.04) \times 1.9 = 0.154 = 15.4\%$ k_s

ST-4. $(0.08 \times 0.2) + (0.12 \times 0.10) + (0.16 \times 0.70) = 0.14 = 14\%$ k_a

ST-5. The break point in the MCC schedule caused by the increase in the cost of debt, BP_d, after $8,000,000 is borrowed, equals $\$8{,}000{,}000 \div 0.40 = \$20{,}000{,}000$.

10

Capital Budgeting Decision Methods

Chapter Objectives

After reading this chapter, you should be able to:

10-1 Explain two decision practices used in the capital budgeting process.

10-2 Describe how to calculate the payback period, net present value, internal rate of return, and modified internal rate of return for a proposed capital budgeting project.

10-3 Define capital rationing and describe how firms decide which projects to select.

10-4 Explain how to measure the risk of a capital budgeting project.

10-5 Explain why risk-adjusted discount rates are used.

"Everything is worth what its purchaser will pay for it."

—Publilius Syrus

WestJet Unveils Its Eastern Expansion Plan

WestJet Airlines Ltd. saw the number of passengers it carried last year jump by 19.1%—ending 2003 with a bang, as traffic soared in December by 22% on a year-over-year basis. Meanwhile, WestJet also unveiled yesterday the first elements of its eastern Canadian expansion plan.

However, WestJet's load factor, or percentage of seats filled on its flights, dropped last year, to 70.6% from 73.2%. This was largely due to a 47.7% increase in capacity, or seats available for sale. For December, the load factor rose, to 73.6% from 72.1%, as capacity grew 37.9%.

Clive Beddoe, WestJet's chief executive, said he is optimistic the airline can improve its load factor and traffic numbers in 2004, largely due to the introduction of satellite TV on its flights. The airline hopes the TV service will lure new passengers. "If we saw our load factor climb by five percentage points, as a result of that, we could see an increase in our margins of 50%," he said in a broadcast interview.

WestJet also said it plans to beef up service and add new routes, which follows up on an announcement last month regarding an aggressive expansion push eastward.

The low-cost carrier will add new daily non-stop service between Moncton, N.B., and Montreal, and increase its non-stop schedule between Calgary and Toronto. Both moves take effect March 4.

WestJet plans to add 11 new aircraft, the Boeing 737-700, to its fleet this year.

Before the WestJet Corporation announced that it planned to acquire 11 new aircraft to support its eastern expansion plans, financial analysts at the WestJet Corporation had to determine whether the proposed expansion project made financial sense for the firm. Because the project was a major risk, the financial analysts could not just recommend that the firm spend many millions of dollars willy-nilly. Analysts decided to accept the project based on objective financial decision methods, concluding that despite the risks, the project's returns would justify the acquisition cost.

In this chapter, you will learn some of the techniques that financial analysts like those at WestJet use to analyze long-term investment opportunities.

Source: Paul Vieira, "WestJet Unveils Its Eastern Expansion Plan," *The National Post*, 28 January 2004.

Chapter Overview

We now look at the decision methods that analysts use to approve investment projects and how they account for a project's risk. Investment projects such as the WestJet expansion project fuel a firm's success, so effective project selection often determines a firm's value. The decision methods for choosing investment projects, then, are some of the most important tools financial managers use.

We begin by looking at the capital budgeting process and three capital budgeting decision methods: *the payback method, the net present value method,* and *the internal rate of return method.* Then we discuss how to select projects when firms limit their budget for capital projects, a practice called *capital rationing.* Finally, we look at how firms measure and compensate for the risk of capital budgeting projects.

The Capital Budgeting Process

All businesses budget for capital projects—an airline that considers purchasing new planes, a production studio that decides to buy new film cameras, or a pharmaceutical company that invests in researching and developing a new drug. **Capital budgeting** is the process of evaluating proposed large, long-term investment projects. The projects may be the purchase of fixed assets, investments in research and development, advertising, or intellectual property. For instance, Microsoft's development of *Windows 98*™ software was a capital budgeting project.

Let us make an important note here. In Chapter 8, we talked about PV and FV calculations and we used i to denote the rate of interest during the period. In this chapter, we use k to denote the discount rate or the required rate of return on the project.

Before we discuss the specific decision methods for selecting investment projects, we briefly examine capital budgeting basics: capital budgeting decision practices, types of capital budgeting projects, the cash flows associated with such projects, and the stages of the capital budgeting process.

Decision Practices

Financial managers apply two decision practices when selecting capital budgeting projects: *accept/reject* and *ranking.* The accept/reject decision focuses on the question of whether the proposed project would add value to the firm or earn a rate of return that is acceptable to the company. The ranking decision ranks competing projects in order of desirability to choose the best one(s).

The accept/reject decision practice determines whether a project is acceptable in light of the firm's financial objectives. That is, if a project meets the firm's basic risk and return requirements, it will be accepted. If not, it will be rejected.

Ranking compares projects to a standard measure and orders the projects based on how well they meet the measure. If, for instance, the standard is how quickly the project pays off the initial investment, then the project that pays off the investment most rapidly would be ranked first. The project that paid off most slowly would be ranked last.

Types of Projects

Firms invest in two categories of projects: independent projects and mutually exclusive projects. **Independent projects** do not compete with each other. A firm may accept none, some, or all from among a group of independent projects. Say, for example, that a firm is able to raise funds for all worthwhile projects it identifies. The firm is considering two new projects—a new telephone system and a warehouse. The telephone system and the warehouse would be independent projects. Accepting one does not preclude accepting the other.

In contrast, **mutually exclusive projects** compete against each other. The best project from among a group of acceptable mutually exclusive projects is selected. For example, if a company needed only one copier, a proposal to buy a Xerox™ copier and a second proposal to buy a Toshiba™ copier would indicate that these two projects are mutually exclusive.

Capital Budgeting Cash Flows

Although decision-makers examine accounting information such as sales and expenses, capital budgeting decision-makers base their decisions on relevant cash flows associated with a project. The relevant cash flows are **incremental cash flows**—cash flows that will occur if an investment is undertaken but will not occur if it is not.

For example, imagine that you are an animator who helps create children's films. Your firm is considering whether to buy a computer to help you design your characters more quickly. The computer would enable you to create two characters in the time it now takes you to draw one, thereby increasing your productivity.

The incremental cash flows associated with the animation project are (1) the initial investment in the computer and (2) the *additional* cash the firm will receive because you will double your animation output for the life of the computer. These cash flows will occur if the new computer is purchased and will not occur if it is not purchased. These are the cash flows, then, that affect the capital budgeting decision.

Estimating cash flows, the subject of Chapter 11, is a major component of capital budgeting decisions, as we see in the next section.

Stages in the Capital Budgeting Process

The capital budgeting process has four major stages:

1. Finding projects
2. Estimating the incremental cash flows associated with projects
3. Evaluating and selecting projects
4. Implementing and monitoring projects

This chapter focuses on stage 3—how to evaluate and choose investment projects. We assume that the firm has found projects in which to invest and has estimated the projects' cash flows effectively.

Take Note

Capital budgeting techniques are usually used only for projects with large cash outlays. Small investment decisions are usually made by the "seat of the pants." For instance, if your office supply of pencils is running low, you order more. You know that the cost of buying pencils is justified without undergoing capital budgeting analysis.

Capital Budgeting Decision Methods

The four formal capital budgeting decision methods we will examine are *payback, net present value, internal rate of return,* and *modified internal rate of return.* Let's begin with the payback method.

The Payback Method

One of the simplest capital budgeting decision methods is the payback method. To use it, analysts find a project's **payback period**—the number of time periods it will take before the cash inflows of a proposed project equal the amount of the initial project investment (a cash outflow). In the WestJet example discussed at the beginning of this chapter, the analysts would determine how many years it would take to recoup the acquisition costs of 11 new aircraft—the Boeing 737-700.

How to Calculate the Payback Period To calculate the payback period, simply add up a project's positive cash flows, one period at a time, until the sum equals the amount of the project's initial investment. The number of time periods required is the payback period.

To illustrate, imagine that you work for a firm called the AddVenture Corporation. AddVenture is considering two investment proposals, Projects X and Y. The initial investment for both projects is $5,000. The finance department estimates that the projects will generate the following cash flows:

Cash Flows

	For Initial Investment	*End of Year 1*	*End of Year 2*	*End of Year 3*	*End of Year 4*
Project X	–$5,000	$2,000	$3,000	$500	$0
Project Y	–$5,000	$2,000	$2,000	$1,000	$2,000

By analyzing the cash flows, we see that Project X has a payback period of two years because the project's initial investment of $5,000 (a cash flow of –$5,000) will be recouped (by offsetting positive cash flows) at the end of year 2. In comparison, Project Y has a payback of three years.

Dogbert gives the hapless MBA exactly what he deserves. This would not have happened if the man with the MBA had asked about the net present value.

Source: DILBERT © 1996 United Feature Syndicate, Inc. Reprinted by permission.

Payback Method Decision Rule To apply the payback decision method, firms must first decide what payback time period is acceptable for long-term projects. In our case, if the firm sets two years as its required payback period, it will accept Project X but reject Project Y. If, however, the firm allows a three-year payback period, then both projects may be accepted if they are independent.

Problems with the Payback Method The payback method is used in practice because of its simplicity, but it does not consider cash flows that occur after the payback period. For example, suppose Project Y's cash flows were $10 million instead of $2,000 in year 4. It would not make any difference. Project Y would still be rejected under the payback method if the company's policy were to demand a payback of no more than two years. Failing to look beyond the payback period can lead to poor business decisions, as shown.

Another deficiency of the payback method is that it does not consider the time value of money. For instance, compare the cash flows of Projects A and B:

Cash Flows

	For Initial Investment	*End of Year 1*	*End of Year 2*
Project A	–$5,000	$3,000	$2,000
Project B	–$5,000	$2,000	$3,000

Assuming the required payback period is two years, we see that both projects are equally preferable—they both pay back the initial investment in two years. However, time value of money analysis indicates that if both projects are equally risky, then Project A is better than Project B because the firm will get more money sooner. Nevertheless, timing of cash flows makes no difference in the payback computation.

Because the payback method does not factor in the time value of money, nor the cash flows after the payback period, its usefulness is limited. Although it does provide a rough measure of a project's liquidity and can help to supplement other techniques, financial managers should not rely on it as a primary decision method.

The Net Present Value (NPV) Method

The project selection method that is most consistent with the goal of owner wealth maximization is the net present value method. The **net present value (NPV)** of a capital budgeting project is *the dollar amount of the change in the value of the firm as a result of undertaking the project.* The change in firm value may be positive, negative, or zero, depending on the NPV value.

If a project has a NPV of zero, it means that the firm's overall value will not change if the new project is adopted. Why? Because the new project is expected to generate exactly the firm's required rate of return—no more and no less. A positive NPV means that the firm's value will increase if the project is adopted because the new project's estimated return exceeds the firm's required rate of return. Conversely, a negative NPV means the firm's value will decrease if the new project is adopted because the new project's estimated return is less than what the firm requires.

Calculating NPV To calculate the net present value of a proposed project, we add the present value of a project's projected cash flows and then subtract the amount of the initial investment.[1] The result is a dollar figure that represents the change in the firm's value if the project is undertaken.

Formula for Net Present Value (NPV), Algebraic Method

$$NPV = \left(\frac{CF_1}{(1+k)^1}\right) + \left(\frac{CF_2}{(1+k)^2}\right) + \cdots + \left(\frac{CF_n}{(1+k)^n}\right) - \text{Initial Investment} \quad (10\text{-}1a)$$

where

CF = Cash flow at the indicated times

k = Discount rate, or required rate of return for the project

n = Life of the project measured in the number of time periods

To use financial tables to solve present value problems, write the NPV formula as follows:

The Formula for NPV, Table Method (10-1b)

$$NPV = CF_1(PVIF_{k,1}) + CF_2(PVIF_{k,2}) + \ldots + CF_n(PVIF_{k,n}) - \text{Initial Investment}$$

where

PVIF = Present Value Interest Factor

k = Discount rate, or required rate of return for the project

n = Life of the project measured in the number of time periods

To use the TI BAII PLUS financial calculator to solve for NPV, switch the calculator to the spreadsheet mode, enter the cash flow values in sequence, then the discount rate, depicted as I on the TI BAII PLUS calculator, then compute the NPV.

For simplicity, we use only the algebraic equation and the financial calculator to calculate NPV. If you prefer using financial tables, simply replace Equation 10-1a with Equation 10-1b.[2]

To show how to calculate NPV, let's solve for the NPVs of our two earlier projects, Projects X and Y. First, note the following cash flows of Projects X and Y:

Cash Flows

	For Initial Investment	*End of Year 1*	*End of Year 2*	*End of Year 3*	*End of Year 4*
Project X	–$5,000	$2,000	$3,000	$500	$0
Project Y	–$5,000	$2,000	$2,000	$1,000	$2,000

[1]We use many of the time value of money techniques learned in Chapter 8 to calculate NPV.

[2]If the future cash flows are an annuity, Equations 10-1a and 10-1b can be modified to take advantage of the present value of annuity formulas discussed in Chapter 8, Equations 8-4a and 8-4b.

Assume the required rate of return for Projects X and Y is 10 percent. Now we have all the data we need to solve for the NPV of Projects X and Y.

Applying Equation 10-1a and assuming a discount rate of 10 percent, the NPV of Project X follows:

$$
\begin{aligned}
NPV_x &= \left(\frac{\$2,000}{(1+0.10)^1}\right)+\left(\frac{\$3,000}{(1+0.10)^2}\right)+\left(\frac{\$500}{(1+0.10)^3}\right)-\$5,000\\
&= \frac{\$2,000}{1.1}+\frac{\$3,000}{1.21}+\frac{\$500}{1.331}-\$5,000\\
&= \$1,818.1818+\$2,479.3388+\$375.6574-\$5,000\\
&= -\$326.82
\end{aligned}
$$

We may also find Project X's NPV with the financial calculator at a 10 percent discount rate as follows:

TI BAII PLUS FINANCIAL CALCULATOR SOLUTIONS PROJECT X NPV

Keystrokes	*Display*
CF	CF_0 = old contents
2nd CLR Work	CF_0 = 0.00
5000 +/− ENTER	CF_0 = −5,000.00
↓ 2000 ENTER	C01 = 2,000.00
↓	F01 = 1.00
↓ 3000 ENTER	C02 = 3,000.00
↓	F02 = 1.00
↓ 500 ENTER	C03 = 500.00
↓	F03 = 1.00
NPV	I = 0.00
10 ENTER	I = 10.00
↓ CPT	NPV = −326.82

The preceding calculations show that at a 10 percent discount rate, an initial cash outlay of \$5,000, and cash inflows of \$2,000, \$3,000, and \$500 at the end of years 1, 2, and 3, the NPV for Project X is –\$326.82.

To find the NPV of Project Y, we apply Equation 10-1a as follows:

$$
\begin{aligned}
NPV_y &= \left(\frac{\$2,000}{(1+0.10)^1}\right)+\left(\frac{\$2,000}{(1+0.10)^2}\right)+\left(\frac{\$1,000}{(1+0.10)^3}\right)+\left(\frac{\$2,000}{(1+0.10)^4}\right)-\$5,000\\
&= \frac{\$2,000}{1.1}+\frac{\$2,000}{1.21}+\frac{\$1,000}{1.331}+\frac{\$2,000}{1.4641}-\$5,000\\
&= \$1,818.1818+\$1,652.8926+\$751.3148+\$1,366.0269-\$5,000\\
&= \$588.42
\end{aligned}
$$

Using the financial calculator, we solve for Project Y's NPV at a 10 percent discount rate as follows:

TI BAII PLUS FINANCIAL CALCULATOR SOLUTIONS PROJECT Y NPV

Keystrokes	*Display*
CF	CF_0 = old contents
2nd CLR Work	CF_0 = 0.00
5000 +/− ENTER	CF_0 = −5,000.00
↓ 2000 ENTER	C01 = 2,000.00
↓ 2 ENTER	F01 = 2.00
↓ 1000 ENTER	C02 = 1,000.00
↓	F02 = 1.00
↓ 2000 ENTER	C03 = 2,000
↓	F03 = 1.00
NPV	I = 0.00
10 ENTER	I = 10.00
↓ CPT	NPV = 588.42

Our calculations show that with a required rate of return of 10 percent, an initial cash outlay of \$5,000, and positive cash flows in years 1 through 4 of \$2,000, \$2,000, \$1,000, and \$2,000, respectively, the NPV for Project Y is \$588.42. If we compare Project X's NPV of –326.82 to Project Y's NPV of \$588.42, we see that Project Y would add value to the business and Project X would decrease the firm's value.

NPV Decision Rules NPV is used in two ways: (1) to determine if independent projects should be accepted or rejected (the accept/reject decision); and (2) to compare acceptable mutually exclusive projects (the ranking decision). The rules for these two decisions are:

- NPV Accept/Reject Decision—A firm should accept all independent projects having NPVs greater than or equal to zero. Projects with positive NPVs will add to the value of the firm if adopted. Projects with NPVs of zero will not alter the firm's value but (just) meet the firm's requirements. Projects with NPVs less than zero should be rejected because they will reduce the firm's value if adopted. Applying this decision rule, Project X would be rejected and Project Y would be accepted.
- NPV Ranking Decision—The mutually exclusive project with the highest positive NPV should be ranked first, the next highest should be ranked second, and so on. Under this decision rule, if the two projects in our previous example were mutually exclusive, Project Y would be ranked first and Project X second. (Not only is Project X second in rank here, but it is unacceptable because it has a negative NPV.)

The NPV Profile The k value is the cost of funds used for the project. It is the discount rate used in the NPV calculation because the cost of funds for a given project is that project's required rate of return. The relationship between the NPV of a project and k is inverse—the higher the k, the lower the NPV, and the lower the k, the higher the NPV.[3]

Because a project's NPV varies inversely with k, financial managers need to know how much the value of NPV will change in response to a change in k. If k is incorrectly specified, what appears to be a positive NPV could in fact be a negative NPV and vice versa—a negative NPV could turn out to be positive. Mutually exclusive project rankings could also change if an incorrect k value is used in the NPV computations.[4]

To see how sensitive a project's NPV value is to changes in k, analysts often create an NPV profile. The **NPV profile** is a graph that shows how a project's NPV changes when different discount rate values are used in the NPV computation.

Building an NPV profile is straightforward. First, the NPV of the project is calculated at a number of different discount rates. Then the results are plotted on the graph, with k values on one axis and the resulting NPV values on the other. If more than one project is included on the graph, the process is repeated for each project until all are depicted. To illustrate, we will build an NPV profile of Projects X and Y. We will plot Project X and then Project Y on the graph.

To begin, we first calculate the NPV of Project X with a number of different discount rates. The different k values may be chosen arbitrarily. For our purposes, let's use 0 percent, 5 percent, 10 percent, 15 percent, and 20 percent. The results of Project X's NPV calculations follow:

Discount Rate	*Project X NPV*
0%	$500.00
5%	$57.77
10%	–$326.82
15%	–$663.68
20%	–$960.65

Now Project X's NPV values may be plotted on the NPV profile graph. Figure 10-1 on page 314 shows the results.

When the data points are connected in Figure 10-1, we see how the NPV of Project X varies with the discount rate changes. The graph shows that with a k of about 5.7 percent, the value of the project's NPV is zero. At that discount rate, then, Project X would provide the firm's required rate of return, no more and no less.

[3]We are assuming here that the project is a typical one, meaning that it has an initial negative cash flow, the initial investment, followed by all positive cash flows. It is possible that if a project has negative cash flows in the future, the relationship between NPV and k might not be an inverse relationship.

[4]The estimation of the cost of funds used for capital budgeting projects was covered in Chapter 9.

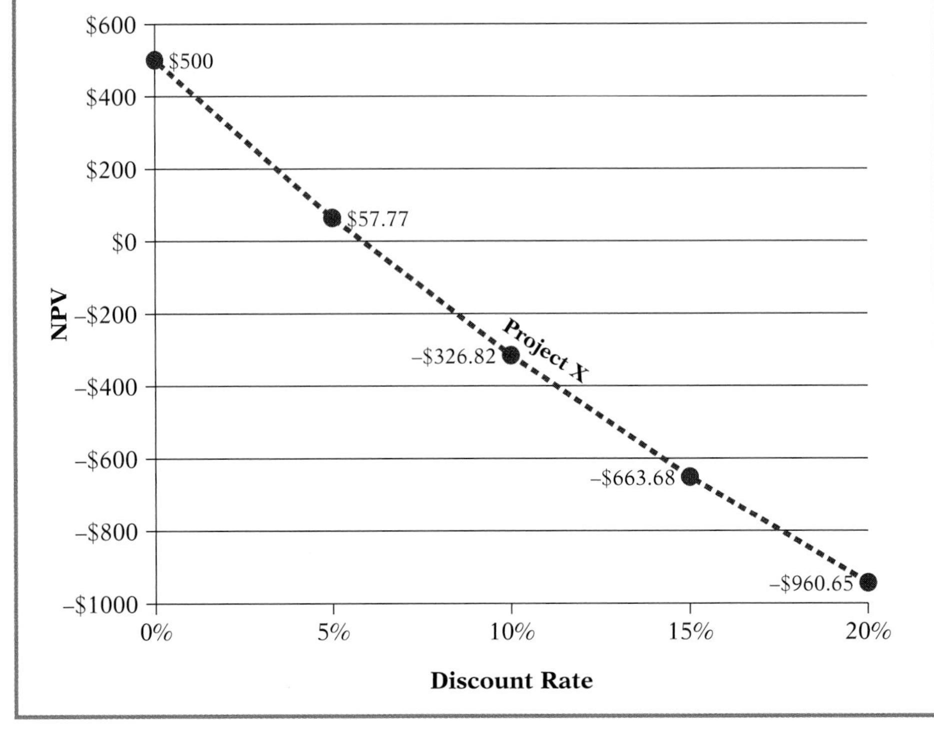

Figure 10-1 NPV Profile of Project X The NPV profile shows how the NPV of Project X varies inversely with the discount rate, k. Project X's NPV is highest ($500) when the discount rate is zero. Its NPV is lowest (–$960.65) when the discount rate is 20 percent.

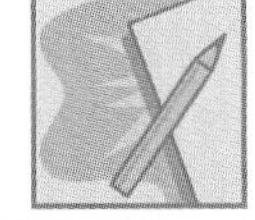

Take Note

The NPV profile line is curved, not straight. The curve is steepest at low discount rates and becomes shallower at higher rates. This shape occurs because discounting is the inverse of the exponential compounding phenomenon, as described in Chapter 8.

Next, we add project Y to the NPV profile graph. We calculate the NPV of Project Y at a number of different discount rates: 0 percent, 5 percent, 10 percent, 15 percent, and 20 percent. The results follow:

Discount Rate	*Project Y NPV*
0%	$2,000.00
5%	$1,228.06
10%	$588.42
15%	$52.44
20%	–$401.23

Figure 10-2 shows these NPV values plotted on the NPV profile graph.

Notice in Figure 10-2 that Project Y's NPV profile falls off more steeply than Project X's. This indicates that Project Y is more sensitive to changes in the discount rate than Project X. Project X's NPV becomes negative and, thus, the project is unacceptable when the discount rate rises above about 6 percent. Project Y's NPV becomes negative and, thus, the project is unacceptable when the discount rate rises above about 16 percent.

Problems with the NPV Method Although the NPV method ensures that a firm will choose projects that add value to a firm, it suffers from two practical problems. First, it is difficult to explain NPV to people who are not formally trained in finance. Few nonfinance people understand phrases such as "the present value of future cash flows" or "the change in a firm's value given its required rate of return." As a result, many financial managers have difficulty using NPV analysis persuasively.

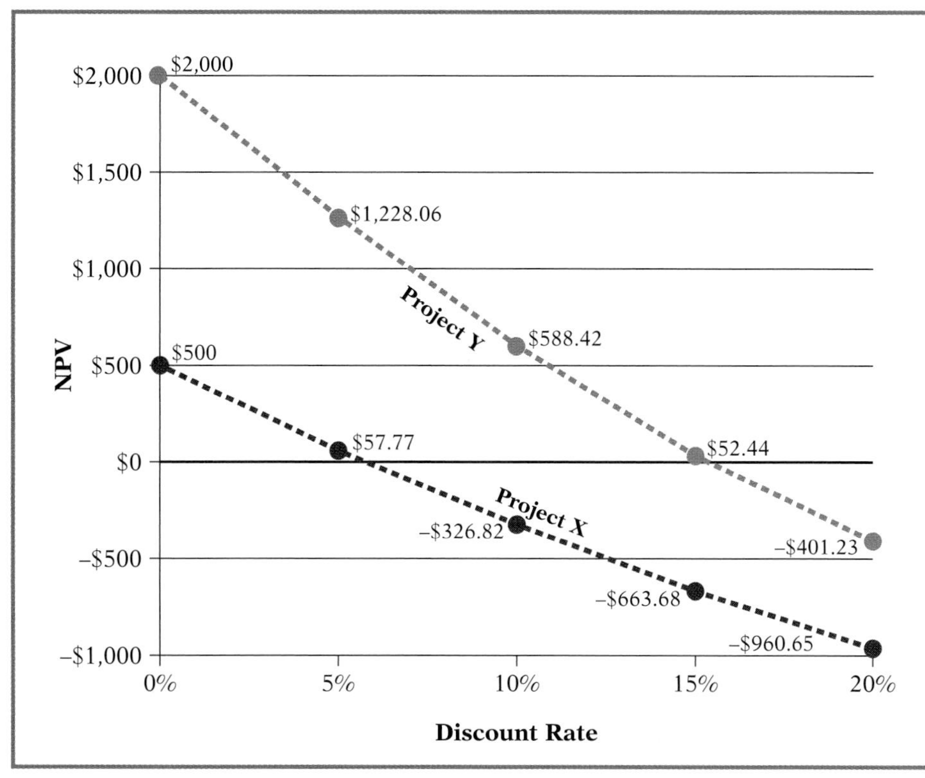

Figure 10-2 NPV Profile of Projects X and Y
This NPV profile shows how the NPVs of two capital budgeting projects, Projects X and Y, vary inversely with the discount rate, k.

A second problem is that the NPV method results are in dollars, not percentages. Many owners and managers prefer to work with percentages because percentages can be easily compared with other alternatives; Project 1 has a 10 percent rate of return compared with Project 2's 12 percent rate of return. The next method we discuss, the internal rate of return, provides results in percentages.

The Internal Rate of Return (IRR) Method

The **internal rate of return (IRR)** is the estimated rate of return for a proposed project, given the project's incremental cash flows. Just like the NPV method, the IRR method considers all cash flows for a project and adjusts for the time value of money. However, the IRR results are expressed as a percentage, not a dollar figure.

When capital budgeting decisions are made using the IRR method, the IRR of the proposed project is compared with the rate of return management requires for the project. The required rate of return is often referred to as the **hurdle rate**. If the project's IRR is greater than or equal to the hurdle rate (jumps over the hurdle), the project is accepted.

Calculating Internal Rate of Return: Trial-and-Error Method If the present value of a project's incremental cash flows were computed using management's required rate of return as the discount rate and the result exactly equalled the cost of the project, then the NPV of the project would be zero. When NPV equals zero, the required rate of return, or discount rate used in the NPV calculation, is the projected rate of return, IRR. To calculate IRR, then, we reorder the terms in Equation 10-1a to solve for a discount rate, k, that results in an NPV of zero.

The formula for finding IRR, Equation 10-2, follows:

Formula for IRR

$$NPV = 0 = \left(\frac{CF_1}{(1+k)^1}\right) + \left(\frac{CF_2}{(1+k)^2}\right) + \cdots + \left(\frac{CF_n}{(1+k)^n}\right) - \text{Initial Investment} \quad (10\text{-}2)$$

To find the IRR of a project using Equation 10-2, fill in the cash flows, the n values, and the initial investment figure. Then choose different values for k (all the other values are known) until the result equals zero. The IRR is the k value that causes the left-hand side of the equation, the NPV, to equal zero.

To illustrate the process, let's calculate the IRR for Project X. Recall that the cash flows associated with Project X were as follows:

Cash Flows

	For Initial Investment	*Year 1*	*Year 2*	*Year 3*	*Year 4*
Project X	–$5,000	$2,000	$3,000	$500	$0

First, we insert Project X's cash flows and the times they occur into Equation 10-2.

$$0 = \left(\frac{\$2{,}000}{(1+k)^1}\right) + \left(\frac{\$3{,}000}{(1+k)^2}\right) + \left(\frac{\$500}{(1+k)^3}\right) - \$5{,}000$$

Next, we try various discount rates until we find the value of k that results in an NPV of zero. Let's begin with a discount rate of 5 percent.

$$\begin{aligned} 0 &= \left(\frac{\$2{,}000}{(1+0.05)^1}\right) + \left(\frac{\$3{,}000}{(1+0.05)^2}\right) + \left(\frac{\$500}{(1+0.05)^3}\right) - \$5{,}000 \\ &= \left(\frac{\$2{,}000}{1.05}\right) + \left(\frac{\$3{,}000}{1.1025}\right) + \left(\frac{\$500}{1.157625}\right) - \$5{,}000 \\ &= \$1{,}904.76 + \$2{,}721.09 + \$431.92 - \$5{,}000 \\ &= \$57.77 \end{aligned}$$

This is close, but not quite zero. Let's try a second time, using a discount rate of 6 percent.

$$\begin{aligned} 0 &= \left(\frac{\$2{,}000}{(1+0.06)^1}\right) + \left(\frac{\$3{,}000}{(1+0.06)^2}\right) + \left(\frac{\$500}{(1+0.06)^3}\right) - \$5{,}000 \\ &= \left(\frac{\$2{,}000}{1.06}\right) + \left(\frac{\$3{,}000}{1.1236}\right) + \left(\frac{\$500}{1.191016}\right) - \$5{,}000 \\ &= \$1{,}886.79 + \$2{,}669.99 + \$419.81 - \$5{,}000 \\ &= -\$23.41 \end{aligned}$$

This is close enough for our purposes. We conclude that the IRR for Project X is slightly less than 6 percent.

Although calculating IRR by trial and error is time-consuming, the guesses do not have to be made entirely in the dark. Remember that the discount rate and NPV are inversely related. When an IRR guess is too high, the resulting NPV value will be too low. When an IRR guess is too low, the NPV will be too high.

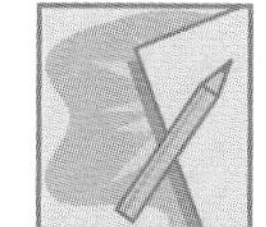

Take Note

We could estimate the IRR more accurately through more trial and error. However, carrying the IRR computation to several decimal points may give a false sense of accuracy, as in the case in which the cash flow estimates are in error.

Calculating Internal Rate of Return: Financial Calculator Finding solutions to IRR problems with a financial calculator is simple. After clearing previous values, enter the initial cash outlay and other cash flows and compute the IRR value.

The TI BAII PLUS financial calculator keystrokes for finding the IRR for Project X are shown next.

TI BAII PLUS FINANCIAL CALCULATOR SOLUTION IRR

Keystrokes	*Display*
CF	CF_0 = old contents
2nd CLR Work	CF_0 = 0.00
5000 +/− ENTER	CF_0 = −5,000.00
↓ 2000 ENTER	C01 = 2,000.00
↓	F01 = 1.00
↓ 3000 ENTER	C02 = 3,000.00
↓	F02 = 1.00
↓ 500 ENTER	C03 = 500.00
↓	F03 = 1.00
IRR	IRR = 0.00
CPT	IRR = 5.71

We see that with initial cash outflow of $5,000 and Project X's estimated cash inflows in years 1 through 3, the IRR is 5.71 percent.

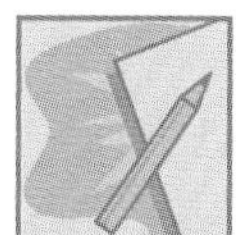

Take Note

If you are using a financial calculator other than the TI BAII PLUS, the calculator procedure will be similar but the keystrokes will differ. Be sure to check your calculator's instruction manual.

IRR and the NPV Profile Notice in Figure 10-2, that the point where Project X's NPV profile crosses the zero line is, in fact, the IRR (5.71 percent). This is no accident. When the required rate of return, or discount rate, equals the expected rate of return, IRR, then NPV equals zero. Project Y's NPV profile crosses the zero line just below 16 percent. If you use your financial calculator, you will find that the Project Y IRR is 15.54 percent. If an NPV profile graph is available, you can always find a project's IRR by locating the point where a project's NPV profile crosses the zero line.

IRR Decision Rule When evaluating proposed projects with the IRR method, those that have IRRs equal to or greater than the required rate of return (hurdle rate) set by management are accepted, and those projects with IRRs that are less than the required rate of return are rejected. Acceptable, mutually exclusive projects are ranked from highest to lowest IRR.

Benefits of the IRR Method The IRR method for selecting capital budgeting projects is popular among financial practitioners for three primary reasons:

1. IRR focuses on all cash flows associated with the project.
2. IRR adjusts for the time value of money.
3. IRR describes projects in terms of the *rate* of return they earn, which makes it easy to compare them with other investments and the firm's hurdle rate.

Problems with the IRR Method The IRR method has several problems, however. First, because the IRR is a percentage number, it does not show how much the value of the firm will change if the project is selected. If a project is quite small, for instance, it may have a high IRR but a small effect on the value of the firm. (Consider a project that requires a \$10 investment and returns \$100 a year later. The project's IRR is 900 percent, but the effect on the value of the firm if the project is adopted is negligible.)

If the primary goal for the firm is to maximize its value, then knowing the *rate* of return of a project is not the primary concern. What is most important is the *amount* by which the firm's value will change if the project is adopted, which is measured by NPV.

To drive this point home, ask yourself whether you would rather earn a 100 percent rate of return on \$5 (\$5) or a 50 percent rate of return on \$1,000 (\$500). As you can see, it is not the rate of return that is important but the dollar value. Why? Dollars, not percentages, comprise a firm's cash flows. NPV tells financial analysts how much value will be created. IRR does not.

A second problem with the IRR method is that, in rare cases, a project may have more than one IRR, or no IRR. This is shown in detail in Appendix 10A.

A third challenge with the IRR method is that it discounts cash flows by smaller discount factors in the early years of the project and by larger discount factors in later years. The IRR method is implicitly biased towards cash flows in early years by making them "more important" to the project. On the other hand, we can perhaps argue that cash flows in later years are more uncertain and should be discounted by larger discount factors. This approach is certainly consistent with the time value of money principle.

Lastly, we can say that all financial forecasts are sensitive to changes in their key parameters. The IRR calculation is no exception. Even small changes in financial forecasts may lead to significant changes in IRR. So, the more accurate the forecasts are, the more reliable the IRR method is as a tool for appraising capital budgeting projects.

The IRR can be a useful tool in evaluating capital budgeting projects. As with any tool, however, knowing its limitations will enhance decision making. We need to appreciate that the end results of the IRR analysis are only as realistic and reliable as the data used to estimate the cash flows and determine the discount rates.

Conflicting Rankings between the NPV and IRR Methods

As long as proposed capital budgeting projects are independent, both the NPV and IRR methods will produce the same accept/reject indication. That is, a project that has a positive NPV will also have an IRR that is greater than the discount rate. As a result, the project will be acceptable based on both the NPV and IRR values. However, when mutually exclusive projects are considered and ranked, a conflict occasionally arises. For instance, one project may have a higher NPV than another project but a lower IRR.

To illustrate how conflicts between NPV and IRR can occur, imagine that the AddVenture Company owns a piece of land that can be used in different ways. On the one hand, this land has minerals beneath it that could be mined, so AddVenture could invest in mining equipment and reap the benefits of retrieving and selling the minerals. On the other hand, the land has perfect soil conditions for growing grapes that could be used to make wine, so the company could use it to support a vineyard.

Clearly, these two uses are mutually exclusive. The mine cannot be dug if there is a vineyard, and the vineyard cannot be planted if the mine is dug. The acceptance of one of the projects means that the other must be rejected.

Now let's suppose that AddVenture's finance department has estimated the cash flows associated with each use of the land. The estimates are presented next:

Time	*Cash Flows for the Mining Project*	*Cash Flows for the Vineyard Project*
t_0	($736,369)	($736,369)
t_1	$500,000	$0
t_2	$300,000	$0
t_3	$100,000	$0
t_4	$20,000	$50,000
t_5	$5,000	$200,000
t_6	$5,000	$500,000
t_7	$5,000	$500,000
t_8	$5,000	$500,000

Note that although the initial outlays for the two projects are the same, the incremental cash flows associated with the projects differ in amount and timing. The Mining Project generates its greatest positive cash flows early in the life of the project, whereas the Vineyard Project generates its greatest positive cash flows later. The differences in the projects' cash flow timing have considerable effects on the NPV and IRR for each venture.

Assume AddVenture's required rate of return for long-term projects is 10 percent. The NPV and IRR results for each project given its cash flows are summarized as follows:

	NPV	*IRR*
Mining Project	$65,727.39	16.05%
Vineyard Project	$194,035.65	14.00%

These figures were obtained with our TI BAII PLUS calculator, in the same manner as shown earlier in the chapter.

The NPV and IRR results show that the Vineyard Project has a higher NPV than the Mining Project ($194,035.65 versus $65,727.39), but the Mining Project has a higher IRR than the Vineyard Project (16.05 percent versus 14.00 percent). AddVenture is faced with a conflict between NPV and IRR results. Because the projects are mutually exclusive, the firm can only accept one.

In cases of conflict among mutually exclusive projects, the one with the highest NPV should be chosen because NPV indicates the dollar amount of value that will be added to the firm if the project is undertaken. In our example, then, AddVenture should choose the Vineyard Project (the one with the higher NPV) if its primary financial goal is to maximize firm value. Venture capitalists refer to this as maximizing the "cash-on-cash" return from a project.

The Modified Internal Rate of Return (MIRR) Method

One problem with the IRR method that was not mentioned earlier is that the only way you can actually receive the IRR indicated by a project is if you reinvest the intervening cash flows in the project at the IRR. If the intervening cash flows are reinvested at any rate lower than the IRR, you will not end up with the IRR indicated at the end of the project.

For example, assume you have a project in which you invest $100 now and expect to receive four payments of $50 at the end of each of the next four years:

t_0	t_1	t_2	t_3	t_4
– 100	+50	+50	+50	+50

The IRR of this investment, calculated using either the trial-and-error or financial-calculator methods, is 34.9 percent. On the surface, this sounds like a fabulous investment. But, as they say, do not count your chickens before they hatch. If you cannot reinvest each $50 payment at the IRR of 34.9 percent, forget it; you will not end up with an overall return of 34.9 percent. To see why, consider what would happen if, for example, you simply put each $50 payment in your pocket. At the end of the fourth year, you would have $200 in your pocket. Now, using Equation 8-6, calculate the average annual rate of return necessary to produce $200 in four years with a beginning investment of $100:

$$\text{Actual return of the investment per Equation 8-6} = (200/100)^{(1/4)} - 1$$

$$= 18.9\% \text{ (not } 34.9\%)$$

Despite the fact that the IRR of the investment was 34.9 percent, you only ended up with an 18.9 percent annual return. The only way you could have obtained an annual return of 34.9 percent was to have reinvested each of the $50 cash flows at 34.9 percent. This is called the *IRR reinvestment assumption.*

To get around the IRR reinvestment assumption, a variation on the IRR procedure has been developed, called the **Modified Internal Rate of Return (MIRR)** method. The MIRR method calls for assuming that the intervening cash flows from a project are reinvested at a rate of return equal to the cost of capital. To find the MIRR, first calculate how much you would end up with at the end of a project, assuming the intervening cash flows were invested at the cost of capital. The result is called the project's *terminal value.* Next, calculate the annual rate of return it would take to produce that end amount from the beginning investment. The rate is the MIRR.

Here is the MIRR calculation for the project in our example, in which \$100 is invested at time zero, followed by inflows of \$50 at the end of each of the next four years. Let us assume for this example that the cost of capital is 10 percent.

Step 1: Calculate the project's terminal value:

Time	*Cash Flow*	*FV of Cash Flow at t_4 If Reinvested @ 10% Cost of Capital (per Equation 8-a)*
t_1	\$50	$FV = \$50 \times (1 + 0.10)^3 = \$66.55$
t_2	\$50	$FV = \$50 \times (1 + 0.10)^2 = \$60.50$
t_3	\$50	$FV = \$50 \times (1 + 0.10)^1 = \$55.00$
t_4	\$50	$FV = \$50 \times (1 + 0.10)^0 = \$50.00$
		Project's Terminal Value: \$232.05

Step 2: Calculate the annual rate of return that will produce the terminal value from the initial investment:

Project's Terminal Value: \$232.05

PV of Initial Investment: \$100

Per Equation 8-6:

$$MIRR = (232.05/100)^{(1/4)} - 1$$

$$MIRR = 23.4\%$$

This is a much more realistic expectation than the 34.9 percent return from the project indicated by the IRR method. Remember, any time you consider investing in a project, you will not actually receive the IRR unless you can reinvest the project's intervening cash flows at the IRR. Calculate the MIRR to produce a more realistic indication of the actual project outcome.

In this section, we looked at four capital budgeting decision methods: the payback method, the net present value method, the internal rate of return method, and the modified internal rate of return method. We also investigated how to resolve conflicts between NPV and IRR decision methods. Next, we turn to a discussion of capital rationing.

Now that you have learned about different methods of analyzing capital projects, let's see how non-business professionals, like engineers, may use these methods. For a discussion of this topic, see Finance at Work 10-1.

Capital Rationing

Our discussion so far has shown that all independent projects with NPVs greater than or equal to zero should be accepted. All such projects that are adopted will add value to the firm. To act consistently with the goal of shareholder wealth maximization, then, it seems that if a firm locates \$200 billion worth of independent positive NPV projects, it should accept all the projects.

FINANCE AT WORK 10-1

Sales Retail Sports Media Technology Public Relations Production Exports

BETTER THAN PAYBACK

In the August 2003 issue, I discussed why it is so important for engineers to start "looking at things like an accountant." My point was that engineers today can no longer satisfy management by ensuring that their decisions are keeping operations running. Today, engineers have to do that and "show the money" to upper management to gain support for their projects. Unfortunately, engineers may not quantify project benefits in the metrics of business and accounting that would be most helpful to their cause.

Here's a review of how to "find" the money to support buying decisions and project needs.

To justify the value of your purchasing decision, it's important to look past the most common measure used by engineers (and management) in predicting if a project should be approved. That measure is Payback Time (PT). According to Robert Dunlap, a former chemical engineer at UOP and now a final-year MBA student at the University of Texas, "PT is flawed because it says nothing about what happens after the project is over and has to be lived with. Also, the time horizon associated with PT is arbitrary, based more on accounting standards' affinity for year-on-year and quarter-on-quarter results. PT associated with these results causes problems if your industry segment does not fluctuate on such an economic cycle. As such, use of PT leads to adverse selection toward projects deemed 'low-hanging fruit.'"

Dunlap favours the use of Net Present Value (NPV) or Internal Rate of Return (IRR). "The NPV of a project involves discounting *all* cash flows the project incurs and summing these discounted values to achieve a final number," he says. "That number is designated the NPV. If it is positive, then the project should be undertaken. IRR is related to NPV a solves for a discount rate that will result in an NPV of 0. T rate is the IRR. If the IRR is greater than the company's ov all cost of capital, then the project should be accepted."

For examples of how to figure the discount rates asso ated with NPV and IRR for your next project, see this colu online www.controleng.com/issues (when you select October 2003 issue, you'll find the link in "Editorial" un "Departments").

"It is important to understand that these methods determining project value are valuable because they m decision-making into a more appropriate area, as opposed being based on temporary output boosts or on projects t appear to be doing well over the short run," says Dunl "Engineers must understand the value of making decisi this way because, in the long run, engineering is ab economics."

Questions to Consider

1. *To what extent should specialists from traditionally n business disciplines have a basic understanding finance principles?*
2. *Discuss advantages and disadvantages of using Payba NPV, and IRR methods in determining the attractiven of capital budgeting projects.*

Source: David Greenfield, "Better Than Payback," *Control Engineering*, October 2003. Reprinted with the permission of the author.

In practice, however, many firms place dollar limits on the total amount of capital budgeting projects they will undertake. They may wish to limit spending on new projects to keep a ceiling on business size or the amount of available cash may limit investment spending. This practice of setting dollar limits on capital budgeting projects is known as **capital rationing**.

If capital rationing is imposed, then financial managers should seek the combination of projects that maximizes the value of the firm within the capital budget limit. For example, suppose a firm called BeLimited does not want its capital budget to exceed $200,000. Seven project proposals, Proposals A to G, are available, as shown in Table 10-1.

Under capital rationing, BeLimited must choose the combination of acceptable Projects A through G that produces the highest total NPV without exceeding its capital budget limit of $200,000.

Note that all the projects in Table 10-1 have positive net present values, so they are all acceptable. However, BeLimited cannot adopt them all because

Project	Initial Cash Outlay	Net Present Value
A	$20,000	$8,000
B	$50,000	$7,200
C	$40,000	$6,500
D	$60,000	$5,100
E	$50,000	$4,200
F	$30,000	$3,800
G	$30,000	$2,000

Table 10-1
BeLimited Project Proposals

that would require the expenditure of more than $200,000, its self-imposed capital budget limit.

Under capital rationing, BeLimited's managers try different combinations of projects seeking the combination that gives the highest NPV without exceeding the $200,000 limit. For example, the combination of Projects B, C, E, F, and G costs $200,000 and yields a total NPV of $23,700. A better combination is that of Projects A, B, C, D, and F, which costs $200,000 and has a total NPV of $30,600. In fact, this combination has the highest total NPV, given the $200,000 capital budget limit (try a few other combinations to see for yourself), so that combination is the one BeLimited should choose.

In this section, we explored capital rationing. In the following section, we will examine how risk affects capital budgeting decisions.

Risk and Capital Budgeting

Suppose you are a financial manager for AddVenture Corporation. You are considering two capital budgeting projects, Project X (discussed throughout the chapter) and Project X2. Both projects have identical future cash flow values and timing, and both have the same NPV, if discounted at the same rate, k, and the same IRR. The two projects appear equally desirable.

Now suppose you discover that Project X's incremental cash flows are absolutely certain, but Project X2's incremental cash flows, which have the same expected value, are highly uncertain. These cash flows could be higher or lower than forecast. In other words, Project X is a sure thing and Project X2 appears to be quite risky. As a risk-averse person, you would prefer Project X over Project X2.

Financial managers are not indifferent to risk. Indeed, the riskier a project, the less desirable it is to the firm. To incorporate risk into the NPV and IRR evaluation techniques, we use the standard deviation and coefficient of variation (CV) measures discussed in Chapter 7. We begin by examining how to measure the risk of a capital budgeting project. Then we explain how to include the risk measurement in the NPV and IRR evaluation.

Measuring Risk in Capital Budgeting

Financial managers may measure three types of risk in the capital budgeting process. The first type is *project-specific risk,* or the risk of a specific new project. The second type is *firm risk,* which is the impact of adding a new project

Take Note

The CV is often chosen as the risk measure because the CV reflects the risk per unit of expected return. Using only the standard deviation makes it more difficult to tell whether the risk is high or low.

to the existing projects of the firm. The third is *market (or beta) risk*, which is the effect of a new project on the shareholders' nondiversifiable risk.

In this chapter, we focus on measuring firm risk. To measure firm risk, we compare the coefficient of variation (CV) of the firm's portfolio before and after a project is adopted. The before-and-after difference between the two CVs serves as the project's risk measure from a firm perspective. If the CAPM approach (discussed in Chapter 7) is preferred, a financial manager could estimate the risk of a project by calculating the project's beta instead of the change in firm risk.

Computing Changes in the Coefficient of Variation Let's reconsider our earlier example, Project X. Recall that the IRR of Project X was 5.71 percent. Now suppose that after careful analysis, we determine this IRR is actually the most likely value from a range of possible values, each with some probability of occurrence. We find the expected value and standard deviation of Project X's IRR distribution using Equations 7-1 and 7-2, respectively. We find that the expected value of the IRR distribution is 5.71 percent and the standard deviation is 2.89 percent.

To see how adding Project X to the firm's existing portfolio changes the portfolio's coefficient of variation (CV), we follow a five-step procedure.

Step 1: **Find the CV of the Existing Portfolio.** Suppose the expected rate of return and standard deviation of possible returns of AddVenture's existing portfolio are 6 percent and 2 percent, respectively. Given this information, calculate the CV of the firm's existing portfolio using Equation 7-3:

$$\begin{aligned} CV &= \frac{\text{Standard Deviation}}{\text{Mean, or Expected Value}} \\ &= \frac{0.02}{0.06} \\ &= 0.3333, \text{ or } 33.33\% \end{aligned}$$

Step 2: **Find the Expected Rate of Return of the New Portfolio (the Existing Portfolio Plus the Proposed Project).** Assume that the investment in Project X represents 10 percent of the value of the portfolio. In other words, the new portfolio after adding Project X will consist of 10 percent Project X and 90 percent of the rest of the firm's assets. With these figures, solve for the expected rate of return of the new portfolio using Equation 7-4. In the calculations, Asset A represents Project X and Asset B represents the firm's existing portfolio.

$$\begin{aligned} E(R_p) &= [w_a \times E(R_a)] + [w_b \times E(R_b)] \\ &= (0.10 \times 0.0571) + (0.90 \times 0.06) \\ &= 0.00571 + 0.05400 \\ &= 0.05971 \text{ or } 5.971\% \end{aligned}$$

Step 3: **Find the Standard Deviation of the New Portfolio (the Existing Portfolio Plus the Proposed Project).** Calculate the standard deviation of the new portfolio using Equation 7-5. Assume the degree of correlation (r) between project X (Asset A) and the firm's existing portfolio (Asset B) is zero. Put another way, there is no relationship between the returns from Project X and the returns from the firm's existing portfolio.

$$
\begin{aligned}
\sigma_p &= \sqrt{w_a^2\sigma_a^2 + w_b^2\sigma_b^2 + 2w_a w_b r_{ab}\sigma_a\sigma_b} \\
&= \sqrt{(0.10^2)(0.0289^2) + (0.90^2)(0.02^2) + (2)(0.10)(0.90)(0.0)(0.000578)} \\
&= \sqrt{(0.01)(0.000835) + (0.81)(0.0004) + 0} \\
&= \sqrt{0.00000835 + 0.000324} \\
&= \sqrt{0.00033235} \\
&= 0.0182, \text{ or } 1.82\%
\end{aligned}
$$

Step 4: **Find the CV of the New Portfolio (the Existing Portfolio Plus the Proposed Project).** To solve for the CV of the new portfolio with Project X included, we use Equation 7-3, as follows:

$$
\begin{aligned}
CV &= \frac{\text{Standard Deviation}}{\text{Mean, or Expected Value}} \\
&= \frac{0.0182}{0.05971} \\
&= 0.3048, \text{ or } 30.48\%
\end{aligned}
$$

Step 5: **Compare the CV of the Portfolio with and without the Proposed Project.** To evaluate the effect of Project X on the risk of the AddVenture portfolio, we compare the CV of the old portfolio (without Project X) to the CV of the new portfolio (with Project X). The coefficients follow:

CV of the Portfolio without Project X	*CV of the Portfolio with Project X*	*Change in CV*
33.33%	30.48%	– 2.85

The CV of the firm's portfolio dropped from 33.33 percent to 30.48 percent with the addition of Project X. This 2.85 percentage point decrease in CV is the measure of risk in Project X from the firm's perspective.

Adjusting for Risk

Most business owners and financial managers are risk averse, so they want the capital budgeting process to reflect risk concerns. Next, we discuss how to adjust for risk in the capital budgeting process—risk-adjusted discount rates. The discount rate is the cost of capital discussed in Chapter 9. A project's risk-adjusted discount rate is the cost of capital for that specific project.

Risk-Adjusted Discount Rates (RADRs) One way to factor risk into the capital budgeting process is to adjust the rate of return demanded for high- and low-risk projects. **Risk-adjusted discount rates (RADRs)**, then, are discount rates that differ according to their effect on a firm's risk. The higher the risk is, the higher the RADR is. The lower the risk is, the lower the RADR is. A project with a normal risk level would have an RADR equal to the actual discount rate.

To find the RADR for a capital budgeting project, we first prepare a risk adjustment table like the one in Table 10-2. We assume in Table 10-2 that the coefficient of variation, CV, is the risk measure to be adjusted for. The CV is based on the probability distribution of the IRR values.

Table 10-2 Risk-Adjustment Table

If Adoption of the Proposed Capital Budgeting Project Would Change the CV of the Firm's Portfolio IRR by the Following Amount:	Then Assign the Project to the Following Risk Category:	And Adjust the Discount Rate for the Project as Follows:
More than a 1 percent increase	High Risk	+2%
Between a 1 percent decrease and a 1 percent increase	Average Risk	0
More than a 1 percent decrease	Low Risk	− 2%

Take Note

The data in Table 10-2 are only for illustration. In practice, the actual amount of risk adjustment will depend on the degree of risk aversion of the managers and shareholders.

Table 10-2 shows how the discount rates for capital budgeting projects might be adjusted for varying degrees of risk. The discount rate of a project that decreased the CV of the firm's portfolio of assets by 2.5 percentage points, for example, would be classified as a low-risk project. The project would be evaluated using a discount rate two percentage points lower than that used on average projects.

This has the effect of making Project X a more desirable project. In other words, financial managers would calculate the project's NPV using an average discount rate that is two percentage points lower, which would increase the project's NPV. If the firm uses the IRR method, financial managers would compare the project's IRR to a hurdle rate two percentage points lower than average, which would make it more likely that the firm would adopt the project.

RADRs are an important part of the capital budgeting process because they incorporate the risk–return relationship. All other things being equal, the more a project increases risk, the less likely it is that a firm will accept the project; the more a project decreases risk, the more likely it is that a firm will accept the project.

SUMMARY

10-1 Explain two decision practices used in the capital budgeting process.

Capital budgeting is the process of evaluating proposed investment projects. Capital budgeting projects may be independent—the projects do not compete with each other—or mutually exclusive—accepting one project precludes the acceptance of the other(s) in that group.

Financial managers apply two decision practices when selecting capital budgeting projects: *accept/reject* decisions and *ranking* decisions. The accept/reject decision is the determination of which independent projects are acceptable in light of the firm's financial objectives. Ranking is a process of comparing projects to a standard measure and ordering the mutually exclusive projects based on how well they meet the measure. The capital budgeting process is concerned only with incremental cash flows; that is, those cash flows that will occur if an investment is undertaken but will not occur if it is not.

10-2 Describe how to calculate the payback period, net present value, internal rate of return, and modified internal rate of return for a proposed capital budgeting project.

The payback period is defined as the number of time periods it will take before the cash inflows from a proposed capital budgeting project will equal the amount of the initial investment. To find a project's payback period, add all the project's positive cash flows, one period at a time, until the sum equals the amount of the initial cash outlay for the project. The number of time periods it takes to recoup the initial cash outlay is the payback period. A project is acceptable if it pays back the initial investment within a time frame set by firm management.

The net present value (NPV) of a proposed capital budgeting project is the dollar amount of the change in the value of the firm that will occur if the project is undertaken. To calculate NPV, total the present values of all the projected incremental cash flows associated with a project and subtract the amount of the initial cash outlay. A project with an NPV greater than or equal to zero is acceptable. An NPV profile—a graph that shows a project's NPV at many different discount rates (required rates of return)— shows how sensitive a project's NPV is to changes in the discount rate.

The internal rate of return (IRR) is the projected percentage rate of return that a proposed project will earn, given its incremental cash flows and required initial cash outlay. To calculate IRR, find the discount rate that makes the project's NPV equal to zero. That rate of return is the IRR. A project is acceptable if its IRR is greater than or equal to the firm's required rate of return (the hurdle rate).

The IRR method assumes that intervening cash flows in a project are reinvested at a rate of return equal to the IRR. This can result in overly optimistic expectations when the IRR is high and the intervening cash flows cannot be reinvested. To produce more realistic results, the Modified Internal Rate of Return (MIRR) method was developed. The MIRR method calls for assuming that the intervening cash flows from a project are reinvested at a rate of return equal to the cost of capital. To find the MIRR, first calculate how much you would end up with at the end of a project, assuming the intervening cash flows were invested at the cost of capital. The result is called the project's *terminal value*. Next, calculate the annual rate of return it would take to produce that end amount from the beginning investment. That rate is the MIRR.

10-3 Define capital rationing and describe how firms decide which projects to select.

The practice of placing dollar limits on the total size of the capital budget is called capital rationing. Under capital rationing, the firm will select the combination of projects that yields the highest NPV without exceeding the capital budget limit.

10-4 Explain how to measure the risk of a capital budgeting project.

To measure the risk of a capital budgeting project, we determine how the project would affect the risk of the firm's existing asset portfolio. We compare the coefficient of variation of possible returns of the firm's asset portfolio with the proposed project and without it. The difference between the two coefficients of variation is the measure of the risk of the capital budgeting project.

10-5 Explain why risk-adjusted discount rates are used.

To compensate for the degree of risk in capital budgeting, firms may adjust the discount rate for each project according to risk. The more risk is increased, the higher the discount rate. The more risk is decreased, the lower the discount rate. Rates adjusted for the risk of projects are called risk-adjusted discount rates (RADRs).

EQUATIONS INTRODUCED IN THIS CHAPTER

Equation 10-1a: NPV Formula, Algebraic Method

$$NPV = \left(\frac{CF_1}{(1+k)^1}\right) + \left(\frac{CF_2}{(1+k)^2}\right) + \cdots + \left(\frac{CF_n}{(1+k)^n}\right) - \text{Initial Investment}$$

where

CF = Cash flow at the indicated times
k = Discount rate, or required rate of return for the project
n = Life of the project measured in the number of time periods

Equation 10-1b: NPV Formula, Table Method

$$NPV = CF_1(PVIF_{k,1}) + CF_2(PVIF_{k,2}) + \ldots + CF_n(PVIF_{k,n}) - \text{Initial Investment}$$

where

PVIF = Present Value Interest Factor
k = Discount rate, or required rate of return for the project
n = Life of the project measured in the number of time periods

Equation 10-2: Formula for IRR Using Equation 10-1a

$$NPV = 0 = \left(\frac{CF_1}{(1+k)^1}\right) + \left(\frac{CF_2}{(1+k)^2}\right) + \cdots + \left(\frac{CF_n}{(1+k)^n}\right) - \text{Initial Investment}$$

where

k = the IRR value

Fill in cash flows (CFs) and periods (n). Then choose values for k by trial and error until the NPV equals zero. The value of k that causes the NPV to equal zero is the IRR.

SELF-TEST

ST-1. What is the NPV of the following project?

Initial investment	$50,000
Net cash flow at the end of year 1	$20,000
Net cash flow at the end of year 2	$40,000
Discount rate	11%

ST-2. What is the IRR of the project in ST-1?

ST-3. You've been assigned to evaluate a project for your firm that requires an initial investment of $200,000, is expected to last for 10 years, and is expected to produce after-tax net cash flows of $44,503 per year. If your firm's required rate of return is 14 percent, should the project be accepted?

ST-4. What is the IRR of the project in ST-3?

ST-5. What is the MIRR of the project in ST-3?

ST-6. Assume you have decided to reinvest your portfolio in zero-coupon bonds. You like zero-coupon bonds because they pay off a known amount, $1,000 at maturity, and involve no other cash flows other than the purchase price. Assume your required rate of return is 12 percent. If you buy some 10-year zero-coupon bonds for $400 each today, will the bonds meet your return requirements? (Hint: Compute the IRR of the investment given the cash flows involved.)

ST-7. Joe, the cut-rate bond dealer, has offered to sell you some zero-coupon bonds for $300. (Remember, zero-coupon bonds pay off $1,000 at maturity and involve no other cash flows other than the purchase price.) If the bonds mature in 10 years and your required rate of return for cut-rate bonds is 20 percent, what is the NPV of Joe's deal?

REVIEW QUESTIONS

1. How do we calculate the payback period for a proposed capital budgeting project? What are the main criticisms of the payback method?
2. How does the net present value relate to the value of the firm?
3. What are the advantages and disadvantages of the internal rate of return method?
4. Provide three examples of mutually exclusive projects.
5. What is the decision rule for accepting or rejecting proposed projects when using net present value?
6. What is the decision rule for accepting or rejecting proposed projects when using internal rate of return?
7. What is capital rationing? Should a firm practise capital rationing? Why?
8. Explain how to resolve a ranking conflict between the net present value and the internal rate of return. Why should the conflict be resolved as you explained?
9. Explain how to measure the firm risk of a capital budgeting project.
10. Why is the coefficient of variation a better risk measure to use than the standard deviation when evaluating the risk of capital budgeting projects?
11. Explain why we measure a project's risk as the change in the CV.
12. Explain how using a risk-adjusted discount rate improves capital budgeting decision making compared with using a single discount rate for all projects.

PROBLEMS

10-1. Three separate projects each have an initial cash outlay of $10,000. The cash flow for Peter's Project is $4,000 per year for three years. The cash flow for Paul's Project is $2,000 in years 1 and 3 and $8,000 in year 2. Mary's Project has a cash flow of $10,000 in year 1, followed by $1,000 each year for years 2 and 3. ◀ Payback

a. Use the payback method to calculate how many years it will take for each project to recoup the initial investment.

b. Which project would you consider most liquid?

10-2. You have just paid $20 million in the secondary market for the winning lottery ticket. The prize is $2 million at the end of each year for the next 25 years. If your required rate of return is 8 percent, what is the net present value (NPV) of the deal? ◀ Net Present Value

10-3. What is the internal rate of return (IRR) of the 6/49 deal in question 2? ◀ Internal Rate of Return

10-4. What is the modified internal rate of return (MIRR) of the 6/49 deal in question 2? ◀ Modified Internal Rate of Return

10-5. RejuveNation needs to estimate how long the payback period would be for their new facility project. They have received two proposals and need to decide which one is best. Project Weights will have an initial investment of $200,000 and generate positive cash flows of $100,000 at the end of year 1, $75,000 at ◀ Payback Period the end of year 2, $50,000 at the end of year 3, and $100,000 at the end of year 4. Project Waters will have an initial investment of $300,000 and will generate positive cash flows of $200,000 at the end of year 1 and $150,000 at the end of years 2, 3, and 4. What is the payback period for Project Waters? What is the payback period for Project Weights? Which project should RejuveNation choose?

NPV ▶ **10-6.** Calculate the NPV of each project in problem 10-5 using RejuveNation's cash flows and a 10 percent discount rate.

NPV and IRR ▶ **10-7.** The Bedford Falls Bridge Building Company is considering the purchase of a new crane. George Bailey, the new manager, has had some past management experience while he was the chief financial officer of the local credit union. The cost of the crane is $17,291.42, and the expected incremental cash flows are $5,000 at the end of year 1, $8,000 at the end of year 2, and $10,000 at the end of year 3.

a. Calculate the net present value if the required rate of return is 12 percent.

b. Calculate the internal rate of return.

c. Should Mr. Bailey purchase this crane?

NPV and IRR ▶ **10-8.** Lin McAdam and Lola Manners, managers of the Winchester Company, do not practise capital rationing. They have three independent projects they are evaluating for inclusion in this year's capital budget. One is for a new machine to make rifle stocks. The second is for a new forklift to use in the warehouse. The third project involves the purchase of automated packaging equipment. The Winchester Company's required rate of return is 13 percent. The initial investment (a negative cash flow) and the expected positive net cash flows for years 1 through 4 for each project follow:

Expected Net Cash Flow

Year	Rifle Stock Machine	Forklift	Packaging Equipment
0	$(9,000)	($12,000)	($18,200)
1	2,000	5,000	0
2	5,000	4,000	5,000
3	1,000	6,000	10,000
4	4,000	2,000	12,000

a. Calculate the net present value for each project.

b. Which project(s) should be undertaken? Why?

NPV and IRR ▶ **10-9.** The Trask Family Lettuce Farm is located in the fertile Okanagan Valley of British Columbia. Adam Trask, the head of the family, makes all the financial decisions that affect the farm. Because of an extended drought, the family needs more water per acre than the existing irrigation system can supply. The quantity and quality of lettuce produced are expected to increase when more water is supplied. Cal and Aron, Adam's sons, have devised two different solutions to their problem. Cal suggests improvements to the existing system. Aron is in favour of a completely new system. The negative cash flow associated with the initial investment and expected positive net cash flows for years 1 through 7 for each project follow. Adam has no other alternatives and will choose one of the two projects. The Trask Family Lettuce Farm has a required rate of return of 12 percent for these projects.

Expected Net Cash Flow

Year	Cal's Project	Aron's Project
0	($100,000)	($300,000)
1	22,611	63,655
2	22,611	63,655
3	22,611	63,655
4	22,611	63,655
5	22,611	63,655
6	22,611	63,655
7	22,611	63,655

a. Calculate the net present value for each project.
b. Calculate the internal rate of return for each project.
c. Which project should Adam choose? Why?
d. Is there a conflict between the decisions indicated by the NPVs and the IRRs?

10-10. Buzz Lightyear has been offered an investment in which he expects to receive payments of $4,000 at the end of each of the next 10 years in return for an initial investment of $10,000 now. ◀ IRR and MIRR

a. What is the IRR of the proposed investment?
b. What is the MIRR of the proposed investment? Assume a cost of capital of 15 percent.
c. Why is the MIRR thought of as a more realistic indication of a project's potential than the IRR?

10-11. Dave Hirsh publishes his own manuscripts and is unsure about which of two new printers he should purchase. He is a novelist living in Brandon, Manitoba. Having slept through most of his Finance 300 course in college, he is unfamiliar with cash flow analysis. He enlists the help of the finance professor at the Brandon University, Dr. Gwen Cash, to assist him. Together they estimate the following expected initial investment (a negative cash flow) and net positive cash flows for years 1 through 3 for each machine. Dave only needs one printer and estimates it will be worthless after three years of heavy use. Dave's required rate of return for this project is 10 percent. ◀ Payback, NPV, and IRR

Expected Net Cash Flow

Year	Printer 1	Printer 2
0	($2,000)	($2,500)
1	900	1,500
2	1,100	1,300
3	1,300	800

a. Calculate the payback period for each printer.
b. Calculate the net present value for each printer.
c. Calculate the internal rate of return for each printer.
d. Which printer do you think Dr. Cash will recommend? Why?
e. Suppose Dave's required rate of return were 16 percent. Does the decision about which printer to purchase change?

10-12. Matrix.com has designed a virtual-reality program that is indistinguishable from real life to those experiencing it. The program will cost $20 million to develop (paid up front), but the pay-off is substantial: $1 million at the end of year 1, ◀ NPV, IRR, and MIRR

$2 million at the end of year 2, $5 million at the end of year 3, and $6 million at the end of each year thereafter, through year 10. Matrix.com's weighted average cost of capital is 15 percent. Given these conditions, what are the NPV, IRR, and MIRR of the proposed program?

Independent and Mutually Exclusive Projects ▶

10-13. Project A has an initial investment of $11,000 and it generates positive cash flows of $4,000 each year for the next six years. Project B has an initial investment of $17,000 and it generates positive cash flows of $4,500 each year for the next six years. Assume the discount rate, or required rate of return, is 13 percent.

a. Calculate the net present value of each project. If Project A and Project B are mutually exclusive, which one would you select?

b. Assume Projects A and B are independent. Based on NPV, which one(s) would you select?

c. Calculate the internal rate of return for each project.

d. Using IRR for your decision, which project would you select if Project A and Project B were mutually exclusive? Would your answer change if these two projects were independent instead of mutually exclusive?

e. Project C was added to the potential capital budget list at the last minute as a mutually exclusive alternative to Project B. It has an initial cash outlay of $17,000, and it generates its only positive cash flow of $37,500 in the sixth year. Years 1 through 5 have $0 cash flow. Calculate Project C's NPV. Which alternative, Project B or C, would you choose?

f. Now calculate the IRR of Project C and compare it with Project B's IRR. Based solely on the IRRs, which project would you select?

g. Because Projects B and C are mutually exclusive, would you recommend that Project B or Project C be added to the capital budget for this year? Explain your choice.

NPV and IRR ▶

10-14. Joanne Crale is an independent petroleum geologist. She is taking advantage of every opportunity to lease the mineral rights of land she thinks lies over oil reserves. She thinks there are many reservoirs with oil reserves left behind by major corporations when they plugged and abandoned fields in the 1960s. Ms. Crale knows that with today's technology, production can be sustained at much lower reservoir pressures than was possible in the 1960s. She would like to lease the mineral rights from George Hansen and Ed McNeil, the landowners. Her net cost for this current oil venture is $5 million. This includes costs for the initial leasing and three planned development wells. The expected positive net cash flows for the project are $1.85 million each year for four years. On depletion, she anticipates a negative cash flow of $250,000 in year 5 because of reclamation and disposal costs. Because of the risks involved in petroleum exploration, Ms. Crale's required rate of return is 16 percent.

a. Calculate the net present value for Ms. Crale's project.

b. Calculate the internal rate of return for this project.

c. Would you recommend the project?

NPV Profit Analysis ▶

10-15. Silkwood Power Company is considering two projects with the following predicted cash flows:

	Hydroelectric Upgrade	Geothermal Upgrade
Initial Investment CFs	($100,000)	($100,000)
End of year 1 CFs	20,000	80,000
End of year 2 CFs	30,000	40,000
End of year 3 CFs	40,000	30,000
End of year 4 CFs	90,000	10,000

a. Which project(s) would be accepted if the company's cost of capital were 6 percent?
b. Which project(s) would be accepted if the company's cost of capital were 15 percent?
c. At what cost of capital would Silkwood value each project equally?
d. At what cost of capital would the hydroelectric project become unacceptable?
e. At what cost of capital would the geothermal project become unacceptable?

10-16. The product development managers at World Series Innovations are about to recommend their final capital budget for next year. They have a self-imposed budget limit of $100,000. Five independent projects are being considered. Vernon Simpson, the chief scientist and CEO, has minimal financial analysis experience and relies on his managers to recommend the projects that will increase the value of the firm by the greatest amount. Given the following summary of the five projects, which ones should the managers recommend?

◀ Challenge Problem

Projects	Initial Cash Outlay	Net Present Value
Chalk Line Machine	($10,000)	$4,000
Gel Padded Glove	($25,000)	$3,600
Insect Repellent	($35,000)	$3,250
Titanium Bat	($40,000)	$2,500
Recycled Base Covers	($20,000)	$2,100

10-17. A project you are considering has an initial investment of $5,669.62. It has positive net cash flows of $2,200 each year for three years. Your required rate of return is 12 percent.

◀ Various Capital Budgeting Issues

a. Calculate the net present value of this project.
b. Would you undertake this project if you had the cash available?
c. What would the discount rate have to be before this project's NPV would be positive? Construct an NPV profile with discount rates of 0 percent, 5 percent, and 10 percent to answer this question.
d. What other method might you use to determine at what discount rate the net present value would become greater than 0?

10-18. The internal rate of return (IRR) of a capital investment, Project B, is expected to have the following values with the associated probabilities for an economic life of five years. Calculate the expected value, standard deviation, and coefficient of variation of the IRR distribution.

◀ Expected IRR

IRR	Probability of Occurrence
0%	0.05
1%	0.10
3%	0.20
6%	0.30
9%	0.20
11%	0.10
12%	0.05

10-19. Four capital investment alternatives have the following expected IRRs and standard deviations.

◀ Capital Budgeting Risk

Project	Expected IRR	Standard Deviation
A	14%	2%
B	16%	6%
C	11%	5%
D	14%	4%

If the firm's existing portfolio of assets has an expected IRR of 13 percent with a standard deviation of 3 percent, identify the lowest- and the highest-risk projects in the preceding list. You may assume the correlation coefficient of returns from each project relative to the existing portfolio is 0.50 and the investment in each project would constitute 20 percent of the firm's total portfolio.

Portfolio Risk ▶

Excel

10-20. Assume that a company has an existing Portfolio A, with an expected IRR of 10 percent and standard deviation of 2 percent. The company is considering adding a Project B, with expected IRR of 11 percent and standard deviation of 3 percent to its portfolio. Also assume that the amount invested in Portfolio A is $700,000 and the amount to be invested in Project B is $200,000.

a. If the degree of correlation between returns from Portfolio A and Project B is 0.90 (r = 0.9), calculate:

- **i.** the coefficient of variation of Portfolio A
- **ii.** the expected IRR of the new combined portfolio
- **iii.** the standard deviation of the new combined portfolio
- **iv.** the coefficient of variation of the new combined portfolio

Coefficient of Variation Risk in Capital Budgeting ▶

b. What is the change in the coefficient of variation as a result of adopting Project B?

c. Assume the firm classifies projects as high risk if they raise the coefficient of variation of the portfolio 2 percentage points or more, as low risk if they lower the coefficient of variation of the portfolio 2 percentage points or more, and as average risk if they change the coefficient of variation of the portfolio by less than 2 percent in either direction. In what risk classification would Project B be?

RADRs ▶

d. The required rate of return for average-risk projects for the company in this problem is 13 percent. The company policy is to adjust the required rate of return downward by 3 percent for low-risk projects and to raise it 3 percent for high-risk projects (average-risk projects are evaluated at the average required rate of return). The expected cash flows from Project B are as follows:

CF of Initial Investment	($200,000)
end of year 1	55,000
end of year 2	55,000
end of year 3	55,000
end of year 4	100,000

Calculate the NPV of Project B when its cash flows are discounted at:

- **i.** the average required rate of return
- **ii.** the high-risk discount rate
- **iii.** the low-risk discount rate

Risk and Capital Budgeting ▶

10-21. Dorothy Gale is thinking of purchasing a London amusement park, Glinda's Gulch. She already owns at least one park in each of the surrounding communities and wants to expand her operations into London. She estimates the IRR from the project may be one of a number of values, each with a certain probability of occurrence. Her estimated IRR values and the probability of their occurrence follow:

Glinda's Gulch

Possible IRR Value	Probability
2%	0.125
5%	0.20
9%	0.35
13%	0.20
16%	0.125

Now Dorothy wants to estimate the risk of the project. Assume she has asked you to do the following for her:

a. Calculate the mean, or expected, IRR of the project.

b. Calculate the standard deviation of the possible IRRs.

c. Assume the expected IRR of Dorothy's existing portfolio of parks is 8 percent with a standard deviation of 2 percent. Calculate the coefficient of variation of Dorothy's existing portfolio.

d. Calculate the expected IRR of Dorothy's portfolio if the Glinda's Gulch project is adopted. For this calculation, assume that Dorothy's new portfolio will consist of 80 percent existing parks and 20 percent new Glinda's Gulch.

e. Again assuming that Dorothy's new portfolio will consist of 80 percent existing parks and 20 percent new Glinda's Gulch, calculate the standard deviation of Dorothy's portfolio if the Glinda's Gulch project is added. Because Glinda's Gulch is identical to Dorothy's other parks, she estimates that the returns from Glinda's Gulch and her existing portfolio are perfectly positively correlated (r = +1.0).

f. Calculate the coefficient of variation of Dorothy's new portfolio with Glinda's Gulch.

g. Compare the coefficient of variation of Dorothy's existing portfolio with and without the Glinda's Gulch project. How does the addition of Glinda's Gulch affect the riskiness of the portfolio?

10-22. Four capital investment alternatives have the following expected IRRs and standard deviations.

◀ Risk and Capital Budgeting

Excel

Project	Expected IRR	Standard Deviation
A	18%	9%
B	15%	5%
C	11%	3%
D	8%	1%

The firm's existing portfolio of projects has an expected IRR of 12 percent and a standard deviation of 4 percent.

a. Calculate the coefficient of variation of the existing portfolio.

b. Calculate the coefficient of variation of the portfolio if the firm invests 10 percent of its assets in Project A. You may assume that there is no correlation between the returns from Project A and the returns from the existing portfolio (r = 0). (Note: In order to calculate the coefficient of variation, you must first calculate the expected IRR and standard deviation of the portfolio with Project A included.)

c. Using the same procedure as in (b) and given the same assumptions, calculate the coefficient of variation of the portfolio if it includes, in turn, Projects B, C, and D.

d. Which project has the highest risk? Which has the lowest risk?

Firm Risk ▶

Excel

10-23. A firm has an existing portfolio of projects with a mean, or expected, IRR of 15 percent. The standard deviation of this estimate is 5 percent. The existing portfolio is worth $820,000. The addition of a new project, PROJ1, is being considered. PROJ1's expected IRR is 18 percent with a standard deviation of 9 percent. The initial investment for PROJ1 is expected to be $194,000. The returns from PROJ1 and the existing portfolio are perfectly positively correlated (r = +1.0).

a. Calculate the coefficient of variation for the existing portfolio.

b. If PROJ1 is added to the existing portfolio, calculate the weight (proportion) of the existing portfolio in the combined portfolio.

c. Calculate the weight (proportion) of PROJ1 in the combined portfolio.

d. Calculate the standard deviation of the combined portfolio. Is the standard deviation of the combined portfolio higher or lower than the standard deviation of the existing portfolio?

e. Calculate the coefficient of variation of the combined portfolio.

f. If PROJ1 is added to the existing portfolio, will the firm's risk increase or decrease?

Risk and Capital Budgeting ▶

10-24. VOTD Pharmaceuticals is considering the mass production of a new sleeping pill. Neely O'Hara, VOTD's financial analyst, has gathered all the available information from the finance, production, advertising, and marketing departments and has estimated that the yearly net incremental cash flows will be $298,500. She estimates that the initial investment for this project will be $2 million. The pills are expected to be marketable for 10 years, and Neely does not expect that any of the investment costs will be recouped at the end of the 10-year period. VOTD's required rate of return for average-risk projects is 8 percent. Two percent is added to the required rate of return for high-risk projects.

a. Calculate the net present value of the project if VOTD management considers it to be average risk.

b. A lot of uncertainty is associated with the potential competition of new drugs that VOTD's competitors might introduce. Because of this uncertainty, VOTD management has changed the classification of this project to high risk. Calculate the net present value at the risk-adjusted discount rate.

c. Assuming the risk classification does not change again, should this project be adopted?

d. What will the yearly net incremental cash flow have to be to have a positive NPV when using the high-risk discount rate?

Comprehensive Problem ▶

Excel

10-25. Aluminum Building Products Company (ABPC) is considering investing in either of the two mutually exclusive projects described as follows:

Project 1. Buying a new set of roll-forming tools for its existing roll-forming line to introduce a new cladding product. After its introduction, the product will need to be promoted. This means that cash inflows from additional production will start some time after (see the table below) and will gradually pick up in subsequent periods.

Project 2. Modifying its existing roll-forming line to increase productivity of its available range of cladding products. Cash inflows from additional production will start immediately and will reduce over time as the products move through their life cycle.

Sarah Brown, project manager of ABPC, has requested that you do the necessary financial analysis and give her your opinion about which project ABPC should select. The projects have the following net cash flow estimates:

Year	Project 1	Project 2
0	($200,000)	($200,000)
1	0	90,000
2	0	70,000
3	20,000	50,000
4	30,000	30,000
5	40,000	10,000
6	60,000	10,000
7	90,000	10,000
8	100,000	10,000

Both these projects have the same economic life of eight years and average risk characteristics. ABPC's weighted average cost of capital, or hurdle rate, is 7.2 percent.

a. Which project would you recommend Ms. Brown accept to maximize value of the firm? (Hint: Calculate and compare NPVs of both projects.)

b. What are the IRRs of each project? Which project should be chosen using IRR as the selection criterion?

c. Draw the NPV profiles of both projects. What is the approximate discount rate at which both projects would have the same NPV? What is that NPV?

d. Does the selection remain unaffected for

i. WACC > 5.4 percent

ii. WACC > 8.81 percent

iii. WACC > 14.39 percent?

e. Further market survey research indicates that both projects have lower-than-average risk and, hence, the risk-adjusted discount rate should be 5 percent. What happens to the ranking of the projects using NPV and IRR as the selection criteria? Explain the conflict in ranking, if any.

f. Answer parts (a), (d), and (e), assuming the projects are independent of each other.

10-26. The following net cash flows are projected for four separate projects. The required rate of return is 20 percent. ◀ Challenge Problem

Year	A	B	C	D
0	$–300,000	$–200,000	$–50,000	$ –25,000
1	0	60,000	100,000	0
2	0	60,000	100,000	0
3	100,000	50,000	100,000	0
4	100,000	40,000	100,000	0
5	200,000	30,000	0	50,000
6	200,000	20,000	0	500,000

a. Calculate the NPV of each project.

b. Calculate the IRR for each project.

c. Which project(s) would you accept and why?

d. Recalculate (a) and (b) assuming that the required rate of return is equal to 10 percent. Which project(s) would you choose and why? Do IRR calculations change from the previous calculations in (b)? Why or why not?

Challenge Problem ▶ **10-27.** The following net cash flows are projected for four separate projects. The required rate of return is 20 percent.

Year	A	B	C	D
0	$-200,000	$-100,000	$-50,000	$-20,000
1	45,000	50,000	10,000	0
2	45,000	50,000	10,000	0
3	90,000	50,000	10,000	0
4	90,000	30,000	10,000	0
5	90,000	20,000	10,000	25,000
6	90,000	10,000	10,000	25,000

a. Calculate the NPV of each project.

b. Calculate the IRR for each project.

c. Which project(s) would you accept and why?

d. Recalculate (a) – (b) assuming that the required rate of return is equal to 10 percent. Which project(s) would you choose and why? Do IRR calculations change from the previous calculations in (b)? Why or why not?

Comprehensive Problem ▶ **10-28.** The balance sheet for the Company XYZ is presented below. The Company's net income is expected to be equal to $432,000 in 2005, $1,644,000 in 2006, and $3,060,000 in 2007. The discount rate is equal to 10 percent. Calculate:

a. The amount of cash from operating activities for the years 2005, 2006, and 2007.

b. Present value of the stream of cash flow from operating activities assuming the discount rate above. Assume that this problem is as at the end of 2004.

Balance Sheet
XYZ
2004–2007

	2004	2005	2006	2007
Assets				
Cash	$ 3,000,000	$ 3,757,000	$ 3,076,000	$ 4,361,000
Marketable Securities	6,000,000	7,000,000	8,000,000	8,000,000
Accounts Receivable	2,000,000	4,000,000	6,000,000	10,000,000
Inventory	4,000,000	4,500,000	6,000,000	7,000,000
Prepaid Expenses	1,500,000	2,000,000	3,000,000	4,000,000
P.P. & E., Gross	14,000,000	14,000,000	14,000,000	14,000,000
Less Accum. Amortization	6,000,000	7,400,000	8,800,000	10,200,000
P.P. & E., Net	8,000,000	6,600,000	5,200,000	3,800,000
Liabilities				
Accounts Payable	3,000,000	6,000,000	8,000,000	11,000,000
Notes Payable	1,000,000	1,000,000	1,000,000	1,000,000
Accrued Expenses	700,000	750,000	800,000	900,000
Long-Term Debt	4,000,000	4,000,000	4,000,000	4,000,000
Shareholders' Equity				
Preferred Shares	4,000,000	4,000,000	4,000,000	4,000,000
Common Shares	500,000	500,000	500,000	500,000
Retained Earnings	11,300,000	11,607,000	12,976,000	15,761,000

10-29. The balance sheet for Company ABC follows. The Company's net income is expected to be equal to $22,200,000 in 2005, $27,660,000 in 2006, and $29,220,000 in 2007. The discount rate is equal to 10 percent. Calculate: ◀ Comprehensive Problem

a. The amount of cash from operating activities for the years 2005, 2006, and 2007. Treat Notes Payable as a part of the financing section of the cash flow statement. (Hint: Do not include it in your calculations.)

b. Present value of the stream of cash flow from operating activities assuming the discount rate given. Assume that this problem is as at the end of 2004.

Balance Sheet
ABC
2004–2007

	2004	2005	2006	2007
Assets				
Cash	$ 3,000,000	$31,300,000	$55,060,000	$85,380,000
Marketable Securities	6,000,000	5,000,000	4,000,000	3,000,000
Accounts Receivable	20,000,000	18,000,000	16,000,000	16,000,000
Inventory	40,000,000	35,000,000	32,000,000	30,000,000
Prepaid Expenses	10,000,000	8,000,000	7,000,000	6,000,000
P.P. & E, Gross	13,000,000	23,000,000	33,000,000	43,000,000
Less Accum. Amortization	6,000,000	8,300,000	11,600,000	15,900,000
P.P. & E., Net	7,000,000	14,700,000	21,400,000	27,100,000
Liabilities				
Accounts Payable	35,000,000	40,000,000	45,000,000	50,000,000
Notes Payable	6,000,000	7,000,000	5,000,000	5,000,000
Accrued Expenses	7,000,000	8,000,000	9,000,000	10,000,000
Long-Term Debt	20,000,000	10,000,000	5,000,000	5,000,000
Shareholders' Equity				
Preferred Shares	6,000,000	6,000,000	6,000,000	6,000,000
Common Shares	10,000,000	20,000,000	20,000,000	20,000,000
Retained Earnings	2,000,000	21,000,000	45,460,000	71,480,000

10-30. You are the Investment Manager at Toronto Financial Services, a venture capital fund focusing on investments in a wide variety of sectors. Your boss, Mr. Kowalski, has asked you to perform an analysis of one of the firm's investment companies, Hamilton Steel and Machinery (HSM). Your firm made a $10 million investment into HSM and acquired a 10 percent stake in January 2004. Mr. Kowalski tells you that he would like you to perform an analysis of the optimal timing to sell this investment. In short, you are expected to sell this investment to maximize IRR. You would consider selling your firm's stake in HSM at the beginning of 2005, 2006, or 2007 (holding period of 1, 2 or 3 years). Mr. Kowalski tells you that companies like HSM are valued on the multiples of the projected net change in cash flow at the end of each period, which is equal to 15 (this is called the "industry average multiple"). He further explains that to arrive at the value of the firm at the end of a particular period, you would need to multiply the "industry average multiple" by the value of net change in cash flow for a particular year. He clarifies further that your firm's proceeds would only be equal to 10 percent of the disposal value as your firm only owns a 10 percent stake in HSM. You also know that the firm plans to pay $350,000 in common share dividends and $175,000 in preferred share dividends every year between 2004 and 2007. The firm's financial statements are presented below. ◀ Comprehensive Problem

Income Statement
Hamilton Steel and Machinery
2004–2007

	2004	2005	2006	2007
Net Sales	$187,000,000	$210,000,000	$234,000,000	$263,000,000
Cost of Goods Sold	121,550,000	130,200,000	142,740,000	157,800,000
Selling and Admin. Expenses	42,000,000	46,000,000	52,000,000	60,000,000
Amortization	1,000,000	1,400,000	1,900,000	2,500,000
Operating Income	22,450,000	32,400,000	37,360,000	42,700,000
Interest Expense	1,900,000	1,700,000	1,700,000	1,900,000
Earnings before Taxes	20,550,000	30,700,000	35,660,000	40,800,000
Income Tax	8,220,000	12,280,000	14,264,000	16,320,000
Net Income	12,330,000	18,420,000	21,396,000	24,480,000

Balance Sheet
Hamilton Steel and Machinery
2004–2007

	2004	2005	2006	2007
Assets				
Cash	$ 3,000,000	$ 7,295,000	$14,566,000	$27,021,000
Marketable Securities	1,000,000	3,000,000	3,500,000	4,000,000
Accounts Receivable	12,000,000	17,000,000	23,000,000	33,000,000
Inventory	12,000,000	15,000,000	22,000,000	25,000,000
Prepaid Expenses	7,000,000	7,000,000	7,000,000	7,000,000
P.P. & E., Gross	10,000,000	14,000,000	19,000,000	25,000,000
Less Accum. Amortization	6,000,000	7,400,000	9,300,000	11,800,000
P.P. & E., Net	4,000,000	6,600,000	9,700,000	13,200,000
Liabilities				
Accounts Payable	6,500,000	7,500,000	10,500,000	14,000,000
Notes Payable	7,000,000	7,000,000	7,000,000	7,000,000
Accrued Expenses	3,000,000	3,000,000	3,000,000	3,000,000
Long-Term Debt	12,000,000	10,000,000	10,000,000	12,000,000
Shareholders' Equity				
Preferred Shares	3,500,000	3,500,000	3,500,000	3,500,000
Common Shares	7,000,000	7,000,000	7,000,000	7,000,000
Retained Earnings	0	17,895,000	38,766,000	62,721,000

a. Generate a full statement of income and retained earnings for 2004, 2005, 2006 and 2007.

b. Generate cash flow statements for HSM for 2005, 2006, and 2007.

c. Find IRRs if your firm were to sell its entire stake in HSM at the beginning of each period in the next three years (i.e., you sell your firm's stake in January of 2005, 2006, and 2007).

d. Suggest the optimal time to sell the investment (i.e., in January of 2005, 2006, or 2007).

e. Calculate the following ratios for the period 2004–2007:

  i. Gross profit margin

  ii. Operating profit margin

  iii. Net profit margin

iv. Return on assets
v. Return on equity
vi. Current ratio
vii. Quick ratio

f. Interpret ratios calculated above.

10-31. Mark Norm is the Investment Manager at a Winnipeg investment firm. His boss, Mr. Cash, has asked him to perform an analysis of one of the firm's investment companies, Toronto Logistics. Mr. Norm's investment firm made a $7 million investment into Toronto Logistics and acquired a 10 percent stake in January 2004. Mr. Cash tells Mark that he needs an analysis of the optimal timing for selling Toronto Logistics. Mark needs to consider selling his investment firm's stake in Toronto Logistics at the beginning of 2005, 2006, or 2007 (holding period of 1, 2, or 3 years). Mr. Cash tells Mark that companies like Toronto Logistics are valued on the multiples of the projected net change in cash flow at the end of each period, which is equal to 20 (this is called the "industry average multiple"). He further explains that to arrive at the value of the firm at the end of a particular period, Mark needs to multiply the "industry average multiple" by the value of net change in cash flow for a particular year. He clarifies further that the investment firm's proceeds would only be equal to 10 percent of the disposal value of Toronto Logistics as the investment firm only owns a 10 percent stake in the firm. Mark knows that the firm does not plan to pay any dividends in the future and it did not pay any in 2004. The firm's financial statements are presented below.

◀ Comprehensive Problem

Income Statement
Toronto Logistics
2004–2007

	2004	2005	2006	2007
Net Sales	$52,000,000	$64,000,000	$72,000,000	$96,000,000
Cost of Goods Sold	38,000,000	50,000,000	56,000,000	74,000,000
S&A Expenses	7,500,000	9,000,000	11,000,000	13,000,000
Amortization	1,000,000	1,300,000	1,600,000	1,900,000
Operating Income	5,500,000	3,700,000	3,400,000	7,100,000
Interest Expense	400,000	755,000	1,245,000	2,530,000
Earnings before Taxes	5,100,000	2,945,000	2,155,000	4,570,000
Income Tax	2,040,000	1,178,000	862,000	1,828,000
Net Income	3,060,000	1,767,000	1,293,000	2,742,000

Balance Sheet
Toronto Logistics
2004–2007

	2004	2005	2006	2007
Assets				
Cash	$ 3,000,000	$15,667,000	$26,310,000	$38,952,000
Marketable Securities	800,000	800,000	800,000	1,000,000
Accounts Receivable	4,500,000	4,500,000	5,000,000	6,000,000
Inventory	7,000,000	7,000,000	7,500,000	11,000,000
Prepaid Expenses	600,000	600,000	800,000	1,000,000
P.P. & E., Gross	10,000,000	13,000,000	16,000,000	19,000,000
Less Accum. Amortization	6,000,000	7,300,000	8,900,000	10,800,000
P.P. & E., Net	4,000,000	5,700,000	7,100,000	8,200,000

Liabilities				
Accounts Payable	5,000,000	11,000,000	12,000,000	15,000,000
Notes Payable	1,000,000	550,000	450,000	300,000
Accrued Expenses	450,000	500,000	550,000	600,000
Long-Term Debt	3,000,000	7,000,000	12,000,000	25,000,000
Shareholders' Equity				
Preferred Shares	2,000,000	2,000,000	2,000,000	2,000,000
Common Shares	3,000,000	6,000,000	12,000,000	12,000,000
Retained Earnings	5,450,000	7,217,000	8,510,000	11,252,000

a. Generate cash flow statements for Toronto Logistics for 2005, 2006, and 2007.

b. Find IRRs if your firm were to sell its entire stake in Toronto Logistics at the beginning of each period in the next three years (i.e., you sell your firm's stake in January of 2005, 2006, and 2007).

c. Suggest the optimal time to sell the investment (i.e., in January of 2005, 2006, or 2007).

d. Calculate the following ratios for the period 2004–2007:
   i. Gross profit margin
   ii. Operating profit margin
   iii. Net profit margin
   iv. Return on assets
   v. Return on equity
   vi. Current ratio
   vii. Quick ratio

e. Interpret the ratios calculated above.

ANSWERS TO SELF-TEST

ST-1. The NPV of the project can be found using Equation 10-1a as follows:

$$\begin{aligned} NPV &= \left(\frac{\$20,000}{(1+0.11)^1}\right) + \left(\frac{\$40,000}{(1+0.11)^2}\right) - \$50,000 \\ &= \left(\frac{\$20,000}{1.11}\right) + \left(\frac{\$40,000}{1.2321}\right) - \$50,000 \\ &= \$18,018 + \$32,465 - \$50,000 \\ &= \$483 \end{aligned}$$

ST-2. To find the IRR, we solve for the k value that results in an NPV of zero in the NPV formula (Equation 10-1a) by trial and error:

Try using k = 11%:

$$
\begin{aligned}
0 &= \left(\frac{\$20,000}{(1+0.11)^1}\right) + \left(\frac{\$40,000}{(1+0.11)^2}\right) - \$50,000 \\
&= \left(\frac{\$20,000}{1.11}\right) + \left(\frac{\$40,000}{1.2321}\right) - \$50,000 \\
&= \$18,018 + \$32,465 - \$50,000 \\
&= \$483
\end{aligned}
$$

The result does not equal zero. Try again using a slightly higher discount rate, k = 11.65%:

$$
\begin{aligned}
0 &= \left(\frac{\$20,000}{(1+0.1165)^1}\right) + \left(\frac{\$40,000}{(1+0.1165)^2}\right) - \$50,000 \\
&= \left(\frac{\$20,000}{1.1165}\right) + \left(\frac{\$40,000}{1.24657225}\right) - \$50,000 \\
&= \$17,913 + \$32,088 - \$50,000 \\
&= \$1
\end{aligned}
$$

Close enough. The IRR of the project is almost exactly 11.65 percent.

ST-3. The NPV of the project must be calculated to see if it is greater or less than zero. Because the project in this problem is an annuity, its NPV can be found most easily using a modified version of Equation 10-1b as follows:

$$NPV = PMT(PVIFA_{k,\,n}) - \text{Initial Investment}$$

We include this problem (and some others that follow) to show you that Equations 10-1a and 10-1b can be modified to take advantage of the present value of an annuity formulas covered in Chapter 8, Equations 8-4a and 8-4b. The problem could also be solved using the basic forms of Equations 10-1a and 10-1b, but those would take longer.

In this problem, the initial investment is \$200,000, the annuity payment is \$44,503, the discount rate, k, is 14 percent, and the number of periods, n, is 10.

$$
\begin{aligned}
NPV &= \$44,503(PVIFA_{14\%,\,10}) - \$200,000 \\
&= \$44,503(5.2161) - \$200,000 \\
&= \$232,132 - \$200,000 \\
&= \$32,132
\end{aligned}
$$

Because the NPV is positive, the project should be accepted.

ST-4. The IRR is found by setting the NPV formula to zero and solving for the IRR rate, k. In this case, there are no multiple cash flows, so the equation can be solved algebraically. For convenience, we use Equation 10-1b modified for an annuity:

$$0 = \$44{,}503(\text{PVIFA}_{k\%,\ 10}) - \$200{,}000$$

$$\$200{,}000 = \$44{,}503(\text{PVIFA}_{k\%,\ 10})$$

$$\frac{\$200{,}000}{\$44{,}503} = \text{PVIFA}_{k\%,\ 10}$$

$$4.49408 = \text{PVIFA}_{k\%,\ 10}$$

Finding the PVIFA in Table IV in the Appendix (page A-4), we see that 4.4941 (there are only four decimal places in the table) occurs in the year 10 row in the 18 percent column. Therefore, the IRR of the project is 18 percent.

ST-5. To calculate the MIRR, first calculate the project's terminal value. Next, calculate the annual rate of return it would take to produce that end amount from the beginning investment. That rate is the MIRR.

For the project in ST-3:

Step 1: Calculate the project's terminal value. Note—The terminal value could be calculated by adding up the future values of each individual cash flow, as in the MIRR explanation. In this case, however, that would be a lengthy procedure because there are 10 cash flows. Recognizing that the cash flows are an annuity, we can make use of the future value of an annuity formula, Equation 8-3a, to calculate the terminal value:

$$\text{FV} = \$44{,}503\left[\frac{(1+0.14)^{10}-1}{0.14}\right]$$

$$\text{FV} = \$44{,}503\left[19.3372951\right]$$

$$\text{FV} = \text{Project's Terminal Value} = \$860{,}568$$

Step 2: Calculate the annual rate of return that will produce the terminal value from the initial investment.

Project's Terminal Value: \$860,568

PV of Initial Investment: \$200,000

Per Equation 8-6:

$$\text{MIRR} = (860{,}568/200{,}000)^{(1/10)} - 1$$

$$\text{MIRR} = 0.1571 \text{ or } 15.71\%$$

ST-6. There are only two cash flows in this problem, a \$400 investment at time 0 and the \$1,000 payoff at the end of year 10. To find the IRR, we set the NPV formula to zero, fill in the two cash flows and periods, and solve for the IRR rate, k, that makes the right-hand side of the equation equal zero. Equation 10-1b is more convenient to use in this case:

$$0 = \$1{,}000(\text{PVIF}_{k\%,\ 10}) - \$400$$

$$\$400 = \$1{,}000(\text{PVIF}_{k\%,\ 10})$$

$$\frac{\$400}{\$1{,}000} = \text{PVIF}_{k\%,\ 10}$$

$$0.4000 = \text{PVIF}_{k\%,\ 10}$$

If we find the PVIF in Table II in the Appendix (page A-2), we see that 0.4000 occurs in the year 10 row between the 9 percent and 10 percent columns. Therefore, the IRR of the project is between 9 percent and 10 percent. (The exact value of the IRR is 9.596 percent.) Because your required rate of return in this problem was 12 percent, the bonds would *not* meet your requirements.

ST-7. Solve for the NPV using Equation 10-1a or b. Equation 10-1a would be the more convenient version for this problem. The cash flows are a \$300 investment at time 0 and a \$1,000 future value (FV) in 10 years. The discount rate is 20 percent.

$$\begin{aligned} NPV &= \left(\frac{\$1,000}{(1+0.20)^{10}}\right) - \$300 \\ &= \left(\frac{\$1,000}{6.191736}\right) - \$300 \\ &= \$161.51 - \$300 \\ &= -\$138.49 \end{aligned}$$

Appendix 10A Wrinkles in Capital Budgeting

In this appendix, we discuss three situations that change the capital budgeting decision process. First, we examine *nonsimple projects,* projects that have a negative initial cash flow, in addition to one or more negative future cash flows. Next, we explore projects that have multiple IRRs. Finally, we discuss how to compare mutually exclusive projects with unequal project lives.

Nonsimple Projects

Most capital budgeting projects start with a negative cash flow—the initial investment—at t_0, followed by positive future cash flows. Such projects are called **simple projects. Nonsimple projects** are projects that have one or more negative future cash flows after the initial investment.

To illustrate a nonsimple project, consider Project N, the expected cash flows for a nuclear power plant project. The initial investment of \$500 million is a negative cash flow at t_0, followed by positive cash flows of \$25 million per year for 30 years as electric power is generated and sold. At the end of the useful life of the project, the storage of nuclear fuel and the shutdown safety procedures require cash outlays of \$100 million at the end of year 31. The timeline depicted in Figure 10A-1 shows the cash flow pattern.

−\$500	25	25	25	. . .	25	−100
t_0	t_1	t_2	t_3	. . .	t_{30}	t_{31}

Figure 10A-1 Cash Flow Timeline for Project N (in millions)

Take Note

The $25 million annual payment for 30 years constitutes an annuity, so we were able to adapt Equation 10-1a by using the present value of annuity formula, Equation 8-4a.

With a 20 percent discount rate, an initial investment of $500 million, a 30-year annuity of $25 million, and a shutdown cash outlay of $100 million in year 31, the NPV of Project N follows (in millions):

$$NPV_n\text{(in millions)} = -\$500\left(\frac{1}{(1+0.20)^0}\right) + \$25\left[\frac{1-\frac{1}{(1+0.20)^{30}}}{0.20}\right] - \$100\left(\frac{1}{(1+0.20)^{31}}\right)$$
$$= (-\$500 \times 1) + (\$25 \times 4.9789364) - (\$100 \times .0035106)$$
$$= -\$500 + \$124.47341 - \$.35106$$
$$= -\$375.87765$$

We find that at a discount rate of 20 percent, Project N has a negative net present value of – 375.878 (in millions), so the firm considering Project N should reject it.

Multiple IRRs

Some projects may have more than one internal rate of return. That is, a project may have several different discount rates that result in a net present value of zero.

Here is an example. Suppose Project Q requires an initial cash outlay of $160,000 and is expected to generate a positive cash flow of $1 million in year 1. In year 2, the project will require an additional cash *outlay* in the amount of $1 million. The cash flows for Project Q are shown on the following timeline in Figure 10A-2:

Figure 10A-2 Cash Flow Timeline for Project Q

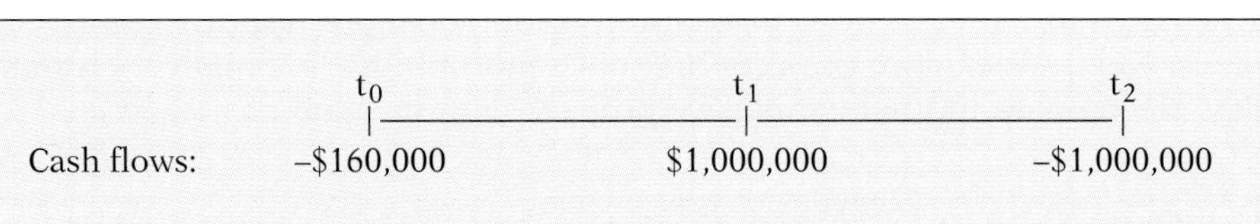

We find the IRR of Project Q by using the trial-and-error procedure, Equation 10-2. When k = 25 percent, the NPV is zero.

$$0 = \left(\frac{\$1{,}000{,}000}{(1+0.25)^1}\right) - \left(\frac{\$1{,}000{,}000}{(1+0.25)^2}\right) - \$160{,}000$$
$$= \$800{,}000 - \$640{,}000 - \$160{,}000$$
$$= \$0$$

Because 25 percent causes the NPV of Project Q to be zero, the IRR of the project must be 25 percent. But wait! If we had tried k = 400%, the IRR calculation would look like this:

$$0 = \left(\frac{\$1{,}000{,}000}{(1+4.00)^1} \right) - \left(\frac{\$1{,}000{,}000}{(1+4.00)^2} \right) - \$160{,}000$$
$$= \$200{,}000 - \$40{,}000 - \$160{,}000$$
$$= \$0$$

Because 400 percent results in an NPV of zero, 400 percent must also be the IRR of the Project Q. Figure 10A-3 shows the net present value profile for Project Q. By examining this graph, we see how 25 percent and 400 percent both make the net present value equal to zero.

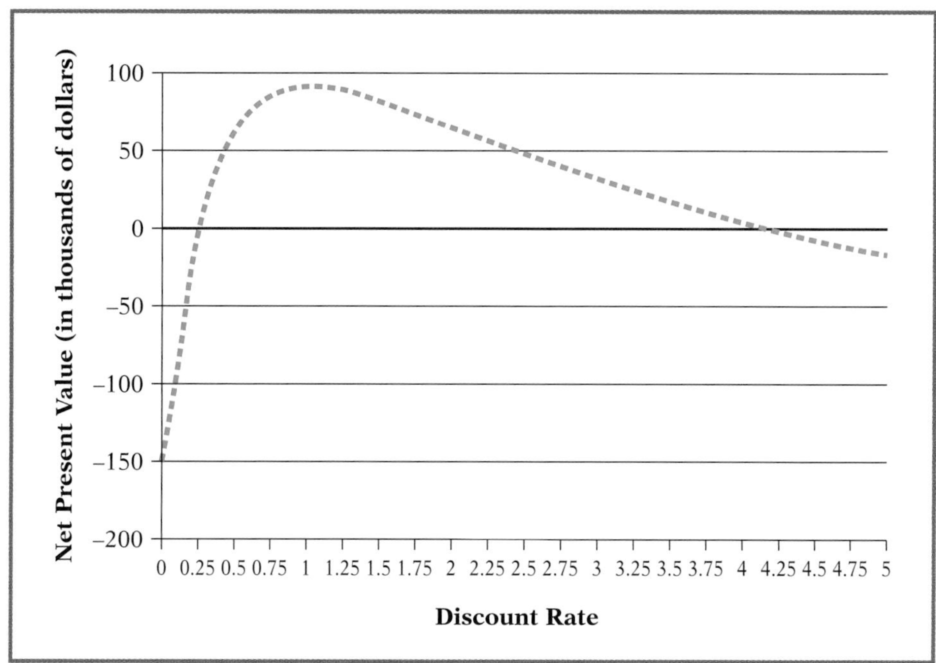

Figure 10A-3 Net Present Value Profile for Project Q
The net present value profile for Project Q crosses the zero line twice, showing that two IRRs exist.

As the graph shows, Project Q's net present value profile crosses the horizontal axis (has a zero value) in two different places at discount rates of 25 percent and 400 percent.

Project Q had two IRRs because the project's cash flows changed from negative to positive (at t_1) and then from positive to negative (at t_2). It turns out that a nonsimple project may have (but does not have to have) as many IRRs as there are sign changes. In this case, two sign changes resulted in two internal rates of return.

Whenever we have two or more IRRs for a project, the IRR method is not a useful decision-making tool. Remember the IRR accept/reject decision rule: Firms should accept projects with IRRs higher than the discount rate and reject projects with IRRs lower than the discount rate. With more than one discount rate, decision-makers will not know which IRR to use for the accept/reject decision. In projects that have multiple IRRs, then, switch to the NPV method.

Mutually Exclusive Projects with Unequal Project Lives

When mutually exclusive projects have different expected useful lives, selecting among the projects requires more than comparing the projects' NPVs. To illustrate, suppose you are a business manager considering a new business telephone system. One is the Cheap Talk System, which requires an initial cash outlay of $10,000 and is expected to last three years. The other is the Rolles Voice System, which requires an initial cash outlay of $50,000 and is expected to last 12 years. The Cheap Talk System is expected to generate positive cash flows of $5,800 per year for each of its three years of life. The Rolles Voice System is expected to generate positive cash flows of $8,000 per year for each of its 12 years of life. The cash flows associated with each project are summarized in Figure10A-4.

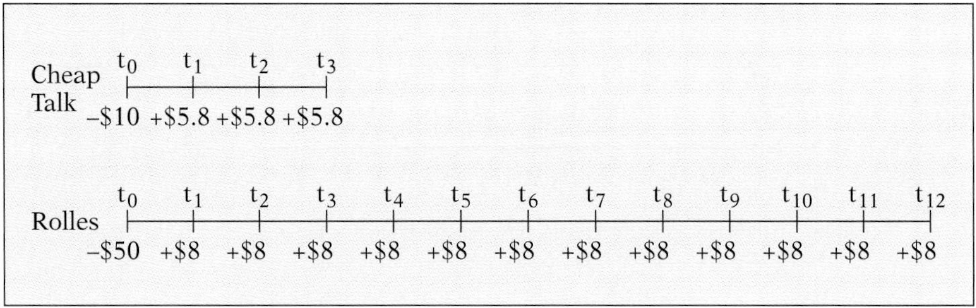

Figure 10A-4
Cash Flows for the Cheap Talk and Rolles Voice Communications Systems (in thousands)
This figure shows the cash flows for two projects with unequal lives, Project Cheap Talk and Project Rolles Voice.

To decide which project to choose, we first compute and compare their NPVs. Assume the firm's required rate of return is 10 percent. We solve for the NPVs as follows:

1. **NPV of Cheap Talk.**

$$NPV_{CT} = \$5,800\left[\frac{1-\dfrac{1}{(1+0.10)^3}}{0.10}\right] - \$10,000$$
$$= \$5,800(2.48685) - \$10,000$$
$$= \$14,424 - \$10,000$$
$$= \$4,424$$

2. **NPV of Rolles Voice.**

$$NPV_{Rolles} = \$8,000\left[\frac{1-\dfrac{1}{(1+0.10)^{12}}}{0.10}\right] - \$50,000$$
$$= \$8,000(6.81369) - \$50,000$$
$$= \$54,510 - \$50,000$$
$$= \$4,510$$

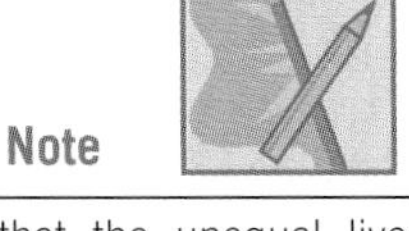

Take Note

Note that the unequal lives problem is only an issue when the projects under consideration are mutually exclusive. If the projects were independent, we would adopt all projects that had NPVs greater than or equal to zero, no matter what the lives of the projects.

We find that Project Cheap Talk has an NPV of $4,424, compared with Project Rolles' NPV of $4,510. We might conclude, based on this information, that the Rolles Voice System should be selected over the Cheap Talk system because it has the higher NPV. However, before making that decision, we must assess how Project Cheap Talk's NPV would change if its useful life were 12 years, not three years.

Comparing Projects with Unequal Lives

Two possible methods that allow financial managers to compare projects with unequal lives are the replacement chain approach and the equivalent annual annuity (EAA) approach.

The Replacement Chain Approach The *replacement chain* approach assumes each of the mutually exclusive projects can be replicated until a common time period has passed in which the projects can be compared. The NPVs for the series of replicated projects are then compared to the project with the longer life. An example illustrates this process. Project Cheap Talk could be repeated four times in the same time span as the 12-year Rolles Voice project. If a business replicated project Cheap Talk four times, the cash flows would look as depicted below in Figure 10A-5:

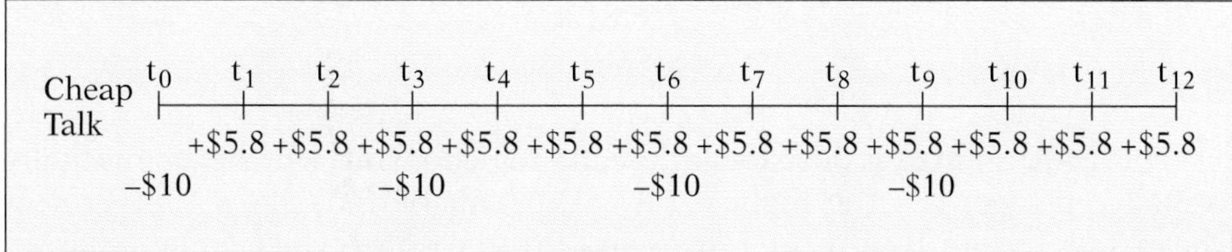

Figure 10A-5 Cash Flows for the Cheap Talk System Repeated Four Times (in thousands)

The NPV of this series of cash flows, assuming the discount rate is 10 percent, is $12,121. Each cash flow, be it positive or negative, is discounted back the appropriate number of years to get the NPV of the four consecutive investments in the Cheap Talk system.

The NPV of $12,121 for Cheap Talk system is the sum of the NPVs of the four repeated Cheap Talk projects, such that the project series would have a life of 12 years, the same life as the Rolles Voice System Project. We are now comparing apples to apples. Cheap Talk's replacement chain NPV is $12,121, whereas the NPV of Project Rolles Voice is $4,510 over the same 12-year period. If a firm invested in project Cheap Talk four successive times, it would create more value than investing in one project Rolles Voice.

The Equivalent Annual Annuity (EAA) The equivalent annual annuity (EAA) approach converts the NPVs of the mutually exclusive projects into their equivalent annuity values. The *equivalent annual annuity* is the amount of the annuity payment that would give the same present value as the actual future cash flows for that project. The EAA approach assumes that you could repeat the mutually exclusive projects indefinitely as each project came to the end of its life.

The equivalent annuity value (EAA) is calculated by dividing the NPV of a project by the present value interest factor for an annuity (PVIFA) that applies to the project's life span.

Formula for an Equivalent Annual Annuity (EAA) (10A-1)

$$EAA = \frac{NPV}{PVIFA_{k,\,n}}$$

where

k = Discount rate used to calculate the NPV

n = Life span of the project

The NPVs of Cheap Talk ($4,424) and Rolles Voice ($4,510) were calculated earlier, assuming a required rate of return of 10 percent. With the project's NPV and the discount rate, we calculate each project's EAA, per Equation 10A-1, as follows:

1. **EAA of Project Cheap Talk**

$$EAA_{CT} = \frac{\$4{,}424}{2.48685} = \$1{,}778.96$$

2. **EAA of Project Rolles**

$$EEA_{Rolles} = \frac{\$4{,}510}{6.81369} = \$661.90$$

The EAA approach decision rule calls for choosing whichever mutually exclusive project has the highest EAA. Our calculations show that Project Cheap Talk has an EAA of $1,778.96 and Project Rolles Voice System has an EAA of $661.90. Because Project Cheap Talk's EAA is higher than Project Rolles's, Project Cheap Talk should be chosen.

Both the replacement chain and the EAA approach assume that mutually exclusive projects can be replicated. If the projects can be replicated, then either the replacement chain or the equivalent annual annuity methods should be used because they lead to the same correct decision. Note in our case that the EAA method results in the same project selection (Project Cheap Talk) as the replacement chain method. If the projects cannot be replicated, then the normal NPVs should be used as the basis for the capital budgeting decision.

Equations Introduced in This Appendix

Equation 10A-1: The Formula for an Equivalent Annual Annuity

$$EAA = \frac{NPV}{PVIFA_{k,\,n}}$$

where

k = Discount rate used to calculate the NPV

n = Life span of the project

11

Estimating Incremental Cash Flows

Chapter Objectives

After reading this chapter, you should be able to:

11-1 **Explain** the difference between incremental cash flows and sunk costs.

11-2 **Identify** three main types of incremental cash flows in a capital budgeting project.

11-3 **Explain** why cash flows associated with project financing are not included in incremental cash flow estimates.

11-4 **Identify** four different scenarios for disposition of assets under the tax reporting regime.

"Never underestimate the value of cold cash."

—Gregory Nunn

Saving Money?

Company X is a large multinational corporation with many facilities throughout Canada and the rest of the world. Employees at a variety of Canadian sites frequently are required to travel to the home office in Headquarters City. On a typical day, there may be a dozen or more employees travelling to Headquarters City from any given satellite city site.

Company X has many corporate jets at airports throughout Canada near the larger satellite cities. Senior executives routinely fly on these corporate jets when travelling to Headquarters City. Middle-level managers fly on commercial aircraft, usually located at a much greater distance from the workplace. The reason for this is that the department of the travelling employee is "billed" $800 if the corporate jet is used. This $800 expense goes into the financial report of that department, which goes to corporate headquarters. Managers can frequently find commercial airfares under $300 for employees travelling to Headquarters City.

Because each department would rather be charged $300 a trip instead of $800 when reporting its financial performance, only a few of the most senior executives fly the corporate jets. This means that each corporate jet typically has a dozen empty seats for its daily flights to Headquarters City. It is clearly in the interest of each department manager to keep his or her expenses down. Is it in the interests of the shareholders to have mostly empty planes fly each day to Headquarters City? The cost of adding an additional passenger or 12 additional passengers to a corporate jet is almost zero. A very small amount of additional fuel would be consumed. The shareholders would save $300 for each additional person who took an otherwise-empty seat on a corporate jet instead of flying on a commercial airline.

Consider the interests of the department managers and those of the shareholders of Company X as you read Chapter 11.

Chapter Overview

In Chapter 10, we applied capital budgeting decision methods, taking the cash flow estimates as a given. In this chapter, we see how financial managers determine which cash flows are incremental and, therefore, relevant to a capital budgeting decision. We define incremental cash flows and distinguish incremental cash flows from sunk costs. We also examine how financial managers estimate incremental initial investment cash flows and incremental operating cash flows in the capital budgeting decision. Finally, we explore how the financing cash flows of a capital budgeting project are factored into the capital budgeting decision.

Incremental Cash Flows

The capital budgeting process focuses on cash flows, not accounting profits. Recall from our discussion in Chapter 1, it is cash flow that changes the value of a firm. Cash outflows reduce the value of the firm, whereas cash inflows increase the value of the firm.

In capital budgeting, **incremental cash flows** are the positive and negative cash flows directly associated with a project. They occur if a firm accepts a project, but they do not occur if the project is rejected.

For instance, suppose that the chief financial officer of the Red Deer Bobcats, Mr. Ball, is analyzing the cash flows associated with a proposed project. He finds that the CEO hired a consultant to assess the proposed project's environmental effects. The consultant will be paid $50,000 for the work. Although the $50,000 fee is related to the project, it is not an incremental cash flow because the money must be paid whether the project is accepted or rejected. Therefore, the fee should not be included as a relevant cash flow of the expansion project decision. Cash flows that have already occurred or will occur whether a project is accepted or rejected are **sunk costs.**

Financial managers carefully screen out irrelevant cash flows such as sunk costs, from the capital budgeting decision process. If they include irrelevant cash flows in their capital budgeting decision, then their calculations of a project's payback period, net present value (NPV), or internal rate of return (IRR) will be distorted and inaccurate. The calculations may be so distorted that they lead to an incorrect decision about a capital budgeting project.

Let's make one note here. As you work through the chapter, we continue to make the distinction that there is a difference between financial reporting and tax reporting, resulting from different treatment of amortization under the two schemes. While under Generally Accepted Accounting Principles companies enjoy some freedom in determining the annual amount of amortization, the *Income Tax Act* sets cost allowance classes and procedures for asset amortization.

What are the implications for this chapter? There are two. Firstly, a manager can apply the financial reporting approach or tax reporting approach to determine the appropriate amount of cash flows. As long as one of the procedures is used consistently across evaluated projects, the resulting calculations and the answer should be correct. Secondly, in terms of problem solving at the end of the chapter, we recommend that you use the financial reporting scheme unless we specifically ask you to calculate the answers by using the tax-reporting regime.

Types of Incremental Cash Flows

To accurately assess the value of a capital budgeting project, financial managers must identify and estimate many types of incremental cash flows. The three main types of incremental cash flows are *initial investment cash flows, operating cash flows,* and *shutdown cash flows.* We examine these three types of incremental cash flows in the sections that follow.

Initial Investment Cash Flows

Generally, financial managers begin their incremental cash flow estimates by assessing the costs of the initial investment. The negative cash flow associated with the initial investment occurs only if the project is accepted. Initial investment cash flows include the purchase price of the asset or materials to produce the asset, the installation and delivery costs, and the additional investment in net working capital.

Purchase Price, Installation, and Delivery Financial managers usually obtain quotes on the purchase price and installation and delivery costs from suppliers. These figures, then, can usually be estimated with a high degree of accuracy.

Changes in Net Working Capital Aside from the setup costs and purchase price of a proposed capital budgeting project, a company may have to invest in changes in net working capital. As explained in Chapter 4, net working capital is defined as current assets (working capital) minus current liabilities. If a proposed capital budgeting project will cause a positive change in net working capital (the most likely scenario), the cash outlay needed to finance this must be included in the cash flow estimates.

Recall that working capital consists of cash, accounts receivable, and inventory, along with other current assets, if any. Companies invest in these assets in much the same way they invest in plant and equipment. Accepting a new project often triggers an increase in cash, accounts receivable, and inventory investments. Working capital investments tie up cash the same way as investment in a new piece of equipment.

A company's current liabilities—such as accounts payable, accrued wages, and accrued taxes—may also be affected if a firm accepts a capital budgeting project. For example, if a plant is expanded, the company may place larger

Dogbert points out that fees for consultants drain cash from the firm. Such fees are not part of the incremental cash flows in a capital budgeting analysis, however. They must be paid whether or not the project is accepted.

Source: DILBERT © 1996 United Feature Syndicate, Inc. Reprinted by permission.

orders with suppliers to accommodate the increased production. The increase in orders is likely to lead to an increase in accounts payable.

Increases in current liabilities create cash inflows. It is unlikely that current liabilities will increase sufficiently to finance all the needed current asset buildup. This is the reason that an investment in net working capital is almost always required.

Table 11-1 shows an example of the incremental changes in net working capital that might occur with a proposed capital budgeting project for the McGuffin Company.

Table 11-1 Change in McGuffin Company Net Working Capital If New Project Is Accepted

Current Asset Changes	Current Liability Changes
$5,000 Increase in Cash	$8,000 Increase in Accounts Payable
$7,000 Increase in Receivables	$2,000 Increase in Accruals
$15,000 Increase in Inventory	
Total Current Asset Changes: $27,000	Total Current Liability Changes: $10,000
Increase in Net Working Capital (NWC): $27,000 – $10,000 = $17,000	
Incremental Cash Flow Due to the Increase in NWC = – $17,000	

As Table 11-1 indicates, the McGuffin Company project has an estimated increase of $27,000 in current assets and a $10,000 increase in current liabilities, resulting in a $17,000 change in net working capital. That is, the firm will have to spend $17,000 to increase its net working capital by this amount—a negative cash flow.

Once financial managers estimate the initial investment incremental cash flows, they analyze the operating cash flows of a capital budgeting project. We turn to those cash flows next.

Operating Cash Flows

Operating cash flows are those cash flows that the project generates after it is in operation. For example, cash flows that follow a change in sales or expenses are operating cash flows. Those operating cash flows incremental to the project under consideration are the ones relevant to our capital budgeting analysis. Incremental operating cash flows also include tax changes, including those due to changes in amortization expense, opportunity costs, and externalities.

Taxes The change in taxes that will occur if a project is accepted is part of the incremental cash flow analysis. Tax effects are considered because a tax increase is equivalent to a negative cash flow and a tax decrease is equivalent to a positive cash flow (tax savings). In a capital budgeting decision, then, financial managers must examine whether and how much tax the firm will pay on additional income that the proposed project generates during a given period. They must also see how much taxes will decrease if the project increases the firm's periodic operating expenses (such as payments for labour and materials), thereby creating additional tax deductions.

Amortization and Taxes Financial managers estimate changes in amortization expense as part of the incremental cash flow analysis because increases in amortization expense may increase a firm's cash flow. How? Amortization expense is deductible for tax purposes. The greater the amortization expense deduction, the less tax a firm must pay in taxes and the less cash it must give to the Canada Revenue Agency. Financial managers estimate the amount of amortization expense that a capital budgeting project will have, therefore, to see how much the firm's taxable income and taxes owed will change.

Incremental amortization expense is the change in amortization expense that results from accepting a proposed capital budgeting project. Incremental amortization expense affects the change in taxes attributable to a capital budgeting project.

To illustrate how incremental amortization expense changes taxes due, recall how we converted after-tax net profits into operating cash inflows in Chapter 4. We added all noncash charges (including amortization) that were deducted as expenses on the firm's income statement to net profits after taxes. Once the tax effects of a project's amortization expense are calculated, we add this incremental amortization expense back to the project's net profits after taxes.

The following example demonstrates how to estimate the incremental amortization expense of a capital budgeting project. Suppose your firm is considering a project that is expected to earn $100,000 in cash sales in year 1. Suppose that, in addition to the sales increase, the project is expected to increase cash operating expenses by $50,000 and incremental amortization expense will be $10,000. Assume your firm's tax rate is 40 percent. First, compute the net operating cash flows from the project for this year, as shown in Table 11-2.

Table 11-2 Net Operating Cash Flows for New Project

1. New Project Sales (cash inflow)	$100,000
2. New Project Cash Operating Expenses (cash outflow)	– 50,000
3. New Project Amortization Expense (noncash expense)	– 10,000
4. Net New Project Taxable Income	40,000
5. Taxes on New Project Income (40%) (cash outflow)	– 16,000
6. Net New Project After-Tax Income	24,000
7. Plus Amortization Expense (added back)	+ 10,000
8. Net Incremental Cash Flow	$ 34,000

Compare line 3 and line 7 in Table 11-2. Note that once we used the new project incremental amortization expense of $10,000 to make the tax change calculations, we added this $10,000 amortization expense back to the new project's after-tax net income to calculate the incremental operating cash flow for this year from the new project. The incremental amortization expense affected cash flow only because of the potential cash flow offered by the tax savings.

Opportunity Costs Sometimes accepting a capital budgeting project precludes other opportunities for the firm. For instance, if an industrial mixer already owned by a toy company is used to make a new product called

Cream 4, then that mixer will not be available to make the Cream 2 currently produced in that mixer. The forgone benefits of the alternative not chosen are opportunity costs.

Opportunity costs are incremental cash flows that financial managers consider in a capital budgeting decision. In our example, the opportunity cost comes from the lost use of the industrial mixer for other products our firm makes. If our cash flows decrease by $30,000 due to the decrease in sales of Cream 2 that we can no longer make, then this $30,000 is the opportunity cost of choosing to produce the new product, Cream 4.

Externalities In estimating incremental operating cash flows, financial managers consider the effect a capital budgeting project might have on cash flows related to other parts of the business. **Externalities** are the positive or negative effects on existing projects if a new capital budgeting project is accepted.

For instance, suppose that a tennis ball manufacturer decides to start making tennis racquets but does not want to hire any additional managers. The current managers may become overworked because the expansion project requires manager time and oversight. This is a negative externality. Existing projects suffer due to manager inattention, but it is difficult to measure the size of those incremental costs because they are qualitative in nature.

On the other hand, the new racquet project may give the company more visibility than it had before and increase sales of its existing tennis ball business, thereby leading to an increase in cash flows. Because these cash flows from the increased tennis ball sales are incremental to the tennis racquet project under consideration, they should be considered in the capital budgeting analysis. This is a positive externality. Here again, however, the qualitative costs associated with the positive externalities are likely to be difficult to measure.

If the impact of externalities can be measured, they should be incorporated in the capital budgeting analysis. If the cost of externalities cannot be measured precisely—as is likely the case—most firms use a subjective analysis of externalities before making a project's final accept or reject decision. For example, if the NPV of a project is only slightly greater than zero, company officials may reject the project if they believe significant unmeasured negative externalities are present.

Finance at Work 11-1 discusses the capital budgeting program at Zellers.

NANCE AT WORK 11-1

les Retail Sports Media Technology Public Relations Production Exports

3C PUTTING HEFT BEHIND ZELLERS UNIT

ts battle with retail titan Wal-Mart, Hudson's Bay Co. is put- a big push on improving its Zellers stores by almost dou- ng its capital spending this year—with more than half of that geted for its discount chain.

HBC, which reported yesterday lower profit last year from previous year, said it will step up the rollout of renovated Zellers stores because the remodelled outlets perform better than the older ones.

Zellers, which has updated just over half of its 312 stores, will have recast 175 of them by the end of this year and all of them within four years, company executives said.

continued

"We are now in a position to be able to invest in our business," chief executive officer George Heller told an analysts' conference call after HBC released year-end results.

Zellers is among a growing number of Canadian retailers being forced to make aggressive moves to counter the Wal-Mart juggernaut.

It is critical for Zellers to quickly revamp its outlets to take on Wal-Mart Canada Corp., which has been stealing business from HBC as well as other retailers, industry watchers say.

"It's the price of admission to stay in the ball game," retailing analyst David Brodie at Research Capital Corp. said in an interview. "Zellers is still under the gun in battling against Wal-Mart."

Zellers has changed its pricing over the past few years, shifting to everyday low pricing, widened assortment and cut costs.

But HBC, which also owns The Bay and Home Outfitters, has been constrained in its capital spending as it paid down debt, reduced inventory levels and generally got its house in order, Mr. Brodie said.

Meanwhile, Wal-Mart hasn't stood still.

It now rings up sales of $430 a square foot, well above the $155 at Zellers, according to Mr. Brodie's estimates of total store space productivity.

Before this year, HBC's capital expenditures had been dropping; last year, they were $138-million.

In 2004, HBC will pour between $200-million and $250-million into the business, and more than half will be directed toward Zellers, analysts were told yesterday. Mr. Heller said Zellers' sales tend to rise 5 percent in its remodelled stores compared with its older outlets.

Mr. Heller said he was pleased with the year-end results in light of the challenging year, which included bouts of SA and a power blackout in Ontario.

For the 12 months ended Jan. 31, profit fell to $69-r lion or 82 cents a share from $111-million or $1.40. Sa climbed to $7.4-billion from $7.38-billion.

When factoring out one-time items—including a $1C million or 15 cents a share charge for higher Ontario inco taxes—"normalized" profit in the latest year was 93 cent share compared with $1.19.

However, excluding the extra week in 2003 (vers 2002), sales slipped 1 percent. Same-store sales at out open a year or more—a key measure in retailing—fell 2.6 p cent at Zellers and 2.3 percent at the Bay. Same-store sa are those in outlets open a year or more and considered important barometer in retailing.

Mr. Heller told analysts that he expects "conservati sales gains for the coming year, although he added that company had "turned a corner" in 2003 and was on-track meet its five-year blueprint for growth.

For 2004, the company forecast "normalized" profit share of between $1.15 and $1.25. HBC shares took o cents to finish at $12.71 on the Toronto Stock Exchange.

Questions to Consider

1. *What relevant information would you select from the for the incremental cash flow analysis?*
2. *What assumptions would you need to make?*
3. *Which method of capital project evaluation is likely to used by HBC and why?*

Source: Marina Strauss, "HBC Putting Heft Behind Zellers Unit," March 2004. Reprinted with permission from *The Globe and Mai*

Shut Down Cash Flows

Financial managers estimate the shutdown cash flows that are expected to occur at the end of the useful life of a proposed capital budgeting project. Shutdown cash flows may include those from the project's residual value, taxes tied to the sale of the used asset, and the reduction of net working capital.

If a project is expected to have a positive residual value at the end of its useful life, there will be a positive incremental cash flow at that time. However, this residual value incremental cash flow must be adjusted for taxes.

In Chapter 4, we made the distinction between calculating amortization expense for financial and tax reporting. We stated that under Generally Accepted Accounting Principles, companies enjoy some freedom in determining the annual amount of amortization expense as long as the principles are applied consistently and relate to the asset's actual useful life. Under the rules of the *Income Tax Act*, a company is not permitted to use the amortization expense calculated by financial accountants for the purpose of calculating taxable income. Instead, the *Act* allows a company to claim capital cost allowance (CCA). Capital cost allowance is used in calculating taxable income regardless of the method chosen by the company for the purpose of financial reporting. In most cases, the amount of capital cost allowance will exceed the amount of amortization expense, especially in the early years. Consequently, the amount of taxes declared by financial accountants would differ from those actually paid. Let's now consider the treatment of asset disposition as considered by financial accountants and by the Canada Revenue Agency.

It may be important here to point out the key differences in the terminology used by financial accountants and those who interpret the *Income Tax Act* in order to avoid confusion. The following table presents a brief comparison of accounting and tax terms.

Taxation Term	*Accounting Term*
Capital Cost	Acquisition Cost
Capital Cost Allowance	Amortization Expense
Undepreciated Capital Cost (UCC)	Net Book Value

Source: Byrd, C., and Chen, I. (2003). *Canadian Tax Principles.* Toronto: Pearson Prentice Hall.

Financial Reporting

Let's consider four possible scenarios and again stress that the amount of any addition to or deduction from taxable income resulting from asset disposition calculated under GAAP is likely to differ from the amount arrived at by using the *Income Tax Act* procedures. At the end of any fiscal year, a company must prepare calculations in accordance with the *Act* to arrive at the "actual" amount of taxes paid to CRA no matter what the financial reports say.

First, the asset may be sold for less than its acquisition cost but for more than its net book value. In this instance, the difference between the proceeds of disposition and the asset's net book value is reported on the financial statements as a gain on disposal. For example, let's assume that we acquire an asset for $1,000,000 and determine that its useful life is five years (amortization at 20 percent per annum). A straight-line method is applied. The calculation of the net book value in Year 4 is presented below. The difference between the gross value of the asset and the accumulated amortization in Year 4 is equal to $200,000 ($1,000,000 – $800,000)—this is the asset's net book value. The difference between the disposal value and the asset's net book value is equal to $300,000 ($500,000 – $200,000). This amount is called a gain on disposal and is added to net income at the year-end.

The table that follows presents the calculation of an asset's net book value and a gain on disposal.

	Year 1	*Year 2*	*Year 3*	*Year 4*
Asset, Gross Value	$1,000,000	$1,000,000	$1,000,000	$1,000,000
Amortization Expense	$200,000	$200,000	$200,000	$200,000
Accumulated Amortization	$200,000	$400,000	$600,000	$800,000
Net Book Value	$800,000	$600,000	$400,000	$200,000
Disposal Value				$500,000
Gain on Disposal				$300,000

Second, the asset may be sold for more than its acquisition cost. The procedure of arriving at a net book value is the same as in the example above. The amount by which the proceeds of disposition exceed the net book value is added to net income. From the asset disposal value (we assume it to be equal to \$1,200,000) we deduct the asset's net book value to arrive at a gain on disposal equal to \$1,000,000 (\$1,200,000 – \$200,000).

Third, the asset may be sold for the amount equal to its net book value. In this case, the asset disposition has no net income effects for financial reporting purposes. However, as already mentioned, we may actually pay taxes as calculated under the *Income Tax Act*.

Fourth, the asset may be sold for less than its net book value. The amount by which the net book value exceeds the proceeds of disposition is treated as a loss on disposal and is deducted from net income for financial reporting purposes.

Tax Reporting

While it is not our objective to exhaustively cover the topic of the disposal of amortizable assets, it is important to discuss the mechanics of calculating changes in taxable income for tax reporting. It is also important to highlight some of the key principles in using the CCA methodology.

Similarly to the financial reporting section above, four cases will be considered. First, we will assume that the asset is sold for less than its Capital Cost, but for more than its Undepreciated Capital Cost (UCC). Secondly, we will consider a case where the asset is sold for more than its Capital Cost. Thirdly, the asset may be sold for the amount equal to the UCC balance. Lastly, we will consider the case where the UCC exceeds the disposition proceeds.

Let's assume that we purchased an asset that falls into CCA Class 43 for \$1,000,000. We further assume that the asset is the only asset in CCA Class 43—this is a critical assumption. The applicable CCA rate is 30 percent. We assume that we sold the asset in Year 4 for \$500,000. In Year 1, we would deduct the amount of CCA equal to \$150,000 from the opening UCC balance according to the half-year rule (\$1,000,000 × 30 percent × 1/2). The UCC ending balance at the end of Year 1 and the opening UCC balance at the beginning of Year 2 would be equal to \$850,000. In Year 2, we would deduct \$255,000 (\$850,000 × 30 percent) from the opening UCC balance to arrive at the closing UCC balance equal to \$595,000. This procedure would continue in Years 3 and 4. In Year 4, we dispose of the asset for \$500,000. In order to calculate the amount added to taxable income from the amount of the opening UCC balance in Year 4, we deduct the lesser of the proceeds from disposal (\$500,000) or Capital Cost (\$1,000,000). The result would equal a negative amount of \$83,500 (\$416,500 – \$500,000 = –\$83,500). This amount is termed Recapture of CCA. It represents excess amortization charged over the proceeds of disposition. Note that we do not deduct CCA in Year 4, the year of asset disposal. Recapture of CCA is added to taxable income for the year.

The following table presents the calculation described in detail above.

	Year 1	*Year 2*	*Year 3*	*Year 4*
Opening UCC	0	$850,000	$595,000	$416,500
Capital Cost	$1,000,000	—	—	—
Proceeds of Disposition	—	—	—	$500,000
CCA	$150,000	$255,000	$178,500	0
CCA Recapture	—	—	—	($83,500)
Ending UCC	$850,000	$595,000	$416,500	—

If the asset were sold for more than its Capital Cost, the procedure would be similar with regards to Years 1–3. The difference would occur in the year of disposal, Year 4. Similar to the procedure described above, from the UCC balance in Year 4, we subtract the lesser of the proceeds of disposition ($1,200,000) or Capital Cost ($1,000,000). Since the amount of Capital Cost is less than the proceeds of disposition, we deduct it from the opening UCC balance ($416,500) in Year 4 to arrive at Recapture of CCA equal to a negative amount of $583,500 ($416,500 – $1,000,000). This amount represents an addition to taxable income in Year 4.

In this instance, we also need to deal with a capital gain because the asset was sold for more than its Capital Cost. According to CRA rules, one-half of the capital gain ($1,200,000 – $1,000,000 = $200,000 × 50 percent = $100,000) is added to taxable income. A total amount of $683,500 ($100,000 + $583,500) is added to taxable income generated in Year 4 and is taxed at a company's applicable provincial and federal tax rate. Similarly, we do not deduct CCA in Year 4.

The table that follows presents the calculations.

	Year 1	*Year 2*	*Year 3*	*Year 4*
Opening UCC	0	$850,000	$595,000	$416,500
Capital Cost	$1,000,000	—	—	—
Proceeds of Disposition	—	—	—	$1,000,000
CCA	$150,000	$255,000	$178,500	0
CCA Recapture	—	—	—	($583,500)
Ending UCC	$850,000	$595,000	$416,500	—

In the event that the asset is sold for the amount equal to the UCC balance in Year 4, no additions or deductions are made to taxable income. No taxes are paid on asset disposal.

Lastly, when the proceeds from disposition of the asset are equal to, let's say, $300,000 in Year 4, this amount would be deducted from the UCC balance in Year 4 resulting in a terminal loss of $116,500 ($416,500 – $300,000), which would be 100 percent deductible from taxable income.

We made simplifications in our calculations. Most importantly, we assumed that the acquired asset is the only asset in CCA Class 43. Realistically, there would likely be other assets in this class. In the event that the proceeds of disposition exceed the UCC balance, the appropriate amount of CCA Recapture (and a capital gain if applicable) is deducted from the UCC balance of the entire class. This would result in the reduction of the UCC balance rather than an immediate inclusion of this amount in calculating taxable income. In turn, the reduction of the UCC balance would reduce the amount of CCA available in future years, hence an increase in future taxable income. Only when no other assets in a particular asset class exist would there be an immediate impact on taxable income.

Comparison between Financial and Tax Reporting

Different scenarios for financial and tax reporting are summarized in Table 11-3. Remember that the rules for tax reporting are based on the assumption that the acquired asset is the only asset in a particular asset class. Otherwise, the treatment of disposal would be more complicated.

Table 11-3
Financial and Tax Reporting in Asset Disposal

Type of Sale	Financial Reporting	Tax Reporting
The asset is sold for more than its purchase price	The difference between the asset's disposal value and its net book value results in a gain on disposal. This amount is added to net income for financial reporting purposes.	The amount added to taxable income equals the difference between the UCC balance and the lesser of: – Proceeds of disposition, or – Capital Cost Additionally, one-half of the difference between the proceeds of disposition and Capital Cost is treated as a capital gain and added to taxable income. The two amounts are taxed at the applicable federal and provincial tax rate.
The asset is sold for less than its purchase price but more than its book value	The difference between the asset's disposal value and its net book value results in a gain on disposal. This amount is added to net income for financial reporting purposes.	The amount added to taxable income equals the difference between the UCC balance and the lesser of: – Proceeds of disposition, or – Capital Cost The two amounts are taxed at the applicable federal and provincial tax rate.
The asset is sold for its book value	There is no net income effects for financial reporting purposes, but the company is likely to pay taxes as determined by tax reporting procedures.	No tax.
The asset is sold for less than its book value	The difference between the asset's net book value and its disposal value results in a loss on disposal.	The difference between the UCC balance and proceeds of disposition would be deducted from taxable income.

Financing Cash Flows

Suppose a company planned to borrow or sell new common shares to raise part or all of the funds needed for a proposed capital budgeting project. The company would receive a cash inflow on receipt of the loan or the sale of new common shares. Conversely, the company must make the interest and principal payments on the loan, or may make dividend payments to shareholders. **Financing cash flows** are the cash outflows that occur as creditors are paid interest and principal and shareholders are paid dividends.

If a capital budgeting project is rejected, financing cash flows will not occur, so they are relevant cash flows in the capital budgeting decision. However, as we saw in Chapter 10, financing costs are factored into the discount rate (required rate of return) in the NPV calculation. Those costs are also included in the hurdle rate of the IRR decision rule. Therefore, to avoid double counting, we do not include financing costs in our operating incremental cash flow estimates when we make capital budgeting decisions. If we did include financing costs as part of the incremental operating cash flows, then the NPV or IRR analysis would be distorted. This distortion could lead in turn to a poor capital budgeting decision.

Figure 11-1 summarizes the cash flow estimation process and its role in capital budgeting.

Figure 11-1 **The Cash Flow Estimation Process**

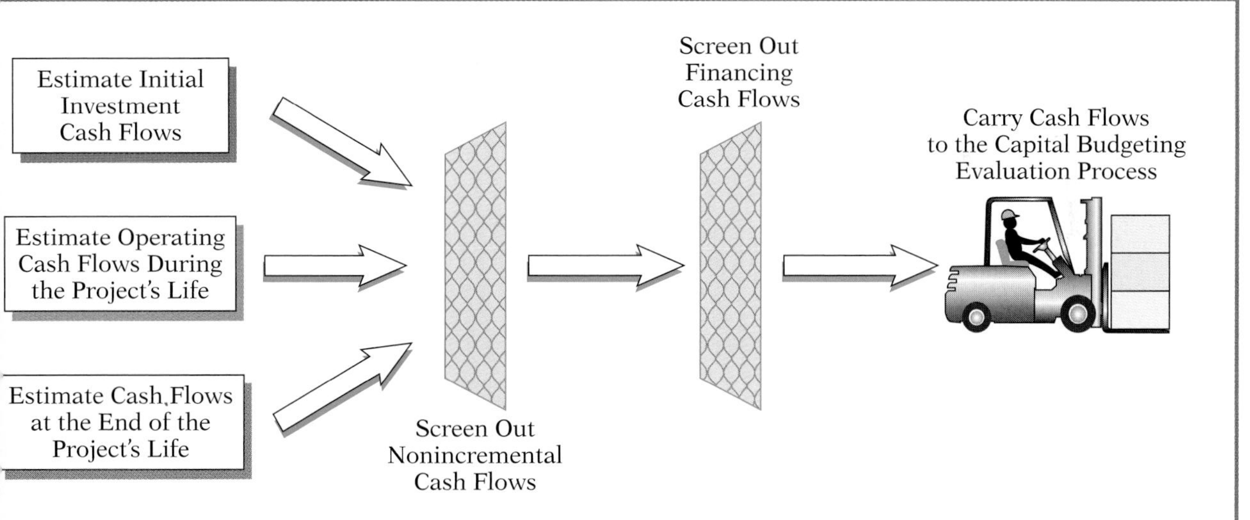

Incremental Cash Flows of an Expansion Project

To practise capital budgeting cash flow estimation, let's examine a proposed expansion project. An expansion project is one in which the company adds a project and does not replace an existing one. Imagine a company called the Red Deer Bobcats, which makes forklifts. It is considering a project to install \$3 million worth of new machine tools in its main plant. The new tools are expected to last for five years. The Bobcats' operations management and marketing experts estimate that during those five years, the tools will result in a sales increase of \$800,000 per year.

The Red Deer Bobcats' CEO has asked Mr. Ball, the company CFO, to identify all incremental cash flows associated with the project and to calculate the project's NPV and IRR. Based on the incremental cash flow analysis and Ball's recommendation, the company will make an accept or reject decision about the project.

Ball's first step is to identify the relevant (incremental) cash flows associated with the project. He begins with the initial investment in the project, then looks at the operating cash flows, and finally the shutdown cash flows.

Initial Investment Cash Flows The cash flows that will occur as soon as the project is implemented (at t_0) make up the project's initial investment. The initial investment includes the cash outflows for the purchase price, installation, delivery, and increase in net working capital.

Ball knows that its tool supplier gave the Bobcats a bid of $3 million to cover the cost of the new tools, including setup and delivery. The Bobcats' inventory and accounting specialists estimate that if the tools are purchased, inventory will need to increase by $40,000, accounts receivable by $90,000, and cash by $10,000. This is a $140,000 increase in current assets (working capital).

Also, the Bobcats' experts estimate that if the tools are purchased, accounts payable will increase by $20,000 as larger orders are placed with suppliers and accruals (wages and taxes) will increase by $10,000—a $30,000 increase in current liabilities. Subtracting the increases in current liabilities from the increases in current assets ($140,000 – $30,000) results in a $110,000 increase in net working capital associated with the expansion project.

Ball concludes after extensive research that he has found all the initial investment incremental cash flows. The cash flows are summarized in Table 11-4.

Table 11-4 Bobcats' Manufacturing Expansion Project Initial Investment Incremental Cash Flows at t_0

Cost of Tools and Setup	$3,000,000
+ Investment in Additional NWC	110,000
= Total Initial Cash Outlay	$3,110,000

Operating Cash Flows Now Ball examines the operating cash flows, those cash flows expected to occur from operations during the five-year period after the project is implemented (at t_1 through t_5). The Bobcats expansion project operating cash flows reflect changes in sales, operating expenses, and amortization tax effects. We assume these cash flows occur at the end of each year.

Ball learns from the vice-president of sales that cash sales are expected to increase by $800,000 per year because the new tools will increase manufacturing capacity. If purchased, the tools will be used to perform maintenance on other equipment at Bobcats, so operating expenses (other than amortization) are expected to decrease by $100,000 per year.

Amortization is a noncash expense, but remember that Ball must use amortization to compute the change in income tax that the Bobcats must pay. After taxes are computed, Ball then will add back the change in amortization in the operating cash flow analysis.

Let's further assume that the new manufacturing tools are amortized at 20 percent, so $600,000 will be charged to amortization expense every year for five years (we ignore a half-year convention rule).

Now Ball summarizes the incremental operating cash flows for the Bobcats' capital budgeting project in Table 11-5.

Ball is not quite through yet. He must include in his analysis additional shutdown cash flows that occur at t_5, the end of the project's life.

Table 11-5 Red Deer Bobcats' Manufacturing Expansion Project Incremental Operating Cash Flows, Years 1–5

	t_1	t_2	t_3	t_4	t_5
+ Change in Sales	+ 800,000	800,000	800,000	800,000	800,000
+ Reduction in Nonamortization Operating Expenses	+ 100,000	100,000	100,000	100,000	100,000
– Amortization Expense	– 600,000	600,000	600,000	600,000	600,000
= Change in Operating Income	= 300,000	300,000	300,000	300,000	300,000
– Tax on New Income (See Note)	– 120,000	120,000	120,000	120,000	120,000
= Change in Earnings after Taxes	= 180,000	180,000	180,000	180,000	180,000
+ Add Back Amortization Expense	+ 600,000	600,000	600,000	600,000	600,000
= Net Incremental Operating Cash Flow	= 780,000	780,000	780,000	780,000	780,000

Note: It may occur that taxes in any given year are negative amounts because of the negative figure at the change in operating income line, which means earnings after taxes for those years are *increased* by the amount of the taxes saved.

Shutdown Cash Flows The Bobcats' company experts estimate that the actual economic life of the tools will be five years, after which time the tools should have a residual value of $800,000. If we assume that the tools are sold at the end of the year, assets are almost amortized to zero, so at t_5 the book value of the new tools is zero. Therefore, if the tools are sold at the end of year 5 for their residual value of $800,000, the Bobcats will realize a taxable gain on the sale of the tools of $800,000 ($800,000 – $0 = $800,000). The income tax on the gain at the Bobcats' tax rate of 40 percent will be $800,000 × 0.40 = $320,000.

The net amount of cash that the Bobcats will receive from the sale of the tools is the residual value minus the tax paid:

$800,000	Residual Value
– 320,000	Taxes Paid
$480,000	Net Proceeds

The net proceeds from the tool sale in year 5, then, are $480,000.

Finally, if the new tools are sold at t_5, Ball concludes (based on sales department information) that the Bobcats' sales will return to the level that they were at before the new tools were installed. Consequently, there will be no further need for the additional investment in net working capital that was made at t_0. When the \$110,000 investment in net working capital is recaptured,[1] it is recovered in the form of a positive cash flow.

The additional incremental cash flows from the sale of the tools and the change in net working capital are summarized in Table 11-6.

Table 11-6 Red Deer Bobcats' Expansion Project Shutdown Cash Flows at t_5

Residual Value	\$800,000
– Taxes on Residual Value	– 320,000
= Net Cash Inflow from Sale of Tools	+ 480,000
+ Cash from Reduction in NWC	+ 110,000
= Total Additional Cash Flows at t_5	= 590,000

Cash Flow Summary and Valuation Tables 11-4, 11-5, and 11-6 contain all the incremental cash flows associated with the Bobcats' proposed expansion project. Ball's next step is to summarize the total incremental net cash flows occurring at each point in time in one table. Table 11-7 shows the results.

Table 11-7 contains the bottom-line net incremental cash flows associated with the Bobcats' proposed expansion project. The initial cash flow at t_0 is –\$3,110,000. The operating cash flows from t_1 to t_5 total \$3,900,000. The sum of all the incremental positive and negative cash flows for the project is \$1,380,000.

Table 11-7 Bobcats Expansion Project Summary of Incremental Cash Flows

	t_0	t_1	t_2	t_3	t_4	t_5
For Purchase and Setup	(3,000,000)					
For Additional NWC	(110,000)					
From Operating Cash Flows		780,000	780,000	780,000	780,000	780,000
From Residual Value Less Taxes						480,000
From Reducing NWC						110,000
Net Incremental Cash Flows	(3,110,000)	780,000	780,000	780,000	780,000	1,370,000

Now Ball is ready to compute the NPV, IRR, and MIRR of the expansion project based on the procedures described in Chapter 10.

Assuming that the Bobcats' discount rate is 10 percent, Ball computes the NPV of the project using Equation 10-1 as follows:[2]

---

[1]Current assets, in the amount by which they exceed current liabilities, are sold and not replaced because they are no longer needed.

[2]The NPV Formula, Equation 10-1a, follows:

$$NPV = \left(\frac{CF_1}{(1+k)^1}\right) + \left(\frac{CF_2}{(1+k)^2}\right) + \cdots + \left(\frac{CF_n}{(1+k)^n}\right) - \text{Initial Investment}$$

	t_0	t_1	t_2	t_3	t_4	t_5
Net Incremental Cash Flows	(3,110,000)	780,000	780,000	780,000	780,000	1,370,000
PV of Cash Flows	$\frac{(3,110,000)}{(1 + 0.10)^0}$	$\frac{780,000}{(1 + 0.10)^1}$	$\frac{780,000}{(1 + 0.10)^2}$	$\frac{780,000}{(1 + 0.10)^3}$	$\frac{780,000}{(1 + 0.10)^4}$	$\frac{1,370,000}{(1 + 0.10)^5}$
	= (3,110,000)	= 709,091	= 644,628	= 586,026	= 532,750	= 850,662

$$NPV = (3,110,000) + 709,091 + 644,628 + 586,026 + 532,750 + 850,662$$

Assuming a discount rate of 10 percent, the NPV of the project is \$213,157.

Next, Ball uses the trial-and-error method described in Chapter 10 to find the IRR of the project.[3] He finds that the IRR, the discount rate that makes the NPV equal to zero, is 12.44 percent.

$$NPV_P = 0 = \frac{-3,110,000}{(1+k)^0} + \frac{780,000}{(1+k)^1} + \frac{780,000}{(1+k)^2} + \frac{780,000}{(1+k)^3} + \frac{780,000}{(1+k)^4} + \frac{1,370,000}{(1+k)^5}$$

$$k = 0.1244, \therefore IRR = 0.1244 = 12.44\%$$

Finally, Ball uses the method described in Chapter 10 to find the MIRR of the project:

Time	*Cash Flow*	*FV of Cash Flow at t_5 If Reinvested @ 10% Cost of Capital (per Equation 8-1a)*
t_1	\$780,000	$\times (1 + 0.10)^4$ = \$1,141,998
t_2	\$780,000	$\times (1 + 0.10)^3$ = \$1,038,180
t_3	\$780,000	$\times (1 + 0.10)^2$ = \$943,800
t_4	\$780,000	$\times (1 + 0.10)^1$ = \$858,000
t_5	\$1,370,000	$\times (1 + 0.10)^0$ = \$1,370,000
		Terminal Value: \$5,351,978
		Initial investment: \$3,110,000
		MIRR per Equation 8-6: 11.47%

Because the project's NPV of \$213,157 is positive, the IRR of 12.44 percent exceeds the required rate of return of 10 percent. Because the MIRR of 11.47 percent exceeds the required rate of return, Ball will recommend that the Bobcats proceed with the expansion project.

In this discussion, we examined how a firm determines the incremental costs of an expansion project and the project's NPV, IRR, and MIRR. We turn next to replacement projects and their incremental costs.

We can use capital budgeting principles to solve a business problem or a personal dilemma. Financial Management and You 11-1 describes how capital budgeting concepts can be applied to a non-business situation.

---

[3]The formula for finding a project's IRR, Equation 10-2, is:

$$0 = \left(\frac{CF_1}{(1+k)^1}\right) + \left(\frac{CF_2}{(1+k)^2}\right) + \cdots + \left(\frac{CF_n}{(1+k)^n}\right) - \text{Initial Investment}$$

FINANCIAL MANAGEMENT AND YOU 11-1

The Incremental Costs of Studying Abroad

Imagine that you want to study international finance at the Universität Heidelberg in Germany during the next academic year. Your college has an exchange agreement with Heidelberg that guarantees tuition and housing at your in-state resident rate. To decide whether to spend the academic year studying abroad instead of at home, you draw up a list of costs in U.S. dollars. Here is what you find:

1. Cost of travel to and from Heidelberg	$1,100.00
2. Cost of student lodging and tuition for academic year	$4,985.00
3. Cost of books and other supplies	$600.00
4. Cost of food ($450 per month for nine months)	$4,050.00
5. Cost of summer travel in Europe (including food, supplies, rail passes, and student hostel charges)	$2,000.00
	$12,735.00

At first glance, the opportunity appears too expensive to consider. Now that you have read this chapter, however, you realize you need to screen out irrelevant costs and consider opportunity costs and externalities. Your new list looks like this:

1. Cost of travel to and from Heidelberg	$1,100.0
2. Cost of tuition and lodging in Heidelberg minus cost of lodging and tuition in the United States	$0.0
3. Cost of books and other supplies ($600) minus cost of same in the United States ($500)	$100.0
4. Cost of food abroad for academic year ($4,050) minus cost of same in the United States ($3,150 with cafeteria pass)	$900.0
5. Cost of summer travel in Europe ($2,000) minus cost of summer room/board/travel in the United States ($1,200)	$800.0
6. Opportunity cost of no summer job abroad (U.S. summer job income of $1,200 minus $0 income abroad)	$1,200.0
	$4,100.0

You estimate that your relevant costs are $4,100 for t year. Although you cannot measure them exactly, you kn the study abroad has positive externalities—it will furth your career plans. Can you afford to accept this opportuni

Source: Air travel, rail passes, and lodging price information retrieved from Saber® Database.

Asset Replacement Decisions

Often a company considers replacing existing equipment with new equipment. A replacement decision is a capital budgeting decision to purchase a new asset and replace and retire an old asset, or to keep the old asset. Financial managers identify the *differences* between the company's cash flows with the old asset versus the company's cash flows if the new asset is purchased and the old asset retired. As illustrated in Figure 11-2, these differences are the incremental cash flows of the proposed new project.

REAL OPTIONS

Externalities and opportunity costs are not the only elements of the capital budgeting decision that are difficult to reduce to an incremental cash flow estimate. Many projects have options embedded in them that add to the value of the project and, therefore, of the firm. For example, a project may provide management with the option to revise a capital budgeting project at a later date. This characteristic is called a **real option**. It is a real option because it is related to a real asset such as a piece of equipment or a new plant. You may already be familiar with financial options (calls and puts) that give the holder the opportunity to buy or sell financial assets such as shares or bonds at a later

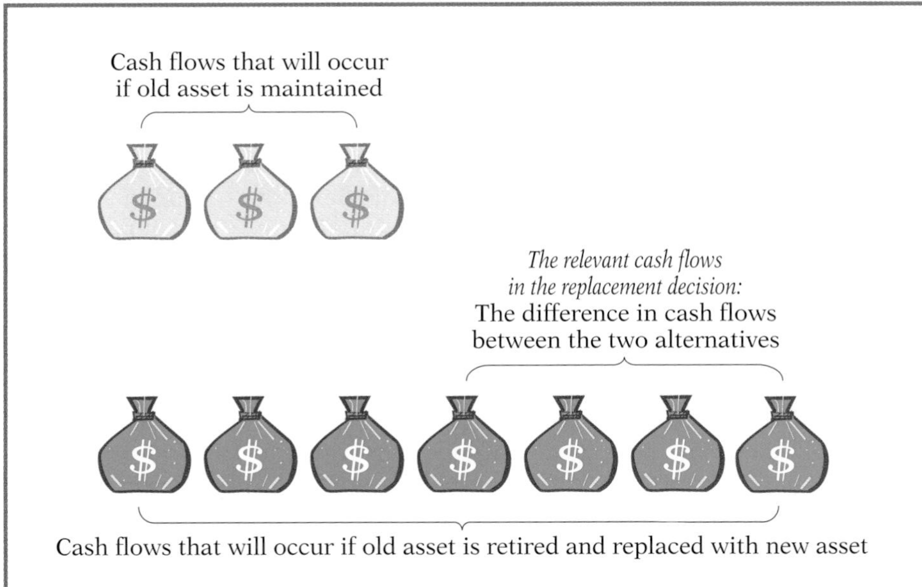

Figure 11-2 Comparing Cash Flows: Replacing an Asset versus Keeping It
Figure 11-2 illustrates how firms compare the difference between the cash flows of replacing an old asset with a new one or keeping the old asset.

date. Real options are similar except that their value is related to the value of real assets rather than to the value of financial assets. Note that the word *option* indicates that the future alternative does not have to be taken. It will be taken only if it is seen as adding value.

The flexibility that is provided by a real option to revise a project at a later date has value. This option may be to expand a project, to abandon it, to create another project that is an offshoot of the current project, or something else. For example, a restaurant with room to expand is more valuable than one that is confined to its original fixed space, other things being equal. A project that can be shut down before its scheduled useful life if it turns out to be a failure is more valuable, other things being equal, than a similar failed project that must continue operating. An investment in a research laboratory that might develop a wonderful new drug that is completely unknown to us now is more valuable, other things being equal, than an investment in another project that has no potential future spinoffs.

Traditional NPV and IRR analysis often overlooks the value that may come from real options because this value cannot be reduced to a simple incremental cash flow estimate. Faced with this difficulty, managers usually omit from capital budgeting analysis, real options that are part of a project. This causes the NPV and IRR figures to be understated. As a result, the value real options add to the firm and the increase in the project rates of return that they provide are not recognized.

The NPV process can be modified to reflect the value that real options add to the firm. This involves computing the traditional NPV and then adding today's value of any real options that may be present. The following paragraphs illustrate the mechanics of the process.

Real options can be incorporated into the capital budgeting process by using *decision trees*. Decision trees show the different paths a project could take, including the various options that may be available. Each place at which the decision tree branches is called a *node*. There are two kinds of nodes, decision nodes and outcome nodes.

- A decision node is one that shows the alternatives available for management at that point in time.
- An outcome node is one that shows the various things that can happen once a decision path is chosen.

Let's go through an NPV analysis using a decision tree and real options to illustrate how the process works. Suppose that Jason and Jennifer are business partners who think their hometown of Hamilton would support a new Mexican restaurant, which they have decided to call Super Marg. Figure 11-3 shows the decision tree for Super Marg Mexican Restaurant. In Figure 11-3, A, C, and D are decision nodes whereas B and E are outcome nodes.

Jason and Jennifer's first expenditure is the $250,000 investment required to build the restaurant. This initial cash outflow is shown at the left side of Figure 11-3. This is decision node A. Once the new restaurant is built, customers will determine how successful it is. According to Jason and Jennifer's estimates, the probability is 0.3 that it will be a smash hit, 0.6 that it will be moderately successful, and 0.1 that it will be a bomb. Outcome node B shows these three possibilities. Note that all the probabilities associated with a node must sum to 1.0. If the restaurant is a smash hit, operating cash flows of $75,000 in year 1 are expected. If it is a smash hit, Jason and Jennifer will expand the business after one year of operation, making an additional investment of $50,000 at t_2. Decision node C indicates where the management decision to expand the business would be made. Paths 1, 2, and 3 show the possible outcomes if the business is expanded. Path 4 indicates the path that would not be taken if the expansion option is pursued. Jason and Jennifer can do better than this if the restaurant is a smash hit.

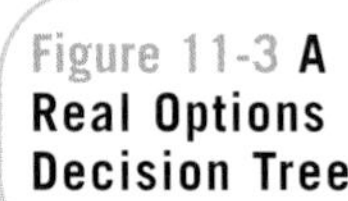
Figure 11-3 **A Real Options Decision Tree**

After expansion, the probability is 0.25 that subsequent operating cash flows will be $110,000, 0.50 that they will be $100,000, and 0.25 that they will be $90,000. Each of these cash flow streams would continue for seven years, until t_9. Outcome node E in Figure 11-3 shows these three possibilities.

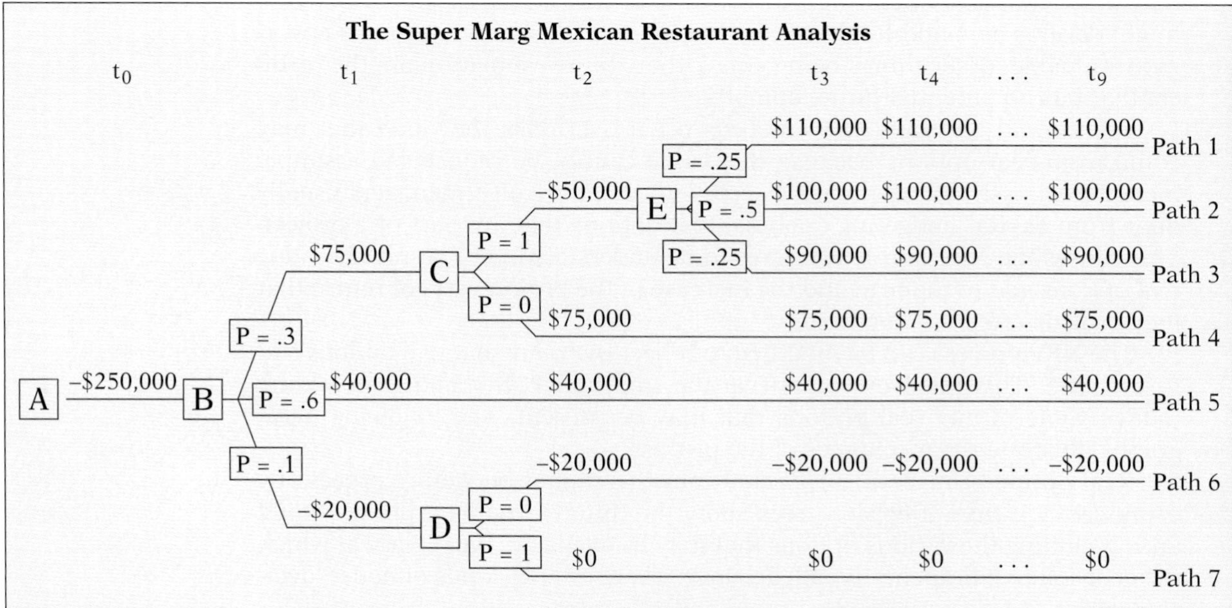

If the restaurant is moderately successful, operating cash flows of $40,000 per year for nine years are expected. Path 5 shows this cash flow stream. If the restaurant bombs, an operating cash flow of –$20,000 at t_1 is expected. This outcome would cause Jason and Jennifer to abandon the business after one year. Decision node D shows this abandonment option. Note that the probability is 1.0 that Jason and Jennifer will abandon the project if cash flows in t_1 are –$20,000. Path 6 shows the negative cash flows from t_2 to t_9 that are avoided if the project is abandoned. Path 7 shows the $0 cash flows that are preferred to the –$20,000 cash flows that would have occurred.

Once all the decisions, outcomes, and probabilities are plotted on the decision tree, the net present value and joint probability of each path can be computed. Note in Figure 11-3 that there are seven possible paths the operation can take. The probabilities associated with each possible path are multiplied together to give a joint probability for that path. The sum of the joint probabilities is 1.0. When the net present value for each path is multiplied by its joint probability and these results added, the expected net present value for the entire deal is obtained.

Table 11-8 on page 372 shows the NPV calculations for the Super Marg Restaurant project, assuming that Jason and Jennifer's required rate of return is 10 percent. The NPV of each of the seven paths is calculated using Equation 10-1a. In the far right-hand column of Table 11-8, the NPVs of each path are multiplied by the joint probability of that path occurring to give a composite score for each path called the *product*. The sum of the products, $15,161, is the expected NPV of the project. Because the expected NPV is greater than zero, the project would be accepted.

SUMMARY

11-1 Explain the difference between incremental cash flows and sunk costs.

Incremental cash flows are the cash flows that will occur if a capital budgeting project is accepted. They will not occur if the investment is rejected. Sunk costs are costs that will occur whether a project is accepted or rejected. Financial managers must screen out sunk costs from the capital budgeting analysis to prevent distortion in cash flow estimates. Any distortion in these estimates will, in turn, lead to inaccurate NPV or IRR values and could result in poor capital budgeting decisions.

11-2 Identify three main types of incremental cash flows in a capital budgeting project.

Financial managers must examine three main types of cash flows to estimate the incremental cash flows of a proposed capital budgeting project. First, they must assess the cost of the initial investment: the purchase price, the installation and delivery costs, and any change in net working capital. Then the financial manager must analyze incremental operating cash flows. These may include tax changes due to changes in sales and amortization expense, opportunity costs, and externalities. Finally, a financial manager must examine the project shutdown cash flows such as those cash flows from the project's residual value, the reduction of net working capital, and the tax-related cash flows from the sale of the used asset.

11-3 Explain why cash flows associated with project financing are not included in incremental cash flow estimates.

Incremental operating cash flows are treated separately from incremental financing cash flows. The latter are captured in the discount rate used in the NPV calculation and

Table 11-8 Super Marg Mexican Restaurant

Real Options NPV Analysis

	Cash Flows										Joint Probability of Occurrence	NPV	Product
	t_0	t_1	t_2	t_3	t_4	t_5	t_6	t_7	t_8	t_9			
Path 1	($250,000)	$75,000	($50,000)	$110,000	$110,000	$110,000	$110,000	$110,000	$110,000	$110,000	0.075	$219,443	$16,458
Path 2	($250,000)	$75,000	($50,000)	$100,000	$100,000	$100,000	$100,000	$100,000	$100,000	$100,000	0.15	$179,208	$26,881
Path 3	($250,000)	$75,000	($50,000)	$90,000	$90,000	$90,000	$90,000	$90,000	$90,000	$90,000	0.075	$138,973	$10,423
Path 4	($250,000)	$75,000	$75,000	$75,000	$75,000	$75,000	$75,000	$75,000	$75,000	$75,000	0	$181,927	$0
Path 5	($250,000)	$40,000	$40,000	$40,000	$40,000	$40,000	$40,000	$40,000	$40,000	$40,000	0.60	($19,639)	($11,783)
Path 6	($250,000)	($20,000)	($20,000)	($20,000)	($20,000)	($20,000)	($20,000)	($20,000)	($20,000)	($20,000)	0	($365,180)	$0
Path 7	($250,000)	($20,000)	$0	$0	$0	$0	$0	$0	$0	$0	0.1	($268,182)	($26,818)
										Sum =	1.0	**Exp NPV = $15,161**	

Required rate of return (k) = 10%

in the hurdle rate used when applying the IRR decision rule. Financial managers do not include financing costs as incremental operating cash flows to avoid distorting the NPV or IRR calculations in the capital budgeting process. Double counting would result if financing costs were reflected in both the operating cash flows and the discount rate.

11-4 Identify four different scenarios for disposition of assets under the tax reporting regime.

Financial reporting differs from tax reporting, resulting from different treatments of amortization under the two reporting regimes. While under Generally Accepted Accounting Principles, companies enjoy some freedom in determining the annual amount of amortization, but the *Income Tax Act* sets cost allowance classes and procedures for asset amortization.

There are four scenarios that are generally considered under financial and tax reporting. First, the asset may be sold for less than its acquisition cost but for more than its net book value. Second, the asset may be sold for more than its acquisition cost. Third, the asset may be sold for the amount equal to its net book value. Fourth, the asset may be sold for less than its net book value.

SELF-TEST

ST-1. Fat Tire Corporation had $20,000 in amortization expense last year. Assume its tax rate is 40 percent. How much are the firm's taxes reduced (and cash flow increased) by the amortization deduction on income tax returns?

ST-2. Skinny Ski Corporation had net income in 2002 of $2 million and amortization expense of $400,000. What was the firm's operating cash flow for the year?

ST-3. Powder Hound Ski Company is considering the purchase of a new helicopter for $1.5 million. The company paid an aviation consultant $20,000 to advise them on the need for a new helicopter. The decision about buying the helicopter has not been made yet. If it is purchased, what is the total initial cash outlay that will be used in the NPV calculation?

ST-4. Rich Folks Ski Area is considering the replacement of one of its older ski lifts. By replacing the lift, Rich Folks expects sales revenues to increase by $500,000 per year. Maintenance expenses are expected to increase by $75,000 per year if the new lift is purchased. Amortization expense would be $100,000 per year. (The company uses the straight-line method.) The old lift has been fully amortized. The firm's tax rate is 38 percent. What would the firm's incremental annual operating cash flows be if the new lift is purchased?

ST-5. Snorkel Ski Company is considering the replacement of its aerial tram. Sales are expected to increase by $900,000 per year and amortization expense is also expected to rise by $300,000 per year. The tax rate is 32 percent. The purchase will be financed with a $900,000 bond issue carrying a 10 percent annual interest rate. What are the annual incremental operating cash flows if this project is accepted?

REVIEW QUESTIONS

1. Why do we focus on cash flows instead of profits when evaluating proposed capital budgeting projects?
2. What is a sunk cost? Is it relevant when evaluating a proposed capital budgeting project? Explain.

3. How do we estimate expected incremental cash flows for a proposed capital budgeting project?
4. What role does amortization play in estimating incremental cash flows?
5. How and why does working capital affect the incremental cash flow estimation for a proposed large capital budgeting project? Explain.
6. How do opportunity costs affect the capital budgeting decision-making process?
7. How are financing costs generally incorporated into the capital budgeting analysis process?

PROBLEMS

Expansion Project, Initial Investment Cash Flows ▶

11-1. Tru-Green Landscaping is shopping for a new lawn mower. The purchase price of the model the company has selected is $6,000. However, Tru-Green plans to add some special attachments that will cost $5,000, and painting the company's name on the side of the mower will cost $300. Building a garage and maintenance facility for the mower and several other items of new equipment will cost $12,000. What is the total cash outflow at t_0 for the mower?

Salvage Value Cash Flows ▶

11-2. An asset amortized at 30 percent was purchased three years ago for $200,000 (its original amortization basis). Calculate the cash flows if the asset is sold now at

a. $60,000

b. $80,000

Assume the applicable tax rate is 40 percent. Do not apply the half-year rule. Use a straight-line method.

Operating Cash Flows ▶

11-3. Mr. Van Orten is evaluating the purchase of new trenching equipment for Scorpio Enterprises. For now, he is only figuring the incremental operating cash flow from the proposed project for the first year. Mr. Van Orten estimates that the firm's sales of earth-moving services will increase by $10,000 in year 1. Using the new equipment will add an additional $3,000 to their operating expenses. Interest expense will increase by $100 because the machine will be partly financed by a loan from the bank. The additional amortization expense for the new machine will be $2,000. Scorpio Enterprises' tax rate is 35 percent.

a. Calculate the change in operating income (EBIT) for year 1.

b. Calculate the cash outflow for taxes associated with this new income.

c. What is the net new after-tax income (change in earnings after taxes)?

d. Calculate the net incremental operating cash flow from this project for year 1.

e. Are there any expenses listed that you did not use when estimating the net incremental cash flow? Explain.

Expansion Project, Operating Cash Flows ▶

11-4. Ever-Fresh Landscaping bought a large-size golf course mower for $20,000. With this new machine, the company was able to increase its business, raising its annual revenue from $250,000 to $350,000 each year. Operating costs went up as well, however, from $70,000 to $100,000 annually. The mower is amortized at 20 percent and the company's tax rate is 35 percent. What is the net incremental operating cash flow in year 1 for the new lawn mower investment? Do not apply the half-year rule.

11-5. Never Brown Landscaping has a lawn mower that it bought three years ago for $10,000. The mower has an actual operating life of six years, at the end of which the mower can be sold for $2,000. Never Brown's income tax rate is 35 percent. What are the terminal cash flows associated with the mower investment? The company uses the straight-line method.

◀ Expansion Project, Terminal Cash Flows

11-6. Mr. Phelps, a financial analyst at Rhodes Manufacturing Corporation, is trying to analyze the feasibility of purchasing a new piece of equipment that has a useful life of five years. The corporation uses the straight-line method and doesn't apply the half-year rule. The amortization rate is equal to 20 percent. The initial investment, including the cost of equipment and its start-up, would be $375,000. Over the next five years, the following earnings before amortization and taxes will be generated from using this equipment:

◀ Estimating Cash Flows

Excel

End of Year	EBDT ($)
1	120,000
2	90,000
3	80,000
4	80,000
5	80,000

Rhodes's discount rate is 13 percent and the company pays 40 percent tax. There is no residual value at the end of year 5. Should Mr. Phelps recommend acceptance of the project?

11-7. Assume the same cash flows, initial investment, amortization rate, discount rate, and income tax rate as given in problem 11-6. Now assume that the resale value of the equipment at the end of five years will be $50,000. Calculate the NPV and recommend whether the project should be accepted.

◀ Estimating Cash Flows

Excel

11-8. George Kaplan is considering adding a new crop-dusting plane to his fleet at North Corn Corner, Inc. The new plane will cost $85,000. He anticipates spending an additional $20,000 immediately after the purchase to modify it for crop-dusting. Kaplan plans to use the plane for five years and then sell it. He estimates that the residual value will be $20,000. With the addition of the new plane, Kaplan estimates revenue in the first year will increase by 10 percent over last year. Revenue last year was $125,000. Other first-year expenses are also expected to increase. Operating expenses will increase by $20,000 and amortization expense will increase by $10,500. Kaplan's tax rate is 40 percent.

◀ Initial Investment, Operating Cash Flows, and Salvage Value

a. For capital budgeting purposes, what is the net cost of the plane? Or, stated another way, what is the initial net cash flow?

b. Calculate the net incremental operating cash flow for year 1.

c. In which year would the salvage value affect the net cash flow calculations?

11-9. Ghost Squadron Historical Aircraft, Inc. (GSHAI) is considering adding a rare World War II B-24 bomber to its collection of vintage aircraft. The plane was forced down in Burma in 1942 and it has remained there ever since. Flying a crew to Burma and collecting the wreckage will cost $100,000. Transporting all the parts to the company's restoration facility in Alberta will cost another $35,000. Restoring the plane to flyable condition will cost an additional $600,000 at t_0.

◀ Evaluating an Expansion Project

Excel

GSHAI's operating costs will increase by $40,000 a year at the end of years 1 through 7 (on top of the restoration costs). At the end of years 3 through 7, revenues from exhibiting the plane at air shows will be $70,000. At the end of year 7, the plane will be retired. At that time the plane will be sold to a museum for $500,000.

The plane is expected to have a useful life of seven years. GSHAI's income tax rate is 35 percent and the company's weighted average cost of capital is 12 percent. Calculate the NPV and IRR of the proposed investment in the plane. The company uses the straight- line method. Also, do not apply the half-year rule.

Changes in Net Working Capital ▶

11-10. The management of the local cotton mill is evaluating the replacement of low-wage workers by automated machines. If this project is adopted, production and sales are expected to increase significantly. Norma Rae, the mill's financial analyst, expects cash will have to increase by $8,000 and the accounts receivable will increase by $10,000 in response to the increase in sales volume. Because of the higher level of production, inventory will have to increase by $12,000 with an associated $6,000 increase in accounts payable. Accrued taxes and wages, even with the decrease in the number of labourers, are estimated to increase by $2,500.

a. Calculate the change in net working capital if the automation project is adopted.

b. Is this change in NWC a cash inflow or outflow?

c. Given the limited information about the duration of the project, in what year should this change affect the net incremental cash flow calculations?

Cash Flows and Capital Budgeting ▶

Excel

11-11. Sunstone, Inc. has entrusted financial analyst Flower Belle Lee with the evaluation of a project that involves buying a new asset at a cost of $90,000. The asset has a useful life of four years and will generate the following revenue stream:

End of Year	1	2	3	4
Revenues ($)	50,000	30,000	20,000	20,000

The asset has a resale value of $10,000 at the end of the fourth year. Sunstone's discount rate is 11 percent. The company has an income tax rate of 30 percent. Should Flower recommend purchase of the asset? The company uses the straight-line method and it does not use the half-year rule.

Replacement Decision and Cash Flows ▶

Excel

11-12. Moonstone, Inc., a competitor of Sunstone, Inc., in problem 11-11, is considering purchasing similar equipment with the same revenue, initial investment, useful life, and resale value. Moonstone's discount rate is 10 percent and its income tax rate is 40 percent. However, Moonstone is considering the new asset to replace an existing asset with a book value of $20,000 and a resale value of $10,000. What would be the NPV of the replacement project?

Changes in Net Working Capital ▶

Excel

11-13. You have just joined Moonstone, Inc. as its new financial analyst. You have learned that accepting the project described in problem 11-12 will require an increase of $10,000 in current assets and will increase current liabilities by $5,000. The investment in net working capital will be recovered at the end of year 4. What would be the new NPV of the project?

Challenge Problem ▶

Excel

11-14. You have been hired by Drs. Venkman, Stantz, and Spenler to help them with NPV analysis for a replacement project. These three New York City parapsychologists need to replace their existing supernatural beings detector with a new, upgraded model. They have calculated all the necessary figures but are unsure about how to account for the sale of their old machine. The original amortization basis of the old machine is $20,000, and the accumulated amortization is $12,000 at the date of the sale. They can sell the old machine for $18,000 cash. Assume that the tax rate for their company is 30 percent.

a. What is the book value of the old machine?

b. What is the taxable gain (loss) on the sale of the old equipment?

c. Calculate the tax on the gain (loss).
d. What is the net cash flow from the sale of the old equipment? Is this a cash inflow or an outflow?
e. Assume the new equipment costs $40,000 and they do not expect a change in net working capital. Calculate the incremental cash flow for t_0.
f. Assume they could only sell the old equipment for $6,000 cash. Recalculate parts (b) through (e).

◀ Cash Flows and Capital Budgeting

Excel

11-15. Mitch and Lydia Brenner own a small factory located in Bodega Bay, California. They manufacture rubber snakes used to scare birds away from houses, gardens, and playgrounds. The recent and unexplained increase in the bird population in northern California has significantly increased the demand for the Brenners' products. To take advantage of this marketing opportunity, they plan to add a new molding machine that will double the output of their existing facility. The cost of the new machine is $20,000. The machine setup fee is $2,000. With this purchase, current assets must increase by $5,000 and current liabilities will increase by $3,000. The economic life of the new machine is four years and it has a useful life of four years. The company uses the straight-line method and does not use the half-year rule. The machine is expected to be obsolete at the end of the fourth year and to have no residual value.

The Brenners anticipate recouping 100 percent of the additional investment in net working capital at the end of year 4. Sales are expected to increase by $20,000 each year in years 1 and 2. By year 3, the Brenners expect sales to be mostly from repeat customers purchasing replacements instead of sales to new customers. Therefore, the increase in sales for years 3 and 4 is estimated to only be $10,000 in each year. The increase in operating expenses is estimated to be 20 percent of the annual change in sales. Assume the tax rate is 40 percent.

a. Calculate the initial net incremental cash flow.
b. Calculate the net incremental operating cash flows for years 1 through 4. Round all calculations to the nearest whole dollar.
c. Assume the Brenners' discount rate is 14 percent. Calculate the net present value of this project. Would you recommend the Brenners add this new machine to their factory?

◀ Cash Flows and Capital Budgeting

Excel

11-16. The RHPS Corporation specializes in the custom design, cutting, and polishing of stone raw materials to make ornate building facings. These stone facings are commonly used in the restoration of older mansions and estates. Janet Weiss and Brad Majors, managers of the firm, are evaluating the addition of a new stone-cutting machine to their plant. The machine's cost to RHPS is $150,000. Installation and calibration costs will be $7,500. They do not anticipate an increase in sales, but the reduction in the operating expenses is estimated to be $50,000 annually. The machine is expected to be obsolete after five years. At the end of five years, Weiss and Majors expect the cash received from the sale of the obsolete machine to offset the shutdown and dismantling costs. The RHPS cost of capital is 10 percent and the tax rate is 35 percent. The Corporation uses the straight-line method. Do not use the half-year rule. The amortization rate equals 20 percent.

a. Calculate the net present value for the addition of this new machine. Round all calculations to the nearest dollar.
b. Would you recommend that Weiss and Majors go forward with this project?

Comprehensive Problem ▶ Excel

11-17. The Chemical Company of Baytown purchased new processing equipment for $40,000 on December 31, 2000. The equipment had an expected life of four years and the company uses the straight-line method. Do not use the half-year rule. Due to changes in environmental regulations, the operating cost of this equipment has increased. The company is considering replacing this equipment with a more efficient process line at the end of 2002. The salvage value of the old equipment is estimated to be $4,000. The tax rate is 40 percent.

a. Calculate the cash flow from the sale of this equipment. Assume the sale occurred at the end of 2002.

b. The new process line has a higher capacity than the old one and is expected to boost sales. As a result, the cash requirement will increase by $1,000, accounts receivable by $5,000, and inventory by $10,000. It will also increase accounts payable by $6,000 and accrued expenses by $3,000. Calculate the incremental cash flow due to the change in the net working capital.

c. The new equipment will cost $180,000, including installation and start-up costs. Calculate the net cash outflow in 2002 if the new process line is installed and is ready to operate by the end of 2002.

d. Beginning in January 2003, this new equipment is expected to generate additional sales of $60,000 each year for the next four years. It will have an economic life of four years. Being more efficient, the new equipment will reduce yearly operating expenses by $6,000. Calculate the net incremental operating cash flows for 2003 through 2006. Assume the tax rate will remain at 40 percent. Round calculations to the nearest whole dollar.

e. At the end of its economic life, the new process line is expected to be sold for $20,000. The cost of capital for the company is 6 percent. Calculate the net present value and the internal rate of return (only if you have a financial calculator) for this project. Round calculations to the nearest dollar. Recommend whether the replacement project should be adopted or rejected. (Hint: Preparation of a summary of incremental cash flows similar to Table 11-5 may be helpful.)

Real Options ▶ Excel

11-18. Joe and Tim are business partners who are considering opening a brewpub in Whistler, British Columbia. It is to be called J&T's Double Diamond Brewhouse. Joe and Tim's first expenditure is the $300,000 investment required to build the brewpub. Once it is built, customers will determine how successful it is. According to Joe and Tim's estimates, the probabilities are 0.25 that it will be a smash hit, 0.50 that it will be moderately successful, and 0.25 that it will bomb.

If the brewpub is a smash hit, operating cash flows of $200,000 at the end of years 1 and 2 are expected. In that case, Joe and Tim will expand the business at the end of year 2 at a cost of $100,000. After expansion, the probabilities are 0.50 that subsequent operating cash flows at the end of year 3 will be $400,000, 0.30 that they will be $200,000, and 0.20 that they will be $90,000. Each of these cash flow streams would continue in years 4 and 5.

If the brewpub is moderately successful, operating cash flows of $100,000 per year at the end of years 1 through 5 are expected. If the brewpub bombs, operating cash flows of –$40,000 per year at the end of years 1 through 5 are expected. This outcome would cause Joe and Tim to abandon the business at the end of year 1. The probability is 1.0 that Joe and Tim will abandon the project if cash flows at the end of year 1 are –$40,000.

a. Plot the decisions, outcomes, and probabilities associated with the new project on a decision tree similar to Figure 11-3.

b. Calculate the NPV and joint probability of each path in the decision tree. Assume that Joe and Tim's required rate of return is 14 percent.

c. Calculate the expected NPV of the entire deal. Again, assume that Joe and Tim's required rate of return is 14 percent.

Operating Cash Flow, CCA

11-19. At the beginning of 2004, Edmonton General Contractors acquired manufacturing and processing assets for the price of $500,000. The acquired assets fall into CCA Class 43 and are amortized at 30 percent (a declining balance method). This newly acquired asset represents the only asset in Class 43. The company sold the assets at the end of 2007.

a. Calculate the effect of disposition on the company taxable income in 2007 under the CRA rules if the asset was sold for $300,000. Assume there are no other assets in Class 43 at disposal.

b. Calculate the effect of disposition on the company taxable income in 2007 under the CRA rules if the asset was sold for $600,000. Assume there are no other assets in Class 43 at disposal.

Operating Cash Flow, CCA

11-20. At the beginning of 2004, Hamilton Office Depot, a newly formed company founded by local entrepreneurs, made a decision to buy furniture for its office for $50,000. The furniture falls into CCA Class 8 and is amortized at 20 percent (a declining balance method). The furniture represents the only assets in Class 8 at Hamilton Office Depot. At the end of 2007, the company decided to move its operations to Calgary and since the furniture would not fit well into their new office, the management decided to dispose of the old furniture.

a. Calculate the effect of disposition on the company taxable income in 2007 under the CRA rules if the asset was sold for $40,000. Assume there are no other assets in Class 8 at disposal.

b. Calculate the effect of disposition on the company taxable income in 2007 under the CRA rules if the asset was sold for $60,000. Assume there are no other assets in Class 8 at disposal.

Operating Cash Flow, CCA

11-21. You purchased a piece of manufacturing equipment for $30,000. The asset falls into CCA Class 43 and is amortized at 30 percent (a declining balance method). According to your financial projections, incremental sales would increase by $10,000 per annum in the first three years and then increase to $30,000 in the following years. The increase in operating expenses is estimated to be 20 percent of the annual change in sales.

With this purchase, current assets will increase by $5,000 and liabilities will increase by $2,000. You are considering the impact of the project in the next five years. At this time, you would sell the equipment for $35,000. You expect to recoup the entire investment in working capital at the end of year 5. You estimate the cost of capital to be equal to 20 percent. Your income tax rate is equal to 40 percent.

a. Calculate the initial net incremental cash flow.

b. Calculate the net incremental operating cash flows for years 1 through 5.

c. Calculate the NPV and IRR of this project. Would you accept this project?

Operating Cash Flow, CCA

11-22. You purchased a piece of furniture for $20,000. The asset falls into CCA Class 8 and is amortized at 20 percent (a declining balance method). According to your financial projections, incremental sales would increase by $5,000 per annum every year and start from the base level of $15,000 in the first year. The increase in operating expenses is estimated to be 40 percent of the annual change in sales.

With this purchase, current assets will increase by $10,000 and liabilities will increase by $4,000. You are considering the impact of the project in the next five years. At this time, you would sell the equipment for $15,000. You expect to recoup the entire investment in working capital at the end of year 5. You estimate the cost of capital to be equal to 20 percent. Your income tax rate is equal to 35 percent.

a. Calculate the initial net incremental cash flow.
b. Calculate the net incremental operating cash flows for years 1 through 5.
c. Calculate the NPV and IRR of this project. Would you accept this project?

Challenge Problem ▶ **11-23.** Philip Mills is an owner of a table tennis club in Winnipeg. In the last few years, the club has been extraordinarily successful with the involvement of one of the leading world table tennis players, Huang Chang from China, who has participated in many training sessions conducted at the club. Mr. Mills senses that he can make additional money from increasing the capacity of his club by purchasing additional tables. The cost of 30 additional tables is equal to $30,000 and there are no set up costs. With this investment, Mr. Mills estimates that he would still need to increase his inventory by $10,000 through the purchase of rackets, rubbers, and balls. He anticipates recouping 100 percent of his investment in additional assets at the end of year 5. Mr. Mills does not anticipate any incremental increases in liabilities. From his coaching experience, Mr. Mills knows that tables will only last for five years after which they become obsolete. They also have no residual value.

With the enlarged capacity to train additional players, Mr. Mills anticipates that he will increase his sales by $20,000 per year in the first two years. In years 3–5, he expects that sales would reach $35,000 per year through increasing the brand awareness of his club in Winnipeg and across Canada. The increase in operating expenses is estimated to be 20 percent of the annual change in sales. Assume that the tax rate is 40 percent and Mr. Mills' discount rate is 20 percent. Additionally, do not apply the half-year convention rule (amortization at 20 percent per year under the straight-line method).

a. Calculate the initial net incremental cash flow.
b. Calculate the net incremental operating cash flows for years 1 through 5.
c. Calculate the NPV and IRR of this project. Would you recommend that Mr. Mills add the new tables to his club?

Challenge Problem ▶ **11-24.** Alexander and Thomas Grey, both business students at Brandon University, want to invest further cash in their successful vending machine operation on the university campus. They plan to introduce a few additional vending machines with health foods at a total cost of $18,000. They estimate that the set-up costs and delivery would incur an additional $2,000. According to their financial projections, incremental sales would increase by $15,000 per annum in the first two years and then begin to decline in subsequent years as the novelty of these machines wear off (Year 3 – $10,000; Year 4 – $8,000; Year 5 – $6,000). The increase in operating expenses is estimated to be 30 percent of the annual change in sales.

With this purchase, current assets will increase by $12,000 and liabilities will increase by $4,000. The economic life of new machines is five years and no residual value is expected at the end of the period. Students expect that changes in working capital will be reversed at the end of year 5 (i.e., they will recoup 100 percent of their investment in current assets and repay 100 percent of their credit from suppliers).

Assume that the marginal tax rate is 20 percent and the discount rate is 15 percent. Additionally, do not apply the half-year convention rule (amortization at 20 percent per year under the straight-line method).

a. Calculate the initial net incremental cash flow.

b. Calculate the net incremental operating cash flows for years 1 through 5.

c. Calculate the NPV and IRR of this project. Would you recommend that they purchase additional vending machines?

ANSWERS TO SELF-TEST

ST-1. $20,000 × 0.40 = $8,000 tax savings

ST-2. $2,000,000 + $400,000 = $2,400,000 operating cash flow

ST-3. $1,500,000 total initial cash outlay. (The $20,000 for the consultant is a sunk cost.)

ST-4. ($500,000 – $75,000 – $100,000) × (1 – 0.38) = $325,000 × 0.62 = $201,500 incremental net income $201,500 + $100,000 amortization expense = $301,500 incremental operating cash flow

ST-5. ($900,000 – $300,000) × (1 – 0.32) = $600,000 × 0.68 = $408,000 incremental net income $408,000 + $300,000 amortization expense = $708,000 incremental operating cash flow. (The finance costs are not part of operating cash flows. They will be reflected in the required rate of return.)

12

Business Valuation

Chapter Objectives

After reading this chapter, you should be able to:

12-1 Explain the importance of business valuation.

12-2 Discuss the concept of business valuation.

12-3 Describe how to compute the market value and the yield to maturity of a bond.

12-4 Explain how to calculate the market value and expected yield of preferred shares.

12-5 Describe two ways to compute the market value per share of common shares.

12-6 Explain three ways to compute the market value of total common equity.

12-7 Define the expected yield on common shares and how to calculate it.

12-8 Describe how to compute the value of a complete business.

"Nowadays we know the price of everything and the value of nothing."

—Oscar Wilde

The Art of Valuation

After Harold Ballard, the colourful but ornery owner of the Toronto Maple Leafs, passed away in 1990, his friend and businessman Steve Stavro decided to purchase controlling interest in Maple Leaf Gardens Ltd., which included the hockey team, the franchise, the players' contracts and the building on Carlton Street in Toronto. But Stavro had a problem. As a trustee of the Ballard estate, and a member of MLG's board of directors since 1981, he had a fiduciary responsibility to ensure MLG received the highest possible price for its shares; as a potential purchaser, he desired the opposite. In other words, Stavro found himself in a serious conflict of interest.

But Stavro was determined. In October 1993, he hired Nesbitt Burns (then called Burns Fry) and RBC Dominion Securities to prepare independent reports on the value of MLG shares. The two agreed that controlling interest in MLG was worth about $32 a share, but to keep shareholders on side, Stavro bumped the price up to $34. However, Susan Himmel, Ontario's Public Trustee who overlooked the charities in Ballard's will, hired valuator Richard Wise to review the opinions of Nesbitt and RBC.

And that's where things blew apart. Wise's findings: Nesbitt Burns and RBC Dominion had substantially underestimated the company's value and erroneously based their opinions on past performance more than on its future potential earnings.

He concluded that the two firms had asked the wrong kind of questions. As Wise of Wise, Blackman in Montreal says, "Valuators from Nesbitt Burns and RBC Dominion didn't take into account the principal sources of revenue–including revenues from broadcasting. They ignored the value of board advertising and the value of concessions."

The MLG case illustrates the complex, often volatile nature of the field called business valuation. Business valuators, like Wise, can be hired to assign a dollar value to anything from a medical practice to a dot-com business. They render their services in matrimonial and shareholder disputes, are called in to calculate injury and damages claims or even to provide litigation support. And it often is a contentious affair, for the obvious reason that the parties involved–generally a buyer and a seller–find it difficult to come to an agreement on a price.

Chapter Overview

In this chapter, we will discuss how to value businesses in a dynamic marketplace. First, we will investigate the importance of business valuation and introduce a general model that analysts and investors use to value assets. Then we will show how to adapt the model to bonds, preferred shares, and common shares. For common shares, we will explore additional valuation techniques.

The Importance of Business Valuation

As Chapter 1 explained, the primary financial goal of financial managers is to maximize the market value of their firm. It follows, then, that financial managers need to assess the market value of their firms to gauge progress.

Accurate business valuation is also a concern when a corporation contemplates selling securities to raise long-term funds. Issuers want to raise the most money possible from selling securities. Issuers lose money if they undervalue their businesses. Likewise, would-be purchasers are concerned about businesses' value because they do not want to pay more than what the businesses are worth.

A General Valuation Model

The value of a business depends on its future earning power. To value a business then, we consider three factors that affect future earnings:

- Size of cash flows
- Timing of cash flows
- Risk

These three factors also determine the value of individual assets belonging to a business, or interests in a business, such as those possessed by bondholders and shareholders.

In Chapter 7, we examined how risk factors affect an investor's required rate of return. In Chapter 8, we learned that time value of money calculations can determine an investment's value, given the size and timing of the cash flows. In Chapters 9, 10, and 11, we learned how to evaluate future cash flows.

Financial managers determine the value of a business, a business asset, or an interest in a business by finding the present value of the future cash flows that the owner of the business, asset, or interest could expect to receive. For example, we can calculate a bond's value by taking the sum of the present values of each of the future cash flows from the bond's interest and principal payments. We can calculate a share's value by taking the sum of the present values of future dividend cash flow payments.

Analysts and investors use a general valuation model to calculate the present value of future cash flows of a business, business asset, or business interest. This model, the **discounted cash flow model (DCF)**, is a basic valuation model for an asset that is expected to generate cash payments in the form of cash earnings, interest and principal payments, or dividends. The DCF equation is shown in Equation 12-1:

The Discounted Cash Flow Valuation Method

$$V_0 = \frac{CF_1}{(1+k)^1} + \frac{CF_2}{(1+k)^2} + \frac{CF_3}{(1+k)^3} + \cdots + \frac{CF_n}{(1+k)^n} \qquad (12\text{-}1)$$

where

V_0 = Present value of the anticipated cash flows from the asset, its current value

$CF_{1,\,2,\,3,\,\text{and}\,n}$ = Cash flows expected to be received one, two, three, and so on up to n periods in the future

k = Discount rate, the required rate of return

The DCF model values an asset by calculating the sum of the present values of all expected future cash flows.

The discount rate in Equation 12-1 is the investor's required rate of return, which is a function of the risk of the investment. Recall from Chapter 7 that the riskier the security, the higher the required rate of return.

The discounted cash flow model is easy to use if we know the cash flows and discount rate. For example, suppose you were considering purchasing a security that entitled you to receive payments of \$100 in one year, another \$100 in two years, and \$1,000 in three years. If your required rate of return for securities of this type were 20 percent, then we would calculate the value of the security as follows:

$$\begin{aligned} V_0 &= \frac{\$100}{(1+0.20)^1} + \frac{\$100}{(1+0.20)^2} + \frac{\$1{,}000}{(1+0.20)^3} \\ &= \$83.3333 + \$69.4444 + \$578.7037 \\ &= \$731.48 \end{aligned}$$

The total of the security's three future cash flows at a 20 percent required rate of return yields a present value of \$731.48.

In the sections that follow, we will adapt the discounted cash flow valuation model to apply to businesses and business components.

Applying the General Valuation Model to Businesses

According to the general valuation model, Equation 12-1, the value of a business asset is the present value of the anticipated cash flows from the asset. The value of a complete business, therefore, is the present value of the cash flows expected to be generated by the business. In order to use the general valuation model to estimate the value of a complete business, we must forecast the cash flows expected to be generated by the business and discount them to the present using the required rate of return appropriate for the business. This sounds relatively simple, but in fact, it is an extremely complex task requiring the cash flow estimation techniques that you learned in Chapter 11 and the cost of capital estimation techniques that you learned in Chapter 9.

Instead of tackling the value of a complete business all at once, we will begin with the present values of the components of the business, as illustrated in Figure 12-1.

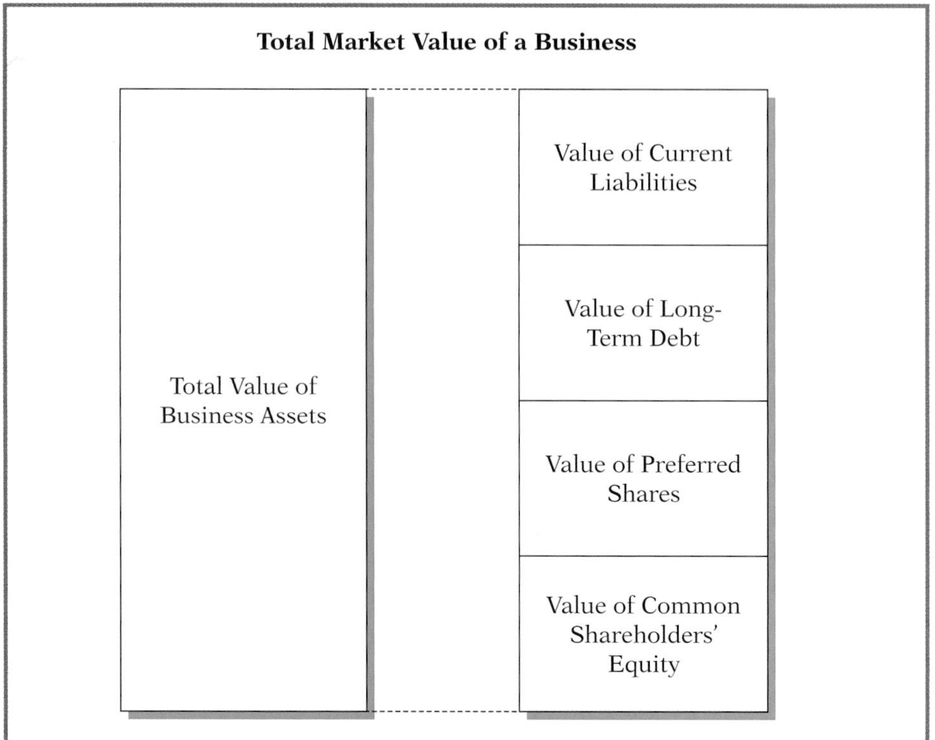

Figure 12-1 Total Market Value of a Business This figure illustrates how the total market value of a business is the sum of the present values of the components of the business.

As Figure 12-1 shows, the value of all of a businesses' assets (i.e., the complete business) equals the sum of the present values of its current liabilities, long-term debt, preferred shares, and common shares. In the remainder of this chapter, we will apply this approach, first examining the valuation of current liabilities and long-term debt (corporate bonds), then preferred shares, and finally common shares. Following those individual discussions, we will show how the same techniques can be used to estimate the total value of a business.

Valuing Current Liabilities and Long-Term Debt

Current liabilities are short-term obligations of a company that are fixed by agreement. Accounts payable, for example, represents amounts that the company has purchased from its suppliers and has agreed to pay for in a specified amount of time. Because the time to maturity of these obligations is not lengthy, the market value of current liabilities is most often taken to be equal to their book value. Therefore, when analysts value the current-liability component of a complete business, they normally just read the value of the current liabilities from the firm's balance sheet.

Long-Term Debt A company's long-term obligations may be long-term loans from a commercial bank or a private investor, corporate bonds, or notes issued to the public. In each case, the value of the debt is the present value of the future cash flows that would accrue to the owner of the debt, as we have explained previously. In this chapter, we will discuss the valuation of long-term debt when it is in the form of bonds.

Bond Valuation

Remember from Chapter 2 that a bond's cash flows is determined by the bond's coupon interest payments, face value, and maturity.

Because coupon interest payments occur at regular intervals throughout the life of the bond, those payments are an annuity. Instead of using several terms representing the individual cash flows from the future coupon interest payments (CF_1, CF_2, and so on), we adapt Equation 12-1 by using one term to show the annuity. The remaining term represents the future cash flow of the bond's face value, or principal, that is paid at maturity. Equation 12-2 shows the adapted valuation model:

The Bond Valuation Formula (Algebraic Method)

$$V_B = INT \times \left[\frac{1 - \frac{1}{(1+k_d)^n}}{k_d} \right] + \frac{M}{(1+k_d)^n} \qquad (12\text{-}2)$$

where

V_B = Current market value of the bond

INT = Dollar amount of each periodic interest payment

n = Number of times the interest payment is received (which is also the number of periods until maturity)

M = Principal payment received at maturity

k_d = Required rate of return per period on the bond debt instrument

The table version of the bond valuation model is shown in Equation 12-3, as follows:

The Bond Valuation Formula (Table Method)

$$V_B = (INT \times PVIFA_{k,\,n}) + (M \times PVIF_{k,\,n}) \qquad (12\text{-}3)$$

where

$PVIFA_{k,\,n}$ = Present Value Interest Factor for an Annuity from Table IV

$PVIF_{k,\,n}$ = Present Value Interest Factor for a single amount from Table II

To use a calculator to solve for the value of a bond, enter the dollar value of the interest payment as [PMT], the face value payment at maturity as [FV], the number of payments as n, and the required rate of return, k_d depicted as [I/Y] on the TI BAII PLUS calculator. Then compute the present value of the bond's cash flows.

Now let's apply the bond valuation model. Suppose Bell Canada Enterprises (BCE) issues a 7 percent coupon interest rate bond with a maturity of 20 years. The face value of the bond, payable at maturity, is $1,000.

First, we calculate the dollar amount of the coupon interest payments. At a 7 percent coupon interest rate, each payment is 0.07 × $1,000 = $70.

Next, we need to choose a required rate of return, k_d. Remember that k_d is the required rate of return that is appropriate for the bond based on its risk, maturity, marketability, and tax treatment. Let's assume that 8 percent is the rate of return the market determines to be appropriate.

Take Note

The determinants of nominal interest rates, or required rates of return, include the real rate of interest, the inflation premium, the default risk premium, the liquidity premium, and the maturity premium. Each person evaluating a bond will select an appropriate required rate of return, k_d, for the bond based on these determinants.

Now we have all the factors we need to solve for the value of BCE's bond. We know that k_d is 8 percent, n is 20, the coupon interest payment is \$70 per year, and the face value payment at maturity is \$1,000. Using Equation 12-2, we calculate the bond's value as follows:

$$
\begin{aligned}
V_B &= \$70 \times \left[\frac{1 - \dfrac{1}{(1+0.08)^{20}}}{0.08}\right] + \frac{\$1{,}000}{(1+0.08)^{20}} \\
&= (\$70 \times 9.8181474) + \left(\frac{\$1{,}000}{4.660957}\right) \\
&= \$687.270318 + \$214.548214 \\
&= \$901.82
\end{aligned}
$$

Notice that the value of BCE's bond is the sum of the present values of the 20 annual \$70 coupon interest payments plus the present value of the one-time \$1,000 face value to be paid 20 years from now, given a required rate of return of 8 percent.

To find the BCE bond's value using present value tables, recall that the bond has a face value of \$1,000, a coupon interest payment of \$70, a required rate of return of 8 percent, and an n value of 20. We apply Equation 12-3 as shown:

$$
\begin{aligned}
V_B &= (\$70 \times PVIFA_{8\%,\,20\text{ yrs}}) + (\$1{,}000 \times PVIF_{8\%,\,20\text{ yrs}}) \\
&= (\$70 \times 9.8181) + (\$1{,}000 \times 0.2145) \\
&= \$687.267 + \$214.500 \\
&= \$901.77
\end{aligned}
$$

We see that the sum of the present value of the coupon interest annuity, \$687.267, plus the present value of the principal, \$214.500, results in a bond value of \$901.77. There is a five-cent rounding error in this example when the tables are used.

Here's how to find the bond's value using the TI BAII PLUS financial calculator. Enter the \$70 coupon interest payment as PMT, the one-time principal payment of \$1,000 as FV, the 20 years until maturity as n (N on the TI BAII PLUS), and the 8 percent required rate of return—depicted as I/Y on the TI BAII PLUS. As demonstrated in Chapter 8 calculator solutions, clear the time value of money TVM registers before entering the new data. Skip steps 2 and 3 if you know your calculator is set to one payment per year and is also set for end-of-period payment mode.

TI BAII PLUS FINANCIAL CALCULATOR SOLUTION

Step 1: Press 2nd CLR TVM to clear previous values.

Step 2: Press 2nd P/Y 1 ENTER , 2nd BGN , 2nd SET . Repeat 2nd SET until END shows in the display, 2nd QUIT to set to the annual interest rate mode and to set the annuity payment to end-of-period mode.

Step 3: Input the values and compute.

1000 FV 8 I/Y 20 N 70 PMT CPT PV Answer: −901.82

The $901.82 is negative because it is a cash outflow—the amount an investor would pay to buy the bond today.

We have shown how to value bonds with annual coupon interest payments in this section. Next, we show how to value bonds with semiannual coupon interest payments.

Semiannual Coupon Interest Payments

In the hypothetical bond valuation examples for BCE, we assumed the coupon interest was paid annually. However, most bonds issued pay interest semiannually (twice per year). With semiannual interest payments, we must adjust the bond valuation model accordingly. If the BCE bond paid interest twice per year, the adjustments would look like this:

	Annual Basis	*Semiannual Basis*
Coupon Interest Payments	$70	÷ 2 = $35 per six-month period
Maturity	20 yrs	× 2 = 40 six-month periods
Required Rate of Return	8%	÷ 2 = 4% semiannual rate

These values can now be used in Equation 12-2, Equation 12-3, or a financial calculator in the normal manner. For example, if BCE's 7 percent coupon, 20-year bond paid interest semiannually, its present value per Equation 12-2 would be:

$$V_B = \$35 \times \left[\frac{1 - \dfrac{1}{(1+0.04)^{40}}}{0.04} \right] + \frac{\$1000}{(1+0.04)^{40}}$$

$$= (\$35 \times 19.792774) + \left(\frac{\$1000}{4.801021} \right)$$

$$= \$692.74709 + \$208.2890$$

$$= \$901.04$$

The value of our BCE bond with semiannual interest and a 4 percent per semiannual period discount rate is $901.04. This compares to a value of $901.82 for the same bond if it pays annual interest and has an 8 percent annual discount rate. Note that a required rate of return of 4 percent per semiannual period is not the same as 8 percent per year. The difference in the frequency of discounting gives a slightly different answer.

The Yield to Maturity of a Bond

Most investors want to know how much return they will earn on a bond to gauge whether the bond meets their expectations. That way, investors can tell whether they should add the bond to their investment portfolio. As a result, investors often calculate a bond's yield to maturity before they buy a bond. **Yield to maturity (YTM)** represents the average rate of return on a bond if all promised interest and principal payments are made on time and if the interest payments are reinvested at the YTM rate given the price paid for the bond.

Calculating a Bond's Yield to Maturity To calculate a bond's YTM, we apply the bond valuation model. However, we apply it differently than we did when solving for a bond's present value (price) because we solve for k_d, the equivalent of YTM.

To compute a bond's YTM, we must know the values of all variables except k_d. We take the market price of the bond, P_B, as the value of a bond, V_B, examining financial sources such as *The Globe and Mail* or *The Financial Post* for current bond prices.

Once you have all variables except k_d, solving for k_d algebraically is exceedingly difficult because that term appears three times in the valuation equation. Instead, we use the trial-and-error method. In other words, we guess a value for k_d and solve for V_B using that value. When we find a k_d value that results in a bond value that matches the published bond price, P_B, we know that the k_d value is the correct YTM. The YTM is the return that bond investors require to purchase the bond.[1]

Here's an illustration of the trial-and-error method for finding YTM. Suppose that *The Globe and Mail* reported that the BCE bond in our earlier example is currently selling for \$1,114.70. What is the bond's YTM if purchased at this price?

Recall the annual coupon interest payments for the BCE bond were \$70 each, the bond had a 20-year maturity, and a face value of \$1,000. Applying the bond valuation model, we solve for the k_d that produces a bond value of \$1,114.70.

$$\$1{,}114.70 = \$70 \times \left[\frac{1 - \dfrac{1}{(1+k_d)^{20}}}{k_d}\right] + \frac{1{,}000}{(1+k_d)^{20}}$$

Although we can try any k_d value, remember that when k was 8 percent, the bond's calculated value, V_B, was \$901.82. Bond prices and yields vary inversely—the higher the YTM, the lower the bond price; and the lower the YTM, the higher the bond price. The bond's current market price of \$1,114.70 is higher than \$901.82, so we know the YTM must be less than 8 percent. If you pay more than \$901.82 to buy the bond, your return will be less than 8 percent.

Because we know that YTM and bond prices are inversely related, let's try 7 percent in our bond valuation model, Equation 12-2. We find that a k_d value of 7 percent results in the following bond value:

$$\begin{aligned} V_B &= \$70 \times \left[\frac{1 - \dfrac{1}{(1+.007)^{20}}}{0.07}\right] + \frac{\$1{,}000}{(1+0.07)^{20}} \\ &= (\$70 \times 10.59401425) + \left(\frac{\$1{,}000}{3.86968446}\right) \\ &= \$741.5809975 + \$258.4190028 \\ &= \$1{,}000.00 \end{aligned}$$

---

[1]In Chapter 9, this required rate of return was called the firm's cost of debt capital, which we adjust for taxes. In this chapter, however, our main focus is finding the value of different types of securities, so k_d is referred to as the investor's required rate of return.

At a k_d of 7 percent, the bond's value is \$1,000 instead of \$1,114.70. We will need to try again. Our second guess should be lower than 7 percent because at $k_d = 7\%$ the bond's calculated value is lower than the market price. Let's try 6 percent. At a k_d of 6 percent, the bond's value is as follows:

$$V_B = \$70 \times \left[\frac{1 - \frac{1}{(1+0.06)^{20}}}{0.06}\right] + \frac{\$1,000}{(1+0.06)^{20}}$$

$$= (\$70 \times 11.46992122) + \left(\frac{\$1,000}{3.20713547}\right)$$

$$= \$802.8944853 + \$311.8047269$$

$$= \$1,114.70$$

With a k_d of 6 percent, the bond's value equals the current market price of \$1,114.70. We conclude that the bond's YTM is 6 percent.[2]

To use the table method to find the YTM of BCE's 7 percent coupon rate, 20-year bond at a price of \$1,114.70, use Equation 12-3 as follows:

First guess: $k_d = 7\%$:

$$V_B = (\$70 \times PVIFA_{7\%, 20 \text{ periods}}) + (\$1,000 \times PVIF_{7\%, 20 \text{ periods}})$$

$$= (\$70 \times 10.5940) + (\$1,000 \times 0.2584)$$

$$= \$741.58 + \$258.40$$

$$= \$999.98$$

\$999.98 is too low. We must guess again. Let's try $k_d = 6\%$, as follows:

$$V_B = (\$70 \times PVIFA_{6\%, 20 \text{ yrs}}) + (\$1,000 \times PVIF_{6\%, 20 \text{ years}})$$

$$= (\$70 \times 11.4699) + (\$1,000 \times 0.3118)$$

$$= \$802.893 + \$311.80$$

$$= \$1,114.69$$

Close enough (to \$1,114.70). The bond's YTM is about 6 percent.

Finding a bond's YTM with a financial calculator avoids the trial-and-error method. Simply plug in the values on the calculator and solve for k_d, as shown:

TI BAII PLUS FINANCIAL CALCULATOR SOLUTION

Step 1: Press 2nd CLR TVM to clear previous values.

Step 2: Press 2nd P/Y 1 ENTER , 2nd BGN , 2nd SET . Repeat 2nd SET until END shows in the display, 2nd QUIT to set to the annual interest rate mode and to set the annuity payment to end-of-period mode.

Step 3: Input the values and compute.

1,114.70 +/− PV 1000 FV 20 N 70 PMT CPT I/Y Answer: 6.00

---

[2]We were lucky to find the bond's exact YTM in only two guesses. Often the trial-and-error method requires four or five guesses.

Using the financial calculator, we find that the YTM of the BCE $1,000 face value 20-year bond with a coupon rate of 7 percent and a market price of $1,114.70 is 6 percent.

The Relationship between Bond YTM and Price

A bond's market price depends on its yield to maturity. When a bond has a YTM greater than its coupon rate, it sells at a *discount* from its face value. When the YTM is equal to the coupon rate, the market price equals the face value. When the YTM is less than the coupon rate, the bond sells at a *premium* over face value.

For instance, in our initial calculations of the BCE bond, we found that the present value of its future cash flows was $901.82. This price was lower than the bond's $1,000 face value. Because its market price was lower than its face value, the bond sold at a discount (from its face value). A bond will sell at a discount because buyers and sellers have agreed that the appropriate rate of return for the bond should be higher than the bond's coupon interest rate. With the BCE bond, investors required an 8 percent rate of return, but the fixed coupon interest rate was only 7 percent. To compensate for a coupon interest rate that is lower than the required rate, investors would be unwilling to pay the $1,000 face value. Instead, they would only be willing to pay $901.82 to buy the bond.

Now recall the trial-and-error calculations for the YTM of the BCE 7 percent coupon rate bond in the previous section. When the YTM was 7 percent, we found that the bond's price was $1,000. This was no coincidence. When the YTM is equal to the coupon interest rate—that is, when the bond is selling at *par*—the bond's price is equal to its face value. We saw that when would-be buyers and sellers of BCE's bond agree that the appropriate yield to maturity for the bond is 6 percent instead of 7 percent, the price is above $1,000.

The change from a 7 percent to a 6 percent YTM results in a market value of $1,114.70. This market value for the bond is higher than the $1,000 face value. Because the market price is higher than the bond's face value, in our case, the bond sells at a *premium*. Why? Investors pay more to receive "extra" interest because the coupon rate paid is higher than the YTM demanded.

In our example, the calculations show that investors were willing to pay $1,114.70 for a bond with a face value of $1,000 because the coupon interest was one percentage point higher than the required rate of return.

Figure 12-2 shows the relationship between YTM and the price of a bond.

The inverse relationship between bond price and YTM is important to bond traders. Why? Because if market YTM interest rates rise, bond prices fall. Conversely, if market YTM interest rates fall, bond prices rise. The suggestion that the Bank of Canada might raise interest rates is enough to send the bond market reeling as bond traders unload their holdings.

In this section, we examined bond valuation for bonds that pay annual and semiannual interest. We also investigated how to find a bond's yield to maturity and the relationship between a bond's YTM and its price. We turn next to preferred share valuation.

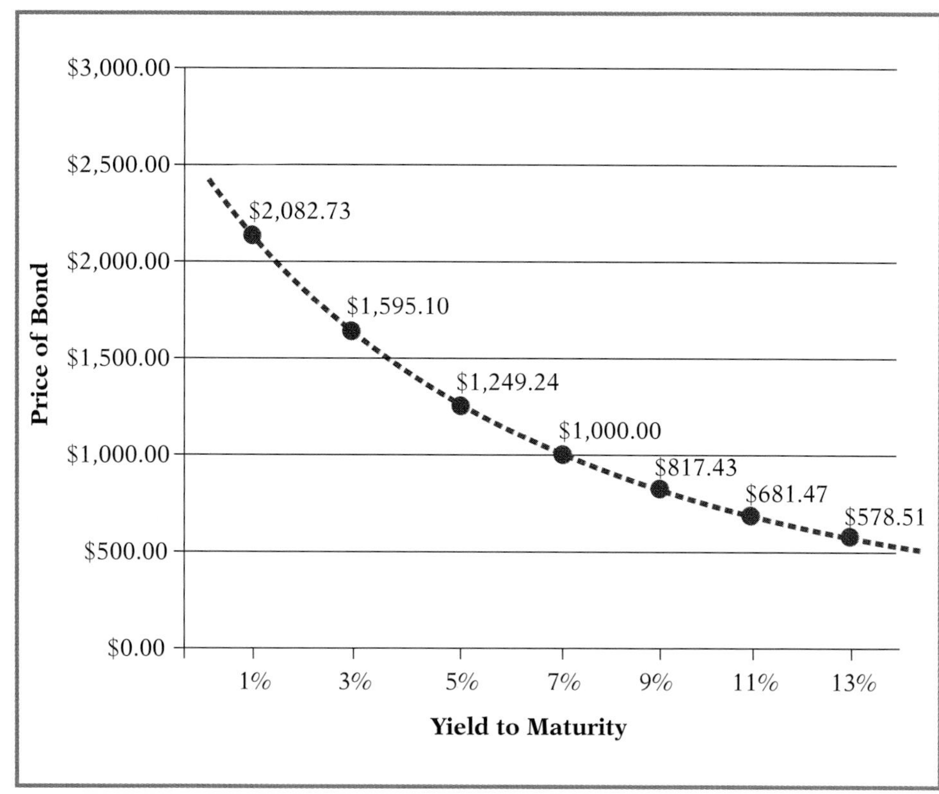

Figure 12-2
Bond YTM versus Bond Price
Figure 12-2 shows the inverse relationship between the price and the YTM for a $1,000 face value, 20-year, 7% coupon interest rate bond that pays annual interest.

Preferred Share Valuation

To value preferred shares, we adapt the discounted cash flow valuation formula, Equation 12-1, to reflect the characteristics of preferred shares. First, recall that the value of any security is the present value of its future cash payments. Second, review the characteristics of preferred shares. Preferred shares have no maturity date, so they have no maturity value. Their future cash payments are dividend payments that are paid to preferred shareholders at regular time intervals for as long as they (or their heirs) own the shares. Cash payments from preferred share dividends are scheduled to continue forever. To value preferred shares, then, we must adapt the discounted cash flow model to reflect that preferred share dividends are a perpetuity.

Finding the Present Value of Preferred Share Dividends

To calculate the value of preferred shares, we need to find the present value of their future cash flows—which are a perpetuity. In Chapter 8, we learned how to find the present value of a perpetuity. We use the formula for the present value of a perpetuity, Equation 8-5, but adapt the terms to reflect the nature of preferred shares.[3]

---

[3]Equation 8-5 is $PV = \frac{PMT}{k}$. In Equation 12-4, V_P substitutes for PV, D_p replaces PMT, and k_p replaces k.

The preferred share valuation calculations require that we find the present value (V_P) of preferred share dividends (D_p), discounted at the required rate of return, k_p. The formula for preferred share valuation follows:

The Formula for the Present Value of Preferred Shares

$$V_P = \frac{D_p}{k_p} \tag{12-4}$$

where

V_P = Current market value of the preferred shares
D_p = Amount of the preferred share dividend
k_p = Required rate of return for this issue of preferred shares

Let's apply Equation 12-4 to an example. Suppose investors expect an issue of preferred shares to pay an annual dividend of $2 per share. Investors in the market have evaluated the issuing company and the market conditions and have concluded that 10 percent is a fair rate of return on this investment. The present value for one preferred share, assuming a 10 percent required rate of return follows:

$$\begin{aligned} V_P &= \left(\frac{\$2}{0.10}\right) \\ &= \$20 \end{aligned}$$

We find that for investors whose required rate of return (k_p) is 10 percent, the value of each share of this issue of preferred shares is $20.

The Yield on Preferred Shares

Take Note

With bonds, an investor's annual percent return on investment is called the yield to maturity, or YTM. With preferred and common shares, an investor's percent return on investment is simply called the yield because preferred and common shares do not have a maturity date.

The yield on preferred shares represents the annual rate of return that investors would realize if they bought the preferred shares for the current market price and then received the promised preferred dividend payments.

Like bond investors, preferred share investors want to know the percentage yield that they can expect if they buy preferred shares at the current market price. That way, investors can compare the yield with the minimum they require to decide whether to invest in the preferred shares.

Fortunately, calculating the yield on preferred shares is considerably easier than calculating the YTM for a bond. To calculate the yield, we rearrange Equation 12-4 so that we solve for k_p. We are not solving for the value of the preferred shares, V_P, but rather are taking the market price of the preferred shares, P_p, as a given and solving for k_p as follows:

Formula for the Yield on Preferred Shares

$$k_P = \frac{D_p}{P_p} \tag{12-5}$$

where

k_p = Yield on investment that an investor can expect if the shares are purchased at the current market price, P_p, and if the preferred dividend, D_p, is paid forever

D_p = Amount of the preferred share dividend
P_p = Current market price of the preferred shares

To illustrate how to find the yield using Equation 12-5, suppose Sure-Thing Corporation's preferred shares are selling for $25 per share today and the dividend is $3 a share. Now assume you are a potential buyer of Sure-Thing's preferred shares, so you want to find the expected annual percent yield on your investment. You know that the current market value of the shares, P_p, is $25 and the dividend, D_p, is $3. Applying Equation 12-5, you calculate the yield as follows:

$$k_p = \frac{D_p}{P_p}$$

$$= \frac{\$3}{\$25}$$

$$= 0.12, \text{ or } 12\%$$

You find that the yield for Sure-Thing's preferred shares is 12 percent. If your minimum required rate of return is less than or equal to 12 percent, you would invest in the Sure-Thing preferred shares. If your required rate of return is greater than 12 percent, you would look for other preferred shares that had a yield of more than 12 percent.

Common Share Valuation

The valuation of common shares is somewhat different from the valuation of bonds and preferred shares. Common share valuation is complicated by the fact that common share dividends are difficult to predict compared with the interest and principal payments on a bond or dividends on preferred shares. Indeed, corporations may pay common share dividends irregularly or not pay dividends at all. Moreover, because owners of more than 50 percent of a corporation's share equity have control over the affairs of the business and can force their will, the value of a controlling interest of common shares is relatively more valuable than the value of one share. This means that different procedures must be used to value controlling interests (or total common shareholders' equity) than are used to value one share. Often, ownership of less than 50 percent of a corporation's common shares can result in control if the percentage owned is significant and if the remaining shares are widely dispersed among investors not working in concert with each other.

In the sections that follow, we examine the most popular methods of valuing individual common shares. We will then illustrate how these methods are applied to the valuation of total common shareholders' equity.

Valuing Individual Common Shares

As with bonds and preferred shares, we value individual common shares by estimating the present value of the expected future cash flows from the common shares. Those future cash flows are the expected future dividends and the expected price of the shares when the shares are sold. The discounted cash flow valuation model, Equation 12-1, adapted for common shares is shown in Equation 12-6:

The DCF Valuation Model Applied to Common Shares

$$P_0 = \frac{D_1}{(1+k_s)^1} + \frac{D_2}{(1+k_s)^2} + \frac{D_3}{(1+k_s)^3} + \cdots + \frac{P_n}{(1+k_s)^n} \qquad (12\text{-}6)$$

where

P_0 = Present value of the expected dividends, the current price per share of the common shares

D_1, D_2, D_3, etc. = Common share dividends expected to be received at the end of periods 1, 2, 3, and so on until the shares are sold

P_n = Anticipated selling price of the shares in n periods

k_s = Required rate of return on this common share investment

In practice, however, using Equation 12-6 to value common shares is problematic because an estimate of the future selling price of a common share is often speculative. This severely limits the usefulness of the model.

Instead, some analysts use models that are a variation of Equation 12-6 that do not rely on an estimate of a share's future selling price. We turn to those models next.

The Constant Growth Dividend Model Common share dividends can grow at different rates. The two growth patterns we examine here are constant growth and nonconstant, or supernormal, growth.

The constant growth dividend model assumes common share dividends will be paid regularly and grow at a constant rate. The constant growth dividend model (also known as the Gordon growth model because financial economist Myron Gordon helped develop and popularize it) is shown in Equation 12-7:

The Constant Growth Version of the Dividend Valuation Model

$$P_0 = \frac{D_1}{k_s - g} \qquad (12\text{-}7)$$

where

P_0 = Current price per share of the common shares

D_1 = Dollar amount of the common share dividend expected one period from now

k_s = Required rate of return per period on this common share investment

g = Expected constant growth rate per period of the company's common share dividends

Equation 12-7 is easy to use if the share dividends grow at a constant rate. For example, assume your required rate of return (k_s) for WestJet's common shares is 10 percent. Suppose your research leads you to believe that WestJet will pay a \$0.25 dividend in one year (D_1) and, for every year after the dividend, will grow at a constant rate (g) of 8 percent a year. Using Equation 12-7, we calculate the present value of WestJet's common share dividends as follows:

$$P_0 = \frac{\$0.25}{0.10 - 0.08}$$
$$= \frac{\$0.25}{0.02}$$
$$= \$12.50$$

We find that with a common share dividend in one year of $0.25, a constant growth rate of 8 percent, and a required rate of return of 10 percent, the value of the common shares is $12.50 per share.

In a no-growth situation, g, in the denominator of Equation 12-7 becomes zero. To value shares that have no growth is particularly easy because the value is simply the expected dividend (D_1) divided by k_s.

The Nonconstant, or Supernormal, Growth Model In addition to the constant growth dividend cash flow pattern that we discussed in the previous section, some companies have very high growth rates, known as supernormal growth of the cash flows. Valuing the common shares of such companies presents a special problem because high growth rates cannot be sustained indefinitely. A young high-technology firm may be able to grow at a 40 percent rate per year for a few years, but this growth must slow down because it is not sustainable given the population and productivity growth rates. In fact, if the firm's growth rate did not slow down, its sales would surpass the gross domestic product of the entire nation over time. Why? The company has a 40 percent growth rate that will compound annually, whereas the gross domestic product may grow at a 4 percent compounded average annual growth rate.

The constant growth dividend model for common shares, Equation 12-7, then, must be adjusted for those cases in which a company's dividend grows at a supernormal rate that will not be sustained over time. We do this by dividing the projected dividend cash flow stream of the common shares into two parts: the initial supernormal growth period and the next period in which normal and sustainable growth is expected. We then calculate the present value of the dividends during the fast-growth time period first. Then we solve for the present value of the dividends during the constant growth period that is a perpetuity. The sum of these two present values determines the current value of the shares.

To illustrate, suppose Supergrowth Corporation is expected to pay an annual dividend of $2 per share one year from now and that this dividend will grow at a 30 percent annual rate during each of the following four years (taking us to the end of year 5). After this supernormal growth period, the dividend will grow at a sustainable 5 percent rate each year beyond year 5. The cash flows are shown in Figure 12-3.

The valuation of a share of Supergrowth Corporation's common shares is described in the following three steps.

Step 1: Add the present values of the dividends during the supernormal growth period. Assume that the required rate of return, k_s, is 14 percent.

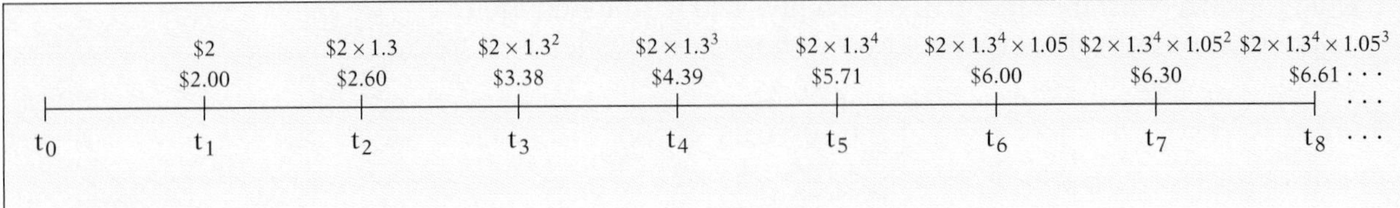

Figure 12-3 Timeline of Supergrowth Common Share Dividend with Initial Supernormal Growth

$$\begin{aligned} \$2.00 \times 1/1.14 &= \$\,1.75 \\ \$2.60 \times 1/1.14^2 &= \$\,2.00 \\ \$3.38 \times 1/1.14^3 &= \$\,2.28 \\ \$4.39 \times 1/1.14^4 &= \$\,2.60 \\ \$5.71 \times 1/1.14^5 &= \underline{\$\,2.97} \\ \Sigma &= \$11.60 \end{aligned}$$

Step 2: Calculate the sum of the present values of the dividends during the normal growth period, from t_6 through infinity in this case. To do this, pretend for a moment that t_6 is t_1. The present value of the dividend growing at the constant rate of 5 percent to perpetuity could be computed using Equation 12-7.

$$P_0 = \frac{D_1}{k_s - g}$$

Substituting our values, we would have:

$$P_0 = \frac{\$6}{0.14 - 0.05} = \$66.67$$

Because the $6.00 dividend actually occurs at t_6 instead of t_1, the $66.67 figure is not a t_0 value but rather a t_5 value.

It, therefore, needs to be discounted back five years at our required rate of return of 14 percent. This gives us $\$66.67 \times 1/1.14^5 = \$34.63$. The result of $34.63 is the present value of the dividends from the end of year 6 through infinity.

Step 3: Finally we add the present values of the dividends from the supernormal growth period and the normal growth period. In our example, we add $11.60 + $34.63 = $46.23. The sum of $46.23 is the appropriate market price of Supergrowth Corporation's common shares, given the projected dividends and the 14 percent required rate of return on those dividends.

The P/E Model Many investment analysts use the price to earnings, or P/E, ratio to value common shares. As we discussed in Chapter 6, the P/E ratio is the price per share of common shares divided by the company's earnings per share:

The P/E Ratio

$$\text{P/E ratio} = \frac{\text{Price per Share}}{\text{Earnings per Share}}$$

The P/E ratio indicates how much investors are willing to pay for each dollar of a firm's earnings per share. So, a P/E ratio of 20 means that investors are willing to pay $20 for $1 of a firm's earnings. A high P/E ratio indicates that investors believe the firm's earnings per share will increase, or that the risk of the shares is low, or both.

Financial analysts often use a P/E model to estimate common share value for businesses that are not public. First, analysts compare the P/E ratios of similar companies within an industry to determine an appropriate P/E ratio for companies in that industry. Second, analysts calculate an appropriate share price for firms in the industry by multiplying each firm's earnings per share (EPS) by the industry average P/E ratio. The P/E model formula, Equation 12-8, follows:

The P/E Model

$$\text{Appropriate Share Price} = \text{Industry P/E Ratio} \times \text{EPS} \qquad (12\text{-}8)$$

To illustrate how to apply the P/E model, let's value the common shares of the Zumwalt Corporation. Suppose that Zumwalt Corporation has current earnings per share of $2 and, given the risk and growth prospects of the firm, the analyst has determined that the company's common shares should sell for 15 times current earnings. Applying the P/E model, we calculate the following price for Zumwalt Corporation's common shares:

$$\begin{aligned}\text{Appropriate Share Price} &= \text{Industry P/E Ratio} \times \text{EPS} \\ &= 15 \times \$2 \\ &= \$30\end{aligned}$$

Our P/E model calculations show that $30 per share is the appropriate price for common shares for a company that has a $2 earnings per share and an industry P/E ratio of 15. The industry P/E ratio would be adjusted up or down according to the individual firm's growth prospects and risk relative to the industry norm.

Valuing Total Common Shareholders' Equity

As we said earlier, different procedures must be used to value total common shareholders' equity than are used to value one common share. The primary reason for this is that owners of some large percentage of a corporation's shares have control over the affairs of the business and can force their will on the remaining shareholders. This makes the value of a controlling interest of common shares relatively more valuable than a noncontrolling interest. Therefore, to value controlling interests of common shares, or total shareholders' equity, we must use models that account for this "control premium." In the sections that follow, we examine the most popular methods of valuing total shareholders' equity.

Book Value One of the simplest ways to value total common shareholders' equity is to subtract the value of the firm's liabilities and preferred shares, if any, as recorded on the balance sheet from the value of its assets. The result is the **book value** or **net worth**.

Book Value of Common Equity

$$\text{Book Value of Common Equity} = \text{Total Assets} - \text{Total Liabilities} - \text{Preferred Share Equity} \qquad (12\text{-}9)$$

The book value approach has severe limitations. The asset values recorded on a firm's balance sheet usually reflect what the current owners originally paid for the assets, not the current market value of the assets. Due to these and other limitations, the book value is rarely used to estimate the market value of common equity.

Liquidation Value The liquidation value and book value valuation methods are similar, except that the liquidation method uses the market values of the assets and liabilities, not book values, as in Equation 12-9. The market values of the assets are the amounts the assets would earn on the open market if they were sold (or liquidated). The market values of the liabilities are the amounts of money it would take to pay off the liabilities.

The **liquidation value** is the amount each common shareholder would receive if the firm closed, sold all assets and paid off all liabilities and preferred shares, and distributed the net proceeds to the common shareholders.

Although more reliable than book value, liquidation value is a worst-case valuation assessment. A company's common shares should be worth at least the amount generated at liquidation. Because liquidation value does not consider the earnings and cash flows the firm will generate in the future, it may provide misleading results for companies that have significant future earning potential.

The Free Cash Flow DCF Model

The Free Cash Flow DCF Model is very similar to the nonconstant, or supernormal, dividend growth model discussed earlier but, instead of discounting dividend cash flows, the free cash flow model discounts the total cash flows that would flow to the suppliers of the firm's capital. Once the present value of those cash flows is determined, liabilities and preferred shares (if any) are subtracted to arrive at the present value of common shareholders' equity.

Free Cash Flows Free cash flows represent the total cash flows from business operations that flow to the suppliers of a firm's capital each year. In forecasts, free cash flows are calculated as follows:

Cash Revenues
– Cash Expenses
= Earnings before Interest, Taxes, and Amortization (EBITA)
– Amortization
= Earnings before Interest and Taxes (EBIT)
– Federal and Provincial Income Taxes
= Net Operating Profit After Tax (NOPAT)
+ Add Back Amortization
– Capital Expenditures
– New Net Working Capital
= Free Cash Flow

Free cash flow represents those amounts in each operating period that are "free" to be distributed to the suppliers of the firm's capital—that is, the debt holders, the preferred shareholders, and the common shareholders. In the previous calculation, you can see that free cash flow is the amount remaining after cash expenses, income taxes, capital expenditures, and new net working capital are subtracted from cash revenues.

An Example.

Let us assume that the time now is July 5, 2005 and you work for a firm that is interested in acquiring Canada Drugs Limited (CDL), a Canadian pharmaceutical company. In support of the acquisition analysis, you have been asked to prepare an estimate of the market value of the firm's common equity. The methodology you have chosen is the discounted free cash flow model.

Following a lengthy analysis of the pharmaceutical market and Canada Drugs' financial statements, you produce the discounted free cash flow forecast and valuation shown in Figure 12-4. In the following paragraphs, we explain the procedure. The forecasting variables that form the basis for the valuation are listed at the top of Figure 12-4 (these are the product of your lengthy analysis). For convenience, we have numbered each line in the figure at the left-hand side.

The "Actual 2005" column in Figure 12-4 contains CD's operating results for the fiscal year ended March 31, 2005. The remaining columns contain the forecast for the next 10 years. Note that the Actual 2005 column is not included in the calculation of the total present value of company operations because these financial results have already occurred and are not future cash flows.

Product revenues (line 12) are expected to accelerate from 30 to 60 percent annual growth over four years, with the growth rate decreasing 10 percentage points a year after that until the tenth year of the forecast when revenue growth settles out at an expected long-term growth rate of 5 percent a year (the growth factor is on line 1). Funded research and development revenue (line 13), on the other hand, is expected to decrease 50 percent a year until it is almost negligible after 10 years (the growth factor is on line 2). These factors produce total revenues (line 14) exceeding \$143 million in 2010 and \$358 million in 2015.

Direct costs of revenues on line 15 are a function of the expected gross profit margin on line 3. In CD's forecast, 2005's gross margin of 70 percent is extended for each year through 2015. This produces gross profits (see line 16) ranging from just over \$21 million in 2006 to over \$251 million in 2015. Given the forecasted gross profit figures, direct costs on line 15 are "plugged" by subtracting gross profit from total revenues.

Research and development expenses (line 17) are expected to grow by 10 percent in 2006 and then to decrease by 10 percent a year through 2015. Selling, general, and administrative expenses (line 18) are forecast as a percentage of revenue, starting at 38 percent of revenue in 2006 (the same percentage as in 2005) and declining to 34 percent in 2015. Subtracting these operating expenses from gross profit leaves earnings before interest, taxes, and amortization (EBITA on line 19) of negative \$15.197 million in 2006, positive \$13.988 million in 2009, and positive \$118.344 million in 2015.

Although they are noncash expenses, amortization is included in discounted free cash flow forecasts in order to calculate income tax expense. In the case of Canada Drugs, amortization expense (line 20) is forecast to be 10 percent of revenue each year. Subtracting amortization expense from EBITA produces earnings before interest and taxes (EBIT), also known as operating income (see line 21).

Figure 12-4 Discounted Free Cash Flow Forecast and Valuation

Canada Drugs Limited

Discounted Free Cash Flow Forecast and Valuation
(In Thousands)

Forecasting Variables

Line		Actual 2005	2006	20
1	Product revenue growth factor	20%	30%	4
2	Research revenue growth factor		–50%	–5
3	Expected gross profit margin	70%	70%	7
4	R&D expense growth factor		10%	–1
5	S, G, & A expense % of revenue	38%	38%	3
6	Amort. % of revenue	12%	10%	1
7	Capital expenditure growth factor		10%	–1
8	Net working capital to sales ratio		10%	1
9	Income tax rate	40%		
10	Assumed long-term sustainable growth rate	5% per year		
11	Discount rate	20%		

Forecast and Valuation

Line		Actual 2005	2006	20
12	Product revenue	$22,017	$28,580	$39,
13	Funded research and development revenue	2,879	1,440	[illegible]
14	**Total Revenue**	**24,896**	**30,020**	**40,6**
15	Direct costs	7,375	9,006	12,
16	**Gross profit**	**17,521**	**21,014**	**28,4**
17	Research and development expenses	22,671	24,938	22,
18	Selling, general, and administrative expenses	9,443	11,273	15,
19	**Earnings before interest, taxes, & amortization (EBITA)**	**(14,593)**	**(15,197)**	**(9,**
20	Amortization	2,968	3,002	4,
21	**Earnings before interest and taxes (EBIT)**	**(17,561)**	**(18,199)**	**(13,**
22	Available tax-loss carryforwards	(51,857)	(69,418)	(87,
23	Net taxable earnings	0	0	
24	Federal and provincial income taxes	0	0	
25	**Net operating profit after tax (NOPAT)**	**(17,561)**	**(18,199)**	**(13,**
26	Add back amortization	2,968	3,002	4,
27	Subtract capital expenditures	(2,555)	(2,811)	(2,
28	Subtract new net working capital		(656)	(1,
29	**Free cash flow**	**($17,148)**	**($18,664)**	**($12,**
30	**Terminal value, 2015**			
31	Present value of free cash flows @ 20%		(15,553)	(8,
32	**Total present value of company operations**	**$158,637**		
33	Plus current assets	106,966		
34	Less current liabilities	(8,967)		
35	Less long-term debt	(368)		
36	Less preferred shares	0		
37	**Net market value of common equity**	**$256,268**		

--------	--------	Forecast	--------	--------	--------	--------	--------
008	**2009**	**2010**	**2011**	**2012**	**2013**	**2014**	**2015**
50%	60%	50%	40%	30%	20%	10%	5%
50%	–50%	–50%	–50%	–50%	–50%	–50%	–50%
70%	70%	70%	70%	70%	70%	70%	70%
10%	–10%	–10%	–10%	–10%	–10%	–10%	–10%
37%	36%	36%	36%	35%	35%	35%	34%
10%	10%	10%	10%	10%	10%	10%	10%
0%	–10%	–10%	–10%	–10%	–10%	–10%	–10%
10%	10%	10%	10%	10%	10%	10%	10%

Years Ending March 31

--------	--------	Forecast	--------	--------	--------	--------	--------
008	**2009**	**2010**	**2011**	**2012**	**2013**	**2014**	**2015**
859	$95,659	$143,304	$200,350	$260,069	$311,582	$342,140	$358,588
360	180	90	45	23	12	6	3
219	**95,839**	**143,394**	**200,395**	**260,092**	**311,594**	**342,146**	**358,591**
066	28,752	43,018	60,119	78,028	93,478	102,644	107,577
153	**67,087**	**100,376**	**140,276**	**182,064**	**218,116**	**239,502**	**251,014**
200	18,180	16,362	14,726	13,253	11,928	10,735	9,662
163	34,919	51,723	71,561	91,950	109,056	118,552	123,008
210)	**13,988**	**32,291**	**53,989**	**76,861**	**97,132**	**110,215**	**118,344**
022	9,584	14,339	20,040	26,009	31,159	34,215	35,859
232)	**4,404**	**17,952**	**33,949**	**50,852**	**65,973**	**76,000**	**82,485**
777)	(107,009)	(102,605)	(84,653)	(50,704)			
0	0	0	0	148	65,973	76,000	82,485
0	0	0	0	59	26,389	30,400	32,994
232)	**4,404**	**17,952**	**33,949**	**50,793**	**39,584**	**45,600**	**49,491**
022	9,584	14,339	20,040	26,009	31,159	34,215	35,859
277)	(2,049)	(1,844)	(1,660)	(1,494)	(1,345)	(1,211)	(1,090)
990)	(3,580)	(4,765)	(5,705)	(5,972)	(5,151)	(3,056)	(1,645)
477)	**$8,359**	**$25,682**	**$46,624**	**$69,336**	**$64,247**	**$75,548**	**$82,615**
							$578,305
591)	4,031	10,321	15,614	19,350	14,942	14,642	106,742

As shown in Figure 12-4, line 22, Canada Drugs has $51.857 million in tax-loss carryforwards at the beginning of 2005. Operating income was a negative $17.561 million in 2005, so $51.857 million + $17.561 million = $69.418 million in tax-loss carryforwards are available at the beginning of 2006. This situation continues until 2012, when the carryforwards are finally used up, and Canada Drugs reports $148,000 in net taxable earnings. After 2012, operating income is fully taxable.

The forecast assumes a combined federal and provincial income tax rate of 40 percent (see line 9). Applying this rate to CD's net taxable earnings (line 23) in 2012, 2013, 2014, and 2015, and $0 to the earlier years, produces the income tax expenses shown on line 24. Subtracting taxes from EBIT produces the company's net operating profit after tax (NOPAT on line 25), which is negative $18.199 million in 2006 rising to positive $49.491 million in 2015.

Once NOPAT has been determined, three further adjustments are necessary to calculate free cash flow. First, on line 26, amortization is added back to NOPAT because these noncash items were subtracted earlier only for the purpose of calculating income tax expense. Next, on line 27, expected capital expenditures are subtracted. Capital expenditures are amounts expected to be spent to procure new plant and equipment. For this forecast, we assume that your research indicates that Canada Drugs will need to spend 10 percent more on plant and equipment in 2006 than it did in 2005 (see line 7), and that this spending may be decreased 10 percent a year in each year after 2006. The resulting capital expenditure budget, shown in Figure 12-4, line 27, peaks at $2.811 million in 2006 and gradually decreases to just over $1.0 million in 2015.

Finally, on line 28, new net working capital investment is subtracted. Net working capital is the difference between current assets and current liabilities that must be financed from long-term capital sources (debt and equity). When businesses grow, they typically need more working capital in the form of cash, inventory, and receivables and not all of it can be financed spontaneously from current liabilities. For this reason, the company's long-term debt and equity holders must invest additional amounts each year to "take up the slack." In the case of Canada Drugs, we will assume that your research indicates that the typical ratio of net working capital to sales in the pharmaceutical industry is 10 percent (see line 8). In other words, for every $10 of new sales a company realizes, $1 of new net working capital will be needed. In Figure 12-4, line 28, this is calculated by multiplying the difference in product revenue each year by 0.10. In 2006, for example, ($28,580 –$22,017) × 0.10 and rounded to even thousands = $656,000 of new net working capital is needed. The remaining years are calculated similarly.

After all the calculations have been completed, the resulting figures on line 29 represent amounts that are free to be distributed to the suppliers of Canada Drug's capital, either in the form of interest to the debt holders or dividends to the shareholders. These free cash flows range from negative $18.664 million in 2006 to positive $82.615 million in 2015.

In the previous paragraphs, we explicitly forecast the free cash flows for 2006 through 2015. However, what about the years after that? After all, Canada Drugs is not expected to suddenly cease operating at the end of 2015 but to continue operating indefinitely into the future as a going concern.

To forecast the free cash flows in the years beyond 2015, we rely on a variation of the constant growth dividend valuation model, Equation 12-7. After

2015, Canada Drug's free cash flows are expected to grow at a constant rate of 5 percent a year indefinitely. We adapt Equation 12-7 to value these constantly growing free cash flows as follows:

Constant Growth Free Cash Flow Valuation Model

$$V_{fcf\,t} = \frac{FCF_t(1+g)}{k-g} \tag{12-10}$$

where

$V_{fcf\,t}$ = Value of future free cash flows at time t
FCF_t = Free cash flow at time t
k = Discount rate
g = Long-term constant growth rate of free cash flows

According to Equation 12-10, and assuming a discount rate of 20 percent (see line 11),[4] the value as of the end of 2015 of CD's free cash flows in years 2016 and beyond, in thousands, would be:

$$V_{fcf\,2015} = \frac{\$82,615(1+0.05)}{0.20-0.05}$$

$$V_{fcf\,2015} = \$578,305$$

The value of the free cash flows at the end of 2015 and beyond is called the **terminal value** of the company's operations at the end of 2015. The amount is shown in Figure 12-4 on line 30.

On line 31, the present value of the free cash flows is calculated using Equation 8-2a, assuming a discount rate of 20 percent. The present values are then summed up on line 32 to produce the total value of CD's operations on July 5, 2005, which is $158.637 million.

Let us say a few words about this value before proceeding. As we said earlier, the present value of the company's free cash flows ($158.637 million in the case of Canada Drugs) represents the market value of the firm's core income-producing operations. In the world of finance and investing, this is sometimes called the firm's *enterprise value.* It is NOT the total market value of the entire company, however, or the total market value of the company's assets because the current, or nonoperating, assets of the company have not yet been accounted for.

We shall have more to say about this issue later in the chapter in the section on valuing complete businesses. For now, just remember that the present value of the company's free cash flows equals the market value of the firm's core income-producing operations (called enterprise value). The relationship is illustrated in Figure 12-5.

In the analysis in Figure 12-4, we have calculated the market value of Canada Drugs' operating, or income-producing assets, as shown in the lower-left portion of Figure 12-5. Observing Figure 12-5, it is clear that to obtain the

---

[4]The discount rate represents the weighted average required rates of return of Canada Drug's debt holders and common shareholders. Calculating this weighted average return was discussed in detail in Chapter 9.

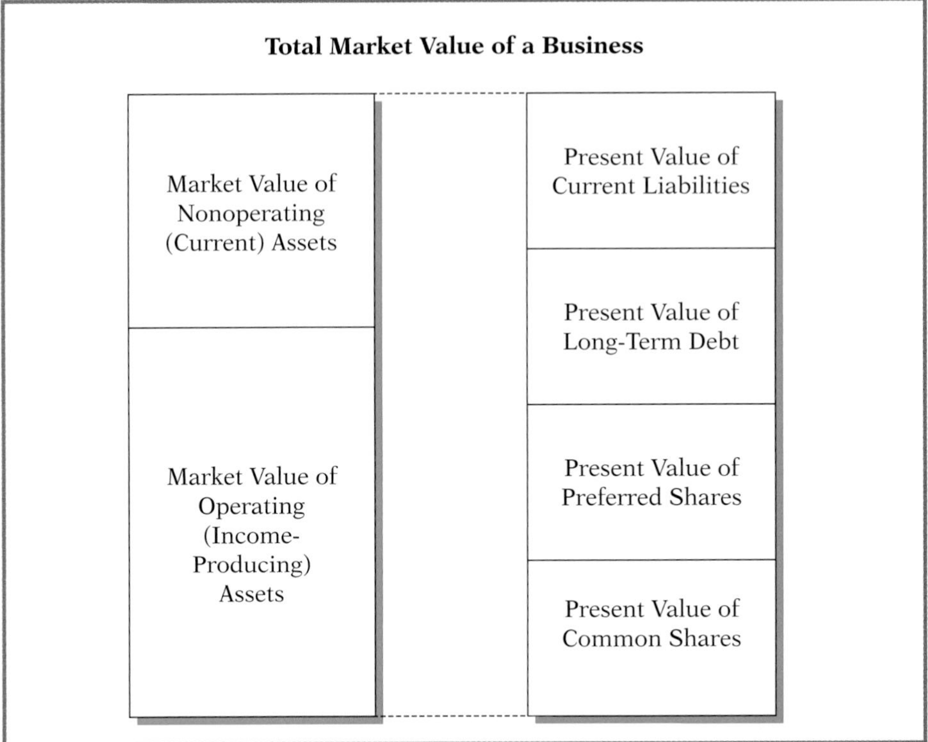

Figure 12-5
Total Market Value of a Business
This figure is an extension of Figure 12-1, showing how total assets are made up of operating (income-producing) assets plus nonoperating (current) assets.

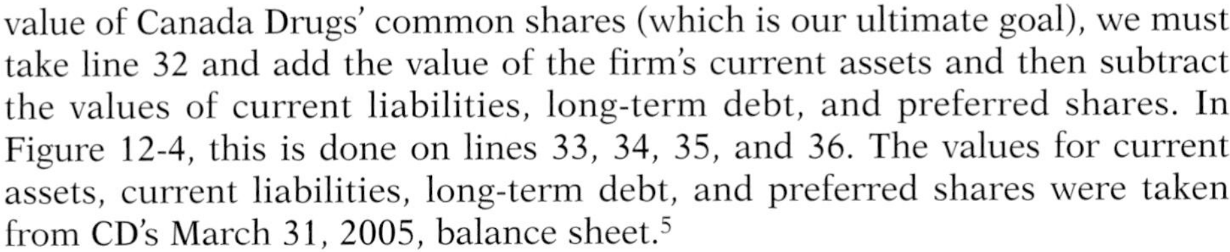

value of Canada Drugs' common shares (which is our ultimate goal), we must take line 32 and add the value of the firm's current assets and then subtract the values of current liabilities, long-term debt, and preferred shares. In Figure 12-4, this is done on lines 33, 34, 35, and 36. The values for current assets, current liabilities, long-term debt, and preferred shares were taken from CD's March 31, 2005, balance sheet.[5]

Line 37 of Figure 12-4 shows the final result after adding Canada Drugs' current assets ($106.966 million) and subtracting current liabilities ($8.967 million), long-term debt ($0.368 million), and preferred shares ($0) from the present value of the firm's operations ($158.637 million). This final result, $256.268 million, is the total market value of Canada Drugs' common equity as of March 31, 2005.[6]

Take Note

Do not confuse the market value of CD's common equity, as calculated here, with the actual price of the firm's common shares on the open market. The $256.268 million is what the company's shares are worth to an investor with a required rate of return of 20 percent a year, given the assumptions in the model in Figure 12-4. Stock traders in the market may be making any number of different assumptions about Canada Drugs and may have different required rates of return. As a result, the actual price of Canada Drugs' shares in the market may be completely different than the *intrinsic* value shown here.[7]

---

[5] To be precise, we should have calculated the *market* values of CD's current assets, current liabilities, and long-term debt before making the adjustments. In practice, however, the book values from the balance sheet are often used instead because the process of valuing the items is difficult and the market values often do not differ materially from the book values.

[6] Ideally we would like to have valued Canada Drugs as of July 5, 2005. However, this would require incorporating quarterly data and fractional years into the forecast. To keep things simple, we stayed with annual data and valued the company as of the date of its most recent balance sheet.

[7] Let's assume that Canada Drugs' shares closed at $15.75 on our valuation date of March 31, 2005, which equates to a total common equity value of $327.138 million, not including a control premium. This is $70.870 million higher than the $256.268 million estimated by our model. Could investors have been overcome by speculative fever on that date? We leave that for you to decide.

The Yield on Common Shares

We calculate the yield for common shares by rearranging the terms in Equation 12-7 to arrive at the constant growth dividend model, as shown in Equation 12-11:

The Yield, or Total Return, on Common Shares

$$k_s = \frac{D_1}{P_0} + g \tag{12-11}$$

where

D_1 = Amount of the common share dividend anticipated in one period

P_0 = Current market price of the common shares

g = Expected constant growth rate of dividends per period

k_s = Expected rate of return per period on this common share investment

Equation 12-11 is also called the formula for an investor's total rate of return from common shares. The share's **dividend yield** is the term D_1/P_0.

To demonstrate how Equation 12-11 works, suppose you found that the price of Telus common shares today was \$52 per share, significantly above its current price. Then suppose you believe that Telus will pay a common dividend next year of \$4.80 a share, and the dividend will grow each year at a constant annual rate of 4 percent. If you buy one share of Telus common shares at the listed price of \$52, your expected annual percent yield on your investment will be:

$$\begin{aligned} k_s &= \frac{D_1}{P_0} + g \\ &= \frac{\$4.80}{\$52} + 0.04 \\ &= 0.0923 + 0.04 \\ &= 0.1323 \text{ or } 13.23\% \end{aligned}$$

If your minimum required rate of return for Telus common shares, considering its risk, were less than 13.23 percent, you would proceed with the purchase. Otherwise you would look for another firm that had an expected return appropriate for its level of risk.

By now you have learned how to perform a discounted cash flow valuation. We used this valuation technique for a company that generated cash flows and had assets and liabilities. Let us imagine for a moment that we are looking at a business, maybe an Internet-based business, which does not have any trading history and no profits. In such circumstances, how would we approach a valuation of such a business? International Perspectives in Finance 12-1 discusses an approach that may be used for valuing Internet or new technology companies.

INTERNATIONAL PERSPECTIVES IN FINANCE 12-1

What Is It Worth? Learning How to Value Internet Stocks

How does one figure out how much an Internet company is worth? Valuation is the underlying principle of investing. The stock market is a mechanism to determine the appropriate value of a company. In the long term, it has proved to be a pretty reliable mechanism. In the short term, it frequently makes mistakes. The smartest investor is the one who can recognize and buy stocks trading at less than their true value and sell them at or above their true value. But if you have no idea what that underlying value is, you're flying blind.

Remember that the price of a share of stock isn't cheap or expensive in a vacuum. A $3 share of company X isn't necessarily "cheaper" than a $50 share of company Y; it depends on how many shares of stock are outstanding and on what annual earnings are in the pipeline. How can we estimate those earnings? There are a number of more or less complicated methods, but the quickest way to get a rough idea is to follow these three steps:

1. Determine the size of the overall market the company is going after—say $4 billion a year in sales.
2. Multiply that by the company's market share (current or expected)—say 25 percent to determine its potential revenue (in this case, $1 billion).
3. Multiply the potential revenue by the amount of money t company earns on each dollar of revenue, the "profit ma gin," such as 21 percent. The result is the potential prc (here, $210 million).

The next step is to look at the company's "price-to-ear ings ratio," a measure of how highly other investors value t stock. Take the stock price, divide it by the company's p share profit—overall earnings divided by the number of shar outstanding—and you have the P/E ratio. Comparing a co pany's P/E with rivals or the overall market is a commonly us way to decide if a stock is cheap on a relative basis.

What if you do all these calculations and the stock s seems expensive? Does that mean you should rule out bu ing it? Not necessarily. If you have years to go before reti ment, you might take it on faith that the company will "gr into" the valuation the market has bestowed on it.

Note: This is excerpted from "NetWorth" by Stephen E. (Steve) Frank, who writes the "Playing the Net" column for *The Wall Stre Journal Sunday*. Mr. Frank is a Journal reporter who also appear on CNBC.

Source: interactive.wsj.com/archive/retrieve.cgi?id= SB991322512288946127.djm (June 8, 2001).

VALUING COMPLETE BUSINESSES

Up to this point in the chapter, we have dealt with the values of business components as shown in the right-hand "pillar" in Figure 12-1. Now we turn our attention to valuing the complete business all at once, or the total value of the business's assets as shown in the left-hand "pillar" in Figure 12-1.

The Free Cash Flow DCF Model Applied to a Complete Business

As it turns out, using the Free Cash Flow Model to value a complete business is quite straightforward once you have learned how to use it to value common share equity. This is because the Free Cash Flow Model values the complete business as a part of the procedure to value common share equity. Refer again to Figure 12-5, which shows that the value of a complete business is the sum of the values of the operating, or income-producing, assets plus the value of the nonoperating, or current, assets. All that is necessary to use the Free Cash Flow Model to value a complete business is to add the value of the company's operations, calculated exactly the same way as in Figure 12-4 for Canada Drugs, to the value of the company's current assets, taken from the most recent balance sheet.[8] Following this procedure, the complete business value for Canada Drugs would be:

Present value of company operations (or *enterprise value*)	\$158.637 million
+ Value of current assets	106.966 million
= Complete business value of Canada Drugs (see Figure 12-4, lines 32 and 33)	\$265.603 million

The Replacement Value of Assets Method

The replacement value of assets valuation method is similar to the liquidation model covered earlier in the chapter. According to the concept underlying the model, the market value of a complete business cannot exceed the amount it would take to buy all of the firm's assets on the open market. For example, you would not be willing to pay the owners of Canada Drugs \$265.603 million for the company if you could buy all the assets necessary to duplicate the company for \$200 million.

Although it is simple in concept, the replacement value of assets method is not often applied to complete business valuations for two reasons:

1. It is frequently very difficult to locate similar assets for sale on the open market.
2. Some of a business's assets are difficult to define and quantify. (How do you quantify a business's reputation, for example, or the strength of its brands?)

Although it is difficult to use the replacement value of assets method to value a complete business, the model can be quite useful for estimating the value of individual assets in a business. For example, the value of a company's nonproprietary software can be estimated by listing the various programs in use and then noting the prices of those programs in retail stores, catalogues, and on the Internet. The sum of the lowest prices at which the programs could be obtained is the replacement value of the company's software. In another example, it is possible to estimate the value of a company's machinery and equipment by calculating what it would cost to replace all the machinery and equipment. This is normally done by noting the prices for machinery and equipment of similar age and in similar condition on the open market. Alternatively, analysts sometimes note the prices of new machinery and equipment and adjust those prices to reflect the age and condition of the machinery and equipment belonging to the company.

Individual asset valuations of this type are most often employed when one business buys another and it is necessary to allocate the purchase price among the assets purchased. In such cases, the "fair market value" of the individual assets is estimated (using the replacement value of assets method, the discounted free cash flow method, or some other method) and any amounts remaining are assigned to "goodwill."

[8]As we said earlier, to be precise, one should use the *market* value of the current assets rather than the book value from the balance sheet. However, because estimating the market value of the current assets is time-consuming and the results are often not materially different from the book value, many analysts simply use the book value in their complete business valuations.

SUMMARY

12-1 Explain the importance of business valuation.

When corporations contemplate selling their businesses, they do not want to undervalue the businesses because they want to raise the most money possible. Likewise, would-be purchasers of businesses use valuation methods to avoid paying more than the businesses are worth.

12-2 Discuss the concept of business valuation.

To value any business, business asset, or security, we apply risk and return and time value of money techniques. In sum, the value of a business, asset, or security is the present value of the expected future cash flows. Bond cash flows are the periodic interest payments and the principal at maturity. Common share and business cash flows come from the future earnings that the assets produce for the firm, usually leading to cash dividend payments.

To value businesses, assets, and securities, investors and financial managers use a general valuation model to calculate the present value of the expected future cash flows. This model incorporates risk and return and the time value of money concepts.

12-3 Describe how to compute the market value and the yield to maturity of a bond.

The market value of a bond is the sum of the present values of the coupon interest payments plus the present value of the face value to be paid at maturity, given a market's required rate of return.

The yield to maturity of a bond (YTM) is the average annual rate of return that investors realize if they buy a bond for a certain price, receive the promised interest payments and principal on time, and reinvest the interest payments at the YTM rate.

A bond's market price and its YTM vary inversely. That is, when the YTM rises, the market price falls, and vice versa. When a bond has a YTM greater than its coupon rate, it sells at a discount to its face value. When the YTM is equal to the coupon rate, the market price equals the face value. When the YTM is less than the coupon rate, the bond sells at a premium over face value.

12-4 Explain how to calculate the market value and expected yield of preferred shares.

The market value of preferred shares is the present value of the stream of preferred share dividends, discounted at the market's required rate of return for that investment. Because the dividend cash flow stream is a perpetuity, we adapt the present value of a perpetuity formula, Equation 8-5, to value preferred shares.

The yield on preferred shares represents the annual rate of return that investors realize if they buy the shares for the current market price and then receive the promised dividend payments on time.

12-5 Describe two ways to compute the market value per share of common shares.

The market value of common shares is estimated in a number of ways, including (1) finding the present value of all the future dividends the shares are expected to pay, discounted at the market's required rate of return for the shares; and (2) finding the price implied, given the level of earnings per share and the appropriate P/E ratio. The dividend growth model and the P/E valuation approaches assume the firm will be a going concern. That is, the models value the future cash flows that a firm's assets are expected to produce. Two versions of the dividend growth model are commonly used, one for situations in which the future growth of the firm's dividends is expected to be constant, and the other for situations in which the future growth of the firm's dividends is expected to be nonconstant, or supernormal. Supernormal growth implies a period of high growth followed by a settling out at the long-term constant growth rate.

12-6 Explain three ways to compute the market value of total common equity.

The market value of total common equity is estimated in a number of ways, including (1) estimating common equity value based on the book value of the firm's assets as recorded on the balance sheet, less all liabilities and preferred shares (if any); (2) estimating the value of the firm's assets if they were to be liquidated on the open market and all claims on the firm were to be paid off; and (3) employing a discounted free cash flow model that calculates the present value of expected free cash flows to the suppliers of the firm's capital. The discounted free cash flow model is similar to the nonconstant dividend growth model in that it involves making a forecast of free cash flows during a specified period (usually 7 to 10 years). This is followed by the calculation of the value of the cash flows expected to be received after the forecast period (called the terminal value). The present values of the free cash flows and the present value of the terminal value are summed to produce the total present value of the firm's operations. This figure, in turn, is adjusted by adding current assets and subtracting current liabilities, long-term debt, and preferred shares (if any) to produce the total value of common share equity.

12-7 Define the expected yield on common shares and how to calculate it.

The yield on common shares is the percentage return investors can expect if they purchase the shares at the prevailing market price and receive the expected cash flows. It is calculated by solving for k in the constant growth dividend model.

12-8 Describe how to compute the value of a complete business.

The market value of a complete business can be found by applying the discounted free cash flow model used to estimate the value of common equity. In the complete business application, current assets are added to the present value of the firm's operations to produce the value of the complete business. Sometimes the value of complete businesses can also be found by calculating the amount that would be required to replace the firm's assets, but this method is usually more effective when applied to the valuation of individual business assets.

EQUATIONS INTRODUCED IN THIS CHAPTER

Equation 12-1: The Discounted Cash Flow Valuation Model

$$V_0 = \frac{CF_1}{(1+k)^1} + \frac{CF_2}{(1+k)^2} + \frac{CF_3}{(1+k)^3} + \cdots + \frac{CF_n}{(1+k)^n}$$

where

V_0 = Present value of the anticipated cash flows from the asset, its current value

$CF_{1,2,3,\text{ and } n}$ = Cash flows expected to be received one, two, three, and so on up to n periods in the future

k = Discount rate, the required rate of return

Equation 12-2: The Bond Valuation Formula (Algebraic Method)

$$V_B = INT \times \left[\frac{1 - \frac{1}{(1+k_d)^n}}{k_d} \right] + \frac{M}{(1+k_d)^n}$$

where

V_B = Current market value of the bond
INT = Dollar amount of each periodic interest payment
n = Number of times the interest payment is received (which is also the number of periods until maturity)
M = Principal payment received at maturity
k_d = Required rate of return per period on the bond debt instrument

Equation 12-3: The Bond Valuation Formula (Table Method)

$$V_B = (INT \times PVIFA_{k,\,n}) + (M \times PVIF_{k,\,n})$$

where

$PVIFA_{k,\,n}$ = Present Value Interest Factor for an Annuity from Table IV
$PVIF_{k,\,n}$ = Present Value Interest Factor for a single amount from Table II

Equation 12-4: The Formula for the Present Value of Preferred Shares

$$V_p = \frac{D_p}{k_p}$$

where

V_p = Current market value of the preferred shares
D_p = Amount of the preferred share dividend
k_p = Required rate of return for this issue of preferred shares

Equation 12-5: The Formula for the Yield on Preferred Shares

$$k_p = \frac{D_p}{P_p}$$

where

k_p = Yield on investment that an investor can expect if the shares are purchased at the current market price, P_p, and if the preferred dividend, D_p, is paid forever
D_p = Amount of the preferred share dividend
P_p = Current market price of the preferred share

Equation 12-6: The DCF Valuation Model Applied to Common Shares

$$P_0 = \frac{D_1}{(1+k_s)^1} + \frac{D_2}{(1+k_s)^2} + \frac{D_3}{(1+k_s)^3} + \cdots + \frac{P_n}{(1+k_s)^n}$$

where

P_0 = Present value of the expected dividends, the current price per share of the common shares
D_1, D_2, D_3, etc. = Common share dividends expected to be received at the end of periods 1, 2, 3, and so on until the shares are sold
P_n = Anticipated selling price of the shares in n periods
k_s = Required rate of return on this common share investment

Equation 12-7: The Constant Growth Version of the Dividend Valuation Model

$$P_0 = \frac{D_1}{k_s - g}$$

where

P_0 = Current price per share of the common shares
D_1 = Dollar amount of the common share dividend expected one period from now
k_s = Required rate of return per period on this common share investment
g = Expected constant growth rate per period of the company's common share dividends

Equation 12-8: The P/E Model for Valuing Common Shares

$$\text{Appropriate Share Price} = \text{Industry P/E Ratio} \times \text{EPS}$$

Equation 12-9: The Book Value of Common Equity

$$\text{Book Value of Common Equity} = \text{Total Assets} - \text{Total Liabilities} - \text{Preferred Share Equity}$$

Equation 12-10: The Constant Growth Free Cash Flow Valuation Model

$$V_{fcf\,t} = \frac{FCF_t(1+g)}{k-g}$$

where

$V_{fcf\,t}$ = Value of future free cash flows at time t
FCF_t = Free cash flow at time t
k = Discount rate
g = Long-term constant growth rate of free cash flows

Equation 12-11: The Yield, or Total Return, on Common Shares

$$k_s = \frac{D_1}{P_0} + g$$

where

D_1 = Amount of the common share dividend anticipated in one period
P_0 = Current market price of the common shares
g = Expected constant growth rate of dividends per period
k_s = Expected rate of return per period on this common share investment

SELF-TEST

ST-1. The Bombardier Corporation has issued a 10.95 percent annual coupon rate bond that matures December 31, 2023. The face value is $1,000. If the required rate of return on bonds of similar risk and maturity is 9 percent, and assuming the time now is January 1, 2003, what is the current value of Bombardier's bond?

ST-2. Bombardier's 10.95 percent coupon rate, 2023 bond is currently selling for $1,115. At this price, what is the yield to maturity of the bond? Assume the time is January 1, 2003.

ST-3. McDonald's is offering preferred shares that pay a dividend of $1.93 a share. The dividend is expected to continue indefinitely. If your required rate of return for McDonald's preferred shares is 8 percent, what is the value of the shares?

ST-4. Quaker Oats Corporation's next annual dividend is expected to be $1.14 a share. Dividends have been growing at a rate of 6 percent a year, and you expect this rate to continue indefinitely. If your required rate of return for these shares is 9 percent, what is the maximum price you should be willing to pay for it?

ST-5. Goodyear Corporation shares are currently selling for $38 per share. The company's next annual dividend is expected to be $1.00 a share. Dividends have been growing at a rate of 5 percent a year and you expect this rate to continue indefinitely. If you buy Goodyear at the current price, what will be your yield, or total return?

REVIEW QUESTIONS

1. Describe the general pattern of cash flows from a bond with a positive coupon rate.
2. How does the market determine the fair value of a bond?
3. What is the relationship between a bond's market price and its promised yield to maturity? Explain.
4. All other things held constant, how would the market price of a bond be affected if coupon interest payments were made semiannually instead of annually?
5. What is the usual pattern of cash flows for preferred shares? How does the market determine the value of a preferred share, given these promised cash flows?
6. Name two patterns of cash flows for a common share. How does the market determine the value of the most common cash flow pattern for common shares?
7. Define the P/E valuation method. Under what circumstances should a share be valued using this method?
8. Compare and contrast the book value and liquidation value methods for common shares. Is one method more reliable? Explain.
9. Answer the following questions about the discounted free cash flow model illustrated in Figure 12-4.
   a. What are "free cash flows"?
   b. Explain the terminal-value calculation at the end of the forecast period. Why is it necessary?
   c. Explain the term *present value of the firm's operations* (also known as *enterprise value*). What does this number represent?
   d. Explain the adjustments necessary to translate enterprise value to the total present value of common equity.
10. Explain the difference between the discounted free cash flow model as it is applied to the valuation of common equity and as it is applied to the valuation of complete businesses.
11. Why is the replacement value of assets method not generally used to value complete businesses?

PROBLEMS

12-1. Owen Meany is considering the purchase of a $1,000 Vancouver Municipal Bond. The city is raising funds for a much-needed advertising campaign to promote its West Coast resort community. The stated coupon rate is 6 percent, paid annually. The bond will mature in 10 years. The YTM for similar bonds in the market is 8 percent.

◀ Bond Valuation

a. How much will the annual interest payments be?

b. What is the market price of the bond today?

c. Is the interest received on a municipal bond generally tax free?

12-2. Assume CBC is offering a corporate bond with a face value of $1,000 and an annual coupon rate of 12 percent. The maturity period is 15 years. The interest is to be paid annually. The annual YTM for similar bonds in the market is currently 8 percent.

◀ Bond Valuation

a. What is the amount of interest to be paid annually for each bond?

b. What is the value of this $1,000 bond today?

c. What would be the present value of the interest and principal paid to holders of one of their bonds if the interest payments were made semiannually instead of annually?

12-3. The Winnipeg Opera Company is offering zero coupon bonds to fund the needed structural repairs to its historic building. A Toronto investment firm is considering the purchase of several of these bonds. The bonds have a face value of $2,000 and are scheduled to mature in 10 years. Similar bonds in the market have an annual YTM of 12 percent. If the investment firm purchases three of these bonds today, how much money will it receive 10 years from today at maturity?

◀ Bond Valuation

12-4. Two best friends, Thelma and Louise, are making long-range plans for a road trip vacation to Mexico. They will embark on this adventure in five years and want to invest during the five-year period to earn money for the trip. They decide to purchase a $1,000 Alberta Oil Company bond with an annual coupon rate of 10 percent with interest to be paid semiannually. The bond will mature in five years. The YTM of similar bonds is 8 percent. How much should they be willing to pay for the bond if they purchase it today?

◀ Bonds with Semiannual Interest Payments

12-5. Assume that Intel Corporation's $1,000 face value 9 percent coupon rate bond matures in 10 years and sells for $1,100. If you purchase the bond for $1,100 and hold it to maturity, what will be your average annual rate of return on the investment?

◀ Expected Rate of Return on a Corporate Bond

12-6. Clancy Submarines, Inc. is offering $1,000 par value bonds for sale. The bonds will mature 10 years from today. The annual coupon interest rate is 12 percent, with payments to be made annually. James Hobson just purchased one bond at the current market price of $1,125.

◀ YTM

Excel

a. Will the YTM of this bond be greater than or less than the coupon interest rate? Answer this part without doing any calculations.

b. To the nearest whole percent, what is the YTM of Mr. Hobson's bond? You will need to crunch some numbers for this part.

c. What would the YTM have to be to make the market price of the bond equal to the face value? No number crunching is needed to answer.

◀ Pricing

YTM ▶ Excel

12-7. A corporate bond has a face value of $1,000 and an annual coupon interest rate of 7 percent. Interest is paid annually. Of the original 20 years to maturity, only 10 years of the life of the bond remain. The current market price of the bond is $872. To the nearest whole percent, what is the YTM of the bond today?

Preferred Share Valuation ▶

12-8. The new Shattuck Corporation will offer its preferred shares for sale in the very near future. These shares will have a guaranteed annual dividend of $10 per share. As you research the market, you find that similar preferred shares have an expected rate of return of 12 percent. If the preferred shares could be purchased today, what price per share would you expect to pay for it?

Preferred Share k ▶

12-9. Lucky Jackson knows that one share of Grand Prix Enterprises preferred shares sells for $20 per share on the open market. From its annual reports, he sees that Grand Prix pays an annual dividend of $1.75 per share on preferred shares. What is the market's required rate of return on Grand Prix's shares?

Preferred Share Valuation ▶

12-10. Tiny Shipping Corporation is planning to sell preferred shares that will pay an annual dividend of $8 per share. The current expected rate of return from similar preferred shares issues is 13 percent.

a. What price per share would you expect to have to pay to purchase these shares?

b. If the shares are actually selling for $50 per share, what is the market's required rate of return for these shares?

Common Share Valuation per Share ▶

12-11. China S. Construction, Inc. is in the business of building electrical power plants in eastern Canada. Jack Godell and the rest of the board members of the firm have just announced a $4 per share dividend on the corporation's common shares to be paid in one year. Because the quality of some of its recent projects is under attack by investigative television reporters, the expected constant dividend growth rate is only estimated to be 1 percent. The required rate of return for similar shares in this industry is 16 percent.

a. What is the present value of the expected dividends from one share of China S. Construction's common shares?

b. What is the share's dividend yield (D_1/P_0)?

Yield on Common Shares ▶

12-12. The current listed price per share of a certain common share is $15. The cash dividend expected from this corporation in one year is $2 per share. All market research indicates that the expected constant growth rate in dividends will be 4 percent per year in future years. What is the rate of return on this investment an investor can expect if shares are purchased at the current listed price?

Common Share Valuation per Share ▶

12-13. Golden Manufacturing Company is expected to pay a dividend of $8 per share of common shares in one year. The dollar amount of the dividends is expected to grow at a constant 3 percent per year in future years. The required rate of return from shares of similar common shares in the present environment is 14 percent.

a. What would you expect the current market price of Golden common shares to be?

b. Assuming the cash dividend amount and the growth rate are accurate, what is the annual rate of return on your investment in Golden common shares if you purchased shares at the share's actual listed price of $65 per share?

Bond Valuation ▶

12-14. Micron issues a 9 percent coupon bond with a maturity of 5 years. The face value of the bond, payable at maturity, is $1,000. What is the value of this bond if your required rate of return is 12 percent?

12-15. Sam wants to purchase a bond that has a par value of $1,000, an annual coupon rate of 7 percent, and a maturity of 10 years. The bond's interest is paid semiannually. Sam's annual required rate of return is 11 percent. What should Sam be willing to pay for this particular bond?

◀ Bond Valuation (Semiannual Interest)

12-16. What is the value of a security that entitles you to receive the following payments if your required rate of return for this type of security is 23 percent?

◀ Discounted Cash Flows (DCF)

$80—end of year 1
$150—end of year 2
$1,500—end of year 3

12-17. Tom expects the issue of InVest preferred shares to pay an annual dividend of $3 per share. He also has researched the company and feels that 12 percent is a fair rate of return for this investment. Calculate the value of each share.

◀ Preferred Share Valuation

12-18. Analysts forecast that Dixie Chicks, Inc. (DCI) will pay a dividend of $2.20 a share at the end of this year, continuing a long-term growth trend of 9 percent a year. If this trend is expected to continue indefinitely and investors' required rate of return for DCI is 18 percent, what is the market value per share of DCI's common shares?

◀ Common Share Valuation, Constant Growth

12-19. PepsiCo (NYSE: PEP) paid a dividend of $0.58 per share this year. Dividends at the end of each of the next five years are expected to be as follows:

◀ Common Share Valuation, Nonconstant Growth

Year 1	$0.70
Year 2	$0.83
Year 3	$0.96
Year 4	$1.09
Year 5	$1.22

After year 5, dividends are expected to grow indefinitely at 10 percent a year. If your required rate of return for PepsiCo common shares is 12 percent, what is the most that you would pay per share for PepsiCo today?

12-20. Regis knows that CRS shares sell for $82 per share, have a growth rate of 7 percent, and a dividend that was just paid of $3.82. What can Regis expect as an annual percent yield if he purchases a share of CRS?

◀ Common Share Yield

12-21. Gwenyth just purchased a bond for $1,250 that has a maturity of 10 years and a coupon interest rate of 8.5 percent, paid annually. What is the YTM of the $1,000 face value bond that she purchased?

◀ Yield to Maturity (YTM)

12-22. Analysts forecast that free cash flows from Dixie Chicks, Inc. (DCI) will be $2.1 million in the coming year, continuing a long-term growth trend of 9 percent a year. If this trend is expected to continue indefinitely and investors' required rate of return for DCI is 18 percent, what will be the total enterprise value of DCI?

◀ Enterprise Value, Constant Growth

12-23. The free cash flow for PepsiCo (NYSE: PEP) this year was $1,026,600,000. Free cash flows at the end of each of the next five years are expected to be as follows:

◀ Enterprise Value, Nonconstant Growth

Year 1	$1,231,920,000
Year 2	$1,453,665,600
Year 3	$1,686,252,096
Year 4	$1,922,327,389
Year 5	$2,153,006,676

After year 5, free cash flows are expected to grow indefinitely at 10 percent a year. If the weighted average cost of capital (WACC) for PepsiCo is 12 percent, what is the enterprise value of the company today?

Book Value ▶ **12-24.** Jack and Frank Baker know that their piano renditions of lounge songs have limited appeal on the night club circuit, so they work part-time as investment consultants. They are researching relatively unknown corporations, one of which is Susie Diamond Enterprises. To get a quick idea of the value of SDE's common shares, they have taken the following numbers from the most recent financial statements.

Total Assets	$675,000
Total Liabilities	$120,000
250,000 Common Shares Authorized	
100,000 Common Shares Outstanding	

What is the book value (net worth) of Susie Diamond Enterprises?

Book Value, Liquidation Value, and P/E Methods ▶ **12-25.** The most recent balance sheet of Free Enterprise, Inc. follows.

Free Enterprise, Inc.
Balance Sheet
December 31, 2004 (thousands of dollars)

Assets		Liabilities + Equity	
Cash	$ 4,000	Accounts Payable	$ 4,400
Accounts Receivable	10,000	Notes Payable	4,000
Inventory	13,000	Accrued Expenses	5,000
Prepaid Expenses	400	Total Current Liabilities	13,400
Total Current Assets	27,400	Bonds Payable	6,000
Property, Plant, and Equipment	11,000	Common Equity	19,000
Total Assets	$38,400	Total Liabilities + Equity	$38,400

a. What was Free Enterprise's book value (net worth) at the beginning of 2005?

b. If the company had 750,000 common shares authorized and 500,000 shares outstanding, what was the book value per common share at the beginning of 2005?

c. Net income of Free Enterprise, Inc. was $5,610,000 in 2004. Calculate the earnings per share of Free Enterprise's common shares.

d. The P/E ratio for a typical company in Free Enterprise, Inc.'s industry is estimated to be 6. Using the EPS from (c), calculate the price of one share of common shares at the beginning of 2005, assuming that Free Enterprise commands a P/E ratio value equal to that of an average company in its industry.

e. What would you infer about the company's total assets shown on the balance sheet when comparing this calculated share price with the company's book value per share?

f. Calculate the liquidation value of Free Enterprise's common shares assuming the market value of the total assets is $50 million and the market value of total liabilities is $20 million, as estimated by your analyst.

Comprehensive Problem ▶ **12-26.** Lucky Jackson is trying to choose the best of the three investment alternatives recommended to him by his full-service investment broker. The alternatives are:

a. The corporate bond of Star Mining Company has a face value of $1,000 and an annual coupon interest rate of 13 percent. The bond is selling in the market at $1,147.58. Of the original 20 years to maturity, only 16 years of the life of the bond remain.

b. The preferred shares of Supernova Minerals Company have a value of $100 per share and it offers an annual dividend of $14 per share. The market price of the shares is $140 per share.

c. The common shares of White Dwarf Ores Company sell in the market at $300 per share. The company paid a dividend of $39 per share yesterday. The company is expected to grow at 3 percent per annum in the future.

Which of the three alternatives should Lucky choose? Remember the priority of claims for bondholders, preferred shareholders, and common shareholders from Chapters 1 and 4.

◀ Nonconstant Dividend Growth Model

Excel

12-27. Suppose Flash in the Pan Corporation is expected to pay an annual dividend of $3 per share one year from now and that this dividend will grow at the following rates during each of the following four years (to the end of year 5): Year 2, 20 percent; Year 3, 30 percent; Year 4, 20 percent; Year 5, 10 percent. After this supernormal growth period, the dividend will grow at a sustainable 5 percent rate each year beyond year 5.

a. What is the present value of the dividends to be paid during the supernormal growth period? Assume that the required rate of return, k_s, is 15 percent.

b. What is the present value of the dividends to be paid during the normal growth period (from year 6 through infinity)?

c. What is the total present value of one share of Flash in the Pan's common shares?

◀ Discounted Free Cash Flow Model for Total Common Equity (Challenge Problem)

Excel

12-28. Assume that you are the owner of a pet foods company and you are interested in acquiring the shares of Hardi-Pets, an up-and-coming company that markets a new type of dog food that causes pets that eat it to never become ill and to never need shots. Selected financial data for Hardi-Pets is shown.

Hardi-Pets, Inc. Selected Financial Data for 2001

Total Revenue	$1,000,000
Cost of Goods Sold	500,000
Gross Profit	500,000
Selling, General, and Administrative Expenses	200,000
Earnings before Interest, Taxes, & Amortization (EBITA)	300,000
Amortization	100,000
Earnings before Interest and Taxes (EBIT)	200,000
Capital Expenditures	15,000
Tax Rate	40%
Current Assets, Dec. 31, 2001	100,000
Current Liabilities, Dec. 31, 2001	80,000
Long-Term Debt, Dec. 31, 2001	500,000
Preferred Shares Outstanding, Dec. 31, 2001	0

Prepare a valuation analysis of Hardi-Pets total common equity using the discounted free cash flow model. Use a spreadsheet format similar to the example shown in Figure 12-4. The following forecasting variables apply. Assume that the time now is January 1, 2002.

	2002	2003	2004	2005	2006	2007	2008	2009	2010	2
Revenue Growth Factor	10%	15%	20%	25%	30%	25%	20%	15%	10%	
Expected Gross Profit Margin	50%	50%	50%	50%	50%	50%	50%	50%	50%	
S., G., & A. Exp. % of Revenue	20%	20%	20%	20%	20%	20%	20%	20%	20%	
Amortization % of Revenue	10%	10%	10%	10%	10%	10%	10%	10%	10%	
Capital Expend Growth Factor	10%	10%	10%	10%	–10%	–10%	–10%	–10%	–10%	–
Net Working Cap. to Sales Ratio	10%	10%	10%	10%	10%	10%	10%	10%	10%	

Tax rate = 40%
Assumed long-term sustainable growth rate = 5% per year after 2011
Discount rate = 20%

Discounted Free Cash Flow Model for Complete Business Valuation (Challenge Problem)

Excel

12-29. The Great Expectations Company just finished its first year of operations in which the company realized $2 million in revenue. Company managers are looking forward to a number of years of rapid growth ahead, and to this end they are seeking $10 million in long-term debt financing from the Capital 4 U Financing Company. However, before the loan can be approved, an independent appraisal of Great Expectations is required to establish the fair market value of the company.

Assume that you are a financial analyst working for Value Plus, Independent Appraisers. Capital 4 U has engaged your firm to estimate the fair market value of Great Expectations as a complete business. Selected financial data for Great Expectations is shown.

Great Expectations, Inc.
Selected Financial Data for 2001

Total Revenue	$2,000,000
Cost of Goods Sold	1,200,000
Gross Profit	800,000
Selling, General, and Administrative Expenses	1,200,000
Earnings before Interest, Taxes, & Amortization (EBITA)	(400,000)
Amortization	200,000
Earnings before Interest and Taxes (EBIT)	(600,000)
Capital Expenditures	1,000,000
Tax Rate	40%
Current Assets, Dec. 31, 2001	500,000

Prepare a valuation analysis of Great Expectations as a complete business using the discounted free cash flow model. Use a spreadsheet format similar to the example shown in Figure 12-4, modified for a complete business. The following forecasting variables apply. Assume that the time now is January 1, 2002.

	2002	2003	2004	2005	2006	2007	2008	2009	2010	2
Revenue Growth Factor	20%	30%	40%	50%	60%	50%	40%	30%	20%	
Expected Gross Profit Margin	50%	51%	52%	53%	54%	55%	56%	57%	58%	
S., G., & A. Exp. % of Revenue	50%	40%	30%	29%	28%	27%	26%	25%	24%	
Amortization % of Revenue	10%	10%	10%	10%	10%	10%	10%	10%	10%	
Capital Expend Growth Factor	40%	35%	30%	25%	20%	–10%	–15%	–20%	–25%	–
Net Working Cap. to Sales Ratio	19%	18%	17%	16%	15%	14%	13%	12%	11%	

Tax rate = 40%
Assumed long-term sustainable growth rate = 5% per year after 2011
Discount rate = 20%

12-30. The free cash inflow for Canadian Wireless Communications (CWC) this year is $100,000. Free cash inflows at the end of each of the next seven years are expected to be as follows: ◀ Enterprise Value

Year	Amount in ($)
1	120,000
2	160,000
3	170,000
4	250,000
5	320,000
6	400,000
7	500,000

a. Assume that after year 7, free cash flows are expected to grow indefinitely at 5 percent per year. If the weighted average cost of capital (WACC) for CWC is 20 percent, what is the enterprise value of the company today?

b. Assume that after year 7, free cash flows are expected to grow indefinitely at 10 percent per year. If the weighted average cost of capital (WACC) for CWC is 20 percent, what is the enterprise value of the company today?

c. Assume that after year 7, free cash flows are expected to grow indefinitely at 5 percent per year. If the weighted average cost of capital (WACC) for CWC is 15 percent, what is the enterprise value of the company today?

d. Assume that after year 7, free cash flows are expected to grow indefinitely at 10 percent per year. If the weighted average cost of capital (WACC) for CWC is 15 percent, what is the enterprise value of the company today?

12-31. The free cash inflow for Brandon Construction (BC) this year is $250,000. Free cash inflows at the end of each of the next seven years are expected to be as follows: ◀ Enterprise Value

Year	Amount in ($)
1	500,000
2	950,000
3	1,200,000
4	700,000
5	450,000
6	600,000
7	450,000

a. Assume that after year 7, free cash flows are expected to grow indefinitely at 5 percent per year. If the weighted average cost of capital (WACC) for BC is 20 percent, what is the enterprise value of the company today?

b. Assume that after year 7, free cash flows are expected to grow indefinitely at 10 percent per year. If the weighted average cost of capital (WACC) for BC is 20 percent, what is the enterprise value of the company today?

c. Assume that after year 7, free cash flows are expected to grow indefinitely at 5 percent per year. If the weighted average cost of capital (WACC) for BC is 15 percent, what is the enterprise value of the company today?

d. Assume that after year 7, free cash flows are expected to grow indefinitely at 10 percent per year. If the weighted average cost of capital (WACC) for BC is 15 percent, what is the enterprise value of the company today?

12-32. Radio Jazz is a Toronto-based network of ten local radio broadcasters located in major metropolitan centres across Canada that focus on jazz music. Mr. Jones, the founder of Radio Jazz, holds an 80 percent stake in the station while Mrs. Queen, the company's managing director, owns 20 percent. Radio Jazz consists ◀ Market Value of Common Equity of ten separate legal entities. The stations broadcast from 1-kW transmitters and each has a technical reach of 1 million listeners. The company's financial statements for the period 2004–2007 are provided below. You expect that the long-term sustainable growth rate would be equal to 5 percent per year after 2007.

Income Statement
Radio Jazz
2004–2007

	2004	2005	2006	2007
Net Sales	$146,000,000	$198,000,000	$234,000,000	$257,000,000
Cost of Goods Sold	94,900,000	122,760,000	142,740,000	154,200,000
S&A Expenses	40,000,000	40,000,000	40,000,000	40,000,000
Amortization	1,600,000	2,300,000	3,300,000	4,800,000
Operating Income	9,500,000	32,940,000	47,960,000	58,000,000
Interest Expense	2,200,000	3,000,000	3,700,000	4,800,000
Earnings before Taxes	7,300,000	29,940,000	44,260,000	53,200,000
Income Tax	2,920,000	11,976,000	17,704,000	21,280,000
Net Income	4,380,000	17,964,000	26,556,000	31,920,000

Balance Sheet
Radio Jazz
2004–2007

	2004	2005	2006	2007
Assets				
Cash	$ 3,000,000	$12,764,000	$29,620,000	$52,340,000
Marketable Securities	2,000,000	4,000,000	4,000,000	6,000,000
Accounts Receivable	10,000,000	16,000,000	22,000,000	24,000,000
Inventory	15,000,000	20,000,000	27,000,000	34,000,000
Prepaid Expenses	7,000,000	8,000,000	9,000,000	9,000,000
P.P. & E., Gross	16,000,000	23,000,000	33,000,000	48,000,000
Less: Accum. Amortization	6,000,000	8,300,000	11,600,000	16,400,000
P.P. & E., Net	10,000,000	14,700,000	21,400,000	31,600,000
Liabilities				
Accounts Payable	6,000,000	8,000,000	13,000,000	15,000,000
Notes Payable	7,000,000	12,000,000	13,000,000	15,000,000
Accrued Expenses	3,000,000	4,000,000	3,500,000	3,000,000
Long-Term Debt	15,000,000	18,000,000	24,000,000	33,000,000
Shareholders' Equity				
Preferred Shares	3,000,000	3,000,000	3,000,000	3,000,000
Common Shares	7,000,000	7,000,000	7,000,000	7,000,000
Retained Earnings	6,000,000	23,464,000	49,520,000	80,940,000

a. Develop a simplified cash flow statement (without the financial section) to arrive at a free cash flow for Radio Jazz for the years 2005, 2006, and 2007. The free cash flow is defined here as the sum of total cash flow from operations and cash used for investment purposes.

b. Calculate the present value of cash flows obtained in (a) by using a 20 percent discount rate. Please note that you are considering the valuation at the beginning of 2005. (Hint: Use cash flows from 2005, 2006, and 2007.)

c. Calculate the terminal value of the cash flow for 2007.

d. Calculate the net market value of common equity for Radio Jazz using the financial data from the balance sheet at the end of 2004.

e. The company paid $350,000 in common share dividends and $150,000 in preferred share dividends every year for the period of 2004–2007. Generate a statement of income and retained earnings for 2004–2007.

f. Calculate the following ratios for the period 2004–2007.
   i. Gross profit margin
   ii. Operating profit margin
   iii. Net profit margin
   iv. Return on assets
   v. Return on equity
   vi. Current ratio
   vii. Quick ratio

g. The industry averages for specific ratios are presented below (both for past and future projections). How do you interpret the company's actual (2004) and projected financial performance?

Industry Average	2004	2005	2006	2007
Gross Profit Margin	26.50%	26.40%	25.60%	26.70%
Operating Profit Margin	15.40%	17.20%	18.20%	19.50%
Net Profit Margin	12.30%	12.80%	12.90%	13.40%
Return on Assets	15.10%	16.20%	16.50%	17.10%
Return on Equity	27.40%	28.30%	28.40%	27.20%
Current Ratio	2.40	2.50	2.40	2.50
Quick Ratio	1.60	1.70	1.60	1.60

12-33. Inter Parts (IP) is the premier distributor of spare parts for passenger cars and trucks in Canada. The company began operations in 1980 and achieved sales of $50 million by the end of 2004. The company is based in Calgary, where it is a dominant supplier. It currently distributes its products to many regions in Canada through informal associations with strong local distributors. The company has grown rapidly in recent years and has grown its profits as well. The company stocks over 100,000 product lines for passenger cars. It also carries a significant amount of product lines for trucks. The company's products are sold through a number of distribution channels (wholesale—52%, workshops—15%, export—30%, and other channels—3%). The company's financial statements for the period 2004–2007 are provided below. The company expects that the long-term sustainable growth rate would be equal to 5 percent per year after 2007. ◀ Market Value of Common Equity

Income Statement
Inter Parts
2004–2007

	2004	2005	2006	2007
Net Sales	50,000,000	65,000,000	76,000,000	92,000,000
Cost of Goods Sold	38,000,000	46,000,000	54,000,000	64,000,000
S&A Expenses	7,500,000	9,000,000	11,000,000	13,000,000
Amortization	1,300,000	1,600,000	1,800,000	2,000,000
Operating Income	3,200,000	8,400,000	9,200,000	13,000,000
Interest Expense	600,000	700,000	675,000	450,000
Earnings before Taxes	2,600,000	7,700,000	8,525,000	12,550,000
Income Tax	1,040,000	3,080,000	3,410,000	5,020,000
Net Income	1,560,000	4,620,000	5,115,000	7,530,000

Balance Sheet
Inter Parts
2004–2007

	2004	2005	2006	2007
Assets				
Cash	3,000,000	4,058,000	3,548,000	5,190,000
Marketable Securities	500,000	500,000	800,000	1,000,000
Accounts Receivable	5,000,000	5,500,000	8,000,000	10,000,000
Inventory	5,000,000	6,000,000	7,500,000	9,000,000
Prepaid Expenses	500,000	600,000	700,000	800,000
P.P. & E., Gross	13,000,000	16,000,000	18,000,000	20,000,000
Less Accum. Amortization	6,000,000	7,600,000	9,400,000	11,400,000
P.P. & E., Net	7,000,000	8,400,000	8,600,000	8,600,000
Liabilities				
Accounts Payable	4,500,000	5,500,000	6,500,000	8,000,000
Notes Payable	1,000,000	1,000,000	750,000	500,000
Accrued Expenses	500,000	500,000	600,000	700,000
Long-Term Debt	5,000,000	6,000,000	6,000,000	4,000,000
Shareholders' Equity				
Preferred Shares	1,500,000	1,000,000	750,000	500,000
Common Shares	1,000,000	1,250,000	1,500,000	1,750,000
Retained Earnings	7,500,000	9,808,000	13,048,000	19,140,000

a. Develop a cash flow statement (without the financial section) to arrive at a free cash flow for Inter Parts for the years 2005, 2006, and 2007. The free cash flow is defined here as the sum of total cash flow from operations and cash used for investment purposes.

b. Calculate the present value of cash flows obtained in (a) by using a 20 percent discount rate. Please note that you are considering the valuation at the beginning of 2005. (Hint: Use cash flows from 2005, 2006, and 2007.)

c. Calculate the terminal value of the cash flow for 2007.

d. Calculate the net market value of common equity for Inter Parts using the financial data from the balance sheet in 2004.

e. The company paid the following amounts of common share dividends (2004—$50,000; 2005—$312,000; 2006—$375,000; 2007—$438,000) and preferred share dividends (2004—$1,500,000; 2005—$2,000,000; 2006—$1,500,000; 2007—$1,000,000). Generate a statement of income and retained earnings for 2004–2007.

f. Calculate the following ratios for the period 2004–2007:
   i. Gross profit margin
   ii. Operating profit margin
   iii. Net profit margin
   iv. Return on assets
   v. Return on equity
   vi. Current ratio
   vii. Quick ratio

g. The industry averages for specific ratios are presented below (both for past and expected). How do you interpret the company's actual (2004) and projected financial performance?

Industry Average	2004	2005	2006	2007
Gross Profit Margin	26.50%	25.40%	25.60%	26.70%
Operating Profit Margin	12.40%	11.50%	10.20%	11.10%
Net Profit Margin	4.90%	4.80%	5.10%	5.50%
Return on Assets	7.20%	7.80%	9.20%	10.10%
Return on Equity	6.70%	7.20%	6.20%	7.20%
Current Ratio	2.40	2.50	2.40	2.50
Quick Ratio	1.60	1.70	1.60	1.50

Market Value of Common Equity

12-34. Given the following information about Company XYZ, calculate the net market value of common equity for the Company using the financial data from the balance sheet in 2004. The company expects that the long-term sustainable growth rate would be equal to 10 percent per year after 2007 and a discount rate of 15 percent. The company does not pay any dividends. Let's assume that you value Company XYZ at the beginning of 2005. (Hint: Use cash flows from 2005, 2006, and 2007. Develop a cash flow statement without the financial section to arrive at a free cash flow for XYZ for the years 2005, 2006, and 2007. The free cash flow is defined here as a sum of total cash flow from operations and cash used for investment purposes.)

Income Statement
Company XYZ
2004–2007

	2004	2005	2006	2007
Net Sales	17,000,000	21,000,000	32,000,000	43,000,000
Cost of Goods Sold	11,050,000	13,440,000	20,480,000	25,800,000
S&A Expenses	3,000,000	3,500,000	4,000,000	7,000,000
Amortization	500,000	500,000	500,000	500,000
Operating Income	2,450,000	3,560,000	7,020,000	9,700,000
Interest Expense	400,000	400,000	400,000	400,000
Earnings before Taxes	2,050,000	3,160,000	6,620,000	9,300,000
Income Tax	820,000	1,264,000	2,648,000	3,720,000
Net Income	1,230,000	1,896,000	3,972,000	5,580,000

Balance Sheet
Company XYZ
2004–2007

	2004	2005	2006	2007
Assets				
Cash	3,000,000	3,396,000	6,868,000	11,948,000
Marketable Securities	5,000,000	5,000,000	5,000,000	5,000,000
Accounts Receivable	2,000,000	3,000,000	4,000,000	5,000,000
Inventory	4,000,000	6,000,000	8,000,000	10,000,000
Prepaid Expenses	1,500,000	1,500,000	1,500,000	1,500,000
P.P. & E., Gross	5,000,000	5,000,000	5,000,000	5,000,000
Less Accum. Amortization	1,000,000	1,500,000	2,000,000	2,500,000
P.P. & E., Net	4,000,000	3,500,000	3,000,000	2,500,000
Liabilities				
Accounts Payable	3,000,000	4,000,000	6,000,000	8,000,000
Notes Payable	1,000,000	1,000,000	1,000,000	1,000,000
Accrued Expenses	1,000,000	1,000,000	1,000,000	1,000,000
Long-Term Debt	3,000,000	3,000,000	3,000,000	3,000,000

Shareholders' Equity				
Preferred Shares	2,000,000	2,000,000	2,000,000	2,000,000
Common Shares	1,000,000	1,000,000	1,000,000	1,000,000
Retained Earnings	8,500,000	10,396,000	14,368,000	19,948,000

Market Value of Common Equity ▶

12-35. Given the following information about Company ABC, calculate the net market value of common equity for the company using the financial data from the balance sheet in 2004. The company expects that the long-term sustainable growth rate would be equal to 5 percent per year after 2007 and a discount rate of 20 percent. The company pays $1 million in common share dividends between 2004 and 2007. Let's assume that you value Company ABC at the beginning of 2005. (Hint: Use cash flows from 2005, 2006, and 2007. Develop a cash flow statement without the financial section to arrive at a free cash flow for XYZ for the years 2005, 2006, and 2007. The free cash flow is defined here as a sum of total cash flow from operations and cash used for investment purposes.)

Income Statement
Company ABC
2004–2007

	2004	2005	2006	2007
Net Sales	123,000,000	155,000,000	182,000,000	221,000,000
Cost of Goods Sold	55,350,000	71,300,000	85,540,000	106,080,000
S&A Expenses	42,000,000	50,000,000	55,000,000	60,000,000
Amortization	1,300,000	1,800,000	2,300,000	2,800,000
Operating Income	24,350,000	31,900,000	39,160,000	52,120,000
Interest Expense	2,600,000	1,700,000	1,000,000	1,000,000
Earnings before Taxes	21,750,000	30,200,000	38,160,000	51,120,000
Income Tax	8,700,000	12,080,000	15,264,000	20,448,000
Net Income	13,050,000	18,120,000	22,896,000	30,672,000

Balance Sheet
Company ABC
2004–2007

	2004	2005	2006	2007
Assets				
Cash	3,000,000	3,920,000	4,116,000	26,588,000
Marketable Securities	6,000,000	7,000,000	8,000,000	5,000,000
Accounts Receivable	20,000,000	20,000,000	25,000,000	30,000,000
Inventory	40,000,000	47,000,000	50,000,000	60,000,000
Prepaid Expenses	10,000,000	8,000,000	7,000,000	6,000,000
P.P. & E., Gross	13,000,000	18,000,000	23,000,000	28,000,000
Less: Accum. Amortization	6,000,000	7,800,000	10,100,000	12,900,000
P.P. & E., Net	7,000,000	10,200,000	12,900,000	15,100,000
Liabilities				
Accounts Payable	35,000,000	40,000,000	35,000,000	40,000,000
Notes Payable	6,000,000	7,000,000	5,000,000	5,000,000
Accrued Expenses	7,000,000	4,000,000	5,000,000	6,000,000
Long-Term Debt	20,000,000	10,000,000	5,000,000	5,000,000
Shareholders' Equity				
Preferred Shares	6,000,000	6,000,000	6,000,000	6,000,000
Common Shares	10,000,000	10,000,000	10,000,000	10,000,000
Retained Earnings	2,000,000	19,120,000	41,016,000	70,688,000

ANSWERS TO SELF-TEST

ST-1. The present value of Bombardier's 10.95 percent 2020 bond can be found using Equation 12-2:

$$V_B = INT \times \left[\frac{1-\frac{1}{(1+k_d)^n}}{k_d}\right] + \frac{M}{(1+k_d)^n}$$

Face value is \$1,000. The coupon interest payment is 10.95 percent of \$1,000, or \$109.50. n is 2023 – 2002 = 21. k_d = 9%.

$$V_B = \$109.50 \times \left[\frac{1-\frac{1}{(1+0.09)^{21}}}{0.09}\right] + \frac{\$1,000}{(1+0.09)^{21}}$$

$$= (\$109.50 \times 9.29224) + \left(\frac{\$1,000}{6.108808}\right)$$

$$= \$1017.50 + \$163.70$$

$$= \$1,181.20$$

So the present value of the bond is \$1,181.20.

ST-2. The bond's YTM is found by trial and error. We know that the bond has a price of \$1,115; face value of \$1,000; coupon interest payment of \$109.50 (10.95% of \$1,000); and matures in 21 years. Now we can find that value of k_d that produces a V_B of \$1,115. Use Equation 12-2 and solve for V_B.

First try k = 9%:

$$V_B = \$109.50 \times \left[\frac{1-\frac{1}{(1+0.09)^{21}}}{0.09}\right] + \frac{\$1,000}{(1+0.09)^{21}}$$

$$= (\$109.50 \times 9.29224) + \left(\frac{\$1,000}{6.108808}\right)$$

$$= \$1017.50 + \$163.70$$

$$= \$1,181.20 > 1,115$$

\$1,181.20 is too high. Try again using a higher yield (remember, bond prices and yields vary inversely).

Second try at k_d = 10%:

$$V_B = \$109.50 \times \left[\frac{1-\frac{1}{(1+0.10)^{21}}}{0.10}\right] + \frac{\$1,000}{(1+0.10)^{21}}$$

$$= (\$109.50 \times 8.64869) + \left(\frac{\$1,000}{7.40025}\right)$$

$$= \$947.03 + \$135.13$$

$$= \$1,082.16 < 1,115$$

$1,082.16 is too low. Try again using a lower yield.

Third try at k_d = 9.65%:

$$V_B = \$109.50 \times \left[\frac{1 - \frac{1}{(1+0.0965)^{21}}}{0.0965}\right] + \frac{\$1{,}000}{(1+0.0965)^{21}}$$

$$= (\$109.50 \times 8.86545) + \left(\frac{\$1{,}000}{6.92120}\right)$$

$$= \$970.77 + \$144.48$$

$$= \$1{,}115.25$$

At k_d = 9.65%, the calculated value of V_B is within $0.25 of the current market price. We conclude the bond's YTM is 9.65 percent.[9]

ST-3. Equation 12-5 is used to find the value of preferred shares as follows:

$$V_P = \frac{D_P}{k_p}$$

D_p is $1.93 and k_p is 8 percent.

$$V_P = \frac{\$1.93}{0.08}$$

$$= \$24.125$$

ST-4. The maximum price you are willing to pay for Quaker Oats is what it is worth to you, or its value. Because the characteristics of the share fit the constant dividend growth model, use Equation 12-7 to compute the value.

$$P_0 = \frac{D_1}{k_s - g}$$

D_1 is $1.14, k_e is 9 percent, and g is 6 percent.

Given these conditions, the value of Quaker Oats shares is:

$$P_0 = \frac{\$1.14}{0.09 - 0.06}$$

$$= \frac{\$1.14}{0.03}$$

$$= \$38$$

ST-5. The yield on common shares can be found using Equation 12-11.

$$k_s = \frac{D_1}{P_0} + g$$

D_1 is $1, P_0 is $38, and g is 5 percent. Given these conditions, the yield on Goodyear common shares is as follows:

[9] The exact YTM, found using a financial calculator, is 9.652590645 percent.

$$
\begin{aligned}
k_s &= \frac{\$1}{\$38} + 0.05 \\
&= 0.0263 + 0.05 \\
&= 0.0763, \text{ or } 7.63\%
\end{aligned}
$$

Comprehensive Cases: Part III

Case 1: New Ventures Limited

New Ventures Limited (NVL) is one of the largest and most experienced private equity fund investment advisors in Canada, serving the Canadian Enterprise Fund, the Canadian Private Equity Funds I & II, and the Canadian Enterprise Fund. Its team of investment professionals and staff has worked together in Canada and the United States since 1990. Funds currently managed exceed $1 billion. The Canadian Enterprise Fund is Canada's government funded non-profit corporation, formed in 1990 with the support of Parliament and capitalized at $250 million. Its aim was to promote private sector development and to stimulate investment in Canada, primarily by making direct equity investments and loans to small and medium-sized companies. By 1992, the Canadian Enterprise Fund had attracted the attention of private investors who wished to invest in Canada but did not have the ability to do so. The Canadian Private Equity funds were established as limited partnerships to stand alongside the Canadian Enterprise Fund. The investors included the leading pension funds and institutional investors, who together have invested a total of $500 million. In 1997, the Canadian Enterprise Fund was established. The fund is an addition to the Canadian Private Equity Funds I & II and has raised $250 million, bringing the combined capital base of three funds for investment in Canada to $1 billion.

NVL originates and evaluates proposals for consideration by the funds' investment committees. The fund's activities are aimed at promoting the development of the Canadian private sector primarily through equity investments, but also through loans and highly focused technical assistance, training, and feasibility studies. NVL is particularly interested in requests from private businesses, companies undergoing privatization, and joint ventures with foreign partners. It has the ability to syndicate much larger investments. To date, NVL has completed 48 transactions and makes approximately 5–10 investments per year. The average size of an investment is equal to $10.7 million, though larger deals are preferred. The largest investment NVL has ever made was equal to about $40 million.

Venture Capital

The definition of venture capital has evolved in recent years, but it generally is considered to be capital provided to new ventures. Venture capitalists are also in the business of provision of capital and "know-how" to companies in order to help companies realize capital appreciation. While the main objective of "making profits" is in line with the goals of other profit-oriented businesses, venture capital funds differ significantly in comparison to other capital providers; they prefer to support companies with strong management teams, have higher risk tolerance, and expect high returns for their capital. Over the long run, a venture capital firm's primary long-term goal is to realize a net return on investment across its portfolio of companies that exceeds the return from alternative investments. In fact, a venture capital firm usually needs to achieve significant, above-average returns to justify the risks and long periods of illiquidity inherent in venture capital investing, as well as to cover the firm's operating expenses and incentive compensation.

Evaluation of NVL's Historical Financial Performance

Mr. Martin Louis has heard some great things about the financial performance of New Ventures Limited and his objective is to provide new capital to the funds for management. Prior to his meeting with NVL's Managing Director, Mr. Louis was thinking about a method of evaluating the financial performance of NVL. He reminded himself that the most commonly used performance measure for venture capital funds is an internal rate of return ("IRR"). He knew that investors rely on internal rates of return to measure past performance, not only because the accounting returns of younger venture capital funds are difficult to verify and interpret but also because fund returns are highly variable. An exceptional return on a single investment can significantly boost the performance of an entire fund. Consequently, high cash returns on earlier funds may reflect good luck more than good judgment, and thus may be an unreliable indicator of the fund manager's skills. He also wondered whether other measures of performance, such as NPV or Payback, could be employed. Alternatively, he also considered another alternative approach to measure past performance on the basis of a purely qualitative assessment of a particular venture capital fund's management skills.

Requirements

1. State your views about employing NPV and Payback methods in this situation.
2. Would using the IRR method be more appropriate? Why or why not?
3. What other aspects of the business should be analyzed to reach a conclusion about the performance of the fund?

CASE 2: PACKAGING PARTNERS

Packaging Partners (PP) is the supplier of printed and laminated plastic packaging and one of Canada's largest producers of polyethylene (PE) films and bags. Most of PP's printed bags and foils are produced in volume runs for individual customers in the food processing and medical industries. Twenty customers account for about 40 percent of sales although there are altogether about 2,000 customers.

In 2004, PP sold 4,410 tonnes of plastic packaging and plastic packaging products, up from 4,107 in 2003. PP derived 56 percent of its 2004 sales from printed packaging—a figure that is expected to increase over time. Foils are used in various packaging machines while bags are generally filled manually or serve as shopping bags. Primarily, the food processing, medicine, and electronic sectors use the bags and foils. Thus the product assortment includes bags suitable for frozen foods, heat shrinkable plastic films, laminated bags and fills for vacuum sealing, shopping bags with advertising, and various types of general plastic packaging. Printing is key to the value added by PP and the company has invested about $1 million in 2002 and 2003 to upgrade its printing technology, specifically in Macintosh technology for print design, Dupont printing technology, and computerized ink mixing technology. The company owns state-of-the-art design and ink mixing facilities and two older six-colour and one four-colour printing machines. PP's customers are impressed with the current print quality, given the age of the machines.

The company's management has two options to consider in terms of the capital budgeting programs. The two options are described as follows:

Capital Program I

Product	Cost (In $ millions)	Purpose	2005	2006	2007	20
8-colour 1,400 mm flexographic press with central cylinder	2.5	Higher-quality printing	X			
1,400 mm solventless laminating machine	0.6	Able to laminate different types of plastic films and print in between layers		X		
1,400 mm cutting machine	1.0	Able to cut increased widths of films produced by new printer and laminator				X
Multilayer coextrusion facility	3.0	Able to produce multilayer films without lamination			X	
Upgrade and modernization plans	1.0	Increase the efficiency and utilization of existing assets		X		
Total	**8.1**					

With the investment shown in this table, the company estimates that inventory levels need to increase by $25 million, but these would be recaptured at the end of 2009. No residual value is expected. PP's sales will increase by $10 million per year in 2005 and 2006. In years 2007, 2008, and 2009 sales would reach $20 million per year. The increase in operating expenses is estimated to be 20 percent of the annual change in sales. Assume that the tax rate is 35 percent and the company's often used discount rate is 15 percent. Additionally, do not apply the half-year convention rule (amortization at 10 percent per year under the straight-line method).

The only difference in Capital Program II compared to Capital Program I comes from the amounts and timing of investments.

Requirements

Which Capital Program should the company adopt? Show your analysis.

Capital Program II

Product	Cost (In $ millions)	Purpose	2005	2006	2007	20
10-colour 2,000 mm flexographic press with central cylinder	4.0	Higher-quality printing		X		
2,000 mm solventless laminating machine	1.5	Able to laminate different machine types of plastic films and print in between layers		X		
2,000 mm cutting machine	2.0	Able to cut increased widths of films produced by new printer and laminator	X			
Multilayer coextrusion facility	3.0	Able to produce multilayer films without lamination				X
Total	**10.5**					

CASE 3: ALUCAN

AluCan is one of the largest aluminum processors in Canada. It is located in Hamilton, Ontario. The company is involved in three distinct business units: casting alloy making, manufacturing extruded and drawn products, and aluminum foil rolling and packaging material manufacturing. Each of these business areas involves different technologies, distinct markets, and different customers groups.

Mr. John Belt, the company's Chief Financial Officer, sat at his desk thinking about costs and benefits of the planned investment program. The company has committed significant financial and human resources to capital budgeting programs in the past and the projects have resulted in a significant increase in the company's sales and profitability. Mr. Belt was less certain about the effects of the newly planned capital budgeting program to be undertaken between 2005 and 2007. Most importantly, a decision had to be made as to whether or not to undertake the project.

Investment Program

In the last three years, the company focused its investment effort on the packaging and extrusion divisions. A detailed breakdown of historical and projected capital investment levels by business unit is provided in the following table:

Capital Investment by Business Unit and by Year (In $ millions)

Business Unit	*2003 Actual*	*2004 Actual*	*2005 Forecast*	*2006 Forecast*	*2007 Forecast*
Casting Alloys	1.0	0.0	0.02	0.08	0.0
Extrusion and Billet Making	3.2	0.4	0.4	14.7	4.1
Packaging	3.3	6.5	1.4	3.9	0.0
Other*	0.1	0.3	1.8	2.1	0.8
Total	7.6	7.2	3.62	20.78	4.9

*Infrastructure, environmental, information technology.

One of the key investments in the extrusion business has been the installation of a powder coating facility to satisfy the demand of the construction sector for painted profiles. The other has been the complete rebuild of one 2,550 tonne press involving the modernization of pumps (to increase reliability), billet heating and cutting (to save energy and improve yields), and the handling of extruded profiles as they come out of the press (to ensure that they do not become bent and suffer surface damage). As a result of these investments, the company has increased the capacity of the rebuilt press, significantly improved the quality and finish of the profiles it supplies to the construction sector as well as achieving better yields and energy savings.

The key area for future investment is the extrusion division, including billet making for the extrusion presses. Additional investment is also planned in the packaging division. The investment in billet making involves the construction of a new semi-continuous casting unit for billets and the partial modernization of one existing billet casting unit. The billet manufacturing plant is currently capacity constrained and suffers from quality problems. The key quality issues include difficulties in achieving completely straight billets and achieving a smooth surface. The lack of straight billets impacts extrusion speed, significantly reducing the efficiency of the extrusion process. The smooth billet surfaces are necessary to produce extruded products with surface finish acceptable for construction applications. As a result of problems with the billet surfaces, the company needs to machine a significant proportion of the billets it produces, increasing costs and reducing yields. The new billet plant is designed to improve billet quality to acceptable levels and increase billet-casting capacity to feed the increased output of the extrusion plant. Modernization of 2,550-tonne presses, along the lines of the modernization program already carried out on one such press, is designed to provide AluCan with significant extruding capacity capable of meeting the quality requirements of the construction market. The last major item planned in the extrusion plant is the installation of a CONFORM process for making aluminum products. The investment in lacquering and adhesive application machines in the packaging division is designed to allow the company to produce aluminum and plastic laminates for box lids, used in yogurt and cheese packaging. The purchase of slitters is to increase the company's capacity in the area of aluminum and plastic-based laminates.

With this investment, Mr. Belt estimates that he would still need to increase inventory levels by $15 million by purchasing additional raw materials. However, he anticipates recouping 100 percent of his additional investment in new assets at the end of 2009. No residual value is expected. Mr. Belt anticipates the company's sales to increase by $15 million per year in 2005 and 2006. In years 2007, 2008, and 2009, he expects that sales increases would reach $45 million per year. The increase in operating expenses is estimated to be 20 percent of the annual change in sales. Assume that the marginal tax rate is 40 percent and the company's often-used discount rate is 10 percent. Additionally, do not apply the half-year convention rule (amortization at 20 percent per year under the straight-line method).

Requirements

Prepare a capital budgeting evaluation to help Mr. Belt with his decision.

Part IV
Long-Term Financing Decisions

CHAPTERS

ENCANA—A TRADE-OFF BETWEEN GROWTH AND DIVIDENDS

www.encana.com

CORPORATE INFORMATION

Headquarters	Calgary, Alberta
Industry	Oil and Gas
Number of Explored Regions	Four
Listed on	TSX, NYSE
Ticker symbol	ECA
President & CEO	Gwyn Morgan

(In $ millions)	2000	2001	2002	2003
Sales	4,366	4,894	6,276	10,216
Profit before Tax	1,633	1,885	1,101	2,616
Net Profit	1,021	1,287	812	2,360
Common Share Dividends	101	1,282	108	139
Current Assets	N/A	1,673	3,810	2,088
Current Liabilities	N/A	1,640	2,692	1,931
Total Assets	N/A	10,800	19,912	24,110
Capital Expenditures	1,466	1,955	3,021	5,115
Shareholders' Equity	N/A	3,979	8,718	11,278

Business

EnCana is one of the world's leading independent oil and gas companies and North America's largest independent natural gas and storage operators. Approximately ninety percent of EnCana's assets are located in North America. The Company's international subsidiaries operate in three regions: U.K. (the operators of a large oil discovery), Ecuador (the largest private oil producer), and Gulf of Mexico (exploration of oil). EnCana was created in April 2002 through a merger of Alberta Energy Company (AEC) and PanCanadian Petroleum Limited (PPL).

Financial Performance

EnCana's numbers present a steady increase in sales. Between 2000 and 2003, the consolidated sales more than doubled. Net profits have been increasing steadily over the years in dollar terms and reached $2.4 billion at the end of 2003. However, the Company's net profit margins declined from 41.2 percent in 2000 to 23.2 percent in 2003. The Company's asset base increased to more than $24 billion reflecting recent acquisitions. The total cumulative capital expenditure program beginning in the year 2001 was equal to $10 billion.

Profits, Capital Expenditure Programs, and Dividends

In spite of a heavy capital expenditure program aimed at sustaining strong growth, EnCana was committed to return some cash to its shareholders. In 2001, an extraordinary one-off dividend of $1.3 billion was paid as part of a business reorganization. In 2002, EnCana paid $108 million or 13.3 percent of net profits in common share dividends. In 2003, the level of common share dividends increased to $139 million, but it decreased to 5.9 percent as a percentage of the Company's net profit. The chief reason for the decline in the dividend payout ratio reflects the fact that the company decided to commit over $5 billion to the capital expenditure program. In fact, the Company's management decided to limit the amount of dividends to its shareholders and focus on the available cash resources to effect acquisitions. This is a very common trade-off made by management teams where a lack of dividends for some time may be traded off against higher growth potential in sales, and eventually profitability. Increased profitability may translate into higher dividends in the future.

In a press release issued on the 26th of February 2004, EnCana reported that its board of directors approved a 33 percent increase in the company's quarterly dividend equal to US$0.10 per share. The previous quarterly dividend was equal to CAD$0.10 per share. The increased dividend followed a stellar performance in 2003 and a strong business outlook for the company in the future.

Sources: www.globeandmail.com, www.cbc.ca, www.encana.com, www.tsx.com. Financial data for 2002 and 2003 from 2003 *Annual Report*, pages 75–77; data from 2001 and 2000 from 2002 *Annual Report*, pages 66–69.

13

Capital Structure Basics

Chapter Objectives

After reading this chapter, you should be able to:

13-1 Define capital structure and describe a central question in finance about it.

13-2 Explain operating, financial, and combined leverage effects and the resulting business and financial risks.

13-3 Describe how to find the breakeven level of sales for a firm.

13-4 Describe the risks and returns of a leveraged buyout.

13-5 Explain how changes in capital structure affect a firm's value.

"The Lord forbid that I should be out of debt, as if, indeed, I could not be trusted."

—François Rabelais

A Popcorn Venture

Jason is a college student who wants to start his own business. Jason's business idea is to sell popcorn from a cart, just as he has seen done in the downtown area of the city in which he lives. The downtown vendor sells about 500 bags of popcorn a day, and Jason thinks he might be able to do as well with a similar popcorn stand near the college in his town.

However, the wagon contains both a popcorn-making machine and a storage room for supplies, so it is not inexpensive. Also, if Jason went into this business, he would need an expensive business operator's license from the city. The downtown vendor charges only $1 for a bag of popcorn, so Jason would have to sell a lot of popcorn to recoup the high price of the wagon and the license, $8,000 and $4,000 respectively. His variable costs are $0.04 per bag.

Is this a viable business idea or not? What are the risks and the potential returns of this business? Is this a better path than taking a McJob, as many of Jason's friends have done? In this chapter we'll look at some of these issues.

Source: Jason's popcorn venture is based on actual events. The entrepreneur's name has been changed and approximate numbers have been used because data about this private company are confidential.

Chapter Overview

In this chapter, we investigate how fixed costs affect the volatility of a firm's operating and net income. We see how fixed operating costs create *operating leverage,* which magnifies the effect of sales changes on operating income. We also examine how fixed financial costs create *financial leverage,* which magnifies the effect of changes in operating income on net income. Then we analyze the risk and return of leveraged buyouts (LBOs). Finally, we see how changes in a firm's capital structure affect the firm's overall value.

Capital Structure

Capital structure is the mixture of funding sources (debt, preferred shares, or common shares) that a firm uses to finance its assets. A central question in finance is what blend of these financing sources is best for the firm. That is, how much of a firm's assets should be financed by borrowing? How much should be financed by preferred shareholders? How much should be financed by the common shareholders? The question is important because each of these financing sources has a different cost, as you learned in Chapter 9, and each of them has a different degree of risk. Therefore, the choice of financing directly affects a firm's weighted average cost of capital and the degree of riskiness in the firm.

The amount of debt that a firm uses to finance its assets creates **leverage**. A firm with a lot of debt in its capital structure is said to be highly levered. A firm with no debt is said to be unlevered. In physics, the term *leverage* describes how a small force can be magnified to create a larger force. For example, if a farmer wants to move a large boulder in a field, he can wedge a long board (a lever) between the large boulder and a small rock (a fulcrum), which gives him enough leverage to push down on the end of the long board and easily move the boulder.

The power of leverage can also be harnessed in a financial setting. Its magnifying power can help or hurt a business. A firm that has leverage will earn or lose more than it would without leverage. In the sections that follow, we investigate specific types of leverage and the risks associated with each type.

Operating Leverage

Operating leverage refers to the phenomenon whereby a small change in sales triggers a relatively large change in operating income (or earnings before interest and taxes, also known as EBIT). Operating leverage occurs because of fixed costs in the operations of the firm. A firm with fixed costs in the production process will see its EBIT rise by a larger percentage than sales when unit sales are increasing. If unit sales drop, however, the firm's EBIT will decrease by a greater percentage than its sales.

Table 13-1 illustrates the operating leverage effect for a firm in which all production costs, a total of $5,000, are fixed. Observe how the presence of the fixed costs causes a 10 percent change in sales to produce a 20 percent change in operating income.

Calculating the Degree of Operating Leverage The degree of operating leverage, or DOL, measures the magnitude of the operating leverage effect. The

Table 13-1 The Operating Leverage Effect—Fixed Costs Only

	Period 1	Period 2	Percent Change
Sales	$10,000	$11,000	10%
Fixed Costs	–5,000	–5,000	
Operating Income	$ 5,000	$ 6,000	20%

degree of operating leverage is the percentage change in earnings before interest and taxes (%ΔEBIT) divided by the percentage change in sales (%ΔSales):

Degree of Operating Leverage (DOL)

$$\text{DOL} = \frac{\%\Delta\text{EBIT}}{\%\Delta\text{Sales}} \tag{13-1}$$

where

%ΔEBIT = Percentage change in earnings before interest and taxes

%ΔSales = Percentage change in sales

According to Equation 13-1, the DOL for the firm in Table 13-1 is:

$$\text{DOL} = \frac{20\%}{10\%} = 2.0$$

We see that, for a firm with a 10 percent change in sales and a 20 percent change in EBIT, the DOL is 2.0. A DOL greater than 1 shows that the firm has operating leverage. That is, when sales change by some percentage, EBIT will change by a greater percentage.

The Effect of Fixed Costs on DOL Table 13-2 shows the projected base-year and second-year income statement for Jason's Popcorn Wagon. The income statement allows us to analyze Jason's operating leverage. (Note that Table 13-2 divides the operating expenses into two categories, fixed and variable.) We see that sales and operating expenses are likely to change in the second and subsequent years. We also see the predicted impact on EBIT, given the sales forecast.

Table 13-2 Jason's Popcorn Wagon Projected Income Statement (Fixed Costs Are $12,000, Variable Costs Are $0.04 per Unit, and Price per Unit Is $1)

	Base Year	Year 2	
Sales	$30,000	$33,000	$\%\Delta = \frac{33{,}000 - 30{,}000}{30{,}000} = 10\%$
–VC	–1,200	–1,320	
–FC	–12,000	–12,000	
= EBIT	$16,800	= $19,680	$\%\Delta = \frac{19{,}680 - 16{,}800}{16{,}800} = 17.1\%$

We see from Table 13-2 that Jason's percentage change in sales is 10 percent and his percentage change in EBIT (or operating income) is 17.1 percent.

We use Equation 13-1 to find Jason's DOL, as follows:

$$\begin{aligned} DOL &= \frac{\%\Delta EBIT}{\%\Delta Sales} \\ &= \frac{(19{,}680 - 16{,}800)/16{,}800}{(33{,}000 - 30{,}000)/30{,}000} \\ &= \frac{0.171}{0.10} \\ &= 1.71 \end{aligned}$$

Our DOL calculations indicate that if Jason's Popcorn Wagon business sales increase by 10 percent from the base year to the next year, EBIT will increase by 17.1 percent. This larger percentage increase in EBIT is caused by the company's fixed operating costs. No matter how much popcorn Jason produces and sells, his wagon and license costs stay the same. The fixed costs cause the EBIT to increase faster than sales. If sales decrease, the fixed costs must still be paid. As a result, the fixed costs cause EBIT to drop by a greater percentage than sales.

The Alternate Method of Calculating DOL Instead of using Equation 13-1, we may also find the DOL by using only numbers found in the base-year income statement. Subtract total variable costs from sales, divide that number by sales minus total variable costs minus fixed costs, and solve for DOL. The formula for the alternate method of finding DOL, Equation 13-2, follows:

Degree of Operating Leverage (DOL) (alternate)

$$DOL = \frac{Sales - VC}{Sales - VC - FC} \tag{13-2}$$

where

VC = Total variable costs

FC = Total fixed costs

From Table 13-2, we know that in the base year, Jason's Popcorn Wagon has sales of $30,000, variable costs of $1,200, and fixed costs of $12,000. Using the alternate formula, we find that Jason has the following DOL:

$$\begin{aligned} DOL &= \frac{Sales - VC}{Sales - VC - FC} \\ &= \frac{30{,}000 - 1{,}200}{30{,}000 - 1{,}200 - 12{,}000} \\ &= \frac{28{,}800}{16{,}800} \\ &= 1.71 \end{aligned}$$

We find a DOL of 1.71, just as we did with Equation 13-1. How did this happen? The alternate formula, Equation 13-2, uses only numbers from the base year income statement, whereas Equation 13-1 requires information from the base year and year 2.[1] Why use two different ways to calculate DOL when they both give the same answer? Because each method reveals different information about operating leverage.

The percentage change version of the DOL formula, Equation 13-1, shows the effect of the leverage—sales change by a certain percentage, triggering a greater percentage change in operating income if the DOL is greater than 1. The percentage change in operating income, then, is the product of the percentage change in sales and this degree of operating leverage.

The alternate DOL formula, Equation 13-2, shows that fixed costs cause the leveraging effect. Whenever fixed costs are greater than 0, DOL is greater than 1, indicating a leverage effect (the percentage change in EBIT is greater than the percentage change in sales). The larger the amount of fixed costs, the greater the leveraging effect.

Taken together, the two formulas demonstrate that leverage has the effect of triggering a greater percentage change in operating income when a percentage change in sales occurs and that fixed costs cause operating leverage. Equation 13-3 shows how changes in sales and DOL combine to determine the change in EBIT.

Percentage Change in EBIT

$$\%\Delta\text{EBIT} = \%\Delta\text{Sales} \times \text{DOL} \tag{13-3}$$

where

$\%\Delta$Sales = Percentage change in sales

DOL = Degree of operating leverage

The Risk of Operating Leverage As we know from Chapter 7, the risk associated with operating leverage is business risk. Recall that business risk refers to the volatility of operating income. The more uncertainty about what a company's operating income will be, the higher its business risk. Volatility of sales triggers business risk. The presence of fixed costs, shown by the amount of DOL, magnifies business risk. The total degree of business risk that a company faces is a function of both sales volatility and the degree of operating leverage.

Dilbert points out to his boss that he undertook some actions to meet budgeted forecasts. He also made some "brave" assumptions about sales.

Source: DILBERT reprinted by permission of United Feature Syndicate, Inc.

[1]Equations 13-1 and 13-2 give the same numeric result when sales price per unit, fixed costs, and variable costs per unit are constant.

Financial Leverage

Fluctuations in sales and the degree of operating leverage determine the fluctuations in operating income (also known as EBIT). Now let's turn our attention to financial leverage. **Financial leverage** is the additional volatility of net income caused by the presence of fixed-cost funds (such as fixed-rate debt) in the firm's capital structure. Interest on fixed-rate debt is a fixed cost because a firm must pay the same amount of interest, no matter what the firm's operating income.

Calculating the Degree of Financial Leverage (DFL) The **degree of financial leverage (DFL)** is the percentage change in net income (%DNI) divided by the percentage change in EBIT (%ΔEBIT). The formula for DFL follows:

Degree of Financial Leverage (DFL)

$$DFL = \frac{\%\Delta NI}{\%\Delta EBIT} \tag{13-4}$$

where

$\%\Delta NI$ = Percentage change in net income

$\%\Delta EBIT$ = Percentage change in earnings before interest and taxes

If net income changes by a greater percentage than EBIT changes, then the DFL will have a value greater than 1, and this indicates a financial leverage effect.[2]

Table 13-3 shows the entire base-year income statement for Jason's Popcorn Wagon and the projections for year 2. Notice that the lower portion of the income statements contains fixed interest expense, so we would expect the presence of financial leverage.

Table 13-3 Jason's Popcorn Wagon Income Statement—Base Year and Projected Year 2

	Base Year	Year 2	
Sales	$30,000	$33,000	$\%\Delta = \frac{33{,}000 - 30{,}000}{30{,}000} = 10\%$
–VC	–1,200	–1,320	
–FC	–12,000	–12,000	
= EBIT	= 16,800	= 19,680	$\%\Delta = \frac{19{,}680 - 16{,}800}{16{,}800} = 17.1\%$
–I	–800	–800	
= EBT	= 16,000	= 18,880	
–Tax (15%)	–2,400	–2,832	
= NI	= 13,600	= 16,048	$\%\Delta = \frac{16{,}048 - 13{,}600}{13{,}600} = 18\%$

[2]Note that the degree of financial leverage calculated using Equation 13-4 will be faced by preferred shareholders and common shareholders together. If you were interested in finding the degree of financial leverage faced by common shareholders only, you would modify Equation 13-4 by subtracting preferred dividends from net income.

As shown in Table 13-3, the percentage change in EBIT from the base year to year 2 is 17.1 percent, and the percentage change in net income from the base year to year 2 is 18 percent. Jason's degree of financial leverage according to Equation 13-4 follows:

$$\begin{aligned} DFL &= \frac{\%\Delta NI}{\%\Delta EBIT} \\ &= \frac{0.18}{0.171} \\ &= 1.05 \end{aligned}$$

Our calculations show that Jason's Popcorn Wagon business has a degree of financial leverage of 1.05.

Another Method of Calculating Financial Leverage Just as with DOL, there are two ways to compute DFL. Instead of using Equation 13-4, the percentage change in NI divided by the percentage change in EBIT, we could instead calculate the DFL using only numbers found in the base-year income statement. By dividing EBIT by EBIT minus interest expense (I), we can find DFL. The equation looks like this:

Degree of Financial Leverage (DFL) (alternate)

$$DFL = \frac{EBIT}{EBIT - I} \tag{13-5}$$

where

EBIT = Earnings before interest and taxes
I = Interest expense

The base-year income statement numbers in Table 13-3 show that Jason's EBIT is $16,800 and his interest expense is $800. To find the degree of financial leverage, we apply Equation 13-5 as follows:

$$\begin{aligned} DFL &= \frac{EBIT}{EBIT - I} \\ &= \frac{16,800}{16,800 - 800} \\ &= \frac{16,800}{16,000} \\ &= 1.05 \end{aligned}$$

Equation 13-5 yields the same DFL for Jason's business as Equation 13-4.[3] Both formulas are important because they give us different but equally important insights about financial leverage. Equation 13-4 shows the effect of financial leverage—net income (NI) will vary by a larger percentage than operating income (EBIT). Equation 13-5 pinpoints the source of financial leverage—

[3]Equations 13-4 and 13-5 give the same DFL value only if the fixed financial costs (interest expense) and the tax rate are constant.

fixed interest expense. The degree of financial leverage, DFL, will be greater than 1 if interest expense (I) is greater than 0. In sum, interest expense magnifies the volatility of NI as operating income changes.

How Interest Expense Affects Financial Leverage To illustrate the financial leverage effect, suppose that to help start his business, Jason borrowed $10,000 from a bank at an annual interest rate of 8 percent. This 8 percent annual interest rate means that Jason will have to pay $800 ($10,000 × 0.08) in interest each year on the loan. The interest payments must be made, no matter how much operating income Jason's business generates. In addition to Jason's fixed operating costs, he also has fixed financial costs (the interest payments on the loan) of $800.

The fixed financial costs magnify the effect of a change in operating income on net income. For instance, even if Jason's business does well, the bank interest payments do not increase, even though he could afford to pay more. If Jason's business does poorly, however, he cannot force the bank to accept less interest simply because he cannot afford the payments.

The Risk of Financial Leverage The presence of debt in a company's capital structure and the accompanying interest cost create extra risk for a firm. As we know from Chapter 7, the extra volatility in NI caused by fixed interest expense is financial risk. The financial risk of the firm compounds the effect of business risk and magnifies the volatility of net income. Just as fixed operating expenses increase the volatility of operating income and business risk, so, too, fixed financial expenses increase the volatility of NI and magnify financial risk. This is shown in Equation 13-6.

Percentage Change in Net Income

$$\%\Delta \text{NI} = \%\Delta \text{EBIT} \times \text{DFL} \tag{13-6}$$

where

$\%\Delta$EBIT = Percentage change in earnings before interest and taxes

DFL = Degree of financial leverage

Now we explore the combined effect of operating and financial leverage next.

Combined Leverage

The combined effect of operating leverage and financial leverage is known as **combined leverage**. Combined leverage occurs when net income changes by a larger percentage than sales, which occurs if there are any fixed operating or financial costs. The following combined leverage formula solves for the net income change due to sales changes that occur when fixed operating and financial costs are present.

The **degree of combined leverage (DCL)** is the percentage change in net income ($\%\Delta$NI) divided by the percentage change in sales ($\%\Delta$Sales), as shown in Equation 13-7:

Degree of Combined Leverage Formula, DCL

$$\text{DCL} = \frac{\%\Delta \text{NI}}{\%\Delta \text{Sales}} \tag{13-7}$$

where

$\%\Delta NI$ = Percentage change in net income

$\%\Delta Sales$ = Percentage change in sales

The alternate DCL formula follows:

Degree of Combined Leverage (DCL) (alternate 1)

$$DCL = \frac{Sales - VC}{Sales - VC - FC - I} \tag{13-8}$$

where

VC = Total variable costs

FC = Total fixed costs

I = Interest expense

We can also calculate the degree of combined leverage (DCL) a third way: multiplying the degree of operating leverage (DOL) by the degree of financial leverage (DFL). The third DCL formula is shown in Equation 13-9.

Degree of Combined Leverage (DCL) (alternate 2)

$$DCL = DOL \times DFL \tag{13-9}$$

where

DOL = Degree of operating leverage

DFL = Degree of financial leverage

Equation 13-10 shows the combined effect of DOL and DFL on net income (NI).

Percentage Change in Net Income (NI)

$$\%\Delta NI = \%\Delta Sales \times DOL \times DFL \tag{13-10}$$

where

$\%\Delta Sales$ = Percentage change in sales

DOL = Degree of operating leverage

DFL = Degree of financial leverage

Equation 13-10 shows how the change in net income is determined by the change in sales and the compounding effects of operating and financial leverage.

Fixed Costs and Combined Leverage Fixed operating costs create operating leverage, fixed financial costs create financial leverage, and these two types of leverage together form combined leverage. If fixed operating costs (FC) and fixed interest costs (I) were both zero, there would be no leverage effect. The percentage change in net income (NI) would be the same as the percentage change in sales. If either, or both, fixed operating costs and fixed financial costs exceed zero, a leverage effect will occur (DCL > 1).

Firms that have high operating leverage need to be careful about how much debt they pile onto their balance sheets, and the accompanying interest costs they incur, because of combined leverage effects. Remember that for

Jason's Popcorn Wagon, the degree of operating leverage (DOL) was 1.71 and the degree of financial leverage was 1.05. The degree of combined leverage for Jason's business according to Equation 13-8 is 1.80 ($1.71 \times 1.05 = 1.80$ rounded to two decimal places). Jason is quite confident that his sales will be high enough so that this high leverage will not be a problem. If the sales outlook were questionable, though, the combined leverage effect could magnify poor sales results.

Leverage is helpful when sales increase (positive percentage changes). Magnifying this positive change benefits the firm. However, leverage is harmful when sales decrease because it magnifies the negative change. Because future sales for most companies are uncertain, most companies view leverage with mixed feelings.

The idea that additional borrowing or leverage may lead to higher sales and profits is not only recognized by the business sector but also by public institutions. Finance at Work 13-1 discusses the uses of leverage by Canadian universities.

NANCE AT WORK 13-1

les Retail Sports Media Technology Public Relations Production Exports

IVERSITIES HOPPING ON BOND ISSUE BANDWAGON

unicipalities, hospitals, airport authorities and other public ·or entities can pay for new facilities and infrastructure by owing huge amounts in the bond market and assuming ;-term debt—in Concordia's case, repayment is over 40 ·s—why not universities?

While the Ottawa-based Canadian Association of versity Business Officers (CAUBO) doesn't specifically k the construction volume and cost of expansion by uniities across Canada, it follows the amounts of their bond es, which reveals something of their scope, says Jacques ıson, CAUBO's executive director.

The total is nearly $2-billion over the past three years, tly to the larger universities, "because if you don't borrow 0-million or more, it isn't worth it," he says. Royal Bank of ada and Bank of Nova Scotia are among the biggest ers to universities.

The University of Toronto, York University, University of British Columbia, Simon Fraser, Concordia, McGill, McMaster, University of Guelph, Queen's, and the University of Ottawa have all gone the bond issue route, he says.

Questions to Consider

1. *How would you approach the analysis of financial performance of a university?*
2. *What may be the key determinants in increasing the debt load by universities?*
3. *Is the trend of university borrowing likely to continue in the future?*

Source: Albert Warson, "Universities Hopping on Bond Issue Bandwagon," *The Globe and Mail*, 23 March 2004. Used with permission. Albert Warson is a Toronto-based freelance writer.

Breakeven Analysis and Leverage

Investments in projects may change a firm's fixed operating and financing costs, thereby affecting firm value. Fixed costs may affect firm value because of *leverage effects* and the resulting risk from those leverage effects.

To understand a firm's potential for risk and return, then, financial managers must understand two types of leverage effects: operating leverage and financial leverage.

Breakeven analysis is a key to understanding *operating leverage*. In breakeven analysis we examine fixed and variable operating costs. Fixed costs are those costs that do not vary with the company's level of production. **Variable costs** are those costs that change as the company's production levels change.

In breakeven analysis, the **sales breakeven point** is the level of sales that a firm must reach to cover its operating costs. Put another way, it is the point at which the operating income (earnings before interest and taxes) equals zero.

A company with high fixed operating costs must generate high sales revenue to reach the sales breakeven point. A company with low fixed operating costs requires relatively low sales revenue to reach its sales breakeven point.

We usually observe a high/low trade-off in breakeven analysis. Firms with high fixed operating costs tend to have low variable costs, and vice versa. A company that automates a factory, for instance, commits to significant fixed costs—the expensive equipment. However, the company's variable labour costs are likely to be low at a highly automated plant that operates with relatively few employees. In contrast, a company that produces handmade pottery with little overhead and hires hourly workers as needed, is likely to have low fixed costs but high variable costs.[4]

To demonstrate the high/low trade-off, we gather data for a sales breakeven chart for two firms. The first firm has high fixed and low variable costs. The second firm has low fixed and high variable costs.

Constructing a Sales Breakeven Chart

A breakeven chart shows graphically how fixed costs, variable costs, and sales revenue interact. Analysts construct the chart by plotting sales revenue and costs at various unit sales levels on a graph. To illustrate, let's construct the breakeven chart for Jason's Popcorn Wagon, featured in the opening of the chapter.

The first step in constructing the breakeven chart is to find the breakeven point for the business. Let's look at some of the numbers for Jason's business and calculate the level of sales Jason must achieve to break even. Recall that at the breakeven point, operating income equals zero. If sales are below the breakeven point, Jason suffers an operating loss. If sales are above the breakeven point, Jason enjoys an operating profit. (Interest and taxes, subtracted after finding operating income, will be discussed in the last section of the chapter.)

Jason wants to know that his business venture has the potential for a positive operating profit, so he is keenly interested in finding his breakeven point. To find this point, we need to know how many bags of popcorn he must sell before the sales revenue contributed by each bag sold just covers his fixed and variable operating costs. The relevant sales breakeven figures for Jason's proposed business are shown in Table 13-4.

The numbers in Table 13-4 show that Jason's fixed costs are high compared with his sales price of $1 per bag of popcorn. The fixed costs include the $8,000

---

[4]Labour costs can be either fixed or variable. If workers are guaranteed pay for a certain minimum number of hours per week, as might be called for in a union contract, the labour costs associated with this minimum guaranteed pay would be fixed costs. The costs associated with hourly worker pay with no guaranteed minimum are variable.

Fixed Costs	
Wagon (annual rental)	$8,000
City License (annual fee)	$4,000
Total	$12,000
Variable Costs per Unit	
One Paper Bag	$0.020
Oil	$0.005
Salt	$0.003
Popcorn	$ 0.012
Total	$0.040
Sales Price per Unit	$1.00

Table 13-4 Jason's Popcorn Wagon Relevant Figures for Breakeven Analysis

annual rental fee for the wagon and the $4,000 annual license fee. Jason must pay these costs no matter how much popcorn he produces and sells.

In contrast to the high fixed operating costs, Jason's variable operating costs per unit are a tiny fraction of his sales price of $1 per unit. The bag, oil, salt, and popcorn that help produce one bag of popcorn cost a total of $0.04. Each bag of popcorn that is sold, then, contributes $0.96 to cover the fixed costs, and ultimately the profit of the business ($1 – $0.04 = $0.96). The sales price per unit minus the variable cost per unit, $0.96 in this case, is the **contribution margin.**

From the numbers presented in Table 13-4, we can calculate the breakeven level of sales for Jason's business. We find the level of sales needed to reach the operating income breakeven point by applying the following formula:

The Breakeven Point in Unit Sales, $Q_{b.e.}$

$$Q_{b.e.} = \frac{FC}{p - VC} \tag{13-11}$$

where

$Q_{b.e.}$ = Quantity unit sales breakeven level
FC = Total fixed costs
p = Sales price per unit
VC = Variable cost per unit

For Jason's business, the total fixed costs are $12,000, the price per unit is $1, and the variable cost per unit is $0.04. According to Equation 13-11, Jason's popcorn business has the following sales breakeven point:

$$\begin{aligned} Q_{b.e.} &= \frac{\$12{,}000}{\$1 - \$0.04} \\ &= \frac{\$12{,}000}{\$0.96} \\ &= 12{,}500 \end{aligned}$$

We find that Jason's sales breakeven point with $12,000 in fixed costs, $0.04 per unit in variable costs, and a $1 per bag sales price, is 12,500 units. At $1 per bag, this is $12,500 in sales to reach the breakeven point.

Now that we know Jason's sales breakeven point, we need revenue and cost information to construct the breakeven chart.

Revenue Data At any given level of unit sales, Jason's total sales revenue can be found using Equation 13-12:

Total Revenue, TR

$$TR = p \times Q \tag{13-12}$$

where

p = Sales price per unit
Q = Unit sales (quantity sold)

Table 13-5 shows how to calculate Jason's sales revenues at different sales levels. For instance, we see that if Jason sells 5,000 bags of popcorn at the price of $1 per bag, his total revenue will be 5,000 × $1 = $5,000. If Jason sells 10,000 bags, his total revenue will be $10,000.

Table 13-5 Sales Revenues at Different Unit Sales Levels

Unit Sales (Q)	×	Price (P)	=	Total Revenue (TR)
0	×	$1	=	$0
5,000	×	$1	=	$5,000
10,000	×	$1	=	$10,000
15,000	×	$1	=	$15,000
20,000	×	$1	=	$20,000
25,000	×	$1	=	$25,000
30,000	×	$1	=	$30,000

Cost Data By definition, Jason's fixed costs will remain $12,000, regardless of the level of unit production and sales. His variable costs, however, increase by $0.04 for each unit sold. Jason's total costs for any given level of unit production and sales can be found using Equation 13-13 as follows:

Total Costs, TC

$$TC = FC + (VC \times Q) \tag{13-13}$$

where

FC = Fixed costs
VC = Variable cost per unit
Q = Units produced

Table 13-6 demonstrates how we use Equation 13-13 to calculate Jason's total costs for different production and sales levels. For instance, we see that if Jason sells 5,000 bags of popcorn at a variable cost of $0.04 per bag and fixed costs of $12,000, his total cost will be $12,200. At 10,000 bags, his total

Fixed Costs (FC)	+	(Variable Cost/Unit (VC)	×	Units Total Produced (Q))	=	Cost (TC)
$12,000	+	($0.04	×	0)	=	$12,000
$12,000	+	($0.04	×	5,000)	=	$12,200
$12,000	+	($0.04	×	10,000)	=	$12,400
$12,000	+	($0.04	×	15,000)	=	$12,600
$12,000	+	($0.04	×	20,000)	=	$12,800
$12,000	+	($0.04	×	25,000)	=	$13,000
$12,000	+	($0.04	×	30,000)	=	$13,200

Table 13-6 Jason's Popcorn Wagon Total Costs for Different Sales Levels

cost will be $12,400. We assume the number of units produced equals the number of units sold.

Plotting Data on the Breakeven Chart Jason's breakeven chart is shown in Figure 13-1. The chart is constructed with units produced and sold (Q) on the horizontal axis and cost and revenue dollars on the vertical axis. Total revenues from Table 13-5 are shown on the TR line and total costs from Table 13-6 are shown on the TC line.

We see from the chart that to break even, Jason has to sell $12,500 worth of popcorn at $1 per bag—a quantity of 12,500 bags.

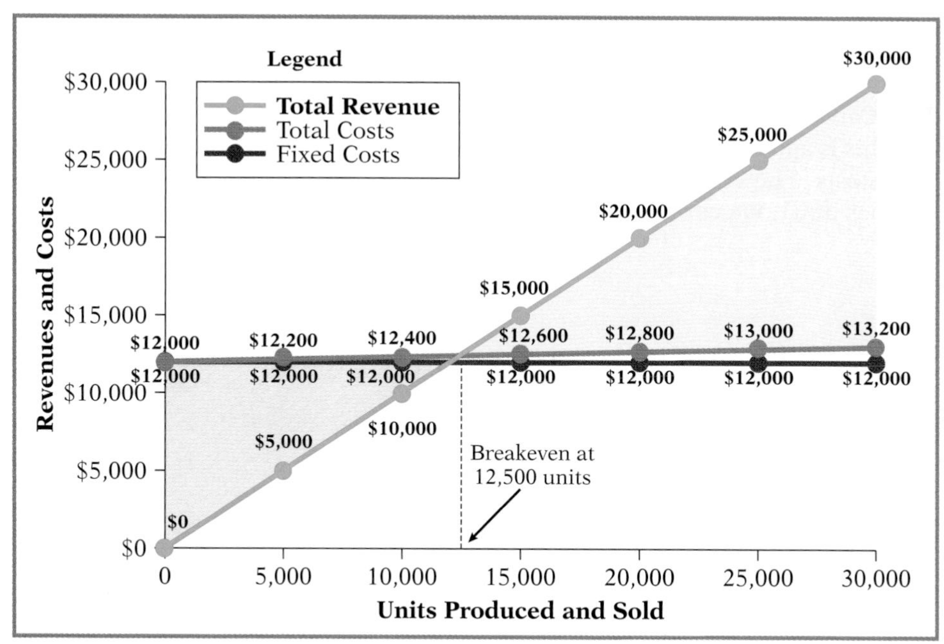

Figure 13-1 Breakeven Chart for Jason's Popcorn Wagon
Figure 13-1 shows the fixed costs, total costs, and total revenues of Jason's Popcorn Wagon at different levels of unit sales. The breakeven sales point, the intersection of the total costs and total revenues lines, is 12,500 units.

Applying Breakeven Analysis

Although 12,500 bags of popcorn may seem like a lot of sales just to break even, Jason has watched another vendor downtown sell, on average, 500 bags of popcorn a day. Jason plans to sell for three months during the summer, four weeks a month, five days a week. He estimates that he could sell 30,000 bags of popcorn (500 bags × 3 months × 4 weeks × 5 days) during the summer. At this sales level, Jason expects $30,000 in gross sales revenue at $1 per bag and $16,800 in operating income [$30,000 total revenue – $12,000 fixed costs – ($30,000 × 0.04 variable costs) = $16,800 operating income]. Not a bad summer job income.

How is it possible to make so much money selling popcorn? Note how once Jason passes the breakeven point in sales, each additional $1 bag of popcorn he sells generates $0.96 of operating profit. The $0.04 in variable costs incurred in the production of that bag of popcorn represents a small part of the $1 in revenue generated. Operating profit rises rapidly as sales climb above the breakeven point of 12,500 units, as shown by Figure 13-1. Were Jason's sales potential not so promising, however, his risk of loss (negative operating income) would be a greater concern. The green area of the graph in Figure 13-1 shows Jason's loss potential.

The breakeven chart allows Jason to see the different sales scenarios to understand his profit and loss potential. Because the total revenue line in Figure 13-1 is much steeper than the total cost line (because the sales price per unit is much greater than the variable cost per unit), the profit potential is great. Because of the high fixed costs, however, the loss potential is great, too. What happens depends on how much popcorn Jason can sell.

To illustrate what happens with a low breakeven business, let's construct a breakeven chart for Carey, another college student, who wants to sell hot-plate mini-cookbooks (only five pages long) to college students.[5]

Because Carey plans to operate from her apartment and use her own recipes for the mini-cookbook, her only fixed cost would be a $1,000 printer's design fee. Her variable costs consist of her paper printing costs at $0.60 per unit. Carey plans to sell her cookbook for $1 per unit.

This is a low-risk business. The design fee is modest and there are no other fixed costs. The contribution margin is $0.40 ($1 sales price – $0.60 variable cost per unit). We can find Carey's breakeven point using Equation 13-11:

$$\begin{aligned} Q_{b.e.} &= \frac{FC}{p - VC} \\ &= \frac{\$1{,}000}{\$1 - \$0.60} \\ &= \frac{\$1{,}000}{\$0.40} \\ &= 2{,}500 \end{aligned}$$

We find that Carey's breakeven point is 2,500 units. Carey figures she can sell to friends in the dorm. Beyond that, however, the sales potential is uncertain. She may or may not reach the breakeven point.

To find Carey's breakeven point, we find her total revenue and total costs at different sales levels and plot them on a breakeven chart.

[5]Believe it or not, Carey's business is also inspired by a true story. Oliver Stone would be proud.

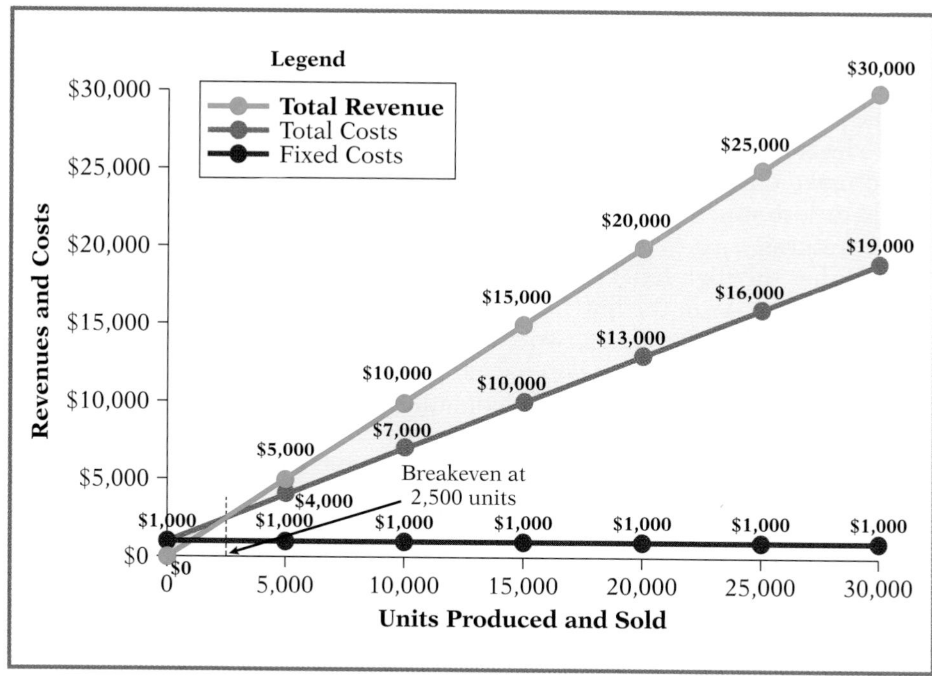

Figure 13-2
Breakeven Chart for Carey's Mini-Cookbooks
Figure 13-2 shows the fixed costs, total costs, and total revenues of Carey's Mini-Cookbooks at different levels of unit sales. The breakeven sales level of 2,500 units is the point at which the total costs line crosses the total revenues line.

Note how small the loss potential is for Carey's business, as shown in the green area in Figure 13-2, compared with Jason's loss potential, shown in the green area in Figure 13-1. Carey's loss potential is small because her breakeven level of sales ($0 operating income) is 2,500 units, compared with Jason's 12,500-unit breakeven point. Even if she sold nothing, Carey would lose only the $1,000 in fixed costs that she had to pay (compared with Jason's $12,000). Table 13-7 shows the profit and loss potential for Jason and Carey.

Table 13-7
Jason's and Carey's Profit and Loss Potential

Units Produced and Sold	Jason			Carey		
	$Total Costs	$Total Revenue	$Operating Income	$Total Costs	$Total Revenue	$Operating Income
0	12,000	0	−12,000	1,000	0	−1,000
5,000	12,200	5,000	−7,200	4,000	5,000	1,000
10,000	12,400	10,000	−2,400	7,000	10,000	3,000
15,000	12,600	15,000	2,400	10,000	15,000	5,000
20,000	12,800	20,000	7,200	13,000	20,000	7,000
25,000	13,000	25,000	12,000	16,000	25,000	9,000
30,000	13,200	30,000	16,800	19,000	30,000	11,000
35,000	13,400	35,000	21,600	22,000	35,000	13,000
40,000	13,600	40,000	26,400	25,000	40,000	15,000

The risk of Jason's business is also evident when we look at sales of 15,000 units for each business. Jason has a profit of only $2,400, whereas Carey would earn a profit of $5,000; at 30,000 units sold, however, Jason earns a profit of

$16,800 and Carey earns only $11,000, as shown in Table 13-7. Jason's profits are much more dependent on selling a large number of units than Carey's.

Now compare the profit potential for the two proposed businesses. Jason has the potential to make much more profit (operating income) than Carey. At a sales level of 30,000, Table 13-7 shows Jason makes $16,800, whereas Carey would make only $11,000. Even though Jason's business has more risk—he stands to lose much more if sales do not go well—he has the potential for greater returns.

Take Note

Long-distance telephone and cable companies are examples of firms with high fixed costs and low variable costs per unit. A consulting firm would be an example of a firm with low fixed costs and high variable costs.

Whether the high fixed cost and low variable cost per unit business (like Jason's) is better than the low fixed cost and high variable cost per unit business (like Carey's) depends on two factors: how many units you think you can sell and how much tolerance you have for risk. High fixed costs and low variable costs per unit mean high profit potential and high loss potential, as in the case of Jason's proposed business. Conversely, low fixed costs and high variable costs per unit mean low profit potential and low loss potential, as in the case of Carey's proposed business.

LBOs

Many publicly owned corporations have been bought out by a small group of investors, including top management of the firm, using a large amount of borrowed money. Such a purchase is called a *leveraged buyout,* or LBO. The leverage referred to is financial leverage.

In an LBO, investment banking firms work to identify attractive target companies. These investment-banking firms solicit investors to acquire the target. To take over the target, the purchasing group raises cash, mostly borrowed, to purchase the common shares from the general public. The share purchase converts the publicly owned corporation to a privately owned one. The investment-banking firm would collect fees for its advice and for underwriting the bond issue that helped raise the additional debt capital.

Because of the dramatic increase in financial leverage, some LBOs have worked out well for investors and others have been disasters. For instance, Kohlberg, Kravis, & Roberts, better known as KKR, made a 50 percent annual rate of return on its $1.34 billion investment after the Beatrice Company LBO. In contrast, the 1986 $1.4 billion LBO of Revco Drug Stores did not fare as well. Two years later the company filed for bankruptcy when it was unable to generate enough cash flow to pay the interest and principal due on its bonds. Other companies purchased through LBOs include Borg-Warner, Montgomery Ward, Safeway, and Southland.

When a company with a normal debt load goes through an LBO, investors holding the company's bonds issued before the LBO are often hurt. The surge in the company's debt results in more financial risk. With higher risk, the market requires a higher rate of return, so the bonds issued before the LBO will see their market interest rates rise—and their market prices fall—after the company announces an LBO.

To illustrate the effects on bondholders, consider the 1989 LBO of RJR Nabisco. Table 13-8 shows how the holders of the RJR Nabisco bonds suddenly had a claim on a much riskier company.

The bondholders, led by Metropolitan Life Insurance Company, sued when the value of the bonds they held dropped precipitously after the firm announced its LBO. The lawsuit was settled out of court in 1991.

Table 13-8 Effect of a Leveraged Buyout on RJR Nabisco

	Before the Buyout (1988)	**After the Buyout (1989)**
Long-Term Debt	$4,975 million	$21,948 million
Total Equity	$5,819 million	$1,237 million
Debt to Equity Ratio	85.5%	1,774%

Source: Value-Line Investment Survey

The risk of an LBO is large because of financial leverage effects. As the Beatrice and Revco examples indicate, potential returns from an LBO may be large positive or negative values because of financial leverage effects. Bondholders may suddenly see the value of their bonds drop precipitously after an LBO announcement. In Chapter 14, we discuss how bondholders can protect themselves against this risk.

Now that we have analyzed how fixed operating and financial costs can create leverage effects and risk, we will consider the optimal capital structure for a firm.

Ethical Connections 13-1 discusses the issues related to the LBO transaction in the case of RJR Nabisco.

ETHICAL CONNECTIONS 13-1
Let's Rip Off the Bondholders?

e board of directors of a corporation is elected by the com-
on shareholders. The bondholders generally have no say
out who serves on the board. If the board is considering a
oposal that will create considerable value for the sharehold-
s, while at the same time raking the bondholders over the
als, what do you think the board will do? Is there anything
ong with this? After all the board members have a fiduciary
sponsibility to the shareholders, not to the bondholders.

The RJR Nabisco bondholders at Metropolitan Life
surance Company, in the example on pages 454–455,
ould not have been shocked that the board of RJR Nabisco
ted to approve the LBO offered to the company. In almost
y takeover a significant premium over the current market
ue is offered to shareholders. You may be able to buy a few
ndred shares at the current market price, but a significant
emium, perhaps 30 percent to 50 percent or more, will
ually have to be paid if you want to buy the whole com-
ny. You are buying real control when you buy the whole
mpany, whereas you are buying an insignificant amount of
ntrol when you buy a few hundred shares.

The directors of RJR Nabisco clearly created extra value
the shareholders. Because the buyout was achieved with
huge amount of borrowed money, the bondholders found
emselves suddenly with a debt claim against a very risky company, whereas the day before the LBO was announced the firm had had a much lower level of risk. High-risk companies have higher interest rates demanded by the market for their bonds. If the market's required rate of return for your bond goes up, the price of your bond goes down.

The bondholders clearly thought that the LBO was unfair so they sued. It was certainly unpleasant even if it was not unfair.

Questions to Consider

1. *Did the RJR Nabisco board members have any responsibility to the bondholders of the company?*
2. *Did RJR Nabisco make any promises that it would not take on more debt after the earlier bonds were sold?*
3. *When you obtain a mortgage loan or car loan, do you promise not to borrow more money in the future?*
4. *If the bondholders wanted protection from future bond issues, should this not have been brought up when those bonds were initially sold rather than years later?*
5. *Is it not true that the bondholders are being taken advantage of by the common shareholders through the latter's representatives on the board of directors?*

Capital Structure Theory

Every time a company borrows, it increases its financial leverage and financial risk. New equity financing decreases financial leverage and risk. Changes in financial leverage, we have seen, bring the potential for good and bad results. How then do financial managers decide on the right balance of debt and equity? Financial managers analyze many factors, including the tax effects of interest payments and how the comparative costs of debt and equity affect firm value.

Tax Deductibility of Interest

Debt in a firm's capital structure can be beneficial. First, debt creates the potential for leveraged increases in net income (NI) when operating income (EBIT) is rising. Second, debt gives the company a tax deduction for the interest that is paid on the debt. In contrast to debt, an issue of common shares to raise equity funds results in no tax break. In short, interest paid on business debt is tax deductible, but dividends paid to common shareholders are not. The tax laws, therefore, give companies an incentive to use debt in their capital structures.

Although the tax deductibility of interest payments on debt is a benefit, debt has costs, too. We know that the financial risk of the firm increases as debt increases. As financial risk increases, including an increasing risk of bankruptcy, a company will incur costs to deal with this risk. For example, suppliers may refuse to extend trade credit to the company, and lawyers' fees may drain funds that could go to either bondholders or common share investors.

Modigliani and Miller

How does a company balance the costs and benefits of debt? In 1958, Franco Modigliani and Merton Miller wrote a seminal paper that has influenced capital structure discussion ever since. Modigliani and Miller (known in economics and finance circles as M&M) concluded that when interest payments are tax deductible to a firm, a capital structure of all debt is optimal.

In reaching this conclusion, M&M assumed the following:

1. There were no transaction costs.
2. Purchasers of a company's bonds or common shares paid no income tax.
3. Corporations and investors can borrow at the same rate of interest.
4. Investors and management have the same information about the firm.
5. Debt the firm issues is riskless.
6. Operating income is not affected by the use of debt.

In such an environment, M&M showed that the tax benefits to the firm from issuing debt were so beneficial that the benefits allowed the company to increase its value by issuing more and more debt. Given the assumptions, a 100 percent debt capital structure is optimal.

The assumptions, of course, do not exist in the real world. Companies do not seek a 100 percent debt capital structure, suggesting that capital structure is not optimal. In the real world, capital structures vary widely.

Toward an Optimal Capital Structure

Firms seek to balance the costs and benefits of debt to reach an optimal mix that maximizes the value of the firm. Figure 13-3 shows the component costs and weighted cost of capital according to the view of most financial managers. Given the way suppliers of capital react in the real world, many financial managers believe this view is more realistic than the M&M model.

Figure 13-3 illustrates what many believe happens to the cost of debt, equity, and the weighted average cost of capital (WACC) as the capital structure of the firm changes. First, the graph shows that debt is less expensive than equity capital. Second, it shows that the weighted average cost of capital equals the cost of equity when the firm has no debt. Third, it shows that at point Z, firms minimize the weighted average cost of capital so, at that point, the capital structure maximizes the value of the firm. The cost advantage that debt has over equity dominates the increasing risk up to point Z. At this point, the greater risk begins to dominate and causes the weighted average cost of capital to begin to turn upward.

We learned in Chapter 9 how to estimate the costs of debt and equity and weighted average figures. Here we study how capital structure changes may affect the firm's cost of capital and its value.

The Lower Cost of Debt Figure 13-3 shows that debt capital has a lower cost than equity capital. Debt is less expensive than equity for two reasons. As mentioned earlier, interest payments made by a firm are tax deductible and dividend payments made to common shareholders are not. Even without the tax break, however, debt funds are cheaper than equity funds. The required rate of return on a bond is lower than the required rate of return on common shares for a given company because debt is less risky than equity to investors.

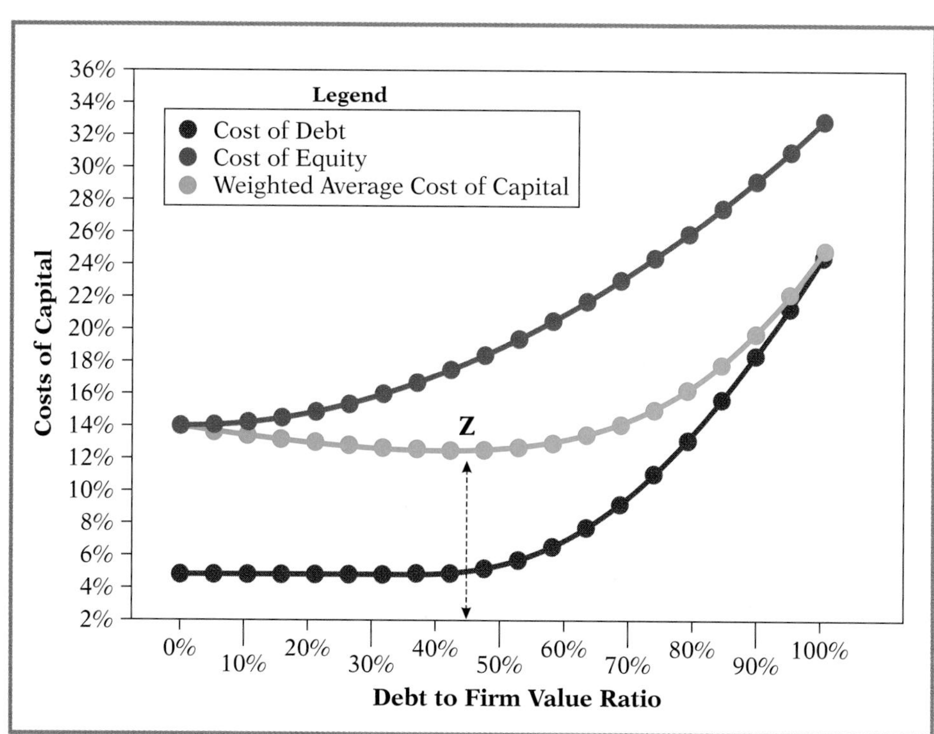

Figure 13-3
Cost of Capital and Capital Structure
Figure 13-3 shows the cost of debt, cost of equity, and weighted average cost of capital (WACC) for different capital structures. The WACC is minimized at point Z.

Debt is less risky because bondholders have a claim superior to that of common shareholders on the earnings and assets of the firm.

How Capital Costs Change as Debt Is Added If we examine the WACC line in Figure 13-3, we see that the weighted average cost of capital equals the cost of equity when the firm has no debt. Then, as debt is added, the cost advantage (to the issuing company) of debt over equity makes the weighted average cost of capital decrease, up to a point, as more of the less expensive debt funds and less of the more expensive equity funds are used. The effect of adding debt to capital structure is shown in Figure 13-3 as we move along the horizontal axis from the origin.

The Effect of Risk What causes the WACC to increase, as shown in Figure 13-3, beyond point Z? As the firm moves to a capital structure with higher debt (moves to the right along the horizontal axis of Figure 13-3), the risk of the firm increases. As financial risk rises with additional debt, the required return of both debt and equity investors increases. Notice that the cost of equity curve starts to climb sooner than the cost of debt curve. This is because common shareholders get paid *after* bondholders.

As both the cost of debt and the cost of equity curves turn upward, the curve depicting the weighted average of the cost of debt and the cost of equity eventually turns upward, too. According to the capital structure view depicted in Figure 13-3, if a firm has less debt than the amount at Z, the WACC is higher than it needs to be. Likewise, if a firm has more debt than the amount at Z, the WACC is higher than it needs to be. Only at the capital structure at point Z do firms minimize the weighted average cost of capital. This is the capital structure, then, that maximizes the value of the firm.

Establishing the Optimal Capital Structure in Practice In the real world, it is unlikely that financial managers can determine an exact point for Z where the WACC is minimized. Many financial managers try instead to estimate Z and set a capital structure close to it. Unfortunately, no formula can help estimate point Z. The optimal capital structure for a firm depends on the future prospects of that firm.

For example, say a company has a product in great demand that is protected by a patent with many years to expiration. The company will find that bond and common share investors are comfortable with a large amount of debt. This firm's Z value will be high. However, a firm in a competitive industry, with some quality control problems and soft demand for its product, is in a different position. It will find that bond and common share investors get nervous (and demand higher returns) when the debt to total value[6] ratio is above even a moderate level. This firm's Z value will be much lower than that of the first firm.

So the answer to the question, "What is the optimal capital structure for a firm?" is, "It depends." With no formula to use to estimate the firm's Z value, management examines the capital structure of similar companies and the future prospects of the firm. Financial managers must balance the costs and benefits of debt and use expertise and experience to develop the capital structure they deem optimal.

---

[6]Total value here refers to the total market value of the firm's outstanding debt and equity.

SUMMARY

13-1 Define capital structure and describe a central question in finance about it.

Capital structure is the mixture of funding sources (debt, preferred shares, or common shares) that a firm uses to finance its assets. A central question in finance is what blend of these financing sources is best for the firm. That is, how much of a firm's assets should be financed by borrowing? How much should be financed by preferred shareholders? How much should be financed by the common shareholders? The question is important because each of these financing sources has a different cost and each of them has a different degree of risk. Therefore, the choice of financing directly affects a firm's weighted average cost of capital and the degree of riskiness in the firm.

13-2 Explain operating, financial, and combined leverage effects and the resulting business and financial risks.

Firms with high fixed costs have high operating leverage—that is, a small change in sales triggers a relatively large change in operating income. Firms with low fixed costs have less operating leverage. The effect of low operating leverage is that small changes in sales do not cause large changes in operating income.

Business risk refers to the volatility of a company's operating income. Business risk is triggered by sales volatility and magnified by fixed operating costs.

If a company uses fixed-cost funds (such as fixed interest rate bonds) to raise capital, financial leverage results. With financial leverage, fixed interest costs cause net income to change by a greater percentage than a given percentage change in EBIT.

The presence of financial leverage creates financial risk for a firm—the risk that the firm will not be able to make its interest payments if operating income drops. Financial risk compounds the business risk already present.

The total effect of operating leverage and financial leverage is called combined leverage. The value of the degree of financial leverage is multiplied by the value of the degree of operating leverage to give the degree of combined leverage (DCL). The DCL gives the percentage change in net income for a given percentage change in sales.

13-3 Describe how to find the breakeven level of sales for a firm.

The costs of operating a business can be categorized as fixed or variable. Operating costs that do not vary with the level of production are fixed; operating costs that do vary with the level of production are variable. High fixed costs are usually tied to low variable costs per unit and low fixed costs are usually tied to high variable costs per unit.

The breakeven point is the level of sales that results in an operating income of zero. At sales levels above the breakeven point, a firm begins to make a profit. A company with high fixed operating costs must generate high sales revenue to cover its fixed costs (and its variable costs) before reaching the sales breakeven point. Conversely, a firm with low fixed operating costs will break even with a relatively low level of sales revenue.

13-4 Describe the risks and returns of a leveraged buyout.

LBOs, or leveraged buyouts, occur when publicly owned corporations are bought out by a small group of investors using mostly borrowed funds. The purchase is leveraged because the investors finance it with a large amount of borrowed money. Consequently, when a firm is purchased in an LBO, it is saddled with a large amount of debt in its capital structure and a large amount of financial leverage and financial risk.

13-5 Explain how changes in capital structure affect a firm's value.

Capital structure theory deals with the mixture of debt, preferred shares, and equity a firm utilizes. Because interest on business loans is a tax-deductible expense, and because lenders demand a lower rate of return than shareholders for a given company (because lending money is not as risky as owning shares), debt capital is less expensive than equity capital. However, the more a company borrows, the more it increases its financial leverage and financial risk. The additional risk causes lenders and shareholders to demand a higher rate of return. Financial managers use capital structure theory to help determine the mix of debt and equity at which the weighted average cost of capital is lowest.

EQUATIONS INTRODUCED IN THIS CHAPTER

Equation 13-1: Degree of Operating Leverage (DOL)

$$DOL = \frac{\%\Delta EBIT}{\%\Delta Sales}$$

where

%ΔEBIT = Percentage change in earnings before interest and taxes
%ΔSales = Percentage change in sales

Equation 13-2: Degree of Operating Leverage (DOL) (alternate)

$$DOL = \frac{Sales - VC}{Sales - VC - FC}$$

where

VC = Total variable costs
FC = Total fixed costs

Equation 13-3: Percentage Change in EBIT

$$\%\Delta EBIT = \%\Delta Sales \times DOL$$

where

%ΔSales = Percentage change in sales
DOL = Degree of operating leverage

Equation 13-4: Degree of Financial Leverage (DFL)

$$DFL = \frac{\%\Delta NI}{\%\Delta EBIT}$$

where

%ΔNI = Percentage change in net income
%ΔEBIT = Percentage change in earnings before interest and taxes

Equation 13-5: Degree of Financial Leverage (DFL) (alternate)

$$DFL = \frac{EBIT}{EBIT - I}$$

where

EBIT = Earnings before interest and taxes
I = Interest expense

Equation 13-6: Percentage Change in Net Income

$$\%\Delta NI = \%\Delta EBIT \times DFL$$

where

%ΔEBIT = Percentage change in earnings before interest and taxes
DFL = Degree of financial leverage

Equation 13-7: Degree of Combined Leverage (DCL)

$$DCL = \frac{\%\Delta NI}{\%\Delta Sales}$$

where

$\%\Delta NI$ = Percentage change in net income
$\%\Delta Sales$ = Percentage change in sales

Equation 13-8: Degree of Combined Leverage (DCL) (alternate 1)

$$DCL = \frac{Sales - VC}{Sales - VC - FC - I}$$

where

VC = Total variable costs
FC = Total fixed costs
I = Interest expense

Equation 13-9: Degree of Combined Leverage (DCL) (alternate 2)

$$DCL = DOL \times DFL$$

where

DOL = Degree of operating leverage
DFL = Degree of financial leverage

Equation 13-10: Percentage Change in Net Income (NI)

$$\%\Delta NI = \%\Delta Sales \times DOL \times DFL$$

where

$\%\Delta Sales$ = Percentage change in sales
DOL = Degree of operating leverage
DFL = Degree of financial leverage

Equation 13-11: The Breakeven Point in Unit Sales, $Q_{b.e}$

$$Q_{b.e.} = \frac{FC}{p - VC}$$

where

$Q_{b.e.}$ = Quantity unit sales breakeven level
FC = Total fixed costs
p = Sales price per unit
VC = Variable cost per unit

Equation 13-12: Total Revenue, TR

$$TR = p \times Q$$

where

p = Sales price per unit
Q = Unit sales (quantity sold)

Equation 13-13: Total Costs, TC

$$TC = FC + (VC \times Q)$$

where

FC = Fixed costs
VC = Variable cost per unit
Q = Units produced

SELF-TEST

ST-1. Mr. Marsalis's firm has fixed costs of $40,000, variable costs per unit of $4, and a selling price per unit of $9. What is Mr. Marsalis's breakeven level of sales (in units)?

ST-2. HAL's computer store has sales of $225,000, fixed costs of $40,000, and variable costs of $100,000. Calculate the degree of operating leverage (DOL) for this firm.

ST-3. HAL's computer store has operating income (EBIT) of $85,000 and interest expense of $10,000. Calculate the firm's degree of financial leverage (DFL).

ST-4. Kane Newspapers, Inc. has an after-tax cost of debt of 6 percent. The cost of equity is 14 percent. The firm believes that its optimal capital structure is 30 percent debt and 70 percent equity and it maintains its capital structure according to these weights. What is the weighted average cost of capital?

ST-5. Johnny Ringo's Western Shoppe expects its sales to increase by 20 percent next year. If this year's sales are $500,000 and the degree of operating leverage (DOL) is 1.4, what is the expected level of operating income (EBIT) for next year if this year's EBIT is $100,000?

ST-6. Marion Pardoo's Bookstore has a degree of operating leverage (DOL) of 1.6 and a degree of financial leverage (DFL) of 1.8. What is the company's degree of combined leverage (DCL)?

REVIEW QUESTIONS

1. What is the operating leverage effect and what causes it? What are the potential benefits and negative consequences of high operating leverage?
2. Does high operating leverage always mean high business risk? Explain.
3. What is the financial leverage effect and what causes it? What are the potential benefits and negative consequences of high financial leverage?
4. Give two examples of types of companies likely to have high operating leverage. Find examples other than those cited in the chapter.
5. Give two examples of types of companies that would be best able to handle high debt levels.
6. What is an LBO? What are the risks for the equity investors and what are the potential rewards?
7. If an optimal capital structure exists, what are the reasons that too little debt is as undesirable as too much debt?

PROBLEMS

Breakeven Point ▶

13-1 Lilies, a flower shop, has the following data for October 2004:

Fixed Costs	$2,300/month
Variable Costs (per unit)	
Packets	$ 0.75
Décor	$ 3
Miscellaneous	$ 2
Sales Price	$50

a. What is Lilies's breakeven point in sales per month?

b. The owner of Lilies is planning on moving to a new location that will cut fixed costs by 30 percent. The price can be lowered to $45 per unit. What is the new breakeven point in sales (per month)?

13-2. ViSorb sells its deluxe cell phone model for $125, its advanced model for $90, and its basic model for $55. The company has fixed costs of $10,000 per month and variable costs are $15 per unit sold. ◀ Total Revenue, Total Costs

a. Calculate the total revenue if 30 units of each model are sold.

b. What are the total costs if 30 units of each model are sold?

c. What is the company's total revenue if it sells 10 deluxe models, 15 advanced models, and 35 basic models?

d. What would its total costs be at the sales level in (c)?

13-3. The following is an income statement for Gabotti Enterprises. ◀ Degree of Operating Leverage

	2001	2002
Net Sales	$15,000,000	$25,000,000
Fixed Costs	3,800,000	3,800,000
Variable Costs	1,980,000	3,300,000
Operating Income	9,220,000	17,900,000
Interest Expense	1,710,000	1,710,000
EBT	7,510,000	16,190,000
Taxes (30%)	2,253,000	4,857,000
Net Income	$5,257,000	$11,333,000

Calculate Gabotti Enterprises' DOL. Use both methods and compare results.

13-4. From the table in problem 13-3, calculate Gabotti Enterprises' DFL using both methods. ◀ Degree of Financial Leverage

13-5. Howard Beal Co. manufactures molds for casting aluminum alloy test samples. Fixed costs amount to $20,000 per year. Variable costs for each unit manufactured are $16. Sales price per unit is $28. ◀ Breakeven Anaylsis

a. What is the contribution margin of the product?

b. Calculate the breakeven point in unit sales and dollars.

c. What is the operating profit (loss) if the company manufactures and sells

   i. 1,500 units per year?

   ii. 3,000 units per year?

d. Plot a breakeven chart using the forgoing figures.

13-6. UBC Company, a competitor of Howard Beal Co. in problem 13-5, has a comparatively labour-intensive process with old equipment. Fixed costs are $10,000 per year and variable costs are $20 per unit. Sales price is the same, $28 per unit. ◀ Breakeven Analysis

a. What is the contribution margin of the product?

b. Calculate the breakeven point in unit sales and dollars.

c. What is the operating profit (loss) if the company manufactures and sells

   i. 1,500 units per year?

   ii. 3,000 units per year?

d. Plot a breakeven chart using the figures in (c).

e. Comment on the profit and loss potential of UBC Company compared with Howard Beal Co.

Operating Leverage ▶

13-7. Use the same data given in problem 13-5 (fixed cost = $20,000 per year, variable cost = $16 per unit, and sales price = $28 per unit) for Howard Beal Co. The company sold 3,000 units in 2002 and expects to sell 3,300 units in 2003. Fixed costs, variable costs per unit, and sales price per unit are assumed to remain the same in 2002 and 2003.

a. Calculate the percentage change in operating income and compare it with the percentage change in sales.

b. Comment on the operating leverage effect.

c. Calculate the degree of operating leverage using

  i. data for 2002 and 2003

  ii. data for 2002 only

d. Explain what the results obtained in (c) tell us.

Financial Leverage ▶

13-8. Use the same data given in problems 13-5 and 13-7 (fixed cost = $20,000 per year, variable cost per unit = $16, sales price per unit = $28, 2002 sales = 3,000 units, and expected 2003 sales = 3,300 units) for Howard Beal Co. Fixed costs, variable costs per unit, and sales price per unit are assumed to remain the same in 2002 and 2003. The company has an interest expense of $2,000 per year. Applicable income tax rate is 30 percent.

a. Calculate the percentage change in net income and compare it with the percentage change in operating income (EBIT).

b. Comment on the financial leverage effect.

c. Calculate the degree of financial leverage using

  i. data for 2002 and 2003

  ii. data for 2002 only

d. Explain what the results obtained in (c) tell us about financial leverage.

Breakeven Analysis ▶

13-9. Tony Manero owns a small company that refinishes and maintains the wood flooring of many dance clubs in Toronto. Because of heavy use, his services are required at least quarterly by most of the clubs. Tony's annual fixed costs consist of amortization expense for his van, polishing equipment, and other tools. These expenses were $9,000 this year. His variable costs include wood-staining products, wax, and other miscellaneous supplies. Tony has been in this business since 1977 and accurately estimates his variable costs at $1.50 per square yard of dance floor. Tony charges a rate of $15 per square yard.

a. How many square yards of dance floor will he need to work on this year to cover all of his expenses but leave him with zero operating income?

b. What is this number called?

c. Calculate the breakeven point in dollar sales.

d. Tony has little competent competition in the Toronto area. What happens to the breakeven point in sales dollars if Tony increases his rate to $18 per square yard?

e. At the $18 per square yard rate, what are Tony's operating income and net income if he completes work on 14,000 square yards this year? Assume his tax rate is 40 percent and he has a $25,000 loan outstanding on which he pays 12 percent interest annually.

Operating Leverage and Breakeven Analysis ▶

13-10. Otis Day's company manufactures and sells men's suits. His trademark grey flannel suits are popular on Bay Street and in boardrooms throughout the East. Each suit sells for $800. Fixed costs are $200,000 and variable costs are $250 per suit.

a. What is the firm's operating income on sales of 600 suits? On sales of 3,000 suits?

b. What is Mr. Day's degree of operating leverage (DOL) at a sales level of 600 suits? At a sales level of 3,000 suits?

c. Calculate Mr. Day's breakeven point in sales units and sales dollars.

d. If the cost of the grey flannel material increases so that Mr. Day's variable costs are now $350 per suit, what will be his new breakeven point in sales units and sales dollars?

e. Considering the increase in variable costs, by how much will he need to increase the selling price per suit to reach the original operating income for sales of 3,000 suits calculated in (a)?

13-11. Company A, Company B, and Company C all manufacture and sell identical products. They each sell 12,000 units annually at a price of $10 per unit. Assume Company A has $0 fixed costs and variable costs of $5 per unit. Company B has $10,000 in fixed costs and $4 in variable costs per unit. Company C has $40,000 fixed costs and $1 per unit variable costs. ◀ Operating Leverage

a. Calculate the operating income (EBIT) for each of the three companies.

b. Before making any further calculations, rank the companies from highest to lowest by their relative degrees of operating leverage. Remember what you read about how fixed costs affect operating leverage.

13-12. Faber Corporation, a basketball hoop manufacturing firm in Red Deer, Alberta, plans to branch out and begin producing basketballs in addition to basketball hoops. It has a choice of two different production methods for the basketballs. Method 1 will have variable costs of $6 per ball and fixed costs of $700,000 for the high-tech machinery, which requires little human supervision. Method 2 employs many people to hand-sew the basketballs. It has variable costs of $16.50 per ball, but fixed costs are estimated to be only $100,000. Regardless of which method CEO Norman Dale chooses, the basketballs will sell for $30 each. Marketing research indicates sales in the first year will be 50,000 balls. Sales volume is expected to increase to 60,000 in year 2. ◀ Operating Leverage

a. Calculate the sales revenue expected in years 1 and 2.

b. Calculate the percentage change in sales revenue.

c. Calculate the earnings before interest and taxes for each year for both production methods.

d. Calculate the percentage change in EBIT for each method.

e. Calculate the year 1 degree of operating leverage for each method, using your answers from (b) and (d).

f. Calculate the degree of operating leverage again. This time use only revenue, fixed costs, and variable costs from year 1 (your base year) for each production method.

g. Under which production method would EBIT be more adversely affected if the sales volume did not reach the expected levels?

h. What would drive this adverse effect on EBIT?

i. Recalculate the year 1 base year EBIT and the degree of operating leverage for both production methods if year 2 sales are expected to be only 53,000 units.

13-13. Three companies manufacture and sell identical products. They each have earnings before interest and taxes of $100,000. Assume Company A is an all-equity company and, therefore, has zero debt. Company B's capital structure is ◀ Financial Leverage

10 percent debt and 90 percent equity. It makes annual interest payments of \$2,000. Company C's capital structure is just the opposite of B. It has 90 percent debt and 10 percent equity. Company C has annual interest expense of \$40,000. The tax rate for each of the three companies is 40 percent.

a. Before making any calculations, rank the companies from highest to lowest by their relative degrees of financial leverage (DFL). Remember what you read about how debt and the interest expense that comes with it affects financial leverage.
b. Calculate the degree of financial leverage for each company. Was your answer to (a) correct?
c. Calculate the net income for each company.

Financial Leverage ▶

Excel

13-14. Michael Dorsey and Dorothy Michaels each own their own companies. They design and supply custom-made costumes for Broadway plays. The income statement from each company shows they each have earnings before interest and taxes of \$50,000 this year. Mr. Dorsey has an outstanding loan for \$70,000 on which he pays 13 percent interest annually. When she started her business, Ms Michaels only needed to borrow \$10,000. She is still paying 9 percent annual interest on the loan. Each company expects EBIT for next year to be \$60,000. The tax rate for each is 40 percent and is not expected to change for next year.

a. Calculate the net income for each company for this year and next year.
b. Calculate the percentage change in net income for each company.
c. Calculate the percentage change in EBIT for each company.
d. Calculate this year's degree of financial leverage for each company using your answers from (b) and (c).
e. Calculate the degree of financial leverage for each company again. This time use only EBIT and interest expense for this year.
f. If earnings before interest and taxes do not reach the expected levels, in which company would net income be more adversely affected?
g. What would drive this adverse effect on net income?
h. Recalculate the degree of financial leverage and the net income expected for next year for both companies if EBIT only increases to \$53,000.

Degree of Combined Leverage ▶

13-15. In 2002, Calaire had net income of \$75,000 and sales of \$230,000. John Mastore, the financial manager, has forecast the 2003 net income to be \$200,000 and sales to be \$400,000. What is Calaire's degree of combined leverage if these numbers become fact?

Challenge Problem ▶

Excel

13-16. Fanny Brice, owner of Funny Girl Comics, has sales revenue of \$200,000, earnings before interest and taxes of \$95,000 and net income of \$30,000 this year. She is expecting sales to increase to \$225,000 next year. The degree of operating leverage is 1.35 and the degree of financial leverage is relatively low at 1.09.

a. Calculate the percentage change in EBIT Ms. Brice can expect between this year and next year.
b. How much will EBIT be next year in dollars?
c. Calculate the percentage change in net income Ms. Brice can expect between this year and next year.
d. How much net income should Ms. Brice expect next year?
e. Calculate this year's degree of combined leverage (DCL).
f. Ms. Brice is considering a price increase. This would mean the percentage change in sales revenue between this year and next year would be 20 percent. If this is true, what net income (in dollars) can she expect for next year?

◀ Degree of Combined Leverage

13-17. Clint Reno owns Real Cowboy, a western wear store that has current annual sales of $2,800,000. The degree of operating leverage (DOL) is 1.4. EBIT is $600,000. Real Cowboy has $2 million in debt on which it pays 10 percent annual interest. Calculate the degree of combined leverage for Real Cowboy.

◀ DOL, DFL, and DCL Interactions

13-18. Chad Gates owns Strings Attached, a store that sells guitars. The company has $5 million in current annual sales, fixed operating costs of $300,000, and $700,000 in variable operating costs for a total EBT of $2.5 million. The firm has debt of $16,666,666.67 on which it pays 9 percent annual interest. The degree of combined leverage (DCL) for Strings Attached is 1.72.

a. Calculate the degree of operating leverage (DOL).

b. What is the degree of financial leverage (DFL) for Strings Attached? Calculate your answer using the EBIT and interest expense figures and your knowledge of how DOL and DFL jointly determine DCL.

c. If sales next year increase by 20 percent, what will be the percent change in net income?

◀ Comprehensive Problem

13-19. Soccer International, Inc. produces and sells soccer balls. Partial information from the income statement for 2002 and 2003 follows.

Soccer International, Inc.
Income Statement for the Year Ended December 31

	2002	2003
Sales Revenue	$560,000	616,000
Variable Costs	240,000	264,000
Fixed Costs	160,000	160,000
EBIT	—	—
Interest Expense	40,000	40,000
EBT	—	—
Income Taxes (30%)	—	—
Net Income	—	—

Soccer International sells each soccer ball for $16.

a. Fill in the missing values in the income statements of 2002 and 2003.

b. Calculate Soccer International's breakeven point in sales units for 2002 and 2003.

c. Calculate the breakeven point in dollar sales for 2002 and for 2003.

d. How many soccer balls need to be sold to have an operating income of $200,000 in 2002?

e. What is the operating profit (loss) in 2002 if the company sells

i. 18,000 balls?

ii. 24,000 balls in 2002?

f. Calculate the degree of operating leverage for 2002 and for 2003.

g. If sales revenue is expected to increase by 10 percent in 2003, calculate the percentage increase in EBIT and the dollar amount of EBIT for 2003.

h. Calculate the degree of financial leverage for 2002 and for 2003.

i. Calculate the percentage change in net income and the dollar amount of net income expected in 2003.

j. Calculate the degree of combined leverage for 2002 and for 2003.

k. Assume Soccer International raises its selling price and that sales revenue increases to $650,000 in 2003. How much net income can be expected in 2003?

Percentage Change in Net Income ▶ **13-20.** Los Amigos has an operating income of $35,000 in 2002 and a projected operating income of $50,000 in 2003. It estimates its DFL to be 1.71. At this estimated DFL, what will be the change in net income?

DOL, DFL, and DCL ▶ **13-21.** The income statement for Company ABC is presented below. For the years 2005, 2006, and 2007, calculate DOL, DFL, and DCL.

Income Statement
Company ABC
2004–2007

	2004	2005	2006	2007
Net Sales	346,000	398,000	434,000	457,000
Cost of Goods Sold	224,900	246,760	264,740	274,200
S&A Expenses	90,000	102,000	115,000	123,000
Amortization	7,600	9,600	11,700	14,200
Operating Income	23,500	39,640	42,560	45,600
Interest Expense	3,200	4,000	4,700	5,800
Earnings before Taxes	20,300	35,640	37,860	39,800
Income Tax	8,120	14,256	15,144	15,920
Net Income	12,180	21,384	22,716	23,880

DOL, DFL, and DCL ▶ **13-22.** The income statement for Company XYZ is presented below. For the years 2005, 2006, and 2007, calculate DOL, DFL, and DCL.

Income Statement
Company XYZ
2004–2007

	2004	2005	2006	2007
Net Sales	15,000	21,000	25,000	28,000
Cost of Goods Sold	6,750	9,660	11,750	13,440
S&A Expenses	6,200	8,000	9,400	10,000
Amortization	1,300	1,500	1,700	1,700
Operating Income	750	1,840	2,150	2,860
Interest Expense	600	700	700	800
Earnings before Taxes	150	1,140	1,450	2,060
Income Tax	60	456	580	824
Net Income	90	684	870	1,236

DOL, DFL, and DCL ▶ **13-23.** Given the following information, calculate DOL, DFL, and DCL for 2005, 2006, and 2007.

	2004	2005	2006	2007
Net Sales	45,000	54,000	65,000	70,000
Cost of Goods Sold	29,250	33,480	39,650	42,000
Gross Margin	15,750	20,520	25,350	28,000
	35.00%	*38.00%*	*39.00%*	*40.00%*
S&A Expenses	12,000	14,000	15,000	16,000
Earning before Interest, Taxes, Amortization (EBITA)	3,750	6,520	10,350	12,000
	8.33%	*12.07%*	*15.92%*	*17.14%*
Amortization	2,000	3,000	4,000	4,500
Earnings before Interest and Taxes (EBIT)	1,750	3,520	6,350	7,500
	3.89%	*6.52%*	*9.77%*	*10.71%*

Interest Expense	1,200	1,000	1,500	1,800
Earnings before Taxes (EBT)	550	2,520	4,850	5,700
Taxes	220	1,008	1,940	2,280
Earnings after Tax (EAT)	330	1,512	2,910	3,420
	0.73%	*2.80%*	*4.48%*	*4.89%*
Preferred Share Dividends	100	100	100	100
Earnings Available to Common Shareholders	230	1,412	2,810	3,320
Common Share Dividends	50	50	50	50
Addition to Retained Earnings	180	1,362	2,760	3,270

13-24. Given the following information, calculate DOL, DFL, and DCL for 2005, 2006, and 2007. ◀ DOL, DFL, and DCL

	2004	2005	2006	2007
Net Sales	124,000	154,000	168,000	210,000
% Growth		*24%*	*9%*	*25%*
Cost of Goods Sold	80,600	95,480	102,480	126,000
Gross Margin	43,400	58,520	65,520	84,000
	35.00%	38.00%	39.00%	40.00%
S&A Expenses	20,000	20,000	20,000	20,000
Earning before Interest, Taxes, Amortization (EBITA)	23,400	38,520	45,520	64,000
	18.87%	*25.01%*	*27.10%*	*30.48%*
Amortization	4,000	4,000	4,000	4,000
Earnings before Interest and Taxes (EBIT)	19,400	34,520	41,520	60,000
	15.65%	*22.42%*	*24.71%*	*28.57%*
Interest Expense	5,400	6,000	6,000	6,000
Earnings before Taxes (EBT)	14,000	28,520	35,520	54,000
Taxes	5,600	11,408	14,208	21,600
Earnings after Tax (EAT)	8,400	17,112	21,312	32,400
	6.77%	*11.11%*	*12.69%*	*15.43%*
Preferred Share Dividends	5,000	5,000	5,000	5,000
Earnings Available to Common Shareholders	3,400	12,112	16,312	27,400
Common Share Dividends	1,000	1,000	1,000	1,000
Addition to Retained Earnings	2,400	11,112	15,312	26,400

ANSWERS TO SELF-TEST

ST-1. Sales breakeven point (in units) = \$40,000 ÷ (\$9 – \$4) = 8,000 units

ST-2. Degree of operating leverage (DOL) = (\$225,000 – \$100,000) ÷ (\$225,000 – \$100,000 – \$40,000) = 1.47

ST-3. Degree of financial leverage (DFL) = \$85,000 ÷ (\$85,000 – \$10,000) = 1.13

ST-4. Weighted average cost of capital, $k_a = (0.3 \times 6\%) + (0.7 \times 14\%) = 11.6\%$

ST-5. Next year's EBIT equals (this year's EBIT × 20% × 1.4) + this year's EBIT = (\$100,000 × 20% × 1.4) + \$100,000 = \$128,000

ST-6. Degree of combined leverage (DCL) = DOL × DFL = 1.6 × 1.8 = 2.88

14

Corporate Bonds, Preferred Shares, and Leasing

Chapter Objectives

After reading this chapter, you should be able to:

14-1 **Describe** three main contract terms of a bond issue.

14-2 **Define** nine types of bonds.

14-3 **Describe** the key features of preferred shares.

14-4 **Compare** and contrast an operating lease versus a capital lease.

14-5 **Explain** how to choose between leasing and buying options.

"The borrower is servant to the lender."

—Proverbs 22:7

An Interview with a Bond Analyst

A leading bond analyst in Toronto described bonds as the turtle in the turtle and the hare story.

"Bonds are great tools to work with. If you're smart, you can make your retirement secure. People choose shares like they choose ice cream; it depends on a lot of things—the weather, their mood, their tastes. Bonds are much easier to evaluate once you know the correct rating. It is one of the few vehicles out there where if the company or government is secure, you know exactly what you will get back and when. Shares can't do that for you. In fact, many cite shares as a better bet, due to their higher potential return. However, people get too greedy, and it only takes one failure to deplete your portfolio. Bonds, though, if played correctly always stay the course."

Source: Anonymous.

Chapter Overview

In Chapter 2, we examined the basic characteristics and terminology of corporate bonds. In Chapter 12, we learned how to estimate the value of bonds. In this chapter, we investigate how corporate bonds and preferred shares play a role in the financing decisions of a corporation. We also explore how leasing decisions affect a firm's finances.

Bond Basics

A **corporate bond** is a security that represents a promise by the issuing corporation to make certain payments to the owner of the bond, according to a certain schedule. The corporation that issues a bond is the debtor and the investor who buys the bond is the creditor.

The **indenture** is the contract between the issuing corporation and the bond's purchaser. It spells out the various provisions of the bond issue, including the face value, coupon interest rate, interest payment dates, maturity date, and other details. The yield to maturity is not in the indenture because it is market determined and changes with market conditions. The major features of bond indentures are described in the next section.

The investment bankers who underwrite the new bond issue help the firm set the terms of that issue. This usually means obtaining a rating for the bonds from one or more of the major rating companies such as Moody's, DBRS, and Standard & Poor's. Bond ratings shown in Table 14-1 reflect the likelihood that the issuer will make the promised interest and principal payments on

Table 14-1
Moody's, DBRS (Dominion Bond Rating Service), and Standard & Poor's Bond Rating Categories

Moody's	Standard & Poor's	DBRS	Remarks
Aaa	AAA	AAA	Best Quality
Aa1	AA+	Aah	
Aa2	AA	AAm	High Quality
Aa3	AA–	AAl	
A1	A+	Ah	Satisfactory Credit Quality
A2	A	Am	Or
A3	A–	Al	Upper Medium Grade
Baa1	BBB+	BBBh	Adequate Credit Quality
Baa2	BBB	BBBm	Or
Baa3	BBB–	BBBl	Low Medium Grade
Ba1	BB+	BBh	
Ba2	BB	BBm	Speculative
Ba3	BB–	BBl	
B1	B+	Bh	
B2	B	B	Highly Speculative
B3	B–	Bl	
Caa	CCC+	CCC	
Ca	CCC	CCC	Extremely Speculative
C	CCC–	C	
	D	D	Default

time. Many institutional investors, the main purchasers of bonds, are prohibited, either by law or by client demands, from purchasing unrated bonds.

Bonds rated Baa3 or above by Moody's, BBBl or above by DBRS, and BBB– or above by Standard & Poor's are called **investment-grade bonds**. Bonds with lower than investment-grade ratings (Ba1 or below by Moody's, BBh or below by DBRS, and BB+ or below by Standard & Poor's) are called **junk bonds**. We will have more to say about junk bonds later in the chapter.

Corporate bonds are a significant source of financing for large businesses. Figure 14-1 shows the 10 largest bond deals in history as of late 2001.

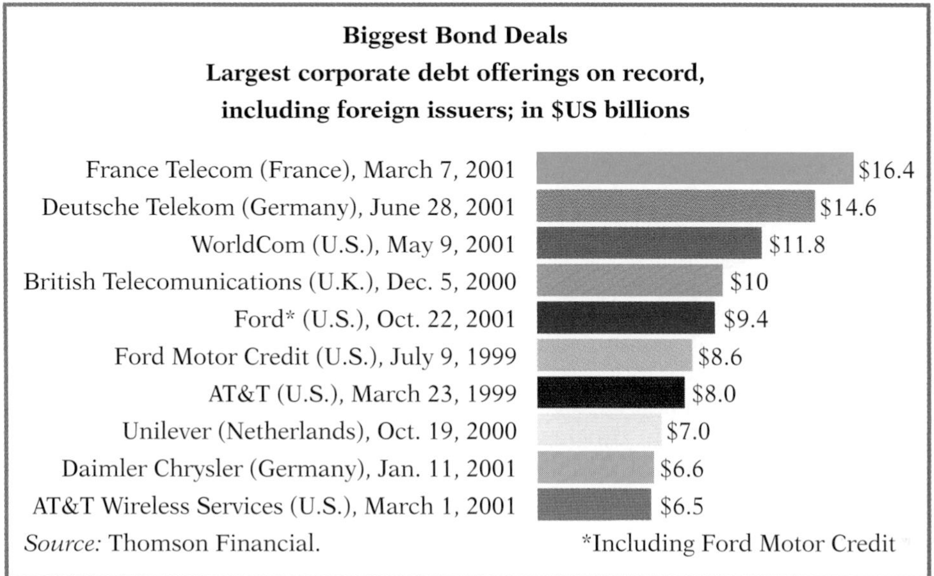

Figure 14-1 **Biggest Bond Deals**
Source: Zuckerman, G. (2001, October 23). Ford's $9.4 Billion Offering Provides Boost for Bonds. *The Wall Street Journal* Interactive Edition.

Features of Bond Indentures

In addition to the basic characteristics of the bond (interest, principal, maturity, and specific payment dates), the bond indenture specifies other features of the bond issue. These features include:

- Any security to be turned over to the bond's owner in the event the issuing corporation defaults
- The plan for paying off the bonds at maturity
- Any provisions for paying off the bonds ahead of time
- Any restrictions the issuing company places on itself to provide an extra measure of safety to the bondholder
- The name of an independent trustee to oversee the bond issue

Thus, every key feature of the bond issue is spelled out in the bond indenture.

Security

A person who buys a newly issued bond is, in effect, lending money to the issuing corporation for a specified period of time. Like other creditors, bondholders are concerned about getting their money back. A provision in the loan agreement (the indenture) that provides security[1] to the lender in case of default will increase the bond's value, compared with a loan agreement without a security provision. The value is higher because the investor has an extra measure of protection. A bond that has a security provision in the indenture is a **secured bond**. A bond that does not pledge any specific asset(s) as security is a **debenture**. Debentures are backed only by the company's ability and willingness to pay.

Plans for Paying Off the Bond Issue

Bonds are paid off, or retired, by a variety of means. Some of the more popular methods include *staggered maturities, sinking funds,* and *call provisions.*

Staggered Maturities Some bond issues are packaged as a series of different bonds with different or staggered maturities. Every few years a portion of the bond issue matures and is paid off. Staggering maturities in this fashion allows the issuing company to retire the debt in an orderly fashion without facing a large one-time need for cash, as would be the case if the entire issue were to mature at once. **Serial payments** pay off bonds according to a staggered maturity schedule.

Sinking Funds Although *sinking* is not an appealing word, sending your debt to the bottom of the ocean has its appeal. When a **sinking fund** provision is included in the bond's indenture, the issuing company makes regular contributions[2] to a fund that is used to buy back outstanding bonds. Putting aside a little money at a time in this fashion ensures that the amount needed to pay off the bonds will be available.

Call Provisions

Many corporate bonds have a provision in their indentures that allows the issuing corporation to pay off the bonds before the stated maturity date, at some stated price. This is known as a **call provision**. The price at which the bonds can be purchased before the scheduled maturity date is the *call price*.

Call provisions allow issuing corporations to refinance their debt if interest rates fall, just as homeowners refinance their mortgage loans when interest rates fall. For example, a company that issued bonds in 2003 with a 9 percent coupon interest rate would be making annual interest payments of 9 percent of $1,000 or $90 on each bond. Suppose that in 2004, the market rate of the company's bonds was 7 percent. If the bond indenture contained a call provision,[3] the company could issue 7 percent bonds in 2004 and use the proceeds from the issue to "call in" or pay off the 9 percent bonds. The company's

---

[1]Chapter 2 used a different definition of security (a financial claim such as a share or bond). Security has another definition, as used here. This definition is any asset (such as a piece of equipment, real estate, or a claim on future profits) that is promised to the investor in the event of a default.

[2]These are called "contributions" in the same sense that the government refers to the money you pay into the CPP (or QPP) as contributions. You have no choice; you must pay. If a company fails to make its required contributions to a sinking fund as described in the indenture, the bond issue can be declared to be in default.

[3]If a bond issue is callable, there is usually a certain amount of time that must pass before the bonds can be called. This is known as a *deferred call provision.* The indenture specifies the *call date.* The issuer can call bonds in from investors on or after this call date.

new interest payments would be only 7 percent of $1,000, or $70, thus saving the company $20 on each bond each year.

When bonds are called, convention is that the call price the issuer must pay is generally more than the face value. This excess of the call price over the face value is known as the **call premium**. The call premium may be expressed as a dollar amount or as a percentage of par.

Issuing new bonds to replace old bonds is known as a **refunding** operation. Remember the option to call a bond is held by the issuing corporation. The owners of the bonds have no choice in the matter. If investors do not turn in their bonds when the bonds are called, they receive no further interest payments.

A company approaches a bond refunding the same way it does any capital budgeting decision. The primary incremental cash inflows come from the interest savings realized when old high-interest debt is replaced with new low-interest debt. The primary incremental cash outflows are the call premium, if any, and the flotation costs associated with the new bond issue. All these variables must be adjusted for taxes and then evaluated by the firm. If the net present value of the incremental cash flows associated with the refunding is greater than or equal to zero, the refunding is done. If the NPV is negative, the company allows the old bonds to remain outstanding. This is the same thing you do when deciding whether to refinance a mortgage loan on a home.

Occasionally, a corporation will refund a bond issue even though there are no significant interest savings to be had. If the outstanding bonds have indenture provisions that the issuing company now finds oppressive or too limiting, the old bonds could be called and new bonds issued without the offending features. Let's go through a typical bond refunding decision.

A Sample Bond Refunding Problem

Suppose the Mega-Chip Corporation has $50 million worth of bonds outstanding with an annual coupon interest rate of 10 percent. However, market interest rates have fallen to 8 percent since the bonds were issued five years ago. Accordingly, the Mega-Chip Corporation would like to replace the old 10 percent bonds with a new issue of 8 percent bonds. In so doing, the firm could save 2 percent × $50 million = $1 million a year in interest payments. The original maturity of the 10 percent bonds was 20 years. The relevant financial data are summarized in Table 14-2.

Table 14-2 Mega-Chip Bond Refunding Problem

Old Bond Issue	$50,000,000; 10% annual interest rate; interest paid annually; 20 years original maturity; 15 years remaining to maturity
Call Premium on Old Bond	5%
Underwriting Costs on Old Bonds When Issued 5 Years Ago	2% of amount issued
New Bond Issue	$50,000,000; 8% annual interest rate; interest paid annually; 15 years to maturity
Underwriting Costs on New Bonds	3% of amount issued
Tax Rate	40%
After-Tax Cost of Debt	AT k_d = 4.8%

The Mega-Chip Corporation will be issuing new bonds having the same maturity as the number of years remaining to maturity on the old bonds (15 years). The *call premium* on the old bonds is the amount specified in the original bond indenture that the company must pay the bond owners if the bonds are called. The call premium is expressed as a percentage of the bond's face value. Thus, in this case, Mega-Chip will have to pay the old bondholders 5 percent of \$50 million, or \$2.5 million, in addition to the face value of the bonds, if it calls the bonds in.

The amount of the underwriting costs and the interest savings realized as a result of the refund are numbers that are essentially certain, so a very low discount rate is called for in this capital budgeting problem. The usual custom is to use the after-tax cost of debt for the discount rate. In this case, the number is 4.8 percent.[4]

$$\begin{aligned}\text{After-Tax } k_d &= \text{Before-Tax } k_d \times (1 - \text{Tax Rate})\\ &= 0.08 \times (1 - 0.40)\\ &= 0.048 \text{ or } 4.8\%\end{aligned}$$

The calculations for this refunding capital budgeting problem are shown in Table 14-3.

The cash outflows in Table 14-3 are fairly straightforward. The 5 percent call premium on the old bonds and the 3 percent underwriting costs on the new bonds add up to a total outflow of \$4 million.

The cash inflows are more complicated. There is an annual interest savings of \$1 million per year for 15 years. This amounts to \$600,000 after taxes. The present value of these after-tax annual savings is \$6,312,840, using the after-tax cost of debt of 4.8 percent as the discount rate. Call premiums are not tax deductible. The tax deductions from the underwriting costs on the old bonds were amortized over a mandated five years. Thus, if the bonds are called now, the entire balance of the underwriting costs not yet claimed as a tax deduction will become immediately deductible. Since five years have gone by, the amount is zero.

The difference between the immediate tax savings from this deduction and the present value of the tax savings that would have been realized over any remaining years is the incremental cash inflow relating to these underwriting costs. We see from our calculations, then, that the present value of the tax savings from the amortization of the underwriting costs on the new bonds is \$522,422.

Netting out all the incremental cash outflows and inflows gives a net present value figure of \$2,835,262. Because this NPV figure is greater than zero, Mega-Chip will accept the project and proceed with the bond refunding.[5]

---

[4]This number was found using Equation 9-1. Mega-Chip's current before-tax cost of debt is 8 percent and its marginal tax rate is 40 percent.

[5]This assumes that the management of Mega-Chip Corporation does not expect interest rates to fall further in the months to come. If managers are confident in a forecast for even lower interest rates to come, they may wait, expecting an even greater NPV in the near future.

Cash Outflows	Calculations	Incremental Cash Flows
Call Premium Paid	$50,000,000 × 0.05 =	$2,500,000
New Bond Underwriting Costs	$50,000,000 × 0.03 =	$1,500,000
Total Outflows		$4,000,000
Cash Inflows		
Interest Savings	Interest on old bonds: $50,000,000 × 0.10 = $5,000,000 Interest on new bonds: $50,000,000 × 0.08 = $4,000,000 $1,000,000 difference each year for 15 years Less taxes on the additional income at 40%: $1,000,000 × 0.40 = ($400,000) Net Savings = $600,000 per year Present value of the net savings for 15 years at 4.8%: $\$600,000 \times \left[\frac{1-\frac{1}{1.048^{15}}}{0.048}\right] = \$600,000 \times 10.5214 =$	$6,312,840
Tax Savings from New Bond Underwriting Costs	($50,000,000 × 0.03)/5 = $300,000 per Year Write-off Tax Savings = $300,000 × 0.4 = $120,000 PV of Tax Savings = $\$120,000 \times \left[\frac{1-\frac{1}{1.048^{5}}}{0.048}\right] =$	$ 522,422
Total Inflows $6,835,262		
Net Present Value =	$6,835,262 – $4,000,000 =	$2,835,262

Table 14-3 **Mega-Chip Bond Refunding Calculations**

Restrictive Covenants

A company that seeks to raise debt capital by issuing new bonds often makes certain promises to would-be investors to convince them to buy the bonds being offered or to make it possible to issue the bonds at a lower interest rate. These promises made by the issuer to the investor, to the benefit of the investor, are **restrictive covenants**. They represent something like a courtship. If the suitor does not give certain assurances about the way that the other party will be treated, there is little chance the relationship will blossom.

In a bond issuer–bond investor relationship, these assurances may include limitations on future borrowings, restrictions on dividends, and minimum levels of net working capital (current assets minus current liabilities) maintained.

Limitations on Future Borrowings Investors who lend money to a corporation by buying its bonds expect that the corporation will not borrow excessively in the future. A company in too much debt may be unable to pay bond principal and interest payments on time. Bond investors would be worried if, after buying the bonds of a firm with a 20 percent debt to total assets ratio, the company then issued $100 million of additional bonds, increasing that ratio to over 90 percent. The new debt would make the earlier-issued bonds instantly more risky and would lower their price in the market.

A restrictive covenant in which the corporation promises not to issue a large amount of future debt would protect the company's current bondholders from falling bond ratings and plunging market prices. A bond issue with this restriction in the indenture will have more value than a bond issue without this guarantee. As a result, the bonds could be issued at a lower coupon interest rate than bonds without the restriction in the indenture.

Restrictions on Dividends An indenture may also include restrictions on the payment of common share dividends if a firm's times interest earned ratio drops below a specified level. This restriction protects the bondholders against the risk of the common shareholders withdrawing value (cash for dividends that may be needed to make future interest payments) from the firm during difficult times. The bondholders are supposed to have priority over common shareholders. A bond issue with this sort of protection for investors can be issued at a lower interest rate than a bond issue without it.

Minimum Levels of Working Capital Current assets can generally be quickly and easily converted to cash to pay bills. Having a good liquidity position protects all creditors, including bondholders. Minimum working capital guarantees in an indenture provide an additional margin of protection for bondholders and, therefore, reduce the interest rate required on such bonds.

The Independent Trustee of the Bond Issue

Violations of any of the provisions included in the indenture could constitute a default. Therefore, an independent **trustee** is named in the indenture to oversee the bond issue and to make sure all the provisions spelled out in the indenture are adhered to.

Most people think a default is a failure to make a scheduled interest or principal payment on time. Actually, this is only one possible type of default because the promise to pay interest and principal on their due dates is only part of the promise made by the bond issuer in the indenture. Failure to keep any of the substantive promises mentioned in the indenture constitutes a default.

Types of Bonds

Some of the more innovative new financial instruments have been developed in the bond market. Let's now look more closely at the many kinds of bonds, both traditional and new.

Secured Bonds

A secured bond is backed by specific assets pledged by the issuing corporation. In the event of a default, the investors in these secured bonds would have a claim on these assets.

Mortgage Bonds A bond backed by real assets (not financial assets) is known as a **mortgage bond**. When you buy a house and finance the purchase with a mortgage loan, you are pledging your house (a real asset) as collateral for that loan. You are issuing a mortgage bond to the lender. That is what corporations do when they pledge real assets, such as airplanes and railroad cars, as collateral for the bonds issued to purchase those assets.

Different mortgage bonds can be issued that pledge the same real assets as collateral. Different classes of mortgage bonds signal the priority each investor has on the asset. An investor in a **first-mortgage** bond has first claim on the proceeds from the sale of the pledged assets if there is a default. A later lender may be an investor in a **second-mortgage** bond. In the event of default, the holder of the second mortgage receives proceeds from the sale of the pledged assets only after the first-mortgage bond investors have received all payments due to them. Similarly, third-mortgage bonds, fourth-mortgage bonds, and so forth can be issued with correspondingly lower priorities.

Unsecured Bonds (Debentures)

A bond that is not backed by any collateral is called a debenture. A debenture is backed only by the ability and willingness of the issuing corporation to make the promised interest and principal payments as scheduled. If a debenture were to go into default, the bondholders would be unsecured creditors. They would only have a general claim on the issuing company, not a right to the firm's specific assets.

There may be different classes of debentures. Certain issues may have a higher priority for payment than others. If bond issue A has priority for payment over bond issue B, according to their respective indentures, then bond issue A is said to be a **senior debenture** and bond issue B is said to be a **subordinated debenture.** A senior debenture has a prior claim to the earnings and liquidation proceeds from the general assets of the firm (those assets not specifically pledged as security for other bonds) relative to the claim of subordinated debenture investors.

Subordinated debentures have a lower-priority claim on the firm's earnings and assets. Because subordinated debentures are riskier than senior debentures, investors demand and issuers pay higher interest rates on them. This higher interest rate is consistent with the risk–return relationship—the greater the risk of a security, the greater the required rate of return. Holders of first-mortgage bonds assume less risk than holders of second-mortgage bonds. Debenture holders have more risk than secured bondholders, and subordinated debenture holders have more risk than senior debenture holders. Preferred share investors take more risk than a bond investor, and common share investors take more risk still for a given company. This risk hierarchy, reflecting the relative priority of claims, is shown in Figure 14-2.

Convertible Bonds

One of the special types of bonds available is called a **convertible bond.** A convertible bond is a bond that may be converted, at the option of the bond's owner, into a certain amount of another security issued by the same company. In the vast majority of the cases, the other security is common shares.[6] This means that the investor who bought the convertible bond may send it back to the issuing company and "convert" it into a certain number of that company's common shares.

[6]Some convertible bonds can be converted into a certain amount of preferred shares or some other security issued by the company.

Figure 14-2 The Risk Hierarchy Figure 14-2 shows the different priorities of claims that creditors and investors have on a company in default. First mortgage bondholders are paid first, whereas common shareholders are paid last.

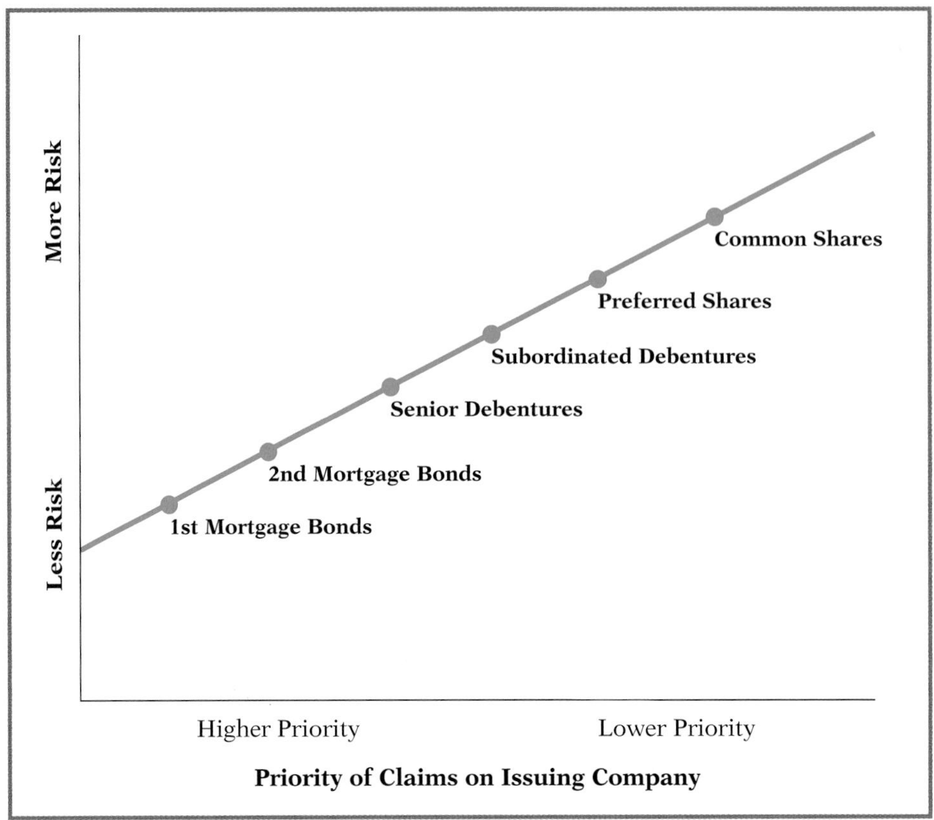

Features of Convertible Bonds Convertible bonds have a face value, coupon rate, interest payment frequency, and maturity spelled out in their indenture, as do regular nonconvertible bonds. The indenture also spells out the terms of conversion if the investor chooses to exercise that option. If the bond's owner elects not to convert the bond, the owner continues to receive interest and principal payments as with any other bond.

The Conversion Ratio.

Each convertible bond has a conversion ratio. The **conversion ratio** is the number of common shares that an investor would get if the convertible bond were converted. For example, Hudson Bay Co. issued a convertible $1,000 bond that matures in 2008 with a conversion ratio of 15.75. This means that the bond's owner can trade in the bond for 5.75 shares of Hudson Bay Co. at any time.

The Conversion Value.

To find the conversion value of a bond, multiply the conversion ratio by the market price per share of the company's common shares, as shown in Equation 14-1:

Conversion Value of a Convertible Bond

$$\text{Conversion Value} = \text{Conversion Ratio} \times \text{Share Price} \tag{14-1}$$

The **conversion value** is the amount of money that bond owners receive if they convert the bond to common shares and then sell the common shares.

Table 14-4 Hudson Bay Company, Convertible Bond Characteristics

Maturity Date	December 1, 2008
Face Value	$1,000
Type of Interest	Semiannual
Coupon Interest Rate	7.5%
Conversion Ratio	5.75

Source: Prospectus, *The Financial Post*, February 10, 2004.

For example, if the Hudson Bay Co. shares were selling for $15, then the conversion value of the convertible bond described in Table 14-4 would be as follows:

$$\begin{aligned}\text{Conversion Value} &= \text{Conversion Ratio} \times \text{Share Price}\\ &= 5.75 \times \$15.00\\ &= \$86.25\end{aligned}$$

Equation 14-1 shows us that at a rate of $15 per common share, the conversion value of the convertible bond is $86.25.

The Straight Bond Value.

If a convertible bond is not converted into shares, then it is worth at least the sum of the present values of its interest and principal payments.[7] The value coming from the interest and principal is called the convertible bond's **straight bond value**. The discount rate used to compute this straight bond value is the required rate of return for a nonconvertible bond having characteristics (risk, maturity, tax treatment, and liquidity) similar to the convertible bond.

As shown in Table 14-4, Hudson Bay Co.'s convertible bond has a coupon interest rate of 7.5 percent and a maturity date of December 1, 2008. With a face value of $1,000, the annual interest payments will be $75 (0.075 × 1,000). Because interest is paid semiannually, actual interest payments of $37.50 ($75 ÷ 2) are made twice a year. If the required rate of return on similar nonconvertible bonds is 8 percent annual interest (4 percent semiannually),[8] then according to Equation 12-2, the bond's straight bond value as of December 1, 2006, follows:[9]

$$\begin{aligned}V_{\text{Bond}} &= \$37.50 \times \left[\frac{1-\dfrac{1}{(1.04)^4}}{0.04}\right] + \$1{,}000 \times \frac{1}{(1.04)^4}\\ &= \$37.50 \times 3.629895 + \$1{,}000 \times 0.854804\\ &= \$136.12 + \$854.80\\ &= \$990.92\end{aligned}$$

[7]Equation 12-2 in Chapter 12 gives the present value of a bond's interest and principal payments.

[8]If 8 percent were the annual required market rate of return, then the corresponding semiannual required rate of return would be 3.923 percent ($1.03923^2 - 1 = 0.08$ or 8 percent) and not 4 percent. We will round this to 4 percent to simplify the calculation.

[9]December 1, 2008 is two years (four semiannual periods) into the future from December 1, 2006.

We find that the present value of a two-year, semiannual convertible bond with a face value of $1,000 and a 7.5 percent annual coupon interest rate is $990.92.

A rational investor may convert a bond if advantageous but will not convert it if disadvantageous. Therefore, a convertible bond is always worth the conversion value or the straight bond value whichever is greater.

Variable-Rate Bonds

Take Note

A convertible bond does not have to be converted to reap the benefits of a high conversion value. The mere fact that the bond could be converted into common shares having a certain value makes the convertible bond worth at least that conversion value.

Although most corporate bonds pay a fixed rate of interest (the coupon interest rate is constant), some pay a variable rate. With a **variable-rate bond**, the initial coupon rate is adjusted according to an established timetable and a market rate index.

The variable bond rates could be tied to any rate, such as a Treasury bond rate or the London Interbank Offer Rate (LIBOR). Bond issuers check this market rate on every adjustment date specified in the indenture and reset the coupon rate accordingly.

The variable rate protects investors from much of the interest rate risk inherent in fixed-rate bonds. Rising inflation hurts investors in fixed-rate bonds because the price of fixed-rate bonds falls as rising inflation increases an investor's required rate of return. In times of rising inflation, the price of a variable-rate bond does not fall as much because the investor knows that a coupon rate adjustment will occur to adjust to new, higher interest rates. However, investors who buy bonds with fixed coupon interest rates will be better off when market interest rates are falling. A variable-rate bond would have its coupon rate drop as market interest rates fell.

An issuing corporation can benefit from issuing variable-rate bonds if market rates are historically high and a drop in rates is expected. Of course, high rates can rise even further, in which case the issuing company could lose money.

Putable Bonds

A **putable bond** is a bond that can be cashed in before maturity at the option of the bond's owner. This is like the callable bond described earlier in the chapter except that the positions of the issuer and the bond's owner with respect to the option have been reversed. Investors may exercise the option to redeem their bonds early when it is in their best interest to do so. Investors usually redeem fixed-rate bonds if interest rates have risen. The existing, lower-interest-rate bond can be redeemed and the proceeds used to buy a new higher-interest-rate bond.

Junk Bonds

Another type of bond that has become popular (and controversial) is the junk bond. Junk bonds, also known as *high-yield bonds,* have a bond rating below investment grade. As shown earlier in this chapter, according to Moody's ratings, a junk bond would have a rating of Ba1 or below. According to Standard & Poor's ratings, it would have a rating of BB+ or below, and according to DBRS's rating it would have a rating of BBh or below. The name *junk* is perhaps unfairly applied because these bonds are usually not trash; they are simply riskier than bonds having an investment grade. For instance, many bonds used to finance corporate takeovers have below-investment-grade ratings.

Some junk bonds start out with investment-grade ratings but then suffer a downgrade—the issuing company may have fallen on hard financial times or may have gone through a major financial restructuring that increased the risk of the outstanding bonds. Such junk bonds are known as *fallen angels*. One example of a fallen angel is the 2002 downgrade of Nortel bonds to junk bond status because the company's financial health had deteriorated considerably.

Bond ratings are a very tricky notion. Bonds are thought to be less risky than shares, but there are many issues that need to be incorporated and even then the process is still difficult, as one can observe in Ethical Connections 14-1. See also International Perspectives in Finance 14-1 on page 484.

International Bonds

An **international bond** is a bond sold in countries other than where the corporate headquarters of the issuing company is located. The bonds may be denominated in the currency of the issuing company's country or in the currency of the country in which the bonds are sold. Foreign corporations issue bonds in Canada, sometimes denominated in their home currencies and

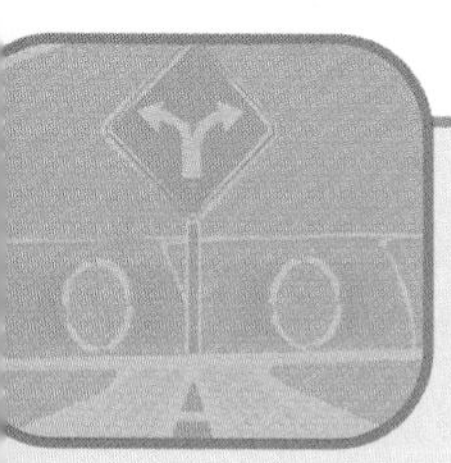

ETHICAL CONNECTIONS 14-1

407 Credit Rating Under Review

ʋo major bond raters—Standard and Poor's Corp. and ɒminion Bond Rating Services—have put the 407's bond ues under review because of the dispute between Ontario d the private highway operator over its right to raise tolls.

Any change in the 407 International Inc.'s ability to se tolls without government approval could have negative plications for the "A" long-term issuer credit and senior cured debt ratings, and the "A–junior" and "BBB" subornated debt ratings, said Standard and Poor's credit analyst ario Angastiniotis.

"When we first rated the 407 debt, what was factored o the rating was the company's ability to raise tolls without tually going to the government for permission," said gastiniotis. "We were assuming it would not be regulated d would not have to ask for any permission for raising tolls. the extent that any government actions hinder that ability raise tolls, that could affect the rating some time in the ure, and that's really the risk we're trying to highlight."

407 International Inc. raised tolls by 1 cent a kilometre Sunday over the objections of the province. The 407, ich has a 99-year lease to operate the highway, says the reement it negotiated with the previous Conservative govnment is ironclad, and gives it the right to raise tolls as long traffic continues to rise on the 407.

The governing Liberals, who campaigned against the s, say a clause in the contract requires the 407 to consult with the government before raising tolls. On Monday, officials from the highway and the government met to try to resolve the issue. At the same time, the Liberals officially put the private operator of Highway 407 on notice of default over toll hikes, a move that could end up costing millions in legal fees but that the Liberals say could return ownership of the lease to the public.

DBRS issued a release late yesterday saying that "theoretically" a default by the 407 could "lead to a loss of the highway concession without compensation," but added that it stands by its previous public statements that based on a reading of the contract, "there is no requirement . . . for the company to obtain the province's consent when increasing toll rates."

Questions to Consider

1. *What implications does a lower bond rating have on a company?*
2. *If 407 International Inc. loses the battle and their cost of borrowing increases, what may the results be anyway? Why?*

Source: "407 Credit Rating under Review" by Kevin McGran. *The Toronto Star*, 4 February 2004. Reprinted with permission – Torstar Syndication Services.

sometimes in Canadian dollars. In turn, Canadian corporations frequently issue bonds outside of Canada. These bonds may be denominated in Canadian dollars or in some other currency.

Eurobonds are bonds denominated in the currency of the issuing company's home country and sold in another country. For example, if General Motors of Canada issued a dollar-denominated bond in Italy, it would be called a Eurobond. Similarly, if Ferrari, an Italian company, issued a euro-denominated bond in Canada, the bond would be called a Eurobond. If the Ferrari bond were denominated in U.S. dollars instead of euros and sold in the United States, it would be referred to as a *Yankee bond*.

Take Note

Be careful not to confuse Eurobonds with Eurodollars. Eurodollars are dollar-denominated deposits in banks outside the United States.

Super Long-Term Bonds

IBM, the Disney Corporation, Coca-Cola, and recently Nacional Electricidad SA, the largest power company in Chile, have issued bonds with a maturity of 100 years, which is a much longer maturity than is typical among corporate bond issuers. Investors who purchase these bonds must have confidence in the future cash flow of these companies.

In this section, we have described types of bonds. Next, we examine preferred shares, their characteristics, and those who purchase them.

INTERNATIONAL PERSPECTIVES IN FINANCE 14-1

Fans of the Pfandbriefe?

Germany's Pfandbriefe could be the ideal product for U.S. investors but they remain hesitant, says Suzanne Miller.

The German Pfandbriefe has been more reliable than a Duracell battery. First issued 230 years ago, the bonds have survived the napoleonic wars, World War II and the collapse of the Berlin Wall with no known defaults, proponents say. Yet most US bond investors have scant interest in the Pfandbriefe, a covered bond collateralized by long-term assets that has traditionally been issued by German mortgage banks. Shouldn't US investors reconsider, given that Pfandbriefe have toughed out one of the worst credit cycles since the Great Depression?

This was what senior German mortgage bankers and a handful of experts and traders were hoping when they met with US investors at a New York conference in May. The message was that the Pfandbriefe can survive just about anything—even Germany's current banking crisis. "Don't believe the German banking system sucks and the Pfandbriefe is part of it. The Jumbo market is the safest and most liquid you can find," the US audience was advised by Christian Ganssmuller, head of German fixed income at Citigroup Global Markets Deutschland AG.

With more than E1100bn outstanding, the Pfandbrie is the biggest segment of the euro-denominated private bo market in Europe, rivalling the size of individual Europe government bond markets. Jumbo loans are the biggest a most liquid issues, with about 300 loans outstanding a averaging E1.6bn in size. The Pfandbriefe is issued to fu loans secured by first-ranking mortgages or loans secured the public sector and are typically rated triple-A. One of big selling points is its reputation of being bulletproof to kinds of risk.

For instance, issuing mortgage banks are legally limit to the mortgage and public sector financing business meaning they're barred from jumping into riskier bu nesses. Moreover, German mortgage borrowers don't ha prepayment options for the first 10 years of their loan, there's little prepayment risk—unlike the US mortgag backed securities market, where prepayment risk is a w of life.

Source: "Fans of the Pfandbriefe?" 6 October 2003. Reprinted w permission of *The Banker*.

PREFERRED SHARES

Preferred shares are so called because owners of preferred shares have a priority claim over common shareholders to the earnings and assets of a corporation. That is, preferred shareholders receive their dividends before common shareholders. Preferred shares are not issued by many corporations except in certain industries, such as public utilities.

The preferred share dividend is usually permanently fixed, so the potential return on investment for a preferred shareholder is not as high as it is for a common shareholder. Common shareholders are entitled to all residual income of the firm (which could be considerable).

Preferred shares are known as a hybrid security. They are hybrids because they have both debt and equity characteristics. Preferred shares are like debt primarily because preferred shareholders do not have an ownership claim, nor do they have any claim on the residual income of the firm. It is also like equity because it has an infinite maturity and a lower-priority claim against the firm than bondholders have.

Preferred Share Dividends

Issuers of preferred shares generally promise to pay a fixed dollar amount of dividends to the investor. This promise, however, does not result in bankruptcy if it is broken. Unlike failure to make a scheduled interest or principal payment to bondholders, failure to pay a scheduled dividend to preferred shareholders is not grounds for bankruptcy of the company that issued the preferred shares.

Occasionally, *participating preferred shares* are issued. This type of preferred share offers the chance for investors to share the benefits of rising earnings with the common shareholders. This is quite rare, however.

Preferred shares can be either *cumulative* or *noncumulative* with respect to its dividends. With cumulative preferred shares, if a dividend is missed, it must be paid at a later date before dividends may resume to common shareholders. Seldom is any interest paid, however, to compensate preferred shareholders for the fact that when dividends are resumed, they are received later than when promised. Noncumulative preferred shares do not make up missed dividends. If the dividends are skipped, they are lost forever to the investors.

Preferred Share Investors

Corporations can generally exclude 100 percent of the dividend income received on preferred shares issued by another corporation from their taxable income.

Because of the favourable tax treatment corporations received on this dividend income, they bid up the price on preferred shares, thus lowering the expected rate of return. The lower expected rate of return is the price they pay for receiving the preferential tax treatment.

Individuals must gross up their dividends by 25 percent, but they receive a tax credit on two-thirds of the grossed-up amount at the federal level. For example, if Bob received \$100 in dividends one year, for tax purposes he would declare \$125 (100×1.25) and receive a credit of \$16.67 ($25 \times 2/3$). Although a little strange in format, dividends generally have better tax advantages than interest on bonds.

Convertible Preferred Shares

Occasionally companies issue preferred shares that are convertible into a fixed number of common shares. The convertible preferred shares may be either cumulative or noncumulative, just like "regular" preferred shares. For example, in 2001, Northgate Exploration Limited raised approximately $90 million from an issue of 6 percent cumulative convertible preferred shares to Trilon Financial Corporation. Each preferred share was convertible into common shares, based on a conversion price of $11.51 per share.[10]

In some cases, convertible preferred shares may also be exchanged for a certain number of convertible bonds with the identical pre-tax cash flow and common share conversion terms. This type of share is called convertible exchangeable preferred shares.

LEASING

Debt is often incurred to acquire an asset. An alternative to borrowing and buying an asset is to lease the asset. A **lease** is an arrangement in which one party that owns an asset contracts with another party to use that asset for a specified period of time, without conveying legal ownership of that asset. The party who owns the asset is known as the lessor. The party who uses the asset is the **lessee**. The lessee makes lease payments to the **lessor** for the right to use the asset for the specified time period.

A lease contract that is long term and noncancellable is very similar to a debt obligation from the perspective of the lessee. There are different types of lease contracts. These different types have different accounting treatments, which we turn to next.

Operating and Capital Leases for Accounting Purposes

An **operating lease** has a term substantially shorter than the useful life of the asset and is usually cancellable by the lessee. A **capital lease** is long term and noncancellable. The lessee uses up most of the economic value of the asset by the end of the lease's term with a capital lease.

If you went on a business trip and leased a car for the week to make your business calls, this would be an operating lease. This same car will be leased again to many other customers, and in one week you will use up a small fraction of the car's economic value. Your company, which is paying your travel expenses, would deduct these lease payments as business expenses on the income statement.

If your company signed a 10-year, noncancellable lease on a $20 million supercomputer, this is likely to be a capital lease. After 10 years the supercomputer is likely to be obsolete. Your company would have used up most, if not all, its economic value by the end of the 10-year lease period. The lessor surely would demand lease payments high enough to recognize this fact and also to compensate for the time value of money that is paid over a 10-year period. The fact that the payments are spread out over time means that the lessor must be compensated for the cost of the asset and for the delay in the receipt of the lease payments.

---

[10]http://northgateexploration.ca, Press Releases, December 20, 2001.

CRA Operating versus Capital Lease

Prior to 2001, CRA (Canada Revenue Agency) was stricter on the terms of capital leases and operating leases. The tax effects to businesses could be severe in some cases. In general, if a lease was considered for tax purposes to be an operating lease, the full amount of the lease was deducted for tax purposes. However, if the lease was classified as a capital lease, it would have the same consequences as buying the item. The business could only therefore deduct the portion of the lease that was interest and deduct the remaining value of the lease according to the CRA capital cost allowance guidelines. (This was briefly outlined in Chapter 4.)

Fortunately for many businesses and corporations, in 2001, CRA IT Bulletin IT-233R was withdrawn. The result of this was that CRA now judges leases according to their form, not their substance. As a consequence of this, most leasing practices are considered by CRA to be fully deductible through the nature of an operating lease.

Accounting Treatment of Leases Both operating and capital lease payments show up on the income statement. Assuming that a lease is genuine, payments made by the lessee to the lessor are shown on the income statement as tax-deductible business expenses for both types of leases. These are costs of doing business for the lessee.

Capital leases have another accounting impact, however, that operating leases do not. A capital lease also shows up on the company's balance sheet because it is functionally equivalent to buying the asset and financing the purchase with borrowed money. If the asset had been purchased and financed with debt, the asset and the liability associated with the debt would both show up on the balance sheet. Because a capital lease is functionally equivalent to a purchase financed with debt, the *CICA Handbook* says that the accounting treatment should be similar.

Failure to make a bond payment can lead to bankruptcy, as can failure to make a contractual lease payment on a noncancellable lease. The leased asset is shown in the asset section of the lessee's balance sheet with a corresponding liability entry in the amount of the present value of all the lease payments owed to the lessor.

A lease is classified as a capital lease if it meets *any one* of the following four criteria:

1. Ownership of the asset is transferred to the lessee at the end of the lease's term.
2. There is an option for the lessee to buy the asset at a bargain purchase price at the end of the lease period.
3. The lease period is greater than or equal to 75 percent of the estimated useful life of the asset.
4. The present value of the lease payments equals 90 percent or more of the fair market value of the asset at the time the lease is originated, using the lower of the lessee's cost of debt or the lessor's rate of return on the lease as the discount rate.

Only if none of these four criteria applies is the lease considered an operating lease, with no balance sheet entry.

FINANCE AT WORK 14-1

Sales Retail Sports Media Technology Public Relations Production Exports

HYBRID FINANCING—MEZZANINE CAPITAL

Mezzanine is a term used to describe debt that is junior in repayment obligation to traditional bank financing or senior debt. The need for this type of financing occurs when a gap exists between the amount the senior lender will provide and the amount of equity capital that is available.

Corporate borrowers often use more than one type of debt. A typical capital structure might include a secured term loan, a secured revolving line of credit from a bank, equipment leases, mezzanine debt, and conventional equity (common and preferred shares). Mezzanine debt (sometimes called second-tier debt) is unsecured subordinated debt in which the lender also receives some rights to acquire equity. It provides an additional layer of financing between the senior debt and the company's equity.

Mezzanine financing may be an attractive way to borrow funds beyond the amount that secured lenders will lend, although at somewhat higher interest rates. Borrowers shou be aware, however, that there are both costs and benefits th are less visible and less susceptible to quantification than t financial considerations such as interest rates, amortizatio security, and equity costs.

Mezzanine investors are subordinate to collateralized sen lenders but are senior to the equity investors. Mezzanine capi therefore, looks like equity to the debtor's commercial ba lender and looks like debt to the company. It combines cash fl and risk characteristics of both senior debt and common shar Mezzanine capital is typically supplied by venture capital limi partnerships and other nonbank financial institutions.

Sources: Batey, D. L. Hidden Costs and Benefits of Mezzanine Level Financing. www.businesscity.com/doc/nvart5.htm and www.norwest.com/business-structfinance/doc/mezz_capital.htm.

Lease or Buy?

Leasing is growing in popularity. Whether an asset should be leased or bought depends on the relative costs of the two alternatives. Leasing is most nearly comparable to a buy–borrow alternative. Because signing a debt contract is similar to signing a lease contract, comparisons are usually made between the lease option and the buy with borrowed funds option.

The alternative that has the lower present value of after-tax costs is usually chosen. The tax factor considered for the lease alternative would be the tax deductibility of the lease payments that would be made (assuming the lease is an operating lease). The tax factors for the buy with borrowed funds alternative would come primarily from two sources. One is the tax deduction that comes with the payment of interest on the borrowed funds. The other is the tax deduction that comes with the capital cost allowance on the purchased asset.

A Lease or Buy Decision Example Let's go through an example of a lease or buy decision to illustrate the computations involved. For our example, we will use Mr. Edward in the car manufacturing company whose project was to install $5 million worth of new machines in the company's main manufacturing plant. The decision about how to finance the acquisition must be made. For simplicity, let us assume that two alternatives are available: (1) The machines can be purchased using the proceeds from a $5 million, five-year, 10 percent after-tax interest rate loan from a bank, or (2) the machines can be leased for $1.1 million a year, payable at the beginning of each of the next five years. At the end of the lease term, the machines would be returned to the lessor for disposal.[11] If the machines are purchased, they cannot be sold for salvage at the end of five years.

[11]For simplicity in this example, we will assume that the lease is a straightforward operating lease, so no other accounting considerations are required.

The cost of leasing is twofold: the amount of the lease that you actually pay (your payment minus any taxes), and the opportunity cost of any tax savings from buying the asset. If these two items together are less than the object you wish to purchase, then you should lease the object. If they are not, you should buy.

The first thing we will deal with is the PV of the TAX savings. (This represents the opportunity cost of not leasing.)

We will assume that the machinery for tax purposes will be classified as class 8 of the CCA rates. This rate assumes that all additions are taxed with the half-year rule initially and that the deduction rate is 20 percent. In our case that means if we were to buy the machine, assuming there is no other machinery in this class at that time, the following would happen in year 1.

UCC class at the beginning of the year	$—
Add: Acquisitions	5,000,000
UCC before half-year rule	$5,000,000
Deduction: half-year rule for new acquisitions	(2,500,000)
Base amount for CCA claim	$2,500,000
Deduct: CCA for the year 20%	(500,000)
UCC class at the end of the year	$4,500,000

The second year would see a CCA deduction of $900,000 (4,500,000 × 0.2), the third year's deduction would be $720,000 [(4,500,000 – 900,000) × 0.2)], the fourth year's deduction would be $576,000, the fifth year's deduction would be $460,800. You should notice that the deductions are decreasing at a rate of 1.25, or you could say that the subsequent deduction is equal to 80 percent of the previous year's deduction. The equation used is 1 – CCA rate, so 1 – 0.20 = 0.80 or 80 percent.

Now we know, from our present value and NPV lessons, that in order to evaluate two alternatives, we need to compare all cash flows to the present time. In the case of tax deductions, assuming the tax deductions are applicable to all years, the following would be the PV of tax savings under CCA deductions (assuming a 40 percent tax rate for our corporation and a 10 percent interest rate) to Year 1 (not Year 0):

Year	*CCA Deduction*	*Tax*	*Tax Savings*	*PV*	*PV of Tax Savings (to Period 1)*
2	$900,000	40%	$360,000	0.90909	$327,273
3	$720,000	40%	$288,000	0.82645	$238,017
4	$576,000	40%	$230,400	0.75131	$173,103
5	$460,800	40%	$184,320	0.68301	$125,893

Of course we have only done the calculation for 5 years; we have not taken into account the full PV of all tax deductions. As we mentioned before, each subsequent deduction falls by (1 – CCA rate), which in our case is 0.8 (1 – 0.2). In terms of an equation, the following can be said where X represents the value of the deduction in the second year, Y represents the amount of all CCA deductions without the tax deductions factored in yet, and R represents that current discount rate.

$$E_1 \quad Y = \frac{X}{(1+R)} + \frac{0.8X}{(1+R)^2} + \frac{0.8^2 X}{(1+R)^3} + \ldots + \frac{0.8^{N-2} X}{(1+R)^{N-1}} + \frac{0.8^{N-1} X}{(1+R)^N}$$

The problem with our deduction is that theoretically the tax deduction can go on forever. We will therefore attempt to reduce the equation to something more manageable. We will first multiply both sides of the equation by 0.8/(1 + R). The new equation is as follows:

$$E_2 \quad Y(\frac{0.8}{(1+R)}) = \frac{0.8X}{(1+R)^2} + \frac{0.8^2 X}{(1+R)^3} + \frac{0.8^3 X}{(1+R)^4} + \ldots + \frac{0.8^{N-1} X}{(1+R)^N} + \frac{0.8^N X}{(1+R)^{N+1}}$$

If you look at both equations, you should notice some items that are identical. We will thus deduct equation E_2 from E_1, eliminating the common factors. The new equation is now:

$$Y - Y\frac{0.8}{(1+R)} = \frac{X}{(1+R)} - \frac{0.8^N X}{(1+R)^{N+1}}$$

Further we can assume that as N gets closer to infinity, $\frac{0.8^N X}{(1+R)^{N+1}}$ gets closer to being equal to zero. Our equation reduces to $Y = \frac{X}{(R+0.2)}$.

We forgot to do one thing, the tax factor. If we assume that the tax rate is 40 percent, our total PV of all tax deductions will be:

$$Y(0.4) = \frac{(0.4)X}{(R+0.2)}$$

Now, the only thing we are going to change is the notation. We will denote our tax rate as T (instead of 0.4), our required rate of return as k_i (instead of R), and our PV of all tax deductions as PV_{tax} [instead of Y(0.4)]. Further, we should notice that 0.2 is the same as 1 – 0.8, and that 0.2 is equal to our original CCA rate. Therefore, we will denote 0.2 as d. Lastly, X was equal to the CCA rate times the amount of the asset, so will we denote this as d times CA (Cost of Asset). Our equation turns into:

$$PV_{TAX} = \frac{TdCA}{(k_i + d)}$$

The last adjustment we need to make is for the fact that we will only get a half-year's deduction in year 1 according to the half-year rule. Our final equation for tax deduction is:

$$PV_{TAX} = \left[\frac{TdCA}{(k_i + d)}\right]\left[\frac{1+0.5k_i}{1+k_i}\right]$$

In our case, the after tax cost of financing is 10 percent [16.66% × (1 – 0.4) = 10%]. So, in our example, the PV of the tax savings would be:

$$PV_{TAX} = \left[\frac{(0.4)(0.2)(5,000,000)}{(0.10 + 0.2)}\right]\left[\frac{1 + 0.5(0.10)}{1 + 0.10}\right]$$

which equals PV_{TAX} = 1,272,727

The second thing we will deal with is the cost of the lease payments. The lease is paid for over several years with consistent payments. This sounds very similar to an annuity, which it is. The PV annuity formula, as you learned from Chapter 8, is:

$$PVA = PMT\left[\frac{\left(1 - \frac{1}{(1+R)^N}\right)}{R}\right]$$

In our case, PMT is the after-tax portion of our lease payment. The last item we need to address is the fact that most leases need to be paid at the beginning of the month—an annuity due. All we need to do is multiply the PVA equation by (1 + R). Thus, the PV of our after-tax lease payments will look like this:

$$PVA = (1 - 0.4)(1,100,000)\left[\frac{\left(1 - \frac{1}{(1+0.1)^5}\right)}{0.1}\right](1 + 0.1)$$

The PV of the after-tax lease payments is 2,752,111.

Now we add these two items together, which equals a total lease cost of \$4,024,838 (\$2,752,111 + \$1,272,727). Is this amount greater than or less than 5 million? The answer is that it is less than, so we lease the machines. The ultimate equation is as follows:

$$NPV_{LEASE} = CA - \left[\left[\frac{TdCA}{k_i + d}\right]\left[\frac{1 + 0.5k_i}{1 + k_i}\right] + (1 - T)L_P\left(\frac{1 - \frac{1}{(1+k_i)^N}}{k_i}\right)(1 + k_i)\right]$$

where

CA = Cost of the asset
T = Tax rate
k_i = The discount rate
L_P = The lease payment
d = The CCA rate

If NPV_{LEASE} is greater than zero, then you lease. If it is less than zero, then you buy. Now let us try some examples to perfect the idea. It is important to remember that the choice to adopt a piece of equipment is independent of how you are going to finance it.

Let us suppose that Bill wishes to buy a new car for his business. We will assume the following mutually exclusive cases. You should notice that the only difference between case 1 and case 2 is the amount and that the only difference between case 1 and case 3 is the rate. We will assume that all cars fall into class 10 and therefore have a CCA rate of 30 percent. The following link is a good one for looking up CCA rates: **http://www.cra-arc.gc.ca/E/pub/tg/rc4060/rc4060-13-e.html**. We will further assume a 40 percent tax rate.

Case 1: Price = $30,000

	Rate	*Monthly Payment*	*Term in Years*	*Value at End of Term*
Buy	0.045	$559.29	5	0
Lease	0.00	$500.00	5	0

Case 2: Price = $20,000

	Rate	*Monthly Payment*	*Term in Years*	*Value at End of Term*
Buy	0.045	$372.86	5	0
Lease	0.00	$333.33	5	0

Case 3: Price = $30,000

	Rate	*Monthly Payment*	*Term in Years*	*Value at End of Term*
Buy	0.04	$552.50	5	0
Lease	0.10	$632.14	5	0

SOLUTION: CASE 1

k = 0.045 × 0.6 = 0.027

$$NPV = 30{,}000 - \left[\left[\frac{0.4 \times 0.3 \times 30{,}000}{0.027 + 0.3}\right]\left[\frac{1 + 0.5 \times (0.027)_i}{1 + 0.027}\right] + (1 - 0.4)632.14\left(\frac{1 - \dfrac{1}{(1 + 0.002)^{60}}}{0.002}\right)(1 + 0.002)\right]$$

NPV = 2,277.49

Therefore, we lease. Note that the rate of buying was used as the interest rate because this is the opportunity cost of leasing instead of buying. What happens if we change the sale price now?

SOLUTION: CASE 2

k = 0.045 × 0.6 = 0.027

$$\text{NPV} = 20{,}000 - \left[\left[\frac{0.4 \times 0.3 \times 20{,}000}{0.027 + 0.3}\right]\left[\frac{1 + 0.5 \times (0.027)_i}{1 + 0.027}\right]\right.$$

$$+(1-0.40)333.33\left(\frac{1-\dfrac{1}{(1+0.00225)^{60}}}{0.00225}\right)(1+0.00225)\Bigg]$$

NPV = 1,518.44 Therefore, we lease.

SOLUTION: CASE 3

k = 0.04 × 0.6 = 0.024

$$NPV = 30,000 - \left[\left[\frac{0.4\times0.3\times30,000}{0.024+0.3}\right]\left[\frac{1+0.5\times(0.024)_i}{1+0.024}\right]\right.$$

$$\left.+(1-0.4)632.14\left(\frac{1-\dfrac{1}{(1+0.002)^{60}}}{0.002}\right)(1+0.002)\right]$$

NPV = –2,448.23

We therefore buy.

For those of you who are interested in what happens if the residual value is not zero, two things happen. First, you cannot claim all the CCA deduction and secondly, when you buy the item, you have something of value. The equation for this calculation is as follows:

$$NPV_{LEASE} = CA - \left[\left[\frac{TdCA}{k_i+d}\right]\left[\frac{1+0.5k_i}{1+k_i}\right] - \left[\frac{1}{(1+k_i)^n}\right]\left[\frac{TdRV}{k_i+d}\right]\right.$$

$$\left.+(1-T)L_P\left(\frac{1-\dfrac{1}{(1+k_i)^n}}{k_i}\right)(1+k_i)+\frac{RV}{(1+k)^n}\right]$$

where

CA = Cost of the asset
T = Tax rate
k_i = The discount rate
L_P = The lease payment
d = The CCA rate
RV = Resale value

If there were a resale value in Case 1 of $5,000, the following adjustment would have been made:

$$NPV_{LEASE} = 2,277.49 - \left[-\left[\frac{1}{(1+0.00225)^{60}}\right]\left[\frac{0.4\times0.3\times5,000}{0.027+0.3}\right]+\frac{5,000}{(1+0.00225)^{60}}\right]$$

The new solution would be –$305.13 and therefore we buy. The full solution would look like the following. As complicated as it seems, it really is punching in numbers and making sure you follow the proper order of operations. Please note that a question in one of the comprehensive cases uses residual value in its calculations.

$$\text{NPV} = 30{,}000 - \left[\left[\frac{0.4 \times 0.3 \times 30{,}000}{0.027 + 0.3} \right] \left[\frac{1 + 0.5 \times (0.027)_i}{1 + 0.027} \right] - \left[\frac{1}{(1 + 0.00225)^{60}} \right] \right.$$

$$\left. \left[\frac{0.4 \times 0.3 \times 5{,}000}{0.027 + 0.3} \right] + (1 - 0.40)500.00 \left(\frac{1 - \dfrac{1}{(1 + 0.00225)^{60}}}{0.00225} \right) (1 + 0.00225) + \frac{5{,}000}{(1 + 0.00225)^{60}} \right]$$

SUMMARY

14-1 Describe three main contract terms of a bond issue.

The indenture is the contract that spells out the terms of the bond issue. A call provision gives the issuer the option to buy back the bonds before the scheduled maturity date. A conversion provision gives the bondholder the option to exchange the bond for a given number of shares. Restrictive covenants may include limits on future borrowings by the issuer, minimum working capital levels that must be maintained, and restrictions on dividends paid to common shareholders.

14-2 Define nine types of bonds.

All bonds are debt instruments that give the holder a liability claim on the issuer. A mortgage is a bond secured by real property. A debenture is an unsecured bond. A convertible bond is convertible, at the option of the bondholder, into a certain number of common shares (sometimes preferred shares or another security).

A variable-rate bond has a coupon interest rate that is not fixed but is tied to a market interest rate indicator. The bondholder can cash in a putable bond before maturity. Bonds that are below investment grade are junk bonds. An international bond, a bond sold in a country other than the country of the corporate headquarters of the issuing company, differs from a Eurobond. A Eurobond is a bond denominated in the currency of the issuing company's home country and sold in another country. A super long-term bond is one that matures in 100 years.

14-3 Describe the key features of preferred shares.

Preferred shares are a hybrid security that has debt and equity characteristics. Preferred shareholders have a superior claim relative to the common shareholders to a firm's earnings and assets, and their dividend payments are usually fixed. Those traits resemble debt. In addition, preferred shares have an infinite maturity and a lower-priority claim to assets and earnings than bondholders.

14-4 Compare and contrast an operating lease versus a capital lease.

Operating leases are usually short term and cancellable. Capital leases are long term and noncancellable. Both operating and capital leases appear on the income statement of the lessee because they are tax-deductible business expenses. Because capital leases are functionally equivalent to a purchase financed with debt, GAAP rules require that businesses treat them similarly for accounting purposes. Capital leases, therefore, appear on the balance sheet.

A lease is an arrangement in which the owner of an asset contracts to allow another party the use of the asset over time. In order for the lease to be genuine, the lessee (the party to whom the asset is leased) must not have an effective ownership of the asset. CRA's current stance is to treat most leases as operating leases.

14-5 Explain how to choose between leasing and buying options.

Leasing comprises three costs: the amount of the lease you actually pay, the opportunity cost of any tax savings if you had bought the item instead, and the present value of the residual value if any. If these three costs are lower than the value of the item, you lease. Otherwise you buy.

EQUATIONS INTRODUCED IN THIS CHAPTER

Equation 14-1: Conversion Value of a Convertible Bond

$$\text{Conversion Value} = \text{Conversion Ratio} \times \text{Share Price}$$

SELF-TEST

ST-1. Explain the features of a bond indenture.

ST-2. What is a callable bond?

ST-3. What is the straight bond value of a convertible bond?

ST-4. What are cumulative preferred shares?

ST-5. Which financial statement(s) would a capital lease affect? Why?

ST-6. What is the conversion value of a convertible bond having a current share price of $15 and a conversion ratio of 20?

REVIEW QUESTIONS

1. How does a mortgage bond compare with a debenture?
2. How does a sinking fund function in the retirement of an outstanding bond issue?
3. What are some examples of restrictive covenants that might be specified in a bond's indenture?
4. Define the following terms that relate to a convertible bond: *conversion ratio, conversion value,* and *straight bond value.*
5. If a convertible bond has a conversion ratio of 20, a face value of $1,000, a coupon rate of 8 percent, and the market price for the company's shares is $15 per share, what is the convertible bond's conversion value?
6. What is a callable bond? What is a putable bond? How do each of these features affect their respective market interest rates?

PROBLEMS

14-1. Sean Thornton has invested in a convertible bond issued by Cohan Enterprises. The conversion ratio is 20. The market price of Cohan common shares is $60. The face value is $1,000. The coupon rate is 8 percent and the annual interest is paid until the maturity date 10 years from now. Similar nonconvertible bonds are yielding 12 percent (YTM) in the marketplace. Calculate the straight bond value of this bond. ◀ Straight Bond Value

14-2. Use the same data given in problem 14-1. Now assume that interest is paid semiannually ($40 every six months). Calculate the straight bond value. ◀ Straight Bond Value

Conversion Value ▶ **14-3.** Using the data in problem 14-1, calculate the conversion value of the Cohan Enterprises convertible bond.

Conversion Value ▶ **14-4.** Jenessa Wilkens purchased 10 convertible bonds from Raingers in 2002 that mature in 2012 with a conversion ratio of 26.5 each. Currently Raingers shares are selling for $32 per share. Jenessa wants to convert six of her bonds. What is the conversion value of these six bonds?

Straight Bond Value ▶ **14-5.** Amear Kyle has a balance in his savings account of $10,000. He wants to invest 10 percent of this amount into a convertible bond issued by the Hamptom Corp. The market price of Hamptom Corp. common shares is $85. The convertible bond has a conversion ratio of 30. This bond has a 9 percent annual coupon rate (paid quarterly), a maturity of 15 years, and a face value of $1,000. Nonconvertible bonds with similar attributes are yielding 15 percent. Calculate the straight bond value for this bond.

Conversion Value ▶ **14-6.** Using the values in problem 14-5, find the conversion value of this bond.

Straight Bond Value ▶ **14-7.** Characteristics of Tanbs, Inc. convertible bonds.

Conversion Ratio	25.885
Face Value	$1,000
Maturity Date	15 years hence
Coupon Interest Rate	6.75% annual
Interest Paid	Semiannually

Calculate Tanbs, Inc.'s straight bond value on its convertible bonds. The current market interest rate on similar nonconvertible bonds is 8 percent.

Sinking Fund ▶ **14-8.** Two years ago a company issued $10 million in bonds with a face value of $1,000 and a maturity of 10 years. The company is supposed to put aside $1 million in a sinking fund each year to pay off the bonds. Dolly Frisco, the finance manager of the company, has found out that the bonds are selling at $800 apiece in the open market now when a deposit to the sinking fund is due. How much would Dolly save (before transaction costs) by purchasing 1,000 of these bonds in the open market instead of calling them in at $1,000 each?

Call Provision ▶ **14-9.** BLK issued bonds in 2000 with a 7 percent coupon interest rate. The bond's indenture stated that the bonds were callable after three years. So, when interest rates fell to 5 percent in 2004, the company called the old bonds and refunded at the 5 percent rate. If BLK issued 30,000 10-year bonds, how much did BLK save in interest per year?

Call Provision ▶ **14-10.** A company where J. B. Brooks works as the vice-president of finance issued 20,000 bonds 10 years ago. The bonds had a face value of $1,000, an annual coupon rate of 10 percent, and a maturity of 20 years. This year the market yield on the company's bond is 8 percent. The bonds are callable after five years at par. If Ms. Brooks decides in favour of exercising the call option, financing it through a refunding operation, what would be the annual savings in interest payments for the company? (Interest is paid annually.)

Call Premium ▶ **14-11.** Use the same information given in problem 14-10. Now assume that the call premium is 5 percent and the bonds were called back today. J. B. Brooks purchased 10 bonds when they were originally issued at $950 per bond. Calculate the realized rate of return for Brooks.

14-12. J. B. Brooks of problem 14-11, after getting her bonds called back by the original issuing company, can now invest in a $1,000 par, 8 percent annual coupon rate, 10-year maturity bond of equivalent risk selling at $950. (Interest is paid annually.) ◀ Total Return on Investment

a. What is the overall return for Brooks over the 20 years, assuming the bond is held until maturity?

b. Compare the overall return with the return on the bonds in problem 14-10 if they had not been called. Did Brooks welcome the recall?

14-13. Captain Nathan Brittles invested in a $1,000 par, 20-year maturity, 9 percent annual coupon rate convertible bond with a conversion ratio of 20 issued by a company six years ago. What is the conversion value of Captain Brittles's investment if the current market price for the company's common shares is $70? (Interest is paid annually.) ◀ Conversion Value

14-14. Use the same information given in problem 14-13. If the current required rate of return on a similar nonconvertible bond is 7 percent, what is the straight bond value for the bond? Should Captain Brittles convert the bond into common shares now? ◀ Straight Bond Value

14-15. Tom Dunston invested in a $1,000 par, 10-year maturity, 11 percent coupon rate convertible bond with a conversion ratio of 30 issued by a company five years ago. The current market price for the company's common shares is $30. The current required rate of return on similar but nonconvertible bonds is 13 percent. Should Mr. Dunston consider converting the bond into common shares now? ◀ Bond Conversion

14-16. Six years ago, Ruby Carter invested $1,000 in a $1,000 par, 20-year maturity, 9 percent annual coupon rate putable bond, which can be redeemed at $900 after five years. If the current required rate of return on similar bonds is 13 percent, should Ruby redeem the bond? What is the realized rate of return after redeeming? (Interest is paid annually.) ◀ Putable Bond

14-17. Five years ago, Diana Troy invested $1,000 in a $1,000 par, 10-year maturity, 9 percent annual coupon rate putable bond, which can be redeemed at $900 after five years. If the current required rate of return on similar bonds is 14 percent, should Diana redeem the bond? What is the realized rate of return after redeeming? If Diana reinvests the sum in a $1,000 par, five years to maturity, 13 percent annual coupon rate bond selling at $900 and holds it until maturity, what is her realized rate of return over the next five years? What is her realized rate of return over the entire 10 years? ◀ Reinvesting Putable Bond

14-18. Hot Box Insulators, a public company, initially issued investment-grade, 20-year maturity, 8 percent annual coupon rate bonds 10 years ago at $1,000 par. A group of investors bought all of Hot Box's common shares through a leveraged buyout, which turned the bonds overnight into junk bonds. Similar junk bonds are currently yielding 25 percent in the market. Calculate the current price of the original bonds. ◀ Challenge Problem

14-19. Profit Unlimited Company is in bankruptcy. The company has the following liability and equity claims: ◀ Priority of Claim

First-Mortgage Bonds	$5 million
Second-Mortgage Bonds	5 million
Senior Debentures	10 million
Subordinated Debentures	4 million
Common Shares	10 million (par value)

Mortgaged assets have been sold for $7 million and other assets for $13 million. According to priority of claims, determine the distribution of $20 million obtained from the sale proceeds.

Bond Refunding ▶ Excel

14-20. Suppose the Builders-R-Us Real Estate Finance Corporation has $60 million worth of bonds outstanding with an annual coupon interest rate of 8 percent. However, market interest rates have fallen to 6 percent since the bonds were issued 5 years ago. Accordingly, Builders-R-Us would like to replace the old 8 percent bonds with a new issue of 6 percent bonds.

The relevant financial data are summarized here:

Old Bond Issue	$60,000,000, 8% annual interest rate, interest paid semiannually, 20 years original maturity, 10 years remaining to maturity
Call Premium on Old Bond	4%
Underwriting Costs on Old Bonds When Issued 5 Years Ago	2% of amount issued
New Bond Issue	$60,000,000, 6% annual interest rate, interest paid semiannually, 10 years to maturity
Underwriting Costs on New Bonds	3% of amount issued
Tax Rate	40%
Discount Rate for Present Value Analysis (After-Tax Cost of Debt)	3.6%

The Builders-R-Us Corporation will be issuing new bonds having the same maturity as the number of years remaining to maturity on the old bonds.

a. What are the total cash outflows that Builders-R-Us will incur at time zero if the company implements the proposed bond-refunding program?

b. What are the annual before-tax savings in interest payments that Builders-R-Us would realize?

c. What are the annual after-tax savings in interest payments that Builders-R-Us would realize?

d. What is the present value of the annual after-tax interest savings?

e. What are the annual tax savings on the call premium that will be paid in the refunding program?

f. What is the present value of the annual tax savings on the call premium?

g. What are the net tax savings from writing off the balance of the old bond underwriting costs?

h. What are the tax savings from the new bond underwriting costs?

i. What is the present value of the tax savings from the new bond underwriting costs?

j. What is the present value of the total cash inflows that will occur if the bond-refunding program is implemented?

k. What is the net present value of the proposed bond-refunding program? Would you advise Builders-R-Us to proceed with the program?

Lease-Buy Analysis ▶ Excel

14-21. Regina Hitechia, the CIO of Aurora Glass Fibers, Inc. is considering whether to lease or buy some new computers in the company's manufacturing plant. The new computers can be purchased for $800,000 with the proceeds from a 4-year,

10 percent interest rate loan, or leased for $250,000 a year, payable at the beginning of each year for the next four years. The computers fall into CCA class 10 at 30 percent and have an expected useful life of four years. The residual value of the computers at the end of the fourth year is zero. If the computers are leased, they will be returned to the leasing company at the end of the fourth year. Aurora's tax rate is 40 percent.

a. What is the present value of the cash flows associated with leasing the computers?
b. Should Ms. Hitechia purchase or lease the new computers?

14-22. Nancy Morrison, sole shareholder of Brains Inc., which specializes in equipment for head trauma victims, had $1,000,000 face value bonds issued 5 years ago for 25 years (i.e., there are 20 years left until maturity). The interest payments paid by Brains Inc. were 10.5 percent. At the time of issuance, the company had a speculative rating of B. In order to sweeten the deal, Nancy was forced to allow each bond to be convertible into 20 shares. She was able to have a call provision placed into the agreement, whereby her company could buy the bonds back at 4 percent. The issuance cost at the time was 3 percent, and this should be the same for future issuances. The current price of the bonds on the open market is $1,705.11 and the company's tax rate is 40 percent. The current share price is $85. BBB bonds are selling at a yield of 6 percent for 20 years until maturity. ◀ Challenge Problem

Excel

Recently, the work done by Brains Inc. has resulted in several discoveries that will produce a consistent flow of heavy income over the foreseeable future. The company's bond rating jumped up to a BBB rating. Nancy was thrilled and was considering what she could do to take advantage of this jump.

a. What should be the effects of the credit rating jump?
b. What could Nancy do to take advantage of the rate jump? What would her savings be?
c. Considering the full description of the bonds, what do you think would happen when Nancy tried to exercise her right to call back the bonds?
d. What relationship do you notice between the share price and the bond price?

14-23. Markus was considering buying or leasing a car for his business. These are the following factors that he had to contend with: ◀ Lease versus Buy

- MRSP $25,000
- CCA Class 10 rate = 30%
- Business tax rate = 30%
- Markus could borrow from a bank at 7percent
- If it were leased, after 5 years the car would be returned. If bought, after 5 years it would be worth nothing. The lease payment assumes a 7 percent implied rate.

a. What is the yearly lease payment (assuming that the lease is paid yearly, not monthly)? What is the present value of the lease payments? In this case, what is the only factor that is different between leasing and buying?
b. If Markus knew that he tended to over-drive his cars, resulting in an estimated extra $5,000 charge at the end of the lease, how would this change things, if any?
c. Assuming the information in (b) and if Markus was offered 0.1 percent financing if he bought the car instead of leasing, how would things change?

Convertible Preferred Share ▶

14-24. Benson Creed had issued several preferred shares several years ago at a very low fixed dividend rate, at a time when low rates were expected. To sweeten the deal, he allowed the issuance of the preferred shares to be structured in such a way that each preferred share could be converted into one common share at any given time. Currently, the preferred shares were priced close to the common share price of $10. Similar preferred shares, without a conversion option, were trading at $5. Benson was very worried. He currently owned 51 percent of the company and did not like the idea of his ownership being reduced.

a. If no restrictions existed, what creative action could Benson take to reduce the chance of the conversion?

b. What sort of restrictions would you like to see if you were a preferred shareholder?

ANSWERS TO SELF-TEST

ST-1. A bond indenture is the contract that spells out the provisions of a bond issue. It always contains the face value, coupon rate, interest payment dates, and maturity date. It may also include terms of security in the case of default, if any; the plan for paying off the bonds at maturity; provisions for paying off the bonds ahead of time; restrictive covenants to protect bondholders; and the trustee's name.

ST-2. A callable bond is a bond that can be paid off early by the issuer at the issuer's option.

ST-3. The straight bond value of a convertible bond is the value a convertible bond would have without its conversion feature. It is the present value of the interest and principal using the required rate of return on a similar nonconvertible bond as the discount rate.

ST-4. Cumulative preferred shares are preferred shares for which missed dividends must be made up (paid) by the issuing company before common share dividends may be resumed.

ST-5. A capital lease would show up on both the income statement and the balance sheet. Lease payments are business expenses that belong on the income statement, and GAAP rules call for capital leases to be reflected on the balance sheet also.

ST-6. $15 market price of the share × 20 conversion ratio = $300 conversion value of the convertible bond.

Common Shares

Chapter Objectives

After reading this chapter, you should be able to:

15-1 **Describe** the characteristics of common shares, including how residual income affects shares.

15-2 **Describe** the process of making shares public.

15-3 **Contrast** majority and cumulative voting rules.

15-4 **Describe** at least two advantages and disadvantages of equity financing.

15-5 **Describe** the features of rights, warrants, and options, while being able to estimate their value in terms of intrinsic value and time value.

"Where your treasure is, there will your heart be also."

—Matthew 6:21

Krispy Kreme IPO Gets Sweet Reception

By Paul Nowell, The Associated Press, April 5, 2000

Winston-Salem, N.C. (AP)—Like a fresh serving of its tasty treats, Krispy Kreme Doughnut Corp.'s reception on Wall Street on Wednesday was hot and sweet, with its shares climbing more than 75 percent in their first day of trading.

The Winston-Salem company's initial public offering was priced at $21 per share yesterday, and opened this morning at $32 on the Nasdaq Stock Market with the ticker symbol KREM. At 4 p.m., the shares stood at $37, after 7 million shares had changed hands during the day.

"It's almost like a dream," president Scott Livengood said in a telephone interview from New York. "It's a culmination of a lot of work for generations."

Livengood remembers selling boxes of Krispy Kreme doughnuts in high school. He's been with the company for 22 years.

Krispy Kreme, founded in 1937 by Vernon Carver Rudolph in a Winston-Salem storefront, is issuing 3 million common shares, putting the value of the IPO at about $63 million.

During the past six years, the Southern institution has ventured into such decidedly un-Southern markets as Manhattan and Las Vegas. Krispy Kreme now has 141 stores in 27 states, from New York to California.

Each store makes and sells about 20 different kinds of doughnuts. But their signature item remains the Hot Original Glazed doughnut. True fans find the urge irresistible to stop at Krispy Kreme when the "Hot Doughnuts Now" sign is on.

Chapter Overview

In this chapter, we explore the characteristics and types of common shares, types of common share owners, and the pros and cons of issuing shares to raise capital. Then we investigate how firms issue common shares. Finally, we examine *rights, warrants,* and *options* and their risk and return features.

The Characteristics of Common Shares

As we learned in Chapter 2, **common shares** are securities that represent an equity claim on a firm. Having an equity claim means that the one holding the security (the common shareholder) is an owner of the firm, has voting rights, and has a claim on the *residual income* of the firm. **Residual income** is income left over after other claimants of the firm have been paid. Residual income can be paid out in the form of a cash dividend to common shareholders, or it can be reinvested in the firm. Reinvesting this residual income increases the market value of the common shares due to the new assets acquired or liabilities reduced.

Corporations sometimes have different classes of shareholders. For example, a corporation's charter may provide for a certain class of shareholders to have greater voting rights than other classes. Or one class of shares may receive its dividends based on the performance of only a certain part of the company.

The Bombardier Company, for example, has two different classes of shares. Class A shares, owned mostly by family members, have 10 times the voting rights of Class B shares. Dual-class share structures are often the case for public corporations, such as Bombardier, that started out as private family businesses and in which family members continue to actively manage the company. (There is no consistent standard, however, about which designation, A or B, has the greater voting rights and which designation the lesser.)

A relatively new special class of shares is sometimes created when a company that has long been in one line of business expands into a new, often riskier line. The company will then issue a new class of common shares that represents a claim only on the new business. These shares are called target shares because their value is targeted toward specific (nontraditional) assets. In 1995, for example, Qwest Communications International (one of the Baby Bells spun off in the AT&T divestiture) issued target shares to finance its venture in cellular, cable, and other nontelephone businesses. The idea is that a different kind of shareholder is likely to be attracted to the newer, nontraditional businesses than the shareholder interested in "plain old telephone service" (POTS).

All classes of shares have values that are determined when those shares are traded from one investor to another at the various stock exchanges and in the over-the-counter market, as was described in Chapter 2. The market takes into account the characteristics of a given class and values each class accordingly.

Common shareholders are paid dividends determined by the ability and willingness of the firm to pay. The board of directors of the corporation makes this dividend decision. Residual income not paid out to the common shareholders in the form of dividends is reinvested in the firm. It benefits the common shareholders there as well (because they are the owners of the corporation). Remember that this "residual" amount is credited to Retained Earnings and has no direct effect on the company's cash account.

Dogbert's deal demonstrates why it is important to read the contract carefully when executing a merger. A business ethics class might be a good idea for Dogbert.

Source: DILBERT © 1996 United Feature Syndicate, Inc. Reprinted by permission.

All corporations issue shares. Some corporations are privately owned, whereas members of the general public own others. The rules for private and public corporations differ, as we see next.

Shares Issued by Private Corporations

Private corporations (also known as closely held corporations) are so called because their common shares are not traded openly in the marketplace. Tax returns, of course, are filed with the CCRA, but this information is confidential. Privately held corporations are usually small, and the shareholders are often actively involved in the management of the firm. The corporate form of organization is attractive to many small firms because the owners face only limited liability.

Shares Issued by Publicly Traded Corporations

Bombardier, BCE Inc., Alcan Inc.—these are just some examples of well-known publicly traded corporations. A **publicly traded corporation** is a corporation the common shares of which can be bought by any interested party and the corporation must release audited financial statements to the public. It is typically run by a professional management team, which likely owns only a tiny fraction of the outstanding common shares.

The professional management team that handles the operations of the firm reports to a group called the **board of directors**. The board of directors, in turn, is elected by the common shareholders to represent their interests. The board is an especially important body for large public corporations because management typically owns such a small percentage of the firm. The agency problem discussed in Chapter 1 described the conflict of interest that can occur when those who run a firm own very little of it. The common shareholders elect the board members, and the board members oversee the management of the company.

Members of the board of directors have a fiduciary responsibility to the common shareholders who elected them. **Fiduciary responsibility** is the legal duty to act in the best interests of the person who entrusted you with property or power. When shareholders elect board members to represent them, they entrust the board members with the management of their company. The board members owe it to the common shareholders to act in the common shareholders' interest. Shareholders may vote directly on some major issues, such as a proposal to merge or liquidate the company.

Institutional Ownership of Common Shares

Institutional investors own many common shares of publicly traded corporations. These investors are financial institutions that invest in the securities of other companies. Money management firms handling pension fund money, trust companies, insurance companies, mutual funds, and the like are major common shareholders. The link between ownership and control is likely to be a loose one in such cases because the individual shareholder is several layers away from the corporation. For instance, a worker may have a claim on a pension fund that is managed by a money management firm that has invested funds in another company's common shares.

In recent years, many institutional investors have begun to take a more active role in overseeing the companies in which they own common shares. Institutional investors usually have substantial amounts of funds, so they can buy a large number of shares and become major shareholders. As a result, they can exercise more control than widely dispersed individual investors. Fidelity Investments, for example, a large U.S. mutual fund company, has been seeking seats on the board of directors of companies in which Fidelity is a major shareholder.

In this section, we investigated common share characteristics, including classes of shares issued by private and public corporations. We also looked at institutional ownership of common shares. Next, we examine the voting rights of common shareholders.

Voting Rights of Common Shareholders

Common shareholders have the power to vote according to the number of shares they own. The general rule is "one vote per share." A shareholder group holding more than 50 percent of the voting shares has a *majority interest* in the firm. The shareholder or group of shareholders that owns enough voting shares to control the board and operations of the firm has a *controlling interest* in the firm. The shareholder group gains control when it elects a majority of its supporters to the board of directors.

In practice, a group can gain control with much less than 50 percent of the voting shares. This can happen if the remaining voting shares are widely distributed among many thousands of shareholders (each of whom owns a tiny percentage of the outstanding voting shares) who do not act in concert with each other. Many firms are controlled by groups of common shareholders owning as little as 5 percent or 10 percent of the voting shares, sometimes less.

Proxies

In large publicly traded corporations, the typical shareholder is likely to be uninterested in the details of the company's operations. It is not worth going to the shareholders' meeting in another part of the country if you hold only a few hundred shares. Such shareholders will typically allow others to vote their shares for them by *proxy*. This means that another group—usually the management of the company, but sometimes a group opposing management—will vote the shares for the shareholder who has given his or her proxy.

To give permission to another to vote your shares, you sign a card sent out by the group seeking this permission. In contested votes, in which several competing groups may solicit shareholder proxies, each group may send out a card of a different colour.

Board of Directors' Elections

Corporate elections typically use one of two different sets of voting rules to fill seats on the board of directors. These are *majority voting* and *cumulative voting* rules. Under majority voting rules, a given number of seats are to be filled in a given election. The number of voting shares held, plus proxy votes held, represents the number of votes a person may cast for a given candidate for each separate seat. If multiple seats are contested, the candidates for a given seat will compete against each other for that seat. The person receiving the greatest number of votes wins that seat. With majority voting, whoever controls the majority of the votes will get their candidates elected to every seat to be filled.

Under cumulative voting rules, all the candidates run against each other but do not run for a particular seat. If there are five seats to be filled in the election, the top five vote getters among all the candidates win those seats. Votes are cast—one vote per share times the number of seats being contested—for as many or as few candidates as a voter wishes. This means that shareholders with shares and proxies for less than a majority of the number of voting shares can "accumulate" their votes by casting them all for only a few candidates (even casting all votes for one candidate).

Cumulative voting makes it more likely that those shareholders with less than a majority of the voting shares will get some representation on the board. With majority voting rules, in which candidates run for specified seats, the majority shareholders in each of these separate elections would outvote minority shareholders.

Suppose Burgerworld Corporation has a ten-member board and terms for three of the ten members are expiring. The firm uses cumulative voting rules. Seven candidates are competing for the right to fill these three seats. There are 100,000 voting shares of common shares outstanding for Burgerworld. This means that 300,000 total votes will be cast (100,000 shares × 3 contested seats = 300,000 total votes).

The shareholders are divided into two camps of differing corporate management philosophy. The majority group controls 60 percent of the voting shares, whereas the minority group of common shareholders controls the other 40 percent. The minority group nominated one of the seven candidates. The minority shareholder group knows that with only 40 percent of the votes, they have no hope of winning two or three of the three seats contested. Does the minority group of shareholders have enough voting power to get their one candidate on the board?

The majority shareholders would like to get three of their people elected to the three seats available. If they want to succeed, they will have to spread their 180,000 votes (60 percent of 300,000) among their three favourite candidates. Spreading the votes evenly among their preferred candidates, each candidate supported by the majority group would receive 60,000 votes (180,000 ÷ 3 = 60,000). If the minority shareholders cast all their votes for their candidate, that person will receive 120,000 (300,000 total – 180,000 majority votes = 120,000 minority votes) votes and win a seat on the board.

The formula for determining the number of directors that a shareholder group could elect, given the number of voting shares they control, is shown next in Equation 15-1.

The Number of Directors Who Can Be Elected under Cumulative Voting Rules

$$\text{NUM DIR} = \frac{(\text{SHARES CONTROLLED} - 1) \times (\text{TOT NUM DIR T.B.E.} + 1)}{\text{TOT NUM VOTING SHARES}} \quad (15\text{-}1)$$

where

NUM DIR = Number of directors who can be elected by a given group

SHARES CONTROLLED = Number of voting shares controlled by a given group

TOT NUM DIR T.B.E. = Total number of directors to be elected in the election

TOT NUM VOTING SHARES = Total number of voting shares in the election

Using the number of shares owned by the minority shareholders described in our Burgerworld example (40,000 of 100,000 shares outstanding), we can calculate the number of directors that this minority group could elect. Recall that the number of directors to be elected is three. The calculations follow:

$$\text{NUM DIR} = \frac{(40{,}000 - 1) \times (3 + 1)}{100{,}000}$$
$$= 1.60$$

This group can elect one of their people to the board out of the three to be elected. Note that we rounded down to get the answer. Because people cannot be divided, the minority group cannot elect 0.6 (60 percent) of a person to the board.

The formula for determining the number of shares needed by a given group to elect a given number of directors is shown next in Equation 15-2.

The Number of Shares Needed to Elect a Given Number of Directors under Cumulative Voting Rules

$$\text{NUM VOTING SHARES NEEDED} = \frac{\text{NUM DIR DESIRED} \times \text{TOT NUM VOTING SHARES}}{\text{TOT NUM DIR T.B.E.} + 1} + 1 \quad (15\text{-}2)$$

where

NUM DIR DESIRED = Number of directors a given group of shareholders desires to elect

TOT NUM VOTING SHARES = Total number of voting shares in the election

TOT NUM DIR T.B.E. = Total number of directors to be elected in the election

For example, to calculate the number of voting shares needed to elect two of the three directors in the election described earlier, we could plug in the appropriate numbers into Equation 15-2. The calculation is shown next:

$$\text{NUM VOTING SHARES NEEDED} = \frac{2 \times 100{,}000}{3+1} + 1$$
$$= 50{,}001$$

We find that a group would need control of 50,001 voting shares to guarantee the election of two of the three directors in this election. This number is equivalent to 150,003 votes spread evenly between two director candidates. This would be 75,001.5 votes per candidate (50,001 voting shares × 3 total directors to be elected ÷ 2 directors sought to be elected). The other shareholders, holding 49,999 voting shares, would have the remaining 149,997 votes (49,999 voting shares × 3 total directors to be elected). If these 149,997 votes were divided between two candidates, that would be only 74,998.5 votes per candidate.

In this section, we reviewed the voting rights of common shareholders. We examine the advantages and disadvantages of equity financing next.

The Pros and Cons of Equity Financing

Selling new common shares has advantages and disadvantages for a corporation. Some disadvantages include dilution of power and earnings per share of existing shareholders, flotation costs, and possible unfavourable market perceptions about the firm's financial prospects. The advantages of a new share issue include additional capital for the firm, lower risk, and the potential to borrow more in the future.

Disadvantages of Equity Financing

Selling new common shares is like taking in new partners (although we are referring to a corporation rather than to a partnership). When you sell new common shares, you must share the profits and the power with the new shareholders. When new common shares are issued, the ownership position of the existing common shareholders is diluted because the number of shares outstanding increases.

The dilution may result in lower earnings per share for a profitable company. Losses, of course, would be shared, too, resulting in a lower negative earnings per share figure for a money-losing company. The voting power of the existing common shareholders would also be diluted. Firms concerned with losing control through diluted voting power often avoid raising funds through a share issue.

Also, when new common shares are sold, **flotation costs** are incurred. As we discussed in Chapter 9, flotation costs are fees paid to investment bankers, lawyers, and others when new securities are issued. The flotation costs associated with new common share issues are normally much higher than those associated with debt.

Another reason that common share issues are often a last resort for many corporations is because of signalling effects. **Signalling** is a message a firm sends, or investors infer, about a financial decision.

It is reasonable to suggest that the internal corporate managers have better insight into a firm's future business prospects than the average outside investor. If we accept this proposition as true, then we would not expect a company to sell additional shares to the general public unless its managers know that the future prospects for the company are worse than is generally believed. How do we know this? Equity financing is expensive and often used as a last resort. The inference drawn by investors who agree with this view is that a corporation issuing new shares wants more "partners" with whom to share future bad times. A company that expected good times would attempt to preserve the benefits for the current owners alone. Instead of issuing new shares, then, the firm would issue more debt securities.

Management may issue new common shares even though the future financial prospects for the firm are bright. However, if the market believes otherwise, the price of the common shares will drop when the new common shares are issued.

Advantages of Equity Financing

Why would any corporation issue new shares? One big reason is that corporations do not pay interest (and are not legally obligated to pay any dividends) to common shareholders. Unlike interest payments on debt, dividends can be skipped without incurring legal penalties. Interest payments on debt reduce a firm's earnings, whereas dividend payments to shareholders do not.

Some firms choose equity financing because they do not like borrowing. Some business people view being "in debt" as undesirable. They avoid it if possible and pay off unavoidable debts as soon as possible. Companies in which managers and owners hold this view will tend to favour equity financing.

A final reason that firms choose equity instead of debt financing is that the firm may have so much debt that borrowing more may be difficult or too expensive. Suppose, for example, that the "normal" ratio of debt to assets in your firm's industry is 20 percent and your firm's debt to assets ratio is 40 percent. If this is the case, lenders may be reluctant to lend your firm any more money at an affordable interest rate or may impose certain restrictive covenants, thus limiting your company's flexibility; your firm might be forced to issue shares to raise funds. In this situation, a new share issue could bring the firm's debt ratios down to more normal industry levels. This would make it easier for the firm to borrow in the future.

In this section, we described the pros and cons of a new share issue. We turn to the process of issuing common shares next.

Issuing Common Shares

When a firm wishes to raise new equity capital, it must first decide whether to try to raise the capital from the firm's existing shareholders or to seek new investors. Private companies usually raise additional equity capital by selling new shares to existing common shareholders. This generally satisfies these shareholders because they continue to exercise complete control over the firm. However, when a large amount of equity capital must be raised, the existing shareholders may find that their only recourse is to sell shares of the firm's shares to the general public. A firm that sells its private shares to the general public "goes public." The issuance of common shares to the public for the first time is known as an **initial public offering (IPO)**. Figure 15-1 describes the Krispy Kreme IPO.

Figure 15-1
IPO of Krispy Kreme

Krispy Kreme Goes Public

In April 2000 Krispy Kreme Doughnut Corporation went public by offering 7 million shares of common stock at $21 per share, $5.25 adjusted for two 2-1 stock splits. J.P. Morgan was the lead underwriter for the IPO. Krispy Kreme had a P/E ratio of 82 in October 2001, when its stock price was $35 per share. Investors were obviously betting on a sweet future for Krispy Kreme. The company trades on the New York Stock Exchange with the ticker symbol KKD.

Krispy Kreme's signature product is the Hot Original Glazed doughnut. It has a cult following similar to that Coors beer had back in the days when that product was available only in Colorado. Krispy Kreme is hoping that its sales and profits can continue to grow as it increases the number of stores. It is hoping that the allure of its "hard to get" image doesn't wear off too quickly.

Institutional investors are major buyers of new equity issues. Investment bankers who try to sell initial shares typically prefer to sell large blocks of shares to institutional investors, as opposed to selling many small blocks of shares to individual investors.

The Function of Investment Dealers

When a corporation does decide to sell shares to the public, its first step is to contact an investment firm to handle the issue. Some of the names of investment dealers that a corporation might contact would include ScotiaMcLeod, Nesbitt Burns, and RBC Capital Markets, to mention only a few.

Investment bankers handle all the details associated with pricing the share and marketing it to the public. A potential investor in a new security must be given a prospectus. A **prospectus** is a disclosure document that describes the security and the issuing company. Investment bankers typically announce a new issue and the availability of the prospectus in a large boxed-in ad.

Underwriting versus Best Efforts Investment bankers take on the job of marketing a firm's shares to the public on one of two bases: **underwriting** or **best efforts**. When an investment banker *underwrites* a share issue, it means the investment banker agrees to buy a certain number of shares from the issuing company at a certain price. Usually, a group of investment bankers will form a temporary alliance called a **syndicate** when underwriting a new security issue. The head of the investment banking syndicate is known as the **manager** or lead underwriter. The manager has the primary responsibility for advising the security issuer. Extra fees are collected for this advice. It is up to the syndicate to sell the shares to the public at whatever price it can get. An underwriting poses the least risk to the firm for which shares are being issued. This is because the firm gets the share issue proceeds from the investment bankers all at once, up front. However, because the investment bankers bear the risk that they might not be able to sell the firm's shares at the price they expect, they charge a rather substantial fee for underwriting.

A less expensive alternative to underwriting is called a *best efforts offering*. In this arrangement, the investment banker agrees to use its "best efforts" to sell the issuing company's shares at the desired price, but it makes no firm promises to do so. If the shares can only be sold at a lower price than was expected, then the issuing firm must either issue more shares to make up the difference or be satisfied with lower proceeds from the share issue. Not surprisingly, the fees investment bankers charge for marketing shares on a best efforts basis are considerably less than those they charge for underwriting.

Finance at Work 15-1 discusses a *bought deal* offering.

Pricing New Share Issues

When new shares in a company are to be sold to the public, someone must decide at what price to offer them for sale. This is not a significant problem when the company's shares are already publicly traded. The new shares are simply sold at the same price as the old shares, or perhaps a little lower.[1] However, if the company is going public, there is no previous market activity to establish what the shares are worth. In this situation, the investment banker, in conjunction with the issuing company's managers, must put a price on the shares and hope that the market will agree that the price represents fair

NANCE AT WORK 15-1

les Retail Sports Media Technology Public Relations Production Exports

IDERWRITERS LOSE MILLIONS ON CAE SHARE ISSUE

ntreal—The underwriting syndicate that helped flight simu- r maker CAE raise $175 million through a recent offering hares now finds itself holding shares that are worth far less n what they paid for them.

The investment banks underwriting the offering bought entire 26.6 million shares CAE was selling. The purchase s a "bought deal." That's where one or two underwriters buy entire issue and then resell the shares to the public.

The share offering, which closed Tuesday, was priced at 58 a share. . . .

At the time the offering was announced on Sept. 11, that med like a good deal, as CAE shares closed on Sept. 11 at 72.

But last Friday, CAE revealed that it had lost out on an 0-million US training contract with the U.S. Army. CAE res fell dramatically on that news. In Tuesday morning trad- , CAE shares were at $5.13.

At $1.45 a share below the offering price, that means the underwriters have a paper loss of $38.57 million on the 26.6 million shares they've bought, because they cannot sell them above the current market price.

At this point, the underwriters have little choice but to park the shares in their own corporate accounts and wait for the stock price to recover to at least $6.58.

Under terms of the original offering, the underwriters have the option of buying an additional 2.66 million shares at $6.58 each until October 30. It's a safe bet that this option will not be exercised unless CAE shares stage a dramatic recovery in the next month.

The underwriting syndicate includes Scotia Capital, RBC Dominion Securities, CIBC World Markets, Dundee Securities, TD Securities, and Griffiths McBurney and Partners.

Source: CBC News Online Staff, "Underwriters Lose Millions on CAE Share Issue." CBC News. www.cbc.ca. 1 October 2003. Reproduced with permission of the Canadian Broadcasting Corporation.

[1]There is usually a small amount of dilution (downward movement) in the price of a company's common shares when new shares are sold.

value. This is a daunting task indeed and frequently investment bankers and firm managers miss the mark. International Perspectives in Finance 15-1 discusses IPOs (initial public offerings) in Canada.

Valuing the Shares of a Company That Is Not Publicly Traded Before investment bankers offer a company's shares for sale to the public, they must have some idea of how the public will value the shares to predict the new issue market price. The trouble is, when a company's shares has not been sold to anyone before, it is perilously difficult to say how much it is worth.

Suppose you have been creating oil paintings for a few years and have become pretty good at it. One day the art club you belong to has a show, and one of your paintings is included. When you deliver the painting to the gallery, you are asked what sale price you wish posted on the painting. Now you face the same question firms and investment bankers face. How much is the painting worth? How much can you get for it?

Naturally, you want to sell the painting for as high a price as possible, but the potential buyers want to pay as low a price as possible. If you post too high an asking price, no one will buy your painting and you will leave empty handed. If you post too low a price, however, someone will snatch it up and may well resell it to someone else for a substantial profit. You can see that if you had previously sold a number of similar paintings you would have an idea of what to ask for this one. The first painting you try to sell is the one that presents the pricing problem.

In Chapter 12, we presented some of the methods that companies and investment bankers use to estimate the market value of a company's shares. These methods include calculating the present value of expected cash flows, multiplying earnings per share by the appropriate P/E ratio, the book value approach, and the liquidation value approach.

Rights, Warrants, and Options

Rights and warrants are securities issued by a corporation that allow investors to buy new common shares. They originate in different ways and have somewhat different characteristics, as explained in the following sections.

Preemptive Rights

When some companies plan to issue new shares, they establish procedures to protect the ownership interest of the original shareholders. The existing shareholders are given securities that allow them to preempt other investors in the purchase of new shares. This security is called a preemptive right. A **preemptive right**, sometimes referred to simply as a *right,* gives the holder the option to buy additional common shares at a specified price (the *subscription price*) until a given expiration date. Current shareholders who do not wish to exercise their rights can sell them in the open market.

The Number of Rights Required to Buy a New Share Suppose that Right Stuff Corporation has 100,000 common shares currently outstanding. An additional 20,000 common shares are to be sold to existing shareholders by means of a rights offering. Because one right is sent out to existing shareholders for each share held, 100,000 rights must be sent out. There are five shares outstanding for each new share to be sold (100,000/20,000 = 5). Five

INTERNATIONAL PERSPECTIVES IN FINANCE 15-1

Why U.S. Abuses on IPOs Wouldn't Happen in Canada

)ecial)—Investors needn't worry that there are serious
uses in initial public offerings (IPOs) of shares in Canada
nilar to those recently exposed by law officials in the
ited States.

If stock prices were to jump dramatically following an
) in Canada as they often do in the United States, things
re might be different. But given the approach taken by
nadian investment dealers in pricing new issues, post-IPO
ce jumps in Canada are rare, and when they do occur,
ey are modest. As a result, there is little incentive here for
questionable practices that have come to light south of
border.

The key difference between the United States and
nada is that individual employees and brokers working in
S. underwriting firms traditionally have been able to buy
t IPOs along with other investors at the issue price. In
ner words, many U.S. brokers also get to participate in the
ce jump.

In Canada, the situation is much different. While bro-
rage employees in Canada can legally buy IPOs, policies
the major brokerage houses allow the purchase of IPOs by
okers only after all customer orders are filled.

Thus, in the case of a hot new issue with customers
mping on the bandwagon, the brokers and other employ-
s of Canadian underwriting firms don't get any shares. The
rporate finance team pricing the issue and the retail bro-
rs selling it can't benefit directly from a post-IPO price
mp.

This means the incentives for pricing new issues are dif-
ent in Canada than in the United States. In Canada, the
centive is to get the highest price possible for the issuing
ent (a company trying to sell stock into the market). By
tting the highest price and generally doing a good job for
e issuing client, the underwriting firm not only earns its fee
t gets a positive reputation that can attract more issuing
ents. The corporate finance officials pricing the new issue
nefit directly through higher bonuses for the fees they
ract.

Over time, this has created a much different set of mar-
t expectations for IPOs in Canada. With a Canadian IPO as
ely to see a price decline as a price increase, the process
esn't invite as much investor speculation or set up a major
centive for abuse.

In the United States, the lead broker in the underwriting instead uses its influence to keep the IPO price as low as possible, thereby yielding a big profit for employees along with other investors as the price doubles or triples after the IPO. The stock-price gains for the corporate finance team and retail brokers participating in the new issue can far exceed the usual 5 to 8 percent underwriting fee.

The fact that stocks often double or triple in the days following an IPO has generated some questionable practices. U.S. underwriting firms have been caught bestowing hot IPOs to senior executives of companies they want investment banking business from. It is a practice known as "spinning." Former star investment banker Frank Quattrone is facing obstruction of justice charges stemming from IPO spinning.

U.S. underwriting firms have defended the spinning practice by saying the executives are simply good clients and that is why they got the shares allocated to them. But the executives on the receiving end are obviously in a conflict of interest position in any subsequent decision-making on which underwriting firms to use.

Another questionable practice of U.S. underwriting firms is known as "laddering," whereby IPO buyers, in exchange for receiving shares at the low IPO price, agree to purchase more shares in the open market at a higher price immediately after the IPO. This, of course, helps drive up the stock price after the IPO and serves to provide buyers at high prices for stock doled out to brokers and their corporate friends.

If stock prices didn't jump so high after an IPO, these practices wouldn't make sense. If the chances of losing were as great as the chances of winning on an IPO, and if the gain when it occurred was usually only 5 or 10 percent, who would want an allocation of shares?

In a market ruled by greed, change the incentives and you'll change the outcome.

Wayne Cheveldayoff is a former investment advisor and professional financial planner currently specializing in financial communications and investor relations at Wertheim + Co. in Toronto.

Source: Wayne Cheveldayoff, "Why U.S. Abuses on IPOs Wouldn't Happen in Canada." 14 November 2003. Reprinted with permission of The Canadian Press.

rights are therefore needed, along with the payment of the subscription price, to purchase a new common share through the rights offering.

The Value of a Right We know that five rights are required to buy a new common share of Right Stuff Corporation through the rights offering. To determine the value of each right, we must also know the subscription price and the market price of Right Stuff's common shares.

This information, along with our knowledge of the number of rights required to buy a new share, will allow us to estimate the value of one of these rights.[2]

Suppose that the current market price of one of Right Stuff Corporation's common shares is \$65 and that the subscription price is set at \$50. This means that you are saving \$15 (\$65 – \$50 = \$15) when you send in your five rights to receive one of the new shares (known as "exercising your rights"). This means that each right would be worth \$3 (\$15 ÷ 5 = \$3) before dilution effects are considered.

The approximate value of a right can be determined by two formulas. The formula used depends on the status of the shares as they trade in the marketplace, relative to the timing of the issuance of the rights. Timing is the key to determining which approximation formula to use.

Rights are generally sent out several weeks after the announcement of the rights offering is made. This initial period is called the **rights-on** period and the shares are said to *trade rights-on* during this time. This means that if the common shares are purchased during the rights-on period, the investor will receive the forthcoming rights.

At the opening of trading on the day following the rights-on period, the shares are said to be trading **ex-rights**. This means that the purchaser buys the shares without (*ex* is Latin for "without") receiving the entitlement to the preemptive rights if the purchase is on or after the ex-rights date.

Trading Rights-On.

If the share is trading rights-on, then we calculate the approximate market value of the right as depicted in Equation 15-3:

Approximate Value of a Right, Share Trading Rights-On

$$R = \frac{M_0 - S}{N + 1} \tag{15-3}$$

where

R = Approximate market value of a right

M_0 = Market price of the common shares, selling rights-on

S = Subscription price

N = Number of rights needed to purchase one of the new common shares

We call R the approximate market value of the right because rights are securities that can be traded just like shares and bonds. Once the rights are sent to the existing common shareholders (those who bought the shares

---

[2]The actual pricing of a right is somewhat more complicated than what we are presenting here. A right is an option to buy the new share at the specified subscription price. The rights valuation presented here should be considered an approximation only.

before they "went ex-rights"), the rights can be traded in the marketplace at the option of the owner. The actual market price of the right may be slightly different than shown in the formulas presented here because of the option characteristics of the rights, which are discussed later.

Table 15-1 shows the calculation of the approximate market value of a Right Stuff Corporation right. This is the value of the right as determined by the rights-on formula, Equation 15-3.

Table 15-1 Right Valuation with Share Selling Rights-On

M_0, Market Price of the Common Shares, Rights-On	\$65
S, Subscription Price	\$50
N, Number of Rights Required to Purchase One New Common Share	5
R, Approximate Market Price of One Right	$R = \frac{\$65 - \$50}{5+1} = \frac{\$15}{6} = \$2.50$

We see from the calculations in Table 15-1 that the market value of one Right Stuff right is \$2.50, given a market price of one common share at \$65, a subscription price of \$50, and five rights required to purchase one new common share.

Selling Ex-Rights.

To find the approximate value of the right when the shares are selling ex-rights, the ex-rights formula must be used. This formula is presented as follows in Equation 15-4:

Approximate Value of a Right, Share Trading Ex-Rights

$$R = \frac{M_X - S}{N} \quad (15\text{-}4)$$

where

R = Approximate market value of a right

M_x = Market price of the common shares, selling ex-rights

S = Subscription price

N = Number of rights needed to purchase one of the new common shares

When the common shares begin trading ex-rights, the entitlement to the forthcoming rights is lost. Thus, the price of the common shares in the marketplace will drop by the value of the right now lost on the ex-rights date (other factors held constant).

Suppose Right Stuff Corporation common shares begin selling ex-rights today. When the opening bell rings on the exchange, the price of Right Stuff common shares will drop by the amount of the value of the right that has been lost. Holding other factors constant (no news overnight to otherwise affect the value of the common shares), the price of the common shares will drop by \$2.50 from \$65 to \$62.50.

Table 15-2 shows the calculation of the approximate market value of the right when the common shares are selling ex-rights, using Equation 15-4.

Table 15-2 Right Valuation with Shares Selling Ex-Rights

M_x, Market Price of the Common Shares, Ex-Rights	\$62.50
S, Subscription Price	\$50
N, Number of Rights Required to Purchase One New Common Share	5
R, Approximate Market Price of One Right	$R = \frac{\$62.50 - \$50}{5} = \frac{\$12.50}{5} = \$2.50$

When the common shares are selling ex-rights, Equation 15-4 gives the approximate market value of a right. The equation reflects the loss of the entitlement of the rights, \$2.50 in our example.

Warrants

A **warrant** is a security that gives its owner the option to buy a certain number of common shares from the issuing company, at a certain exercise price, until a specified expiration date. The corporation benefits from issuing warrants because the issue raises funds. It also creates the possibility of a future increase in the company's number of common shares. The investor values warrants because of the option to buy the company's shares.

Warrants are similar to rights except they are sold to investors instead of given away to existing shareholders. They typically have longer maturities than rights and are often issued with bonds as part of a security package. It is important to note also that the warrant price is at a premium to today's share price.

Warrant Valuation Warrants have value only until the expiration date, at which time they become worthless. Before a warrant expires, its value depends on how the price of the common shares compares to the warrant's *exercise price*—the price the firm sets for exercising the right to buy common shares—and on other factors, described next.

To value warrants, investors must be able to find the exercise value. The exercise value is the amount saved by purchasing the common shares by exercising the warrant rather than buying the common shares directly in the open market. If there is no saving, the exercise value is zero.

The formula for calculating the exercise value of a warrant is described in Equation 15-5 as follows:

The Exercise Value of a Warrant

$$XV = (M - XP) \times \# \tag{15-5}$$

where

XV = Exercise value of a warrant

M = Market price of the shares

XP = Exercise price of a warrant

$\#$ = Number of shares that may be purchased if the warrant is exercised

Suppose that the McGuffin Corporation warrant entitles the investor to purchase four shares of common shares, at an exercise price of $50 per share, during the next three years. If the current common share price is $60, the exercise value according to Equation 15-5 follows:

$$XV = (M - XP) \times \#$$
$$= (\$60 - \$50) \times 4$$
$$= \$40$$

Our calculations show that the exercise value is $40.

If the market price of the common share were $50 or less, the exercise value of the warrant would be zero. This is because you would have an option to buy the common shares at a price that is no better than the regular market price of the share. You would have no reason to exercise the warrant, and a rational investor would not do so.

Note that the time remaining until the expiration of the warrant does not affect the exercise value. For the McGuffin Corporation warrants, the investor saves $10/share on four common shares, creating an exercise value of $40.

As long as there is still time remaining until expiration, the actual market price of a warrant will be greater than the exercise value. The difference between the market price and the exercise value is called the warrant's time value. Warrants have time value because if the price of the common shares goes up, the exercise value increases with leverage and without limit (because of the fixed exercise price). If, on the other hand, the price of the common shares fall, the exercise value cannot dip below zero. Once the common share price is at or below the exercise price, no further damage can be done to the exercise value.

The exercise value is zero if the common share price is at or below the exercise value, but it can never be negative. Table 15-3 shows the exercise value for a McGuffin Corporation warrant for different possible share values.

No matter how much below $50 the market price of the common share goes, the exercise value stays at zero. As the share value goes above $50, however, the exercise value increases at a much faster rate than the corresponding

Table 15-3 McGuffin Corporation Warrant Exercise Value

Market Price of One Common Share	Exercise Price	Number of Shares	Value
$100	$50	4	$200
$ 90	$50	4	$160
$ 80	$50	4	$120
$ 70	$50	4	$ 80
$ 60	$50	4	$ 40
$ 50	$50	4	$ 0
$ 40	$50	4	$ 0
$ 30	$50	4	$ 0
$ 20	$50	4	$ 0

increase in the share price. The difference between the potential benefit if the share price increases (unlimited and leveraged) and the potential loss (limited) is what gives a warrant its time value.

Because of this time value, warrants are seldom exercised until they near maturity, even when the exercise value is high. This is because if a warrant is exercised, only the exercise value is realized. If the warrant is sold to another investor, the seller realizes the exercise value plus the time value. The time value approaches zero as the expiration date nears. A warrant approaching its expiration date, having a positive exercise value, would be exercised by the investor before the value goes to zero on the expiration date.

The greater the volatility of the share price, and the greater the time to expiration, the greater the market value of the warrant. If the share price is volatile, the share price could easily increase. This would give the warrant owner the benefit of an even greater increase due to leverage. If the common share price decreases, no more than the price paid can be lost. The more time left before expiration, the better the chance for a major share price change, up or down. Again, the warrant value upside is substantial if the share price moves up, and the downside potential is limited if the share price decreases. The asymmetry of the warrant's upside and downside potential gives the warrant greater value.

Options

There are two basic types of options, call options and put options. Call options give the owner the right, but not the obligation, to buy a share at a certain price, which is called the exercise price. Put options give the owner the right, but not the obligation, to sell a share at a certain price. The valuation of these options is very similar to that of warrants. In fact, one can view warrants as being extremely long call options. Options, like warrants, have both intrinsic value and time value. For example, if a share were trading for $55 and a call option existed at $7 to buy the share at $50, the intrinsic value would be $5 (55 – 50) and the time value would be equal to the real price of the option minus the intrinsic value of the option. In this case, the time value would be $2 (7 – 5). The time value of the option will corrode as the option comes closer to expiring, similar to warrants, except that their expirations are much shorter in duration. As well, much like options, the more volatile the underlying security is, the higher the time value of the option will be. This is due to the fact that the most an investor can lose is the cost of the premium, but the gain is unlimited. Premiums are what investors pay when they buy an option. Therefore, the greater the volatility, the greater the chance that at any given time the option will fall dramatically (good for put options) or rise dramatically (good for call options).

Put options are the opposite of call options. They give the possessor the right to sell a share at a certain level, the exercise price. In this case, you make money when the share value falls. Imagine that the current share price was $15 and you owned a put option stating the right to sell the share at $20. The put option may be selling at $6. The intrinsic value would be $5 (20 – 15) and the time value would therefore be $1. If the share were, for example, to fall to $10 per share tomorrow, the intrinsic value of your put option would have actually increased to $10 (20 – 10). This is because of your right to sell the share at the higher exercise price. Investors can use put options to make money when they think a share will fall in value, but they can also use put options to save money.

Options are usually purchased rather than given and the price you pay for an option is known as a premium. Suppose, for example, you own a share of BCE Inc. and you are afraid that the share price will go down soon. However, you really do not want to sell the share. You could protect your share by purchasing a put option. Let us suppose that the current price of BCE is $25 and a put option exists on BCE for a premium of $1.50 with an exercise price of $26. The option expires in 3 months.

Let us suppose that, in 3 months, the share drops to $20. What is your loss?

	Current	*3 Months later*	*Loss/Gain*
Share price	25	20	–5
Option value	–1.5	6	4.5
Total loss or gain			–0.5

Notice that, in 3 months, the put option has no more time value because the option is about to expire. Ignoring commissions and bid ask spreads, you could exercise your option and sell your share at $26. If you wished, you could at the same time buy back the share for $20, making your total loss equal to $0.50. What would happen if the share dropped to $15 in three months?

	Current	*3 Months later*	*Loss/Gain*
Share price	25	15	–10
Option value	–1.5	11	9.5
Total loss or gain			–0.5

We should notice that with a put option, our loss is limited. Obviously, there must be a downside. If we are wrong about the share price and it actually climbs to, for example $40, the following would happen.

	Current	*3 Months later*	*Loss/Gain*
Share price	25	40	15
Option value	–1.5	0	–1.5
Total loss or gain			13.5

Our put option would be worth zero at the end of 3 months and this would have the effect of reducing our total gain by the original cost of the premium.

Let us suppose that Jennifer was interested in protecting a share that she held. She currently owns ten shares of BCE valued at $26 each. She does not want to sell the share but has heard rumours that a trade dispute may take place in the next few months. She would like to protect her shares such that the most she would lose would be 10 percent. The premium for put options right now is $1.60 per option, where the strike price is set at $25. Suppose for simplicity that the BCE shares can go down to $10 a share or, if the trade dispute is truly a rumour, that the shares will soar to $35 a share. Assume the put would expire the day the share falls but afterwards Jennifer was able to take advantage of the share change. (In other words, ignore the time value portion of the put option and only focus on its intrinsic value.)

a. How many options does Jennifer need to protect her shares of BCE?

b. How much would Jennifer lose if the trade dispute were untrue?

Answer

a. The value of Jennifer's shares are $260 (10 × $26). She is willing to lose 10 percent, so she is willing to lose $26. In other words, if the share price falls below the 10 percent, she needs the put options to exactly offset that loss.

Share price	$26.00
Acceptable loss value per share	$23.40
If rumour is true, share price falls to	$10.00
Difference between loss and acceptable loss	$13.40
Total difference between 10 shares	$134.00
Option strike price	$25.00
If rumour is true, share price falls to	$10.00
Value of put, no time value	$15.00
Premium	–$1.60
Total gain	$13.40
Total number of options needed	10

Let us test this out, assuming the share price falls.

	Price	*Number of Shares*	*Total Value*
Shares	10	10	100
	Value	*Number of Puts*	
Put option	15	10	150
Premium	–1.6	10	–16
Total value			234
	Price	*Number of Shares*	
Shares original	26	10	260
Total loss			–10%

Seems good.

b. If the shares went the other way, Jennifer would simply lose the equivalent of the premiums she paid.

	Price	Number of Shares	Total Value
Shares	35	10	350
	Value	*Number of Puts*	
Put option	0	10	0
Premium	–1.6	10	–16
Total value			334

SUMMARY

15-1 Describe the characteristics of common shares, including how residual income affects shares.

Common shares are securities that represent ownership claims on a corporation. The shareholders are entitled to the residual income of the firm, resulting in a high-risk position relative to other claimants and a relatively high-return potential. Common shares may come in different classes with different voting rights or dividend payments.

15-2 Describe the process of making shares public.

Once a firm decides that the benefits outweigh the costs of issuing shares, the firm almost always seeks the help of an investment banking firm. The investment banker usually underwrites the new issue, which means that it purchases the entire issue for resale to investors. Sometimes the investment banker will try to find investors for the new common shares without a guarantee to the issuing company that the shares will be sold. This arrangement is known as a best efforts offering.

15-3 Contrast majority and cumulative voting rules.

The professional management team that handles the operations of the firm reports to the board of directors. The board of directors, in turn, is elected by the common shareholders to represent their interests. Because the shareholders have entrusted the board to represent their interests, board members have a fiduciary duty to act on shareholders' behalf. Shareholders usually vote according to the number of shares held. The two main types of voting rules are the majority voting rules, under which candidates run for specific seats, and the cumulative voting rules, under which all the candidates run against each other but do not run for a particular seat.

15-4 Describe at least two advantages and disadvantages of equity financing.

Equity financing has several advantages. It reduces the risk of a firm because common shareholders, as opposed to debtors, have no contractual entitlement to dividends. Equity financing can also increase the ability to borrow in the future. Disadvantages of equity financing include the dilution of existing shareholder power and control, flotation costs incurred when new common shares are sold, and the negative signal investors often perceive (rightly or wrongly) when new common shares are sold.

15-5 Describe the features of rights, warrants, and options, while being able to estimate their value in terms of intrinsic value and time value.

Rights are securities given to existing common shareholders that allow them to purchase additional shares at a price below market value. Corporations issue rights to safeguard the power and control of existing shareholders in the event of a new share issue. Warrants are securities that give the holder the option to buy a certain number of common shares of the issuing company at a certain price for a specified period of time. Warrants have high-return potential because, if the share price increases, the value of the warrant increases at a much higher rate due to leverage. The downside risk of a warrant is limited because the maximum loss potential is the price of the warrant. As a result of the high-return and low-risk potential, warrants have time value that is greatest when the share price is volatile and the time to maturity is great. A warrant is very similar to a very long duration call option. Call options give the owner the right, but not the obligation, to buy a share at the exercise price while put options give the owner the right, but not the obligation, to sell a share at the exercise price. Put options can be used to protect the value of your current shares.

EQUATIONS INTRODUCED IN THIS CHAPTER

Equation 15-1: The Number of Directors Who Can Be Elected under Cumulative Voting Rules

$$\text{NUM DIR} = \frac{(\text{SHARES CONTROLLED} - 1) \times (\text{TOT NUM DIR T.B.E.} + 1)}{\text{TOT NUM VOTING SHARES}}$$

where

NUM DIR = Number of directors who can be elected by a given group
SHARES CONTROLLED = Number of voting shares controlled by a given group
TOT NUM DIR T.B.E. = Total number of directors to be elected in the election
TOT NUM VOTING SHARES = Total number of voting shares in the election

Equation 15-2: The Number of Shares Needed to Elect a Given Number of Directors Under Cumulative Voting Rules

$$\text{NUM VOTING SHARES NEEDED} = \frac{\text{NUM DIR DESIRED} \times \text{TOT NUM VOTING SHARES}}{\text{TOT NUM DIR T.B.E.} + 1} + 1$$

where

NUM DIR DESIRED = Number of directors a given group of shareholders desires to elect
TOT NUM VOTING SHARES = Total number of voting shares in the election
TOT NUM DIR T.B.E. = Total number of directors to be elected in the election

Equation 15-3: Approximate Value of a Right, Share Trading Rights-On

$$R = \frac{M_0 - S}{N + 1}$$

where

R = Approximate market value of a right
M_0 = Market price of the common shares, selling rights-on
S = Subscription price
N = Number of rights needed to purchase one of the new common shares

Equation 15-4: Approximate Value of a Right, Share Trading Ex-Rights

$$R = \frac{M_X - S}{N}$$

where

R = Approximate market value of a right
M_x = Market price of the common shares, selling ex-rights
S = Subscription price
N = Number of rights needed to purchase one of the new common shares

Equation 15-5: The Exercise Value of a Warrant

$$XV = (M - XP) \times \#$$

where

XV = Exercise value of a warrant
M = Market price of the shares
XP = Exercise price of a warrant
$\#$ = Number of shares that may be purchased if the warrant is exercised

SELF-TEST

ST-1. What is residual income and who has a claim on it?

ST-2. Is a new common share issue usually perceived as a good or bad signal by the market? Explain.

ST-3. What does it mean when a company's common shares are said to be trading ex-rights?

ST-4. If a company's common shares are selling at \$80 per share and the exercise price is \$60 per share, what would be the exercise value of a warrant that gives its holder the right to buy 10 shares at the exercise price?

REVIEW QUESTIONS

1. What are some of the government requirements imposed on a public corporation that are not imposed on a private, closely held corporation?
2. How are the members of the board of directors of a corporation chosen and to whom do these board members owe their primary allegiance?
3. What are the advantages and the disadvantages of a new share issue?
4. What does an investment banker do when underwriting a new security issue for a corporation?
5. How does a preemptive right protect the interests of existing shareholders?
6. Explain why warrants are rarely exercised unless the time to maturity is small.
7. Under what circumstances is a warrant's value high? Explain.
8. How can put options be used to protect the value of your current shares? What similarities are there between call options and warrants?

PROBLEMS

Ownership Claim ▶ **15-1.** Sonny owns 20,000 common shares in QuickFix Company. The company has one million shares outstanding at a market value of $50 per share. What percentage of the firm does Sonny own?

If the company issues 500,000 new shares at $50 per share to new shareholders, how does Sonny's ownership change?

Valuation of IPO ▶ **15-2.** Terence Mann is considering buying some common shares of an initial public offering by NewAge Communications Corporation. The privately held company is going public by issuing 2 million new shares at $20 per share. Terence gathered the following information about NewAge:

Total assets	$200 million (historical cost)
Total liabilities	$150 million (market value)
Number of shares retained by pre-IPO owners	3 million (5 million shares outstanding after IPO)
Estimated liquidation value	$250 million
Estimated replacement value of assets	$400 million
Expected dividend in one year	$2 per share
Expected dividend growth rate	8%

The required rate of return for Terence from a common share for this type of company is 13 percent.

Compare the selling price of the share with its value as obtained from different valuation methods. Would you recommend that Terence buy the shares?

Number of Directors ▶ **15-3.** Danali Corporation has 2,500,000 common shares outstanding. Danali has a 15-member board and five will leave at the end of this year. There are nine candidates for these five open seats. The minority group of shareholders controls 45 percent of the shares and the majority group control the other 55 percent. What is the maximum number of directors who definitely can be elected by each of the following under cumulative voting rules?

a. The minority group

b. The majority group

Number of Voting Shares Needed ▶ **15-4.** Using the information in the previous problem, how many voting shares would be needed to elect the specified directors?

a. 1 director

b. 3 directors

c. 5 directors

Number of Directors ▶ **15-5.** Alliances are shifting and Danali Corporation (described in the previous two problems) now has 35 percent of the voting shares controlled by the minority group and 65 percent by the majority.

a. How many directors can now be elected for the minority group?

b. How many voting shares would be needed if the minority group wanted two directors under the revised group breakdown?

Term of Board Members ▶ **15-6.** Iowa Corn Corporation has nine board members. Three of these seats are up for election every three years. What is the length of the term served by each board member?

15-7. The shareholders of Blue Sky, Inc. are divided into two camps of different corporate management philosophy. The majority group controls 65 percent and the minority group controls 35 percent of the voting shares. The total number of common shares outstanding is 1 million. The total number of directors to be elected in the near future is four. What is the maximum number of directors the minority group can possibly elect, assuming that the company follows cumulative voting procedures?

◀ Cumulative Voting

15-8. Ms. O'Niel owns 26,000 common shares of Tri Star Corporation out of 200,000 shares outstanding. The board has seven members and all seven seats are up for election now. Ms. O'Niel has long wanted to serve as a member of the board. Assuming that the company follows cumulative voting procedures, can Ms. O'Niel get herself elected to the board on the strength of her own votes?

◀ Cumulative Voting

15-9. The Rainbow Corporation had traditionally been a constant dollar-dividend paying company, with the board enjoying the support of retired investors holding 65 percent of the voting shares. A dissident group of high-salaried young investors holding 30 percent of the voting shares prefers reinvestment of earnings to save personal taxes and, hence, wants to elect board members supportive of its cause. The company has 600,000 shares outstanding and the board has 13 members—all to be reelected shortly.

◀ Dividend Group and Cumulative Voting

a. How many directors can the young shareholders elect under:

i. cumulative voting rules?

ii. majority voting rules?

b. What percentage of voting shares and/or proxies must the dissident group have to be able to elect seven out of the 13 board members?

15-10. Fargo Corporation has 500,000 common shares currently outstanding. The company plans to sell 50,000 more shares to the existing shareholders through a rights offering. How many rights will it take to buy one share?

◀ Rights Offering

15-11. A company with 2 million common shares currently outstanding is planning to sell 500,000 new shares to its existing shareholders through a rights issue. Current market price of a share is $65 and the subscription price is $55. If the shares are selling rights-on, calculate the value of a right.

◀ Value of Rights

15-12. Use the same information given in problem 15-11. Now calculate the value of a right if the shares are selling ex-rights.

◀ Value of Rights

15-13. Fillsulate Products, a manufacturer of refractory powders, is about to declare a rights issue. The subscription price is $65. Seven rights in addition to the subscription price are required to buy one new share. Rights-on market price of one share is $77. Calculate the value of one right. Also calculate the new share price once it goes ex-rights.

◀ Value of Rights

15-14. Johnny Rocco owns 700 common shares of East-West Tobacco Company, which is offering a rights issue to its existing shareholders. To buy one new share, Johnny will need four rights plus $60. Rights-on market price of the shares is $72.

◀ Rights Offering

a. Calculate the value of a right.

b. What is the maximum number of new shares Johnny can buy?

c. How much would he have to spend if he decides to buy all the new shares he can?

d. If he decides not to buy the new shares, how much would he be able to sell his rights for?

Rights Value (Rights-On) ▶ **15-15.** Kelsery Products is planning on selling 300,000 new shares to existing shareholders through a rights issue. The company currently has 1,500,000 outstanding shares at a market price of $40 and a subscription price of $25. The share is selling rights-on. What is the value of one right?

Rights Value (Ex-Rights) ▶ **15-16.** Using the data from problem 15-15, calculate the value of one right if the shares are selling ex-rights.

Challenge Problem ▶ **15-17.** Armand Goldman owns 60 shares of East Asia Shipping Company and has $750 in cash for investment. The company has offered a rights issue in which purchasing a new share would require four rights plus $50 in cash. Current market value of one share is $62.

a. Calculate the value of a right if the shares are selling rights-on.

b. Should Armand participate in the rights offering by buying as many shares as he can or sell his rights and keep the shares he already owns at a diluted value?

Warrants ▶ **15-18.** The current market price of a common share of SkyHigh, Inc. is $100. The company had issued warrants earlier to its new bond investors that gave the investors an option to buy five common shares at an exercise price of $85. Calculate the exercise value of a warrant. What happens to the exercise value of the warrant if the share price changes to:

a. $110?

b. $80?

Comprehensive Problem ▶ Excel **15-19.** The current market price of Digicomm's common shares are $40 per share. The company has 600,000 common shares outstanding. To finance its growing business, the company needs to raise $2 million. Due to its already high debt ratio, the only way to raise the funds is to sell new common shares. Alvin C. York, the vice-president of finance of Digicomm, has decided to go ahead with a rights issue, but he is not sure what price the existing shareholders would be willing to pay. Digicomm's investment banker has suggested that an analysis based on a wide range of possible prices be carried out and the subscription prices agreed upon were $36, $33, $29, and $26 per share. Digicomm's net income for the year is $1 million.

Based on the preceding information, Mr. York has asked you to carry out the following analysis:

a. For each of the possible subscription prices, calculate the number of shares that would have to be issued and the number of rights required to buy one new share.

b. For each of the possible subscription prices, calculate the earnings per share immediately before and immediately after the rights offering.

c. Guy Hamilton owns 10,000 shares of Digicomm. For each of the possible subscription prices, calculate the maximum number of new shares Guy would be able to buy. Under each of these cases, calculate Guy's total claim to earnings before and after the offering.

Option Valuation ▶ **15-20.** Fill in the blanks. Assume that the time value for a call option and a put option in the same row are identical.

Share Price	Put Option Premium	Call Option Premium	Exercise Price
30	5		33
25		3	24
15		2	17
10	1	1	
52	4		52

15-21. Tony, a portfolio manager, owns two options: a put option and a call option on the same share. The put option had a premium of $2 and the call option had a premium of $3. The exercise price for the call option was $20 and the exercise price for the put option was $25.

◀ Option Valuation

Excel

a. If the options were about to expire tomorrow, what would you argue the current market value of the share to be? Why?

b. What is the maximum loss that Tony can have despite the economic outcome of the underlying security? What is the maximum gain?

c. Create a worksheet showing how the value of your options change as the security values moves from $5, $15, $25, $35.

15-22. Blow Your Own Horn Inc. was recently thinking of expanding its business and its needs for the future are $2.5 million. There are currently 100,000 shares outstanding. The directors have several choices, and they are not bound by any restrictions. The company has decided that its best course of action would be to issue rights or to issue bonds with a warrant attachment. If the rights were issued, they would be given at a 1:1 ratio, where a right would be given for one share per share of current ownership. The current share price is $35 (ex-rights) and each right allows the owner to buy one share at $25. The current market yield on bonds is 8.5 percent and the corporation has decided that it can only afford to pay an annual 7 percent interest payment for 25 years. To sweeten the deal, a warrant option will exist for each bond purchased, allowing 5 shares to be purchased per bond at an exercise price of $30.70.

◀ Comprehensive Problem

Excel

a. How many bonds will need to be issued to fund the future requirement? Assume that all warrants will be exercised.

b. Analyze the two situations and use your knowledge of dilution of shares to figure out which situation will place the shareholders in the best situation. Assume that all the rights and warrants are exercised.

c. In terms of the current shareholders, what are the drawbacks to issuing rights? What are the drawbacks to issuing bonds with warrant attachments?

15-23. Sarah and Pascal were the sole owners of Tooth Prevent, Inc.; they produced special new toothbrushes. Their company had grown to an estimated value of several million dollars and they were interested in taking the company public. They currently have an equal amount of shares in the company. There were 1,000,000 shares outstanding between them. Both Sarah and Pascal had some concerns about the public offering.

◀ Comprehensive Problem

a. Sarah wanted to know what methods existed for taking the company public and which would give them the highest amount of money. What can you say to help Sarah out?

b. Further, Pascal did not know how much of the company they should sell to the public. To keep control of the company, Pascal wanted to make sure that he and Sarah had enough shares to ensure they would both be guaranteed director positions. There will be a total of three directors for the corporation.

How would you respond to this in terms of the two different sets of voting rules you learned about in this chapter?

c. What other options could you think of? (Hint ... Bombardier)

Security Basics ▶ **15-24.** You are the financial advisor for a large, well-known investment company and you have been asked to explain the characteristics of common shares, preferred shares, and bonds. These are the most common responses you give. Fill in each space with the proper term.

____

are inherently more risky than

____

because of their unguaranteed return and their reliance on residual income. Both

____

and

____

have fixed payments, but only

____

have payments that are tax-deductible to the company. For this reason,

____

are considered to be quasi products, having the characteristics of both debt and equity. While

____

may have the least default risk, the value of this holding may still fluctuate with the market. One important feature of

____

is to make sure that their payments are cumulative; this is a measure to make sure that these holders are not taken advantage of by the holders of

______________________________.

Comprehensive Problem ▶ Excel **15-25.** Amy has several thousand shares of Bombardier and she is nervous about the immediate future of the company. She does not want to lose money but, by the same token, she does not want to sell her shares just in case her predictions about the company's future are incorrect. The current value of one share is \$6.50. She thinks that the share may fall to \$4 within the next 3 months but that would be the limit of the loss. However, there is a chance that the share price may bounce up to \$10 per share based upon some speculation of new aerospace contracts being won. The current call option, with an expiry date of 3 months and an exercise price of \$6.50, has a premium of \$1.25 per option.

a. Assuming that a three-month call option has a time value of \$1 above a three-month put option, what would you expect to pay today for a three-month put option with an exercise price of \$7?

b. If Amy owns 15,000 shares and she wants to limit her maximum dollar loss to \$5,000, how many options should she buy (including premiums)? Assume that a share would not fall lower than \$4 per share.

c. How many options of both calls and puts would Amy need if she wanted to limit her maximum dollar loss to \$5,000 (including premiums), but with the condition that if the share went up to \$10, she would double her straight share return (not including the premiums)? Assume that the lowest price is \$4 per share and that the highest value is \$10 per share.

ANSWERS TO SELF-TEST

ST-1. Residual income is income that is left over after all claimants, except for common shareholders, have been paid. This leftover income belongs to the common shareholders, who receive this income either in the form of a dividend or by having it reinvested in the corporation that they own.

ST-2. The market usually infers bad news when new common shares are issued. Investors ask themselves why the current owners would want to share their profits with new owners if management expected good news ahead. The market often infers (rightly or wrongly) that there must be bad news coming and the management of the firm wants to "share" with new shareholders. New shares issued are, therefore, usually perceived as a negative signal.

ST-3. A share is selling ex-rights when the purchase of that share no longer carries with it entitlement to the rights that are soon to be sent out to shareholders.

ST-4. (\$80 share price – \$60 exercise price) × 10 shares purchased per warrant = \$200 exercise value of the warrant

16

DIVIDEND POLICY

CHAPTER OBJECTIVES

After reading this chapter, you should be able to:

16-1 Explain how dividend policy affects shareholders' positions.

16-2 Describe dividends in respect to five different dividend theories.

16-3 Outline the process of how dividends get into the shareholders' hands.

16-4 Understand the effects of stock dividends and stock splits.

"Finance is the art of passing currency from hand to hand until it finally disappears."

—Robert W. Sarnoff

A Share Analyst Was Asked What He Thought about Dividends

"Dividends are a necessary evil. If the company is good, you would rather your money stay in there. But dividends are a measure of a company's real financial health. It is like when a cook takes a sip of the soup. The cook does it to evaluate the progress of the meal. The same can be said for dividends and the health of the company. Are the dividends constant? Are they stable? Surprise ups or downs in dividend policies without proper explanation can lead to dramatic effects on the shares. The underlying point is that dividends tell a story; and some stories are better than others."

Source: Anonymous.

Chapter Overview

In this chapter, we explore the importance of dividends, the factors that determine a firm's dividend policy, and leading dividend policy theories. We then examine how a firm makes dividend payments to shareholders. We finish by identifying alternatives to paying cash dividends.

Dividends

Dividends are the cash payments that corporations make to their common shareholders. Dividends provide the return common shareholders receive from the firm for the equity capital they have supplied.[1] Even companies that do not currently pay dividends reinvest in the firm the earnings they generate. In this way, they increase the ability of the firm to pay dividends in the future.

The board of directors decides what dividend policy best serves the common shareholders of the firm. Should a dividend be paid now, or should the earnings generated be reinvested for the future benefit of the common shareholders? If dividends are paid now, how much should be paid? These are some of the questions addressed in the following sections.

Although only corporations officially pay dividends to owners, sole proprietorships and partnerships also distribute profits to owners. Many of the same considerations examined in this chapter for corporate dividend policy can also be used to help make proper profit distribution decisions for these other forms of business organization.

Why a Dividend Policy Is Necessary

Why does a company need a strategic policy relating to dividend payments? Why not just "wing it" each year (or quarter, or other span of time) and pay the dividend that "feels right" at that time? Because market participants (current and potential shareholders) generally do not like surprises. An erratic dividend policy means that those shareholders who liked the last dividend cannot be sure that the next one will be to their liking. This uncertainty can result in a drop in the company's share price. When shareholders do not get what they expect, they often show their displeasure by selling their shares. A well-planned policy, appropriate for the firm and its business strategy, can prevent unpleasant surprises for market participants and protect the share price.

Factors Affecting Dividend Policy

Dividend policy is based on the company's need for funds, the firm's cash position, its future financial prospects, shareholder expectations, and contractual restrictions with which the firm may have to comply.

---

[1]You may wonder about this statement because common share investors can always receive a return by selling their shares. Remember, however, when investors sell their shares that other investors pay them, not the corporation. Except when a corporation buys back its own shares, (which is a form of dividend payment), the only cash corporations pay to investors is a dividend payment.

Need for Funds

Dividends paid to shareholders use funds that the firm could otherwise invest. Therefore, a company running short of cash or with ample capital investment opportunities may decide to pay little or no dividends. Alternatively, there may be an abundance of cash or a dearth of good capital budgeting projects available. This could lead to very large dividend payments.

Management Expectations and Dividend Policy

If a firm's managers perceive the future as relatively bright, on the one hand, they may begin paying large dividends in anticipation of being able to keep them up during the good times ahead. On the other hand, if managers believe that bad times are coming, they may decide to build up the firm's cash reserves for safety instead of paying dividends.

Shareholders' Preferences

Reinvesting earnings internally, instead of paying dividends, would lead to higher share prices and a greater percentage of the total return coming from capital gains. *Capital gains* are profits earned when the price of a capital asset, such as common shares, increases.

Common shareholders in high tax brackets may prefer to receive their return from the company in the form of capital gains instead of dividends. Some shareholders prefer capital gains because the federal income tax inclusion rate on capital gains is limited to 50 percent. If the shares are not sold, capital gains taxes can be postponed indefinitely. If, however, the shareholders are mainly retired people looking for current income from their investments, then they may prefer a high dividend payment policy. The board of directors should consider such shareholder preferences when establishing the firm's dividend policy.

Restrictions on Dividend Payments

A firm may have dividend payment restrictions in its existing bond indentures or loan agreements. For example, a company's loan contract with a bank may specify that the company's current ratio cannot drop below 2.0 during the life of the loan. Because payment of a cash dividend draws down the company's cash account, the current ratio may fall below the minimum level required.[2] In such a case, the size of a dividend may have to be cut or omitted. In addition, the net profits' rule prohibits dividend payments if they would create negative retained earnings on the balance sheet. In other words, dividends can only be paid from current and past incomes. Further, the insolvency rule states that a company cannot give out dividends if they are insolvent or if the dividend will make them insolvent. These restrictions are a prohibition against "raiding the initial capital." Figure 16-1 summarizes the factors that influence the dividend decision.

---

[2]Recall that the current ratio is found by dividing current assets (of which cash is a part) by current liabilities. Thus, decreasing cash to pay a dividend will lower the ratio.

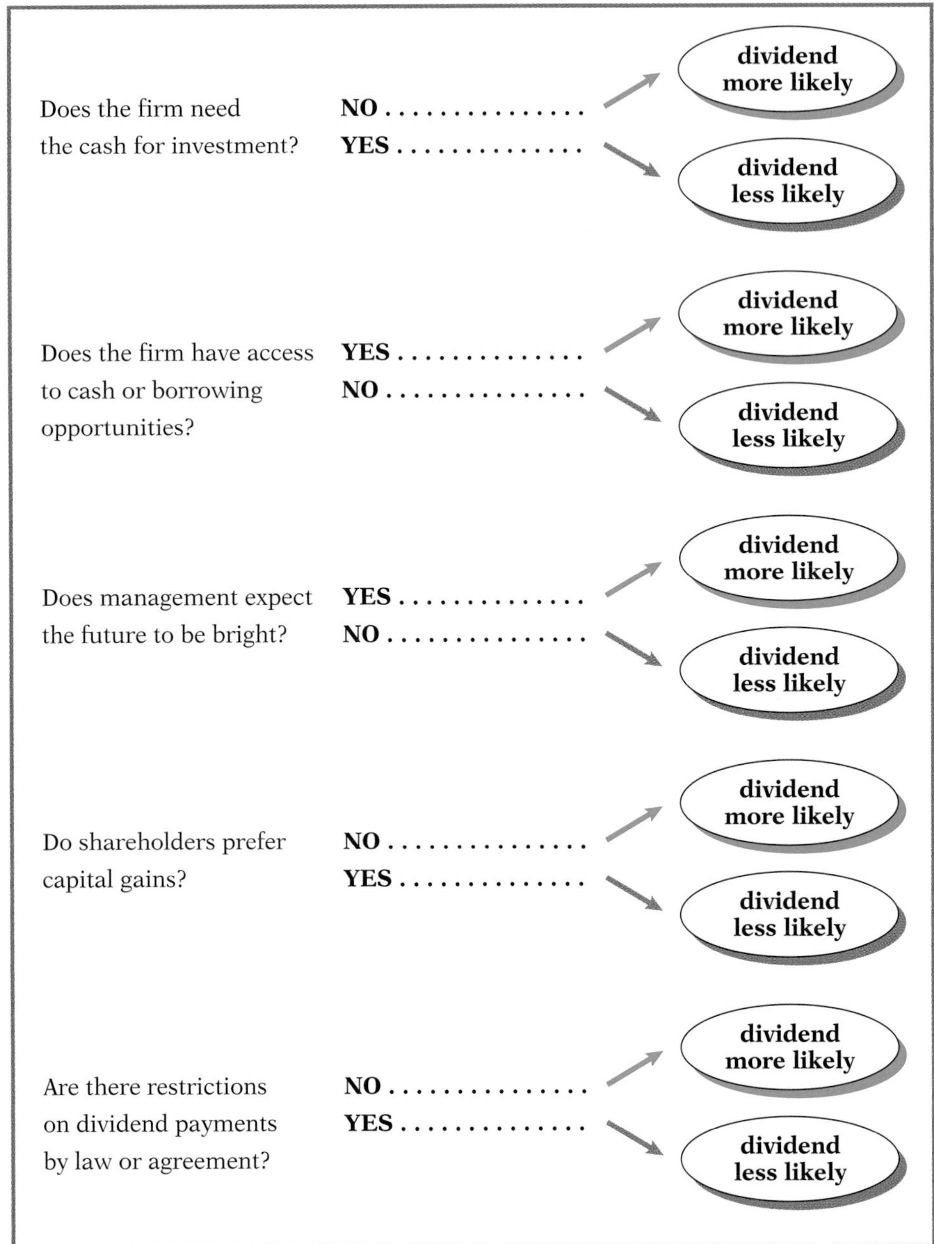

Figure 16-1 Dividend Decision Factors
This figure identifies key elements that make a dividend payment more or less likely.

Cash versus Earnings

Dividends are often discussed in relation to a firm's earnings. The dividend payout ratio is often cited as an indicator of the generosity (or lack thereof) of the firm's dividend policy. The dividend payout ratio is calculated by dividing the total dollar amount of dividends paid by net income, as seen in Equation 16-1.

Dividend Payout Ratio

$$\text{Dividend Payout Ratio} = \frac{\text{Dividends Paid}}{\text{Net Income}} \qquad (16\text{-}1)$$

If Calvin Corporation, for example, earns a net income of \$10,000 and pays \$3,000 in dividends, then its dividend payout ratio will be as follows:

$$\text{Dividend Payout Ratio} = \frac{\$3{,}000}{\$10{,}000}$$
$$= 0.30, \text{ or } 30\%$$

We see from our calculations that Calvin Corporation has a dividend payment ratio of 30 percent. This is not the same as dividend yield, which is calculated as:

$$\frac{\text{Dividends per Share}}{\text{Price per Share}}$$

A caution, however: by focusing on reported earnings and the dividend payout ratio, we ignore the key to paying dividends. The key is *cash*. When a company generates earnings, this usually results in cash flowing into the firm. The earnings and the cash flows do not necessarily occur at the same time, however. Table 16-1 illustrates these timing differences.

Table 16-1 shows us that Easy Credit Corporation reported \$600,000 of earnings this year but did not receive any cash. Unless cash was acquired from previous earnings, the firm could not pay dividends.

Table 16-1 Easy Credit Corporation Selected Financial Data for Current Year

Sales (all on credit, payments due in next year)	\$1,000,000
Total expenses	400,000
Net income	600,000
Cash received this year	\$0

Even if the company reported negative earnings, it could pay dividends if it had, or could raise, enough cash to do so. If a company believed that a certain dividend payment was critical to the preservation of the firm's value, it might even choose to borrow to obtain the cash needed for the dividend payment. Corporate borrowing to obtain cash for a dividend payment happens occasionally, when the dividend payment expected by the common shareholders is believed to be crucial.

Leading Dividend Theories

We have investigated how corporations consider many different factors when they decide what their dividend policies should be. Financial experts attempt to consolidate these factors into theories about how dividend policy affects the value of the firm. We turn to some of these theories next.

The Residual Theory of Dividends

The residual dividend theory is widely known. The theory hypothesizes that the amount of dividends should not be the focus of the company. Instead, the primary issue should be the amount of earnings it generates. The amount of earnings retained, according to this view, depends on the number and size of acceptable capital budgeting projects and the amount of earnings available to finance the equity portion of the funds needed to pay for these projects. Any earnings left after these projects have been funded are paid out in dividends. Because dividends arise from residual, or leftover earnings, the theory is called the *residual theory*. Table 16-2 shows how to apply this theory.

Table 16-2
Residual Corporation—Applying the Residual Dividend Theory

Investment Needed for New Projects	$10,000,000
Optimal Capital Structure	30% Debt – 70% Equity
Equity Funds Needed	70% × $10,000,000 = $7,000,000
Earnings Available	$12,000,000
Residual	$12,000,000 – $7,000,000 = $5,000,000
Amount of Dividends to Be Paid	$5,000,000

We see in Table 16-2 that Residual Corporation needs $10 million to finance its acceptable capital budgeting projects. It has earnings of $12 million. It needs equity funds in the amount of 70 percent of the $10 million needed, or $7 million. This leaves residual earnings of $5 million for dividends.

If the earnings available had been $20 million instead of $12 million, then the dividend payment would have been $13 million ($20 million – $7 million). However, if earnings available had been $6 million instead of $12 million, then no dividends would have been paid at all. In fact, $1 million in additional equity funding would need to be raised by issuing new common shares. The amount of dividends to be paid is an afterthought, according to this theory. Its total earnings drive the value of the firm, not how these earnings are distributed.

The residual dividend theory focuses on the optimal use of earnings generated from the perspective of the firm itself. This may appeal to some, but it ignores shareholders' preferences about the regularity of and the amount of dividend payments. If a firm follows the residual theory, when earnings are large and the acceptable capital budgeting projects small and few, dividends will be large. Conversely, when earnings are small and many large, acceptable projects are waiting to be financed, there may be no dividends if the residual theory is applied. The dividend payments will be erratic and the amounts will be unpredictable.

The Clientele Dividend Theory

The **clientele dividend theory** is based on the view that investors are attracted to a particular company in part because of its dividend policy. For example, young investors just starting out may want their portfolios to grow in value from capital gains rather than from dividends, so they seek out companies that retain earnings instead of paying dividends. Share prices tend to increase as earnings are retained and the resulting capital gain is not taxed until the shares are sold. If they are sold, they are taxed at a maximum inclusion rate of 50 percent.

Elderly investors, in contrast, may want to live off the income their portfolios provide. They would tend to seek out companies that pay high dividends rather than reinvesting for growth. According to the clientele dividend theory, each company, therefore, has its own clientele of investors who hold the shares in part because of its dividend policy.

If the clientele theory is valid, then it does not much matter what a company's dividend policy is so long as it has one and sticks to it. If the policy is changed, the clientele that liked the old policy will probably sell their shares. A new clientele will buy the shares based on the firm's new policy. When a dividend policy change is contemplated, managers must ask whether the effect of the new clientele's buying will outweigh the effect of the old clientele's selling. The new clientele cannot be sure that the most recent dividend policy implemented will be repeated in the future.

The Signalling Dividend Theory

The **signalling dividend theory** is based on the premise that the management of a company knows more about the future financial prospects of the firm than the shareholders do. According to this theory, if a company declares a dividend larger than that anticipated by the market, this will be interpreted as a signal that the future financial prospects of the firm are brighter than expected. Investors presume that management would not have raised the dividend if it did not think that this higher dividend could be maintained. As a result of this signal of good times ahead, investors buy more shares, causing a jump in the share price.

Conversely, if a company cuts its dividend, the market takes this as a signal that management expects poor earnings and does not believe that the current dividend can be maintained. In other words, a dividend cut signals bad times ahead for the business. The market price of the share drops when the firm announces a lower dividend because investors sell their shares in anticipation of future financial trouble for the firm.

If a firm's managers believe in the signalling theory, they will always be wary of the message their dividend decision may send to investors. Even if the firm has some attractive investment opportunities that should be financed with retained earnings, management may turn them down if adopting them would prevent paying the expected dividend and send an unfavourable signal to the market.

The Bird-in-the-Hand Theory

The **bird-in-the-hand theory** claims that shareholders prefer to receive dividends instead of having earnings reinvested in the firm on their behalf. Although shareholders should expect to receive benefits in the form of higher future share prices when earnings are retained and reinvested in their company, there is uncertainty about whether the benefits will actually be realized. However, if the shareholders were to receive the earnings now, in the form of dividends, they could invest them now in whatever they desired. In other words, "a bird in the hand is worth two in the bush."

If the bird-in-the-hand theory is correct, then shares of companies that pay relatively high dividends will be more popular—and, therefore, will have relatively higher share prices—than shares of companies that reinvest their earnings.

Modigliani and Miller's Dividend Theory

Franco Modigliani and Merton Miller (commonly referred to as M&M) theorized in 1961 that dividend policy is irrelevant.[3] Given some simplifying

[3]Miller, M., and Modigliani, F. (1961). Dividend Policy, Growth, and the Valuation of Shares. *Journal of Business*, 411–33.

assumptions, M&M showed how the value of a company is determined by the income produced from its assets, not by its dividend policy. According to the **M&M dividend theory**, the way a firm's income is distributed (in the form of future capital gains or current dividends) does not affect the overall value of the firm. Shareholders are indifferent as to whether they receive their return on their investment in the firm's equity from capital gains or dividends—so dividends do not matter.

M&M's arguments have been critiqued for decades. Most often, financial theorists who disagree with M&M maintain that M&M's assumptions are unrealistic. The validity of a theory, however, lies with its ability to stand up to tests of its predictions. The results of these tests are mixed and modern financial theorists continue to argue about what dividend policy a company should pursue.

The Mechanics of Paying Dividends

We have seen how the board of directors decides whether the firm will pay a dividend. Next, let's consider what happens when companies pay dividends and the timing of those payments.

The board's decision to pay a dividend is called *declaring* a dividend. This occurs on the **declaration date**. On that date, a liability called **dividends payable** is created on the firm's balance sheet.

Because the common shares of public corporations typically are traded every day in the marketplace, the board of directors must select a cutoff date, or **date of record**, to determine who will receive the dividend. At the end of business on this date, the company shareholder records are checked. All owners of the common shares at that time receive the forthcoming dividend.

When shares are traded on an exchange or in the over-the-counter market, it takes several days to process the paperwork necessary to record the change of ownership that occurs when the share changes hands. On the date of record, then, the company's transfer agent will not yet know of stock trading that occurred in the days immediately preceding the date of record.

The **transfer agent** is the party that keeps the records of shareholder ownership for a corporation. The transfer agent pays dividends to the appropriate shareholders of record after the company has deposited the required money with the transfer agent.

Because it takes time for news of a stock trade to reach the transfer agent, the rules of trading dictate that two days before the date of record, common shares that have an upcoming dividend payment will begin to trade **ex-dividend**. (The prefix *ex* is a Latin word meaning "without.") Investors who buy the shares on or after the ex-dividend date will be buying it "without" entitlement to the forthcoming dividend. The two-day period gives exchange officials enough time to notify the transfer agent of the last batch of stock trades that occurred before the ex-dividend period. The extra time ensures that the shareholder records will be correct on the date of record.

A few weeks after the date of record, the cheques are mailed out to the common shareholders. The date of mailing is called the **payment date**.

Figure 16-2 shows a time line for the dividend payment sequence.

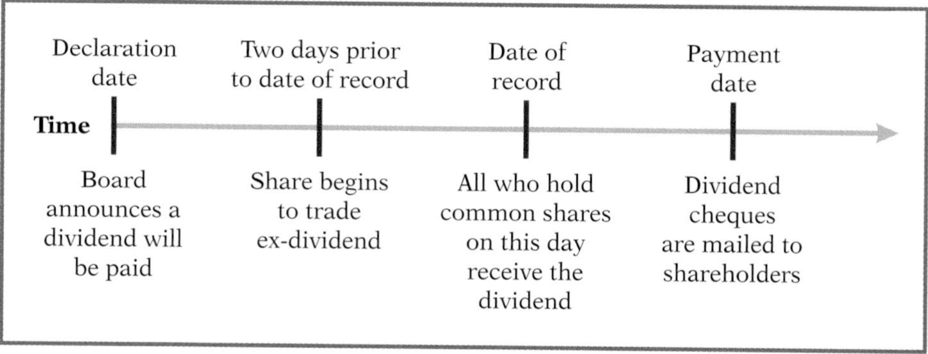

Figure 16-2 The Dividend Payment Time Line
This figure shows the sequence of events for a dividend payment.

Dividend Reinvestment Plans

Many corporations offer a **dividend reinvestment plan (DRIP)**, under which shareholders reinvest their dividends rather than receive them in cash. DRIPs are popular because they allow shareholders to purchase additional shares without incurring the commission costs that accompany regular share purchases made through a stockbroker. The new shares, including fractional shares, are purchased at the price prevailing in the market at that time. The amount of the dividend paid and reinvested is still taxable income to the shareholder. See Financial Management and You 16-1.

Alternatives to Cash Dividends

Sometimes corporations want to give something to the shareholders even though there is insufficient cash available to pay a cash dividend. At other times, corporations do not want to pay a cash dividend because they want to build up their cash position. Let's look at some of the options available for giving shareholders something without using precious cash.

Stock Dividends and Stock Splits

Instead of sending out cheques to shareholders, the firm could issue additional shares. Many shareholders view the receipt of these extra shares as a positive event, similar to the receipt of a cheque. In the sections that follow, we will question the validity of this widely held view.

New common shares can be distributed to existing shareholders with no cash payment in two different ways: stock dividends and stock splits. Both increase the number of shares outstanding and neither raises additional equity capital. There is an accounting difference between them, however. Let's examine these two alternatives to cash dividends next.

Stock Dividends When a **stock dividend** is declared, the existing common shareholders receive new shares, proportionate to the number of shares currently held. This is usually expressed in terms of a percentage of the existing holdings, such as 5 percent, 10 percent, or 20 percent but usually less than 25 percent. For example, if a 20 percent stock dividend were declared, one new share would be sent out to existing shareholders for every five currently owned. The following example illustrates how the process works and how the transaction would be accounted for on the firm's balance sheet.

FINANCIAL MANAGEMENT AND YOU 16-1

Dividend Reinvestment Records Can Avoid Tax Headaches

If you sign up for a dividend reinvestment plan, be sure to keep good tax records. The CRA treats the dividends reinvested in new shares as though you had received the cash and used that cash to buy the shares. Here are some record-keeping tips to help you avoid tax headaches.

1. *Know how often your dividends are reinvested.* Most companies that pay dividends do so quarterly. This means that under a reinvestment plan, you will be buying new shares every quarter, including fractional shares.
2. *Know how each share is taxed.* When you sell your shares, you will have a capital gain in the amount of the sales price minus the basis for each share, includi fractional shares. Over 10 years you could have shar with 40 different tax bases (10 years times four quart per year), not including the basis of the original shar you bought. Keep track of each basis.
3. *Keep your records.* You should never throw away t records establishing the basis for your dividend reinve ment shares until you sell them (and not for several ye after that in case you get audited). These records may in your files for decades.

Suppose that Bob and Bill own a chain of bed and breakfast lodges called BB Corporation. Now suppose the BB Corporation declares a 20 percent stock dividend so that each shareholder receives 20 new shares for every 100 shares they hold. This will increase the total number of shares outstanding from 100,000 to 120,000. Assume that the market price of one of BB's shares at the time of this stock dividend is $24. The equity section of BB's balance sheet, before and after the 20 percent stock dividend, is shown in Table 16-3.

Table 16-3

BB Corporation Capital Account as of December 31, 2004

Common Shares (100,000 shares)	$1,000,000
Retained Earnings	$5,000,000
Total Shareholders' Equity	$6,000,000

BB Corporation Capital Account as of January 1, 2005 (after a 20% stock dividend)

Common Shares (120,000 shares)	$1,480,000
Retained Earnings	$4,520,000
Total Shareholders' Equity	$6,000,000

First, note in Table 16-3 that after the 20 percent stock dividend, the common shares account changed from $1,000,000 to $1,480,000, an increase of 20 percent or $480,000.

Finally, note that the retained earnings account changed from $5 million to $4,520,000, a decrease of $480,000. This change reflects the transfer of $480,000 to the common shares account. Retained earnings must decrease because the 20 percent stock dividend did not alter the shareholders' position.

Thus, we see that a share dividend is just an accounting transfer from retained earnings to common shares. The number of shares increased by

20,000 in this case, but the overall economic effect was zero. Neither profits nor cash flows changed, nor did the degree of risk in the firm. The firm's ownership "pie" was cut into more pieces, but the pie itself was the same size.

On receiving their new shares in the mail, some shareholders may think they have received something of economic value because they have new share certificates for which they did not pay. However, who issued these new share certificates? The corporation did. Who owns the corporation? The shareholders do. The shareholders have given themselves new shares, but they continue to hold the same percentage of the firm as they held before the stock dividend.

The price per common share will drop because of the increase in the number of shares outstanding. The price decrease happens or the total market value of the common shares will increase (price per share × number of shares outstanding) while no economically significant event has occurred.

Many investors feel smug, as PJ does here, when the shares they own split. Is PJ better off than his sister because he has twice as many "shares" of sandwich?

Source: Reprinted with special permission of King Features Syndicate.

Adjustment of a Share's Market Price after a Stock Dividend. Investors in the stock market generally recognize that a stock dividend simply increases the number of shares of a firm and does not otherwise affect the total value of the firm. After a firm declares a stock dividend, then, the market price of the firm's shares will adjust accordingly. Table 16-4 illustrates the expected share price adjustment for BB Corporation.

Table 16-4 BB Corporation Share Price Adjustment in Response to a 20% Stock Dividend

	Number of Shares Outstanding	×	Price per Share	=	Total Value of the Shareholders' Positions
Before Stock Dividend	100,000	×	\$24	=	\$2,400,000
After Stock Dividend	120,000	×	\$20	=	\$2,400,000

With the information from Table 16-4, we can find the new price of one of BB's shares as follows:

New number of shares: 120,000
Total value of firm's shares: \$2,400,000

Now let X = the new share price. We solve for the new share price as shown:

$$120{,}000X = \$2{,}400{,}000$$

$$X = \$20$$

Here's the key to solving for the new share price after a stock dividend: remember that the total value of all the firm's shares remains the same as it was before the stock dividend. There may be a positive effect on the share price due to expectations about the cash dividend. We explore this effect later in the chapter.

Stock Splits When an increase of more than 25 percent in the number of common shares outstanding is desired, a corporation generally declares a *stock split* instead of a stock dividend. The firm's motivation for declaring a stock split is generally different from that for a stock dividend. A stock dividend appears to give shareholders something in place of a cash dividend. A **stock split** is an attempt to bring the firm's share price into what management perceives to be a more popular trading range.

Stock splits are usually expressed as ratios. A 4–1 *(four-for-one) stock split,* for example, indicates that new shares are issued such that there are four shares after the split for every one share before the split. In a 3–2 split, there would be three shares after the split for every two outstanding before the split.

Table 16-5 BB Corp. Capital Account as of Dec. 31, 2004 (before a 4–1 stock split)

Common Shares (100,000 shares)	\$1,000,000
Retained Earnings	\$5,000,000
Total Shareholders' Equity	\$6,000,000

BB Corp. Capital Account as of Jan. 1, 2005 (after the 4–1 stock split)

Common Shares (400,000 shares)	\$1,000,000
Retained Earnings	\$5,000,000
Total Shareholders' Equity	\$6,000,000

The accounting treatment for a stock split is simpler than for a stock dividend. Table 16-5 shows how the BB Corporation would account for a 4–1 stock split.

In Table 16-5, note that only the common shares entry in the equity section of the balance sheet is affected by the stock split. The entry indicates that after the stock split, there are four times as many common shares outstanding as before the split. It also implies that the book value of each share is one-fourth the value it was before. The total dollar value of $1,000,000 remains the same. Retained earnings is completely unaffected by a stock split.

Adjustment of a Share's Market Price after a Stock Split.

As with a stock dividend, investors in the stock market recognize that a stock split simply increases the number of shares of a firm and does not otherwise

Table 16-6 BB Corporation Share Price Adjustment Due to a 4–1 Stock Split

	Number of Shares Outstanding	×	Price per Share	=	Total Value of the Shareholders' Positions
Before Stock Dividend	100,000	×	$24	=	$2,400,000
After Stock Dividend	400,000	×	$ 6	=	$2,400,000

affect the total value of the firm. Therefore, the market price of the firm's share will adjust accordingly following a stock split. Table 16-6 illustrates the share price adjustment for the BB Corporation in response to the 4–1 stock split.

We see in Table 16-6 that, just as with the stock dividend, no economically significant event has occurred. The common share ownership "pie" has been cut into four times as many pieces as before, but the size of the pie is the same. As Table 16-6 shows, after the 4–1 split, each share will trade in the market at approximately one-fourth the price it commanded before the split.

Sometimes the cash dividend is increased at the same time as a stock split or a stock dividend. In our 4–1 stock split example, if the cash dividend per share is decreased by less than three-fourths, shareholder cash dividends received would increase. A $1 per share cash dividend, for instance, could be cut to $0.30 instead of the $0.25 value that would leave total cash dividends unchanged. The market sometimes anticipates such an increase in the cash dividend, leading to a possible increase in the total market value of the common shares.

The Rationale for Stock Splits.

One of the most famous stock splits is the Berkshire Hathaway stock split of 1996. Before the split, Berkshire Hathaway shares were selling for $34,000 a share. Because the shares soared in value from $18 per share in 1965 to $34,000 in 1996, institutional investors began to offer—for a fee—thousand-dollar securities based on Berkshire shares. To halt others from making money off of the company's shares, Berkshire decided to offer some Baby Berkshire shares in a 30–1 stock split.[4]

[4]Allan Sloan, "Stop Kicking Yourself," *Newsweek* (April 8, 1996): 47.

Unlike Berkshire, which split some of its shares to prevent nonowners from dealing in Berkshire securities, many companies split shares to increase its value. This may have been the case when Canadian Natural Resources announced its intention for a 2 for 1 stock split on February 25, 2004. Its shares went up $2.23 to close at $68.63. Managers believe that as the market price per common share increases over time, it gets too expensive for some investors. Management perceives that a stock split will decrease the price per share, thereby increasing the number of potential investors who can afford to buy it. More potential investors might create additional buying pressure, which would result in an increase in share price. This argument is less persuasive, however, as the percentage of share ownership and trading activity by institutional investors (mutual funds, pension funds, insurance companies, and so on) continues to increase. These investors can afford to pay a very high price per share. Managers, however, continue to use stock splits to adjust the share price to a lower level to make it more affordable.

International Perspectives in Finance 16-1 discusses stock splits.

INTERNATIONAL PERSPECTIVES IN FINANCE 16-

Corporate Optimism Prompts More U.S. Stock Splits

New York—If the current trend continues, 2004 could become known as "The Year of the Split."

Stock splits can increase when corporate directors think their stock is poised to move higher, signaling bullishness.

But directors can also approve a split because a stock's price has already soared or because management is trying to increase investor diversification in a given stock.

This year, 81 companies have already divided their shares or announced plans to do so by March 31, according to research firm Thomson First Call (News—Websites). That compares with 55 splits during the first quarter of last year.

The previous big year for splits was 2000.

In the first quarter of 2000—with the tech bubble yet to burst and the stock market at all-time highs—140 companies split their shares, leading to 449 splits for the year.

The large number so far this year is a sign that companies are more optimistic about rising stock prices than in the past four years, investors say.

The immediate effect of a split is to increase the number of shares available and to push prices lower. For that reason, directors are unlikely to split their stock when they expect a sustained decline lies ahead. The idea behind splits is to sanction a price cut because each share has become too expensive from a marketing point of view.

"Did you ever know of a company whose stock w going down and then they split?" asked Cumm Catherwood, a portfolio manager with Philadelphia-bas Rutherford, Brown & Catherwood, which oversees $700 lion. "You only ever split when you think the stock is gc up."

While the sheer number of companies splitting sha this year is up, the trend is all the more impressive beca it is not restricted to one or two sectors. Companies in a w range of businesses are splitting.

This quarter's list included Eaton Corp. (NYSE:ETN News), a maker of hydraulic systems, vehicle parts and e trical equipment; men's clothing seller Jos. A. Bank Cloth Inc. (NasdaqNM:JOSB—News); and regional bank N York Community Bancorp. (NYSE:NYB—News).

"It contrasts to the late '90s when most of the com nies were telecom, technology and Internet-related," s Mark Foster, portfolio manager with Columbus, India based Kirr, Marbach & Co. which oversees $460 million. the extent that it's more broad-based, it's a much healt situation."

Source: Nick Olivari, "Corporate Optimism Prompts More U.S. Stock Splits." February 10, 2003. Reprinted with the permissio Reuters Limited © 2004. All rights reserved.

SUMMARY

16-1 Explain how dividend policy affects shareholders' positions.

Share prices often change dramatically when a dividend change is announced, indicating that the market believes dividends affect value. The dividend decision, then, must be carefully planned and implemented. Factors that influence dividend decisions are a company's need for funds, its future financial prospects, shareholder preferences and expectations, and the firm's contractual obligations.

Although dividends are often discussed in the context of a firm's earnings, dividends are paid in cash. As a result, a firm's cash flow is a crucial factor affecting its dividend policy.

16-2 Describe dividends in respect to five different dividend theories.

The major dividend theories that help guide dividend policy include the residual theory of dividends, the clientele theory, the signalling theory, the bird-in-the-hand theory, and the Modigliani and Miller theory.

The residual theory posits that the amount of dividends matters less than the amount of earnings retained. If a firm enacts a residual policy, its dividend payments are likely to be unpredictable and erratic.

The clientele dividend theory assumes that one of the key reasons investors are attracted to a particular company is its dividend policy. Under this theory, it does not matter what the dividend policy is so long as the firm sticks to it.

The signalling dividend theory is based on the premise that management knows more about the future finances of the firm than do shareholders, so dividends signal the firm's future prospects. A dividend decrease signals an expected downturn in earnings; a dividend increase signals a positive future is expected. Managers who believe the signalling theory will be conscious of the message their dividend decision may send to investors.

The bird-in-the-hand theory assumes that shareholders prefer to receive dividends instead of having earnings reinvested in the firm on their behalf. If correct, shares of companies that pay relatively high dividends will be more popular and, therefore, will have relatively higher share prices than shares of companies that reinvest their earnings.

The Modigliani and Miller theory claims that earnings from assets, rather than dividend policy, affect firm value, so dividend policy is irrelevant.

16-3 Outline the process of how dividends get into the shareholders' hands.

The corporate board of directors declares dividends. Shareholders on the date of record are entitled to the declared dividend. Investors who buy the share before the ex-dividend date (two days before the date of record) will receive the dividend declared by the board. Investors who buy the share on or after the ex-dividend date have bought the share too late to get the dividend.

16-4 Understand the effects of stock dividends and stock splits.

Corporations sometimes award shareholders stock dividends (additional shares) and stock splits instead of cash dividends. Both stock splits and stock dividends increase the number of outstanding shares and decrease the price per share. Although neither of these actions is a real substitute for a cash dividend, many investors perceive these events as good news even though earnings do not increase nor does risk decrease.

EQUATIONS INTRODUCED IN THIS CHAPTER

Equation 16-1: The Dividend Payout Ratio

$$\text{Dividend Payout Ratio} = \frac{\text{Dividends Paid}}{\text{Net Income}}$$

SELF-TEST

ST-1. A company pays \$4 per share in dividends and has 100,000 shares outstanding. The company has net income of \$1 million. Its market price per share is \$100. What is its dividend payout ratio?

ST-2. Is the amount of the dividend to be paid the primary focus of the board of directors if the board is guided by the residual theory of dividends? Explain.

ST-3. Does a company following the clientele theory of dividends pay high or low dividends? Explain.

ST-4. When paying dividends, what is the date of record?

ST-5. If a company share has a \$2 market value, what will be the effect of a 4–1 stock split? (Assume there is no signalling effect.)

REVIEW QUESTIONS

1. Explain the role of cash and of earnings when a corporation is deciding how much, if any, cash dividends to pay to common shareholders.
2. Are there any legal factors that could restrict a corporation in its attempt to pay cash dividends to common shareholders? Explain.
3. What are some of the factors that common shareholders consider when deciding how much, if any, cash dividends they desire from the corporation in which they have invested?
4. What is the Modigliani and Miller theory of dividends? Explain.
5. Do you believe an increased cash dividend can send a signal to the common shareholders? If so, what signal might it send?
6. Explain the bird-in-the-hand theory of cash dividends.
7. What is the effect of stock (not cash) dividends and stock splits on the market price of common shares? Why do corporations declare stock splits and stock dividends?

PROBLEMS

Payout Ratio ▶ **16-1.** After discussion with the board of directors of the company, Lionel Mandrake, founder and chairman of Mandrake, Inc. decided to retain \$600 million from its net income of \$1 billion. Calculate the payout ratio.

Payout Ratio ▶ **16-2.** The net income of Harold Bissonette Resorts, Inc. was \$50 million this past year. The company decided to have a 40 percent payout ratio. How much was paid in dividends and how much was added to the retained earnings?

Dividend Payout Ratio ▶ **16-3.** Charleston Industrial revised its dividend policy and decided that it wants to maintain a retained earnings account of \$1 million. The company's retained earnings account at the end of 2003 was \$750,000 and it had earnings available to common shareholders of \$800,000 in 2004. What is Charleston Industrial's dividend payout ratio for 2004?

Payout Ratio ▶ **16-4.** Delenburk had net income of \$4 million for 2004 and it has a policy of maintaining a dividend payout ratio of 35 percent. Calculate the amount that was paid to shareholders in 2004. If the company had a retained earnings account of \$1.2 million at the end of 2003, what is the balance in the retained earnings account at the end of 2004?

16-5. Hannah Brown International maintains a dividend policy with a constant payout ratio of 30 percent. In the last three years, the company has had the following earnings.

◀ Constant Payout Ratio and Retained Earnings

	Year 1	Year 2	Year 3
Net Income ($ million)	30	20	25

What is the total addition to retained earnings over the last three years?

16-6. Use the same data given in problem 16-5. Now, if the company followed a constant dollar dividend policy and paid $10 million in dividends each year, compute the dividend payout ratios for each year and the total addition to retained earnings over the last three years.

◀ Constant Dollar Dividend Policy

16-7. Eliza Doolittle, the chief financial officer of East West Communications Corporation, has identified $14 million worth of new capital projects that the company should invest in next year. The optimal capital structure for the company is 40 percent debt and 60 percent equity. If the expected earnings for this year are $10 million, what amount of dividend should she recommend according to residual theory?

◀ Residual Theory of Dividend Policy

16-8. Use the same data given in problem 16-7. Now, what would be the amount of dividend that could be paid if East West's net income for this year is:

◀ Residual Theory of Dividend Policy

a. $16 million?

b. $6 million?

16-9. DreamScapes Entertainment's financial managers have determined that the company needs $12 million to fund its new projects for next year. It has an optimal capital structure of 20 percent debt and the rest is equity. This year the company has $24 million in earnings available to common shareholders and 20,000,000 shares outstanding. According to the residual theory, what is the dividend per share paid to common shareholders?

◀ Residual Theory

16-10. Jan Brady, chief accountant of Mulberry Silk Products, is trying to work out the feasibility of a 20 percent stock dividend. The equity section of the balance sheet follows:

◀ Stock Dividend

	($ 000s)
Common Shares (2 million shares)	$10,000
Retained Earnings	10,000
Total Shareholders' Equity	20,000

The current market price of the company's share is $31. Is it possible to pay a 20 percent stock dividend? Is it possible to pay a 10 percent stock dividend? Explain.

16-11. Use the same data given in problem 16-10. After payment of a 10 percent stock dividend, what will be the expected market price of the share? Also, show how the equity section of the balance sheet will change.

◀ Stock Dividend

16-12. Malea Liberty has 800,000 common shares outstanding. It has decided to declare a 30 percent stock dividend. Before the declared dividend, the retained earnings account was $60,000,000 and the common shares account was $13,600,000. The current share price is $40. Calculate the new values for the following items:

◀ Stock Dividend

a. Number of common shares

b. Common shares account

c. Retained earnings

Stock Dividend ▶ **16-13.** Malea Liberty's market price before the declared stock dividend was $40 per share. What would be the market price after the declared stock dividend described in problem 16-12? (Assume the total value of the shareholders' positions remains the same.)

Stock Split ▶ **16-14.** Wesley Crusher, chief accountant of Blue Sky Cruise Lines, is trying to figure out the effect of a 3–1 stock split. The equity section of the balance sheet follows:

	($ 000s)
Common Shares (3 million shares)	$12,000
Retained Earnings	8,000
Total Shareholders' Equity	20,000

The current market price of one company share is $33. If Blue Sky Cruise Lines decided to have a 3–1 stock split, how would the equity section change after the split? What would be the share's market price?

Stock Split ▶ **16-15.** Use the same information given in problem 16-14. If Blue Sky Cruise Lines' net income is $800,000, what is the earnings per share before and after the 3–1 stock split? Will there be any change in the price to earnings ratio before and after the stock split?

Stock Split ▶ **16-16.** Sumner Outdoor Equipment Company decided to go for a 5–1 stock split. The common shareholders received a dividend of $1.33 per share after the split.

a. If the dollar amount of dividends paid after the split is the same as that paid last year before the split, what was the dividend per share last year?

b. If the dollar amount of dividends paid after the split is 10 percent higher than what was paid last year before the split, what was the dividend per share last year?

Challenge Problem ▶ **16-17.** The market price of one of Linden Landscaping Company's shares is $30 the day before the shares go ex-dividend. The earnings of the company are $10 million and the company follows a dividend policy with a constant payout ratio of 40 percent. There are 1 million common shares outstanding. What would be the new ex-dividend price of the shares?

Long-Term Dividend (Residual Theory) ▶ **16-18.** In its strategic plan for the next five years, Springfield Manufacturing Company has projected the following net income and capital investments (figures in $000s):

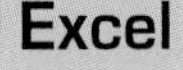

Year	Net Income	Investments
2003	1,000	800
2004	1,100	1,000
2005	1,200	2,000
2006	1,300	800
2007	1,400	1,000

The capital structure the company wishes to maintain is 40 percent debt and 60 percent equity. There are currently 500,000 common shares outstanding. If you own 500 common shares, calculate the amounts you would receive in dividends over the next five years (2003 to 2007), assuming that the company uses the residual dividend theory each year to determine the dividend to be paid to its common shareholders.

16-19. Use the same data given in problem 16-18. Now assume that the company plans to issue 100,000 new common shares in 2008 at $6 per share. What will be the dividend that you receive in 2008, 2009, and 2010, assuming your common share holding remains the same at 500 shares?

◀ Long-Term Dividend (Residual Theory)

16-20. The equity section of the balance sheet of Cafe Vienna is given next:

◀ Comprehensive Problem

Excel

	($ 000s)
Common Shares (500,000 shares)	1,500
Retained Earnings	8,500
Total Common Equity	10,000

The company earned a net income of $3 million this year. Historically, the company has paid dividends with a constant payout ratio of 50 percent. The share will sell at $47 after the ex-dividend date.

William Riker, the vice-president of finance for Cafe Vienna, is considering all possible ways to increase the company's earnings per share (EPS). One possibility he is weighing is to buy back some of the company's outstanding common shares from the market using all the net income earned this year without paying any dividend to common shareholders.

a. Determine the repurchase price of the common shares.

b. Calculate the number of shares that could be repurchased using this year's net income.

c. Show the changes in the equity section of the balance sheet after the repurchase.

d. If net income next year is expected to be $4 million, what would be the EPS next year with and without the repurchase?

e. If you own 50 common shares of the company, would you like the company's decision of buying back shares instead of paying a dividend?

16-21. Blue Jays wants to bring its share price down to a more attractive level. In order to do this, Blue Jays wants to implement a 4–1 stock split. Before the split, the company has 300,000 shares outstanding at $4 par that were issued at a market price of $9 per share; retained earnings is $10,000,000. Fill in the values before and after the split.

◀ Stock Split

Before the Split	
Number of Shares	________
Common Shares (account total)	________
Retained Earnings	________
Total Shareholders' Equity	________

After the Split	
Number of Shares	________
Common Shares (account total)	________
Retained Earnings	________
Total Shareholders' Equity	________

16-22. Kristine, Matthew, and Rufus were the three directors of High Earning Company, Inc. They had a stellar first year of operations. Earnings were really high and they thought that the shareholders would be really pleased. Most of the shareholders are from the Baby Boom generation and many of them are beginning to retire. Further, many of the shareholders prefer that their investment

◀ Dividend Policy

provide the lowest reasonable risk possible. High Earning Company has several amazing growth prospects, but they will need funds in order to get them started.

a. What conflicts of interest can you think of that may exist between the shareholders' desires and the company's growth opportunities?

b. In terms of dividends, what should the directors do according to residual theory, clientele dividend theory, and the bird-in-the-hand theory?

c. Can you think of an idea that would attempt to make a compromise between the potential problems of the shareholders and the future prospects of the company?

Dividend Policy ▶ **16-23.** Paul and the other directors of Bigchange Corp. have always followed the policy of a constant payout dividend. That is to say, they will always pay out 40 percent of their earnings per share when it is positive and zero otherwise. For example, if the EPS for one year were 5.5, the dividend would be $2.2 for that year. Bigchange Corp. has been a relatively stable company over its last 30 years of operations, but there are some years which were off pattern. Here is the following EPS for the last 5 years.

2000	2001	2002	2003	2004
5.00	3.50	–5.80	0.25	3.75

a. What would be the dividend payouts for the years 2000–2004?

b. What are the advantages and disadvantages of using this policy?

c. According to the signalling theory, state what shareholders would be thinking throughout years 2000–2004?

d. From your response to (c), can you think of a better dividend policy than a constant payout ratio policy?

Stock Splits Comprehensive ▶ **16-24.** Your best friend, Fred, was thinking about investing in more shares of a particular company that had just split. He concluded that stock splits were profitable because a shareholder would receive more shares. Before the split, Fred owned 100 shares with a market value of $20 each. His total portfolio was $2000. Fred was excited after the split, arguing that his current 200 shares were worth $4000, doubling his return. You are becoming very angry at his constant obnoxious attitude and you want to show Fred how wrong he actually is. Fred was never good with numbers, but he loved food, so you both ordered a pizza and split the cost 50–50. The pizza cost $20 and was cut into 8 pieces. Fred was very unhappy, but you only smirked as you tossed a quarter of the pizza to your friend and began to dine on the other three-quarters. Your argument was that Fred had only paid for 4 pieces and so that was all the pizza that he was going to get.

a. How did you use Fred's own words against him?

b. Can you find similarities between the pizza purchase and the value of a company?

Dividends Comprehensive ▶ **16-25.** Being a little upset with you over the pizza in problem 16-24, Fred pointed out that his shares were going to go up because of their huge dividends. You shake your head and tell Fred that it is impossible for shares to go up just because of their dividend policy. Fred miffs you again, implying that he needs another lesson. Therefore, you bet Fred that he can secretly pick any number between 1 and 100 and you can guess it. Fred agrees to the challenge. You and Fred each put $50 into a jar and then cut up 100 pieces of paper, each representing an equal portion of the jar's contents ($100 in total). You take all the papers. Each round, two dollars are taken out of the jar and one dollar is given to each of you. Then

Fred writes down a number between 1 and 100 on a piece of paper. If you guess it incorrectly, you must trade 2 pieces of paper for the dollar just given to Fred and if you win, you simply take Fred's dollar. Fred seems okay with this, deducing that $\$100/100 \times 2 = \$2$. Therefore, every time you lose, he gains \$1 (2 pieces of paper worth \$2 minus the dollar he pays out from his round payment). Fifty rounds pass and you lose each time. Fred is thrilled to have all the pieces of paper, representing 100 percent ownership of the jar's contents. You just smirk as you walk away with \$100.

a. Explain how the game worked.

b. Can you relate this to how stock dividends affect shareholders' positions?

c. If dividends should have no affect on the value of a share, why could share prices go up with an unexpected dividend?

16-26. The directors of company Wearegoingbankruptrealsoon Corp. (WB for short) did not have enough cash to give the shareholders their regular dividend this year. The directors were trying to be creative and think of a way to give the shareholders something without using their cash. They came up with two potential ideas; offer a \$5 per share dividend to all shareholders with a mandatory requirement of a dividend reinvestment, or offer a 10 percent stock dividend (the current market value of a share is \$50). A feud erupted between the directors as to which policy to follow. Assume the following accounts summarize the WB balance sheet. ◀ Dividend Policy

Cash	100,000	Liabilities	900,000
A/R	1,750,000	Common Shares	
		(100,000 outstanding)	100,000
		Retained Earnings	850,000
Total Assets	1,850,000	Total Liabilities and Shareholders' Equity	1,850,000

a. What would be the effects on the accounts with a \$5 mandatory reinvestment policy? How did the shareholders' position change?

b. What would be the effects on the accounts with a 10 percent stock dividend? How did the shareholders' position change?

c. Which policy, using your results from (a) and (b), would you say is the best for shareholders?

d. Further, assume that there is an effective tax rate of 30 percent on all dividends issued to shareholders. What is the effect of (a) and (b)?

16-27. Sam and Samantha were the directors of a large company and wanted to issue a \$3 per share dividend. You told them they could not. Why? The following is the company's balance sheet. ◀ Dividend Policy

Cash	225,000	Liabilities	100,000
A/R	160,000	Common Shares	
		(100,000 outstanding)	10,000
		Retained Earnings	275,000
Total Assets	385,000	Total Liabilities and Shareholders' Equity	385,000

ANSWERS TO SELF-TEST

ST-1. Dividend payout ratio = dividends paid ÷ net income = ($4/share × 100,000 shares) ÷ $1,000,000 = $400,000 ÷ $1,000,000 = 0.40 = 40%

ST-2. No. According to the residual theory of dividends, the amount of earnings that should be retained is determined first. Whatever amount is not retained is paid out in dividends.

ST-3. A company following the clientele theory of dividends might have either high or low dividend payments. If the shareholders preferred high dividends, this is what would be paid. If they preferred low dividends, this would be the policy.

ST-4. The date of record is the date on which a company checks its shareholder records. Investors listed in the records on that date are entitled to receive the dividend that was recently declared.

ST-5. $2 original market value ÷ 4 (4 for 1 split) = $0.50 market value

COMPREHENSIVE CASES: PART IV

CASE 1: WIRELESS ALBERTA LIMITED

Wireless Alberta Limited (WAL) is one of the leading operators of GSM telephony in Alberta and British Columbia. WAL launched its services in 2004, with the expectation of gaining approximately 35,000 subscribers by the end of the year. It has reached 112,300 subscribers and continues to grow its business. The company set up its network infrastructure with equipment supplied by Alcatel and Motorola and concentrated its efforts on building a large coverage of national roads. WAL decided on a strategy to out-build its competitors and achieve a greater geographic coverage throughout the two provinces. Subsequent building out resulted in the coverage of 30 main population centres across the provinces. The company now has around 6,000 kilometres of road coverage.

In 2004, Wireless Alberta Limited had operating revenues of $41 million, of which $28 million came from service revenues and $13 million came from handset sales. $25 million of the service revenues can be attributed to recurrent revenues, such as monthly fees, national and international airtime, and roaming and interconnection revenues. The remainder of the revenue comes from connection fees. Handset sales are not a part of Wireless Alberta's core business, but it takes time for dealers to develop their own import channels. In the meantime, WAL has to supply handsets directly or indirectly in order to acquire customers.

The Company's historical financials and forecasts follow. The data for 2004 are real; the data for 2005–2008 are estimates.

(In $ millions)	*2004*	*2005*	*2006*	*2007*	*2008*
Revenues	41.2	170.6	291.7	375.9	406.1
EBITDA	(44.7)	4.2	95.1	152.6	186.8
Net Income	(48.8)	(54.1)	6.4	51.7	76.4
Number of Subscribers	112,300	306,400	506,300	686,900	838,800

The management forecasts that the company will be EBITDA positive in 2005 and will be profitable as of 2006. In 2007, the company is projected to generate $376 million in revenues and an EBITDA of $153 million, representing an EBITDA margin of 41 percent. A margin of 40–50 is considered standard in the industry.

Mr. James Conroy, a veteran of the telecommunications industry in Canada, was one of the newly appointed directors of the board and represented the largest shareholders in the company, holding a 55 percent stake in the business. He spent over 25 years working for various international mobile telephone operators in India and China as well as for Bell Canada's fixed network and Bell Mobility's cellular operations.

Mr. Conroy was contemplating providing a memo to his fellow board members, as well as to the management team, outlining his thoughts for the establishment of a dividend policy for the company. From the financial projections, which he regarded as quite conservative, he was able to see that the company was likely to generate strong profits in 2007. These profits would likely increase in the future as the company builds its customer bases and is able to provide a number of complementary services. Mr. Conroy was contemplating two approaches:

1. To allow management to make decisions with respect to the dividend policy for the company. In other words, management would decide on the financial needs for the company and direct any unused profits towards shareholders.
2. To provide shareholders with the main decision-making capability with respect to the amount of dividends paid every year. The shareholders would determine the dividend policy every year, considering the financial projections and the company's capital needs.

Requirements

1. Mr. Conroy, interrupted by a telephone call, quickly wrote on his notepad that he must review the advantages and disadvantages of the two approaches from the point of view of both management and the shareholders. He also made a note to consider what other factors would need to be taken under consideration in these circumstances. What advantages and disadvantages of the two approaches would Mr. Conroy list?
2. What other factors would Mr. Conroy need to take under consideration?

CASE 2: CANDY CORP.

Tom, Dick, and Harry are the 3 directors of Candy Corp. Candy Corp. began in 1985, producing several different brands and types of sugar treats. Their first brand was something called Nutty-Crunz. It took the popularity of a chocolate bar and put it into a ball form. Unknown to the company, health enthusiasts jumped on the idea; the ball form had the illusion of being smaller than a chocolate bar. In reality, the Nutty-Crunz had three times the calories of any normal-sized chocolate bar, but people did not look at it that way.

Adding to its success, Candy-Bunch was introduced in 1987. The name, Candy-Bunch, was soon changed as the market decided that the term Candy-Brunch would be more appropriate. Unexpectedly, Candy-Brunch became a popular after-breakfast treat. Some enthusiasts even said that because the Candy-Brunch was so sweet it actually reduced hunger, thus making Candy-Brunch part of a wholesome breakfast.

In 1991, the company launched its best and currently its most popular candy, called the Candy-Man. It was specially designed and marketed as a health bar for bodybuilders. Bodybuilders need an immense amount of calories during the day. Therefore, Candy-Man was marketed as a vital source of energy and, by throwing some vitamins into it, the company was able to show that the vitamins per calorie of intake were far greater than any other food supplement. In 1995, the Health Commission in Canada forced Candy Corp. to put a warning label on the chocolate bar. Several people who had eaten the bar regularly had since become extremely obese due to their belief that the bar would make them strong with little if any training. Being clever, Candy Corp. did issue a warning label that stated, "The government has demanded that we put this warning on our labels. In cases of over-consumption of Candy-Man, the bar has been known to give extreme mass to the person in question. Both arm and pectoral size will increase dramatically."

New products have always been a source of great revenue for the company, and many of its original shareholders from the company's inception almost two decades ago are still invested with the company. For a strange reason, the only people two decades ago who were interested in the company were people in their 40s. This was later determined to be a type of mid-life crisis issue and that buying into a candy company may be a way of reliving some of those youthful days at the candy store. Those original 40-year-olds are reaching the age of retirement. Twenty years have passed and each one of them held the dream of creating an original Candy store.

In the last two decades or so, the growth potential from new products has completely overcome the idea of receiving dividends. In fact since inception, the company has not declared one single dividend. The shareholders seem to have been fine with this over the years, but are now in a dilemma. The shareholders do not want to sell their shares but retirement is coming up. Tom, Dick, and Harry have always been receptive to the needs of their shareholders, but find that a dividend may hurt the company's future performance. A new product has already been test-marketed and well received by the focus groups. This new candy, called the Candy-NoCarb, is expected to be a great success. Candy Corp. has created a chocolate bar with zero calories from carbohydrates, which fits in perfectly with the idea of a no-carb diet program. They are able to granulate fat and use that as a substitute for the carbs. The following summarizes the company's expected partial balance sheet after the first year of Candy-NoCarb.

Partial Balance Sheet after First Year of Operations with Candy-NoCarb

	Before Candy-NoCarb	*After Candy-NoCarb*
Assets		
Cash	$ 550,000	$ 450,000
Accounts Receivable	25,000	35,000
Inventory	35,000	90,000
Net Candy Machines	350,000	400,000
Candy Projects	1,000,000	1,500,000
Liabilities		
Accounts Payable	20,000	51,000
Equity		
Common Shares	50,000	50,000
Retained Earnings	1,890,000	2,374,000

Notes: Any increase in Retained Earnings is due to an increase in net income. Candy Projects are the investments in the development of ideas and their associated costs.

Requirements

1. Summarize the different dividend policies and other ways of getting cash to the shareholders.
2. Construct a situation that will help the shareholders get some money while the company retains its opportunity to promote Candy-NoCarb.
3. Develop a dividend policy for future years, the book's or your own, that will satisfy the current shareholders while providing room for future expansion projects.

CASE 3: ECON-CAR

Econ-Car is a local business that rents cars as its major revenue. It was originally solely owned by Michelle Tucon. Econ-Car has been in business for three years, and has made several mistakes over the last couple of years. Tucon failed to hire a lawyer to manage the company's contracts, believing that she could do it by herself since a contract is a contract. Unfortunately she omitted several key factors in the contract that clients were able to take advantage of, and then not pay anything. As an incentive to take the extra insurance, Tucon offered free insurance if the mileage driven was less than 30 kilometres. Unfortunately she forgot to separate the insurance policy from the rest of the contract, making it seem that everything was free if the mileage was less than 30 kilometres.

Mitch, her brother, was equally foolish when he bought into the business a year after start-up. He thought it was the greatest idea in the world to print flyers and give them to brand new 16-year-old drivers. He failed to realize that his company had a policy of renting out cars to adults only, who had to be a least 18 years of age. Not only did Econ-Car waste money on the flyers, but they also incurred opportunity costs due to frustrated potential clients who were unable to rent cars because they were supposedly not available, while the young drivers were angry because they had been offered the opportunity to rent a car and now discovered they could not.

Learning their lessons, both Michelle and Mitch decided to seek the help of an expert on their current issue. Michelle and Mitch have always been taught that buying is better than leasing because you owned the item in question. That is why when they were both teenagers their parents told them that whatever Michelle and Mitch could save up for a car the parents would match, as long as the vehicle would be fully paid when purchased. They have followed this policy in their business as well, only growing as fast as their cash was received. Their current basic strategy is to save up money from daily rentals. They will then put the money in a short-term investment account that returns about 3.5 percent per year (daily compounding). At the point in which they have enough money to buy a new car, they will expand their fleet. They have recently been approached by an accountant who says that there are tax advantages to leasing. Further, the accountant suggests that they are probably losing business by not increasing their fleet.

Econ-Car only has three vehicles on the lot, and the three cars are constantly in use. This suggests that the accountant may be right about the loss of potential clients. Both Michelle and Mitch are nervous about leasing a car or borrowing money to purchase one; they still like the idea of saving up for something so that they could own it. In any case, the accountant did some research for them. The vehicles are to be placed in class 10, with a maximum capital cost allowance of 30 percent per year. The company has a 40 percent tax rate. The accountant has summarized three vehicles that he believes Econ-Car should purchase. This would double their fleet size and hopefully increase sales. Econ-Car has a line of credit that it could use to finance the cars at 7 percent, or it could use financing from the dealerships, which changes from car to car.

In any event, the following summarizes the results of the accountant's research:

Price $ 25,000

	Rate	Monthly Payment	Term in Years	Value at End of Term
Buy	0.05	$471.78	5	5,000
Lease	0.07	$492.16	5	0

Price $ 29,000

	Rate	Monthly Payment	Term in Years	Value at End of Term
Buy	0.04	$293.61	10	1,000
Lease	0.05	$306.31	10	0

Price $ 15,000

	Rate	Monthly Payment	Term in Years	Value at End of term
Buy	0.07	$297.02	5	500
Lease	0.06	$288.55	5	0

The accountant's research suggests that Econ-Car should consider both buying and leasing options for these cars, and it is just a matter of selecting the best payment option for each car. Further, the accountant highlights the fact that the term for each vehicle matches the warranty of the respective vehicle. This makes sense because Econ-Car is in the business of renting cars, not fixing them.

Requirements

1. Summarize the situation in point form.
2. Identify which cars should be leased (if any) and which cars should be bought (if any).
3. Following the mentality of Michelle and Mitch, suggest what course of action should be taken. Can you adjust the solution in requirement 2, making a partial compromise to this mentality?

Part V
Short-Term Financing Decisions

CHAPTERS

BARRICK GOLD CORPORATION—A FOCUS ON LIQUIDITY

www.barrick.com

CORPORATE INFORMATION

Headquarters	Toronto, Ontario
Industry	Mining
Number of Mines	12
Listed on	TSX, NYSE, other exchanges
Ticker symbol	ABX
President & CEO	Gwyn Morgan

Year Ended 31 January (In US$ millions)	**1999**	**2000**	**2001**	**2002**	**2003**
Sales	1,421	1,936	1,989	1,967	2,035
Profit / (Loss) before Tax	441	(1,375)	83	177	222
Net Profit / (Loss)	331	(1,189)	96	193	200
Current Assets	744	1,166	1,014	1,322	1,365
Current Liabilities	304	530	590	483	350
Total Assets	5,353	5,293	5,202	5,261	5,362
P.P. & E. Capital Expenditure	620	710	607	228	322
Long-Term Debt	525	901	793	719	761
Shareholders' Equity	4,154	3,190	3,192	3,334	3,494

Business

Barrick Gold Corporation ("Barrick") is one of Canada's largest gold companies and the world's third largest producer. The Company is involved in the production and sale of gold, and its operations include related mining activities such as exploration, development, and processing. Barrick operates a portfolio consisting of twelve mines and four major development projects around the world. Sixty percent of total production came from North America (Canada and the United States), 20 percent from South America (mainly Chile and Argentina), 12 percent from Australia, and 7 percent from East Africa. In 2003, Barrick produced approximately 150 tonnes of gold.

Financial Performance

The company's financial performance has been steady in the last few years. Barrick's sales have been flat since the year 2000, hovering around the US$2.0 billion mark. The company's profitability, though, has evolved over time. In 2000, the company made a loss of US$1.2 billion; in 2002 and 2003, it made a profit of around US$ 200 million. In an effort to become the industry's world leader, the company embarked on a mission to extend its international footprint into Russia. In 2003, Barrick invested US$153.4 million to acquire a 29 percent stake in a publicly traded British company, Highland Gold Mining Limited, that is mining gold in Russia. This has been coupled with the appointment of a new Chief Operating Officer, Peter Kniver, who is expected to focus on strategic operational issues and increased operating efficiency. Most importantly, the strengthened management team expects to focus on creating sustained earnings growth, which has been lacking in the past.

Liquidity Management at Barrick

At Barrick, management defines liquidity as the company's ability to generate adequate amounts of cash to meet its short term needs. This also includes a focus on reliable and cost effective sources of cash that are available to satisfy current and prospective cash commitments. Management regards the management of liquidity risk as critical to the protection of its existing capital, maintenance of market and investor confidence, and realization of investment opportunities. The liquidity measures reflect this focus. The company's current ratio has been improving, equalling 2.4 in 1999 and 3.9 in 2003. At Barrick, liquidity analysis and management is performed by the Corporate Treasury function, which is responsible for developing liquidity strategies and policies as well as implementing the liquidity measures. The Finance Committee, comprising members of the management team and members of the board of directors, oversees the liquidity function and reports on the company's liquidity position. Historically, Barrick has relied on its net cash flow from operating activities, available cash resources, and various short-term debt instruments. The company also recently issued publicly traded debentures as an additional liquidity buffer.

Sources: Financial data for 2003 and 2002 from 2003 *Annual Report*, pages 64–67; data for 2001 and 2000 from 2001 *Annual Report*, pages 58–61; data for 1999 from 1999 *Annual Report*, pages 41–49.

Working Capital Policy

Chapter Objectives

After reading this chapter, you should be able to:

17-1 **Explain** what working capital is.

17-2 **Discuss** how permanent current assets differ from temporary current assets.

17-3 **Explain** the optimal working capital level in terms of profitability versus liquidity.

17-4 **Contrast** the aggressive, moderate, and conservative methods of financing working capital.

"Ready money is Aladdin's lamp."

—Lord Byron

When Push Comes to Shove

The temptation to delay payments to suppliers may be especially hard to resist during an economic downturn, says Stephen Payne, president of REL Consultancy Group. "The short-term, knee-jerk reaction is to take as long as you can to pay," he points out.

But, Payne warns, that approach "can bite you in the rear end." He explains that when you next order product, suppliers treated in this fashion may simply increase their prices to "offset the abuse." After all, while the tactic decreases your days of payables outstanding, it increases your suppliers' days of receivables outstanding.

To be sure, he notes, "the whole idea behind supply-chain improvement is to get somebody else to carry the can." But buyers can manage that only if they're in a stronger position than their suppliers. "It all depends on your clout," says Payne.

Still, "if you want a genuine partnership," he adds, "it may be worth it to carry that debt." How to weigh the trade-offs involved? Much depends on whether you're focusing on top-line growth or profitability. For that reason, says Payne, companies that are new or trying to gain market share should be less draconian with suppliers, while those focusing on the bottom line may be better off taking a firmer approach. –R.F.

Source: Excerpted from the July 2001 issue of *CFO*. © 2001 CFO Publishing Corp. For more information about reprints from *CFO*, contact PARS International Corp. at 212-221-9595.

Chapter Overview

In this chapter, we examine *working capital policy*—the management of a firm's current assets and its financing. First, we will see why firms manage working capital carefully, why they accumulate it, and how to classify current assets. We then investigate what determines a firm's working capital policy and look at different types of policies.

Managing Working Capital

Working capital refers to a firm's current assets. By "current" we mean those assets that the firm expects to convert into cash within a year. Current assets include *cash; inventory,* which generates cash when the items are sold; and *accounts receivable,* which produces cash when customers pay off their credit accounts. Current assets are considered liquid because they can be transformed into cash in a relatively short time.

Net working capital is the firm's current assets minus current liabilities. Current liabilities are business obligations (i.e., debts) that the firm plans to pay off or otherwise satisfy within a year. Examples include *accounts payable*—bills due soon—and *bank loans payable* in less than a year.

Table 17-1 shows the working capital and net working capital for Green World Lawn Care Products Company, which manufactures lawn and gardening products and sells them to retailers.

Table 17-1 Green World Lawn Care Products Company Balance Sheet, as of December 31, 2004

Cash	$ 2,000	Accounts Payable	$ 7,000
Accounts Receivable	1,000	Notes Payable	4,000
Inventory	10,000	Total Current Liabilities	11,000
Total Current Assets	13,000	Other Liabilities	7,000
Other Assets	32,000	Common Shares	27,000
Total Assets	$45,000	Total Liabilities and Equity	$45,000

In Table 17-1, we see that Green World has $13,000 in current assets (working capital), $11,000 in current liabilities, and $2,000 in net working capital ($13,000 – $11,000 = $2,000). Net working capital is important to firms. It represents the amount of current assets remaining if they were liquidated to pay the company's short-term debts.

Working capital policy is the firm's policy about its working capital level and how its working capital should be financed. For instance, a firm needs to make decisions about how much to keep in its cash account, what level of inventory to maintain, and how much to allow accounts receivable to build up. The firm must also decide whether to finance current assets with short-term funds, long-term funds, or some mixture of the two. Together, the level and financing decisions make up the firm's working capital policy.

Why Businesses Accumulate Working Capital

Why do firms accumulate working capital and why does its level vary over time? In this section, we examine the answers to these two questions.

Fluctuating Current Assets

Many factors affect a firm's working capital policy. For instance, a service firm may require a different level of current assets than a manufacturing firm. Or a business like Jason's Popcorn Wagon, which makes and sells popcorn during the summer months only, has different working capital needs than a firm that makes products year-round.

To illustrate the principles of working capital policy, we focus on a manufacturing firm that has level production—that is, it produces the same amount of product every month, year-round. However, its sales are seasonal—the firm sells more in certain time periods than in others. Many businesses are seasonal. (For instance, a swimwear manufacturer may sell many more swimsuits at the start of summer than it does in other months. A lawn care products manufacturer will probably have more sales at the start of the gardening season than it will in other months.)

If a business has level production but not level sales, inventory increases when production exceeds sales. Inventory then falls when sales exceed production. The firm's other current assets may fluctuate during the year as well. Accounts receivable, for example, will rise when new credit sales exceed customer payments and will fall when customer payments exceed new credit sales. Cash will accumulate as sales revenues are collected and will decline when bills are paid. Thus, the current assets of the business will fluctuate over time.

Permanent and Temporary Current Assets

Although the level of current assets in the firm may fluctuate, it rarely reaches zero. The firm will nearly always have some cash on hand, hold some inventory in stock, and be owed some amount of money. Current assets thus reach various temporary levels but will rarely fall below some minimal permanent level. This effect is illustrated for Green World Lawn Care Products Company in Figure 17-1 on page 564.

Figure 17-1 shows three categories of business assets that affect a firm's working capital policy:

1. **Temporary current assets** represent the level of inventory, cash, and accounts receivable that fluctuate seasonally.
2. **Permanent current assets** represent the base level of inventory, cash, and accounts receivable, which tends to be maintained.
3. **Capital assets** represent the land, buildings, equipment, and other assets that would not normally be sold or otherwise disposed of for a long period of time.

Permanent current assets tend to build up on a firm's balance sheet year after year. Cash collections increase as the business grows, accounts receivable grow as the list of credit customers lengthens, inventory on hand rises as new

Take Note

The term *permanent current assets* may sound like an oxymoron (like "jumbo shrimp"), but it is not. A portion of a firm's current assets is likely to remain on a firm's balance sheet indefinitely.

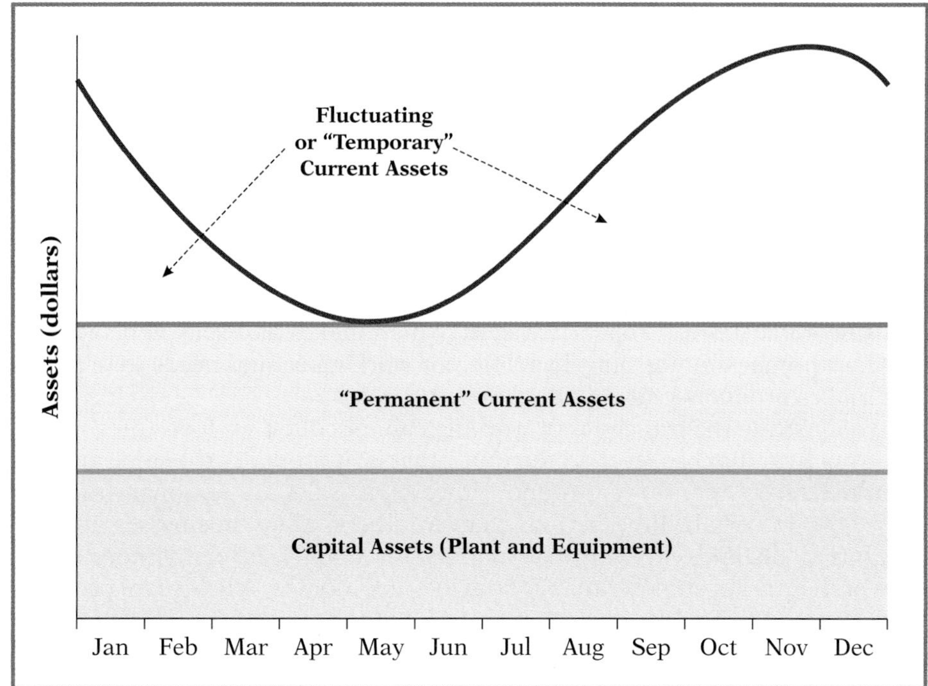

Figure 17-1 The Variation in Current Assets over Time for Green World Lawn Care Products
Figure 17-1 shows how the current assets of a company tend to fluctuate over time but never fall below a permanent level of current assets.

facilities are opened, and so on. Figure 17-2 shows how Green World Lawn Care Product's current assets might vary over several years.

As Figure 17-2 shows, businesses have two tasks: First, they must contend with current assets that fluctuate through their business cycle. Second, they

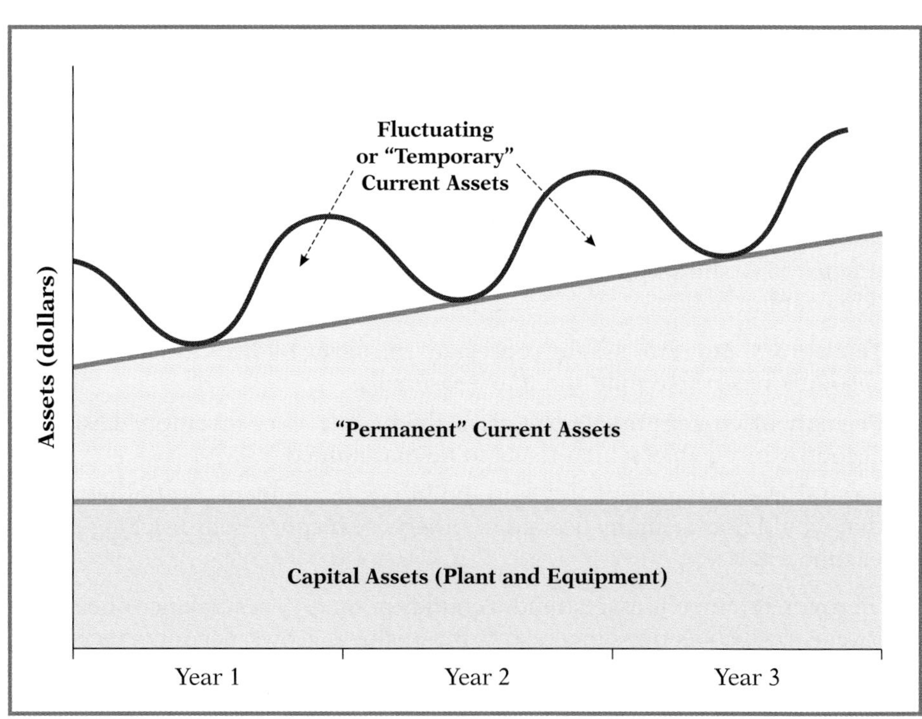

Figure 17-2 The Variation in Current Assets over Several Years for Green World Lawn Care Products
Figure 17-2 shows how a typical firm's current assets tend to build up from year to year, while fluctuating within each year. The effect occurs because as firms grow, they accumulate more cash, accounts receivable, and inventory over time.

must manage permanent current asset growth due to long-term business growth over time. In the sections that follow, we discuss how firms do this.

Liquidity versus Profitability

Lenders would like a company to have a large excess of current assets over current liabilities. However, the owners do not necessarily feel the same way. Think about it. Current assets—in the form of cash, accounts receivable, and inventory—do not earn the firm a very high return. Cash is usually held in a chartered bank chequing account that pays little to no interest. Accounts receivable earns no return because it represents money that customers owe to the firm that the firm does not have yet. Inventory earns no return until it is sold. (Inventory being held by the firm is just material sitting in a warehouse, earning nothing.) These assets have the advantage of being liquid (although inventory must first be sold to customers), but holding them is not very profitable.

Now consider the company's noncurrent assets—its land, buildings, machinery, equipment, and long-term investments. These assets can earn a substantial return. The company's land, buildings, machinery, and equipment are used to turn raw material into products that can be sold for a profit. Long-term investments (such as investments in subsidiaries) generally produce greater returns than current assets. These noncurrent assets may be profitable, but they are usually not very liquid. Lenders are reluctant to let firms use them for collateral (protection in the event of a default) for short-term loans. Why? Because lenders will have to spend more time and incur more expense to sell noncurrent assets if firms default on their loans and the lenders become the asset owners. As a result, lenders prefer that firms use liquid assets as loan collateral.

Firms, then, are faced with a trade-off in their working capital management policy. At one extreme, they can seek liquidity, holding a lot of cash and other current assets in case cash is needed soon. At the other extreme, they can seek profitability, holding a low level of current assets and investing primarily in long-term, high-return-producing assets. This was one of the reasons Nortel crumbled. It invested too heavily for the long term, resulting in a liquidity crisis when its predictions were found to be incorrect. Under this approach, sales performance may ultimately be hampered by inventory stockouts and/or strained customer relations brought on by strict credit terms.

In practice, no firm would actually choose either of these extreme positions. Instead, managers seek a balance between liquidity and profitability that reflects their desire for profit and their need for liquidity.

Establishing the Optimal Level of Current Assets

The search for a balance between liquidity and profitability serves as a general guide for financial managers looking for an optimal level of current assets. However, the level managers eventually achieve is actually a result of their efforts to maintain optimal levels of each of the *components* of the current asset group. In other words, a firm's optimal level of current assets is reached when the optimal level of cash, inventory, and accounts receivable[1] is achieved. Each asset account is managed separately and the combined results produce the actual level of current assets. Here is a description of the attempt to find the optimal level for each current asset account:

- *Cash:* Managers try to keep just enough cash on hand to conduct day-to-day business, while investing extra amounts in short-term marketable securities. We discuss cash in detail in Chapter 18.
- *Inventory:* Managers seek the level that reduces lost sales due to lack of inventory, while at the same time holding down inventory costs. We discuss inventory management in Chapter 19.
- *Accounts receivable:* Firms want to enhance sales but hold down bad debt and collection expenses through sound credit policies. We discuss credit policies in Chapter 19.

Once financial managers set policies to attain the optimal level of current assets, they must turn their attention to the flip side of working capital management: managing current liabilities. As we will find in the following case, those that do not manage their current liabilities well can find their companies in dire straits.

Managing Current Liabilities: Risk and Return

A firm's current asset fluctuations and any long-term build-up of current assets (its working capital) must, of course, be financed. The question facing financial managers is whether to obtain the financing from short-term borrowing, long-term borrowing, contributions from the owners (equity financing), or some mixture of all three.

As is so often the case, the choice of the firm's working capital financing blend depends on managers' desire for profit versus their degree of risk aversion. Short-term debt financing is generally less expensive than long-term debt and always less expensive than equity financing. Recall from Chapter 2 that short-term interest rates are usually lower than long-term interest rates. Short-term loans, however, are more risky because a firm may not have enough cash to repay the loans (due to cash flow fluctuations) or interest rates may increase and increase the cost of short-term funds as loans are renewed. Long-term debt and/or equity financing is less risky from the firm's perspective because it puts repayment off (forever, in the case of shares) and locks in an interest rate for a long time period in the case of long-term debt.

Take Note 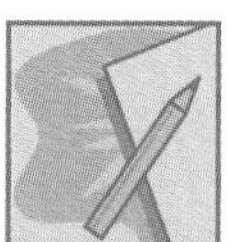

In our discussion we assume that a firm has all available financing alternative options. In practice, however, some firms may have limited financing options. For example, small firms usually have limited access to long-term capital markets.

The balance between the risk and return of financing options depends on the firm, its financial managers, and its financing approaches. We discuss several financing approaches next.

[1]Along with any other current assets the firm possesses, of course. In this book, we concentrate on these three major categories of current assets.

NANCE AT WORK 17-1

ales Retail Sports Media Technology Public Relations Production Exports

DGE CALLS ON UNION, STELCO TO CO-OPERATE

ey'll have to wait.

Underlining the need for co-operation, a judge reserved decision yesterday on the United Steelworkers' bid to cind Stelco Inc.'s ability to operate under court protection. tario Superior Court Justice James Farley told the sides that gardless of the case's outcome, co-operation is necessary in der to improve upon the steel giant's problems. "You've got start now, and starting on an adversarial basis is not good," told a courtroom full of lawyers, company representatives d a busload of retirees and current workers who travelled m Hamilton.

"It is incumbent on everybody to try to find a solution to t problem. There's no reason why you shouldn't be operat-, even now, before I give my decision, to see how matters n be improved," Farley said.

Stelco, the country's largest steel maker in shipment ton-ge, gained court protection under the Companies' Creditors angement Act on Jan. 29 after saying it could no longer erate without relief from creditors and other stakeholders.

But the union claims the company is not actually insol-nt, despite facing financial problems. It's worried that with elco designated as insolvent, protection from the CCAA uld cost jobs, wages and pension benefits. Union lawyer vid Jacobs stuck to those arguments yesterday afternoon, iming that an affidavit signed by Hap Stephen, who was pointed in January as the company's restructuring officer, uld require "mathematical gymnastics" to come up with its nclusions.

Stephen's affidavit supported the insolvency claim, stating at obtaining new credit was unlikely outside CCAA protection. ephen said Stelco could not meet obligations as they become e, and the value of its assets could not cover its liabilities.

The company faced a "looming liquidity crisis" before it s granted court protection, he added.

Jacobs said Stelco had positive working capital Jan. 29 when Farley approved the company's request for creditor protection, adding that the company underestimated Stelco's worth and consistently made estimates that attempted to "undersell itself to this court."

He said the company, which has 8,000 employees and some 13,000 pensioners, mistakenly compared itself to American steel companies in order to determine its worth and how much its "legacy costs," or pension obligations to retirees, amounted to. Jacobs also said that the company's claim of insolvency should have been based on its ability to repay obligations as of Jan. 29, not in the future.

In trying to convince Farley that the company should remain under creditor protection, Stelco's lawyer argued that under CCAA, it's up to the courts to define the meaning of insolvent and that Farley has the ability to extend Stelco's protection while it restructures. Michael Barrack argued that insolvency should also be based on assets and liabilities, not just working capital.

He added that the company was acting "responsibly" by seeking creditor protection while it is still viable, and said if the company can't operate under creditor protection it will likely go into receivership later this year.

"Not a single expert has come forward from the (Steelworkers) and said that Stelco is not facing a liquidity crisis. In fact, they have said just the opposite."

A tense and testy morning session saw Farley chastise both sides for a lack of co-operation before making this decision to hear the motion.

Source: "Judge Calls on Union, Stelco to Co-operate" by Neco Cockburn. *The Toronto Star*, 4 February 2004. Reprinted with permission—Torstar Syndication Services.

THREE WORKING CAPITAL FINANCING APPROACHES

The three primary working capital financing approaches are the *aggressive* approach, the *conservative* approach, and the *moderate* approach. A firm that takes an aggressive approach uses more short-term financing to finance current assets. Firm risk increases, due to the risk of fluctuating interest rates, but the potential for higher returns increases because of the generally low-cost financing. A firm that implements the conservative approach avoids short-term financing to reduce risk but decreases the potential for maximum value creation because of the high cost of long-term debt and equity financing. The moderate approach tries to balance risk and return concerns.

The Aggressive Approach

We know that short-term interest rates are normally lower than long-term interest rates. We also know that borrowing short term is riskier than borrowing long term because the loan must be paid off or refinanced sooner rather than later.

The **aggressive working capital financing approach** involves the use of short-term debt to finance at least the firm's temporary assets, some or all of its permanent current assets, and possibly some of its long-term capital assets. The aggressive approach is shown graphically in Figure 17-3.

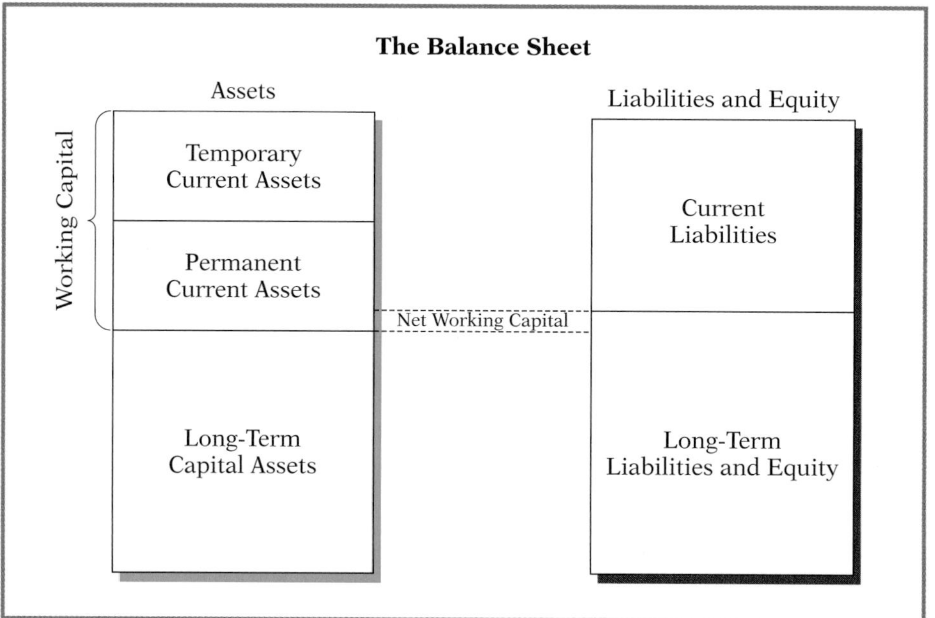

Figure 17-3 The Aggressive Working Capital Financing Approach
Figure 17-3 shows the firm's assets on the left and liabilities and equity on the right. Subtracting current liabilities from current assets shows that this firm's working capital financing strategy is to finance nearly all current assets with current liabilities, resulting in a small amount of net working capital.

If we compare current assets and current liabilities in Figure 17-3, we see that all the firm's temporary current assets and most of its permanent current assets are being financed with short-term debt (the current liabilities). As a result, the firm has very little *net* working capital. Depending on the nature of the firm's business, this small amount of net working capital can be risky. There is little cushion between the value of liquid assets and the amount of debt due in the short term.

Firms may be more aggressive than the firm depicted in Figure 17-3. If the firm's managers financed *all* working capital from short-term debt, then current assets would equal current liabilities and the firm would have zero net working capital—no cushion at all. Managers may go even further and finance a portion of the firm's capital assets (plant and equipment) with short-term debt, creating a *negative* net working capital. However, such an approach is *very* risky. (Think what would happen to a firm using that approach if short-term interest rates rose unexpectedly.)

What tempts financial managers to take the aggressive approach and use a relatively large amount of short-term debt for working capital financing? Usually, lower interest rates tempt them. Managers will take a risk if the promise of return is high enough to justify it. However, the downside could be disastrous, as was the case for the former president of EuroBizNet, a small-sized company in Quebec that attempted to sell European music over the Internet. Paul Mcdonald lost everything when his aggressive approach bankrupted his company.

The Conservative Approach

Borrowing long-term is considered less risky than borrowing short-term. This is because the borrower has a longer time to use the loan proceeds before repayment is due. Furthermore, if interest rates should go up during the period of the loan, the long-term borrower has another advantage. The long-term borrower has locked in a fixed interest rate and may end up paying less total interest than the short-term borrower, who must renew the loan each time it comes due—at a new, higher interest rate. If market rates fall, the long-term borrower can usually refinance.

The **conservative working capital financing approach** involves the use of long-term debt and equity to finance all capital assets and permanent current assets, in addition to some part of temporary current assets. The conservative approach is shown graphically in Figure 17-4.

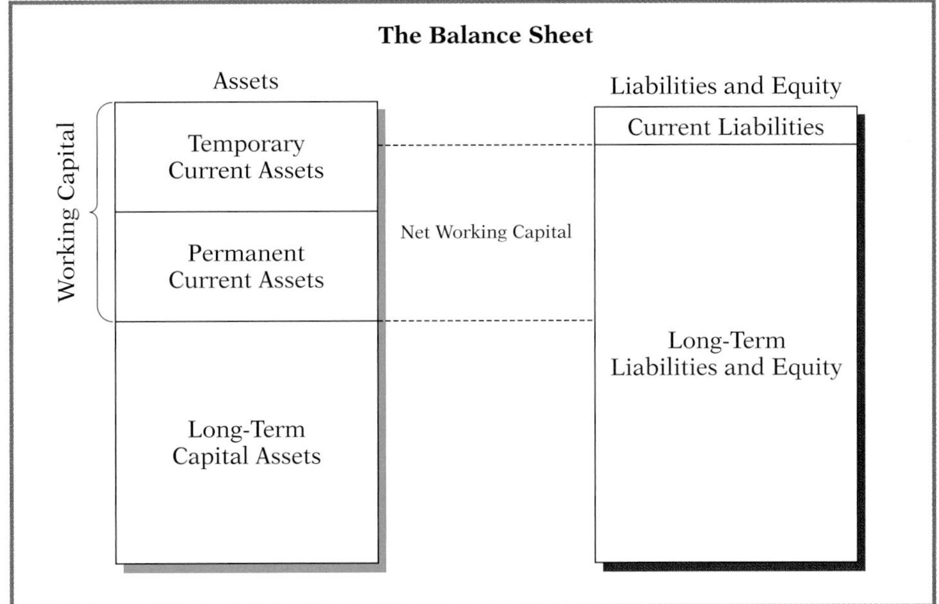

Figure 17-4 The Conservative Working Capital Financing Approach
The relative size of the current asset and current liability accounts in Figure 17-4 reveals the firm's working capital financing strategy. The figure shows that this firm is financing nearly all current assets with long-term liabilities and equity, resulting in a high level of net working capital.

Compare current assets with current liabilities in Figure 17-4. Note that all the firm's permanent current assets and most of its temporary current assets are being financed with long-term debt or equity. As a result, current assets exceed current liabilities by a wide margin and the firm has a large amount of *net* working capital. Having a large amount of net working capital is a relatively low-risk position because the firm has many assets that could be liquidated to satisfy short-term debts.

A financial manager who applies an ultra-conservative approach would use cash from the owners to finance all asset financing needs (high cash balance supported by equity) and incur no debt. By using only equity capital, the firm would also have the maximum amount of net working capital possible because it would have no current liabilities.

The safety of the conservative approach has a cost. Long-term financing is generally more expensive than short-term financing. Long-term interest rates are higher than short-term rates when there is an upward-sloping yield curve, the normal yield curve described in Chapter 2. Also, the cost of equity is greater than the cost of either long-term or short-term debt, as described in Chapter 9. So relying on long-term debt and equity sources to finance working capital consumes funds that could otherwise be put to more productive use.

The Moderate Approach

An accounting concept known as the *matching principle* states that the cost of an asset should be recognized over the length of time the asset provides revenue, or benefit, to the business.

The concept of the matching principle can be applied to define a moderate position between the aggressive and the conservative working capital financing approaches. According to the matching principle, temporary current assets that are only going to be on the balance sheet for a short time should be financed with short-term debt—that is, current liabilities. Permanent current assets and capital assets that are going to be on the balance sheet for a long time should be financed from long-term debt and equity sources. The **moderate working capital financing approach** is shown in Figure 17-5.

Figure 17-5 The Moderate Working Capital Financing Approach
In Figure 17-5, we see that this firm's approach to working capital financing policy is to finance its permanent current assets with long-term debt and equity and its temporary current assets with current liabilities. This results in a moderate level of net working capital.

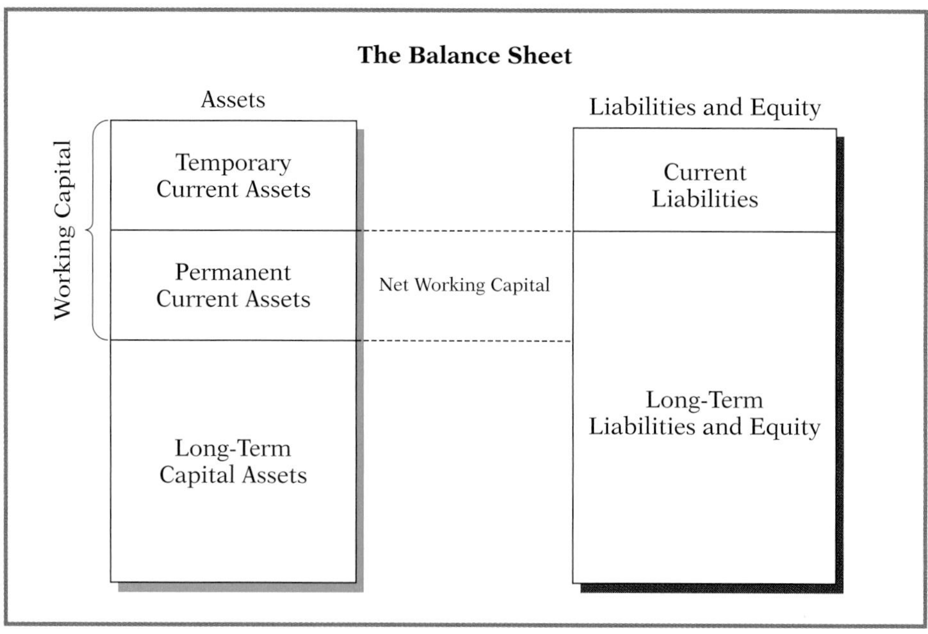

If we look at current assets and current liabilities in Figure 17-5, we see that the firm has matched its short-term temporary current assets to its current liabilities. It has also matched its long-term permanent current assets and capital assets to its long-term financing sources. This policy gives the firm a moderate amount of net working capital. It calls for a relatively moderate amount of risk balanced by a relatively moderate amount of expected return.

Now that we have described three working capital financing policies, we turn to an analysis of the effect of such policies on a firm.

Working Capital Financing and Financial Ratios

The use of *ratio analysis* highlights how the three approaches to working capital financing policy can affect the risk and return potential of a firm. In Table 17-2, we compare selected financial ratios for three different firms that differ only in the manner in which they finance their working capital. Firm A takes the aggressive approach, Firm C takes the conservative approach, and Firm M takes the moderate approach.

Table 17-2 Ratio Analysis of Approaches to Working Capital Financing Policy (in thousands)

Data as of the End of the Last Fiscal Year	Firm A Aggressive	Firm C Conservative	Firm M Moderate
Temporary Current Assets	$ 200	$ 200	$ 200
Permanent Current Assets	$ 400	$ 400	$ 400
Capital Assets	$ 600	$ 600	$ 600
Total Assets	$1,200	$1,200	$1,200
Current Liabilities	$ 300	$ 100	$ 200
Long-Term Debt	$ 300	$ 500	$ 400
Shareholders' Equity	$ 600	$ 600	$ 600
Total Liabilities and Equity	$1,200	$1,200	$1,200
Net Income for the Year	$ 126	$ 114	$ 120
Net Working Capital	$ 300	$ 500	$ 400
Current Ratio	2.0	6.0	3.0
Total Debt to Total Assets Ratio	50%	50%	50%
Return on Equity	21%	19%	20%

Notice in Table 17-2 that Firm A, which follows an aggressive financing approach, has the highest net income, smallest amount of net working capital, the lowest current ratio, and the highest return on shareholders' equity of any of the three firms. This is consistent with the relationship between risk and return (the more risk a firm takes, the more it can potentially earn). There is no guarantee, of course, that net income will be positive.

Firm C, which follows the conservative financing approach, has the lowest net income, the largest amount of net working capital, the highest current ratio, and the lowest return on shareholders' equity of the three firms. This reflects its relatively lower risk and lower return potential.

Firm M, which follows the moderate approach of matching its short-term temporary current assets to its current liabilities is, of course, in a position between the other two.

Table 17-3 summarizes the cost and risk considerations of the aggressive, conservative, and moderate approaches to working capital financing.

Table 17-3 The Three Approaches to Working Capital Financing Policy—Cost and Risk Factors

	Aggressive	Conservative	Moderate
Cost	Low	High	In-Between
Risk	High	Low	In-Between

In the real world, of course, each firm must decide on its balance of financing sources and its approach to working capital management based on its particular industry and the firm's risk and return strategy. Often, recessions are viewed as a negative occurrence. There is, however, an upside. Working capital managers must employ more efficient management techniques. Some of these are outlined in International Perspectives in Finance 17-1.

INTERNATIONAL PERSPECTIVES IN FINANCE 17-1

We Can Work It Out—The 2002 Working Capital Survey

A recession can bring out the best and the worst in corporate finance. The worst has been splattered across newspaper front pages for months now. Some of the best is happening in back offices, where companies continue to find ways to mine working capital—the amount of money they have tied up in operations—to increase cash flow. In a recession, however, the traditional methods companies use to extract that cash—calling in overdue payments, stretching out their own, and relentlessly paring down inventories—can lead to a gigantic, circular squeeze in which no one wants to cut a cheque to anyone else. This year's working capital survey, our sixth conducted jointly with REL Consultancy Group, finds signs that companies are exploiting creative tactics to reduce working capital and improve cash flow without alienating customers or stringing out suppliers—much. But these methods pose challenges of their own.

Don't Break the Chain

We noted a year ago that squeezing customers too hard might drive them into the arms of a competitor. This year, companies seem more worried about driving their suppliers into bankruptcy—particularly at a time when they need those suppliers to help them reduce inventory. "If you grow your supplier payments by too many days, that impedes your ab ity to work with them to manage your inventory," notes Pa Inc. CFO Judy Bruner, whose days payable outstandi (DPO) dropped 13 days last year. And inventory turns are far more lucrative source of working capital than payable says REL Americas president Stephen Payne, because fi ished inventory has a higher value than the raw materi represented by payables.

Palm isn't alone in treating suppliers well on payable Across all industries, average DPO dropped by 5 days 2001 to 32 days. "We don't believe it is good business pra tice to extend payables," says Kenneth A. Goldman, CFO Siebel Systems Inc., whose DPO dropped from an alrea diminutive 5 days in 2000 to just 3 last year. "We did make our cash flow on the backs of our vendors." Softwa companies have no inventory, so most of Siebel's payab are consulting fees, capital expenditures, and ordina expenses such as rent and utilities. "Clearly we are going pay those on time," he says.

Securitization Blanket

Such solicitousness toward suppliers does not necessar imply a tougher line with customers, however. To be su erage days sales outstanding (DSO) dropped last year from ; days to 47 days, as companies like Siebel, Palm, Lear, and exus all reported beefed-up collections. But much of the provement in the manufacturing sector appears to have me not from dunning customers, but from a surge in alter- tive financing techniques. As capital markets dried up, mpanies looking for cash turned, often for the first time, to chniques such as securitization of receivables. That can use the DSO number in the survey to plummet even if a mpany's collection activity has not improved at all.

Of course, companies that opt to securitize usually main responsible for collecting the receivables, and the chniques can be addictive if a company's business doesn't improve, simply because it represents a one-time income gain. "Once you get into the securitization world, it's hard to get out of it," warns Peak. "Once you get on that treadmill and start recording gains on your income statement, it's hard to jump off." That's made all the more likely by the upfront costs of securitizations. They must be amortized, so any event that forces a company to unwind securitization before its time carries a high price. Finally, there are growing questions about how companies report securitization activity.

Source: Excerpted from the August 2002 issue of *CFO*. © 2002 CFO Publishing Corp. For more information about reprints from *CFO*, contact PARS International Corp. at 212-221-9595.

SUMMARY

17-1 Explain what working capital is.

A firm's current assets—such as cash, inventory, and accounts receivable—are referred to as working capital. Managing the levels and financing of working capital effectively is necessary to keep the firm's costs and risk under control while maintaining a firm's returns and cash flow over the long term.

Firms accumulate working capital because of fluctuations in sales, production, and cash or credit payments. For instance, cash accumulates as accounts are collected and declines when bills are paid. Inventory builds when production exceeds sales and falls when sales exceed production. Accounts receivable rises as credit sales are made and falls when customers pay off their accounts. The combined effect of changes in each current asset account causes working capital to fluctuate. Furthermore, working capital will gradually build up over time unless the firm takes some concrete action to either reinvest the funds in long-term assets or distribute them to the firm's owners.

17-2 Discuss how permanent current assets differ from temporary current assets.

Temporary current assets represent the level of current assets that fluctuates and permanent current assets represent the level of current assets a firm keeps regardless of periodic fluctuations.

17-3 Explain the optimal working capital level in terms of profitability versus liquidity.

Current asset management involves a trade-off between the need for liquidity and the desire for profitability. The more current assets a firm holds, the more liquid the firm, because the assets can be converted to cash relatively quickly. However, tying up funds to sustain a certain level of current assets prevents the funds from being invested in long-term, high-return-producing assets. Firms reach an optimal level of current assets when the optimal level for each individual current asset account (mainly cash, inventory, and accounts receivable) is achieved. Separate techniques exist for managing each of the current asset accounts. The techniques for managing each current asset account are described in Chapters 18 and 19.

17-4 Contrast the aggressive, moderate, and conservative methods of financing working capital.

Short-term interest rates are usually lower than long-term interest rates, so financing working capital with short-term debt generally lowers the firm's financing costs.

However, using short-term debt increases the risk that cash will not be available to pay the loans back and the firm may have to renew its loans at higher interest rates. Relying on long-term debt and/or equity sources to finance working capital decreases risk because firms repay such obligations in the long term and firms lock in an interest rate. A firm's return suffers, however, because long-term financing costs are normally higher than short-term costs.

The aggressive approach to working capital policy consists of financing all temporary current assets and some or all long-term permanent current assets, and possibly a portion of capital assets with short-term debt. The conservative approach to working capital policy consists of financing all permanent current assets and some short-term temporary current assets with long-term debt and/or equity financing. The moderate approach consists of financing temporary current assets with short-term debt and financing long-term permanent current assets with long-term debt and/or equity.

SELF-TEST

ST-1. Explain the liquidity–profitability trade-off associated with working capital management.

ST-2. How is the optimal level of working capital established?

ST-3. Using the following financial data, draw a diagram showing the company's temporary current assets, permanent current assets, and capital assets during this last year.

Selected Financial Data for the Past Fiscal Year ($000s)

	Jan 1	Mar 31	Jun 30	Oct 31	Dec 31
Total Assets	$580	$480	$280	$400	$580
Capital Assets	$100	$100	$100	$100	$100

ST-4. As of today, a company has $100,000 of temporary current assets, $50,000 of permanent current assets, and $80,000 of capital assets. If the company follows the moderate approach to working capital financing, how much of its assets will be financed with short-term debt (current liabilities) and how much will be financed with long-term debt and/or equity as of today?

REVIEW QUESTIONS

1. What is working capital?
2. What is the primary advantage to a corporation of investing some of its funds in working capital?
3. Can a corporation have too much working capital? Explain.
4. Explain how a firm determines the optimal level of current assets.
5. What are the risks associated with using a large amount of short-term financing for working capital?
6. What is the matching principle of working capital financing? What are the benefits of following this principle?
7. What are the advantages and disadvantages of the aggressive working capital financing approach?
8. What is the most conservative type of working-capital financing plan a company could implement? Explain.

PROBLEMS

17-1. WPS International has the following balance sheet. Twenty-five percent of its current assets are temporary and the remainder is permanent current assets. ◀ Working Capital

Cash	$150,000	Accounts Payable	$100,000
Inventory	120,000	Notes Payable	90,000
Accounts Receivable	80,000	Long-Term Debt	120,000
Capital Assets	500,000	Shareholders' Equity	540,000
Total Assets	$850,000	**Total Liabilities and Equity**	$850,000

a. What is WPS International's working capital?

b. What is WPS International's net working capital?

c. Calculate the temporary current assets.

d. Calculate the permanent current assets.

17-2. Compare the following two firms and decide which has more liquidity. Explain why. ◀ Liquidity

Firm 1

Cash	$10,000
Inventory	$3,000
Accounts Receivable	$2,500
Capital Assets	$15,000
Accounts Payable	$7,500
Notes Payable	$4,000
Long-Term Debt	$7,000
Shareholders' Equity	$12,000

Firm 2

Cash	$8,000
Inventory	$6,000
Accounts Receivable	$3,500
Capital Assets	$13,000
Accounts Payable	$3,500
Notes Payable	$11,000
Long-Term Debt	$9,000
Shareholders' Equity	$7,000

17-3. Consider the following two companies: ◀ Assessing Liquidity

	Company A	Company B
Cash	$1,000	$ 80
Accounts Receivable	400	880
Capital Assets	1,500	1,620
	$2,900	$2,580
Accounts Payable	$ 900	$ 600
Long-Term Debt	800	1,100
Shareholders' Equity	1,200	880
	$2,900	$2,580

Which of the two firms is more liquid? Why?

Current Assets: Current Liabilities and Net Working Capital

17-4. Capt. Louis Renault's Hikewell Outdoor Equipment Company has the following balance sheet accounts as of the end of last year. One-half current assets are permanent and one-half are temporary.

Cash	$ 30,000	Accounts Payable	$100,000
Accounts Receivable	15,000	Notes Payable	60,000
Inventory	130,000	Long-Term Debt	90,000
Capital Assets	500,000	Shareholders' Equity	425,000
	$675,000		$675,000

a. What is the amount of the company's current assets, its working capital?
b. What is the amount of the company's current liabilities?
c. What is the amount of the company's net working capital?
d. What percentage of temporary current assets is financed by current liabilities? Would you consider this an aggressive approach or a conservative approach?

Conservative Working Capital Financing Approach

17-5. Alexander Sebastian, the finance manager of Hikewell Outdoor Equipment Company of problem 17-4, thinks that the way the company is financing its current assets is too risky. By the end of next year, he would like the *pro forma* balance sheet to look as follows:

Cash	$ 30,000	Accounts Payable	$ 30,000
Accounts Receivable	15,000	Notes Payable	20,000
Inventory	130,000	Long-Term Debt	150,000
Capital Assets	500,000	Shareholders' Equity	475,000
	$675,000		$675,000

a. What is the amount of the company's projected current assets, its working capital?
b. What is the amount of the company's projected current liabilities?
c. What is the amount of the company's projected net working capital?
d. What percentage of temporary current assets is projected to be financed by current liabilities? Would you consider this an aggressive approach or a conservative approach?

Assessing Working Capital Policy

17-6. Consider the following balance sheet for Lulu Belle's Killer Guard Dogs, Inc.:

Assets		Liabilities and Equity	
Cash	$ 50	Accounts Payable	$ 80
Accounts Receivable	40	Short-Term Debt	90
Inventories	70	Long-Term Debt	210
Capital Assets	530	Shareholders' Equity	310
	$690		$690

a. How much working capital does Lulu Belle have?
b. How much net working capital does Lulu Belle have?
c. What working capital financing policy (aggressive, moderate, or conservative) is Lulu Belle following?
d. Explain what actions Lulu Belle could take to increase the company's liquidity.

17-7. Laroux Products has the following balance sheet. Its temporary current assets are 30 percent of the current assets and the remaining are permanent current assets.

◀ Conservative Approach to Working Capital

Cash	$ 100,000
Inventory	$ 200,000
Accounts Receivable	$ 150,000
Capital Assets	$ 550,000
Total Assets	$1,000,000

Accounts Payable	$ 600,000
Notes Payable	$ 200,000
Long-Term Debt	$ 150,000
Shareholders' Equity	$ 50,000
Total Liabilities and Equity	$1,000,000

The company would like to change its financing approach to a more conservative one. Create a new balance sheet using the conservative approach that the company could adopt. Laroux estimates the asset amounts will remain the same.

17-8. Tony Reynolds, CFO for Ridgeway Building Supplies, has determined that the company would run best if it used the moderate approach to financing. Recently, the company has thought about switching to this approach. The following is a partial balance sheet stating its assets. Permanent current assets are assumed to be 60 percent of the current assets.

◀ Moderate Approach to Working Capital

Cash	$ 50,000	Accounts Payable	________
Accounts Receivable	25,000	Notes Payable	________
Inventory	150,000	Long-Term Debt	________
Capital Assets	475,000	Shareholders' Equity	________
	$700,000		

What would the company's financing look like if Tony switched to the moderate approach? Calculate for the following scenarios:

a. Accounts payable is $40,000; shareholders' equity is $200,000.

b. Accounts payable is $30,000; shareholders' equity is $425,000.

17-9. Using the information given in problem 17-8, what would Ridgeway Building Supplies' financing look like if Tony decided to use an aggressive approach instead? Accounts payable is $180,000 and shareholders' equity is $200,000.

◀ Aggressive Approach to Working Capital

17-10. Marian Pardoo, the chief financial officer of Envirosafe Chemical Company, believes in a moderate approach to financing following the matching principle. Some of the projected balance sheet accounts of the company for the end of next year follow:

◀ Moderate Working Capital Financing Approach

	Current and Capital Assets	Permanent Current Assets
Cash	$ 30,000	$15,000
Accounts Receivable	15,000	5,000
Inventory	130,000	80,000
Capital Assets	500,000	
Total Assets	$675,000	

Liabilities	
Accounts Payable	$ 20,000
Short-Term Debt	?
Long-Term Debt	?
Shareholders' Equity	450,000
Total Liabilities and Equity	$675,000

How much should Marian finance by short-term debt and long-term debt to conform to the matching principle?

Aggressive Working Capital Financing Approach ▶

17-11. Use the same data given in problem 17-10. Marian's boss, Ann Lowell, is the vice-president of finance of Envirosafe Chemical Company and she expects interest rates to decrease in the future. Therefore, she would like to follow a very aggressive policy using a large amount of short-term debt and a small amount of long-term debt. She would also like to decrease net working capital to $25,000. How much should Ann finance by short-term debt and how much by long-term debt to conform to her aggressive approach?

Different Working Capital Financing Approaches ▶

17-12. Comparative data at the end of this past year for three firms following aggressive, moderate, and conservative approaches to working capital policy follow (in thousands of dollars):

	Aggressive	Moderate	Conservative
Temporary Current Assets	$ 75	$ 75	$ 75
Permanent Current Assets	100	100	100
Capital Assets	500	500	500
Total Assets	675	675	675
Current Liabilities	160	75	50
Long-Term Debt	90	150	150
Shareholders' Equity	425	450	475
Net Income	70	70	70

Calculate, compare, and comment on the current ratios, total debt to asset ratios, and returns on equity of the three firms.

Challenge Problem ▶

17-13. Greenplanet Recycling Company is considering buying an additional facility at a cost of $500,000. The facility will have an economic life of five years. The company's financial officer, Karen Holmes, can finance the project by:

a. A five-year loan at an annual interest rate of 13 percent, or

b. A one-year loan rolled over each year for five years

Compare the total interest expenses for both the preceding alternatives under the following assumptions and calculate the savings in the interest expenses by choosing one of two alternatives:

i. The one-year loan has a constant interest rate of 11 percent per year over the next five years.

ii. The one-year loan has an annual interest rate of 11 percent in the first two years, 14 percent in the third and fourth years, and 16 percent in the fifth year.

The Matching Principle ▶

Excel

17-14. To analyze your company's working capital financing policy, you have gathered the following balance sheet data for the past 12 months (in thousands of dollars):

Date	Total Assets	Capital Assets
Jan 31	$45	$14
Feb 28	46	14
Mar 31	34	14
Apr 30	48	14
May 31	40	14
Jun 30	30	14
Jul 31	28	14
Aug 31	39	14
Sep 30	45	14
Oct 31	39	14
Nov 30	52	14
Dec 31	50	14

Plot these data on a trendline graph. Indicate the amount of your firm's current liabilities each month if you follow the matching principle.

17-15. Milton Warden, the finance manager of WinHeart Gift Company, is analyzing past data on the firm's capital assets, permanent current assets, and temporary current assets for each month over the last five years. The company maintains level production, but its sales are seasonal. He found that the monthly level of the three types of assets over the last five years could be closely approximated by the following patterns (in thousands of dollars):

◀ Comprehensive Problem

Excel

- Capital assets remained constant at 39 each month over the last five years.
- Permanent current assets were equal to 2 in January of year 1 and had grown 0.16 per month each month over the last five years.
- Temporary current assets followed the same pattern each year, starting at 0 in January. Then each year they increased by 1 monthly until July and reduced by 1 monthly until they reached 0 again in January of the next year.

a. On a graph similar to the one shown in Figure 17-2, plot these data.

b. On the graph, calculate and identify the level of temporary current assets, permanent current assets, and capital assets in:

   i. The month of September of year 4

   ii. The month of August of year 5

c. Now calculate the levels of current liabilities in those months if the company followed:

   i. An aggressive working capital financing approach

   ii. A moderate working capital financing approach

   iii. A conservative working capital financing approach

Assume that the shareholders' equity remained constant at 20 over those five years.

17-16. Buddy Love, a finance officer of Christmas Tree Ornaments and Gifts Company, is analyzing past data on the capital assets, permanent current assets, and temporary current assets of the company each month over the last several years. The company maintains level production, but its sales peak at the end of the year. He found that the monthly level of the three types of assets over the last five years could be closely approximated by the following equations (in thousands of dollars):

◀ Comprehensive Problem

Excel

- Capital assets were equal to 55 and remained constant each month over the last five years.

- Permanent current assets were equal to 10 in January of year 1 and had grown 0.30 per month each month over the last five years.
- Temporary current assets = m(m – 1)/4, where m = 1, 2, ... , 12 for Jan, Feb, ... , Dec, respectively.

a. Plot these data on a graph similar to the one shown in Figure 17-2.

b. On your graph, calculate and identify the level of temporary current assets, permanent current assets, and capital assets at the following times:
   i. The month of September of year 2
   ii. The month of October of year 4
   iii. Year 5's minimum and maximum levels of total assets and the months those levels occurred

c. Now calculate the levels of current liabilities in the months described in (b) of this problem if the company followed:
   i. An aggressive working capital financing approach
   ii. A moderate working capital financing approach
   iii. A conservative working capital financing approach

Assume that the shareholders' equity remained constant at 30 over those five years.

Net Working Capital Strategies ▶

17-17. Samuel was analyzing the working capital for his company. The economy had been performing poorly in the last several years. Both Samuel's clients and suppliers had been feeling the effects of a long recession. Due to the sluggish economy, the Bank of Canada had been lowering its Target for the Overnight Rate, leading to the lowest borrowing rates in several decades. Investors have been pushing for a greater return for the last several years, but Samuel has not been able to deliver. Trying to be creative, Samuel has asked you to think of some creative ways to increase his net income.

a. Describe some of the net working capital strategies you think Samuel could follow in order to increase net income.

b. What are the drawbacks?

c. Assume that the current low borrowing rates will not continue and that they are perceived to rise in the coming year. What effects could this have on the decision process?

Ratios and Net Working Capital ▶

17-18. The manager of Multi-Software Company has recently been inquiring about getting a loan from the Royal Bank. Unfortunately, Multi-Software must have a current ratio of 2.4 and a quick ratio of 1.2 in order for the bank to accept them. Multi-Software has come to you for advice. The company right now has a current ratio of 1.5 and a quick ratio of 1.5. Multi-Software Company satisfies the quick ratio but not the current ratio.

a. Before even attempting to increase the current ratio, you try to explain the reason why your current ratio is so low and that the quick ratio is a much better indicator of liquidity for your client's type of business. What arguments could you make?

b. What are the drawbacks to having too high a current ratio and quick ratio?

c. List some strategies that could be used in order to increase the current ratio. Is it possible to increase the current ratio without increasing the quick ratio for this type of company?

Fluctuating Working Capital ▶

17-19. Toomuchcash Golf Corp. (TGC for short) has way too much cash during some periods of the year. During the beginning of summer, cash restraints are high due to the need for large amounts of cash for inventory purchases. By the end of the summer, cash restraints are low because inventory purchases are low. All other cash outputs are nominal relative to the inventory purchases. TGC generally pays all its purchases off within 10 days, 20 days earlier than required. The average age of the receivables is 55 days. TGC is upset by the amount of cash that must be kept on hand, thinking that if the fluctuations in cash over the year were reduced, then more money could be used in more profitable ways. The current cost of short-term borrowing is 7 percent. The current rate of investment is 4 percent.

a. Right off the bat, what could you suggest that TGC can do to reduce its cash fluctuations?

Excel

b. There has been a strong push for TGC to accept MasterCard and Visa payments. TGC has been hesitant to do this, due to the credit cards demanding 5 percent of each sale. Numerically, could you argue that the credit card proposal would save money?

c. TGC's suppliers have recently created a payment plan for companies that would rather pay monthly instead of in a lump sum. All outstanding balances will be charged 3 percent with a monthly payment plan. Numerically, could you justify that TGC should take this offer?

◀ Working Capital Approaches

17-20. Ups and Downs Corp. (UPD for short) has been considering the change from a conservative approach to an aggressive approach when dealing with the financing of its current assets. Interest rates are currently extremely high. Further, it is expected that rates will drop in the near future.

a. What is the effect of borrowing more short-term debt in terms of your liquidity ratios, in your ability to borrow further, and in the shareholders' perspective?

b. If rates were to fall within 1 year, what is the upside to UPD's decision? If UPD were to be extremely aggressive, what could the company do in terms of financing its capital assets?

c. When a company has negative working capital, what in effect is it doing? Logically speaking, when would companies be more tempted to employ more aggressive approaches?

◀ Working Capital Approaches

17-21. Ups and Downs Corp. has benefited from an aggressive approach to managing its working capital. Rates have fallen dramatically over the last few years and because UPD has been financing through a continued falling rate, its profit ratios have been slightly higher than average. Right now, rates are the lowest they have been in several decades and UPD is considering the modification of its working capital approach.

a. When do you think companies will be tempted to favour a more conservative approach?

b. Assuming that rates cannot go lower and that they will rise soon, what are the disadvantages to following a conservative approach?

c. When do you think a company would be tempted to implement a moderate approach?

ANSWERS TO SELF-TEST

ST-1. Working capital (i.e., current assets in the form of cash, accounts receivable, inventory, and so on) can normally be exchanged for cash, or liquidated, in a relatively short time. Therefore, the more working capital a company can maintain, the easier it is to raise cash quickly. However, maintaining working capital costs money and ties up funds that could otherwise be used to invest in long-term, income-producing assets, so profits and returns suffer. For this reason, we say that managing working capital involves balancing liquidity and profitability.

ST-2. The optimal level of working capital is achieved when the optimal levels of each current asset account—cash, inventory, accounts receivable, and any others—are reached. Each current asset category is managed separately and the combined results produce the optimal level of current assets.

ST-3.

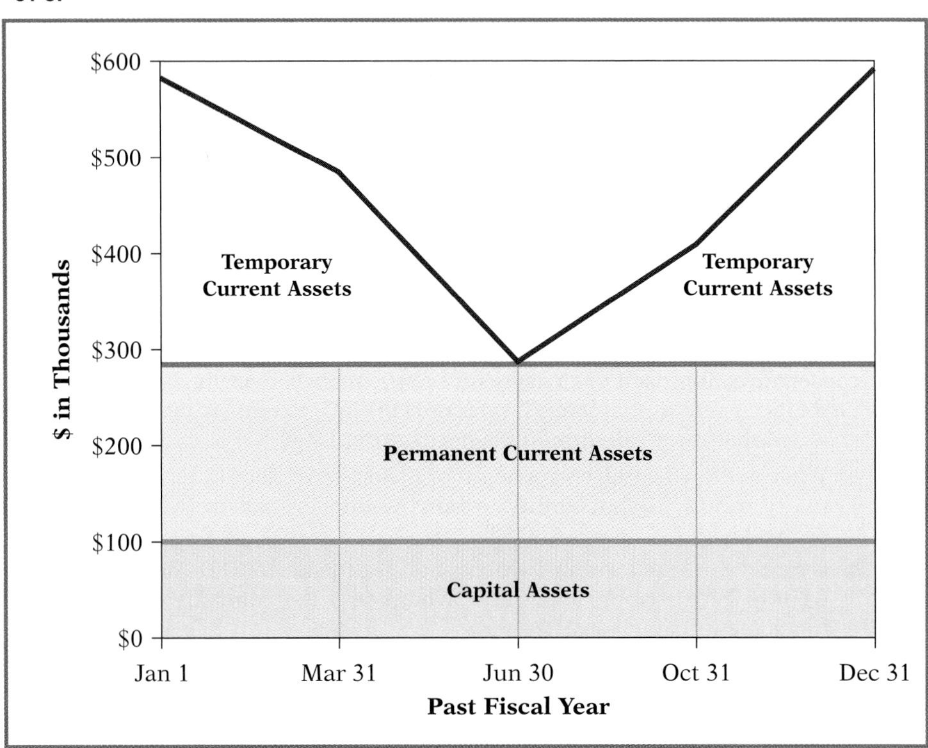

ST-4. Following the moderate approach, the company will finance its temporary current assets with short-term debt and the rest of its assets with long-term debt and equity. Therefore, as of today, the company will have on its balance sheet:

Current Liabilities	$100,000
Long-Term Debt and Equity	$130,000

18

Managing Cash

Chapter Objectives

After reading this chapter, you should be able to:

18-1 List three factors that affect a company's desired minimum cash balance.

18-2 List three factors that affect a company's maximum cash balance.

18-3 Discuss how the Miller-Orr model solves for a target optimal cash balance.

18-4 Explain the purpose of a cash budget.

18-5 Explain how firms manage their cash inflows and outflows to maximize value.

"I've never been poor, but I've been broke."

—Mike Todd

Waterfront Corp. Near Shutdown

The corporation responsible for turning Toronto's waterfront from derelict to delightful is 26 days away from bankruptcy because the federal government hasn't paid its bills.

The Toronto Waterfront Revitalization Corp. stopped all new spending in January and is so broke that it doesn't have money to pay employees or the rent on its office, the board of directors was told at a meeting yesterday.

The federal government owes the corporation $10 million, and if it doesn't turn over at least $6.6 million before March 15, the "shut-down plan," which involves stopping all projects and laying off staff, begins.

Source: Excerpt from "Waterfront Corporation Starved for Cash, May Fold," by Kerry Gillespie. *The Toronto Star*, 5 March 2004. Reprinted with permission—Torstar Syndication Services.

Chapter Overview

In this chapter, we look at how firms manage cash. Cash flow management can even mean electronic cash. Here we start by exploring factors that affect a company's optimal cash balance and learn how to estimate the optimal balance. Then we examine how firms forecast their cash needs, develop a cash budget, and manage cash inflows and outflows.

Cash Management Concepts

Whether they work in a large multinational corporation or a small business, financial managers need to know how much cash to keep on hand. Cash management may sound simple. Should businesses not accumulate as much cash as possible? It is not that easy. Recall from Chapter 17 that cash earns no return for the business owners. In fact, a business that accumulated as much cash as possible and did not invest in any assets would fail because it would earn no return for the shareholders.[1] Cash, then, should not be obtained for its own sake. Rather, it should be considered the "grease" that enables the machinery of the firm to run. Cash management is the process of controlling how much of this grease is needed and where and when to apply it. Nortel Networks has been promising tighter cash controls in order to raise its share price.

Take Note

In this chapter, the term *cash* refers to dollar amounts in the firm's chequing account at a chartered bank and the coin and currency in the cash drawer. Interest is not generally paid on business chequing accounts and, of course, coin and currency earn no interest when it is in the cash drawer.

Determining the Optimal Cash Balance

To determine how much cash a firm should keep on hand, financial managers must:

- Maintain enough in the cash account to make payments when needed (minimum balance)
- Keep just the needed amount in the cash account so that the firm can invest excess funds and earn returns (maximum balance)

Let's examine the factors that affect the minimum cash balance and the maximum cash balance.

The Minimum Cash Balance

The size of a firm's minimum cash balance depends on three factors: (1) how quickly and inexpensively a firm can raise cash when needed, (2) how accurately the firm's managers can predict when cash payment requirements will occur, and (3) how much precautionary cash the firm's managers want to keep to safeguard against emergencies. The effect of these three factors on the minimum cash balance is shown in Figure 18-1. We examine the three factors that affect a firm's minimum cash balance in the following sections.

Raising Cash Quickly When Needed If a firm's managers could obtain cash instantly whenever they needed it, at zero cost, they would not need to maintain any balance in the cash account at all. All the firm's funds could be

[1] In fact, because there would be no investment in earning assets, such a business would never accumulate more cash than was originally contributed by the founders.

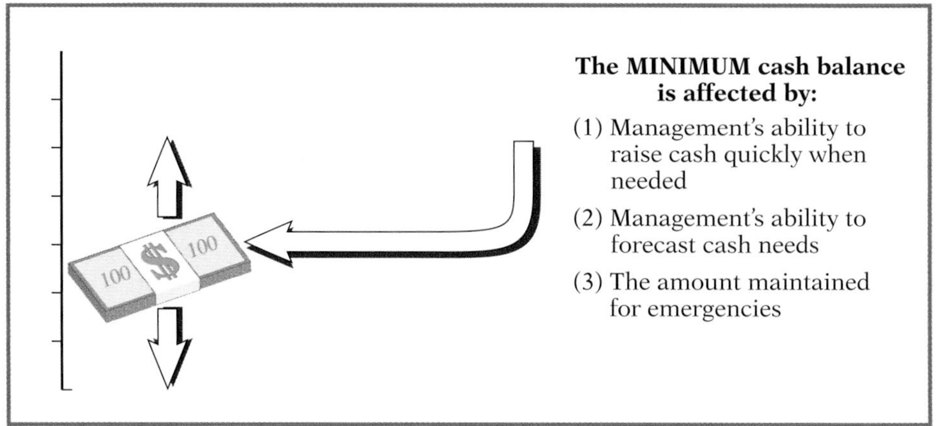

Figure 18-1
Factors Affecting the Minimum Cash Balance
Figure 18-1 shows the three factors that determine the minimum amount a firm will keep in its cash account.

invested in short-term income-producing securities as soon as received. In the real world, of course, neither firms nor anyone else can borrow or sell assets to raise all the cash they want anytime, instantly, at zero cost. In practice, obtaining cash usually takes time and has a positive cost. Therefore, businesses maintain at least some cash in their chequing accounts.

The question is how much cash is enough? The answer is, only experience will tell. The more difficult or expensive it is to get cash when needed, the more a firm needs to keep in its chequing account. At most—if cash were very difficult to obtain because the firm had no liquid assets, or if short-term interest rates were very high—the firm would want to keep enough cash on hand to cover all foreseeable needs until the next time the firm expects to receive more cash.

Predicting Cash Needs Cash flows can be volatile because of the business environment or the risk of the business. For instance, in a weak economy, people and firms pay bills more slowly. So even though sales may be strong, a firm may not have much cash. Also, in an economy with interest rate fluctuations or inflation, cash flow needs can vary suddenly because of economic factors. To protect against an uncertain business environment, firms may maintain extra cash to cover cash needs.

Similarly, the cash flows of a start-up or high-risk business may vary because the company grows at uneven, often unpredictable rates. Managers, then, may have a tough time estimating the firm's cash needs with certainty. Such firms often keep extra cash to act as a buffer against cash flow volatility.

How much extra cash a firm keeps in its coffers to protect against uncertainty depends on two factors: how difficult and expensive it is to raise cash when needed and how volatile the firm's cash flow patterns are.

Coping with Emergencies Most cash payments are expected and planned. However, unforeseen emergencies may occur: storms, fires, strikes, computer system failures, and, most often, failure of business plans to materialize. These emergencies can cause unexpected, sometimes large, drains on a firm's cash. Insurance can help, but there is no substitute for having cash ready when you need it. Managers, then, assess the likelihood of potential emergencies and how quickly and easily cash can be obtained in case of an emergency. They adjust their cash balances accordingly. The more *risk averse* managers are, the more precautionary cash they try to keep on hand for emergencies.

Insurance companies in and out of Canada had to dish out about 40 billion U.S. dollars because of September 11.

The Maximum Cash Balance

Suppose that a firm's managers decide they wish to keep at least $20,000 in the firm's cash account. The next question is, how much should be allowed to accumulate in the cash account before the excess is withdrawn and invested in something that produces a return? If the balance in the cash account is $20,001, for example, should a dollar be withdrawn and invested? Should $30,000 be allowed to accumulate before any is withdrawn and invested? The answer depends on three factors: (1) the available investment opportunities, (2) the expected return from these opportunities, and (3) the transaction cost of withdrawing cash and making an investment. The factors that affect a firm's maximum cash balance are summarized in Figure 18-2. We describe the three factors affecting the maximum cash balance in detail next.

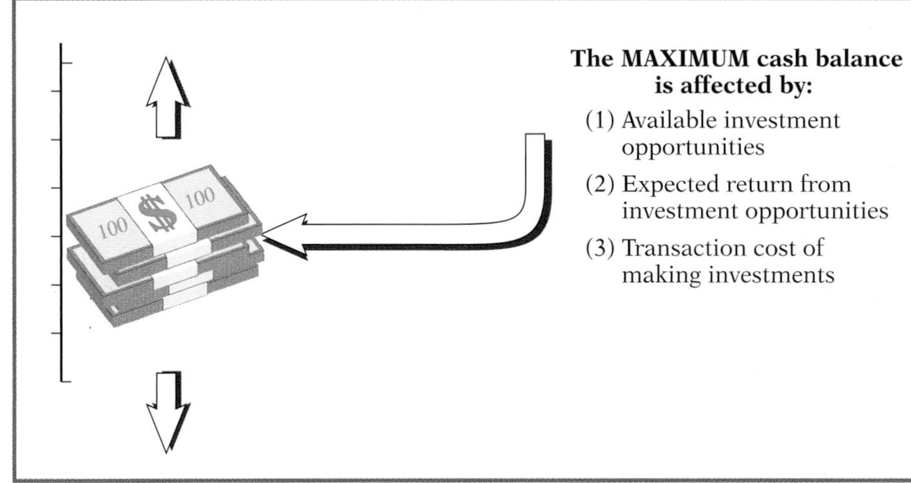

Figure 18-2 Factors Affecting the Maximum Cash Balance
Figure 18-2 shows the three factors that affect a firm's maximum cash balance.

Available Investment Opportunities All businesses have at least a few (and some have many) alternative short-term income-producing investments in which they could invest their cash. These range from money market mutual funds and CDs to Eurodollars and commercial paper. The more opportunities a firm has, the sooner it will invest rather than allow cash to simply accumulate in the firm's chequing account.

Expected Return on Investments The potential return on investments is just as important as the number of investments. If the expected return is relatively high, firms will be quick to invest excess cash. If the expected return is relatively low, however, firms might let more cash accumulate before investing.

The rates in Canada have been exceptionally low in the last few years, making the opportunity cost of investments fairly low compared to historic averages.

Transaction Cost of Making Investments Investing has costs. For instance, when you deposit money in a savings account, someone must search for information about and arrange for the transfer of the funds to the savings account. The search and implementation efforts take time and that time has a cost.

Monetary and other costs of transferring cash into an investment are **transaction costs** —the costs associated with the transaction. Managers are interested in transaction costs because if the potential income from an investment does not exceed the cost of making the investment, then the investment is not worthwhile. Transaction costs also affect the frequency of a firm's investments. If transaction costs are relatively low, the firm will invest often and will let only a small amount of excess cash accumulate in the cash account. Conversely, if transaction costs are relatively high, the firm will make fewer investments, letting a larger amount of cash accumulate in the meantime.

In this section, we have seen that firms determine some minimum and maximum amount to keep in their cash accounts. The minimum amount is based on how quickly and inexpensively firms can raise cash when needed, how accurately cash needs can be predicted, and how much precautionary cash a firm keeps for emergencies. The maximum amount depends on available investment opportunities, the expected returns from the investments, and the transaction costs of withdrawing the cash and making the investment.

Determining the Optimal Cash Balance

Financial theorists have developed mathematical models to help firms find an optimal "target" cash balance between the minimum and maximum limits that balances liquidity and profitability concerns. In the following sections, we discuss one of these models, the Miller–Orr model.

The Miller–Orr Cash Management Model In 1966, Merton Miller and Daniel Orr developed a cash management model that solves for an optimal target cash balance about which the cash balance fluctuates until it reaches an upper or lower limit.[2] If the upper limit is reached, investment securities are bought, bringing the cash balance down to the target again. If the lower limit is reached, investment securities are sold, bringing the cash balance up to the target. Figure 18-3 shows the operation of the model.

The formula for the target cash balance, Z, shown in Figure 18-3 follows:

Miller–Orr Model

Formula for the Target Cash Balance (Z)

$$Z = \sqrt[3]{\frac{3 \times TC \times V}{4 \times r}} + L \tag{18-1}$$

where

TC = Transaction cost of buying or selling short-term investment securities

V = Variance of net daily cash flows

r = Daily rate of return on short-term investment securities

L = Lower limit to be maintained in the cash account

Remember, to take the cube root of a number, you raise the number to the 1/3 power.

[2]Miller, M., and Orr, D. (1966). A Model of the Demand for Money by Firms. *Quarterly Journal of Economics*, 413–35.

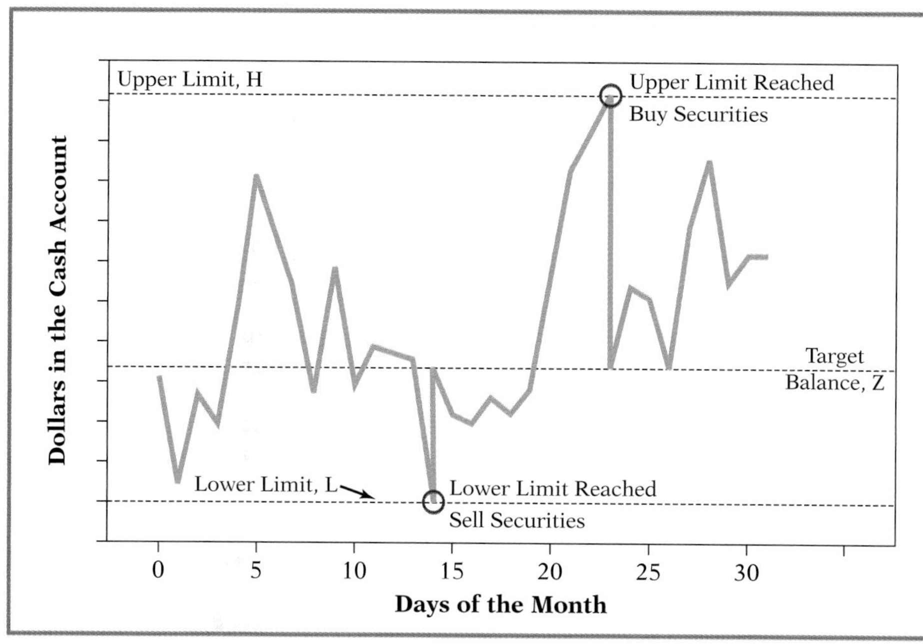

Figure 18-3
Cash Balances in a Typical Month Using the Miller–Orr Model
Figure 18-3 shows a firm's fluctuating cash flows, and its upper, lower, and optimal cash balances according to the Miller–Orr model.

Notice in Figure 18-3 that the target cash balance, Z, is one-third of the way between the lower limit, L, and the upper limit, H. The Miller–Orr formula for the upper limit, H, is as follows:

Miller–Orr Model

Formula for the Upper Limit for the Cash Account

$$H = 3Z - 2L \qquad (18\text{-}2)$$

In the Miller–Orr model, management, according to the minimum cash, sets the lower limit, L, balance concerns that were discussed earlier.

To illustrate how the Miller–Orr model works, assume that short-term investment securities are yielding 4 percent per year and that it costs the firm $30 each time it buys or sells investment securities. Now assume that the firm's cash inflows and outflows occur irregularly and that the variance of the daily net cash flows has been found to be $90,846. Management wants to keep at least $10,000 in the cash account for emergencies, so L = $10,000. Under these circumstances, the firm will have the following target cash balance, according to Equation 18-1:

$$\begin{aligned} Z &= \sqrt[3]{\frac{3 \times 30 \times \$90{,}846}{4 \times (0.04/365)}} + \$10{,}000 \\ &= \sqrt[3]{\frac{\$8{,}176{,}140}{0.00043836}} + \$10{,}000 \\ &= \$2{,}652 + \$10{,}000 \\ &= \$12{,}652 \end{aligned}$$

With a 4 percent annual return (converted to a daily figure), a lower limit of $10,000, transaction costs of $30, and a variance of $90,846, we see that the firm's target cash balance, Z, is $12,652.

According to Equation 18-2, the firm's upper limit for the target cash balance will be:

$$H = (3 \times \$12{,}652) - (2 \times \$10{,}000)$$
$$= \$37{,}956 - \$20{,}000$$
$$= \$17{,}956$$

According to the Miller–Orr model, then, the firm in this example will seek to maintain \$12,652 in its cash account. If the cash balance increases to \$17,956, the firm will buy \$5,304 worth of investment securities to return the balance to \$12,652. If the cash balance falls to \$10,000, the firm will sell \$2,652 worth of investment securities to raise the cash balance to \$12,652. By finding the optimal cash balance, the firm seeks to accommodate its cash needs, given the volatility of cash inflows and outflows, and maximize its investment opportunities. We see, then, that the Miller–Orr model can help firms find their optimal cash balance.

Now that we have examined factors that affect a firm's minimum, maximum, and optimal cash balances and described how a firm may find its target cash balance, we next look at how a firm can forecast its cash needs.

Forecasting Cash Needs

Financial managers must frequently provide detailed estimates of their firm's future cash needs. The primary purpose of such estimates is to identify when excess cash will be available and when outside financing will be required to make up cash shortages.

Financial managers cannot base future cash estimates on *pro forma* income statements for the appropriate time period. Why? Because income and expenses are not always received and paid for in cash. Remember, if a firm is using an accrual-based accounting system, revenues and expenses may be recognized in one accounting period, but cash may not change hands until another period.

One technique that can be used to estimate true future cash needs is to develop a cash budget. A **cash budget** is a detailed budget plan that shows where cash is expected to come from and where it is expected to go during a given period of time.

The best way to learn about cash budgets is to practice creating one. In the following sections, we will develop a cash budget for Bulldog Batteries that shows detailed cash flows from month to month throughout the upcoming year.

Developing a Cash Budget

The first step in developing a monthly cash budget is to identify sales revenue for each month of the period covered by the budget. Assume that it is the end of December 2003 and that Bulldog Batteries' 2004 sales are expected to occur as follows:

Sales (in thousands of dollars)	
Nov 2003 (reference)	$ 13,441
Dec 2003 (reference)	13,029
Jan 2004	12,945
Feb 2004	14,794
Mar 2004	16,643
Apr 2004	18,492
May 2004	20,341
Jun 2004	22,191
Jul 2004	24,040
Aug 2004	22,191
Sep 2004	20,341
Oct 2004	18,492
Nov 2004	16,643
Dec 2004	14,794
2004 Total	$221,907

Next, assume all of Bulldog's sales are on credit, so no cash is received immediately when a sale is made. Experience from past sales reveals that 30 percent of Bulldog's customers will pay off their accounts in the month of sale, 60 percent will pay off their accounts in the month following the sale, and the remaining 10 percent of the customers will pay off their accounts in the second month following the sale. Given this payment pattern, Bulldog's actual cash collections on sales throughout the year will follow the pattern shown in Table 18-1 on page 592.

In Table 18-1, we computed January's cash collections (in thousands) as follows:

30% of January 2004's Sales:	0.30 × $12,945 =	$ 3,884
+ 60% of December 2003's Sales:	0.60 × $13,029 =	7,817
+ 10% of November 2003's Sales:	0.10 × $13,441 =	1,344
= Total Collections in January 2004:		$13,045

Collections for the other months are computed similarly.

The next step in developing the cash budget is to turn to cash outflows. Assume that Bulldog Batteries' cost of materials is 27 percent of sales. Bulldog manufactures batteries expected to be sold in February, one month ahead of time in January and it orders all the materials it needs for January's production schedule one month ahead of time in December. This schedule repeats for each month of the year. Bulldog makes all its purchases on credit and pays for them in cash during the month following the purchase. Therefore, December's purchase orders will be paid for in January, and so on.

If Bulldog follows the production schedule illustrated in Figure 18-4 throughout 2004, its cash outflows for materials purchases will be as shown in Table 18-2 on page 592. (Materials purchases for November and December of 2004 are based on sales forecasts for January and February 2005 of $14,342,000 and $14,794,000, respectively.)

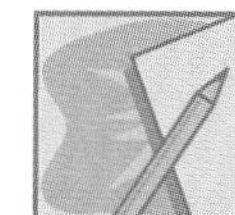

Take Note

If Bulldog's managers expected other cash receipts during 2004, they would add them to sales collections in the appropriate month to obtain the total cash inflows for each month, as shown in Table 18-1.

Table 18-1 Bulldog's Actual Cash Collections (in thousands)

	2003		2004											
	Nov	Dec	Jan	Feb	Mar	Apr	May	Jun	Jul	Aug	Sep	Oct	Nov	Dec
Cash Inflows														
Sales (reference only; not a cash flow)	$13,441	$13,029	$12,945	$14,794	$16,643	$18,492	$20,341	$22,191	$24,040	$22,191	$20,341	$18,492	$16,643	$14,794
Cash collections on sales:														
30% in month of sale			$ 3,884	$ 4,438	$ 4,993	$ 5,548	$ 6,102	$ 6,657	$ 7,212	$ 6,657	$ 6,102	$ 5,548	$ 4,993	$ 4,438
60% in first month after sale			7,817	7,767	8,876	9,986	11,095	12,205	13,315	14,424	13,315	12,205	11,095	9,986
10% in second month after sale			1,344	1,303	1,295	1,479	1,664	1,849	2,034	2,219	2,404	2,219	2,034	1,849
Total collections			$13,045	$13,508	$15,164	$17,013	$18,862	$20,711	$22,561	$23,300	$21,821	$19,971	$18,122	$16,273
Other cash receipts			0	0	0	0	0	0	0	0	0	0	0	0
Total Cash Inflows			$13,045	$13,508	$15,164	$17,013	$18,862	$20,711	$22,561	$23,300	$21,821	$19,971	$18,122	$16,273

Table 18-2 Bulldog's Cash Outflows for Sales and Materials Purchased (in thousands)

	2003		2004											
	Nov	Dec	Jan	Feb	Mar	Apr	May	Jun	Jul	Aug	Sep	Oct	Nov	Dec
Sales (reference only; not a cash flow)	$13,441	$13,029	$12,945	$14,794	$16,643	$18,492	$20,341	$22,191	$24,040	$22,191	$20,341	$18,492	$16,643	$14,794
Materials puchases (27% of sales two months ahead—reference only, not a cash flow)		$ 3,994	$ 4,494	$ 4,993	$ 5,492	$ 5,992	$ 6,491	$ 5,992	$ 5,492	$ 4,993	$ 4,494	$ 3,994	$ 3,872	$ 3,994
Payments for material purchases:														

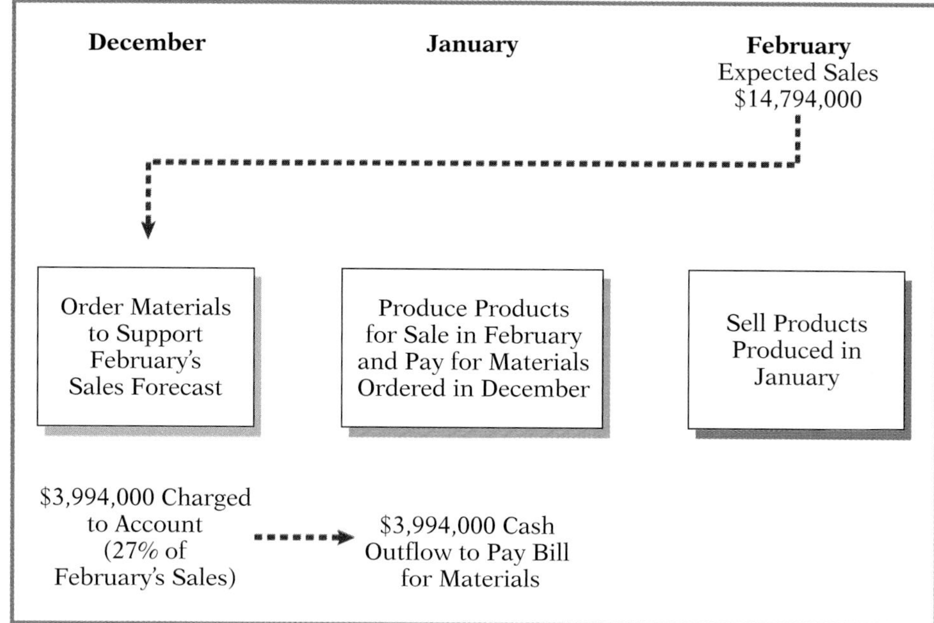

Figure 18-4
Timing for Bulldog Batteries' Cash Payments for Purchases
Figure 18-4 shows Bulldog Batteries' production and cash flow schedule.

For the sake of simplicity, assume Bulldog's remaining cash outflows are all direct expenses paid for in the month incurred as follows:

- Production expenses other than purchases are equal to purchases. (Bulldog's production costs are split evenly between materials cost and other production costs.)
- Sales and marketing expenses are 18.025 percent of sales each month.
- General and administrative expenses are $903,000 each month.
- Interest expense is expected to be $2,971,000 for the year. We assume that expense will be paid all at one time in December 2004.
- Bulldog's expected income tax bill for 2004 is $19,980,000. The bill will be paid in four installments in April, June, September, and December.
- Bulldog expects to declare four quarterly dividends of $6,098,000 in 2004. These will be paid in March, June, September, and December.

Bulldog's total cash outflows, including the preceding expenses and payments for materials purchases, are shown in Table 18-3 on page 594.

After all the cash inflows and outflows for each month are accounted for (as we have done in Tables 18-1, 18-2, and 18-3), the next step is to summarize the *net* gain (or loss) for each month in 2004. Table 18-4 on page 594 contains the summary.

The final step in developing the cash budget is to summarize the effects of the monthly net cash flows on monthly cash balances and list any external financing required. The procedure for January 2004 is shown in Table 18-5 on page 595. We assume a cash balance of $65,313,000 at the beginning of January, a desired target cash balance of $65,000,000, and short-term loans of $302,000 outstanding at the beginning of the month.

Table 18-3
Bulldog's Total Cash Outflows (in thousands)

	2003	2004											
	Dec	Jan	Feb	Mar	Apr	May	Jun	Jul	Aug	Sep	Oct	Nov	Dec
Cash Outflows													
Materials purchases (reference only; not a cash flow)	$3,994	$ 4,494	$ 4,993	$ 5,492	$ 5,992	$ 6,491	$ 5,992	$ 5,492	$ 4,993	$ 4,494	$ 3,994	$ 3,872	$ 3,994
Payments for materials purchases: 100% in month after purchase		$ 3,994	$ 4,494	$ 4,993	$ 5,492	$ 5,992	$ 6,491	$ 5,992	$ 5,492	$ 4,993	$ 4,494	$ 3,994	$ 3,872
Other cash payments:													
Production costs other than purchases		3,994	4,494	4,993	5,492	5,992	6,491	5,992	5,492	4,993	4,494	3,994	3,872
Selling and marketing expenses		2,333	2,667	3,000	3,333	3,666	4,000	4,333	4,000	3,667	3,333	3,000	2,667
General and administrative expenses		903	903	903	903	903	903	903	903	903	903	903	903
Interest payments													2,971
Tax payments					4,995		4,995			4,995			4,995
Dividend payments				6,098			6,098			6,098			6,098
Total Cash Outflows		$11,225	$12,557	$19,987	$20,215	$16,553	$28,978	$17,219	$15,887	$25,649	$13,223	$ 11,892	$25,378

Table 18-4
Bulldog's Cash Inflows and Outflows and Net Cash Flows (in thousands)

	2004											
	Jan	Feb	Mar	Apr	May	Jun	Jul	Aug	Sep	Oct	Nov	Dec
Total Cash Inflows	$13,045	$13,508	$15,164	$17,013	$18,862	$20,711	$22,561	$23,300	$21,821	$19,971	$18,122	$16,273
Total Cash Outflows	11,225	12,557	19,987	20,215	16,553	28,978	17,219	15,887	25,649	13,223	11,892	25,378
Net Cash Gain (Loss)	$ 1,820	$ 951	($ 4,823)	($ 3,203)	$ 2,309	($ 8,267)	$ 5,341	$ 7,413	($ 3,828)	$ 6,748	$ 6,230	($ 9,105)

Table 18-5 **Cash Flow and Financing Requirements Summary, January 2004**

Cash Flow Summary	(in thousands)
1. Cash balance at the start of the month	$65,313
2. Net cash gain (loss) during the month	1,820
3. Cash balance at the end of the month before financing	67,133
4. Minimum cash balance desired	65,000
5. Surplus cash (deficit) (line 3 – line 4)	$ 2,133
External Financing Summary	
6. External financing balance at the start of the month	$ 302
7. New financing required (negative amount on line 5)	0
8. Financing repayments (positive amount on line 5*)	302
9. External financing balance at the end of the month	0
10. Cash balance at the end of the month after financing (balance on line 3 + new financing on line 7 – repayments on line 8)	$66,831

*If the positive amount on line 5 exceeds the external financing balance on line 6, enter the external financing balance on line 6.

The procedure is repeated for February using January's cash balance at the end of the month after financing as the starting cash balance for February. Table 18-6 on page 596 contains the 12-month summary for Bulldog Batteries.

After filling out the cash budget through December 2004, Bulldog's managers can see that the firm will have surplus cash in January and February, but external financing will be needed in March, April, June, and September.

According to the budget, the loans can be fully paid off by October and $66,598 will be in the cash account at the end of the year. Armed with this information, Bulldog's managers would approach their banker to establish a line of credit with a limit higher than $11,201,000—the largest anticipated loan balance.

For your convenience, Bulldog's complete cash budget for 2004 is shown in Table 18-7 on pages 597–598. We have described how to forecast a firm's short-term cash needs by constructing a cash budget. Next, we explore ways to manage a firm's short-term cash flow.

Managing the Cash Flowing in and out of the Firm

People who manage a firm's cash should focus on four objectives: (1) to increase the flow of cash into the business, (2) to decrease the flow of cash out of the business, (3) to receive cash as quickly as possible, and (4) to pay cash out as slowly as possible, without missing the due date. This gives you more time to put cash to work earning a return. In the sections that follow, we discuss ways to accomplish the four objectives of cash flow management. Figure 18-5 on page 599 illustrates these objectives.

Table 18-6
Bulldog's 12-Month Summary of Cash Flow and Financing Requirements (in thousands)

	Dec	Jan	Feb	Mar	Apr	May	Jun	Jul	Aug	Sep	Oct	Nov	Dec
		2004											
Cash Flow Summary													
1. Cash balance at start of month		$65,313	$66,831	$67,782	$65,000	$65,000	$65,000	$65,000	$65,000	$66,554	$65,000	$69,473	$75,704
2. Net cash gain (loss) during month		1,820	951	(4,823)	(3,203)	2,309	(8,267)	5,341	7,413	(3,828)	6,748	6,230	(9,105)
3. Cash balance at end of month before financing (line 1 + line 2)		$67,133	$67,782	$62,959	$61,797	$67,309	$56,733	$70,341	$72,413	$62,725	$71,748	$75,704	$66,598
4. Minimum cash balance desired		65,000	65,000	65,000	65,000	65,000	65,000	65,000	65,000	65,000	65,000	65,000	65,000
5. Surplus cash (deficit) (line 3 – line 4)		$ 2,133	$ 2,782	($2,041)	($3,203)	$ 2,309	($8,267)	$ 5,341	$ 7,413	($2,275)	$ 6,748	$10,704	$ 1,598
External Financing Summary													
6. External financing balance at start of month		$ 302	$ 0	$ 0	$ 2,041	$ 5,243	$ 2,934	$11,201	$ 5,860	$ 0	$ 2,275	$ 0	$ 0
7. New financing required (negative amount from line 5)		0	0	2,041	3,203	0	8,267	0	0	2,275	0	0	0
8. Financing repayments (positive amount from line 5 up to the amount on line 6)		302	0	0	0	2,309	0	5,341	5,860	0	2,275	0	0
9. External financing balance at end of month	$302	0	0	2,041	5,243	2,934	11,201	5,860	0	2,275	0	0	0
10. Cash balance at end of month after financing (line 3 + line 7 – line 8)		$66,831	$67,782	$65,000	$65,000	$65,000	$65,000	$65,000	$66,554	$65,000	$69,473	$75,704	$66,598

Table 18-7 Bulldog's Complete Cash Budget (in thousands)

	2003		2004											
	Nov	**Dec**	**Jan**	**Feb**	**Mar**	**Apr**	**May**	**Jun**	**Jul**	**Aug**	**Sep**	**Oct**	**Nov**	**Dec**
Cash Inflows														
Sales (reference only; not a cash flow)	$13,441	$13,029	$12,945	$14,794	$16,643	$18,492	$20,341	$22,191	$24,040	$22,191	$20,341	$18,492	$16,643	$14,794
Cash collections on sales:														
30% in month of sale			$ 3,884	$ 4,438	$ 4,993	$ 5,548	$ 6,102	$ 6,657	$ 7,212	$ 6,657	$ 6,102	$ 5,548	$ 4,993	$ 4,438
60% in first month after sale			7,817	7,767	8,876	9,986	11,095	12,205	13,315	14,424	13,315	12,205	11,095	9,986
10% in second month after sale			1,344	1,303	1,295	1,479	1,664	1,849	2,034	2,219	2,404	2,219	2,034	1,849
Total collections			$13,045	$13,508	$15,164	$17,013	$18,862	$20,711	$22,561	$23,300	$21,821	$19,971	$18,122	$16,273
Other cash receipts			0	0	0	0	0	0	0	0	0	0	0	0
Total Cash Inflows			$13,045	$13,508	$15,164	$17,013	$18,862	$20,711	$22,561	$23,300	$21,821	$19,971	$18,122	$16,273
Cash Outflows														
Materials purchases (reference only; not a cash flow)		$ 3,994	$ 4,494	$ 4,993	$ 5,492	$ 5,992	$ 6,491	$ 5,992	$ 5,492	$ 4,993	$ 4,494	$ 3,994	$ 3,872	$ 3,994
Payments for materials purchases:														
100% in month after purchase			$ 3,994	$ 4,494	$ 4,993	$ 5,492	$ 5,992	$ 6,491	$ 5,992	$ 5,492	$ 4,993	$ 4,494	$ 3,994	$ 3,872
Other cash payments:														
Production costs other than purchases			3,994	4,494	4,993	5,492	5,992	6,491	5,992	5,492	4,993	4,494	3,994	3,872
Selling and marketing expenses			2,333	2,667	3,000	3,333	3,666	4,000	4,333	4,000	3,667	3,333	3,000	2,667
General and administrative expenses			903	903	903	903	903	903	903	903	903	903	903	903
Interest payments														2,971
Tax payments						4,995		4,995			4,995			4,995
Dividend payments					6,098			6,098			6,098			6,098
Total Cash Outflows			$11,225	$12,557	$19,987	$20,215	$16,553	$28,978	$17,219	$15,887	$25,649	$13,223	$11,892	$25,378
Net Cash Gain (Loss)			$ 1,820	$ 951	($ 4,823)	($ 3,203)	$ 2,309	($ 8,267)	$ 5,341	$ 7,413	($ 3,828)	$ 6,748	$ 6,230	($ 9,105)

Table 18-7 (continued)

	2003	2004											
	Dec	**Jan**	**Feb**	**Mar**	**Apr**	**May**	**Jun**	**Jul**	**Aug**	**Sep**	**Oct**	**Nov**	**Dec**
Cash Flow Summary													
1. Cash balance at start of month		$65,313	$66,831	$67,782	$65,000	$65,000	$65,000	$65,000	$65,000	$66,554	$65,000	$69,473	$75,704
2. Net cash gain (loss) during month		1,820	951	(4,823)	(3,203)	2,309	(8,267)	5,341	7,413	(3,828)	6,748	6,230	(9,105)
3. Cash balance at end of month before financing (line 1 + line 2)		$67,133	$67,782	$62,959	$61,797	$67,309	$56,733	$70,341	$72,413	$62,725	$71,748	$75,704	$66,598
4. Minimum cash balance desired		65,000	65,000	65,000	65,000	65,000	65,000	65,000	65,000	65,000	65,000	65,000	65,000
5. Surplus cash (deficit) (line 3 – line 4)		$ 2,133	$ 2,782	($ 2,041)	($ 3,203)	$ 2,309	($ 8,267)	$ 5,341	$ 7,413	($ 2,275)	$ 6,748	$10,704	$ 1,598
External Financing Summary													
6. External financing balance at start of month		$ 302	$ 0	$ 0)	$ 2,041	$ 5,243	$ 2,934	$11,201	$ 5,860	$ 0	$ 2,275	$ 0	$ 0
7. New financing required (negative amount from line 5)		0	0	2,041	3,203	0	8,267	0	0	2,275	0	0	0
8. Financing repayments (positive amount from line 5 up to the amount on line 6)		302	0	0	0	2,309	0	5,341	5,860	0	2,275	0	0
9. External financing balance at end of month	$ 302	0	0	2,041	5,243	2,934	11,201	5,860	0 2,275	0	0	0	
10. Cash balance at end of month after financing (line 3 + line 7 – line 8)		$66,831	$67,782	$65,000	$65,000	$65,000	$65,000	$65,000	$66,554	$65,000	$69,473	$75,704	$66,598

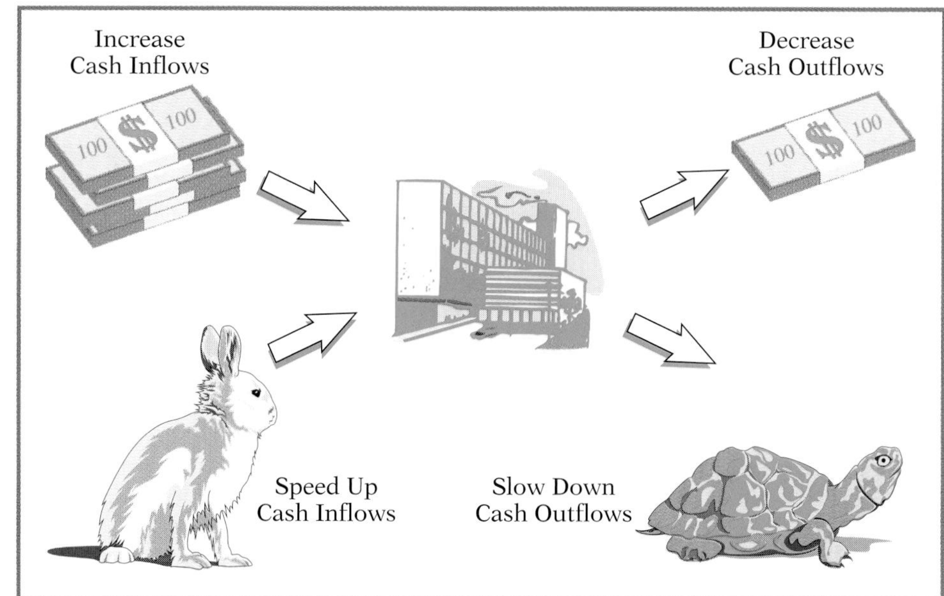

Figure 18-5
Managing the Cash Flowing in and out of the Firm
Figure 18-5 shows the four objectives of cash flow management.

Increasing Cash Inflows

There are really only two ways to increase the amount of cash flowing into a business during any given time period. First, the firm can do more of whatever it is that makes money—that is, a manufacturing business can sell more products or a service business can serve more people. Of course, when sales increase, costs increase too. Hopefully, however, the sales increase will be larger than the cost increase. Second, firms can increase the return that the company's assets are earning—that is, firms can find ways to produce more money with the same amount of assets.

Take Note

Because the financing is only needed for a short time, it is typically obtained from a line of credit or short-term notes.

Decreasing Cash Outflows

Managers can also increase the *net* amount of cash flowing into their firms during any given time period by decreasing the amount of cash flowing out. How? By cutting costs.

Finding the proper balance between short-term and long-term considerations is a subject that business managers must grapple with every day. There are no easy answers.

A less obvious way to decrease cash outflows from the business is to decrease the *risk* of doing business. Risk in business equates to uncertainty and a business that faces a lot of uncertainty must keep a lot of cash on hand to deal with unexpected events. If a firm could somehow reduce the degree of risk of doing business, the number of unexpected events would drop and the amount needed in the cash account could be reduced.

Speeding Up Cash Inflows

Most business managers would agree that, other things being equal, they would rather have cash earlier than later. This makes sense. The earlier a firm receives cash, the earlier it can put it to work earning a return. Accordingly, managers try to figure out how to speed the flow of cash into their firms.

Collecting funds from the firm's customers more quickly speeds cash inflow. The ideal situation, from a business firm's point of view, would be for all customers to pay for the products or services they buy immediately. However, the realities of the marketplace demand that credit be extended.[3] Given that credit often must be extended, the business firm's goal is to encourage customers to pay off their accounts as quickly as possible. The firm might even offer customers a *discount* if they pay their bills early, say, within 10 days. This technique works and the firm's managers hope that the return they can earn by getting the cash early outweighs the amount lost through the discount.[4]

Another way to speed up cash inflows is to make use of computerized fund transfers wherever possible. An **electronic funds transfer** is the act of crediting one account and debiting another automatically by a computer system.

Electronic transfer is much faster than cheques, which can take over a week to mail and clear.

Take Note

Be wary of cost-cutting measures that hurt the business in the long term. For example, a drug company might boost profits now by cutting research and development spending (an expense). However, that action will rob the company of new products that would generate extra value later.

Another method of speeding cash collections is a lockbox system. A **lockbox** system allows customers to send cheques to a nearby post office box. The firm arranges for these funds to be deposited in a bank in or near the customer's city for electronic transfer to the receiving firm's account. Here's how a lockbox system works. A Montreal-based business that has customers nationwide rents post office boxes in major cities all around the country. The firm directs its customers to send payments for their bills to the post office box in the city nearest them. The firm arranges for a bank in each city to pick up the mail from the post office box at least once a day and to deposit any payments received in the firm's account at the bank. From that point on, the funds are immediately available for the firm's use, either from the individual banks directly or by having the banks electronically transfer the funds to the firm's bank in Montreal. By using the lockbox system, the firm can receive cash two to five days faster than if customers mailed all their payments to Montreal.[5]

Slowing Down Cash Outflows

Just as speeding up the flow of cash into the firm gives managers more time to earn a return on the cash, so does slowing down the flow of cash out of the firm. Either way, the idea is to increase the amount of time that the firm has possession of the cash. One obvious way to slow down cash outflows is to delay paying bills as long as possible. However, the firm must take great care not to overstep the bounds of good sense and fair play in applying this principle. Imagine what would happen if a firm did not pay its employees on time or delayed paying suppliers. Its business operations would suffer or it might not stay in business at all. Firms should not pay bills that are due at the end of the month on the first of the month, but neither should they take unfair advantage of creditors by making late payments. Stressful times often tempt companies into taking unfair advantage of their creditors. The following feature summarizes some of the effects of September 11.

---

[3]A quick example illustrates why businesses must grant credit: Suppose two firms in town both sold office supplies. One will let you, a business owner, order supplies over the phone any time you want and you are billed once a month. The other demands that you go to the store and pay cash each time you want to buy supplies. How long do you think the second store will be able to stay in business?

[4]This subject is discussed more fully in Chapter 19.

[5]Before implementing such a system, of course, the firm would have to evaluate whether the extra amount that could be earned on the funds collected two to five days early is greater than the cost of maintaining the lockbox system.

INTERNATIONAL PERSPECTIVES IN FINANCE 18-1

Grant Thornton

e destructive attacks of Septempter 11 left an enormous ark on what was an already uncertain economic vironment.

In striving to keep U.S. industry moving in these dis- ssing times, business leaders need to swiftly evaluate their cumstances in light of the increased anxiety brought about those events.

Although the survey discussed in this article reflects atti- des prior to the disruptive events, the management sponses to a slowing economy outlined are seen as even ore critical for consumer and industrial products (CIP) mpanies to consider in today's business climate.

As the most recent Grant Thornton Business Owners uncil (BOC) Survey confirms, CIP companies had been eling the economic slowdown dramatically.

"CIP industry executives have concerns about their sinesses, and those concerns are causing them to focus ore of their attention on working capital and how to prove it," says John Desmond, partner-in-charge of Grant ornton's Long Island, N.Y., office.

As a result, they're managing their businesses to come ough the downturn as intact as possible. More than half ported paying more heed to cash management, and one- rd reported refinancing debt while interest rates are low, cording to Grant Thornton's latest BOC poll.

"CIP companies typically are the first to be affected by economic decline," says Terry Phipps, a management nsulting services senior manager with Grant Thornton's nsas City, Mo., office. "They're also the first to come out. rviving the downturn is one thing, but the key is getting epared for the growth cycle that will inevitably follow."

Cash management and increased working capital are portant components of survival and long-term success, smond and Phipps agree.

"One strategy that was pointed out in the BOC Survey sponses is to improve relationships with banks," says smond.

"Sit down with the banker and find out what's available enhance cash flow. Also, many companies are keeping nks well informed so there won't be any surprises. It's a fensive move so bankers will continue to work with them oughout the hard times."

At the same time, CIP companies should be taking very g, hard looks at their inventory management, accounts yable, and accounts receivable procedures.

"Shortening the cash collection cycle, moving inventory, d extending payment terms a few days could easily generate an additional $1 million or $2 million in cash flow for a $50 million company," says Phipps.

Some fairly easy steps he recommends are:

Make sure billings are sent out correctly the first time, to avoid giving cash-strapped customers a reason to delay payment.

Evaluate procuring and sourcing materials. If suppliers don't ship on time or have frequent backorders, the lowest-priced goods may not come at the lowest cost.

Compare current and historical performance measures to determine whether inventory is being properly managed. Review where inventory decisions are being made. The fact that manufacturers can keep equipment running and people busy doesn't justify their making a warehouse full of products that can't be sold.

Work with financial institutions to reduce fees and take advantage of sweep, zero-balance and cash concentration accounts, and lockboxes as appropriate.

Examine order fulfillment from the time orders come in until the time customers pay their bills. Customer satisfaction and retention are more critical than ever, and internal efficiencies and improvements help create long-term satisfied customers.

Adopt a more efficient maintenance program based on hours of use rather than date since last services. Be sure good parts aren't being replaced simply for the sake of convenience.

Companies might also want to consider using the extra time a slow economy often brings by considering major improvement initiatives.

"Look at the plant layout to see if it's as efficient as it can be," Phipps says. "Information technology takes some major expenditures, but it's something everyone should certainly be considering. The first step is implementing an enterprise resource planning system, even if some modules are deferred until the economy is more robust."

Finally, Desmond says, CIP owners and chief executive officers are working harder and staying more attuned to customers as they attempt to continue the path to prosperity.

"That's not a new strategy, but it wasn't as necessary in the last decade," he says. "This economy was pretty good for eight or 10 years, and one tends to forget the ugly times. It's time to remember."

Source: www.grantthornton.ca/corporate/conveyor_fall_01.pdf. Reprinted with permission of Grant Thornton's Conveyor, Vol. 12 No. 4, Fall 2001.

SUMMARY

18-1 List three factors that affect a company's desired minimum cash balance.

Having a minimum balance ensures that enough money is maintained in the cash account to make payments when needed. The base level to be maintained is affected by: (1) how quickly and inexpensively the firm can raise cash when needed, (2) how accurately the firm can predict cash needs, and (3) how much extra the firm wants to keep in the cash account for emergencies.

18-2 List three factors that affect a company's maximum cash balance.

Having a maximum balance ensures that firms limit the cash balance so that the firms invest and earn a return on as much cash as possible. The maximum amount to be maintained is affected by three factors: (1) available investment opportunities, (2) expected returns from these opportunities, and (3) the transaction costs of withdrawing the cash and making the investments.

18-3 Discuss how the Miller–Orr model solves for a target optimal cash balance.

The Miller–Orr model recognizes that a firm's cash balance might fluctuate up and down in an irregular fashion over time. The model solves for an optimal target cash balance about which the cash balance fluctuates until it reaches an upper or lower limit. If the upper limit is reached, short-term investment securities are bought, bringing the cash balance down to the target again. If the lower limit is reached, short-term investment securities are sold, bringing the cash balance up to the target.

18-4 Explain the purpose of a cash budget.

Managers use a cash budget to estimate detailed cash needs for future periods. Cash budgets are necessary because *pro forma* income statements and balance sheets do not indicate the actual flow of cash in and out of the firm. A monthly cash budget shows detailed cash flows from month to month throughout the year and how much over or short the firm's cash account will be at the end of each month. By using a cash budget, managers can estimate when it will be necessary to obtain short-term loans from their bank.

18-5 Explain how firms manage their cash inflows and outflows to maximize value.

The four objectives of cash management are to increase the flow of cash into the business, to decrease the flow of cash out of the business, to receive cash more quickly, and to pay cash out more slowly.

Ways to increase the flow of cash into the firm include selling more products, serving more customers, and increasing the return earned by the firm's assets. Ways to reduce the flow of cash out of the business include cutting costs and decreasing the degree of risk in the business. Ways to speed up the flow of cash into the business include helping customers pay off their credit accounts more quickly and using electronic funds transfer or lockbox techniques. Ways to slow down the flow of cash out of the firm include taking advantage of credit terms whenever possible.

EQUATIONS INTRODUCED IN THIS CHAPTER

Equation 18-1: Formula for Miller–Orr Model Target Cash Balance

$$Z = \sqrt[3]{\frac{3 \times TC \times V}{4 \times r}} + L$$

where

TC = Transaction cost of buying or selling short-term investment securities
V = Variance of net daily cash flows
r = Daily rate of return on short-term investment securities
L = Lower limit to be maintained in the cash account

Equation 18-2: Formula for the Upper Limit in the Miller–Orr Model

$$H = 3Z - 2L$$

where

Z = Target cash balance
L = Lower limit to be maintained in the cash account

SELF-TEST

ST-1. Assume that short-term investment securities are yielding 5 percent and it costs a firm \$20 each time it buys or sells investment securities. The variance of the firm's daily net cash flows has been found to be \$20,000. Management wants to keep at least \$1,000 in the cash account for emergencies. Given these conditions, what is the firm's target cash balance?

ST-2. What is the maximum amount that the firm in question ST-1 will let accumulate in its cash account before investing excess cash in marketable securities?

ST-3. Continuing with the firm in ST-1 and ST-2, how much will the firm invest in marketable securities if the upper limit in ST-2 is reached?

ST-4. Assume a company has \$1,000 in its cash account at the beginning of a month and short-term loan balances of \$3,500. If the company experiences a \$14,000 net cash inflow during the month and its desired target cash balance is \$3,000, how much of the outstanding loans can be paid off this month?

REVIEW QUESTIONS

1. What are the primary reasons that companies hold cash?
2. Explain the factors affecting the choice of a minimum cash balance amount.
3. What are the negative consequences of a company holding too much cash?
4. Explain the factors affecting the choice of a maximum cash balance amount.
5. What is the difference between *pro forma* financial statements and a cash budget? Explain why *pro forma* financial statements are not used to forecast cash needs.
6. What are the benefits of "collecting early" and how do companies attempt to do this?
7. What are the benefits of "paying late" (but not too late) and how do companies attempt to do this?
8. Refer to the Bulldog Batteries Company's cash budget in Table 18-7. Explain why the company would probably not issue \$1 million worth of new common shares in January to avoid all short-term borrowing during the year.

PROBLEMS

18-1. Your company wants to have a minimum cash balance of \$3,000 and an upper-limit cash balance equal to \$9,000. What would be your target cash balance? ◀ Miller–Orr Model

Miller–Orr Model ▶

18-2. Selena Rogers, the financial analyst of Keep-Fit Health Equipment Company, has a short-term investment yield of 3 percent and transaction cost of $40 per transaction. The cash inflows and outflows have traditionally been irregular with a variance of daily net cash flows equal to $39,000. Management of the company wants a minimum cash balance of $2,200. Calculate:

a. The target cash balance

b. The upper limit of cash balance

Miller–Orr Model ▶

18-3. Will Clark, the financial analyst of Get-Fit Health Equipment Company, a competitor of Keep-Fit of problem 18-2, has the same yield and transaction cost. However, the variance of daily net cash flows is equal to $52,000. Management of the company wants a minimum cash balance of $3,900. Calculate:

a. The target cash balance

b. The upper limit of cash balance

Miller–Orr Model ▶

18-4. Nire Ltd. has determined that its short-term investments are yielding 5 percent annually and the cost is $25 each time it buys and sells securities. Nire's total assets amount to $150,000, its variance of net daily cash flows is estimated to be $65,580, and it wants to keep a minimum 10 percent of total assets in a cash account. What is the firm's target cash balance according to the Miller–Orr model?

Miller–Orr Model ▶

18-5. Using the information in problem 18-4, find Nire's upper limit for the cash account according to the Miller–Orr model.

Cash Inflows ▶

Excel

18-6. Marion Crane, a financial analyst of Lifelong Appliances Company, is trying to develop a cash budget for each month of 2004. The sales are expected to occur as follows:

Month	Sales (in thousands of dollars)
Nov 2003 (reference)	$131
Dec 2003 (reference)	129
Jan 2004	126
Feb 2004	133
Mar 2004	139
Apr 2004	143
May 2004	191
Jun 2004	226
Jul 2004	242
Aug 2004	224
Sep 2004	184
Oct 2004	173
Nov 2004	166
Dec 2004	143
Jan 2005 (reference)	136
Feb 2005 (reference)	139

Assume all of Lifelong's sales are on credit, so no cash is received immediately when a sale is made. It is expected that 20 percent of Lifelong's customers will pay off their accounts in the month of sale, 70 percent will pay off their accounts in the month following the sale, and the remaining 10 percent of the customers will pay off their accounts in the second month following the sale. Given this payment pattern, help Marion to calculate Lifelong's actual monthly cash collections throughout 2004.

18-7. Use the same sales data given in problem 18-6. To improve the cash collections, Marion has decided to undertake stricter credit terms. With this change she expects that 40 percent of Lifelong's customers will pay off their accounts in the month of sale, 55 percent will pay off their accounts in the month following the sale, and the remaining 5 percent of the customers will pay off their accounts in the second month following the sale. Given this payment pattern, what would be Lifelong's actual monthly cash collections throughout 2004?

◀ Cash Inflows

18-8. The following is an estimate of sales revenues for 2004 for Kcir, Inc.

◀ Cash Inflows

Excel

	Sales
January	$17,956
February	16,523
March	18,366
April	19,500
May	22,890
June	22,980
July	23,157
August	23,000
September	21,650
October	19,250
November	18,920
December	19,069

All sales are made on credit. History shows that 45 percent of customers will pay off their accounts in the month the purchase is made, 40 percent of customers will pay off their accounts the month following the purchase month, and the remaining 15 percent will pay off their accounts in the second month following the purchase month. Find the cash collections for:

a. March

b. June

c. September

18-9. Kcir, Inc. has estimated expenses as follows (use the table in Problem 18-8 for sales figures needed to calculate expenses).

◀ Cash Outflows

Excel

- General and administrative: $2,000/month
- Material purchases: 5 percent of sales (paid the month following the purchase)
- Interest expense: $750/year (paid in monthly installments)
- Income tax: $4,500/year (paid in quarterly installments at end of quarter)

Find the cash outflows for the following months.

a. February

b. June

c. November

18-10. Use the same sales data given in problem 18-6. Assume that Lifelong's cost of materials is 30 percent of sales. Appliances that are expected to be sold in February will be manufactured one month ahead of time in January, and all the materials needed for January's production schedule will be ordered one month ahead of time in December. This schedule repeats for each month of the year. Lifelong makes all of its purchases on credit and pays for them in cash during the month following the purchase. That is, December's purchase orders are paid for in January, and so on. Assume Lifelong's remaining cash outflows are all direct expenses paid for in the month incurred as follows:

◀ Challenge Problem

Excel

- Production expenses other than purchases are equal to 80 percent of purchases.
- Sales and marketing expenses are 19 percent of sales each month.
- General and administrative expenses are $11,000 each month.
- Interest expense is expected to be $31,000 for the year. Assume it will be paid all at once in December 2004.
- Lifelong's income tax bill for 2004 is expected to be $100,000. The bill will be paid in four equal installments in April, June, September, and December.
- Two semiannual dividends of $50,000 each are expected to be declared in 2004. These will be paid in June and December.

Calculate Lifelong's total cash outflows, including the preceding expenses and payments for materials purchases.

Cash Outflows ▶

Excel

18-11. Use the same data given in problem 18-10, except for the payment schedule for materials purchased. Now assume that Lifelong pays for the material purchased in the following manner: 30 percent is paid in cash in the month of purchase and the remaining 70 percent is paid in cash during the month following the purchase. That is, 30 percent of December's purchase orders are paid for in December and the balance of 70 percent is paid in January, and so on. With this change, calculate Lifelong's total cash outflows, including the preceding expenses, dividends, and payments for materials purchases.

Comprehensive Problem ▶

Excel

18-12. Rose Sayer, a financial analyst of Fit-and-Forget Fittings Company, is trying to develop a cash budget for each month of 2004. The sales are expected to occur as follows:

Month	Sales (in thousands of dollars)
Nov 2003 (reference)	$2,266
Dec 2003 (reference)	2,230
Jan 2004	2,116
Feb 2004	2,300
Mar 2004	2,402
Apr 2004	2,420
May 2004	3,390
Jun 2004	3,909
Jul 2004	4,164
Aug 2004	3,933
Sep 2004	3,163
Oct 2004	2,912
Nov 2004	2,886
Dec 2004	2,424
Jan 2005 (reference)	2,353
Feb 2005 (reference)	2,442

Assume that all of Fit-and-Forget's sales are on credit, so no cash is received immediately when a sale is made. It is expected that 30 percent of Fit-and-Forget's customers will pay off their accounts in the month of sales, 65 percent will pay off their accounts in the month following the sale, and the remaining 5 percent of the customers will pay off their accounts in the second month following the sale.

Assume that Fit-and-Forget's cost of materials is 20 percent of sales. Fit-and-Forget manufactures fittings expected to be sold in February one month ahead of time, in January. They order all the materials they need for January's production schedule one month ahead of time, in December. This schedule repeats for each month of the year. Fit-and-Forget makes all purchases on credit and pays for the material purchased in the following manner: 20 percent is paid in cash in the month of ordering and the balance of 80 percent is paid in cash during the month following the purchase. That is, 20 percent of December's purchase orders are paid for in December and the balance of 80 percent is paid in January, and so on. Assume Fit-and-Forget's remaining cash outflows are all direct expenses paid for in the month incurred as follows:

- Production expenses other than purchases are equal to 14 percent of purchases.
- Sales and marketing expenses are 16 percent of sales each month.
- General and administrative expenses are $180,000 each month.
- Interest expense is expected to be $500,000 for the year. Assume it will be paid all at once in December 2004.
- Fit-and-Forget's income tax bill for 2004 is expected to be $1,600,000. The bill will be paid in four equal installments in April, June, September, and December.
- Two semiannual dividends of $855,000 each are expected to be declared in 2004. These will be paid in June and December.

Assume a cash balance of $1,133,000 at the beginning of January, a desired target cash balance of $1,110,000, and short-term loans of $50,000 outstanding at the beginning of the month. Calculate total cash inflows, total cash outflows, net cash gain (loss), cash flow summary, and external financing (if any) summary in the same format as Table 18-7.

18-13. The workers at NorthTome Inc. were complaining about several factors, including the lack of benefits, late payments, and the lack of a sufficient wage. Management is expecting a strike very soon, where management will be forced to pay contract workers to replace the striking ones. The contract workers will need to be paid on a daily basis if the strike comes about. This differs from a bi-weekly payment plan for the staff employees. However, because the contract workers will not be considered employees, the company will not have to pay the employer's portion of Employment Insurance and the Canada Pension Plan. The interest rate for borrowing and lending money is currently 5 percent. The CPP employee deduction rate is 4.95 percent and the EI employee deduction rate is 2.1 percent. These rates are deducted from each employee's pay (certain upper and lower limits have been relaxed for this question) and are given to the government each quarter. Along with the employees' deductions, NorthTome Inc. must pay an equal amount of CPP and 1.4 times the EI deduction. The company is open 7 days a week. ◀ Comprehensive Problem

Excel

a. How does the mere possibility of a strike potentially change the cash budget?

b. Assuming a strike does occur, how will the new cash budget be affected?

c. Would NorthTome Inc. suffer much from a strike? Contrast the short-run with the long-run effects.

18-14. Which of these companies would you argue has the greatest variance of net daily cash flows? Why? ◀ Variance of Cash Flows

a. MultiBig Corp. is a well-established company with several decades of experience in basic food distribution. Its target market is major grocery stores throughout Canada. Since each supplier of MultiBig Corp. has had a strong business relationship with the food giant for several decades, the suppliers tend to provide very loose payment plans.

b. Quick and Easy Corp. is a subsidiary of its parent company, PetroClean. It prepares and produces cleaning products. Quick and Easy has several suppliers and clients, but its major supplier is Chemics (another subsidiary of PetroClean) and its major client is the parent company itself. Quick and Easy has been in operation for 3 months.

Miller–Orr Model ▶

Excel

18-15. Mark Simon is in charge of the company's cash flow. He uses the Miller-Orr model to set his target cash level. The current cost of cash is 4 percent and the current short-term investment rate is 2.5 percent. Mark has been using BigBank to transfer cash back and forth, from the company's short-term investment account and its business chequing account. The average cost of transaction has been about \$30. However, after further investigation, Mark has discovered that CompuBank is offering a very similar service, but the transaction fees would only average \$20 a transaction.

a. If Mark went to CompuBank, how would this change the company's target cash budget?

b. Assume that Mark needs X amount of dollars. Further, assume that he could take out cash from the short-term investment account or he could borrow the money from the line of credit at 4 percent. (Assume daily compounding.) At what amount of money would Mark be indifferent between taking cash out of the short-term investments or the line of credit? (Assume that new money equal to X will be coming in 5 days.)

Comprehensive Problem ▶

18-16. NoRun, Inc. is a company that has one major client, the government. NoRun's job is to fix roads and bridges for automobiles nationwide. NoRun invests large sums of cash in equipment and materials. The government is supposed to pay NoRun bi-monthly. In addition to materials and equipment, NoRun's other major expenses are salaries.

a. What is NoRun's major risk?

b. If salaries are not paid, employees will not work. If suppliers are not paid, suppliers will not provide additional materials. Can you develop a situation where a downward spiral of negative effects can occur?

c. Can you think of any possible solutions for NoRun?

Managing Cash Flow ▶

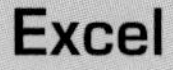

18-17. For every dollar that Maxcor Inc. needs but does not have available, it will cost 4 percent annually (assume daily compounding). Suppliers are paid quickly and clients are asked to pay within 30 days. Clients always pay just on time. Maxcor has forecasts of spending \$40,000 on interest payments this year if things do not change. Maxcor has a fixed amount of cash outstanding, \$1 million dollars at all times, and it knows that it can reduce this amount to \$500,000 by simply paying its suppliers on time instead of earlier. As for the other half, Maxcor has asked for your help.

a. Can you develop some strategies in order for Maxcor to quicken its cash receipts?

b. Assuming that Maxcor offers a 2 percent discount for payments paid before 10 days, would this be advantageous to solving Maxcor's problem?

c. Which idea do you like the most?

ANSWERS TO SELF-TEST

ST-1. Per Equation 18-1, the firm's target cash balance per the Miller–Orr model is

$$Z = \sqrt[3]{\frac{3 \times 20 \times \$20{,}000}{4 \times (0.05/365)}} + \$1{,}000$$
$$= \sqrt[3]{\frac{\$1{,}200{,}000}{0.000547945}} + \$1{,}000$$
$$= \$1{,}299 + \$1{,}000$$
$$= \$2{,}299$$

ST-2. Per Equation 18-2, the upper limit will be

$$H = (3 \times \$2{,}299) - (2 \times \$1{,}000)$$
$$= \$6{,}897 - \$2{,}000$$
$$= \$4{,}897$$

ST-3. If the upper limit is reached, the firm will invest the amount necessary to bring the cash balance back down to the target balance level. This amount is

$$\$4{,}897 - \$2{,}299 = \$2{,}598$$

ST-4. A summary of the company's cash flows and external financing is shown next:

1. Cash balance at the start of the month	$ 1,000
2. Net cash gain (loss) during month	14,000
3. Cash balance at the end of the month before financing	15,000
4. Minimum cash balance desired	3,000
5. Surplus cash (deficit) (line 3 – line 4)	12,000
External Financing Summary	
6. External financing balance at the start of the month	$ 3,500
7. New financing required (negative amount on line 5)	0
8. Financing repayments (the entire loan balance)	3,500
9. External financing balance at the end of the month	0
10. Cash balance at the end of the month after financing (Balance on line 3 + new financing on line 7 – repayments on line 8)	$11,500

As shown on line 8 of the preceding summary, the company can pay off the entire $3,500 short-term loan balance this month.

19

Accounts Receivable and Inventory

Chapter Objectives

After reading this chapter, you should be able to:

19-1 **Describe** how the management of accounts receivable and inventory affect profitability and liquidity.

19-2 **Describe** a three-step process used to find the optimal level of accounts receivable and inventory.

19-3 **Name** and **describe** two different inventory management approaches.

19-4 **Explain** five different characteristics evaluated by a credit policy.

19-5 **Describe** seven different approaches to dealing with overdue accounts.

"Everybody likes a kidder, but nobody lends him money."

—Arthur Miller

When Collections Become Too Aggressive

It was rumoured that a woman received a bill for $0.00 from a local telephone company, for an account that had been cancelled. Thinking that it was an error, she would throw the bills away, only to receive several subsequent bills for the same amount, including interest on the $0.00 amount. Even after calling the telephone company several times, the bills kept coming in, each demanding the $0.00 she owed them. She finally issued a cheque for $0.00.

Source: Anonymous.

Chapter Overview

A key component of working capital policy is managing accounts receivable and inventory. In this chapter, we see that accounts receivable and inventory are necessary investments that affect a firm's profitability and liquidity. Then we investigate how financial managers determine the optimal level of these current assets. Finally, we examine inventory management techniques and collection policies.

This man confronts the daily challenges faced by companies that extend trade credit to customers.
Source: From *The Wall Street Journal*—Permission, Cartoon Features Syndicate.

Why Firms Accumulate Accounts Receivable and Inventory

As we saw in Chapter 4, accounts receivable represent money that customers owe to the firm because they have purchased goods or services on credit. Accounts receivable, therefore, are assets that have value.[1] Nonetheless, any time a firm accumulates accounts receivable, it suffers opportunity costs because it is unable to invest or otherwise use the money owed until customers pay. A firm may also incur a direct cost when it grants credit because some customers may not pay their bills at all. The ideal situation, from a firm's point of view, is to have customers pay cash at the time of the purchase.[2]

---

[1]In fact, firms sometimes sell their customers' "IOUs" to other businesses for cash. This process, known as *factoring* accounts receivable, is discussed later in this chapter.

[2]Individuals are the same way. For example, if you sell your car to another student, which would you prefer: to be paid in cash at the time of sale or to let the buyer pay you a little bit each month?

In the real world, of course, it is unrealistic to expect customers always to pay cash for products and services. Who would buy lumber from a firm that insisted all its customers pay cash if other lumber companies offered credit? Like it or not, for most firms, granting credit is an essential business practice. The real question managers must answer is, how much credit should the firm grant and to whom? Offering more credit enhances sales but also increases costs. At some point the cost of granting credit outweighs the benefits. Financial managers must manage accounts receivable carefully to make sure this asset adds to, rather than detracts from, a firm's value.

The situation with inventory is similar. Inventory is costly to accumulate and maintain, so firms generally want to hold as few products in inventory as possible. For most firms, however, operating without any inventory is impractical—can you imagine a grocery store with no food on display? Most firms that sell products accumulate some inventory. Financial managers must find the best level of inventory. They do this by weighing the risk of losing sales due to unavailable products against the cost savings produced by reducing inventory.

Accounts receivable and inventory are investments because both tie up funds and have opportunity costs, but both can add to the firm's value. Be careful not to be confused by the term *investment*. Investment usually implies something desirable—a long-term venture specifically planned and implemented for profit. Instead, accounts receivable and inventory may be viewed as necessary evils. Most firms need accounts receivable and inventory to do business, but less is generally better. Managing accounts receivable and inventory, then, ought to be done with an eye toward reducing these assets to the lowest level possible consistent with the firm's goal of maximizing value. An Ontario fencing company felt the sting of poor accounts receivable management when they went bankrupt after 10 years of operations from one overdue account that became uncollectible. It accounted for 70 percent of the receivable account.

How Accounts Receivable and Inventory Affect Profitability and Liquidity

Holding different levels of accounts receivable and inventory can affect a company's profitability and liquidity. To illustrate, consider Firms A and B in Table 19-1, on page 614. Firm A sells all its products for cash and keeps no inventory. Firm B gives its customers 30 days to pay and maintains a large product inventory. Assuming every other factor is equal, including the firms' capital structures, Firm A can earn more than twice the return on its shareholders' equity as Firm B simply by eliminating accounts receivable and inventory (and any associated current liabilities and long-term debt).

The comparison between Firms A and B in Table 19-1 illustrates the liquidity, profitability, and risk of each firm. Observe that although Firm A is more *profitable* than Firm B as measured by return on equity (14.3 percent versus 7.1 percent), it is much less *liquid,* as measured by the current ratio[3]

---

[3]Current Ratio $= \dfrac{\text{Current Assets}}{\text{Current Liabilities}}$

Table 19-1 Comparison of Accounts Receivable and Inventory Policies, Selected Financial Data for Firms A and B (In 000s)

	Firm A	Firm B
Data as of December 31	Sells Products for Cash and Holds No Inventory	Sells Products for Credit and Accumulates Inventory
Cash	$ 100	$ 100
Accounts Receivable	0	200
Inventory	0	400
Capital Assets	500	500
Total Assets	$ 600	$1,200
Current Liabilities	$ 50	$ 100
Long-Term Debt	200	400
Shareholders' Equity	350	700
Total Liabilities and Equity	$ 600	$1,200
Sales	$2,433	$2,433
Expenses	2,383	2,383
Net Income for the Year	$ 50	$ 50
Current Ratio	2.0	7.0
Quick Ratio	2.0	3.0
Return on Equity	14.3%	7.1%

(2.0 versus 7.0). If the managers of Firm A needed to raise more than $100,000 cash in a hurry, they would have no recourse but to seek outside financing or sell some of their capital assets. The managers of Firm B, however, could collect cash from customers, draw down inventory, or both.

However, Firm B's business practice of accumulating inventory adds risk to the firm if the inventory is hard to liquidate. Some inventory may not be sold, or it may be sold for a low value. Note how, when using the quick ratio[4] to compare firm liquidity, we see that Firm A's quick ratio is the same as its current ratio (2.0), but Firm B's quick ratio is 3.0 compared with its current ratio of 7.0. When using the quick ratio, then, we see that Firm A is less liquid than Firm B (2.0 versus 3.0) but how much less depends on the liquidity of the inventory.

Most firms accumulate some accounts receivable and inventory. Because these current assets can affect the profitability and liquidity of the firm, financial managers try to find the amounts of both assets that maximize firm value. In the following section, we examine how to find the optimal level of these current assets.

FINDING OPTIMAL LEVELS OF ACCOUNTS RECEIVABLE AND INVENTORY

The conclusions drawn from Table 19-1 assumed that sales for both firms were $2,433,000. This may not be a reasonable assumption. Firm B may have

[4] $\text{Quick Ratio} = \dfrac{\text{Current Assets Less Inventory}}{\text{Current Liabilities}}$

greater sales than Firm A because it grants credit and has inventory immediately available for purchase. Depending on how well customers respond to Firm B's decision to grant credit and maintain inventory, the resulting increase in sales and net income might boost Firm B's return on equity beyond that of Firm A.

However, bad debts and inventory costs are likely to drive up Firm B's expenses, possibly causing its net income to fall. The net result could be a *decrease* in Firm B's return on equity.

Conflicting forces make it more difficult to assess the situation. For accounts receivable, the forces are sales that increase as more generous credit terms are offered *versus* costs that increase with collections, bad debts, and opportunity costs from forgone investments. For inventory, the conflicting forces are sales that increase as more products are made available *versus* storage costs that increase as more inventory is accumulated.

In the following sections, we discuss how to find a balance between these conflicting forces in order to determine the optimal levels of accounts receivable and inventory.

The Optimal Level of Accounts Receivable

To find the best level of accounts receivable, financial managers must review the firm's credit policies, any proposed changes in those policies, and the incremental cash flows of each proposed credit policy. We must then compute the net present value of each policy.

Credit Policy A firm's credit terms and credit standards make up the firm's **credit policy**. Remember, accounts receivable are created by customers taking advantage of the firm's credit terms. These terms generally offer a discount to credit customers who pay off their accounts within a short time and they specify a maximum number of days that credit customers have to pay off the total amount of their accounts. An example of such terms is "2/10, n30." This means that credit customers will receive a 2 percent discount if they pay off their accounts within 10 days of the invoice date and the full net amount is due within 30 days if the discount is not taken.

For example, suppose you purchase $1,000 worth of camping supplies on credit July 1. If you pay the bill before July 11, you receive a 2 percent discount and the equipment will only cost you $980. If you pay the bill between July 11 and July 31, you will owe the full amount—$1,000. The bill is past due if you do not pay it by July 31.

Some firms offer credit without a discount feature, simply giving their customers so many days to pay. An example would be "n90"—net 90, pay the invoice amount within 90 days.

Individual customers receive credit from the firm if they meet the firm's **credit standards** for character, payment history, and so on.[5] Taken together, the credit terms and credit standards constitute the firm's credit policy.

A firm that wishes to change its level of accounts receivable does so by changing its credit policy. *Relaxing* the credit policy—by adopting less stringent credit standards or extending the net due period—will tend to cause accounts receivable to increase. *Tightening* the credit policy—by adopting

Take Note

In real life, the firm's credit policy may be limited by marketplace constraints. A new, small firm attempting to sell to large, well-established customers may have to offer credit terms that match those of competitors in the industry.

[5]We will discuss credit standards more fully later in this chapter.

more stringent credit standards or shortening the net due period—will tend to cause accounts receivable to decrease. The discount percent or time period could also be changed. This may either increase or decrease accounts receivable, depending on the reaction of customers to competing influences. Table 19-2 summarizes the effects of tightening credit policy on accounts receivable.

Table 19-2 The Effects of Tightening Credit Policy

Action	Effect on Accounts Receivable
Raise standards for granting credit	Fewer credit customers Fewer people owing money to the firm at any given time Accounts receivable goes down
Shorten net due period	Accounts paid off sooner Less money owed to the firm at any given time Accounts receivable goes down
Reduce discount percent	Fewer credit customers, *but* Some customers who previously took discount now do not Net effect on accounts receivable depends on whether the number of customers lost will be more than the number of those now forgoing the discount and paying the higher net amount
Shorten discount period	Same as above; some credit customers will leave, others will forgo the discount and pay the higher net amount. Net effect on accounts receivable is indeterminate

Analyzing Accounts Receivable Levels To decide what level of accounts receivable is best for the firm, we follow this three-step process:

1. Develop *pro forma* financial statements for each credit policy under consideration.
2. Use the *pro forma* financial statements to estimate the incremental cash flows of the proposed credit policy and compare them to the current policy cash flows.
3. Use the incremental cash flows and calculate the net present value (NPV) of each policy change proposal. Select the credit policy with the highest NPV.

To demonstrate how the three-step credit policy evaluation works, let's analyze a proposed credit policy for a fictional firm, Bulldog Batteries. Assume Bulldog Batteries currently offers credit terms of 2/10, n30, and Jackie Russell, the vice-president for marketing, thinks the terms should be changed to 2/10, n40. Doing so, she says, will result in a 10 percent increase in sales but only a small increase in bad debts. Should Bulldog make the change?

For the sake of simplicity, we make the following additional assumptions:

- Ms. Russell is correct that sales will increase by 10 percent if the new credit policy is implemented.
- Cost of goods sold and other operating expenses on the firm's income statement, and all current accounts on the balance sheet, will vary directly with sales. So each of these accounts will increase by 10 percent with the change in credit policy.

- All of Bulldog's sales are made on credit.

Suppose further that Ms. Russell produced the following data on Bulldog's customers' historical payment patterns:

- 45 percent of Bulldog's customers take advantage of the discount and pay off their accounts in 10 days.
- 53 percent of Bulldog's customers forgo the discount but pay off their accounts in 30 days.
- The remaining 2 percent of Bulldog's customers pay off their accounts in 100 days.[6]

Ms. Russell expects that under the new credit policy:

- 45 percent of Bulldog's customers will still take advantage of the discount and pay off their accounts in 10 days.
- 52 percent of Bulldog's customers will forgo the discount and pay off their accounts in 40 days.
- 3 percent of Bulldog's customers will pay off their accounts in 100 days.

With this information, we calculate the weighted average of the customers' payment periods (average collection period, or ACP) under the old and new credit policies. We weight the averages for each scenario by multiplying the percentage of customers who pay times the number of days they take to pay. Then we total each scenario result, as follows:

Under the old credit policy:

$$\begin{aligned} \text{ACP} &= (0.45 \times 10 \text{ days}) + (0.53 \times 30 \text{ days}) + (0.02 \times 100 \text{ days}) \\ &= 22.4 \text{ days} \end{aligned}$$

Under the new credit policy:

$$\begin{aligned} \text{ACP} &= (0.45 \times 10 \text{ days}) + (0.52 \times 40 \text{ days}) + (0.03 \times 100 \text{ days}) \\ &= 28.3 \text{ days} \end{aligned}$$

Based on Ms. Russell's information, we know that under the current credit policy, bad debt expenses are 2 percent of sales; under the new policy, they will climb to 3 percent of sales. Bulldog's CFO has informed us that any increases in current assets resulting from the policy change will be financed from short-term notes at an interest rate of 6 percent. The CFO also tells us that the firm's effective tax rate is 40 percent and that the cost of capital is 10 percent. The long-term interest rate is 8 percent.

Step 1: Develop the *Pro Forma* Financial Statements.

The first step is to develop the *pro forma* financial statements that reflect the effects of the proposed credit policy change. We begin by reviewing the firm's current income statement and balance sheet and then we create new statements that incorporate the changes. The statements for Bulldog Batteries are shown in Figure 19-1. The left-hand column shows Bulldog's financial

---

[6]In real life, many of these customers will never pay off their accounts, creating bad debts. Assume here, however, that they do pay off their accounts eventually. If we do not make that assumption, our mathematical average will include a certain percentage of customers taking an infinite amount of time to pay. As a result, we get an infinite average collection period (ACP) and that will not provide usable information.

Figure 19-1
Bulldog Batteries Financial Statements
Figure 19-1 shows the *pro forma* financial statements for Bulldog Batteries with the current collection policy and with the proposed collection policy.

Income Statements

	With Old Credit Terms 2/10, n30	With New Credit Terms 2/10, n40	Remarks
Sales (all on credit)	$201,734	$221,907	10% increase assumed
Cost of Goods Sold	107,280	118,008	Increase in proportion with sales (10%
Gross Profit	94,454	103,899	
Bad Debt Expense	4,035	6,657	Old: 2% of sales New: 3% of sales
Other Operating Expenses	43,229	47,552	Increase in proportion with sales (10%
Operating Income	47,190	49,660	
Interest Expense	1,221	1,223	Notes Payable × 0.06 + LTD × 0.08
Before-Tax Income	45,969	48,467	
Income Taxes (tax rate = 40%)	18,388	19,387	
Net Income	$ 27,581	$ 29,080	

Balance Sheets as of December 31

	With Old Credit Terms 2/10, n30	With New Credit Terms 2/10, n40	Remarks
Assets			
Current Assets			
Cash and Marketable Securities	$ 65,313	$ 71,844	Increase in proportion with sales (10%)
Accounts Receivable	12,380	17,205	See Note 1
Inventory	21,453	23,598	Increase in proportion with sales (10%)
Total Current Assets	99,146	112,647	
Capital Assets	92,983	92,983	No change
Total Assets	$192,129	$205,630	
Liabilities and Equity			
Current Liabilities			
Accounts Payable	$ 26,186	$ 28,805	Increase in proportion with sales (10%)
Notes Payable	302	332	Increase in proportion with sales (10%)
Total Current Liabilities	26,488	29,137	
Long-Term Debt	15,034	15,034	No change
Total Liabilities	41,522	44,171	
Common Shares	67,100	67,100	No change
Retained Earnings	83,507	85,006	Old RE + 1,499 net income difference
Total Shareholders' Equity	150,607	152,106	
Total Liabilities and Equity	$192,129	$196,277	
Additional Funds Needed		9,353	See Notes 2 and 3
		$205,630	

Note 1: Accounts Receivable (AR) = Credit sales per day × ACP. Under the old credit policy: AR = ($201,734/365) × 22.4 $12,380. Under the new credit policy: AR = ($221,907/365) × 28.3 = $17,205

Note 2: $9,353 is the amount of additional financing needed (AFN) to balance the balance sheet. It is the amount that must be obtained from outside sources to undertake the proposed credit policy change. Therefore, $9,353 may be viewe as the net investment required at time zero for the project.

Note 3: If $9,353 is borrowed to make up for AFN, Bulldog will incur new interest charges. If included in the income sta ment, these interest charges will reduce the net income and retained earnings—throwing the balance sheet off balance again and changing the amount of AFN. If the problem is solved using an electronic spreadsheet, the financial statemen can be recast several times until the additional interest expense becomes negligible. Here, however, we will use the origi nal interest rate to simplify the calculations.

statements before the credit policy change, the middle column shows them after the change, and the right-hand column shows how the new figures were calculated, given our assumptions.

Step 2: Compute the Incremental Cash Flows.

Now it is time to compute the incremental cash flows that occur as a result of the credit policy change. Table 19-3 contains these cash flows. Table 19-3 shows that Bulldog's initial investment cash flow is $9,352 and its net incremental cash flows from t_1 through infinity are $1,499 per year.

Step 3: Compute the NPV of the Credit Policy Change.

Now that we have all the incremental cash flows, we can calculate the NPV of the proposed credit terms change. We learned in Chapter 10 that NPV is calculated by summing the present value (PV) of all a project's projected cash flows and then subtracting the amount of the initial investment.[7] In our example, we have a net incremental cash outflow (the initial investment) that occurs at time t_0 of $9,353 followed by net incremental cash inflows occurring from time t_1 through infinity of $1,499 per year. The PV of the $1,499 per year from time t_1 through infinity can be found using the formula in Chapter 8 for the present value of a perpetuity (PVP):

$$\text{PVP} = \text{PMT} \times \left(\frac{1}{k}\right)$$

where

PMT = Cash flow per period

k = Required rate of return

1. Net Incremental Cash Outflow at Time Zero (t_0)	
External Financing Required from the Projected Balance Sheet	$ 9,353
2. Incremental Cash Flows Occurring in the Future	
Incremental Cash Inflow	
Increase in Sales	$20,173
Incremental Cash Outflows	
Increase in Cost of Goods Sold	$10,728
Increase in Bad Debt Expenses	2,622
Increase in Other Operating Expenses	4,323
Increase in Interest Expense	2
Increase in Taxes	999
Total Incremental Cash Outflows	$18,674
Net Incremental Cash Flows Occurring from Time (t_1) through Infinity: $20,173 – $18,674 =	$ 1,499 per year

Table 19-3 Incremental Cash Flows Associated with Changing Bulldog Batteries' Credit Policy from 2/10, n30 to 2/10, n40

[7] See Equation 10-1a in Chapter 10.

According to our assumptions, Bulldog Batteries' cost of capital is 10 percent. Applying Equation 8-5, we find the PV of an endless stream of payments of \$1,499 discounted at 10 percent as follows:

$$\begin{aligned} \text{PVP} &= \text{PMT} \times \left(\frac{1}{k}\right) \\ &= \$1{,}499 \times \left(\frac{1}{0.10}\right) \\ &= \$14{,}990 \end{aligned}$$

Take Note

Remember that this analysis depends on the accuracy of our assumptions. In this case, we assumed that sales would increase 10 percent, bad debts would increase to 3 percent of sales, and customers would pay according to the pattern described. If these assumptions are invalid, the credit policy analysis will also be invalid.

We see that the present value of the \$1,499 perpetuity with a 10 percent required rate of return is \$14,990.

To complete the NPV calculation, we now need to subtract the \$9,353 net cash outflow that occurs at time t_0—the initial investment—from the present value of the \$14,990 perpetuity, as shown next:

$$\begin{aligned} \text{NPV} &= \$14{,}990 - \$9{,}353 \\ &= \$5{,}637 \end{aligned}$$

We find that the net present value of the credit policy change is \$5,637. Because the NPV is positive, the credit terms change proposal should be accepted. Doing so will increase the value of Bulldog Batteries by \$5,637.[8]

Any credit policy change proposal can be evaluated using this framework. Managers may try any number of discount amounts, discount periods, and net due periods until they discover the combination with the greatest NPV.

The Optimal Level of Inventory

Firms may be able to stimulate sales by maintaining more inventory, but they may drive up costs as well. The financial manager's task is to figure out what level of inventory produces the greatest benefit to the firm. Financial managers first estimate the costs that are associated with inventory.

The Costs of Maintaining Inventory The two main costs associated with inventory are carrying costs and ordering costs. *Carrying costs* are those costs associated with keeping inventory on hand—warehouse rent, insurance, security expenses, utility bills, and so on. Carrying costs are generally expressed in dollars per unit per year.

Ordering costs are those costs incurred each time an order for inventory materials is placed—clerical expense, telephone calls, management time, and

[8]Given all the information presented so far, we could also calculate the internal rate of return (IRR) of the credit terms proposal. We simply solve the PV of a perpetuity formula for k, which represents the IRR:

$$\text{k, or IRR} = \text{PMT/PVP}$$

In our example: $\text{IRR} = \$1{,}499/\$9{,}353 = 0.1603 \text{ or } 16.03\%$

Because 16.03 percent exceeds Bulldog's cost of capital of 10 percent, the credit terms change proposal should be accepted.

so on. Ordering costs tend to be fixed no matter what the size of the order, so they are generally expressed in dollars per order.

Although you would think financial managers would like to minimize these two costs, it is not so easy. Carrying costs tend to rise as the level of inventory rises, but ordering costs tend to fall as inventory rises (because less ordering is necessary). Firms that minimize carrying costs by keeping no inventory have to order materials every time they want to produce an item, so they actually maximize ordering costs. Likewise, firms that minimize ordering costs by ordering all materials at once have sky-high carrying costs.

Complicating the situation is the possibility that a larger stock of inventory might increase sales. More inventory on display means more opportunities to catch the customer's eye and more inventory on hand means fewer sales lost due to not having the correct size or model available. The fact that more inventory might translate into more sales means the lowest-cost level of inventory might not be the optimal level of inventory. To find the optimal level, managers have to balance the costs and benefits of various inventory levels.

Analyzing Inventory Levels To maximize the value created from the firm's investment in inventory, use a three-step process similar to the one used to find accounts receivable levels. First, generate *pro forma* income statements and balance sheets for each proposed inventory level. Second, observe the incremental cash flows that occur with the change. Third, compute the NPV of the incremental cash flows. The following example illustrates the three-step process.

Dealin' Dan, the owner of Cream Puff Used Cars, wants to determine the optimal number of cars to display on his lot. Dan knows that increasing the number of cars on display will probably cause sales to increase, but it would also increase his inventory carrying costs. Dan also knows that decreasing the number of cars on display will save him inventory costs but might also cost him sales. As a result, Dan is not sure how a change in his planned average inventory level from 32 cars to 48 cars will affect the value of his firm.

We will make the following assumptions about Cream Puff's financial condition:

1. Cream Puff's inventory ordering costs are $100 per order. (Each time Dealin' Dan takes action to obtain cars, whether from other dealers or from trade-ins, he incurs $100 in processing costs.)
2. Inventory carrying costs are $500 per car per year.
3. Because Dealin' Dan does not expect to keep cars on the lot more than a few weeks, he finances all the firm's inventory with short-term debt. The short-term interest rate available to Cream Puff is 6 percent.
4. Cream Puff pays $5,000, on average, for each car it purchases for resale. The firm's average selling price per car is $6,000.
5. Cream Puff displays, on average, about 32 cars on its lot. Sales occur regularly throughout the year and Dan expects to sell 200 cars this year.
6. Based on his business experience, Dan believes that the relationship between inventory and Cream Puff's car sales is direct, as shown in Figure 19-2. According to the graph, an increase in inventory from 32 to 48 cars should produce an increase in the number of cars sold per year from 200 to 232.

Figure 19-2
Cream Puff Used Cars Inventory versus Number of Cars Sold
Figure 19-2 shows the direct relationship between inventory and sales. As inventory increases, sales increase; as inventory decreases, sales decrease.

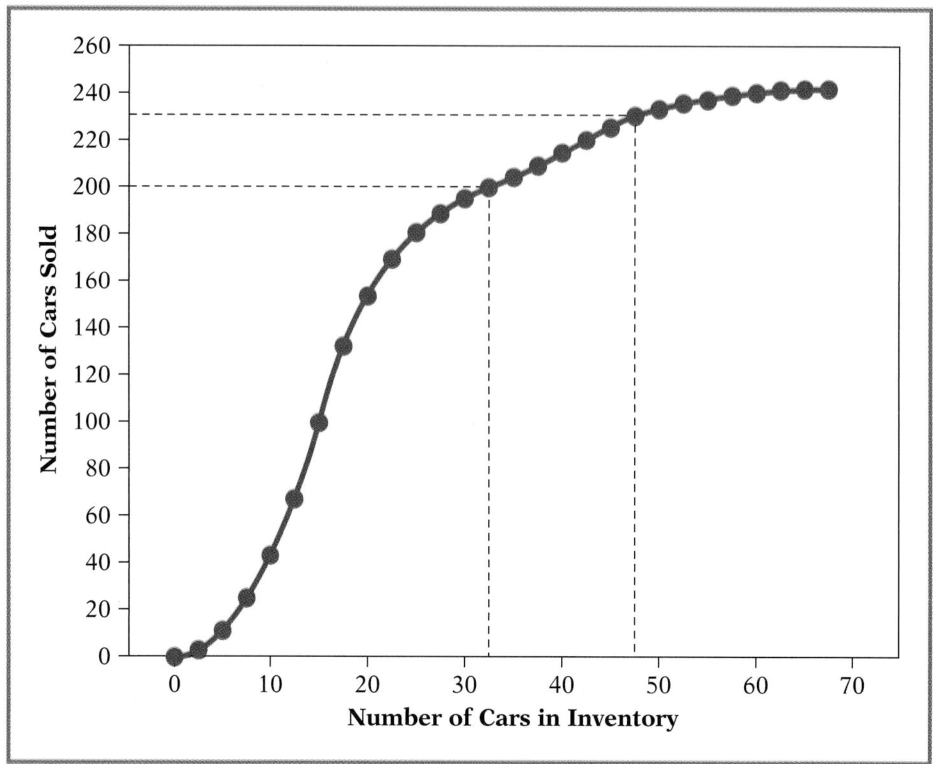

Dan uses the *economic order quantity* (EOQ) model to compute the number of cars to order from wholesale dealers when he replenishes his inventory.[9] According to the EOQ model, the optimal order size follows:

Formula for Economic Order Quantity Model

$$OQ = \sqrt{\frac{2 \times S \times OC}{CC}} \qquad (19\text{-}1)$$

where

OQ = Order quantity
S = Annual sales volume in units
OC = Ordering costs, per order
CC = Carrying costs, per unit per year

We may use the model to see what order size Cream Puff should have. We know that sales are 200 cars per year, ordering costs are $100 per order, and the carrying costs are $500 per year. According to Equation 19-1, the ordering quantity for Cream Puff is as follows:

[9]The EOQ model computes the inventory order size that, if certain other conditions are met, will minimize total inventory costs for the year. For a complete discussion of the model, refer to a production management text.

$$OQ = \sqrt{\frac{2 \times 200 \times 100}{500}}$$
$$= \sqrt{80}$$
$$= 8.94 \text{ (round to 9)}$$

We find that the ordering quantity that minimizes inventory costs is nine cars per order. Cream Puff's sales occur regularly, so Dan orders nine replacement cars at even intervals throughout the year. The sales forecast calls for 200 cars to be sold this year, so the number of orders for replacement cars will be 200/9 = 22.22 (round to 22).[10] Each order for replacement cars costs $100, so Cream Puff's total ordering cost—assuming 22 orders are made—is $2,200.

Under the current inventory policy, Cream Puff's average inventory level is 32 cars. Carrying costs are $500 per car per year, so total carrying costs are 32 × $500 = $16,000. We sum the ordering and carrying costs to find the total inventory costs for Cream Puff. The total costs are $2,200 + $16,000 = $18,200.

We assume in our example that other operating expenses on Cream Puff's income statement and all current accounts on the balance sheet vary directly with sales, so each of these accounts will increase (or decrease) proportionally with sales. We also assume that the interest rate on short-term debt is 6 percent and the rate on long-term debt is 8 percent. Finally, assume that Cream Puff's effective tax rate is 40 percent and the firm's cost of capital is 10 percent.

Now we are ready to apply the three-step process to determine the optimal level of inventory for Cream Puff Used Cars.

Step 1: Develop *Pro Forma* Financial Statements.

Let's see how Dealin' Dan's proposed inventory change from 32 cars to 48 cars will affect the business. The left-hand column in Figure 19-3 shows Cream Puff's projected 2005 income statement and balance sheet. It also shows selected financial ratios, given our assumptions, current inventory policy of 32 cars, and the total inventory costs of $18,200. The right-hand column contains revised statements and ratios assuming average inventory is raised to 48 cars. The remarks column explains how the various numbers were computed.

If Dealin' Dan's assumptions are correct, increasing the number of cars on display at the Cream Puff used car lot to 48 will produce a $192,000 increase in sales (32 extra cars). Inventory costs and other expenses will increase too, of course, but only by a total of $186,534, so profits should rise by $5,466. On the surface, it looks like Dan should go ahead with the inventory change, does it not? Perhaps, but let's see how the change will affect the value of Dan's firm by computing the incremental cash flows associated with the change and the NPV of those incremental cash flows.

Step 2: Compute the Incremental Cash Flows.

Drawing the necessary information from the *pro forma* statements shown in Figure 19-3, Table 19-4 lists the incremental cash flows of changing the average inventory level from 32 cars to 48 cars. See pages 624 and 625.

---

[10]Astute readers will note that, after rounding, 22 × 9 = 198. So Dealin' Dan will not actually order the exact number of cars he expects to sell this year. However, this small discrepancy will not materially affect our analysis.

Figure 19-3
Dealin' Dan's Cream Puff Used Cars Inventory Analysis
Figure 19-3 shows the *pro forma* financial statements with Cream Puff's current average inventory policy of 32 cars and with the new inventory policy of 48 cars

Income Statements

	Current Inventory Policy	New Inventory Policy	Remarks
Sales	$1,200,000	$1,392,000	32-car increase × $6,000 each
Cost of Goods Sold	1,000,000	1,160,000	32-car increase × $5,000 each
Gross Profit	200,000	232,000	
Inventory Costs	18,200	26,300	See Note 1
Other Operating Expenses	85,000	98,600	16% increase (same as sales)
Operating Income	96,800	107,100	
Interest Expense	11,040	12,230	CL × 0.06 + LTD × 0.08
Before-Tax Income	85,760	94,870	
Income Taxes (tax rate = 40%)	34,304	37,948	
Net Income	$ 51,456	$ 56,922	

Balance Sheets, as of December 31

	Current Inventory Policy	New Inventory Policy	Remarks
Assets			
Current Assets			
Cash and Securities	$ 47,000	$ 54,520	Change in proportion with sales (16% increase)
Accounts Receivable	63,000	73,080	Change in proportion with sales (16% increase)
Inventory	160,000	240,000	16-car increase (48 – 32) × $5,000 ea
Total Current Assets	270,000	367,600	
Capital Assets	72,000	72,000	No change
Total Assets	$ 342,000	$ 439,600	
Liabilities and Equity			
Current Liabilities			
Accounts Payable	$ 50,000	$ 58,000	Change in proportion with sales (16% increase)
Notes Payable	74,000	85,840	Change in proportion with sales (16% increase)
Total Current Liabilities	124,000	143,840	
Long-Term Debt	45,000	45,000	No change
Total Liabilities	169,000	188,840	
Common Shares	69,000	69,000	No change
Retained Earnings	104,000	109,466	Old RE + $5,466 net income difference
Total Shareholders' Equity	173,000	178,466	
Total Liabilities and Equity	$ 342,000	$ 367,306	
Additional Funds Needed		72,294	To be obtained from external sources
		$ 439,600	

Note 1: The new total inventory costs were computed as follows:

$$\text{New Order Quantity per the EOQ} = \sqrt{\frac{2 \times 232 \times \$100}{500}}$$
$$= 9.63 \text{ (round to 10)}$$

Number of orders this year	= 232/10 = 23.2 (round to 23)
New total ordering cost	= 23 × $100 = $2,300
New average inventory level	= 48
New total carrying cost	= 48 × $500 = $24,000
New total inventory cost	= $2,300 + $24,000 = $26,300

$8,100 increase.

Table 19-4 Incremental Cash Flows If Cream Puff Changes Inventory Level from 32 to 48 Cars

1. Incremental Cash Outflows at (t_0)	
Additional Funds Needed from the Projected Balance Sheet	$ 72,294
2. Incremental Cash Flows Occurring in the Future	
Incremental Cash Inflows:	
Increase in Sales	$192,000
Incremental Cash Outflows	
Increase in Cost of Goods Sold	$160,000
Increase in Inventory Costs	8,100
Increase in Other Operating Expenses	13,600
Increase in Interest Expense	1,190
Increase in Taxes	3,644
Total Incremental Cash Outflows	$186,534
Net Incremental Cash Flows Occurring from Time (t_1) through Infinity: $192,000 – $186,534 =	$5,466 per year

We see in Table 19-4 that the initial investment cash flows of changing Dealin' Dan's inventory policy are $72,294. We also find that the net cash flows associated with changing the average inventory level are $5,466 per year.

Step 3: Compute the NPV of the Inventory Policy Change.

We are ready now to calculate the NPV of the inventory policy change just as we did for accounts receivable. First, we compute the present value of the net cash inflows occurring from time t_1 through infinity from Table 19-4 ($5,466 per year) using Equation 8-5, the formula for the present value of a perpetuity:

$$\begin{aligned} PVP &= PMT \times \left(\frac{1}{k}\right) \\ &= \$5{,}466 \times \left(\frac{1}{0.10}\right) \\ &= \$54{,}660 \end{aligned}$$

We find that the present value of the net cash flow perpetuity is $54,660.

Next, we subtract the present value of the net cash outflows at t_0 (the initial investment) to find the NPV of the inventory policy change. From Table 19-4, we see the net cash outflow that occurs at t_0 is $72,294. So, the NPV of Dealin' Dan's Cream Puff Used Cars inventory change proposal is as follows:

$$\begin{aligned} NPV &= \$54{,}660 - \$72{,}294 \\ &= (\$17{,}634) \end{aligned}$$

We find that the net present value of the inventory change proposal is –$17,634. Because the NPV is negative, the inventory change proposal should be rejected. Accepting it would decrease the value of the Cream Puff Used Cars company by $17,634.[11]

In the preceding analysis, we used one possible inventory level and observed the effect on the value of the Cream Puff firm. By repeating this procedure a number of times, we could eventually find one inventory level, or a range of levels, at which the firm's value was maximized. We would then have found the true optimal level of inventory for the firm.

Inventory Management Approaches

Managing inventory is more than just determining the optimal level of items to keep on hand. Remember, the task is to hold down inventory costs without sacrificing sales too much. Techniques for doing this abound, but two approaches deserve special mention: the ABC classification system and the just-in-time (JIT) system. Inventory management must also be flexible. Such is the case for northern Ontario's declining wood supply due to fuel prices, a higher dollar, and trade disputes (2004).

The ABC Inventory Classification System

The **ABC system** of inventory classification is a tool used to lower inventory carrying costs. The system classifies inventory according to value. In many firms, inventory items may range in value from relatively expensive to relatively inexpensive. Generally, firms have fewer expensive items and more inexpensive items. In such a situation, it does not make sense to use one inventory control system to manage all inventory items because the firm would waste a lot of time and effort monitoring the relatively inexpensive items. For example, imagine the inventory system of a bicycle store. Its inventory would probably include several custom-designed racing bicycles; standard 10-speed and mountain bikes; and cycling helmets, water bottles, and other cycling equipment. Would it not waste time and effort to assign serial numbers to all items in inventory and keep them all locked up in glass cases?

Under the ABC system, firm managers classify the relatively few, very expensive items as group A, the larger number of less expensive items as group B, and the rest of the relatively inexpensive items as group C.[12] Then different inventory control systems are designed for each group, appropriate for the value of that group. For example, the owner of a bicycle shop might assign custom-designed racing bikes to group A, less expensive standard bicycles to group B, and the rest of the inventory to group C. Then the owner could apply inventory control techniques appropriate for each group, as follows:

- *Group A:* Assign serial numbers to each item. Keep in secure storage. Check inventory daily. Keep fixed number on display, ordering replacements as each is sold.

---

[11]The internal rate of return (IRR) of the inventory proposal is k, or IRR = PMT/PV (initial investment) IRR = 5,466/72,294 = 0.0756 or 7.56%. Because 7.56 percent is less than Dealin' Dan's cost of capital of 10 percent, the inventory change proposal should be rejected.

[12]Of course, the classifications are not limited to just A, B, and C. Depending on the firm's product lines, some companies might have D, E, and F as well. However, the guiding principle is the same.

- *Group B:* Assign serial numbers to each item. Keep in secure storage. Check inventory monthly. Manage levels of each type per the EOQ model.
- *Group C:* Check inventory annually. Reorder when visual checks of shelves indicate need.

This technique allows the bicycle storeowner to concentrate his or her time and effort on those items that deserve it. Unnecessary carrying costs on the rest of the inventory items are thus avoided.

Just-in-Time Inventory Control (JIT)

The **just-in-time (JIT)** inventory system, developed in Japan, is useful when storage space is limited and inventory carrying costs are high. The system attempts to operate the firm on little or no inventory.

Here is an example of how JIT works. A firm that makes kitchen cabinets needs wood, brass handles and knobs, screws, and varnish. All these items constitute the firm's raw materials inventory. On the one hand, the firm could order these raw materials once a month and keep them in storage areas until needed in the manufacturing process (incurring inventory carrying costs as a result). On the other hand, the firm might strike a deal with its raw materials suppliers to deliver just the number of items needed immediately upon request. The items would thus arrive just in time to be used. The firm would not need to store materials and inventory-carrying costs would be eliminated.[13]

In addition to lowering inventory-carrying costs, just-in-time systems tend to force quality into the manufacturing process. Any defect in materials will force the entire production line to shut down until the firm can obtain replacement materials.

Carrying little or no inventory can have drawbacks, however. (See International Perspectives in Finance 19-1 on page 628.) Suppliers that are late or produce poor-quality products jeopardize the firm's customer relations. Little or no inventory means that the business does not have a buffer when a work slowdown occurs due to illness, natural disaster, or a labour dispute.

For instance, General Motors had an inventory system similar to JIT. When 3,000 workers at two brake plants in Dayton, Ohio went on strike in early 1996, the ripple effects were staggering. Without the brake parts in inventory, workers at other GM plants could not complete car assembly, so eventually 177,775 GM workers were idled. The labour dispute virtually shut down GM's North American operations.[14]

Recall that the JIT inventory system was developed in Japan, where labour unions do not exist. Clearly, firms that employ organized labour should carefully consider the risks of JIT, as evidenced by the GM strike. The following feature provides an instance of a problem when inventory was limited.

---

[13]You can see that, in effect, the requirement to store materials (and the attendant carrying costs) is passed on to the suppliers. Presumably, the suppliers would adopt such systems as well until a closely coordinated chain from original suppliers to final customers developed.

[14]Blumenstein, R., and Christian, N. (1996, March 25). Parts Dispute to Remain Despite GM–UAW Accord. *The Wall Street Journal*; Byrne, J. (1996). Has Outsourcing Gone Too Far? *Business Week*.

INTERNATIONAL PERSPECTIVES IN FINANCE 19-

BSP May Halt Production Soon

Steel production in Bhilai Steel Plant (BSP) belonging to Steel Authority of India Ltd. (SAIL), is likely to come to a halt within a day or two because of acute coal shortage.

According to sources, the coal inventory of BSP has dropped to 20,000–22,000 tonnes from the average level of 1–1.5 lakh tonnes and it is likely to meet only a day's requirement. The plant management has already ordered production cut to the extent of 30 percent.

"With the current level of coal stock, we can just manage for one more day or half, despite cutting down the average production levels. And with financial year-end round the corner, this coal shortage will deal a huge blow to the fortunes of BSP," sources said.

BSP's average hot metal production is 14,500 tonnes per day. It was first reduced to 10,000 tonnes per day and now to 9,000 tonnes per day. Out of the six blast furnaces, one has stopped functioning and another is operating at half its capacity.

A senior official of SAIL confirmed that the plant was facing a coal shortage and "adjustments" had been made in production levels. "The situation is tight but there is no reason to panic," the official told *Business Line.*

Plant level officials held a different view. According to them, BSP's daily coal requirement is 12,500 tonnes and the practice is to maintain seven days of stock. Of the total coal requirement, BSP imports approximately 80 percent, which is around 10,000 tonnes. The rest is domestic coal.

Unlike other SAIL plants, BSP is heavily dependent on imported coal because of two reasons. First, it is located far away from the coal belt of India and nearer to the Vizag p So, importing coal made sense. Secondly, imported coal i better alternative for the plant.

The three Australian coal majors, namely BHP, M and Anglo Coal, had long term contracts for supplying c to BSP. "Out of these three, supplies from two had stopp long back. It was supposed to resume from February b nothing much had happened," sources said.

BSP officials at the plant level are quite lost. They a not too sure of the plans of the SAIL headquarters. They a more worried as production cuts of this nature will affect t health of the plant.

Sources added that production of billets, which is c rently fetching good prices on the export market, was down by 50 percent. The merchant mill has stopped p duction. Similarly production at the rolling mill was sh down from Tuesday.

Out of two steel melting shops, one is catering only plates and rails and the other for the billets, merchant m and wire rod production. "We have not hampered our pl and rail production," sources said.

Two sinter machines have already been closed dov The daily coke oven pushing rate was first reduced from 6 to 580 and now to 540. Even at the current production lev BSP needs 9,000 tonnes of coal per day.

Source: "BSP may halt production soon," March 11, 2004. Reprinted with permission of Sify.com.

MAKING CREDIT DECISIONS

Earlier in this chapter, we said that individual customers receive credit from the firm if they meet the firm's credit standards. Credit standards are those requirements each individual customer must satisfy in order to receive credit from the firm. They are tests, in other words, of a person's creditworthiness.

Firms often base their credit standards on the *Five Cs of Credit:* character, capacity, capital, collateral, and conditions.

1. *Character:* the borrower's *willingness to pay.* Lenders evaluate character by looking at the borrower's past payment patterns. A good payment record in the past implies willingness to pay debts in the future.
2. *Capacity:* the borrower's *ability to pay,* as indicated by forecasts of future cash flows. The more confidence a lender has that a borrower is going to receive cash in the future, the more willing the lender will be to grant credit now.

3. *Capital:* how much wealth a borrower has to fall back on, in case the expected future cash flows with which the borrower plans to pay debts do not materialize. Lenders feel more comfortable if borrowers have something they could liquidate if necessary to pay their debts.
4. *Collateral:* what the lender gets if capacity and capital fail, and the borrower defaults on a loan. Collateral is usually some form of tangible asset, such as the firm's inventory, buildings, manufacturing equipment, and so on that has been pledged as security by the borrower.
5. *Conditions:* the business conditions the borrower is expected to face. The more favourable business conditions appear to be for the borrower, the more willing lenders are to grant credit.

To evaluate potential credit customers (in terms of the Five Cs of Credit, or any other criteria), firms find some way to quantify how well the customers compare to the measurement criteria. Some firms use a method known as credit scoring. **Credit scoring** works by assigning points according to how well customers meet indicators of creditworthiness. For example, statisticians have determined that established businesses tend to pay their debts more faithfully than new businesses. So, a credit applicant might be awarded points for each year that the applicant's firm has been in business. A sample of a simplified credit score sheet is shown in Figure 19-4 for Wishful Thinking Company.

We cannot overemphasize the importance of investigating creditworthiness carefully before granting credit. Not doing so is a quick way to end up with lots of accounts receivable and no cash!

Collection Policies to Handle Bad Debts

Sometimes, despite precautions, a firm ends up with customers who do not pay their bills. You thought your firm did a good job of scoring customers. But some of them are not paying their bills on time, and a few have not paid at all. Now what?

Slow or no payment is bound to happen to any credit-granting business. Firms establish a **collection policy** to cope with the problem. For instance, what do you do if one of your long-time customers fails to pay a bill on the due date? Send it to a collection agency the next day? Ignore the situation and hope for the best? Send a reminder notice? Start charging interest? It helps to have a collection policy in place. That way, both the firm and its customers know what to expect once credit has been granted.

No single collection policy will be best for all firms and for all customers. The best policy depends on the business situation, the firm's tolerance for abuse, and the relationship it has with customers. However, most firms consider one or more of the following collection policies:

- *Send reminder letters.* Send one or more letters, each one becoming less friendly in tone. Certainly, the first letter should not sound threatening. (How often have you simply misplaced a bill and not realized it until you received a reminder notice?)
- *Make telephone calls.* If gentle reminders in the mail do not produce results, call the customer to see what the problem is. If there is a good reason why the customer has not paid the bill, you may choose to take no action or

Figure 19-4
Sample Items on a Credit Scoring Worksheet for Wishful Thinking Company
Figure 19-4 shows an example of items on a credit-scoring sheet that determines an applicant's credit-worthiness. No attempt is made here to determine the amount of credit that may be extended.

CRITERIA		SCORE
1. Length of time since missing a payment on any loan		______
More than four years	4 points	
Three to four years	3 points	
Two to three years	2 points	
One to two years	1 point	
Less than one year	0 points	
2. Length of time in business		______
More than four years	4 points	
Three to four years	3 points	
Two to three years	2 points	
One to two years	1 point	
Less than one year	0 points	
3. Net income		______
More than $200,000	4 points	
$100,000 to $200,000	3 points	
$50,000 to $100,000	2 points	
$25,000 to $50,000	1 point	
Less than $25,000	0 points	
4. Net worth		______
More than $1 million	4 points	
$500,000 to $1 million	3 points	
$100,000 to $500,000	2 points	
$50,000 to $100,000	1 point	
Less than $50,000	0 points	
5. Market value of tangible assets		______
More than $1 million	4 points	
$500,000 to $1 million	3 points	
$100,000 to $500,000	2 points	
$50,000 to $100,000	1 point	
Less than $50,000	0 points	
6. Expected business growth rate in next five years		______
More than 20 percent	4 points	
15 to 20 percent	3 points	
10 to 15 percent	2 points	
5 to 10 percent	1 point	
Less than 5 percent	0 points	
	Total Score:	______

Approved for credit if score = 12 or more

make accommodating arrangements. Make sure that any alternative payment plan is specific so that the firm can follow up early if the customer fails to pay again.

- *Hire collection agencies.* When all efforts to collect are unsuccessful, you may want to turn to professional collection agencies. This action should be used sparingly for two reasons. First, it will probably cost the firm any future business from this customer. Second, the price of the collection agency service may be very high, often 50 percent of the uncollected debt.
- *Sue the customer.* Legal action is a last resort. A lawsuit is even more expensive than using a collection agency, so firms should determine whether the

court action is worth the trouble. Remember the "lawyers first" rule: Lawyers almost always get paid first.

- *Settle for a reduced amount.* A firm should keep in mind that trying too hard to collect from a customer may force the customer into bankruptcy. Once the client is in bankruptcy, the firm may not receive any money. In such a case, settling for a reduced amount, or a stretched-out payment schedule, may be the firm's best option.
- *Write off the bill as a loss.* In other words, forget it. This may be a firm's best alternative if the amount owed is relatively small or too costly to collect. Firms may have to write off all or part of the bill as a loss anyway if efforts to collect are unsuccessful.
- *Sell accounts receivable to factors.* Selling accounts receivable to some other person or business is known as **factoring**. Businesses that make money by buying accounts receivable from other firms, at less than their face value, are called **factors**. Suppose your firm had 100 customers who owed you a total of $10,000. Rather than wait for the customers to pay, you might sell the "IOUs" to a factor for $9,000 in cash. The factor discounts the accounts by an amount that both generates a return and compensates for the risk that some customers will not pay. Your firm no longer has to manage the accounts, plus it has cash to put to use elsewhere.

When granting credit to customers, it is best to remember the old saying, "An ounce of prevention is worth a pound of cure." In other words, crafting credit standards that avoid frequent collections can save a firm time and money. The following feature describes the stance that RBC takes when applying credit scores. To a potential borrower, this would be very important.

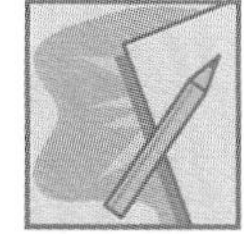

Take Note

A firm that frequently writes off uncollected amounts needs to tighten its standards for granting credit.

INANCE AT WORK 19-1

ales Retail Sports Media Technology Public Relations Production Exports

HAT'S YOUR CREDIT SCORE?

some point in their lives, just about everyone applies for a edit card or loan yet most people don't know the process t is used to approve or decline a loan. The process of risk sessment and evaluation is called credit scoring. Here's how tistical experience and analysis is used to evaluate credit uests at Royal Bank Financial Group.

: What is credit scoring?

en you apply for credit, be it a loan or a credit card, the ancial institution reviews all of the factors that indicate ether or not you would be a good candidate for credit. edit scoring analyzes an applicant's characteristics to pre- t future credit behaviour. Most financial institutions have tistical information to build mathematical models. When fill in the credit application form, the questions about your nk relationship and job and residential stability are com- ed to database samples of others with similar characteris- s. If this is the first time you have applied for credit, the financial institution usually looks at things like your savings account, how you manage your chequing account—are there a lot of overdrafts?—and your history in paying monthly bills and other financial commitments. If this isn't your first credit application, the financial institution looks at your credit bureau report and at how you manage your other credit cards and loans. Then, based on a credit scoring formula, you and your repayment risk are evaluated and ranked. This is your Credit Score.

Q. How can a mathematical formula determine whether or not I will be a good credit risk?

These mathematical equations predict who is statistically likely to repay their loan or credit card. Credit scoring eliminates any bias. There is no discrimination; it boils down to financial management. A lender can look at the application, verify that all credit policies are met and then rank the risk statistically. The

continued

models are tested and updated constantly. Credit scoring allows for faster service on your credit application.

Q. If my score is low, will my request automatically be declined?

The credit scoring process is designed to restrict automatic declines. If a low score appears, someone is assigned to look at the application to re-evaluate the information. Often an application can fall into a "grey" zone. Applications that are marginal are automatically reexamined.

Q. Is credit scoring used on just personal loans and credit card applications?

Credit scoring is also used for small business credit applications because how you manage your personal finances often indicates how you will manage your business finances. Since the most common major purchases a borrower makes are a home and car, credit scoring looks at their payment record as a good indication of how they will handle any other credit payments.

Q. I'm self-employed. Will that show up as a negative when I apply for a loan?

The strength of credit scoring is that it does not look at any s gle characteristic. It's the combination of an applicant's p sonal and financial history that is significant. Be self-employed is not seen as a negative.

Q. What can I do to help my application achieve a h score?

Make sure you complete the application accurately and in from how long you've lived at your present address to y employment history and financial circumstances. Each pi of information will form part of the credit-scoring formula, s complete application will result in a clear overall picture.

You may also want to verify information the lender obta from other sources, for example, your credit bureau rep Does your report accurately reflect your personal financial s tus, including credit repayment history? You can obtain a c of your credit report by calling Equifax at 1-800-465-7166 Trans Union at 1-800-663-9980.

Source: Ombudsman Advice Columns, Credit Scoring, 1998. Excerpted from Royal Bank of Canada. www.rbc.com/ombudsman advice_columns /1998/ac1998_credscore.html. Reprinted with th permission of the Royal Bank of Canada.

SUMMARY

19-1 Describe how the management of accounts receivable and inventory affect profitability and liquidity.

Granting credit and maintaining inventory are necessary business practices. Offering more credit and increasing inventory enhance sales. However, both accounts receivable and inventory tie up cash and incur opportunity costs—the cost of not having funds that could generate returns. The financial manager's task is to balance (1) the risk of losing sales due to not granting credit or having products available against (2) the savings produced by collecting cash immediately or maintaining inventory at a reduced level.

19-2 Describe a three-step process used to find the optimal level of accounts receivable and inventory.

The optimal level of accounts receivable or inventory may be found by using a three-step process: (1) create *pro forma* financial statements for alternative credit or inventory policies; (2) use the *pro forma* data to estimate the incremental cash flows associated with the proposed changes; and (3) compute the net present value of each alternative. When this process is complete, managers compare the NPVs of each alternative to see which policy produces the most favourable effect on the value of the firm.

19-3 Name and describe two different inventory management approaches.

Two popular inventory management approaches are the ABC and just-in-time (JIT) inventory systems. The ABC system classifies inventory items into categories according to their relative value. Management's time, money, and effort can then be directed to those inventory items in the proportions that they deserve.

The JIT inventory system calls for close coordination between manufacturers and suppliers to ensure that parts and materials used in the manufacturing process arrive just in time to be used. If the coordination is close enough, raw materials inventories at the manufacturing firm can be eliminated.

19-4 Explain five different characteristics evaluated by a credit policy.

Firms evaluate the creditworthiness of their customers by applying the following Five Cs of Credit:

- *Character*—a borrower's willingness to pay
- *Capacity*—a borrower's ability to pay
- *Capital*—how much wealth a borrower has to fall back on, in case the expected future cash flows with which the borrower plans to pay debts do not materialize
- *Collateral*—what the lender gets if capacity and capital fail and the borrower defaults on a loan
- *Conditions*—the business conditions a borrower is expected to face

To evaluate potential credit customers, firms use a credit scoring procedure that assigns numerical values to the various indicators of creditworthiness.

19-5 Describe seven different approaches to dealing with overdue accounts.

A firm's collection policy includes the actions the firm plans to take in the event that credit customers do not pay their bills on time. Policy actions include reminder letters, telephone calls, use of collection agencies, court action, settling for partial payment, factoring the accounts, and writing off the bills as a loss.

EQUATIONS INTRODUCED IN THIS CHAPTER

Equation 19-1: The Economic Order Quantity for Inventory

Formula for Economic Order Quantity Model

$$OQ = \sqrt{\frac{2 \times S \times OC}{CC}}$$

where

OQ = Order quantity
S = Annual sales volumes in units
OC = Ordering costs, per order
CC = Carrying costs, per unit per year

SELF-TEST

ST-1. Assume Cash & Carry, Inc. is considering offering credit to its customers. Management estimates that if it does so, sales will increase 10 percent, expenses will increase 5 percent, accounts receivable will increase to \$200,000, cash will decrease by \$50,000, and current liabilities will increase to \$300,000. No other accounts on the financial statements will be affected. Compute the company's return on equity (ROE) ratio and current ratio if it adopts the proposal. Base your calculations on Cash & Carry's latest financial statements.

Selected Financial Data for Cash & Carry, Inc. (In 000s)

	Prior to Granting Credit	After Granting Credit
Cash	$ 100	
Accounts Receivable	0	
Total Current Assets	100	
Current Liabilities	50	
Total Equity	2,000	
Sales	2,500	
Expenses	2,300	
Net Income for the Year	200	

ST-2. Your firm sells inventory at an even rate throughout the year. Sales volume this year is expected to be 100,000 units. Inventory ordering costs are $30 per order and inventory carrying costs are $60 per unit per year. Given these conditions, what is the most economical inventory order quantity (EOQ)?

ST-3. Refer to the Dealin' Dan's Cream Puff Used Cars example in the text. Continue with the assumptions given and compute the NPV of raising the company's average inventory level of cars to 60. Assume the inventory change would cause unit sales to increase to 240 per year.

ST-4. Your firm uses the credit scoring worksheet in Figure 19-4 to evaluate potential credit customers. If an applicant has never missed a loan payment, has been in business for two and a half years, has net income of $75,000, has a net worth of $90,000, has tangible assets worth $120,000, and has an expected business growth rate of 12 percent a year, will the applicant be granted credit?

REVIEW QUESTIONS

1. Accounts receivable are sometimes not collected. Why do companies extend trade credit when they could insist on cash for all sales?
2. Inventory is sometimes thought of as a necessary evil. Explain.
3. What are the primary variables being balanced in the EOQ inventory model? Explain.
4. What are the benefits of the JIT inventory control system?
5. What are the primary requirements for a successful JIT inventory control system?
6. Can a company have a default rate on its accounts receivable that is too low? Explain.
7. How does accounts receivable factoring work? What are the benefits to the two parties involved? What are the risks?

PROBLEMS

Accounts Receivable, ACP ▶

19-1. Compu-Chip Co. had annual credit sales of $8,030,000 and an average collection period (ACP) of 22 days in 2004. What is the company's accounts receivable for the year? Assume 365 days in a year.

Accounts Receivable, ACP ▶

19-2. If Compu-Chip Co. of problem 19-1 is expected to have annual credit sales of $7,600,000 and an average collection period of 26 days in 2005, what would be the company's accounts receivable? Do you think that the company is relaxing or tightening its credit policy in 2005, compared to its policy in 2004?

Accounts Receivable, ACP, Credit Policy ▶

19-3. Fitzgerald Company has credit terms of 2/15, n60. The historical payment patterns of its customers are as follows:

- 40 percent of customers pay in 15 days.
- 57 percent of customers pay in 60 days.
- 3 percent of customers pay in 100 days.

Annual sales of tools is $730,000. Assume there are 365 days in a year.

a. Calculate the average collection period (ACP).

b. What is the accounts receivable (AR) assuming all goods are sold on credit?

19-4. If Fitzgerald in problem 19-3 decides to adopt more stringent credit terms of 2/10, n30, sales are expected to drop by 10 percent but the following improved payment pattern of its customers is expected:

◀ Accounts Receivable, ACP, Credit Policy

- 40 percent of customers will pay in 10 days.
- 58 percent of customers will pay in 30 days.
- 2 percent of customers will pay in 100 days.

Calculate the new average collection period (ACP) and accounts receivable (AR) assuming all goods are sold on credit.

19-5. Tuscany Style, a furniture company, has a current credit policy of 2/10, n20. It estimates under this policy that 25 percent of its customers will take advantage of the discount, 60 percent will pay within 20 days, and the remaining customers will pay within 30 days. What is its average collection period (ACP)?

◀ Accounts Receivable, ACP

19-6. Tuscany Style, described in problem 19-5, is planning on revising its credit policy in an attempt to shorten its average collection period. Its new policy is 3/10, n30. Under this new policy, 32 percent of customers are expected to take advantage of the discount, 67 percent will pay within 30 days, and 1 percent will pay within 45 days. Calculate the new ACP. Should Tuscany Style adopt the new policy or keep the old one? Explain.

◀ Accounts Receivable, ACP

19-7. Elwood Blues, vice-president of sales for East-West Trading, Inc. wants to change the firm's credit policy from 2/15, n40 to 2/15, n60, effective January 1, 2005. He is confident that the proposed relaxation will result in a 20 percent increase over the otherwise expected annual sales of $350,000 with the old policy. All sales are made on credit. The historical payment pattern under the present credit terms is as follows:

◀ Effect of Change of Credit Policy

Excel

Under the old policy:

- 40 percent of the customers take advantage of the discount and pay in 15 days.
- 58 percent of the customers forgo the discount and pay in 40 days.
- The remaining 2 percent pay in 100 days.

Under the new credit policy, the payment pattern is expected to be as follows:

- 40 percent of the customers will take advantage of the discount and pay in 15 days.
- 57 percent of the customers will forgo the discount and pay in 60 days.
- The remaining 3 percent will pay in 100 days.

Bad debt expenses are expected to rise from 2 percent to 3 percent with the change in credit policy. Assume (i) any increase in current assets will be financed by short-term notes at an interest rate of 7 percent; (ii) long-term interest rate is 10 percent; (iii) income tax rate is 40 percent; (iv) cost of capital for East-West is 11 percent; (v) cost of goods sold is 80 percent of sales; (vi) other operating expenses are $10,000 under the old policy.

The *pro forma* balance sheet items of the company, excluding accounts receivable, under the old policy would be as follows:

Cash and Securities	$ 15,000	Accounts Payable	$14,918
Inventory	50,000	Notes Payable	35,000
Capital Assets	120,000	Long-Term Debt	30,000
Common Shares	85,000		
Retained Earnings	50,000		

Also assume that the cost of goods sold and other operating expenses in the income statement and all current asset and current liability items, except accounts receivable, vary directly with sales.

a. Calculate average collection periods and accounts receivable under the old and the new policies.

b. Develop *pro forma* income statements and balance sheets under the old and the new policies.

c. Calculate the incremental cash flows for 2005 and the subsequent years.

d. Advise Mr. Blues if he should adopt the new policy.

Effect of Change of Credit Policy ▶ Excel

19-8. Use the same information given in problem 19-7 with the following changes. Mr. Blues asked Mr. Scott Hayward, the general manager of sales of East-West, to recheck the payment patterns and credit history of East-West's customers to be absolutely sure that the change in credit policy would indeed be beneficial to the company. A strict scrutiny by Mr. Hayward resulted in the following changes in the expected payment pattern and bad debts:

Under the old policy:

- 40 percent of the customers take advantage of the discount and pay in 15 days.
- 58 percent of the customers forgo the discount and pay in 40 days.
- The remaining 2 percent pay in 100 days.

Under the new credit policy, the payment pattern is expected to be as follows:

- 30 percent of the customers will take advantage of the discount and pay in 15 days.
- 60 percent of the customers will forgo the discount and pay in 60 days.
- The remaining 10 percent will pay in 100 days.

Bad debt expenses are expected to rise from 2 percent to 4 percent with the change in credit policy. Under this changed scenario, is adoption of the new credit policy advisable?

Challenge Problem ▶ Excel

19-9. Tom Jackson, the vice-president of sales for A-Z Trading, Inc. wants to change the firm's credit policy from 3/10, n40 to 3/15, n30, effective January 1, 2005. He is confident that, although the proposed tightening will result in a 10 percent decrease over the otherwise expected annual sales of $2 million with the old policy, it will increase the profitability and value of the firm. All sales are made on credit. The historical payment pattern under the present credit terms is as follows:

Under the old policy:

- 30 percent of the customers take advantage of the discount and pay in 10 days.
- 60 percent of the customers forgo the discount and pay in 40 days.
- The remaining 10 percent pay in 100 days.

Under the new credit policy, the payment pattern is expected to be as follows:

- 42 percent of the customers will take advantage of the discount and pay in 15 days.
- 57 percent of the customers will forgo the discount and pay in 30 days.
- The remaining 1 percent will pay in 100 days.

Bad debt expenses are expected to decrease from 3 percent to 1 percent with the change in credit policy. Assume (i) any decrease in the current assets will be used to pay off short-term notes currently outstanding at an interest rate of 8 percent;

(ii) long-term interest rate is 11 percent; (iii) income tax rate is 40 percent; (iv) cost of capital for A-Z is 13 percent; (v) cost of goods sold is 80 percent of sales; and (vi) other operating expenses are $60,000 under the old policy.

The *pro forma* balance sheet items of the company, excluding accounts receivable, under the old policy would be as follows:

Cash and Securities	$ 86,000	Accounts Payable	$ 84,740
Inventory	285,000	Notes Payable	200,000
Capital Assets	652,000	Long-Term Debt	171,000
Common Shares	485,000		
Retained Earnings	285,000		

Also assume that the cost of goods sold and other operating expenses in the income statement and all current account items in the balance sheet vary directly with sales.

a. Calculate average collection periods and accounts receivable under the old and the new policies.

b. Develop *pro forma* income statements and balance sheets under the old and the new policies.

c. Calculate the incremental cash flows for 2005 and the subsequent years.

d. Advise Mr. Jackson if he should adopt the new policy.

19-10. Windhome and Drake Co., a dealer in building products, has the following costs associated with its business in 2004:

Economic Order Quantity

Ordering Cost	$250 per order
Carrying Cost	$300 per unit per year
Annual Sales	500 units

Calculate the EOQ, the number of orders placed per year, and total ordering cost for 2004.

19-11. Use the same data for problem 19-10, except that the carrying cost is expected to increase by 10 percent in 2005 due to increase in rentals of warehouse space. Recalculate the EOQ, number of orders placed per year, and total ordering cost for 2005.

Economic Order Quantity

19-12. TrailCrazer is updating its ordering strategy. Business has been increasing dramatically and it cannot keep up with its current strategy. Executives have decided to implement the EOQ model to determine its ordering quantities and cycles. In 2004, TrailCrazer had the following costs:

Economic Order Quantity

Annual Sales	1,200 units
Carrying Costs	$100 per unit
Ordering Costs	$250 per unit per year

Calculate:

a. The EOQ

b. Number of orders to be placed each year

19-13. Jamison Electronics is forecasting next year's optimal order size. In 2004, annual sales are 200 units, with a carrying cost of $150 per unit and ordering costs of $50. However, its 2005 forecast is that annual unit sales will increase by 25 percent and that both ordering and carrying costs will increase by 10 percent. What will Jamison's optimal order size be for 2005 if these numbers are correct?

Economic Order Quantity

Credit Scoring ▶ Excel

19-14. Mr. Danny Fisher's firm uses the credit scoring sheet in Figure 19-4 to evaluate the creditworthiness of its customers. An applicant missed a loan payment three and a half years back, has been in business for six years, has a net income of $143,000, a net worth of $1.5 million, a market value of $550,000 in tangible assets, and a business growth rate of 14 percent. Would Mr. Fisher approve credit to the applicant?

Credit Scoring ▶ Excel

19-15. Kierna Jesup is the financial manager for Rummer International. She determines which customers are extended credit and how much. The following is a sample-scoring sheet that her company uses to grant credit:

Criteria	Points	Score
Length of Time Since Last Delinquent Payment		
Greater than 2.5 years	4	______
2–2.5 years	3	______
1.5–2 years	2	______
1–1.5 years	1	______
Less than 1 year	0	______
Length of Time in Business		
Greater than 5 years	4	______
4–5 years	3	______
3–4 years	2	______
2–3 years	1	______
Less than 2 years	0	______
Net Income		
Greater than $100,000	4	______
$75,000–$100,000	3	______
$50,000–$75,000	2	______
$25,000–$50,000	1	______
Less than $25,000	0	______

Approved with a score at or above 8

Companies will receive the following credit with a score of
8 = 10% total assets
9 = 20% total assets
10 = 30% total assets
11 = 40% total assets
12 = 50% total assets

TWI has sent in an application for credit. It has been in business since 1992 and has never had a late payment. In 2004, its assets are $1.2 million, EBT was $100,000, and its tax rate is 40 percent. Will Kierna approve TWI for credit? If so, for how much?

Effect of Change of Inventory Policy ▶ Excel

19-16. Mr. Homer Smith is the vice-president of sales for Sunrise Corporation, which buys and sells mobile homes. He is sure that increasing the number of homes on display will cause sales to increase. He thinks that an increase in inventory effective January 1, 2005, from the present level of 60 units to 100 units will boost sales from 350 units per year to 450 units per year. Assume the ordering cost to be $200 per order, the carrying cost to be $600 per unit per year, unit sales price to be $10,000, unit purchase price to be $8,000, and applicable income tax rate to be 40 percent. Also assume that any increase in the current assets will be financed by short-term notes at an interest rate of 7 percent, long-term interest rate is 10 percent, cost of capital for Sunrise is 11 percent, cost of goods sold is 80 percent of sales, and other operating expenses are $100,000 under the old policy. The *pro forma* balance sheet items of the company under the old policy would be as follows:

Cash and Securities	$ 55,000	Accounts Payable	$100,000
Accounts Receivable	105,000	Notes Payable	95,000
Capital Assets	100,000	Long-Term Debt	65,000
Common Shares	280,000		
Retained Earnings	200,000		

Also assume that the cost of goods sold and other operating expenses in the income statement and all current asset and current liability items vary directly with sales.

a. Calculate the EOQ, number of orders issued per year, and inventory cost.

b. Develop *pro forma* income statements and balance sheets under the old and the new policies.

c. Calculate the incremental cash flows for 2004 and the subsequent years.

d. Advise Mr. Smith if he should adopt the new policy.

◀ Effect of Change of Inventory Policy

19-17. Use the same information given in problem 19-16, except that Ms. Judy Benjamin, the general manager of sales for Sunrise, thinks that increasing the inventory level from 60 to 90 will increase sales from 350 to 390 units per year. With other assumptions remaining the same as in problem 19-16, evaluate this change in the inventory policy.

◀ Comprehensive Problem

19-18. Ms. Terry McKay is the vice-president of sales for Windermere Corporation, which sells hot air balloons. She is sure that increasing the number of balloons on display will cause sales to increase. She thinks that an increase in inventory effective January 1, 2005, from the present level will boost sales to higher levels in 2005 as shown:

		Inventory Level (Units)	Sales (Units)
Present		70	340
Future (2005)	(1)	80	375
	(2)	90	390
	(3)	100	400

Assume ordering costs are $160 per order, carrying costs are $400 per unit per year, unit sales price is $16,000, unit purchase price is $12,800, and applicable income tax rate is 40 percent. Also assume that any increase in the current assets will be financed by short-term notes at an interest rate of 7 percent, the long-term interest rate is 11 percent, cost of capital for Windermere is 13 percent, cost of goods sold is 80 percent of sales, and other operating expenses are $130,000 under the present policy. The *pro forma* balance sheet items of the company under the present policy would be as follows:

Cash and Securities	$ 65,000	Accounts Payable	$110,000
Accounts Receivable	114,000	Notes Payable	95,000
Capital Assets	113,000	Long-Term Debt	65,000
Common Shares	400,000		
Retained Earnings	518,000		

Also assume that the cost of goods sold and other operating expenses in the income statement and all current account items in the balance sheet vary directly with sales.

Find out for Ms. McKay what level of inventory maximizes value of the firm by doing the following and comparing the net present values of the cash flows associated with each level of inventory:

a. Calculate the EOQ, number of orders issued per year, and inventory cost.
b. Develop *pro forma* income statements and balance sheets under the present and the future policies.
c. Calculate the incremental cash flows for 2005 and the subsequent years.
d. Advise Ms. McKay whether she should change the present inventory policy. If so, which inventory level should she adopt?

JIT Inventory ▶

19-19. Jennifer and Norma are in charge of managing some of the working capital components. Jennifer is saying that JIT inventory would save the company money because the storage costs would be minimal, while Norma is stating that this may not increase total profits. Jennifer is confused because if storage costs went down, she believed that net income must go up.

a. Give Norma's reasons for arguing that the net income may not go up.
b. If the company in question took orders solely over the Internet (customers come to the company's online display to choose from products), how may Jennifer counter a portion of Norma's argument?
c. Under what conditions would the use of JIT increase net income?

Comprehensive Inventory Management ▶

19-20. James has just begun a ranching business. He intends to buy cows and bulls in order to sell the offspring for profit once they reach the age of one year. James began his business about 3 months ago and has already invested a sizeable amount of money in the business.

a. What does inventory include? In this unique situation, what would be considered inventory? What sort of timing issues could you think of?
b. In this case, what are the carrying costs? What are the ordering costs?
c. What other problems can you think of in terms of inventory management?
d. Be creative. By using the knowledge from this chapter, can you develop a plan to manage this type of inventory, while thinking of ways to minimize costs?

Accounts Receivable Collection ▶

19-21. Poppy and Bill are in charge of collections for a local corporation. Recently, the company's average age of receivables had been increasing while the potential for bad debts is on the rise. Poppy and Bill are concerned for their jobs and are thinking of ways to lower the average age of receivables, while decreasing bad debts as much as possible. Poppy suggests that they give a discount to clients who pay early, but Bill prefers the idea of factoring out the receivables as a quick way of getting cash. The company's receivables are split into two types of groups. The first group tends to pay things off within 35 days, while the second group tends to pay things off in about 120 days. Just about all of the bad debts occur within the second group.

a. What are the pros and cons of
   i. giving a trade discount?
   ii. factoring receivables?
b. In this situation, which approach do you feel would most probably be the best solution?
c. Can you develop a better solution?

Accounts Receivable Collection ▶

19-22. Under current production limitations, Poppy and Bill learned that inventory production is working at maximum speed, and that most clients have been placed on a waiting list several months long. It is unfortunate that opportunity costs are being incurred, but Poppy and Bill found a potential silver lining.

a. How could Poppy and Bill take advantage of the current situation to partially solve the problem in the previous question? (Hint: Think about the latter part of the chapter.)

b. How long can this strategy survive? What are the long-term effects?

c. What will be the short-term effects?

19-23. Thompson & Thompson (T & T) is a new family-run business. Positive forecasts were generated, but Thompson is having difficulty convincing suppliers to send them goods on credit. Having to write out a cheque every time T & T wanted to buy a pencil was very inconvenient and costly, both in actual transaction fees and missed opportunities. They have come to you for help. ◀ Credit Scoring

a. What factors would a company look at before giving T & T credit terms?

b. How could T & T improve their credit score?

ANSWERS TO SELF-TEST

ST-1.

Selected Financial Data for Cash & Carry, Inc. (In 000s)

	Prior to Granting Credit	After Granting Credit
Cash	$ 100	$ 50
Accounts Receivable	0	200
Total Current Assets	100	250
Current Liabilities	50	300
Total Equity	2,000	2,000
Sales	2,500	2,750
Expenses	2,300	2,415
Net Income for the Year	200	335
Current Ratio	\$100/\$50 = 2	\$250/\$300 = 0.833
Return on Equity	\$200/\$2,000 = 0.10	\$335/\$2,000 = 0.1675

ST-2. Per Equation 19-1, the EOQ model:

$$OQ = \sqrt{\frac{2 \times 100{,}000 \times 30}{60}}$$
$$= \sqrt{100{,}000}$$
$$= 316.228 \text{ (round to 316)}$$

ST-3. Use the three-step process to compute the NPV of raising the average inventory to 60 cars:

- *Step 1:* Create *pro forma* financial statements for the new inventory policy:

Dealin' Dan's Cream Puff Used Cars Inventory Analysis
Income Statements

	Current Inventory Policy	New Inventory Policy	Remarks
Sales	$1,200,000	$1,440,000	Unit sales × price each, from assumptions
Cost of Goods Sold	1,000,000	1,200,000	Unit sales × cost each, from assumptions
Gross Profit	200,000	240,000	
Inventory Costs	18,200	32,400	See Note 1
Other Operating Expenses	85,000	102,000	Increase in proportion with sales
Operating Income	96,800	105,600	
Interest Expense	11,040	12,528	ST & LT Debt × Costs of Debt
Before-Tax Income	85,760	93,072	
Income Taxes (rate = 40%)	34,304	37,229	
Net Income	$ 51,456	$ 55,843	

Balance Sheets as of December 31

	Current Inventory Policy	New Inventory Policy	Remarks
Assets			
Current Assets:			
Cash and Securities	$ 47,000	$ 56,400	Change in proportion with sales
Accounts Receivable	63,000	75,600	Change in proportion with sales
Inventory	160,000	300,000	Average inventory × cost of each, from assumptions
Total Current Assets	270,000	432,000	
Capital Assets	72,000	72,000	No change
Total Assets	$342,000	$504,000	
Liabilities and Equity			
Current Liabilities:			
Accounts Payable	$ 50,000	$ 60,000	Change in proportion with sales
Notes Payable	74,000	88,800	Change in proportion with sales
Total Current Liabilities	124,000	148,800	
Long-Term Debt	45,000	45,000	No change
Total Liabilities	169,000	193,800	
Common Shares	69,000	69,000	No change
Retained Earnings	104,000	108,387	Old RE + net income change
Total Shareholders' Equity	173,000	177,387	
Total Liabilities and Equity	$342,000	$371,187	
Additional Funds Needed		132,813	Obtained from external sources
		$504,000	

Note 1: The new total inventory costs were computed as follows:

$$\text{New Order Quantity per the EOQ} = \sqrt{\frac{2 \times 240 \times \$100}{500}}$$
$$= 9.8 \text{ (round to 10)}$$

Number of orders this year = 24/10 = 2.4
New total ordering cost = 24 × \$100 = \$2,400
New average inventory level = 60
New total carrying cost = 60 × \$500 = \$30,000
New total inventory cost = \$2,400 + \$30,000 = \$32,400

- *Step 2:* Compute the incremental cash flows:

Incremental Cash Flows Associated with Changing Cream Puff Used Cars Inventory Level from 32 Cars to 60 Cars

1. Incremental Cash Outflows at Time Zero (t_0):	
Additional Funds Needed from the Projected Balance Sheet	\$132,813
2. Incremental Cash Flows Occurring in the Future	
Incremental Cash Inflows:	
Increase in Sales	\$240,000
Incremental Cash Outflows:	
Increase in Cost of Goods Sold	\$200,000
Increase in Inventory Costs	14,200
Increase in Other Operating Expenses	17,000
Increase in Interest Expense	1,488
Increase in Taxes	2,925
Total Incremental Cash Outflows:	\$235,613
Net Incremental Cash Flows Occurring from Time t_1 through Infinity:	\$ 4,387 per year

- *Step 3:* Compute the NPV of the Inventory Policy Change:

PV of the net cash inflows occurring from time t_1 through infinity (\$4,387 per year) using Equation 8-5:

$$\begin{aligned} PVP &= PMT \times \left(\frac{1}{k}\right) \\ &= \$4{,}387 \times \left(\frac{1}{0.10}\right) \\ &= \$43{,}870 \end{aligned}$$

Subtract the PV of the net cash outflows at t_0 (\$132,813) to obtain the NPV of the inventory policy change:

$$\begin{aligned} NPV &= \$43{,}870 - \$132{,}813 \\ &= -\$88{,}943 \end{aligned}$$

Because the NPV is negative, the inventory change proposal should be rejected.

ST-4. The applicant's completed credit scoring worksheet from Figure 19-4 is shown next.

Credit Scoring Worksheet for (applicant)

Criteria		Score
1. Length of time since missing a payment on any loan		4
More than four years	4 points	
Three to four years	3 points	
Two to three years	2 points	
One to two years	1 point	
Less than one year	0 points	
2. Length of time in business		2
More than four years	4 points	
Three to four years	3 points	
Two to three years	2 points	
One to two years	1 point	
Less than one year	0 points	
3. Net income		2
More than $200,000	4 points	
$100,000 to $200,000	3 points	
$50,000 to $100,000	2 points	
$25,000 to $50,000	1 point	
Less than $25,000	0 points	
4. Net worth		1
More than $1 million	4 points	
$500,000 to $1 million	3 points	
$100,000 to $500,000	2 points	
$50,000 to $100,000	1 point	
Less than $50,000	0 points	
5. Market value of tangible assets		2
More than $1 million	4 points	
$500,000 to $1 million	3 points	
$100,000 to $500,000	2 points	
$50,000 to $100,000	1 point	
Less than $50,000	0 points	
6. Expected business growth rate in next five years		2
More than 20 percent	4 points	
15 to 20 percent	3 points	
10 to 15 percent	2 points	
5 to 10 percent	1 point	
Less than 5 percent	0 points	
	Total Score:	13

Approved for credit if score = 12 or more
Result for applicant: Approved

20

Short-Term Financing

Chapter Objectives

After reading this chapter, you should be able to:

20-1 **Describe** two reasons why external short-term financing may be required.

20-2 **Differentiate** between long-term financing and short-term financing.

20-3 **Describe** two common types of short-term business loans.

20-4 **Define** trade credits and explain how to compute their cost.

20-5 **Define** commercial paper and explain how to compare its percent cost to that of a bank loan.

20-6 **Describe** how to compute the effective interest rate of a loan and compare it to the loan's stated interest rate.

20-7 **Explain** how accounts receivable and inventory can be used as collateral.

"If you would know the value of money try to borrow some."

—Benjamin Franklin

CANADA SMALL BUSINESS FINANCING PROGRAM: BUY OR LEASE—NOW THE CHOICE IS YOURS

One of the Government of Canada's best programs for small businesses has just become a whole lot better. And that means more opportunities for you.

Since 1961, hundreds of thousands of small businesses have obtained financing that might not otherwise have been available to them—thanks to the Small Business Loans Program and its successor, the Canada Small Business Financing (CSBF) Program.

Today the Program continues to help Canadian small firms get business improvement loans. But as of April 1, 2002, it also helps them access financing to lease new or used equipment under the five-year Capital Leasing Pilot Project.

The Canada Small Business Financing Program seeks to increase the availability of loans and capital leases for establishing, expanding, modernizing and improving small businesses. It does this by encouraging financial institutions and leasing companies to make their services available to small businesses.

Under the Program, a small business must apply for a loan or lease to the financial institution (bank, credit union or caisse populaire) or the participating leasing company of its choice. If the application is granted, the federal government will guarantee 85 percent of the lender's losses in the event of default.

Source: Canada Small Business Financing Program: Buy or Lease—Now the Choice Is Yours. http://strategis.ic.gc.ca/epic/internet/incsbfp-pfpec.nsf/en.la01215e.html. Reproduced with the permission of the Minister of Public Works and Government Services, 2004.

Chapter Overview

The credit card is perhaps the best-known source of short-term financing. However, businesses use many other types of short-term financing to sustain their business operations. In this chapter, we discuss the advantages and disadvantages of short-term financing, sources of that financing, and methods for calculating the cost of each source. We also show how loan terms can affect a loan's effective interest rate and how accounts receivable and inventory can be used as short-term loan collateral.

The Need for Short-Term Financing

Businesses rely on short-term financing from external sources for two reasons. The first is growth—profits may simply not be high enough to keep up with the rate at which the company is buying new assets. Imagine a convenience store chain that wished to open one new store a month. If each new store cost $100,000, the company would have to be *very* profitable to be able to do this without obtaining external financing.

The second reason that businesses rely on external short-term financing is choice. Rather than waiting to save enough money from net profits to make their desired purchases, many firms would rather borrow the money at the outset and make their purchases on time. People make the same choices in their personal lives. For example, you could save a little money each month until you saved enough to buy a car with cash. This might take a long time, however, and in the meantime you would be without transportation. Alternatively, you could borrow the money to buy the car and have it to drive around while you are paying off the loan. People—and businesses—often choose the latter alternative.

Clearly, the ability to obtain external financing is crucial for most businesses. Without it, most businesses could never even get started.

Short-Term Financing versus Long-Term Financing

Two factors influence the duration of external financing that businesses seek. The first, of course, is availability. A firm may want to take out a 10-year loan to finance its inventory purchases, but it may find no one willing to make such a loan. In general, businesses can usually find financing for short time periods. It is more difficult to find long-term financing.

The second factor influencing the length of time that firms finance for is the risk–return, or liquidity–profitability, trade-off discussed in Chapter 17.

In the context of financing alternatives, here is how the trade-off works:

- *Short-term financing* is usually less expensive than long-term financing because short-term interest rates are normally lower than long-term interest rates.[1] Therefore, the desire for profitability (return) pushes firms toward short-term financing.

[1]Remember from Chapter 2 that a normal yield curve is upward sloping.

- *Long-term financing* is regarded as less risky than short-term financing for the borrower because the borrower locks in the agreed-on interest rate for a long period of time. No matter how interest rates change during the life of the loan, the borrower's interest costs are certain. Furthermore, the borrower does not have to incur the transaction costs of obtaining new financing every few months. So, the desire to avoid risk encourages firms to use long-term financing.

The length of time that firms finance for depends on whether they want "to eat well or sleep well."[2] Returns generally increase, as financing maturities grow shorter but so does risk. Risk decreases as financing maturities grow longer but so do returns. The blend of financing maturities that a firm selects reflects how aggressive or conservative the firm's managers are.

Figure 20-1 summarizes the factors that influence the sources of external financing. External financing can come from short-term or long-term sources. We discuss short-term financing sources next.

SHORT-TERM FINANCING ALTERNATIVES

When most businesses need money for a short time—that is, for less than one year—they usually turn to two sources: short-term loans and trade credit (the process of delaying payments to suppliers). Large, well-established businesses may make use of a third financing source: commercial paper. In the sections

Figure 20-1 External Financing Source-Selection Process
This flow chart illustrates the external financing source-selection process. A firm first determines the need for external financing and then considers several factors before selecting the short-term financing sources.

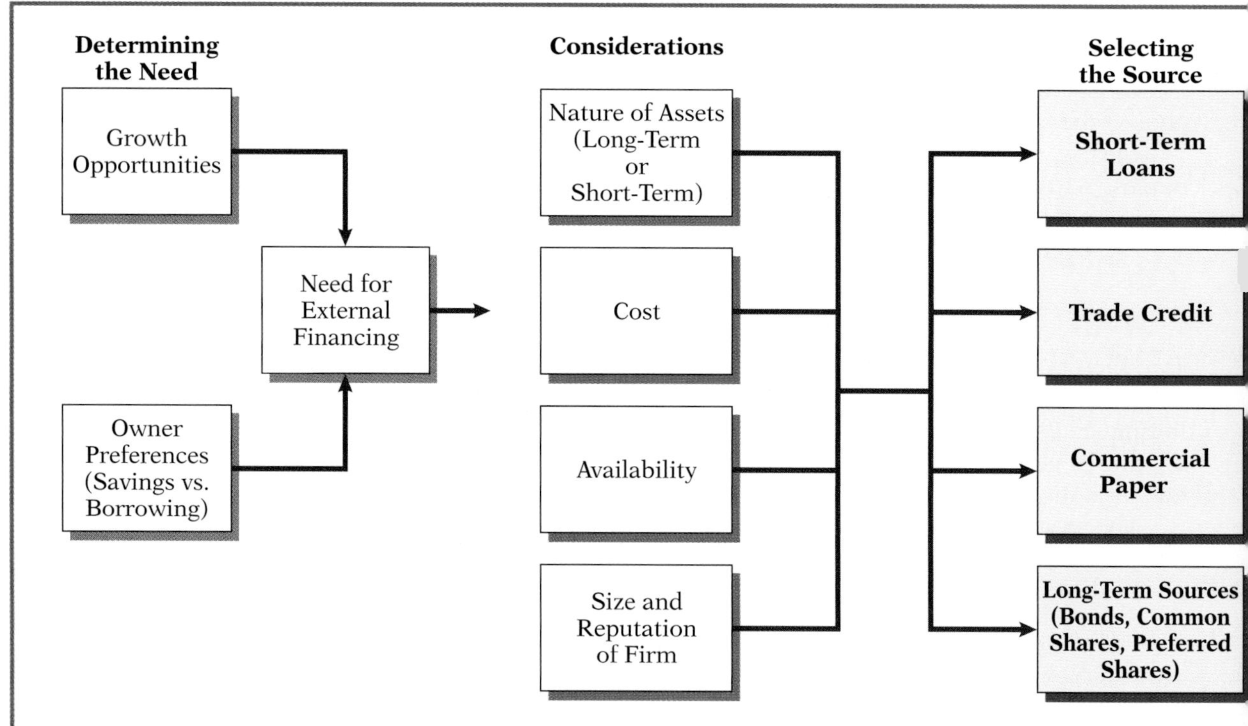

[2]The phrase is adapted from a remark by J. Kenfield Morley, who said, "In investing money, the amount of interest you want should depend on whether you want to eat well or sleep well."

that follow, we discuss the various aspects of obtaining money from these three sources.

Short-Term Loans from Banks and Other Institutions

Financial institutions offer businesses many types of short-term loans. No matter what the type of loan, however, the cost to a borrower is usually measured by the percent interest rate charged by the lender. The annual interest rate that reflects the dollars of interest paid divided by the dollars borrowed is the **effective interest rate.**

Often, the effective interest rate differs from the interest rate advertised by the bank, which is known as the **stated interest rate.**

Two common types of short-term loans are the *self-liquidating loan* and the *line of credit.* We examine these loan alternatives next. No matter what type of loan a firm uses, the firm must sign a promissory note. A **promissory note** is the legal instrument that the borrower signs and is the evidence of the lender's claim on the borrower.

Self-Liquidating Loans Many of the short-term loans obtained from banks are self-liquidating. A **self-liquidating loan** is one in which the proceeds of the loan are used to acquire assets that will generate enough cash to repay the loan. An example is a loan used to finance a seasonal increase in inventory, such as the purchase of swimwear to sell during the summer months. The sale of the inventory generates enough cash to repay the loan.

The Line of Credit As we now know, each time a firm borrows money from a bank, it signs a promissory note. However, a firm may have more than one promissory note outstanding at any one time. Indeed, a firm could have a substantial number of promissory notes outstanding, all with overlapping terms of payment. To keep loans under control, banks may specify the maximum total balance that firms may have in outstanding short-term loans. A **line of credit** is the borrowing limit a bank sets for a firm. A line of credit is an informal arrangement. The bank may change a firm's credit limit or withdraw it entirely at any time. This may happen when business conditions change, but the bank does not need a reason to reduce or eliminate a firm's line of credit.

In contrast, a *revolving credit agreement* is a formal agreement between a bank and a borrower to extend credit to a firm up to a certain amount for some period of time (which may be for several years). The agreements are usually set forth in a written contract and firms generally pay a fee for the revolving credit.

Trade Credit

When a company purchases materials, supplies, or services on credit instead of paying cash, that frees up funds to be used elsewhere just as if the funds had been borrowed from a bank. **Trade credit** is the act of obtaining funds by delaying payment to suppliers. The longer a company delays paying for purchases, the more trade credit the firm is said to be using.

Even though trade credit is obtained by simply delaying payment to suppliers, it is not always free. Next, we explain the cost of trade credit and how to compute it so that it can be compared to the cost of a bank loan or other credit source.

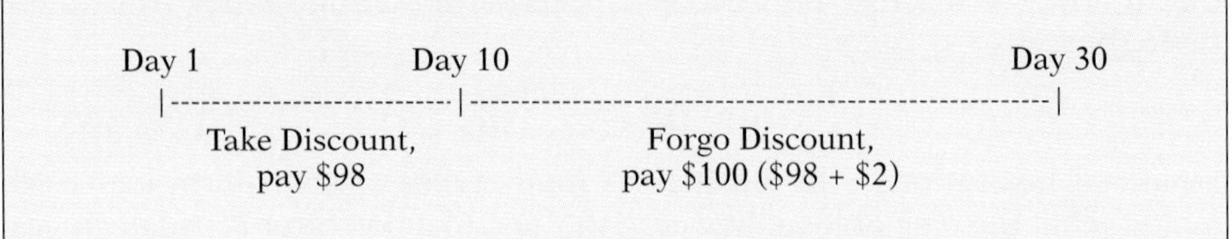

Figure 20-2
Payment Schedule with 2/10, n30 Credit Terms
Figure 20-2 shows the purchaser's payment schedule for a $100 purchase from a supplier who offers 2/10, n30 credit terms.

Computing the Cost of Trade Credit If a supplier charges a firm interest on credit balances, then computing the cost of trade credit is easy—simply read the interest rate charges on the supplier's account statements, much as we would read a credit card's interest charges.

Most wholesale suppliers, however, do not charge interest on credit balances. Instead, they simply give their customers so many days to pay and offer them a discount on the amount of the purchase if they pay early. A typical example of such credit terms is 2/10, n30—if customers pay their bills within 10 days of the invoice date, they will receive a 2 percent discount; if not, the net amount of the bill is due within 30 days.[3] Figure 20-2 diagrams a purchaser's payment deadlines for a $100 purchase on credit terms of 2/10, n30.

We see from Figure 20-2 that if a firm takes the discount, it can obtain the use of $98 for up to 10 days without any cost. In this case, the trade credit the firm receives is free. However, suppose a firm does not take the discount? Look at Figure 20-2 again and think of the situation this way: Instead of paying $98 on the tenth day, the firm can pay $98 any time during the next 20 days as long as it pays a "fee" of $2 for delaying payment. In essence, the firm is "borrowing" $98 for 20 days at a cost of $2. Assuming that the firm pays its bill on day 30, we can compute the effective annual interest rate of the trade credit using the following equation:

Trade Credit Effective Annual Interest Rate Formula

$$k = \left(1 + \frac{\text{Discount \%}}{100 - \text{Discount \%}}\right)^{\left(\frac{365}{\text{Days to Pay} - \text{Discount Period}}\right)} - 1 \qquad (20\text{-}1)$$

where

k = Cost of trade credit expressed as an effective annual interest rate

Discount % = Percentage discount being offered

Days to Pay = Time between the day of the credit purchase and the day the firm must pay its bill

Discount Period = Number of days in the discount period

The number 365 in the equation represents the number of days in a year. We also multiply the result, k, by 100 to express it as a percentage.

In our example, the discount percentage is 2 percent, the total number of days to pay is 30, and the number of days in the discount period is 10. We use Equation 20-1 to solve for k as follows:

[3]Credit terms of this type were introduced in Chapter 19 from the point of view of the supplier granting the credit. Here, we discuss the terms from the purchaser's point of view.

$$
\begin{aligned}
k &= \left(1+\frac{2}{100-2}\right)^{\left(\frac{365}{30-10}\right)}-1\\
&= (1+0.020408)^{(18.25)}-1\\
&= (1.020408)^{(18.25)}-1\\
&= 1.4458-1\\
&= 0.4458 \text{ or } 44.58\%
\end{aligned}
$$

As the calculation shows, the firm's trade credit—the use of $98 for an additional 20 days—costs the firm an effective annual percentage rate of interest of nearly 45 percent! Why would any reasonable financial manager pay such high rates? Most reasonable financial managers would not, unless very unfavourable circumstances forced them to or they did not realize that they were doing it.

Instead, because bank loan rates are much lower than 45 percent, most reasonable financial managers would borrow $98 from the bank and use it to pay the supplier on the tenth day to take advantage of the discount. Twenty days later, the financial manager would repay the loan plus the interest charges, which would be considerably less than $2. Either way, a firm can obtain the use of $98 for 20 days, but borrowing from a bank is usually the much less expensive alternative.

Commercial Paper

Firms can sell **commercial paper**—unsecured notes issued by large, very creditworthy firms for up to 270 days—to obtain cash. Selling commercial paper is usually a less expensive alternative to getting a short-term loan from a bank. Remember that only large, creditworthy corporations sell commercial paper because only they can attract investors who will lend them money for lower rates than banks charge for short-term loans.

Calculating the Cost of Commercial Paper Commercial paper is quoted on a *discount basis.* So, to compare the percent cost of a commercial paper issue to the percent cost of a bank loan, we first convert the commercial paper **discount yield** to an effective annual interest rate. We use the following three-step process to find this rate.

1. Compute the discount from face value using Equation 20-2, the formula for the dollar amount of the discount on a commercial paper note:

   Dollar Amount of the Discount on a Commercial Paper Note

$$
D=\frac{DY\times Par\times DTG}{360} \qquad (20\text{-}2)
$$

   where

   D = Dollar amount of the discount
   DY = Discount yield
   Par = Face value of the commercial paper issue; the amount to be paid at maturity
   DTG = Days to go until maturity

2. Compute the price of the commercial paper issue by subtracting the discount (D) from Par, as shown in Equation 20-3:

Price of a Commercial Paper Note

$$\text{Price} = \text{Par} - \text{D} \tag{20-3}$$

3. Compute the effective annual interest rate using the following formula, Equation 20-4:

Effective Annual Interest Rate of a Commercial Paper Note

$$\text{Effective Annual Interest Rate} = \left(\frac{\text{Par}}{\text{Price}}\right)^{\left(\frac{365}{\text{DTG}}\right)} - 1 \tag{20-4}$$

To illustrate the three-step process, imagine you are a financial analyst at GMACCL (General Motors Acceptance Corporation of Canada, Limited) and your commercial paper dealer[4] has informed you that she is willing to pay 3.3 percent discount yield for a $1 million issue of GMACCL 90-day commercial paper notes. What effective annual interest rate does the 3.3 percent discount yield equate to?

Step 1: **Compute the discount using Equation 20-2.**

$$\begin{aligned} D &= \frac{DY \times Par \times DTG}{360} \\ &= \frac{0.033 \times \$1{,}000{,}000 \times 90}{360} \\ &= \frac{\$2{,}970{,}000}{360} \\ &= \$8{,}250 \end{aligned}$$

We see that with a 3.3 percent discount rate, $1 million face value, and 90 days to go until maturity, the dollar amount of the discount on the commercial paper note is $8,250.

Step 2: **Compute the price using Equation 20-3.**

$$\begin{aligned} \text{Price} &= \text{Par} - \text{D} \\ &= \$1{,}000{,}000 - \$8{,}250 \\ &= \$991{,}750 \end{aligned}$$

Our calculations show that the price of the 90-day commercial paper note with a face value of $1 million at a discount price of $8,250 is $991,750.

Step 3: **Compute the effective annual interest rate using Equation 20-4.**

$$\begin{matrix}\text{Effective Annual} \\ \text{Interest Rate}\end{matrix} = \left(\frac{\text{Par}}{\text{Price}}\right)^{\left(\frac{365}{\text{DTG}}\right)} - 1$$

[4]GMACCL sells commercial paper directly to the public. Others sell it through dealers.

$$= \left(\frac{\$1{,}000{,}000}{\$991{,}750}\right)^{\left(\frac{365}{90}\right)} - 1$$
$$= (1.00832)^{4.056} - 1$$
$$= 1.0342 - 1$$
$$= 0.0342 \text{ or } 3.42\%$$

Applying Equation 20-4, we find that the effective annual interest rate of a $1 million, 90-day commercial paper note with a price of $991,750 is 3.42 percent. Now, you can compare the 3.42 percent effective annual interest rate GMACCL would pay for commercial paper to the various loan rates available and choose the best deal.

The following graph, Figure 20-3, summarizes the returns from corporate paper during mid-1999 to mid-2004. Due to corporate paper's similar quality amongst company borrowers, the graph provides a good picture of what an investor could have made during that period.

In the next section, we examine the effect of loan terms on the effective interest rate.

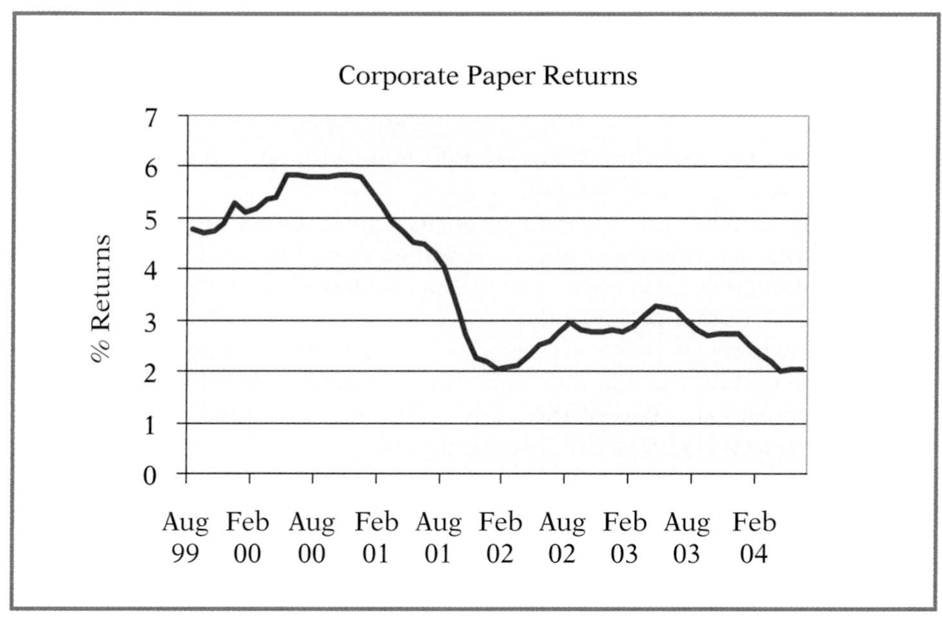

Figure 20-3 Returns from Corporate Paper (mid-1999–mid-2004)

Source: Corporate Paper Returns, August 1999 to June 2004. Data adapted from the Bank of Canada, Prime corporate paper rate 1 month, specific series B14039 (V122509). www.bankofcanada.ca/en/interest-look.htm. Reprinted with permission of the Bank of Canada.

How Loan Terms Affect the Effective Interest Rate of a Loan

The effective interest rate of a bank loan may not be the same as the stated interest rate advertised by the bank because of a lender's loan terms. In the following sections, we describe how to find the effective interest rate and what terms affect the effective interest rate.

The Effective Interest Rate

Some loans have the same effective rate of interest as the stated rate of interest because the bank places no terms on the loan other than the amount of interest and the amount borrowed. In these cases, finding the effective interest rate per period is straightforward. We divide the interest paid on the loan by the amount of money borrowed during the period of the loan (and afterwards multiply the result by 100 to obtain a percent). Equation 20-5 shows the effective interest rate formula:

Effective Interest Rate of a Loan

$$\text{Effective Interest Rate k} = \frac{\text{\$ Interest You Pay}}{\text{\$ You Get to Use}} \tag{20-5}$$

For example, suppose you borrow $10,000 from a bank for one year and your promissory note specifies that you are to pay $1,000 in interest at the end of the year. We use Equation 20-5 to find the effective interest rate for the loan as follows:

$$\begin{aligned} k &= \frac{\$1{,}000}{\$10{,}000} \\ &= 0.10 \\ \times 100 &= 10\% \end{aligned}$$

The calculations show that for a $10,000 loan with $1,000 in interest, the effective interest rate is 10 percent.

Effective interest rates are customarily expressed as annual rates. If a loan's maturity is for one year and there are no complicating factors, computing effective interest rates is quite simple, as we have just seen. Equation 20-5 gives the effective rate per period.

For many loans, however, things are not so simple. Lenders have a variety of terms and conditions that they apply to loans and many of them affect the effective interest rate. Two of the more common loan terms, *discount loans* and *compensating balances,* are discussed next.

Discount Loans

Sometimes a lender's terms specify that interest is to be collected up front, at the time the loan is made, rather than at maturity. When this is the case, the loan is referred to as a **discount loan**. In a discount loan, the amount the borrower actually receives is the principal amount borrowed minus the interest owed. So the amount the borrower may use is lower than if the loan were a standard loan with interest paid annually at year's end. As a result, the borrower's effective interest rate is higher than it would be for a standard loan.

Let's return to our earlier one-year, $10,000 loan example to see what happens if it is a discount loan. Instead of paying $1,000 in interest at the end of the year (the equivalent of an effective interest rate of 10 percent), the $1,000 in interest must be paid at the beginning of the year. According to Equation 20-5, the effective interest rate is as follows:

$$k = \frac{\$ \text{ Interest You Pay}}{\$ \text{ You Get to Use}}$$
$$= \frac{\$1,000}{\$10,000 - \$1,000}$$
$$= \frac{\$1,000}{\$9,000}$$
$$= 0.1111 \text{ or } 11.11\%$$

Note that by collecting the $1,000 interest on the loan at the start of the year, the effective rate of interest rose from 10 percent to 11.11 percent, solely because of the timing of the interest payment. The stated interest rate, then, is lower than the borrower's effective rate of interest.

Compensating Balances

Sometimes a lender's loan terms will specify that while a loan is outstanding, the borrower must keep some minimum balance in a chequing account at the lender's institution. The amount required is called a **compensating balance.**

The lender would say that this minimum balance is its compensation for granting the borrower favourable loan terms (even though the terms may not be especially favourable). Because the borrower cannot allow the balance in the chequing account to fall below the required minimum during the life of the loan, the borrower may not use these funds during the life of the loan. As a result, the borrower's effective interest rate is higher than it would be without a compensating balance requirement. This assumes that the borrower would not have kept the required compensating balance funds in the chequing account if the loan were a standard loan.

Let's add a compensating balance requirement to our one-year, $10,000 loan with a year-end interest payment of $1,000. The stated rate of interest is 10 percent. Assume the bank requires a compensating balance of 12 percent of the amount borrowed in a chequing account during the life of the loan. This compensating balance requirement would be referred to as a "12 percent compensating balance requirement." We quickly figure out that 12 percent of $10,000 is $1,200. Then we use Equation 20-5 to find the following effective interest rate:

$$k = \frac{\$ \text{ Interest You Pay}}{\$ \text{ You Get to Use}}$$
$$= \frac{\$1,000}{\$10,000 - \$1,200}$$
$$= \frac{\$1,000}{\$8,800}$$
$$= 0.1136 \text{ or } 11.36\%$$

We find that the effect of the bank's 12 percent compensating balance requirement is to raise the effective interest rate to the borrower by 1.36 percentage points. Instead of paying 10 percent, the borrower actually pays 11.36 percent. The effect of the compensating balance requirement is to increase the effective rate of interest, 11.36 percent, compared with the stated rate of interest of 10 percent.

Figure 20-4 shows how changing the terms of a one-year loan can affect the effective interest rate. The chart summarizes the effect of simple interest, discount interest, and compensating balances. Figure 20-4 demonstrates that loan terms such as discount interest and compensating balances reduce the amount the borrower gets to use, thus raising the effective interest rate.

Figure 20-4
How Changing the Terms of a Loan Can Affect the Effective Interest Rate
Figure 20-4 shows the impact of loan terms on the effective interest rate (the amount you pay to obtain the loan divided by the amount you get to use during the life of the loan).

Simple Interest Rate	$\frac{\text{\$ interest you pay}}{\text{\$ you get to use}}$	$\frac{\$1{,}000}{\$10{,}000}$	= .10, or 10%
Discount Interest	$\frac{\text{\$ interest you pay}}{\text{\$ you get to use}}$	$\frac{\$1{,}000}{\$10{,}000 - \$1{,}000 = \$9{,}000}$	= .1111, or 11.11%
Compensating Balance (12%)	$\frac{\text{\$ interest you pay}}{\text{\$ you get to use}}$	$\frac{\$1{,}000}{\$10{,}000 - \$1{,}200 = \$8{,}800}$	= .1136, or 11.36%

Loan Maturities Shorter Than One Year

Another term that affects the effective interest rate is a loan maturity that is less than one year. In such cases, we modify Equation 20-5 to convert the effective interest rate of the loan that is for less than a year into an annual rate. We find the annual rate so that we can compare that rate with those from other lenders, almost all of which are expressed as annual rates. Annualizing the rates allows a comparison of apples to apples, rather than apples to oranges. An example demonstrates this point.

Suppose you are borrowing $10,000 for one *month* and paying $1,000 in interest at the end of the *month* (with no other conditions). The effective interest rate of this loan is 10 percent, according to Equation 20-5. However, remember that the rate is 10 percent *per month.* It would be inaccurate to say that the interest rate on this loan was the same as a 10 percent loan from another financial institution. Why? Because the 10 percent stated rate from the other institution is an annual rate and you are comparing it to a monthly rate. For one month, the other institution's stated rate would be 10 percent divided by 12 months, which equals 0.83 percent, an amount that is considerably less than the 10 percent monthly interest on your loan.

Annualizing Interest Rates We can modify Equation 20-5 so that it annualizes interest rates that are not paid yearly. The modified formula, Equation 20-6, follows:

Effective Annual Interest Rate (20-6)

$$\text{Effective Annual Interest Rate } k = \left(1 + \frac{\text{\$ Interest You Pay}}{\text{\$ You Get to Use}}\right)^{\left(\begin{smallmatrix}\text{Loan Periods}\\ \text{in a Year}\end{smallmatrix}\right)} - 1$$

We then multiply the result by 100 to find the percentage rate.

Now let's use Equation 20-6 to annualize the $10,000 loan with interest of $1,000 a month. Remember, the *monthly* interest rate for this loan is 10 percent and there are 12 monthly loan periods in a year. The calculations follow:

$$
\begin{aligned}
k &= \left(1+\frac{\$1,000}{\$10,000}\right)^{12} - 1 \\
&= (1+0.10)^{12} - 1 \\
&= (1.10)^{12} - 1 \\
&= 3.1384 - 1 \\
&= 2.1384 \text{ or } 213.84\%
\end{aligned}
$$

We find that the interest rate is more than 213 percent. Surely there is a more inexpensive alternative at another bank. Suppose you find one in which the *stated* annual interest rate for a $10,000 one-month loan is 12 percent. What's the *effective* annual interest rate for this loan? In order to apply Equation 20-6 to find out, we first compute the dollar amount of interest to be paid:

- The stated rate for one year, or 12 months, is 12 percent, so the rate for one month is 12 percent/12 = 1 percent.[5]
- 1 percent of $10,000 is $10,000 × 0.01 = $100.
- So, the amount of "dollars you pay" to get this loan is $100.

Because the loan is for one month, we know that there are 12 loan periods in a year. Now we are ready to plug these numbers into Equation 20-6 as shown next:

$$
\begin{aligned}
k &= \left(1+\frac{\$\text{ Interest You Pay}}{\$\text{ You Get to Use}}\right)^{\left(\text{Loan Periods in a Year}\right)} - 1 \\
&= \left(1+\frac{\$\,100}{\$\,10,000}\right)^{12} - 1 \\
&= (1+0.01)^{12} - 1 \\
&= (1.01)^{12} - 1 \\
&= 1.1268 - 1 \\
&= 0.1268 \text{ or } 12.68\%
\end{aligned}
$$

The effective annual rate, 12.68 percent, is a little higher than the bank's stated rate of 12 percent because of the compounding effect of adding "interest on interest" for 12 months.

Beware the payday loan terms of Money-Marts. If $100 were borrowed for the normal two-week period, a cheque for $120 dated two weeks hence would have to be turned over to Money-Mart by the borrower. This reflects the repay-

[5]If the loan's term is one week, divide by 52. If it is one day, divide by 365, and so on.

ment of the \$100 principal plus the \$20 "fee" charged. Treating the fee as interest we get:

$$k = \left(\$1 + \frac{\$20}{\$100}\right)^{26} - 1$$
$$= 1.20^{26} - 1$$
$$= 114.47546 - 1$$
$$= 113.47546 \text{ (expressed as a decimal)}$$
$$= 11{,}347.546\%$$

The exponent was 26 because there are 26 two-week periods per year (52 weeks per year divided by 2). The effective annual rate for this loan is 11,347.546 percent.

We have seen how discount loans, compensating balances, and loans that have maturities less than a year affect the effective annual interest rate. Next, we work through an example of a loan with more than one complicating term.

A Comprehensive Example

Let's consider a loan that includes all the complicating factors discussed in the preceding sections. Suppose you want to borrow \$5,000 for one week and the bank's terms are 8 percent interest, collected on a discount basis, with a 10 percent compensating balance. What is the effective annual interest rate of this loan?

Computing the Interest Cost in Dollars The bank's stated rate of interest for one year, or 52 weeks, is 8 percent, so the rate for one week is 8 percent/52 = 0.1538 percent.

$$0.1538 \text{ percent of } \$5{,}000 \text{ is } \$5{,}000 \times 0.001538 = \$7.69$$

So, the amount of dollars in interest that you pay to obtain this loan is \$7.69.

Computing the Net Amount Received Because this is a discount loan, the interest will be collected up front. This means that \$7.69 will be deducted from the \$5,000 loan.

The loan also has a 10 percent compensating balance requirement, so 10 percent of the \$5,000, or \$500, must remain in a chequing account at the bank, denying you the use of it during the life of the loan.

The net amount of money that you will get to use during the life of the loan is \$5,000 – \$7.69 – \$500 = \$4,492.31.

Computing the Effective Annual Interest Rate We use Equation 20-6, the formula for annualizing a loan with a term of interest payments less than a year, to find the effective annual interest rate for this loan. The calculations follow:

$$
\begin{aligned}
k &= \left(1+\frac{\$\text{ Interest You Pay}}{\$\text{ You Get to Use}}\right)^{\left(\begin{smallmatrix}\text{Loan Periods}\\ \text{in a Year}\end{smallmatrix}\right)}-1\\
&= \left(1+\frac{\$7.69}{\$4,492.31}\right)^{52}-1\\
&= (1+0.001712)^{52}-1\\
&= (1.001712)^{52}-1\\
&= 1.093-1\\
&= 0.093 \text{ or } 9.3\%
\end{aligned}
$$

We see that the effective annual interest rate for a one-week, \$5,000 discounted loan with an interest rate of 8 percent and a 10 percent compensating balance requirement is 9.3 percent. The effective rate of interest, 9.3 percent, is higher than the 8 percent stated rate of interest.

Computing the Amount to Borrow

In the preceding comprehensive example, you tried to borrow \$5,000. Presumably that was the amount you needed to use for a week. However, as shown, if the bank collected \$7.69 in interest up front and made you keep \$500 in a chequing account during the term of the loan, you would only receive \$4,492.31. Clearly, given the bank's terms, you will have to borrow some amount greater than \$5,000 to end up with the \$5,000 you need. So the question is, how much do you have to borrow to walk out of the bank with \$5,000?

We solve this question algebraically. Let X = the amount to borrow. Now, because the loan is a discount loan, the bank will collect one week's worth of interest or (0.08/52) times X at the beginning of the week. Furthermore, 10 percent of X must remain in a chequing account at the bank as a compensating balance. When these two amounts are subtracted from X, the remainder must equal \$5,000. Here is the equation describing the situation:

$$X-\left(\frac{0.08}{52}\right)X-0.10X=\$5,000$$

We then solve for X as follows:

$$
\begin{aligned}
X-\left(\frac{0.08}{52}\right)X-0.10X &= \$5,000\\
X-0.001538X-0.10X &= \$5,000\\
0.8985X &= \$5,000\\
X &= \$5,564.83
\end{aligned}
$$

We find that if you borrow \$5,564.83 for one week at 8 percent, discount interest, with a 10 percent compensating balance requirement, you will leave the bank with \$5,000.[6]

---

[6]In case you are wondering, the effective annual interest rate for this loan, per Equation 20-2, is 9.3 percent.

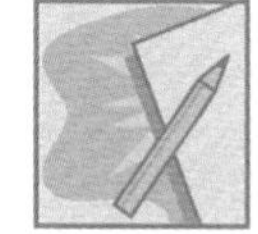

Take Note

Loans for which collateral is required are called *secured loans*. If no collateral is required, the loan is unsecured.

We have examined how loan terms can affect the effective interest rate. Now we turn to types of collateral that are used to secure short-term loans.

The importance of keeping high-quality commercial paper standards has been a cornerstone to North-American money markets. Other countries also find that they have a need for quality assurances. International Perspectives in Finance 20-1 identifies some issues that prevailed in India.

INTERNATIONAL PERSPECTIVES IN FINANCE 20-

RBI Revisits Commercial Paper Guidelines

As part of its consultative process, the Reserve Bank of India (RBI) has released a status paper on commercial paper (CP) inviting comments.

CP is a negotiable short-term unsecured promissory note with fixed maturities issued by well-rated companies. CP is a low cost alternative to bank loans from institutional investors. The last review of the CP guidelines was undertaken in October 2000. Periodically, market participants have suggested various modifications in the guidelines and the RBI has carefully sifted through these suggestions to avoid any mishaps.

When CP was introduced in January 1990, only highly rated corporate borrowers were allowed to issue CP to diversify their short-term borrowings, but over time there has been a diluting of the norms. Initially, CP had a maximum maturity of three-six months, but in 1993 the maximum maturity was raised to less than one year. Subsequently, in 1998, the minimum maturity was reduced to 15 days. Inter-country comparison shows that in the US there is no prescribed maturity period, but as a matter of practice it is limited to 270 days; the most popular period is, however, 1–7 days.

In India, the minimum rating was initially P1+ of CRISIL but was subsequently, softened to P1 (April 1990) and P2 (May 1992). In the UK, US and France rating is not compulsory but generally only the highest rating evinces investor interest.

...

It is recommended that the minimum credit rating be brought down to P3 of CRISIL to provide a choice to issuers and investors. Enough is enough on diluting norms. By making P3 the minimum, the CP market can get a bad name by selling the paper of companies which are close to junk status. It would take only one failure to make investors and, therefore, the RBI should not further dilute the m mum rating.

...

It is suggested that assets backed commercial pa should be introduced to deepen the CP market. Such a m ification would enable riskier firms to access the CP mar The RBI should stay away from such assets backed CP.

In order to improve transparency, the discussion pa states that it should be made mandatory to report all deals on the NDS platform within 15 minutes of underta the transactions so that benchmarking becomes m appropriate. This should be implemented.

...

The total amount outstanding under CP at the en March 2004 was a little over Rs 9,100 crore. The CP ma has, over the last 14 years, been free from glitches. The cussion paper put out by the RBI shows signs of daredev which the RBI would do well to avoid.

Dropping CP minimum rating, *reducing the CP to a c day maturity* and asset backed CP are avoidable measu The RBI has an immaculate record of carefully nurtu money market instruments. One fails to understand why RBI is willing to be led down a hazardous path. The must know that it will take just one CP failure to collapse CP market which it has so assiduously developed over last 14 years. Why is the RBI taking the risk of sullying name even if it is only in a discussion paper?

Source: "RBI Revisits Commercial Paper Guidelines" by Mr S. Tarapore. Reprinted with the permission of Indian Express Newspapers (Bombay) Ltd.

Collateral for Short-Term Loans

The promissory note that specifies the terms of the loan often includes the type of **collateral** used to secure the loan.

For secured short-term loans, lenders usually require that the assets pledged for collateral be short term in nature also. Lenders require short-term assets because they are generally more liquid than long-term assets and are easier to convert to cash if the borrower defaults on the loan. The major types of short-term assets used for short-term loan collateral are accounts receivable and inventory.

Accounts Receivable as Collateral

Accounts receivable are assets with value because they represent money owed to a firm. Because of their value, a lender might be willing to accept the accounts as collateral for a loan. If so, the borrowing firm may *pledge* its accounts receivable. The pledge is a promise that the firm will turn over the accounts receivable collateral to the lender in the case of default.

Loan agreements that use accounts receivable as collateral usually specify that the firm is responsible for the amount of the accounts receivable even if the firm's credit customers fail to pay. In short, the borrowing firm still has to pay even if its customers do not.

Lenders try to safeguard against accounts receivable that fluctuate so much that the value of the account becomes less than the value of the loan. Accounts receivable fluctuate because some credit customers may send in payments on their outstanding accounts receivable, others may make new charges, and some may be late with payments. If accounts receivable are pledged as short-term loan collateral, lenders usually require a loan payment plan that prevents the value of the accounts from dropping below the value of the loans. For instance, a bank may require a borrower to send payments received on pledged accounts to the lender to apply against the loan balance. Sending payments as received decreases the balance of the loan as the value of accounts receivable decreases, thereby protecting the lender.

Inventory as Collateral

Like accounts receivable, inventory represents assets that have value, so it can be used as collateral for loans. The practice of using inventory as collateral for a short-term loan is called **inventory financing.**

A major problem with inventory financing is valuing the inventory. If a borrowing firm defaults on a loan secured by inventory, the lender wants to know that the inventory can compensate for the remaining loan balance. To illustrate how important valuing inventory is, suppose you were a banker who lent a firm $200,000 for six months. As collateral, the firm put up its entire inventory of Alien Angels dolls, based on characters in a soon-to-be-released major motion picture. Unfortunately, once the movie was released, it was a bust. The firm was unable to repay its loan and you as the banker have ended up with 10,000 dolls no one wants. It is small comfort to you now that the firm said the angels were worth $20 each when they were offered as collateral.

To compensate for the difficulties in valuing inventory, lenders usually lend only a fraction of the stated value of the inventory. If the inventory consists of fairly standard items that can be resold easily, like 2 × 4s, then the lender might be willing to lend up to 80 percent of the inventory's stated value. In contrast, if the inventory consists of perishable or specialized items, like the Alien Angels in our example, then the lender will only lend a small fraction of their value, or might not be willing to accept them as collateral at all.

Inventory depletion is an additional concern for lenders who allow borrowers to use inventory as short-term loan collateral. The borrowing firm can sell the pledged inventory and use the cash received for other purposes, leaving the lender with nothing if the borrower defaults. This can happen when the lender has only a general claim, or *blanket lien*, on the borrower's inventory in the event of a default. Therefore, when inventory is used as collateral for a loan, the lender will often insist on some procedures to safeguard its interests.

One procedure to safeguard the interests of the lender is for the borrower to issue trust receipts to the lender. A *trust receipt* is a legal document in which specifically identified assets, inventory in this case, are pledged as collateral for the loan. Automobiles, railroad cars, and airplanes are often financed this way. The lender can make surprise visits to the borrower's business, checking to be sure that the pledged assets are on hand as they should be. There is often a unique identification number (a car's VIN, vehicle identification number, for example) on these assets.

Another procedure to control pledged inventory is to use a *public warehouse* where the inventory cannot be removed and sold without permission of the lender. When the inventory is sold (with the lender's permission), the proceeds are sent to the lender and used to reduce the outstanding loan balance. Although this arrangement gives the lender control, it is expensive for the borrowing firm. Usually the borrowing firm must pay for the warehouse and seek the lender's permission each time it wants to sell some inventory.

We have seen that short-term secured loans generally have short-term liquid assets pledged as collateral, such as accounts receivable or inventory. Lenders often add loan terms to protect against problems such as fluctuating accounts receivable and overvalued or depleted inventory.

The following feature discusses APR, APY, and EAR.

FINANCIAL MANAGEMENT AND YOU 20-1

APR, APY, and EAR

Your credit card cites interest rates in terms of the annual percentage rate, APR. Financial institutions pay interest on deposits in terms of annual percentage yield, APY. In this chapter, we showed you how to compute the equivalent annual rate, EAR, which reflects the effect of compounding. Here we show the differences among these three percentage calculations.

If your credit card company charges you 1.5 percent per month, then the APR reported would be 18 percent. The APR is simply the quoted rate per period times the number of time periods per year. Because there are 12 months per year, the monthly rate of 1.5 percent is multiplied by 1[illegible] obtain the APR of 18 percent.

$$\begin{aligned} \text{APR} &= \text{Rate per Period} \times \text{Number of Periods per Y[illegible]} \\ &= 1.5\% \times 12 \\ &= 18\% \end{aligned}$$

When banks advertise the interest rates they pa[illegible] depositors, they quote the interest rate in terms of APY. [illegible] formula is:

$$\text{APY} = 100 \times [(1 + \$\ \text{Interest}/\$\ \text{Principal})^{(365/\text{days in term})} \ldots$$

For example, if a firm pays 6 percent annual interest mpounded monthly, a six-month $1,000 GIC would earn erest of $30.38. Assume that the GIC is for January ough June, a period having 181 days. The annual interest e of 6 percent divided by 12 gives a monthly interest rate 0.5% or 0.005 expressed as a decimal. The calculations the interest earned and for the APY are:

$$\begin{aligned} \text{Interest} &= 1.005^6 \times \$1{,}000 - \$1{,}000 \\ &= \$1{,}030.38 - \$1{,}000 \\ &= \$30.38 \\ \text{APY} &= 100 \times [(1 + \$30.38 / \$1{,}000)^{(365/181)} - 1] \\ &= 0.0622 \text{ or } 6.22\% \end{aligned}$$

The EAR presented in this chapter is the annual rate that would be paid if interest were compounded each stated period for a full year.

$$\text{EAR} = (1 + \$\ \text{Interest}/\$\ \text{You Get to Use})^{(\text{Loan Periods in a Year})} - 1$$

For example, a firm pays 1 percent interest per month on a one-month $1,000 loan. Also assume that there is a 15 percent compensating balance requirement. The interest is 0.01 × $1,000, which equals $10. The amount the borrower gets to use is $1,000 × (1 – 0.15), which equals $850. There are 12 months in a year. The EAR would be:

$$\begin{aligned} \text{EAR} &= (1 + \$10/\$850)^{12} - 1 \\ &= 1.0118^{12} - 1 \\ &= 1.1512 - 1 \\ &= 0.1512 \text{ or } 15.12\% \end{aligned}$$

SUMMARY

20-1 Describe two reasons why external short-term financing may be required.

Firms rely on short-term financing from outside sources for two reasons:

- *Growth:* Profits simply may not be high enough to keep up with the rate at which they are buying new assets.
- *Choice:* Rather than save enough money to make desired purchases, many firms borrow money at the outset to make their purchases.

20-2 Differentiate between long-term financing and short-term financing.

Short-term financing is usually a less expensive option than long-term financing because of its generally lower interest rates. However, short-term financing is riskier than long-term financing because, unlike long-term financing, the loans come due soon, the lender may not be willing to renew financing on favourable terms, and short-term interest rates may rise unexpectedly.

20-3 Describe two common types of short-term business loans.

Two common types of short-term business loans are a self-liquidating loan and a line of credit. A self-liquidating loan is a loan for an asset that will generate enough return to repay the loan balance. A line of credit is a maximum total balance that a bank sets for a firm's outstanding short-term loans.

20-4 Define trade credits and explain how to compute their cost.

Trade credit is obtained by purchasing materials, supplies, or services on credit. By buying on credit, the firm has use of the funds from the time of the purchase until the account is paid. To calculate the cost of trade credit, divide the amount of the discount offered by the supplier by the amount the buyer owes. The result is annualized for comparison with other financing sources.

20-5 Define commercial paper and explain how to compare its percent cost to that of a bank loan.

Commercial paper consists of unsecured notes issued by large, creditworthy corporations for periods up to 270 days. The cost of commercial paper is quoted as a discount yield. To compare the percent cost of a commercial paper issue to the percent cost of a bank loan, the commercial paper's discount yield must be converted to an effective annual interest rate.

20-6 Describe how to compute the effective interest rate of a loan and compare it to the loan's stated interest rate.

The cost of a loan is normally measured by dividing the amount paid to obtain the loan by the amount the borrower gets to use during the life of the loan. The result is converted to a percentage. The stated interest rate on a loan is not always the same as the loan's effective annual interest rate. If the lender collects interest up front (a discount interest loan) or requires the borrowing firm to keep a fraction of the loan in an account at the lending institution (a compensating balance), then the amount of money the borrower gets to use is reduced. As a result, the effective rate of interest the borrower is paying is increased.

20-7 Explain how accounts receivable and inventory can be used as collateral.

Short-term loans are often secured by short-term liquid assets, such as accounts receivable and inventory. When accounts receivable are used for collateral, the borrower pledges to turn over its accounts receivable to the lender if the borrower defaults. When inventory is used for collateral, the borrowing firm often sets aside the inventory that has been identified for collateral in a separate warehouse. When the inventory is sold, the cash received is forwarded to the lender in payment for the loan.

EQUATIONS INTRODUCED IN THIS CHAPTER

Equation 20-1: Trade Credit Effective Annual Interest Rate Formula

$$k = \left(1 + \frac{\text{Discount \%}}{100 - \text{Discount \%}}\right)^{\left(\frac{365}{\text{Days to Pay} - \text{Discount Period}}\right)} - 1$$

where

k = Cost of trade credit expressed as an effective annual interest rate
Discount % = Percentage discount being offered
Days to Pay = Time between the day of the credit purchase and the day the firm must pay its bill
Discount Period = Number of days in the discount period

Equation 20-2: Dollar Amount of the Discount on a Commercial Paper Note

$$D = \frac{DY \times Par \times DTG}{360}$$

where

D = Dollar amount of the discount
DY = Discount yield
Par = Face value of the commercial paper issue; the amount to be paid at maturity
DTG = Days to go until maturity

Equation 20-3: Price of a Commercial Paper Note

$$\text{Price} = \text{Par} - D$$

where

Par = Face value of the note at maturity
D = Dollar amount of the discount

Equation 20-4: Effective Annual Interest Rate of a Commercial Paper Note

$$\text{Effective Annual Interest Rate} = \left(\frac{\text{Par}}{\text{Price}}\right)^{\left(\frac{365}{\text{DTG}}\right)} - 1$$

where

Par = Face value of the note at maturity
Price = Price of the note when purchased
DTG = Number of days until the note matures

Equation 20-5: Effective Interest Rate of a Loan

$$\text{Effective Interest Rate } k = \frac{\$\text{ Interest You Pay}}{\$\text{ You Get to Use}}$$

Equation 20-6: Effective Annual Interest Rate

$$\text{Effective Annual Interest Rate } k = \left(1 + \frac{\$\text{ Interest You Pay}}{\$\text{ You Get to Use}}\right)^{\left(\begin{array}{c}\text{Loan Periods}\\ \text{in a Year}\end{array}\right)} - 1$$

SELF-TEST

ST-1. Your company's suppliers offer terms of 3/15, n40. What is the cost of forgoing the discount and delaying payment until the fortieth day?

ST-2. A commercial paper dealer is willing to pay a 4 percent discount yield for a $1 million issue of Pennzoil 60-day commercial paper notes. To what effective annual interest rate does the 4 percent discount yield equate?

ST-3. A bank is willing to lend your company $20,000 for six months at 8 percent interest with a 10 percent compensating balance. What is the effective annual interest rate of this loan?

ST-4. Using the loan terms from ST-3, how much would your firm have to borrow in order to have $20,000 for use during the loan period?

REVIEW QUESTIONS

1. Companies with rapidly growing levels of sales do not need to worry about raising funds from outside the firm. Do you agree or disagree with this statement? Explain.
2. Banks like to make short-term, self-liquidating loans to businesses. Why?
3. What are compensating balances and why do banks require them from some customers? Under what circumstances would banks be most likely to impose compensating balances?
4. What happens when a bank charges discount interest on a loan?
5. What is trustworthy collateral from the lender's perspective? Explain whether accounts receivable and inventory are trustworthy collateral.
6. Trade credit is free credit. Do you agree or disagree with this statement? Explain.
7. What are the pros and cons of commercial paper relative to bank loans for a company seeking short-term financing?

PROBLEMS

Simple and Discount Loans ▶

20-1. Harold Hill is planning to borrow $20,000 for one year, paying interest in the amount of $1,600 to a bank. Calculate the effective annual interest rate if the interest is paid:

a. At the end of the year

b. At the beginning of the year (discount loan)

Loans with Compensating Balance ▶

20-2. Chad Gates is planning to borrow $40,000 for one year, paying interest of $2,400 to a bank at the beginning of the year (discount loan). In addition, according to the terms of the loan, the bank requires Chad to keep 10 percent of the borrowed funds in a non-interest-bearing chequing account at the bank during the life of the loan. Calculate the effective annual interest rate.

Challenge Problem ▶

20-3. Ralph Bellamy is considering borrowing $20,000 for a year from a bank that has offered the following alternatives:

a. An interest payment of $1,800 at the end of the year

b. An interest payment of 8 percent of $20,000 at the beginning of the year

c. An interest payment of 7.5 percent of $20,000 at the end of the year in addition to a compensating balance requirement of 10 percent

i. Which alternative is best for Ralph from the effective-interest-rate point of view?

ii. If Ralph needs the entire amount of $20,000 at the beginning of the year and chooses the terms under (c), how much should he borrow? How much interest would he have to pay at the end of the year?

Loans with a Life of Less than a Year ▶

20-4. If Joyce Heath borrows $14,000 for three months at an annual interest rate of 16 percent paid up-front with a compensating balance of 10 percent, compute the effective annual interest rate of the loan.

Discount Loans with Compensating Balance for Less than a Year ▶

20-5. You are planning to borrow $10,000 from a bank for two weeks. The bank's terms are 7 percent annual interest, collected on a discount basis, with a 10 percent compensating balance. Compute the effective annual interest rate of the loan.

Commercial Paper ▶

20-6. Bud Baxter is planning a $1 million issue of commercial paper to finance increased sales from easing the credit policy. The commercial paper note has a 60-day maturity and 6 percent discount yield. Calculate:

a. The dollar amount of the discount

b. The price

c. The effective annual interest rate for the issue

Commercial Paper ▶

20-7. Carmen Velasco, an analyst at Smidgen Corporation, is trying to calculate the effective annual interest rate for a $2 million issue of a Smidgen 60-day commercial paper note. The commercial paper dealer is prepared to offer a 4 percent discount yield on the issue. Calculate the effective annual interest rate for Carmen.

Trade Credit ▶

20-8. Beth Everdene, the sales manager of Gordon's Bakery, Inc., wants to extend trade credit with terms of 2/15, n45 to your company to boost sales. Calculate the cost of forgoing the discount and paying on the forty-fifth day.

20-9. Calculate the cost of forgoing the following trade credit discounts and paying on the last day allowed:

◀ Trade Credit

a. 3/10, n60

b. 2/15, n30

Recalculate the costs assuming payments were made on the fortieth day in each of the preceding cases without any penalty. Compare your results.

20-10. Legacy Enterprises received an invoice from its supplier. The terms of credit were stated as 3/15, n45. Calculate the effective annual interest rate on the trade credit.

◀ Trade Credit

20-11. Callaway Krugs issues $2,000,000 in commercial paper for 90 days at a 3.8 percent discount yield. Calculate each of the following.

◀ Commercial Paper

a. Dollar amount of the discount

b. Price of the commercial paper

c. Effective annual interest rate on the commercial paper

20-12. Mr. Daniels wants to buy a new car. The bank has offered him a $20,000 discount interest loan at 6.5 percent. What is the effective interest rate?

◀ Effective Interest Rate

20-13. National Bank requires that all its borrowers have a compensating balance of 13 percent of the amount borrowed. If you need to take out a small-business expansion loan for $30,000 at 10 percent, what would be your effective interest rate on this one-year loan?

◀ Compensating Balance

20-14. You are the financial manager for Talc Ltd. and the owner has just asked you to compute the effective annual interest rate on the loans the company currently has outstanding. The following is a list of these loans:

◀ Annualizing Interest Rates

a. $50,000; 0.5% monthly rate, maturity: 1 month

b. $150,000, 0.6% monthly rate, maturity: 3 months

c. $75,000, 0.75% monthly rate, maturity: 1 month

d. $120,000; 0.8% monthly rate, maturity: 6 months

20-15. To sustain its growth in sales, Monarch Machine Tools Company needs $100,000 in additional funds next year. The following alternatives for financing the growth are available:

◀ Comparing Costs of Alternative Short-Term Financing

a. Forgoing a discount available on trade credit with terms of 1/10, n45 and, hence, increasing its accounts payable

b. Obtaining a loan from a bank at 10 percent interest paid up front

Calculate the cost of financing for each option and select the best source.

20-16. If the bank imposes an additional requirement of a 12 percent compensating balance on Monarch in problem 20-15 and the company could negotiate more-liberal credit terms of 1/15, n60 from its supplier, would there be any change in Monarch's choice of short-term financing?

◀ Comparing Costs of Alternative Short-Term Financing

20-17. Ms. Johnson has just finished her company's *pro forma* financial statements and has concluded that $1.5 million in additional funds are needed. To cover this cash shortage, her company is going to take out a loan. HomeLand Bank has offered them a 9 percent discount interest loan with a 12 percent compensating balance. How much does Ms. Johnson's company need to borrow with these stated terms to leave the bank with $1.5 million in usable funds?

◀ Amount to Borrow

Financing ▶ Excel

20-18. Company ABC is increasing its sales terms from n45 to n60. In the long term, this new policy would create more sales and increase profit. However, one of the drawbacks in switching to this new policy is that there would be a greater need for financing inventory production. This is due to new sales and customers would be slower in paying back their debts. We will assume that all customers pay on the final possible date. Under the old policy, the amount of sales was $25,000 per day. Under the new system, the amount of sales would be $35,000 per day. The gross profit is 30 percent. ABC needed to finance all additional inventory. They had two choices. They could issue commercial paper at a discount of 3.5 percent for a ninety-day note, or they could use a line of credit from the bank at an annual yield of 3.5 percent (compounded daily).

a. If your goal were to choose the least expensive source of financing, which would you choose?

b. What would happen if you were forced to keep 1 percent of all that would be borrowed on the line of credit, in a chequing account earning 0 percent?

Financing ▶ Excel

20-19. Company ABC is pausing to reflect on their decision in problem 20-18.

a. Using your answers from (a) in problem 20-18, try to see what the NPV of the change is. Assume that all additional inventory must be financed through short-term borrowing.

b. How would including ABC's tax rate of 30 percent change things?

Financing ▶ Excel

20-20. Brother Corp. is analyzing one of its supplier's new credit terms. The supplier's old credit terms were 0.5/10, n30. With the current cost of borrowing, Brother had been indifferent between waiting 30 days to pay off the debt or borrowing at day 10 and saving the 0.5 percent discount. The new credit term is 1/15, n60.

a. Should Brother Corp. take advantage of the new credit terms?

b. Assume the cost of borrowing for Brother is linked to the prime rate. If all impacts of Brother's borrowing rate are proportional to the prime rate, by how much would the prime rate have to change in order for you to come to a different conclusion than the one chosen within (a)?

Secured Loans ▶

20-21. BigBank is about to give a secured loan to one of its clients, based on the client putting the value of the receivables up as collateral. Your boss at BigBank wants to make sure that the preferred rate you are about to give is justified.

a. What sort of provisions would you create in order to protect BigBank's position?

b. What could your client do that could negate the reality of the loan being secured?

c. How would bad debts and the average age of the receivables affect your position?

Financing ▶

20-22. Your client is extremely risk-adverse and would like to guarantee his payments as much as possible. He has come to you for suggestions as to creating a net income that would fluctuate the least, month after month. Your client's company is being offered a 4 percent (monthly compounding) line of credit or a fixed 10-year loan at 5.5 percent for all financing needs. The line of credit is a variable rate linked to Prime. The company has been offering payment plans to those that cannot pay within the required 30 days. Fifty percent of sales come about because of the company's payment plan. The other fifty percent of sales are classified as receivables with an n30 payment period. The company's average age of receivables is 34 days. Bad debts have fluctuated throughout the months, averaging anywhere from 10 to 15 percent. Both the payment plan and the receivables need to be financed.

Assuming sales stay constant month-to-month, create a situation that would be the least volatile with the goal of obtaining the most profit as possible.

ANSWERS TO SELF-TEST

ST-1. The cost is found using Equation 20-1. The discount percentage is 3 percent, the discount period is 15 days, and payment is to be made on the fortieth day. The calculations follow:

$$
\begin{aligned}
k &= \left(1+\frac{3}{100-3}\right)^{\left(\frac{365}{40-15}\right)}-1 \\
&= (1+0.0309278)^{14.6}-1 \\
&= (1.0309278)^{14.6}-1 \\
&= 1.56-1 \\
&= 0.56 \text{ or } 56\%
\end{aligned}
$$

ST-2. Use the three-step process described in the text to find the effective annual interest rate as follows:

- *Step 1:* Compute the discount using Equation 20-2.

$$
\begin{aligned}
D &= \frac{DY \times Par \times DTG}{360} \\
&= \frac{0.04 \times \$1,000,000 \times 60}{360} \\
&= \frac{\$2,400,000}{360} \\
&= \$6,667
\end{aligned}
$$

- *Step 2:* Compute the price using Equation 20-3.

$$
\begin{aligned}
\text{Price} &= \text{Par} - D \\
&= \$1,000,000 - \$6,667 \\
&= \$993,333
\end{aligned}
$$

- *Step 3:* Compute the effective annual interest rate using Equation 20-4.

$$
\begin{aligned}
\text{Effective Annual Interest Rate} &= \left(\frac{\text{Par}}{\text{Price}}\right)^{\left(\frac{365}{DTG}\right)}-1 \\
&= \left(\frac{\$1,000,000}{\$993,333}\right)^{\left(\frac{365}{60}\right)}-1 \\
&= (1.00671)^{6.083}-1 \\
&= 1.0415-1 \\
&= 0.0415 \text{ or } 4.15\%
\end{aligned}
$$

ST-3. The amount your firm would pay in interest with the loan is

$$0.08/2 = 0.04 \text{ for six months}$$
$$0.04 \times \$20{,}000 = \$800$$

The amount your firm would be able to use during the life of the loan is the principal less the compensating balance:

$$\$20{,}000 - (0.10 \times \$20{,}000) = \$18{,}000$$

The loan is for six months, so we use Equation 20-6 to solve for the effective annual interest rate:

$$\begin{aligned} k &= \left(1 + \frac{\$800}{\$18{,}000}\right)^2 - 1 \\ &= (1 + 0.0444)^2 - 1 \\ &= (1.0444)^2 - 1 \\ &= 1.0908 - 1 \\ &= 0.0908 \text{ or } 9.08\% \end{aligned}$$

ST-4. Let X = the amount to borrow.

$$\begin{aligned} X - 0.1X &= \$20{,}000 \\ 0.9X &= \$20{,}000 \\ X &= \$22{,}222 \end{aligned}$$

COMPREHENSIVE CASES: PART V

CASE 1: BREAD, INC.

Bread, Inc. has been operating for 10 years delivering new types of bread products to the public every couple of years. Its first product was simply labelled SuperBread. It offered more vitamins and had an extremely high amount of calcium in it. However, about 5 years ago, Bread, Inc. almost went bankrupt because of its concept of variety breads. The company offered different flavoured breads to the public according to the type of sandwich that they wanted to eat. The four major sellers were BalonyBread, HamburgerBread, TunaBread, and SpamBread. The idea was to put trace amounts of the particular sandwich meat inside the bread as it was baking. The problem occurred when the bread was put on the shelves. It went bad within a day. Worse, several lawsuits were issued against Bread, Inc. for food poisoning. It took Bread, Inc. almost 5 years to recover and they are now ready to venture into a new product line. The company's most recent product is called MoreBagel, which really looks like a super-sized bagel. It was developed as the Canadian version of the Philadelphia pretzel. Bread, Inc. is very proud of this new product and is contemplating restructuring in order to incorporate this new idea. The following is Bread, Inc.'s current partial balance sheet:

Partial Balance Sheet (In millions)

Assets	
Cash	$ 250,000
Accounts Receivable	90,000
Inventory	75,000
Net Machines	10,000
Liabilities	
Accounts Payable	5,000
Bonds Payable	300,000
Equity	
Common Shares	50,000
Retained Earnings	70,000

Bread, Inc. has a gross margin of 30 percent and currently has net daily sales of 1,000. With the introduction of MoreBagel, the company expects that its revenue will go through the roof. After a couple of months of initial set-up, it is expected that the revenue stream will begin to flow in a consistent manner for an infinite time into the future. Bread, Inc. also tends to pay most of its bills with cash, thinking that paying on account will hurt its reputation.

Bread, Inc. first went to its corporate financial advisor to see if more bonds could be issued to the public. The financial advisor called the investment-banking unit of the bank the company has dealt with for several years and it declined even the notion of creating a new bond issue. Bread, Inc.'s debt ratio is too high, way too high to consider lending money to it

Then the financial advisor asked the same question of someone that she knew in a local chartered bank. After she showed powerful data suggesting that the success of MoreBagel was imminent, this banker decides to offer Bread, Inc. a deal. The bank is willing to offer a short-term rate of 3 percent lower than what the company currently pays on its bonds. The cost of calling the bonds has been included in the financing rate. The bank is willing to lend money up to a debt ratio of 80 percent, which is extremely high, but the bank believes in the idea of MoreBagel.

Bread, Inc. needs cash and as much as possible. Each dollar that they do not have is a dollar expected to be lost in sales. There is no limit to the expansion possibilities. Each dollar put into Bread, Inc. can be expected to double within a year.

Another consideration is that Bread, Inc. has always followed the policy of a 50 percent dividend approach. This means that each year the company gives out 50 percent of its earnings in the form of dividends. In years that the money did not exist, Bread, Inc. borrowed to finance the dividend. The shareholders have gotten used to this; receiving the dividend is proof that the company is still doing well. The more money that they received in any year, the better they believed the company was doing.

Another interesting situation also exists for Bread, Inc. Because the company has been paying cash for so many years on most of its purchases, the suppliers have consistently reduced the price of their products by 2 percent. Although this policy may remain in place for the immediate future, Bread, Inc. believes that it will lose out on this deal if it starts paying on account for the long term. However, for the first three months, it does not expect the suppliers to notice any change.

Requirements

1. Analyze the situation and make notes about the major points of the situation.
2. Suggest several courses of action that will maximize the amount of cash flow available to Bread, Inc.
3. Knowing that Bread, Inc. has a history of potentially bad decisions, can you create a backup plan in case MoreBagel returns only 10 percent of what it is supposed to in profit? Or if MoreBagel only breaks even? Or if MoreBagel loses money?

CASE 2: YO-YO, INC.

Yo-Yo, Inc. was founded in 1965 when it began producing yo-yos for the general public. The yo-yo philosophy then was for each yo-yo company to make its own product. Production costs were $0.15 a yo-yo and each year those costs increased by 4 percent. Yo-Yo has also increased its price by the same amount. When the business was new, the original gross margin on the sale of each yo-yo was 20 percent. Over the last several decades, the company has been extremely successful at selling yo-yos, selling these toys worldwide and expanding production requirements by at least 10 percent each year. The growth in its production has been mentioned in top Canadian business journals and Yo-Yo has been named the most consistent growth company of the decade.

Recently, however, a new Chinese yo-yo company has entered the market and is selling its yo-yos well below Yo-Yo's price. Matching the competing company's price is a necessity in order to keep the growth stream the same as it has been in the past. However, this will eat into profits and Yo-Yo, Inc. does not like the idea. However, it seems to be necessary at this point; the growth of the company is still more important than any short-term gain. Currently, the yo-yos from China are selling at 10 percent below Yo-Yo's selling price. This is an unsatisfactory situation for Yo-Yo, Inc. After several decades of producing yo-yos, the company may need to outsource their production to another company who can produce the items less expensively. In this sense, Yo-Yo, Inc. will be exclusively in the retail business.

Consequently, Yo-Yo, Inc. is investigating three such manufacturers. The cost of storing yo-yos is $0.10 per unit per year and annual sales are expected to be 1.5 million units at the going rate. Sales are fairly constant each day, but Yo-Yo, Inc. likes to keep at least 2 days' worth of units on hand at all times.

The representatives of each potential supplier visited the company to argue their cases. Yo-Yo, Inc. used one of the suppliers' student-workers to take notes and summarize the important information in each company's offer. This seems to be a necessity considering the size of the account at hand and the abilities of each supplier to push aside the cost factor and focus on the relationship aspect. Having a good relationship with a supplier is important, but right now money talks. A good relationship is expected when an account that can be worth several millions of dollars is to be dealt with. The following summarizes the notes from the student-worker.

Arms Length, Inc.

Arms Length, Inc. is a company that has been in business for 10 years. It has a defective rating of 15 percent, which means 15 out of every 100 yo-yos manufactured are defective. Because of the heavy defect rate, Yo-Yo, Inc. would need to hire someone to monitor the yo-yos at an extra cost of $100,000 per year. The shipping and ordering costs are $125 per shipment. Further, an additional charge for shipping will be associated with the 15 defective units that need to be returned. Each 15-unit shipping will cost $10. (Note: At any given time, because yo-yos are tested the same day, only 85 percent of the original order will be in stock at any given time.) The cost per unit will give Yo-Yo, Inc. a 35 percent gross margin off the current market price.

Mr. Perfect, Inc.

Mr. Perfect, Inc. is a company that has been in business for 25 years. It has a defective rating of 0 percent, which means for each 100 yo-yos they produce, 0 are defective. The shipping and ordering costs are $160 per shipment. The cost per unit will give Yo-Yo, Inc. a 15 percent gross margin off the current market price. Yo-Yo likes this company because it believes that it will save testing salaries. For example, Yo-Yo will save $100,000 per year by using Mr. Perfect, Inc. instead of Arms Length, Inc.

SuperFly, Inc.

SuperFly, Inc. is a company that has been in business for 15 years. It has a defective rating of 5 percent, which means for each 100 yo-yos manufactured, 5 are defective. Yo-Yo, Inc. will need to hire someone to test for defects; this will cost the company about $50,000 a year. The shipping and ordering costs are $150 per shipment. SuperFly absorbs any costs associated with defects. (Note: At any given time, because yo-yos are tested the same day, only 95 percent of the original order will be in stock.) The cost per unit will give Yo-Yo, Inc. a 30 percent gross margin off the current market price.

Yo-Yo, Inc. is really concerned with its future course of action. The company is faced with so many options that it is not sure what to do. Yo-Yo needs to analyze which company they should use. Further, it may still be more profitable for Yo-Yo, Inc. to manufacture the yo-yos themselves, but it seems unlikely.

Requirements

1. Using the EOQ model, develop the best order quantity for each supplier.
2. Assess each company in terms of ordering costs, unit costs, and storing costs.
3. Make a decision in terms of both the short term and the long term. Make your decision with regard to future sales growth prospects.

CASE 3: CANADIAN TRIBUNE

The *Canadian Tribune* is a nationwide paper that has sold subscriptions in Canada for the last 23 years. Founded by Tomas Troy, the newspaper grew in popularity due to its honest and unbiased perspective on current issues. Not swayed by popular media, reporters at the *Tribune* were always told to write the truth as they saw it and the way that someone else would see it. The *Tribune* was one of the first papers that printed angry letters, addressing certain perspectives that were generally perceived as improper.

The company originally started with 5 employees and has now grown to 5,000 employees nationwide, offering the best benefits possible compared to the norm. The *Tribune* has always believed in people and that honesty and integrity should be the key to any newspaper. This is why it is having so many problems now. The *Tribune* has always focused itself on being a newspaper of the people and not of business, allowing people to pay when they felt like it. The idea is if the *Tribune* gives good service to the people, they will pay their respective fees on time and in good faith. Unfortunately, it seems as if this policy has been taking advantage of. The *Tribune*'s bad debts currently run at about 50 percent of its sales. This has forced it to raise prices by 50 percent to cover the cost of delinquent subscribers. Current-paying customers are becoming upset by constant increases and, ironically, are thinking that the *Tribune* is becoming just another money-grabbing company. Something needs to change.

One thing is for sure, the price of the paper must fall by at least 40 percent. It is not a free society if people cannot even afford reading material. Currently, there are two deals offered by the *Tribune*. The weekend deal costs $7 a week, offering the newspaper only on Saturdays and Sundays. The all-week deal costs $10 a week, offering the newspaper seven days a week. The current subscription rate is 50 million readers nationwide and is expected to increase dramatically in the next couple of years if the price of the paper falls. This is consistent with the *Tribune's* point of view. Everyone who wants a paper, or who would like a paper, should be able to receive one. It is unfortunate that its current prices seem to negate that policy. Further, by lowering subscription prices and thereby increasing subscription levels, the *Tribune* believes that it will be able to employ more writers and offer even better benefits to their employees.

The *Tribune* has been toying around with the idea of offering a discount to readers who pre-pay subscriptions. The company is not entirely sure how much of a discount it should give their subscribers, or even if it is worth it. An effective annual interest rate of a 2 percent discount is outrageously high.

Another consideration that subscribers may be offered is to have the newspaper pre-authorized to deduct each month's payment from a credit card of the reader's choice. The cost of this is 5 percent per dollar earned. Only 50 percent of the subscribers would even consider this option.

Another issue that has arisen is that many corporate subscribers ask for the paper but either they do not realize that they should pay, believing the paper is free, or they simply do not pay at all, thinking that it is not worth the hassle. Developing a credit policy for the general public may limit the idea of free speech, but corporations too lazy to pay may be another issue altogether. The *Tribune* has heard about credit policies but never having implemented one or believed in one, it has no clue where it should begin.

The last type of subscriber that the *Tribune* has is various bodies of government. These bodies do pay but in their own sweet time, sometimes up to two years late. Governments will not pay through a credit card and are indifferent to trade discounts. Paying off a newspaper quickly is like saving a penny in ten years; it is not important enough to them. The *Tribune* is not certain how to handle this and a creative solution may be needed.

The following breaks down the subscription percentage of each type of reader.

Subscribers	*Percentage*
Residential	60%
Corporate	25%
Government	15%
Total	100%

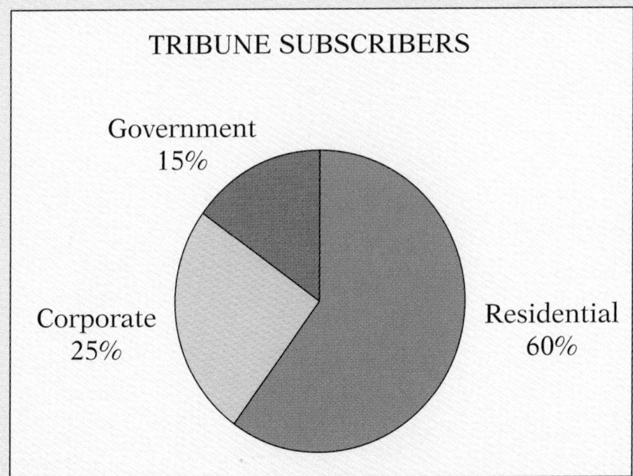

Requirements

1. Analyze the situations.
2. Develop a trade discount for residential readers that you believe will benefit the *Tribune*.
3. Develop a credit policy to deal with corporate readers.
4. Develop a creative solution to deal with government readers.
5. Summarize and explore different options that may exist.

APPENDIX

Table I

Future Value Interest Factors, FVIF, Compounded at i Percent for n Periods: $FVIF_{i,n} = (1 + i)^n$

Interest Rate, i

Number of Periods, n	0%	1%	2%	3%	4%	5%	6%	7%	8%	9%	10%	12%	14%	16%	18%	20%	25%	30%	35%	40%	45%	50%
0	1.0000	1.0000	1.0000	1.0000	1.0000	1.0000	1.0000	1.0000	1.0000	1.0000	1.0000	1.0000	1.0000	1.0000	1.0000	1.0000	1.0000	1.0000	1.0000	1.0000	1.0000	1.0000
1	1.0000	1.0100	1.0200	1.0300	1.0400	1.0500	1.0600	1.0700	1.0800	1.0900	1.1000	1.1200	1.1400	1.1600	1.1800	1.2000	1.2500	1.3000	1.3500	1.4000	1.4500	1.5000
2	1.0000	1.0201	1.0404	1.0609	1.0816	1.1025	1.1236	1.1449	1.1664	1.1881	1.2100	1.2544	1.2996	1.3456	1.3924	1.4400	1.5625	1.6900	1.8225	1.9600	2.1025	2.2500
3	1.0000	1.0303	1.0612	1.0927	1.1249	1.1576	1.1910	1.2250	1.2597	1.2950	1.3310	1.4049	1.4815	1.5609	1.6430	1.7280	1.9531	2.1970	2.4604	2.7440	3.0486	3.3750
4	1.0000	1.0406	1.0824	1.1255	1.1699	1.2155	1.2625	1.3108	1.3605	1.4116	1.4641	1.5735	1.6890	1.8106	1.9388	2.0736	2.4414	2.8561	3.3215	3.8416	4.4205	5.0625
5	1.0000	1.0510	1.1041	1.1593	1.2167	1.2763	1.3382	1.4026	1.4693	1.5386	1.6105	1.7623	1.9254	2.1003	2.2878	2.4883	3.0518	3.7129	4.4840	5.3782	6.4097	7.5938
6	1.0000	1.0615	1.1262	1.1941	1.2653	1.3401	1.4185	1.5007	1.5869	1.6771	1.7716	1.9738	2.1950	2.4364	2.6996	2.9860	3.8147	4.8268	6.0534	7.5295	9.2941	11.3906
7	1.0000	1.0721	1.1487	1.2299	1.3159	1.4071	1.5036	1.6058	1.7138	1.8280	1.9487	2.2107	2.5023	2.8262	3.1855	3.5832	4.7684	6.2749	8.1722	10.5414	13.4765	17.0859
8	1.0000	1.0829	1.1717	1.2668	1.3686	1.4775	1.5938	1.7182	1.8509	1.9926	2.1436	2.4760	2.8526	3.2784	3.7589	4.2998	5.9605	8.1573	11.0324	14.7579	19.5409	25.6289
9	1.0000	1.0937	1.1951	1.3048	1.4233	1.5513	1.6895	1.8385	1.9990	2.1719	2.3579	2.7731	3.2519	3.8030	4.4355	5.1598	7.4506	10.6045	14.8937	20.6610	28.3343	38.4434
10	1.0000	1.1046	1.2190	1.3439	1.4802	1.6289	1.7908	1.9672	2.1589	2.3674	2.5937	3.1058	3.7072	4.4114	5.2338	6.1917	9.3132	13.7858	20.1066	28.9255	41.0847	57.6650
11	1.0000	1.1157	1.1234	1.3842	1.5395	1.7103	1.8983	2.1049	2.3316	2.5804	2.8531	3.4785	4.2262	5.1173	6.1759	7.4301	11.6415	17.9216	27.1439	40.4957	59.5728	86.4976
12	1.0000	1.1268	1.2682	1.4258	1.6010	1.7959	2.0122	2.2522	2.5182	2.8127	3.1384	3.8960	4.8179	5.9360	7.2876	8.9161	14.5519	23.2981	36.6442	56.6939	86.3806	129.7463
13	1.0000	1.1381	1.2936	1.4685	1.6651	1.8856	2.1329	2.4098	2.7196	3.0658	3.4523	4.3635	5.4924	6.8858	8.5994	10.6993	18.1899	30.2875	49.4697	79.3715	125.2518	194.6195
14	1.0000	1.1495	1.3195	1.5126	1.7317	1.9799	2.2609	2.5785	2.9372	3.3417	3.7975	4.8871	6.2613	7.9875	10.1472	12.8392	22.7374	39.3738	66.7841	111.1201	181.6151	291.9293
15	1.0000	1.1610	1.3459	1.5580	1.8009	2.0789	2.3966	2.7590	3.1722	3.6425	4.1772	5.4736	7.1379	9.2655	11.9737	15.4070	28.4217	51.1859	90.1585	155.5681	263.3419	437.8939
16	1.0000	1.1726	1.3728	1.6047	1.8730	2.1829	2.5404	2.9522	3.4259	3.9703	4.5950	6.1304	8.1372	10.7480	14.1290	18.4884	35.5271	66.54171	21.7139	217.7953	381.8458	656.8408
17	1.0000	1.1843	1.4002	1.6528	1.9479	2.2920	2.6928	3.1588	3.7000	4.3276	5.0545	6.8660	9.2765	12.4677	16.6722	22.1861	44.4089	86.5042	164.3138	304.9135	553.6764	985.2613
18	1.0000	1.1961	1.4282	1.7024	2.0258	2.4066	2.8543	3.3799	3.9960	4.7171	5.5599	7.6900	10.5752	14.4625	19.6733	26.6233	55.5112	112.4554	221.8236	426.8789	802.8308	1477.8919
19	1.0000	1.2081	1.4568	1.7535	2.1068	2.5270	3.0256	3.6165	4.3157	5.1417	6.1159	8.6128	12.0557	16.7765	23.2144	31.9480	69.3889	146.1920	299.4619	597.63041	164.1047	2216.8378
20	1.0000	1.2202	1.4859	1.8061	2.1911	2.6533	3.2071	3.8697	4.6610	5.6044	6.7275	9.6463	13.7435	19.4608	27.3930	38.3376	86.7362	190.0496	404.2736	836.6826	1687.9518	3325.2567
25	1.0000	1.2824	1.6406	2.0938	2.6658	3.3864	4.2919	5.4274	6.8485	8.6231	10.8347	17.0001	26.4619	40.8742	62.6686	95.3962	264.698	705.641	1812.78	4499.88	10819.3	2525.2
30	1.0000	1.3478	1.8114	2.4273	3.2434	4.3219	5.7435	7.6123	10.0627	13.2677	17.4494	29.9599	50.9502	85.8499	143.371	237.376	807.794	2620.00	8128.55	24201.4	69349.0	191751
35	1.0000	1.4166	1.9999	2.8139	3.9461	5.5160	7.6861	10.6766	14.7853	20.4140	28.1024	52.7996	98.1002	180.314	327.997	590.668	2465.19	9727.86	36448.7	130161	444509	1456110
40	1.0000	1.4889	2.2080	3.2620	4.8010	7.0400	10.2857	14.9745	21.7245	31.4094	45.2593	93.0510	188.884	378.721	750.378	1469.77	7523.16	36118.9	163437	700038	2849181	11057332
45	1.0000	1.5648	2.4379	3.7816	5.8412	8.9850	13.7646	21.0025	31.9204	48.3273	72.8905	163.988	363.679	795.444	1716.68	3657.26	22958.9	134107	732858	3764971	18262495	83966617
50	1.0000	1.6446	2.6916	4.3839	7.1067	11.4674	18.4202	29.4570	46.9016	74.3575	117.391	289.002	700.233	1670.70	3927.36	9100.44	70064.9	497929	3286158	0248916	117057734	637621500

Table II

Present Value Interest Factors, PVIF, Discounted at i Percent for n Periods: $PVIF_{i,n} = \frac{1}{(1+i)^n}$

Discount Rate, i

Number of Periods, n	0%	1%	2%	3%	4%	5%	6%	7%	8%	9%	10%	12%	14%	16%	18%	20%	25%	30%	35%	40%	45%	50%
0	1.0000	1.0000	1.0000	1.0000	1.0000	1.0000	1.0000	1.0000	1.0000	1.0000	1.0000	1.0000	1.0000	1.0000	1.0000	1.0000	1.0000	1.0000	1.0000	1.0000	1.0000	1.0000
1	1.0000	0.9901	0.9804	0.9709	0.9615	0.9524	0.9434	0.9346	0.9259	0.9174	0.9091	0.8929	0.8772	0.8621	0.8475	0.8333	0.8000	0.7692	0.7407	0.7143	0.6897	0.6667
2	1.0000	0.9803	0.9612	0.9426	0.9246	0.9070	0.8900	0.8734	0.8573	0.8417	0.8264	0.7972	0.7695	0.7432	0.7182	0.6944	0.6400	0.5917	0.5487	0.5102	0.4756	0.4444
3	1.0000	0.9706	0.9423	0.9151	0.8890	0.8638	0.8396	0.8163	0.7938	0.7722	0.7513	0.7118	0.6750	0.6407	0.6086	0.5787	0.5120	0.4552	0.4064	0.3644	0.3280	0.2963
4	1.0000	0.9610	0.9238	0.8885	0.8548	0.8227	0.7921	0.7629	0.7350	0.7084	0.6830	0.6355	0.5921	0.5523	0.5158	0.4823	0.4096	0.3501	0.3011	0.2603	0.2262	0.1975
5	1.0000	0.9515	0.9057	0.8626	0.8219	0.7835	0.7473	0.7130	0.6806	0.6499	0.6209	0.5674	0.5194	0.4761	0.4371	0.4019	0.3277	0.2693	0.2230	0.1859	0.1560	0.1317
6	1.0000	0.9420	0.8880	0.8375	0.7903	0.7462	0.7050	0.6663	0.6302	0.5963	0.5645	0.5066	0.4556	0.4104	0.3704	0.3349	0.2621	0.2072	0.1652	0.1328	0.1076	0.0878
7	1.0000	0.9327	0.8706	0.8131	0.7599	0.7107	0.6651	0.6227	0.5835	0.5470	0.5132	0.4523	0.3996	0.3538	0.3139	0.2791	0.2097	0.1594	0.1224	0.0949	0.0742	0.0585
8	1.0000	0.9235	0.8535	0.7894	0.7307	0.6768	0.6274	0.5820	0.5403	0.5019	0.4665	0.4039	0.3506	0.3050	0.2660	0.2326	0.1678	0.1226	0.0906	0.0678	0.0512	0.0390
9	1.0000	0.9143	0.8368	0.7664	0.7026	0.6446	0.5919	0.5439	0.5002	0.4604	0.4241	0.3606	0.3075	0.2630	0.2255	0.1938	0.1342	0.0943	0.0671	0.0484	0.0353	0.0260
10	1.0000	0.9053	0.8203	0.7441	0.6756	0.6139	0.5584	0.5083	0.4632	0.4224	0.3855	0.3220	0.2697	0.2267	0.1911	0.1615	0.1074	0.0725	0.0497	0.0346	0.0243	0.0173
11	1.0000	0.8963	0.8043	0.7224	0.6496	0.5847	0.5268	0.4751	0.4289	0.3875	0.3505	0.2875	0.2366	0.1954	0.1619	0.1346	0.0859	0.0558	0.0368	0.0247	0.0168	0.0116
12	1.0000	0.8874	0.7885	0.7014	0.6246	0.5568	0.4970	0.4440	0.3971	0.3555	0.3186	0.2567	0.0276	0.1685	0.1372	0.1122	0.0687	0.0429	0.0273	0.0176	0.0116	0.0077
13	1.0000	0.8787	0.7730	0.6810	0.6006	0.5303	0.4688	0.4150	0.3677	0.3262	0.2897	0.2292	0.1821	0.1452	0.1163	0.0935	0.0550	0.0330	0.0202	0.0126	0.0080	0.0051
14	1.0000	0.8700	0.7579	0.6611	0.5775	0.5051	0.4423	0.3878	0.3405.	0.2992	0.2633	0.2046	0.1597	0.1252	0.0985	0.0779	0.0440	0.0254	0.0150	0.0090	0.0055	0.0034
15	1.0000	0.8613	0.7430	0.6419	0.5553	0.4810	0.4173	0.3624	0.3152	0.2745	0.2394	0.1827	0.1401	0.1079	0.0835	0.0649	0.0352	0.0195	0.0111	0.0064	0.0038	0.0023
16	1.0000	0.8528	0.7284	0.6232	0.5339	0.4581	0.3936	0.3387	0.2919	0.2519	0.2176	0.1631	0.1229	0.0930	0.0708	0.0541	0.0281	0.0150	0.0082	0.0046	0.0026	0.0015
17	1.0000	0.8444	0.7142	0.6050	0.5134	0.4363	0.3714	0.3166	0.2703	0.2311	0.1978	0.1456	0.1078	0.0802	0.0600	0.0451	0.0225	0.0116	0.0061	0.0033	0.0018	0.0010
18	1.0000	0.8360	0.7002	0.5874	0.4936	0.4155	0.3503	0.2959	0.2502	0.2120	0.1799	0.1300	0.0946	0.0691	0.0508	0.0376	0.0180	0.0089	0.0045	0.0023	0.0012	0.0007
19	1.0000	0.8277	0.6864	0.5703	0.4746	0.3957	0.3305	0.2765	0.2317	0.1945	0.1635	0.1161	0.0829	0.0596	0.0431	0.0313	0.0144	0.0068	0.0033	0.0017	0.0019	0.0005
20	1.0000	0.8195	0.6730	0.5537	0.4564	0.3769	0.3118	0.2584	0.2145	0.1784	0.1486	0.1037	0.0728	0.0514	0.0365	0.0261	0.0115	0.0053	0.0025	0.0012	0.0006	0.0003
25	1.0000	0.7798	0.6095	0.4776	0.3751	0.2953	0.2230	0.1842	0.1460	0.1160	0.0923	0.0588	0.0378	0.0245	0.0160	0.0105	0.0038	0.0014	0.0006	0.0002	0.0001	0.0000
30	1.0000	0.7419	0.5521	0.4120	0.3083	0.2314	0.1741	0.1314	0.0994	0.0754	0.0573	0.0334	0.0196	0.0116	0.0070	0.0042	0.0012	0.0004	0.0001	0.0000	0.0000	0.0000
35	1.0000	0.7059	0.5000	0.3554	0.2534	0.1813	0.1301	0.0937	0.0676	0.0490	0.0356	0.0189	0.0102	0.0055	0.0030	0.0017	0.0004	0.0001	0.0000	0.0000	0.0000	0.0000
40	1.0000	0.6717	0.4529	0.3066	0.2083	0.1420	0.0972	0.0668	0.0460	0.0318	0.0221	0.0107	0.0053	0.0026	0.0013	0.0007	0.0001	0.0000	0.0000	0.0000	0.0000	0.0000
45	1.0000	0.6391	0.4102	0.2644	0.1712	0.1113	0.0727	0.0476	0.0313	0.0207	0.0137	0.0061	0.0027	0.0013	0.0006	0.0003	0.0000	0.0000	0.0000	0.0000	0.0000	0.0000
50	1.0000	0.6080	0.3715	0.2281	0.1407	0.0872	0.0543	0.0339	0.0213	0.0134	0.0085	0.0035	0.0014	0.0006	0.0003	0.0001	0.0000	0.0000	0.0000	0.0000	0.0000	0.0000

Table III

Future Value Interest Factors for an Annuity, FVIFA, Compounded at i Percent for n Periods: $FVIFA_{i,n} = \sum_{t=1}^{n}(1+i)^{n-t} = \frac{(1+i)^n - 1}{i}$ **(for non-zero i)**

Interest Rate, i

Number of Annuity Pmts., n	0%	1%	2%	3%	4%	5%	6%	7%	8%	9%	10%	12%	14%	16%	18%	20%	25%	30%	35%	40%	45%	50%
1	1.0000	1.0000	1.0000	1.0000	1.0000	1.0000	1.0000	1.0000	1.0000	1.0000	1.0000	1.0000	1.0000	1.0000	1.0000	1.0000	1.0000	1.0000	1.0000	1.0000	1.0000	1.0000
2	2.0000	2.0100	2.0200	2.0300	2.0400	2.0500	2.0600	2.0700	2.0800	2.0900	2.1000	2.1200	2.1400	2.1600	2.1800	2.2000	2.2500	2.3000	2.3500	2.400	2.4500	2.5000
3	3.0000	3.0301	3.0604	3.0909	3.1216	3.1525	3.1836	3.2149	3.2464	3.2781	3.3100	3.3744	3.4396	3.5056	3.5724	3.6400	3.8125	3.9900	4.1725	4.3600	4.5525	4.7500
4	4.0000	4.0604	4.1216	4.1836	4.2465	4.3101	4.3746	4.4399	4.5061	4.5731	4.6410	4.7793	4.9211	5.0665	5.2154	5.3680	5.7656	6.1870	6.6329	7.1040	7.6011	8.1250
5	5.0000	5.1010	5.2040	5.3091	5.4163	5.5256	5.6371	5.7507	5.8666	5.9847	6.1051	6.3528	6.6101	6.8771	7.1542	7.4416	8.2070	9.0431	9.9544	10.9456	12.0216	13.1875
6	6.0000	6.1520	6.3081	6.4684	6.6330	6.8019	6.9753	7.1533	7.3359	7.5233	7.7156	8.1152	8.5355	8.9775	9.4420	9.9299	11.2588	12.7560	14.4384	16.3238	18.4314	20.7813
7	7.0000	7.2135	7.4343	7.6625	7.8983	8.1420	8.3938	8.6540	8.9228	9.2004	9.4872	10.0890	10.7305	11.4139	12.1415	12.9159	15.0735	17.5828	20.4919	23.8534	27.7255	32.1719
8	8.0000	8.2857	8.5830	8.8923	9.2142	9.5491	9.8975	10.2598	10.6366	11.0285	11.4359	12.2997	13.2328	14.2401	15.3270	16.4991	19.8419	23.8577	28.6640	34.3947	41.2019	49.2578
9	9.0000	9.3685	9.7546	10.1591	10.5828	11.0266	11.4913	11.9780	12.4876	13.0210	13.5795	14.7757	16.0853	17.5185	19.0859	20.7989	25.8023	32.0150	39.6964	49.1526	60.7428	74.8867
10	10.0000	10.4622	10.9497	11.4639	12.0061	12.5779	13.1808	13.8164	14.4866	15.1929	15.9374	17.5487	19.3373	21.3215	23.5213	25.9587	33.2529	42.6195	54.5902	69.8137	89.0771	113.330
11	11.0000	11.5668	12.1687	12.8078	13.4864	14.2068	14.9716	15.7836	16.6455	17.5603	18.5312	20.6546	23.0445	25.7329	28.7551	32.1504	42.5661	56.4053	74.6967	98.7391	130.162	170.995
12	12.0000	12.6825	13.4121	14.1920	15.0258	15.9171	16.8699	17.8885	18.9771	20.1407	21.3843	24.1331	27.2707	30.8502	34.9311	39.5805	54.2077	74.3270	101.841	139.235	189.735	257.493
13	13.0000	13.8093	14.6803	15.6178	16.6268	17.7130	18.8821	20.1406	21.4953	22.9534	24.5227	28.0291	32.0887	36.7862	42.2187	48.4966	68.7596	97.6250	138.485	195.929	276.115	387.239
14	14.0000	14.9474	15.9739	17.0863	18.2919	19.5986	21.0151	22.5505	24.2149	26.0192	27.9750	32.3926	37.5811	43.6720	50.8180	59.1959	86.9495	127.913	187.954	275.300	401.367	581.859
15	15.0000	16.0969	17.2934	18.5989	20.0236	21.5786	23.2760	25.1290	27.1521	29.3609	31.7725	37.2797	43.8424	51.6595	60.9653	72.0351	109.687	167.286	254.738	386.420	582.982	873.788
16	16.0000	17.2579	18.6393	20.1569	21.8245	23.6575	25.6725	27.8881	30.3243	33.0034	35.9497	42.7533	50.9804	60.9250	72.9390	87.4421	138.109	218.472	344.897	541.988	846.324	1311.68
17	17.0000	18.4304	20.0121	21.7616	23.6975	25.8404	28.2129	30.8402	33.7502	36.9737	40.5447	48.8837	59.1176	71.6730	87.0680	105.931	173.636	285.014	466.611	759.784	1228.17	1968.52
18	18.0000	19.6147	21.4123	23.4144	25.6454	28.1324	30.9057	33.9990	37.4502	41.3013	45.5992	55.7497	68.3941	84.1407	103.740	128.117	218.045	371.518	630.925	1064.70	1781.85	2953.78
19	19.0000	20.8109	22.8406	25.1169	27.6712	30.5390	33.7600	37.3790	41.4463	46.0185	51.1591	63.4397	78.9692	98.6032	123.414	154.740	273.556	483.973	852.748	1491.58	2584.68	4431.68
20	20.0000	22.0190	24.2974	26.8704	29.7781	33.0660	36.7856	40.9955	45.7620	51.1601	57.2750	72.0524	91.0249	115.380	146.628	186.688	342.945	630.165	1152.21	2089.21	3748.78	6648.51
25	25.0000	28.2432	32.0303	36.4593	41.6459	47.7271	54.8645	63.2490	73.1059	84.7009	98.3471	133.334	181.871	249.214	342.603	471.981	1054.79	2348.80	5176.50	11247.1990	24040.7	50500.3
30	30.0000	34.7849	40.5681	47.5754	56.0849	66.4388	79.0582	94.4608	113.283	136.308	164.494	241.333	356.787	530.312	790.948	1181.88	3227.17	8729.99	23221.6	60501.1	154107	383500
35	35.0000	41.6603	49.9945	60.4621	73.6522	90.3203	111.435	138.237	172.317	215.711	271.024	431.663	693.573	1120.71	1816.65	2948.34	9856.76	32422.9	104136	325400	987794	2912217
40	40.0000	48.8864	60.4020	75.4013	95.0255	120.800	154.762	199.635	259.057	337.882	442.593	767.091	1342.03	2360.76	4163.21	7343.86	30088.7	120393	466960	1750092	6331512	22114663
45	45.0000	56.4811	71.8927	92.7199	121.029	159.700	212.744	285.749	386.506	525.859	718.905	1358.23	2590.56	4965.27	9531.58	18281.3	91831.5	.447019	2093876	9412424	40583319	167933233
50	50.0000	64.4632	84.5794	112.797	152.667	209.348	290.336	406.529	573.770	815.084	1163.91	2400.02	4994.52	10435.6	21813.1	45497.2	.280256	1659761	9389020	50622288	260128295	1275242998

Table IV

Present Value Interest Factors for an Annuity, PVIFA, Discounted at i Percent for n Periods:

$$PVIFA_{i,n} = \sum_{t=1}^{n} \frac{1}{(1+i)^t} = \frac{1 - \frac{1}{(1+i)^n}}{i} = \frac{1}{i} - \frac{1}{i(1+i)^n} \quad \text{(for non-zero i)}$$

Discount Rate, i

Number of Annuity Pmts., n	0%	1%	2%	3%	4%	5%	6%	7%	8%	9%	10%	12%	14%	16%	18%	20%	25%	30%	35%	40%	45%	50%
1	1.0000	0.9901	0.9804	0.9709	0.9615	0.9524	0.9434	0.9346	0.9259	0.9174	0.9091	0.8929	0.8772	0.8621	0.8475	0.8333	0.8000	0.7692	0.7407	0.7413	0.6897	0.6667
2	2.0000	1.9704	1.9416	1.9135	1.8861	1.8594	1.8334	1.8080	1.7833	1.7591	1.7355	1.6901	1.6467	1.6052	1.5656	1.5278	1.4400	1.3609	1.2894	1.2245	1.1653	1.1111
3	3.0000	2.9410	2.8839	2.8286	2.7751	2.7232	2.6730	2.6243	2.5771	2.5313	2.4869	2.4018	2.3216	2.2459	2.1743	2.1065	1.9520	1.8161	1.6959	1.5889	1.4933	1.4074
4	4.0000	3.9020	3.8077	3.7171	3.6299	3.5460	3.4651	3.3872	3.3121	3.2397	3.1699	3.0373	2.9137	2.7982	2.6901	2.5887	2.5616	2.1662	1.9969	1.8492	1.7195	1.6049
5	5.0000	4.8534	4.7135	4.5797	4.4518	4.3295	4.2124	4.1002	3.9927	3.8897	3.7908	3.6048	3.4331	3.2743	3.1272	2.9906	2.6893	2.4356	2.2200	2.0352	1.8755	1.7366
6	6.0000	5.7955	5.6014	5.4172	5.2421	5.0757	4.9173	4.7665	4.6229	4.4859	4.3553	4.1114	3.8887	3.6847	3.4976	3.3255	2.9514	2.6427	2.3852	2.1680	1.9831	1.8244
7	7.0000	6.7282	6.4720	6.2303	6.0021	5.7864	5.5824	5.3893	5.2064	5.0330	4.8684	4.5638	4.2883	4.0386	3.8115	3.6046	3.1611	2.8021	2.5075	2.2628	2.0573	1.8829
8	8.0000	7.6517	7.3255	7.0197	6.7327	6.4632	6.2098	5.9713	5.7466	5.5348	5.3349	4.9676	4.6389	4.3436	4.0776	3.8372	3.3289	2.9247	2.5982	2.3306	2.1085	1.9220
9	9.0000	8.5660	8.1622	7.7861	7.4353	7.1078	6.8017	6.5152	6.2469	5.9952	5.7590	5.3282	4.9464	4.6065	4.3030	4.0310	3.4631	3.0190	2.6653	2.3790	2.1438	1.9480
10	10.0000	9.4713	8.9826	8.5302	8.1109	7.7217	7.3601	7.0236	6.7101	6.4177	6.1446	5.6502	5.2161	4.8332	4.4941	4.1925	3.5704	3.0915	2.7150	2.4136	2.1681	1.9653
11	11.0000	10.3676	9.7868	9.2526	8.7605	8.3064	7.8869	7.4987	7.1390	6.8052	6.4951	5.9377	5.4527	5.0286	4.6560	4.3271	3.6564	3.1473	2.7519	2.4383	2.1849	1.9769
12	12.0000	11.2551	10.5753	9.9540	9.3851	8.8633	8.3838	7.9427	7.5361	7.1607	6.8137	6.1944	5.6603	5.1971	4.7932	4.4392	3.7251	3.1903	2.7792	2.4559	2.1965	1.9846
13	13.0000	12.1337	11.3484	10.6350	9.9856	9.3936	8.8527	8.3577	7.9038	7.4869	7.1034	6.4235	5.8424	5.3423	4.9095	4.5327	3.7801	3.2233	2.7994	2.4685	2.2045	1.9897
14	14.0000	13.0037	12.1062	11.2961	10.5631	9.8986	9.2950	8.7455	8.2442	7.7862	7.3667	6.6282	6.0021	5.4675	5.0081	4.6106	3.8241	3.2487	2.8144	2.4775	2.2100	1.9931
15	15.0000	13.8651	12.8493	11.9379	11.1184	10.3797	9.7122	9.1079	8.5595	8.0607	7.6061	6.8109	6.1422	5.5755	5.0916	4.6755	3.8593	3.2682	2.8255	2.4839	2.2138	1.9954
16	16.0000	14.7179	13.5777	12.5611	11.6523	10.8378	10.1059	9.4466	8.8514	8.3126	7.8237	6.9740	6.2651	5.6685	5.1624	4.7296	3.8874	3.2832	2.8337	2.4885	2.2164	1.9970
17	17.0000	15.5623	14.2919	13.1661	12.1657	11.2741	10.4773	9.7632	9.1216	8.5436	8.0216	7.1196	6.3729	5.7487	5.2223	4.7746	3.9099	3.2948	2.8398	2.4918	2.2182	1.9980
18	18.0000	16.3983	14.9920	13.7535	12.6583	11.6896	10.8276	10.0591	9.3719	8.7556	8.2014	7.2497	6.4674	5.8178	5.2732	4.8122	3.9279	3.3037	2.8443	2.4941	2.2195	1.9986
19	19.0000	17.2260	15.6785	14.3238	13.1339	12.0853	11.1581	10.3356	9.6036	8.9501	8.3649	7.3658	6.5504	5.8775	5.3162	4.8435	3.9424	3.3105	2.8476	2.4958	2.2203	1.9991
20	20.0000	18.0456	16.3514	14.8775	13.5903	12.4622	11.4699	10.5940	9.8181	9.1285	8.5136	7.4694	6.6231	5.9288	5.3527	4.8696	3.9539	3.3158	2.8501	2.4970	2.2209	1.9994
25	25.0000	22.0232	19.5235	17.4131	15.6221	14.0939	12.7834	11.6536	10.6748	9.8226	9.0770	7.8431	6.8729	6.0971	5.4669	4.9476	3.9849	3.3286	2.8556	2.4994	2.2220	1.9999
30	30.0000	25.8077	22.3965	19.6004	17.2920	15.3725	13.7648	12.4090	11.2578	10.2737	9.4269	8.0552	7.0027	6.1772	5.5168	4.9789	3.9950	3.3321	2.8568	2.4999	2.2222	2.0000
35	35.0000	29.4086	24.9986	21.4872	18.6646	16.3742	14.4982	12.9477	11.6546	10.5668	9.5442	8.1755	7.0700	6.2153	5.5386	4.9915	3.9884	3.3330	2.8571	2.5000	2.2222	2.0000
40	40.0000	32.8347	27.3555	23.1148	19.7928	17.1591	15.0463	13.3317	11.9246	10.7574	9.7791	8.2438	7.1050	6.2335	5.5482	4.9966	3.9995	3.3332	2.8571	2.5000	2.2222	2.0000
45	45.0000	36.0945	29.4902	24.5187	20.7200	17.7741	15.4558	13.6055	12.1084	10.8812	9.8628	8.2825	7.1232	6.2421	5.5523	4.9986	3.9998	3.3333	2.8571	2.5000	2.2222	2.0000
50	50.0000	39.1961	31.4236	25.7298	21.4822	18.2559	15.7619	13.8007	12.2335	10.9617	9.9148	8.3045	7.1327	6.2463	5.5541	4.9995	3.9999	3.3333	2.8571	2.5000	2.2222	2.0000

GLOSSARY

ABC system An inventory system in which items are classified according to their value for inventory control purposes.

actuaries People who use applied mathematics and statistics to predict claims on insurance companies and pension funds.

additional funds needed The additional external financing required to support asset growth when forecasted assets exceed forecasted liabilities and equity.

after-tax cost of debt (AT k_d) The after-tax cost to a company of obtaining debt funds.

agency costs Costs incurred to monitor agents to reduce the conflict of interest between agents and principals.

agency problem The possibility of conflict between the interests of a firm's managers and those of the firm's owners.

agent A person who has the implied or actual authority to act on behalf of another.

aggressive working capital financing approach The use of short-term funds to finance all temporary current assets, possibly all or some permanent current assets, and perhaps some fixed assets.

amortization basis The total value of an asset upon which amortization expense will be calculated, a part at a time, over the life of the asset.

amortized loan A loan that is repaid in regularly spaced, equal installments, which cover all interest and principal owed.

annuitant A person who is entitled to receive annuity payments.

annuity A series of equal cash payments made at regular time intervals.

arbitrage The process whereby equivalent assets are bought in one place and simultaneously sold in another, making a risk-free profit.

average tax rate The amount of tax owed, divided by the amount of taxable income.

balance sheet The financial statement that shows an economic unit's assets, liabilities, and equity at a given point in time.

Bank Act The legislation by which all banks are regulated.

Bank of Canada The BOC is Canada's central bank. One of its chief purposes is to adjust the money supply through the Target for the Overnight Rate.

banker's acceptance A security that represents a promise by a bank to pay a certain amount of money if the original note maker does not pay.

bearer The owner of a security.

best efforts basis An arrangement in which the investment banking firm tries its best to sell a firm's securities for the desired price, without guarantees. If the securities must be sold for a lower price, the issuer collects less money.

beta (β) The measure of nondiversifiable risk. The stock market has a beta of 1.0. Betas higher than 1.0 indicate more nondiversifiable risk than the market, and betas lower than 1.0 indicate less. Risk-free portfolios have betas of 0.0.

bird-in-the-hand theory A theory that says investors value a dollar of dividends more highly than a dollar of reinvested earnings because uncertainty is resolved.

board of directors A group of individuals elected by the common shareholders to oversee the management of the firm.

bond maturity date The date on which the final payment is promised by the bond issuer.

bonds Securities that promise to pay the bearer a certain amount at a time in the future and may pay interest at regular intervals over the life of the security.

bond value The value coming from the interest and principal is called the convertible bond's *straight bond value*.

book value, net worth The total amount of common shareholders' equity on a company's balance sheet.

broker A person who brings buyers and sellers together.

business risk The uncertainty a company has due to fluctuations in its operating income.

caisses populaires Financial institutions that have members and operate similarly to credit unions.

call premium The premium the issuer pays to call in a bond before maturity. The excess of the call price over the face value.

call provision A bond indenture provision that allows the issuer to pay off a bond before the stated maturity date at a specified price.

capital Funds supplied to a firm.

capital Assets that would not normally be sold or otherwise disposed of for a long period of time.

capital assets The land, buildings, equipment, and other assets that would not normally be sold or otherwise disposed of for a long period of time.

capital asset pricing model (CAPM) A financial model that can be used to calculate the appropriate required rate of return for an investment project, given its degree of risk as measured by beta (β).

capital budget A document that shows planned expenditures for major asset acquisitions items such as equipment or plant construction.

capital budgeting The process of evaluating proposed projects.

capital cost allowance (CCA) A method of allocating the cost of an asset under the *Income Tax Act*.

capital (financial) lease A lease that is generally long-term and noncancellable, with the lessee using up most of the economic value of the asset by the end of the lease's term.

capital gains The profit made when an asset price is higher than the price paid.

capital lease A lease that is long-term and noncancellable.

capital market The market where long-term securities are traded.

capital rationing The process whereby management sets a limit on the amount of cash available for new capital budgeting projects.

capital structure The mixture of sources of capital that a firm uses (e.g., debt, preferred shares, and common shares).

cash budget A detailed budget plan that shows the cash flows expected to occur during specific time periods.

chief financial officer The manager who directs and coordinates the financial activities of the firm.

clientele dividend theory The theory that says a company should attempt to determine the dividend wants of its shareholders and maintain a consistent policy of paying shareholders what they want.

coefficient of variation The standard deviation divided by the mean. A measure of the degree of risk used to compare alternatives with possible returns of different magnitudes.

collateral Assets a borrower agrees to give to a lender if the borrower defaults on the terms of a loan.

collection policy The firm's plans for getting delinquent credit customers to pay their bills.

combined leverage The phenomenon whereby a change in sales causes net income to change by a larger percentage because of fixed operating and financial costs.

commercial paper A short-term, unsecured debt instrument issued by a large corporation or financial institution.

common share A security that indicates ownership of a corporation.

compensating balance A specified amount that a lender requires a borrower to maintain in a non-interest-paying account during the life of a loan.

component cost of capital The cost of raising funds from a particular source such as bondholders or common shareholders.

compound interest Interest earned on interest in addition to interest earned on the original principal.

conservative working capital financing approach The use of long-term debt and equity to finance all long-term fixed assets and permanent current assets in addition to some part of temporary current assets.

continuous compounding A process whereby interest is earned on interest every instant of time.

contribution margin Sales price per unit minus variable cost per unit.

controller The manager responsible for the financial and cost accounting activities of a firm.

conversion ratio The number of shares (usually of common shares) that the holder of a convertible bond would receive if he or she exercised the conversion option.

conversion value The value of the share that would be received if the conversion option on a convertible bond were exercised.

convertible bond A bond that may be converted, at the option of the bond's owner, into a certain amount of a different type of security issued by the company.

corporate bond A security that represents a promise by the issuing corporation to make certain payments, according to a certain schedule, to the owner of the bond.

corporation A predominant business vehicle chartered by the province that is a separate legal entity having some, but not all, of the rights and responsibilities of a natural person.

correlation The degree to which one variable is linearly related to another.

correlation coefficient The measurement of degree of correlation, represented by the letter r. Its values range from +1.0 (perfect positive correlation) to –1.0 (perfect negative correlation).

cost of debt (k_d) The lender's required rate of return on a company's new bonds or other instrument of indebtedness.

cost of equity from new common shares (k_n) The cost of external equity, including the costs incurred to issue new common shares.

cost of internal common equity (k_s) The required rate of return on funds supplied by existing common shareholders through earnings retained.

cost of preferred shares (k_p) Investors' required rate of return on a company's new preferred shares.

credit policy Credit standards a firm has established and the credit terms it offers.

credit scoring A process by which candidates for credit are compared against indicators of creditworthiness and scored accordingly.

credit standards Requirements customers must meet in order to be granted credit.

credit unions Financial institutions owned by members who receive interest on shares purchased and who obtain loans.

cross-sectional analysis Comparing variables for different entities (such as ratio values for different companies) for the same point in time or time period.

current assets Liquid assets of an economic entity (i.e., cash, accounts receivable, inventory, etc.) usually converted into cash within one year.

current liabilities Liabilities that are coming due soon, usually within one year.

date of record The date on which shareholder records are checked for the purpose of determining who will receive the dividend that has been declared.

dealer A person who makes his or her living buying and selling assets.

debenture A bond that is unsecured.

declaration date The date on which the board of directors announces a dividend is to be paid.

declining balance method An amortization method by which a fixed amortization rate is multiplied by the book value of an asset in order to determine the amortization expense in that period.

default risk premium The extra interest lenders demand to compensate for assuming the risk that promised interest and principal payments may be made late or not at all.

degree of combined leverage (DCL) The percentage change in net income divided by the percentage change in sales.

degree of financial leverage (DFL) The percentage change in net income divided by the percentage change in operating income.

degree of operating leverage (DOL) The percentage change in operating income divided by the percentage change in sales.

demander of capital A government, business, or household unit with expenditures greater than its income.

discounted cash flow (DCF) model A model that estimates the value of an asset by calculating the sum of the present values of all future cash flows.

discount loan A loan with terms that call for the loan interest to be deducted from the loan proceeds at the time the loan is granted.

discount rate The interest rate used to calculate a present value representing the required rate of return.

discount yield The return realized by an investor who purchases a security for less than face value and redeems it at maturity for face value.

diversification effect The effect of combining assets in a portfolio such that the fluctuations of the assets' returns tend to offset each other, reducing the overall volatility (risk) of the portfolio.

dividend reinvestment plan (DRIP) An arrangement offered by some corporations where cash dividends are held by the company and used to purchase additional shares for the investor.

dividend yield A share's annual dividend divided by its current market price.

dividends Payments made to shareholders at the discretion of the board of directors of the corporation.

dividends payable The liability item on a firm's balance sheet that reflects the amount of dividends declared but not yet paid.

economic value added (EVA) The amount of profit remaining after accounting for the return expected by the firm's investors.

effective interest rate The annual interest rate that reflects the dollar interest paid divided by the dollar obtained for use.

electronic funds transfer The act of crediting one account and debiting another automatically by a computer system.

equity multiplier The total assets to total common shareholders' equity ratio.

excess financing The amount of excess funding available for expected asset growth when forecasted liabilities and equity exceed forecasted assets.

ex-dividend A characteristic of common shares such that it is trading *without* entitlement to an upcoming dividend.

ex-rights A characteristic of common shares such that it is trading *without* the entitlement to an upcoming rights offering.

externalities Positive or negative effects that will occur to existing projects if a new capital budgeting project is accepted.

face value, or **par value,** or **principal** The amount the bond issuer promises to pay to the investor when the bond matures. The terms *face value, par value,* and *principal* are often used interchangeably.

factors Businesses that make money by buying accounts receivable from other firms, at less than their face value.

factoring The practice of selling accounts receivable to another firm.

fiduciary responsibility The legal requirement that those who are managing assets owned by someone else do so in a prudent manner and in accordance with the interests of the person(s) they represent.

financial intermediaries Institutions that facilitate the exchange of cash and securities.

financial leverage The phenomenon whereby a change in operating income causes net income to change by a larger percentage because of the presence of fixed financial costs.

financial markets Exchanges or over-the-counter mechanisms where securities are traded.

financial ratio A number that expresses the value of one financial variable relative to the value of another.

financial risk The additional volatility of a firm's net income caused by the presence of fixed financial costs.

financing cash flows Cash flows that occur as creditors are paid interest and principal and shareholders are paid dividends.

first-mortgage bond A mortgage bond (a bond secured by real property) that gives the holder first claim on the real property pledged as security if there is a foreclosure.

fixed costs Costs that do not vary with the level of production.

flotation cost A fee that companies pay (to investment bankers and to others) when new securities are issued.

future value The value that money or another asset will have in the future.

future value interest factor for an annuity (FVIFA) The factor which, when multiplied by an expected annuity, gives you the sum of the future values of the annuity stream:

$$\frac{1-\frac{1}{(1+i)^n}}{i}$$

future value interest factor for a single amount (FVIF) The $(1 + i)^n$ factor that is multiplied by the original value to solve for future value.

going concern value The value that comes from the future earnings and cash flows that can be generated by a company if it continues to operate.

Guaranteed Investment Certificate A low-risk investment offered by banks and similar institutions.

horizontal analysis A comparative analysis of financial statements over time that financial analysts often perform. It normally entails an analysis of the items in the financial statements from year to year or over a period of time.

hurdle rate The minimum rate of return that management demands from a proposed project before that project will be accepted.

income statement A financial statement that presents the revenues, expenses, and income of a business over a specified period of time.

incremental amortization expense The change in amortization expense that a company will incur if a proposed capital budgeting project is accepted.

incremental cash flows Cash flows that will occur only if an investment is undertaken.

indenture The contract between the issuing corporation and the bond's purchaser.

independent projects A group of projects such that any or all could be accepted.

industry comparison The process whereby financial ratios of a firm are compared to those of similar firms to see if the firm under scrutiny compares favourably or unfavourably with the norm.

inflation premium The extra interest that compensates lenders for the expected erosion of purchasing power of funds due to inflation over the life of the loan.

initial public offering (IPO) The process whereby a private corporation issues new common shares to the general public, thus becoming a publicly traded corporation.

institutional investors Financial institutions that invest in the securities of other companies.

interest The compensation lenders demand and borrowers pay when money is lent.

interest rate spread The rate a bank charges for loans minus the rate it pays for deposits.

intermediation The process that occurs when funds flow from suppliers of capital to a financial institution to demanders of capital.

internal rate of return (IRR) The estimated rate of return for a proposed project, given the size of the project's incremental cash flows and their timing.

international bonds Bonds that are sold in countries other than where the issuer is domiciled.

inventory financing A type of financing that uses inventory as loan collateral.

investment-banking firm A firm that helps issuers sell their securities and that provides other financial services.

investment-grade bonds Bonds rated Baa3 or above by Moody's bond rating agency and BBB– or above by Standard & Poor's.

junk bonds Bonds with ratings that are lower than investment grade (Ba1 or below by Moody's, BBh or below by DBRS, and BB+ or below by Standard & Poor's).

just-in-time (JIT) An inventory system in which inventory items are scheduled to be delivered "just in time" to be used as needed.

lead underwriter or **manager** The head of an investment banking syndicate.

lease A contract between an asset owner (lessor) and another party who uses that asset (lessee) that allows the use of the asset for a specified period of time, specifies payment terms, and does not convey legal ownership.

lessee The party in a lease contract who uses the asset.

lessor The party in a lease contract who owns the asset.

leverage Something that creates a magnifying effect, such as fixed operating or fixed financial costs that cause a magnifying effect on the movements of operating income or net income.

leverage effect The result of one factor causing another factor to be magnified, such as when debt magnifies the return shareholders earn on their invested funds over the return on assets.

liability insurance Insurance that pays obligations, which may be incurred by the insured as a result of negligence, slander, malpractice, and similar actions.

limited liability companies LLCs are hybrids between partnerships and corporations that are taxed like the former and have limited liability for the owners like the latter.

limited liability partnership LLPs are business entities usually formed by professionals such as doctors, lawyers, or accountants and provide limited liability for the partners.

limited partnerships LPs are partnerships that include at least one partner whose liability is limited to the amount invested. They usually take a less active role in the running of the business than do general partners.

line of credit An informal arrangement between a lender and borrower in which the lender sets a limit on the maximum amount of funds the borrower may use at any one time.

liquidation value The amount that would be received by the owners of a company that sold all its assets at market value, paid all its liabilities and preferred shares, and distributed what was left to the owners of the firm.

liquidity risk premium The extra interest lenders demand to compensate for holding a security that is not easy to sell at its fair value.

lockbox A way station (typically a post office box) at which customers may send payments to a firm.

M&M dividend theory A theory according which the way a firm's income is distributed (in the form of future capital gains or current dividends) does not affect the overall value of the firm.

manager or **lead underwriter** The head of an investment banking syndicate.

managing investment banker The head of an investment banking underwriting syndicate.

marginal cost of capital (MCC) The weighted average cost of capital for the next dollar of funds raised.

marginal tax rate The tax rate applied to the next dollar of taxable income.

market efficiency The relative ease, speed, and cost of trading securities. In an efficient market, securities can be traded easily, quickly, and at low cost. In an inefficient market, one or more of these qualities is missing.

market risk premium The additional return above the risk-free rate demanded by investors for assuming the risk of investing in the market.

market value added (MVA) The market value of the firm, debt plus equity, minus the total amount of capital invested in the firm.

maturity date The date the bearer of a security is to be paid the principal, or face value, of a security.

maturity risk premium The extra (or sometimes lesser) interest that lenders demand on longer-term securities.

mixed ratio A financial ratio that includes variables from both the income statement and the balance sheet.

moderate working capital financing approach An approach in which a firm finances temporary current assets with short-term funds and permanent current assets and fixed assets with long-term funds.

modified internal rate of return (MIRR) The estimated rate of return for a proposed project for which the projected cash flows are assumed to be reinvested at the cost of capital rate.

Modigliani and Miller dividend theory A theory developed by financial theorists Franco Modigliani and Merton Miller that says the amount of dividends paid by a firm does not affect the firm's value.

money market The market where short-term securities are traded.

mortgage bond A bond secured by real property.

multinational corporation (MNC) A corporation that has operations in more than one country.

municipal bonds Bonds issued by a province, city, county, or other nonfederal government authority, including specially created municipal authorities such as a toll road or industrial development authority.

mutually exclusive projects A group of projects that compete against each other; only one of the mutually exclusive projects may be chosen.

net present value (NPV) The estimated change in the value of the firm that would occur if a project is accepted.

net working capital The amount of current assets minus the amount of current liabilities of an economic unit.

nominal interest rate The rate observed in the financial marketplace that includes the real rate of interest and various premiums.

nominal risk-free rate of interest The interest rate without any premiums for the uncertainties associated with lending.

nondiversifiable risk The portion of a portfolio's total risk that cannot be eliminated by diversifying. Factors shared to a greater or lesser degree by most assets in the market, such as inflation and interest rate risk, cause nondiversifiable risk.

nonsimple project A project that has a negative initial cash flow and also has one or more negative future cash flows.

NPV profile A graph that displays how a project's net present value changes as the discount rate, or required rate of return, changes.

open-market operations The buying and selling of Canadian Treasury securities or foreign currencies to achieve some economic objective.

operating lease A lease that has a term substantially shorter than the useful life of the asset and is usually cancellable by the lessee.

operating leverage The effect of fixed operating costs on operating income; because of fixed costs, any change in sales results in a larger percentage change in operating income.

opportunity cost The cost of forgoing the best alternative to make a competing choice.

optimal capital budget The list of all accepted projects and the total amount of their initial cash outlays.

option The right, but not the obligation, to buy or sell a security at a certain price.

over-the-counter market A network of dealers around the world.

partnership An unincorporated business owned by two or more people.

payback period The expected amount of time a capital budgeting project will take to generate cash flows that cover the project's initial cash outlay.

payment date The date the transfer agent sends out a company's dividend cheques.

pension fund A financial institution that takes in funds for workers, invests those funds, and then provides for a retirement benefit.

permanent current assets The minimum level of current assets maintained.

perpetuity An annuity that has an infinite maturity.

portfolio A collection of assets that are managed as a group.

preemptive right A security given by some corporations to existing shareholders that gives them the right to buy new common shares at a below-market price until a specified expiration date.

present value Today's value of promised or expected future value.

present value interest factor for a single amount (PVIF) The $1/(1 + i)^n$ factor that is multiplied by a given future value to solve for the present value.

present value interest factor for an annuity (PVIFA) The factor which, when multiplied by an expected annuity payment, gives you the present value of the annuity stream:

$$\frac{(1+i)^n - 1}{i}$$

primary market The market in which newly issued securities are sold to the public.

primary reserves Vault cash and deposits at the Bank of Canada that go toward meeting a bank's reserve requirements.

principal A person who authorizes an agent to act for him or her.

private corporation A corporation that does not offer its shares to the general public and that can keep its financial statements confidential.

***pro forma* financial statements** Projected financial statements.

promissory note A legal document that the borrower signs indicating agreement to the terms of a loan.

proprietorship A business that is not incorporated and is owned by one person.

prospectus A disclosure document given to a potential investor when a new security is issued.

publicly traded corporations Corporations that have common shares, which can be bought in the marketplace by any interested party and that must release audited financial statements to the public.

pure time value of money The value demanded by an investor to compensate for the postponement of consumption.

putable bonds Bonds that can be redeemed before the scheduled maturity date, at the option of the bondholder.

real option A valuable characteristic of some projects where revisions to that project at a later date are possible.

real rate of interest The rate that the market offers to lenders to compensate for postponing consumption.

refunding Issuing new bonds to replace old bonds.

required reserve ratio The percentage of deposits that determines the amount of reserves a financial institution is required to hold.

residual income Income left over and available to common shareholders, after all other claimants have been paid.

restrictive covenants Promises made by the issuer of a bond to the investor, to the benefit of the investor.

rights-on A characteristic of common shares such that it is trading *with* the entitlement to an upcoming right.

risk The potential for unexpected events to occur.

risk-adjusted discount rate (RADR) A required rate of return adjusted to compensate for the effect a project has on a firm's risk.

risk aversion A tendency to avoid risk that explains why most investors require a higher expected rate of return the more risk they assume.

risk-free rate of return The rate of return that investors demand in order to take on a project that contains no risk other than an inflation premium.

risk–return relationship The positive relationship between the risk of an investment and an investor's required rate of return.

sales breakeven point The level of sales that must be achieved such that operating income equals zero.

second-mortgage bond A mortgage bond (a bond secured by real property) that gives the holder second claim (after the first-mortgage bondholder) on the real property pledged as security.

secondary market The market in which previously issued securities are traded from one investor to another.

secured bond A bond backed by specific assets that the investor may claim if there is a default.

security A document that establishes the bearer's claim to receive funds in the future.

self-liquidating loan A loan that is used to acquire assets that generate enough cash to pay off the loan.

senior debenture An unsecured bond having a superior claim on the earnings and assets of the issuing firm relative to other debentures.

serial payments A mode of payment in which the issuer pays off bonds according to a staggered maturity schedule.

share Certificates of ownership interest in a corporation.

share dividend A firm sends out new shares to existing shareholders and makes an accounting transfer from retained earnings to the common share and capital in excess of par accounts of the balance sheet.

short-term financing decisions Financial decisions relating to raising funds for a short period of time from sources such as bank loans, trade credit, and commercial paper.

signalling The message sent by managers, or inferred by investors, when a financial decision is made.

signalling dividend theory A theory that says dividend payments often send a signal from the management of a firm to market participants.

simple project A project that has a negative initial cash flow, followed by positive cash flows only.

sinking fund A method for retiring bonds. The bond issuer makes regular contributions to a fund that the trustee uses to buy back outstanding bonds and retire them.

stakeholder A party having an interest in a firm (e.g., owners, workers, management, creditors, suppliers, customers, and the community as a whole).

standard deviation A statistic that indicates how widely dispersed actual or possible values are distributed around a mean.

stated interest rate The interest rate advertised by the lender. Depending on the terms of the loan, the stated rate may or may not be the same as the effective interest rate.

statement of retained earnings A financial statement that shows how the value of retained earnings changes from one point in time to another.

stock dividend See ***share dividend***.

stock split A firm gives new shares to existing shareholders.

straight bond value The value a convertible bond would have if it did not offer the conversion option to the investor.

straight-line amortization method An amortization rule that allows equal amounts of the cost of an asset to be allocated over the asset's life.

subordinated debenture An unsecured bond having an inferior claim on the earnings and assets of the issuing firm relative to other debentures.

sunk cost A cost that must be borne whether a proposed capital budgeting project is accepted or rejected.

suppliers of capital A government, business, or household unit with expenditures less than its income.

syndicate A temporary alliance of investment banking firms that is formed for the purpose of underwriting a new security issue.

Target for the Overnight Rate This rate is the main tool used by the Bank of Canada to conduct monetary policy.

tariff A tax imposed by one country on imports from another country.

temporary current assets The portion of current assets that fluctuates during the company's business cycle.

terminal value The predicted value of a company's projected free cash flows at a specified future point in time from that point in time to perpetuity.

time value of money The phenomenon whereby money is valued more highly the sooner it is received.

trade credit Funds obtained by delaying payment to suppliers.

transaction cost The cost of making a transaction, usually the cost associated with purchasing or selling a security.

transfer agent A party, usually a chartered bank, that keeps track of changes in stock ownership, collects cash from a company, and pays dividends to its shareholders.

treasurer The manager responsible for financial planning, fund raising, and allocation of money in a business.

Treasury bills Securities issued by the federal government in minimum denominations of $10,000 in maturities of three, six, or twelve months.

Treasury bonds and notes Securities issued by the federal government that make semiannual coupon interest payments and pay the face value at maturity. Treasury notes come in maturities of one to ten years. Treasury bonds come in maturities of more than ten years.

trend analysis An analysis in which something (such as a financial ratio) is examined over time to discern any changes.

trust companies Financial institutions that take in deposits and make loans (primarily mortgage loans).

trustee The party that oversees a bond issue and makes sure all the provisions set forth in the indenture are carried out.

uncertainty The chance, or probability, that outcomes other than what are expected will occur.

underwriting The process by which investment banking firms purchase a new security issue in its entirety and resell it to investors. The risk of the new issue is transferred from the issuing company to the investment bankers.

variable costs Costs that vary with the level of production.

variable-rate bonds Bonds that have periodic changes in their coupon rates, usually tied to changes in market interest rates.

vertical analysis A common-size analysis of financial statements, used as a way to gain insight into a financial statement.

warrant A security that gives the holder the option to buy a certain number of common shares of the issuing company, at a certain price, for a specified period of time.

weakening currency A currency that is now convertible into a smaller number of units of another currency than previously was the case.

wealth Assets minus liabilities.

weighted average cost of capital (k_a or WACC) The average of all the component costs of capital, weighted according to the percentage of each component in the firm's optimal capital structure.

working capital Another name for the current assets on a firm's balance sheet.

yield to maturity (YTM) The investor's return on a bond, assuming that all promised interest and principal payments are made on time and the interest payments are reinvested at the YTM rate.

zero-coupon bonds Bonds that pay face value at maturity and that pay no coupon interest.

INDEX

Note: Key terms and the pages on which they are defined are in bold face; *f* refers to figures and *t* refers to tables.

D

E

F

G

H

I

N

O

P

T

U

V

W

Y

Z